THE ROUTLEDGE COM JANE AUSTEN

First published anonymously, as 'a lady', Jane Austen is now among the world's most famous and highly revered authors. *The Routledge Companion to Jane Austen* provides wide-ranging coverage of Jane Austen's works, reception, and legacy, with chapters that draw on the latest literary research and theory and represent foundational and authoritative scholarship as well as new approaches to an author whose works provide seemingly endless inspiration for reinterpretation, adaptation, and appropriation. The *Companion* provides up-to-date work by an international team of established and emerging Austen scholars and includes exciting chapters not just on Austen in her time but on her ongoing afterlife, whether in the academy and the wider world of her fans or in cinema, new media, and the commercial world. Parts within the volume explore Jane Austen in her time and within the literary canon; the literary critical and theoretical study of her novels, unpublished writing, and correspondence; and the afterlife of her work as exemplified in film, digital humanities, and new media. In addition, the *Companion* devotes special attention to teaching Jane Austen.

Cheryl A. Wilson is Professor of English and Dean of the School of Humanities & Social Sciences at Stevenson University. In 2012, she participated in the NEH Summer Seminar 'Jane Austen and Her Contemporaries' with Devoney Looser and several other *Routledge Companion* contributors. She is the author of *Literature and Dance in Nineteenth-Century Britain* (2009), *Fashioning the Silver Fork Novel* (2012), and *Jane Austen and the Victorian Heroine* (2017).

Maria H. Frawley is a Professor of English at The George Washington University in Washington, DC, where she teaches courses in nineteenth-century British literature. She is the author of *A Wider Range: Travel Writing by Women in Victorian England*; *Anne Brontë*; an edition of Harriet Martineau's *Life in the Sick-Room*, and *Invalidism and Identity in Nineteenth-Century Britain*, in addition to essays on nineteenth-century women writers, including Jane Austen. She is at work on a book titled *Keywords of Jane Austen's Fiction*.

ROUTLEDGE LITERATURE COMPANIONS

Also available in this series:

The Routledge Companion to Transnational American Studies
Edited by Nina Morgan, Alfred Hornung and Takayuki Tatsumi

The Routledge Companion to Victorian Literature
Edited by Dennis Denisoff and Talia Schaffer

The Routledge Companion to Health Humanities
Edited by Paul Crawford, Brian Brown and Andrea Charise

The Routledge Companion to Crime Fiction
Edited by Janice Allan, Jesper Gulddal, Stewart King and Andrew Pepper

The Routledge Companion to Literature and Trauma
Edited by Hanna Meretoja and Colin Davis

The Routledge Companion to Literature and Disability
Edited by Alice Hall

The Routledge Companion to Death and Literature
Edited by Daniel K. Jernigan, Neil Murphy and W. Michelle Wang

The Routledge Companion to Australian Literature
Edited by Jessica Gildersleeve

The Routledge Companion to Jane Austen
Edited by Cheryl A. Wilson and Maria H. Frawley

For more information on this series, please visit: www.routledge.com/literature/series/RC4444

THE ROUTLEDGE COMPANION TO JANE AUSTEN

Edited by Cheryl A. Wilson and Maria H. Frawley

First published 2022
by Routledge
605 Third Avenue, New York, NY 10158

and by Routledge
2 Park Square, Milton Park, Abingdon, Oxon, OX14 4RN

Routledge is an imprint of the Taylor & Francis Group, an informa business

© 2022 selection and editorial matter, Cheryl A. Wilson and Maria H. Frawley; individual chapters, the contributors

The right of Cheryl A. Wilson and Maria H. Frawley to be identified as the authors of the editorial material, and of the authors for their individual chapters, has been asserted in accordance with sections 77 and 78 of the Copyright, Designs and Patents Act 1988.

With the exception of Chapter 42, no part of this book may be reprinted or reproduced or utilised in any form or by any electronic, mechanical, or other means, now known or hereafter invented, including photocopying and recording, or in any information storage or retrieval system, without permission in writing from the publishers.

Chapter 42 of this book is available for free in PDF format as Open Access from the individual product page at www.routledge.com. It has been made available under a Creative Commons Attribution-Non Commercial-No Derivatives 4.0 license.

Trademark notice: Product or corporate names may be trademarks or registered trademarks, and are used only for identification and explanation without intent to infringe.

Library of Congress Cataloging-in-Publication Data
A catalog record for this title has been requested

ISBN: 978-0-367-02729-2 (hbk)
ISBN: 978-1-032-01327-5 (pbk)
ISBN: 978-0-429-39815-5 (ebk)

DOI: 10.4324/9780429398155

Typeset in Bembo
by MPS Limited, Dehradun

CONTENTS

List of Figures	*x*
Notes on Contributors	*xii*
List of Abbreviations	*xx*
Introduction	1

PART I
Jane Austen's Works   **9**

1	*Northanger Abbey* and the Functions of Metafiction *Jodi L. Wyett*	11
2	*Sense and Sensibility*, Novel and Phenomenon *Peter Graham*	23
3	*Pride and Prejudice*: Not Altogether 'Light & Bright & Sparkling' *Susan J. Wolfson*	40
4	The Novelty of *Mansfield Park* *Emily Rohrbach*	58
5	Emma, a Heroine *George Justice*	65
6	The Politics of Friendship in *Persuasion* *Michael D. Lewis*	75

Contents

7   The Historical and Cultural Aspects of Jane Austen's Letters   95
    Jodi A. Devine

8   'Setting at Naught All Rules of Probable or Possible': Jane Austen's
    'Juvenilia'   106
    John C. Leffel

PART II
Historicising Austen: A Sampling   **125**

9   Touching upon Jane Austen's Politics   127
    Devoney Looser

10 'A Picture of Real Life and Manners'? Austen, Burney, and Edgeworth   133
    Linda Bree

11 Jane Austen and the Georgian Novel   145
    Elaine Bander

12 From Samplers to Shakespeare: Jane Austen's Reading   158
    Katie Halsey

13 Pedestrian Characters and Plots: *Persuasion* and *The Heart of Midlothian*   170
    Tara Ghoshal Wallace

14 From Jewelled Toothpick-Cases to Blue Nankin Boots: Austen,
    Consumerist Culture, and Narrative   180
    Laura M. White

15 'Bringing Her Business Forward': Jane Austen and Political Economy   193
    Sarah Comyn

16 Material Goods in Austen's Novels   205
    Sandie Byrne

17 Jane Austen and Music   218
    Laura Vorachek

18 'All the Egotism of an Invalid': Hypochondria as Form in Jane Austen's
    Sanditon   229
    Sarah Marsh

Contents

19 Jane Austen and the Whitewashed Past   246
    Olivia Murphy

20 They Came Before *and* After Olivia: Cats, Black Ladies and Political
    Blackness in Eighteenth-Century British Literature and Austen   259
    Lyndon J. Dominique

PART III
Critical Approaches to Austen: A Sampling   **275**

21 Hearing Voices in Austen: The Representation of Speech and Voice in the
    Novels   277
    Adela Pinch

22 Being Plotted, Being Thrown: Austen's Catch and Release   296
    William Galperin

23 Austen's Literary Time   306
    Amit Yahav

24 Austen, Masculinity, and Romanticism   318
    Sarah Ailwood

25 Jane Austen Likes Women: Self-Worth, Self-Care, and Heroic Self-
    Sacrifice   333
    Kathleen Anderson

26 'Queer Austen' and *Northanger Abbey*   342
    Susan Celia Greenfield

27 'A Perfectly Swell Romance': Jane Austen and Fred Astaire: A Case Study
    in Analogy Criticism   358
    Paula Marantz Cohen

28 Translating Jane Austen: World Literary Space and Isabelle de Montolieu's
    La Famille Elliot (1821)   368
    Rachel Canter

29 Jane Austen and the Social Sciences   379
    Wendy Jones

Contents

PART IV
Austen's Communities: A Sampling   **397**

30 *Persuasions: The Jane Austen Journal* and *Persuasions On-Line*: 'Formed for [an] Elegant and Rational Society'   399
    Susan Allen Ford

31 'It is Such a Happiness When Good People Get Together': JAS and JASNA   409
    Alice Marie Villaseñor

32 Live Austen Adaptation in the Age of Multimedia Reproduction   422
    Christopher C. Nagle

33 'You Do Not Know Her or Her Heart': Minor Character Elaboration in Contemporary Austen Spin-Off Fiction   439
    Kylie Mirmohamadi

34 Jane Goes Gaga: Austen as Celebrity and Brand   446
    Marina Cano

35 Global Jane Austen: Obstinate, Headstrong Pakistanis   468
    Laaleen Sukhera

36 Race, Class, Gender Remixed: Reimagining *Pride and Prejudice* in Communities of Colour   481
    Sigrid Michelle Anderson

37 Writing Community: Some Thoughts about Jane Austen Fanfiction   490
    Melanie Borrego

PART V
Teaching Jane Austen: A Sampling   **497**

38 Teaching Jane Austen in the Twenty-First Century   499
    Michael Gamer and Katrina O'Loughlin

39 Close Reading and Close Looking: Teaching Austen Novels and Films   509
    Martha Stoddard Holmes

40 Myth, Reality, and Global Celebrity: Teaching Jane Austen Online   523
    Gillian Dow and Kim Simpson

Contents

41 Epistemic Injustice in *Pride and Prejudice* and *Mansfield Park*; Or, What Austen Teaches Us about Mansplaining and White Privilege   535
    Tim Black and Danielle Spratt

42 Race, Privilege, and Relatability: A Practical Guide for College and Secondary Instructors   547
    Juliette Wells

43 Austen's Belief in Education: Sōseki, Nogami, and Sensibility   559
    Kimiyo Ogawa

44 Teaching Jane Austen through Public Humanities: The Jane Austen Summer Program   571
    Inger S. B. Brodey, Anne Fertig, and Sarah Schaefer Walton

Index   *586*

LIST OF FIGURES

12.1	Sampler by Ann Upton, 1725, given by Miss Agnes Fry, 1949 © Bristol Culture, by kind permission of Bristol Museums and Archives	163
12.2	The Caricature Shop. Courtesy of the Lewis Walpole Library, Yale University	165
12.3	Beauty in Search of Knowledge. Courtesy of the Lewis Walpole Library, Yale University	166
30.1	*Persuasions* No.1 1979. Photo by Kim Rushing	400
30.2	*Persuasions* No.2 1980. Photo by Kim Rushing	401
30.3	*Persuasions* No.20 1998. Photo by Kim Rushing	405
34.1	Poster of Fundraising Campaign *Reimagining Jane Austen's 'Great House'*. Courtesy of the designer Jackson Bone and Chawton House Library	448
34.2	Jane Austen Engraving in Evert A. Duyckinck's *Portrait Gallery of Eminent Men and Women of Europe and America* (1873)	449
34.3	Poster for Jane Austen Bodleian Libraries Exhibition. The Bodleian Libraries, The University of Oxford	451
34.4	Moment of Unveiling the Austen Wax Figure at The Jane Austen Centre in Bath, 2014. Photograph courtesy of ITV West Country	452
34.5	The 1796 Shakespeare Exhibition, North Wall. Part of the e-gallery *What Jane Saw*. Courtesy of Janine Barchas, creator of *What Jane Saw*	454
34.6	*Old Steine, Brighton, from the North*, 1796, by Jacob Spornberg. Watercolour painting. Courtesy of The Royal Pavilion & Museums, Brighton & Hove	455
34.7	*Walking Dress, seafront*, 1818. Hand-coloured aquatint. From Rudolph Ackermann's *The Repository of Arts, Literature, Commerce, Manufactures, Fashions and Politics*. Courtesy of the University of Sussex	456
34.8	*Bathing Machines*, 1790, Aquatint by Thomas Rowlandson, Tinted by Henry Alken. Published by Messrs Robinsons Paternoster Row. Courtesy of The Royal Pavilion & Museums, Brighton & Hove	457
34.9	Landing Page of the e-library *Reading with Jane*. Courtesy of the artist Jessica Irene Joyce	458
34.10	Austen Book Bench *Once Upon a Time in Steventon* by Sian Storey. Part of the project *Sitting with Jane*. Image courtesy of the organizers Destination Basingstoke	460

List of Figures

34.11	Austen Book Bench *A Fine Day to Sit and Look Upon Verdure* by Lynsey Brecknell and Kieron Reilly. Part of the project *Sitting with Jane*. Image courtesy of the organizers Destination Basingstoke	460
34.12	E-wall from the Fundraising Campaign *Brick by Brick*. Courtesy of Chawton House	461
34.13	Austen's Gold Ring, Set with a Turquoise Stone. Courtesy of Jane Austen's House Museum, Chawton	462
34.14	*The Darcy Look* Enacted by the Local Authorities of Alton, Hampshire, in July 2017. Photograph courtesy of Chawton House	465
44.1	Carl Rose, 'The Two Camps of Austen Devotees', *New York Times,* October 23, 1949	572
44.2	NC counties. Counties represented by JASP Teacher Scholars are shaded	579
44.3	Demographic Breakdown from JASP 2019—Race & Ethnicity	581
44.4	Demographic Breakdown from JASP 2019—Age	582

CONTRIBUTORS

Sarah Ailwood is Senior Lecturer in the School of Law at the University of Wollongong. She is the author of *Jane Austen's Men: Rewriting Masculinity in the Romantic Era* (Routledge, 2019) and the co-editor of *Katherine Mansfield and Literary Influence* (Edinburgh University Press, 2015), and has published on women's writing, gender, and Romanticism. She has wide research interests in literature, law, and humanities, and is currently working on women's life writing, sexual harassment and the #MeToo moment, and eighteenth-century women's legal memoirs.

Kathleen Anderson is the author of *Jane Austen's Women: An Introduction* (SUNY Press, 2018), and co-author of *Jane Austen's Guide to Thrift* (Berkley Books, 2013). Her numerous essays have appeared in publications as diverse as *The Huffington Post, Persuasions: The Jane Austen Journal, The Chronicle of Higher Education, Women's Studies, Christianity Today*, and *ISLE*. Anderson earned her A.B. at Harvard and her M.A. and Ph.D. at University of Iowa. Formerly Professor of English and Research Fellow in the Arts and Humanities at Palm Beach Atlantic University, she decided to leave academia to focus on her writing and other creative work.

Sigrid Michelle Anderson is the Librarian for English Language and Literature and a lecturer in American Culture at the University of Michigan. Her research focuses on race and gender in print culture and new media. She is the author of *Fictions of Dissent: Reclaiming Authority in Transatlantic Women's Writing of the Late Nineteenth Century* (2010), and her work has appeared in *Studies in the Novel, American Periodicals, Victorian Literature and Culture, Neo-Victorian Studies, College & Research Libraries,* and *portal: Libraries and the Academy*.

Elaine Bander, retired from the English Department of Dawson College (Montreal), has published many essays on Jane Austen, Frances Burney, and other late Georgian writers. Recent publications include: 'JASNA and the Academy: The Anxiety of Affiliation', in *Persuasions* 39 (2017); '"Books Universally Read and Admired": Mrs. Smith in *Northanger Abbey*', in *Persuasions* 41 (2019); 'Jane Austen's Artless Heroines: Catherine Morland and Fanny Price', in *Art and Artifact in Austen*, edited by Anna Battigelli (Newark: University of Delaware Press, 2020); and 'Reason, Romanticism, or Revolution? Jane Austen rewrites Charlotte Smith in *Catharine, or the Bower*', in *Persuasions* 42 (2020).

Contributors

Tim Black is Professor and Chair of Philosophy at California State University, Northridge. He has published widely in epistemology and in the history of philosophy, including 'Action and Luck in the Kierkegaardian Ethical Project' in the *International Philosophical Quarterly* (2018).

Melanie Borrego is a Professor of English and the Associate Dean for Undergraduate Education at Brandman University. Her interest in cultural studies began during her dissertation on the literary responses to *Uncle Tom's Cabin,* and her focus on fanfiction began not long after. She has presented on Jane Austen fan fiction (JAFF) in many venues, including the first Fan Studies Network North America Conference in Chicago.

Linda Bree has written widely on women writers of the late eighteenth and early nineteenth centuries. As Editorial Director for Literature and later Head of Humanities at Cambridge University Press she oversaw the publication of The Cambridge Edition of the Works of Jane Austen and co-edited (with Janet Todd) the *Later Manuscripts* volume (2008). She has edited *Persuasion* (1998) and co-edited (with Peter Sabor and Janet Todd) *Jane Austen's Manuscript Works* (2013) for Broadview, and her Oxford World's Classics edition of Maria Edgeworth's *Belinda* was published in 2020.

Inger S. B. Brodey is Associate Professor in English and Comparative Literature at the University of North Carolina at Chapel Hill and co-founder and director of the award-winning Jane Austen Summer Program and its offshoots, including a virtual public education arm called Jane Austen and Co. Her books, book essays, and articles are centred in literature, political philosophy, and intellectual history. She is a frequent speaker at Jane Austen events around the world and board member of the North American Friends of Chawton House.

Sandie Byrne is Associate Professor in English at the University of Oxford and a Fellow of Kellogg College, Oxford. She is the author of a number of books and articles on nineteenth- and twentieth-century writing, including *Jane Austen*, Mansfield Park and *Jane Austen's Possessions and Dispossessions: The Significance of Objects.*

Marina Cano is Associate Professor of English at Volda University College, Norway. She has also taught at the University of Limerick (Ireland), the University of St Andrews and Edinburgh Napier University (Scotland). She is the author of *Jane Austen and Performance* (Palgrave, 2017) and the co-editor of *Jane Austen and William Shakespeare: A Love Affair in Literature, Film and Performance* (Palgrave 2019). During 2013–2016, she was a researcher in the international, interdisciplinary project 'Travelling Texts 1790–1914: Transnational Reception of Women's Writing at the Fringes of Europe' (European Commission, HERA).

Rachel Canter is a Ph.D. student at George Washington University. She focuses in late eighteenth and early nineteenth-century British Literature, with a particular interest in women novelists and translation.

Paula Marantz Cohen is Distinguished Professor of English and Dean of the Pennoni Honors College at Drexel University where she is host of the TV interview show, *The Civil Discourse*. She is the author of five non-fiction books and five novels, including *Jane Austen in Boca* and two other Jane Austen updates. Her latest book, *Of Human Kindness: What Shakespeare Teaches Us About Empathy,* was recently published with Yale University Press.

Contributors

Sarah Comyn is an Assistant Professor and Ad Astra Fellow in the School of English, Drama and Film at University College Dublin. She is the author of *Political Economy and the Novel: A Literary History of "Homo Economicus"* (Palgrave, 2018) and co-author of *Early Public Libraries and Colonial Citizenship in the British Southern Hemisphere* (Palgrave, 2019: with Lara Atkin, Porscha Fermanis and Nathan Garvey).

Jodi A. Devine is a Research & Instruction Librarian at Bryant University. She has taught writing and literature classes to traditional and continuing education students at Providence College, Brown University, the University of Delaware, and Kent State University. She earned her Ph.D. from the University of Delaware, and her dissertation, 'Epistolary Revelations: Reading Letters in Nineteenth-Century British Novels', explores how fictional correspondence reflects the historical and cultural practices of letter writing, and in some cases, offers a critique of social constructions of behaviour.

Lyndon J. Dominique is Associate Professor of English and Africana Studies at Lehigh University in Pennsylvania where he specializes in eighteenth-century British literature and issues related to critical race studies, colonialism and transatlanticism, gender, and social justice. He received his B.A. with honours in Comparative American Studies from The University of Warwick in England and his Ph.D. in English from Princeton University. He is the editor of the anonymously published 1808 novel *The Woman of Colour* (2007) and the author of a monograph, *Imoinda's Shade: Marriage and the African Woman in Eighteenth-Century British Literature, 1759–1808* (2012).

Gillian Dow is an Associate Professor in the English Department at the University of Southampton. She has been associated with Chawton House since 2005, serving as Executive Director from 2014 to 2019. Gillian has published widely on Austen and her contemporaries. Edited collections include *Women's Writing, 1660–1830: Feminisms and Futures* (Palgrave, 2016), co-edited with Jennie Batchelor; *Uses of Austen: Jane's Afterlives* (Palgrave, 2012), co-edited with Clare Hanson; *Readers, Writers, Salonnières: Female Networks in Europe, 1700–1900* (Peter Lang, 2011), co-edited with Hilary Brown. She is currently writing a book on women translators in Romantic-period Britain and France.

Anne Fertig is a doctoral candidate in the Department of English and Comparative Literature at the University of North Carolina at Chapel Hill. Her research interests include the Scottish Enlightenment, women's historiography, and political sovereignty. Her publications include the book, *A Song of Glasgow Town: The Collected Poems of Marion Bernstein* (ASLS 2015). She has volunteered with the Jane Austen Summer Program for many years, and she is the founder of Jane Austen and Company, a free public humanities series that explores the experiences and writings of Jane Austen and her female contemporaries.

Susan Allen Ford has been Editor of *Persuasions* and *Persuasions On-Line* since 2006 and is an active member of JASNA. She is Professor of English Emerita at Delta State University and has published essays on Jane Austen and her contemporaries, the gothic, detective fiction, and Shakespeare. She is slowly working on a book on what Austen's characters are reading, 'Jane Austen's "Great Readers": When Characters Read Books'.

Maria Frawley is a Professor of English at The George Washington University in Washington, DC, where she teaches courses in nineteenth-century British literature. She is the author of *A Wider Range: Travel Writing by Women in Victorian England*; *Anne Brontë*; an edition of Harriet Martineau's *Life in the Sick-Room*, and *Invalidism and Identity in Nineteenth-Century Britain*, in addition to essays on

xiv

nineteenth-century women writers, including Jane Austen. She is at work on a book titled *Keywords of Jane Austen's Fiction.*

William Galperin is Distinguished Professor of English at Rutgers University. He is the author of *The Historical Austen* (2003) and, most recently, *The History of Missed Opportunities: British Romanticism and the Emergence of the Everyday* (2017), which features a discussion of *Emma, Mansfield Park,* and Austen's correspondence.

Michael Gamer is Professor of English and Comparative Literature at the University of Pennsylvania and British Academy Global Professor of English and Drama at Queen Mary University of London. His books include *Romanticism and the Gothic: Genre, Reception, and Canon Formation* (Cambridge University Press, 2000) and *Romanticism, Self-Canonization, and the Business of Poetry* (Cambridge University Press, 2017). With Angela Wright, he is General Editor of *The Cambridge Edition of the Works of Ann Radcliffe,* and is currently at work on a digital and scholarly project called *Romantic Melodrama: Feeling in Search of Form,* sponsored by the British Academy.

Peter Graham is Professor Emeritus of English at Virginia Tech. His publications on nineteenth-century British literature and culture include *Jane Austen & Charles Darwin: Naturalists and Novelists, Byron's Bulldog, Don Juan and Regency England, Articulating the Elephant Man* (with Fritz Oehlschlaeger), and *Darwin's Sciences* (with Duncan Porter).

Susan Celia Greenfield is Professor of English at Fordham University, editor of *Sacred Shelter: Thirteen Journeys of Homelessness and Healing* (2019), author of *Mothering Daughters: Novels and the Politics of Family Romance, Frances Burney to Jane Austen* (2002, 2003), and co-editor of *Inventing Maternity: Politics, Science and Literature, 1650–1865* (1999). She has also published many scholarly articles, op-eds, and short stories.

Katie Halsey is Senior Lecturer in Eighteenth-Century Literature at the University of Stirling, and Director of its Centre for Eighteenth-Century Studies. Her publications include *Jane Austen and her Readers, 1786–1945* (Anthem, 2012), and she is currently Principal Investigator of the project 'Books and Borrowing 1750–1830: An Analysis of Scottish Borrowers' Registers', funded by the Arts and Humanities Research Council.

Martha Stoddard Holmes is Professor of Literature and Writing Studies at California State University, San Marcos. A Brakebill Distinguished Professor, she teaches British literature, creative writing, and health humanities. Her publications include *Fictions of Affliction: Physical Disability in Victorian Culture* (University of Michigan Press, 2004/2009) and several co-edited works: with Joyce L. Huff, *The Cultural History of Disability in the Long Nineteenth Century* (Bloomsbury, 2020); with Diane P. Freedman, *The Teacher's Body* (SUNY Press, 2003); and special issues of *J. Medical Humanities, Literature and Medicine,* and *Nineteenth-Century Gender Studies.* She is writing and drawing a graphic narrative of ovarian cancer.

Wendy Jones is an independent scholar, psychotherapist, and English/Writing instructor who has published widely in both academic and popular venues. Her essays have appeared in *Persuasions, ELH,* and *Eighteenth-Century Fiction.* She blogs regularly for *Psychology Today* (Intersubjective: what literature tells us about our minds https://www.psychologytoday.com/us/blog/intersubjective) and has been a guest blogger on other sites. She is the author of two books, *Jane on the Brain: Exploring the Science of Social Intelligence* and *Consensual Fictions: Women, Liberalism, and the English Novel.* Her essay 'The Map of Love in *Mansfield Park*' is included in Routledge's *Jane Austen and Sciences of the Mind.*

Contributors

George Justice is Professor of English at Arizona State University. He specializes in eighteenth-century British literature, particularly writings by women. He also writes on issues of higher education. His latest book is *How to Be a Dean*, and he is currently working on an edition of Frances Burney's novel, *Camilla* (1796).

John C. Leffel is Associate Professor of English at SUNY-Cortland. He has published numerous essays and reviews on Jane Austen, Maria Edgeworth, Elizabeth Hamilton, and other Romantic-era women writers. He is currently working on several projects concerning 'speculators' and the rhetoric of 'speculation' in late-eighteenth-century British literature and popular culture.

Michael D. Lewis is an Associate Professor at Washington and Jefferson College, where he teaches English and gender and women's studies. He has published on Victorian novels and periodicals, including articles on Elizabeth Gaskell and mutiny, *Punch* and the Second Reform Act, and Charles Dickens and female homoeroticism. He's currently completing a book on democracy and violence in industrial fiction.

Devoney Looser, Regents Professor of English at Arizona State University, has authored or edited nine books—including *The Making of Jane Austen* and *The Daily Jane Austen: A Year in Quotes*—and published essays in the *Atlantic*, the *New York Times, Salon*, the *TLS*, and the *Washington Post*. As a Guggenheim Fellow and NEH Public Scholar, Looser is completing *Sister Novelists: Jane and Anna Maria Porter in the Age of Austen* for Bloomsbury.

Sarah Marsh teaches at American University in Washington, DC, where she is jointly appointed in the Department of Literature and the Department of Critical Race, Gender, and Culture Studies. Her book project, *Constituting White Supremacy*, identifies the 'ancient constitution'—an early modern English ideal of racial liberty—as a major source of white supremacy in the anglophone Atlantic.

Kylie Mirmohamadi is an adjunct Senior Research Fellow at La Trobe University, Melbourne, Australia. She has published widely in the areas of literary studies, cultural studies, and Australian history. She is the author of *The Digital Afterlives of Jane Austen: Janeites at the Keyboard* (Palgrave Pivot, 2014).

Olivia Murphy recently completed a Postdoctoral Research Fellowship at the University of Sydney, where she is now an Honorary Associate of the English Department. She is the author of *Jane Austen the Reader: The Artist as Critic* and the co-editor of *Romantic Climates: Literature and Science in an Age of Catastrophe* and *Anna Letitia Barbauld: New Perspectives*. Research for this chapter was begun while she was a Visiting Research Fellow at Chawton House Library.

Christopher C. Nagle is Associate Professor of English and Gender & Women's Studies at Western Michigan University. He is the author of *Sexuality and the Culture of Sensibility in the British Romantic Era* (Palgrave Macmillan), and essays on Cleland, Sade, and a wide range of eighteenth- and nineteenth-century women writers, including Austen, Owenson, Landon, and Cristall. He is currently working on a book-length study of affect and the intermedial life of Austen adaptation, with a focus on live performance, and has new work on Austen forthcoming in several other collections.

Kimiyo Ogawa is Professor in the Department of English Studies at Sophia University, Japan. She is currently interested in how advances in medical and physiological science informed representations of mind and human behaviour in a range of eighteenth-century novels.

Her recent publications include an edited collection (with Mika Suzuki) titled *Johnson in Japan* (Bucknell University Press, 2020), book chapters on Charlotte Lennox in *British Romanticism in European Perspective* (Eds. Steve Clark and Tristanne Connolly, Palgrave, 2015), and on Jane Austen and Yaeko Nogami in *British Romanticism in Asia* (Eds. Alex Watson and William Laurence, Palgrave, 2019).

Katrina O'Loughlin is Lecturer in English (Romantic and Nineteenth-Century Literature) at the University of Brunel London, and co-author and Vice-Chair of the four-year interdisciplinary COST Action project *People in Motion: Entangled Histories of Displacement across the Mediterranean (1492–1923)*. She has published on eighteenth- and nineteenth-century women writers; travel, displacement, encounter, and exchange; and the history of emotion, including *Women, Writing, and Travel in the Eighteenth Century* (Cambridge University Press, 2018).

Adela Pinch is Professor of English and Women's Studies at the University of Michigan. She is the author of *Strange Fits of Passion: Epistemologies of Emotion, Hume to Austen* (Stanford University Press, 1996), and *Thinking about Other People in Nineteenth-Century British Writing* (Cambridge University Press, 2010), as well as numerous articles on eighteenth- and nineteenth-century British literature and culture. She is currently completing a third monograph, *Victorian Fiction and the Location of Experience*.

Emily Rohrbach teaches English literature at Durham University. Her first book, *Modernity's Mist: British Romanticism and the Poetics of Anticipation*, was published in the Lit Z series of Fordham University Press in 2016; it includes a chapter on time in Austen's *Persuasion*. Her essay on Austen's *Emma*, 'Without You I Am Nothing: On the Counterfactual Imagination in *Emma*', was published in 2018 in the journal *Textual Practice* and is part of her second book, provisionally entitled *Codex Poetics: Romantic Books and the Politics of Reading*.

Kim Simpson is the Chawton House Postdoctoral Fellow, and lectures in eighteenth-century literature at the University of Southampton. Her research interests include seduction narratives, eighteenth-century women's writing, anonymity and the body, and she also has a keen interest in public engagement and heritage.

Danielle Spratt is an Associate Professor of English at California State University, Northridge, where she teaches eighteenth-century literature with a focus on the history of science and medicine, public and digital humanities, and social justice. With Bridget Draxler, she is the author of *Engaging the Age of Jane Austen: Public Humanities in Practice* (U of Iowa P, 2018). Her most recent work has appeared or is forthcoming in *Profession* and *British Women Satirists in the Long Eighteenth Century* (Cambridge UP). She is currently completing a manuscript on reproduction, empire, and the rise of the novel.

Laaleen Sukhera is a writer and consultant. She's the founder of the Jane Austen Society of Pakistan and has participated in panels, podcasts, and features including the BBC, NPR, *The Economist*, British Council Arts, the Galle Literary Festival, and JASNA's AGM. Laaleen curated *Austenistan*, an anthology published by Bloomsbury set among Lahore wedding parties, Karachi salons, Islamabad ballrooms, and Surrey estates. She counts an hour spent in the company of Colin Firth as 'the most enjoyable and simultaneously surreal' evening of her life and is elated to have contributed a quilt patch to a certain beloved house museum in Chawton.

Contributors

Alice Marie Villaseñor is an Associate Professor of English at Medaille College in Buffalo, NY, where she earned the Brian R. Shero Teaching Excellence and Campus Leadership Award. A Life Member of the Jane Austen Society of North America, she serves on both the JASNA International Visitor Program Committee and the JASNA Equity, Diversity, and Inclusion Committee. Previously, she was a JASNA International Visitor and a board member of JASNA and JASNA-SW. She has published on the Austen family, Austen's fiction, and Austen film adaptations, and she is currently working on a project about Victorian women's responses to Austen's work.

Laura Vorachek is Associate Professor of English at the University of Dayton and specializes in nineteenth-century British literature. She has published articles on Jane Austen and on Victorian musical culture in *Persuasions*, *The Routledge Handbook to Nineteenth-Century British Periodicals and Newspapers* (2016), *Victorian Periodicals Review*, *Victorian Literature and Culture*, *Victorians: A Journal of Culture and Literature*, and *Clio: A Journal of Literature, History, and the Philosophy of History*.

Tara Ghoshal Wallace is a Professor Emerita of English at George Washington University, specializing in eighteenth- and nineteenth-century British literature. Her books include *Jane Austen and Narrative Authority*; *Imperial Characters: Home and Periphery in Eighteenth-Century Literature*; *Women Critics, 1660–1820* (co-editor, with the Folger Collective); and Frances Burney's *A Busy Day* (editor). She has published articles on Jane Austen, Frances Burney, Elizabeth Hamilton, Samuel Johnson, Alexander Pope, Walter Scott, Tobias Smolett, and Mary Wollstonecraft. Her current project is on Walter Scott's representations of monarchy.

Sarah Schaefer Walton is a Ph.D. student at the University of North Carolina—Chapel Hill, focusing on Romantic and Victorian travel literature. She is the Associate Director of the Jane Austen Summer Program, a member of the board, Co-Director of JASP+, and Project Manager for Jane Austen's Desk. She has a B.A. in literature and creative writing and an M.A. in English with a concentration in women's and gender studies from Virginia Tech. Her research interests include fan cultures, the digital humanities, and the history of tourism.

Juliette Wells is Elizabeth Conolly Todd Distinguished Professor of English at Goucher College in Baltimore, Maryland, USA. She is the author of two histories of Austen's readers—*Reading Austen in America* (2017) and *Everybody's Jane: Austen in the Popular Imagination* (2011), both published by Bloomsbury Academic—and is working on a third, tentatively titled *Americans for Austen: Landmarks in Biography, Criticism, and Collecting*. For Penguin Classics she created 200th-anniversary annotated editions of *Persuasion* (2017) and *Emma* (2015). Most recently, her chapter 'Intimate Portraiture and the Accomplished Woman Artist in *Emma*' appeared in *Art and Artifact in Jane Austen* (2020).

Laura M. White is the John E. Weaver Professor of English at the University of Nebraska-Lincoln. She publishes widely in nineteenth-century interdisciplinary topics, and is the author of two monographs on Jane Austen and the editor of a critical edition on the same. Her latest book is on Carroll's adult satires in the Alice books, *The Alice Books and the Contested Ground of the Natural World* (Routledge, 2017). She is also the PI of the website *Austen Said: Patterns of Diction in Austen's Novels*, which allows users to track forms of narration, including free indirect narration, phrase by phrase (*austen.unl.edu*).

Cheryl A. Wilson is Professor of English and Dean of the School of Humanities & Social Sciences at Stevenson University. In 2012, she participated in the NEH Summer Seminar 'Jane Austen and Her Contemporaries' with Devoney Looser and several other *Routledge Companion* contributors. She is the author of *Literature and Dance in Nineteenth-Century Britain* (Cambridge University Press, 2009),

Fashioning the Silver Fork Novel (Pickering & Chatto, 2012), and *Jane Austen and the Victorian Heroine* (Palgrave, 2017).

Susan J. Wolfson, Professor of English at Princeton University, is a specialist in Long Romanticism. Among her many publications, the ones on Austen include the award-winning *Annotated Northanger Abbey* (Harvard University Press, 2014), 'Re: Reading *Pride and Prejudice*: "What think you of books?"' in *The Blackwell Companion to Jane Austen,* ed. Claudia L. Johnson & Clara Tuite (2009), 'Boxing Emma: the Reader's Dilemma at Box Hill', in 'Re-reading Box Hill: Reading the Practice of Reading Everyday Life', ed. William Galperin, *Romantic Circles Praxis Series* (2000), and, with Claudia L. Johnson, the Longman Cultural Edition of *Pride and Prejudice* (2003).

Jodi L. Wyett is Professor of English at Xavier University, where she teaches eighteenth-century British literature and culture, women's literature, film, and gender theory. She has published on Jane Austen, Frances Brooke, Charlotte Lennox, animal studies, and pedagogy, particularly related to the use of adaptations and multi-genre courses. She is currently working on a book about women novelists' use of the female quixote trope to address anti-novel discourse as well as a project on Frances Burney, Catholic tolerance, and human rights.

Amit Yahav is Associate Professor at the University of Minnesota, Twin Cities. She published articles on the intersections of liberalism, nationalism, and early novels and a book, *Feeling Time: Eighteenth-Century Sensibility and the Novel*, on the literary dimensions of temporal phenomenology. Her current project explores the political stakes of literary leisure in eighteenth- and nineteenth-century Britain.

LIST OF ABBREVIATIONS

E   *Emma*
MP   *Mansfield Park*
NA   *Northanger Abbey*
P   *Persuasion*
PP   *Pride and Prejudice*
SS   *Sense and Sensibility*

INTRODUCTION

Cheryl A. Wilson and Maria H. Frawley

WILSON: STEVENSON UNIVERSITY
FRAWLEY: GEORGE WASHINGTON UNIVERSITY

A 'Companion'

Scholarly collections of essays take many forms. Whether pitched as 'miscellanies' or as volumes designed to situate their subject 'in context', they share an aspiration to be wide-ranging, even while staying within the bounds prescribed (overtly or by implication) by the volume's announced focus. A 'companion' is no exception to this rule. The term has long denoted a collection of essays or entries that collectively function as a handbook, an accessible guide to the topic. Still, its more familiar meaning as simply 'a person who one spends time with, or travels with', invites additional consideration, particularly in light of Jane Austen's own writing.

When Jane Austen invokes this more common meaning of 'companion' she most frequently does so simply to signal the persons with whom a character converses, interacts, or travels. But, as is so often the case with her writing, Austen found the term a useful one for discriminating among people, for making social judgements, or for evaluating one character's utility in relation to another, as when Fanny Price early on in her time at Mansfield experiences herself as 'avowedly useful as her aunt's companion' (28) or when Catherine Morland is recognised for the 'good humour and cheerfulness' that had made her 'a valuable companion' (111) to the Allens. We learn in *Emma* that while Emma 'dearly loved her father … he was no companion for her. He could not meet her in conversation, rational or playful' (6). By contrast, the Gardiners in *Pride and Prejudice* are identified as well matched for travel with Elizabeth. As the narrator, channelling Elizabeth's thoughts, explains, 'One enjoyment was certain—that of suitableness as companions; a suitableness which comprehended health and temper to bear inconveniences—cheerfulness to enhance every pleasure—and affection and intelligence, which might supply it among themselves if there were disappointments abroad' (212-3). Readers of *Sense and Sensibility* learn of the intense value of a well chosen companion when Elinor contemplates Colonel Brandon escorting her mother from her home to [Cleveland, the home of the Palmers], where Marianne lies gravely ill: 'The comfort of such a friend at that moment as Colonel Brandon—of such a companion for her mother,—how gratefully was it felt!—a companion whose judgment would guide, whose attendance must relieve, and whose friendship might sooth her!—as far as the shock of such a summons *could* be lessened to her, his presence, his manners, his assistance, would lessen it' (235). While we cannot possibly hope that this 'companion' will be all of that for our readers (!), we do hope the essays gathered in this collection function in just the ways that Austen herself envisioned when representing suitable or ideal companions. In other words, we hope they are valuable, whether as guides to particular novels, or as representations of new ways of studying

DOI: 10.4324/9780429398155-NaN-1

Austen, or as pedagogical inspiration for those who teach Austen, or as illustrations of the multifarious ways that Austen's reach has been extended through her fandom.

Ours is not the first 'Companion' to Jane Austen, and, given how long-lived has been Jane Austen's 'moment', it will not be the last. Indeed, the varied approaches taken in previous essay collections on Austen inevitably shaped our sense of what our volume might do as well as what it need not do. Demonstrating well the myriad ways that social histories inform Austen's writing, the 2005 *Jane Austen in Context* edited by Janet Todd (Cambridge) provides useful and discrete chapters on topics such as 'Manners', 'Money', 'Dress', and 'Religion', serving as a resource for understanding her fiction and reflecting the value of reading Austen within the social and cultural contexts of her time. When Edward Copeland and Juliet McMaster compiled *The Cambridge Companion to Jane Austen* in 1997, they sought—as volume editors often do—to situate their subject within her own world as well as within contemporary critical discourse with chapters on Austen's works accompanied by chapters on topics such as class, style, and literary tradition, and closing with Claudia Johnson's masterful 'Austen's Cults and Cultures'. With the second edition in 2011, the editors aimed to include 'the new interests of the twenty-first century', including a dedicated chapter on *Lady Susan, The Watsons*, and *Sanditon* and another on film adaptations (xi). Their gesture reflects the distinctive ways that Jane Austen's writing can be made to speak to historical moments, whether understood broadly (as in 'the twenty-first century') or more narrowly (as in 'the #MeToo movement'), a topic we address in more detail below.

The *Cambridge Companion*, as well as the volume of essays collected by Janet Todd, are the tip of the iceberg in terms of Jane Austen collections that aspire to the comprehensiveness we associate with reference books. Consider, for example, the following sources: *A Jane Austen Companion: A Critical Survey and Reference Book*, by R. B. Pinion (1973); *The Jane Austen Companion*, edited by J. David Grey, A. Walton Litz, and B. C. Southam (1986); *A Companion to Jane Austen Studies*, edited by Laura C. Lambdin and Robert T. Lambdin; *A Critical Companion to Jane Austen*, by William Baker (2008); *Student Companion to Jane Austen*, by Debra Teachman (2000); *Jane Austen: A Companion*, by Josephine Ross (2003); and *Readings on Jane Austen* by Clarice Swisher (1997). The delightfully titled *The Bedside, Bathtub & Armchair Companion to Jane Austen* (edited by Carol Adams, Douglas Buchanan, and Kelly Gesch) even suggests that one need not be in a library to find oneself wanting to take recourse to a collection of this sort!

As of the publication of this volume, the Austen Cambridge *Companions* also include individual volumes dedicated to *Pride and Prejudice* (2013) and *Emma* (2015). Published to coincide with the novels' bicentenaries, the volumes include both literary and historical contexts as well as several essays each on adaptations and reception, reflecting the widening range of Jane Austen's circulation in contemporary culture, a topic this volume addresses as well. Indeed, the covers of the Cambridge Companions devoted to *Pride and Prejudice* and *Emma* feature stills from the 1990s Austen film and television boom (Jennifer Ehle and Colin Firth and Emma Thompson and Jeremy Northam, respectively).

Published in 2012, Claudia L. Johnson and Clara Tuite's *A Companion to Jane Austen* (Wiley-Blackwell) also has a section on reception and adaptation. Far more attention, however, is devoted to textual studies and book history, reflecting the influence of studies of reading and readership as well as book history by scholars such as Kathryn Sutherland, William St. Clair, Kate Flint, and others.

The continuing interest in 'companions' to Austen, like the proliferation of scholarly monographs and articles on the writer, testify to the long-standing assumptions about her centrality to the canon of British literature as well as to perceptions of her continuing 'relevance'. In his essay 'Jane Austen is Everything', written for *The Atlantic* in September of 2017, Nicholas Dames argued that her 'vision of personal flourishing' was one that 'still feels thoroughly modern'. In the few years during which we worked on compiling the essays for this volume, we witnessed new variations on

Introduction

the theme of Austen and her relevance, with ideals of 'personal flourishing' often replaced by realities of oppression and struggle as foci of consideration. #MeToo became a viral hashtag shortly after revelations of sexual abuse by Harvey Weinstein came to light, and op-eds written with headlines such as 'Jane Austen: A role model for the #MeToo generation' followed in short order. In fact, Paula Marantz Cohen, a contributor to this volume, wrote a widely read piece titled 'What Jane Austen Can Teach Us About Sexual Harassment' for the *Wall Street Journal* (January 2018). Even more recently, the COVID-19 pandemic spawned its fair share of commentary reflecting on the ways Austen's fiction purportedly prepares one for the radically altered lifestyles brought on by the pandemic. To cite just a few examples, in 'Sense and social distancing', written for *The Guardian* in late April of 2020, Josephine Tovey wrote that 'lockdown has given me a newfound affinity with Jane Austen's heroines'. Similarly, writing for *Marie Claire* in May 2020, Jessica M. Goldstein warned readers that 'the single life under COVID-19 is eerily Jane Austen-esque'.

If these (and dozens of similar) articles suggest a propensity to find Austen immediately adaptable to and useful for any given moment in a cultural conversation, other recent work has profitably sought to unsettle and complicate the assumptions we bring to Jane Austen. An essay titled 'On Reading and Teaching, but Not Loving, Jane Austen' written for *The Atlantic* (2017) by Patricia A. Matthew, brings much-needed attention to the numerous ways that Austen's fame, as well as a narrowly conceived canon of Romantic-era literature, converge to obscure important works written by her contemporaries. These are writings that represent, for example, interracial marriage and the experiences of biracial women and that grapple with debates about transatlantic slavery and abolition. They are, to use Matthew's words, 'stories [that] show the fuller range of British culture in the 1800s'. Raising questions about race and representation here and elsewhere, Matthew and other scholars of the period have encouraged us to reframe the way we situate Austen within her own era, and many have begun this work, as evidenced in 'The Battle Over Jane Austen's Whiteness: Past Meets Present', an article by Jasmin Malik Chua featured in February 2020 in *The Daily Beast*. Work by Olivia Murphy, Juliette Wells, Lyndon Dominique, Sigrid Michelle Anderson, and Tim Black and Danielle Spratt in our volume demonstrates well the earnest engagement of Austen scholars and teachers in taking up this crucial conversation.

Design and Scope

As anyone who has curated a volume of essays aspiring in some way toward comprehensiveness knows, gaps in coverage are inevitable. Early on in the planning for *A Companion to Jane Austen,* we realised that we would likely *not* allocate space to an essay focused on Jane Austen's biography. Readers and critics alike have engaged with Jane Austen's biography since her brother Henry published the posthumous 'Biographical Notice' alongside *Northanger Abbey* and *Persuasion* in 1818. Austen biography has ranged widely over the past 200-plus years, despite the relative dearth of primary source materials. As the *Companion* was evolving, we noted interesting biographical threads emerging. Austen's reading practices and her access to different texts are discussed in essays by Katie Halsey, Elaine Bander, and Linda Bree, for example. Devoney Looser illuminates Austen's mid-Victorian reception through the lens of the political beliefs assigned to her by some of her early biographers. Access to Austen's letters, too, has been shaped by editors and biographers, as Jodi A. Devine demonstrates, and the letters, revealing so much of what Devine calls 'the process of [Austen's] life' continue to serve as valuable source material for readers and critics. Finally, Austen's biography is a continuing source of inspiration for the adaptations, reimaginings, and fan fiction discussed in the 'Austen's Communities' section of the volume.

These threads demonstrate the profound debt of contemporary scholars to the work of Austen biographers. From early works by Victorian critics and family members, to John Halperin's *The Life of Jane Austen (1984),* Park Honan's *Jane Austen: Her Life* (1987), Jan Fergus's *Jane Austen: A Literary*

Life (1991), Claire Tomalin's *Jane Austen: A Life* (1997) and more recent biographies or biographically-focused studies, including Emily Auerbach's *Searching for Jane Austen* (2004), Paula Byrne's *The Real Jane Austen: A Life in Small Things* (2014), and Helena Kelly's *Jane Austen, the Secret Radical* (2017), these sometimes-controversial works demonstrate that interest in the author's life is not waning. Extensive biographical work on the Austen family has also been undertaken by scholars, most notably by Deirdre LeFaye in her extensive annotations to what has become the authoritative edition of *Jane Austen's Letters* (4th edition 2014) as well as *Jane Austen: a Family Record* (2003), and *A Chronology of Jane Austen and Her Family 1600–2000* (2013). In short, the wealth of excellent, accessible research on Austen's biography led us to conclude that the best way to represent that work in the *Companion* was via scholarship that engages biographical elements and that builds on this strong foundation of seminal and recent scholarship.

In planning for *The Routledge Companion*, we issued deliberately broad invitations to potential contributors whose work on Austen we knew and admired as well as to emerging scholars we were just beginning to 'meet' or who had been recommended by colleagues in the field. Rather than be overly-prescriptive, we encouraged them to suggest approaches to Austen that engaged with earlier foundational work but that simultaneously illuminated emerging interests and new directions in the field of Jane Austen Studies. Revealing trends emerged in the essays we received in response, in some cases demonstrating the solidification of certain ways of historicising Austen (as for example around colonialism and imperialism in her time period) and in other cases revealing new focuses (as for example in the currently robust attention to *Sanditon*). No matter what their chosen topics or approaches, the majority of our contributors have multiple Austen identities: we are teachers, scholars (both affiliated and independent), and members of Austen communities. Engagement with students, other researchers, Austen fans, and members of creative communities inspired by Austen surely impacts the ways in which we view Austen and the elements of her writings that we are drawn to explore. In deference to our multiple identities and commitments, we encouraged our contributors to use their own writerly styles and allowed them to use the edition of Austen's work that best served the purpose of the essay. We are also fortunate to have several editors of Austen editions among our contributors: Linda Bree (*Later Manuscripts*, Cambridge; *Jane Austen's Manuscript Works*, Broadview), Sandie Byrne (*Mansfield Park*, Macmillan) George Justice (*Emma*, Norton), Devoney Looser (*Sense and Sensibility*, Penguin Classics), Juliette Wells (*Emma, Persuasion*, Penguin Classics), and Susan J. Wolfson (*Northanger Abbey: An Annotated Edition*, Harvard UP; *Pride and Prejudice*, Longman).

The Routledge Companion to Jane Austen is divided into five sections: Jane Austen's Works; Historicising Austen: A Sampling; Critical Approaches to Austen: A Sampling; Austen's Communities: A Sampling; and Teaching Jane Austen: A Sampling. Although divisions inevitably create challenges of overlap, we believe the organisation will benefit a wide range of readers. As such, we have included the designator 'a sampling' to remind readers that comprehensive coverage is beyond the scope of a single volume as well as to encourage readerly sampling, moving among the essays and sections in a non-linear order to experience—to 'sample'—the variety of approaches to and understandings of Austen.

For those approaching this *Companion* with interest in learning more about a single work, we begin with single-focus essays on each of the six completed novels, the juvenilia, and the letters. These essays are designed in different ways to offer readers a point of entry into the critical conversations around each text while also reflecting ways the author's own interpretation of the novel draws on and pushes forward the critical tradition. Jodi L. Wyett approaches the metafictional manoeuvres of *Northanger Abbey* by looking at the novel's engagement with the eighteenth-century literary traditions of satire, sentiment, and the gothic. With *Sense and Sensibility*, Peter Graham considers the novel in its original context as well as in its contemporary iterations and adaptations to uncover how it has engaged, and continues to engage, new and returning readers. In her essay on *Pride and Prejudice*, Susan J. Wolfson 'uses a hybrid method: reading the literary manifestations of the

Introduction

material data-field, and reading material manifestations for literary, not just circumstantial, significance. Nobody escapes the contours, including the narrator, whose opening lob, for all its crafty wit, arcs into sober material conclusions'. Emily Rohrbach's essay on *Mansfield Park* considers how Austen's reader—perhaps fresh from reading *Pride and Prejudice*—must, like Fanny Price herself, become 'reconcile[d] … to the novelty of Mansfield Park'. *Emma*, in the hands of George Justice, is situated in its eighteenth-century context as a novel that in both subject and form explores ideas of heroism and how 'the word "heroine" is charged in the literature of the period as well as in Jane Austen's own oeuvre'. And, Michael D. Lewis' reading of *Persuasion* looks at the bonds of female friendship and Austen's exploration of these relationships throughout the text. This section also includes Jodi A. Devine's essay on the history and fortune of Jane Austen's letters and the various uses to which they have been put by contemporary scholars. Finally, John C. Leffel's essay on the juvenilia concludes the *Companion*'s opening section with an exploration of moments of transgression in these early works.

The next section 'Historicising Austen: A Sampling' includes twelve essays that foreground a range of ways that historical perspectives illuminate Austen's writing. While the act of historicising Austen is not new, the ways in which we historicise her and the historical moments and topics that capture the attention of scholars are constantly evolving. For contributions to this section, we encouraged authors to do a 'deep dive' into topics that situate Austen in her world (whether social, literary, commercial, cultural) and, in doing so, model for our student readers the function and importance of this form of scholarship.

Beginning with an analysis that is both topical and evergreen in its content and approach, Devoney Looser 'touches upon' Jane Austen's politics, with particular attention to the ways in which Austen's life and writings were shaped by critical and biographical works in the middle of the nineteenth century. Linda Bree, Elaine Bander, Katie Halsey, and Tara Goshal Wallace all put Austen in the context of her literary contemporaries. Bree's essay looks at the distinct influences of Maria Edgeworth and Frances Burney on Austen's writings, and Bander looks at Austen as a discriminating reader of eighteenth-century texts and the ways in which these texts manifest in Austen's own work. Calling Austen a 'magpie reader', Katie Halsey, too, looks at Austen's reading, focusing on the impact of 'material now considered ephemeral or unimportant' on her writing. Tara Goshal Wallace reads acts of female pedestrianism in Austen's *Persuasion* alongside Walter Scott's 1818 novel *The Heart of Midlothian*. Scholars' attention to the commercial world of Austen and her characters was an interesting theme that emerged in this volume's creation. Laura M. White explores the parallel worlds of commercial and marriage markets in working through some of Austen's scenes of shopping and consumerism in the novels. Sarah Comyn's essay considers 'the changing political economic context Austen was writing' and 'how Austen's novels implicitly engage with and critique the relationship between economic and moral values'. Sandie Byrne, too, examines the interplay of economics and morality with specific attention to ideas of property and the legal status of women at the end of the eighteenth century. Additional cultural and historical lenses are deployed in Laura Voracheck's essay on music and women's musical instruction during the period and Sarah Marsh's investigation of hypochondria and how it informs Austen's final unfinished novel, *Sanditon*. The section concludes with two essays on race in Austen. Olivia Murphy analyses how Austen's world 'has for many people come to be a kind of shorthand for an all-white England of conservative values and decorous feminine behaviour' and how contemporary re-imaginings of the period are working to counteract this narrative. And, Lyndon Dominique, too, looks at Austen's world in his essay on 'political blackness' in the literature of the period.

The sampling of essays in the section on Critical Approaches to Austen is also designed to serve as a model for scholarly work in a range of areas. To a certain extent, the essays in this section reflect the ways in which critical trends have moved away from single-application readings (for example, a feminist reading of *Emma*) to more integrated and nuanced analyses. The essays in this section undertake complex readings of Austen's style and form as informed by a range of critical and theoretical perspectives and put forth innovative approaches to Austen's texts and textuality. Adela Pinch, for instance, 'assesses the significance of the astonishing diversity of Austen's methods for representing speech and voice' as an important contribution to the development of the novel. William Galperin dives into Austen's plot structures in his essay, 'Being Plotted, Being Thrown: Austen's Catch and Release', observing, 'For the moment it is worth noting that virtually everything that Austen felt about plot, if only on the evidence of her earliest readers, is embedded in her most famous sentence at the beginning of her most beloved novel'. And, Amit Yahav scrutinises Austen's engagement with time and temporality, particularly as it applies to leisure and reading. Not surprisingly, many scholars continue to find productive ways to study Austen through the lens of gender ideology. Sarah Ailwood looks at Austen's men and Romantic conceptions of masculinity, with particular attention to *Pride and Prejudice* and *Persuasion*. Kathleen Anderson's essay considers Austen's heroines and their construction as complex, self-realised women. 'Queer Austen' is the topic of Susan Celia Greenfield's essay, which offers both an overview of this critical lens and a close reading of *Northanger Abbey* that considers the 'queerness of the heroine's gothic obsessions'. Interdisciplinary approaches, too, continue to offer much to Austen studies, and this section offers several examples of this kind of work. Jane Austen's affinities with Fred Astaire are the subject of Paula Marantz Cohen's essay on 'analogy criticism', in which she explores 'the relationship between and among works as they operate within postmodern culture'. Rachel Canter looks at a different kind of analogy in her close analysis of the work of one of Austen's early translators, Isabelle de Montolieu, and her 1821 French translation of *Persuasion*. Concluding this section, Wendy Jones approaches both Austen as a writer and her works themselves from the perspective of the social sciences, specifically from psychology and cognitive literary criticism.

Recognising that twenty-first-century Austen has expanded beyond film and television adaptations, as well as the ways that Austen societies have cultivated a shared understanding of Jane Austen, we allocated space for a section on 'Austen's Communities'. where we could showcase studies of forums for Austen readers and scholars, as well as spin-off fiction, live theatre, Austen societies, global reactions, and young adult fiction. The Jane Austen Society (UK) and Jane Austen Society of North America (JASNA) are the focus of Alice Marie Villaseñor's essay on the development and activity of these foundational and influential organisations, as well as the way in which members engage with Jane Austen, her works, and one another. In a revealing bit of data, she reports that links to eleven other societies, spread across the globe, can be found on JASNA's home page, 'with more being formed all the time'. JASNA's publications, *Persuasions* and *Persuasions On-line* are the subject of the essay by *Persuasions* editor Susan Allen Ford, which reveals how 'what was imagined for both JASNA and its journal was oxymoronic: sportive thought or serious fun'. Additional essays in this section are rich with the seeds of new and emerging scholarly pursuits. For instance, Marina Cano delves into Austen's celebrity, taking readers through a rich array of exhibitions and events (online and in-person). She finds that 'the instability and ephemeral quality of some of these spaces and events—either made of pixels or with a short life-span—add to the anarchic and unpredictable quality' of what she calls 'Gaga Austen'. The simultaneous engagement by both fans and scholars with these varied projects—what Melanie Borrego refers to as the 'porous boundaries' between scholar and fan in her study of fanfiction communities—is a theme throughout the essays in this section. The ways in which Austen's novels, and the phenomenon that is 'Jane Austen', create community is another commonality addressed by several of our authors. Journalist Laaleen Sukhera brings together the voices and 'variegated perspectives' of Pakistani readers of Austen and members of the Jane Austen Society of Pakistan in recounting the creation of and response to her 2017 book *Austenistan*.

While the phrase 'Austen adaptation' was, for some time, synonymous with Colin Firth in a wet shirt, the scope has significantly expanded since 1995, fuelled by what Rachel Brownstein in *Why*

Jane Austen? memorably referred to as 'Jane-o-mania' and what Marina Cano dubs 'Gaga Austen'. Austen's minor characters, Kylie Mirmohamadi explains, offer rich source material for contemporary authors. Arguing that 'contemporary, cultural, literary, and market trends' shape 'the ever changing parameters of fan activity', her essay invites readers to consider the many reimaginings of Mary Bennet. Such reimaginings often offer opportunities to foreground social and political inequalities, as Sigrid Michelle Anderson demonstrates in her discussion of recent novels that set *Pride and Prejudice* in communities of colour. Anderson situates this work within 'a larger cultural conversation about making space for writers of colour, representation, and cultural capital'. Theatre Studies informs Chris Nagle's essay on 'live' Austen, which makes the case that 'more people than ever will encounter [Austen's] work first in an adapted form' and examines some of the scripted and improvisational theatre pieces that have been inspired by Austen and her works.

These new directions also yield new audiences for Jane Austen's works and, we hope, new students in courses devoted exclusively to Jane Austen or those incorporating Austen alongside other topics of study. From the beginning stages of planning for this *Companion*, we were committed to including a section on teaching Austen, particularly as doing so enabled us to demonstrate the many ways that critical and historical scholarship and emerging areas of study directly inform classroom practice. One theme that emerged in the essays on Austen and Pedagogy was the decentralisation of the instructor and of Jane Austen herself in favour of a focus on the students—what they bring to the conversation and what they need. Whether they are studying as part of a college curriculum, electing to spend part of their summer at Jane Austen Camp, or part of a global community of online learners, the students of Austen are a vibrant and diverse group, and their experiences and contributions, along with those of their instructors, are reflected in this section.

Martha Stoddard Holmes reminds us that we are learners as well as teachers in discussing the evolution of her course on Austen and Film. Her chapter evidences the value of using film adaptations to provide 'pathways' for 'reluctant readers' and presents a compelling case for appreciating how teaching the 'visual, verbal, and auditory grammar of a filmed scene leads us back to the page'. Writing about their experiences developing and teaching a Massive Open Online Course (MOOC) devoted to Austen and offered for free on the Future Learn platform, Gillian Dow and Kim Simpson reveal a similar keen concern with teaching Austen in 'an academic age of public outreach' and using available tools to challenge persistent myths about Austen, in their case by going back to source materials with their students. Tim Black and Danielle Spratt share the fascinating experience of teaching Austen to and with first generation students of colour at Cal State, Northridge, where they explore ways that Austen's works, especially *Pride and Prejudice* and *Mansfield Park*, attend to forms of injustice; their pedagogical approach and innovate assignments (such as a podcast series) demonstrate the value of authorising students to direct the learning process. Their inclusive stance resonates well with that taken by Juliette Wells, who in her wonderfully useful 'guide' for teachers of Austen emphasises the need to welcome 'the entire continuum of [her students'] reactions to Austen's novels: from confusion to hostility, to unabashed fandom and professions of "relatability"'. Michael Gamer and Katrina O'Loughlin, too, acknowledge the opportunities that emerge when instructors are willing to reframe and expand our approaches. Like the other teachers of Austen featured in this section of the companion, they advocate a foregrounding of differences in readers and a recognition of 'the power of analogical thinking to create points of entry and overlap'. In developing their summer programme devoted to Austen, Inger Brody, Anne Fertig, and Sarah Schaefer Walton came to a similar conclusion, finding that Austen's seeming 'omnipresence' and her 'cultural capital' could be experienced as 'strengths rather than liabilities' for a 'public humanities enterprise'.

If essays within sections of the companion speak to one another, so too is there generative overlap across the boundaries suggested by subdivisions within our Table of Contents.

Indeed, one of the most delightful aspects of working with contributors and reading their essays-in-progress was the discovery of unanticipated connections that emerged across their work. The reception by international audiences, outside the United Kingdom and Unied States, for instance, connects Kimiyo Ogawa's essay on teaching, Laaleen Sukhera's on journalism, and Rachel Canter's on French translation. Matters of textuality and Austen's style, too, are taken up by authors discussing a range of topics from plotting (Galperin), to voice (Pinch), to invalidism (Marsh). Scholarly interest in the history of reading inflects and creates productive interconnections between the essays by Amit Yahiv (on reading and 'entertainment purposes' in his study of Austen and literary time), Katie Halsey (on how Austen's reading shaped her creative practice), and Adela Pinch (on the 'concerns of elocutionists' and the representation of voice as central to Austen's vision of the novel). Gender studies has long been central to Austen studies and is represented in this companion by essays on Romantic masculinity (Sarah Ailwood), queering *Northanger Abbey* (Susan Greenfield), female friendship (Michael Lewis), and the art of the heroine (George Justice, Sigrid Anderson, Kathleen Anderson). Working in and engaging with the tradition of foundational feminist scholarship, such as Gilbert and Gubar's *The Madwoman in the Attic,* these essays demonstrate why such analyses continue to offer rich sources for critical study.

In the end, though, attempts to map the network of ideas connecting individual essays within this companion prove impossible, perhaps because 'Jane Austen' as a field of study is so heterogeneous and fluid. The adjective 'kaleidoscopic' works well to convey the potential interconnections between the chapters in this volume as well as the ever-shifting terrain of Jane Austen Studies more generally. As our volume takes its place in a genealogy of 'companions' and 'collections' devoted to Jane Austen, our greatest hope is that the next generation of scholars, students, and general readers will find new questions to ask and new directions to take, ensuring that future scholarship will be as robust and generative as all that we have benefited from.

Works Cited

Austen, Jane. *Emma,* edited by James Kinsley. With an Introduction and Notes by Adela Pinch. Oxford UP, 2008.

Austen, Jane. *Mansfield Park,* edited by James Kinsley. With an Introduction and Notes by Jane Stabler. Oxford UP, 2008.

Austen, Jane. *Northanger Abbey, Lady Susan, the Watsons, Sanditon,* edited by James Kinsley and John David. With an Introduction and Notes by Claudia L. Johnson. Oxford UP, 2008.

Austen, Jane. *Pride and Prejudice,* edited by James Kinsley. New Introduction by Isobel Armstrong, Oxford UP, 1990.

Austen, Jane. *Sense and Sensibility,* edited by James Kinsley. With an Introduction by Margaret Anne Doody and Notes by Claire Lamont. Oxford UP, 2008.

Brownstein, Rachel. *Why Jane Austen?* Columbia UP, 2011.

Chua, Jasmin Malik. 'The Battle over Jane Austen's Whiteness: Past Meets Present.' *The Daily Beast,* 22 Feb. 2020.

Cohen, Paul Marantz. 'What Jane Austen Can Teach Us About Sexual Harassment.' *Wall Street Journal,* 1 Jan. 2018.

Dames, Nicholas. 'Jane Austen is Everything.' *The Atlantic,* vol. 320.2, Sept. 2017, pp. 92–103.

Edward, Copeland, and Juliet McMaster, editors. *The Cambridge Companion to Jane Austen.* Cambridge UP, 1997.

Goldstein, Jessica M. 'Sense and Social Distancing.' *Marie Claire,* 29 May 2020.

Matthew, Patricia A. 'On Teaching, but not Loving, Jane Austen.' *The Atlantic,* 23 Jul. 2017.

Tovey. Josephine. 'Sense and Social Distancing: "Lockdown Has Given Me a Newfound Affinity with Jane Austen's Heroines."' *The Guardian,* 29 Apr. 2020.

PART I

Jane Austen's Works

1

NORTHANGER ABBEY AND THE FUNCTIONS OF METAFICTION

Jodi L. Wyett

XAVIER UNIVERSITY

Northanger Abbey, first sold (in 1803 to Richard Crosby, who never published it) and last published (bound with *Persuasion* and Henry Austen's treacly biographical sketch of his sister as a pious, unambitious spinster), may well be the black sheep of the Austen novel family. It not only proves most likely of the six novels to be cut from the syllabi of Austen-dedicated university seminars, but also suffers from some denigrating critical commonplaces: an early, immature work that Austen never had the chance to fully revise; a near-burlesque of the fashionable Gothic fiction of the 1790s; a disjointed text that suffers from the fits and starts of its composition. Even Susan Wolfson, the editor of the lovingly prepared Belknap Press annotated edition of the novel, calls it 'an odd repository of strange, uneven power' (10). Some of the ambivalence about *Northanger Abbey* seems to stem from Austen's own testimony in a letter penned to her niece, Fanny Knight, just months before her death that, 'Miss Catherine is put upon the Shelve for present, and I do not know that she will ever come out' (348). Yet even while she had shelved *Northanger Abbey*, its bookish content tugged at Jane Austen till the last. The unfinished novel manuscript, 'Sanditon', shares more themes, settings, and character types with *Northanger Abbey* than any of the previously published works: a resort town, a heroine on the move, quixotic characters, fashionable obsessions, the power of books. Indeed, *Northanger Abbey* serves as synecdoche for the state of the novel at the turn of the nineteenth century. The parodic and metafictional qualities that initially marked the novel for dismissal for some readers are the same that reveal a rich, complex network of meaning inflected by gender and influenced by eighteenth-century satirical, Gothic, and sentimental writing. At the same time, the novel's interplay between past and present portends the nineteenth-century novel's obsession with history. Consequently, *Northanger Abbey* gives us insight not only into Austen's understanding of and position in the long eighteenth-century novel marketplace, but also into her work's enduring appeal. This chapter will consider the early publication history of *Northanger Abbey*, survey its critical reception, and then build upon that critical tradition to explore how the novel's metafictionality operates. The critical history of oppositional readings of all of Austen's famously slippery works manifests in *Northanger Abbey*'s dizzying paradoxes that course with the magic of the entire Austen oeuvre: traditional and progressive politics, pious and impertinent morality, comfortably conventional and breathtakingly original narrative form.

From 'Susan' to *Northanger Abbey*: Composition, Publication, and Early Reception

The composition and publishing history of *Northanger Abbey* spans the whole of Austen's professional career. Cassandra Austen's notes on her sister's work indicate that the manuscript, initially called

DOI: 10.4324/9780429398155-1-3

'Susan', was drafted between 1798 and 1799.[1] References within the novel suggest Austen made revisions after the family's move to Bath in 1801, upon her father's retirement from his position as rector of Steventon. In 1803, 'Susan' was sold to London publisher Crosby and Co. by then-banker Henry Austen's lawyer. The book was advertised but never appeared. It was not until 1809, four years after her father's death and just months before settling with her mother and sister at the Chawton cottage offered by her brother, Edward Austen Knight, that Austen would write to Crosby and Co. using the pen name 'Mrs. Ashton Dennis', abbreviated with recognisable Austenian acidity as M.A.D., to inquire after their intentions to publish. Austen's parry to send another copy of the manuscript to a different publisher was met by the counter thrust of legal action with the caveat that she could buy back her work for the original £10 selling price. Presumably unable to pay the sum, Austen's negotiation died there.[2] Only after revising her other early epistolary works, 'Elinor and Marianne' and 'First Impressions', published as *Sense and Sensibility* (1811) and *Pride and Prejudice* (1813) respectively, and then composing and publishing both *Mansfield Park* (1814) and *Emma* (1815), would Austen return to the 'Susan' manuscript. Henry bought back the copyright in 1816 and, according to the 1870 *Memoir of Jane Austen* published by Austen's nephew, James Edward Austen-Leigh, purportedly exulted in the post-deal revelation that the publisher had failed to bring out an early work by the author of *Pride and Prejudice* (30). Narelle Shaw argues for a substantial revision of the novel upon its reacquisition in 1816 on the basis of Austen's use of free indirect discourse. Austen also changed her heroine's name in light of another recently advertised novel called *Susan* and wrote a prefatory advertisement explaining why the text might seem somewhat dated given changes in 'places, manners, books, and opinions' in the years that it had languished at a bookseller who inexplicably never brought it out (11). She clearly intended to seek out publication again.

But Jane Austen was unable to bring 'Catherine' off the shelf. She died in July 1817 at the age of 41. Rechristened *Northanger Abbey* by either Henry or Cassandra, the novel was published posthumously by John Murray in December of 1817, with an 1818 date stamp on the title page. The volume that included *Persuasion* and Henry Austen's 'Biographical Notice of the Author' was reviewed favourably by three periodicals in 1818. *The British Critic* ranked *Northanger Abbey* not only above *Persuasion* but also as 'one of the very best of Miss Austen's productions' (301). *The Gentleman's Magazine*, perhaps following from the *British Critic,* also gave preference to *Northanger Abbey* over *Persuasion,* both for its story and its moral. The May 1818 *Edinburgh Magazine and Literary Miscellany* piece focused on Austen's life as characterised by Henry's biographical notice. Praising Austen's works in general for their firm footing in the realistic and quotidian when many literary productions were embracing the tumult of the times, the *Edinburgh Magazine* ultimately offered no specific commentary on *Northanger Abbey* or *Persuasion* beyond 'The first is the more lively, and the second the more pathetic'; 'as stories', we are told, 'they are nothing in themselves' (454). Nevertheless, the reviewer presciently predicts that when reading tastes change, Austen 'will be one of the most popular of English novelists' (454).

While Austen's reputation as one of the most popular of English novelists did grow steadily throughout the nineteenth century, *Northanger Abbey's* fortunes seemed to have declined, particularly after the publication of James Edward Austen-Leigh's *Memoir*. In 1821, The Rev. Richard Whately, writing anonymously for the *Quarterly Review*, proclaimed that though novels generally had improved of late, particularly in terms of possessing greater realism and 'more solid sense', *Northanger Abbey* was 'decidedly inferior to [Austen's] other works' (352, 367). G.H. Lewes shot back in 1859 with a defense of 'the charming novel', *Northanger Abbey,* as 'written with unflagging vivacity' and 'two characters no one else could have equalled—Henry Tilney and John Thorpe' (100). By 1870, as Barbara M. Benedict and Deirdre Le Faye note in their introduction to the Cambridge edition of *Northanger Abbey,* Austen-Leigh propagated a notion that his aunt preferred poetry to most novels, 'thus once again marginalising *Northanger Abbey* and indeed linking it with her teenage writings' as well as giving rise to the critical commonplace yoking Austen's pioneering of a new form of moral fiction to her purported dismissal of the popular novels of her day (xlvi).

Complicating *Northanger Abbey*: Modern Critical Reception

The twentieth-century turn toward sustained scholarly treatment of Austen's work is generally credited with the release of R.W. Chapman's Oxford University Press editions in the 1920s and 30s, yet Rebecca West's 1932 preface to *Northanger Abbey* may well be considered the first serious feminist treatment of the novel. West redeems *Northanger Abbey* for its merits as the vehicle of Austen's conscious critique of a society whose literature hoodwinked women into believing they were all-powerful when, in reality, they were largely valued as objects with exchange value, just as General Tilney treats Catherine Morland, not as intelligent subjects. Consequently, Isabella Thorpe's coquetry reflects back upon her society's skewed values that offer women no means of independence from the marriage market.

West's interpretation was relatively singular; much mid-twentieth-century criticism took up the question of the purported disjunction between the first (realistic) and second (parodic) volumes of the novel, a persistent critical concern that contributes to the characterisation of *Northanger Abbey* as a transitional text between the juvenilia and the 'mature' fiction as first suggested by Austen-Leigh. Frank Kearful begins his analysis with the proclamation that 'The most important—and most interesting—critical problem concerning *Northanger Abbey* is the question of its aesthetic unity' (511). Ultimately, Kearful concludes that the novel's 'disunity' is in fact its structure and purpose: parodic and realistic elements paradoxically work together to challenge readers' ideas about reality and 'overly facile distinctions between illusions and delusions' (520–21, 527). In 'Regulated Hatred: An Aspect of the Work of Jane Austen,' D.W. Harding argues that the only thin thread holding the two volumes together is Catherine exchanging John and Isabella Thorpe for Henry and Eleanor Tilney (138). Harding's enduring argument that all of Austen's work is marked by her irrepressible disdain for her society begins with Henry Tilney's 'paranoid' and 'bitter' turn of phrase characterizing the improbability of Catherine's suspicion that his father is a murderer because in England, 'every man is surrounded by a neighbourhood of voluntary spies' (7–8). In his extended analysis of *Northanger Abbey,* Harding posits that Catherine's recovery from Gothic reverie is significantly less important than her recognition of Isabella's true motives and (lack of) character, marking her psychological growth rather than social promotion. In *Jane Austen: A Study of Her Artistic Development*, A. Walton Litz, arguing that *Northanger Abbey* is Austen's earliest work, describes its two volumes as 'detachable units' (59). Litz cites Henry Tilney's shifting roles between ambiguous hero and Austen's authorial proxy as indicative of the novel's lack of narrative sophistication and cohesion. Thematically, though, Litz acknowledges the novel's complexity, as Catherine learns to regulate her uncontrolled sympathetic imagination and, subsequently, to read not only the Gothic novel but also the illusions of security that abound in her reality.

While more recent scholarship on *Northanger Abbey* at times trades in these old-saw diminutions of the novel based on form and function, it largely moves beyond to offer a remarkable breadth of insight into topics as diverse as Austen's politics and uses of history, the Gothic, reading, and the novel genre itself as well as gender. The latter has become a key focus of critical attention to the novel from feminist readings in defense of women's writing to considerations of Catherine Morland and Henry Tilney as perhaps Austen's most manifestly queer couple, at turns insipid and/or wise (Catherine) and pedantic and/or charming (Henry).

The questions of style that dominated mid-twentieth-century scholarship on *Northanger Abbey* persist. Lloyd Brown's *Bits of Ivory: Narrative Techniques in Austen's Fiction* focuses on Austen's use of language with particular attention to Henry Tilney's preoccupation with the changing usage of the word 'nice' during the walk round Beechen Cliff while Cynthia Wall connects psychological complexity to punctuation, specifically Austen's use of dashes. Building on B.C. Southam's foundational contention that *Northanger Abbey* was Austen's first extensive use of direct rather than epistolary narration, William Galperin's treatment of *Northanger Abbey* argues for the novel's 'completeness' and 'stability' as opposed to *Sense and Sensibility* and *Pride and Prejudice*, both of which underwent wholesale revision from their original epistolary formats (138). The use of free indirect discourse in the novel, he argues, both signals a stylistic improvement and a failure of narrative omniscience that accounts for the novel's 'unevenness of tone' (139).

Austen's parody of Gothic fiction is another significant locus of critical attention to *Northanger Abbey's* style. George Levine argues for the form of *Northanger Abbey* not as a crude precursor to better things to come, but instead as the 'essential form of most of the major novels' (337). Parody, Levine contends, is central to the process whereby a protagonist learns to accept quotidian reality as unlike fantasy. Tara Ghoshal Wallace considers Austen's use of parody to conclude that Austen 'mocks and undermines her own chosen method—parodic discourse—so that both narrative and reader are kept off-balance' (262). The resulting narrative instability forces the reader both to participate in and battle with the narrator for control of meaning in the text. Bharat Tandon suggests that *Northanger Abbey* deploys convention and surprise at turns, parodying then transposing Gothic form, scattering double ironies everywhere, and generally refusing to do what readers expect, thereby enabling Austen's trenchant critique of her society and opening up possibilities rather than closing them down.

Even while *Northanger Abbey*'s parody of the Gothic novel and its second volume setting have often been considered heavy-handed burlesque out of sync with the first volume, Austen's uses of the Gothic have long fascinated critics. Benedict and Le Faye go so far as to argue that interest in *Northanger Abbey*'s parody has memorialized the Gothic novel of Austen's time (lix). While Marvin Mudrick contends that the novel's characters function rigidly as anti-types of recurring figures in Gothic novels (with the partial exception of Henry Tilney), Tony Tanner holds that during the course of the novel Gothic horror transfers from the house to its owner, General Tilney, as a reminder that the Georgian social structure itself does not and cannot provide security. Working from her own definition of the concept of Gothic feminism, Diane Hoeveler argues that Austen both undercuts and deploys its key components, which are predicated on Mary Wollstonecraft's characterisation of women as morally superior, innocent victims of patriarchal corruption. On the other hand, Maria Jerinic argues that reading *Northanger Abbey* as a simple parody of the Gothic novel assumes women are unable to read critically and unfairly relegates Catherine Morland to victim status when, in fact, the target of Austen's parody is male presumptions to tell women what and how to read. Subsequently, Jerinic sees *Northanger Abbey* as an imitation rather than a rejection of the Radcliffian Gothic. Critics such as Judith Wilt have paid particular attention to the relationship between *Northanger Abbey* and Anne Radcliffe's extremely popular rational Gothic novel *The Mysteries of Udolpho* (1794). For Wilt, Radcliffian Gothic elements serve as metaphors for multiple aspects of Catherine's reality. Eleanor Ty reads the influence of not only Radcliffe's work but also 'more radical and political Gothic novels' that point to how the female body sites the political anxieties of the era and highlights women's marginality in a patriarchal context (259). The extended list of 'horrid novels' found in *Northanger Abbey* are also of keen interest. Bette B. Roberts suggests that the Gothic novels referenced in *Northanger Abbey* were chosen as exemplars of the worst of their kind, but Natalie Neill argues to the contrary that Austen's culminating achievement was her ability to revise and adapt her literary inheritance. Neill identifies the tropes in the books Austen parodies, now known collectively as the 'Northanger Novels', to illustrate how Austen's metafictional repackaging of these tropes valorises realism and denigrates didacticism.

Of course, literary traditions beyond the Gothic are key influences on *Northanger Abbey* as well. Mary Lascelles, among the first scholars to note how the novel engages with the eighteenth-century women's literary tradition beyond simply naming Frances Burney and Maria Edgeworth in the chapter 5 defense of novels, deems Catherine Morland an inversion of Charlotte Smith's impossibly perfect titular heroine in *Emmeline* (1788). Mary Waldron agrees that Catherine is surely a response to Emmeline's perfect, innate composure as well as to Arabella, Charlotte Lennox's comically delusional heroine of *The Female Quixote* (1752), to argue that the novel leaves readers uncertain whether to sympathise with or judge Catherine. George Justice treats *Northanger Abbey* as an anti-courtship novel while Penny Gay's *Jane Austen and the Theatre* explores generic crossovers, arguing that *Northanger Abbey* owes much structurally and thematically to the methods and tropes of theatricality and urban sophistication. Devoney Looser maintains that in a marketplace where authors of genres as diverse as history and the novel competed for readers, Austen validates her own writing by co-opting historical writing's claims to authority and moral edification. Arguing about canonicity and Austen's place in the development of the genre of the novel, Clifford Siskin predicates the elevation of Austen's writing on her refusal to participate in the sentimental tradition or contribute to the periodical press; both, he argues, are parodied in *Northanger Abbey*.

With its settings in resort-town social culture and the carefully modernised country seat of the commodity-conscious General Tilney, *Northanger Abbey* is also a valuable record of material culture in Bath, from the pump room to the assembly room, as well as fashionable consumerism, from spotted muslin to Wedgwood china. 'The pleasures and pains of living in a market economy consume the characters in Austen's novel, and Catherine Morland is hardly immune to the appeal of shopping', Susan Zlotnick states, exploring parallels between reading and shopping as sites of women's agency (277). Alistair Duckworth contends that Austen uses irony to expose the threat of mercenary interests and consumerist values to a morally ordered society, but, ultimately, the experiment to marry a novel of manners to a parody of the Gothic falls flat as the ironic resolution of the novel does not offer a wholly satisfactory moral outcome. In *Unbecoming Conjunctions,* Jillian Heydt-Stevenson queers Austen's uses of contemporary fashion as well as the metaphors of dress, cross-dressing, and dressage (re: horses) to interrogate the ideology of the 'natural' and expose gender as performative. Robert Merret sees *Northanger Abbey's* simultaneous critique and embrace of fashionable consumerism figured in British-French cultural exchange as expressive of Austen's measured response to reactionary fear of French influence. For Lauren Miskin, Henry Tilney's taste in fashion, specifically 'true Indian muslin', is not only indicative of his patriarchal privilege but also his enactment of British imperialist regulatory values, which extend from cloth to women.

Among the fashionable pursuits of the leisured classes was, of course, reading. The famous defense of novels in chapter 5 subverts the powerful cultural association between a weak woman and the desire to read novels and, further, inverts the trope to valorise novels and novel reading. At the outset, Janet Todd's *Cambridge Introduction to Jane Austen* declares *Northanger Abbey* not only to be '[a]bout the seduction of the reader, fictional and real' but also about the joys and pitfalls of novel reading as well as its epistemological functions (36). Exploring how circulating libraries mitigated the expense of books and thus made reading fashionable if socially ambivalent, Lee Erickson argues that in *Northanger Abbey* Austen portrays books as necessary luxuries, both dangerous and worthy. Jan Fergus argues that as the heroine is instructed, so too the reader, whereas Robert W. Uphaus contends that Austen's fiction sanctioned the moral authority of women and novels by providing 'both story and reflection' (336). Barbara Benedict characterises Catherine's reading as a commodified site of moral conflict in a commercial culture where self is defined by taste while Katie Halsey characterises *Northanger Abbey* as both indebted to and resistant to conduct literature for women, with its defense of the novel explicitly aimed at Fordyce's recommendations of periodical essay moralising over novels in his *Sermons to Young Women*, mocked in *Pride and Prejudice* as well. Reading and experience are at turns aligned and opposed by scholars who consider education to be a key theme in *Northanger Abbey,* such as Jocelyn Harris, who argues for Catherine's autodidacticism as fundamentally Lockean in nature. Laura Mooneyham also sees Catherine Morland's education as empirical and self-directed, a weaning from a complex maze of fictions ranging from Gothic novels to other characters' lies catalysed by her increasing ability to understand linguistic cues at the same time she remains a paradoxically blank slate onto which Henry Tilney projects his pedantry.

Despite a persistent desire among many Austen fans to see her work as apolitical, many readers of *Northanger Abbey* have recognised how the political and geographical exigencies of the late eighteenth and early nineteenth centuries impinge upon the text. Marilyn Butler's influential scholarship argues that *Northanger Abbey* provides an anti-Jacobin disapproval of selfishness, as figured in Isabella Thorpe. Claudia L. Johnson counters that Austen's critique of her society is distinctly feminist. Henry Tilney thus figures as a charming bully who dismisses the violent realities represented by Gothic fictions to preserve patriarchal power. Ronald Paulson, Gary Kelly, and Warren Roberts all make the case for the influence of the French Revolution on Austen's work as manifested in *Northanger Abbey* in specific. For Paulson, for example, the Gothic functions as a metaphorical coping mechanism for coming to grips with the unfathomably horrific realities of the French Revolution. Robert Hopkins unequivocally deems *Northanger Abbey* both 'political' and a product of its composition in the 1790s during a period of significant civil unrest illustrated by Henry Tilney's references to enclosures and riots during the walk round Beechen Cliff as well as his affirmation of the presence of 'voluntary spies' among the English when he reprimands Catherine for supposing his father a murderer. Hopkins makes the case for General Tilney as a villain, a 'voluntary sp[y]' whose late-night reading of political pamphlets serves the Pitt regime's repressive tactics to quell radicalism (214). Stemming from debates surrounding Catholic Relief in 1790s and figured in Catherine's fantasy of Northanger as a convent before the Reformation, Beth Kowaleski-Wallace sees the spectre of Catholic history in Britain haunting *Northanger Abbey*. On the other hand, Janine Barchas posits Austen as a writer attuned to her contemporary moment, deeply informed, and at times even prurient, in contrast to the image of the retired maiden aunt painting in tiny brush strokes on 'the little bit (two Inches wide) of Ivory on which I work' (*Letters* 337). Barchas argues that *Northanger Abbey* maps the geographical contours of its Bath setting with painstaking detail as well as incorporates the oft-shocking deeds of actual historical figures who inhabited Austen's contexts. Toby R. Benis connects the geographical to the political in *Northanger Abbey* via an analysis of neighbourhoods—Bath's lack of them and the social ties that bind as well as Northanger's totalitarian destruction of any distinctions in place or space in the name of General Tilney's tyranny.

Gender-based analyses have been central to recent critical work on *Northanger Abbey,* even when other methods and foci take precedence. Gilbert and Gubar's foundational work in *The Madwoman in the Attic* includes an influential reading of *Northanger Abbey* as 'an indictment of patriarchy', suggesting that Austen uses and transforms the fictional conventions of her day to dramatize women's inability to escape patriarchal conventions (128). Margaret Kirkham, arguing for enlightenment feminism's influence on Austen, surmises that 'Susan' was suppressed by Crosby because of the gendered defense of novels within. Yet other critics see *Northanger Abbey*'s hero and heroine as indicative of Austen's recognition of the social construction of gender, such as Joseph Litvak's argument that while Henry's charming satirical wit is predicated on class privilege, the novel's queer energies are mirrored in the complex interplay of history and fiction that mark Catherine Morland's ascension to the upper-middle class. Emma Clery also notes the queering of Henry and Catherine at the outset of the novel before offering that the central concern of Austen's works is an epistemological problem resolved by the hero and heroine coming to know each other's minds.

Doubly Critical: *Northanger Abbey's* Metafictional Functions

Queer, disjointed, parodic, political *Northanger Abbey* provides an exemplar of metafiction's ability to critique society at the same time that it illustrates the power of representation in the increasingly influential genre of the novel. Metafiction is fiction that points out its own status as an artificial construct using techniques such as knowing references to generic conventions, digressions that break from the action of the plot, satirical and ironic narratorial asides (or satire and irony in any guise), allusions to other fictions, and self-conscious references to reading and writing. In *Northanger Abbey*, while social constructs such as female sensibility and patriarchal authority prove to be imaginative fictions tied to novelistic conventions such as sentimental romance and Gothic horror, they nevertheless also prove to have consequences in the real(istic) world. Bharat Tandon has argued for how Austen's double ironies enable her social critique. Indeed, Austen's uses of foiling and doubling allow for deconstruction of the very binaries she presents, imaginary constructs deployed in opposing pairs that not only negate but also implode when juxtaposed with one another, pointing to the fictions that underpinned Jane Austen's social reality while also, in falling back in on themselves, revealing the intractability of their social functions.

Northanger Abbey's opening chapter signals its status as a parody of Gothic fiction but also illustrates its metafictional technique. The opening line, 'No one who had ever seen Catherine Morland in her infancy, would have supposed her born to be an heroine', assumes readers come to the text with a predetermined notion of what a heroine is, and the description that follows confirms that the definition comes from existing novel conventions (13). Catherine has a kind father and a healthy mother, quite to the contrary of Gothic novel precepts that insist upon despotic patriarchs and dead mothers. Yet the novel also offers a cruelly authoritarian patriarch and a dead, martyred mother in General Tilney and his late wife. While Austen takes pains to describe the General's tyranny in realistic terms as often petty—he has exacting standards for food and décor and demands militaristic attention to timeliness from his children—he is nonetheless a tyrant. The General is not a murderer, but indeed, 'always a check upon his children's spirits' and the man who callously throws Catherine out of his home when he learns she is not the heiress John Thorpe made her out to be (156).

To be sure, Catherine's journeys and her maturation place *Northanger Abbey* squarely in the tradition of *bildungsroman*, or a coming-of-age story, such as Frances Burney's wildly popular novel *Evelina* (1788), subtitled 'a young lady's entrance into the world'. The novel tradition that Austen inherited proves to be another locus of meaning illuminated by her use of metafictional technique. *Northanger Abbey* both reflects upon its predecessors and innovates, helping to forge a new path for the novel genre. Samuel Johnson's *Rambler* number 4 is often cited as articulating the ideal characteristics for fiction in the mid-eighteenth century. Based on Classical dictates that literature should both entertain and instruct, Johnson champions realistic fiction, works that 'exhibit life in its true state', as the ideal vehicles for 'convey[ing] the knowledge of vice and virtue' (19, 21). At the same time, Johnson notes that novels are potentially dangerous not only for their content but also because young, inexperienced readers may become too absorbed and influenced by realistic fiction. Johnson subsequently recommends all novels clearly depict moral lessons and provide endings that exhibit poetic justice. *Northanger Abbey* both mocks and upholds Johnson's dictates for fiction, perhaps most readily illustrated in its ending, prefaced by the narrator's address to her readers, 'who will see in the tell-tale compression of the pages before them, that we are all hastening together to perfect felicity' (250). Eleanor Tilney receives a late-breaking wealthy suitor to assuage her father's greed and reward her level-headed friendship to Catherine, cheekily figured in the stock language of 'the most charming young man in the world … instantly before the imagination of us all' (251). Yet the satirical final line surely mocks Johnson's wish for conclusions that deliver clear morals and poetical justice. The obtrusive narrator's coy anti-moral refers to how General Tilney's mistreatment of Catherine goads Henry into breaking with his father and declaring himself to her: 'I leave it to be settled by whomsoever it may concern, whether the tendency of this work be altogether to recommend parental tyranny, or reward filial disobedience' (252). Such mockery of existing dictates that delimit the function of the novel begins the work of carving out a place for fiction to evince broader values and ask more questions, and certainly to be regarded more highly than it had hitherto been in the literary hierarchy.

Northanger Abbey's complex relationship to the traditions Austen inherits and subsequently both accepts and rejects must be remembered if we are tempted to read the novel as a simple attack on unrealistic fiction in order to champion realism. While Catherine and Isabella's fervent Gothic novel reading is parodied in Catherine's mistaken assumptions based on those fictional conventions and Isabella's utterly disingenuous use of shallow sentimental conventions that prove to have no foundation in true feelings or friendship, as I have noted above, *Northanger Abbey* also clearly deploys Gothic conventions for its own purposes and does so from a position of great intimacy with those conventions. Furthermore, realistic literary forms do not emerge from the novel unscathed. Chapter 5's defense of novels validates the novel as a vehicle 'in which the greatest powers of the mind are displayed, in which the most thorough knowledge of human nature, the happiest delineation of its varieties, the liveliest effusions of wit and humour, are conveyed to the world in the best-chosen language' (38). Novel readers, including novel heroines who read novels, are also redeemed in this long narrative digression, but other more celebrated forms of moral literature are mocked. Austen makes space for the novel as a legitimate vehicle of entertainment and instruction by questioning the inherent value of literary miscellanies that reprinted popular extracts, the periodical press, which will come back in the end of the novel as Mrs Morland runs to fetch an old issue of *The Mirror* in hopes of curing Catherine's post-excursion malaise, and history, as Devoney Looser has noted, which also returns as a topic of discussion during the walk round Beechen Cliff. Indeed, history and fiction prove to be just as slippery a pairing as the Tilney and Thorpe siblings. Catherine, the reluctant reader of history, notes how historiography often ascribes invented language, thoughts, and motives to historical figures; 'the chief of all this must be invention', Catherine declares (108). Eleanor, who enjoys reading history, replies that she is 'very well contented to take the false with the true', a statement as easily applied to the necessary suspension of disbelief required of realistic fiction (109). Just as history can be fiction, *Northanger Abbey* illustrates how fiction can be true in both its moral and representational integrity. Novel reading, even Gothic novel reading, is further redeemed in the characterisation of the charming yet pedantic Henry Tilney, who of course reads *Udolpho* with great attention, while his foil *and* double,[3] the callow boor John Thorpe, dismisses novel-reading outright, aside from prurient books by Henry Fielding and Matthew 'Monk' Lewis. Thorpe cannot even identify a title by the celebrated Frances Burney, who numbers among the novelists championed in chapter 5 of *Northanger Abbey*. Subsequently, novel reading clearly functions as a legitimate vehicle of entertainment and instruction, but it proves to be only one potential locus for acquisition of understanding.

Indeed, *Northanger Abbey* contemplates at length multiple ways of knowing, especially as they are gendered by both access to education and worldly experience. Epistemological questions, as E.J. Clery has argued, dominate Austen's works. This emphasis is clearly evidenced in the novel's wordplay as well as its self-conscious reflection on tricks of language such as that moment explicated by Lloyd Brown, Henry Tilney's derision of the new, watered-down usage of the word 'nice' as synonymous with pleasant, when it, ironically, formerly denoted particularity or scrupulousness, and 'was applied only to express neatness, propriety, delicacy, or refinement' (108). So, too, Isabella's declaration that *Sir Charles Grandison* must be 'an amazing horrid book' because deemed so boring as to be unreadable by her friend, Miss Andrews (41). Of course, Miss Andrews has also supplied the list of 'horrid' novels Catherine and Isabella plan to read together, wherein Catherine uses 'horrid' as a synonym for the titillating Gothic. Narratorial asides function similarly to unmoor easy conclusions, such as the truth and absurdity in the narrator's observation upon Catherine's ignorance as a positive attribute:

> Where people wish to attach, they should always be ignorant. To come with a well-informed mind is to come with an inability of administering to the vanity of others, which

a sensible person would always wish to avoid. A woman especially, if she have the misfortune of knowing anything, should conceal it as well as she can.

… I will only add, in justice to men, that though to the larger and more trifling part of the
sex, imbecility in females is a great enhancement of their personal charms, there is a portion
of them too reasonable and too well informed themselves to desire anything more in
woman than ignorance. (110–11)

It is certainly true that many would-be lovers have been won over by having their superior abilities
flattered by an admirer. But does the narrator really believe women to be imbecilic, or is she calling
out her culture's devaluation of women's abilities? The passage is laced with irony, making the latter
seem more likely, yet Catherine Morland is certainly ignorant. On the other hand, Catherine's
instincts about General Tilney prove to be true. The only certainty in the passage may be its
illustration of the slippery, arbitrary nature of language.

While such ricocheting insights may create confusion, they also serve the ends of all good satire:
to expose and ridicule a society's shortcomings. Subsequently, imbecility in women cannot be taken
for granted in a novel that deploys multiple gendered reversals and paradoxes, as scholars such as
Clery, Heydt-Stevenson, and Litvak have previously explored. Recall that novel-hungry Catherine
Morland grew up rough and tumble, 'fond of all boys' plays' (13). The stranglehold of middle- and
upper-middle-class female propriety manifests throughout Austen's oeuvre, in the shock of country-
lane tromping Elizabeth Bennet's refusal of not one but two perfectly eligible suitors despite the
impending doom the girl-heavy Bennet family faces as their patriarch and their maiden daughters
both age out of their utility to the social system via death and impoverished spinsterhood. Like
Elizabeth Bennet before her, even while Catherine Morland is 'abducted' by John Thorpe and
unceremoniously cast onto the streets in the early hours of a morning not previously set for her
departure from General Tilney's domains, she insists upon more physical mobility than her heroic
sistren. Catherine's athletic exuberance becomes the locus of General Tilney obsequiously 'admiring
the elasticity of her walk, which corresponded exactly with the spirit of her dancing', much to
Catherine's delight, so that she might walk away 'as she concluded, with great elasticity, though she
had never thought of it before' (103). Indeed, Catherine is not afraid of a walk in the rain or round
Beechen Cliff, a tumble down a hillside, or asserting herself to disentangle from the grasp of the
odious Thorpes to run through the streets of Bath and burst into the lodgings of the Tilneys,
unannounced even, unlike poor Evelina Anville before her, all too often trapped by those who
would manipulate her and the sentimental conventions to which she often adheres.

Similarly, *Northanger Abbey*'s unconventional hero, mansplaining Henry Tilney, knows muslin
and novels while his wordplay and satirical wit make him at turns a misogynist and/or a proto-
feminist. Henry's wry conflation of marriage and dancing sets Catherine's scatter-brained queru-
lousness at odds with her somehow innate moral practicality even while it keeps readers guessing
about whether, as his sister insists, 'he must be entirely misunderstood, if he can ever appear to say an
unjust thing of any woman at all' (114). Catherine cannot make sense of Henry's riddle comparing
marriage to a country dance: 'But they are such very different things!' (76). Yet Henry's observation
serves to expose the ways in which even simple customs disempower women in patriarchal contexts,
'You will allow, that in both, man has the advantage of choice, woman only the power of refusal'
(77). Here, as elsewhere in the novel, the observation doubles back upon itself, when Henry notes
that in dancing the gendered duties within marriage, where men support women and women make
happy homes for men, 'are exactly changed; the agreeableness, the compliance are expected from
him, while she furnishes the fan and the lavender water' (77). In the end, in yet another reversal of
gendered expectation, Henry proves to have misjudged the heights of his father's avarice and

potential for cruelty while clueless Catherine, whose moral purity shines through her in her credulousness, proves to have been right about General Tilney after all.

To be sure, *Northanger Abbey* presents readers with puzzles much more harrowing than those Frank Churchill slides to Emma Woodhouse. The tricks of language Austen deploys in the novel reflect the epistemological mind games and the social pitfalls faced by young women of modest means in a stifling English patriarchal context pulled even more taut by the threats of revolutionary reform from both within and abroad. Catherine Morland's rather mundane journey, from Fullerton to Bath and Northanger before returning to Fullerton again in a post-chaise, not only leaves readers wondering whether to endorse 'patriarchal tyranny' over 'filial disobedience' but also uncertain about the arbitrary nature of reality, caught in the debate between what is 'horrid' versus what is 'nice' and luxuriating in the novel's exemplum of the complex, chameleon qualities embodied by all of Jane Austen's work.

Notes

1 For Cassandra's note, see *The Novels of Jane Austen*, vol. VI, plate facing p. 242.
2 See Mandal for more on Crosby's potential reasons for not publishing *Northanger Abbey* after buying the copyright.
3 While Tilney and Thorpe appear to be opposites, attractive and intelligent and repulsive and ignorant in turn, they are both pushy in their own ways, complicating an overly simplistic valuation of the hero over the graceless John Thorpe with his self-professed 'Well hung' gig (46). Wild-driving John Thorpe 'abducts' Catherine in said well-hung gig when she wishes to walk with the Tilneys, but Henry also holds Catherine with his teasing tale of the Gothic horrors that purportedly await her at Northanger even while he steadily and soberly directs his curricle toward the estate.

Works Cited

Austen, Jane. *Jane Austen's Letters*, edited by Deirdre Le Faye, 4th ed. Oxford UP, 2011.
Austen, Jane. *The Novels of Jane Austen*, edited by R. W. Chapman, 3rd ed., vol. V. Oxford UP, 1932–1934.
Barchas, Janine. *Matters of Fact in Jane Austen: History, Location, and Celebrity*. Johns Hopkins UP, 2012.
Benedict, Barbara M. 'Jane Austen and the Culture of Circulating Libraries: The Construction of Female Literacy.' *Revising Women: Eighteenth-Century "Women's Fiction" and Social Engagement*, edited by Paula Backscheider. Johns Hopkins UP, 2000, pp. 147–199.
Benedict, Barbara, and Deirdre Le Faye. 'Introduction.' *Northanger Abbey*, by Jane Austen, 1818, Cambridge UP, 2006, pp. xxiii–lxi.
Benis, Toby R. 'The Neighborhoods of *Northanger Abbey*.' *The Eighteenth Century: Theory and Interpretation*, vol. 56, no. 2, 2015, pp. 179–192.
British Critic, new series, vol. 9, Mar. 1818, pp. 293–301.
Brown, Lloyd W. *Bits of Ivory: Narrative Techniques in Austen's Fiction*. Louisiana State UP, 1973.
Butler, Marilyn. *Jane Austen and the War of Ideas*. Clarendon, 1975.
Clery, E. J. 'Gender.' *The Cambridge Companion to Jane Austen*, edited by Edward Copeland and Juliet McMaster, 2nd ed. Cambridge UP, 2011, pp. 159–175.
Duckworth, Alistair M. *The Improvement of the Estate: A Study of Jane Austen's Novels*. Johns Hopkins, 1971.
Edinburgh Magazine and Literary Miscellany, a New Series of the Scots Magazine, vol. 2, May 1818, pp. 453–455.
Erickson, Lee. *The Economy of Literary Form: English Literature and The Industrialization of Publishing, 1800–1850*. Johns Hopkins UP, 1996.
Fergus, Jan S. *Jane Austen and the Didactic Novel: Northanger Abbey, Sense and Sensibility, and Pride and Prejudice*. Barnes & Noble, 1983.
Galperin, William H. *The Historical Austen*. U of Pennsylvania P, 2003.
Gay, Penny. *Jane Austen and the Theatre*. Cambridge UP, 2002.
Gentleman's Magazine, vol. 88, Jul. 1818, pp. 52–53.
Gilbert, Sandra M., and Susan Gubar. *The Madwoman in the Attic: The Woman Writer and the Nineteenth-Century Literary Imagination*. Yale UP, 1979.

Halsey, Katie. *Jane Austen and her Readers, 1786–1945*. Anthem, 2012.

Harding, Denys Clement Wyatt. *Regulated Hatred and Other Essays on Jane Austen*, edited by Monica Lawlor. Athlone, 1998.

Harris, Jocelyn. *Jane Austen's Art of Memory*. Cambridge UP, 1989.

Heydt-Stevenson, Jillian. *Austen's Unbecoming Conjunctions: Subversive Laughter, Embodied History*. Palgrave Macmillan, 2005.

Hoeveler, Diane. 'Vindicating *Northanger Abbey*: Mary Wollstonecraft, Jane Austen, and Gothic Feminism.' *Jane Austen and Discourses of Feminism*, edited by Devoney Looser. St. Martin's, 1995, pp. 117–135.

Hopkins, Robert. 'General Tilney and Affairs of State: The Political Gothic of *Northanger Abbey*.' *Philological Quarterly*, vol. 57, 1978, pp. 213–224.

Jerinic, Maria. 'In Defense of the Gothic: Rereading *Northanger Abbey*.' *Jane Austen and Discourses of Feminism*, edited by Devoney Looser. St. Martin's, 1995, pp. 137–149.

Johnson, Claudia L. *Jane Austen: Women, Politics, and the Novel*. U of Chicago P, 1990.

Johnson, Samuel. *The Rambler*, no. 4, 1750, pp. 19–24.

Justice, George. '*Northanger Abbey* as Anti-Courtship Novel.' *Persuasions: Journal of the Jane Austen Society of North America*, vol. 20, 1998, pp. 185–195.

Kearful, Frank, 'Satire and the Form of the Novel: The Problem of Aesthetic Unity in *Northanger Abbey*.' *ELH: English Literary History*, vol. 32, no. 4, 1965, pp. 511–527.

Kelly, Gary. 'Jane Austen and the English Novel of the 1790s.' *Fetter'd or Free? British Women Novelists, 1670–1815*, edited by Mary Anne Schofield and Cecilia Macheski. Ohio UP, 1986, pp. 285–306.

Kirkham, Margaret. *Jane Austen, Feminism and Fiction*. Barnes & Noble, 1983.

Kowaleski-Wallace, Beth. ''Penance and mortification for ever': Jane Austen and the Ambient Noise of Catholicism.' *Eighteenth-Century Women and English Catholicism, special issue of Tulsa Studies in Women's Literature*, vol. 31, no. 1/2, 2012, pp. 159–180.

Lascelles, Mary. *Jane Austen and Her Art*. Oxford UP, 1939.

Levine, George Lewis. *The Realistic Imagination: English Fiction from Frankenstein to Lady Chatterley*. U of Chicago P, 1981.

Lewes, G.H. 'The Novels of Jane Austen.' *Blackwood's Magazine*, vol. 86, 1859, pp. 99–113.

Litvak, Joseph. *Strange Gourmets: Sophistication, Theory, and the Novel*. Duke UP, 1997.

Litz, A. Walton. *Jane Austen: A Study of Her Artistic Development*. Oxford UP, 1965.

Looser, Devoney. 'Reading Jane Austen and Rewriting "Herstory."' *Critical Essays on Jane Austen*, edited by Laura Mooneyham White. Prentice Hall International, 1998, pp. 34–66.

Mandal, A. A. 'Making Austen Mad: Benjamin Crosby and the Non-Publication of "Susan".' *The Review of English Studies*, vol. 57, no. 231, 2006, pp. 507–525.

Merrett, Robert. 'Consuming Modes in *Northanger Abbey*: Jane Austen's Economic View of Literary Nationalism.' *Persuasions: Journal of the Jane Austen Society of North America*, no. 20, 1998, pp. 222–235.

Miskin, Lauren. '"True Indian Muslin" and the Politics of Consumption in Jane Austen's *Northanger Abbey*.' *Journal for Early Modern Cultural Studies*, vol. 15, no. 2, 2015, pp. 5–26.

Mooneyham, Laura G. *Romance, Language and Education in Jane Austen's Novels*. Macmillan, 1988.

Mudrick, Marvin. *Jane Austen: Irony as Defense and Discovery*. Princeton UP, 1952.

Neill, Natalie. '"The Trash with Which the Press Now Groans": *Northanger Abbey* and the Gothic Best Sellers of the 1790s.' *Eighteenth-Century Novel*, vol. 4, 2004, pp. 163–192.

Paulson, Ronald. 'Gothic Fiction and the French Revolution.' *ELH: English Literary History*, vol. 48, no. 3, 1981, pp. 532–554.

Roberts, Warren. *Jane Austen and the French Revolution*. Palgrave Macmillan, 1979.

Shaw, Narelle. 'Free Indirect Speech and Jane Austen's 1816 Revision of *Northanger Abbey*.' *SEL Studies in English Literature, 1500-1900*, vol. 30, no. 4, 1990, pp. 591–601.

Siskin, Clifford. 'Jane Austen and the Engendering of Disciplinarity.' *Jane Austen and Discourses of Feminism*, edited by Devoney Looser, St. Martin's, 1995, pp. 51–67.

Southam, B. C. *Jane Austen's Literary Manuscripts*. Oxford UP, 1964.

Tandon, Bharat. *Jane Austen and the Morality of Conversation*. Anthem, 2003.

Tanner, Tony. *Jane Austen*. Harvard UP, 1986.

Todd, Janet. *The Cambridge Introduction to Jane Austen*, 2nd ed. Cambridge UP, 2015.

Ty, Eleanor. 'Catherine's Real and Imagined Fears: What Happens to Female Bodies in Gothic Castles.' *Persuasions: Journal of the Jane Austen Society of North America*, vol. 20, 1998, pp. 248–260.

Uphaus, Robert W. 'Jane Austen and Female Reading.' *Studies in the Novel*, vol. 19, no. 3, 1987, pp. 334–345.

Waldron, Mary. *Jane Austen and the Fiction of Her Time*. Cambridge UP, 1999.

Wall, Cynthia. '"The Little Words": The Close Reading of Really Small Things.' *Wordsworth Circle*, vol. 47, no. 2-3, 2016, pp. 114–118.

Wallace, Tara Ghoshal. '*Northanger Abbey* and the Limits of Parody.' *Studies in the Novel*, vol. 20, no. 3, 1988, pp. 262–273.

West, Rebecca. Preface. *Northanger Abbey*, by Jane Austen, 1818, Jonathan Cape, 1932, pp. v–xi.

Whateley, Richard. '*Northanger Abbey*, and *Persuasion*.' *Quarterly Review*, vol. 24, 1820/21, pp. 352–376.

Wilt, Judith. *Ghosts of the Gothic: Austen, Eliot, & Lawrence*. Princeton UP, 1980.

Wolfson, Susan. Introduction. *Northanger Abbey: An Annotated Edition*, by Jane Austen, 1818, Belknap Press of Harvard UP, 2014, pp. 1–60.

Zlotnick, Susan. 'From Involuntary Object to Voluntary Spy: Female Agency, Novels, and the Marketplace in *Northanger Abbey*.' *Studies in the Novel*, vol. 41, no. 3, 2009, pp. 277–292.

2
SENSE AND SENSIBILITY, NOVEL AND PHENOMENON

Peter Graham

VIRGINIA POLYTECHNIC INSTITUTE AND STATE UNIVERSITY

Not just an Austen novel but also a significant cultural artifact, *Sense and Sensibility* is arguably one of its author's most perplexing works. Much of what's perplexing about it derives from a tension between the novel's embodiment of contingencies and conventions from its own time and the values or expectations of present-day readers. Except perhaps for *Northanger Abbey, Sense and Sensibility* is the Austen novel most strongly eighteenth century, rather than Regency, in its attitudes, tropes, values, and conventions. Like *Northanger Abbey* (originally *Susan*) and *Pride and Prejudice* (initially *First Impressions*), *Sense and Sensibility* was drafted in the 1790s, when its author was in her twenties. No manuscript survives to provide conclusive evidence, but Deirdre Le Faye, Kathryn Sutherland, and other scholars have opined that *Sense and Sensibility* was probably first written in epistolary form in or around 1795 and titled *Elinor and Marianne*. Jocelyn Harris in *Jane Austen's Art of Memory* speculates intriguingly and specifically about Austen's revision of the manuscript and argues that in various ways it borrows from and even rewrites works of eighteenth-century fiction by Henry Fielding, Frances Burney, and above all Austen's favourite, Samuel Richardson.

Two hundred years later, or thereabouts, the 1995 film of *Sense and Sensibility*, directed by Ang Lee and with a screenplay by Emma Thompson, became the first movie adaptation of an Austen novel since *Pride and Prejudice* in 1940. The *Sense and Sensibility* film, closely followed by the films *Persuasion* and *Clueless* (*Emma* brilliantly re-envisioned in a Beverly Hills high school) and the wildly popular tv mini-series of *Pride and Prejudice* starring Jennifer Ehle and Colin Firth as Elizabeth Bennet and Fitzwilliam Darcy, introduced a new audience to Austen's novels and gave turn-of-the-21st-century legs to Austen's turn-of-the-19th-century texts. But what readers find on Austen's pages doesn't always correspond to their present-day sense or sensibility. As Devoney Looser points out in her lively introduction to the 2018 Penguin edition of *Sense and Sensibility*, present-day 'readers who love *Sense and Sensibility* are rarely describing their first encounter with the book' (xi) but instead are re-readers. Similarly, readers displeased by the novel are often comparing it to a version of the story first known to them from film or TV adaptations.

In recent decades, scholarship on *Sense and Sensibility* has tended to focus on a number of distinct but overlapping themes all relevant in their different ways to this tension between Austen-era realities and contemporary values and expectations: the financial situation of the Dashwood women and what their plight says about the economic status of women in Austen's time, the moral ambiguity discernible in certain characters and the darkness of various plot incidents, the dissonance between the novel's well-developed, deeply satisfying sisterly relationship of its two heroines and

DOI: 10.4324/9780429398155-2-4

their arguably less satisfying romances and marriages, the novel's point of view and how it changed from the novel-in-letters format Austen is said to have first employed, and the meanings, relations between, and thematic uses of the important late-eighteenth-century terms constituting the novel's alliterative title: 'sense' and 'sensibility'. The ensuing chapter will take up these topics that have proven interesting to twentieth- and twenty-first-century Austen scholars in hopes both of suggesting what Austen's novel may have meant in its own time and of appraising how our own time understands and values *Sense and Sensibility*, now a pop-culture phenomenon as well as a three-volume novel published in 1811.

Sense and Sensibility in Short

Like all her other novels, *Sense and Sensibility* centres on the lives, loves, and marital fates of young, marriageable girls: in this case the Dashwood sisters, nineteen-year-old Elinor and seventeen-year-old Marianne. (A significant alteration in the Emma Thompson screenplay for the Ang Lee film adds about a decade to Elinor's age to make her being played by thirty-five-year-old Thompson more plausible.) Austen's recurrent method is to introduce novelty and new people into the socially limited 'three or four families in a country village' lives of her heroines, either by bringing in new characters as in *Pride and Prejudice*, *Emma*, and *Persuasion* or by taking the heroine into different environments as in *Northanger Abbey*, *Pride and Prejudice*, *Mansfield Park*, and *Persuasion*. *Sense and Sensibility* is initially a novel of displacement. After a concise backstory of the 'family of Dashwood … long settled in Sussex', (1) the novel's action begins with the Dashwood women, a widow and her three daughters, feeling obliged to leave their home Norland Park when their husband and father dies after only a year as incumbent of the estate and his son John, half-brother to Elinor, Marianne, and Margaret, inherits.[1] But the bereaved Dashwood women don't leave before Elinor and Edward Ferrars, the brother of her rude, mercenary, inhospitable sister-in-law Fanny, have become interested in one another.

Kept within their limited means by the prudent and practical Elinor, the Dashwood women settle three counties west in rural Devonshire at Barton Cottage, a modest residence offered to them on reasonable terms by Mrs Dashwood's generous, affable cousin Sir John Middleton. Their reduced economic circumstances and isolated new neighbourhood mean that their social life centres on the Middletons' house Barton Park, where they become acquainted with Colonel Brandon, a brooding bachelor friend of Sir John's who is attracted to Marianne—as is Willoughby, a dashing sportsman paying his yearly visit to an old aunt whose estate, Allenham, he is to inherit. Further additions to the milieu are Lady Middleton's mother, the jovial, rich London widow Mrs Jennings, Mrs Jennings' amiably airheaded younger daughter Charlotte and her rudely sarcastic husband Mr Palmer, and Lucy and Anne Steele, downmarket cousins of Mrs Jennings, the former quick and shrewd, the latter a garrulous dullard. Edward Ferrars's awkwardly reticent regard for Elinor seems real, but Lucy Steele confides to Elinor that she and Edward, who met when he was being privately educated at her uncle's house, have for some time been secretly engaged. Meanwhile, the candid, unrestrained Marianne has been behaving in ways that broadcast her strong attachment to Willoughby—though no engagement is avowed either before or after his abrupt and unexplained departure from Devonshire.

Mrs Jennings invites the two oldest Dashwood sisters to stay with her in London during the winter season, and in the metropolis they encounter almost everyone of their acquaintance: Brandon, the John Dashwoods, Edward Ferrars and eventually his mother and younger brother, the Palmers, and the Steele sisters. Willoughby unaccountably keeps his distance, which is agony for Marianne, whose correspondence with him suggests to Elinor the likelihood or certainty of their being engaged. In fact he is about to marry an heiress, Miss Grey. Marianne takes the news badly and behaves histrionically, but still more outrageous drama ensues when the ambitious Ferrars family learns of Edward's secret engagement to Lucy. Edward honourably refuses to break it, so his furious mother disinherits him. Nonetheless, Colonel Brandon's generously offering Edward the clerical living of the parish associated with his estate Delaford will give him the bare minimum for starting married life as a clergyman.

En route home to Barton with Mrs Jennings, the Dashwood sisters break their journey at Cleveland, the estate of Mr Palmer. Here Marianne falls dangerously ill after wandering recklessly in wet weather. Colonel Brandon and Mrs Jennings show their worth and stand by the sisters as Marianne's life is in jeopardy. When settled back at Barton Cottage and convalescing, a chastened Marianne resolves to model her behaviour on her older sister's—and Colonel Brandon's faithful devotion eventually wins her heart and hand. As for Elinor, she is able to follow her feelings and marry Edward Ferrars because when Mrs Ferrars disinherits him and in her fit of parental pique settles the Ferrars estate on his foppish younger brother Robert, the mercenary Lucy breaks the engagement and successfully sets her cap for the new heir. Thus the Dashwood sisters eventually end up married and established at Delaford Park and its parsonage, two houses as physically close to one another as Elinor and Marianne are in spirit.

The personal contrasts between the older and the younger sister in this devoted pair bespeak Jane Austen's tendency as a fledgling novelist in the 1790s to begin on familiar ground. The other two manuscripts she drafted in this decade also start with domestic situations she knew well. *Northanger Abbey* features the heroine whose family background is closest to the Austen's. Catherine Morland, though unlike Jane (number six of eight) an oldest sibling, comes from a clergyman's large family comparable to George and Cassandra Austen's brood. Uniquely among the parents of the six novels' heroines, the senior Morlands are like the Austens: solid, sensible, and competent as individuals and as a unit—and, a rarity for competent parents in Austen's novels, both are alive. *Pride and Prejudice*, like *Sense and Sensibility*, presents a pair of sisters closely bonded as the Austen sisters were, and with the elder more sober and restrained like Cassandra, the younger edgier and witty like Jane. The women of the Bennet household, like the Dashwoods, live under the threat of eventual eviction from their settled home. But unlike the Dashwood and Austen women, they do not actually experience it in the novel. The initial problem the Dashwoods face in *Sense and Sensibility* is just what the Austen women might have anticipated in the 1790s and what they actually experienced when George Austen retired in 1800 and the eldest son James succeeded to his clerical livings of Steventon and Dean. The three Austen women followed the retired rector to Bath and then after his death in 1805 lived provisionally in various rented lodgings on their own modest funds supplemented by Jane's brothers' contributions until Edward Austen settled his mother and sisters in Chawton Cottage on his Hampshire estate of the same name in 1809. It is hardly surprising that Jane Austen's resurgence of literary energy coincided with her return to settled life in a country village—and *Sense and Sensibility* was published two years later in 1811, with *Pride and Prejudice* closely following in 1812. Then she was on to the mature period of creativity that resulted in *Mansfield Park*, *Emma*, and *Persuasion*, the latter published posthumously with *Northanger Abbey*, which had been retrieved from a publisher who had bought the manuscript and then sat upon it for years.

'Sense?' 'Sensibility?'

Many of the intriguing perplexities of *Sense and Sensibility* rise directly or indirectly out of two matters unrelated to plot or character: Jane Austen's turning a late-eighteenth-century epistolary novel into the third-person narrative published in 1811 and changing the story's title from *Elinor and Marianne* to *Sense and Sensibility*. Interestingly, all three of the manuscripts Austen drafted in the 1790s were eventually published under different titles; and it is debatable whether or not the change of titles was in each case an improvement. The alliterative enigma of *Pride and Prejudice* appeals to the ear, eye, and mind more richly than does *First Impressions*. Although the earlier title is less ambiguous, few readers keen on determining who is proud, who is prejudiced, and to what extent the qualities might be distributed between heroine and hero would count that as much of an advantage. *Susan* was published as *Northanger Abbey*, perhaps because the latter title foregrounds the novel's status as a mock Gothic. But to call the story after its heroine (her name is Catherine, not Susan, in the published version) would in fact be truer to what goes on in the novel, much less than half of which happens within the walls of Northanger Abbey, an edifice not glimpsed, explored, and temporarily inhabited by the ingenue heroine until more than half way through the tale of her maturation. Like *Northanger Abbey, Elinor and Marianne* is a novel whose main subject is best characterised by its protagonists' names; and some dissatisfactions readers feel with the novel might derive from the fact that though the novel ends with Elinor's and Marianne's arguably less-than-romantically-satisfying marriages it is mainly about their sisterhood. In this way *Sense and Sensibility* contrasts with *Pride and Prejudice,* for however deep and devoted the sisterly bond between Jane and Elizabeth Bennet may be, the story line centres on the developing bond between Elizabeth and Darcy, powerfully attractive equals each improved by the other.

A text called *Elinor and Marianne* would almost demand that readers privilege the sisterly relationship over the developing romances and, as Enit Steiner puts it, would highlight the discursive and communicative nature of the story. Changing the title to the contrasting conceptual terms *Sense and Sensibility* shifts attention from the feminine and familial to the arguably masculine and abstract. Because 'sense' and 'sensibility' are both terms understood somewhat differently in Austen's day and ours, the words themselves can perplex. Further, the temptation to identify one Dashwood (Elinor) as 'sense' and the other (Marianne) as 'sensibility' may keep readers from recognising the emotional and mental complexities of the two sisters—and from appraising the presence, absence, balance, or imbalance of sense and sensibility in other characters, a repaying critical exercise, as Margaret Anne Doody among others has shown.

Most readers' first instinct is to view Elinor Dashwood as the 'sense' sister, the one who clearly discerns the impressions gathered by her senses and her social intelligence and whose qualities of mind and character equip her to deal reasonably with what she discerns. The contrast makes Marianne the 'sensibility' sister, the one whose personal reaction to impressions is lively, acute, candid, unrestrained—and continually revealed in verbal outbursts or bodily responses such as blushing or going pale, becoming faint, bursting into tears, or falling seriously ill. A consequence of this readerly tendency that the title encourages has been a host of articles and monographs either considering the literary and philosophical legacy of the terms 'sense' and 'sensibility' or questioning the validity of interpreting Austen's novel using this binary. Inger Sigrun Brodey's 'Making Sense of Sensibility' exemplifies the critical rewards of applying a historicist approach to the interrelated terms, while Claudia Johnson's *Sense and Sensibility* chapter in *Jane Austen: Women, Politics, and the Novel* is a seminal text in the debate about the legitimacy of mapping sensibility onto Marianne and sense onto Elinor. The critical consensus in the extensive, evolving sense vs. sensibility debate seems to be that a polarised or binary reading is reductive and that both joint protagonists exhibit elements of each concept.

Recent scholarship has also argued that the tendency to read *Sense and Sensibility* reductively is the consequence of the novel's complicated point of view—the way Austen's narrator has the novel's audience see much of the story through Elinor's eyes. For Rebecca Richardson, reading *Sense and Sensibility* as a confessional text reveals the extent to which Elinor shapes readers' experience of the novel: 'These [confessional] scenes literalize the focalization of the novel through Elinor: Elinor receives, holds, and eventually repackages back-stories for other characters'. As 'confidante, confessor, analyst, and interrogator', Elinor is the character on stage most (226–27). If we read the novel this way, Elinor's perspective becomes the reader's perspective. Her perspective seems reasonable—sensible—because it seems to convey a truthful account of the events unfolding. Elinor *becomes* 'sense', and Marianne by default becomes 'sensibility'—more precisely, sensibility seen through the lens of sense. James O'Rourke goes further in examining the effect of reading the events of *Sense and Sensibility* largely through Elinor's eyes and suggests that even the assumption that Elinor's perspective is a 'sensible' one is faulty. Summarising his intentions for 'What Never Happened: Social Amnesia in *Sense and Sensibility*', O'Rourke asserts that on a formal level the novel 'masks a subtle but persistent narrative bias that favors its central character, Elinor'. What O'Rourke calls the 'Elinorcentric' narrative both draws readers in and gives them reasons to question her values (774). Elinor, seen in this light, is not necessarily so objective or sensible as the narrative might encourage readers to conclude, but the focalisation of the text makes that this point easy for readers to miss.

Marcia McClintock Folsom offers one of the subtlest assessments of what distinguishes the *Sense and Sensibility* narrator's voice. As Folsom sees it in 'The Narrator's Voice and the Sense of *Sense and Sensibility*', the narrator is 'strangely contentious', a subtle blended voicing of not just Elinor's values and tastes but also Marianne's, and something beyond both, 'as though the narrator herself is angry at the mediocrity of some of her characters or the exhausting triviality of social life' (29). Seen from this vantage point, the sharp observations that give an intermittent biting edge to the tone of *Sense and Sensibility*, need not be Elinor's mediated musings. Rather, they articulate the irritation that any woman possessing healthy amounts of both sense and sensibility might feel, be she diplomatic Elinor, blunt Marianne, or Jane Austen herself, as she views the absurdities of human behaviour in general and the injustices of her patriarchal culture in particular. Sometimes these contentious observations are specific, like the write-off of Robert Ferrars's 'face of strong, natural, sterling insignificance' (192) after the Dashwood sisters have seen him belabour the particulars of a jewel-encrusted bespoke toothpick case. But at other times they are more sweeping. When Lady Middleton fatuously falls for the Steele sisters' clumsy flattery of her children, the narrator jumps from this particular case to a general truth: 'a fond mother, though, in pursuit of praise for her children, the most rapacious of human beings, is likewise the most credulous; her demands are exorbitant, but she will swallow anything' (103). Here, the almost contemptuous feelings expressed may be both Elinor's and Marianne's—but the unfiltered formulation sounds like Jane Austen venting a bad mood in her most personal letters.

From Epistolary to Third Person

Austen, when first composing the novel, seemingly determined that sisterhood (the relationship of a pair similar to herself and Cassandra, who like Elinor was two years older, more restrained in demeanour, and adept in drawing) would be central to her story. The fact that this early version was also epistolary would by dint of its structure arguably have foregrounded sisterhood even more clearly than does its later third-person iteration. Without a mediating narrator, the story would unfold mainly in the words of sisters writing to one another. Such a generic choice would have given Elinor's and Marianne's perspectives equal weight and would have shown the latter more directly than a narrative often focalised through Elinor does.

Besides being intimate in a way that third-person narration cannot be, the epistolary form was considered characteristically feminine, as a number of scholarly works from throughout the twentieth century have observed. Among others, Mary Favret's *Romantic Correspondence: Women, Politics, and the Fiction of Letters* is a key text for understanding the relationship between the epistolary form and women's lived experience. But recent scholarship from Enit Karafili Steiner and Rebecca Richardson has deviated from the somewhat traditional interpretation of the epistolary as a feminine genre. Instead, these scholars consider how *Sense and Sensibility*'s shift from the epistolary to third person also reflects Austen's political environment and anticipates developments in her writing style. Steiner, in 'Between Cohesion and Reform in *Sense and Sensibility*' considers the possible impact the 1795 'Gagging Acts' (the Treason Act, which extended the definition of high treason to include speech and thought even if untranslated into action, and the Seditious Meetings Act, which banned public meetings of over fifty unless certified by a magistrate) might have had on a 1790s story centering on secrets and communication. At the time when Austen was drafting the novel, Steiner argues, sociability became a contested and suspect value. Conversation, abandoned for silence and concealment, was policed in a culture of censure and censorship (463).

The original epistolary form, in short, may have further complicated an already complex exploration of the role of honesty in public discourse and social interaction. By shifting to third person Austen could better convey that communication (or its absence) was central to her characters' stories. Indeed the sisters themselves, verbally intimate but each reticent about something important, recognize this point, as is evident in their brief quarrel about confiding, a word-duel Marianne concludes with an unfair but penetrating thrust: 'We have neither of us any thing to tell; you, because you communicate, and I, because I conceal nothing' (147). Richardson in her turn hypothesises that *Sense and Sensibility's* epistolary past had an important residual impact on its final third-person form. In 'Dramatizing Intimacy: Free Indirect Discourse in *Sense and Sensibility*', Richardson focuses on the role of confession in the novel. She argues that it serves to reveal key points of the plot and, more significantly, nuances of narrative perspectives and voices—which is to say that confession ushers in the beginnings of Austen's signature use of free indirect discourse (243).

It is intriguing to wonder if, far from being a mere accident of literary fashion, Austen's decision to change the narrative structure of the novel was an intellectual and artistic one. But such an evolution in narrative form could, following up on an argument made magisterially by Jocelyn Harris in *Jane Austen's Art of Memory,* very well be a straightforward matter of a maturing writer moving away from formative influences whose novels might, in the early drafts of what eventually became *Sense and Sensibility*, have been too obviously emulated or too heavily borrowed from. Surveying the eighteenth-century antecedents of *Sense and Sensibility*, Harris points out various ways that it derives from, and sometimes outright copies, one of her favourite writers, Samuel Richardson, author of the epistolary novels *Pamela*, *Clarissa*, and *Sir Charles Grandison*, supposedly Jane Austen's favourite. Some details—among them Brandon's name and the paratextual stories of the two Elizas—could have come right out of Richardson. The move out of epistolary style might be a more mature Austen's declaration of independence from him and from other epistolary predecessors who influenced her profoundly, novelists whose eighteenth-century epistolary presence lingers in *Sense and Sensibility* despite the change of narrative form.

The Sisters

As to the sisters Elinor and Marianne: whether it's their letters or their intimate conversations that move the plot forward, whether one of them is 'sense' and one 'sensibility' or they both display ever-varying degrees and mixtures of both qualities, their relationship constitutes the core of the novel. For this reason it seems likely that the plot changed markedly with the shift out of epistolary format. It is almost impossible to imagine a novel written in letters without a single exchange of correspondence between its two heroines (and title characters in the earliest draft)—but *Sense and Sensibility* is unique among Austen's novels in featuring sisters who never spend a night apart. The mutual devotion of Jane and Elizabeth Bennet is the only instance of sisterly feeling rivalling the Dashwoods' in the Austen canon, and the Bennet sisters' paths diverge from time to time, occasionally for weeks. Their intermittent separations require both correspondence and explanatory conversation. The Dashwood duo, never apart, has no need for writing letters to one another—and as mentioned above, despite being in constant contact each sister withholds important information from the other (in Elinor's case, that Lucy and Edward are engaged; in Marianne's, that she and Willoughby correspond despite not being engaged) though for very different reasons.

Elinor and Marianne first appear in a comparison and contrast in which the narrator also includes their mother. Elinor is introduced as advisor to her mother. She's a precociously mature nineteen-year-old 'counsellor' whose 'strength of understanding' and 'coolness of judgment' permit her 'frequently to counteract, to the advantage of them all, that eagerness of mind in Mrs Dashwood which must have generally led to imprudence. She had an excellent heart;—her disposition was affectionate, and her feelings were strong; but she knew how to govern them: it was a knowledge which her mother had yet to learn, and which one of her sisters had resolved never to be taught' (4).

A short paragraph devoted to the sister who is resolved not to learn to govern her feelings follows—and it seems hardly coincidental that in the 1790s Austen would confer on this unrestrained romantic the name given to the female personification of the French Revolution, a name Austen never reused for another character: 'Marianne's abilities were, in many respects, quite equal to Elinor's. She was sensible and clever; but eager in every thing; her sorrows, her joys, could have no moderation. She was generous, amiable, interesting: she was every thing but prudent. The resemblance between her and her mother was strikingly great' (4–5). As Inger Sigrun Brodey convincingly demonstrates in *Ruined by Design*, Marianne is a female counterpart to Goethe's young Werther, the Romantic-era prototype of excessive sensibility (168-72).

Several points deriving from these introductory sentences, ideas simple but easily forgotten, are worth noticing. First, the initial presentation of the sisters clearly asserts that neither Elinor nor Marianne has a deficiency of either sense (if by that we mean the capacity to think) or of sensibility (in contrast, if we're setting the qualities in contrast, the capacity to feel). What's happened thus far, as I have argued in *Jane Austen and Charles Darwin: Naturalists and Novelists*, is that these sisters' personalities, like those of sibling group members in the other novels, have been developing in relation to the distinctive circumstances of their family environment. Lacking a mother with an inclination to govern feelings and give adult credence to the claims of prudence and practicality, Elinor has necessarily developed the prudent, practical, parental side of her character—perhaps earlier in conscious emulation of her late father but now certainly to step in for him as the rational grownup in the female household. Marianne, two years younger, has filled a family niche not occupied by Elinor: she has emulated their mother, who has encouraged her in doing so (an intergenerational feedback loop we see later in Mrs Bennet and Lydia of *Pride and Prejudice*). But the sisters are only nineteen and seventeen. If we compare their ages to those of the heroines of Austen's other novels, incrementally building a cohort of marriageable female protagonists and supporting characters, Elinor and Marianne are old enough to be out in society, the latter barely so. But neither of them is old enough to be seen as a fully formed adult woman, however articulate they both are and however mature Elinor's values may be—and she does have the seeming *gravitas* of often being the wisest woman (or person) in the room. Among the women older than Elinor, Mrs Dashwood lacks her restraint and practicality, Mrs Jennings her manners and discernment, Lady Middleton her depth, Fanny Dashwood and Mrs Ferrars her principled behaviour and altruism, Mrs Palmer and Miss Steele her mature deportment, and Lucy Steele her education and ethical soundness.

Like Catherine Morland, Fanny Price, and even Elizabeth Bennet and Emma Woodhouse, the last two being twenty as their respective novels begin, the Dashwood sisters' characters are still developing in important ways. Throughout *Sense and Sensibility* what we see, sometimes savour, and sometimes deplore, are very specific instances of how these two engaging siblings respond with sense or with sensibility—to appropriate or inappropriate degrees—as the contingencies of their lives unfold. From time to time they are inclined to disagree over matters of conduct, Marianne calling Elinor cold or reserved for declining to avow 'love' for Edward, Elinor seeing Marianne as rash, discourteous, or worse, whether she's ignoring the customary niceties of guest behaviour at Barton Park or at Mrs Jennings's London house or spending undue amounts of time in Willoughby's company, thinking that she can accept his proffered gift of a horse, or corresponding with him—the last a conventional signal of being engaged. But the sisters' love and respect for one another is unmissable. Indeed, their mutually involved dyad is so strong a bond that Margaret, the 'good-humoured, well-disposed' third sister, seems an afterthought, as her cursory description in the last sentence of the novel's first chapter makes clear: 'as she had already imbibed a good deal of Marianne's romance, without having much of her sense, she did not, at thirteen, bid fair to equal her sisters at a more advanced period of life' (5). In contrast to the novel, the Emma Thompson screenplay makes far fuller use of Margaret as an engaging innocent whose questions reveal the absurdities of adult gentility, whose earnest curiosity evokes warm and lively responses from re-pressed Edward, and whose tomboy ways offer a playful version of Regency girlhood that is ap-pealing to present-day audiences.

During the two years that take readers from the Dashwood sisters' displacement from Norland Park to their putting down roots at Delaford—Elinor marries Edward and moves in at the parsonage well before Marianne finds herself as lady of Brandon's manor 'submitting to new attachments, entering on new duties, placed in a new home, a wife, the mistress of a family, and the patroness of a village' (333)—there are ample trials of their characters and tests of their values. As Sarah Emsley explains in *Jane Austen's Philosophy of the Virtues*, these trials and tests involve delicately reconciling amiability and tact with honesty in the social world while cultivating the heroic virtue of fortitude and the Christian virtue of love (58). In their personal and social interactions, one or the other of the sisters often falls short. As Emsley sees it, both sisters need to learn how to balance honesty with civility, though they deviate from a desirable mean in opposite directions. Marianne often displays rudeness to others and respects only her own feelings; Elinor is capable of the polite lie, active or passive, in the interest of respecting the feelings of others.

Elinor's imbalances, as Emsley sees it, are in any case self-aware and thus moral weakness rather than vice. Her behaviours are likelier than are her younger sister's to be amiable and often downright admirable. Notable among such behaviours: Elinor's restraint in respecting Lucy's confidential disclosures and her disinterest in furthering Brandon's goal of setting up Edward Ferrars, the man she loves, so that he will have the money to marry Lucy, whom she loathes for good reasons in her discreet way. But as a realistic young woman rather than a paragon, Elinor is capable of moments of erring, for instance when the narrator's access to her thoughts exposes what might look like a grim delight in encouraging confidential remarks that reveal Lucy Steele's innate vulgarity and ignorance. A more serious if far briefer lapse comes after the crisis in Marianne's illness, when Elinor reluctantly receives Willoughby's visit and momentarily falls for his charisma. Neither justifying Willoughby's conduct nor approving his marital choice, she nonetheless feels tenderness for the rogue and regret for how things have turned out, dreads what the effect of informing Marianne might be, 'and for a moment wished Willoughby a widower' (294). But her objectifying Willoughby's bride as an in-convenient obstacle instantly gives way to remembering faithful Colonel Brandon. Elinor feels that 'to *his* sufferings and *his* constancy far more than his rival's, the reward of her sister was due' (294); and here she reifies her sister Marianne, though in a far more benevolent way. These passing thoughts offer evidence that Elinor's moral danger is of being too heavily influenced by her society's values, in this specific case the reduction of women to marriage-market commodities.

Marianne is less self-aware than is Elinor, so her shortcomings are more serious. As Susan Morgan observes in *In the Meantime: Character and Perception in Jane Austen's Fiction*, Marianne's self-vaunted integrity 'is a luxury, an indulgence of self at the expense of those around her' (127). Confident that her personal tastes and judgements are correct, she lives what Kierkegaard would call an aesthetic life, self-involved as opposed to Elinor, whose life is ethical, related to and defined by other people. This self-involvement repeatedly leads Marianne into mistakes: she takes Willoughby's superficial charm for more substantial excellence and writes off both Mrs Jennings and Colonel Brandon because of superficial attributes that blind her to deeper ones. Trusting in her own infallibility, she refuses to acknowledge how wrong she's been to walk surreptitiously through Mrs Smith's house at Allenham with Willoughby, imagining the improvements she would make. Alerted to this mistake by Elinor, Marianne responds with typical moral solipsism: 'if there had been any real impropriety in what I did, I should have been sensible of it at the time …' (59). But if Marianne's opinions and behaviors are often wrong, love, good intent, and sobering experience incline her to correct them. Recovered from illness, she recognizes her conduct when under Willoughby's spell as 'nothing but a series of imprudence toward myself, and want of kindness to others' (303).

Individually errant though Elinor and Marianne may be at different times, in different ways, and to different degrees, the great constant in their characters is sisterly devotion. Nothing shakes their bond of love, just as nothing in the action of the novel physically separates them. Whatever Austen's readers think of the Dashwood sisters' marriages, the last words of *Sense and Sensibility* declare that a consequence of these unions is their prospect of life-long sisterly togetherness. The *Sense and Sensibility* narrator, often inclined toward waspishness, phrases this affirmation negatively: 'among the merits and happiness of Elinor and Marianne, let it not be ranked as the least considerable, that though sisters, and living almost within sight of each other, they could live without disagreement between themselves, or producing coolness between their husbands' (335). But readers should recognise that any scepticism or irony here is directed at sisters in general. For Elinor and Marianne, life lived side by side will be a blessing, perhaps life's best one.

Inheritance, Money, and Power

From its first sentences *Sense and Sensibility* announces itself a novel of inheritance: 'The family of Dashwood had long been settled in Sussex. Their estate was large, and their residence was at Norland Park, in the centre of their property, where, for many generations, they had lived in so respectable a manner, as to engage the general good opinion of their surrounding acquaintance' (1). But what's a family? The word as Austen uses it here is dynastic rather than domestic—a surname (Dashwood) enduring in a place (Norland Park, Sussex) over time. For her readers, however, it means something more immediate: the widow Dashwood and her three daughters. The initial problem, both for readers and for the female quartet including the two heroines Elinor and Marianne, is that things work smoothly and conventionally for 'family' in the one sense but at the expense of a 'family' in the second sense. An estate remains intact and economically solvent, indeed enhanced, in the patriarchal bloodline at the cost of uprooting and displacing a mother and her daughters.

So dearly do the Dashwood daughters love Norland Park that it is easy to forget that none of them was born there. With their parents the Henry Dashwoods, the sisters moved to Norland ten years before the death of the bachelor incumbent of the estate, when the loss of a sister left him alone. Austen describes Henry Dashwood as 'the legal inheritor of the Norland estate, and the person to whom he [the bachelor uncle] intended to bequeath it' (1)—that is, the rightful heir to Norland if the uncle were to die intestate but also the heir designated by terms of his will. Norland Park, like a number of the other estates in *Sense and Sensibility*, is not entailed as the story opens. But the uncle's will controls the estate intergenerationally by settling it on Henry Dashwood for his lifetime and subsequently securing it to John Dashwood and his four-year-old son. Henry Dashwood is thus left without discretionary power to provide for his wife and daughters either by the sale of the park's valuable timber or 'by any charge on the estate' (2). In the notes to his edition of *Sense and Sensibility* R. W. Chapman points out that Austen's phrasing in the first edition was 'by any division of the estate' (383)—'division of' suggesting a far more radical way of equalising distribution of the estate's assets than 'charge on' does. Changing the verb shows her interest in the precise legal nature of the bequest.

Not surprisingly, there has been a great deal of discussion from a feminist point of view of John Dashwood's inheritance of Norland and his stepmother and half-sisters' removal from their established home—the latter event cunningly precipitated by John's wife Fanny, who could be seen as a perfect example of the 'cold-hearted, narrow-minded woman' Wollstonecraft in *Vindication of the Rights of Woman* imagines manipulating a man who inherits an estate at the expense of his sisters.

'Jealous of the little kindness which her husband shows to his relations', and 'displeased at seeing the property of HER children lavished on a helpless sister' (63—Wollstonecraft's words, not Austen's), Fanny Dashwood is just the sort of selfish married woman who according to Wollstonecraft ruthlessly plays any card to drive out rival females. John Dashwood, 'not an ill-disposed young man, unless to be rather cold hearted, and rather selfish, is to be ill disposed' (Austen's narrator's sarcastic words, not Wollstonecraft's) and uxoriously fond of a wife who's 'a strong caricature of himself—more narrow-minded and selfish' (3), readily capitulates to Fanny's wishes. The brilliantly bitter second chapter of *Sense and Sensibility* is nothing but a step-by-step discussion wherein Fanny Dashwood progressively diminishes her husband's initial plan for satisfying the deathbed promise he made to look after his stepmother and half-sisters by the minimally generous act of settling a thousand pounds on each sister. At Fanny's urging, John's notion of appropriate fraternal generosity dwindles first to five hundred pounds per sister, then to a hundred-pound annuity for their mother, next to 'a present of fifty pounds now and then', and finally to practical help with their move and 'occasional presents of fish and game', a gesture rendered impossible by their eventual move from Sussex to Devonshire (9).

Just as indignant as Wollstonecraft was at patriarchal injustice, modern-day feminist critics of *Sense and Sensibility* have tended to emphasise the historical constraints on women's inheritance as a springboard for considering Austen's perspective on the legal status of women. Though severe on Austen at some other moments, Sandra Gilbert and Susan Gubar, in their now-classic *The Madwoman in the Attic* (1979), cite *Sense and Sensibility* and the other two earliest-begun novels to argue that Austen seriously considers contemporary economic and legal restrictions women of her time faced:

> [Austen explores] the specific ways in which patriarchal control of women depends on women being denied the right to earn or even inherit their own money. From *Sense and Sensibility*, where a male heir deprives his sisters of their home, to *Pride and Prejudice*, where the male entail threatens the Bennet girls with marriages of convenience [...] Austen reminds her readers that the laws and customs of England may, as Henry Tilney glowingly announces, insure against wife-murder (II, chap. 10), but they do not offer much more than this minimal security for a wife not beloved, or a woman not a wife. (136)

While many of the financial readings of the novel continue in this vein, often as a method for either granting or denying Austen a feminist intent, several recent interpretations push the conversation about money in *Sense and Sensibility* in a new direction. Either by foregrounding the financial independence or power of certain female characters in *Sense and Sensibility* or by appraising the commercial underpinnings of marriage, these critics ask readers to reconsider the economic framework of the novel. In 'Amatory Gifts in *Sense and Sensibility*', Lauren Wilwerding applies gift theory, which posits that 'where commodities are exchanged for other things or money, gifts are exchanged to establish or maintain relationships, social bonds, and commitments' to the romantic pairings in Austen's text (2). Taking Marianne's repulsion at a marriage based on 'commercial exchange' as a point of departure, Wilwerding asks, 'In the companionate model of marriage, do women still function as gifts? Can women participate in gift exchange with men?' and claims that *Sense and Sensibility* '[addresses] these questions through heroines who deploy different gifting strategies and illustrates the consequences of these strategies for readers' (2). Jackie Mijares considers a more concretely particular version of female financial power in 'Mrs Jennings and 'The Comfortable Estate of Widowhood', or the Benefits of Being a Widow with a Handsome Jointure'. Noting that 'whether a woman was left richer or poorer, one tradeoff for losing one's husband was regaining one's self according to the law', Mijares traces the legal and lived consequences of widowhood using the fiscal stability of Mrs Jennings as a model and ultimately showing that Mrs

Jennings's effective home management is one of several clues from Austen about the competence and practical virtue of a character that some readers, like Marianne Dashwood, might be otherwise inclined to dismiss as absurd (para 2; para 19).

Connecting a practical concern for money with the concept of 'sense' and a charitable and happy disposition with 'sensibility' Kathleen Anderson and Jordan Kidd claim that Mrs Jennings and (more controversially) her daughter Mrs Palmer represent a perfect balance of the two, in part because of their financial stability. In 'Mrs Jennings and Mrs Palmer: The Path to Female Self-Determination in Austen's Sense and Sensibility', Anderson and Kidd argue that Mrs Jennings's financial and emotional independence, rooted as it is in a love of her family and sociability, gives her self-assurance and happiness. They likewise note that Charlotte Palmer is prosperous but not mercenary and interpret her lack of concern with money or with society's perception of her as setting Charlotte apart from women with either too much sensibility or too much 'cold, material sense'. For Anderson and Kidd, the latter quality distinguishes the villainesses of the novel, such characters as Mrs Ferrars, Fanny Dashwood, and Lucy Steele. Mrs Ferrars has both widowed autonomy and considerable financial power; her daughter Fanny Dashwood holds the whip hand over a husband weaker than she is; and Lucy Steele possesses the shrewdness and focused drive to rise significantly above her situation to attain a financial status far beyond that accorded to the deserving Elinor; so all three could be viewed as having escaped the patriarchal control condemned by Gilbert and Gubar. But none is admirable, two because of how unwisely and selfishly they respectively wield economic power, the other for how ruthlessly she pursues such power. In a novel that foregrounds female characters' unjust financial plights, it is sadly unsatisfying but all too true to life to see that some, though not all, of the women possessing economic power misuse it.

An empirical approach to issues of money, inheritance, and economic clout can prove especially rewarding, as *Sense and Sensibility* is a novel grounded in financial particulars. We know just where the Dashwood women have started, living at Norland Park, an estate worth 4000 pounds a year, and just what they have by way of their own assets: 7000 pounds Henry Dashwood had 'in his own disposal', an additional 1000 pounds each settled on his three daughters, personal property such as china, plate, linen, and Marianne's pianoforte, and 'the offer of a small [furnished] house on very easy terms' (19), Barton Cottage. We also know Elinor and Marianne's professed opinions on money. Elinor asserts that 'wealth' has much to do with happiness; Marianne disagrees and claims that 'beyond a competence' money can offer no satisfaction. But it becomes clear, as Elinor has wryly and rightly suspected, that her idea of 'wealth' and Marianne's of 'competence' are much the same: 1800–2000 pounds a year (78).

We also learn the material circumstances of Elinor and Marianne's suitors, among other characters. Edward Ferrars initially has 2000 pounds in his own right and is heir to an estate (significantly, not an entailed one) worth 1000 a year that he loses to his younger brother when their mother finds out about his engagement to Lucy Steele. Edward is offered the clerical living at Delaford (200 pounds a year plus a small rectory) by Colonel Brandon and eventually receives 10,000 pounds, the equivalent of his sister Fanny's dowry, from his semi-relenting mother. John Willoughby has one estate, Combe Magna, worth 600–700 pounds a year according to Sir John Middleton but lives beyond his means, as he is also presumptive heir to a second estate, Allenham Court, belonging to his aged aunt Mrs Smith. Colonel Brandon's Delaford is an estate worth 2000 a year—the very figure that constitutes 'wealth' to Elinor and 'competence' to Marianne.

In 'Money in Jane Austen', a meticulous and penetrating analysis of the economic basis of Austen's novels put into telling comparison with the financial underpinnings of her own life, Robert D. Hume explores the 'brutal contrast between the tiny sums that were painfully important in Austen's own life' and the 'giant sums' we encounter in her fiction (290). Hume also approximates what those 'giant sums' might mean in terms of present-day buying power. He explains that an income of 2000 pounds a year would, in the early nineteenth century, have put its possessor in the top .018% of the population. In other words both Colonel Brandon and his fellow 2000-pounds-a-year estate-holder Mr Bennet, who seems far from rich in *Pride and Prejudice*, would be better off than more than 999 out of a thousand English contemporaries. The total income with which Edward and Elinor will start married life, approximately 850 pounds a year, puts them far above the figures variously identified as 'nominal' or 'reasonable' for turn-of-the-century English clergymen (between 150 and 238 pounds)—and even well above the roughly 600 pounds a year on which the Rev George Austen, a pluralist holding the livings of Steventon and Dean and supplementing his clerical income by taking in paid pupils, supported a wife and eight children.

As W. H. Auden trenchantly observed in his poem 'Letter to Lord Byron', Jane Austen's novels, *Sense and Sensibility* among them, do indeed 'Reveal so frankly and with such sobriety/ The economic basis of society' (Part 1: 9). Nonetheless it is useful to remember (as Hume points out) that in *Sense and Sensibility* and her other works, she is imagining lives based on fortunes far grander than her own modest economic circumstances. Such fortunes did exist in her day, of course—and similarly, despite the generally restricted access to money (even their own fortunes) and to financial independence available most women of her day, nineteenth-century English women could and sometimes did wield economic power. That is the case in *Sense and Sensibility*, as some of the feminist scholarship noted above has acknowledged. But, as is her empirical wont, Austen resists generalising on the matter. Miss Grey, a 50,000-pounder who has come of age and has control of the largest specified female fortune in Austen's novels, uses her money to buy Willoughby, a spendthrift who clearly loves another woman. As a married woman, Fanny Dashwood's money legally belongs to her husband, but she uses her stronger character and more determined will to control his economic choices, notably to squelch his feeble impulses of generosity and to encourage his narrowly dynastic selfishness. Fanny's equally small-minded mother, who has the legal power to determine who will inherit the Ferrars estate, chooses badly: she disinherits the worthy Edward for honouring his engagement to Lucy, designates his foolish, foppish brother the heir, and ends up with the predatory Lucy as daughter-in-law anyway. But set against her are two other widows with ample resources, sound financial sense, and strong moral sensibilities: Mrs Jennings, whose silly surface belies her competence, compassion, generosity, and right judgment, and Mrs Allen, 'an exemplary version of authority', in Claudia Johnson's phrase (70). Mrs Smith refuses to excuse Willoughby's seductions on learning of them and accordingly, acting as a sort of moral opposite to Mrs Ferrars, intends to disinherit an *unengaged* man for a *good* reason. But she eventually forgives Willoughby, 'stating his marriage with a woman of character, as the source of her clemency', a strong reason for him to suspect that 'had he behaved with honour towards Marianne, he might have been happy and rich' (334).

Dull Marriages, Dark Doings, and a Conclusion That Fails to Satisfy Some Readers

The abuse of financial and domestic power by some women able to wield it connects to one of the other major areas of scholarly interest: the novel's multi-marriage ending, so potentially exasperating to *Sense and Sensibility* readers who prefer to see virtue rewarded and vice punished in fiction and for a different reason to those who, having loved the Ang Lee version first, favour the film's more rom-com denouement: triumphant music, clearly joyful Marianne, radiant Brandon in scarlet regimentals tossing coins to the crowd, cinematic images so compelling that they gloss over the twenty-nine-year disparity in the actors' ages. Kate Winslet and Alan Rickman were twenty and forty-nine when the film came out. That's a decade more than the age gap that makes seventeen-year-old Marianne initially dismiss thirty-six-year-old Brandon, the one person of the Barton Park set who appreciates her musical performance with true taste and pleasure, as aged, infirm, and long past the sensation of love—a man who should have 'nothing to do with matrimony' (32).

Such moral or romantic readers might gnash their teeth at Lucy Steele prospering through ruthlessness and rapacity, might object to Marianne settling for a much older man, and might think that Elinor marries Austen's most tepid male protagonist, a low-energy depressive who is heroic only in abiding by an engagement no matter what. For many scholars, however, the reader-frustrating marital conclusion is what separates Austen's more realistic storytelling from the sentimental romances she arguably satirises: the moments least satisfying as the conclusion of a romantic fiction feel the truest to life. In 'Secret Sharing and Secret Keeping: Lucy Steele's Triumph in Speculation', Lynda A. Hall makes the claim that Austen means her readers to be dissatisfied by Lucy's success: 'Through her characterization of this 'monstrous pretty' speculator, Jane Austen reveals an unsavory truth: speculative behavior, however unscrupulous it might be, is rewarded in a consumer-driven society' (171). In economic and social ways Lucy, by marrying the heir to the Ferrars estate (even though he is the inferior brother in every other way) seems to triumph over the far more deserving Elinor, who gains a first son socially and economically demoted to second-son status—and gains him only because Lucy has jilted him. For Hall and other critics, this conclusion so unattractive to readers who would prefer for Elinor's match to surpass Lucy's in every way shows a truth about how society works.

Marianne's marriage, too, is sometimes interpreted as a comment on the social realities of Austen's time, another example of moral realism that speaks both to the historical contingencies of Austen's moment and to the timeless traits of her nuanced, complex characters. In '"Describing What Never Happened": Jane Austen and the History of Missed Opportunities', William Galperin argues that it is not so much Marianne and Colonel Brandon's marriage that forces readers into the position of considering its unsatisfactory realness as it is Willoughby's reaction to it: '*Sense and Sensibility* is forever haunted by the specter of John Willoughby, whose own reflections at the novel's close—in particular the 'pang' he experiences at the thought of Marianne Dashwood's marriage to Colonel Brandon—are less a retributive instrument than a darkling echo of earlier prospects' (355). Willoughby, in short, does not receive what he deserves in a morally retributive sense but instead gets what might be practically expected as long-term emotional consequences of the mercenary matrimonial bargain he's made: some interludes of disappointment, regret, and longing for what might have been.

Austen the realist does not, however, allow readers keen for emotional justice to imagine Willoughby inconsolable, habitually gloomy, or broken hearted: 'He lived to exert, and frequently to enjoy himself. His wife was not always out of humour, nor his home always uncomfortable; and in his breed of horses and dogs, and in sporting of every kind, he found no inconsiderable degree of domestic felicity' (334). Surprising though it might at first seem, this fast-forward into Willoughby's married future shows him, as far as consolations go, a kindred spirit to Sir John Middleton. The true Willoughby turns out to be less the aesthete Marianne imagined him than the sporting country gentleman he had been from the moment he appeared on the scene, with a gun and two pointers, to become Marianne's 'preserver'. Readers of *Sense and Sensibility*, like Austen's narrator, seem to feel little if any concern for Miss Grey, the heiress Willoughby married for her 50,000 pounds; but it is not unlikely that things turn out for the Willoughbys much as they do for the temperamentally incompatible Middletons, the warm-hearted, undiscriminating sportsman Sir John yoked to a cold-hearted, conventionally elegant mere mother. In this sort of marriage, each ill-matched individual can take some satisfaction in embracing a culturally determined gender role even if denied a congenial partner. But that is cold comfort for characters in the oeuvre of the novelist widely credited with being the most popular and accomplished fictive presenter of companionate marriage, a cultural ideal that arose in Austen's time and endures through ours.

A persistent problem for present-day readers is the notable difference in when women embark upon companionate marriages in Austen's novels and when they typically do now. As Shannon Chamberlain points out in 'What Jane Austen Thought Marriage Couldn't Do', modern readers might justifiably observe that Austen novels such as *Sense and Sensibility* 'focus too much on younger women at the expense of making older ones either irrelevant or ridiculous'. Given this focus, many or most Austen heroines enter into marriage before present-day readers, not inclined to accept Regency mores while reading about Regency manners, would consider them old enough to do so. One such reader, Shawn Lisa Maurer, argues in 'At Seventeen: Adolescence in *Sense and Sensibility*' that the Brandon marriage frustrates present-day readers because Marianne's adolescence has been realistically represented throughout the novel. In Maurer's view, Marianne is 'a distinctly modern adolescent figure, whose transformation into 'a wife, the mistress of a family, and the patroness of a village', evokes in many readers a deep sense of the lost possibilities inherent in the adolescent state' (723–24). There may be present-day advocates for perpetual adolescence, but a harsher potential critique comes from feminist readers such as Carol Lazzaro-Weis, who take umbrage at what happens in the 'female *bildungsroman*' when adolescent girls have indeed grown into womanhood: 'suppression and defeat of female autonomy, creativity, and maturity by patriarchal gender norms' (17).

Marianne, viewed from these present-day perspectives, may seem to have been quickly and perhaps artificially pushed into an adulthood oppressive to strong female identity. Her early actions, intemperate opinions, and reckless passions can be understood as the natural consequences of her age and emotional maturity. Thus even though the bride is two years older and wiser and the narrator assures readers that Marianne's loving heart 'became, in time, as much devoted to her husband, as it had once been to Willoughby' the marital conclusion, reported rather than dramatically presented, can seem both abrupt and unsuitable. The problem, however, may be less with the conclusion of *Sense and Sensibility* itself than with the mismatch between present-day expectations and the real circumstances in which many young Regency women married. As Chamberlain might put it, Marianne's marriage at nineteen is something readers of today might see as more appropriate for women of twenty-seven or so—but then seventeen-year-old Marianne pronounced of such mature specimens, 'A woman of seven and twenty ... can never hope to feel or inspire affection again' (32) though Elinor and the novel's narrator obviously believe otherwise. As observations like Galperin's, Chamberlain's, Lazaro-Weis's, and Maurer's suggest, if the novel's ending proves frustrating, the frustrations may stem in various ways from what readers want for Austen's characters.

Sense and Sensibility, though a fiction, is filled with believably imperfect people: Mrs Jennings is a practical manager and a happy, generous, good woman, but she is also nosy, silly, and vulgar; Lady Middleton is elegant but cold and insubstantial, her sister Charlotte Palmer warm, good-natured, dim-witted, and in possession (as Elinor notes) of an irritating laugh. The Jennings sisters are married to men whose characters are similarly mixed but particularly ill-suited to their respective spouses': warm-hearted, welcoming, undiscriminating Sir John seems as wrong for Lady Middleton as sardonic Palmer, whose caustic remarks and insulting behaviours conceal sound judgement and a generous heart, seems for Charlotte. As in the real world, the good people of *Sense and Sensibility* are not necessarily the most amusing or good-natured ones, while the charming ones are not necessarily trustworthy or kind. Nowhere is this distinction between surface and substance clearer than in the characters of Willoughby and Edward Ferrars, who have both attracted their share of critical attention. Moreland Perkins' in-depth analysis of *Sense and Sensibility* shows that the complexity of these two characters rests in their aesthetic or sexual appeal. Edward, in Perkins' view, is an unsatisfying Austen hero because his best characteristics are not conventionally masculine: 'his modesty, his quiet reticence, his "open, affectionate heart"', the fact that 'all his wishes centered in domestic comfort and the quiet of private life' are virtues his culture construed as typically feminine (40).

Elinor can easily value these low-key traits, but characters like Marianne struggle to interpret Edward as a viable romantic partner. Willoughby's romantic dash, in contrast, is nearly universally acknowledged, in large part because he's a more obviously manly man. Hall, in 'Jane Austen's Attractive Rogues: Willoughby, Wickham, and Frank Churchill', claims that Willoughby 'possesses the first, and perhaps the most important trait of the attractive rogue—he fulfills the heroine's idea of good looks and romance' (186). Interestingly, though, Willoughby's most potent appeal is more than superficial. He can rival Marianne in being a person of sensibility—unlike the prosaic Edward Ferrars, whose deficiencies in appreciating the picturesque, the sublime, and the aesthetic appeal of art, whether Cowper's poetry or Elinor's drawing, evoke Marianne's pity.

But in fact neither of these two younger candidates for romantic hero can match thirty-five-year-old Colonel Brandon, a true man of feeling whose backstory involves having loved and lost, planned a failed elopement, fought a duel, felt deep melancholy, wrestled with jealousy of an unworthy rival, kept and then revealed dark secrets, and displayed true devotion—all despite the flannel waistcoats seventeen-year-old Marianne deplores and the nineteen-year age difference between him and the woman he loves. Austen encourages her readers to go beyond young Marianne's merely aesthetic sensibility in *Sense and Sensibility*. Perhaps in part due to the female focalisation of the novel, she uses male characters in particular to draw attention to how manners and style can mask intentions, values, or natures. We, like the Dashwood sisters, must look beneath the surface to discern the true worth of Edward Ferrars, Willoughby, Colonel Brandon, Mr Palmer, or Sir John Middleton. Perhaps only selfish John Dashwood and foolish Robert Ferrars, male characters who act as they are deep down, are exceptions to this rule.

Such disparities between surface and substance, between aesthetic appeal and ethical substance, like the realistic but perhaps ungratifying marital conclusions, stand out in Austen's oeuvre because they gesture toward a darker world than is usually more than hinted at in her other novels (with the exception, perhaps, of *Mansfield Park*). Many scholars, most notably Claudia Johnson and Mary Poovey, have addressed the paratextual darkness of *Sense and Sensibility*. Calling it a 'disenchanted novel', Johnson argues in *Jane Austen: Women, Politics, and the Novel* that such off-stage actions as Willoughby's seduction and abandonment of the under-age Eliza Williams and the duel he fights with Colonel Brandon reveal the sexual violence and irresponsibility implicit in the lives of country gentlemen and thereby force readers to consider the legitimacy of social codes that insist on marriage:

> Whereas conduct books teach young women the social codes they must adopt if they are to live acceptably as wives and daughters [...*Sense and Sensibility*] makes those codes and communities that dictate them the subject of its interrogation, and what is at stake finally is not propriety, but survival [...] If Marianne has resisted the codes which not only require but reward calculation and coldheartedness, she has submitted without resistance to those which dictate desolation and very nearly death as the price of feeling. (50)

Marianne escapes the sexual violence or debasement that might befall heroines found in sentimental romances, the sad fates of Colonel Brandon's beloved cousin Eliza (who has suffered far more and sunk far lower than any other woman mentioned in an Austen novel) and her illegitimate daughter (rescued from a similar fate by Colonel Brandon). But Marianne nearly dies of grief and self-inflicted illness and in the end either settles for or welcomes what the narrator calls 'an extraordinary fate. She was born to discover the falsehood of her own opinions, and to counteract, by her conduct, her most favorite maxims' (333). That fate entails a commitment very different from what she would have envisioned or chosen at the start of the novel. Jane Schmidt, in her recent article '"Had I Died, It Would Have Been Self-Destruction": Indulged Sensibility and Retaliatory Illness in Austen's *Sense and Sensibility*', interprets Marianne's illness as a kind of last-resort expression of autonomy, wherein Marianne takes control of her emotional response to heartbreak and channels it into 'a suicide fantasy through which she punishes the duplicitous beloved and the society that inculcates the restrictions to the woman's role in romantic relationships' (422). Anne Richards, in 'The Passion of Marianne Dashwood: Christian Rhetoric in *Sense and Sensibility*', argues that Marianne's illness is not simply a turning point in her romantic inclinations but a 'Christian rebirth', thus locating Austen and her novel within an enduring turn-of-the-nineteenth-century evangelical literary tradition: '*Sense and Sensibility* is a novel about Marianne Dashwood—not for the reasons Romantically inclined readers might like to give, but because Marianne's *Christian* passion is the focus of the dramatic action of the novel' (152). For Maurer, Marianne's illness is less an indictment of marriage or a comment on Austen's socio-religious context than it is an example of Austen's psychological realism: 'we might attribute Marianne's physical and mental distresses to the volatility and emotional susceptibility associated with adolescence' (742).

The darkness in *Sense and Sensibility*—especially that surrounding Marianne, her two suitors, and the ruined young women whose lives might have been Marianne's—is not always interpreted as evidence of social realism though. In *The Proper Lady and the Woman Writer: Ideology as Style in the Works of Mary Wollstonecraft, Mary Shelley, and Jane Austen,* Mary Poovey views the second-hand accounts of how the two Elizas were betrayed, abused, seduced, and abandoned as borrowed 'romantic' tropes that undercut the novel's prevailing social realism. But Poovey sees that realism as going only so far: 'in *Sense and Sensibility,* Jane Austen will no more pursue the criticism of patriarchy […] than she will pursue the grim reality that is implicit in the narrator's account of the Dashwoods' economic situation' (192–93). In *Irony as Defense and Discovery* Marvin Mudrick makes a harsher but similar claim that the Elizas episode is sentimental fluff, and Jocelyn Harris argues that the subplots featuring Eliza senior and junior are not simply abstracted borrowings of romantic or sentimental tropes but more precisely unassimilated matter taken from Samuel Richardson: 'Jane Austen adopted the stories of Eliza Brandon and her daughter Eliza Williams—the surname probably came from a runaway daughter in *Grandison*—with very little change from *Clarissa*. They are the worse for it. Even the confusing repetition of the name Eliza reveals how cursorily she thought the episode through' (57). Bonnie G. Nelson, acknowledging Harris's and Mudrick's critiques, addresses this problem of realism versus romance in her article 'Rethinking Marianne Dashwood's Very Strong Resemblance to Eliza Brandon'. Nelson believes that this dramatic episode subverts the novel's realism even as it serves to focus the social critiques of 'mercenary marriage, familial coercion, female vulnerability, loss of home, parental failure, primogeniture, and disinheritance' (165).

The ambivalent critical response to the Eliza episodes runs parallel to other previously discussed interpretative difficulties *Sense and Sensibility* imposes on readers hoping for internal consistency, realistic representation of Austen's milieu, or conformity with their own culture's values and expectations. Are the novel's dissonances a mark of inexperience, the occasional infelicities we might expect to find in a first published book? Or are they artful and intentional? Do they reflect Jane Austen's ties to the more robust novels of the eighteenth century, ties that weaken as she establishes her own voice as a Regency novelist? Is the novel's economic particularity a reflection of social realism or of personal fantasy? Does the conclusion endorse the institution of marriage, problematise it, or foreground the fictive nature of the genre's obligatory 'happy ever after'? How do the patterns and practices found in *Sense and Sensibility* endure through the subsequent five completed and published novels? How does Austen vary her patterns and alter her practices as her art evolves? Even if *Sense and Sensibility* weren't the delightful and edifying book most readers and re-readers come to find it, these enduring, substantial questions and others like them would suffice to hold the attention of scholarly and popular audiences alike.

Note

1 Jane Austen, *Sense and Sensibility*, ed. James Kinsley, with a new Introduction by Margaret Anne Doody. Oxford: Oxford UP, 1970. Subsequent citations will refer to this text, substantially based on a collation of R. W. Chapman's first and second editions of the novel, and will be parenthetical.

Works Cited

Anderson, Kathleen, and Jordan Kidd. 'Mrs. Jennings and Mrs. Palmer: The Path to Female Self-Determination in Austen's *Sense and Sensibility*.' *Persuasions: The Jane Austen Journal*, vol. 30, 2008, 135–148.

Austen, Jane. *Sense and Sensibility*, edited by James Kinsley, introduction by Margaret Anne Doody. Oxford UP, 1970.

Auden, W. H. *Letter to Lord Byron*, 1936; Letters from Iceland. Random House, 1937.

Brodey, Inger Sigrun. 'Making Sense of Sensibility.' *Persuasions: The Jane Austen Journal*, vol. 37, 2015, 62–80.

Brodey, Inger Sigrun. *Ruined by Design: Shaping Novels and Gardens in the Culture of Sensibility*. Routledge, 2008.

Chamberlain, Shannon. 'What Jane Austen Thought Marriage Couldn't Do.' *Atlantic Monthly*, 3 Oct. 2019.

Chapman, R.W., editor. *Sense and Sensibility*. Oxford UP, 1933, rpt. 1971.

Doody, Margaret Anne. Introduction. *Sense and Sensibility* by Jane Austen, 1811, Oxford UP, 1970.

Emsley, Sarah. *Jane Austen's Philosophy of the Virtues*. Palgrave Macmillan, 2005.

Favret, Mary. *Romantic Correspondence: Women, Politics, and the Fiction of Letters*. Cambridge UP, 2008.

Folsom, Marsha McClintock. 'The Narrator's Voice and the Sense of *Sense and Sensibility*.' *Persuasions: The Jane Austen Journal*, vol. 33, 2011, 29–39.

Galperin, William. '"Describing What Never Happened": Jane Austen and the History of Missed Opportunities.' *ELH*, vol. 73, no. 2, 2006, 355–382.

Gilbert, Sandra M., and Susan Gubar. *The Madwoman in the Attic: The Woman Writer and the Nineteenth-Century Literary Imagination*. Yale UP, 1979.

Graham, Peter W. *Jane Austen & Charles Darwin: Naturalists and Novelists*. Ashgate, 2008.

Hall, Lynda A. 'Jane Austen's Attractive Rogues: Willoughby, Wickham, and Frank Churchill.' *Persuasions: The Jane Austen Journal*, vol. 18, 1996, 186–190.

Hall, Lynda A. 'Secret Sharing and Secret Keeping: Lucy Steele's Triumph in Speculation.' *Persuasions: The Jane Austen Journal*, vol. 33, 2011, 166–171.

Harris, Jocelyn. *Jane Austen's Art of Memory*. Cambridge UP, 1989.

Hume, Robert D. 'Money in Jane Austen'. *Review of English Studies*, new series, vol. 64, no. 264, 2013, 289–310.

Johnson, Claudia L. *Jane Austen: Women, Politics, and the Novel*. U of Chicago P, 1988.

Looser, Devoney. Introduction. *Sense and Sensibility* by Jane Austen, 1811, Penguin, 2019.

Maurer, Shawn Lisa. 'At Seventeen: Adolescence in *Sense and Sensibility*.' *Eighteenth-Century Fiction*, vol. 25, no. 4, spring 2013, pp. 721–750.

Mijares, Jackie. 'Mrs. Jennings and "The Comfortable State of Widowhood," or the Benefits of Being a Widow with a Handsome Jointure.' *Persuasions On-Line*, vol. 38, 2017.

Morgan, Susan. *In the Meantime: Character and Perception in Jane Austen's Fiction*. U of Chicago P, 1980.

Mudrick, Marvin. *Jane Austen. Irony as Defense and Discovery*. Princeton UP, 1952.

Nelson, Bonnie G. 'Rethinking Marianne Dashwood's Very Strong Resemblance to Eliza Brandon.' *Persuasions: The Jane Austen Journal*, vol. 34, 2012, 164–178.

O'Rourke, James. 'What Never Happened: Social Amnesia in *Sense and Sensibility*.' *Studies in English Literature*, vol. 54, no. 4, 2014, 773–791.

Perkins, Moreland. *Reshaping the Sexes in Sense and Sensibility*, U of Virginia P, 1998.

Poovey, Mary. *The Proper Lady and the Woman Writer: Ideology as Style in the Works of Mary Wollstonecraft, Mary Shelley, and Jane Austen*, U of Chicago P, 1984.

Richards, Anne. 'The Passion of Marianne Dashwood: Christian Rhetoric in *Sense and Sensibility*.' *Persuasions: The Jane Austen Journal*, vol. 25, 2003, 141–154.

Richardson, Rebecca. 'Dramatizing Intimacy: Free Indirect Discourse in Sense and Sensibility.' *ELH*, vol. 81, no. 1, 2014, 225–244.

Schmidt, Jane. '"Had I Died, It Would Have Been Self-Destruction": Indulged Sensibility and Retaliatory Illness in Austen's Sense and Sensibility.' *English Studies*, vol. 100, no. 4, 2018, 422–437.

Steiner, Enit Karafili. 'Between Cohesion and Reform in *Sense and Sensibility*.' *Women's Writing*, vol. 22, no. 4, 2015, 1–17.

Wilwelding, Lauren. 'Amatory Gifts in Sense and Sensibility.' *Persuasions: The Jane Austen Journal*, vol. 37, 2015, 208–217.

Wollstonecraft, Mary. *Vindication of the Rights of Woman, with Strictures on Political and Moral Subjects*. The Scott Library, 1891. Google Books, https://www.google.com/books/edition/A_Vindication_of_the_Rights_of_Woman/K1ZYAAAAcAAJ?hl=en&gbpv=1&dq=mary+wollstonecraft+a+vindication+of+the+rights+of+women&printsec=frontcover. Accessed 1 July 2020.

3

PRIDE AND PREJUDICE: NOT ALTOGETHER 'LIGHT & BRIGHT & SPARKLING'

Susan J. Wolfson

PRINCETON UNIVERSITY

Masterplot and Data-field

The now famous first sentence-paragraph of *Pride and Prejudice* comes as a proverb, with a wry twist: 'It is a truth universally acknowledged, that a single man in possession of a good fortune, must be in want of a wife' (5).[1] So appealing is this signature wit that Austen's dissatisfaction with her novel as 'rather too light & bright & sparkling;—it wants shade' seems perverse.[2] Sparkle has been the durable delight for generations. I'm not about to cloud, let alone sour, this; but I want to help Austen out by proposing that her distinct pleasure in unorthodox Elizabeth Bennet—'I think her as delightful a creature as ever appeared in print', she cooed to her sister (29 January 1813; *Letters* 201)—may have blinded her insight to the penumbra on the larger creation, both literary and empirical. My essay is an experiment on this field of inference.

Precisely because of the consensus, whether Janeite-fanned or countercast critique, that this is Austen's most sparkling novel—by force of both verbal wit and 'romance' satisfactions—a careful close reading is needed to assay the extraordinariness of her achievement on more than a surface of assured narrative authority. Historicist critiques have had a tendency to flatten literary formings, while a too-curated literary formalism can suppress a historicity of material facts and formations. My method is hybrid: reading the literary manifestations of the material data-field and reading material manifestations for literary, not just circumstantial, significance. Nobody escapes the contours, including the narrator, whose representation doesn't pick up everything that the narrative presents.

Take that opening aphorism. An assured authorial wit mocks the very discourse, winking at the ontology of 'universal' as an inflated specific for misses and their mothers. It is a jest, but a jest a little-too-ready-made to flatter a reader's pride in getting it. If we have jumped on board, the rest of the chapter rattles the ride, by taking seriously the looming shade over son-less Mrs Bennet and her five daughters, to be abjected by male entail, and lose in a stroke home, property, and Longbourn rents, to shift as they might.[3] The witty rhyme of narrative desire and social desire—*in possession of* and *in want of*—wrests *good fortune* from a romance-gloss to a cash registered marriage plot. And here, a slight fissure between *wit* and *want:* the wry *must* for a man is raw grammar for misses, a down-trending market of about ten years to secure the best deal. The next paragraph, also one brilliantly cut sentence, operates less as a sequel or elaboration than as a meta-lexical riff on the contingency of 'truth':

40

DOI: 10.4324/9780429398155-3-5

However little known the feelings or views of such a man may be on his first entering the neighborhood, this truth is so well fixed in the minds of the surrounding families, that he is considered as the rightful property of some one or other of their daughters (5).

Men do not know this because most property is rightfully theirs, a fixture of fact across Austen's ringing of 'fixed' for just about every sense in Johnson's *Dictionary*—from transfixed, fixated, to settled, unvarying fact (I:808).[4] If the ironising lights shine clear these days, it was still possible in 1936 to be unsettled by Austen's exposure of the economic base of romance. Only slightly archly, W. H. Auden affects distress in *Letter to Lord Byron* about this she-calculus—one that Byron, a man of good title in want of a wife in possession of a good fortune, had firmly in hand:

> It makes me most uncomfortable to see
>   An English spinster of the middle class
>   Describe the amorous effects of 'brass',
> Reveal so frankly and with such sobriety
> The economic basis of society. (part I: 9)

Unregaled in brass but with amorous glamour around his economic straits, Byron imprints the romance plot of *Pride and Prejudice* (as we will see later). In its economic lexicon, 'fortune' and its synonym, 'happiness' (*hap* is fortune), are never less than frankly material matters. What Auden describes as a revealed material basis Mark Schorer tracks as a visible 'stylistic sub-structure … under the surface of manners' and an inescapable recognition in its lexicon (xvi).

While all Austen's novels are so shaded, rather darkly at times, *Pride and Prejudice* has seemed such a fun holiday that 'fairy tale' is a frequent genre-tag, with negative couplings as foils to the central sparkle.[5] That's a structural function, but it is pressed at the edges by the data-field that remains unorganised toward this end. Auden's contemporary Virginia Woolf caught the way Austen's writing 'stimulates us to supply what is not there'. She meant 'much deeper emotion than appears upon the surface' (146). Half a century on, Sandra Gilbert and Susan Gubar discerned exposures right upon the surface, reading 'Austen's cover story' (their chapter title) as a syntax of proprieties plastered over depths of authorial conflict and alienation (154).

My argument is that data 'upon the surface', often dispersed but never swept away, needs no ironic distance, no intuition of symptomatic absence, deformation, or dark linings (though all this is in play). It is a legible litter on the literary surface, loose ends that resist tying up into fictional or social coherence, what Schorer values as 'aesthetic and moral precision' in the achievement of an 'integrated' thematic 'whole' (xix) and, in this compass, Reuben Brower's insistence that 'it is only the complex persons, the "intricate characters," that require and merit interpretation' (172). These paradigms have their latest iteration in Alex Woloch's *The One and the Many,* in which 'the many' secondary and peripheral characters function to bolster one 'achieved structure' (44). I do appreciate his cast and casting well beyond Brower's dramatis personae, and his widening of the sphere that Alistair Duckworth draws: a movement 'from an initial condition of potential social fragmentation to a resolution in which the grounds of society are reconstituted as the principal characters come together in marriage'. The Duckworth-grounds privilege the gentry 'drawing room' as host to 'widely separate outlooks and social positions' that 'mirror … social distances outside' (116–17)—a map 'generally agreed' on (he is sure) by all readers.[6] To this he adds a codicil from Lionel Trilling's liberal imagination: 'female vivacity' must find accommodation to 'strict male syntax' as a matter of 'high moral import' (118n, Trilling 222).

We could historicise the older stories of concord (and Brower's social compact of irony) as post-war, mid-century desiderata, but it is telling that 1980s feminist Mary Poovey can cite *Pride and Prejudice* as fairy tale, subtly skilled and motivated. Even with its array of 'dissatisfying' peripheral marriages, in this 'most idealistic of all of her novels, marriage remains … the ideal paradigm of the most perfect fusion between the individual and society' (204). Abetted by Austen's wit and irony, aesthetic gratifications displace 'social realism and criticism', attesting both 'to the power of her artistry and to the magnitude of our own desire to deny the disturbing ideological contradictions that have made such imaginative compensation necessary' (206–7). What Poovey credits to aesthetic mastery, Woloch assigns to a textual structure homologous to 'the social structure of capitalism' (124): *Pride and Prejudice* corrals 'the dispersion and fragmentation of the many' into 'one unified, although asymmetric field', the novel's 'controlling structure and final representation'.[7]

Without denying Austen's tonal and formal artistry of containment, I am interested in the dispersions and fragmentations: not only odd complexities in seemingly simple characters, but also weaves of words, names, locations. These adhere to those secondary characters about whom Brower is sure 'there can be no disagreement' in 'a proper way of thinking' (174; he is echoing Elizabeth); and it disarrays Woloch's totalising, controlling structure, to slant into Austen's textual surface with indexes of untold stories, back stories, spectral alterities, foreshortened futures, and unresolved equivocations. These aren't mysteries awaiting revelation (like the impresario of Pip's 'great expectations') but present, unorganised material. Karen Newman nicely tracks the unstable binary of romance and realism in 'visible seams' where 'contradictory materials' and 'rival versions of a single set of facts' coexist in this novel's characters 'without final reconciliation or resolution'—either in sentence-craft or plotlines (694–95).[8] This is a text that can dilate, as William Galperin scans it, 'to complicated … often antithetical ends' (*Historical Austen* 1). There is no recuperation to a dialectic of subversion and containment, or a dynamic of resistance to containment. It is an unpolished panorama of shade and sparkle that Austen leaves to her readers to determine. Such information clutters the formation of her first, crisp chapter.

Mr & Mrs Bennet, née Miss Gardiner

Pride and Prejudice concludes with one vibrant marriage (the Darcys), one pale pairing (the Bingleys), one travesty (the Wickhams), and a cascade of 'happy', 'happily', 'happiest', and 'happiness' washing over them all, so conspicuously—notwithstanding tonal layering—as to court a banality of the sort that John Keats camps up in the third stanza of *Ode on a Grecian Urn*: 'More happy love! more happy, happy love!' A happy master-plotting that keeps Elizabeth from derailing into a family-friendly bargain with her first suitor, William Collins, heir to the Longbourn entail. He has agreeably proposed making a match with one of the daughters, a practical generosity, but in the romance plot for Elizabeth, a noncontender. His chief service to Austen is sustainable fuel for Mr Bennet's satire. The narrator provides an advance cartoon: 'altogether a mixture of pride and obsequiousness, self-importance and humility' for his station in life (I.15/68). Mr Bennet gives a remix, with a value-added jab at his wife:

> An unhappy alternative is before you, Elizabeth. From this day you must be a stranger to one of your parents.—Your mother will never see you again if you do not marry Mr. Collins, and I will never see you again if you *do*. (I.20/103)

Such nicely styled wit floats no wisp that both parents might see to her security after he has shuffled off his mortal coil. It's not that Elizabeth should marry Mr Collins; it's that Mr Bennet is careless of the consequences when he really will never see Elizabeth again—'as soon as Mr. Bennet were dead', in his wife's future-cast (I.23/118). In the shadows is Miss Jane Austen having to shift, as soon as Revd Austen were dead, with her mother and sister on meagre economy. Mr Bennet is so much fun, however, that we may well share Brower's alliterated pleasure in his 'perversity' and the wife's 'petulance' (165). Across Volume I, the narrator leagues with the fun. The narrator's report of the wife 'really in a most pitiable state … an agony of ill humour' serves to set-up the husband's jest that her only relief will be a state of 'insensibility' (I.23/118–19)—no negligible negative in a novel whose title page reads 'by the Author of "Sense and Sensibility"'. The serious version is Elizabeth's rue at Charlotte Lucas's 'insensibility of danger' in catching Collins on the rebound, sacrificing 'security for happiness' (II.1/122).

Narration is one thing, authorial registration another. In a notorious essay titled 'Regulated Hatred', flung in the face of wartime Janeite adulation (*Scrutiny* 1940), D. W. Harding pressed at the instability of Austen's caricatures, even Mr Collins, a 'comic fantasy' he sees wavering into a 'fantastic nightmare' of how 'economic and social institutions' claim 'power over the values of personal relationships' (352–53). He advanced a 'deliberately lop-sided' illumination of Austen's under-reported imagination of 'things and people which to her, and still are, hateful' (362). Harding's 'still are', like Auden's socio-economic Austen, casts a line beyond the frisson of fiction. Appreciating his edgy accounting, ever contrarian William Empson dissented only to say that what Harding imagined unearthing in her social 'unconsciousness' was quite visible in the 'sunlight of her writings' (124).[9]

Harding's cast of hatefuls includes Mrs Bennet and Lady Catherine. There is more to say about Mr Collins. For now I want to focus on these women as no nightmares, but everyday deposits of social credit. As characters, both are delegitimised: Lady Catherine as imperious, arrogant, and manipulative, Mrs Bennet as ridiculous and hysteric. But both inhabit a fissure between narrator-prejudice and the narrated world that entertains their logic. Chapter 1 presents Mr Bennet, an 'odd … mixture of quick parts, sarcastic humour, reserve, and caprice', bonded to a wife 'of mean understanding, little information, and uncertain temper'. Some qualifying narrative data are recessive, but not absent: a 23-year marriage (trying for a male heir) has issued five girls and, as soon as the third year, a case of chronic 'nerves' in the wife. 'The business of her life was to get her daughters married; its solace was visiting and news' is the last sentence of this first chapter (7–8). No fritter of busyness, *business* draws on a range of respectable definitions in Johnson's *Dictionary:* 'employment', 'serious engagement', 'something required to be done' (I:305).

The little more information on the Bennets—a superannuated marriage plot now at dead end—comes sporadically, in casual data, usually during other narrative business. In the throes of the Lydia-crisis is a mention of their separate apartments (III.5/243–44). When Mrs Bennet's brother (Mr Gardiner) visits, we're told he is 'sensible' and 'superior to his sister' both by 'nature' and 'education' (II.2/124). She, apparently, was not given his education, and so thwarted in resources for becoming more 'sensible' and remanded by 'nature' to childbearing. If Mary Wollstonecraft (not alone) berates female miseducation, the Lydia-crisis makes it clear that 'sensible' has not exactly been Mr Bennet's strong suit. His retreats to his library, a redoubt of 'leisure and tranquillity' from 'folly and conceit in every other room of the house' (I.15/69), seem no less a deformation than Mrs Bennet's nerves. Unfolding events desparkle his wit: it is cruel in 'exposing his wife to the contempt of her own children' (II.19/203–4) and its neglect of family fortunes. Elizabeth, the narrator says, has long felt the 'evil' of his 'laughing at' his daughters (II.14/184; 18/199). Trilling lets him off with just a light rap: his 'irony of moral detachment is shown to be the cause of his becoming a moral nonentity' (181)—ineffectual but not culpable.

What brought this father to this pass? It's not until Volume II's last chapter (19) that we get the story. Young Mr Bennet, 'captivated by youth and beauty, and that appearance of good humour, which youth and beauty generally give', cooled quickly on the discovery of no great wit. 'Respect, esteem, and confidence, had vanished for ever; and all his views of domestic happiness were overthrown' (203). Wollstonecraft's ledger might throw him into the grievance column for the wrongs to a wife. For her part, Mrs Bennet knows that her stock has fallen since the days of 'her share of beauty' (I.1/6) and knows, too, that this came with a financial share, an inheritance of £4000 (I.7/31), twice the annual Longbourn revenue—considerable cents to sensibility. That's the extent of Mr Bennet's business mindedness. Planning on a male heir, daily 'economy was held to be perfectly useless'. Then five daughters, and despite efforts 'for many years' after Lydia, no son; 'it was then too late to be saving'. 'Mr. Bennet had very often wished … that, instead of spending his whole income', he had budgeted 'for the better provision of his children, and of his wife, if she survived him' (III.8/261).[10] But he regards his daughters as 'all silly and ignorant like other girls', allowing only 'little Lizzy' some 'quickness' (I.1/7). If the narrator doesn't call him 'selfish and improvident', Austen makes this deducible. Not even Lizzy and Jane seem sufficiently educated for a good position as governess, 'well placed out', as Lady Catherine puts it (II.6, 146)—the bleak last stop for marriage-market remainders.

This is Mr Bennet's course in home economics, with a pass from the narrator:

> To his wife he was very little otherwise indebted, than as her ignorance and folly had contributed to his amusement. This is not the sort of happiness which a man would in general wish to owe to his wife; but where other powers of entertainment are wanting, the true philosopher will derive benefit from such as are given. (203)

To true 'philosopher' Wollstonecraft (the persona of *Rights of Woman*), this is a male case of what culture labels 'female': 'led by their senses' rather than 'sense' (35). Elizabeth's sad reckoning of a waste of 'talents' and 'respectability' is on the same page (204). It's a post-nuptial plot of debts, contribution, owings, wanting, and what's 'given'. Ledger-woman Lady Catherine knows the laws of 'given'. In want of Elizabeth's promise 'never to enter into … an engagement' with her nephew Mr Darcy, she stands her ground on this word: 'I shall not go away until you have given me the assurance I require' (III.14/302). The novel's final iteration of 'given' is attached to Lydia, whose only assets are 'the claims to reputation which her marriage had given her' (III.19/327).

Mr Bennet's double in delinquency is Wickham's father, the Darcys' trusty steward. This, too, is no narrative but textual litter. The steward, 'always poor from the extravagance of his wife' (no businesswoman, she), was unable to provide his son with an education (II.12/173). As charming as he is amoral, he tries and fails at fortune-hunting, and winds up with Lydia, another wife with extravagant tastes, on low returns: £100/annum, then at the decease of both her parents, a lump sum of £1000 (for £50/annum). For his part, Mr Bennet counts this as *his* good fortune, a relief from an anxiety that the lad might have sought more, to the ruination of the other daughters (III.7/258). At this, Austen lets even the narrator's partisanship run out of wit: 'his chief wish was to have as little trouble in the business as possible' (8/262)—that word again, recalling his wife's better care for *business*. Into this slant Austen already had enlisted Elizabeth's indirect discourse for Wickham:

> he might imagine, from my father's behaviour, from his indolence and the little attention he has ever seemed to give to what was going forward in his family, that *he* would do as little, and think as little about it, as any father could do. (III.5/240)

In Chapter 8, the narrator gives the sequel: the mess having been managed by other men 'with so little inconvenience to himself', Mr Bennet 'naturally returned to all his former indolence' (262): *natural* indolence, just above the ground-zero of 'insensible' he's so easily satirises.

This reflex has worn thin by the time Mr Bennet declares his expected delight in 'the impudence and hypocrisy of my son-in-law' (III.15/308). But these guys escape full narrative censure, in their whirl of amusement and qualified pity: bad actors but good company. Polishing up its appreciation of Austen's 'moral' force, the *Quarterly Review* put 'a load of indolence and insensibility' into Mr Bennet's account-sheet (Scott, 194). Yet it is telling that the *Critical Review* could praise 'our sensible author' for giving him the consolations of satiric philosophy (319).[11] That 'many such silly women as Mrs. Bennet may be found' does 'great credit to the sense and sensibility of the authoress', it quipped with an Austenian wink (324). *British Critic* was even willing to reverse the information before its very eyes: Mr Bennet is 'reserved, acute, and satirical, but not indolent' (190).

'Not Sensible': Mr Collins' Sensitivity, Miss Lucas's Sense, Mrs Collins' Sensibility

By fortune of entail, Mr Collins takes the place of the Bennet women. This may be sly wit on Austen's part, flashed by Wollstonecraft's lights, to read a 'female' social structure: servile, dependent, obsequious (28). He is 'Wollstonecrafted' just this way: 'not a sensible man', a 'deficiency of nature' (character) 'little assisted by education or society'. With 'a weak head, living in retirement, and the consequential feelings of early and unexpected prosperity', his 'fortunate' event is a recommendation to a powerful woman, Lady Catherine de Bourgh, who granted the living at Hunsford (I.15/68). Who would disagree with Elizabeth's dismayed character-report for Charlotte to take to 'heart': 'a conceited, pompous, narrow-minded, silly man' (II.1/121)?

Austen, briefly. She cracks open this countour to a fleeting aperture for pity. When Mr Collins praises Lady Catherine's having 'always spoke to him as she would to any other gentleman' (I:14/65), we can hear a vibe of social insecurity.[12] We then hear, from the narrator directly, that 'the greatest part' of his life was 'spent under the guidance of an illiterate and miserly father'. The upshot was 'a great deal of humility in manner', so awkward that he could not form any 'useful acquaintance' at university. What he learned was 'a mixture of pride and obsequiousness, self-importance and humility' (I.15/68), legible in the 'servility and self-importance' of his letter of introduction to Mr Bennet (13/63). While the marriage plot needs Collins to leverage Elizabeth's better desert, Austen scripts his proposal with some complexity. Aware that his 'fortune' equals Bennet-misfortune, his 'olive-branch' is a 'plan of amends—of atonement': marrying one of the daughters, an 'excellent' plan, he declares, 'excessively generous and disinterested' (I.15/68–69).[13] Hyperbolic, but unarguable: after all, with the connection to Rosings and certainty of entail, he could have aimed higher, say at a Miss Gardiner. Then Austen closes this aperture as the olive branch proves a thorny rod. Assuring Elizabeth that he will 'make no demand' of settlement, Collins recites the meagre math on her value: 'one thousand pounds in the 4 percents … after your mother's decease' (£40/annum), an oafish bouquet whose promise that 'no ungenerous reproach shall ever pass my lips' (19/99) has just been perfumed with contradiction.

It's clear that all the Bennet girls court this reproach—as does Charlotte Lucas. If Collins has a 'plan', Charlotte has a 'scheme' (I.22/111). To Elizabeth, it is disgrace, humiliation, and certain unhappiness (115); 'unaccountable! in every view it is unaccountable!' (II.1/121). But Austen summons other accountings into our regard. She was Elizabeth's age when she began the novel (in 1796). By the time she finished it, she was Charlotte's, almost a 'spinster' (at 27, one year away from this official status). Charlotte is aware that her brothers live in 'apprehension' of having to maintain an 'old maid' and that her sisters can't come out (be courted) before she is settled (1.22/112). In another narratology, her account could be self-sacrificing heroism. In *Pride and Prejudice* it is social realism.[14] 'Happiness in marriage is entirely a matter of chance' is a sentence Austen writes for her well before Collins materializes (I.6/26). When 'every thing was settled between them to the satisfaction of both', Charlotte felt 'the good luck' of this 'preservation from want' (I.22/112). How deftly these words echo the novel's opening sentence with a female difference: not 'good fortune', just 'good luck'; 'want' as a nightmare female future, not open male opportunity. The 'good fortune', Elizabeth will come to see, is Mr Collins's. Charlotte is 'one of the very few sensible women who would have accepted him, or have made him happy' (II.9/136). Two senses of happiness: pleasant satisfaction for him; for her, a lucky resolution to a family problem. Austen's textual surface lets these words tell the differential story in 'a prudential light' (II.9/136), neither bright nor sparkling.

Not consigning Charlotte to a narratological un-Elizabeth, Austen's lets her words weave a sociology, a woman's need for 'establishment' for her security and her family's relief (II.1/122). Wollstonecraft saw this 'desire of establishing themselves,—the only way women can rise in the world,—by marriage' as a vast social disease (*RW* 8–9). Charlotte's parents know this. Behind the façade of their aspirational titles, Sir William and Lady Lucas are able 'to give little fortune' to their daughters and likely to set their pack of sons to fortune-hunt. Mr Collins registering as 'a most eligible match' on the 'exceedingly fair' prospect of his entail, the Lucases begin 'directly to calculate with more interest than the matter had ever excited before, how many years longer Mr. Bennet was likely to live' (I.22/112). Collins's 'disinterested' plan and Charlotte's 'disinterested desire' are positive glows against this rapacious actuarial 'interest'.

To judge Charlotte only on a scale of romance, trading self-respect for security, is to neglect what Austen knew, was haunted by. 'Anything is to be preferred or endured rather than marrying without Affection', she wrote to a lively niece the year after *Pride and Prejudice* appeared (18 November 1814; *Letters* 280). The deftly rhymed 'preferred or endured' could well have begun a non-marriage-plot in this key. 'Nothing can be compared to the misery of being bound without Love', she wrote a few weeks on (286). This is her underlining, sending the legal 'bond of marriage' into a life-sentence of bondage. Impoverished spinsterhood is a reciprocal nightmare. She was writing *Emma* at the time, this doom embodied in Miss Bates, Austen's middle-age coeval and the heroine's binary: she 'neither young, handsome, rich' (I.3/36), Emma debuted as 'handsome, clever, and rich' and 'twenty-one' (I.1/1). 'A single woman, with a very narrow income, must be a ridiculous, disagreeable, old maid!' exclaims Emma—with no interest in marriage, because 'a single woman, of good fortune, is always respectable' (I.X/179–80). This is plot-coded as her not yet knowing what's good for her, but outside the plot it looms as a utopian vision.[15] A year or so after finishing *Emma* (signed, 'the Author of "Pride and Prejudice"'), Austen submits the hegemony of the marriage plot to jesting illogic, 'Single Women have a dreadful propensity for being poor—which is one very strong argument in favour of Matrimony' (13 March 1817; *Letters* 332). Or the sole one.

For most women in Austen's day, even gentlewomen, romance is a luxury in novels like *Pride and Prejudice*. Hence Wollstonecraft's censure in *Rights of Woman* of the deleterious effects of novels: not just churns of sensation and facile sentiment, but vehicles of improbable social expectation, inimical to 'rational' content with one's 'own station' (131). However much she despised Dr John Gregory's strictures on the female delicacy of not displaying 'good sense' and 'any learning' in the company of men, she was on the same page about the delusive diet of novels.[16] In Austen's novel, Elizabeth gets to call herself a 'rational creature' in declining Collins' proposal (1.19/101), but so too Charlotte may claim rational satisfaction in 'her home and her housekeeping, her parish and her poultry' (II.13/187)—another witty run of Austenian alliteration for the book of the unromantic everyday. In a para-plot trajectory, we may realise her pressured future as the next mistress of Longbourn and heir to Mrs Bennet's business: the need to produce a son and to establish any daughters. When Mrs Collins returns for a visit to Lucas Lodge, she is pregnant—spoofed by Mr Bennet as her olive branch, no less (III.15/308).[17]

Lord Byron, no slouch on satire, could concede the unlucky lot of all women: 'Condemned to child-bed' (*Don Juan* XIV.XXIII)—no blessed event, too often a death sentence, the invisible, unhappy codicil to the marriage bond. Austen knew it on the ledger of her own family, in which all her brothers (except childless Henry) outlived a first wife, at the end of several exhausting, often suspenseful pregnancies. Edward Knight's wife died about two weeks after delivering her eleventh child. Frank Austen's wife also died at this mark. It was a common case.[18] As Byron wrote up the invoice in 1823 on the 'real sufferings of their she-condition' (*Don Juan* XIV.XXIII),

> Man's very sympathy with their estate
> Has much of selfishness and more suspicion.

Their love, their virtue, beauty, education,
But form good housekeepers to breed a nation. (XXIIV)

What 'their estate' is not (in *Pride and Prejudice* anyway) is *entail.*--

He-Entail and its She-Discontents

Pride and Prejudice concentrates 'nation' into rural gentry, 'gentleman-like' trades and professions, and an elite that is sometimes gracious, sometimes not. *Noblesse oblige* is the code that sustains the status quo, with satires of ignoble actors (snobs and rogues) serving as its safety valves. In the patrilineal entail, the male heirs were lifetime tenants of the estates (Pemberley, Rosings, Longbourn), the she-condition unanchored.[19] Edmund Burke's *Reflections on the Revolution in France* (1790) gave male entail a glow of national pride. It is his master-trope for mystifying and naturalizing vast systemic inequalities 'as *an inheritance from our forefathers*' (44). The italics are his, repeated on the next page, in anticipation of this (now famous) argument:

> it has been the uniform policy of our constitution to claim and assert our liberties, as an *entailed inheritance* derived to us from our forefathers, and to be transmitted to our posterity; as an estate specially belonging to the people of this kingdom ... By this means our constitution preserves an unity in so great a diversity of its parts. We have an inheritable crown; an inheritable peerage; and a house of commons and a people inheriting privileges, franchises, and liberties, from a long line of ancestors.
>
> This policy appears to me to be the result of profound reflection; or rather the happy effect of following nature, which is wisdom without reflection, and above it. (47)

For such wisdom, Burke's synonym is *prejudice*: 'the prejudice of ages ... operates as an instinct to secure property, and to preserve communities in a settled state' (205), a homologous grammar for landed entail. This is 'a prejudice ... of reason', involved in 'profound and extensive wisdom' (136). Austen's linking of *Pride* and *Prejudice* is legibly Burkean this way. Burke distinguishes rational pride from the puffery of 'personal pride and arrogance' (68). It is 'a noble pride' (71), pride of class, 'manly pride' (118). Austen's marriage plot chastens Mr Darcy from the negative to the positive end of the scale: a pride and prejudice in the custodial care of Pemberley by male entail, the iconic formation to which Elizabeth's pride and prejudice is happily reformed.[20] Burke's ideology gets a local habitation and a household name.

Austen's use of Lady Catherine as decoy for aristocratic power, attracting its insolence and arrogance, as Claudia Johnson remarks, preserves its luster in the better-mannered Mr Darcy and affirms 'the majesty of Pemberley' (*Jane Austen* 88-9). Questioning of this system is given to this contaminated Lady and her fellow decoy, petulant Mrs Bennet. The Lady is forthright (even at the expense of protégé Collins). 'I see no occasion for entailing estates from the female line', she declares (II.6/145), with an 'authoritative manner' allowed by 'rank and fortune', in a snide report by Wickham that is pretty much an establishing shot (I.16/80). Austen further undercuts her conceit with some odd ironies of nomenclature. The Lady and her deceased sister (Darcy's mother) were née Fitzwilliam, one of the wealthiest aristocracies, fount of Mr Darcy's forename, Fitzwilliam.[21] This, moreover, is the family of the Earl to whom Burke addressed his *Letter to a Noble Lord*, his sequel to *Reflections,* published in 1796, when Austen first drafted the novel that would become *Pride and Prejudice.* As wife of Sir Lewis de Bourgh, she remains Lady, because her title is inherited, not acquired by marriage (e.g., Lady Lucas). But her married name is weirdly loaded: de Bourgh is the Anglo-Norman line of a branch for which the Irish line is 'Burke'. So even as Lady Catherine proclaims that strict male entail 'was not thought necessary in Sir Lewis de Bourgh's family' (II.6/145), Austen gives her a *Burke*-allied surname. So, too, her full title, 'the Right Honourable' (I:13/61), also Burke's title. Austen leaves the complexities of nomenclature as an unorganised glitter of informational litter.

Compared to Lady Catherine, Mrs Bennet is an impotent squeak, but with higher stakes. 'I am sure if I had been you', she grumps to Mr Bennet, 'I should have tried long ago to do something or other about it' (I.13/60). He may have; Collins's letter opens with a mention of some 'breach' between his father and Mr Bennet (61). Austen's narrative obscures this backstory and instead deploys rational daughters to 'explain' to their querulous mother 'the nature of an entail'.

> They had often attempted it before, but it was a subject on which Mrs. Bennet was beyond the reach of reason: and she continued to rail bitterly against the cruelty of settling an estate away from a family of five daughters, in favour of a man. (60–61)

This is Lady Catherine, in a different tone. Austen allows the question (not least its gloss as 'natural') to hang beyond its satirised speakers. Mrs Bennet's spectrum of insensibility has a sensible claim, 'how any one could have the conscience to entail away an estate from one's own daughters'. To this, Mr Bennet says (at the pregnant close of volume I), 'I leave it to yourself to determine' (1.23/119).

That women can determine nothing is beyond irony. Austen's text, if not her narrative, casts the rhetorical vector of *yourself* past Mrs Bennet to a reader's reach of reason. To Claudia Johnson, Lady Catherine is 'every bit as ludicrous as Mrs Bennet' (*Jane Austen* 88), but I'll argue that on this score, Austen allows Mrs Bennet to be every bit as sensible as Lady Catherine: characterology does not dictate moral judgement.[22] While Austen has Jane and Elizabeth invoke 'nature' to endorse the norm and put quarrels 'beyond … reason', a satirist such as Austen knows the contingency of such value-laden words, and how a grievance can leverage a norm into a question. Lady Catherine's remark to Elizabeth that 'Daughters are never so much consequence to a father' is a categorical shot beyond the immediate situation (about whether Elizabeth really needs to return to Longbourn from her long stay at Rosings). It lands at a periphery with bearing on the matter of male entail, gossip about one of Mr Wickham's recent targets for fortune-hunting, a royally named Miss Mary King, heiress of her grandfather's fortune (II.4/135).

Lady Catherine's point is not negated by conceit, and in so far as caricature is a device of displacement, a displacement is still a place from which to speak. Sandra Gilbert and Susan Gubar caught this force in their groundbreaking revaluation of vilified women, *The Madwoman in the Attic* (1979): 'Opposed to the very basis of patriarchy, the exclusive right of male inherit[a]nce, Lady Catherine quite predictably earns the vilification always allotted … to the representatives of ma-triarchal power' (172). Austen's investment in Lady Catherine has more going on than even this critical force and her dramatic utility as Elizabeth's antagonist.[23] The first two syllables of 'authoritative'—Wickham's slur, internalized by Elizabeth (II.6/143)—are *author*, Austen's allonym ('Author of …') on *Pride and Prejudice*'s title page. Austen enjoyed writing for her as much as she did Elizabeth. On a measure of self-possession, sarcasm, of social perspicuity, she livens every page on which she appears. Lady Catherine's legal entail is nothing to her durable literary entail.

Not a character but a discourse, Miss King focuses a related question, about the fortune-hunting of men with no entail. While Elizabeth recoils from Charlotte's 'scheme', she's rather more liberal with men of necessity. When Wickham's flirtation with her (they've bonded in contempt of Darcy) shifts to 'the most remarkable charm' of Miss King's 'ten thousand pounds'—a crude metonym—Austen's narrator invites us to think afresh about Charlotte's case in Elizabeth's view of these men: she 'did not quarrel with … his wish of independence', no earned self-sufficiency, even, just well-funded leisure.[24] 'Nothing, on the contrary', continues the narrator's collaborative indirect style, 'could be more natural' (II.3/132–33)—that word again: as *natural* as male entail it seems. No 'difference in matrimonial affairs between the mercenary and the prudent motive' is Elizabeth's woke market analysis (4/135). The license flashes again with another almost-beau, Darcy's amiable cousin Colonel Fitzwilliam, 'the younger son of an Earl' and so a dim chance of entail. Poor lad, brought up in 'habits of expence', he cannot 'afford to marry without some consideration to money' (II.10/160). Austen lets Elizabeth allow this, but also lets her readers think that such a son may have much of the world all before him, from family connections—not least, Darcy and Lady Catherine.[25] Wollstonecraft censured this class of 'idle' military, 'superficial young men, whose only occupation is gallantry' (flirting), 'whose polished manners' and 'ornamental drapery … of fashion' provide fashionable cover for 'vice' (fortune-hunting, gaming, running up debts) and furthermore structured them as deformations of rational manliness (26–27). Colonel Fitzwilliam is yet another magnet for siftable litter, this in a narrative mode that Gerald Prince calls *disnarrated:* 'all the events that *do not* happen but, nonetheless, are referred to (in a negative or hypothetical mode) by the narrative text' (2), indexing stories not told, unrealised, but potential, possible, tellable.

The Indexed Historical World: Histrionic Evil and Wretched Events

A larger social topography of *Pride and Prejudice* is scattered, but not invisible. Austen began this novel in 1796 and published it in 1813, a Napoleonic wartime in which gentry homes and grand estates were far from 'universal', held by less than 2% of England's population. The House of Lords was hereditary; in 1800, only 5% of men (of property) even had the right to elect representatives to the House of Commons. Great landowners like Mr Darcy controlled districts with populations of a few hundred, while new manufacturing cities (Liverpool, Manchester, Birmingham, Leeds) had no representatives, despite burgeoning populations of abjectly exploited workers. Such towns are not even in the periphery of *Pride and Prejudice.* The 'civilised sensibility of Jane Austen's social standards', comments Arnold Kettle, is a 'particular form of social organization' that permits 'sensitive values … to be applicable only to one person in ten or twenty', a 'privileged social position' that entails 'the exploitation of … inferiors' and 'the condemnation to servility and poverty of hundreds of unnamed … human beings'.[26] In a prestigious, canonizing essay on Austen for *The Quarterly Review,* Sir Walter Scott celebrates her registration of 'common occurrences' such as 'occupy the ordinary walks of life', in contrast to improbable 'romantic incident' (193). He hails this as the ground of Austen's 'moral' force, but the 'paths of common life' he surveys are class-exclusive. Take, for example, all those mentions of a 'liberty' of sport-hunting on gentry grounds. Without this liberty, it is poaching, a capital crime, often in hungry desperation. If Austen leaves it to her readers to fill in this picture, her textual surface indexes numerously named human instruments: a shop-boy, a waiter, a private, soldiers, tenant farmers and farmworkers, cottagers, villagers, tithe-paying parishioners, housekeepers, personal maids and household drudges, cooks, footmen, carriage-men, man-servants, butlers, porters—all invisible to Scott.

And almost in Austen's text, where their exertions are given in brief utilities of passive verbs and effaced agency: horses are brought, meals are served, tables cleared; girls are dressed; doors are opened to usher in visitors; servants prepare homes for their residents, are sent to fetch, and are sent for; an apothecary is summoned; tenant farmers, whose rents (and depressed wages for labour) sustain the estate, are never named.[27] Shoe-roses are got by proxy in weather too rainy for Kitty and Lydia to venture (I.17/84). Debts to tradesmen are not 'debts of honour' (III.6, 253). If the latter are not legally enforceable, the former often go unpaid, with scant legal recourse. At Rosings 'all the servants, and all the articles of plate' are beheld in parallel syntax and a conjunction of equivalence (II.6/144). At presumably less ostentatious Pemberley luncheon appears in a parade 'of servants with cold meat, cake, and a variety of all the finest fruits of the season' (III.3/228), as if by the magic of Ariel in *The Tempest.* 'An express came at twelve last night' (III.4/232), on the long road from London to Longbourn, as if by its own agency. As Darcy and Elizabeth endure its 'dreadful news' and 'wretched suspense' (about Wickham and Lydia), they can command a nameless 'servant' and 'maid' for immediate tasking (235).

This is not a tide that washes only over the novel's snobs (Caroline Bingley and Lady Catherine); it is everyday presumption in decent characters. Household stalwarts get clipped or go nameless. Mr Bingley calls his cook 'Nicholls' (I.11/55); it is a humbler Mrs Phillips who accords the courtesy 'Mrs. Nicholls' (III.11/53). The legal muscle set on Wickham is just named 'Haggerston'—this, by sensible, educated 'Edw/E' Gardiner (III.7/257; 8/266)—the former a crude stereotype ('hacker'), while Esq. 'Edward Gardiner' is coded 'guardian of the riches'.[28] As for the Bennets: Lydia and Kitty's gossip about military brutality ('a private had been flogged') is equivalent to nuptial news (I.12/59).[29] Mrs Bennet, in high distress at Lydia's elopement, assumes a license to 'vent all her feelings' on a housekeeper (III.5/245). Discovered, recovered Lydia can order a generic 'Sally' to get her gown mended (5/248)—presumably the 'Sarah' in Mrs Bennet's summons for the ladies' dress and coiffure (13/291). Her senior housekeeper is just 'Hill' (I.13/60). Jane and Elizabeth, moral center of the household, are just as crude, in contrast to Austen's narrator, in the very next sentence, speaks of 'Mrs. Hill' (III.7/255), again in the next two chapters (261, 269). This narrator always refers to Pemberley's housekeeper as 'Mrs. Reynolds' (III.1/211–14)—in contrast to Mr Wickham's rude reference to 'Reynolds' (III.10/ 278). Elizabeth's surprise at finding a 'respectable-looking … and civil' woman (III.1/209) may signify her Darcy-prejudice softening, but not without a whiff of class prejudice.[30] Nothing is made of this, plot-wise, but as data on the surface it's there for us to consider as a norm of behaviour towards one's 'inferiors'.

So, too, the way a lexicon of misery is foregrounded for theatrics or theatrical pathos, universally divorced from material misery. A rare exception are two reports of Darcy being liberal and 'affable to the poor' (III.1/213, 226) but on page 213 the noun is immediately replayed as sentiment in good Mrs Gardiner's calling Wickham 'our poor friend'. The language of *dreadful* and *wretched* is invoked for gentry distresses: whether in pathos, ironised theatrics, or stupid myopia, the words are universally unlinked to actual social misery. Notions of *evil* are similarly curated. It names humiliations and faults of character: the Bingleys' snubbing of Jane (II.10/163); the behaviors of Mr Bennet (III.6/254) and Mr Darcy (III.10/273). It is Darcy who gives the first definition in this key: 'There is, I believe, in every disposition a tendency to some particular evil, a natural defect, which not even the best education can overcome' (I.11/57). He sounds like Prince Hamlet, issuing Wittenberg philosophy: 'So oft it chances in particular men/That for some vicious mole of nature in them—/As in their birth (wherein they are not guilty,/Since nature cannot choose his origin)' (*Hamlet* 1.4). *Evil* is how Elizabeth imagines her family will view her union with Darcy (17/315). Lydia's 'wild giddiness' (II.14/184) and her 'disdain of all restraint' are 'general evils' (18/199–200). Her elopement detonates into Elizabeth's alarm at 'dreadful news', 'wretched suspense', 'horror', 'deepest disgrace', 'distress', 'misery', 'anguish', 'wretched business' (III.4/235–37; 5/242, 246), a lexicon that Austen pours, in rare concord, into Collins's crude sermonizing about all this (6/252). Even when this 'evil' and a feared 'dreadful sequel' (III.5/246) are averted by marriage, it is a 'misery' to be endured (11/285–6). This discourse may be general issue in sentimental fiction, Austen's angle of irony is hard to gauge, but the material is there.

Edgy Advantage: Elizabeth Bennet, Mrs Fitzwilliam Darcy

Lydia's 'infamous elopement' and 'patched-up business'—the indelible entry in Lady Catherine's ledger (III.14/303)—persists as an 'evil' blot, smeared into a narrative postscript of a husband who was never into her, always off to Bath and to card tables. The elopement conjures an infamous sign of alternative marriage-plots: Gretna Green (III.4/233), first village over the border in Scotland, where English law forbidding the marriage of minors without parental consent evaporated. After Lord Hardwicke's 'Act for the Better Preventing of Clandestine Marriages' of 1754, 'Gretna Green' was a metonym for marriage Scottish style in various plots of cultural and domestic rupture, erotic liberty and rebellion against patriarchy. The debates in Parliament, far from any dry proceeding, read like prompts for novels: dastardly fortune-hunting; social mobility and the distribution of wealth; compassion for those unable to afford British legal mandates; sympathy for human passions; parental distress ranging from tyranny and dynastic self-interest, to a pathos of exclusion; teleologies of domestic harmony and social improvement; catastrophes of national consequence.[31]

While Gretna Green is only a peripheral panic in *Pride and Prejudice,* its signpost puts the Elizabeth-Darcy estrangement back on track. Learning of Darcy's secret ministry in discovering the elopers and forcing a marriage, Elizabeth sees 'that he was exactly the man, who, in disposition and talents, would most suit her' (III.8/50–51). When wealthy heiress Anne Isabella Milbanke read *Pride and Prejudice,* this paradigm seemed exportable. She had met Lord Byron in the pride of his first fame, in March 1812, at a party given by Caroline Lamb, first among Byron fan-girls. 'I made no offering at the shrine of Childe Harold', she commented of his celebrity allonym, yet a curiosity lingered: 'I shall not refuse the acquaintance if it comes my way' (Elwin 106). It did, with a fortune-hunting eye, and by October 1812, Byron sent a proposal of marriage through the offices of her aunt and his friend, Lady Melbourne. When Miss Milbanke refused, Lady Melbourne, eager to keep Byron on the horizon, wrote a letter to her niece as a proxy suit:

> He desires me to say, how much obli[d] he is to you for the candour, & fairness, with which you have told him your Sentiments,—that although unfavourable to his hopes, or more properly to his Wishes, for hopes he declares he had not, your conduct on this occasion has encreased the high opinion he had before entertain'd of your abilities, & excellent qualities & encreases the regret he feels at your decision, as well as his admiration for your character … He says to me, 'I cannot sufficiently thank you for the trouble you have taken on my Account … I never will renew a Subject which I am convinced would be hateful to her'. (Elwin 156)

The next January, *Pride and Prejudice,* with its story of an improvable Darcy was out, and by the spring Miss Milbanke was telling her mother: 'I really think it the most probable fiction I have ever read … the interest is very strong, especially for Mr. Darcy' (Elwin 159). Byron was also reading the novel (Murray, *Letters* 512), and may have sensed a happy emissary.

Elizabeth Bennet spurned a first proposal from proud Mr Darcy; then rereading his follow-up letter (an unsuspected novella in itself) and reading 'Pemberley' as a sequel, she is primed to renew the subject. When Jane asks her, 'Will you tell me how long you have loved him?' she answers in a heartbeat, 'from my first seeing the beautiful grounds at Pemberley' (III.17/316). Scott wittily marked this as the pivot when the lady's 'prudence had begun to subdue her prejudice' (*Quarterly* 194).[32] The avatar is a portrait of Darcy in its gallery. Elizabeth 'stood before the canvas … and fixed his eyes upon herself' (III.1/208-9). Byron's portraits were charged this way, too. Darcy returned his credit to Byron. Enchanted by the idea of reforming notoriously 'bad' Byron, Miss Milbanke began a correspondence in August 1813 to test this out. A little more than a year into this, Byron renewed the 'Subject' and Miss Milbanke hazarded the 'romance' that a reformed rake makes the best husband.

It didn't work out that way, famously. A caution was Byron's sigh of relief, after the first refusal, at having escaped (he confessed to Lady Melbourne) 'a cold collation, & I prefer hot suppers'—(*Letters and Journals* 2:246). A reheated collation was solemnised on 2 January 1815, and went cold a year on, devolving into an international Separation Scandal, heated by rumours of Byron's misdeeds and abuse, and prosecuted by him in literary post-nuptials, most immediately best-seller *Childe Harold's Pilgrimage, Canto III* (1816). 'His allusions to me … are cruel and cold'; Lady Byron wrote to a friend, seeing the design 'to attract all sympathy to himself (Stowe, 53).[33]

Brainy and literate, Miss Milbanke has no real counterpart in *Pride and Prejudice,* except in ovo in the most peripheral of the Bennet daughters.

"What say you, Mary?"

When Lady Catherine suggests that the Bennet girls' education, an asset on the marriage market, has been 'neglected', Elizabeth replies that they 'were always encouraged to read' and had 'necessary' tutors (II.6/146). This is the only mention, however; Elizabeth is never seen to study, even to read. The only book Austen gives her is a prop to provoke the Bingley sisters and prompt a conversation with Darcy. Her sister Mary is routinely ridiculed for her reading and musical studies. Awkward or obtuse at home and in society, an autodidactic with a love of maxims and moralising, her remarks ridiculed as 'thread-bare' as Kitty-Lydia gossip, she is her mother's least favourite, so also Austen's. The novel's postscript, far from a fairy tale of an ugly duckling harboring swan DNA, metes out her deserts, with sarcasm (III.19/326): as 'the only daughter who remained at home', she was required to relinquish her 'pursuit of accomplishments' to be her mother's keeper (Miss Bates's lot, too), and for relief 'to mix more with the world', with ever new material to 'moralize over'. Taking a cue from the narrator's mean-spirited ledger, that what Mary lacks in 'genius' and 'taste' is matched by 'vanity', 'application' and a 'conceited manner' (28), *Critical Review* (issuer of that pass on Mr Bennet's indolence) applauded Austen's satire of 'a female pedant, affecting great wisdom, yet saturated with stupidity' (320), the typical reading. Austen later gave this mean sketch of Mary's future: she 'obtained nothing higher than one of her uncle Philip's clerks, and was content to be considered a star in the society of Meriton' (Austen-Leigh 148)—a parody of sparkle in the slant-punned merit of 'Mary-town'.

Such dark wit seems an overdetermined defense against what Thomas De Quincey calls a Dark Interpreter, the 'phantasm' of 'your own lurking thoughts' (750). No real necessity for the plot of *Pride and Prejudice,* Mary inhabits its pages as a supererogatory deformation of female intellectual aspiration. Having 'heard herself mentioned ... as the most accomplished girl in the neighborhood'(I.4/16), she is also painfully aware of 'being the only plain one in the family'—'plain' a euphemism (II.3/133). To balance the deficit, she 'worked hard for knowledge and accomplishments', and is eager 'for display'. I've stitched together this disnarrated Mary from Austen's scrap-heap in order to question the 'undertow of condescension' that readers such as Pat Rogers find unquestionable in Austen's conspicuous plotting against her (467n13).[34] After performing 'a long concerto' (no mean feat) at an evening party, Mary 'was glad to purchase praise and gratitude by Scotch and Irish airs, at the request of her younger sisters', eager to dance with the young men there (I.6/28). Mary misses the score, which is not about her skill but about energetic flirtation and its proxy for the marriage market on which she has small 'purchase'. At another party, obtuse to Elizabeth's policing 'eyes', she is filled with delight at the 'opportunity of exhibiting' and (in the narrator's mean pun) is 'disconcerted' when her father, reading the room, intervenes to end her display. Elizabeth is 'sorry' only for the embarrassments (I.18/94). What is 'mortification' to her (94) is a social death sentence for Mary, with no commutation by study and learning.

I think Austen is rather more divided about this sentencing. This is latent in that mode of disnarrated: 'unrealized possibility ... unfulfilled expectations, unwarranted beliefs ... crushed hopes' (Prince 3). Here is a young woman, with a love of learning, usually to be 'found ... deep in the study' of improvisational musical harmony, 'human nature' and copying 'new extracts' from her reading (I.12/59). I don't find this is reducible to mockery.[35] Austen herself 'practised regularly every morning' on her instrument (Le Faye 178). Imprisoned by her family's ridicule and embarrassment, abject Mary is alertly interested in the 'olive branch' offered by Mr Collins (I.13/63): 'there was a solidity in his reflections which often struck her, and though by no means so clever as herself, she thought that if encouraged to read and improve himself by such an example as her's, he might become a very agreeable companion' (I.22/114)—eligible for a companionate marriage, in which her learning might not be ridiculed. They both love maxims: something to share. Absenting herself from giddy-girl 'pleasures' that would 'doubtless be congenial with generality of female minds', Austen has her say, with perfect Wollstonecraft chops, 'I should infinitely prefer a book' (II.16/192). On Jane's engagement to Bingley, her first 'interest' is a prospect of 'happiness' in 'the use of the library at Netherfield' (III.13/295).

You can see how, on the panorama beyond the plot, Austen zigs and zags around Mary, tripping on the fissures between narrator and narrative, presentation and representation. The narrative levels Mary's bibliophilia, in the very same sentence, with Kitty's lobbying for Netherfield balls. The only library to which Mary has any access is Clarke's in Meryton, this mentioned only in Kitty-Lydia gossip as a site of social mixing (I.7/33). 'I am *not* a great reader', Elizabeth protests to Caroline Bingley's barb on this score (I.8/39). When Mr Bingley offers the library to her, she declines, and the conversation turns to the more impressive one at Pemberley. Darcy is no great reader either, just a curator for whom 'buying books' is patriarchal cultural capital: 'the work of many generations' (40), less read than ready for display. Already expensive, books were lavishly bound in estate livery: ornamented, embossed leather covers, marbled endpapers, and gilded trim. Quipped Robert Southey in 1809, 'they are chiefly purchased as furniture by the rich. It is not a mere antithesis to say that they who buy books do not read them, and that they who read them do not buy them'.[36]

One great reader, from girlhood on, is Jane Austen, beneficiary of her father's library though (before its sad dispersal when his health required the family' diminished removal to Bath). So, too, Mary Bennet, never invited into her father's library. In the novel's postscript, this father smirks that she probably welcomed being the sole daughter at home, 'no longer mortified by comparisons between her sisters' beauty and her own' (III.19/326). *Mortified:* that social death by everyday prejudice, paternally endorsed. Her debut in the novel is her father's teasing, 'What say you, Mary? you are a young lady of deep reflection I know, and read great books and make extracts'. Austen's narrator follows up: 'Mary wished to say something very sensible, but knew not how' (I.2/9). This could have been free indirect style: 'there is some pathos in her yearning', comments Spacks (37n). Austen plants this as the novel's first instance of 'sensible', for the narrator to torque a satire.

Other contourings of Mary, however, glimpse Austen as secret sharer. She curates extracts from her reading. When Elizabeth comments of Darcy's rude behavior at the assembly, 'I could easily forgive *his* pride, if he had not mortified *mine*,' mistress of mortification Mary tries to help out by calling on her (and Austen's) study of Hugh Blair[37]:

> 'Pride', observed Mary, who piqued herself upon the solidity of her reflections, 'is a very common failing I believe. By all that I have ever read, I am convinced that it is very common indeed, that human nature is particularly prone to it, and that there are very few of us who do not cherish a feeling of self-complacency on the score of some quality or other, real or imaginary. Vanity and pride are different things, though the words are often used synonimously. A person may be proud without being vain. Pride relates more to our opinion of ourselves, vanity to what we would have others think of us'. (I.5/24)

Everyone ignores her, but her desynonimisation, piqued, flat and wordy as it is, is pretty much the moral landscape of *Pride and Prejudice*.

When Austen winced at *Pride and Prejudice* as 'rather too light & bright & sparkling', she meant its comedy of manners; what was wanted (desired and lacked) was 'contrast' from some 'shade ... stretched out here & there', by 'something unconnected with the story' as a foil 'to the playfulness & Epigrammatism of the general stile'. An 'Essay on Writing, a critique on Walter Scott, or the history of Buonaparte' might do this (*Letters* 203).[38] Even so, *Pride and Prejudice* has plenty of shades, if not 'stretched out' ones. 'The more I see of the world, the more I am dissatisfied with it', sighs Elizabeth at some early turns of events (II.1/121); Austen leaves it unclear whether this is a temporary mood. Another short-sketch is the truth universally acknowledged that 'married women have never much time for writing' (III.11/280). This is Lydia, excusing herself for not writing thank-you notes, but it sounds like material for Austen epigrammatic 'stile'. Such are *Pride and Prejudice*'s uncanny, legible haunts—also its possibility. Mary Bennet glints unsparkled as a slighted marker of another story. The prospect that Austen's novel forecloses is not closed to recognition.

Put it this way: un-heroine Mary Bennet, leveraged for self-possession, might have 're-stiled' the first sentence of *Pride and Prejudice* for a single woman with no want to be a wife, only to have a room of her own for the pleasures of work. Austen's intelligence is always at work on these slants, these extra glints to its 'sparkling unities'. A great, clear-eyed writer brings her darkness with her, if only in the three-dimensionality stressed by differential levels of light-hearted ambivalence. What results is an intricate tapestry, rich not in spite of but by force of its loose ends and frayed edges.

Notes

1 Quotations follow the publication of 1813, noting, in order, volume and chapter there; then page number(s) in the *Longman Cultural Edition*. For advice and conversation, I'm grateful to Garrett Stewart, William Galperin, Jeff Nunokawa, and Ron Levao.

2 Letter to Cassandra Austen, 4 February 1813; *Letters* 203. My chapter-title alludes to this reservation and to Reuben Brower's canonical, celebratory essay, 'Light and Bright and Sparkling', on Austen's skills as Popean satirist, deftly balancing ironic dialogue and dramatic development in 'the Elizabeth-Darcy narrative' (167).

3 For a sharply nuanced reading of this launch, see William Galperin, *Historical Austen*, 125. Austen may have market-edged the surname *Bennet*: *bene* is an old noun for *prayer, petition, boon* (OED); *benet* as verb means *ensnare* (as with a net, Dr Johnson's *Dictionary* I:232).

4 Karen Newman nicely discusses *fixed*, in this launch and throughout the novel (700–703).

5 Claudia Johnson gives the genre-logic, framed and qualified (*Jane Austen* 73-6). Darryl Jones gives it straight up (93), aligning Austen's skilled retail with his praise of Brower's essay as the 'single finest' on the novel (110).

6 This is a reiterated theme in accounts that limit the class census to aristocracy, gentry, and trade: see Warren Roberts's endorsement of Duckworth (50). But even this circumscribed structure of romance, remarks Patricia Meyer Spacks, does not erase the 'uncomfortable actualities' Austen's text has revealed (24).

7 Minor characters serve 'narrative totality' by lodging negative examples and parodies that reflect the lustre of the main characters (55-6).

8 Johnson seems unaware of Newman's essay, but her view of Austen's forestalling of generalisations and moral codes is on the same page: 'virtually every argument can be undercut with a countervailing argument' (*Jane Austen* 77).

9 Letter to the editor of *Scrutiny*, never sent. 'This left-wing-intellectual approach to the lady, the idea that Tories think she is praising the present system, but we pink boys know that her heart is with the rebels' was just so much stage-setting for Harding to flaunt his excavation of 'Unconscious Psychology' (123). For the impact of Harding on the cult of 'genteel Jane' in the wartime 1940s, see Johnson's *Jane Austen Cults and Cultures*, 141–50. The fount is Henry Austen's 'Biographical Notice', reporting that his sister's 'keenest relish for wit' never stooped to unkindness' (xi–xii).

10 In addition to Miss Gardiner's £4000, a marriage settlement of £5000 was secured to the daughters after the decease of both parents (III.7/257). Income from the 4% funds (£200/year) would scarcely maintain a smaller family in basic gentility (Duckworth 87-8); the three Austen women struggled on £200/year after Revd Austen's death, before the brothers helped out. See also Rogers (li-lii). Bingley's 'four or five thousand a year' (I.1, from an inheritance of £100,000) puts him in the top 1%; Darcy's doubling at £10,000/annum is elite.

11 Schorer's classroom edition consolidates the ledger: 'Mrs Bennet is a transparently scheming boor' while 'Mr Bennet, for all his amiable intelligence and wit, is a demoralized man' (xiii).

12 Spacks nicely notes the indirect discourse (103n6); Woloch (and not alone) refuses any sympathy (83–88).

13 The ethical accent is perhaps inflected by Austen's knowing her father's benefit from the kindness of relatives. Left an orphan, an uncle secured him a scholarship at Oxford. A wealthy cousin, Sir Thomas Knight, granted him two decent church livings. No wonder that 'Knightley' is the hero's name in *Emma*—especially after Sir Thomas's adopted son, Jane's brother Edward, took the surname 'Knight' in 1812.

14 Tave 132-7 and Duckworth more briefly (120n) allow this pass to Charlotte, and Spacks succinctly advocates her case against Elizabeth's 'unrealistic' standards (175-6nn13–14).

15 Galperin sees this utopia conjured in the opening sentence of *Pride and Prejudice*, a canny recognition of 'the subordination that drives [women] to marriage in the first place' (*ELH* 374). In 'Boxing Emma', I discuss the overdetermination of Miss Bates as a spectre in this recognition.

Pride and Prejudice

16 For Gregory's advice see 31-2; for Wollstonecraft's 'animadversions', see chapter 5, section III. Gregory cautions: 'without an unusual share of natural sensibility, and very peculiar good fortune, a woman in this country has very little probability of marrying for love' (80). This 'good fortune' means chance, but the wording is identical to what attracts fortune hunters adept in the cant of love gleaned from novels.

17 For the transition of this friend to Mrs Collins, with near erasure from the novel after Elizabeth leaves Hunsford, see Eric Walker, 164-65.

18 About one friend who had delivered her eighth child in eleven years, Austen exclaimed to her sister, 'poor Woman! How can she be honestly breeding again?' (1 October 1808; *Letters* 140). Venturing at least three more pregnancies, this categorical, exhausted 'Woman' would die ten years after her last delivery, at age 45 (578n).

19 Rogers gives a succinct account (xlix-liii) with a sympathy to Mrs Bennet's protest and an argument for Austen's informed grasp of the system.

20 Duckworth reads 'Fitzwilliam Darcy' as a Burkean hero, bearer of positive 'prejudice', 'social destination', and 'traditional customs and usages'—and a care for Pemberley as an entailed responsibility and legitimising display (128–29).

21 For historical detail on the nomenclature of 'Darcy' and 'Fitzwilliam' and the 'pompous pride' of the elder Darcy drawing his son's forename from his wife's aristocracy, see Doody 81–82, 112, 117. For more on the name 'Fitzwilliam' see Greene, 1024–25—also, more generally, for Austen's literacy in the great names and great houses.

22 Spacks's judgement of Mrs Bennet's 'invincible ignorance' (99nn5–6)—is usual, but not, I think, inevitable.

23 Gilbert and Gubar note affiliations by structural ironies. Lady Catherine is the plot device that seals Elizabeth and Darcy's union (it's no stretch for Galperin to dub her as the novel's real aristocratic hero; *Historical* 196). As Mrs Darcy, moreover, Elizabeth gets the slot Lady Catherine reserved for her daughter, and so doubles as 'daughter' (*Madwoman* 172–73).

24 Wickham was foiled by her alert uncle, who took her off to Liverpool. Fortune-hunters often schemed elopement precisely to evade articles of marriage that would protect a wife from impoverishment after a husband gained legal possession of her fortune. Wickham's early target was Georgiana Darcy's £30,000.

25 For the opportunities, see Rogers 504n2. A colonel's salary might be 'five or six thousand a year' (Mrs Bennet's rational calculus; I.7/32) and a younger son may rise to inheritance on the decease of a sonless elder. Even Rosings may be on this cousin's horizon of whim.

26 He's writing about *Emma* (94–95) but *Pride and Prejudice* qualifies. Unfortunately cut from the Norton Critical Edition of *Emma* after the first edition, this trenchant essay challenges Duckworth's shallow celebration of the achieved unity of *Pride and Prejudice* on a census of 'three classes … nobility, gentry, and trade', Pemberley its unifying hub (132).

27 For a good account, see G. E. Mingay. From 1790 to 1812, landlords grew 'enormously rich' as rents for tenant farmers swelled as much as five-fold, and wages for labour plummeted (Hammond 151). Gentry romance, notes Raymond Williams, battens on 'the brief and aching lives of … the field labourers whom we never by any chance see', and 'all the men and women whose land and work paid their fares and provided their spending money' (54).

28 For both these alert name-catches I am indebted to Doody (116).

29 A frequent form of discipline, with officers' class contempt for the noncommissioned; see Spacks 97n and Shapard 115n12.

30 Johnson's reading of *Pride and Prejudice* as the high tide of Austen's equation of 'the business of life' with 'pursuing happiness' (*Jane Austen* 80) elides the workers whose lives serve this pursuit, even its plot developments. It is even a chambermaid who sends Elizabeth to Pemberley on a mistaken assurance of Darcy's absence there (208).

31 House of Commons 'Debates on the Clandestine Marriage Bill', Sixth Session of the Tenth Parliament, 26 George the Second, 1752 (Hansard's, vol. 15); for annotated selections, see *Pride and Prejudice* ed. Johnson and Wolfson 352-66.

32 Family curator Austen-Leigh protested this audit (132).

33 He wasn't done: there was a sequel caricature in *Don Juan* Canto I (1819) and coded sympathy for himself in *Sardanapalus* (1821). In *Romantic Interactions*, I discuss the uncanny role of *Pride and Prejudice* in the courtship (213-36). In the background nomenclature is the elopement of Lady Amelia D'Arcy and Byron's father, mad, bad Captain Jack Byron in 1778 (Doody 117). Byron had an affair with their daughter (his half sister) during his second courtship of Miss Milbanke, a rumoured cause of their breakup. Captain Jack fortune-hunted his second wife, wealthy heiress Catherine Gordon, Byron's mother, soon impoverished by his profligacy.

34 Schorer's classroom edition delivers it without inflection: 'Mary is a foolishly pontificating young bore' of obvious 'tastelessness and weakness' (xiii). Woloch's extended reading of her discursive function reaches the same bottom line, her static utility as 'monotonous' foil to Elizabeth's lively intelligence (69–74). Spacks generously reports Stephen Scott's passionate defense of Mary (227) but is 'unpersuaded' (429n7).

35 Rogers again: 'skewered in a single phrase', in mockery of 'pedantic study and overweening ambition to shine' (lxxv; 483n).

36 Vol. III: *Letter* LVI. Southey's next sentence could have been Austen's: 'I have heard of one gentleman who gave a bookseller the dimensions of his shelves, to fit up his library; and of another; who, giving orders for the same kind of furniture, just mentioned that he must have Pope, and Shakespere and Milton. "And hark'ye", he added, "if either of those fellows should publish any thing new, be sure to let me have it, for I choose to have all their works"' (42).

37 Blair, 'Lecture X: Precision in Style': 'Pride, makes us esteem ourselves; Vanity, makes us desire the esteem of others' (I:229). Tave (142) and Rogers (xxxix) allow *Lectures* as a likely volume in Reverend Austen's library. Spacks's comment on Mary's 'hackneyed judgments and sentiments' (52n) seems insufficient, both about Mary and the material.

38 The author's first-person frame-break in *Northanger Abbey*, in defense of 'novels' (I.V), emerges from this prospect.

Work Cited

Auden, W. H. *Letter to Lord Byron*, 1936; Letters from Iceland. Random House, 1937.

[Austen, Henry]. 'Biographical Notice of the Author.' 1817; *Northanger Abbey: and Persuasion*, 4 vols. London: John Murray, 1818, I: iii–xix.

[Austen, Jane]. *Pride and Prejudice: A Novel*. London: T. Egerton, 1813.

[Austen, Jane]. *Emma: A Novel*, 3 vols. London: John Murray, 1816.

Austen, Jane. *Emma*, Norton Critical Edition, edited by Stephen M. Parrish. W. W. Norton, 1972.

Austen, Jane. *Jane Austen's Letters*, edited by Deirdre Le Faye, 3rd edited by Oxford UP, 1995.

Austen, Jane. *Pride and Prejudice: A Longman Cultural Edition*, edited by Claudia L. Johnson and Susan J. Wolfson. Pearson Education, 2003.

Austen-Leigh, J. E. *A Memoir of Jane Austen*, 1870. London: Richard Bentley and Son, 1872.

Blair, Hugh. *Lectures on Rhetoric and Belles Lettres*, 6th ed., 3 vols. London: A. Strahan, T. Cadell & c, 1796.

British Critic. Review of *Pride and Prejudice*, vol. 41, no. 2, 1813, pp. 189–190.

Brower, Reuben Arthur. 'Light and Bright and Sparkling: Irony and Fiction in "Pride and Prejudice".' *The Fields of Light: An Experiment in Critical Reading*. Oxford UP, 1951, pp. 164–181.

Burke, Edmund (the Right Honourable). *Reflections on the Revolution in France*. London: J. Dodsley, 1790.

Burke, Edmund (the Right Honourable). *A Letter from The Right Honourable Edmund Burke to a Noble Lord*. London: J. Owen, 1796.

Byron, Anne Isabella, Lady. 'Letter to Lady Anne Barnard, ~1816–1817.' *Stowe*, pp. 50–54.

Byron, George Gordon, Lord. *Byron's Letters and Journals*, edited by Leslie A. Marchand, 12 vols. Harvard UP, pp. 1973–1982.

Byron, George Gordon, Lord. *Don Juan, Cantos XII–XIII and XIV*. London: John Hunt, 1823.

Critical Review: Or, Annals of Literature, Series 4, vol. 3. Article X, on Pride and Prejudice, Mar. 1813, pp. 318–324.

De Quincey, Thomas. 'The Apparition of the Brocken. Suspiria de Profundis: Being a Sequel to the Confessions of an English Opium-Eater. Part I.' *Blackwood's Edinburgh Magazine*, vol. LVII, Jun. 1845, pp. 747–750.

Doody, Margaret. *Jane Austen's Names: Riddles, Persons, Places*. U of Chicago P, 2015.

Duckworth, Alistair M. *The Improvement of the Estate: A Study of Jane Austen's Novels*. Johns Hopkins UP, 1994.

Elwin, Malcolm. *Lord Byron's Wife*. Harcourt, Brace & World, 1962.

Empson, William. 'Letter to the editor of *Scrutiny* in Response to D. W. Harding's Essay.' *Selected Letters of William Empson*, edited by John Haffenden. Oxford UP, 2006, pp. 122–125.

Galperin, William. '"Describing What Never Happened": Jane Austen and the History of Missed Opportunities.' *ELH*, vol. 73, no. 2, 2006, pp. 355–382.

Galperin, William. *The Historical Austen*. U of Pennsylvania P, 2003.

Gilbert, Sandra, and Susan Gubar. 'Jane Austen's Cover Story (and Its Secret Agents)'. *The Madwoman in the Attic: The Woman Writer and the Nineteenth-Century Literary Imagination*. Yale UP, 1979, pp. 146–183.

Greene, D. J. 'Jane Austen and the Peerage.' *PMLA*, vol. 68, no. 5, 1953, pp. 1017–1031.

Gregory, Dr. John. *A Father's Legacy to His Daughters*, 1774 New Edition. London: Strahan and Cadell, 1793.

Hammond, John L., and Barbara Hammond. *The Village Labourer, 1760–1832: A Study in the Government of England before the Reform Bill*. Longmans, Green, 1920.

[Hansard]. *Parliamentary History of England*, XV [A.D. 1753–1765]. Longman, T. C. Hansard & C, 1813.

Harding, D. W. 'Regulated Hatred': An Aspect of the Work of Jane Austen.' *Scrutiny*, vol. 8, no. 4, 1940, pp. 346–362.

Johnson, Claudia L. *Jane Austen: Women, Politics, and the Novel*. U of Chicago P, 1988.

Johnson, Claudia L. *Jane Austen's Cults and Cultures*. U of Chicago P, 2012.

Johnson, Samuel. *A Dictionary of the English Language*, 2 vols. London: Longman, 1755.

Jones, Darryl. *Critical Issues: Jane Austen*. Palgrave, 2004.

Kettle, Arnold. 'Jane Austen.' *An Introduction to the English Novel*, 2 vols. Hutchinson's University Library, 1951, pp. 90–94.

Le Faye, Deirdre. *Jane Austen: A Family Record*, 2nd ed. Cambridge UP, 2004.

Mingay, Gordan Edmond. *English Landed Society in the Eighteenth Century*. Routledge & Kegan Paul, 1963.

Murray, John. *The Letters of John Murray to Lord Byron*, edited by Andrew Nicholson. Oxford UP, 2007.

Newman, Karen. 'Can This Marriage Be Saved: Jane Austen Makes Sense of an Ending.' *ELH*, vol. 50, 1983, pp. 693–710.

Poovey, Mary. *The Proper Lady and the Woman Writer: Ideology as Style in the Works of Mary Wollstonecraft, Mary Shelley, and Jane Austen*. U Chicago P, 1984.

Prince, Gerald. 'The Disnarrated.' *Style*, vol. 22, no. 1, 1988, pp. 1–8.

Roberts, Warren. *Jane Austen and the French Revolution*. Macmillan, 1979.

Rogers, Pat, editor. *Pride and Prejudice: The Cambridge Edition*. Cambridge UP, 2006.

Schorer, Mark. Introduction. *Pride and Prejudice*, by Jane Austen, 1813, Riverside P, 1956, pp. v–xxi.

Scott, Stephen D. 'Making Room in the Middle.' *The Talk in Jane Austen*, edited by Bruce Stovel and Lynn Weinros Gregg. U of Alberta P, 2002, pp. 225–236.

[Scott, Walter]. 'Essay on Austen's novels.' *Quarterly Review*, vol. XIV, no. 27, 1815, pp. 188–201.

Shapard, David M., editor. *The Annotated Pride and Prejudice: A Revised and Expanded Edition*. Random House/ Anchor P, 2004.

[Southey, Robert]. *Letters from England: by Manuel Alvarez Espriella. Translated from the Spanish*, 1807, 2nd ed., 3 vols. London: Longman &c, 1808.

Spacks, Patricia Meyer, editor. *Pride and Prejudice*. Harvard UP/Belknap P, 2010.

Stowe, Harriet Beecher. *Lady Byron Vindicated: A History of the Byron Controversy, from Its Beginning in 1816 to the Present Time*. London: Macmillan, 1870.

Tave, Stuart M. *Some Words of Austen*. U of Chicago P, 1973.

Trilling, Lionel. *The Opposing Self*. Viking P, 1955.

Walker, Eric C. *Marriage, Writing, and Romanticism*. Stanford UP, 2009.

Williams, Raymond. *The Country and the City*. Oxford UP, 1973.

Wolfson, Susan J. 'Boxing Emma: the Reader's Dilemma at Box Hill.' 'Re-reading Box Hill: Reading the Practice of Reading Everyday Life.' *Romantic Circles Praxis Series*, ed. William Galperin. 2000. https:// romantic-circles.org/praxis/boxhill

Wolfson, Susan J. *Romantic Interactions: Social Being & the Turns of Literary Action*. Johns Hopkins UP, 2010.

Wollstonecraft, Mary. *A Vindication of the Rights of Woman: With Strictures on Political and Moral Subjects*, 2nd ed. London: J. Johnson, 1792.

Woloch, Alex. 'Narrative Asymmetry in *Pride and Prejudice*.' *The One vs. the Many: Minor Characters and the Space of the Protagonist in the Novel*. Princeton UP, 2003, pp. 43–124.

Woolf, Virginia. 'Jane Austen.' *The Common Reader*, 2nd ed. Harcourt Brace Jovanovich, 1925, pp. 168–183.

4

THE NOVELTY OF
MANSFIELD PARK

Emily Rohrbach

DURHAM UNIVERSITY

Written between 1811 and 1813 and published in 1814, *Mansfield Park* is the first novel that Austen composed in the 1810s, following a decade of publishing hiatus and just prior to writing *Emma* (publ. 1815) and then *Persuasion* (publ. 1818). Lengthier, darker, and more psychologically and stylistically complex than any of the novels initially written in the 1790s, *Mansfield Park* has posed fascinating challenges for readers. Following the easy-to-love novel *Pride and Prejudice* (begun in the 1790s; publ. 1813), for instance, Fanny Price—heroine of *Mansfield Park*—appears as quietly recessive in her disposition as the beloved Elizabeth Bennet is delightfully forthright. Fanny is, furthermore, altogether lacking in the wit and humour that the sparkling heroine of *Pride and Prejudice* shares in abundance with Austen's narrator. Despite Fanny Price's recessive nature, the narrative voice of *Mansfield Park* is, by contrast, as witty and incisive as that of *Pride and Prejudice*, creating a seemingly intractable tension between the novel's narrator and its main character. Moreover, unlike Elizabeth Bennet, Fanny is significantly marginalised in the social world she enters; beneath Sir Thomas's roof she is often forgotten by characters and narrator alike. Related to that marginalisation is Fanny's moral character, which is serious, steady, and already intact from the narrative beginning. With these distinctive features of Fanny in mind, when the narrator describes in Chapter Two of *Mansfield Park* how time was necessary 'to reconcile Fanny to the novelty of Mansfield Park', one might think of the novel's protagonist as a parallel for Austen's reader familiar with Austen's previously written and published works, who now holds *Mansfield Park* in hand and opens it for the first time, not quite knowing what to make of it. The novel presents a complex set of moral and aesthetic values that has been hard for readers to reconcile with a wider love for Austen's novels. How to get the mind around this literary 'novelty' of Austen's oeuvre?

Three strands of criticism have been particularly effective at articulating the novel's peculiar challenges. These readings do not so much explain what the novel means as they help us see why readers frequently find it so unsettling. The first strand I will discuss focuses on Fanny Price's subjectivity—that is, her reticence and recessive nature. The second emphasises the awkward relation between the narrator's voice and the voice of the heroine. The third calls attention to the relation between the Mansfield Park estate and the slave plantation in Antigua that supports the English estate financially.

Fanny's Recessive Disposition

Morally serious, consistent, and perceptive, Fanny Price is nevertheless unassertive in her views; she is often reticent in conversation and physically withdrawn from social activity and interactions. The most conspicuous example of her typical inconspicuousness may be when, called upon almost forcibly by her cousins to join their domestic theatricals, she states that she 'cannot act'. But that moral seriousness—in part, a reluctance to participate in an activity that conflicts with the authority of Sir Thomas, whom Fanny rightly assumes would not approve—makes her social role and standing among the family unclear for most of the narration. Fanny is neither immediate family nor servant, exactly. The question of her place is literalised in the desire of various characters to locate her spatially: 'Edmund, looking around, said, "But where is Fanny?"' (51); 'Sir Thomas was at that moment looking round him, and saying "But where is Fanny?"' (123); and the narrator informs us, '"where is Fanny?" became no uncommon question' (141)—in fact, a question so recurrent it nearly becomes a linguistic tic of the novel. Descriptions of rooms further illustrate the question of Fanny's subject position. When Fanny first arrives at Mansfield, after some debate Mrs Norris advises Lady Bertram to 'put the child in the little white attic ... Indeed, I do not see that you could possibly place her any where else' (10). Her room in the house is chosen not so much for her clearly belonging there as for her not belonging anywhere else. Fanny is hard to place—meaning both to locate physically and to define socially; this difficulty is exacerbated by her habits of withdrawal.

Fanny's dispositional reluctance to assert her perspective by voicing her thoughts to those around her, together with the Bertram family's tendency to misunderstand her when not overlooking her entirely, are features that have been explored most profoundly, in philosophical and aesthetic terms, by Anne-Lise François in her book *Open Secrets: The Literature of Uncounted Experience*. Drawing to some extent on Nina Auerbach's astonishing reading of the novel, François makes the remarkable observation that Austen reserves the happy ending in *Mansfield Park* for the only character who does not act. For unlike other characters, Fanny never makes a habit of taking actions that would advance her desires or wishes. She pointedly refuses to act in two key moments: the refusal to participate in the staging of the play and her refusal of Henry Crawford's marriage proposal. Ultimately, her deepest desires are all fulfilled for doing nothing—for not expressing her desires or acting on her own behalf. She is permanently elevated above her Portsmouth life of material indigence by virtue of her 'spiritual recessiveness' and physical withdrawal from the vibrant social activity around her; her alliance remains steadfast with things as they are.

Against models of the Enlightenment and industrial capitalism, *Mansfield Park* presents an ethos of 'freeing desire from the demands of goal-oriented action and forming it to laws of its own' (François xviii). This formation of Fanny's desire, her differently lived relation to her desire, means that quieting her passion for Edmund can be consistent with an 'intrinsic pleasure of not having to assert oneself' (François 233). In this novel, Austen suddenly sets aside, as A. Walton Litz put it, 'the principle of growth and change which animates most English fiction' (129).

Fanny's quiet stillness and her curious relation to desire, free from goal-oriented action, are wonderfully exemplified in the outing at Sotherton, where the Bertrams, Crawfords, Mrs Norris, and Mr Rushworth all venture out into the Rushworth estate's 'wilderness, which was a planted wood of about two acres' (65). The buildings already explored from inside, the pleasure seekers soon become restless,

> When the young people, meeting with an outward door, temptingly open on a flight of steps which led immediately to turf and shrubs, and all the sweets of pleasure-grounds, as by one impulse, one wish for air and liberty, all walked out. (64)

Although Fanny *is* part of the group, this characterisation of the 'young people' scarcely includes one who is as inward, unimpulsive, and quick to tire as she. It is as if the narrator herself, like all her characters, has a habit of forgetting the heroine.

Outside, as the group breaks into threes, Fanny's spiritual steadiness becomes literalised. Fanny sits apart from the seekers and strivers—from Mary and Henry Crawford to Julia and Maria Bertram, as well as her Aunt Norris. Feeling tired, she has a seat on a bench while the worldly others swirl around her, physically pursuing their desires as they move about the wood. Her walking companions, Mary and Edmund, leave her behind to find further amusement. For all her inaction, however, Fanny is the one who ultimately finds happiness with Edmund, while Mary ends up unwed, living with Mrs Grant and

> long in finding among the dashing representatives, or idle heir apparents, who were at the command of her beauty, and her 20,000*l*. any one who could satisfy the better taste she had acquired at Mansfield, whose character and manners could authorise a hope of the domestic happiness she had there learnt to estimate, or put Edmund Bertram sufficiently out of her head. (318)

Remaining on the bench in the Sotherton 'wilderness' while Julia and Maria Bertram, Mr Rushworth, and Mary Crawford aggressively pursue their desires, Fanny—by doing nothing, by making no move to wrest Edmund's attention from Mary Crawford's charms—gains, in the end, virtually everything she has longed to attain. At the end of the day at Sotherton, Mrs Norris, with her abiding 'spirit of activity' (6), comes away with significant spoils—pheasants' eggs and a cream cheese 'spunged' from the housekeeper, as Maria puts it, and a heath from the gardener—but it is Fanny who wins the long game (75).

The Narrator and Her Protagonist

However flawed Austen's heroines may be, they are never anti-heroines. From Catherine Morland and Elizabeth Bennet to Fanny Price and Emma Woodhouse, they conjure sympathy from readers and narrator alike. It is Austen's special power to make it so even when, externally, their lives can look so frivolous. And yet, in *Mansfield Park*, sitting awkwardly alongside that narrative sympathy, and at odds with Fanny's place and her outlook, are the confidence, composure, and sense of humour that consistently enliven Austen's narrative voice.

Consider, for instance, the opening sentences of *Mansfield Park* in which the narrative voice abounds in all these things:

> About thirty years ago, Miss Maria Ward of Huntingdon, with only seven thousand pounds, had the good luck to captivate Sir Thomas Bertram, of Mansfield Park, in the county of Northampton, and to be thereby raised to the rank of a baronet's lady, with all the comforts and consequences of a handsome house and large income. All Huntingdon exclaimed on the greatness of the match, and her uncle, the lawyer, himself, allowed her to be at least three thousand pounds short of any equitable claim to it. She had two sisters to be benefited from her elevation; and such of their acquaintance as thought Miss Ward and Miss Frances quite as handsome as Miss Maria, did not scruple to predict their marrying with almost equal advantage. But there are certainly not so many men of large fortune in the world, as there are pretty women to deserve them. (5)

These sentences are infused with numbers: 'thirty years', 'seven thousand pounds', 'two sisters', etc. In setting the scene, the narrator appears obsessed with counting, pairing, calculating, and balancing, as those activities permeate the perspective both thematically and stylistically. While Miss Maria Ward is paired up with Sir Thomas Bertram in the narrator's little history, a noun pair forms of 'comforts and consequences', qualities linked by the social world and the grammatical conjunction 'and'. That twosome is followed by the stylistically balanced pairing of an adjective-noun phrase ('handsome house') with another ('large income'). The narrator's exceedingly precise scrutiny of the numbers shaping social relations scarcely foreshadows Fanny Price's preoccupations. After all, she is the heroine who turns down a marriage proposal from Henry Crawford. Rather, the social calculations on display reflect the strategic numerical evaluations of a Mary Crawford, and perhaps Fanny's Aunt Norris. These calculations appear intensified by the uneven numbers observed: 'But there are not so many of large fortune in the world, as there are pretty women to deserve them'—a numerical imbalance observed with an epigrammatic statement in which the men occupy the independent clause while the women follow in a formulation that is both socially and grammatically subordinate.

When the narrator describes the uncle lawyer's perspective on the initiating marriage, however, there is a subtle sense of humour—laughing, a little rebelliously, at his authority—that is characteristic only of Mary Crawford: 'the lawyer, himself, *allowed her* to be at least three thousand pounds short of any equitable claim to it' (emphasis added). That the lawyer should generously give permission for Miss Maria Ward (Lady Bertram) to consider herself unworthy, as if it were a blessing, is comedy lost on all but the narrator and the subtle reader in this opening paragraph, but it is the kind of comic perspective, irreverent of ruling authorities, shared within the novel perhaps only with Mary Crawford.

That sense of humour often includes wit, a clever playing with language, and such a taste and capacity for wit largely distinguish Mary Crawford and the narrator from other characters. For instance, during the outing at Sotherton, Mary Crawford mistakenly (or playfully) presumes that Edmund will have thought of the same pun she has but is quickly corrected when Edmund explains his mind is not attuned to that sort of linguistic play. When Mary proposes that Edmund go into law as a profession rather than the clergy, their conversation clarifies the matter:

EDMUND: [:] 'Go into the law! with as much ease as I was told to go into this wilderness'.
MARY: [:] 'Now you are going to say something about the law being the worst wilderness of the two, but I forestall you; remember I have forestalled you'.
EDMUND: [:] 'You need not hurry when the object is only to prevent my saying a bon-mot, for there is not the least wit in my nature. I am a very matter of fact, plain spoken being, and may blunder on the borders of a repartee for half an hour together without striking it out' (67).

Austen's own narrative wit calls for a mind like Mary Crawford's to appreciate *its* 'bon-mots'. Consider, for instance, the description in the first chapter of Fanny Price's mother, who bears 'such a superfluity of children, and such a want of almost every thing else' that she is compelled to write to her sisters to ask for help (6). The narrator informs us: 'The letter was not unproductive', as if her abundance of biological fertility is matched by the productivity of her letter. Austen could have put the idea another way ('The letter received a response', 'The letter inspired her sisters' generosity', etc.), but the suggestion of Mrs Price's fertility seeping into her epistolary gesture, to be called 'not unproductive', makes a bit of fun, through language, at Mrs Price's expense. It's a joke that, within the novel, perhaps only Mary Crawford would appreciate.

The novel's heroine, Fanny Price, by contrast, is never in on the joke. How to make sense of the apparent rift between the novel's plot and its narrative voice? While Fanny's morality wins the day, the narrator's style is forever at odds with what D. A. Miller identifies as the heroine's lack thereof. In his book *Jane Austen, or The Secret of Style*, Miller has few words about Fanny Price, except to say:

In *Mansfield Park,* [...] where its thematic condemnation of style was harshest, the narration may have had the goodness to choose a heroine devoid of style, and the kindliness to shelter her under the cloak of its own eloquence and authority, but never did it dream of taking charity to the point of partaking in her self-mistrust, much less her linguistic indigence. (68–69)

The 'Style' to which Miller refers is the absolute authority and beauty of expression that characterise Austen's narrative voice, which comes to us without the specifications of a social self that would situate the source of the voice as a person: 'Austen's work most fundamentally consists in *dematerializing* the voice that speaks it' (6–7). Miller theorises that this dematerialisation is a function of the fact that the novelist lived her life without marrying, and so she wrote about a social world whose prevailing values and preoccupations worked to exclude or diminish precisely herself—an unmarried woman with a sharp critical eye, a remarkable facility with language, and an abundant sense of humour. The narrative voice, therefore, comes across, in Miller's words, as 'thrillingly inhuman' (2). Although Emma Woodhouse displays the qualities of Austen's narrative voice for the majority of the novel, the Box Hill episode puts Emma's wit on shameful display; her moral transformation that follows prepares her to experience marriage to Mr Knightley precisely as a chastening of her style. In *Mansfield Park,* stylish Mary Crawford fails to feel the shame and consequently ends the novel unwed: 'she is the saint and martyr of Austen Style' (54). What can be unsettling for readers of *Mansfield Park*, then, is that they embrace Austen's novels for the very qualities of the narrative voice that cannot be found in the heroine, and yet the novel presents Fanny Price as deeply deserving of our sympathy.[1]

The Place of Antigua

Yet another interpretive problem concerns what to make of the novel's scant references to Antigua, where Sir Thomas travels in the first volume to manage his slave plantation, a colonial possession that financially supports the life at Mansfield Park. In a novel so overtly preoccupied with moral values and everyday life, what to make of the fact that the way of life on display is made possible by the violence and oppression of slavery in which Sir Thomas appears directly involved, though only ever at the edges of Austen's narrative? In a domestic scene with the whole Bertram family in attendance, Fanny's attempt to broach the subject of the slave trade with her uncle, upon his return from Antigua, is met with a 'dead silence' (136). Is the Bertrams' silence on the subject also Austen's? What are its moral and historical implications?

Prior to the publication of Edward Said's critical study *Culture and Imperialism* (1993), critics of Austen, too, were virtually silent on the topic of slavery in *Mansfield Park*. In that book, Said's chapter on 'Jane Austen and Empire' performs what he calls a 'contrapuntal reading' (79). That is, in his reading of the novel, Said centres what appears at its formal periphery, the place of Antigua visible only in scant references to Sir Thomas' trip abroad for the purpose of 'tending his colonial garden' (Said 102). Said's reading of *Mansfield Park* starts to take account of the history of colonialism, slavery, and the burgeoning British empire. It sheds light on what is alluded to only obliquely in Austen's novel, and what Austen's critics had for the most part ignored: that life at Mansfield Park is sustained financially by Sir Thomas' overseas possession, a slave plantation in the West Indies. The novel's formal subordination of colony to metropole carries political implications for the moral trajectory of its plot, which lands Fanny as spiritual mistress of the English estate.

Said's analysis draws a provocative parallel between two movements of expansion: the colonial ventures of Sir Thomas's travel to Antigua and Fanny's move from her crowded family home in Portsmouth into the spacious halls of her relatives in Northampton. The relative stability achieved at the novel's end is due to the 'wealth of Antigua and the imported example of Fanny Price'—financial and moral forces, respectively, brought in to shore up the domestic advantages that such a place can afford. '[T]he morality [that Fanny represents] in fact is not separable from its social basis: right up to the last sentence, Austen affirms and repeats the geographical process of expansion involving trade, production, and consumption that predates, underlies, and guarantees the morality' (111). Put more bluntly, the colonial possession of a slave plantation appears necessary to sustaining moral life in England. Said proposes that, at the outset of the nineteenth century, 'the novel steadily, if unobtrusively, opens up a broad expanse of domestic imperialist culture without which Britain's subsequent acquisition of territory would not have been possible' (114). There is a fundamental interdependence, then, between the moral plot at the centre of Austen's novel and the colonial ventures 'scarcely mentioned in its brilliant pages' (Said 116).

Fanny's brief return to her Portsmouth home reveals her 'newly enlarged sense of what it means to be *at home*' (Said 105), which requires larger and better regulated spaces, more sociable attention to everyone than what she finds there. Said's argument makes it possible to read even the spaces Fanny inhabits at Mansfield Park and how she inhabits them in a new light, for, as Said puts it, '*Mansfield Park* encodes experiences and does not simply repeat them' (116). While Sir Thomas is away, managing his colonial possession abroad, Fanny's own space in the Bertram home significantly expands, and that expansion comes into view as she contemplates a moral quandary regarding the private theatricals being prepared for in Sir Thomas' absence:

> The little white attic, which had continued her sleeping room ever since her first entering the family, proving incompetent to suggest any reply, she had recourse, as soon as she was dressed, to another apartment, more spacious and more meet for walking about in, and thinking, and of which she had now for some time been almost equally mistress. It had been their school-room [...]—The room had then become useless, and for some time was quite deserted, except by Fanny, when she visited her plants, or wanted one of the books, which she was still glad to keep there, from the deficiency of space and accommodation in her little chamber above;—but gradually, as her value for the comforts of it increased, she had added to her possessions, and spent more of her time there; and having nothing to oppose her, had so naturally and so artlessly worked herself into it, that it was now generally admitted to be her's. (105–6)

Fanny's acquisition of more space, her taking over of what they call the 'East room', might encode the larger territorial expansion of British land possessions. That the taking over of new territory (by Fanny, by Sir Thomas and his class) happens 'so naturally' would imply no opposition to these acts of geographical expansion, which of course belies historical facts regarding the colonies at this time, when the success of the slave revolt in Haiti in 1804 and the formal British abolition of the slave trade in 1807 had weakened the power of people like the Bertrams in the Caribbean (Said 112–13). In light of Said's contrapuntal perspective on the novel, we can see that Fanny's takeover of the East room affords her, however tenuously, the comfort on an individual scale that British colonial expansion and its wealth afford the family at Mansfield Park.[2]

★★★

There are, of course, an extensive number of other issues to take up in *Mansfield Park*. The question of Austen's attitude to social gender roles in this novel has been fascinatingly debated by Marilyn Butler and Claudia Johnson, for instance, while Alastair Duckworth took the novel as his starting point for a study of how the English estate in Austen's novels encodes ideas of moral and social improvement.[3] But no critical questions are as specific to one of Austen's novels as are the three issues addressed above with regard to *Mansfield Park*. A recessive heroine, her antipathy to style, and the financial grounds of her affiliation with the Bertrams extending into the West Indies—these qualities of *Mansfield Park* define its novelty.

What the three approaches to the novel examined above further have in common is that they each shed light, in distinct ways, on how *Mansfield Park* builds a narrative around the unspoken. For Fanny Price, to not have to speak or pursue her desires is to have her desires answered fully. In a world unaccommodating to witty, unmarried women, the narrator's social place remains un-speakable and entirely at odds with the quiet morality of Fanny Price. The financial means of sustaining the moral life at Mansfield Park come from the family's slave plantation in Antigua, which cannot be represented because no language to imagine fully the social and moral relations between the two places exists. The narrative force of Austen's most challenging novel derives precisely from the things that it obliquely tells us cannot be said.

Notes

1 For prior approaches to some of the questions of style that Miller addresses, see D. W. Harding's essay 'Regulated Hatred', Marvin Mudrick's *Jane Austen: Irony as Defense and Discovery*, and Mary Poovey's *The Proper Lady and the Woman Writer*.

2 For further considerations of colonialism and space in *Mansfield Park*, see, for instance, Miranda Burgess's essay 'Fanny Price's British Museum', which focuses especially on the East Room, and Patricia Matthew's essay 'Jane Austen and the Abolitionist Turn'.

3 On social gender roles, see also Devoney Looser's edited collection *Jane Austen and Discourses of Feminism*.

Works Cited

Auerbach, Nina. 'Jane Austen's Dangerous Charm: Feeling As One Ought about Fanny Price.' *Jane Austen: New Perspectives*, ed. Janet Todd. Holmes and Meier, 1983, pp. 208–223.

Austen, Jane. *Mansfield Park*, edited by Claudia Johnson. New York: Norton Critical, 1998.

Burgess, Miranda. 'Fanny Price's British Museum: Empire, Genre, and Memory in Mansfield Park.' *Recognizing the Romantic Novel: New Histories of British Fiction, 1780–1830*, edited by Charlotte Sussman and Jill Heydt-Stevenson. Liverpool UP, 2008.

Butler, Marilyn. *Jane Austen and the War of Ideas*. Oxford UP, 1975.

Duckworth, Alastair. *The Improvement of the Estate: A Study of Jane Austen's Novels*. Johns Hopkins UP, 1994.

François, Anne-Lise. 'Fanny's 'Labour of Privacy' and the Accommodation of Virtue in Austen's *Mansfield Park*.' *Open Secrets: The Literature of Uncounted Experience*. Stanford UP, 2008, pp. 218–268.

Harding, D. W. 'Regulated Hatred: An Aspect of the Work of Jane Austen.' *Scrutiny*, vol. 8, 1940, pp. 346–362.

Johnson, Claudia. '*Mansfield Park*: Confusions of Guilt and Revolutions of Mind.' *Jane Austen: Women, Politics, and the Novel*. U of Chicago P, 1988, pp. 94–120.

Litz, A. Walton. *Jane Austen: A Study of Her Artistic Development*. Oxford UP, 1965.

Looser, Devoney, editor. *Jane Austen and Discourses of Feminism*. Palgrave Macmillan, 1995.

Matthew, Patricia A. 'Jane Austen and the Abolitionist Turn.' *Texas Studies in Literature and Language*, vol. 61, no. 4, 2019, pp. 345–361.

Miller, D. A. *Jane Austen, or the Secret of Style*. Princeton UP, 2003.

Mudrick, Marvin. *Jane Austen: Irony as Defense and Discovery*. Princeton UP, 1952.

Poovey, Mary. *The Proper Lady and the Woman Writer: Ideology as Style in the Works of Mary Wollstonecraft, Mary Shelley, and Jane Austen*. U of Chicago P, 1984.

Said, Edward. *Culture and Imperialism*. London: Vintage, 1994.

5

EMMA, A HEROINE

George Justice

ARIZONA STATE UNIVERSITY

James Edward Austen-Leigh quoted his aunt Jane Austen describing the main character of her novel *Emma* as 'a heroine whom no one but myself will much like' (119). Assuming Austen actually said this, we need to interpret what this description might mean. Is it a simple statement of fact? An aggressive taunt, almost daring readers to try to like Emma Woodhouse? For the writer who created Elizabeth Bennet, who vies for supremacy with Shakespeare's Beatrice as perhaps the most loved character in English literature, the decision to create a character that she imagined her readers not liking might constitute a bold artistic decision (as well as potential commercial disaster).

Interpretations of Emma's character have tried to place this novel, as well as Austen's other novels, in the context of conservative literature of the period that humbles proud characters, re-integrating them into a morally upright (and politically static) Britain. Marilyn Butler's analysis in *Jane Austen and the War of Ideas* has still not been surpassed in its description of the way Emma's humiliation at Box Hill finally helps her understand who she is and what her place is in the world. Other analysis, represented by Claudia Johnson's writing about *Emma* in *Jane Austen: Women, Politics, and the Novel* and *Equivocal Beings*, emphasises the positive elements of Emma's intellectual power—her imagination—and suggests that the character is attractive, if not necessarily 'likable'—for the way she inhabits her world and exercises her mind.

In adaptations, in classrooms, and at meetings of the Jane Austen Society of North America, the character of Emma is still widely discussed and debated. Without claiming to settle the question, this essay focuses specifically on the nature of Emma as *heroine*. The word 'heroine' is charged in the literature of the period as well as in Jane Austen's own oeuvre. To accept Emma as a heroine is to understand her in the context of a history of what Hollywood might call 'strong female leads'. Austen mocked the early-nineteenth century version in the 'Plan of a novel …', composed while *Emma* was in press: 'Heroine a faultless Character herself—, perfectly good, with much tenderness & sentiment, & not the least Wit—very highly accomplished …' (358). This doesn't describe Emma, of course, but it is consistent with Mr Weston's embarrassing wordplay on Box Hill: 'M.A.', letters that 'express perfection' (256). Emma is a strong female lead, but in no way is she 'faultless', or representative of 'perfection'.

Austen's toying with notions of heroism relates not only to the novel's protagonist but to its very form. The move is simultaneously literary and anti-literary: even as the novel uses free indirect discourse to present the main character's train of thought in a believable way, erasing the overt literariness of the romance genre, the foregrounding of the notion of the 'heroine' refers directly and self-consciously to literary tradition.[1] Who is Emma? Or, as Mr Knightley exclaims, 'I wonder what

DOI: 10.4324/9780429398155-5-7

65

will become of her!' (30). This is a novel about a heroine who is both entirely fictional and entirely real. The novel is about her and pulls us into her thinking, whether we like it or not. None of Austen's other novels is as directly tied to its main character as is *Emma*.

In closely tying our reading experience to Emma, Austen was following authors who centred long, comprehensive narratives upon a young woman's life and thoughts. These novels were often, like *Emma*, titled after their main characters. Examples include *Pamela* and *Clarissa* (Samuel Richardson), *Amelia* (Henry Fielding), *Evelina*, *Cecilia*, and *Camilla* (Frances Burney), and *Belinda* (Maria Edgeworth), just to name a few that Austen would have read and that would have shaped expectations for her readers. These earlier novels create a heroic plot line out of character development for a woman in a society that does not overall support intellectual, financial, or personal autonomy, transforming the external, fantastical heroism of prose romance into the development of consciousness in a contemporary, realistically described world. The heroic feminism of the eighteenth-century eponymous women's novel pits self against society, typically with ambivalent conclusions that underscore social inequity while providing some level of satisfaction to the individual protagonist. The 'faults' of a character like Burney's Evelina stem from the character's understandable ignorance about the debased 'World' into which she enters at the cusp of adulthood. These faults are linked to the character's moral rectitude, and the (temporary) difference between her manners and the manners expected by the world around her, but, at the same time, show how bad the world is. The heroic—even 'romantic' in an eighteenth-century sense—allegiance to truth and morality is justified by the novel's happy ending. (Burney's *Cecilia* and *Camilla* complicate the happy ending, suggesting that reconciliation between a heroic goodness and worldly corruption truly might be a matter for *romance*—in a literary sense—rather than the realistic novel.)

While clearly composed in the pattern of these novels, *Emma* is different. Austen's novel, more so than the novels above mentioned or even the novels Austen wrote prior to *Emma*, prods its readers to think through the implications, positive and negative, of putting one character first, foremost, and against the world. Emma's humiliations are primarily personal and internal, and only secondarily societal. Emma escapes all her problems, and the suffering even of Harriet Smith is relegated to the sidelines at the novel's end. Instead of overtly challenging the world's corruptions, the ending of the novel seems to affirm an uneasy stasis. The conventional (and more romantic) 'fair heroine' role in the novel is relegated to a tertiary female character, Jane Fairfax, whose thoughts are not only not depicted, but are shielded even from the sympathetic understanding of other characters in the novel. As I discuss below, the phrase 'fair heroine', describing Jane Fairfax with a hint of mockery, is key to understanding how the novel *Emma* rejects the female 'heroism' of both literary romance and recent realistic novels in favour of a complicated, but direct engagement within (and not against) culture. Emma, the 'heroine whom no one but myself will much like', signals a critical turn toward psychological realism of character and literary realism of novelistic form. Emma is a character defined by living within society rather than fighting against it. Yet 'living within' society for Emma also involves putting an imprint upon her world through the active agency of her creative imagination. Emma lives as a feminist, rather than merely talking as one.

We might first ask why Austen even used the word 'heroine' with her nephew in describing the protagonist of *Emma*. The word has a distinctly cultural valence, even for times in history that might have believed in heroism as a fact of the world. The *Oxford English Dictionary*'s first definition associates the word with heightened traits and activity: 'A woman distinguished by the performance of courageous or noble actions; a woman generally admired or acclaimed for her great qualities or achievements'. It's not that there are not moments of genuine heroism in Austen's fiction. Think of Elizabeth Bennet tromping through the mud to be with her sick sister Jane at Netherfield—that is special physical activity done in pursuit of a moral good. Bingley's sisters, rooted in the day-to-day world of manners, mock her departure from 'decorum' even if Bingley and Darcy themselves are drawn to the way the exercise has heightened Elizabeth's physical attractions. Or, consider Anne

Elliot in *Persuasion* calmly taking care of the unconscious Louisa Musgrove after her fall from the Cobb in Lyme Regis. The kind of 'heroism' in the world of the realistic novel is quiet and based on adherence to higher codes of decency and the common good at the (seeming) expense of personal self-interest, even when tied to physical activity.

Separate from a determination of heroic activity in her novels would be Austen's actual use of the word. The works containing multiple uses of 'heroine' are *Northanger Abbey* (22 times) and *Sanditon* (3 times). These novels, bookending the core of Austen's career of writing realistic fiction, differ in narrative style from the other novels (although they have aspects in common with Austen's Juvenilia). They contain exaggeration verging on the burlesque and are self-consciously engaged with the worlds of literature and culture. Austen's use of the word to describe Emma warns us that the world of *Emma* shares some of its world view with the Juvenilia, *Northanger Abbey*, and *Sanditon* even as it seems more closely to resemble *Sense and Sensibility, Pride and Prejudice, Mansfield Park,* and *Persuasion*. Indeed, *Emma* brings together the satiric and overtly literary writing of the Juvenilia, *Lady Susan, Northanger Abbey,* and *Sanditon* with the realism and depth of genuine emotion that characterise Austen's core successes in the genre.

Before discussing female heroism in Austen's fiction, though, it may be useful to understand better the context in which she was writing. This essay began with the place of *Emma* in the history of realistic fiction titled eponymously. At the same time, female heroism was present in a different strain of fiction by, and about, women. The most obvious influence is Charlotte Lennox's *The Female Quixote* (1752), a novel that Jane Austen loved even upon re-reading. In a letter to her sister Cassandra in January, 1807, Austen describes the family rejecting the recently published *Alphonsine* of Madame de Genlis: 'we changed it for the "Female Quixotte", which now makes our evening amusement; to me a very high one, as I find the work quite equal to what I remembered it' (116).

The novel's main character Arabella, like Don Quixote before her, imbibes an outdated world view from the reading of romances. Romance ideology comes into conflict with the realities of the modern world, and the novel's humour derives from a conflict between a fictional view of the world being actuated by high principle and low skullduggery and the modern facts of life experienced by a privileged young woman in a community that expects adherence to an arbitrary set of behaviors—i.e., 'manners'. Book II, Chapter 10, is entitled 'In which our Heroine is engaged in a very perilous Adventure' (1:103). This is the first instance in *The Female Quixote* in which the word 'heroine' is applied to Arabella rather than to a character in one of the books she is reading.

At this point in the narrative, relationships among a foursome have been set: Mr Glanville admires Arabella, but his sister Miss Glanville, who lives entirely within the customs of the day, is jealous of Arabella as she hopes to attract Sir George, who is, unfortunately for Miss Glanville, attracted by the unself-conscious charms of 'our Heroine'. The word 'heroine' then distinguishes Arabella as a creature made out of literature but, at the same time, a character who actually tries to live up to a higher standard of behaviour. The joke is on her in this particular moment when she misinterprets a gardener as a would-be lover planning to abduct her; but the joke is on the world when Miss Glanville cannot believe that another woman would compliment her without the statement being a sarcastic assertion of self-interest. For the quixotic heroine, misinterpretation of the world around her leads to genuine problems for herself and those who care about her, but that misinterpretation stems from adherence to a standard of behaviour that is in many ways superior to the low standard conveniently obeyed by her social equals. The Quixote role, therefore, is made explicit in Lennox's novels, where it becomes sublimated in a novel like Burney's *Evelina*. *Emma*, it turns out, makes the role more explicit again.

The ending of Lennox's *Female Quixote* is brutal. The final use of the word 'heroine' to describe Arabella occurs in Book IX, Chapter 9, when, after hundreds of pages of ridiculous behaviour, Arabella finally crosses a line. Out with a set of ladies, she fears that they are all about to be ravished, and she gives a beautifully heroic speech:

Fortune, which has thrown us into this Exigence, presents us with the Means of gloriously escaping: And the Admiration and Esteem of all Ages to come, will be the Recompence of our noble Daring. Once more, my fair Companions, If your Honor be dear to you, if an immortal Glory be worth your seeking, follow the Example I shall set you, and equal with me the *Roman Clelia*. (2:219)

She is saved by Mr Glanville but develops a fever. Physicians heal the body, but Arabella needs more. The novel introduces a 'pious and learned Doctor [of divinity]', (2:223) perhaps modelled on Lennox's friend Samuel Johnson. The Doctor deprograms (to use an anachronistic word) Arabella, bringing her belief system into some consistency with the real world through a set of dialogues in which the Doctor talks Arabella out of her chivalric beliefs.

The association of quixotism, heroines, and even Clelia continues in the eighteenth century, suggesting that the trope would have been prominent in culture when Austen wrote *Emma*. For example, a play called *Angelica; or Quixote in Petticoats* was printed in 1758. (The dedication to the famous actor, playwright, and theatrical manager David Garrick thanks Garrick for revisions even though the play was refused for performance.) The anonymous author notes that 'The author of the following sheets thinks himself under an indispensable obligation to inform the public that the character of Angelica and the heroic part of Carless, is not only borrow'd, but entirely taken, from the female Quixote, of the ingenious Mrs Lenox' ('Advertisement').

The Female Quixote is only the most prominent of novels that presents a so-labelled 'heroine' at its centre. My research assistant Alexandra Rios used *Eighteenth Century Collections Online* to get a sense of the prominence of the word in the landscape of prose fiction. The word 'heroine' is used in 6323 novels in the database. Limiting it to the full phrase used in *Emma*, 'fair heroine' appears 91 times between 1740 and 1799 within the Literature and Language subject area of the database. Furthermore, a total of 14 novels contain the word 'heroine' within their title.

Alexandra discovered some particular interesting uses for the purpose of understanding *Emma*. In *Maria* by Elizabeth Blower (1785) the quixotic element is highlighted.

'Oh, I am glad you are come, my dear Miss Mordaunt', cried her ladyship, 'my lord's stories are generally so profusely adorned, that we are fiercely ever able to distinguish reality from ornament; be so kind, therefore, fair heroine of the adventure, as to inform us whether your night excursion was really as Quixotic as his lordship described it'. (51)

In *Agitation: or, Memoirs of George Woodford and Lady Emma Melvill* the narrator uses the labelling of 'my fair heroine' to establish connection with the reader and a pause to establish sympathy with the character.

In this manner, she would reason, and sometimes almost resolve to forget him; but his fight would instantaneously banish such an idea, and some newly discovered agreement would make her regard him more than ever. Some of my readers may condemn my fair heroine for this; but they must consider they had been brought up together from children, and always regarded one another as brother and sister. (137)

(Notice not only the foreshadowing of the characters' names but what Mr George Knightley says to Emma about the propriety of their dancing together: 'Brother and sister! no, indeed' [228].)

In eighteenth-century fiction, then, the use of the word 'heroine', and in particular the use of the phrase 'fair heroine', creates connection between the narrator and reader and makes literary characters who inhabit realistic (rather than literary-romance) worlds. It is not precisely a term of mockery, however. We can see in *Adventures of Jemima Russell, an Orphan* (1799) that the main character is referred to as a heroine only in the beginning and at the end, being known more frequently in the novel as 'unhappy sufferer'. Her success in the material world has her labeled 'heroine' only when she becomes 'wise and virtuous' (53), wisdom and virtue being traits of the female heroism of Austen's Emma Woodhouse, as well.

The 'heroines' of eighteenth-century novel culture were, in sum, realistic characters whom their writers wish to pull out of their realistic context in some way in order to reassert simultaneously the literariness of their writing and the genuine achievement (within a realistic social context) of their characters. There's a range between ironic mockery and genuine admiration for overcoming obstacles. It's a range that Austen exploits fully in her own writing.

Lady Susan gives us a main character who is also a narrator, as Lady Susan Vernon's letters give us her particular realistic/distorted narration of the world around her. As with *Emma*, the title (and main) character is not the one labelled 'heroine'. Instead, Lady Susan applies the word mockingly to her daughter. In trying (vainly) to control a rapidly disintegrating set of circumstances, Lady Susan tells her sister-in-law Catherine Vernon about the 'warm' disposition of Catherine's brother Reginald De Courcy, who had tried to intervene on behalf of the sixteen-year-old Frederica, whom Lady Susan was trying to pawn off on the vapid Sir James Martin. Lady Susan tells Catherine that Reginald 'came to expostulate with me, his compassion all alive for this ill-used Girl, this Heroine in distress!' (247–48) The word, as is typical in Austen, places the person it describes in a world of Romance rather than (in this case) the brutal real world of power and interpersonal manipulation personified by Lady Susan, whose view of the world seems warped but is instead realistic expression of personal power that rejects the social values of decency and kindness, which, to her, are just as ridiculous as the world of Romance into which she mockingly places her daughter. Indeed, Emma might be seen as a toned-down version of Lady Susan, a woman with imaginative energies trying to control circumstances around her: very much different from the 'artless' Frederica or the put-upon Jane Fairfax, the novel's 'fair heroine'.

As I noted at the outset, Austen apparently used the word 'heroine' privately to describe the main character of *Emma*. Jane Fairfax is labeled 'fair heroine' approximately midway through the novel, in Volume II, Chapter 8 (152). This is a moment of intense free indirect discourse in which the novel's narrator seems to be voicing Emma's thoughts—they are, as I mention above, together and yet separate. This is the evening of Mr Cole's party—to which Emma secured an invitation after overcoming her snobby (and false) internal refusal, which was followed by internal mortification that she was excluded. It is a large party, and it would become even larger with the after-dinner arrival of 'the worthy females … with Miss Bates, Miss Fairfax, and Miss Smith'. Before then, 'that very dear part of Emma, her fancy, received an amusing supply' (148) from conversation with Mrs Cole, who relates that a 'large, square pianoforté' has mysteriously arrived at the Bates' house. Mrs Cole goes on to describe her pleasure that Jane Fairfax, who plays so well, did not have an instrument while the Coles were in possession of their own new grand pianoforté.

The invocation of Emma's 'fancy' should warn the reader that she may be moving into a moment of self-delusion. In this case, she's egged on by Frank Churchill, who has not discouraged Emma from suspecting that Mr Dixon has provided the instrument to Jane as a token of his passion for Jane. This passion is rendered adulterous by Mr Dixon's marriage to the daughter of Jane's patron, Col. Campbell. Condensing this fantastical plot into two sentences highlights its quixotism. Emma's version of quixotism here is not that of Lennox's Arabella, derived from extensive reading. We know that Emma never really got very deep in her own reading list, which was in any case much more judiciously assembled than that of Arabella, who was indoctrinated in romance from the books on the shelves of her father's library. Nor is it Lady Susan's, which was a faux-quixotism in service of mocking her daughter. Lady Susan can always tell fact from fiction. Instead, Emma's quixotism stems from the generative power of her 'dear' fancy upon the real-life material provided by

Mrs Cole in conversation. Emma is a would-be novelist, spinning out her own (cheapish) plot about crossed love affairs. It is important to quote the passage in full:

> In so large a party it was not necessary that Emma should approach [Jane Fairfax]. She did not wish to speak of the pianoforté, she felt too much in the secret herself, to think the appearance of curiosity or interest fair, and therefore purposely kept at a distance; but by the others, the subject was almost immediately introduced, and she saw the blush of consciousness with which congratulations were received, the blush of guilt which accompanied the name of 'my excellent friend Col. Campbell'.

> Mrs Weston, kind-hearted and musical, was particularly interested by the circumstance, and Emma could not help being amused at her perseverance in dwelling on the subject; and having so much to ask and to say as to tone, touch, and pedal, totally unsuspicious of that wish of saying as little about it as possible, which she plainly read in the fair heroine's countenance. (152)

Austen's technique of free indirect discourse occludes the creator of the phrase 'fair heroine', which, as we have seen, was a stock phrase used widely in the eighteenth-century novel, emphasising ironic distance between a narrative and a female character of beauty (and delusion). If we assume that in this very realistic novel the phrase 'fair heroine' indicates ironic distance—then who is being distanced from whom or what?

Is there ironic distance between Emma and Jane? Between the narrator and Jane? Between the narrator and Emma? For sure, Emma is already deep within her recently concocted fantasy of Jane Fairfax's illicit love affair with Mr Dixon. If the word is Emma's, then there is irony attached to it. Emma likely is correct in interpreting Jane's face as indicating that Jane did not wish to discuss the piano (which she surely knew had been the gift of Frank Churchill). Emma understands the surface, but she misattributes the cause. She is right about the 'blush of consciousness' but wrong about 'the blush of guilt'. Emma has too quickly deluded herself into believing that her senses have confirmed what her 'dear' (both *highly valued* and *too expensive* in eighteenth-century meanings of 'dear') fancy created: a narrative in which Jane is the object of Mr Dixon's illicit love.

When Emma cannot help something, readers should be on the lookout. 'Emma could not resist', the narrator tells us about her rude put-down of Miss Bates at Box Hill (256). Here 'Emma could not help being amused' at Mrs Weston's 'perseverance in dwelling on the subject'. Emma's focus on Mrs Weston's perseverance—rather than on Jane Fairfax's suffering from it—is only casually pushed by the narrative technique, and most readers will miss it the first time through the novel. The fictional narrative (somewhat like a scandalous novel written by Delarivier Manley) that Emma is creating about Jane Fairfax, Col. Campbell, Mr Dixon, and Mrs Dixon is a cruel one that makes Jane miserable without any clear legal hope for a happy resolution. The only thing that could happen in Emma's narrative to make her 'fair heroine' Jane Fairfax happy would be Mrs Dixon's death and Mr Dixon's subsequent legal transfer of love and marriage to Jane. In Emma's usage, then, the word 'heroine' is ironic: the Jane Fairfax in love with her best friend's husband is likely doomed to perpetual misery.

But the ambiguous nature of free indirect discourse opens the possibility that it is the narrator who labels Jane Fairfax a 'heroine' here. The formal separation between the narrator and Emma prevents the character Emma from falling into the cynicism of Lady Susan, whose power is concentrated into the narrator of the book, famously both within Emma's mind and separate from it. There are good reasons that the narrator would want to use the phrase, perhaps simultaneously ironically (as above) and non-ironically. And perhaps readers *should* see Jane Fairfax as a real heroine. The merit, the suffering, and the triumph of Jane Fairfax much more come to the standard and the pattern of Burney's *Cecilia* or *Camilla*. Jane Fairfax fits the pattern of Jane Austen's own Elinor Dashwood, Elizabeth Bennet, and Fanny Price. Neglected merit suffers but ultimately triumphs in a material world that grinds on through the confluence of social status, male domination, marriage law, property law, and sheer bad luck. The triumph of merit represents an exception to the rule of a society that deserves satire. The novel of manners ends happily because that's what readers want, not because the world really works that way.

Whether the ending of Jane Austen's *Emma* provides a happy ending for Jane Fairfax is a matter of interpretation, guided by Emma's and Mr Knightley's own differing analyses of Frank Churchill's final letter to Mrs Weston. For Emma, the letter shows that 'he had been less wrong than she had supposed', and 'could he have entered the room, she must have shaken hands with him as heartily as ever' (305). Mr Knightley's as-it-happened analysis while reading the letter provides a more real-world judgement: 'Very bad—though it might have been worse.—Playing a most dangerous game. Too much indebted to the event for his acquittal.—No judge of his own manners by you.—Always deceived in fact by his own wishes, and regardless of little besides his own convenience.—Fancying you to have fathomed his secret. Natural enough!—his own mind full of intrigue, that he should suspect it in others—' (306–7). In other words, Mr Knightley attributes to Frank Churchill the role of quixotic hero, his understanding of the world 'deceived' by his 'own wishes', in this case not the result of reading romance but 'his own convenience'.

Emma's own quixotism is, here and throughout the novel, shaped by a disconnection between her overactive imagination and a personal role as a heroine. She certainly wants to be 'first' (and is distraught when the odious Mrs Elton claims a precedence as newlywed even endorsed by Mr Woodhouse). But she is realistic about herself (not 'personally vain', Mr Knightley tells Mrs Weston [29]) and about charitable actions. Most recent adaptations of the novel in fact seemingly cannot bear the brutal element of Emma's realism that accepts that her fantastical friendship with Harriet Smith must die away in the face of accepting a social order that dictates socialization within rather than across its class structure: 'The intimacy between [Harriet] and Emma must sink; their friendship must change into a calmer sort of goodwill; and fortunately, what ought to be, and must be, seemed already beginning, and in the most gradual, natural manner' (332). That is a lot of 'must' for a short passage, the real world bulldozing the 'heroism of sentiment' (296) that Emma rejected when she first realised that she loved Mr Knightley and would accept no prior claim of Harriet to Mr Knightley's hand. Emma's rejection of Harriet at the end of the novel constitutes a direct, if understated, rejection of the norms of sentimental fiction in favour of a realistic depiction of the way social class functioned in the time period of the novel. Given that most readers of typical novels in 1816—as well as most viewers of film adaptations in 2020—are closer in class status to Harriet than to Emma, it is unsurprising to see Harriet Smith and Robert Martin beaming at the wedding of Emma and Mr Knightley in Autumn de Wilde's film, which otherwise attempts to be historically scrupulous. Films are expensive to produce and need to please paying audiences. Austen's rejection of a falsely sentimental continuation of friendship between Emma and Harriet shows that the author could, and did, value art over popularity. Even as modern readers, we might not like Emma, but, if we are discerning enough, we must admire *Emma*.

Emma and Jane Fairfax are, of course, not the last of Jane Austen's heroines. Austen bought back the copyright to *Susan* in January of 1816, the month after *Emma* was printed and published. If Emma had been a heroine she feared no one but herself would like, Susan—rechristened Catherine Morland—was, simply, a heroine, dubbed as such from the opening pages of the novel. Both Emma and Catherine are quixotic characters, but Emma's quixotism resulted from the application of her powerful imagination upon her observations of the world, Catherine Morland, like Arabella in Lennox's novel, misapplies reading to the circumstances of daily life in modern England. Catherine's reading is updated from Arabella, who had followed Cervantes' *Don Quixote* in reading traditional heroic romances. Catherine's reading material are the Gothic novels of the 1790s (admitted as outdated in the author's 'Advertisement' prefacing the novel). Most prominent of these is Ann Radcliffe's wildly popular *Mysteries of Udolpho*. In that novel, the main character, Emily St. Aubert, goes through adventures that defy the realistic world faced by Emma or Catherine Morland. And yet Radcliffe was herself a proponent of the 'explained supernatural', itself an assertion of a romantically tinged real world.

> 'You may find, perhaps, Signor', said Emily, with mild dignity, 'that the strength of my mind is equal to the justice of my cause; and that I can endure with fortitude, when it is in resistance of oppression'.

> 'You speak like a heroine', said Montoni, contemptuously; 'we shall see whether you can suffer like one'. (3:111–12)

Like Catherine Morland, Emily St. Aubert is well-read, and her understanding of the world has been shaped by poetry. Emma, on the other hand, we learn early, reads too little. Emma's misunderstanding of the world around her is an outcome—perhaps inevitable and rooted in the social structure—of a powerful mind disappointed by the limited opportunities afforded to women of her particular social status. If Jane Austen's authorship is an example of what a Catherine Morland, daughter of an ordinary clergyman, could do in life with encouragement and a drive to read, observe, and write, Emma's boredom results from constraints faced by Mr Woodhouse's daughter, for whom a life of authorship was materially unlikely.

Austen's last-written complete novel, posthumously published with *Northanger Abbey*, contains accounts of true heroism. *Persuasion*'s Anne Elliot herself meets real-world heroes, specifically in the instance of upright, fearless characters of naval officers, including Admiral Croft, Captains Harville and Benwick, and, of course, Anne's true, abiding love, Captain Frederick Wentworth. Mrs Croft, living with her husband on board the ships he commands, lives a life of real-world adventure, if not heroism, as she describes the travels that have taken her around the globe. But the novel also suggests—at least in Anne's own semi-quixotic analysis—that some women can directly witness, and relate, genuine heroism. Anne imagines that Nurse Rooke, who has been a main carrier of gossip, is a real-life novelist of contemporary heroism:

> Women of that class have great opportunities, and if they are intelligent may be well worth listening to. Such varieties of human nature as they are in the habit of witnessing! And it is not merely in its follies, that they are well read; for they see it occasionally under every circumstance that can be most interesting or affecting. What instances must pass before them of ardent, disinterested, self-denying attachment, of heroism, fortitude, patience, resignation: of all the conflicts and all the sacrifices that ennoble us most. A sick chamber may often furnish the worth of volumes. (110)

Mrs Smith demurs, and it is unclear whether the novel is endorsing or mildly mocking Anne's imagining a woman encountering genuine heroism. Left unstated, but perhaps implied, is the opportunity for genuine female heroism in professional nursing—but that would have to wait for Florence Nightingale, born three years after the publication of *Persuasion*.

If in some ways *Persuasion* represents the apex of Austen's formal experiments in literary realism, the fragment of *Sanditon*, a novel left incomplete at her death, takes up again the hyper-literary mode of writing seen in her juvenilia and in *Northanger Abbey*.[2] As in *Emma*, there is a distinction between the main character Charlotte Heywood and the character in the novel set out as a 'heroine', the impecunious niece of the novel's Lady Denham, Clara Brereton. Charlotte 'could see in [Clara] only the most perfect representation of whatever Heroine might be most beautiful and bewitching, in all the numerous volumes they had left behind them on Mrs Whi[t]by's shelves—… she could not separate the idea of a complete Heroine from Clara Brereton. Her situation with Lady Denham so very much in favour of it!—She seemed placed with her on purpose to be ill-used.—Such Poverty and Dependance joined to such Beauty and Merit, seemed to leave no choice in the business.—These feelings were not the result of any spirit of Romance in Charlotte herself. No, she was a very sober-minded young Lady, sufficiently well-read in Novels to supply her Imagination with amusements, but not at all unreasonably influenced by them' (349). The narrator denies any quixotism on the part of Charlotte (soon dubbed 'my Heroine' by the narrator [353]). Both women are caught up in fictional plots in the way that Emma and Jane are both included in Frank Churchill's escapades. In this case, the novel's rake character, corresponding to Frank, is the almost cartoony villain, Sir Edward Denham, who bests even *Sense and Sensibility*'s Willoughby for the most outlandish anti-hero that Austen created. But of Charlotte the narrator writes, 'If there are young Ladies in the World at her Time of Life, more dull of Fancy and more careless of pleasing, I know them not, and never wish to know them'. One can imagine that the status of female heroism might have been fully determined in *Sanditon* by the contrast of realistic Charlotte and fantastical Clara. Or maybe not.

This brings us back to Emma Woodhouse and Jane Fairfax. In the context of *Sanditon*, Emma would seem to play the Charlotte role and Jane the heroine role akin to Clara: little money, but with beauty and education, and subject to attention from a rake of a superior social and economic situation. The narrator pays more attention to Emma and to Charlotte, and Jane and Clara are potential victims in real life who might play the role of 'heroine' in a romance-tinged interpretation of their situations. But unlike Charlotte, 'dull of fancy and careless of pleasing' (353), Emma is defined by her imagination, her fancy. And while it might be a mistake to suggest that the use, or in Emma's case overuse, of imagination is heroic, it is, within the social situations so meticulously described in *Emma*, an expression of laudable female power.

Thus it is that whether anybody other than Austen 'likes' Emma, she is a heroine for the modern world: using her imagination as the direct aspect of her intellectual power, doing good in the world where she can, and, a Lady Susan without personal vanity, shaping her circumstances while, unlike Lady Susan, acting within moral codes.

Feminism reimagines the relationship of women to the world. Feminism is related to our status as human beings in the material world—it opposes itself to fantastical narrativizing of our daily lives, putting forward instead a world of (as Elizabeth Bennet would have it) 'rational creatures' rather than 'elegant females'. At the same time, feminism is, and very much was in the time of Mary Wollstonecraft and Jane Austen, the creation of women of great creative powers: the imagination. Perhaps, in *Emma*, Jane Austen was creating 'a heroine no one but myself will much like'. But she was also creating the protagonist of her own story, unabashed to put herself at the centre of her own story. It would have been truly fantastical to create her as a heroine who had already figured it all out. Instead, 'handsome, clever, and rich', Emma is a heroine for modern times.

Notes

1   'Free indirect discourse' is the phrase most commonly used to describe one of Austen's characteristic literary techniques, in which the thoughts of a character are described accurately by a third-person narrator but without the use of quotation marks. In its most sophisticated usage, the line between the narrator's seemingly objective account of the world and the character's subjective thoughts and perceptions are nearly indistinguishable. For a good summary of the history of the term and its applicability to *Emma*, see Gunn, 'Free Indirect Discourse and Narrative Authority in *Emma*'.

2   What 'literary realism' is and how it came to be is a highly contentious topic of literary criticism. Some useful accounts include E. M Forster, *Aspects of the Novel*; Ian Watt, *The Rise of the Novel*; Nancy Armstrong, *Desire and Domestic Fiction*; David Lodge, *The Art of Fiction*; and Lennard Davis, *Resisting Novels*. In different

ways, these books—and many others—describe how the illusion of real life is carried out in the form of the novel and how the developing literary form relates to the world in which novels were written and were read.

Works Cited

Adventures of Jemima Russell, an Orphan. A True and Pathetic History. London, 1799. Eighteenth Century Collections Online, Gale. Arizona State University AULC, 10 Mar. 2020.

Agitation: Or, Memoirs of George Woodford and Lady Emma Melvill. In Three Volumes. Dedicated (by Permission) to the Honourable Mrs Lionel Damer. By the Author of the Ring, and the False Friends ... Vol. 1. A New Edition. London, [1788]. Eighteenth Century Collections Online, Gale. Arizona State University AULC, 10 Feb. 2020.

Angelica; Or Quixote in Petticoats. A Comedy, in Two Acts. London, 1758. Eighteenth Century Collections Online, Gale. Arizona State University AULC, 20 May 2020.

Armstrong, Nancy. *Desire and Domestic Fiction*. Oxford UP, 1987.

Austen, Jane. *Emma*, edited by George Justice. W.W. Norton, 2012.

Austen, Jane. 'Lady Susan.' *Jane Austen's Manuscript Works*, edited by Linda Bree, Peter Sabor, and Janet Todd. Broadview, 2013.

Austen, Jane. *Persuasion*, edited by Patricia Meyer Spacks. W.W. Norton, 2013.

Austen, Jane. 'Plan of a Novel, According to Hints from Various Quarters.' *Emma*, edited by George Justice. W.W. Norton, 2012.

Austen, Jane. 'Sanditon.' *Jane Austen's Manuscript Works*, edited by Linda Bree, Peter Sabor, and Janet Todd. Broadview, 2013.

Austen-Leigh, James Edward. *A Memoir of Jane Austen and Other Family Recollections*, edited by Kathryn R. Sutherland. Oxford UP, 2002.

Blower, Elizabeth. *Maria: A Novel. In Two Volumes. By the Author of George Bateman. Vol. 2. Dublin, M.DCC.LXXXVII*. [1787]. Eighteenth Century Collections Online, Gale. Arizona State University AULC, 10 Feb. 2020.

Butler, Marilyn. *Jane Austen and the War of Ideas*. Clarendon P, 1975.

Davis, Lennard J. *Resisting Novels: Ideology and Fiction*. Methuen, 1987.

Forster, E. M., *Aspects of the Novel*. Harcourt, Brace, and World, 1954.

Gunn, Daniel P. 'Free Indirect Discourse and Narrative Authority in *Emma*.' *Narrative*, vol. 12, no. 1, 2004, p. 35–54. *Project MUSE*, doi:10.1353/nar.2003.0023.

Johnson, Claudia L. *Jane Austen: Women, Politics, and the Novel*. U Chicago P, 1990.

Johnson, Claudia L. *Equivocal Beings: Politics, Gender, and Sentimentality in the 1790s*. U of Chicago P, 1995.

Le Faye, Deirdre, edited by *Jane Austen's Letters*, 3rd ed. Oxford UP, 1995.

Lennox, Charlotte. *The Female Quixote: Or, the Adventures of Arabella. In Two Volumes*, Vol. 1. Dublin, MDCCLII. [1752]. Eighteenth Century Collections Online, Gale. Arizona State University AULC, 20 May 2020.

Lodge, David. *The Art of Fiction*. Penguin Books, 1992.

Radcliffe, Ann Ward. *The Mysteries of Udolpho, a Romance; Interspersed with Some Pieces of Poetry*. The second edition. In four volumes. London, 1794. Eighteenth Century Collections Online, Gale, Arizona State University AULC, 20 May 2020.

Watt, Ian. *The Rise of the Novel*. U of California P, 1957.

Wollstonecraft, Mary. *A Vindication of the Rights of Woman: With Strictures on Political and Moral*. London, 1792. Eighteenth Century Collections Online, Gale. Arizona State University AULC, 20 May 2020.

6

THE POLITICS OF FRIENDSHIP IN
PERSUASION

Michael D. Lewis

WASHINGTON & JEFFERSON COLLEGE

As a young writer, Jane Austen entered, perhaps stumbled, into a longstanding question in Western philosophy: what makes a good friend? In 'Love and Freindship' (1790), Laura writes a series of letters to Marianne, the daughter of her childhood friend, warning her against impetuous behaviour by describing her own. After leaving her family home with her new husband Edward—new in that she met and married him on the same day!—Laura met Sophie. Laura informs Marianne, 'After having been deprived during the course of 3 weeks of a real freind (for such I term your Mother) imagine my transports at beholding one, most truly worthy of the Name' (*Catharine* 83). Now, the young Austen treats this enthusiasm satirically; Laura had just set eyes on Sophie and immediately determined her 'most truly worthy'. And, yet, Sophie did prove a real friend after their husbands vanished and they fended for themselves in a series of absurd adventures. Friendship interested Austen from the start to the end of her writings. Her mature writing meditates, more intentionally and less satirically, on the nature and function of friendship. In *Persuasion* (1818), Mrs Smith laments, 'There is so little real friendship in the world!' (149). Through Laura and Mrs Smith, Austen addresses questions fundamental to the Western philosophy of friendship: are real friends few or many? Should a person's friends be like or unlike them in terms of class, gender, and moral character? Does friendship resemble familial relations, especially male ones—so that friendship and fraternity become synonyms—or does the logic of friendship counter the logic of kinship? I consider *Persuasion* in relation to these questions that persist across centuries, even millennia, arguing that friendship is most robust and transgressive in Austen's final novel. Laura's superlatives and effusive praise suffuse the novel, which contrasts supportive friendship with vacuous family. Friendship fills the void left by family, as Anne Elliot receives intense feeling and equitable exchange from those remarkably unlike her aristocratic family, thereby gesturing toward new relations—personal, political, literary.

That Austen's fiction ponders personal relations and weighs in on philosophical debates isn't news. Before offering my interpretation, I review major critical treatments of this wonderful novel, summarising what they argue about personal relationships, political issues, and the relation between the two. Along the way, we will encounter topics that range from feminism to style, from war to time. I then turn to my reading of friendship in *Persuasion*, which, I hope, continues the critical conversation in new and insightful ways.

Critical Overview

I begin my critical overview in the 1970s. The 1970s witnessed the emergence of major critical schools with lasting influence on scholarship in subsequent decades and even today. After the

DOI: 10.4324/9780429398155-6-8

75

political turbulence of the 1960s, critics brought political questions to cultural texts, considering art's relationship to patriarchy, capitalism, and imperialism. Austen scholars interrogated the novels' politics, laying the foundation for contemporary Austen studies. In the last half century, *Persuasion*'s readers have approached some recurring questions. Is it a revolutionary or reactionary novel? Feminist or patriarchal? Does it channel Wollstonecraft or Burke, Hume or Adam Smith? Does it continue or radically depart from preceding fiction—both other writers' and Austen's own? Does it look back to the eighteenth century or confidently step into the nineteenth? I focus on three periods: the first between 1970 and 1986, which marks a golden age of Austen scholarship. In this period, critics position Austen in one political camp or another: she either upholds or overturns the status quo. In the next period I take up, however, the novel's politics become murkier, expressing competing impulses and creating tension. Writing between 1988 and 2005, this group of critics offers renewed attention to literary form and adds political issues of nationalism and war to meditations on patriarchy and society. I close with scholars publishing in the last decade and focusing on new philosophers, such as Adam Smith, and turning gender studies toward masculinity.

In *The Improvement of the Estate* (1971), Alistair M. Duckworth gives us an Austen committed to both tradition and reforms that would guarantee traditional society's survival. The work considers the estate 'a metonym for other inherited structures' (ix), such as society, morality, and language. Due to the interlocking relationship among these systems, Austen strives to ensure the estate's continuance. From the start, Duckworth acknowledges *Persuasion* as an exception to her fiction's general pattern of improvement. After all, this novel's estate is abandoned, not reformed, by the Elliots. This novel's heroine does not find herself safely ensconced in a reformed estate, after a period of precarity. The novel's ending forecasts a professional, not traditional, future. Despite these modifications, *Persuasion* still expresses Austen's 'ethically conservative impulse' (183). Anne consistently confirms conservative principles. First, she rejects Wentworth's initial proposal, which Duckworth connects to a contemporary debate. Our leading woman and man disagree over whether to submit to duty or the heart, and so did the era's leading commentators. Radicals like Mary Wollstonecraft encouraged daughters to privilege feelings over parental advice, while conservatives like Hannah More emphasised daughterly obedience. Anne's rejection sides with More. Second, Anne exhibits 'self-control rather than self-assertion' (198). Third, Anne demonstrates a Burkean commitment to preserving tradition. She copies Kellynch's library holdings, carrying her class's principles and culture with her, transporting them on her travels from Kellynch to Uppercross to Bath. That these affirmations do not take place on the family's estate—as they did at Pemberley and Mansfield Park—does not, for Duckworth, alter the novel's essential conservatism.

Nina Auerbach locates very different politics in *Persuasion*. Where Duckworth saw Burke, Auerbach sees Wollstonecraft. Where he saw tradition, she sees revolution. Where he saw self-control, she sees self-exertion. Where he saw continuity, even in the face of difference, she sees a novel that 'transforms themes and motifs introduced earlier in the author's canon' (112). In 'O Brave New World: Evolution and Revolution in *Persuasion*' (1972), Auerbach compares *Persuasion* to Austen's earliest novels to consider how far the author—her heroines, plots, values—has travelled across her career. In *Northanger Abbey*, Catherine Morland is blinded by Bath and must learn to perceive it as only a dazzling prison. Anne proves immune to Bath's baubles. Anne is both a wiser Catherine and a tempered and narrator-approved Marianne Dashwood. For the latter, 'nature and feeling were dangerous' ('O Brave' 116) and to be avoided. But evasion transitions to embrace, as Anne privileges nature and feeling. It is an injustice that the Bennets will lose Longbourn; it is justice that the Elliots must rent Kellynch. The novel thus rethinks personal temperament and social order. The rethinking of the latter becomes most clear in the navy's role and its 'enormous revolutionary potential' (119) and 'utopian hopes' (120). Wentworth is a harbinger of the future, unlike earlier romantic heroes who remain rooted in and sheltered by a landed estate, whether Pemberley or Donwell Abbey. Auerbach makes more of this difference than Duckworth. The sailors reflect a new emphasis on fulfilling labour, and exertion and agency are shared by naval wives. Mrs Croft shares globetrotting and driving duties with her husband, and she critiques her brother's refusal to treat women as 'rational creatures' (124). In Mrs Croft's rhetoric, Auerbach uncovers Wollstonecraft's, and it's Anne, alone among Austen's heroines, who embodies Wollstonecraft's dream of rational women. In her debate with Harville over whether men or women remain most constant in love, the heroine channels the *Vindication of the Rights of Woman* and its emphasis on unequal educational opportunities. For Auerbach, then, *Persuasion* abandons Austen's earlier plots and politics, rewriting heroines and heroes, attitudes toward land and labour.

The political pendulum swings back to the right, from revolution to preservation, as Marilyn Butler stresses Austen's conservatism. Echoing Duckworth at its start, *Jane Austen and the War of Ideas* (1975) confidently asserts that 'Austen's novels belong decisively' (3) to a canon of conservative novels, as they lay stress on individual reform and 'an ideal order' (2). At its end, however, the book presents *Persuasion* as not so decisive and partisan. *Persuasion* recycles the earlier novels' conservative materials but introduces new techniques. The novel exhibits a conservative distrust of Captain Wentworth and his modern emphasis on self. Butler's Wentworth is Duckworth's, not Auerbach's. He deploys 'Godwinian phraseology' and expresses 'revolutionary optimism and individualism' (275) in his confident belief in his earning potential and in his disappointment in Anne giving way to Lady Russell. Wentworth gives up these modern notions, accepting Anne's initial choice and reversing course as Austen's earlier heroines did. The 'problem' (276), for Butler, is that the novel contains more than the conservative critique of self-reliant Wentworth or self-indulgent Sir Walter: new is the extent of Anne's consciousness. Butler admires the narration of the heroine's subjectivity, declaring that 'nothing in subjective writing in any earlier English novel [can] compare in subtlety of insight or depth of feeling' (278). But Austen fails to coordinate subjective writing with objective satire of the Elliots. This disjunction proves 'the weakness of *Persuasion*' (279), as the novel creates generic vertigo by moving toward the nineteenth-century novel of interiority and backward to the eighteenth-century novel of social comedy, toward George Eliot's heroines and Austen's earliest ones. Despite this lack of coordination, Butler nevertheless finds 'a striking intellectual consistency' across Austen's oeuvre, as the late novels exhibit 'a firmer conception than ever of middle-class duty' (286). Butler's *Persuasion* resembles Duckworth's, as they catalogue both the novel's profound difference and persistent devotion to conservative ideals.

In 1979, Sandra M. Gilbert and Susan Gubar published their groundbreaking *The Madwoman in the Attic*, a major contribution to feminist literary studies. The book meditates on the association, perhaps identity, of authorship and male authority, analysing the ways that nineteenth-century women writers attempted to liberate themselves from men's idealised images of women. Considering Gilbert and Gubar's emphasis on male domination of and through literature, it is not surprising Anne Elliot emerges within their first few pages. The feminist critics cite the debate between Anne and Harville, the heroine's insistence on men's unfair advantage in telling all the stories, and her famous assertion that 'the pen has been in their hands' (6–7). The first of six references to Anne in their introduction underscores Austen's awareness of how 'patriarchy and its texts subordinate and imprison women' (13) and revels in Anne's 'refusal … to be fixed or "killed" by an author/owner, her stubborn insistence on her own way' (16). Gilbert and Gubar's title invokes *Jane Eyre*, but their introduction repeatedly invokes *Persuasion*, as they make Austen's last novel central to this feminist watershed.

Gilbert and Gubar characterise *Persuasion* as the story of a heroine without a story. Years after the broken engagement, Anne is a nobody socially and narratively—a woman without marriage or a marriage plot. Throughout their work, Gilbert and Gubar discuss the ways that the female self is fractured into different characters, and *Persuasion* surrounds Anne with the selves she might have been. If she marries William Walter Elliot, she will become Lady Elliot, an iteration of her mother. If she had accepted Charles Musgrove, she would have become Mary. Analyzing these alternative lives and selves, 'Austen illustrates how growing up female constitutes a fall from freedom, autonomy, and strength into debilitating, degrading, ladylike dependency' (177). Louisa's literal fall physically manifests this degradation. Anne is surrounded by fallen selves and by characters who want to direct her toward a similar fall. Anne must reject these narratives, tell her own story, determine her own life. In doing so, she rejects her father's patriarchal principles and 'refuses to become a lady' (181). Anne thus figures Austen herself, as the heroine authors and authorises her own life, defying others' wishes and demonstrating Auerbach's self-exertion rather than Duckworth's self-control.

Tony's Tanner's simply titled *Jane Austen* (1986) stresses *Persuasion*'s departures—social and stylistic—from the earlier novels. He calls it a 'new kind of novel' (212), a 'unique novel' (221), and a second novel—one that begins years after Anne's and Wentworth's first and foiled courtship, which would've been the material of an earlier Austen novel. The second novel starts with Anne's second life, where she must move from prudence to romance, reversing the course taken by earlier heroines. She and Wentworth successfully revitalise their love, but society fares less successfully, proving unable to resuscitate the order championed by Austen's earlier fictions, as Duckworth argues. In *Persuasion*, society undergoes 'a crisis of values' (217) and cannot find 'any real centre or principle of authority' (210). All that is solid in earlier works melts into air. Rank, manners, property prove unsound, even meaningless. Only naval ranks provide true leadership; manners reveal neither Wentworth's worth nor Mr Elliot's evil; Sir Walter abandons his property. Reliable social foundations dissipate. If Anne is 'the girl on the threshold' (209), then the social world is suspended between an outmoded order and an unknown future. The novel, Tanner contends, also looks forward to later, even much later fiction. The novel's affection for sea and navy anticipates Melville's and Conrad's; the novel's opening, with its reader opening to the same words Sir Walter reads in the baronetage, offers 'the kind of teasing regression which we have become accustomed to in contemporary writers' (208). Austen even takes up questions of twentieth-century philosophy. He reads the pivotal scene where Wentworth ostensibly writes to Benwick while writing his declaration of love to Anne, as suggesting that 'All "writing" or communication is potentially double' and that 'There is ultimately no single, definitively correct "address"' (242). 'The problems and difficulties which Anne and Wentworth have to negotiate are not a function of early nineteenth-century English society. They are inherent in language and communication itself' (242). Tanner's Austen resembles Jacques Derrida who devoted a career to the instability of meaning. Austen gestures toward these concerns in the novel.

To this point, critics have given largely black and white portraits of *Persuasion*. They all attend to nuance, but some deliver a conservative Austen, others a radical one. Two different Austens occupy the far poles of the political spectrum. This clear binary gives way in my second period of *Persuasion* critics, publishing from the late 1980s to the first decade of the twenty-first century. With her important *Jane Austen: Women, Politics, and the Novel* (1988), Claudia Johnson relocates these complexities in the texts themselves. Situating Austen within the context of women's political novels, Johnson rejects the idea that Austen's works are as doctrinaire as Butler insisted or as revolutionary as Auerbach did. She argues instead that both progressive and conservative discourses rely on the same rhetoric, this reliance producing political instability and confusion. Her main example is the characterisation of Wentworth whom she casts as 'a complex figure … of ideological contradiction' (149). Duckworth and Butler identified tension between conservative narrator and newfangled character, but Johnson finds plenty of tension within the portrait itself. When Wentworth recommends nutlike firmness to women, he sounds like a progressive fellow, a strong man desiring a strong woman. When arguing with Mrs Croft, however, he casts women as too delicate to travel on his ship, striking a patriarchal chord. Johnson sees not a new kind of man but a Janus with one face toward the future and one toward the past. Painting a more complex portrait than Butler or Auerbach by considering Wentworth in terms of gender, her reading illustrates the vital influence of feminist criticism on Austen studies.

Johnson also stresses the centrality of gender to the novel's critique of Walter Elliot's self-importance and insularity. This critique reveals *Persuasion*'s progressive impulses and differentiates it from its predecessors. Only here does 'Austen portray the provinciality of her characters as a disadvantage' (158). Conservatives celebrated the neighbourhood as providing strong roots for its inhabitants, but *Persuasion* sees the neighbourhood as rotting, not rooted, as Kellynch suffocates women. Johnson makes this point by recourse to other sites of debate in eighteenth-century thought. Whereas liberal psychology and Samuel Johnson recommend 'change of place' (159) to men, *Persuasion* extends this recommendation to women, as Mrs Croft sails around the world and Anne suffers at home. Whereas Maria Edgeworth criticised but upheld social arrangements, *Persuasion* wonders 'whether women's happiness may not be better served by cutting loose from these arrangements' (160). But even as this sounds like an unambiguous step forward, it is not. Anne's break from the past is both decisive and unimpeachable because silent, the novel 'frown[ing] upon, overt rebellion' (163). Johnson's interpretation thus threads a nuanced needle between Auerbach and Butler, offering a reading sensitive to tension and contradiction.

In the middle of the next decade, Adela Pinch reads the novel in terms of consciousness and feeling, knowing oneself and knowing others, and the experience of reading. *Strange Fits of Passion: Epistemologies of Emotion, Hume to Austen* (1996) shows how the novel's concern with feminine feeling engages eighteenth-century debates, both literary and philosophical. The novel of manners depicted less emotional heroines than Gothic romances, while David Hume encouraged his readers to channel passions into aesthetic taste. Juxtaposing Austen and Hume, Pinch extends the philosophical context beyond Burke and Wollstonecraft. The novel probes feelings both social and emotional. How does consciousness apprehend others? How does Anne apprehend Wentworth? In both cases, 'the presences of other people are apprehended as insistently sensory phenomena' (145). Consciousness encounters others through senses, struck by sounds and bodies, Anne's mind coming to feel 'crowded' (147), confined, claustrophobic. She feels pinched by Mrs Musgrove's large body and her nephew's hanging on her back. Anne's encounters with Wentworth intensify these shocks to the point that 'the presence of her love is apprehended as invasive' (154). The social and the romantic are similarly sensory and shocking, and the romantic includes the additional elements of memory and repetition, as Anne 'practices sustained and conscious recollection' (152). This recalling of the past rewrites plots and philosophy, as Austen gives us a heroine who isn't an ingénue and gives us a consciousness informed by past and present. Anne's absorption resembles the reader's, and *Persuasion* exhibits an ambiguous attitude toward reading. Sir Walter's reading consoles but in the service of narcissism; Anne recites verses about autumn, but she cannot remember one after eavesdropping on Wentworth's sermon on the firm mind; Benwick recites poetry to Louisa when her mind is weakest, suggesting poems are pap. The novel offers its most metafictional moment when Wentworth drops his pen, calling attention to Austen's own. While drawing attention to literature's failures or weaknesses, the novel nevertheless presents it as limited and inevitable, restrictive and emancipatory, impinging and resistant. Literature and lovers, feelings and others, both weigh down and uplift the heroine. Pinch follows Tanner in emphasising Austen's anticipation of postmodern style and Johnson in stressing the tension inherent to the text.

Thus far, I have discussed studies of *Persuasion* that have been largely historicist, critics recreating various contexts: philosophical treatise, political debate, literary genre. This methodological preference follows the trend of literary studies in the 1980s and 1990s. But some Austen critics pursued different paths. Narratologist Robyn R. Warhol, for example, characterises Austen as a feminist novelist, as Gilbert and Gubar do, but she reaches this conclusion by zeroing in on narration. Warhol focuses on 'Austen's management of focalization, that is, her use of Anne Elliot as the central consciousness through which the story gets transmitted' (6). Where Butler saw this centrality and subjectivity as a flaw, Warhol sees them as the means by which Austen meditates on the gaze and the body. Men's looks objectify women's bodies; Anne's looks interpret others' interiority, empowering herself and her perspective. Reading the exterior to get to the interior is, in this novel, 'a distinctly feminine thing to do' (9).

Warhol qualifies this argument. First, she suggests that, unlike Sir Walter and his objectifying obsession with looks, the admirable men in the book, such as Croft and Wentworth, don't pay attention to bodies. Thus, Warhol reframes Wentworth's failure to note Anne's changed looks as a virtue, not a slight. Second, empowering looking only belongs to the middle class. The workers who come to Louisa's aid at Lyme look but are not looked at, not differentiated, not named. Warhol thus offers a less optimistic reading of labour than Auerbach. Third, looking allows the female body to be empowered, but this body experiences both strength and suffering. Anne's desire for Wentworth causes agitation and pain, as Pinch stressed. Anne experiences more positive physical sensations toward the end of the novel, reversing Marianne Dashwood's trajectory from exuberance to sickness. Warhol's rich reading thus adds narratological complexity to the issues often treated by historical critics: gender, labour, the body, and stresses tension, as Johnson and Pinch do.

Like Warhol, D. A. Miller pursues narrative questions in his stunning *Jane Austen, or The Secret of Style* (2003). He focuses on Austen's narrator and praises her achievement of 'a truly out-of-body voice' that lacks body, 'psyche, history, social position' (2), and personality. This voice, devoid of social markers and authorial character, Miller contends, 'may well be the *only* English example' (31), as Fielding, Thackeray, and even Eliot create a voice of human authority rather than 'godlike authority' (31). One secret is her style's concealment of her social identity, as the spinster who writes expertly of marriage. Miller contrasts the heroines' style (little 's') with Austen's Style (big 'S'). The heroines demonstrate style and wit, but they must abandon such style in order to become a person, woman, wife. Austen's Style, however, always remains impersonal, neuter (33), exempt from social norms and laws. Always, that is, until *Persuasion*. The last completed novel is noticeably absent in the first half of Miller's book. The 'typical heroines' (42) include Lizzie, Emma, and Mary Crawford, not Anne. When Miller turns to *Persuasion*, he scorns it as a failure, even betrayal of, Austen's striking accomplishment of the depersonalised voice. The preceding novels keep heroine and narrator apart—even in *Emma* which exhibits Austen's deepest identification with her protagonist—but, in *Persuasion*, that boundary buckles and breaks. Whereas the previous novels give us heroines unlike Austen in that they are young and marriageable, the last one gives us a twenty-seven-year-old spinster whose marital status resembles the author's. Thus, while readers like Tanner enjoy the second novel of the older heroine as an advance in her imagination and plotting, Miller laments it as the disintegration of her cohesive voice. The personality of this narrative voice results from Anne usurping the narrator's usual functions. Whereas the narrator mortifies and ironises and 'slap[s] silly' and 'batter[s]' (71) the earlier heroines, Anne mocks and mortifies herself. The narrator masters the earlier heroines but submits to this one. Miller has strong feelings about this altered relationship. *Persuasion* constitutes 'the great false step of Austen style' (68), reveals the omnipotent narrator 'turned suicidal' (69) and its 'fall' (69) from Edenic narrative. What Miller calls Anne's 'unique absorption of Austen's narration' (69) earned Butler's ire and Warhol's praise. From a very different vantage, Miller echoes Butler, as both critics see the change not as an advance but a failure. Indeed, Miller considers it 'depressing to hear the new vulnerability of *Persuasion* hailed as an extended "reach" for the novelist, when in fact it amounts to the retraction of her great world-historical achievement' (75). Miller sees steps back, dark feelings, and failure whereas Auerbach and Warhol saw progress, light, and success.

At the same time that Miller considered deeply formal issues, other critics turned toward questions of war and nationalism. American wars in Afghanistan and Iraq played a role in this turn, explicitly so in Mary A. Favret's exciting 'Everyday War' (2005). The Napoleonic Wars seem peripheral to *Persuasion*, more background than foreground. In Favret's view, the wars are not peripheral but central, pervading the character's actions and affects, rhetoric and consciousness. This centrality destabilises the boundary between everyday domesticity and distanced enmity. Favret places this boundary in literary and intellectual histories. The former catalogues how eighteenth-century poets—Wordsworth, Coleridge, and Austen's beloved Cowper—strive but fail to distance war from domestic comforts. The latter considers how twentieth-century theorists—Lefebvre, Foucault, Certeau—reveal deep interconnections between wartime and peacetime. Austen thus resembles contemporary Romanticism and anticipates French theory, as Tanner implied. The novel blurs the boundary between war and peace in various ways. Austen sets her novel in 1814, a time of fleeting or false peace. When Anne informs her family that Admiral Croft fought at Trafalgar, her intimate knowledge in 1814 of the 1806 battle blurs boundaries between present peace and past strife, public history and private psyche. War haunts the present and protagonist. Favret reads Austen's novel beside a sailor's diary, *The Adventures of John Wetherell*, this juxtaposition generating remarkable parallels. The most exciting, perhaps, arrives when Favret quotes Wetherell describing various falls—intentional and accidental, suicidal and criminal (attempting to jump ship, literally and metaphorically)—that create 'alarm and accident' (626) aboard his ship. Favret then turns to consider the discussion of Dick Musgrove and the subsequent fall suffered by Anne's nephew Charles Musgrove. Perhaps Dick fell. Perhaps Charles's fall transfers alarm from uncertain sea to stable ground. From there, of course, there's Louisa Musgrove's (in)famous fall at Lyme. Veteran sailors return safely. Landlubbers encounter significant anxiety. This inversion, Favret offers, creates 'an uncanny, unclaimed sense of war rest[ing] beneath these accidents, particularly the otherwise avoided sense of war as violent injury' (627), Austen attempting 'a history of war' (607) that speaks to her own time and to our own.

I now turn to my third and final period of *Persuasion* studies. In the last decade, critics have continued to extend the philosophical contexts for, formal innovations of, and gender politics in *Persuasion*. In *Sympathetic Realism in Nineteenth-Century British Fiction* (2012), Rae Greiner considers nineteenth-century novels in light of Adam Smith's moral philosophy. Her second chapter positions Austen's novel in relation to not only Smith but Jeremey Bentham. Greiner thus enlarges the group of late eighteenth- and early nineteenth-century philosophers who illuminate Austen's thought, as Pinch did with Hume. Greiner's analysis of Smith explores his conception of history and the historian's attention to external and internal facts, to social events and personal sentiments. Smith, like twentieth-century historian R. G. Collingwood after him, 'makes past mentalities come alive by setting them into motion in the minds of the present' (55). Anne Elliot follows Smith from the beginning, reviving, as early as the fourth chapter, her personal history, inhabiting and evaluating the years-old rejection of Wentworth, and concluding with regret at calling it off. She follows Smithian sympathy in putting herself in Wentworth's shoes, inhabiting and evaluating his years of silence, and concluding with regret and resentment that she would've gotten back in touch as soon as he started to earn his fortune. The most spectacularly Smithian moment, however, comes after Anne's and Wentworth's reuniting at novel's end. They have reunited, and he invites her to consider his recent suffering as he feared Lady Russell persuading her to marry Mr Elliot. Anne refuses. Instead, she angrily insists that the two cases are different, that she needed to heed Lady Russell as a teenager but needn't now. She returns to this difference in the evening. 'Anne is clearly waffling' (73), as she complexly adjudicates Lady Russell and her own past and future selves: she was right to be persuaded; Lady Russell was right and wrong; but Anne would never in the future give the same advice to a young woman in her position. In Greiner's fine reading, Anne generates an impartial spectator to evaluate her actions; she sympathises with herself, as Smith demands; and she imagines and sympathises with a future Anne having to weigh the demands of love and filial duty. This sympathy directed to past and future, to self and other, tells us something about Austenian sympathy and realism. 'Such acts of projection make the processes of sympathy intrinsic to the realist enterprise. The ability to imagine unseen people, alternative selves, is the foundation on which our sense of our own reality derives' (Grenier 79). Anne's sympathetic imagining is thus another metafictive moment to add to the ones outlined by Tanner and Pinch. But why do Wentworth and Anne argue and assess *after* they are certain of happiness? Because, the novel insists, the case is never closed, the past is never past.

If the past is never past in *Persuasion*, then the novel also considers how the present becomes the past and how it will function in the future as memory, in Emily Rohrbach's recent reading. While Pinch and others discuss Anne's nostalgic turns to the past, Rohrbach's *Modernity's Mists: British Romanticism and the Poetics of Anticipation* (2016) stresses how frequently Anne looks to the future and looks forward to future nostalgia. In moments of 'anticipated retrospection' (106) Anne imagines the present as a future memory. Meditating on Mrs Clay's designs on her father, she contemplates warning Elizabeth and anticipates recalling the warning, even if futile, as a consolation. Such projections help Anne deal with emotional difficulties, transforming the difficult present into a delightful memory and granting her agency to control current moment and mood. Attention to the future is provoked by pain but also pleasure. Anne no sooner accepts Wentworth's proposal than she turns from present elation to future recollection. Such time travel underscores the reunion's temporary happiness but also allows Anne to avoid delusion. These projected recollections, however, never come to pass. Austen does not plot Anne's future recollections. In Rohrbach's account, this gap between character's and creator's designs indicates Austen's insistence on an unknowable future, for even this most reflective heroine. This inability to forecast the future informs Anne's consciousness and Austen's conception of history. Austen sets *Persuasion* during the temporary peace before Waterloo and the reigniting of international conflict. Her characters appear secure in this temporary peace, but her post-Waterloo readers know it to be short-lived. Positing the impossibility of knowing the future, Austen rejects the 'causal logic so central to Enlightenment historiography' (121), and this rejection becomes clear in Rohrbach's contrast of Austen's historical novel with the first historical novel proper, *Waverley*. Scott, the Regency's other towering novelist who has not played much of a role in the criticism I have summarised here, gives fictional form to the Enlightenment stadial theory of history. Like Adam Smith and others, Scott sees history as stages naturally and inevitably marching toward capitalism, his novel confidently eschewing the unpredictable; Austen foregrounds the unpredictable and eschews clearly unfolding stages. Scott derives character from history; Austen makes history a philosophical question approached through character. Offering Austen as 'a theorist of philosophical modernity' (109), Rohrbach situates *Persuasion* in terms of the Scottish Enlightenment as Greiner did and presents Austen as a keen reckoner with the effect of the Napoleonic Wars on philosophy, history, psyche as Favret did.

Greiner and Rohrbach extend our sense of the philosophical touchstones—thinkers and ideas—relevant to *Persuasion*, and there's also been an expansion of gender readings that focus primarily on masculinity. Such analysis isn't new, of course—debating Wentworth's gender goes back to Duckworth and Butler in this account—but masculinity studies have taken off from feminist and queer studies. I close with Taylor Walle's 2016 article on Wentworth's blushes because it revisits literary and philosophical contexts that we have encountered and produces intriguing insights. Like Greiner, Walle turns to Adam Smith, noting his ambiguous relation to feeling: good sympathy produces social bonds, while bad feelings threaten them. Eighteenth-century debates about feeling's dangers also include the sentimental novel, where men of feeling experience Smithian bad feeling and become antisocial, and Wollstonecraft, who warns against excessive feeling for women. 'Echoing' Smith, Austen rethinks the position of both the sentimental novel and Wollstonecraft's feminism (49). Walle notes that only Anne and Wentworth blush in the entire novel, which makes them a woman and man of feeling. But, contra Wollstonecraft (and the earlier depiction of Marianne Dashwood), Austen depicts Anne as intensely feeling and also profoundly practical, suggesting that women can be emotional *and* rational, as Anne demonstrates when Louisa falls. And, contra the literature of sentiment and Henry Mackenzie, Wentworth blushes and remains masculine, making him engaged, not cut off from the world. His sensibility 'has a muted quality' and makes him 'a revised man of feeling' (58). Benwick is the most traditional man of feeling: morose, self-absorbed, and ultimately inconstant; Wentworth proves more selfless and true to Anne. But, ultimately, Anne and Wentworth, for Walle, are not the union of a woman and man of feeling, because their shared sensibility works to undermine gender difference, leading to 'a genderless sensibility' or 'de-gendering of sensibility' (52) and 'the triumph of Austen's dismantled binary' (66). We have seen Austen anticipate twentieth-century novelists and French theorists, and in Walle's account, she anticipates the feminist and queer theorists critiquing their essentialist predecessors.

Friendship in *Persuasion*

We have seen excellent readers position *Persuasion* in relation to political and philosophical debates over society, gender, and feeling. I want to expand this philosophical context and to consider how friendship is another route for Austen to rethink gender, feeling and family, class and social hierarchy. Let's return to Laura's and Mrs Smith's comments about friendship. The former stresses friendship's reality; the latter its rarity. Austen's characters affirm philosophers' characterisation of true friendship as infrequent. Aristotle, for example, characterises friendship based on virtue as 'not something that extends to a large number' (120), and Montaigne agrees, in what reads like a personals ad: 'I am seeking the companionship and society of such men as we call honourable and talented: my ideal of those men makes me lose all taste for the others. It is, when you reflect on it, the rarest of all forms' (928). Laura, Mrs Smith, and Austen herself enter this philosophical tradition, but most participants bar their entry. Montaigne is desperately seeking 'such *men*'. He later explicitly defines friendship as the exclusive province of men: 'Reasoning powers, wisdom and the offices of loving-friendship are rather to be found in men: that is why they are in charge of world affairs' (931). With 'loving-friendship', Montaigne emphasises the emotional intensity that Laura expresses in 'Love and Freindship' and denies that she (and Anne after her) can experience such affective connection.

Montaigne's misogynistic message ties together three issues central to the Western philosophy of friendship: gender, class, and politics. From Plato and Aristotle to Nietzsche, these philosophers equate friendship with masculinity and with nobility—nobility of status or ethics—and they connect friendship to politics. Misogyny and hierarchy surface throughout the tradition. In Plato's *Lysis*, Socrates wanders into Hippothales and 'some other young men' (69). This group of 'good-looking' (69) men debates who 'has more noble blood' (73), and Socrates assumes the friend to be a noble man (82); he discusses women only as mothers (75). Plato gives the dialogue an exclusively male and aristocratic setting and substance. In the *Eudemian Ethics*, Aristotle follows his teacher, defining friends as men, women as mothers or wives but never friends. 'The pleasure of friendship is the pleasure derived from the friend *himself* in *himself*; for *he* is loved for *himself* and not for being something else' (119, emphases mine), or 'Friendship between kinsfolk comes in several kinds, one between siblings, another between father and sons' (130). 'Siblings' sounds unrestricted by gender, but they're not: friendship 'may be proportional, as in the paternal case, or arithmetical, like that of brothers' (130). Like the *Lysis*, the *Eudemian Ethics* gives us women only in their capacity as mothers or wives, and their subordinate status is clear: 'friendship between father and son is not the same as that between husband and wife, for the latter is between ruler and subject' (122). As he celebrates patriarchal rule, Aristotle uses friendship and kinship interchangeably, creating a parallel between the marital and political and suggesting a correspondence between private and public relations. The Greeks bequeath this same-sex conception of friendship to Montaigne's Renaissance essay, and the family tree doesn't stop there.

Jacques Derrida analyses the patriarchal assumptions underpinning this canon of philosophical treatises. From the outset of *The Politics of Friendship* (1995), the philosopher identifies 'the figure of the friend, so regularly coming back on stage with the features of the *brother*' (viii). And this fraternal figure did not exit after his Renaissance run, reprising this role through the ages. Of Kant, Derrida asks, 'why did he not speak of the sister?' (262). Of Carl Schmitt, he complains, 'Not a woman in sight' (155). Such questions run throughout his analysis. 'And what about the sister?' Derrida asks, 'Where has she gone?' (96). Austen's novels, we might answer, with irritation.[1] When Derrida later asks, 'Will it be said once again, in conclusion, that the sister is altogether mute in this interminable and eloquent dialectic of inimical brothers?' (165), we might remember that Austen's sisters are rarely mute. In the early novels, heroines break their silence first with their literal sisters before giving their future husbands a piece of their mind. In these first novels then, friendship exists within family ties—'friendship between kinsfolk' as Aristotle defined it—but Austen substitutes sorority for the fraternity celebrated by male philosophers.

Derrida offers another point that illuminates the function of friendship in *Persuasion*. As I have said, Plato and Aristotle's friendship obeys a logic of homogeneity: same sex, same class, same moral standing. For Derrida, Nietzsche revolutionarily reorients this tradition away from self to other. Nietzsche interrupts the pattern or order established by his predecessors, urging friendship to seek out what, Derrida says 'can be called the other, the revolution, or chaos' (29) in order to find or found 'friendship without proximity, without presence, therefore without resemblance, without attraction' (35). It is no accident, I think, that Austen and Nietzsche belong to the same century. Derrida's summary of Nietzsche's philosophy might pass for a summary of *Persuasion*'s plot. Anne's first friend (Lady Russell) is a Kellynch neighbour and her later friend (Mrs Smith) a fellow resident of Bath, Anne leaving the house to reach the first and the neighbourhood to reach the second, just as she will have to leave the country to join her husband at sea. This novel condemns the characters who value proximity and celebrates those who reject it. Sir Walter loves Elizabeth because she resembles him and scorns Anne because she does not. He makes much of looks or 'attraction', scorning sailors' leathered skin. His opposite, Admiral Croft complains about all the mirrors in Kellynch: 'oh Lord! there was no getting away from one's self' (119). Croft strikes a quasi-Nietzschean chord in insisting on getting away from self, from Elliotian narcissism. Derrida finds in Nietzsche 'an upheaval here, and we would like to perceive, as it were its seismic waves, the geological figure of a political revolution which is more discreet—but no less disruptive—than the revolutions known under that name' (27). The paradox of discreet disruption seems Austenian. As Johnson argues, the novel doesn't advocate absolute revolt. I think we find revolutionary turbulence in *Persuasion*'s ocean waves, which carry not only a new profession and renewed engagement but new personal connections into the novel. Yes, these waves bring Wentworth, but they also bring friends who reorganise Anne's social relations.

Austen scorns the logic of presence and proximity, resemblance and attraction from the opening page, which foregrounds Austen's contrast between family and friendship. The reader opens *Persuasion* to see Sir Walter opening the baronetage: 'ELLIOT OF KELLYNCH-HALL. "Walter Elliot, born March 1, 1760, married, July 15, 1784, Elizabeth, daughter of James Stevenson, Esq. of South Park, in the county of Gloucester; by which lady (who died 1800) he has issue Elizabeth, born June 1, 1785; Anne, born August 9, 1787; a still-born son, Nov. 5, 1789; Mary, born Nov. 20, 1791"' (5). Various crimes gather here, and not just dull details! Aristocratic scripture privileges birth over life, men over women, rank over character, family over friendship, self over other. Using Derrida's terms, proximity couldn't be closer, as Sir Walter reads his own name, reads of Kellynch inside Kellynch. Not much difference can emerge in the gap between Sir Walter and his printed self, between the walls that encase him and the description of the estate. Differences of gender, however, are profound. Lady Elliot descends from a father but not a mother; is the object, not agent, of her own marriage; dies in a parenthesis, a short-lived reference denying the long-term trauma Anne suffers. The daughters are the same, undifferentiated by character or action, passions or principles. Still-born son occupies the same space as living sisters. And, of course, the still-born son is the greatest loss in terms of primogeniture, greater than the loss of his mother. As the entry goes on, it does not get much better with 'the history and rise of the ancient and respectable family, in the usual terms' (5), Austen suggesting that aristocratic stories are all the same, replicating a basic narrative that neither evolves nor excites. Sir Walter has written in William Walter Elliot as the heir, which offers a profound example of repetition and resemblance, as the addition replicates, perhaps clones, the series of Walters for its latest entry. Sir Walter's entry, like the baronetage, does not tell us anything about character. It does not describe how the heir enkindled only to extinguish Elizabeth's hopes of an intrafamily marriage. It doesn't describe the heir's mistreatment of Mrs Smith. Only the novel will provide these details and scandals, the characters' virtues and vices, their social relations beyond family ties, as Austen carefully defines her middle-class novel against the aristocratic volume.

Quickly compensating for such silence, the narrator provides details of character. Vanity, for Austen, defines Sir Walter, not his property or power. She also counters the baronetage by giving greater detail about Lady Elliot. Breaking the confines of and allowing her to expand beyond a parenthesis, Austen inverts gender hierarchy. Sir Walter's looks earned 'a wife of very superior character to any thing deserved by his own. Lady Elliot had been an excellent woman, sensible and amiable' (6). Austen fills the baronetage's silences and rejects its aristocratic and patriarchal values, as she delineates the wife's superiority. And, if Austen compensates for the baronetage, then Lady Elliot compensates for the baronet: 'She had humoured, or softened, or concealed his failings, and promoted his real respectability' (6). She accepts and covers his inadequacies as spouse and parent. Austen proceeds to offer the most damning indictment of the baronetage, Sir Walter, and the aristocracy: 'though not the very happiest being in the world herself, [she] had found enough in her duties, her friends, and her children, to attach her to life, and make it no matter of indifference to her when she was called on to quit them' (6). These truths are harrowing. Not the 'happiest', Lady Elliot suffered emotional poverty amidst material luxury. We have seen two forms of compensation: narrator for baronetage and Lady Elliot for Sir Walter. There is a third. Lady Elliot 'found enough in her duties, her friends, and her children'. This is a wonderful reconfiguring of a woman's life, shifting her attention away from her husband to her children but also to her friends. Austen dismisses Sir Walter's significance to Lady Elliot as unhesitatingly as the aristocratic text dismissed Lady Elliot from life. In Derridian terms, Austen orients Lady Elliot away from husband and resemblance to nursery and neighbour. Proximity and marriage are not enough.

More emphatic criticism follows: 'Three girls, the two eldest sixteen and fourteen, was an awful legacy for a mother to bequeath; an awful charge rather, to confide to the authority and guidance of a conceited, silly father' (6). Taking aim at the baronetage's emphasis on the transmission of land, Austen redefines 'legacy' as people, not property, as matrilineal bequeathing. The reference to 'authority' is significant, as Austen's era conferred quite a bit of authority on Sir Walter, his rank and gender. But that authority did nothing for his wife. Lady Elliot's emotional wants must be supplied by friendship: 'She had, however, one very intimate friend, a sensible deserving woman, who had been brought, by strong attachment to herself, to settle close by her, in the village of Kellynch; and on her kindness and advice, Lady Elliot mainly relied for the best help and maintenance of the good principles and instruction which she had been anxiously giving her daughters' (6–7). Focusing on the friends' moral and affective values, Austen privileges bountiful friendship over bankrupt marriage. This 'strong attachment' contrasts with the anaemic, perhaps nonexistent, bond with her spouse, and it echoes without the least irony the intense language of 'Love and Freindship'. Continuing to reorient this Lady's life, Austen has Lady Elliot find emotional satisfaction and counsel in her friend and extricates kinship from consanguinity. Lady Russell and Lady Elliot coparent the latter's children, the former becoming surrogate parent for her children outside the home. Lady Russell 'settle[d] close by her', which might be my favourite detail. In Austen's time, an upper-class woman moved when her father or husband said so. But a widow possessed decision-making power. Austen accords Lady Russell agency and self-determination to relocate not for or with a man but for and near a 'very intimate friend'. In our own time, Judith Butler laments marriage's monopoly on affect, with the effect that 'those who live outside the conjugal frame or maintain modes of social organization for sexuality that are neither monogamous nor quasi marital are more and more considered unreal' (26). I am not pursuing a queer reading of ladies Elliot and Russell where I discover underground lesbian desire, but I am saying that they gesture toward an alternative 'mode of social organization' for affect and support, if not sexuality. Austen sees this supportive relationship as more real than the traditional marriage. Austen's depiction of the women's friendship bears remarkable resemblance to Sara Ahmed's description of lesbianisim: 'a redirecting of women's energies away from the labor of maintaining relationships with men as our primary relationships' (225). Lady Elliot's primary relationship is with Lady Russell, without the sex.[2]

The novel's opening foregrounds the concerns of my reading: books, friendship, and the social order. Caroline Levine has discussed the relationship between social and aesthetic forms, asking how they interact. For certain schools of criticism, the social order determines or dominates literary form, producing texts that support the existing social structure, as Duckworth and Butler argue. For other schools, literary forms transgress or resist social power, as Auerbach argues. Levine sees the interaction between social and literary forms as more complicated or unpredictable: 'Instead, literary forms participate in a destabilizing relation to social formations, often colliding with social hierarchies rather than reflecting or foreshadowing them. Literary forms, that is, trouble and remake political relationships in surprising, aleatory, and often confusingly disorderly ways' (626). For Levine, a literary form can sustain or subvert social forms or even do both at the same time, producing tension as Johnson and Pinch contend. I am interested in the interaction among literary form (Sir Walter's baronetage versus Austen's novel), social forms (upper-class power and feudalism and the transition to middle-class power and capitalism), and personal forms (family versus friendship). My argument is that *Persuasion* 'trouble[s] and remake[s] political' and personal relationships. Austen presents the baronetage, the aristocracy, and marriage as collaborating forms that protect the status quo. The novel, I contend, calls potently and persuasively for new literary forms, new social forms, and new personal forms. *Persuasion* wants middle-class novels that celebrate the move from feudalism to capitalism, from family to companionship. To be sure, Austen doesn't so much give up on as reconceptualise marriage. The novel does so by having Anne choose Wentworth over William Walter Elliot, choose the industrious over the idle suitor. But friendship corroborates, even introduces, the moral of the marriage plot, playing a more significant role in *Persuasion* than the preceding novels. Elinor Dashwood has Marianne. Elizabeth Bennet has Jane. These sisters surely suffer a few shortcomings, but they enjoy real emotional ties and do not have to leave the house, as Lady Elliot does, for support, advice, companionship. In the early novels, Austen extends Aristotle's 'friendship between kinsfolk' from brothers and from fathers and sons to sisters. *Sense and Sensibility* initiates a career challenging patriarchal theories of friendship. In the later novels, family fails. Fanny Price has cold cousins. Emma Woodhouse lacks siblings. But Anne Elliot is still more radically isolated. Fanny finds love in her cousin. Emma's father, while fussy, loves her. Anne Elliot, however, lacks such attachments. Her family might consider her 'nobody' (7), but father and sister are nobody of significance in her emotional life. Like her mother, Anne finds compensation in friends, both women and men, aristocrats and bourgeois.[3] Austen's friendships—both consanguine and chosen—resemble the philosophers' friendships between men, in that they tell us something about Austen's reformation of literary form and social order.[4] Anne's greater reliance on friends is another way that Austen expresses growing dissatisfaction with the landed family and the social order it represents.

One does not have to search far for family's failure and Anne's alienation from her kin. Just consider what Elizabeth says of and to Anne. She tells Mary, 'Anne had better stay, for nobody will want her in Bath' (32); she curtly rebuffs Anne's concerns regarding Mrs Clay's possible designs on their father, 'I think it rather unnecessary in you to be advising me' (34). This rejection of 'advising'

The Politics of Friendship in Persuasion

invokes the scenes of advice in the Dashwood and Bennet homes. In those cases, attempted advising proved sometimes successful, sometimes futile—in Lydia's case, spectacularly—but they demonstrated clear sororal concern. Elizabeth's rejection of advising also echoes the opening chapter where Lady Elliot must seek advice outside her family circle, finding it with Lady Russell. Elizabeth shows absolute want of sisterly regard, and Anne must find wise counsel from friends.

For successive generations of Elliot women, friendship provides the comfort and affection missing from the family. Anne follows her mother's lead in looking outside the estate, starting with her surrogate mother. The first chapter depicts Lady Russell offering Lady Elliot what she lacked in her marriage, and it indicates that Lady Russell does the same for Anne. If Anne 'was nobody with either father or sister' (7), she fares better outside the home: 'To Lady Russell, indeed, she was a most dear and highly valued god-daughter, favourite and friend' (7). This sequence recurs throughout the novel: familial indifference followed by friendly compassion. When Anne is initially scheduled to go to Bath, Lady Russell recognises the family disease and prescribes herself as antidote. 'Lady Russell, convinced that Anne would not be allowed to be of any use, or any importance ... was very unwilling to have her hurried away so soon, and wanted to make it possible for her to stay behind, till she might convey her to Bath herself after Christmas' (32). All too familiar with this family and its want of warmth, Lady Russell wants to keep Anne close, just as she kept close to Anne's mother. Austen again reorganises an Elliot woman's affective life, extricating her from family and fostering friendship and moving proximity from kin to friend, from blood to elective bonds.

Anne shows herself conscious of this friendship's importance. Considering returning to Kellynch, she fears encountering Wentworth but doubts they will actually cross paths, concluding that 'upon the whole, she believed she must, on this interesting question, be the gainer, almost as certainly as in her change of domestic society, in leaving poor Mary for Lady Russell' (87). Balancing family, friendship, and romance, her calculus assigns more value, 'certainly', to mentor than to sister. Meditating on her father's possible marriage to Mrs Clay, Anne considers escape routes: 'she might always command a home with Lady Russell' (137). Like Lady Russell's moving to be near Lady Elliot, Anne imagines changing homes, not due to marriage, not due to becoming an orphan, not due to becoming a widow, but because her relation to her living father is dead. This imagined future involves same-sex friendship rather than family, marriage, and reproduction; it lacks the retrospection element studied by Rohrbach but affords the agency she describes. Anne's actual future offers many friends, spaces, and social dynamics anathema to her family.

Praising friendship and Lady Russell, I have left aside one obvious problem. If Lady Russell had not persuaded Anne to reject Wentworth, Anne would never have suffered her family's indifference. Lady Russell's objection rested on Wentworth's inferior class status and uncertain earning power. Lady Russell challenges and compensates for upper-class husband, father, and family, but she also maintains class hierarchy and prejudice. It is useful, I think, to recall Levine's point that forms can have contradictory relationships to other forms. This friendship subverts patriarchal authority and sustains aristocratic authority, whereas later friendships challenge both and present flaws of their own. Austen stresses the tension between Lady Russell's conservative and contumacious behaviour from the start. When Lady Russell, Anne, and Sir Walter's agent consider what to do about the baronet's financial challenges, the narrator offers this summary of her character: 'She had a cultivated mind, and was, generally speaking, rational and consistent—but she had prejudices on the side of ancestry; she had a value for rank and consequence, which blinded her a little to the faults of those who possessed them' (12). The balanced assessment presents Lady Russell as perspicacious and blind. Her 'cultivated mind' resonates with Wollstonecraft's radical vision of women as rational agents, while her 'value for rank' resonates with Burke's conservative vision of an unchanging society. Burkean ideology leaves her uncultivated in terms of the future, the value of work, and the world outside the estate, even as her personal relations testify to the need for a future beyond the estate and marriage.

A number of characters follow Lady Russell as Anne's friends, and they, significantly, are outside her class and lack aristocratic prejudice. These later relations offer a more directly Derridian turn from self to other, resemblance to difference. Anne immediately cultivates fellow-feeling with Admiral and Mrs Croft—a connection that would upset her father enough. She not only consorts with the highest naval ranks but finds warmth in an even lower social sphere. At Lyme, the Harvilles show immediate affection. Austen calls Captain Harville 'a perfect gentleman, unaffected, warm, and obliging. Mrs Harville, a degree less polished than her husband, seemed however to have the same good feelings; and nothing could be more pleasant than their desire of considering the whole party as friends of their own, because the friends of Captain Wentworth' (91). Austen's reference to gentility fires a salvo at the aristocracy. When Sir Walter scorns Wentworth's curate brother, he offers a restrictive definition of a gentleman, 'You misled me by the term *gentleman*. I thought you were speaking of some man of property: Mr Wentworth was nobody, I remember; quite unconnected' (24). The narrator applies this contested term to Harville, expansively defining it, not as a 'man of property' or hierarchy, but as a man of principle and hospitality. Austen further challenges aristocratic prejudice, insisting that Mrs Harville possesses worth despite lacking polish. As the aristocratic family turns inward, forging connections only with relations, like Mr Elliot and the Dalrymples, Anne and the navy turn outward toward an ever-expanding circle of friends, whose lack of polish and connection underscores their difference from Anne.

Revelling in difference, Anne prefers these friends' simpler lifestyle, finding 'bewitching charm in a degree of hospitality so uncommon, so unlike the usual style of give-and-take invitations, and dinners of formality and display' (91). Quiet Anne offers a bold rejection of upper-class materialism and ritual, preferring informal but substantive friendship. When Anne and Mr Elliot debate the definition of good company, she defines it as 'the company of clever, well-informed people, who have a great deal of conversation' (140). Anne's definition does not refer to class or gender or family connection, denying their significance. She values 'well-informed', not well-groomed, people and substantive exchange rather than elegant insipidness. Her definition owes a great deal, I think, to what she has gained from the company of the Crofts and Harvilles. Indeed, she comes to value these ties more than family ones. When she returns to Lady Russell from Uppercross, 'Anne would have been ashamed to have it known, how much more she was thinking of Lyme, and Louisa Musgrove, and all her acquaintance there; how much more interesting to her was the home and the friendship of the Harvilles and Captain Benwick than her own father's house in Camden Place or her own sister's intimacy with Mrs Clay' (116). This remarkable passage addresses the novel's central concerns: personal relations, class differences, property. Anne would rather stay in the Harville's home than her father's Camden Place house, rather socialise with a naval man than a nobleman, rather converse with and about friends than family.[5] Acquaintance trumps resemblance. The next sentence is extraordinary: 'She was actually forced to exert herself, to meet Lady Russell with any thing like the appearance of equal solicitude, on topics which had by nature the first claim on her' (116). Family, supposedly 'by nature', takes priority, but she must 'exert herself' and *force* exertion, revealing that she doesn't naturally revere kinship. Such respect is social(ised). This phrase suggests that social friendship can (and does) matter more than ties of natural kinship.

When the Musgroves arrive in Bath at novel's end, friendship continues to compensate for family. Anne reschedules a rendezvous with Lady Russell 'to see again the friends and companions of last autumn, with an eagerness of good will which many associations contributed to form' (206). The passage depicts an emotional intensity her blood relations cannot reach. The existence of many friends rejects the Aristotelian elitism that true friends remain few and resemble oneself. Anne's excitement proves well-founded, as she enjoys 'Mrs Musgrove's real affection, … a heartiness, and a warmth, and a sincerity which Anne delighted in the more, from the sad want of such blessings at home' (207). Anne has a quasi-family-relationship to Mary's mother-in-law, but Austen positions Mrs Musgrove more with the Harvilles, explicitly in the concluding contrast and implicitly in the emotional terms Austen uses to describe her and the Harvilles. When Anne's family barges in, they shatter sincerity and serenity: their 'entrance seemed to give a general chill. Anne felt an instant oppression, and, wherever she looked, saw symptoms of the same. The comfort, the freedom, the gaiety of the room was over, hushed into cold composure, determined silence, or insipid talk, to meet the heartless elegance' (211). This passage relies on different languages, some familiar and some new. It deploys the familiar language of emotion and warmth and emphasises conversation, contrasting 'insipid talk' with Anne's 'great deal of conversation'. It emphasises aristocratic superficiality, 'heartless elegance' echoing the discourse of 'formality' from the Harvilles' gathering. New, however, is the political rhetoric of 'freedom' and 'oppression'. In the wake of the French Revolution and the Napoleonic Wars, this is charged and dangerous language. It forcefully indicates the novel's and Anne's rejection of and resistance to aristocratic power and spaces, affects and social ties—or, more precisely the lack of social ties. Friendship and the navy are the vehicles for that resistance. But they are camouflaged vehicles. Surrounding revolutionary rhetoric with the rhetoric of affect, conversation, elegance, Austen suggests the importance of feeling to revolution but also achieves the discreet revolution described by Derrida and the less than overt rebellion described by Johnson.

Anne's friendship with Mrs Smith follows a logic similar to the one informing her ties to Lady Russell and the Harvilles. When Anne went to school after Lady Elliot's death, Mrs Smith, then Miss Hamilton, 'had been useful and good to her in a way which had considerably lessened her misery' (143), suggesting how a mourning daughter found more solace in classmate than kin. In Bath, Mrs Smith appears as quite an unusual character in Austen's dramatis personae. 'She was a widow, and poor … and was now in lodgings near the hot-baths, living in a very humble way, unable even to afford herself the comfort of a servant, and of course almost excluded from society' (143–44). Mrs Smith lacks everything that Sir Walter respects: comfortable residence, retinue of servants, well-connected society. These deficiencies, of course, do not faze Anne. And lacking material property, Mrs Smith possesses mental qualities that Anne and Austen respect. Mrs Smith holds up under financial and physical hardship with 'that elasticity of mind, that disposition to be comforted, that power of turning readily from evil to good, and of finding employment which carried her out of herself, which was from Nature alone' (145). Austen consistently describes the minds of the heroine and her female friends. Anne possesses 'elegance of mind' (7). Lady Russell a 'cultivated mind'. Here, Mrs Smith's elasticity demonstrates flexibility in meeting the demands of circumstance in ways that Sir Walter cannot. Middle-class adaptability contrasts with upper-class stagnancy. Depth, complexity, and resilience belong only to those who lack various forms of power. The characters 'preeminent for elasticity of mind', Johnson notes, are by 'the standards set in Austen's fiction, … unusual, and by those set in conservative fiction, far too marginal to be the models they are here' (161–62). The location of these traits in Mrs Smith, in friend, not family, in the resourceful, not ranked, on the fringe, not heart, of respectable society, encapsulates this novel's daringness.

These mental qualities, of course, don't merit Sir Walter's respect. He scornfully asks,

> who is Miss Anne Elliot to be visiting in Westgate-buildings?—A Mrs Smith. A widow Mrs Smith,—and who was her husband? One of the five thousand Mr Smiths whose names are to be met with every where. And what is her attraction? That she is old and sickly.—Upon my word, Miss Anne Elliot, you have the most extraordinary taste! Every thing that revolts other people, low company, paltry rooms, foul air, disgusting associations are inviting to you. (148)

Sir Walter hits upon usual issues: class, residence, neighbourhood, the body's (dis)ability. Anne perceives her friend's self-reliance, but Sir Walter confines her to marital and social status. Less familiar are two words: 'taste' and 'revolts'. Austen might've had Sir Walter say everything that 'repulses', 'disgusts', 'horrifies', or 'nauseates' other people. There were other options, but Austen chose 'revolts', which has a clear political valence. By visiting a place that 'revolts' others, Anne revolts against their prejudice and hierarchy. And her revolt is a matter of aesthetics, Sir Walter suggests with his reference to her 'extraordinary taste'. Politics and aesthetics go hand in hand, as *Persuasion* rethinks political structure and literary art and gestures toward an aesthetics of commonness and non-familial relations. If we return briefly to the baronetage, we see that Austen gives the stillborn son quite the rebellious birthdate: November 5, 1789. Austen unites two revolts: the Gunpowder Plot and the French Revolution, Guy Fawkes and the Bastille. The son's death disrupts the patriarchal process, and in the space of that disruption, Anne, friendship, and the novel walk in to challenge aristocracy.

Mrs Smith has another friend: Nurse Rooke, who presumably has even fewer advantages. But she has a more important resource: knowledge or gossip. Mrs Smith describes her: 'She is a shrewd, intelligent, sensible woman. Hers is a line for seeing human nature; and she has a fund of good sense and observation which, as a companion, make her infinitely superior to thousands of those who having only received "the best education in the world", know nothing worth attending to' (146). Mrs Smith's praise echoes the class critique embedded in Anne's appreciation of the Harvilles. Nurse Rooke proves 'infinitely superior' to those formally educated, declaring insight into human nature can belong to those without educational privileges restricted by class and gender. The novel again upends hierarchy. It extends the Wollstonecraftian emphasis on intellectually capable women to the most socially precarious character in the novel and perhaps Austen's oeuvre. The dismissal of prejudiced perception continues, ramps up, in the next sentence: 'Call it gossip if you will … she is sure to have something to relate that is entertaining and profitable, something that makes one know one's species better' (146). Nurse Rooke becomes storyteller, narrator. Mrs Smith describes both Nurse Rooke and Austen herself, in a metafictional moment of the sort Tanner locates at the novel's opening, thus associating her creator's novelistic art with a lower-class woman. Being 'entertaining and profitable', seeing human nature, and offering sense and observation constitute Austen's realism.[6] Gilbert and Gubar call Nurse Rooke 'a wonderful portrait of Austen herself' (182). Literary form and greatest insight come from below. Anne makes this association even more explicit, when she says that nurses are 'well read' in more than follies. 'A sick chamber may often furnish the worth of volumes' (146). Holding a novel in two volumes, Austen's reader is encouraged to see a connection between nurse and novelist, among women, the déclassé, and novel.

Nurse Rooke tells Mrs Smith stories or gossip, and Mrs Smith relays stories to Anne.[7] As with Lady Russell, there is an elephant in my argumentative room. Nurse Rooke has bad intel. She erroneously tells Mrs Smith that Anne accepted Mr Elliot. Mrs Smith encourages Anne to marry Mr Elliot, who, Mrs Smith knows, is a scoundrel. How do we account for these missteps of Lady Russell and Mrs Smith, respectively preventing a good marriage and pleading for a bad one? Mrs Smith goes so far as to say, rather lie, that Anne is 'safe in his character' (185)! Mrs Smith is a lightning rod for intense responses, from my students to Janeites to critics. The encouragement to marry Mr Elliot is unquestionably suspect and leads to unforgiving characterisations, such as William Galperin's: 'a manipulative and mendacious person' (232). Greiner agrees: 'her "interest" is self-interest only' (81). I agree with these assessments of her self-interest, but one-dimensional descriptions don't capture the complex layers of Austen's portrait. K. K. Collins offers a balanced view: 'This scene therefore juxtaposes, but does not treat as equal, Mrs Smith's completely undisguised desire for gain and her care for her friend' (395). That care, which leads her to describe Mr Elliot's villainy at length, shouldn't be underestimated. The real villains in this novel, in Anne's family tree, proffer no caregiving at all. Mrs Smith's potentially harmful mistake affirms Austen's sense that no relationship is perfect, as suggested by Lady Russell's encouragement to reject Wentworth. Austen's realism insists that few characters lack self-interest entirely, that everyone merits censure. As Austen famously wrote Fanny Knight, 'pictures of perfection as you know make me sick & wicked' (*Letters* 350). That Mrs Smith and Lady Russell

The Politics of Friendship in Persuasion

have flaws is not a reason to discard them but to accept them as verisimilar portraits, with tension of the sort found in Austen by Johnson and by Levine in literature in general.

Finally persuaded that Anne will not marry her cousin, Mrs Smith intimates, 'you ought to be made acquainted with Mr Elliot's real character. Though I fully believe that, at present, you have not the smallest intention of accepting him, there is no saying what may happen. You might, some time or other, be differently affected towards him. Hear the truth, therefore, now, while you are unprejudiced' (187). Sir Walter's emendation to the family entry describes his nephew as 'heir presumptive', but Mrs Smith's narrative reveals a pompous narcissist. 'Mr Elliot is a man without heart or conscience, a designing, wary, cold-blooded being, who thinks only of himself; who, for his own interest or ease, would be guilty of any cruelty[.] … He has no feeling for others' (187). William Walter is Sir Walter on steroids, exhibiting and extending his self-absorption. Mrs Smith, like Austen, focuses on the Elliot men's lack of emotion and ethics, focusing on destructive self-interest. Mrs Smith initially promotes but ultimately prevents a union between Anne and Mr Elliot—the marriage devoutly to be wished by the aristocratic logic of self and resemblance.

Anne considers Mrs Smith a storyteller, associating her with Austen. Responding to this true crime story, Anne thinks, 'I have heard nothing which really surprises me. I know those who would be shocked by such a representation' (194–95). The word 'representation' has long played a role in aesthetic theory, going back to Plato and Aristotle. Mrs Smith's 'representation' joins Sir Walter's 'taste' in underscoring the novel's self-reflective attention to artistic form and its relation to social logic. And Mrs Smith joins Austen in representing Mr Elliot's malfeasance. Indeed, when she produces a letter of his, she transforms *Persuasion*, briefly, into the epistolary fiction with which the novel and Austen grew up.[8] Anne mentions those who might be incredulous, acknowledging the aristocratic prejudices that lead Lady Russell to prefer Mr Elliot. The lower-class friend offers the most accurate understanding. In the next chapter, Anne continues to consider this new story and feels 'most thankful for her own knowledge of him. She had never considered herself as entitled to reward for not slighting an old friend like Mrs Smith, but here was a reward indeed springing from it!—Mrs Smith had been able to tell her what no one else could have done' (199). These thoughts reject the aristocratic logic assaulted throughout the novel. First, Mrs Smith alone possesses knowledge and narrative that Anne needs, just as Austen alone possesses the narrative of *Persuasion*, which we need. Second, the passage reconceptualises debt. Mrs Smith's possession of character leaves Anne indebted and 'thankful' to the woman without possession or portion. Anne briefly considers the possibility of telling her father and sister, but she bypasses them and plans to tell Lady Russell, knowing that she might change her views. Family is irredeemable. Friends are not.

How does the concluding marriage fit into this argument about friendship? D. A. Miller calls marriage 'the institution whose discursive insistence overshadows Austen's entire world' (12). Does *Persuasion*'s marriage consign friendship to darkness and doom? I think not. Friendship proves essential to marriage. In the famous episode where Wentworth drops his pen and writes his letter declaring his love, Anne is surrounded by friends. First, she, Mrs Musgrove, and Mrs Croft debate the ideal length of engagement, and then Anne and Captain Harville have their important debate about (in)constancy. These frank, impassioned, rational debates testify to friendship's power and possibility. Its unreserved exchange—what Anne called 'a great deal of conversation'—helps bypass the restricted discourse between unmarried lovers. Mrs Croft and Harville are not the only friends here. There's one present in absentia. When Anne offers her famous rejoinder against books— 'Men have had every advantage of us in telling their own story. Education has been theirs in so much higher a degree' (220)—she invokes Mrs Smith in two ways. First, Mr Elliot's advantage in telling his own story has been challenged by Mrs Smith's true account. Second, Anne's reference to education echoes her friend's sharp undermining of education: Nurse Rooke is 'infinitely superior to thousands of those who having only received "the best education in the world", know nothing' (146). Oxbridge men know little, but friends (and Austen) much. Friends provide the speech situation and the substance of Anne's speech, as she addresses friend and lover. Duckworth writes that Austen 'emphasize[s] the private, largely non-linguistic nature of the communication between the lovers' (204). It is not public in the way a street or square is, but it is also not private in the sense that it exists between only the two of them. It exists in language and in a community of friends.

This community of friends and paucity of familial affection persist to the novel's end. The book's penultimate paragraph presents a triangulated affect: Mrs Smith's 'recent good offices by Anne had been enough in themselves; and their marriage, instead of depriving her of one friend, secured her two. She was their earliest visitor in their settled life' (235). This triangle consists of two sides of friendship and one side of marriage, which, I think, approximates the importance the novel has assigned to these relations. Mrs Smith, not Sir Walter and Elizabeth, visits first. Mrs Smith also enjoys pride of place in the final paragraph. Austen divides its six sentences equally between Mrs Smith and Anne, and Anne and Wentworth: three for women's friendship and three for marriage to Wentworth. The paragraph's first half celebrates Mrs Smith's 'acquisition of such friends to be often with', emphasises again her 'mental alacrity', and concludes joyfully that 'Her spring of felicity was in the glow of her spirits, as her friend Anne's was in the warmth of her heart' (236). Earlier novels combined family and marriage in their concluding images. The closing paragraph of *Sense and Sensibility* describes the 'strong family connection' that leads to 'constant communication' (353) between the newly married sisters. Not so here, as connection and communication exist only between spouses and among friends.

In *Persuasion*, truth and support come from below, and from outside, from a poor woman and a widowed woman, from relations of friendship. The novel, in its youth, was viewed with suspicion because, it, too, came from below, written for and by the disenfranchised, for and by middle-class women. In *A Room of One's Own*, Virginia Woolf calls for 'rewriting history'; more important than war, Woolf contends, is the fact that 'The middle-class woman began to write. For if *Pride and Prejudice* matters, and *Middlemarch* and *Villette* and *Wuthering Heights* matter, then it matters far more than I can prove in an hour's discourse that women generally, and not merely the lonely aristocrat shut up in her country house among her folios and her flatterers, took to writing' (65). Don't let Sir Walter know there should be books by and for people beneath him (or that he exists only by virtue of one!). Don't tell him that women like Mrs Smith have stories and rooms of their own. A 'lonely aristocrat', Sir Walter contentedly gazes at himself in his mirrors, book, and relatives who resemble him. But, in *Persuasion*—which perhaps matters as much as *Pride and Prejudice*—Austen is done with the lonely aristocrat, extending her imagination to poorer characters and allowing Mrs Smith and Nurse Rooke to become storytellers in their own right. Woolf sees the development of the novel as a kind of collaboration among 'women generally'. I am not sure that Austen considers *Persuasion* the outcome of collaboration. But *Persuasion* certainly represents 'women generally' from baroness to admiral's wife to nurse, and it depicts collaboration among women and between classes. Ladies Elliot and Russell collaborate to raise the former's children. Anne's intuition about Mr Elliot collaborates with Mrs Smith's confirmation of it. Harville and Anne debate and unwittingly collaborate to get the truth to Wentworth. As the world of the 'lonely aristocrat' and his baronetage narrows and withdraws from the outside world, Austen, as Woolf writes elsewhere, 'is beginning to discover that the world is larger' (*Common* 144). The world of *Persuasion* extends outward and forward to a world propelled and narrated by the novel, the navy, and the nurse, by friends and storytellers.

Notes

1   Derrida briefly discusses Mary Shelley (288). If only he had read her contemporary, he'd have seen the sister and female friend hiding in plain sight.
2   For a more properly queer reading, see Kozaczka, who argues that Anne's piano playing is autoerotic and takes her outside of heterosexual time.

3   See Todd for an alternative account of Austen's career: 'she moves from attraction to outright rejection of close female friendship' (32). I find it difficult to see anything approaching 'outright rejection' in *Persuasion*.
4   Readings of *Persuasion* have noted in passing the importance of friendship in it. Johnson describes the novel as 'Peopled more with friends than family' (163), and Tanner writes that 'other values, such as friendship and hospitality, are coming to seem more important' (225) than elegance and education. But Tanner also includes 'the care and concern of friendship' among his catalogue of bankrupt 'traditional sources of authority' (210). For me, friendship does have more authority than family, and I seek to expand these critics' brief mentions of friendship.
5   Kozaczka calls Lyme 'a queer, liminal space' as the episode is suspended between heteronormative and queer time, but it is also a queer space in being founded on community and friendship rather than family. Pinch characterises the Harville home as a constrictive, claustrophobic space (146), but, for me, the restricted space of their home also emancipates Anne from the confining logic of family.
6   Imagining if Austen had lived longer, Woolf imagines her spending time in London and returning to the country with 'a hoard of observations to feast upon' and with new literary techniques to 'hold all that she now perceived of the complexity of human nature' (*Common* 145).
7   Miller describes Mrs Smith's 'proto-novelistic love of news, of managing its acquisition and distribution' (73).
8   Galperin offers an intriguing argument about Austen's revisions that abandoned her initial drafts' epistolary form. The novels' newer form turned out 'an especially sinister instrument of coercion' that created 'the 'new' novel's complicity with certain social formations' (10). Mrs Smith's producing Mr Elliot's letter counters the social formation of intra-class marriage for accruing or holding rank and property.

Works Cited

Ahmed, Sara. *Living a Feminist Life*. Duke UP, 2017.
Aristotle. *The Eudemian Ethics*, Translated by Anthony Kenny. Oxford UP, 2011.
Auerbach, Nina. 'O Brave New World: Evolution and Revolution in *Persuasion*.' *ELH*, vol. 39, no. 1, 1972, pp. 112–128.
Austen, Jane. *Catharine and Other Writings*, edited by Margaret Anne Doody. Oxford UP, 2009.
Austen, Jane. *Jane Austen's Letters*, 4th ed., edited by Deirdre Le Faye. Oxford UP, 2014.
Austen, Jane. *Persuasion*, edited by Gillian Beer. Penguin, 2003.
Austen, Jane. *Sense and Sensibility*, edited by Ros Ballaster. Penguin, 2003.
Butler, Judith. *Undoing Gender*. Routledge, 2004.
Butler, Marilyn. *Jane Austen and the War of Ideas*. Oxford UP, 1975.
Collins, K. K. 'Mrs Smith and the Morality of *Persuasion*.' *Nineteenth-Century Fiction*, vol. 30, no. 3, 1975, pp. 383–970.
Derrida, Jacques. *The Politics of Friendship*, Translated by George Collins. Verso, 2006.
Duckworth, Alistair M. *The Improvement of the Estate: A Study of Jane Austen's Novels*. Johns Hopkins UP, 1971.
Favret, Mary A. 'Everyday War.' *ELH*, vol. 72, no. 3, Fall 2005, pp. 605–633.
Galperin, William H. *The Historical Austen*. U of Pennsylvania P, 2003.
Gilbert, Sandra M., and Susan Gubar. *The Madwoman in the Attic: The Woman Writer and the Nineteenth-Century Literary Imagination*, 2nd ed. Yale UP, 2000.
Greiner, Rae. *Sympathetic Realism in Nineteenth-Century British Fiction*. Johns Hopkins UP, 2012.
Johnson, Claudia. *Jane Austen: Women, Politics, and the Novel*. U of Chicago P, 1988.
Kozaczka, Edward. 'Queer Temporality, Spatiality, and Memory in Jane Austen's *Persuasion*.' *Persuasions On-Line*, vol. 30, no. 1, Winter 2009, http://jasna.org/persuasions/on-line/vol30no1/kozaczka.html. 1 Jun. 2020.
Levine, Caroline. 'Strategic Formalism: Toward a New Method in Cultural Studies.' *Victorian Studies*, vol. 48, no. 4, Summer 2006, pp. 625–657.
Miller, D. A. *Jane Austen, or The Secret of Style*. Princeton UP, 2003.
Montaigne, Michel de. *The Complete Essays*. Translated by M. A. Screech. Penguin, 1987.
Pinch, Adela. *Strange Fits of Passion: Epistemologies of Emotion, Hume to Austen*. Stanford UP, 1996.
Plato. Meno *and Other Dialogues*. Translated by Robin Waterfield. Oxford UP, 2009.
Rohrbach, Emily. *Modernity's Mist: British Romanticism and the Poetics of Anticipation*. Fordham UP, 2016.
Tanner, Tony. *Jane Austen*. Harvard UP, 1986.

Todd, Janet M. 'Female Friendship in Jane Austen's Novels.' *The Journal of Rutgers University Libraries*, vol. 39, no. 1, 1977, pp. 29–43.

Walle, Taylor. '"He Looked Quite Red": *Persuasion* and Austen's New Man of Feeling.' *Eighteenth-Century Fiction*, vol. 29, no. 1, Fall 2016, pp. 45–66.

Warhol, Robyn R. 'The Look, the Body, and the Heroine: A Feminist-Narratological Reading of *Persuasion*.' *NOVEL: A Forum on Fiction*, vol. 26, no. 1, Autumn 1992, pp. 5–19.

Woolf, Virginia. *The Common Reader.* Harcourt, 1925.

Woolf, Virginia. *A Room of One's Own.* Harcourt, 1981.

7

THE HISTORICAL AND CULTURAL ASPECTS OF JANE AUSTEN'S LETTERS

Jodi A. Devine

BRYANT UNIVERSITY

In publishing Jane Austen's letters, her relatives presented to the world their version of their aunt. In some instances, the letters were trimmed of sections that the relative thought perhaps Jane Austen would not have wanted revealed to the public, or words were altered to reflect a more refined Victorian temperament and thus glossed over a coarser Regency word choice. In some cases, their edits and omissions reflected more of their sensibilities than Jane Austen's. Patricia Meyer Spacks states, 'Collected letters have a special value as autobiography because they record not the distillation but the dynamic of experience. Formal autobiography presents itself as the product of a life reflected upon. The sort of informal autobiography amassed in a published accumulation of letters represents the process of life (and especially of relationship) rather than a product' (*Boredom* 93). Jane Austen's letters, especially those to her sister Cassandra, do reflect the 'process of life' with news of visits, balls, illnesses, travel, writing, and relationships. Using historical methodologies and digital humanities tools, this chapter provides a brief historical survey of approaches to Jane Austen's letters as well as discussions of the materiality of the letters and select cultural aspects of her time period.

Jane Austen's brother Henry Austen, in his 1818 'Biographical Notice of the Author', which was included in the posthumous publication of *Northanger Abbey* and *Persuasion*, states, 'The style of her familiar correspondence was in all respects the same as that of her novels. Everything came finished from her pen; for on all subjects she had ideas as clear as her expressions were well chosen. It is not hazarding too much to say that she never dispatched a note or letter unworthy of publication' (qtd. in Amy[1] 18). Her brother clearly has an idealised version of his sister, understandable given how soon after her death he wrote these words. However, readers can easily discern from the corrections in Jane Austen's collection of letters, that she did re-read and edit her letters before mailing them. Jo Modert's *Jane Austen's Manuscript Letters in Facsimile* (1990) provides facsimiles of Jane Austen's letters, thus allowing researchers to see Austen's edits and additions. Tieken-Boon Van Ostade states that the corrections '[show] that Jane Austen rarely put a letter into the post without going over it to correct errors of writing' (24). In this age of spell check and autocorrect, many people do not proofread before sending their words out electronically; however, reviewing and editing is standard practice for many people, especially those like Jane Austen who loved words and was careful to be clear and correct.

Jane Austen's niece Caroline Mary Craven Austen wrote her memories of her aunt in 1867 to help her brother Edward Austen-Leigh with his biography; Caroline's memories were later published as *My Aunt Jane Austen: A Memoir* in 1952. Caroline, who is the daughter of Jane's brother James and was twelve when her aunt died, wrote her recollections of her aunt when she was in her early sixties, so her memories are through the double lenses of a child and time. She does recall that

DOI: 10.4324/9780429398155-7-9

95

Jane Austen's desk was in the drawing room and that 'she wrote very fully to her Brothers when they were at sea, and she corresponded with many others of her family' (Amy 38). Caroline does not believe the public would be interested in the content of the letters as 'they detailed chiefly home and family events: and she seldom committed herself *even* to an *opinion*—so that to strangers they could be *no* transcript of her mind—they would not feel that they knew her any the better for having read them' (Amy 38). However, readers of the letters may learn about daily experiences, cultural objects and practices, and the general way in which the gentry lived during the transition from the 18th to the 19th century. It is from Caroline that we learn that Jane's sister Cassandra 'burnt the greater part [of Jane Austen's letters], (as she told me), 2 or 3 years before her own death' (Amy 39). Chapman, in his Introduction to *Jane Austen's Letters to Her Sister Cassandra and Others*, states 'Doubtless this suppression has cost us much that we should value. But we may suspect that it has not materially affected the impression we should have received from a richer survival' (xxxix). He explains that it would not have been in the 'sisters' temperament ... to exchange letters of sentiment or disquisition' (xl). David Cecil in *A Portrait of Jane Austen* echoes both of these sentiments (9). Given the cost of mail, they would not have used valuable space on their writing paper with their known views on religion or politics, 'but news could not wait' (Chapman xl).

In the first biography of Jane Austen—*A Memoir of Jane Austen* (1869)—James Edward Austen-Leigh includes extracts from some of his aunt's letters, warning the reader 'not to expect too much from them' (Amy 79). He further explains:

> With regard to accuracy of language indeed every word of them might be printed without correction. The style is always clear, and generally animated, while a vein of humour continually gleams through the whole; but the materials may be thought inferior to the execution, for they treat only of the details of domestic life. There is in them no notice of politics or public events; scarcely any discussions of literature, or other subjects of general interest. (Amy 79)

Austen-Leigh had no way of anticipating how Jane Austen's popularity would have grown to such an extent that people would be fascinated by how she lived her life and that those interested in history, woman writers, or material culture would all be able to learn things from Jane Austen's 'details of domestic life'. Roger Sales argues 'that Austen-Leigh tries to allay ... anxieties about his aunt's Regency associations by transforming her into a Victorian proper lady' (5). Sales supports his point by analyzing the 'offending' portions of some of Jane Austen's letters that Austen-Leigh silently deleted from his *Memoir* fearing, according to Sales, that they are 'coarse', and 'too gossipy and discursive' (6–8). Stephanie Moss states that with Austen-Leigh's *Memoir*, 'the romanticization of Austen's world intensified' (261).[2]

Lord Brabourne (1829–1893)—Edward Hugessen Knatchbull Hugessen—was the son of Fanny Knatchbull, who was the daughter of Jane's brother Edward Knight (né Austen). Brabourne discovered, upon his mother's death in 1882 'a box containing ninety-six letters written by Jane Austen and the original manuscript of the short story Lady Susan' (Amy 156). In the Introduction to his *Letters of Jane Austen Edited with an Introduction and Critical Remarks* (1884), Brabourne states:

> [The letters] contain the confidential outpourings of Jane Austen's soul to her beloved sister, interspersed with many family and personal details which, doubtless, she would have told to no other human being. But to-day, more than seventy long years have rolled away since the greater part of them were written; no one now living can, I think, have any possible cause of annoyance at their publication, whilst, if I judge rightly, the public never took a deeper or more lively interest in all that concerns Jane Austen than at the present moment. (Amy 159)

Brabourne explains how the letters that Jane Austen sent to Cassandra must have been divided among Jane's nieces in the Austen-Leigh and Knight families after Cassandra's death and that the letters in his possession were not known to Austen-Leigh when he wrote his *Memoir*. Brabourne thus presents 'entirely new matter, from which may be gathered a fuller and more complete knowledge of Jane Austen … than could otherwise have been obtained' (Amy 160). He continues that the letters will be of interest and that 'although they form no continuous narrative and record no stirring events, it will be remarked that, amid the most ordinary details and most commonplace topics, every now and then sparkle out the same wit and humour which illuminate [her novels]' (Amy 160–61). Sales asserts that Brabourne, like Austen-Leigh, was 'troubled by Regency coarseness and edits out what he takes to be its worst excesses', such as criticism of family members and anatomical references (9).

Brabourne's two volumes contain a biography, a few chapters on her novels, and the recently found letters. Brabourne included the biography because he himself likes to know as much about the people and places he is introduced to when he reads collections of letters written by others (Brabourne 3–4). Even after providing a detailed history of the extended Austen family and places of residence, Brabourne subdivides the letters by date, giving an overview of their contents, identifying people and places mentioned, and adding additional familial anecdotes. This extended glossing of the letters—which seems superfluous to a twentieth-century reader—provides useful context, especially to some of the more obscure people whom Jane Austen mentions.

As Jane Austen's popularity continued to grow and as more letters came to light, two additional relatives—William Austen-Leigh and Richard Arthur Austen-Leigh—published *Jane Austen: Her Life and Letters A Family Record* in 1913, in an effort to 'remove some misconceptions which had arisen about her' (Amy 470). William Austen-Leigh was the son of James Edward Austen-Leigh and Richard was William's nephew. William's sister Mary Augusta Austen-Leigh contributed re-collections as well. The two male Austen-Leighs warn their readers against 'extract[ing] more out of the letters than they will yield' (81). They recognise that the letters to Cassandra were sent on the occasions of the sisters being apart and that letters are missing, either by accident or destroyed purposefully. They state, 'The Austens had a great hatred and dread of publicity. Cassandra felt this with especial force, and the memory of Jane was to her so sacred that to allow the gaze of strangers to dwell upon the actions or the feelings of so precious a being would have seemed to her nothing short of profanation' (82). They believe that Cassandra never thought that the letters would be published but rather used in research and burnt those letters that 'were specially dear to herself, feeling confident that the remainder would not be disturbed' (82). The Austen-Leighs offer to readers sound and reasonable advice as to what to expect from the letters:

> We must also remember that the correspondence was between sisters who knew, each of them, what the other was thinking, and could feel sure that nothing one might say would be misapprehended by the other; and the sort of freemasonry which results from such a situation adds to the difficulty of perfect comprehension by outsiders. Jane, too, was a mistress of subtle irony: the inveterate playfulness which is constantly cropping up in her books appears also in her letters. Secure of her correspondent, she could pass criticism, impute motives, and imagine circumstances which would have been very far from her nature had she thought it possible that any less perfectly informed third person could see them. (82–83)

Jane Austen's letters reveal details of household activities, balls, and dress making, along with witticisms on events and people she encountered. Her letters were not meant for the greater public's consumption, and Jane knew that Cassandra was skilled in discerning which parts of her letters were meant to be read out loud to the family and which were meant only for her eyes.

Mary Augusta Austen-Leigh, sister of William Austen-Leigh, addressed the other side of this issue in *Personal Aspects of Jane Austen* (1920), stating that Cassandra, in destroying Jane's letters, left behind nothing 'excepting that which even she deemed to be altogether negligible' (Amy 510). Mary Augusta Austen-Leigh attempts to discredit writers who used Jane Austen's letters to critique her on the grounds that '[Jane Austen] did not write of them, therefore she did not care for them' (Amy 508). The 'them' here refers to public affairs in general and more specifically to patriotism and the Napoleonic Wars. Mary Augusta Austen-Leigh's argument stems from the nature of the correspondence between the two sisters—why write of public matters when they would have had long periods of discussing them privately when they were together?—and the length of time it took for news of the war, and their brothers' part in it, to reach them. At a young age, Austen reveals her penchant for reading the newspaper; in a 15–16 September 1796 letter to her sister Cassandra,[3] she reports, 'his royal Highness Sir Thomas Williams has at length sailed—; the Papers say "on a Cruize"' (Le Faye 10). Then in an 8–9 November 1800 letter to Cassandra, she writes, 'Mr Holder's paper tells us that sometime in last August, Capt: Austen & the Petterell were very active in securing a Turkish Ship … from the French.—He was forced to burn her however' (Le Faye 57). There are examples of Austen following her brothers' military careers, of which she keeps Cassandra apprised, including letters from 18 September 1796; 1–2 December 1798; 24–26 December 1798; 28 December 1798; 5–6 May 1801; 14 September 1804; 21–23 April 1805; 18–20 April 1811; and 9 February 1813, among others. Keeping the branches of the family abreast of the news of the naval brothers in war time would have been of utmost importance, while most likely, the Austen sisters shared their views on the war itself in private.

R. W. Chapman, in his Preface to the first edition of *Jane Austen's Letters to Her Sister Cassandra and Others*, states that he is bringing together in one volume all known letters by Jane Austen (v) and that he was 'able to do a good deal in addition and correction, as well as in the restoration of Jane Austen's spelling and punctuation' (vii). In his Introduction, Chapman acknowledges that people have both praised and negatively critiqued Jane Austen's letters (xxxix). Chapman, however, values the letters, even if they had not been written by a famous person, for 'they yield a picture of the life of the upper middle class of that time which is surely without rival' (xl). For Chapman, the letters are 'alive' and full of 'vividness' (xlii). Chapman argues that Austen, in her letters, 'makes the small change of her life important, amusing, and endearing', and he does not quite comprehend those who find the letters 'hard and cold' (xliii).

In 1990, Jo Modert published *Jane Austen's Manuscript Letters in Facsimile: Reproductions of Every Known Extant Letter, Fragment, and Autograph Copy, with an Annotated List of All Known Letters*; Modert presents facsimiles of the letters in Chapman's *Letters*, thus allowing readers to see the letters in Jane Austen's handwriting. In 1995, Deirdre Le Faye updated Chapman's *Letters* with additional letters, fragments, scholarship, and numbering to publish the new, third edition of *Jane Austen's Letters*; in 2011, she published the fourth edition which includes new scholarship on Jane Austen's life and family that helps to clarify some of the previously unclear references in the letters but does not include any new letters. In her 1995 Preface, Le Faye delineates Jane Austen's recipients and the respective style she used in addressing them. Le Faye compares Jane's letters to Cassandra as 'the equivalent of telephone calls …—hasty and elliptical, keeping each other informed of domestic events' (xvii). To her brother Frank, Jane's letters are 'in a more regular and considered style, giving a bulletin of information about all members of the family' (xvii). As her nieces and nephews grow up, she offers advice on 'affairs of the heart' to Fanny Knight and to Anna, advice on 'how a natural and credible story should be composed' (xvii). Her letters to the younger nieces and nephews contain 'cheerful teasing' and 'little joking notes', while Jane writes a 'crisp business correspondence' with her publishers (xvii). Like Chapman, who asserts that the letters are 'alive', Le Faye postulates that Austen's letters '*are* real, and as we read them we too can watch the daily business of herself, her family, and friends passing before our eyes' (xviii).

Scholarship on Austen reflects a range of perspectives on her letters, particularly with regard to their value for readers. Deborah Kaplan prioritises Austen's letters over her novels in order 'to consider them on their own terms' and to explore Austen's 'dual cultural contexts' of being a member of the gentry and a woman (212).[4] Some, like Elizabeth Fay, posit that Austen's letters illustrate women's experiences that may have led to a 'poverty of spirit or restricted experience' (64); Fay continues that 'it is our mistake to view her comments as unproductive gossip rather than political critique' (64). Spacks claims that 'personal letters' provide 'women a means of agency' (*Gossip* 164). Along similar lines, Susan A. Whealler claims that Austen was very much aware of her lack of power in the male dominated world, but her letters 'chronicle her attempts to exert private control over certain parts of her life' (198). While Cassandra was away, Jane was forced to step into the role of housekeeper; her letters keep Cassandra up-to-date on the running of the house, while at the same time, they contain satire and critiques of people, events, and the trivialities of running a house.

In discussing the everyday, William H. Galperin comments upon the repetitive nature of the daily and common activities that Austen writes about in her letters. He calls her letters 'a disappointment' and accuses her, when writing to Cassandra, of having 'taken the day off' and calling them 'largely gossip—the comings and goings of family and friends, births, deaths, illnesses, marriages, and meals, along with numerous social and domestic gatherings' (91). However, Galperin does see value in the accounting of everyday events and uses the prosaic nature of Austen's letters to support her depiction of daily, commonplace events in her novels (91–92).

Mixing Austen's personal letters with her fiction borders on the error of conflating a first-person narrator in a work of fiction with the author, but many critics do this, especially by reading the fictional characters' comments on letter writing as Austen's own views. Mary Augusta Austen-Leigh in her *Personal Aspects of Jane Austen* (1920) set the precedent for comparing events in Jane Austen' letters with scenes in her novels. However, Austen, in writing her letters and her novels, had two distinct audiences in mind: the addressee of the letter and if to a family member, the larger family circle present, and the general public, respectively. While it is tempting to read her letters and think, 'oh, that is similar to what happened in *Pride and Prejudice*', we can never know for certain how much Austen wrote into her novels the observations she took from life, how much she invented, and how often she mixed the two. To expect Austen's personal correspondence to be as consistently as polished, as witty, and as entertaining as her novels, is to disregard both the purpose of letters to keep family members up-to-date and Austen's role within the larger family circle.

Roger Sales discusses the letters to Cassandra as a space where Austen could allow herself to laugh or remove the straight face she needed to keep in public.[5] Depending on her audience, Austen knew 'letters were frequently treated in this period as being like newspapers, to be read and widely discussed throughout a particular social circle' (Sales 33). In a 30 November 1814 letter, Jane Austen directs her niece Fanny Knight to include information that could be shared with the larger family circle: 'I shall be most glad to hear from you again my dearest Fanny, but it must not be later than Saturday, as we shall be off on Monday long before the Letters are delivered—and write *something* that may do to be read or told' (Le Faye 286–87). In a 14–15 October 1813 letter to Cassandra, Jane writes, 'You have given many particulars of the state of Chawton House, but still we want more.—Edward wants to be expressly told that all the Round Tower &c. is entirely down, & the door from the Best room stopt up;—he does not know enough of the appearance of things in that quarter' (Le Faye 237). And in an 8–9 November 1800 letter to her sister, Austen writes, 'I have two messages; let me get rid of them, & then my paper will be my own' (Le Faye 55). Not only are contents of letters shared, as in this example of Cassandra's letter lacking in detail per Edward's taste, but letters are vehicles to pass on comments and notes to and from other members of the household.

William May provides an overview of the reception of Chapman's 1932 *Jane Austen's Letters to Her Sister Cassandra and Others* and Deirdre Le Faye's 1995 revised edition. He sees the reception more as a reflection of contemporary readers' views—opposing or otherwise—and 'competing expectations' of the letters than as a path to learning more about Jane Austen (117–20). He advocates for '[reading] Austen's letters more widely as creating their own artful fictions. They create a Miss Austen at odds with the Angel in the House, and one that seems to preoccupy women writers who feel otherwise ill at ease with her novelistic legacy' (127). In *Romantic Correspondence*, Favret critiques the acceptance of the letters as feminine and that 'we accept too readily the notion that the letter allows us a window into the intimate, and usually feminine self' and how this 'disguises, in part, a revolutionary politics' (10) present in letters.

While not writing specifically of Jane Austen, Spacks in *Gossip* states that 'gossip belongs to the realm of private, "natural," discourse, it often violates "the claims of civility"' (6). This defines Austen's letters quite accurately. She did not write her letters for posterity but rather to convey news to her siblings or advice to her nieces and nephews. Spacks discusses the thrall personal letters have on readers years later: 'We read them out of interest in their writer, they enable speculation about that writer. Thrust into exciting intimacy with someone we do not know, we savor secrets never intended for us, allowed to encounter aspects of another's experience not ordinarily divulged' (*Gossip* 74). Perhaps some of the criticism of Jane Austen's letters is derived from the feeling that we *know* her based on her novels; when the letters 'violate the claims of civility' we are 'shocked' or experience a sense of cognitive dissonance at the disconnection between her novels and her letters.

Many critics comment on one of Jane Austen's self-referential statements on writing letters. In a letter from Steventon dated 3–5 January 1801 to her sister Cassandra, she writes, 'I have now attained the true art of letter writing, which we are always told, is to express on paper exactly what one would say to the same person by word of mouth; I have been talking to you almost as fast as I could for the whole of the letter' (Le Faye 68). Anderson and Ehrenpreis, in their discussion of familiar letters written by eighteenth-century authors, state that the letter writer 'liked to compare his letters with polite conversation' which they go on to define as 'an informed, entertaining exchange carried on between persons belonging to a circle of familiar acquaintances, who shared a common knowledge of literature, history, and what we might clumsily call social institutions' (274). Raised in the last quarter of the eighteenth century, and an avid reader, Jane Austen would most likely have been aware of this tradition. Austen may also have been commenting upon the advice commonly given in letter-writing manuals of the time period which was to write a letter as if it were a conversation.[6] While these manuals were mainly written for the lower and middle classes, Austen may have been familiar with them—Samuel Richardson, author of the epistolary novels *Clarissa* and *Pamela*, wrote a letter-writing manual titled *Familiar Letters on Important Occasions* (1741)—and by calling attention to writing as if she were speaking, she satirizes the convention. Kaplan asserts that the newsy element of Austen's letters, especially those written to Cassandra, which are often set off by dashes, 'evokes ... a verbal communication, face-to-face gossip' and represent shifts in Austen's membership in the 'gentry culture' and 'women's culture' (216).

As Le Faye states, there are many ways to approach Jane Austen's letters, one of which is to look for cultural references and gain some of Jane Austen's—and presumably other women's—lived experiences. The writing desk, paper, and pen are material elements of letter writing, while handwriting and franking are important as well.[7] As stated above, Caroline Mary Craven Austen in *My Aunt Jane Austen: A Memoir* recalls her aunt's writing desk, which 'lived in the drawing room' (Amy 38).[8] Jane Austen received the writing desk as a gift from her father in 1794 ('Jane Austen's Writing Desk'); however, it was almost lost while she was travelling. In a letter Jane Austen wrote to Cassandra from Dartford on 24 October 1798, she provides details: 'After we had been here a quarter of an hour it was discovered that my writing and dressing boxes had been by accident put into a chaise which was just packing off as we came in, and were driven away towards Gravesend in their way to the West Indies ... in my writing-box was all my worldly wealth, 7*l*' (Le Faye 15). Luckily, the desk and Austen's other boxes were retrieved. Austen mentions her writing desk again in a letter to Cassandra, written from Southampton, 8–9 February 1807: 'she is now talking away at my side & examining the Treasures of my Writing-desk drawer;—very happy I beleive [sic];—not at all shy of course' (Le Faye 119). Austen is referring to Catherine Foote, daughter of Capt. Foote. While these are the only two specific mentions in her letters of her writing-box, Tieken-Boon Van Ostade believes that when Jane Austen visited relatives, she took her writing-box with her (43).

Austen mentions 'paper' in multiple letters, which is sometimes a reference to the physical paper and other times a metonym for the letter itself. Since the recipient had to pay for the cost of mailing a letter, Jane Austen's comments indicate that she wanted to fill her page so that the recipient received their money's worth, to use a phrase from today. In a letter to her sister Cassandra, written from Steventon, 27–28 October 1798, Jane Austen writes, 'Your letter was a most agreeable surprise to me to day & I have taken a long sheet of paper to shew my Gratitude' (Le Faye 15). In a letter to Cassandra, written from Ibthrop, 30 November–1 December 1800, Jane starts the letter on a Sunday and asks Cassandra if she should expect to hear from Jane on Wednesday, to which Jane answers her own question, 'I think you will, or I should not write, as the three days & half which have passed since my last letter was sent, have not produced many materials towards filling another sheet of paper' (Le Faye 63–64). In another example, to Cassandra from Castle Square, 9 December 1808: 'I am extremely foolish in writing all this unnecessary stuff, when I have so many matters to write about, that my paper will hardly hold it all. Little matters they are to be sure, but highly important' (Le Faye 156). And later in the same letter, 'Having now cleared away my smaller articles of news, I come to a communication of some weight' (Le Faye 157). The highly important little matters include the receipt of bracelets, lists of visitors, plans to attend balls, comments on the latest fashion at the ball—referring to the young women without partners '& each of them with two ugly naked shoulders!'—her dance partner, and visits to others (Le Faye 156–57). The news of weight is that 'my Uncle & Aunt are going to allow James £100. a year … as a Compensation for his loss in the Conscientious refusal of the Hampstead Living' (Le Faye 157). It seems as if Jane Austen needed to dispense with the trivial matters first before reporting on the more worldly matter of James's improved financial security.

Expenses and the cost of items are common themes throughout Austen's letters, and no less so when it comes to the rising costs associated with writing and mailing letters. In a letter to Cassandra, written from London, 16 September 1813, Austen writes, 'I have rejoiced more than once that I bought my Writing paper in the Country', which is perhaps a reference to higher prices in London (Le Faye 223). Austen tells her brother Frank, in a letter written from Godmersham Park, 25 September 1813: 'I am very much obliged to you for filling me so long a sheet a [sic] paper, you are a good one to traffic with in that way, You pay most liberally' referring no doubt to the practice of the recipient of a letter paying for the postage (Le Faye 229). Postal rates kept increasing during Jane Austen's lifetime. The Post Office Act of Parliament defined a 'Single Letter' as a 'Letter consisting of one sheet or piece of paper under the weight of one ounce' (Robertson 57). Prior to 1805, the cost of sending a single letter 'not above 15 miles' was three pennies (3d.) and 'from 15 to 30 miles' four pennies (4d.). From 1805 to 1812, the two rates went up to 4d. and 5d., respectively. The longer the distance, the higher the postal rates. After 1812, the distance chart changed, so sending a letter 'above 15 but not exceeding 20 miles' cost 5d., while 'above 20 but not exceeding 30 miles', cost 6d. The rates were higher for Double Letters (two sheets of paper) and Treble Letters (more than two sheets of paper) (Robertson 58–59). As Austen and Cassandra tried to write to each other every three days or so, and were typically apart for a month or two, their correspondence became quite expensive; they had a 'letter expence' covered by their father while he was alive (see letter 28 December 1798, Le Faye 32). However, Austen does not think of the expense when she teases her niece Caroline Austen in a letter written from Chawton, 23 January 1817: '[I] have now I beleive [sic] two or three Notes to thank you for; but whatever may be their Number, I mean to have this Letter accepted as a handsome return for all, for you see I have taken a complete, whole sheet of Paper, which is to entitle me to consider it as a very long Letter whether I write much or little' (Le Faye 325).

One way to save the expense of postage was to have a letter franked by a government official with the privilege of sending mail for free. Jane Austen mentions the practice of franking in a few letters, including a letter to Cassandra from Sloan Street, 30 April 1811, 'I had sent off my Letter yesterday before Yours came, which I was sorry for; but as Eliza has been so good as to get me a frank, your questions shall be answered without much further expense to you' (Le Faye 185). In another letter to Cassandra, written from Godmersham Park 14–15 October 1813, Jane complains of guests who are unwanted, to her at least: 'I wish there were not Wigrams & Lushingtons in the way to fill up the Table & make us such a motley set.—I cannot spare Mr. Lushington either because of his frank, but Mr. Wigram does no good to anybody' (Le Faye 238). Austen seems willing to put up with the guests who are 'certainly no addition' if she can get a frank for her letter.

Two letters specifically refer to the piece of paper on which the letter was written. Writing to her brother Charles on 6 April 1817 after the death of their uncle, James Leigh-Perrot (their mother's brother), Jane Austen writes, 'I have forgotten to take a proper-edged sheet of Paper' referring to the practice of writing on paper with a black edge to indicate mourning (Le Faye 339). A 14 September 1804 letter to Cassandra from Lyme provides an example of Austen's sarcasm in her reference to 'this fine striped paper', which Le Faye's note clarifies: 'The paper of this letter is rather thin, so that the laid lines are slightly more visible than usual' (Le Faye 92, 380). Lynch reminds us that during Jane Austen's time, 'paper continued to be manufactured, at great expense, from cloth rags exclusively' (83–84).

The process of making paper involves letting moistened linen rags set in a 'damp heap' to rot, then mincing the rags into a pulp, and then pouring the whole into a large vat where it is diluted 'with water to the appearance and consistency of liquid porridge' (Gaskell 57). The 'laid lines' to which Austen refers come from the papermaking moulds, which 'were oblong rectangular wire sieves mounted on wooden frames' (Gaskell 57–58). The papermaker would dip the mould about a third of the way into the vat of liquid pulp, remove it, and then shake the mould so that the pulp would be evenly distributed. The paper picked up the chain and wire pattern at this step of the papermaking process, which required 'great skill' to 'produce sheets of uniform texture and strength'[9] (Gaskell 58–59).

Ink and pens, of course, were essential for written correspondence. Jane Austen mentions 'ink' for letter writing twice in her letters, both to Cassandra. In speaking about her brother Frank's promotion and then his six week or longer wait to be assigned to a new ship, Austen, in her 21–22 January 1801 letter from Steventon, states, 'Poor fellow! to wait from the middle of November to the end of December, & perhaps even longer! it must be sad work!—especially in a place where the ink is so abominably pale' (Le Faye 75). In her 14–15 October 1813 letter from Godmersham Park, in the middle of asking Cassandra to fill her in on the details of entertaining, Jane states, 'I wonder whether the Ink bottle has been filled' (Le Faye 239).

While having dark ink and a full ink bottle are important, having a pen that works to her satisfaction seems difficult to come by. In a letter to Cassandra from Godmersham, 20–22 June 1808, Jane writes, 'I am sick of myself, & my bad pens'. 'Sick of myself' perhaps referring to the preceding line: 'such a sad stupid attempt at Wit, about Matter, that nobody can smile at it' (Le Faye 131). Again to Cassandra from London, 15–16 September 1813, Austen states, 'I must get a softer pen.—This is harder' (Le Faye 218). Presumably, Cassandra would have been able to notice a slight difference in the penmanship with the change of pens. And in her 3 November 1813 letter to Cassandra from Godmersham Park, in addition to handwriting, Jane Austen refers to her pens: 'as my pen seems inclined to write large I will put my Lines very close together', and later in the same letter, set off by dashes, 'The day seems to improve. I wish my pen would too' (Le Faye 247, 248). As a writer, Austen would most likely have had a preference in her pens and the letters reveal some of the idiosyncrasies of writing with a quill pen.

Clear handwriting is an essential part of letter writing, and Jane Austen, while not above criticising others' handwriting, most frequently criticised her own hand. In a letter to Cassandra, written from Steventon, 14–16 January 1801, she critiques her brother James' letter to Edward, as he 'filled three sides of paper, every line inclining too much towards the North-East, & the very first line of all scratched out' (Le Faye 72). Not only is James wasting Edward's money by not filling the fourth side of the paper, his handwriting is slanted, and his letter offers a messy, first impression. Jane Austen does praise Frank's and Cassandra's penmanship. In a letter to her brother Frank, written from Godmersham Park, 25 September 1813, she states, 'you write so even, so clear both in style & Penmanship, so much to the point & give so much real intelligence that it is enough to kill one' (Le Faye 229). And in her letter to Cassandra, written from Godmersham Park, 3 November 1813, Austen writes, 'I took up your Letter again to refresh me, being somewhat tired; & was struck with the prettiness of the hand; it is really a very pretty hand now & then—so small & so neat!—I wish I could get as much into a sheet of paper' (Le Faye 249). Favret states that due to high cost of postage, 'correspondents set a high value on the ability to pack loads of information onto a single page and to write neatly, with a small hand' (135). Caroline Austen, in her 1867 *Memoir*, has a different memory of Jane Austen's handwriting:

> Her handwriting remains to bear testimony to its own excellence; and every note and letter of hers, was finished off *handsomely*—There was an art *then* in folding and sealing—no adhesive envelopes made all easy—some people's letters looked always loose and untidy—but *her* paper was sure to take the right folds, and *her* sealing wax to drop in the proper place'. (Amy 37, italics in original)

The quality of the paper, ink, and pens made a difference in the appearance of the letter and the handwriting. Favret claims that the letter was 'a very material object for Jane Austen' (135) and Austen's comments on the physical elements of letter writing attest to this. Since the letters were paid for by their recipient, they 'were expected to look appealing to the reader' and 'should look as if they were worth the cost of postage' (Favret 136).

While tracing the material objects used in writing letters through Jane Austen's letters to learn about period-specific practices is one way to use Austen's letters, another method is to employ technological advances of the twenty-first century. With the advent of digital humanities projects and scholarship, Ingrid Tieken-Boon Van Ostade has utilized electronic versions of Jane Austen's letters to conduct a sociolinguistic analysis of Austen's letters; her study 'aims to throw a light on Jane Austen's linguistic identity in as far as it can be reconstructed from her letters' (5). Tieken-Boon Van Ostade used the electronic version of Jane Austen's letters in the English Letters Collection provided by the series InteLex Past Masters; she then analyzed the letters using WordSmith Tools, 'a concordancing program … [that] allows for the compilation of frequency and alphabetical lists, for studying words within the context in which they occur' (23).

Tieken-Boon Van Ostade studies Austen's spelling, word choice, grammar, punctuation, and use of capital letters, among other elements of her letters, to provide a book-length study of Jane Austen's language. In her analysis of Austen's self-corrections to her letters, Tieken-Boon Van Ostade notes that Austen's formal letters to such people as her editor contain no errors as was to be expected; however, in her informal letters to her sister Cassandra, Austen's corrections show her 'letter-writing habits' and how she 'formulated her sentences' (Tieken-Boon Van Ostade 92). She concludes that 'Jane Austen's letters, particularly the informal ones, take us as closely to her own spoken language as it is possible to get' (Tieken-Boon Van Ostade 92–93).

If one were to leaf through Le Faye's *Jane Austen's Letters*, then one would soon notice the abundance of dashes, which is another element of Austen's letter writing that Tieken-Boon Van Ostade studies. Her analysis shows that Austen used 'about 43.4 dashes per 1,000 words' and that the frequency of the dash varied by who had copied her letters (Tieken-Boon Van Ostade 100). As with all of her analysis, Tieken-Boon Van Ostade provides charts generated by WordSmith Tools and specific examples from the letters to illustrate the various uses of the linguistic element under discussion.

In her analysis of Austen's word choice and vocabulary, Tieken-Boon Van Ostade notes that Austen's small social and familiar circle and her lack of travel influenced her word choice and vocabulary, stating 'there are aspects of her grammar that are conservative in relation to the time in which she lived' (77). Austen is credited with forty-three first quotations in the *Oxford English Dictionary*, with fifteen of these words from her letters (see Tieken-Boon Van Ostade, Table 6.1, 137); however, Tieken-Boon Van Ostade argues that six of these fifteen should be removed for various reasons and other words from Austen's letters could be added (137–39). Tieken-Boon Van Ostade concludes from studying her letters that Austen's 'language was not particularly innovative … [and] her vocabulary was probably not particularly large' (164). However, the approach taken by Tieken-Boon Van Ostade reveals many new linguistic elements of Austen's letter and novel writing, including a 'linguistic date for *The Watsons*' of '1805–1806' as evidenced by 'her changing writing habits' (227). The use of digital humanities tools provides a useful method to analyse Austen's letters and allows for a level of analysis difficult to do by hand.

There is little agreement among Jane Austen's relatives and critics regarding how to best categorise and use Jane Austen's letters. Are they gossip? Or comparable to phone conversations? Or confidential outpourings of her soul? On one hand, they flit from topic to topic. On the other hand, the letters sent to family members provide information about daily events that would have been of interest to the recipient and would have been discussed if Austen and the recipient were in the same household. From a cultural and historical perspective, they contain valuable information, not only on the material culture of letter writing, but on household responsibilities, fashion, balls, and women's lack of agency in travelling without a male escort, among other topics. Readers who are looking for Jane Austen the *author* in the letters are usually disappointed; however, having a view of Jane Austen the *woman*, with her wit, compassion, sarcasm, joy, sadness, and excitement, is a boon indeed.

Notes

1   In *The Jane Austen Files: A Complete Anthology of Letters & Family Recollections* (2015), Helen Amy has compiled family writings and Jane Austen's letters in one place. I use this anthology as my source for most of the family recollections.
2   See Stephanie Moss for more on the reception of Jane Austen in the latter half of the nineteenth century.
3   All numbering, dates, and quotations from Jane Austen's letters are from *Jane Austen's Letters*, 3rd ed., collected and edited by Deirdre Le Faye.
4   Mary A. Favret looks at Austen's letters and novels in an opposite way, stating 'Public fiction takes precedence over private communication' because the novels can be read on their own, while the letters need 'a critical gloss' to be understood (135).
5   See Roger Sales, *Jane Austen and the Representations of Regency England,* for a brief overview of critical analysis of Austen's letters from 1956 to 1988.
6   See my unpublished dissertation 'Epistolary Revelations: Reading Letters in Nineteenth-Century British Novels' (2007).
7   I wrote this section on the material and cultural aspects of letter writing based on how I teach literature classes. I then discovered that Tieken-Boon Van Ostade has covered similar concepts; for a more detailed account of the materiality of letters and cultural aspects of letter writing, see pp. 36–50 of her *In Search of Jane Austen*.
8   Deidre Lynch in 'The Art of the Letter' in *Jane Austen: Writer in the World*, edited by Kathryn Sutherland includes a photograph of Jane Austen's writing desk, p. 76. The desk is held by the British Library, which on its website, not only has static images of the desk and of Jane Austen's spectacles, but also 3D images which provide views of the desk from all angles: https://www.bl.uk/collection-items/jane-austens-writing-desk
9   For more details on the paper-making process, see Philip Gaskell's *A New Introduction to Bibliography*, pp. 57–77.

Works Cited

Amy, Helen. *The Jane Austen Files: A Complete Anthology of Letters & Family Recollections.* Amberley Publishing, 2015.

Anderson, Howard, and Irvin Ehrenpreis. 'The Familiar Letter in the Eighteenth Century: Some Generalizations.' *The Familiar Letter in the Eighteenth Century*, edited by Howard Anderson, Philip B. Daghlian, and Irvin Ehrenpreis. UP of Kansas, 1968, pp. 269–282.

Austen-Leigh, William, and Richard Arthur Austen-Leigh. *Jane Austen: Her Life and Letters A Family Record*, 2nd ed., Russell & Russell, 1965.

Brabourne, Edward, Lord. *Letters of Jane Austen Edited with an Introduction and Critical Remarks*, 2 vols. London: Richard Bentley & Sons, 1884. https://hdl.handle.net/2027/hvd.32044011609351

Cecil, David. *A Portrait of Jane Austen.* Hill and Wang, 1978.

Chapman, R. W. *Jane Austen's Letters to Her Sister Cassandra and Others*, 2nd ed. Oxford UP, 1952.

Devine, Jodi A. 'Epistolary Revelations: Reading Letters in Nineteenth-Century British Novels.' PhD Diss. U of Delaware, 2007.

Favret, Mary A. *Romantic Correspondence: Women, Politics and the Fiction of Letters.* Cambridge UP, 1994.

Fay, Elizabeth A. *A Feminist Introduction to Romanticism.* Blackwell, 1998.

Galperin, William H. *The History of Missed Opportunities: British Romanticism and the Emergence of the Everyday.* Stanford UP, 2017.

Gaskell, Philip. *A New Introduction to Bibliography.* Oxford UP, 1972.

'Jane Austen's Writing Desk and Spectacles.' *British Library.* https://www.bl.uk/collection-items/jane-austens-writing-desk.

Kaplan, Deborah. 'Representing Two Cultures: Jane Austen's Letters.' *The Private Self: Theory and Practice of Women's Autobiographical Writings*, edited by Shari Benstock. U of North Carolina P, 1988, pp. 211–229.

Le Faye, Deirdre, editor. *Jane Austen's Letters*, 3rd ed. Oxford UP, 1997.

Lynch, Deidre. 'The Art of the Letter.' *Jane Austen: Writer in the World*, edited by Kathryn Sutherland. Bodleian Library, 2017, pp. 76–93.

May, William. 'Letters to Jane: Austen, the Letter and Twentieth-Century Women's Writing.' *Uses of Austen: Jane's Afterlives*, edited by Gillian Dow and Clare Hanson. Palgrave Macmillan, 2012, pp. 115–131.

Modert, Jo, ed. *ane Austen's Manuscript Letters in Facsimile: Reproductions of Every Known Extant Letter, Fragment, and Autograph Copy, with an Annotated List of All Known Letters.* Southern Illinois UP, 1990.

Moss, Stephanie. 'Jane Austen's Letters in the Nineteenth Century: The Politics of Nostalgia.' *Companion to Jane Austen Studies*, edited by Laura C. Lambdin and Robert T. Lambdin. E-book, Greenwood, 2000, pp. 259–274.

Robertson, Alan W. *Great Britain Post Roads, Post Towns, and Postal Rates 1635-1839.* Privately Printed, 1961.

Sales, Roger. *Jane Austen and the Representations of Regency England.* E-book, Routledge, 1992.

Spacks, Patricia Meyer. *Boredom: The Literary History of a State of Mind.* U of Chicago P, 1995.

Spacks, Patricia Meyer. *Gossip.* U of Chicago P, 1986.

Tieken-Boon Van Ostade, Ingrid. *In Search of Jane Austen: The Language of the Letters.* Oxford UP, 2014.

Whealler, Susan A. 'Prose and Power in Two Letters by Jane Austen.' *Sent as a Gift: Eight Correspondences from the Eighteenth Century*, edited by Alan T. McKenzie. U of Georgia P, 1993.

8

'SETTING AT NAUGHT ALL RULES OF PROBABLE OR POSSIBLE': JANE AUSTEN'S 'JUVENILIA'

John C. Leffel

SUNY CORTLAND

I have always thought it remarkable that the early workings of her mind should have been in burlesque, and comic exaggeration, setting at nought all rules of probable or possible—when of all her finished and later writings, the exact contrary is the characteristic.
—*Caroline Austen (1869?)*

An innocent Heart I will ever preserve/and will never from Virtue's dear boundaries swerve.
—*Austen, Henry and Eliza*

The child author Jane Austen is a kind of immoralist—that is, she seems to regard many moral truisms as clichés, and to find pleasure in the habits of the voracious animals of her world.
—*Margaret Doody (2005)*

By the time she began her first literary experiments around the seasoned age of twelve, Jane Austen had already read widely and deeply, building a remarkable familiarity with the conventions and customary formal and stylistic elements of the English novel. In her youthful manuscripts, commonly referred to as the 'juvenilia', Austen gleefully mimics, comically distorts, and parodies those 'novelisms', targeting whatever strikes her as silly, improbable, hackneyed, or simply amusing.[1] Austen's parodic exploration of, and keen experimentation with, genre, narrative, form, and style demonstrate her commitment from a very young age to dissecting the constitutive elements of the English novel precisely in order to rework them; as Mary Waldron suggests, Austen's first writings are bold attempts to 'refashion fiction as she knew it' (16).

Though Austen's experimental early manuscripts have long been overshadowed by the celebrated published novels, they finally appear to be having their moment. Recent years have witnessed an uptick in critical and popular attention as evidenced by the publication of an authoritative scholarly edition (Sabor, 2006/2013); several compact teaching volumes perfectly suited for classroom use (Bree, Sabor, and Todd, 2013; Alexander, 2014; Sutherland and Johnston, 2017); illustrated artist books of individual texts (Johnson and Steinmetz, 2018); and the first critical monograph to focus exclusively upon the juvenilia (McMaster, 2016). We can add to this list a growing body of academic articles and of conference presentations and panels—the *Jane Austen Society of North America* (JASNA), for instance, devoted its 2020 annual meeting entirely to scholarship on the early writings.

In this chapter, I offer a concise survey of the juvenilia's composition, publication, and reception history; examine the prominent role of 'transgression' in the early works' formal, stylistic, and generic construction and orientation as well as in Austen's creation of characters and plots; and offer

106

DOI: 10.4324/9780429398155-8-10

succinct critical readings of specific texts, including *Henry and Eliza*, *The Beautifull Cassandra*, *Jack and Alice*, and *Catharine, or the Bower*, to highlight the early writings' spirited engagement with many of the social and political issues and concerns—particularly those relating to the intersections among money, marriage, mobility, and women's subjectivity and agency—that scholars have analysed in Austen's published novels. In so doing, I hope to extend the critical conversation as well as to suggest new inroads for future inquiry.

★★★

While they are garnering increased attention and enthusiasm now, Jane Austen's deliciously unbridled early writings haven't always been so celebrated by scholars and literary critics, by readers, or even by Austen's own inheritors. After the novelist's death in 1817, Cassandra Austen (in)famously resigned the bulk of her sister's letters and papers to the flames, presumably in an effort to safeguard family privacy and to keep prying eyes out. The fact that Cassandra elected to spare the three early manuscript notebooks that Austen had entitled with mock seriousness 'Volume the First', 'Volume the Second', and 'Volume the Third' is a testament to the family's regard for this ragtag assortment of experimental novels and 'tales'; dramatic sketches and miniature plays; epistles and 'collections of letters'; fragments and 'unfinished performance[s]'; and even a parodic *History of England, from the reign of Henry the 4th to the death of Charles the 1st*. But while the family may have cherished the early manuscripts for *private* enjoyment within the family circle, circulating or publishing them was another matter entirely. In fact, Cassandra safeguarded these literary gems for almost thirty years till her own passing in 1845, upon which the first and second volumes were bequeathed to two of the Austen brothers (Charles and Frank), and the third went to Jane Austen's beloved nephew, James Edward Austen-Leigh. The juvenilia then remained stowed away in family possession for another two and a half decades, unknown to all but a select group of relations and family friends, and 'safe', as many of them believed, precisely because of that obscurity.

But in late 1869 James Edward let the proverbial cat out of the bag when, in the first edition of his *A Memoir of Jane Austen*, he noted the existence of 'an old copy-book containing several tales, some of which seem to have been composed while [his aunt] was quite a girl' (59). Despite being 'disingenuous', as Peter Sabor points out, about the number of notebooks and, thus, the volume of the unreleased materials, James Edward nonetheless provided the first *public* acknowledgment of the juvenilia's existence (xxxviii). When he began preparing shortly thereafter for the second edition of his *Memoir*, Austen's nephew pondered an even bolder move: might he include a sample from the early writings to which he had so tantalisingly alluded in the first edition, perhaps as an appendix? He wrote to his sister, Caroline Austen, to gauge her reaction and to seek her advice as to possible candidates for inclusion. The pair's correspondence demonstrates how the extended Austen family viewed the riotous, boldly experimental first writings as a potential threat to the cherished image of the novelist as an eminently decorous, straight-laced writer of realistic fiction that, beginning with Henry Austen's angelic scripting of his sister in his 1817 'Biographical Notice' (appended to the posthumously published edition of *Northanger Abbey* and *Persuasion*), they had eagerly sought to construct and were determined to maintain.[2] Caroline was virulent that only some of the 'light' verses and perhaps the unfinished novel *Evelyn* (from 'Volume the Third') 'might'—and note how she stresses that qualification twice in the full passage—be appropriate:

> As to the 'stuffing' of the projected volume, [...] some of her light nonsensical verses *might* take—[...] & I have thought that the story, I believe in your possession, all nonsense, *might* be used. I don't mean Kitty's Bower, but the other [i.e., *Evelyn*] [...]. I have always thought it remarkable that the early workings of her mind should have been in burlesque, and comic exaggeration, setting at nought all rules of probable or possible—when of all her finished and later writings, the exact contrary is the characteristic. The story I mean is

clever nonsense, but one knows not how it might be taken by the public, tho' *some*thing must *ever* be risked. What I should deprecate is publishing any of the 'betweenities' when the nonsense was passing away, and before her wonderful talent had found it's [sic] proper channel. Lady Knatchbull has a whole short story [i.e., *Lady Susan*] they were wishing years ago to make public—but were discouraged by others—& I hope the desire has passed away. (qtd. in Sutherland 186, emphases in original)

Caroline's expressed concern over how these 'clever' but reputedly 'nonsens[ical]' early works could be 'taken by the public'[3] reveals how the extended family was determined to control Austen's public image and reception by strictly controlling the circulation and publication of her manuscripts. Caroline employs equally illuminating language when she encourages her brother to rectify what she calls 'this *vexed* question between the Austens and Public' (emphasis added), thereby setting, via her choice of adjective, the family and the reading public once again at odds (186). 'I am sure you will do justice to what there *is*', she goes on to remark of the works in her brother's possession, 'but I feel it must be a difficult task to dig up the *materials*, so carefully have they been buried out of our sight by the past generat[ion]' (186–87, emphases in original). If the previous generation of family members and relatives worked to 'bur[y]' Austen's early writings and other papers, Caroline and James Edward view themselves as representatives of a new generation of guardians, carefully selecting and releasing only a selective sampling of what they deem to be acceptable or 'proper' texts to satiate readers' (and scholars') appetite for more Austen writing, and withholding any that don't conform to the family's carefully constructed image of their esteemed relative. The siblings strive, in other words, to guarantee that their aunt will be remembered for the later, realistic novels, and not the so-called 'nonsense' that preceded them.[4]

And the family had good reason to be apprehensive, for the juvenilia abound with examples of more than just 'clever nonsense', spirited parody, and burlesque: they are replete with unabashedly indecorous—and in some instances, blatantly criminal—content: risqué jokes, allusions, and charades; pervasive binge drinking and eating; elopements and illicit unions; theft; physical violence; suicide; and even murder. Such vestiges of a robust, bawdy, decidedly un-sentimental literary tradition (more Fielding or Swift than Richardson or Burney), the family seem to have fretted, would do no service to the reputation of the author of *Pride and Prejudice* and *Emma*. Thus, the trend started by James Edward and Caroline of strategically releasing excerpts from a small sampling of only the most innocuous early writings, and of downplaying the literary interest and merit of the youthful works *tout court*, would carry on until the early decades of the next century. In 1913, James Edward's son and grandson published *Jane Austen: Her Life and Letters, A Family Record*, in which they revealed for the first time the names of additional items from the early notebooks (*Evelyn* and *Catharine, or the Bower* from 'Volume the Third'); transcribed the opening paragraph of the latter; and provided short descriptions of both works, opining, in language strikingly reminiscent of James Edward's and Caroline's correspondence from more than forty years earlier, that they 'seem to mark a second stage in [Austen's] literary education' when she was 'hesitating between burlesque and immature storytelling, and when indeed it seemed as if she were first taking note of all the faults to be avoided, and curiously considering how she ought *not* to write before she attempted to put forth her strength in the right direction' (v–vi). This passage from *A Family Record* furthermore establishes one of the most frequent critical appraisals of the early works—and particularly such 'betweenities' as the unfinished *Catharine*—by situating them in a trajectory of development ('immature'). The early writings are not significant on their own terms, this argument goes, but only insofar as they reveal directions the young author elected *not* to take.[5]

Between 1922 and 1954, portions of Austen's early manuscripts would finally be published piecemeal, beginning with the release in 1922 of the contents of 'Volume the Second' under the title *Love & Freindship and other Early Works*, edited and with a preface by the novelist and scholar G. K.

Chesterton. The following year, editor R. W. Chapman released his landmark scholarly edition of the *Works of Jane Austen*, but he decided to omit all of the youthful writings as well as related manuscript works such as *Lady Susan* from the set. After a long delay, Chapman did go on to release stand-alone editions of 'Volume the First' and 'Volume the Third' in 1933 and 1951, respectively, but he balked at their merit and dismissed them in his prefaces and published reviews: in his Clarendon Press edition of 'Volume the First' (1933), for instance, Chapman made a point of noting that 'it will always be disputed whether such effusions as these ought to be published; and it may be that we have enough already of Jane Austen's early scraps' (qtd. in Sabor li). It wasn't until 1954 that Chapman finally included the full gamut of these so-called 'scraps' as *Minor Works*, the sixth and final volume of his collected edition. More than a century-and-a-half after they were written, Jane Austen's earliest writings were for the first time widely accessible to scholars, critics, common readers, and 'Janeites' alike. Chapman's choice of title for the newly added volume, however, offers a gauge of how he (and many readers) continued to view these works: as amusing, but decidedly 'minor', literature.

★★★

Despite James Edward's and Caroline Austen's concerted efforts, the juvenilia's publication *did* in fact inspire the earliest commentators to pose the very questions about the novelist and her work that they and other relatives and heirs had been anxious to forestall. Both Chesterton and Virginia Woolf, for instance, raised the distinct possibility that the Austen everyone *thought* they knew was not, in fact, the only or even the 'real' Jane Austen. In the preface to his edition of *Love & Freindship* [sic] in 1922, Chesterton provocatively suggested that Austen be placed alongside Rabelais and Dickens, claiming that her inspiration was that 'of Gargantua and of Pickwick; *it was the gigantic inspiration of laughter*' (xiv–xv; emphasis added). 'These pages', Chesterton writes, 'betray her secret; which is that she was naturally exuberant [...]':

> And her power came, as all power comes, from the control and direction of exuberance. But there is the presence and pressure of that vitality behind her thousand trivialities; she could have been extravagant if she liked. She was the very reverse of a starched or starved spinster; she could have been a buffoon like the Wife of Bath if she chose. This is what gives an infallible force to her irony. This is what gives a stunning weight to her under-statements. (xiii–xv)

Similarly emphasizing Austen's carnivalesque 'exuberance' and the 'gigantic' force of her satire, Virginia Woolf wrote in her expanded essay on Austen (which was included in her collection of essays *The Common Reader* [first series]) that 'nothing is more obvious than that this girl of fifteen, sitting in her private corner of the common parlour, was writing not to draw a laugh from brothers and sisters, and not for home consumption. She was writing for everybody, for nobody; for our age, for her own' (222–23). And 'what is this note', Woolf ponders, which 'sounds distinctly and penetratingly all through the volume? It is the sound of laughter. The girl of fifteen is laughing, in her corner, at the world' (223). In their emphasis on the destabilising power of 'laughter'; on the indecorousness of Austen's early protagonists and their Rabelaisian appetites and illicit behaviours; and on the un-mistakable 'vitality' and 'exuberance' of the juvenilia at large, Chesterton and Woolf established a groundwork for later commentators by emphasising the ways in which Austen's experimental early works problematise the very criteria by which we judge both the author and her oeuvre.

Austen specialists and academic critics initially took a more reserved approach, often focusing on textual studies and on what the early manuscripts reveal about Austen's process and development as an author. B. C. Southam (1964) and A. Walton Litz (1965) spearheaded serious scholarly analysis of the juvenilia, offering seminal accounts of the young author's satirical methods and targets, as well as some of the first sustained critical readings of her early writings. As Southam notes, much of Austen's satire in the first two volumes of juvenilia is best characterized as a direct form of burlesque in which 'the target is ridiculed by a mocking imitation, which emphasizes the weaknesses and conventions of the original by exaggeration, diminution, or rearrangement' (3). Accordingly, we find the young Austen taking aim at specific genres or subgenres of novels, as in her famous burlesque of the sentimental novel (or novel of Sensibility) in *Love and Freindship*. In other instances, she targets particular narrative forms or structures, such as the epistolary novel in *Amelia Webster* and *The Three Sisters*. But she also ranges outside of novels, spoofing dramatic conventions in 'The Mystery' and 'The Visit', and historiography in her outrageous *History of England* ('By a Partial, Prejudiced, and Ignorant Historian'). Like Southam, A. Walton Litz prioritizes Austen's experimentation with, and parody of, identifiable literary genres, forms, and conventions, making a compelling case for the juvenilia to be read collectively as a sustained 'act of criticism' (3). Countering the widely held assumption, championed most famously by Henry James, that Austen was an 'unconscious' artist, somehow unaware of her own intentions and methods, Litz paints a very different picture, arguing that she 'was a supremely conscious artist, and the best evidence of her awareness lies in her incisive criticism of the fiction of her own age, a criticism not found in letters or prefaces but in the burlesques and parodies of her early career' (3).

While there is much to admire in these pioneering studies, both scholars set an unfortunate trend by characterizing Austen's early fictions as little more than apprentice work: even as Southam concedes that 'the [later] novels are intimately related to the juvenilia', for instance, he still undermines the early writings' merit, insisting that 'the focus of critical attention' should 'remain[n] on the novels, beside which the early works are relatively unimportant' (2). Indeed, Southam asserts that of all the youthful writings, only *Love and Freindship* and *The History of England* can 'stand on their own' (2). Litz, meanwhile, blatantly discourages scholars from seeking out specific influences or inspirations (literary or otherwise) that may have inspired and/or helped shape Austen's first writings, doubling down on the idea that these manuscripts 'are chiefly important in relation to the major novels', and that 'an assessment of their place in Jane Austen's artistic career should take precedence over any search for "sources"' (18).

Beginning in the 1970s and 1980s, scholars of a new generation brought different priorities and methodologies to their analyses of Austen's juvenilia, reviving and building upon many of Woolf's and Chesterton's trailblazing insights from decades earlier, and rejecting the narrow focus on development that dominated much of the early criticism. In *The Madwoman in the Attic* (1979), Sandra M. Gilbert and Susan Gubar advance an influential feminist interpretation of *Love & Freindship*, foregrounding and celebrating the early heroines' 'exuberant assertiveness' and 'exploration and exploitation' of their world (115). The novelist and critic Margaret Drabble, in her forward to the first edited collection of essays to examine the youthful writings, finds in the juvenilia alluring 'hints of [...] a fiercer, wilder, more outspoken, more ruthless writer, with a dark vision of human motivation [...] and a breathless, almost manic energy' (xiii, xiv). And in her introduction to the debut *Oxford World's Classics* edition of the early works, entitled *Catharine and other Writings* (1993), Margaret Anne Doody delineates 'an impish and formally daring' young author 'who is most fascinated by the formal qualities of fiction itself, and by the fictionality of fiction' (xxxii). Explicitly rebuffing the well-parroted contention that Austen rejected or grew out of her youthful style and subject-matter, Doody boldly suggests an alternative interpretation: that the demands of getting published (and of polite society) forced Austen to go in 'another direction'. In order to see her works in print, that is, Doody argues that Austen 'had to become genteel, and act like a lady' (xxxviii).

As Juliet McMaster observes, Austen's early writings 'are not merely signposts pointing the way to a destination; they are destinations in themselves [...]' (xiii). Following the lead of many of the pioneering critics mentioned above, literary scholars have begun analysing Austen's earliest literary productions with the same degree of seriousness and gusto that they have devoted to interpretations of her cherished published novels.

One fruitful trend in recent scholarship has involved contextualizing and/or historicizing Austen's early writings in relation to contemporary literary, social, and historical texts and contexts.[6] The large body of influential conduct books and didactic novels whose prescriptions Austen's youthful heroines so blatantly defy proves to be particularly illuminating in this regard.[7] It is no coincidence that the comic exuberance, assertiveness, acquisitiveness, and spirited physicality (among other traits) that readers and critics find so intriguingly characteristic of Austen's earliest protagonists are the very qualities that eighteenth- and early nineteenth-century conduct books, etiquette guides, and other didactic texts sought to discourage and repress in young women readers. Moreover, the very laughter that Woolf identified as the hallmark of Austen's early writings was itself a target of gender-specific attempts at regulation and suppression during the author's lifetime, with both 'women and comedy', as Audrey Bilger summarises, 'seen as potentially disruptive to the social order' (15). Take Dr. Gregory, who in his influential 1774 conduct manual *A Father's Legacy to his Daughters*, dismisses women's humour and 'wit' as not just 'dangerous' but repulsive:

> *Wit* is the most dangerous talent you can possess. [...] Wit is so flattering to vanity, that they who possess it become intoxicated, and lose all self-command [...]. Humour is a different quality. It will make your company much solicited; but be cautious how you indulge it.—It is often a great enemy to delicacy, and a still greater one to dignity of character. It may sometimes gain you applause, but will never procure you respect. (18)[8]

Through his diction, Gregory unwittingly highlights here many of Austen's early heroines' defining traits: wit, vanity and self-regard, scorn of 'good sense' and 'self-command', a penchant for 'intoxica-[tion]' and violence, a 'dangerous' potentiality, and so on—all of which he tethers to female wit and laughter. Invoking yet another defining trait of Austen's early protagonists, Gregory proceeds to dismiss female physicality of any kind, remarking in the same work that 'When a woman speaks of her great strength, her extraordinary appetite, her ability to bear excessive fatigue, we recoil at the description in a way she is little aware of' (30). Austen's early protagonists would thus appear to be *doubly* dangerous in that their physicality—manifested in cartoon-like displays of 'strength', unfettered mobility, and seemingly insatiable 'appetite[s]'—frequently provides the very foundation for Austen's authorial expression of wit and humour even as it undergirds her bold literary and social satire. Well-versed in such moralising, prescriptive discourses, the young Jane Austen, as Jill Heydt-Stevenson suggests, *laughs at all of it*: 'at the advice from conduct books, philosophical tracts, sermons, and medical manuals; at the idea that women's sexuality should be closely guarded; that private pleasures should be controlled; that gender should dictate behaviour; and that any conceivable appetite—sexual, criminal, alimentary, and liquid—should be governed' (par. 1).

Far from embodying the delicate, demure young women that the conduct books and prescriptive fiction promulgated and tried to shape—and that Caroline, James Edward, and Austen's relations worked so hard to convince readers that Austen herself exemplified—Austen's early heroines more often resemble the 'dominant, secure, thrill-seeking, free-wheeling, arrogant females, who consider themselves fit to rule the universe' (70) that Valerie Solanas identified as 'SCUM' in her infamous 1968 radical feminist manifesto. Take Anna Parker, from Austen's 'A Letter from a Young Lady [...]', who casually confesses to an astonishing array of crimes and transgressions:

> I murdered my father at a very early period of my Life, I have since murdered my Mother, and am now going to murder my Sister. I have changed my religion so often that at present I have not an idea of any left. I have been a perjured witness in every

public tryal for these last twelve Years, and I have forged my own Will. In short there is scarcely a crime that I have not committed—But I am now going to reform. Colonel Martin of the Horseguards has paid his Addresses to me, and we are to be married in a few days. (222)[9]

If Parker's announcement of her impending marriage seems to imply that she will abandon her criminal ways and commence a new period of reformed behavior (à la Moll Flanders), Austen explodes such prospects in Parker's brilliantly deadpan sign-off to her letter: 'I am now going to murder my Sister. Yours Ever, Ann Parker' (222). Or consider Sophia and Laura's (from *Love and Freindship*) foiled attempt to rob the good-natured cousin who has hospitably taken them in. When the kind Macdonald interrupts Sophia in the act of (according to Laura's admiring narration of events) 'majestically removing the 5th Bank-note' from his desk, and confronts her, the unabashed Sophia 'instantly put on a most forbidding look, and darting an angry frown on [him], demanded in a haughty tone of voice "Wherefore her retirement was thus insolently broken in on?"' (126). 'Wretch', Sophia continues, 'hastily replacing the Bank-note in the Drawer [...], "how darest thou to accuse me of an Act, of which the bare idea makes me blush?"' (126). Of course, the irony is that Sophia—despite her and Laura's repeated protestations of their 'trembling' sensibility—does *not* blush; it is far more likely *the reader* who blushes at the shameless, self-interested, and self-absorbed behaviour of Austen's first literary characters. Responding to examples such as these, readers have been moved to describe the juvenilia's protagonists as 'Monsters' (Greene), and to characterize Austen's youthful fictions as 'startling in their hostility and cold detachment' (Halperin 30).

Thus, while my invocation of Solanas is quite purposefully perverse, even outrageous, that doesn't make the analogy any less serious or apt: if we consider the young Austen as employing aggressive wit, comic violence and excess, and pointed literary and social satire, strategically 'overlapping representational modes', in Heydt-Stevenson's words, 'in order to highlight the absurdity of women's condition in this culture' (par. 2), then Austen is not, in this respect at least, all that unlike Solanas, who adopted many of the same representational and rhetorical tactics to articulate her frustration, sense of disenfranchisement, and feminist rage. According to Avital Ronell, 'Solanas punctuates her transmissions with laughter, breaking up totalities, bursting established social systems with *the disruptive laugh* that she calls *SCUM Manifesto*' (12, italics added). Ultimately, I'm suggesting that the young Jane Austen's 'disruptive laugh' also targets established 'systems', repressive 'totalities', and regulatory structures—both literary and social/political.

In fact, the 'violation' that Claudia Johnson finds the young novelist committing against 'inherited' forms, genres, and styles ('Kingdom' 48) is just one aspect of Austen's youthful fascination with *transgressions* of all kinds. With its etymological and conceptual ties to movement and mobility (a 'passing or going over') and the negotiation and/or 'violation' of literal and figurative spaces and domains, 'transgression' offers the perfect organising trope for analysing both the content as well as the form and style of Austen's early writings. As I have already begun to outline, and will explore in more detail in the remainder of this chapter, in her juvenilia Austen consistently and quite purposefully transgresses the limits of gender and genre[10]; she crosses lines, blurs boundaries, and breaks rules, 'setting at nought' the established literary genres, conventions, tropes, and plots that she inherited, as well as the social, economic, and political structures that gave rise to and maintained them.

★★★

In the opening pages of *Henry and Eliza: a novel*, written when Austen had just turned thirteen, the titular heroine takes respite before embarking on her journey to the market town of 'M.' and 'amuse[s]' herself for 'some hours' by sitting beneath a tree and 'making and singing the following Lines':

> Though misfortunes my footsteps may ever attend
> I hope I shall never have need of a Freind [sic]
> as an innocent Heart I will ever preserve
> *and will never from Virtue's dear boundaries swerve.* (39, italics added)

Other than Austen's comic exaggeration (Eliza sings for *several hours*), the scene reads like something out of the pages of the sentimental novels and gothic romances that the young author devoured so voraciously: a sensitive young female protagonist, beset by 'misfortunes' and calamities, struggles to 'preserve' an 'innocent Heart' and to guard her 'Virtue'. But Eliza coos this lyric affirmation of her unwavering, 'conscious knowledge of her own Excellence', just moments after she has been 'detected in stealing a banknote of 50£' from her adoptive parents, and been 'turned out of doors by her inhuman Benefactors' (39, 38). Both the narrative setup and Eliza's wonderfully ironic lyric establish transgression as a central focus. Despite her professed intention to stay the path of virtue, as the novel continues, the banished Eliza repeatedly 'swerves' from or transgresses the prescribed bounds of acceptable conduct and conventional morality: captivating and eloping with another woman's fiancé; embarking upon an orgy of conspicuous consumption and ruinous expenditure on the continent, which comes to an end only after Henry's death ('They had lived [...] at the rate of 12,000£ a year, of which Mr Cecil's estate being rather less than the twentieth part, they had been able to save but a trifle [...]' [41]); and, perhaps most outrageously, escaping from 'a snug little Newgate' (in which she had been imprisoned by the vengeful mother of the young woman whose fiancé she had stolen) by giving her infant children 'strict Charge not to hurt themselves' and throwing them out the window before climbing down herself (42). Having escaped from her prison, the indefatigable Eliza proceeds to walk '30 [miles] without stopping', after which she is reconnected with her estranged foster parents, who, in a delightfully outrageous and improbable reconciliation scene, are revealed to be her true birth parents.

But Austen's denouement veers away from any reabsorption of the heroine back into the safe confines of the domestic sphere as the irrepressible Eliza cannot resist satisfying one final desire—that for revenge against her enemy: '[Eliza] raised an Army, with which she entirely demolished the Dutchess's Newgate, snug as it was, and by that act, gained the Blessings of thousands, and the Applause of her own Heart' (45). With its felonious, peripatetic, and eminently self-satisfied heroine as well as its absurd plot, stylistic excess, and narrative panache, *Henry and Eliza* evidences many of the hallmarks of the juvenilia. The young Austen clearly delights in creating characters who transgress the prescribed bounds of acceptable behaviour and morality, just as she takes pleasure in constructing experimental novels that defy protocol and subvert the reader's expectations.

One of the most provocative examples of Austen's approach in this regard comes in *The Beautifull Cassandra; A novel in twelve Chapters*, the very title of which establishes the work's generic identity (novel) and unexpected narrative compression (just twelve chapters). This innovative novel, which traces the titular heroine's misadventures on the streets of London, takes the miniaturizing tendency evidenced in Austen's other early works—what Southam describes as 'a comedy of abridgement' (3)—to a fascinating extreme, spanning only three pages (or approximately forty lines) of printed text. Many of the chapters are comprised of a single sentence; the longest has just four. Austen draws even more attention to her diminution of novel form, moreover, by constructing the work as a recognizable type (or sub-genre) of novel: the traditionally expansive 'picaresque'.[11]

In the opening chapters of Austen's miniaturized, female mock-picaresque,[12] sixteen-year-old Cassandra, 'lovely and amiable', casually purloins a bonnet her mother had just finished for an unnamed Countess, 'place[s] it on her gentle Head', and walks out of her parents' shop 'to make her Fortune' (42). What possibilities (or plots), Austen prods the reader to consider, would be available to a single young woman setting out to 'make her Fortune' during this era? And why does Cassandra steal the bonnet? Is the stolen hat to be sold or exchanged, thereby providing an illicit ground for potential future prosperity? What is clear is that Cassandra's conduct right from the beginning shatters the strict notions of female decorum prevalent during Austen's time; her determination to venture forth into London unaccompanied (and with stolen goods) in order to 'make her fortune' could easily *un-make* her, or compromise her reputation. This type of apprehension is validated when the first character Cassandra encounters on her adventures is a 'young Man'—a Viscount, 'no less celebrated for his Accomplishments and Virtues, than for his Elegance and Beauty' (54).[13] But handsome young men with titles apparently play no part in Cassandra's present schemes: she merely 'curtsey[s] and walk[s] on' (54). What *is* she after?

In the next several chapters, the reader gains new perspective as the exhilarating freedoms of unhindered and unsupervised movement take a fascinatingly defiant and destructive edge when Cassandra turns to violence, theft, and other transgressive acts that contribute to the larger topos of female transgression and rebellion witnessed throughout Austen's juvenilia. Thus, in the fourth chapter, Cassandra 'proceed[s] to the Pastry-cooks' where she 'devour[s] six ices', refuses to pay for them, and then attacks the pastry chef, 'knock[ing]' him down before calmly 'walk[ing] away' (54). Cassandra does not eat politely but *devours* the treats she lacks the money to pay for, exhibiting a consumptive fixation that aligns her with other early heroines such as *Lesley Castle*'s Charlotte Lutterell, with her ambitious 'Devouring Plan' (147) for tackling the food left over from a cancelled wedding dinner, or the characters from the comic drama 'The Visit', who join in 'tossing off a bumper' before tucking in to a comically robust (and rather un-appetizing) repast of 'fried Cowheel', 'red herrings', 'Tripe', 'Liver and Crow', and 'Suet Pudding' (66, 67).

Having fled the scene of her crime, Cassandra next 'ascend[s] a Hackney Coach' and orders it to suburban Hampstead, where 'she was no sooner arrived than she ordered the Coachman to turn round and drive her back again' (55). By travelling alone, without a chaperone, Cassandra thumbs her nose at social rules governing female mobility and decorum. More surprising are her actions after returning to 'the same spot of the same Street she had sate out from': she not only refuses to pay the coachman, but, when challenged, defiantly 'place[s] her bonnet on his head' and escapes (55). By brazenly adorning him with a woman's bonnet, Cassandra ridicules and emasculates the man. Peter Sabor has noted how acts of theft in the juvenilia are 'often accompanied by preening self-congratulation, combined with contempt for the victim' (lxiii). Cassandra's apparent 'contempt' for the coachman is further registered here by the fact that she finally 'pays' him with stolen goods—the pilfered bonnet from her mother's shop.

Cassandra concludes her transgressive journey and returns in the final two chapters to 'her paternal roof in Bond Street from which she had now been absent nearly 7 hours' (56). It is only in the final chapter that Cassandra finally speaks—but only to herself: 'She entered [...] and was pressed to her Mother's bosom by that worthy Woman. Cassandra smiled and whispered to herself "This is a day well spent"' (56). Having achieved her desires via theft, violence, and cunning, the novel's enigmatic final line, hinging on Cassandra's coy smile and the obvious pun in the concluding verb, emphasises her unapologetic *satisfaction* with her day's misadventures. Like a true comic rogue, Cassandra gets away with it.[14] *The Beautifull Cassandra* offers one of the most compelling examples of the young Austen's interrogation of the formal, aesthetic, and social/political ideologies and assumptions governing the novel. By adapting and revising the picaresque; by literally 'miniaturizing' the novel; and by depicting a heroine who boldly and unapologetically pursues her desires and flaunts gender restrictions, social codes, and even laws, the young Austen compels readers to rethink what constitutes a novel at the same time that she challenges her era's stifling restrictions on female bodies and minds.

★★★

Issues pertaining to mobility, money, and marriage consistently intersect in the early writings. Given the centrality of marriage and the 'marriage plot' to her later published novels, it is not surprising to find the young Austen directing her satiric and comic energies at the institution from the very beginning of her career. Indeed, as even a cursory glance demonstrates, Austen proves herself from an astonishingly young age to be a keen and eminently critical observer of the institution and particularly its domineering impact on all aspects of a young woman's life. In the well-conceived fragment *The Three Sisters*, for example, Austen employs the epistolary format to great comic impact, utilising each of the characters' first-person letters to layer different accounts of (and conflicting perspectives on) the same events—namely, the eldest Stanhope sister's (Mary) handling of a marriage offer from Mr Watts. Though she detests her suitor, Mary is so fixated upon the prospect of (to use her own favourite word) 'triumphing' over her two sisters and local competitors by marrying first and to the greatest advantage, that she contemplates accepting Watts' offer despite her pronounced aversion to the man:

> He is quite an old Man, about two and thirty, very plain *so* plain that I cannot bear to look at him. He is extremely disagreable [sic] and I hate him more than anybody else in the world. He has a large fortune and will make great Settlements on me, but then he is very healthy. In short I do not know what to do. (74)

Convinced that she can use Watts' initial offer to aggressively negotiate for a more substantial marriage settlement, Mary proceeds to deliver a ludicrously over-the-top list of demands to her suitor:

> And Remember I am to have a new Carriage hung as high as the Duttons', and blue spotted with silver; and I shall expect a new Saddle horse, a suit of fine lace, and an infinite number of the most valuable Jewels. Diamonds such as never were seen! And Pearls, Rubies, Emeralds, and Beads out of number. You must set up your Phaeton which must be cream coloured with a wreath of silver flowers round it, You must buy 4 of the finest Bays in the Kingdom and you must drive me in it every day. This is not all; You must entirely new furnish your House after my Taste, You must hire two new Footmen to attend me, two Women to wait on me, must always let me do just as I please [...]. You must build me an elegant Greenhouse, and stock it with plants. You must let me spend every Winter in Bath, every Spring in Town, Every Summer in taking some Tour, And every Autumn at a Watering Place [...]. (82–83)

'And pray Miss Stanhope', the astonished Mr Watts inquires at the end of Mary's harangue, 'What am I to expect from you in return for all this', to which his would-be bride replies with blunt self-assurance, 'Expect? Why you may expect to have me pleased' (83).

Mary's over-the-top demands represent an attempt to take some control in determining her own self-worth in a conjugal market that overtly objectifies women and calculates their value in stark financial terms (most obviously, via their portion or dowry). Though comically hyperbolic, Mary's acquisitive turn to material objects (carriages, clothes, jewels, and so on) constitutes a reaction to her own disenfranchisement and objectification as she attempts to seize for herself some degree of agency, control, and self-determination. But while Mary shoots high in her negotiations, she quickly discovers that she lacks any bargaining strength, as Mr Watts makes abundantly clear: '[...] I can offer [my hand] else where', he tells Mary, 'for as I am by no means guided by a particular preference to you above your Sisters it is equally the Same to me which I marry of the three' (82). Mary is forced to accept a severely abridged settlement, consisting of little more than an 'inconsiderable' lot of the family jewelry and 'a Saddle horse', but only upon the stipulation that 'she is not to expect to go to Town or any other public place for these three Years' (84). Though her gains are nominal at best, Mary still finds a way to laud her engagement and to 'triumph'—if only in her own imagination—over her sisters and neighbours before the novel fragment concludes. Through Mary's repeated use of the verb 'to triumph', Austen strategically invokes the connotation of a battle or fight to compel the reader to question exactly what it means—not to mention, *what it takes*—for a young woman like Mary to 'succeed' or 'win' when the cards are so clearly stacked against her favor, and 'victory' often brings little contentment other than in supplying (to invoke *Pride and Prejudice*) a woman's 'pleasantest preservation from want' (138 [Vol. I, Chapter 22]). And given the negative characterisation of Mr Watts, we might well question how 'pleasant' that 'preservation' might be for Mary.

In the rambunctious *Jack and Alice*, competition among the novel's marriageable women is even more fierce. Not only is there a serious lack of eligible men in the world of the novel, but there are hardly any men at all. Such unpromising matrimonial prospects drive the young women of 'Pammydiddle'—including the titular Alice, the three Simpson sisters, and the newcomer, Lucy—to embrace outlandish and extreme methods in their pressing quests to secure an establishment. The sole eligible bachelor in the novel is the coquettish Charles Adams, brilliantly described as an 'amiable, accomplished and bewitching young Man; of so dazzling a Beauty that none but Eagles could look him in the Face' (14). The narrator's description highlights how Charles Adams basks in the security and freedom that his wealth, privilege, youth, physical attractiveness, and, of course, his sex, afford him: he assumes a comically god-like figure in the eyes of his dazzled admirers. The apparent dearth of eligible bachelors gives him even more power. When the titular Alice becomes 'sole inheritress of a very large fortune' after the unexpected death of her brother (who, despite the novel's title, makes no other contribution than in having his alcohol-fueled death announced by the narrator), she entertains 'fresh Hopes of rendering herself acceptable as a wife to Charles Adams', and boldly sends her father to solicit the union (27). Yet Adams rejects the proposal in outrageously blunt terms: 'Your daughter sir, is neither sufficiently beautifull [sic], sufficiently amiable, sufficiently witty, nor sufficiently rich for me—. I expect nothing more in my wife than my wife will find in me—Perfection' (28). An overstocked conjugal 'market' so drives up his asking price that Charles can demand—and patiently hold out for—'Perfection'. Alice is devastated but manages her disappointment in her usual fashion: 'She flew to her Bottle and it was soon forgot' (29).

In burlesquing and comically literalising the cutthroat (pun intended, as we shall see) nature of the marriage market, Austen foregrounds how economic necessity and the pressure to marry advantageously promote a climate of rivalry, aggression, and outright hostility between women. The memorably sketched character of Lady Williams ('a widow with a handsome Jointure and the remains of a very handsome face' [14]), for instance, assumes the role of mature confidante and adviser for the love-struck Alice, only to torment her young charge with passive-aggressive jabs at her shortcomings (such as her 'too red' [19] complexion and related predilection for strong drink) and amusingly trite platitudes that masquerade as advice ('Preserve yourself from a first Love and you need not fear a second' [18]). Another of the novel's eligible young women, Lucy, resolutely stalks Charles Adams all the way from her home in Wales (where he owns an estate) to Pammydiddle, only to become ensnared in a 'man-trap' (a large steel trap intended to catch human poachers rather than game) whilst sneaking onto his grounds. There is perhaps no more apt symbol for the risky, unforgiving nature of the marriage scramble in all of Austen; the discovery prompts Alice to employ one of the young author's much-loved rhetorical figures (the zeugma) as she hilariously interjects, 'Oh! cruel Charles to wound the hearts and legs of all the fair' (25).

Clearly unable to satisfy Adams' inflated and exorbitant standards for a spouse, most of the novel's young women travel to the spa-town of Bath—a hotbed for matrimonial speculation in the period's literature and popular culture—in search of better prospects. Caroline Simpson winds up marrying an elderly though rich Duke, but only *after* his first choice (Lucy) is murdered by a jealous rival: Caroline's sister, the 'envious and malevolent' Sukey (30). With Caroline 'rais[ed] to the rank of a Dutchess' and Sukey 'speedily raised to the Gallows', that leaves only Cecilia, the 'beautifull [sic] but affected' youngest sister, who refuses to be outshone by her older sister:

> Cecilia was too sensible of her own superior charms, not to imagine that if Caroline could engage a Duke, she might without censure aspire to the affections of some Prince—and knowing that those of her native Country were cheifly [sic] engaged, she left England and I have since heard is at present the favourite Sultana of the great Mogul. (32)

With the English Princes already 'engaged' (a sly pun, certainly, given the Royals' rather scandalous conduct at the time), the determined Cecilia instead sets sail for India, where she becomes the 'favourite Sultana' of the Indian emperor in Delhi (32). Driven by her self-regard, ambition, and competitiveness to make a market of her body in the East Indies, Cecilia actually ends up realising the role of 'Sultana' that her rival sister, Caroline, had enacted at the masquerade ball described at the beginning of the novel. The title heroine, meanwhile, remains unattached till the end, with presumably only her ubiquitous bottle of wine to console her. As for Charles Adams, the last line of the novel reveals a shocking twist: the announcement of his impending marriage to none other than Alice's supposed confidante and ally, Lady Williams.

In *Jack and Alice* Austen comically depicts the ways in which the demands of the marriage market create impossible expectations and standards for the young women whose lives and future happiness depend almost exclusively upon their successful negotiation of it. The extreme, hyperbolic demands ('Perfection') of Charles and men like him inspire equally extreme, over-the-top behaviours and tactics from Austen's characters—whether Alice's embrace of the bottle in order to escape her reality and 'forget' her unrequited passion; Lucy's marathon trek across the country in pursuit of Charles Adams; Sukey Simpson's jealous murder of a rival; or her sister's risky decision to relocate to the burgeoning Indian empire in search of a rich husband.[15]

Other early works likewise demonstrate how Austen harnesses bold comedy and satire to interrogate numerous aspects of the marriage market and to undercut its governing structures and ideologies. In *Frederic and Elfrida*, the demands of maintaining rigid standards of 'propriety' prohibit any action at all: the central couple, despite 'lov[ing] with mutual sincerity', are so 'determined not to transgress the rules of Propriety by owning their attachment, either to the object beloved, or to any one else', that they remain entirely silent on the subject for years, thereby missing out on their prime (4). In 'Letter the First' of *A Collection of Letters*, Austen subjects the ritual of a young woman's 'coming out' into society (thereby formally announcing her eligibility in the marriage market) to a risible demystification, ultimately exposing the hand-wringing that surrounds the much-ballyhooed event as *much ado about nothing*.[16] Writing to her friend, a mother expresses her anxiety over her daughters' 'first entrée into Life', divulging her hope that 'their education has been such as will not disgrace their appearance in the World, and *they* will not disgrace their Education' (191). She continues to employ overblown (and hackneyed) language in fretting over the prospect of her daughters being 'seduced' and 'contaminated' by so much 'dissipation'; it is only at the end of her letter that it is revealed to readers that 'This mighty affair' entailed nothing more than the daughters drinking tea with a 'Mrs Cope' and her daughter (192, 193, 192). While we as readers laugh at the mother's fussiness and persistent use of hyperbolic language to characterise such an insignificant outing, the letter reinforces how, given such high-stakes, even the most apparently trivial blunder or faux-pas could jeopardise a young women's chance to successfully navigate the unforgiving path to marriage and the financial stability it secures. In 'Letter the Third' from the same work, meanwhile, Austen offers a powerful first-person account of 'a young Lady in distress'd Circumstances', who vividly describes being subjected to a humiliating attack from a wealthy neighbour who chaperones her to a local ball. Austen emphasises how the protagonist's poverty fuels Lady Greville's insolent (and passive-aggressive) condescension, which she masks as charity. When Greville notices that Maria is wearing a new dress to the ball, for instance, she proceeds to lecture her young companion on the 'needless […] expence' before conceding, 'But I suppose you intend to make your fortune tonight—; Well, the sooner the better; and I wish you success' (198). Maria finds that defending herself and protesting her disinterestedness prove useless: as far as Lady Greville is concerned, Maria's poverty necessitates that she must be a 'Fortune-hunter' seeking to ensnare a rich husband by any means necessary (199). Greville then wilfully mis-interprets Maria's every action as evidence of her mercenary intentions. 'Such', the mortified Maria writes, 'is the humiliating Situation in which I am forced to appear […]' (199). Ultimately, Austen draws attention here to pervasive double-standards and hypocrisy: like the vast majority of young women, Maria's establishment in life depends upon her marrying well. Yet Lady Greville ridicules and demeans her as a 'fortune-hunter' precisely *because* her poverty necessitates that she marries well.

Austen's most ambitious and sustained exploration of the complex of issues I have been tracing comes in her regrettably unfinished novel *Catharine, or the Bower*. Revealingly deemed a 'betweenity' by Caroline Austen for its notable progression beyond parody and burlesque to a more realistic form of comedic satire,[17] *Catharine* brings together Austen's early explorations of female manners, education, mobility, marriage, and transgression into a coherent (albeit incomplete) plot revolving around the misguided parenting and educational methods of an overzealous guardian and their impact on her intelligent, spirited ward. Several scholars have noted the ways in which *Catharine* is replete with social and political references and engagements that reflect the turbulent era in which it was penned.[18] While the question of 'political' readings of Austen's novels—let alone of her youthful manuscripts—remains a vexed one for some, Claudia Johnson persuasively frames the issue by arguing that 'the political import of much of Austen's juvenile as well as mature fiction still remains unacknowledged because it focuses on subjects we define as essentially private and apolitical':

> I am referring, of course, to female experience, and the conventions structuring it. As the works of Burke, Wollstonecraft, More, Godwin, Edgeworth, Rousseau, and Burney (to name only a very few) attest, throughout the 1790s, the formative years of Austen's career, there were few subjects *more* anxiously debated as central to national well-being than female manners. Thus, portions of the juvenilia likely to appear to us variously as the most cute, slight, and precocious are often, in fact, the most laden with controversy. ('The Kingdom' 51)

Perhaps better than any of the early writings, *Catharine* clearly supports Johnson's insight, as Austen works to spotlight and satirically deflate her culture's undue investment in, and overzealous attempts to regulate and control, the politicised female body.

In the novel, Catharine (or 'Kitty', as she is also referred to) is an orphan being raised by a paranoid maiden aunt (Mrs Percival, also listed as 'Mrs Peterson' in the manuscript) with a penchant for spouting conservative platitudes about female virtue, moral decline, and the entire kingdom going to 'rack and ruin' (251). Kitty is almost unique among Austen protagonists in that she is an heiress; but her financial stability, far from shielding her from the pressures and demands of marriage, seems only to heighten her aunt's anxiety about preserving her 'virtue' and drives Mrs Percival to extreme methods so as to ensure that Kitty does not 'marry imprudently' (246). Indeed, Mrs Percival 'watch[es] over' Catharine's conduct 'with so scrutinizing a severity, as to make it very doubtful to many people, and to Catharine amongst the rest, whether she loved her or not' (242). Paranoid that even the slightest contact with a young man will precipitate her niece's (and ultimately, as we shall see, the nation's) ruin, Mrs Percival denies Catharine the opportunity to socialise with other young people in the neighbourhood and prohibits her from visiting male cousins and relatives (or them from visiting her), all the while plying Catharine with conduct literature, sermons, and conservative novels by authors such as Hannah More. Mrs Percival so rigorously seeks to monitor and control her niece's movements and freedoms that she seems to embody Bentham's famed 'panopticon'—a symbol of total surveillance and aggressive regulation.

The titular 'bower', however, functions as a sanctuary, offering Catharine temporary respite from her aunt's 'helicopter' parenting and stultifying scrutiny:

> To this Bower, which terminated a very pleasant and retired walk in her Aunt's Garden, she always wandered whenever anything disturbed her, and it possessed such a charm over her senses, as constantly to tranquilize her mind and quiet her spirits—Solitude and reflection might perhaps have had the same effect in her Bed Chamber, yet Habit had so strengthened the idea which Fancy had first suggested, that such a thought never occurred to Kitty who was firmly persuaded that her Bower alone could restore her to herself. (243)

In her descriptions here and elsewhere, Austen clearly draws upon established literary conventions (vis-à-vis Shakespeare, Spenser, and other poets) in representing the bower as a highly gendered space—indeed, the passage above ('her Bower alone could restore her to herself') as well as Austen's choice of title notably collapse Catharine's subjectivity with the bower.[19] *Catharine* thus offers a unique *prose* example of a longstanding poetic subgenre that Rachel Crawford has coined 'bower poems', which typically foreground 'an enclosed green space as the site of a tryst between a man who enters it and a female character [...] who is an integral part of its terrain' (225). Though *Catharine* is unfinished, it ultimately adheres to established bower conventions and plots by featuring a male incursion into (or transgression of) the garden space, but only after Austen sets the pattern (and expectations) by staging a series of anticipatory 'transgressions'—encompassing the term's connotations of both spatial trespasses and violations of conduct—involving Catharine's cousin, Edward Stanley, who arrives unexpectedly, and against Mrs Percival's orders, while his parents and sister are visiting.

Edward's unanticipated arrival precipitates a series of mild breaches in etiquette on Catharine's part that feed her mistrustful guardian's trepidations and ultimately incite an overblown—though revealing—verbal tirade from Mrs Percival. Not feeling well, Catharine elects to stay home from a ball hosted by a neighbour and attended by her aunt as well as her visiting aunt, uncle, and cousin, Camilla Stanley. While at home, Catharine begins to feel better and to regret her decision when she is interrupted by her excited maid, who informs her that a handsome gentleman has just arrived at the house and inquired for her. Catharine is subsequently introduced to Camilla's brother, Edward, a charming young man with (for Kitty) a seductive disregard for rules of propriety. Despite knowing how her aunt might overreact, Catharine's agrees at Edward's urging to accompany him, alone and without a chaperone, to the neighbouring ball—an act she knows, in strictest terms, to be socially unacceptable, but that she embraces precisely because her aunt's strict parenting methods have lent such instances of defiance an exciting *frisson*. During the ride, the pair immediately hit it off, playfully engaging in suggestive dialogue concerning the appropriateness of their conduct. Upon arrival, Edward presses Kitty to commit another breach in decorum by entering the ballroom alone with him (rather than sending in word of her arrival to Mrs Percival). Despite Catharine's hesitancy, Edward persists, impishly insinuating that such an entrance will cause a titter and thereby ensure that they 'shall be the whole talk of the Country' (272). Catharine's resists, wittily responding that, 'To *me* [...] that would certainly be a most powerful inducement; but I scarcely know whether my Aunt would consider it as such—. Women at her time of life, have odd ideas of propriety you know' (272), thereby poking fun at her aunt's overzealous standards. But Edward scoffs at Catharine's reservations, exclaiming that she should 'break' her aunt of her starchy notions: 'And why', he continues, 'should you object to entering a room with me where all our relations are, when you have done me the honour to admit me without any chaperone [sic] into your Carriage? Do not you think your Aunt will be as much offended with you for one, as for the other of these mighty crimes' (272).[20] The pair's dialogue reinforces the significance of transgression to the novel's plot, as Austen highlights two anticipatory spatial transgressions and attendant breaches of conduct in order to strategically set the reader up for a third and final one: Edward's 'crossing' into, or transgression of, the private confines of the titular bower.

The climactic event occurs shortly after the events of the ball have put Catharine's aunt on high alert, and even prompted her to plead with Edward's father to send him away lest, as she claims outrageously, Kitty's 'scandalous' behavior and 'impudent' conduct set everything at 'sixes and sevens' (282). Struck by Kitty's aunt's 'ridiculous apprehensions', Edward seizes upon an opportunity to torture her: fully aware that Mrs Percival is closely watching them (as usual), he 'passionately' kisses Catharine's hand and 'r[uns] out of the arbour' (283, 286). This staged, final transgression triggers a violent, overblown verbal tirade from Mrs Percival, who places all culpability on the innocent Catharine and interprets the harmless kiss as conclusive evidence of her niece's supposed 'profliga[cy]':

> Well; *this* is beyond anything I could have supposed. *Profligate* as I *knew* you to be, I was not prepared for such a sight. This is beyond any thing you ever did *before*; beyond any thing I ever heard of in my Life! Such Impudence, I never witnessed before in such a Girl! And this is the reward for all the cares I have taken in your Education; [...] All I wished for, was to breed you up virtuously; [...] I bought you Blair's Sermons, and Coelebs in Search of a Wife, I gave you the key to my own Library, and borrowed a great many good books of my Neighbours for you, all to this purpose. [...]—Oh! Catharine, you are an abandoned Creature, and I do not know what will become of you. [...] But I plainly see that every thing is going to sixes and sevens and all order will soon be at an end throughout the Kingdom. (287, emphases in original)

The mere prospect of a playful kiss is enough for Mrs Percival to condemn Kitty as 'an abandoned Creature'—a 'fallen' woman, or prostitute. A shocked and exasperated Kitty challenges her aunt's clichéd moralising and unfair stigmatisation, and debunks the notion that her alleged 'impudence' threatens national security, by insisting, 'I have done nothing this evening that can contribute to overthrow the establishment of the kingdom', to which Mrs Percival responds, 'You are Mistaken Child, [...] the welfare of every Nation depends upon the virtue of it's [sic] individuals, and any one who offends in so gross a manner against decorum and propriety, is certainly hastening it's [sic] ruin. You have been giving a bad example to the World, and the World is but too well disposed to receive such' (287-8). The comic misunderstandings that drive the plot of *Catharine* thus take on an increasingly urgent cast when we acknowledge that they also serve to mark Austen's protagonist as morally deprived, sexually deviant, or even 'lost', to her conservative aunt.

Mrs Percival's emphasis on 'Education' in her harangue—and particularly her reference to Hannah More's (infamous) didactic novel, *Coelebs in Search of a Wife* (1808)—puts the political implications of Austen's unfinished novel into sharper focus. Indeed, the illuminating link between Mrs Percival's social, educational, and political views and those of influential Evangelical writer and activist Hannah More is solidified by the fact that Austen updated the reference in the manuscript in 1809, almost twenty years after the novel was begun.[21] By making this editorial change, Austen affirms the connection between Mrs Percival's obsessive preoccupations over her niece's 'virtue' and her oft-repeated political platitude that 'every thing is going to sixes and sevens' (287).[22] That is to say, by having the extremist Mrs Percival link Kitty's purportedly 'scandalous' (282) behaviour with the potential downfall of the state ('everything will be sixes and sevens'), Austen satirically deflates the 'domino-effect' theory of female transgression and national degradation frequently articulated by conservative commentators in the tense period following the French Revolution. As Robert Hole usefully summarizes, More and other conservatives (or 'Anti-Jacobins') repeatedly hammered down the basic political point that 'female sexual indulgence dissolves morality, which dissolution in turn destroys religion, the removal of which allows the overthrow of order in the state' (Hole xxxii).[23]

Critics such as Waldron, Johnson, Doody, and Leffel have noted how, by targeting More and her novel in her editorial revision, Austen clearly establishes her disagreement with More's conservative advocacy of dated and often hypocritical notions of female decorum as well as her rather Burkean insistence on directly linking the proper deportment and virtuous conduct of women with the health and safety of the nation.[24] In the end, by parodying Mrs Percival's favourite moralising platitude, Austen assails the idea that proper governance or regulation of the female body equates with proper governance of the state (the 'body politic'). In so doing, she clearly rejects misguided, gender-specific educational regimes rooted in aggressive surveillance, sequestration, and censorship.

Austen's strategic invocation of Hannah More to frame and convey the terms of her critique, moreover, puts her in unlikely (or at least, unexpected) company with the 'mad, bad, and dangerous to know' Romantic-era poet, Lord Byron. In canto one of *Don Juan*, Byron employs an allusion to More's *Coelebs in Search of a Wife* toward remarkably similar ends as Austen does in *Catharine*. Characterizing Juan's overprotective mother, Byron refers to her as a 'walking calculation', like 'Coelebs' Wife set out in quest of lovers', before caricaturing Hannah More as 'Morality's prim personification/In which not envy's self a flaw discovers./To other's share let female errors fall,/For she had not even one—the worst of all' (Canto I, stanza 16). That Byron's playful broadside against More appears in a stanza describing Don Juan's mother is significant, for like Austen's Mrs Percival, the character of Donna Inez represents repressive moral authority and faulty educational methods: 'But that which Donna Inez most desired/And saw into herself each day before all/The learnèd tutors whom for him she hired/Was that [Juan's] breeding should be strictly moral':

> The languages, especially the dead,
> The sciences, and most of all the abstruse,
> The arts, at least all such as could be said
> To be the most remote from common use,
> In all these he was much and deeply read,
> But not a page of anything that's loose
> Or hints continuation of the species
> Was ever suffered, lest he should grow vicious. (Canto I, st. 39, 40)

Fearful that her son will encounter 'loose' descriptions in his study of the classics, Donna Inez procures for him editions '[e]xpurgated by learnèd men, who/place Judiciously from out the schoolboy's vision/The grosser parts, but fearful to deface/Too much their modest bard by this omission/[...] They only add them all in an appendix,/Which saves in fact the trouble of an index' (Canto I, st. 44). As Byron playfully suggests, expurgated editions such as those used by Juan's mother and teachers, which relegate sexual materials to an appendix tucked away at the back of the book in a misguided attempt to control readerly access (and promote easy censorship on the part of anxious guardians), simply make it easier for young readers like Juan to get to the 'grosser parts': 'For there we have them all at one fell swoop,/Instead of being scattered through the pages' (Canto I, st. 45). An apt depiction of an editorial return-of-the-repressed, Byron satirises educational attempts like Donna Inez's (and Mrs Percival's) which try to regulate and control sexuality. Thus, while we generally do not think of Austen and Byron as sharing social and political concerns, in this case, both deploy pointed references to Hannah More and her controversial novel in order to question the efficacy of conduct books, didactic treatises, and repressive sexual discourses and educational practices.

★★★

Few would now agree with Chapman's sweeping generalization that Austen's 'immature or fragmentary fictions call for hardly any comment' ('Preface' v). In her manuscript writings we observe the young novelist experimenting with and rethinking the conventions and governing assumptions that structure the various formal and generic incarnations of the novel, while at the same time employing burlesque, aggressive wit and comedy, and pointed social satire to interrogate young women's position in her culture and world. By populating her early works with bold, unapologetic heroines whose transgressive actions and frequently criminal activities subvert and assault the patriarchal structures dictating and controlling late eighteenth-century women's experience of 'the real', Austen compels the reader to connect her heroines' jubilantly outlandish conduct—whether it involves drinking, binging, gratuitous theft, or verbal and even physical violence—with the social, political, and literary agendas that, in fact, inspire and instigate them.

Notes

1 I am indebted to Margaret Doody's formulation, worth quoting here: 'As a teenager she was already an expert in English fiction, and more than that, a student of what might be called "novelism" or "novelizing". She picks up the constituent elements and disarranges them, takes them deliberately apart, wrenching them away from the smooth underlying organization and constructed arrangements in which they are at home' ('Disconcerting' 112).

2 As Southam notes, 'In point of fact Austen-Leigh had wanted to include some of the childhood pieces in the first edition, but this plan was opposed in the family. It may have been felt that Jane Austen's reputation would not be served by making public her immature works, particularly as these contained a lively strain of eighteenth-century humor offensive to Victorian taste' (2).

3 Caroline voices the same apprehension with regard to *Lady Susan* in another letter to James (undated; ca. July 1871): '[…] I have never felt quite sure how it would be taken by the public […]'. See Sutherland 191.

4 For a consideration of Caroline Austen's repeated use of the term 'nonsense' to characterize the juvenilia, see White.

5 On this point, see also Sabor's critical introduction, to which I am indebted.

6 See especially Johnson ('Kingdom'); Kent; Looser; Heydt-Stevenson ('Pleasure'); Waldron; Tuite; Leffel ('Everything'); and Krueger.

7 As Janet Todd notes, 'conduct books, written mainly by men for women, showed a woman how to act so that she would be found attractive enough for a man to marry her, and how to comport herself in this achieved marriage by balancing the domestic and personal, the care of house and husband. Above all, they urged her to learn how to control and, if possible, eradicate her desires, especially those for independence, close female friendship, personal wealth and involvement in power' (xiv).

8 Waldron points out that 'Jane Austen had certainly read this, for she refers to it in *Northanger Abbey*' (18).

9 All references to Austen's juvenilia correspond to Peter Sabor's scholarly edition as part of *The Cambridge Edition of the Works of Jane Austen* (2013).

10 I am echoing here Gilbert and Gubar's memorable phrasing from the title to their chapter on *Love and Freindship*: 'Shut up in prose: Gender and Genre in Austen's Juvenilia'.

11 Characterised by its loose, episodic plot structure; reliance upon chance encounters, mistaken identities, and improbable reversals of fortune; detailed negotiation of diverse (and often disreputable) social settings and milieus; and raucous, frequently bawdy content, the picaresque novel originated from Miguel de Cervantes' *Don Quixote* (c. 1605–1615) and thrived in eighteenth-century England thanks in large part to the immense popularity of Henry Fielding's *Joseph Andrews* (1742) and *Tom Jones* (1749). It was a traditionally male-centred (not to mention, male-penned) novel, which makes the young Austen's appropriation and revision of it all the more compelling. On the links between crime and transgression and the picaresque form, see Gladfelder.

12 See Leffel ('Miniature') for a more developed reading. In the present chapter, I have drawn upon ideas and arguments first presented in the earlier article.

13 Intriguingly, Austen emphasises traits commonly applied to (and valued in) young women: 'beauty', 'accomplishments', and so on. She makes the same type of gesture throughout the early works.

14 On female roguery in the early works, see Monteiro.

15 For more on the historical and literary contexts of the Indian marriage market, see Leffel ('Conjugal').

16 The work is structured as an assemblage of occasional letters in the tradition of Samuel Richardson's *Letters Written to and for Particular Friends on the Most Important Occasions* (1741).

17 As Southam notes of the novel, 'burlesque is intermingled with [Austen's] first experiments in realistic social comedy and more flexible narrative forms' (246).

18 These critics have interpreted the novel as an intervention into topical debates on the subject of 'female manners' (Johnson 'Kingdom' 51); as a 'direct negative response to the sort of pontification about the proper behaviour of young girls' found in the era's conduct literature (Waldron 19); and as a bold examination of adolescent female sexuality and pathological social fears concerning the ungoverned female imagination and body (Heydt-Stevenson 'Pleasure'; Tuite; Leffel 'Everything').

19 On this point see Leffel ('Everything').

20 In response to Catharine's claim that there is 'no reason I should offend against Decorum a second time, because I have already done it once', Edward raises the bar by making an explicit allusion, as Heydt-Stevenson notes (*Unbecoming* 171), to the irrecoverable loss of her virginity: 'On the contrary', he replies, 'that is the very reason which makes it impossible for you to prevent it, since you cannot offend for the *first time* again' (272; Austen's emphasis).

21 Austen's original choice of text here was the Archbishop Thomas Secker's *Lectures on the Catechism of the Church of England* (1769).

22 See also p. 251: 'Mrs P, who was firmly of opinion that the whole race of Mankind were degenerating, said that for her part, Everything she believed was going to rack and ruin, all order was destroyed over the face of the World [...]'.

23 Alan Richardson notes further how 'More sees the issues of women's education, manners, and social role as inherently political' (180), as evidenced in her claim in *Strictures on Female Education* that 'the general state of civilized society depends [...] on the prevailing sentiments and habits of women' (180).

24 For further analysis, see Leffel ('Everything'). In this section, I have drawn (and expanded) upon ideas and arguments first made in the earlier article.

Works Cited

Austen, Jane. *Catharine, and Other Writings*, edited by Margaret Anne Doody and Douglas Murray. Oxford UP, 1998.

Austen, Jane. *Juvenilia*, edited by Peter Sabor. Cambridge UP, 2013.

Austen, Jane. *Love and Freindship and Other Youthful Writings*, edited by Christine Alexander. Penguin, 2014.

Austen, Jane. *Manuscript Works*, edited by Linda Bree, Peter Sabor, and Janet Todd. Broadview, 2013.

Austen, Jane. *Pride and Prejudice*, edited by Pat Rogers. Cambridge UP, 2013.

Austen, Jane. *Teenage Writings*, edited by Kathryn Sutherland and Freya Johnston. Oxford UP, 2017.

Austen, Jane. *The Beautifull Cassandra*, afterward by Claudia Johnson. Princeton UP, 2018.

Austen-Leigh, James Edward. *A Memoir of Jane Austen*. London, Richard Bentley, 1870.

Austen-Leigh, William, and Richard Arthur. *Jane Austen: Her Life and Letters, a Family Record*. London, Smith & Elder, 1913.

Bilger, Audrey. *Laughing Feminism: Subversive Comedy in Frances Burney, Maria Edgeworth, and Jane Austen*. Wayne State UP, 1998.

Byron, Lord. *Don Juan*, edited by T. G. Steffan, E. Steffan, and W. W. Pratt. New York: Penguin Books, 2004.

Chapman, R. W. Preface. *Minor Works. The Works of Jane Austen*, edited by R. W. Chapman. Oxford UP, 1954.

Chesterton, G. K. Preface. *Love & Freindship and Other Early Works*, by Jane Austen, edited by G. K. Chesterton. London: Chatto & Windus, 1922.

Crawford, Rachel. *Poetry, Enclosure, and the Vernacular Landscape, 1700-1830*. Cambridge UP, 2002.

Doody, Margaret Anne. Introduction. *Catharine, and Other Writings*, by Jane Austen, edited by Margaret Anne Doody and Douglas Murray. Oxford UP, 1998.

Doody, Margaret Anne. 'Jane Austen, That Disconcerting "Child".' *The Child Writer from Austen to Woolf*, edited by Christine Alexander and Juliet McMaster. Cambridge UP, 2005, pp. 101–121.

Drabble, Margaret. Forward. *Jane Austen's Beginnings*, edited by J. David Grey. Ann Arbor: UMI, 1989, pp. xii–xiv.

Gilbert, Sandra M., and Susan Gubar. *The Madwoman in the Attic: The Woman Writer and the Nineteenth-Century Literary Imagination*. Yale UP, 1979.

Gladfelder, Hal. *Criminality and Narrative in Eighteenth-Century England*. Johns Hopkins UP, 2001.

Greene, Donald. 'Jane Austen's Monsters.' *Jane Austen Bicentenary Essays*, edited by John Halperin. Cambridge UP, 1975, 262–278.

Gregory, J. *A Father's Legacy to his Daughters*. London: W. Strahan and T. Cadell, 1774.

Grey, J. David, editor. *Jane Austen's Beginnings: The Juvenilia and Lady Susan*. UMI, 1989.

Halperin, John. 'Unengaged Laughter: Jane Austen's Juvenilia.' *Jane Austen's Beginnings: The Juvenilia and Lady Susan*, edited by J. David Grey. UMI, 1989, pp. 29–44.

Heydt-Stevenson, Jill. *Austen's Unbecoming Conjunctions: Subversive Laughter, Embodied History*. Palgrave Macmillan, 2005.

Heydt-Stevenson, Jill. '"Pleasure Is Now, and ought to Be, Your Business": Stealing Sexuality in Jane Austen's *Juvenilia*.' *Historicizing Romantic Sexuality*, edited by Richard Sha. *Romantic Circles Praxis*, Jan. 2006 (n.p.). https://romantic-circles.org/praxis/sexuality/heydt/heydt.html

Hole, Robert, editor. *Selected Writings of Hannah More*. London: William Pickering, 1996.

Johnson, Claudia. '"The Kingdom at Sixes and Sevens": Politics and the Juvenilia.' *Jane Austen's Beginnings: The Juvenilia and Lady Susan*, edited by J. David Grey, UMI, 1989, pp. 45–59.

Kent, Christopher. 'Learning History with, and from, Jane Austen.' *Jane Austen's Beginnings: The Juvenilia and Lady Susan*, edited by J. David Grey, UMI, 1989, pp. 59–72.

Krueger, Misty. 'From Marginalia to Juvenilia: Jane Austen's Vindication of the Stuarts.' *The Eighteenth Century*, vol. 56, no. 2, 2015, pp. 243–259.

Leaska, Mitchell Alexander, editor. *The Virginia Woolf Reader*. Harcourt Brace Jovanovich, 1984.

Leffel, John C. 'Conjugal Excursions, at Home and Abroad, in Austen's "Juvenilia" and *Sanditon*.' *Jane Austen's Geographies*, edited by Robert Clark. Routledge, 2018, pp. 28–51.

Leffel, John C. '"Everything is Going to Sixes and Sevens": Governing the Female Body (Politic) in Jane Austen's *Catharine, or the Bower* (1792).' *Studies in the Novel*, vol. 43, no. 2, 2011, pp. 131–151.

Leffel, John C. 'Jane Austen's Miniature "Novel": Gender, Politics, and Form in *The Beautifull Cassandra*.' *Persuasions*, no. 32, 2010, pp. 184–195.

Litz, A. Walton. *Jane Austen: A Study of her Artistic Development*. Oxford UP, 1965.

Looser, Devoney. 'Reading Jane Austen and Rewriting "Herstory".' *Critical Essays on Jane Austen*, edited by Laura Mooneyham White. New York: G. K. Hall & Co., 1998, pp. 34–66.

McMaster, Juliet. *Jane Austen, Young Author*. Routledge, 2016.

Monteiro, Belisa. 'Comic Fantasy in Jane Austen's Juvenilia: Female Roguery and the Charms of Narcissism.' *Persuasions*, no. 27, 2005, 129–134.

Richardson, Alan. *Literature, Education, and Romanticism: Reading as Social Practice, 1780-1832*. Cambridge UP, 1994.

Ronell, Avital. 'The Deviant Payback: The Aims of Valerie Solanas.' *SCUM Manifesto*, edited by Valerie Solanas. Verso, 2004, pp. 1–34.

Sabor, Peter. Introduction. *Juvenilia*, by Jane Austen, edited by Peter Sabor. Cambridge UP, 2013, pp. xxiii–lxvii.

Solanas, Valerie. *SCUM Manifesto*, edited by Avital Ronell. London: Verso, 2004.

Southam, Brian. *Jane Austen's Literary Manuscripts*, New Edition. Athlone P, 2001.

Sutherland, Kathryn, editor. *A Memoir of Jane Austen and Other Family Recollections*. Oxford UP, 2002.

Todd, Janet, editor. *Female Education in the Age of Enlightenment: Volume I*. London: William Pickering, 1996.

Tuite, Clara. *Romantic Austen: Sexual Politics and the Literary Canon*. Cambridge UP, 2002.

Waldron, Mary. *Jane Austen and the Fiction of Her Time*. Cambridge UP, 1999.

White, Donna R. 'Nonsense Elements in Jane Austen's Juvenilia.' *Persuasions On-Line*, vol. 39, no. 1, 2018. http://jasna.org/publications/persuasions-online/volume-39-no-1/nonsense-elements-in-jane-austens-juvenilia/

PART II

Historicising Austen: A Sampling

9

TOUCHING UPON JANE AUSTEN'S POLITICS

Devoney Looser

ARIZONA STATE UNIVERSITY

What were Jane Austen's political beliefs? Ask ten different scholars, and get ten different answers. My view is that Austen's fiction suggests she was a political liberal on issues of gender and, to some degree, on class, especially what we would now call the middle class. Her positions on race, racism, and slavery also seem to lean liberal, at least in comparison to those held by other educated whites of her time. I see in her fiction evidence of a commitment to reform and to building greater social and economic access to existing institutions. If past is prologue, however, my views may say as much about me as about her writings.

When it comes to making sense of Austen's politics, most critics do see eye to eye on one thing. There is widespread agreement that her early biographers—especially her male family members and collateral descendants—laid the foundation for a powerful, partial, and largely conservative portrait of the author. They presented her as a modest spinster-paragon who was intentionally and happily disconnected from the masculine, public world.[1]

Most often, when Austen's politics were acknowledged in these early biographical accounts, they were said to centre on one word: Tory. That label has been used for many years to argue for Austen's conservatism. But re-examining early sources suggests we have often missed or downplayed further political cues, contexts, and qualifications. Such a reexamination may not get us any closer to pinning down Austen's beliefs on a particular issue. (Her fiction certainly suggests that any positions she took were unlikely to be unbending.) Looking at the earliest biographical sources about her with a fresh eye may help us better to grasp the ways in which the novelist has been handed down in unfortunately limited political terms.

In this essay, I grapple with Austen's reputation from the 1850s to the 1870s, a formative period for her literary afterlife, in order to review previous claims and to deepen our understanding of her political legacy. I examine how categorizing Austen's politics took shape, solidified, and shifted, by turning to her nephew James Edward Austen-Leigh's descriptions of his aunt's party affiliation in *A Memoir of Jane Austen* (1870). I argue for the need to see his description of her in the messy context of mid-century labels, descriptions that may (once again, predictably) give us more insight into his own positions than into hers.

It is well known that Victorian Britain was undergoing significant change in the 1850s, as political winds shifted dramatically from what they were even in Austen's volatile 1810s. Political labelling, too, had destabilised in the intervening years, after riots, incremental (if slow) reform, and mass migration to industrialising cities. Crucially important, too, was the fact that a man's being without a political label was increasingly seen as an oddity. As a source from 1855 put it, 'It is a matter about which a political

DOI: 10.4324/9780429398155-9-12

satirist might make merry, that in our party nomenclature we have lost all provision for designating mere disinterested patriotism, and solitary conscientiousness'. Instead, the author suggests, 'a public man belonging to no party becomes quite unintelligible' (Cyples 2).

Unsurprisingly, these new rules applied differently for women, who were still believed by many to have a better claim on gentility if they were situated outside of the political realm. The question for Austen's collateral descendants, then, seems to have been how to make her (and their) politics intelligible, following a historical shift to a more factionalized political period. Literary critics today may imagine that the political history of nineteenth-century Britain consisted largely of Radicals, Whigs, and Tories. But by the 1850s it was becoming both increasingly difficult to label oneself neatly within these three terms or to ascribe these labels to others. In part, that's because politicians themselves were changing parties—and creating factions and new parties—with stunning frequency. A lifetime affiliation to one party label was no longer a given.

In other words, the choices as to what to call yourself politically—or with whom or which party to affiliate—were multiplying. One essay from 1858 sorts politicians into four categories—Whig, Tory, Radical, or Neutral—seeking, with the latter term, to signal disinterestedness ('List', 1858, 263–64). Yet these four labels were hardly robust enough to describe the available possibilities. This was, after all, an era that admitted the category of 'Tory Radical', in order to suggest a commitment to conservatism and traditional structures, coupled with an anti-capitalist desire to halt in-dustrialisation and urban living for the middle and working classes. Political categorisation to make sense of individuals then was, and is, complex. When an 1859 source set out to classify the 'politics and principles' of hundreds of London, English provincial, Welsh, and Scottish newspapers, it used the following labels: Conservative, Liberal Conservative, Whig, Liberal, Liberal and Independent, Independent, Neutral, Commercial, Radical, Radical and Religious, Palmerstonian, and Undefinable, as well as National, Colonial, Scientific, Horticulturalist, Sporting, Temperance, Biblical, Protestant, Religious, Evangelical, High Church, Anglo-Catholic, Baptist, Secular, and Social ('List', 1859, 112–27). By the mid-nineteenth century, labelling someone or something politically was becoming compulsory. At the same time, the possible terms were proliferating. It is perfectly understandable that many individuals would shift their party allegiances in such a context.

Before turning back to Austen, it may be useful to chart a few high-profile individuals' political shifts. The label 'Palmerstonian' in the aforementioned list is itself telling and deserves unpacking. Lord Palmerston, who became Prime Minister (1859–65), had started out as a Tory, changed to a Whig, and gone on to lead the new Liberal party. He embraced labels all along the political spectrum. He was not alone. William Ewart Gladstone (1809–98), too, began as a High Tory but joined Robert Peel's Conservative faction, as it controversially partnered with Whigs. Then Gladstone shifted to affiliate with the Liberals. By the time he became Prime Minister in 1868, Gladstone was known as a reformer. These sorts of political changes sowed confusion for those who thought that one should have a lifelong membership to a particular political party, not to mention to supporters of particular politicians (e.g., 'Palmerstonians'). This political fluidity or changeability is a phenomenon with important implications for considering Austen's political legacy in the late nineteenth century and thereafter.

It is easily documented, but perhaps still little known, that political confusion, and even strife, played out in the Austen family in the Victorian era. This is evident in the life of James Edward Austen-Leigh, the novelist's nephew. A conservative clergyman, he was author of the first full-length biography, *A Memoir of Jane Austen* (1870). It is in his daughter's memoir of him, however, that we learn of his political dilemmas. She writes that one such dilemma occurred just after Gladstone had affiliated with the Liberal party. James Edward Austen-Leigh's daughter, Mary Augusta Austen-Leigh, writes, 'our father [who went by Edward], who had hitherto supported Mr. Gladstone, now determined not to vote' (M. Austen-Leigh 334). As a prominent church leader with influence in the community, Edward was approached by two close friends who asked him to change his mind about supporting Gladstone. Edward refused. He was said to have wanted to 'preserve the Balance of our Constitution in Church and State and, most especially, the union of the two', so he 'remained unmoved and took no part in the election' (M. Austen-Leigh 335). Edward was said to have 'clear and decided views'—conservative ones—but he 'did not love controversy' (M. Austen-Leigh 336). Going against his friends' wishes was apparently painful. His response to the dilemma was to remove himself from the election, rather than to support the opposition. This anecdote, about a situation he faced one year before he completed his memoir of his aunt, is one we ought to keep at the fore when examining his account of her in the *Memoir*.

Austen-Leigh expresses in the *Memoir* what appear to be conflicting impulses for treating the subject of his aunt's politics. He seeks both to deny and to provisionally to label them. Austen-Leigh first claims that Austen 'never touched upon politics' in her writings, a view that fell well within the bounds of properly apolitical Victorian womanhood and of a supposedly old-fashioned neutrality, said then to be fading from view. This is also an obvious conclusion to reach for a man who allegedly disliked controversy (J. Austen-Leigh 14).

But Austen-Leigh later argues in the opposite direction for labelling his aunt, writing that 'Jane, when a girl, had strong political opinions'. He claims that her views arose from 'an impulse of feeling' rather than from 'enquiry' and 'evidences'—so from appropriately feminine emotion rather than quasi-masculine rationality. Her political opinions were said to have fallen away, however, as she matured. He writes, 'As she grew up, the party politics of the day occupied very little of her attention, but she probably shared the feeling of moderate Toryism which prevailed in her family' (J. Austen-Leigh 84). His claim is that she avoided adult politics, although she then obediently, or carelessly, assented to whatever position prevailed among the men in her clergy-saturated, nominally Tory family.

We ought to do far more to parse Austen-Leigh's key sentence here, however. It has been repeatedly quoted, often without the qualifier and without the implied doubt, by generations of subsequent critics. It is important to notice that Austen-Leigh is far from definitive. The description of her as having '*probably* shared' is tepid, as is her '*moderate* Toryism' (emphasis added). Austen-Leigh shows a commitment to being non-controversial by making no declarative statements about the novelist's politics, especially through the use of the word 'probably'. At the same time, he, like so many before and after him, seeks to claim Austen for his chosen faction—in his case, Toryism. The 'moderate' label may be said to serve as a distancing mechanism from Radical Toryism and High Toryism or to continue a bid for neutrality.

There is even more that we might notice about the kind of Toryism that Austen-Leigh ascribes to his aunt. He and his family did not shun Liberals. His daughter Mary Augusta goes to great pains to mention that her brother Cholmeley Austen-Leigh had been 'coached' in his reading by Mr (afterward Sir) Osborn Morgan, who became 'a well-known Liberal M.P. and distinguished himself by carrying the Married Women's Property Act' (M. Austen-Leigh 230). It is unclear if this seeming endorsement ('distinguished') represents the position of Mary Augusta, James Edward, or Cholmeley Austen-Leigh—or all three. But such approving mentions of Liberals are a rarity in the father's Memoir. Far more often, Edward connects himself—and is connected biographically by others—to high-profile Conservatives. This is most evident in Edward's 'very real and strong friendship' with Bishop Samuel Wilberforce (1805–73), the Tory son of anti-slavery campaigner and MP William Wilberforce (Burns; M. Austen-Leigh 174).

Bishop Wilberforce, Edward's ecclesiastical superior and mentor, was a noted public speaker who considered himself early in life a 'very high Tory', and afterwards a 'Liberal Tory', but always an opponent of 'modern liberalism'. Prince Albert is said to have warned the Bishop to abstain from politics, but in private, the churchman referred to the Whigs as 'shabby, word-eating, pocket-picking … sacrilegious villains' (Burns). He famously spoke in opposition to Charles Darwin's theories at the Oxford Evolution debates of 1860. The Bishop allegedly asked if any of Darwin's proponents there present would claim descent from a monkey on his grandmother's side; Wilberforce believed he had 'got the better of the exchange' (Burns). Nevertheless, Edward Austen-Leigh so admired the Bishop that this mentor's portrait was placed near Edward's coffin at his funeral (M. Austen-Leigh 300). This is a strong—almost a stunning—demonstration of personal and political affiliation and legacy.

As these anecdotes suggest, James Edward Austen-Leigh remained lifelong-loyal to traditional Church of England positions and to the Tories. In literature, he was an avowed fan of Tory-affiliated novelist and poet Sir Walter Scott, described as his 'favourite author' (M. Austen-Leigh 102). Mary Augusta writes about her father's visit to Scott's home at Abbotsford in 1841, a decade after Scott's death, as if it were a pilgrimage. She describes that her father, 'as a nephew of Jane Austen, was allowed to take down her works from the shelf in the Abbottsford library, when he observed from their condition how much they had been read' (M. Austen-Leigh 102–3). In other words, James Edward Austen-Leigh was devoted to literature. In addition to reading aloud from his aunt's works to his family—apparently with skill—he read aloud from Scott, 'an author whose writings gave him extreme pleasure' (M. Austen-Leigh 162).

Austen-Leigh also told his children stories of family encounters with the relatives of Scott, including a visit he had made to Scott's grandmother, Mrs Smith. Austen-Leigh found out that a particular chair the novelist had sat in was marked out by the Scott family as an important relic (M. Austen-Leigh 162). Edward was also said to have had John Gibson Lockhart's biography of Scott 'constantly' in his hand (M. Austen-Leigh 162). Lockhart, Scott's son-in-law, was himself a family biographer. It is an interesting piece of information, given Edward's later choosing—and allegedly with some reluctance—to become a family biographer himself (M. Austen-Leigh 261). Edward's love of Scott and Lockhart may have informed his decision to memorialise his 'Aunt Jane' Austen as he did.

Edward's worship of Scott had its limits, however. His 'admiration' of Scott was 'so profound' that when he learned of Scott's 'unfortunate connexion with the firm of Ballantyne'—the publishing house that Scott helped to drive into and keep in debt—he is said to have removed Scott's last three 'unworthy' novels from the shelf. Mary Augusta claims that 'it distressed him even to have them in the house' (163). That Edward Austen-Leigh blamed Ballantyne, and not Scott, for the author's financial ruin and literary decline shows that he, like many, remained unaware of the ways in which Scott himself was financially implicated in the failure of that publishing business. It may also be no small matter that Ballantyne had quarrelled with Scott over the Reform Bill (which Ballantyne supported) and that the publisher had become Whig-affiliated. Publisher Ballantyne had been memorialized by Lockhart in an 'unfairly critical portrayal' (Ragaz). A more detailed comparison of Lockhart's memoir of Scott with Edward's memoir of Austen is certainly called for, on the basis of these anecdotes alone.

What they all point to is the likelihood that Edward's brand of conservative politics shaped not just his portrayal of his Aunt Jane Austen as an idealised Victorian spinster but also of his specific, if tentative, political labelling of her. Edward seems to have considered himself a moderate Tory, in the tradition of his mentor, Bishop Wilberforce. Whatever the case, the label he chose for his author-aunt stuck, almost from the first. Biographers echoed Edward's political assessment of her, even when they took issue with it. For instance, historian and biographer Goldwin Smith (1823–1910), in his *Life of Jane Austen* (1890), describes the novelist as 'a mild Tory' by 'tradition' (Smith 45). (The table of contents lists this subsection of his text as describing her as 'a mild conservative' whose novels 'accurately depict the social life of the time'.) Smith admits doubt about the appropriateness of his conservative label, writing 'Whatever her opinions were they were pretty sure to be mild', as, he claims, the daughter of a clergyman was likely to be (45). 'Mild' is not moderate but surely gets at the spirit of what Austen-Leigh himself was communicating. Smith further opines that Austen was certainly 'not a Radical of the school of [William] Godwin' (45).

Yet, just after this statement, Smith twice claims that Austen shows 'a flash of something like Radical sympathy for the oppressed governess' in *Emma* and declares her 'a little Radical' in *Persuasion* (48, 47). One is tempted to suggest, repurposing Smith's own manufactured terms, that he finds Austen to be 'a mild Radical'. If so, this would be in keeping with Smith's own politics. He had Radical sympathies and was best known for his pamphleteering work in (successful) attempts to convince the British to ally with the American North, rather than the slave-holding South, in the Civil War. Smith later moved to the United States and Canada, countries that he believed ought to unite. Smith was known for positions fluctuating between liberalism and radicalism (Kent).

What these and other examples point to is the need for a long-term pattern of vision for identifying Austen's politics. Her politics have all too frequently been said to match the personal politics of the person doing the interpreting. The specific example of politician William Gladstone is also instructive. When questioned about whether he admired 'Miss Austen', he replies, 'Certainly … But I am not so enthusiastic about her as some people are' (Tollemache 132). He claims that is because, to him, Austen can neither dive nor soar. He says that she is a first-rate actor in a third-rate piece. He concludes that Austen is parochial, while Sir Walter Scott is 'world historical' (Tollemache 133).

Gladstone, who had at one time seemed a supporter of extending the franchise to females, later came out against women's suffrage. Perhaps he imagined all educated women—as he did Austen—as creatures who could neither dive nor soar. They were rightly relegated to being first-rate actors in their own necessarily (and to him, appropriately) third-rate domestic lives. Gladstone's assessment of Austen would be echoed in the early twentieth century by the elite clubman and critic, Walter Frewen Lord, whose arguments were dismantled in print by writer and schoolteacher Annie Gladstone, as I have argued elsewhere (Looser 141–78). Fractious debates over Austen's politics were common a century and more ago.

Those who have approved of, and admired, Austen also engage in what we might call political mirroring. Many have located in her life or writings their own views. Conservative G. K. Chesterton (1874–1936) finds in Austen a ratification of his conservatism and of the value of traditional marriage (Chesterton 1004). Feminist Rebecca West (1892–1983) finds in Austen a decided feminism, in novels that lay bare the economics of marriage, in order to 'shatter the conception of romantic love' (West ix). We might ask of these early twentieth-century Austen commentators, 'Are they even reading the same books?' Their polarising differences add to our sense of the long history of Austen's fiction as having provided readers with an ink-blot test on which to project their deeply held political opinions.

It ought to go without saying that Austen's fiction itself does much more. Her life and writings have long served to open up, rather than foreclose, political conversation across a wide spectrum of belief. This alone is remarkable for any work of literature or any author's oeuvre. By extension, studying her political legacy may also prompt us to ask better questions of ourselves and others, whether on a local or a global stage. There is nothing remotely 'mild' or 'moderate' about that cultural achievement.

Note

1   The political affiliations that were grafted onto Austen in the nineteenth century were generally derived from the views said to be held on her maternal side. It was said that Austen upheld the Leigh family tradition of supporting the Stuarts. For excellent essays on Austen's history writing, its play with genre, its grappling with predecessors, and its support of the Stuarts, see Johnston and Brophy. For books on Austen's politics that seek to reframe the conversation, see Neill and Knox-Shaw. For a recent book on the subject, geared toward a popular audience, see Kelly, which offers readers a copious amount of what the author calls 'truthful fictions'.

Works Cited

Austen-Leigh, James Edward. *A Memoir of Jane Austen*. London: Richard Bentley, 1870.

Austen-Leigh, Mary Augusta. *James Edward AustenLeigh: A Memoir by His Daughter*. For Private Circulation, 1911.

Brophy, Brigid. 'Jane Austen and the Stuarts.' *Critical Essays on Jane Austen*, edited by Brian Charles Southam. Routledge, Kegan, & Paul, 1969, pp. 21–39.

Burns, Arthur. 'Wilberforce, Samuel (1805–1873).' *Oxford Dictionary of National Biography*, 23 Sep. 2004, https://doi-org.ezproxy1.lib.asu.edu/10.1093/ref:odnb/29385

Chesterton, Gilbert Keith 'June 1, 1929: Jane Austen and the General Election.' *The Collected Works of G. K. Chesterton*, vol. 35, *The Illustrated London News, 1929–1931*, edited by Lawrence J. Clipper. Ignatius P, 1991, pp. 100–104.

Cyples, W. *The Question is Mr Urquhart a Tory or a Radical? Answered by His Constitution for the Danubian Principalities*. Sheffield: Isaac Ironside, 1856.

Johnston, Freya. 'Jane Austen's Past Lives.' *Cambridge Quarterly*, vol. 39, no. 2, 2010, pp. 103–121.

Kelly, Helena. *Jane Austen, the Secret Radical*. Knopf, 2017.

Kent, Christopher A. 'Smith, Goldwin (1823–1910).' *Oxford Dictionary of National Biography*, 23 Sep. 2004. https://doi-org.ezproxy1.lib.asu.edu/10.1093/ref:odnb/36142

Knox-Shaw, Peter. *Jane Austen and the Enlightenment*. Cambridge UP, 2004.

'List of London Newspapers.' *The Literary and Educational Year Book for 1859*. London: Kent & Co, 1859, pp. 112–127.

'List of the Minority on Mr Cayley's Motion on the Currency.' *Academica: An Occasional Journal*. Cambridge: Macmillan, 1858, pp. 263–264.

Looser, Devoney. *The Making of Jane Austen*. Johns Hopkins UP, 2017.

Neill, Edward. *The Politics of Jane Austen*. Palgrave, 1999.

Ragaz, Sharon Anne. 'Ballantyne, James (1772–1833).' *Oxford Dictionary of National Biography*, 23 Sep. 2004. https://doi-org.ezproxy1.lib.asu.edu/10.1093/ref:odnb/1228

Smith, Goldwin. *The Life of Jane Austen*. London: Walter Scott, 1890.

Tollemache, Lionel Arthur. *Talks with Mr Gladstone*. London: Longmans, Green, and Co., 1898.

West, Rebecca. *The Strange Necessity: Essays by Rebecca West*. Doubleday, 1928.

10

'A PICTURE OF REAL LIFE AND MANNERS'? AUSTEN, BURNEY, AND EDGEWORTH

Linda Bree

In the 'Biographical Notice' of Jane Austen which accompanied the posthumous publication of *Northanger Abbey* and *Persuasion* late in 1817, Henry Austen gave an account of his sister's favourite authors. 'It is difficult to say at what age she was not intimately acquainted with the merits and defects of the best essays and novels in the English language', he wrote. 'Richardson's power of creating, and preserving the consistency of his characters' particularly appealed to her, while she 'did not rank any work of Fielding quite so high … Neither nature, wit, nor humour, could make her amends for so very low a scale of morals' (330).

But in the years of Austen's writing career Samuel Richardson and Henry Fielding, the most prominent novelists of the mid-eighteenth century, were no longer the main touchstones of quality. When Henry Austen wished to praise Austen's writing in its own time he claimed that her novels 'by many have been placed on the same shelf as the works of a D'Arblay and an Edgeworth' (327); and when Austen herself, in *Northanger Abbey*, presented a comprehensive compliment to the novel as a form of writing 'in which the greatest powers of the mind are displayed, in which the most thorough knowledge of human nature, the happiest delineation of its varieties, the liveliest effusions of wit and humour are conveyed to the world in the best chosen language', she chose, as examples of the heights the novel could achieve, not any of the works of Richardson or Fielding, but 'Cecilia, or Camilla, or Belinda' (31).

Cecilia: Or Memoirs of an Heiress (1782) and *Camilla: Or, A Picture of Youth* (1796) were the second and third novels of Frances Burney (who wrote after 1793 under her married name of Madame D'Arblay), following her earliest success of *Evelina: Or the History of a Young Lady's Entrance into the World* (1778); and *Belinda* (1801) was written by Maria Edgeworth. Around the turn of the eighteenth–nineteenth centuries, it was Burney and Edgeworth who were the most prominent, and admired, contemporary novelists in Britain.

Although she cited *Cecilia*, *Camilla*, and *Belinda* together, Austen's literary relationship to Burney and Edgeworth differed widely. Burney was born in 1752, when Henry Fielding and Samuel Richardson were in their prime, and she was heavily influenced by them in her own novelistic development. She drew on Richardson in the epistolary style of *Evelina*, and more generally in her scenes of social life among the aristocracy and gentry. Much of her comedy, however, was influenced by Fielding; 'I describe not Men, but Manners; not an Individual, but a Species', Fielding had famously declared in *Joseph Andrews* (1742) (2.5). Similarly, Burney stated in the Preface of *Evelina* that her aim was 'To draw characters from nature, though not from life, and to mark the manners of

DOI: 10.4324/9780429398155-10-13

the times'. It was conventional—not to mention sensible—for novelists of the time to disclaim any resemblance between their characters and real-life individuals, but Burney was also reflecting a widespread sense that art should be about more than simply copying characters and situations of 'real life'. 'Sentiments, which are merely natural, affect not the Mind with any Pleasure, and seem not worthy to engage our attention … What an insipid Comedy shou'd we make of the Chit-chat of a Tea-table, copy'd faithfully and at full Length?' wrote David Hume in 1742 ('Of Simplicity and Refinement', 2.193). Such notions of privileging a heightened and shaped form of 'nature' led Burney to her distinctive presentation of 'type'-like characters, figures behaving in an entirely predictable way according to the characteristics they embody, and producing comic or dramatic effects when set in comparison or collision with each other in vivid and well-realised scenes and situations.

Austen grew up with Burney's work—*Evelina* was published when she was two, *Cecilia* when she was six—and it is easy to see how Burney's broad comedy, dramatic (sometimes melodramatic) situations and lively dialogue might appeal to the young Austen, as she began to develop her own literary skills. Along with many other readers and reviewers, Austen particularly relished Burney's comic characters, which lent themselves readily to reading aloud: decades later Caroline Austen still had a vivid childhood memory of her aunt Jane reading out the scenes in *Evelina* featuring the vulgar, embarrassing Branghton family, 'and I thought it was like a play' (174). 'Miss J. Austen, Steventon' was a subscriber to Burney's long-awaited third novel *Camilla* in 1796 and she and her sister Cassandra read it immediately, trading quotations from it in their letters to each other that summer.[1]

In addition to her praise of the novel alongside *Cecilia* and *Belinda* Austen refers to *Camilla* in another scene in *Northanger Abbey*. The boastful and stupid John Thorpe, after declaring that all novels except *Tom Jones* (Fielding's most famous work, published in 1749 and by 1800 regarded by many as immoral) and *The Monk* (Matthew Lewis's tale of Gothic horror, notorious since its publication in 1796) are 'the stupidest things in creation', refers particularly to 'that other stupid book, written by that woman they make such a fuss about, she who married the French emigrant'. 'I suppose you mean Camilla?' Catherine Morland ventures.

> Yes, that's the book; such unnatural stuff!—An old man playing at see-saw! … as soon as I heard she had married an emigrant, I was sure I should never be able to get through it … the horridest nonsense you can imagine; there is nothing in the world in it but an old man's playing at see-saw and learning Latin; upon my soul there is not. (43)

Since the incidents mentioned by Thorpe occur in the opening chapters of *Camilla*, Austen was strongly implying that he had read no further; she expects readers to understand both the joke, and the compliment made to Burney's novel as something the John Thorpes of this world are unable to appreciate. Her implicit condemnation of the casual racism of Thorpe's comment about Burney's personal circumstances—with its assumption that *Northanger Abbey*'s readers would know of her marriage to Alexandre D'Arblay—is also telling. And Austen makes a neat compliment to the well-observed domestic scenes early in the novel, which were similar in some ways to those she was offering in *Northanger Abbey*.

But Austen was not an uncritical admirer of Burney's work in *Camilla*. Its essentially straight-forward plot is spun out to immense length by the device of having Dr Marchmont, the hero's mentor, repeatedly frustrating through his cautious advice the possibility of the hero and heroine coming to an understanding with each other; and it seems that Austen, like many other readers, grew impatient with the constant deferrals involved. In one letter Austen tartly advises Cassandra to tell one of their friends that 'I wish whenever she is attached to a young Man, some <u>respectable</u> Dr Marchmont may keep them apart for five Volumes' (5 September 1796; *Letters* 9); and at the end of her copy of the novel she wrote a tiny, testy sequel: 'Since this work went to the Press a Circumstance of some Importance to the happiness of Camilla has taken place, namely that Dr Marchmont has at last died'.[2]

In her own juvenile writings, Austen evidently enjoyed burlesquing, as much as copying, Burney's novels: the hilarious multi-recognition scene in 'Love and Freindship', for example ('Another Grand-child! What an unexpected Happiness is this! to discover in the space of 3 minutes, as many of my Descendants!' [121]), is an exaggerated version of an all-too-frequent situation in the novels of the time, but it appears most obviously as a wicked send-up of the highly sentimental acknowledgement of Evelina by her long-estranged father Sir John Belmont towards the end of Burney's novel.

And although in those of Austen's novels which were first drafted in the 1790s there are echoes of Burneyesque characters—not least John Thorpe himself—Burney's creative achievements did not in the end contribute substantially to Austen's own mature fictional practice. Austen wrote herself out of any serious attempt to emulate Burney in her first published novel *Sense and Sensibility* (1811). Here several characters begin with the potential to provide Burneyesque comedy. Mrs Jennings, for example, the wealthy but vulgar City widow, a source of embarrassment and a figure of fun, is at first sight a plausible descendant of *Evelina*'s Madame Duval. Yet as the novel progresses, the presentation of Mrs Jennings takes an unpredictable turn: she becomes a friendly if not very effective protector to the Dashwood girls, and during Marianne's illness she shows 'a kindness of heart which made Elinor really love her' (348)—and all this without losing any of her vulgarity. Mr Palmer, too—who, like many of Burney's idle young men, cultivates a rude and thoughtless character in order to make himself appear interesting—is found in his own home to be 'very capable of being a pleasant companion', despite still being determined to hide his good qualities as far as possible, so that Elinor 'liked him ... upon the whole much better than she had expected' (345). In each case, in making these relatively minor figures more complex, and creating a thoughtful social relationship between them and Elinor, Austen reduces the 'type' element and disciplines the tone of her narrative from a tendency to caricature into a more gentle comic mode.

Strikingly, Burney distanced herself from the idea that she was writing novels at all. In the late eighteenth century the genre, particularly when attempted by women, was regarded as likely to be of negligible literary merit. Burney clearly wished to avoid being regarded as a novelist, using instead a variety of euphemisms for her fictions, as when she described *Camilla*—with spectacular inaccuracy, considering its five hefty volumes—as 'this little Work' (*Camilla*, Advertisement.)

Austen had no embarrassment about being associated with reading or writing novels. When in 1798 she was invited to subscribe to a local library she wrote scornfully of the proprietor's insistence that she would be stocking not only novels but 'every kind of literature &c &c—She might have spared this pretension to our family, who are great Novel-readers & not ashamed of being so' (18–19 December 1798; *Letters* 27). Long before this, Austen had described various items of her own juvenile writings as novels.[3] And her letters show her enthusiastic enjoyment of a wide range of fictions of all kinds and qualities. She was quite prepared to enter into the spirit of the most preposterous Gothic romance if it were well done: 'We are now in Margiana, & like it very well indeed.—We are just going to set off for Northumberland to be shut up in Widdrington Tower, where there must be two or three sets of Victims already immured under a very fine Villain', she wrote with relish of Henrietta Sykes's now largely forgotten *Margiana: or, Widdrington Tower. A Tale of the Fifteenth Century* (1808) (10–11 January 1809; *Letters* 171). And she had a particular liking for novels that satirised fictional conventions, including Charlotte Lennox's *The Female Quixote* (1752), her 'evening amusement' in January 1807 ('to me a very high one'), and Eaton Stannard Barrett's *The Heroine* (1814): 'I have torn through the 3d vol. ... It is a delightful burlesque, particularly on the Radcliffe style' (7–8 January 1807, 2–3 March 1814; *Letters* 120, 267).

What she found much less easy to tolerate were novels that claimed to be concerned with ordinary life but failed to fulfil any such promise. Sarah Harriet Burney's *Clarentine* (1796) was a major disappointment, 'full of unnatural conduct & forced difficulties, without striking merit of any kind'. So too Laetitia-Matilda Hawkins's *Rosanne: Or, a Father's Labour Lost* (1814): 'There are a thousand improbabilities in the story'. And she was particularly scornful about Mary Brunton's *Self-Control*, perhaps because it was published to much praise in 1811 while her own *Sense and Sensibility* was with the printer: there is surely relief as well as condemnation in her verdict that it was 'an excellently-meant, elegantly-written Work, without anything of Nature or Probability in it' (8–9 February 1807,? late February-early March 1815, 11–12 October 1813; *Letters* 126, 301, 244).

In 1814 Austen's teenage niece Anna was writing a novel of her own and sent a series of draft chapters to her grandmother and aunts Jane and Cassandra, a formidable team of critics, for comment. 'Aunt Jane' responded in a series of letters, and in the process shared some important insights into her own practices as a novelist. In line with her comments on other novels she praises Anna for characters and details that are 'natural' or 'probable'. And she has a particularly sharp eye for language that she condemns as 'thorough novel slang': 'I do not like a Lover's speaking in the 3^d person', she writes; 'it is too much like the formal part of Lord Orville, & I think is not natural' (28 September 1814, mid-July 1814; *Letters* 289, 278).

This critical reference to the speaking style of the hero of Burney's *Evelina* is made, pointedly, on the basis of its lack of 'naturalness'. Alongside the broad comedy of some of her characters, Burney has a tendency, already evident in *Evelina* and increasingly prevalent in her later work, towards ornate and overblown language. The rhetoric of Mortimer Delvile, as he urges Cecilia Beverley to marry him (and after speaking of her, to her face, in the third person), is typical: 'Speak then, my Cecilia! relieve me from the agony of this eternal uncertainty, and tell me your word is invariable as your honour, and tell me my mother gives not her sanction in vain!' (5.195). This is not the kind of language Austen uses in any of her novels: indeed at moments of high drama—as when Emma Woodhouse, hearing Harriet Smith give all-too-plausible reasons for believing that she has gained Mr Knightley's love—Austen's language becomes the reverse of ornate: 'the moment she was gone, this was the spontaneous burst of Emma's feelings: "Oh God! that I had never seen her!"' (448).[4] And while Austen does occasionally employ some of the melodramatic plot twists beloved of Burney, as they had been of Richardson—seductions, abandonments and adultery all feature in her novels—they are described rather than represented, a matter of report rather than part of the main narrative. It is a very Austen touch, for example, that the secret engagement of Frank Churchill and Jane Fairfax, though its tensions are carefully delineated, is never exploited for melodrama between the pair, and is fully revealed only when all its miseries have been resolved, at which point a reaction of Highbury towards the revelation is mild resentment at having been collectively misled. It is all very different from Burney's larger-than-life fictional world.

★★★

Maria Edgeworth, born in 1768, and like Austen an admirer of Burney from childhood, was not herself in print at an early enough age to influence Austen's formative writings: by the time her first semi-fictional work, *Letters for Literary Ladies*, appeared in 1795, Austen had already filled her three notebooks of juvenilia and might have drafted her epistolary novella 'Lady Susan'; and before her full-length fictions were published Austen had produced the early versions of *Sense and Sensibility*, *Pride and Prejudice* and *Northanger Abbey*, and had reached a mature understanding of her own literary craft.

Moreover, Edgeworth and Austen were both finding their fictional voice in a late-eighteenth-century context quite different from that of Burney's youth. Clara Reeve's 1785 definition of fiction as 'a picture of real life and manners, and of the times in which it is written' is well known; less frequently cited is her subsequent comment that such novels should aim 'to represent every scene, in so easy and natural a manner, and to make them appear so probable, as to deceive us into a persuasion (at least while we are reading) that all is real' (1.111). This association of probability with seeming reality is a significant pointer to a development in fictional fashion which, as the century drew to a close, increasingly favoured situations and events which a middle- and upper-class readership could recognise as likely circumstances in their own lives: hence 'natural', 'truthful' and 'probable' become terms of high praise. Along with this came a move to reject the highly dramatic or melodramatic or romantic plots and caricatured 'type' characters which had flourished in the eighteenth century, including in the heightened period of political turmoil in the 1780s and early 1790s in favour of a more closely observed representation of contemporary life, involving characters of increasing psychological complexity (though Edgeworth, at least, never entirely lost the temptation to borrow from melodrama and romance traditions).

Edgeworth was a more formidably intellectual figure than Burney or Austen, and in the early 1800s was widely admired for a range of writing, in both fictional and non-fictional modes. Following *Letters for Literary Ladies* she produced, with her father Richard Lovell Edgeworth (a prominent figure in nearly all her literary activities until his death in 1817), *Practical Education* (1798), a two-volume book of advice on the instruction of children, and *Castle Rackrent* (1800), an original, accomplished, and very funny, fictional account of Irish family fortunes, told through the idiosyncratic voice of a blinkered old steward, Thady Quirk. Then came *Belinda*, her first novel about the activities of the English aristocracy and gentry, which contrasted the brittle glare of London society with more worthwhile domestic ways of life. After *Belinda* she produced a succession of highly popular tales for young and older children, and a series of adult narratives, concerning contemporary life and situations, including notably sympathetic accounts of French gentry and aristocrats both during, and in exile because of, the French Revolution. She became best known, however, for her informative, educational and witty fictions of life in her native Ireland: she specialised in vivid pictures both of the local, all-too-often-absentee, landowning class, and their peasant dependents, who display a distinctly national exuberance while living a bare hand-to-mouth existence. These tales were a revelation in presenting both an engaging fictional narrative and an informed, acutely observed, appraisal of the distinctive Irish social system and the day-to-day lives of those affected by it. Her work influenced many novelists, most notably Walter Scott, who in his own first novel, *Waverley*, went out of his way to identify the difference between 'the admirable Irish portraits drawn by Miss Edgeworth' and the caricatures of Irishmen, 'the "dear joys" who so long, with the most perfect family resemblance to each other, occupied the drama and the novel' (376).

Such portraits could only have been created from a detailed knowledge of originals, which Edgeworth, long settled at Edgeworthstown, the family estate sixty miles inland from Dublin, clearly had. It is no coincidence that when, in 1814, Austen warned her niece to write only about what she knew she chose Ireland as her example: 'Let the Portmans go to Ireland, but as you know nothing of the Manners there, you had better not go with them. You will be in danger of giving false representations' (10–18 August 1814; *Letters* 280). This advice is well in line with Austen's principles in writing fiction, but it is during the course of the same exchange of letters that Austen declares to Anna that 'I have made up my mind to like no Novels, really, but Miss Edgeworth's, Yours & my Own', and she would have been well aware how Edgeworth poured scorn on those who wrote about Ireland from ignorance or prejudice (28 September 1814; *Letters* 289). (This exchange with Anna also surely leads to an in-joke in *Emma*—the novel on which Austen was working during those same months—when Jane Fairfax returns to Highbury instead of going with the Dixons to Ireland, a location ignorance of which allows ample room for lurid speculation from members of the Highbury community, including Emma herself.)

Edgeworth offered Austen a strong example of the power of writing of what she knew. Much of the popularity of *Belinda* came from what was widely recognised as its accurate depiction of the speech and habits of the English gentry and aristocracy in their everyday lives. Moreover, the narrative of *Belinda* not only offered a convincing picture of 'high life', but also engaged with issues more often faced in real life than within the pages of a novel. One such topic was illness, and horror of illness, explored by Edgeworth with sensitivity through the travails of the socialite Lady Delacour. Another was the question of the importance of a first love in a woman's life. In the novel one of the reasons for Lady Delacour's unhappiness is that she compares her husband unfavourably with the memory of her first, lost, love, Mr Percival. But—though Lady Delacour finds this impossible to credit—Percival, having once loved her sincerely, has gone on to have a very happy marriage with someone else. During the course of the novel Belinda herself, having found to her regret that the man to whom she is attracted, Clarence Hervey, does not seem willing or likely to propose marriage, is courted by another suitor, Augustus Vincent. This prompts a serious exploration of the issue of the power of first and subsequent loves, initially through a long discussion between Belinda and Lady Anne Percival, who is supporting Augustus' suit, and then through a series of events in which Belinda gradually comes to believe that respect can be the foundation of affection and agrees to marry Vincent.

Belinda discovers, on the eve of her wedding, that Vincent is addicted to gambling; at the same time Hervey is released from a youthful entanglement to reveal his love for Belinda; and so the first loves are reunited. Despite this, the reviewers—otherwise generally positive about both the novel and its author—were horrified. 'Old as we are … we have still so much romance within us, as to deem the virgin's first love an almost sacred bond', declared the *Monthly Review*, 'we should have been better pleased to have seen [Belinda] in the weeds of widowed affection, than in the gay attire of a second courtship' (368–74). The *Critical Review* sniffed that Belinda 'transfers her affections from Mr Hervey to Mr Vincent, and from Mr Vincent back again to Mr Hervey, with as much *sang froid* as she would unhang her cloak from one peg and hang it upon another' (235–37). Both reviewers regarded Belinda's actions as a fatal blot on her character, and therefore on the novel as a whole. Astonishingly, Edgeworth was so stung by these criticisms that in later editions of *Belinda* she made revisions—at considerable cost to the internal coherence of the narrative—to show that her heroine, despite the encouragement and good intentions of Lady Anne, was never able to alter her affections sufficiently to allow her to accept a second suitor.

The sacred nature of a 'first love' was a firmly established fictional convention (it is unquestioned in the case of the heroines of Burney's four novels), and the gap between 'truth to nature' or 'probability' and fictional acceptability is graphically apparent here. The question is one which must often have been faced by real young women—and men—at a time when, by convention, a woman was not supposed to express any affection for a lover unless and until he first expressed affection for her, and when many a first love must have withered in a mist of ignorance and misunderstanding. It is significant, therefore, that when Austen took on the topic too in *Sense and Sensibility*, just possibly (at least in her revision stages) with *Belinda* in mind, she sidestepped the issue of what might be acceptable in a fictional heroine by her much lighter narrative touch and a breezy assumption of common understanding.

The subject is raised in conversation between Elinor Dashwood and Colonel Brandon, who, attracted to Elinor's sister Marianne, sees with regret Marianne's obvious love for Willoughby:

> 'Your sister, I understand, does not approve of second attachments.'
> 'No', replied Elinor, 'her opinions are all romantic.'
> 'Or rather, as I believe, she considers them impossible to exist.'
> 'I believe she does. But how she contrives it without reflecting on the character of her own father, who had himself two wives, I know not.' (66)

Having thus established, almost in passing, the illogicality of fetishising 'first love', the narrative goes on to show that the tragic failure of Marianne's love for Willoughby—a warm and genuine passion—does not blight her life. The narrator even takes a teasing tone, in an echo of the fictional burlesques at which Austen had become so adept: 'Instead of falling a sacrifice to an irresistible passion, as once she had fondly flattered herself with expecting', Marianne turns after all to Brandon:

> Marianne Dashwood was born ... to discover the falsehood of her own opinions, and to counteract, by her conduct, her most favourite maxims. She was born to overcome an affection formed so late in life as at seventeen, and with no sentiment superior to strong esteem and lively friendship, voluntarily to give her hand to another ... (429)

But the narrator's final comments on Marianne's turn from her first love to a second are, though measured, quite free of irony. Having married Brandon, Marianne's 'whole heart became, in time, as much devoted to her husband, as it had once been to Willoughby' (430).

The difference in the treatment of the theme by the two authors may be related to Edgeworth's earnest insistence on *Belinda* as a 'Moral Tale', and the requirement therefore for her heroine to offer a moral example. Throughout her writing career Edgeworth saw her fictions as, to a very large extent, vehicles for moral lessons which she intended to have practical effects on her readers. This was of course by no means unusual, but Edgeworth was a much more skilful writer than other didactic novelists of the time and had a much greater talent for entertaining the reader more interested in an engaging tale than a moral message. The extent to which she was able to maintain this tricky balance in her writing is judged in a perceptive comment from the critic Francis Jeffrey, reviewing her achievements in 1812:

> if we were to select any one of the traits that are indicated by her writings as peculiarly characteristic, and peculiarly entitled to praise, we should specify the singular force of judgment and self-denial, which has enabled her to resist the temptation of being the most brilliant and fashionable writer of her day, in order to be the most useful and instructive. (*Edinburgh Review* 103)

This may seem to the modern reader a very back-handed compliment, yet it catches something essential about a writer steering a course between the well-established idea of fiction being a suitable vehicle for entertaining moral improvement and newer notions of fiction being a valuable end in itself in being able to represent the psychological complexity of modern life. The inevitable contradictions between these two aims are often evident in Edgeworth's fiction. She had a fondness for including in her novels the kind of aphorism that may tend to make a modern reader feel coerced—'How wisely has Providence made the benevolent and generous passions the most pleasurable!' (397) is a typical example from *Belinda*—and at the ends of her novels the good, or repentant, triumph and the evil, or errant, or those who cannot overcome their own weaknesses, inevitably come to a miserable end.

Austen's approach is quite different. Aphorisms in her novels, where they appear, tend to be ironic: 'My Emma, does not every thing serve to prove more and more the beauty of truth and sincerity in all our dealings with each other?' (486) is not only put into the mouth of Mr Knightley rather than made with the authority of the narrator, but it is undercut by the knowledge—on the part of both Emma and the reader—that Mr Knightley is not the beneficiary of 'truth and sincerity' in the circumstances he is commenting upon, thus rendering the comment, and the sentiment, slightly foolish. And while nothing could be more morally powerful, in its way, than—say—Emma's reflections on her conduct with regard to Miss Bates, or the verdict on the education of the Bertram sisters in *Mansfield Park*, Austen's moral intentions press much less insistently on her narratives than do those of Edgeworth. Indeed, it is striking that the ample list of qualities with which Austen dignifies the novel in *Northanger Abbey*, while prominently including 'the most thorough knowledge of human nature', does not mention morality. At the end of *Mansfield Park* the narrator is 'impatient to restore every body, not greatly in fault themselves, to tolerable comfort, and to have done with all the rest' (533). In *Sense and Sensibility* she goes further, associating moralising with fictional convention and turning her back on both: Willoughby, who has seduced and abandoned Colonel Brandon's ward and betrayed Marianne's love and trust, is doomed indeed to a loveless marriage; 'But that he was for ever inconsolable, that he fled from society, or contracted an habitual gloom of temper, or died of a broken heart, must not be depended on ... His wife was not always out of humour, nor his home always uncomfortable' (430). And in the final chapter of *Persuasion* the narrator admits, of the outcome, 'This may be bad morality to conclude with, but I believe it to be truth' (270), which is about as neat a distillation as could be offered of how Austen regarded the rival claims of the two concepts, in the context of the novels she was writing.

But Edgeworth's fiction was not always dominated by insistent moral intention either. Take, for example, the opening of *Belinda*:

> Mrs. Stanhope, a well-bred woman, accomplished in that branch of knowledge, which is called the art of rising in the world, had, with but a small fortune, contrived to live in the highest company. She prided herself upon having established half a dozen nieces most happily; that is to say, upon having married them to men of fortunes far superiour to their own. One niece still remained unmarried—Belinda Portman, of whom she was determined to get rid with all convenient expedition. (7)

Such an opening does not seem likely to herald a heavy-handed moral tale: and so it largely proves. The distinctive narrative voice is here ironic rather than didactic. The deceptively authoritative proposition of the first sentence (which shares something of the tone of the famous opening of *Pride and Prejudice*, 'It is a truth universally acknowledged, that a single man in possession of a good fortune, must be in want of a wife'), the shift from Mrs Stanhope's expressed pride in her achievement to the revealingly gross 'get rid', and the neat way the initial circumstance of the novel is outlined, and the heroine introduced, all suggest that a novelist of wit and skill is at work. Throughout the novel, human nature and human failings are frequently observed with amusement, as when Annabella Luttridge, keen to transfer Vincent's attentions from Belinda to herself, ostentatiously expresses sadness at his departure: 'It would be injustice to omit, that she did all that could be done by a cambric handkerchief, to evince delicate sensibility in this parting scene' (389).

Above all there is the figure of Lady Delacour, one of the most impressive and interesting characters in the fiction of the time. Lady Delacour is the society hostess with whom Belinda spends a winter season, and through whom she comes to see the hollowness of brilliant social success, if achieved without the solid support of a happy domestic existence. Belinda's moral journey is seemingly devoid of much temptation to deviate, and its conclusion is a conventionally moral one, which would not in itself be out of place in many other novels of the period equally concerned to condemn the public display of high life in favour of modest and private domestic happiness (a common trope around the turn of the eighteenth-nineteenth century, closely related to the increasingly domestic tendencies of the novel itself). But any coercive sense of didacticism in the tale as a whole is removed by Lady Delacour herself, who dominates every scene in which she appears, with her wit, her cynicism, her brilliance and her mercurial temperament—not to mention her exuberant pleasure in words and wordplay (a feature which must have particularly appealed to Austen). It is true that she bears some of the force of the moral of the novel—eventually repenting and reforming, and becoming physically healed from the 'cancer' in her breast in the process—but the force of her personality wrenches the narrative out of any moral straitjacket. 'I must confess to you', she tells Belinda, that during these last four years I should have died of ennui if I had not been kept alive by my hatred of Mrs Luttridge, and of my husband—I don't know which I hate most—O, yes I do—I certainly hate Mrs Luttridge the most—for a woman can always hate a woman more than she can hate a man, unless she has been in love with him—which I never was with poor Lord Delacour.—Yes! I certainly hate Mrs Luttridge the most—I cannot count the number of extravagant things I have done on purpose to eclipse her. (57)

The unpredictable movement of Lady Delacour's quick mind as reflected in the volatile rhythms of her speech, the daring and deliberate iconoclasm of her sentiments, the passing sense of self-reflection and even self-criticism, the layers of meaning behind the throwaway 'poor' to describe her husband, all contribute to the overall effect of the workings—however perverse—of an intelligent and lively mind. The nearest thing to this in Austen's works is probably Lady Susan, almost certainly created before Austen read any Edgeworth ('My dear Alicia, of what a mistake were you guilty in marrying a Man of his age!—just old enough to be formal, ungovernable & to have the Gout—too old to be agreable, & too young to die' ['Lady Susan' 62]), but for all Lady Susan's brilliance Lady Delacour is by far the more complex character in psychological terms, not least because beneath her faults and errant behaviour she has warm affections, a fine intellect, and a conscience, all of which demand to be taken seriously.

As part of her design Edgeworth took great pains to establish the authenticity of her characters and situations. She did this partly through buttressing her fictions with a substantial quantity of fact. In *Castle Rackrent* she even offers a glossary of terms to give evidence and information about words and situations in her narrative with which her non-Irish readers may be unfamiliar. In *Belinda* she sets her characters firmly in a detailed presentation of contemporary life: reference is made to a wide range of actual places and events of the London of the late 1790s; current and classic literature popular with the elite of the time is cited; newspapers of the day are quoted; and the narrative contains a number of footnotes averring that a particular saying or situation is 'A fact!' (416) or 'Taken from real life' (137).

But, as Edgeworth discovered, factual correctness can be a treacherous commodity in a novel that aims at probability as well as truth to nature, and the relationship of fact to fiction was something that troubled her throughout her writing life. She once admitted that 'Wherever I brought in *bodily* unaltered, as I have sometimes done, facts from real life, or sayings, or recorded observations of my own, I have almost always found them objected to by good critics as unsuited to the character, or in some way *de trop*' (*A Memoir of Maria Edgeworth*, 3.150). (Her father complained in the same vein that several of the incidents in *Belinda* 'which were founded on fact, have always been blamed as improbable' [25 July 1809; Letter to Etienne Dumont].)

Edgeworth's most direct confrontation with the issue of fact versus fictional plausibility came in her 1814 novel *Patronage*. One of the main strands of the plot is dramatically resolved in a courtroom scene, where the coin under the seal of a punitive contract is found to be of more recent date than the contract itself, thereby proving the document a forgery and vindicating the protagonist's family. *Patronage* was not as successful as most of Edgeworth's earlier fictions, with reviewers criticising particularly both her inaccurate knowledge of the law, and the incident of the coin, which was dismissed as implausible. Edgeworth protested that the coin incident was true: indeed, it had happened to her own grandfather.[5]

Austen, attempting like Edgeworth to write fictions more 'like life' than their predecessors, faced the same challenge in the relationship between accuracy, truth, probability and plausibility. She worked hard to ensure factual accuracy in the smallest detail in her novels. When she felt she had got the Dashwoods' rather complicated legal situation in the early pages of *Sense and Sensibility* muddled, she checked her facts and quietly adjusted wording in the second edition of the novel. In commenting on Anna Austen's draft chapters she was equally scrupulous: Anna's characters 'must be <u>two</u>

days going from Dawlish to Bath; They are nearly 100 miles apart'; and 'the Introduction between Lord P. & his Brother, & Mr Griffin' should be deleted since 'A Country Surgeon ... would not be introduced to Men of their rank' (10–18 August 1814; *Letters* 280). Like Edgeworth, Austen sets her fictions in the contemporary world, among the classes of people with whom, and with whose thoughts and activities, she is familiar. Like Edgeworth, she supports the plausibility of the characters and plots by setting them in known locations, including not only London and Bath, but also Lyme, Portsmouth and even a local beauty spot such as Box Hill. Complex social relationships are carefully drawn: the supercilious ridiculing of the Irish social climber Lady Clonbrony by the English aristocracy in Edgeworth's *The Absentee* (1811), for example, has much in common with the ridiculing of Mrs Bennet by the Bingley sisters. But Austen does not back up her statements with an authorial or narratorial assertion of factual truth (indeed, her narrators rarely take on a tone of authority); and on the relatively few occasions that she reaches outside her fictions to other literature—as in John Thorpe's reference to *Camilla* or Captain Benwick in *Persuasion* feeding his grief by reading the poetry of Scott and Byron—the references arise naturally from the conversation and situations of the characters concerned.

And when it comes to balancing fact and fictional plausibility, Austen's instinct is more sure than Edgeworth's. As she wrote to Anna, referring to an incident comparable to that of the coin in *Patronage*:

> I have scratched out Sir Tho: from walking with the other Men to the Stables &c the very day after his breaking his arm—for though I find your Papa did walk out immediately after his arm was set, I think it can be so little usual as to appear unnatural in a book. (10–18 August 1814; *Letters* 280)

★★★

Austen had a copy of *Emma* sent to Edgeworth, but any hopes she may have had that her new novel would impress the more famous novelist were not fulfilled. Edgeworth wrote to her brother and sister-in-law that the first volume had arrived ahead of the others and, having read it, she had no desire for more. She found it dull:

> ... there was no story except that Miss Emma found the man whom she designed for Harriet's lover was an admirer of her own—and he was affronted at being refused by Emma—and Harriet wore the willow—and <u>smooth thin water gruel</u> is according to Emma's father's opinion a very good thing & it is very difficult to make a cook understand what you mean by <u>smooth thin water gruel</u>! (January 1816; *Maria Edgeworth's Letters* 199)

Of course Edgeworth, since she had not read volumes two and three of *Emma*, had no idea of the deeper game Austen was playing in the novel; but her comment (unnervingly reminiscent of John Thorpe's verdict on *Camilla*) shows how carefully the representation of 'ordinary' life had to be balanced against entertainment value in fiction, even for a reader sympathetic to the principles involved, if 'probability' were not to degenerate into outright 'dullness'. Yet Edgeworth had enjoyed *Mansfield Park* (the beginning of which she had found 'like real life and very entertaining') (December 1814; *Maria Edgeworth's Letters* 188). And though she later dismissed *Northanger Abbey* as 'one of the most stupid nonsensical fiction[s] I ever read (excepting always the praises of myself and Lady Delacour)', criticising General Tilney's actions in sending Catherine home as 'quite outrageously out of nature', she responded warmly to *Persuasion*, which 'appears to me in all that relates to poor Anne & her loves to be exceedingly interesting & natural—The love & lover admirably well drawn so that we feel it is quite real' (21 February 1818; *Maria Edgeworth's Letters* 224). And she changed her mind about *Emma*: exactly twenty years after her comments on *Northanger Abbey* and *Persuasion*, when she was entering her 70s, and Austen was long dead, she wrote that her niece 'has read in the evenings Emma all through & Pride & Prejudice—And I liked them better than ever' (21 February 1838; *Maria Edgeworth's Letters* 369).

Austen would surely have been gratified at these compliments offered to her work by the most prominent novelist of her day. But by the time of Edgeworth's death in 1849 late eighteenth and early nineteenth century literary reputations had begun to alter. When, in 1870, Austen's nephew, the by-then elderly James Edward Austen-Leigh, remarked that if the Austen family's neighbours 'had known that we, in our secret thoughts, classed her with Madame D'Arblay or Miss Edgeworth … they would have considered it an amusing instance of family conceit', his view, to most of his readers, would have seemed quaint (Austen-Leigh 167). In 1881 John Cross, in writing the life of his recently dead wife George Eliot, began with a summary of literary life in 1819, the year of her birth:

> Byron had four years, and Goethe had thirteen years, still to live. The last of Miss Austen's novels had been published only eighteen months, and the first of the Waverley series only six years before. (1.6)

The British novelists who now helped define the period were Walter Scott and Jane Austen.

In fact, the huge popularity of Scott's writing, containing a much larger element of romance, along with a more muscular sense of public life and historical forces, than anything in Burney, Edgeworth or Austen, single-handedly turned the novel in another new direction from 1814, to a large extent eclipsing the novel of domestic realism in the process. Yet Scott had been influenced by Edgeworth and was himself an early admirer of Austen. His article on *Emma* in the *Quarterly Review* of October 1815 is the first authoritative appreciation of Austen's work as a novelist, and pondering her achievement more privately in 1826, after reading *Pride and Prejudice* 'for the third time at least', he wrote that she 'had a talent for describing the involvements, and feelings, and characters of ordinary life, which is to me the most wonderful I ever met with. The big Bow-Wow strain I can do myself like any now going; but the exquisite touch, which renders ordinary commonplace things and characters interesting, from the truth of the description and the sentiment, is denied to me' (Lockhart 6.264). Scott here identified precisely the qualities—at the same time modest and highly ambitious—that Austen worked so hard and so unobtrusively to achieve, and which were instrumental in her work being increasingly admired and read while the names of Burney and Edgeworth, the novelists she herself learned from and admired, sank into relative obscurity.

Notes

1 The subscribers paid a guinea in advance, to cover the costs of publication, and received their copies immediately on publication; their names were listed in the front of the volume. Subscribers to *Camilla* included Maria Edgeworth as well as Jane Austen.

2 Jane Austen's copy of *Camilla* is held in the Bodleian Library, Oxford. The comment was made in pencil, and the words cannot now easily be deciphered, even with the assistance of a magnifying glass.

3 See for example the first two pieces in Volume the First of her juvenilia, 'Frederic and Elfrida, a novel' and 'Jack and Alice, a novel', tentatively dated 1787 and 1790 respectively by Peter Sabor (*Juvenilia* 4, 13, xxviii).

4 The echo of Wordsworth's declaration, in the preface to the second edition of *Lyrical Ballads* (1800), that 'all good poetry is the spontaneous overflow of powerful feelings' associates Austen with a later and quite different register of language and thought from that employed by Burney.

5 The incident is described in an early section of *Memoirs of Richard Lovell Edgeworth, Esq. … Concluded by His Daughter* (2 vols, 1820), 1.16–18, written before the publication of *Patronage*.

Works Cited

Austen, Caroline. 'My Aunt Jane Austen: A Memoir' (1867), reproduced in J. E. Austen-Leigh, *A Memoir of Jane Austen and Other Family Recollections*, edited by Kathryn Sutherland. Oxford UP, 2002.

Austen, Henry. 'Biographical Notice of the Author.' *Northanger Abbey and Persuasion* (1817), reproduced in *Persuasion*, edited by Janet Todd and Antje Blank. Cambridge UP, 2006.

Austen, Jane. *Emma*. 1816, edited by Richard Cronin and Dorothy McMillan. Cambridge UP, 2005.

Austen, Jane. *Jane Austen's Letters*, 4th ed., edited by Deirdre Le Faye. Oxford UP, 2011.

Austen, Jane. 'Love and Freindship.' *Juvenilia*, edited by Peter Sabor. Cambridge UP, 2006.

Austen, Jane. 'Lady Susan' in *Later Manuscripts*, edited by Janet Todd and Linda Bree. Cambridge UP, 2008.

Austen, Jane. *Mansfield Park*. 1814, edited by John Wiltshire. Cambridge UP, 2005.

Austen, Jane. *Northanger Abbey*. 1817, edited by Barbara M. Benedict and Deirdre Le Faye. Cambridge UP, 2006.

Austen, Jane. *Sense and Sensibility* (1811), edited by Edward Copeland. Cambridge UP, 2006.

Austen-Leigh, James Edward. *A Memoir of Jane Austen*. London: Richard Bentley, 1870.

Burney, Frances. *Camilla or a Picture of Youth*. London: Payne, Cadell and Davies, 1796.

Burney, Frances. *Cecilia, or Memoirs of an Heiress*. London: Payne and Cadell, 1782.

Burney, Frances. *Evelina, or the History of a Young Lady's Entrance into the World*. London: Thomas Lowndes, 1778.

Cross, J. W. *George Eliot's Life, as Related in Her Letters and Journals*. London: William Blackwood and Sons, 1885.

Edgeworth, Frances Beaufort. *A Memoir of Maria Edgeworth, with a Selection from Her Letters*, edited by her children. Unpublished, 1867.

Edgeworth, Maria. *Belinda* (1801), edited by Linda Bree. Oxford UP, 2020.

Edgeworth, Maria. *Maria Edgeworth's Letters from Ireland*, selected and edited by Valerie Pakenham. Lilliput P, 2018.

Edgeworth, Richard Lovell. 'To Etienne Dumont, 25 July 1809.' ms Dumont 33. ii.f.22v, Bibliothèque de Genève.

Edgeworth, Richard Lovell, and Maria Edgeworth. *Memoirs of Richard Lovell Edgeworth, Esq. … Concluded by his Daughter*. London: R. Hunter and Baldwin, Cradock, and Joy, 1820.

Fielding, Henry. *The History of the Adventures of Joseph Andrews and His Friend Mr Abraham Adams*. London: Andrew Millar, 1742.

Hume, David. 'Of Simplicity and Refinement.' *Essays, Moral and Political*. Edinburgh: Alexander Kincaid, 1742.

Jeffrey, Francis. 'Miss Edgeworth's *Tales of Fashionable Live*.' *Edinburgh Review*, 1812, vol. 20, pp. 100–126.

Lockhart, John Gibson. *Memoirs of the Life of Sir Walter Scott*. Edinburgh: R. Cadell, 1837–1838.

'Review of *Belinda*.' *The Monthly Review, or Literary Journal, Enlarged*, vol. 37. London: R. Griffiths, April 1802, pp. 368–374.

'Review of *Belinda*.' *The Critical Review, or Annals of Literature*, 2nd series, vol. 34. London: W. Simpin and R. Marshall, February 1802, pp. 235–237.

Reeve, Clara. *The Progress of Romance*. Colchester: W. Keymer, 1785.

Scott, Walter. 'A Postscript That Should Have Been a Preface.' *Waverley, or 'Tis Sixty Years Since* (1814), edited by Claire Lamont. Oxford UP, 1986.

11

JANE AUSTEN AND THE GEORGIAN NOVEL

Elaine Bander

DAWSON COLLEGE

Jane Austen, born a generation after the publication of the first great English novels of Samuel Richardson and Henry Fielding, was fortunate in her family. Like Catherine Morland in *Northanger Abbey*, she had a clever mother who encouraged her reading; like Elizabeth Bennet in *Pride and Prejudice*, she enjoyed access to her scholarly father's extensive library and shared her thoughts with a beloved older sister. Her sophisticated older brothers, James and Henry, students at Oxford, guided her reading and formed her taste much as Edmund Bertram did for his young cousin Fanny Price in *Mansfield Park* (Austen-Leigh et al. 54). Clearly Jane Austen was nurtured within a family of serious, reflective readers.

The evidence of Austen's fiction and letters shows, moreover, that in addition to being widely read in the respectable 'improving' genres of history, biography, poetry, travels, essays, moral philosophy, and sermons, the Austen family also happily consumed popular novels at a time when critics, educators, moralists, and even most novelists treated the genre with disdain. Austen's gossipy letters to her sister Cassandra regularly report on the popular novels that the Austen ladies read aloud after dinner as their 'evening amusement' (7 January 1807; *Letters* 120). Even her clergyman father, like Henry Tilney in *Northanger Abbey*, had pleasure in a good novel, for Jane Austen mentions his enjoying a library copy of Francis Lathom's 1798 'German [i.e. gothic] story', *The Midnight Bell*, while the Austens were travelling during October 1798 (24 October 1798; *Letters* 15). Shortly after her twenty-third birthday the following year, Austen derides the local lending-library organiser's claims 'that her Collection is not to consist only of Novels, but of every kind of Literature &c &c', boasting, 'She might have spared this pretension to our family, who are great Novel-readers & not ashamed of being so;—but it was necessary I suppose to the self-consequence of half her Subscribers' (18 December 1798; *Letters* 27).

Around the time that Austen made that remark, she was working on an early version of *Northanger Abbey*, published posthumously in 1818 (LeFaye xvii–xviii), in which she mocks the pretensions of those whose self-consequence is less robust. Her narrator denounces 'the common cant' that dismisses as mere 'trash' those novels 'in which the greatest powers of the mind are displayed, in which the most thorough knowledge of human nature, the happiest delineation of its varieties, the liveliest effusions of wit and humour are conveyed to the world in the best chosen language', illustrating such 'common cant' with a dialogue in which a 'young lady' is asked, 'And what are you reading, Miss_____?', to which she replies, "'Oh! it is only a novel!"'… while she lays down her book with *affected indifference*, or *momentary shame*' (*NA* 31, my emphasis). Remarkably, the Austen family neither affected indifference nor expressed shame about enjoying novels.

DOI: 10.4324/9780429398155-11-14

All novels, however, were not equal. Jane Austen read widely but not indiscriminately. Margaret Anne Doody notes that while Austen was no scholar (for her novels are uniquely devoid of classical references, nor does she, like other novelists, quote 'Ariosto, Tasso, or Metastasio'),[1] prose fiction was another matter: 'Her letters move easily into allusions to novels, often in matters so minute as to prove an extraordinary knowledge' (Doody 555–57). Austen alludes to popular novels much like male writers cite the classics by quoting Latin and Greek tags. Without Latin or Greek herself, Doody argues, Austen's critical energies were focused on her rigorous analysis of novels: 'For her a whole judgment does not get made on a first reading; novels are allowed a second trial and are supposed to bear the weight of reperusal' (Doody 357). Thus Austen reports to Cassandra, 'We are reading Clarentine [Sarah Harriet Burney's 1796 novel], & are surprised to find how foolish it is. I remember liking it much less on a 2^d reading than at the 1st & it does not bear a 3^d at all. It is full of unnatural conduct & forced difficulties, without striking merit of any kind' (8 February 1807; *Letters* 125–26). While Austen read other, more 'serious', works, novels provoked her highest critical and creative energies. Doody concludes, 'Read aloud, then reread, novels formed her mind so that she could re-form the novel' (Doody 357–58).

Kathryn Sutherland similarly points out how popular novels intellectually empowered women like Austen: 'Denied access to serious institutions of learning, women discovered in the novel at this time a space for informed social comment and political engagement, as well as for entertainment'. Moreover, she argues, 'If Austen's fiction is a sustained dialogue with and allusive critique of the contemporary novel, it is so on terms which endorse the genre's high social and moral purpose even as they satirize its more extravagant effects' (Sutherland, 'Invention' 250). Novels were in effect Austen's academy, affording her rigorous intellectual engagement with the world of ideas.

Ever thrifty, Austen found uses even for poorly written novels. Living as they did on a restricted income in a quiet country neighbourhood, the Austen family were in the habit of turning otherwise tiresome books and neighbours into sources of entertainment, as Jane demonstrates in a letter to Cassandra written while she was working on *Emma*: 'Miss Milles was queer as usual & provided us with plenty to laugh at. She undertook in three words to give us the history of Mrs Sudamore's reconciliation, & then talked on about it for half an hour, using such odd expressions & so foolishly minute that I could hardly keep my countenance' (26 October 1813; *Letters* 255). A silly novel, like a silly person, also had its uses, although perhaps not the uses its author intended. Austen tells her sister, 'I am looking over Self Control again, & my opinion is confirmed of its' being an excellently-meant, elegantly-written Work, without anything of Nature or Probability in it' (11 October, 1813; *Letters* 244). Austen chooses to reread Mary Brunton's 1811 novel even though, since 'Nature' and 'Probability' are among her highest criteria for novels, she believes it risible. Later she mocks *Self Control* in a letter to her niece Anna Lefroy, jokingly promising to write 'a close Imitation of "Self-control" as soon as I can;—I will I improve upon it;—my Heroine shall not merely be wafted down an American river in a boat by herself, she shall cross the Atlantic in the same way, & never stop till she reaches Gravesent' (24 November 1814; *Letters* 295). Living in a world with few novelties or diversions, Austen was prepared to mend-and-make-do by transforming a silly novel into an entertaining burlesque.

Her habit of repurposing bits of novels carries over into her earliest writings. As Isobel Grundy observes, 'From an early age she read like a potential author. She looked for what she could use—not by quietly absorbing and reflecting it, but by actively engaging, rewriting, often mocking it' (Grundy 190). Her first compositions therefore take the form of amusing parodic responses to her family's shared reading, while in her later published novels, she presumes that her readers share her familiarity with the conventional plots, rhetoric, and characters of other novelists even as she undermines their expectations that her own novels will follow those conventions.

By the time Austen began composing her own works, the plots of sentimental or courtship novels had become as conventional as those of a Golden Age detective novel: a genteel, accomplished, principled, country-bred young lady of sixteen or seventeen, often of obscure or apparently illegitimate birth, enters the fashionable world where her striking loveliness attracts eager suitors, some desirable, some dangerous; the heroine sheds copious tears and endures many vicissitudes of courtship and seduction, hindered by her dubious social status or complicated by her untrustworthy guardians, sometimes in consequence of attacks upon her person and reputation by predatory men and jealous women. Often she succumbs to fainting, serious illness, or temporary madness. These adventures test her virtue and fortitude, provoking her to high-minded speeches. She endures the agony of having to choose between love and duty until, after three, four, or five volumes, her enemies are exposed and punished while she is discovered to be of high birth and of unimpeachable virtue, whereupon she is restored to family and fortune and safely and happily wed to the handsome, high-born, worthy, and usually wealthy young man whom she has loved since the first volume. These novels, moreover, frequently contained embedded narratives: digressions sometimes several chapters long in which secondary characters recount tales of their lives and tribulations.[2] With some variation from novel to novel, such was the novel-plot that Austen mocked throughout her lifetime, even as she adopted, domesticated, tested, and remade it.[3]

Were the novels of the long eighteenth century to disappear, their existence and characteristics could be inferred from Austen's own writing. Her personal letters are full of one-sentence parodic plots such as her remark to Cassandra explaining why she has had to pass up an opportunity to travel with her brother Frank as the necessary escort, a plan that depended on her being able to stay unannounced with friends: 'for if the Pearsons were not at home, I should inevitably fall a Sacrifice to the arts of some fat Woman who would make me drunk with Small Beer' (18 September 1796; *Letters* 12); or her congratulations to her nephew upon his leaving Winchester College: 'Now you may own, how miserable you were there; now, it will gradually all come out—your Crimes & your Miseries—how often you went up by the Mail to London & threw away Fifty Guineas at a Tavern, & how often you were on the point of hanging yourself' (16–17 December 1816; *Letters* 336–37). Austen is quick to note conventions, tropes, and clichés to be incorporated into her own comic writing.

Her earliest exuberant juvenilia, probably composed between 1787 and 1792 to entertain her family and closest friends (Sabor xxviii–xxiv), were filled with hilariously inappropriate passions that mock some of the wilder elements of libertine seduction tales by early women writers. First appearing during the Restoration, these so-called amatory novels by popular, prolific female authors like Aphra Behn (1640–1689), Delarivier Manley (1663?–1724), and Eliza Haywood (1693–1756) were unabashed tales of sexual adventures in high life, often called 'secret histories' or 'true histories' because, like the seventeenth-century French romances by Madeleine de Scudéry (1607–1701) from which they were derived, their characters were sometimes based on public figures disguised as historic or invented ones. These tales from a more libertine age were largely forgotten by the mid-eighteenth century, their scandalous adventures replaced by more realistic, bourgeois fiction with explicit moral purpose.[4] Austen's late juvenilia novella, *Lady Susan,* according to Ros Ballaster, is thus a 'relic of late seventeenth- and early eighteenth-century amatory fiction' (210). Only in the second half of the twentieth century have feminist scholars restored these amatory writers, famous in their own day, to renewed prominence in the history of the English novel.[5]

Austen's frequently violent, logic-defying plots in her juvenilia spoof the episodic, digressive, bawdy novels of Henry Fielding (1707–1754) and Tobias Smollett (1721–1771), whose picaresque plots contain romance-like improbable coincidences and feature flawed but good-natured, attractive heroes, called 'mixed' because they were neither exemplary models of virtue nor entirely evil villains. Still other works of Austen's juvenilia mock the emotional excesses of characters in sentimental novels by writers like Samuel Richardson (1689–1781), Laurence Sterne (1713–1768), Henry Brooke (1703–1783), Henry Mackenzie (1745–1831), and Frances Burney (1752–1840).[6]

Austen's first known attempt at realist fiction with a recognisably Austenian heroine is the fragment 'Catharine, or the Bower', the final work in *Volume the Third* of Austen's juvenilia, dated

1792 in the manuscript and slightly amended in subsequent years (Sabor xxxii). 'Catharine' also contains an allusion to popular poet and novelist Charlotte Turner Smith (1749–1806).[7] Young Catharine Percival (sometimes spelled 'Catherine'—she is also called 'Kitty Peterson') is an orphan living with her overly protective maiden aunt Mrs Percival (sometimes called 'Mrs Peterson') whose morbid 'apprehension of her marrying imprudently' keeps Catharine socially isolated (*Juvenilia* 246). Catharine therefore looks forward to meeting Camilla Stanley, an expensively but shallowly educated young lady whose family, distant relations, have come to visit Mrs Percival. Camilla, the narrator relates, had 'an Understanding unimproved by reading and a Mind totally devoid either of Taste or Judgement … . She professed a love of Books without Reading' (*Juvenilia* 248), as Catharine soon discovers:

> 'You have read Mrs Smith's Novels, I suppose?' said she to her Companion—. 'Oh! Yes, replied the other, and I am quite delighted with them—They are the sweetest things in the world—' 'And which do you prefer of them?' 'Oh! dear, I think there is no comparison between them—Emmeline is *so much* better than any of the others—'

> 'Many people think so, I know; but there does not appear so great a disproportion in their Merits to *me*; do you think it is better written?'

> 'Oh! I do not know anything about *that*—but it is better in *everything*—Besides, Ethelinde is so long—' 'That is a very common Objection I beleive, said Kitty, but for my own part, if a book is well written, I always find it too short'.

> 'So do I, only I get tired of it before it is finished'. 'But did not you find the story of Ethelinde very interesting? And the Descriptions of Grasmere, are not they Beautiful?' 'Oh! I missed them all, because I was in such a hurry to know the end of it—' (*Juvenilia* 249)

Camilla then changes the topic to her family's upcoming tour to the Lakes, and Mrs Smith's novels are forgotten.

Smith, significantly, is the only contemporary author cited in Austen's juvenilia (Southam 10), and not once but twice, because in her 'History of England' Austen refers to 'Frederic Delamere', the impetuous, self-indulgent, passionate suitor (among many) of the eponymous heroine of Smith's first novel *Emmeline*. Discussing the reign of Elizabeth I in her 'History', young Austen laments the fate of 'Robert Devereux Lord Essex', claiming, 'This unfortunate young Man was not unlike in Character to that equally unfortunate one *Frederic Delamere*' (*Juvenilia* 185). Only in recent decades have scholars recognised the pervasive influence of Smith's novels upon Austen's, revising the long-established critical belief, summarised by Isobel Grundy, that 'Austen's best-loved authors are those with Augustan affinities: … Richardson, Johnson, Cowper, and Burney' (Grundy 197). Scholars increasingly now suggest that Smith's influence may in fact have been greater than Burney's.[8]

Perhaps 'Catharine, or the Bower' was Austen's attempt to write something like Smith's *Emmeline, the Orphan of the Castle* (1788) or *Ethelinde, or the Recluse of the Lake* (1789), sentimental courtship novels infused with strong social satire and lush descriptions of romantic scenery darkened by gothic shadows. We cannot tell how Austen might have developed her fragment, but in the extant opening chapters her heroine, like Smith's, is raised in isolation and obscurity and, like Smith's heroines, is attached to a site of rural tranquillity, in Catharine's case her garden bower rather than a remote castle in Wales or an isolated cottage in Grasmere. Perhaps, like Smith's heroines, Catharine would have embarked upon distant adventures, accompanying the romantically named Camilla[9] and her family on their travels to the Lakes, observing Camilla's follies while negotiating her own courtship challenges.

Loraine Fletcher catalogues the common elements in Smith's *Emmeline* and *Ethelinde* as consisting of:

> self-possessed, reflective heroines, conflicting family relationships, ascerbic radical satire, acceptance that marriage is a woman's goal but that great caution is necessary in achieving it, a more tolerant attitude to extramarital sex and the 'fallen' woman than is usually found in English novels of the eighteenth and nineteenth centuries, threatening castles emblematic of gender and natural hierarchies, and contrasting locations including sublime mountain landscape. (Fletcher 10)

These elements do not immediately suggest Austen's mature novels, but Smith's third novel *Celestina* (1791) is more promising as an Austen influence, for *Celestina*'s deeply romantic, sentimental hero is a man of feeling named Willoughby. He almost succumbs to family pressure to abandon his poor, obscurely born, but virtuous and talented fiancée, Celestina, fearing she might be his half-sister, in order to marry his wealthy, disagreeable cousin. Jacqueline Labbe sees Smith's Willoughby 'as a bridge between Sir Clement Willoughby, the rake in [Burney's] *Evelina*, and [Austen's] John Willoughby, whose mysterious transformation from lover in sensibility mode to selfish gold-digger with a libertine past has disturbed many readers'. She adds that Austen's 'contemporary readers, well versed in their Burney and their Smith, may thus have had a forewarning [in *Sense and Sensibility*] of Willoughby's unstable status subsequently lost to later readers for whom Smith was not so much a closed as an unknown book' (Labbe 'Party' 'Narrating Seduction' 113–14).

Smith's fourth novel *Desmond* was published early in the summer of 1792, possibly in time for Austen to have read it while writing 'Catharine'. In *Desmond,* Smith exploits the epistolary mode, unusual for her, in order to express her radical views supporting the constitutional phase of the French Revolution through the voice of her idealistic hero Desmond, who fiercely refutes Edmund Burke's conservative *Reflections on the Revolution in France* (1790). Austen's politics were more Burkean than radical, but other passages in Smith's novel would certainly have resonated with the young author and will surely strike readers familiar with Austen's novels.

Desmond's hero is unhappily in love with a married woman, the beautiful, virtuous Geraldine, a victim, like Smith herself, of an abusive, unfaithful, profligate husband; separated from him, she is desperate to support her small children.[10] Her younger unmarried sister Fanny complains that their mother 'proscribes every species of reading, and murmurs when she cannot absolutely prohibit the fashionable, insipid novel' (*Desmond* 215). Denied more challenging works, Fanny is restricted 'to such mawkish reading as is produced ... in the soft semblance of letters, "from Miss Everilda Evelyn to Miss Victorina Villars"', a clear dig at Burney's *Evelina* whose eponymous heroine's guardian is named Villars (*Desmond* 216). Fanny adds, 'I might, indeed, read history; but whenever I attempt to do so, I am, to tell you the truth, driven from it by disgust.—What is it, but a miserly mortifying detail of crimes and follies?—of the guilt of a few, and the sufferings of many ... ?' (*Desmond* 216). Austen, writing six years later, gives Catherine Morland the same sentiments expressed in almost the same words.[11]

Geraldine's vigorous 'defence of novel-reading' (her words, *Desmond* 226) refutes the anti-novel arguments of moralists like Samuel Johnson much as Desmond's letters challenge Burke's politics. In 1750, Johnson had warned in *The Rambler* about the moral dangers of the new realistic, domestic novels. Unlike earlier romances set in far-away and long-ago places and filled with fairy-tale elements, he argued, these newer works were dangerous precisely because they were set in the reader's own, contemporary society and contained more believable ('probable') characters and events. Moreover, Johnson cautioned in terms that became commonplace,

These books are written chiefly to the young, the ignorant, and the idle; to whom they serve as lectures of conduct, and introductions to life. They are the entertainment of minds unfurnished with ideas, and therefore easily susceptible of impressions; not fixed by principles, and therefore easily following the current of fancy; not informed by experience, and consequently open to every false suggestion and partial account. (26)

Johnson feared that realistic fiction would cause vulnerable youth to emulate the vicious rather than the virtuous qualities of attractive 'mixed' characters such as Fielding's Tom Jones (29).

Geraldine, however, argues that 'in every well-written novel' characters who commit errors are subject 'to remorse, regret, and punishment', which is more, she points out, than occurs in actual life: 'in reading the world, a girl must see a thousand very ugly blots, which frequently pass without any censure at all' (*Desmond* 223). Geraldine favourably contrasts those excellent novels 'which represent human life nearly as it is' to the 'wild and absurd writings, that describe in inflated language, beings that never were, nor ever will be', a sentiment that surely agreed with Austen's own taste for the probable and natural, as would Geraldine's amusing parody of such 'absurd' novels that she confects for her sister (*Desmond* 223–24).

Smith's fictional debate about novels may have inspired Austen. In *Desmond*, Smith uses a discussion about novel-reading to reveal her characters' natures. Whatever 'Catharine' might have become had Austen finished it, the fragment marks her strategic shift in her deployment of her own critical understanding of novels, for in 'Catharine' she moves from burlesquing novels by comically exaggerating their elements, as she does throughout the juvenilia, to having her psychologically realistic characters Catharine and Camilla discuss novels in order to reveal *themselves* through *their* comments about novels, as Smith's characters do in *Desmond* (Bander, 'Books', 165–66).

Austen would employ this strategy again in both her first and her last mature novels. In *Northanger Abbey*, Isabella Thorpe appears as a reinvented Camilla Stanley, and John Thorpe condemns himself as a fool when he talks about novels, while in *Sanditon*, the novel that Austen was writing when she died, Sir Edward Denham is an unreliable, egregious misreader who declares, like Thorpe, 'I am no indiscriminate novel-reader. The mere trash of the common circulating library, I hold in the highest contempt' (*Later Manuscripts* 181). The narrator explains, 'He read all the essays, letters, tours and criticisms of the day—and ... gathered only hard words and involved sentences from the style of our most approved writers'. More dangerously, he 'had read more sentimental novels than agreed with him. His fancy had been early caught by all the impassioned and most exceptionable parts of Richardson's'. Having perversely learned the wrong lessons from Richardson's *Clarissa*, his 'great object in life was to be seductive' (*Later Manuscripts* 183). Contemporary readers would have recognised Sir Edward as a quixote, a character derived from Cervantes's *Don Quixote,* whose distracted hero misreads ordinary life as though it were a fabulous romance.

The theme of quixotic reading disorders thus absorbed Jane Austen from first to last, uniting her preoccupations as a reader with her ambitions as a writer. Early in 1807, for example, she recounts how the Austen ladies had found their library copy of Madame de Genlis's *Alphonsine* (1806), a novel about an unwed mother, too indelicate to read aloud ('We were disgusted in twenty pages'), so they 'changed it for the "Female Quixotte", which now makes our evening amusement; to me a very high one, as I find the work quite equal to what I remembered it' (7–8 January 1807; *Letters* 120). *The Female Quixote*, Charlotte Lennox's satiric novel about the dangers of novel-reading, subtitled *The Adventures of Arabella*, was published in 1752 with the patronage of both Samuel Richardson and Samuel Johnson. Arabella, in her sixteenth year, lovely, high-born, educated, and virtuous, lives in the countryside with her reclusive father, where she studies her deceased mother's copies of the extravagantly improbable, elaborately rhetorical, and immensely long heroic French romances of Scudéry in 'very bad Translations' (Lennox 7). Contradicting Johnson's argument that such improbable fairy tales were harmless, Arabella in fact mistakes these romances for conduct books—that is, as practical guides to proper behaviour—and begins to live as though she inhabits one of Scudéry's tales of imperilled maidens and heroic passions. After many 'adventures' Arabella is 'cured' of her delusions: she sadly accepts the diminished world of reality and marries her devoted suitor.

Austen also enjoyed reading Eaton Stannard Barrett's 1813 novel *The Heroine, or, adventures of a fair romance reader*, which spoofs the 1790s gothic novels of Ann Radcliffe much as Lennox mocked the seventeenth-century romances of Scudéry. Austen reports to her sister in March 1814: 'I have torn through the 3^d vol. of the Heroine, & do not think it falls off.—It is a delightful burlesque, particularly on the Radcliffe style' (*Letters* 267). Both of these novels probably influenced her when she began writing *Emma* in 1814, as might have Walter Scott's 1814 *Waverley*, also a kind of quixotic novel, for Scott's naïve hero, Edward Waverley, the scion (like several of Smith's heroes) of an English Jacobite family, joins the ill-fated 1745 Jacobite Rebellion, inspired by the romantic political ideals he has imbibed from a youth spent reading chivalrous romances. Uncharacteristically, Austen shared the romantic Jacobite sentiments of young Waverley, but Scott's satiric inventory of cliché novel plots on the opening page of *Waverley* reads like Austen's own burlesques.[12]

Jane Austen's lifelong concern with ways of reading and misreading is also manifest in her profound interest in the reactions of her own readers. With the help of family and friends she collected readers' responses to *Mansfield Park* and *Emma*, compiling them into her 'Opinions of *Mansfield Park*' and 'Opinions of *Emma*'. She knew that her own novels would undermine readers' expectations and challenge their judgements, and she was keen to see how her readers would negotiate those challenges: to know whether they would read as critically and reflectively as herself.

Kathryn Sutherland describes Austen's novels 'as a form of critical engagement—with society and social relations but also with the genre itself', arguing, 'she recalibrated the novel to the real as she saw it, at the same time questioning the basis in human psychology of any sustainable reality, of any permanent escape from romance and illusionment' (*Textual Lives* 353). Sutherland adds, 'Her spare conversational narratives read like nothing her contemporaries produced. They represent her ambition to take the novel in a new direction …' (353).

One striking new direction was Austen's wholehearted embrace of the term 'novel', for only Haywood, Smollett, and Smith, among serious novelists, had allowed their books to be so designated.[13] Rather, the earliest English novelists took great pains to deny that they wrote novels. On their title pages and in their prefaces they proclaimed that their 'works' were not in fact novels but rather true stories or 'true histories', or else collections of private letters simply 'edited' by the author and presented to the reading public not for diversion but as *exempla* intended to illustrate moral precepts advocating filial obedience or prudence over passion.

Thus Daniel Defoe complains, in the Preface to his second novel *Moll Flanders* (1722): 'The World is so taken up of late with Novels and Romances, that it will be hard for a private History to be taken for Genuine, where the Names and other Circumstances of the Person are concealed' (22). With his dismissive remark about 'Novels and Romances', Defoe was hoping to distinguish his works from the sexually frank tales of the amatory novelists. Forty years later Richardson called his chatty, accessible fictional letters 'a new species of writing' that 'might possibly turn young people into a course of reading different from the pomp and parade of romance-writing, and dismissing the improbable and marvellous, with which novels generally abound, might tend to promote the cause of religion and virtue' (Richardson, 'Letter to Aaron Hill'). Frances Burney, too, rejected the designation 'novel', preferring to call her books 'works', as did Maria Edgeworth (1768–1849), whose 'Advertisement' for her second novel *Belinda* (1801), one of the three novels cited approvingly by the narrator of *Northanger Abbey*, states: 'Every author has a right to give what appellation he may think proper to his works … . The following work is offered to the public as a Moral Tale—the author not wishing to acknowledge a Novel' (2).

Austen may be the only serious novelist apart from Smith to write a novel that includes a defence of novel-reading,[14] and her novels, like her letters, mock pretentious characters who disdain novels. So common were anti-novel sentiments that Catherine Morland, the unlikely heroine of *Northanger Abbey*, assumes that Henry Tilney must not read novels, 'Because [she sadly concedes] they are not clever enough for you—gentlemen read better books' (107). Catherine is thinking of what John Thorpe had boasted earlier: 'I never read novels; I have something else to do' (*NA* 43). In assigning this anti-novel speech to Thorpe, Austen thoroughly discredits both the attitude and the speaker. Henry Tilney, in contrast, surely reflects the more liberal views of Austen's own clergyman father and brothers when he replies to Catherine, 'The person, be it gentleman or lady, who has not pleasure in a good novel, must be intolerably stupid. I have read all Mrs Radcliff's works, and most of them with great pleasure' (107–08). It was unusual in the 1790s for a serious clergyman to praise novels (think of stupid, pompous Mr Collins in *Pride and Prejudice* choosing to entertain the Bennet sisters with Fordyce's *Sermons*), but extraordinary indeed to admit without apology that he enjoys a popular gothic romance by Ann Radcliffe (1764–1823), whose books were all the rage while Austen was first writing *Northanger Abbey* in the late 1790s.

Austen particularly targets the hypocrisy of novel-writers who themselves contribute to anti-novel sentiment. The narrator of *Northanger Abbey* declares:

> I will not adopt that ungenerous and impolitic custom so common with novel-writers, of degrading by their contemptuous censure the very performances, to the number of which they are themselves adding ... and scarcely ever permitting them to be read by their own heroine, who, if she accidentally take up a novel, is sure to turn over its insipid pages with disgust. (30)

In support of this spirited defence, the narrator cites three novels as outstanding examples of the genre: 'It is only Cecilia, or Camilla, or Belinda'; or, in short, only some work in which the greatest powers of the mind are displayed, in which the most thorough knowledge of human nature, the happiest delineation of its varieties, the liveliest effusions of wit and humour are conveyed to the world in the best chosen language' (*NA* 31). *Cecilia* (1782) and *Camilla* (1796) were Frances Burney's second and third novels, and *Belinda* (1801) was Maria Edgeworth's second novel. Austen greatly admired both Burney and Edgeworth.

Ironically, however, *Belinda's* exemplary heroine disdains popular novel-reading while a secondary character goes morally astray because she reads romances. Belinda Portman, yet another lovely, lively, accomplished, virtuous, country-bred young lady of seventeen without much in the way of family or fortune, lives first with her aunt Mrs Stanhope, then becomes a protégée of the brilliantly witty, fashionable, but unhappy Lady Delacour, and finally finds a safe home with the virtuous domestic goddess Lady Anne Percival. Throughout three volumes Belinda is courted by three men. During her time with Lady Delacour, Belinda prudently retreats from the dangers of the fashionable world into the Delacour library 'where', as Heather MacFadyen observes, 'instead of the romances and novels typically condemned by the trope of female reading, Belinda reads nonfiction by Adam Smith, Jean de La Bruyere, Anna Laetitia Barbauld, and John Aiken. When she does read fiction she picks up the blameless moral tales of Jean-François Marmontel and John Moore ...' (MacFadyen 427). Belinda's virtuous suitor Mr Percival, realising that she is unfortunately in love with apparently unavailable Clarence Hervey, condemns the idea inculcated by '"unjust novel writers" that "delicacy"' forbids a woman from forming a second attachment, even if she must marry another than her first love: 'Pernicious doctrine! false as it is pernicious! The struggles between duty and passion may be the charm of romance, but must be the misery of real life' he wisely advises her (*Belinda* 256). Eventually, Belinda reforms Lady Delacour, restoring her to domestic happiness, and herself marries her first attachment: the rich, clever, and fundamentally good Clarence Hervey.

Their courtship had been complicated because he had been secretly raising a young girl in social isolation, on Rousseauian principles, to be his wife: he calls her 'Virginia St. Pierre' after the heroine of Jacques-Henri Bernadin de St-Pierre's 1788 novel *Paul et Virginie,* who is raised in an innocent state of nature only to be corrupted by contact with society, the same fate that awaits Hervey's Virginia after her over-indulgence in sentimental novels stimulates her sexuality and raises her romantic expectations, leaving her prey to a seducer. Happily, Virginia's quixotic novel-induced fall from innocence frees Hervey to marry novel-rejecting Belinda.

Burney and Edgeworth were much admired by the literary establishment and highly praised by moralists; both avowedly wrote to encourage prudence and virtue in their readers. Austen was on safe grounds naming their novels as works 'in which the greatest powers of the mind are displayed' (*NA* 31). The novels that Catherine Morland and Isabella Thorpe actually read, however, are neither Burney's nor Edgeworth's, but rather, gothic novels (Catherine calls them '"horrid"'), specifically Radcliffe's 1798 *The Mysteries of Udolpho.* Surprisingly, though, despite their gothic trappings of rugged romantic scenery, decayed castles, sinister noblemen, mysterious sounds in the night, and threats of imprisonment, rape, incest, or murder, Radcliffe's novels follow roughly the same conventional sentimental courtship plots as do Smith's, Burney's, and Edgeworth's.

These writers were in turn following the sentimental paradigm of Richardson's third novel, *The History of Sir Charles Grandison* (1753), the old-fashioned novel that Catherine Morland's mother 'often reads', that Isabella Thorpe proclaims to be 'an amazing horrid book', and that Catherine Morland, to her credit, finds 'very entertaining' despite its familiarity ('new books do not fall in our way'), and that Austen knew intimately (*NA* 35; Austen-Leigh et al. 54). *Sir Charles Grandison* features a complex double courtship plot with a noble, idealised hero (satirised as 'Charles Adams' in Austen's 'Jack and Alice', *Juvenilia* 14–15), two attractive heroines, the hero's spirited sister, a dastardly villain, and numerous debates about, and object lessons in, virtuous conduct under a variety of trying circumstances. Richardson was the acknowledged—indeed, the self-proclaimed—pioneer of the domestic novel, a term that overlaps with 'sentimental' novel and 'courtship' novel.[15] His phenomenally successful yet controversial first novel *Pamela; or, Virtue Rewarded* (1740) tells, through a series of letters, the story of Pamela Andrews, a clever, virtuous sixteen-year-old servant maid who resists the elaborate seduction schemes of her rakish employer Mr B until at last her virtue (that is, her chastity) is rewarded with marriage to Mr B and elevation to the gentry. Richardson's second novel, *Clarissa; or, the History of a Young Lady* (1747–1748), like *Pamela* an epistolary seduction tale but with a tragic conclusion, was intended, 'To warn the Inconsiderate and Thoughtless of the one Sex, against the base arts and designs of specious Contrivers of the other' (Preface xiii), although to Richardson's chagrin, his charismatic, complex villain Lovelace perversely attracted admirers such as Austen's Sir Edward Denham in *Sanditon.*

Radcliffe's novels, no less than Smith's, Burney's, and Austen's, are indebted to Richardson. Like their sentimental predecessors, Radcliffe's heroines are genteel, accomplished, principled, lovely, country-bred young ladies of sixteen or seventeen who, despite inhabiting an earlier century and the wilder parts of the Continent, possess Georgian sensibilities and behave with impeccable propriety until they are saved from peril by, and marry, the young men whom they have loved since the first volume.

The difference between *Udolpho* on the one hand and *Grandison* or *Cecilia* on the other is one of intent: Radcliffe's aim is to provoke pleasurable sensations rather than serious reflections, to entertain by heightening suspense rather than to educate or reform through exemplary tales, yet she, too, scrupulously endorses conventional morality, punishing vice and rewarding virtue, and her heroines travel similar trajectories. The vicissitudes experienced by Radcliffe's heroines—threats of abduction, confinement, rape, incest, and murder—go far beyond the embarrassing violations of ballroom decorum, careless or spendthrift guardians, rejecting fathers, surplus suitors, apparent rivals, misleading appearances, semantic confusions, harmful gossip, or empty purses that plague the heroines of the domestic courtship novel (although occasionally these heroines too must witness painful deathbeds or suicides, or descend into physical declines and madness), but the difference is one of degree, not kind. Slyly Austen implies in *Northanger Abbey* that distinctions between those novels 'in which the greatest powers of the mind are displayed' versus 'the trash with which the press now groans' are arbitrary and unstable (30–31; Bander, 'Reading').

Reading the novels that Jane Austen admired, novels by Richardson, Fielding, Smollett, and Lennox, by Burney, Smith, Edgeworth, and Radcliffe, reveals just how different hers are from everyone else's, and how much of those elements that appear in the novels of just about everyone else she chooses to leave out of her own. Her 'quixotic' characters never believe *themselves* to be heroic: Catherine Morland is only briefly led astray by Henry Tilney to imagine that she may have wandered into someone else's horrid tale, and even so, she's not far off the mark; Emma Woodhouse imagines romances for other people, with herself as author; Anne Elliot's brief melancholic indulgence in poetry merely delays her recognition of her own returning spring. Austen offers no beautiful heroines to collect an embarrassment of admirers, no dissolute aristocrats determinedly ruining their vast fortunes through extravagance and gaming; no dastardly fortune-hunters or sexual predators trying to abduct the heroine (except for Mr Elton's attack upon Emma in the carriage); no unprincipled women defaming her (merely Lady Catherine de Bourgh's anger at Elizabeth Bennet); no digressive embedded narratives (except for Colonel Brandon's tale of the two Elizas and Mrs Smith's personal history); no picturesque travels to foreign parts (merely Elizabeth Bennet's tour to Derbyshire and Anne Elliot's journeys to Lyme and Bath); no extravagantly worded speeches of passion from the heroines (unless we count Marianne Dashwood's); no violent suicides (apart from Dr. Grant's overeating); no revelations about birth (except Harriet Smith's); no sudden reversals of fortune (except for hapless Edward Ferrars and fortunate Frank Churchill). Only Marianne Dashwood, Elizabeth Bennet, and Emma Woodhouse marry gentlemen of fortune in possession of estates. Austen's other heroines marry professional men: parsons or sailors. Nor do her novels contain any of the stilted, unnaturally formal, or heroic narration and dialogue found in many other Georgian novels. Furthermore, Austen refuses to distribute the ritual poetic justice of rewards and punishments: her villains often live prosperous if dissatisfied lives, her heroines fail to inherit fortunes, and her solemn pronouncements of moral lessons are deeply ironic.

Austen's novels were doing something new. Walter Scott, in his 1816 unsigned review in the *Quarterly Review*, recognised that in Austen's *Emma* 'there are cross purposes enough (were the novel of a more romantic cast) for cutting half the men's throats and breaking all the women's hearts' (Scott 67), but rendered in terms appropriate to everyday Surrey village life. Indeed, the 'Opinions' that Austen collected show how her first readers were struck by the comparative intimacy and familiarity of her story-telling. Lady Gordon is reported as saying of *Mansfield Park*: 'there is scarcely an Incident a conversation, or a person that you are not inclined to imagine you have at one time or other in your life been a witness to, born a part in, & been acquainted with' ('Opinions of *Mansfield Park*', *Later Manuscripts* 234) while Mrs Cage, a family connection, writes about *Emma*: 'I am at Highbury all day, & I ca'nt help feeling I have just got into a new set of acquaintants' ('Opinions of *Emma*', *Later Manuscripts* 238). To her first readers, Austen's novels did not seem like constructed fictions. They seemed like life.

Jane Austen took the novels of Richardson, Fielding, Smollett, Lennox, Burney, Smith, Edgeworth, and even Radcliffe, and scaled down their plots to what might be found 'in the midland counties of England' among the middle ranks of people neither 'spotless as an angel' nor with 'the dispositions of a fiend' (*NA* 205). She wrote against the grain of readerly expectations, deliberately undermining fictional conventions and challenging categorical judgements. Her purpose was neither to stimulate intense sensations nor to inculcate a fixed moral precept. It was, through her exploration of '3 or 4 Families in a Country Village' (9 September 1814; *Letters* 287), to delight her readers with clever, witty, well-expressed narratives in whose everyday plots and characters, containing what she

Notes

1 See, however, Isobel Grundy, who does 'not accept that she dislikes scholarship', pointing out that while Austen 'dislikes pedantry', she is meticulous about accuracy (194–95). Both Grundy and Doody are of course attesting to the scholarly attention that Austen brings to popular fiction.

2 Barbara Benedict, commenting upon the popularity of sentimental passages extracted from their contexts, suggests that such passages might have 'better suited readers whose cultural education inclined them toward sympathetic identification than readers whose cultural education inclined them to seek irony', thus explaining the prevalence of embedded tales, which allow novels to appeal simultaneously to different styles of reading (7). Katherine Binhammer, noting that 'Embedded tales … are ubiquitous', argues that they highlight the narrative act, prompting readers to question narrative authority and context, and thus are 'intentional metafictions' (188–89).

3 Her own 'Plan of a Novel' written at the end of her life remains one of the very best burlesques of sentimental novel clichés.

4 See Stephen Ahern's account of 'the shift that occurred as England moved from a culture of libertinism during the Restoration and its aftermath to a culture of sentimentalism from the mid-eighteenth century through the beginnings of Romanticism' (12).

5 According to Ros Ballaster's feminist reading, Behn and Manley developed their 'feminocentric' fictions from earlier fairy-tale-like French seventeenth-century romances, attempting 'to privilege the female writer as a political agent, precisely by virtue of her position at the margins of the political order', and indulging 'in a complex form of (auto)biographizing that constructs the woman writer as an erotic enigma for her male and female readers', whereas the youngest of the three, Eliza Haywood, responded to changing tastes by adapting her fiction to a more restrained age; thus, Ballaster concludes, 'Eliza Haywood's romances of the 1720s and 1730s, by contrast, refuse such autobiographical impulses and bring us closer to the conventions of domestic fiction' (3).

6 Ahern argues that the publication of *Sense and Sensibility* in 1811 'signaled a new direction in the history of sensibility narrative', with Austen developing Burney's 'sentimental novel of bourgeois manners' but rejecting gothic excesses in order 'to promote domestication of feeling as a necessary feature of companionate marriage', and, by imposing her 'commonsense and often satirical ethos onto the frame of romance', revealing some ambivalence toward romantic sensibility (203).

7 Parts of this discussion of Charlotte Smith's influence upon Austen appear, in an earlier version, in my essay '"Books Universally Read and Admired": Mrs Smith in *Northanger Abbey*'.

8 One of the first was William Magee. See also Labbe, Introd., for a history of Smith's critical reception as she moves 'from minor to central' in the canon (2–3). In 'What Happens at the Party', Labbe summarises the history of critical recognition of Smith by Austen scholars, making a strong case for Smith's pervasive influence. Her *Reading Jane Austen after Reading Charlotte Smith* (Palgrave, 2020) was published too late for me to consult for this essay.

9 The name 'Camilla' seems prescient, for Austen was a subscriber to, and a huge fan of, Frances Burney's third novel *Camilla*, not published until 1796, four years after Austen transcribed her fair copy of 'Catharine' into *Volume the Third*—and in any case, in Burney's earlier drafts of *Camilla*, her heroine had a different name. I thank Susan Allen Ford for suggesting that Pope's allusion to Virgil's 'swift Camilla' in his 'Essay on Criticism' (II.372) was Austen's probable source for the name.

10 Smith described herself as one 'who must live to write & write to live' (Letter to Joseph Cooper Walker, 20 April 1794).

11 Jillian Heydt-Stevenson argues for *Desmond*'s extensive influence upon *Northanger Abbey*, claiming that the older novel is 'embedded in the later' (140).

12 Her 'History of England' is strongly pro-Stuart. Austen joked that she feared that she would like *Waverley* but would prefer to dislike it, because in publishing a good novel the famous poet was 'taking the bread out of other' novelists' mouths (28 September 1814; *Letters* 289). Doody points out that young Waverley's reading tastes are a 'caricature' of Scott's own, just as Catherine Morland's 'mirror' Austen's (Doody 351).

13 See Alexander Pettit, Margaret Case Croskery, and Anna C. Patchias, who suggest that Eliza Haywood was just about the only early novelist other than Smollett to accept the designation 'novel' (19). Ros Ballaster argues that post-mid-century 'women writers of the novel were forced to go to sometimes extraordinary

lengths to avoid' identification with risqué, politically strident writers like Behn, Manley, and Haywood; they preferred to be identified with their virtuous heroines, to which end they published anonymously (208) and strategically avoided associating their names with 'novels'.

14 Although see Jodi L. Wyett, who construes Smith, especially in *Emmeline*, as an anti-novel novelist, and Emmeline as 'an anti-quixote' (261–64).

15 According to received literary history, Richardson and Fielding between them set the stage for the subsequent development of the English novel, but as Brian Corman has recently suggested, while they differed about almost everything else, they agreed in promoting their own novels as 'a new species of writing', to be preferred to those older 'romances' which they decried as old-fashioned, feminised, and morally suspect, thus contributing to the suppression of the earlier female-centric amatory novels and leaving later scholars to overlook significant female authors who wrote between Richardson and Austen (Corman 9–10). One of those authors, Charlotte Smith, creates a heroine, Geraldine, who refers to Richardson and Fielding admiringly as 'the two first of our classics' (*Desmond* 223).

Works Cited

Ahern, Stephen. *Affected Sensibilities: Romantic Excess and the Genealogy of the Novel, 1680–1810.* AMS P, 2007.

Austen, Jane. *Jane Austen's Letters*, edited by Deirdre Le Faye, 4th ed. Oxford UP, 2011.

Austen, Jane. *Juvenilia*, edited by Peter Sabor. Cambridge UP, 2006.

Austen, Jane. *Later Manuscripts*, edited by Janet Todd and Linda Bree. Cambridge UP, 2008.

Austen, Jane. *Northanger Abbey*, edited by Barbara M. Benedict and Deirdre le Faye. Cambridge UP, 2006.

Austen-Leigh, William, Richard Austen-Leigh, and Deirdre Le Faye. *Jane Austen, a Family Record.* British Library, 1989.

Ballaster, Ros. *Seductive Forms: Women's Amatory Fiction from 1640 to 1740.* Clarendon P, 1992.

Bander, Elaine. '"Books Universally Read and Admired": Mrs Smith in *Northanger Abbey.*' *Persuasions*, vol. 41, 2019, pp. 165–181.

Bander, Elaine. 'Reading Mysteries at Bath and Northanger.' *Persuasions*, vol. 32, 2010, pp. 47–59.

Benedict, Barbara M. *Framing Feeling: Sentiment and Style in English Prose Fiction, 1745–1800.* AMS P, 1994.

Binhammer, Katherine. 'Later Fiction.' *The Cambridge Companion to Women's Writing in Britain, 1660–1789*, edited by Catherine Ingrassia. Cambridge UP, 2015, pp. 180–195.

Corman, Brian. *Women Novelists before Jane Austen: The Critics and Their Canons.* U of Toronto P, 2008.

Croskery, Margaret Case, and Anna C. Patchias. Introduction. *Fantomina and Other Works*, by Eliza Haywood, edited by Alexander Pettit, Margaret Case Croskery, and Anna C. Patchias. Broadview P, 2004.

Defoe, Daniel. Preface. *The Novels of Daniel Defoe. Vol. 6: The Fortunes and Misfortunes of the Famous Moll Flanders (1771)*, edited by Liz Bellamy. Pickering & Chatto, 2009, pp. 23–26.

Doody, Margaret Anne. 'Jane Austen's Reading.' *The Jane Austen Handbook*, edited by J. David Grey. Athlone P, 1986, pp. 347–363.

Edgeworth, Maria. *Belinda*, edited by Kathryn J. Kirkpatrick. Oxford UP, 1994.

Fletcher, Loraine. Introduction. *Celestina*, by Charlotte Smith. Broadview P, 2004.

Grundy, Isobel. 'Jane Austen and literary traditions.' *The Cambridge Companion to Jane Austen*, edited by Edward Copeland and Juliet McMaster. Cambridge UP, 1997, pp. 189–210.

Heydt-Stevenson, Jillian. '*Northanger Abbey, Desmond,* and History.' *The Wordsworth Circle*, vol. 44, no. 2-3, 2013, pp. 140–148.

Johnson, Samuel. *The Rambler*, 2nd ed., vol. 1. Edinburgh: Sands, Murray, and Cochran, 1751, pp. 24–32.

Labbe, Jacqueline. Introduction. *Charlotte Smith in British Romanticism*, edited by Jacqueline Labbe. London: Routledge, 2016, pp. 1–11.

Labbe, Jacqueline. 'Narrating Seduction: Charlotte Smith and Jane Austen.' *Charlotte Smith in British Romanticism*, edited by Jacqueline Labbe. London: Pickering and Chatto, 2008, pp. 113–128.

Labbe, Jacqueline. 'What Happens at the Party: Jane Austen Converses with Charlotte Smith.' *Persuasions On-Line*, vol. 30, no. 2, Spring 2010, unpaginated.

Le Faye, Deirdre. Chronology. *Northanger Abbey*, edited by Barbara M. Benedict and Deirdre le Faye. Cambridge UP, 2006, pp. xv–xxi.

Lennox, Charlotte. *The Female Quixote, or, the Adventures of Arabella*, edited by Margaret Dalziel. Oxford UP, 1970.

MacFadyen, Heather. 'Lady Delacour's Library: Maria Edgeworth's *Belinda* and Fashionable Reading.' *Nineteenth-Century Literature*, vol. 48, no. 4, 1984, pp. 423–439.

Magee, William. 'The Happy Marriage: The Influence of Charlotte Smith on Jane Austen.' *Studies in the Novel*, vol. 7, 1975, pp. 120–132.

Richardson, Samuel. 'Letter to Aaron Hill, 1 Feb. 1741.' *The Cambridge Edition of the Correspondence of Samuel Richardson. Vol. 1: Correspondence with Aaron Hill and the Hill Family*, edited by Christine Gerrard. Cambridge UP, 2013, p. 90.

Richardson, Samuel. Preface to the Third Edition. *Clarissa. Or, the History of a Young Lady*, 3rd ed., vol. 1. London: S. Richardson, 1751, pp. i–vii.

Sabor, Peter. Introduction. *Juvenilia*, by Jane Austen, edited by Peter Sabor. Cambridge UP, 2006, pp. xxiii–lxvii.

Scott, Walter. 'Walter Scott, an Unsigned Review of *Emma*, *Quarterly Review*, Dated October 1815, Issued March 1816, xiv, 188-201.' *Jane Austen: The Critical Heritage*, edited by Brian Southam. Routledge, 1968, pp. 58–69.

Smith, Charlotte. *Celestina*, 1791, edited by Loraine Fletcher. Broadview, 2004.

Smith, Charlotte. *Desmond*, 1792, edited by Antje Blank and Janet Todd. Broadview, 2001.

Smith, Charlotte. *The Collected Letters of Charlotte Smith*, edited by Judith Phillips Stanton. Indiana UP, 2003.

Southam, Brian. *Jane Austen's Literary Manuscripts*. Oxford UP, 1964.

Sutherland, Kathryn. 'Jane Austen and the Invention of the Serious Modern Novel.' *The Cambridge Companion to English Literature, 1740–1830*, edited by Thomas Keymer and Jon Mee. Cambridge UP, 2004, pp. 244–262.

Sutherland, Kathryn. *Jane Austen's Textual Lives*. Oxford UP, 2007.

Wyett, Jodi L. 'Female Quixotism Refashioned: *Northanger Abbey*, the Engaged Reader, and the Woman Writer.' *The Eighteenth Century*, vol. 56, no. 2, 2015, pp. 261–276.

12

FROM SAMPLERS TO SHAKESPEARE: JANE AUSTEN'S READING

Katie Halsey

UNIVERSITY OF STIRLING

Making use of new digital resources (such as the recent digitisation of the Godmersham Park Library catalogue at readingwithausten.com) and other new scholarship, in this chapter I revisit the question of Jane Austen's literary influences in the context of a discussion of her reading practices. Recent scholarship by Isobel Grundy, Jocelyn Harris, Peter Knox-Shaw, Olivia Murphy, Janine Barchas, Peter Sabor and others has conclusively proven that Austen's reading was more daring, more demanding, and more eclectic than previous generations of critics had thought. In addition to 'the old guides' (Johnson, Cowper, Crabbe, Richardson, Goldsmith, Hume, and Robertson), named by her first biographers (Austen-Leigh 70), we now know that Austen read both deeply and widely in a variety of genres and forms, from socially sanctioned conduct books and histories to titillating French novels such as *Les Liaisons Dangereuses* (1782) and the latest scandal-sheets. In this chapter, I suggest that a careful consideration of material now considered ephemeral or unimportant can illuminate our thinking about Austen's creative practice in new ways.

Austen was a magpie reader; everything she read was grist to her creative mill, lending itself to parody, satire, and critical re-working. As Jocelyn Harris suggests, Austen's reading energised her creative practice in fundamental and exciting ways (*Art of Memory* x). Austen was, Olivia Murphy puts it, a 'riotous and anarchic' parodist ('The Queerness and the Fun' 32), and she was also, as Kathryn Sutherland has persuasively argued, an inveterate recycler of characters, plots, and ideas (126–27). Drawing on these insights, in this chapter I consider how an increased understanding of her wider reading habits both within and outside the family circle should now inform our literary criticism of the novels, juvenilia, and unfinished works.

'He can read, & I must get him some books', wrote Jane Austen to her sister Cassandra, anxious that their manservant James should be 'quiet & happy' during the family's stay at Lyme Regis in January of 1805. Learning that James had already read the first volume of *Robinson Crusoe* (1719), she determined to 'take care to lend him' the 'Pinckards Newspaper' (14 September 1804; *Letters* 95). Presumably, Jane Austen had in the house a copy of vol. 1 of *Robinson Crusoe* which she could have given or lent to James, but his existing knowledge of the book made this impractical. We must assume that the household had no other books deemed suitable for him, and so the newspaper, already passed on from the Pinckard family, is lent once again, this time to James. Unimportant in itself, this trivial event is nonetheless characteristic both of the importance attached to books (the *must* is telling), and of the frequent difficulty in getting hold of them, in Jane Austen's household—and indeed in those of many others of the middling sort—in the early years of the nineteenth century. It also shows us how, in the absence of books, newspapers could take on an

158

DOI: 10.4324/9780429398155-12-15

almost equal importance. It hence offers some insight into the ways in which books and other reading matter circulated within the Austen family and their wider circle of relatives, friends, and acquaintances.

Jane Austen had different kinds of access to books at different points in her life. Her letters abound with mentions of getting, having, reading, passing on, lending, and borrowing books, as well as her sometimes frustrating and abortive attempts to get hold of the most recent publications. In February, 1807, writing to Cassandra from Southampton for example, she recommended Elizabeth Grant's *Letters from the Mountains* (1807) as a present for their friend Martha Lloyd, adding 'what they are about, nor how many volumes they form I do not know, having never heard of them but from Miss Irvine, who speaks of them as a new & admired work, & as one which has pleased her highly.—I have enquired for the book here, but find it quite unknown' (20–22 February 1807; *Letters* 123). In April of 1811, similarly, she wrote to Cassandra, 'We have tried to get Self-Controul [Mary Brunton's *Self Control*, published 1811], but in vain' (30 April 1811; *Letters* 186). Sometime between then and October of 1813 she did manage to get it, writing to Cassandra that she was 'looking over Self Control again'—a phrase that suggests a re-reading (11–12 October 1813; *Letters* 234). For Austen, a writer keenly and attentively attuned both to the literary market for her own books and the dangers of competition from authors seen to be doing the same thing, the inability to keep up with the latest novels was particularly frustrating.

Very rarely does she discuss buying books, though on one notable occasion she mentions selling them, when, on the move from Steventon, her own books were sold along with her father's 'above 500 Volumes' (Jane to Cassandra Austen, 14–16 January 1801; *Letters* 74). Austen records her glee at selling 'Dodsley's Poems' [Robert Dodsley's *A Collection of Poems in Six Volumes by Several Hands* (1758)] for ten shillings: 'Ten shillings for Dodsley's Poems however please me to the quick, & I do not care how often I sell them for as much' (Jane to Cassandra Austen, 21–22 May 1801; *Letters* 88).[1] David Gilson notes that all but one of the twenty books he was able to trace as having actually belonged to Jane Austen date from the Steventon period, which suggests that this was the last time in her life that book ownership was financially practicable for her (Gilson 431). Austen's letters incessantly record the economical expedients she practised (willingly or otherwise) in every area of her life, and it is clear that her access to reading matter was similarly curtailed and limited by what she called 'Vulgar Economy' (Jane to Cassandra Austen, 30 June–1 July 1808; *Letters* 139), particularly after her father's death in January 1805. As a child, as Gilson rightly says, 'her first recourse would have been to her father's library' (Gilson 431), but after the dispersal of his books, and her own, she almost never again had such free and unfettered access to printed matter, although her life was punctuated by periods of intense and enjoyable cultural richness. Austen's letters vividly document her pleasure in having the freedom of her brother Edward's library at Godmersham Park during her visits there, as well as the whirlwind of trips to theatres and exhibitions she enjoyed on visits to her brother Henry in London. It is easy, too, to imagine her delight when, in 1815, the 'civil rogue', John Murray, offered to lend her 'any book of his', and followed this up with a series of loans of his latest publications (Jane to Cassandra Austen, 24 November 1815; *Letters* 298).

What might otherwise seem extraordinarily eclectic reading choices begin to make more sense within a broader understanding of both the richness, and the poverty, of Austen's cultural *milieux* at different stages of her life. As Peter Knox-Shaw brilliantly shows in his *Jane Austen and the Enlightenment* (2004), Jane Austen grew up in an atmosphere of philosophical enquiry, rigorous critical thinking, and literary openness. George Austen, Knox-Shaw argues, 'was of the sect that delighted in the many new—and still opening—fields of inquiry that were giving greater definition to the created world' (8). The young Jane Austen received an education that was no less rigorous for being informal, in the traditions of critical enquiry promoted by the Anglo-Scottish Enlightenment thinkers such as Hume, Smith, Ferguson, and Robertson.[2] Steventon Rectory was also a place where Austen's brothers brought back the latest scientific, philosophical, and literary ideas from

Oxford and where the family together engaged in putting on plays, for which James Austen wrote prologues that are notable for their acute social and literary commentary. The choice of plays is remarkable for its broad-mindedness, including the 'exceptionally risqué' *The Chances*, by John Fletcher, in the Duke of Buckingham's 1682 adaptation; Henry Fielding's hilarious parody *Tom Thumb* (1730), Susanna Centlivre's proto-feminist *The Wonder: A Woman Keeps a Secret* (1714), and others of a similar ilk (Knox-Shaw 28). Knox-Shaw suggests that the habits of mind inculcated by this progressive and critically informed upbringing stayed with Austen for the rest of her life. Her reading of the liberal historians in particular, he suggests, gave her a lifelong scepticism of dogma, prejudice, and the claims of party or politicians. These mental habits of dispassionate critical enquiry and humane scepticism, Knox-Shaw argues, allow Austen to keep in simultaneous play a number of conflicting moral and political positions in her novels, giving her work its 'taut contrapuntal flavour' (128).

Knox-Shaw is undoubtedly correct, and his account of Austen's literary influences during her youth does an extremely valuable service both in highlighting the continuing importance of the Enlightenment—particularly in its Anglo-Scottish incarnations—on Austen's thinking and writing, and in emphasising the breadth of her reading and the essentially exploratory nature of her engagement with literary texts. Austen's letters record her reading a hodgepodge of material, across a very wide variety of genres, subjects, and political positions. She read both the Whiggish *Morning Chronicle* and the Tory *Quarterly Review*. She was 'in love with' the very different writers George Crabbe, Charles Pasley, Thomas Clarkson, and Claudius Buchanan. She read both the radical (and proto-feminist) Helen Maria Williams, and the anti-Jacobin patriotic conservative Jane West. She owned the Godwinian Robert Bage's *Hermsprong; or, Man as he is not* (1796), despite expressing her sense of Godwin's followers as disreputable elsewhere in her letters: '*He* is as raffish in his appearance as I would wish every Disciple of Godwin to be' (Jane to Cassandra Austen, 21–22 May 1801; *Letters* 89). Alongside her reading of respectable (indeed required) novelists such as Samuel Richardson and Frances Burney, Austen recorded her voracious reading of the latest sentimental, Gothic, and melodramatic novels, such as Sydney Owenson's *Ida of Athens* (1800), Francis Lathom's *The Midnight Bell* (1798), and Eaton Stannard Barrett's *The Heroine* (1814), which she 'tore through' in two evenings (Jane to Cassandra Austen, 2–3 March 1814; *Letters* 255–56). As well as Evangelical writings by Hannah More, her cousin Edward Cooper and Mary Brunton, Austen read the juridical sermons of Thomas Sherlock, conduct books by Thomas Gisborne and James Fordyce, and poetry by the scandalous Byron and Burns as well as the morally irreproachable Cowper.

The books known to have been owned by Austen are of a similarly heterogeneous nature. The anonymous *Fables Choisis* and *The History of Little Goody Two-Shoes*, along with Arnaud Berquin's *L'Ami de L'Adolescence* and *L'Ami des Enfans* are standard children's books of the period, the latter known to have been read also by Maria Edgeworth and Frances Burney (Gilson 439). John Bell's *Travels from St Petersburg in Russia, to diverse parts of Asia* (1764) suggests an early taste for literature about other cultures and nations, later reflected in her reading of Joseph Baretti's *An Account of the Manners and Customs of Italy* (1768), Helen Maria Williams's *A Narrative of the Events which have lately taken place in France* (1815), and Lord Macartney's *Embassy to China* (1807), among others. The presence of both a 6-volume David Hume's *History of England* (1759–1762) and Oliver Goldsmith's 4-volume *The history of England, from the earliest times to the death of George II* (1771), the latter heavily and often critically annotated in Jane Austen's hand, bear witness to her reading of history, and the analytical spirit with which she approached it. Austen's bookshelf also contained various novels: Samuel Johnson's *Rasselas* (1759), Frances Burney's *Camilla* (1796), to which Jane Austen was a subscriber, and Richardson's *Sir Charles Grandison* (1754), the work claimed by her brother Henry and nephew James Edward to be her favourite. The outlier among her novel collection, at least in terms of its politics, is the aforementioned *Hermsprong; or, Man as he is not*. Poetry is represented by the *Works of James Thomson* (1773), the *Poems and Plays* of William Hayley (1785), and Ariosto's well-known epic *Orlando Furioso*, in a translation by John Hoole (5 vols, 1783). Austen also owned Isaac D'Israeli's *Curiosities of Literature* (1791), a small volume of trivia containing a cornucopia of anecdotes, stories, character sketches, and notes on literary themes, and one volume of Addison and Steele's *Spectator* (1744), a work she would later denigrate in *Northanger Abbey's* famous defence of the novel. The sole work of natural history was Goldsmith's *An history of the earth, and animated nature*, in 8 volumes (1774), and she also owned the *Works* of the French salonnière and progressive educationalist Anne Thérèse, Marquise de Lambert. It is perhaps not surprising that the parson's daughter also owned *A companion to the altar: shewing the nature & necessity of a sacramental preparation in order to our worthy receiving the Holy Communion, to which are added Prayers and meditations* (1793), or that such a walker as Jane Austen should have been the family member to inherit Richard Warner's *Excursions from Bath* (1801) on her father's death in 1805.

No records of George Austen's library remain, with the exception of one book, sold at auction in 1974 which contained his bookplate (Charlotte Brooke's *Reliques of Irish Poetry* [1788]), and the *Excursions from Bath* noted above, also containing his bookplate. Reconstructing his library of 500 books is, therefore, impossible, but we can hypothesise that it contained, at the very least, the standard works of the Classical authors that he would have needed to teach the young men who attended his small school, and the sermons of Thomas Sherlock, Hugh Blair and others. No eighteenth-century gentleman's library would have been complete without a copy of the *Spectator*, and probably the *Rambler* and *Idler* too. It would almost certainly have contained Hugh Blair's *Lectures on Rhetoric and Belles Lettres*, Buffon's *Natural History*, and the histories of Edward Gibbon, Charles Rollin, David Hume, and William Robertson, alongside Shakespeare's plays, and the poetry of Pope, Dryden, Akenside, Gray and Collins. The novels of Henry Fielding, Samuel Richardson and Frances Burney, and Goldsmith's *The Vicar of Wakefield* might well also have featured. Beyond that, we probably should not speculate further, although it is tempting to think that copies of Voltaire, Rousseau, and the other major deists might also have been on the shelves. Certainly, a copy of Voltaire's *The History of Charles XII King of Sweden* was signed by either James or Jane Austen, and is, according to Gilson, still in the possession of the family (434). While a library of 500 volumes is neither particularly large nor unusual in the period, it clearly provided sufficient seed for a fertile mind to harvest, since Austen's juvenilia, collected together in three fair-copy manuscript notebooks, show a deep familiarity not only with novels, from the melodramatic to the didactic, but also with a large variety of other genres. These short works distil and satirise plays, poetry, sentimental novels, travelogues, conduct books, epistolary novels, regional novels, didactic novels, and histories, among others, giving particular attention to the works of the most popular novelist of her period, Samuel Richardson. According to the extant documentary record, then, Austen's access to books in her youth was both unfettered and relatively extensive.

After the family's move to Bath in 1801, the dispersal of George Austen's books and Jane's own, and their subsequent moves between lodgings in Bath and then Southampton, Austen's access to books was much more dependent on temporary accommodations; namely circulating and subscription libraries and the country-house libraries of her friends and relatives. Evidence for Austen's membership and use of such libraries is limited, but it is clear that she continued to read the latest publications whenever she could and that she took advantage of whatever means she had at her disposal to get hold of books. The reading society formed at Chawton, for example, seems to have been one such conduit for books, while lengthy visits to friends and relatives such as the Lefroys at Ashe, the Leighs at Adlestrop and Stoneleigh Abbey, the Coopers at Harpsden and Hamstall Ridware, the Cookes at Great Bookham, the Lloyds at Ibthorpe, the Fowles at Kintbury, and the Bigg-Withers at Manydown, were good opportunities to rove through others' book collections. Austen writes, for example, of the 'thick Quarto Volumes, which one always sees in the Breakfast parlour' at Manydown (Jane to Cassandra Austen, 9 February 1813; *Letters* 204). The most important of these collections, though, was undoubtedly her brother Edward Austen Knight's library at

Godmersham Park (of the *c*.200 directly traceable allusions in Austen's novels and letters, 64 of these [32%, or nearly 1/3] were held in the Godmersham Library collection).[3] Austen's letters from London while staying with her brother Henry clearly show her taking full advantage of the theatrical performances available in the capital, and her visits to London provided her with an opportunity to keep up with newly published books, particularly in the last three years of her life, when she was able to take up John Murray's offer, and often borrowed books from him. But she never again had continued free and unfettered access to a collection that she could treat as her own, and it is notable that throughout her lifetime, many of Austen's allusions hark back to the books of her youth. The final, unfinished novel, *Sanditon*, for example, returns to Richardson for its sustained critique of Georgian gender stereotypes. In that novel, Sir Edward Denham longs to be a rake 'in the line of the Lovelaces'—a direct allusion to Richardson's rake-villain, Lovelace, in *Clarissa* (1748)—and plans to abduct Clara Brereton, carrying her off to 'some solitary house' in 'the neighbourhood of Tombuctoo' (*Later Manuscripts* 184), just as Lovelace carries off Clarissa, and, indeed, in another of Richardson's novels, as Mr B. abducts Pamela and incarcerates her in his Bedfordshire estate.

The reading tastes formed in Austen's youth were thus important throughout her life and do much to dispel any remaining sense of Austen as intellectually isolated from the great political and philosophical debates of her time.[4] But books are not the only sources of reading matter, of course, and recent scholarship by Janine Barchas and Jocelyn Harris persuasively argues that Austen was also keenly interested in the 'celebrities, scandals and controversies' of her own day, and that 'these were just as significant for her creativity' as the books she read (Harris, *Satire, Celebrity and Politics* xvii). I would suggest that this was even more the case once she no longer had such easy access to actual books, when ephemeral materials such as newspapers, magazines, and pamphlets became increasingly important to her. Austen's reading of the kind of ephemeral materials in which celebrity news appears is harder to trace, and thus to document, than her reading of books, but scattered references in the letters do note the habitual reading of newspapers (as in the case of the Pinckards' newspaper with which I began this chapter), as well as occasionally alluding to periodicals and magazines. Most of the evidence for such reading rests, however, on the internal evidence provided by allusions and references in the novels, juvenilia, and unfinished works. As early as 1923, R. W. Chapman identified a number of allusions and references to newspapers, periodicals, newspapers and ephemeral works in the novels and minor works.[5] These included *The Agricultural Reports* in *Emma*, *The Morning Post* and the *Kentish Gazette* in *Sanditon*, along with *The Mirror, Rambler* and *Spectator* (*Northanger Abbey*) and the *Idler* and *Quarterly Review* (*Mansfield Park*). Chapman also identified a number of songs and riddles, including Mr Woodhouse's poorly remembered 'Kitty a Fair but Frozen Maid' (by Garrick) and *Robin Adair* (both in *Emma*), and 'The Je ne scai Quoi', quoted in *Mansfield Park*.

An allusion that Chapman was unable to trace in *Northanger Abbey* 'by unwearied diligence they gained' (*NA* 13) is identified by the editors of the Cambridge Edition as coming from 'a couplet from a popular old schoolbook, *A Guide to the English Tongue*' (*NA* 303), but it could equally well have been known to Austen because it was a relatively well-known verse commonly stitched by young girls on samplers. Deirdre Le Faye first hypothesised that this was the case in *Notes & Queries* in 1999, and I have identified five such samplers, dating from 1721 to 1814, with only small variants from the verse suggested by Le Faye.[6] One such appears in Figure 12.1. It seems to me more likely that Austen had a sampler, rather than an 'old schoolbook', in mind, given the emphasis on dress, fashion, and needlework in the paragraph within which this appears, as well as the preceding one. These are the paragraphs which pithily establish Mrs Allen's character ('Dress was her passion' [*NA* 12]), comment on both Catherine and her chaperone's clothing in some detail, and note wryly that Mrs Allan has 'more care for the safety of her new gown than for the comfort of her protegée' (*NA* 13). If it is indeed the case that Austen had a sampler in mind when she made the allusion, it is doubly appropriate, since the allusion would then underscore the juxtaposition of a serious moral

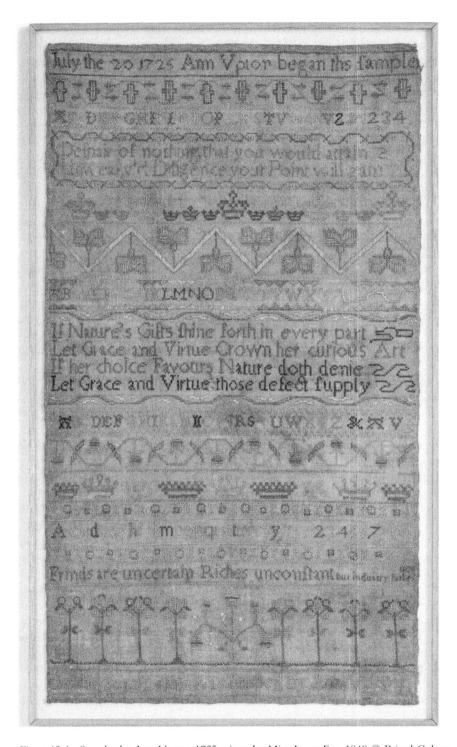

Figure 12.1 Sampler by Ann Upton, 1725, given by Miss Agnes Fry, 1949 © Bristol Culture, by kind permission of Bristol Museums and Archives.

register ('care', 'safety', and 'unwearied diligence') with a concern with the frivolous and the domestic, manifested here through needlework.

In addition to Chapman's identifications of Austen's allusions to ephemeral materials, Edward Copeland first noticed references to the *Lady's Magazine* in *Sense and Sensibility*, and Jennie Batchelor has recently conclusively demonstrated that in fact a large variety of plots, names, and textual echoes from the *Lady's Magazine* appear, recycled and reworked, in a number of Austen's novels.[7] Jocelyn Harris makes an excellent case for Austen's interest in public controversies such as the Regency Crisis, the war with France, the slave trade, and the court-martial of Sir Home Popham, as well as for her fascination with celebrities, naming Lord Byron, Captain Cook, Lord Nelson, stage stars Dorothy Jordan, Sarah Siddons, and Edmund Kean, and 'new-minted celebrity William Shakespeare' as of particular consequence to Austen (*Satire, Celebrity and Politics* xviii). Harris also identifies allusions to 'women who were briefly the talk of the town, heiress Catherine Tylney-Long and Sara Baartman, the so-called Hottentot Venus', and reminds us of Austen's mockery of the dissipation of the Prince Regent and the 'feckless folly' of Prince William (*Satire, Celebrity and Politics* xviii). It is clear that Austen followed the long-running and distasteful domestic battle between the Prince Regent and Caroline of Brunswick, writing in a letter of 16 February 1813, 'Poor Woman, I shall support her as long as I can, because she *is* a Woman, & because I hate her Husband' (Jane Austen to Martha Lloyd, 16 February 1813; *Letters* 208). Harris suggests that Austen followed this, and other controversies, primarily through the 'reports, highlights, compilations, abridgement, and extracts' found in 'newspapers and magazines' (*Satire, Celebrity and Politics* 75). She also draws on a large number of pamphlets, occasional poetry, reports of theatrical performances, broadsheets, and advertisements to show Austen's engagement with the whole of the print culture of her time.

News also appears, of course, not only in textual, but in visual form, and Harris also reminds us of the pervasive culture of visual satire of Austen's period. We know that Austen attended art exhibitions whenever she could, famously looking for a picture of Elizabeth Bennet in the 1814 exhibition of Sir Joshua Reynolds's paintings, but she would also have been faced with satirical images of newsworthy events every time she passed the window of a print shop in any of the towns that she visited. As Rachel Brownstein has noted, print shop windows 'counted among the entertaining spectacles of London' and suggests, as in Figure 12.2, that they were 'a species of street theatre that drew heterogeneous urban audiences' (Brownstein 90).

Such a phenomenon was not limited to London; the print shops in Winchester, Southampton, Bath, Lyme Regis, and Cheltenham—all towns Austen is known to have visited—doubtless had a similar function, while circulating libraries and bookshops also often carried prints as well as books, as shown in Figure 12.3. Austen could therefore hardly have avoided seeing political and celebrity news, even had she wished to do so. As a writer keenly interested in satire in her own practice, it seems probable that she enjoyed seeing satirical prints, and made the most of opportunities to do so.

Janine Barchas suggests that visual materials of all kinds were indeed important to Austen's artistic practice, presenting incontestable evidence of Austen's use of maps and travel guides to plot her novels. She also gives an excellent example of Austen's use of such material for comic purposes, contending that Austen's allusion to Blaize Castle in *Northanger Abbey* depends for its comedy on the widespread knowledge, hilariously shared by none of the characters, that it was a sham—a faux-Gothic folly built by Thomas Farr in 1766, and represented as such in the many guides to Bath produced in the period. Austen's ownership of Richard Warner's *Excursions from Bath* (1801) takes on new importance in this context.

In the light of the accumulated evidence for Austen's reading of ephemeral materials, it is worth remembering Simon Eliot's contention that, in the nineteenth century:

> the book was not the predominant form of text and, more than likely, was not therefore
> the thing most commonly or widely read. By 1907, as the first Census of Production makes

Figure 12.2 The Caricature Shop. Courtesy of the Lewis Walpole Library, Yale University.

clear, books in terms of net value were worth some 14% of the total value of print production (and that included manuscript books and ledgers). The two areas of largest value were, in ascending order, jobbing printing and periodical printing. The most common reading experience, by the mid-nineteenth century at latest, would most likely be the advertising poster, all the tickets, handbills and forms generated by an industrial society, and the daily or weekly paper. Most of this reading was, of course, never recorded or commented upon for it was too much a part of the fabric of everyday life to be noticed. (Eliot para 10)[8]

Such reading is, as Eliot rightly notes, unlikely to be recorded in diaries or letters, but it does become part of the mental world that the reader inhabits. If we are to understand Austen's allusive writing practice properly, therefore, we must think seriously about the ways in which allusions to such ephemeral reading intersect with those to books in Austen's works.

Jane Austen was, as Kathryn Sutherland has argued in another context, a writer who recycled, transposed, and re-used incidents and themes between and within her novels (*Jane Austen's Textual Lives* 126–27). Her recycling of news, gossip, and celebrity scandal is as present, we now know, in the novels, as it is obvious in the letters. But Austen is more, of course, than the re-teller of second-hand scandals, and the question with which most Austen critics are preoccupied is therefore less with what she read than the astonishingly innovative ways in which she used it. It would be easy to assume a more sustained and serious engagement with works we now consider to be important and

Figure 12.3 Beauty in Search of Knowledge. Courtesy of the Lewis Walpole Library, Yale University.

canonical, and a more light-hearted or frivolous engagement with ephemera. But such a conclusion is not supported by the evidence. Austen often treats literary heavyweights with dismissive casualness, making Pope, for example, the subject of a light-hearted pun: '"Whatever is, is best".—There has been one infallible Pope in the World' (Jane to Cassandra Austen, 26 October 1813; *Letters* 244), and likening her own verses comically to those of 'Homer & Virgil, Ovid & Propria que Maribus' (Jane to Cassandra Austen, 24 January 1809; *Letters* 170). She helped to condense Richardson's monumental five-volume novel *Sir Charles Grandison* into a playful skit for the entertainment of nieces and nephews, and ruthlessly mocked the character of Sir Charles himself in the early 'Jack and Alice'.[9] Her famous defence of the novel in *Northanger Abbey* also gives such reading short shrift, rejecting Milton, Pope, Prior, Sterne, and the *Spectator* in favour of the female-authored novel. Conversely, she is perfectly prepared to use works with little to no cultural capital attached to make a serious point, as we saw in her use of the quotation from the sampler in *Northanger Abbey*. In this total disregard for reputation or status, we see a levelling impulse not usually attributed to Austen, in particular by those critics who consider her to be a conservative or anti-Jacobin novelist.[10]

As I've argued elsewhere, however, Austen is a complex and subversive writer, and she is probably never more complex and subversive than in her use of allusion (Halsey, 'The Books Sir Edward Denham Doesn't Read' 54). A number of critics, from Kenneth Moler in 1968 to Olivia Murphy in 2013, have considered Austen's literary allusions in intelligent and illuminating ways. But few—with the notable exceptions of Barchas and Harris—have wished to consider what we might call her *non*-literary allusions—those moments when Austen reaches out to the wider print culture of her day—in any depth. If we are to think seriously about the intellectual world that Austen inhabited, though, further consideration not just of the Enlightenment tradition that she inherited, but also of the kinds of reading not normally considered to be important or influential—songs, ballads, newspapers, pamphlets, magazines, walking guides, and so on—is vital. We also need to take seriously Austen's interest in the visual and material, remembering that maps, prints, paintings—including landscapes and cityscapes—portraits, samplers, and even dress fabrics are also texts of various kinds, lending themselves to interpretation and, in Austen's case, re-use for literary purposes.

In Chapter 9 of *Emma* (1815), with Emma's help, Harriet Smith engages in 'collecting and transcribing all the riddles of every sort that she could meet with, into a thin quarto of hot-pressed paper, made up by her friend, and ornamented with cyphers and trophies' (*E* 74). Canvassing their particular friends and relatives for riddles and charades, Harriet and Emma of course end up eliciting Mr Elton's riddle on 'Courtship', intended by him for Emma herself, but assigned by Emma to Harriet, and interpreted by her as describing his intentions towards Harriet: 'Very well, Mr Elton, very well indeed. I have read worse charades. *Courtship*—a very good hint. I give you credit for it. This is feeling your way. This is saying very plainly—"Pray, Miss Smith, give me leave to pay my addresses to you. Approve my charade and my intentions in the same glance"' (*E* 76). Harriet fails to comprehend any part of the charade, but as soon as Emma has finished interpreting it for Harriet's benefit, she muses complacently to her: 'There does seem to be a something in the air of Hartfield which gives love exactly the right direction, and sends it into the very channel where it ought to flow. "The course of true love never did run smooth—" A Hartfield edition of Shakespeare would have a long note on that passage' (*E* 80). Emma is, of course, wrong in assuming that her 'Hartfield edition' would counteract Shakespeare's lines, since the remainder of the novel nicely demonstrates precisely the opposite, with continual difficulties and obstacles appearing in the way of the various 'true love' matches that the novel eventually brings about. This episode is important in a variety of different ways, but my point here is simply to show how Austen treats Mr Elton's flimsy charade and the line from Shakespeare as exactly equivalent in terms of their cultural authority.[11] In both cases, Emma imposes her own (incorrect) interpretation upon the lines, blithely assuming that her explanation must be the true one. What is important here is that *both* texts serve precisely the same purpose in exposing Emma's 'imaginist' tendencies, her egotism, and her inability to differentiate between facts and fiction (*E* 362). Sandwiched between Mr Elton's charade, and Garrick's 'Kitty, a fair but frozen maid', mis-remembered and misquoted by Mr Woodhouse when he enters three pages later, *A Midsummer Night's Dream* becomes just another text to plunder to bolster Emma's own erroneous worldview.

From Shakespeare to samplers, Austen's magpie versatility—her ability to take what she needed from diverse sources irrespective of their provenance, and to turn it into delicate ironic social commentary—is in my view at the heart of her artistic technique. As Olivia Murphy suggests in her account of Austen's creative practice, 'it is through her critical reading that Austen produced her creative contribution to the novel' (*Jane Austen the Reader* 29). Murphy suggests that Austen learned her craft as a novelist through mocking the language and conventions that she knew best—those of the sentimental novel—and her technique did not fundamentally change, although it was honed and perfected in the writing of the six mature novels and unfinished works. Murphy's elegant analysis of the ways in which Austen dissected and then reassembled the conventions of the sentimental novel to create her own unique form illuminates both Austen's technique and its effects. It is my contention here that analysis of Austen's interactions with the conventions of sensationalist newspaper articles, political pamphlets, and magazine stories (as a beginning) sheds similar new light on some old topics, such as Austen's irony, her politics, and her proto-feminism. If we take seriously my suggestion, borne out in the example from *Emma*, that Austen's allusive practice allocates a similar weight of cultural authority to both lasting and ephemeral materials, we must then consider its implications. Austen starts to appear to us as an even trickier, more ironic, and more subversive writer than we had previously thought.

Notes

1 See also letters of 14–16 January 1801 (*Letters* 74) and 12–13 May 1801 (*Letters* 84), where Austen discusses the arrangements for the dispersal of the books.

2 Michele Cohen has recently argued vigorously for the rigour and breadth of a so-called 'domestic' education; see her 'The pedagogy of conversation in the home: 'familiar conversation' as a pedagogical tool in eighteenth and nineteenth-century England'. *Oxford Review of Education* 41 (2015), 447–63, and '"To think, to compare, to combine, to methodise": Girls' Education in Enlightenment Britain'. *Women, Gender and Enlightenment*, edited by S. Knott and B. Taylor, Palgrave Macmillan, 2005, pp. 224–42.

3 While this statistic is not in itself proof that Austen was drawing her allusions from the copies of books held in the Godmersham Library, it is suggestive of the extent to which she took advantage of this collection.

4 There is a long and important tradition of Austen criticism, dating back to her brother Henry's 'Biographical Notice', appended to the posthumous first edition of *Northanger Abbey and Persuasion* (1818), and developed and perpetuated in her nephew James Edward Austen-Leigh's *Memoir of Jane Austen* (1869), which presents her as fundamentally uninterested in politics. 'The politics of the day occupied very little of her attention', asserted Austen-Leigh in 1869, and this became a critical orthodoxy for successive biographers, critics, and readers until Butler's *Jane Austen and the War of Ideas* decisively shifted the grounds of debate in 1987 (Austen-Leigh 71). Similarly, both Henry and James Edward suggested that Jane's reading had been extremely limited and circumscribed, naming only Goldsmith, Hume, Robertson, Fielding, Richardson, Johnson, Crabbe, Cowper, and Scott. Such a list pays no attention at all not only to the wide reading in philosophy, natural history, politics, and travel documented in her letters to Cassandra, but also to what seems to have been the majority of Austen's reading of books—the female-authored novel. They certainly make no reference to her interest in scandal and satire.

5 R. W. Chapman's indexes to his edition of *Northanger Abbey and Persuasion* and the *Minor Works* have been collated and are now available on www.pemberley.com, supplemented with citations from *A Jane Austen Dictionary* by George L. Apperson.

6 For example, in the Fitzwilliam Collection in Cambridge, one such sampler is in the G. W. L. Glaisher collection, Object Number: T.122-1928. The inscription reads 'AS YOU EXPect That men should DeaL BY YOU/SO Deal BY Them And Give Each man His Due/Better It Is To GAIn Great Reputation Then to/Be RICH For That never Wants VexatioN/Constraint in ALL Thimgs makes The Pleasur/Less Sweet is The love That COMeS With/Willingness/DesPair OF NOthing That YOU WOULd Attain/Unwearied DILIgence YOUR POInt WILL Gain/Experience Best Is Gained Without Much Cost Read Men And/ Books Then Practise What Thou Knowest/They That Are Proud And Other men Disdain Do Often Meet/With Hate And Scorn Again. Mary Wheeler Her Work Done in ninth/Year Of Her Age 1721'. Le Faye suggests the alternative 'Despair of nothing that you would obtain/Unwearied diligence your point will gain/Great blessings ever wait on virtuous deeds/An tho' a late a sure reward succeeds (Le Faye, *Family*

Record), p. 60. Another, pictured in Figure 12.1, in the Bristol Museums and Archives collections, reads 'Despair of nothing, that you would attain/Unweari'd Digligence your Point will gain'. Thanks to Jennie Batchelor for helping me to identify these samplers.

7 See Copeland 153–71, and Batchelor, *The Lady's Magazine (1770–1832) and the Making of Literary History* (Forthcoming). I am very grateful to Jennie Batchelor for allowing me to read her work in MS.

8 Although Eliot is primarily focussed on the later nineteenth century, as his terminus date of 1907 suggests, his contention holds mainly true for the Regency period as well.

9 The manuscript of Austen's version of *Sir Charles Grandison* is held at Chawton House Library. Family tradition holds that the manuscript was dictated to Jane Austen by her niece Anna, and that it was designed to be acted in front of the family, who knew the original well. 'Jack and Alice' appears in *Volume the First* of the manuscript juvenilia.

10 Marilyn Butler first articulated this position in her seminal *Jane Austen and the War of Ideas* (1987), a work that remains influential even while much recent criticism either explicitly or implicitly challenges her interpretation of Austen's political position.

11 It is important to remember that by 1815, Shakespeare was acknowledged as the National Bard, feted by Garrick in his famous Stratford Jubilee of 1769, and, according to Kate Rumbold, 'invested with an enduring emotional and moral authority' through the quotations found in contemporary novels (Rumbold 50). Indeed, Austen elsewhere acknowledges Shakespeare's authority, describing him as 'part of an Englishman's constitution', and suggesting that 'we all talk Shakespeare, use his similes, and describe with his descriptions' (*MP* 390–91).

Works Cited

Austen, Jane. *Juvenilia*, edited by Peter Sabor. Cambridge UP, 2006.

Austen, Jane. *Later Manuscripts*, edited by Janet Todd and Linda Bree. Cambridge UP, 2008.

Austen, Jane. *Northanger Abbey*, edited by Barbara M. Benedict and Deirdre Le Faye. Cambridge UP, 2006.

Austen-Leigh, James Edward. *A Memoir of Jane Austen*, edited by Kathryn Sutherland. Oxford Worlds Classics, 2002.

Barchas, Janine. *Matters of Fact in Jane Austen: History, Location and Celebrity*. Johns Hopkins UP, 2012.

Batchelor, Jennie, *The Lady's Magazine (1770–1832) and the Making of Literary History*. Forthcoming.

Brownstein, Rachel M. 'Caricatures and Characters: James Gillray and Jane Austen.' *Textus: English Studies in Italy*, vol. 30, no. 3, 2017, pp. 71–93.

Butler, Marilyn. *Jane Austen and the War of Ideas*. Clarendon P, 1975.

Copeland, Edward. 'Money Talks: Jane Austen and the *Lady's Magazine*.' *Jane Austen's Beginnings: The Juvenilia and Lady Susan*. Ann Arbor: UMI Research P, 1989, pp. 153–171.

Eliot, Simon, 'The Reading Experience Database; or, What Are We to Do about the History of Reading?' http://www.open.ac.uk/Arts/RED/redback.htm

Gilson, David. *A Bibliography of Jane Austen*. Oak Knoll P, 1997.

Halsey, Katie. 'The Books Sir Edward Denham Doesn't Read: Jane Austen's Literary Jokes.' *Textus: English Studies in Italy*, vol. 30, no. 3, 2017, pp. 53–69.

Harris, Jocelyn. *Jane Austen's Art of Memory*. Cambridge UP, 1989.

Harris, Jocelyn. *Satire, Celebrity, and Politics in Jane Austen*. Bucknell UP, 2018.

Knox-Shaw, Peter. *Jane Austen and the Enlightenment*. Cambridge UP, 2004.

Le Faye, Deirdre. *Jane Austen's Letters*, 3rd ed. Oxford UP, 1995.

Le Faye, Deirdre. *Jane Austen: A Family Record*, 2nd ed. Cambridge UP, 2004.

Moler, Kenneth L. *Jane Austen's Art of Allusion*. U of Nebraska P, 1968.

Murphy, Olivia. *Jane Austen the Reader: The Artist as Critic*. Palgrave Macmillan, 2013.

Murphy, Olivia. 'The 'Queerness and the Fun': Reading Jane Austen's *Volume the First.*' *Textus: English Studies in Italy*, vol. 30, no. 3, 2017, pp. 31–51.

Rumbold, Kate. *Shakespeare and the Eighteenth-Century Novel: Cultures of Quotation from Samuel Richardson to Jane Austen*. Cambridge UP, 2016.

Sutherland, Kathryn. *Jane Austen's Textual Lives from Aeschylus to Bollywood*. Oxford UP, 2005.

13

PEDESTRIAN CHARACTERS AND PLOTS: *PERSUASION* AND *THE HEART OF MIDLOTHIAN*

Tara Ghoshal Wallace

GEORGE WASHINGTON UNIVERSITY

In perhaps the most symbol-laden scene Jane Austen wrote, the 'young people' in *Mansfield Park*, after spending a weary morning touring the grandeurs of Sotherton house, 'as by one impulse, one wish for air and liberty', walk out into the grounds. The results of their perambulations are memorable: the Bertram sisters shake off social constraints in their pursuit of erotic satisfaction, and Mary Crawford captivates Edmund Bertram with her seductive defiance of the logic of time and distance. The episode is so freighted with significance that readers may forget that all this wandering occurs within the confines of a 'wilderness' consisting of 'a planted wood of about two acres' and lasts 'an hour and a half'; the walk that carries so much disruptive meaning extends no further than the cultivated grounds of Sotherton or the allotted time for rambling before dinner. The circumscribed and physically un-demanding nature of this walk through a contrived wilderness are thrown into relief internally in the debate between Edmund and Mary as to whether they have 'walked at least a mile' or 'not half a mile' (90–103)[1] and intertextually in a pair of novels published in the same year (1814) by Austen's more famous contemporaries: Walter Scott's *Waverley*, in which the hero evolves from a dreamy bookish boy to a seasoned young veteran of two armies 'who now equaled any Highlander in endurance of fatigue' after a series of forced marches through a Scotland in the throes of the Jacobite rebellion of 1745 (280); and Frances Burney's *The Wanderer*, in which the dazzlingly beautiful and almost im-possibly accomplished and virtuous Juliet Granville flees her persecutors, contending with the 'pain and difficulty' afflicting 'her wearied limbs' as she navigates on foot not only the thickets of New Forest but also the brutalities and ideological contradictions of a politically unstable nation at the historical moment of the French Revolution (668).[2] In comparison to the rigorous journeys under-taken against a background of momentous political events that these two novels trace, the exertions and flirtations of the Bertram party at Sotherton look mild indeed.

While Burney never produced another novel, Scott and Austen (in a posthumous publication) re-visited, four years later, the issue of mobility and character. *The Heart of Midlothian* and *Persuasion* (both 1818) provide new ways of considering female pedestrianism, especially in the context of a series of 1790s novels which portray 'a kind of deep homelessness'—like Wollstonecraft's *Maria: or the Wrongs of Woman* (1792), Mary Hays's *The Victim of Prejudice* (1799), and *The Wanderer*, which Ingrid Horrocks, echoing Margaret Anne Doody, labels 'a belated 1790s novel … part of a tradition of writing about women's movement concentrated in the last decade of the eighteenth century' (Horrocks 2, 169; Doody, 318). Scott and Austen address nuances and variations of women's mobility omitted from those earlier feminist texts. Neither Anne Elliot nor Jeanie Deans fits into the category of women wanderers studied by Horrocks or Trish Bredar—women whose 'movement

170   DOI: 10.4324/9780429398155-13-16

continues to be figured as strongly associated with work or suffering' (Horrocks 20) or inherently transgressive women in 'an impossible position, one that dramatizes the psychological effects of particular social constraints while calling attention to the material realities of moving about in a gendered body' (Bredar 150) Neither heroine belongs in the collection of victimised women, epitomised by Burney's Juliet, who are forced to endure involuntary and painful walking. They represent instead the reflections of two innovative, confident (and now canonical) authors who explore, complicate, and sometimes collapse the space between privileged/male walking and victimised/female wandering.

★★★

Austen and Scott introduce the novel-reading public to two unconventional heroines who voluntarily undertake pedestrian activity. Anne Elliot is a twenty-seven-year-old spinster, long past her bloom, so 'faded and thin' that Sir Walter harbours no hope of a respectable marriage for her, and so 'wretchedly altered' that Wentworth would not have known her again (6, 61). Jeanie Deans is a 'rustic heroine' of whom 'the historian, with due regard to veracity', must say that her 'personal attractions were of no uncommon description … short, and rather too stoutly made for her size', with a face 'somewhat freckled, and not possessing regular features' (76, 319).[3] Failing to meet even minimal standards of the beauty required of Romantic heroines, Anne and Jeanie must depend on inner, moral qualities to engage readers. Anne, whom Austen thought 'almost too good for me' (23 March 1817; *Letters* 335), is meant to win our allegiance because of her 'elegance of mind and sweetness of character' (6); and Jeanie, who is too good for everybody, earns our admiration through a 'veneration for truth' (244) and a deep altruism that far outshines her merely pretty sister Effie: declining to exonerate Effie of the capital crime of infanticide by telling a small lie, Jeanie decides to walk from Edinburgh to London to secure a royal pardon for her feckless sibling, who has been convicted of bearing a child, now mysteriously lost and presumed dead.[4] This essay connects those inner virtues with their literally pedestrian activities. Jeanie's heroic march seems a world away from Anne's difficulties in managing the two-mile walk to Winthrop, but I argue that *within context*, their ambulatory capabilities can be seen as congruent, especially in the promptitude with which they undertake pedestrian duties. Moreover, both women, in the course of their walks, undergo traumatic experiences which threaten and suspend their mobility, but which provide them (and readers) with important information and set in motion a series of éclaircissements and plot developments crucial to the final outcomes of the two novels.

Since I want to consider correlations more than contrasts, I begin by attending to some essential differences between Jeanie Deans and Anne Elliot: class, historical context, and nationality. Jeanie is a Scottish peasant lass, embarking on her epic walk at a time (1736) when the Union of 1707 has not yet reconciled political and cultural differences between Scotland and Hanoverian England; Anne belongs to the English gentry class dealing with disruptive social changes in the wake of the Napoleonic wars. These socio-chronotropical differences put Anne's walks within Robin Jarvis's category of 'Pedestrianism and the Picturesque' (35) while they relegate Jeanie to the vulnerable position, outlined by Anne D. Wallace, of lower-class women who faced 'special difficulties … especially if they walked alone, because their peripateia translated as sexual wandering … the latent sexual content of the activity combined with its class content and standard prejudices about women's "nature" and proper roles in society to make women's walking, even on local footpaths, unusually perilous to their reputation' (29–30). Traces of this class-based suspicion are discernible in Mary's complaint that Mrs Musgroves' maids 'are always tempting her [Mary's maid, Jemima] to take a walk with them' and Mrs Musgrove's reciprocal accusation that Jemima 'is always upon the gad' (43). The decorous walks of upper-class women, whether to visit Lady Russell or along the Cobb in Lyme, are apparently free from such scandalous imputations, though we may remember that in *Pride and Prejudice*, Elizabeth's Bennet's trek across muddy fields to Netherfield elicits a socio-sexual condemnation from Miss Bingley: 'To walk ... alone, quite alone! ... It seems to me to shew an abominable sort of conceited independence, a most country town indifference to decorum' (36). Despite their different class positions, neither Anne nor Jeanie encounters the kind of sexual predation suffered by Burney's Juliet Granville, who, walking alone on the outskirts of the New Forest, is 'now assailed with coarse compliments upon her pretty face; now by jocose propositions to join company; and now by free solicitations for a salute'; at one point she even incurs 'the danger of personal and brutal insult' (i.e., imminent rape) from a pair of woodcutters (669, 688). Nor are these heroines subject to the indignities aimed at the German traveler Karl Philipp Moritz, whose indispensable account of walking in eighteenth-century Britain describes multiple episodes of hostility, including being refused housing and even food at inns because 'A traveler on foot in this country seems to be considered as a sort wild man, or an out-of-the-way being, who is stared at, pitied, suspected, and shunned by everybody that meets him' (122). Anne, protected by her class markers even when she perambulates alone, stays at an inn (at Lyme) only when accompanied by a highly respectable entourage—Mr Elliot's admiring glances at Anne are so far from leers that Austen's characteristic free indirect discourse informs us that 'he was a man of exceedingly good manners' (104–5). Jeanie, doubly disadvantaged by class and gender, manages to avoid the kind of abuse visited on Moritz in part because her native good sense counsels her to choose, 'with anxious circumspection, such places of repose as looked at once most decent and most sequestered' (250) and in part because 'her own simple and quiet manners' invite courtesy from innkeepers and fellow travellers.

Another essential difference between Anne and Jeanie's peregrinations lies in what Franco Moretti calls 'anthropological' chronotropism, characteristic of historical novels which describe journeys into the geography of the past—he cites Waverley's journey across internal borders to visit the clan culture of the Scottish Highlands (37–38). When Jeanie crosses into England, she notes disparities in religion, sociability, and agricultural practices: she finds, for example, 'the common people of England, although inferior in courtesy to strangers ... yet, upon the whole, by no means deficient in the real duties of hospitality', but writes disapprovingly of 'twa men that were ministers following hunds ... . A sorrowfu' sight to behold!' (251). Anne, circulating within a narrow range of familiar spaces, has no such access to 'internal unevenness' (Moretti 40), though perhaps her bemused observation of the Musgroves' family dynamics may constitute something like an anthropological study—we note Anne's 'lesson, in the art of knowing our own nothingness beyond our own circle' when she moves from Kellynch to Uppercross (42). Jeanie, responding to taunts generated by her bare feet, 'conformed to the national [English] extravagance of wearing shoes and stockings for the whole day, though she 'confessed afterwards that 'besides the wastrife, it was lang or she could walk sae comfortably with the shoes as without them' (249). We may recall Keats remarking on the Scottish practice of women walking 'barefoot, with their Shoes and clean stockings in hand, ready to put on and look smart in the Towns' (163) and connect Wallace's sociosexual argument with Richard M. Griffith's conclusion that 'we depersonalize our feet with shoes', and that a woman's impractical shoe 'symbolizes all confinement ... . Representing as it does the giving up of strictures, the naked foot of the female may incite an erotic response' (281, 286). In *Persuasion*, working-class women in Bath, far from exposing bare feet to pavements and male gazes, add 'the ceaseless clink of pattens' to the cacophony of urban sounds (135). Although there is nothing in *Persuasion* to match the specific cultural difference represented by Scottish and English protocols about being shod, Roger Michell's 1995 film may be teasing out a latent code in the text when he focuses his camera on the Musgrove ladies' delicate shoes as they carefully pick their way along the Cobb while a local urchin races by in his sensible foot-ware.

Both Jarvis and Wallace delineate clear distinctions between those who walk to experience the aesthetic pleasures of Romantic nature and those who walk because they must. Horrocks, especially in her chapter on *The Wanderer*, draws on this earlier work to distinguish between leisured travelers 'in search of aesthetically pleasing or culturally informative sites' and the 'reluctant' women wanderers who are the subject of her book, and who have little to do with Romantic pedestrianism (183). While the narrator of *Midlothian* concedes that 'there was something of romance in Jeanie's venturous resolution' (247) to journey four hundred miles on foot to save her sister, Jeanie remains an almost paradigmatically (even parodically) unromantic heroine—Jane Millgate points out that she is 'marked off from the outset by the absence of any tinge of the romantic in either her appearance or her perspective' (152). She barely registers any picturesque elements of the landscape she traverses. Her Scottish and peasant identity responds to English landscape only by expressing relief at the approach of a hill because 'baith my sight and my very feet are weary o' sic tracks of level ground—it looks a' the way between this and York as if a' the land had been trenched and levelled, whilk is very wearisome to my Scots een' (257). This topographical analysis, and her surprise at the number of windmills dotting the countryside around York constitute the sum of Jeanie's reflections on landscape, and she locates pastoral pleasure not in picturesque views of nature but on the discovery of a cure for sick cattle (251). Indeed, the single appreciative invocation of the connection between Romantic poetry and nature in *The Heart of Midlothian* occurs when mad Madge Wildfire, having announced that 'It's a dainty thing to be in the woods on a fine morning like this', leads Jeanie to a 'hillock of moss, such as the poet of Grasmere has described', which turns out to contain, as in Wordsworth's 'The Thorn', the grave of a baby possibly killed by a betrayed and insane mother (272–73). Jeanie, even less schooled in picturesque views than Catherine Morland and certainly lacking Anne Elliot's easy access to poetry, overlooks the aesthetic pleasure of contemplating a picturesque village, 'one of those beautiful scenes which are so often found in merry England' (279), to concentrate on tidying herself up before approaching its inhabitants for help. Significantly, the only Romantic walker in the text is the self-centered Effie, who, after Jeanie secures her pardon, marries her seducer George Staunton and thereby rises into the upper class, only to become 'listless and unhappy', finding solace only 'while in the open air, and amid the mountain landscapes' (440).

Anne, who famously 'learned romance as she grew older' (30), deliberately, almost theatrically, subscribes to Jeffrey C. Robinson's formulation of the Romantic walk, which 'may be said to code the dialectics of wonderment or consolation and critical thought, or of spiritual transcendence or realization and social historical encounter, or of aesthetic disinterestedness and sensuous engagement' (6). Early in the novel, she walks 'along a favourite grove' to meditate on the possibility that soon Wentworth, too, 'may be walking here' and requires 'many a stroll and many a sigh' to overcome her agitation at that prospect (25, 30); and after the episode at Lyme, she enjoys 'stroll[s] of solitary indulgence in her father's grounds' (133), though her thoughts then seem to turn on Captain Benwick rather than on Wentworth, perhaps because her last walk with him around picturesque Lyme had reactivated their dialogue about responses to the Romantic poetry of Scott and Byron. Even in the urban spread of Bath, Anne can indulge in precious memories of her happy encounter with Wentworth at a concert, allowing the reader to share Austen's gentle mockery of such Romantic pedestrianism: 'Prettier musings of high-wrought love and eternal constancy, could never have passed along the streets of Bath, than Anne was sporting with from Camden-place to Westgate-buildings. It was almost enough to spread purification and perfume all the way' (192). And of course, on that consequential walk to Winthrop, she self-consciously seeks solace from 'the view of the last smiles of the year upon the tawny leaves and withered hedges' while 'repeating to herself some few of the thousand poetical descriptions extant of autumn' before Wentworth's eager appreciation for Louisa's equally romantic assertion that nothing could separate her from the man she loved prevents Anne from 'immediately fall[ing] into a quotation again' (84–85). Like Juliet Granville entering the New Forest while fleeing from her persecutors, 'as unmoved by its beauties, as unobservant of its prospects, as the "Dull Incurious" who pursue their course but to gain the place of their destination' (*Wanderer* 674),[5] Anne momentarily fails to inhabit her cultured and Romantic sensibilities.[6]

Jeanie's fortuitous meeting with the Stauntons brings to an end her sojourn on foot, but it should be noted that she has covered most of the four hundred miles without any discernible fatigue because her natural peasant hardiness and 'uncommonly strong and healthy temperament, free from all nervous affection and every other irregularity' bless her with the stamina that so impresses Queen Caroline that Her Royal Highness admits, 'I thought I was a good walker … but this shames me sadly' (72–73, 339). While Jeanie's pedestrian feat does not quite match that of John Stokes, who, in 1815, walked fifty miles a day for twenty days in order 'to counter a tendency to "excessive cor-pulency"', nor that of Sarah Hazlitt's astonishing thirty-two miles in one day while walking in Scotland to escape the stress of her divorce from William (Jarvis 1, 155–56), Jeanie Deans is clearly an indefatigable walker who strategically explains her extraordinary stamina to Queen Caroline by hoping that 'May your Leddyship never hae sae weary a heart, that ye canna be sensible of the weariness of the limbs' (339). Anne, alas, enjoys no such physical vigour or mental serenity, lacking the elasticity that Catherine Morland exults in once General Tilney has complimented it (103), or the Dashwoods' energetic rambles on the 'high downs' near Barton cottage (40), or Elizabeth Bennet's athletic ease in covering the three miles to Netherfield, 'crossing field after field at a quick pace, jumping over stiles and springing over puddles with impatient activity' (32). Enervated by the two-mile excursion to Winthrop, Anne, 'really tired herself, was glad to sit down', with Mary, subsequently needing Charles Musgrove's arm during the return walk, and tremblingly grateful for Wentworth's 'perception of her fatigue' that saves her a further mile of walking (87, 91).

On the other hand, Anne is no Fanny Price either, as thoroughly prostrated by less than half a mile of strolling through Sotherton's 'sweet wood' (94) as by 'four days together' without access to her gentle exercise on horseback (74). In fact, I would suggest, Austen carefully positions Anne, in her own context, as both physically able and active. As John Wiltshire has pointed out, 'In each of the novel's main locales is found someone who is disabled as a result of injury or disease, or occurs an incident that serves to remind us of the vulnerability or fragility of the body … . *Persuasion* is a novel of trauma: of broken bones, broken heads, and broken hearts' (165). In the context of Captain Harville's lameness, which 'prevented him from taking much exercise' and which precludes him from joining the Uppercross group's last stroll through Lyme because he 'would have quite walking enough by the time he reached home' (99, 108); in the context of Louisa Musgrove's fall in the course of that 'last ill-judged, ill-fated walk to the Cobb' (116) that leaves her incapacitated for months; in the context of Mrs Smith's illness which has 'made her for the present a cripple' (152)[7]: in light of these disabilities Anne is as hale as Jeanie is in comparison to her lover Reuben Butler, whom she dissuades from accompanying her to London because 'your very limbs tremble with standing for ten minutes on the floor; how would you undertake a journey as far as Lunnon?' (247). Jeanie's hyper-able body exceeds even the restlessly active George Staunton, whom she encounters during her last stage on foot, lying 'like a crushed snake, writhing with impatience at my incapacity for motion' (296).[8] In *Narrative Prosthesis: Disability and the Dependencies of Discourse*, David Mitchell and Sharon Snyder correlate disability with 'gender, sexuality, and race, as a constructed category of discursive investment', de-ployed to show how 'the deficient body, by virtue of its insufficiency, serves as baseline for the articulation of the normal body' (2, 7). Their work joins other literature in disability studies to counter 'a homogenizing scheme of a people's shared attributes', advancing a theory of 'disability as a narrative device—an artistic prosthesis—that reveals the pervasive dependency of artistic, cultural, and philo-sophical discourses upon the powerful alterity assigned to people with disabilities' (44, 51). It is not part of my purpose here to undertake a disability studies reading of *Persuasion*, nor even to attempt to summarize Mitchell and Snyder's complex and rich arguments; it is worth pointing out, however, that the list of disabled bodies cited by Wiltshire—and I would include Mrs Croft's temporary immobility when 'tied by the leg' because of a blister (170)—provides a kind of narrative prosthesis: a device allowing the text to construe Anne, despite the fragility she demonstrates during the Winthrop epi-sode, as a body that meets or even exceeds normative standards of abled activity.

The text offers multiple examples of Anne as a frequent and ready walker. Early in the novel, we are told that Anne undertakes an 'almost daily walk to Lady Russell's' (32), a half-mile distance from Kellynch, meaning that she walks at least a mile a day in addition to her perambulations in her favourite grove—perhaps it is worth citing a recent article in *The Washington Post* which reports that the concept of the daily mile, initiated at a primary school in Stirling, Scotland, has been shown to be 'part of the solution to child health and well being' (14 August 2018, E6). At Uppercross, there are similar regular visits to the Great House, described at separate times as being 'about a quarter of a mile' from the cottage (36) and 'half a mile distant' (58)—it may be that the longer distance, expressed through Anne's consciousness of Wentworth dining at the 'Great House' while she remains at home with little Charles, represents her sense of distance from her former lover (36). At Bath, she easily manages the walk from Camden Place to Westgate Buildings, from Milsom Street to Camden Place, and even the 'toilsome walk' (227) between Camden Place and the White Hart inn. Especially in comparison to Lady Russell, Sir Walter and Elizabeth Elliot, who seem dependent on carriages to convey them around Bath, Anne emerges as an excellent candidate for a Fitbit.

While Anne in no way accrues the physical and moral superlatives Jeanie earns by undertaking her journey from Edinburgh to London on behalf of her sister, even her more limited mobility signals superiority of character. Holly E. Pike finds in *Persuasion* a link between social and physical movement, 'connecting outdoor activity and vehicular travel to the characters' ability to look beyond the limits of their own social group and to assess people on qualities other than appearance and status', adding that 'Anne is explicitly associated with the outdoors', thus metaphorically signaling her acceptance of the kind of social mobility so abhorrent to Sir Walter (39). Melissa Soderman emphasizes how Austen locates Anne in public spaces, concluding that she 'has moved away from the psychologically damaging insularity of Kellynch' (798). I would argue for the literal as well as figurative valence of Anne's outdoor activity: she can summon the physical stamina and the mental determination to mobilise her body when either duty or desire calls. After Sir Walter and Elizabeth leave Kellynch, Anne undertakes the most 'trying' task of 'going to almost every house in the parish, as a sort of take-leave' (39), a duty clearly accomplished on foot since she subsequently depends on Lady Russell's carriage to convey her to Uppercross. Her daily mile to and from Lady Russell's house provides a welcome respite from being 'nobody with either father or sister' to bask in the company of one to whom she is 'a most dear and highly valued god-daughter, favourite and friend' (5–6). Her frequent visits to Mrs Smith may have originated in gratitude and pity but become a source of real friendship and social pleasure, until superseded by the 'keener interest' that takes her on foot to the White Hart, where she hopes to meet Wentworth (229). That consequential walk to Winthrop belongs in the categories of both duty and desire: the Musgrove girls, having failed to dissuade Mary from joining them by announcing that 'they were going to take a *long* walk', extend 'a much more cordial invitation' to Anne, who accedes in the first instance because her presence might deflect Mary's interference in their plans; when Charles and Wentworth join them, she chooses, 'from some feelings of interest and curiosity', to remain a member of the party, although she concedes that 'Her *pleasure* in the walk must arise from the exercise and the day' rather than from any sociability. Significantly, no one imagines that the walk would tax Anne's stamina—it is Mary who bristles because 'Every body is always supposing that I am not a good walker' (83–84). In other words, neither Anne nor her walking companions anticipate that the woman who is in the habit of regular perambulatory exercise could find the four-mile walk to Winthrop and back beyond her physical capacity.

★★★

So why does Anne succumb to an uncharacteristic frailty during that walk to Winthrop? Why does she find it so taxing that she needs not only to grasp the opportunity to ride back with Admiral and Mrs Croft but also to be 'glad to sit down' with her sister when Mary, out of pure snobbishness, finds herself 'too excessively tired' to visit the Hayters (85–87)? I suggest that Anne's physical debilitation stems from psychological blows suffered during that walk: Wentworth's eager admiration for Louisa's 'character of decision and firmness' and their seemingly inevitable march toward marriage, as well as Louisa's equally disquieting communication to him that Lady Russell had 'persuaded Anne to refuse' Charles Musgrove's proposal because he is not 'not learned and bookish enough'. These overheard confidences, so distressing to her feelings, immobilise her body: after Louisa and Wentworth move out of earshot, Anne's 'own emotions still kept her fixed. She had much to recover from, before she could move' because 'she had heard a great deal of very painful import … which must give her extreme agitation' (89). Megan Quinn proposes that in *Persuasion*, Austen 'makes a case that it is language itself, rather than its representation of characters, that excites her reader's immediate physical sensations' (260). Whether or not we as readers share Anne's nervous paralysis during the Winthrop episode, her momentary stasis amply demonstrates the effect of words on Anne's material body, and we discern a parallel manifestation when Wentworth's epistolary declaration of love leaves her so visibly agitated by her secret 'overpowering happiness' that Mrs Musgrove forbids her to walk at all and Charles insists that she cannot walk back to Camden Place without the support of a male arm—note that she rapidly recovers enough energy for an hour of explanatory perambulation with Wentworth once Charles eagerly hands her off to her lover (238–39). Anne's robust constitution, attested to by her multiple pedestrian undertakings at Kellynch, Uppercross, Lyme, and Bath, abandons her only when under pressure from strong emotions.

Jeanie Deans, neither overcome by physical exertion nor susceptible to overwhelming emotions, undergoes her own version of psychological alarm and physical immobility. Although she writes to Reuben Butler that she is 'not wearied with walking, but the better for it' (251)—indeed, when accommodated with 'a pillion and post-horse' for a portion of the journey, 'She was a good deal fatigued by a mode of travelling to which she was less accustomed than to walking' (256)—she is so '[m]uch surprised, and somewhat alarmed' when she learns that two mysterious women had inquired about 'a Scotchwoman, going to London upon justice business', that she for once tries to avoid walking (257). Forced to continue on foot when unsuccessful in her attempt to hire posthorses for the next stage, she is accosted by Madge and her mother Meg Murdockson, whose coded threats leave her 'stupified with undefined apprehension' until she recollects 'the affectionate and dutiful errand on which she was engaged' (259), much as Anne marshals her energies to say farewell to tenants at Kellynch or visit the disabled Mrs Smith. There is nothing immaterial or psychological about Jeanie's immobility when the two ruffians engaged by Meg kidnap and imprison her, but, like Anne behind the hedgerow, trapped and silent while overhearing a conversation that troublingly enlightens, Jeanie, confined to a recess in the thieves' den, hears Meg articulate her determination to thwart Jeanie's mission in order to prevent Staunton from marrying Effie, who would then 'hold my daughter's place' as wife of their common seducer (268). In both cases, momentary immobility initiates a cascade of enlightenment that ultimately unravels mysteries and, albeit circuitously, advances intricate plot developments necessary to the novels' resolutions.

In a recent article, Yoon Sun Lee proposes a fascinating re-reading of Austen's plots, suggesting that 'Filiation is practically rejected, as is the idea that an event has an author or even a single cause' (309). My reading both expands and complicates her argument, since I argue that in *Persuasion*, as in *The Heart of Midlothian*, both character and plot are driven by a specific set of events connected with the heroines' mobility and moments of enforced stasis. A sprint through the plot twists of the two novels serves to illustrate my proposition that the pedestrian activities of the heroines mobilise multiple narrative threads. Jeanie, during her forced (imprisoned) immobility, overhears Meg accuse Madge of throwing Effie's child into a lake. Madge's anger at her mother's lie propels her to play 'a fine jink … we will awa' out and tak a walk … and it will be some fun and fresh air' (271), during which hike she recounts a garbled version of her own seduction and betrayal by George Staunton before she drags Jeanie to the Reverend Staunton's church. The Reverend, certain there is 'something extraordinary' in Jeanie's demeanor, summons her to his rectory, where Jeanie encounters George, who relays his conviction that the Murdocksons were responsible for the infant's disappearance (302–4). While remaining deeply disapproving of George's narrative of seduction and criminality, Jeanie, now aware of his intention to surrender to authorities in order to save Effie, writes to him of her success in winning the pardon, thereby leaving him free to spirit the liberated Effie away and marry her. Meanwhile, the Duke of Argyle, deeply impressed that Jeanie has 'come up from Edinburgh on foot, to attempt this hopeless solicitation for your sister's life' (323), not only stage-manages her successful appeal to Queen Caroline, but sends her back to Scotland in his carriage, accompanied by his servants Archibald and Dolly Dutton. At Carlisle, they learn that Meg has been hanged and witness mob violence against Madge, whereupon Jeanie, wishing that 'she could have requited the service Madge had conferred upon her' during her captivity (286), halts their journey to be at Madge's deathbed, an interval during which Archibald and Dolly come into possession of a broadside containing Meg's detailed confession. After more than a decade, this confession finds its way to Jeanie as wrapping for cheese, since Dolly had kept the paper for its 'useful purposes' (368). Jeanie, having read confirmation of Effie's innocence as well an intimation that the child lives, forwards the document to Effie, thus activating Staunton's search for his son, culminating with the patricide which concludes the main plot. When Jeanie, almost immobilized after her frightening encounter with Meg and Madge, resumes her walk after recollecting 'the affectionate and dutiful errand on which she was engaged' (259), she little knows that her courageous decision to proceed on foot will determine the outcome of so many lives ... and plot threads.[9]

The developments launched by the walk to Winthrop may not be as dramatic as those enabling resolution in *The Heart of Midlothian*, but they too drive the novel's course. Louisa's delight in the sensation of jumping into Wentworth's arms, ending in that calamitous fall that culminates in her engagement to Benwick, dates from the pleasure she derived from having Wentworth 'jump her from the stiles' (109) as well as from his praise for the firmness of character that he later condemns as 'the obstinacy of self-will' (242). As for Anne, convinced in the course of that excursion that 'Every thing now marked out Louisa for Captain Wentworth' (90), she not only overcomes the 'extreme agitation' that led to nervous decrepitude—'so much more hardened to being in Captain Wentworth's company than she had at first imagined' (99) that she happily joins the expedition to Lyme—but also becomes more responsive to other men. After 'a very good impulse of her nature' (100) rouses Benwick out of his melancholy, he becomes sufficiently open to a 'second attachment' (28) to win Louisa's heart through the very poetry Anne had warned him against, thus freeing Wentworth to pursue his reawakened love for Anne, which he recounts while supporting an Anne perceived to be too fragile to walk unaided after reading his impassioned letter. It is worth noting that his renewed appreciation for Anne's looks—despite his disingenuous assertion that 'to my eye you could never alter' (243)—is triggered by Mr Elliot's visible admiration for the 'bloom and freshness of youth restored' (104) by sea air while she strolls with a Henrietta eager to share her plans for a future with Charles Hayter, a future assured by that communal walk to Winthrop.

The recuperative readings of literary critics like Horrocks and Bredar, following up the work of cultural historians like Wallace, Jarvis, and Robinson, have provided a welcome and necessary reconsideration of Romantic/male tropes of walking. This essay seeks to supplement rather than challenge their analyses by postulating that Austen and Scott, each in their sixth completed novels, respond to the 1790s *zeitgeist* of fraught feminine pedestrianism by modifying and individualising the perils and rewards encountered by women walkers, requiring readers not to disregard questions of gender and class, but rather insisting on calibrations. At the same time, Austen and Scott make transparent the strategic value of pedestrianism and its consequences as a socio-cultural element deployed in constructing plots. The happy marriages which close *Persuasion* have their roots in what seems to be a quotidian walk to Winthrop, while Jeanie's determination to endure a four-hundred mile walk to London rather than tell a lie to save her sister mobilises a range of events that resolve the multiple complexities of a narrative rooted within the messy matter of Anglo-Scottish history. When Jeanie and Anne exert their respective (and relative) energies by walking in the service of others, they earn their status as heroines; their peregrinations show readers that women walking not only represent socio-cultural trends but also activate formal elements that constitute novelistic plotting.

Notes

1 All references to Austen's novels are from *The Novels of Jane Austen*, ed. R. W. Chapman. Page numbers are incorporated in the text.
2 Austen was certainly aware of both novels sharing readership with *Mansfield Park*; in September 1814 she wrote to Anna Austen that 'Walter Scott has no business to write novels, especially good ones.—It is not fair.—He has Fame & Profit enough as a Poet, and should not be taking the bread out of other people's mouths.—I do not like him, & do not mean to like *Waverley* if I can help it …' (28 September 1814; *Letters* 277). There is no such clear indication that she had read *The Wanderer*, though she writes to Cassandra Austen on 16 September 1813 that the Reverend Dr Isham 'is sure he shall not like Mde Darblay's new Novel half so well' as he likes *Pride and Prejudice* (227). Ingrid Horrocks writes that '*The Wanderer* was eagerly awaited by nineteenth-century readers from Lord Byron to Jane Austen' (169). Scott is dismissive of Burney's last novel, assuring the publisher Constable that it 'is scarce worth including' in a projected series of reprints (*Letters* 7.15).
3 Walter Scott, *The Heart of Midlothian*, ed. David Hewitt and Alison Lumsden. All further references are to this edition and incorporated in the text.
4 Scottish law dictated that a woman who concealed her pregnancy and subsequently lost the child was guilty of a capital crime. For details about how Scott deploys this 1690 statute in his plot, see Tara Ghoshal Wallace, '"This right of mercy": The Royal Pardon in *The Heart of Midlothian*'.
5 The 'Dull Incurious' alludes to James Thomson's *The Seasons*.
6 *Persuasion* and *Midlothian* bifurcate what Burney combines in *The Wanderer*. Juliet, at first repulsed by her rural companions' indifference to bucolic scenes, learns that romantic appreciation of pastoral beauties is precluded by the labouring life, which conflates, perforce, the 'vivid field' with the image of the scythe which must mow it, the 'shady tree' with the axe which must fell it, and the 'the joy that is excited by the view of the twilight' with what 'sends him [the labourer] home to the mat of straw, that rests, for the night, his spent and weary limbs' (701).
7 One could speculate that the Mrs Smith of *Persuasion*, impoverished by her husband's improvidence, bodily disabled and forced to find work to support herself, invokes Charlotte Smith. Bredar connects Charlotte Smith's *Elegiac Sonnets* to the author's biography: 'Smith gestures to the unceasing series of legal, marital, and financial frustrations that plagued her throughout nine years of composition … . Smith spent much of her life battling the consequences of her husband's reckless spending … . Her liberty—including her ability to move freely—was thus significantly curtailed by her situation' (153).
8 For a deeper understanding of this concept, I am indebted to Samuel Yates, whose PhD dissertation, 'Cripping Broadway: Neoliberal Performances of Disability in the American Musical' (George Washington University, 2019), explores how the hyper-capable bodies of multi-talented actors produce a kind of normative standard when they perform disabled bodies.
9 Moreover, Argyle's admiration of Jeanie causes him to provide both a farm for her father and a living for the somewhat feeble Reuben, thus allowing Jeanie to marry her lover.

Works Cited

Austen, Jane. *Jane Austen's Letters*, edited by Deirdre Le Faye. Oxford UP, 1997.
Austen, Jane. *The Novels of Jane Austen*, edited by Robert William Chapman, 3rd ed., 5 vols. Oxford UP, 1932–34.
Bredar, Trish. 'Wild Wanderings: Gender and Pedestrian Travel in Charlotte Smith's *Elegiac Sonnets*.' *European Romantic Review*, vol. 30, no. 2, 2019, pp. 149–164.
Burney, Frances. *The Wanderer: Or, Female Difficulties*, edited by Margaret Anne Doody, Robert J. Mack, and Peter Sabor. Oxford UP, 1991.
Doody, Margaret Anne. *Frances Burney: The Life in the Works*. Rutgers UP, 1988.

Griffith, Richard M. 'Anthropodology: Man A-Foot.' *The Philosophy of the Body: Rejections of Cartesian Dualism*, edited by Stuart F. Spicker. Quadrangle Books, 1970, pp. 274–292.

Horrocks, Ingrid. *Women Wanderers and the Writing of Mobility, 1784–1814*. Cambridge UP, 2017.

Jarvis, Robin. *Romantic Writing and Pedestrian Travel*. Houndmills, Macmillan P, 1997.

Keats, John. *The Letters of John Keats*, edited by Maurice Buxton Forman. Oxford UP, 1952.

Lee, Yoon Sun. 'Austen's Swarms and Plots.' *European Romantic Review*, vol. 30, no. 3, 2019, pp. 307–314.

Millgate, Jane. *Walter Scott: The Making of the Novelist*. U of Toronto P, 1984.

Mitchell, David T., and Sharon L. Snyder. *Narrative Prosthesis: Disability and the Dependencies of Discourse*. U of Michigan P, 2000.

Moran, Colin, Naomi Brooks, and Ross Chesham. 'Fitness Can Go Far in 15 Minutes a Day.' *The Washington Post*, 14 Aug. 2018, E6.

Moretti, Franco. *Atlas of the European Novel, 1800–1900*. Verso, 1998.

Moritz, Karl Philipp. *Travels, Chiefly on Foot, through Several Parts of England, in 1782. Described in Letters to a Friend*. Translated from the German, by a Lady. London: G. G. and J. Robinson, 1795. Gale ECCO reprint.

Pike, Holly E. 'Mobility, the Outdoors, and Social Position in *Persuasion*.' *Persuasions*, vol. 39, 2017, pp. 235–242.

Quinn, Megan. 'The Sensation of Language in Jane Austen's *Persuasion*.' *ECF*, vol. 30, no. 22, 2018, pp. 243–263.

Robinson, Jeffrey C. *The Walk: Notes on a Romantic Image*. U of Oklahoma P, 1989.

Scott, Walter. *The Heart of Midlothian*, edited by David Hewitt and Alison Lumsden. Edinburgh UP, 2004.

Scott, Walter. *The Letters of Sir Walter Scott*, edited by Herbert John Clifford Grierson, 12 vols. Constable, 1932–37.

Scott, Walter. *Waverley*, edited by P. D. Garside. Edinburgh UP, 2007.

Soderman, Melissa. 'Domestic Mobility in *Persuasion* and *Sanditon*.' *Studies in English Literature, 1500–1900*, vol. 45, no. 4, 2005, pp. 787–812.

Wallace, Anne D. *Walking, Literature, and English Culture: The Origins and Uses of Peripatetic in the Nineteenth Century*. Clarendon P, 1993.

Wallace, Tara Ghoshal. '"This Right of Mercy": The Royal Pardon in *The Heart of Midlothian*.' *Yearbook of English Studies*, vol. 47, 2017, pp. 203–223.

Wiltshire, John. *Jane Austen and the Body: 'The Picture of Health'*. Cambridge UP, 1992.

Yates, Samuel. *Cripping Broadway: Neoliberal Performances of Disability in the American Musical*. PhD Diss. George Washington U, 2019.

14

FROM JEWELLED TOOTHPICK-CASES TO BLUE NANKIN BOOTS: AUSTEN, CONSUMERIST CULTURE, AND NARRATIVE

Laura M. White

UNIVERSITY OF NEBRASKA-LINCOLN

Jane Austen wrote in an age in which Britain suffered constant economic upheaval, a series of disruptions caused by the war with France, an ungovernable national debt, banking crises, agricultural depressions, currency debasement, and inflation. This period of economic instability was also marked by dramatic changes in cultural attitudes about consumerism—this was the era in which modern notions of fashion, shopping, and the self as consumer emerged with force among Britain's growing middle classes. While Austen's fiction addresses economic questions only in oblique and partial ways (absent, for instance, are the period's bank failures, which touched her and her family very nearly when her brother Henry's bank crashed in 1816), her works do show significant traces of the age's economic self-fashioning.[1] In particular, Austen's many scenes of shopping and her depiction of characters as forms of *homo economicus* show that Austen was clearly aware of the moral pitfalls shopping and fashion can occasion. Austen exposes most of her shoppers as foolish and vain, whether they dawdle over ribbons, as Harriet does in *Emma*, or dither over jewelled toothpick-cases, as does Robert Dashwood in *Sense in Sensibility*. Characters who are more virtuous and wiser can shop appropriately, as when *Mansfield Park*'s Fanny Price uses her pocket money in Portsmouth to choose books for her sister's improvement or when Charlotte Heywood decides against wasting her money in Sanditon's lending library. This last of Austen's work, *Sanditon*, offers a particularly rich array of market concerns, as the new sea resort is itself on offer and almost everyone seems to be potentially for sale. *Sanditon* makes even more explicit the notion that runs through the other novels, that market choices, shopping, and fashion have a dark parallel in the marriage market.[2]

Shopping had become a modern occasion of display by the middle of the eighteenth century, as Neil McKendrick et al. have shown in detail in their *The Birth of a Consumer Society: The Commercialization of Eighteenth-Century England*. Shops, malls, and arcades mushroomed in Georgian England. As Roy Porter notes, by mid-century, 'a staggering 150,000 retail outlets … [served] a population of not much over six million (one shop per forty people!)' (7). Despite the ongoing economic uncertainty about speculation, labour, prices, bubbles, and failures, this new consumerist culture of the late Georgian and Regency periods featured an explosion of goods, including luxury goods, and tempting access to them. As McKendrick notes, 'commerce increasingly took over the manipulation and direction of fashion. Men and women increasingly had to wear what fashion dictated, had to raise or lower their hems and their heels at the dictates of cloth manufacturers and shoe sellers' (40–41; quoted in Ford 217).

180

DOI: 10.4324/9780429398155-14-17

Austen thus was born into a society with 'buying and selling, the pleasures and pains of acquisitiveness, on the brain and on the tip of the tongue' (Porter 8).[3] She was herself immersed in the markets of her day; her letters, particularly to Cassandra, reveal both her care not to waste money and her mocking assessment of herself as one sometimes lured into unwise expenditures by the 'demands' of fashion.[4] No ascetic, Jane Austen was instead an enthusiastic if sceptical consumer. As Susan Allen Ford notes, she was a woman 'educated in the competing impulses of thrift and desire' (216).[5] She always had cause to watch her pennies, even in the last years of her life when her book profits amplified her meagre income, and her letters testify to her frugality. Nonetheless, she never shunned the marketplace and instead took pride in the canniness of her purchases and their alignment with the latest fashions. In fact, once her means were ampler after the publication of her first novels, she was wealthy enough to shop in Bond Street, the center of fashionable shopping in London, where she indulged herself with 'fashionable muslins' at Grafton House (Porter 9).[6]

When we turn to Austen's fictional accounts of shopping, we find both her keen satire and her awareness that shopping reveals character, or its lack. Her first depicted 'consumer' appears in 'The Beautifull Cassandra' from *Volume the First* of her Juvenilia.[7] This tale, told in twelve chapters of one or two sentences each, offers 'Cassandra', a mock homage to Austen's sister, to whom the work is dedicated. A seeming prodigy of 'loveliness' and 'amiability', Cassandra rockets from chapter to chapter, leaving a trail of theft and violence in the course of her reckless day, stealing a bonnet, ices, and coach-fare and assaulting a pastry cook. As John Leffel notes, 'Cassandra's theft introduces [a] defining element of the Juvenilia, for throughout these works young heroines sabotage the male-driven economy by stealing commodities, services, and sums of money large enough to send them to the gallows' (189–90). Cassandra ends where she began, in her mother's millinery shop in Bond Street. It is as if the temptations of Bond Street and its luxury goods, coupled with her modest circumstances as the daughter of a milliner, have driven her to run amok. The last chapter has Cassandra telling herself, 'It was a day well spent' (47), a self-satisfied conclusion ludicrously at odds with the anarchy of her day's activity (she has not actually 'spent' anything at all). This early spoof shows the raw desires occasioned by the world of consumer goods; Cassandra's thievery seems to begin as a primal response to the lures of a beautiful bonnet.

The novels leave the anarchy of the Juvenilia behind and explore the more subtle role of consumerist desire through the mode of moral realism. In *Northanger Abbey*, it is the minor character Mrs Allen who represents the foolishness of fashionable display; the narrator tells us 'Dress was her passion' (20). As a character, Mrs Allen lies on the verge of caricature, for Austen implies that anyone so consumed by dress must be a negligible figure. Nonetheless, Austen is at pains to show that Mrs Allen's 'most harmless delight in being fine' leads her into the moral lapse of being an inadequate chaperone to Catherine (20). It is telling that on the occasion of Catherine's first entrance into a ballroom in Bath, Mrs Allen shows 'more care for the safety of her new gown than for the comfort of her protegée' (21); here her attention to her clothes and inattention to Catherine prefigure the lapses of oversight she will make when Catherine is pursued by the rapacious John Thorpe. Further, as Lauren Miskin has argued, 'despite her excessive attention to her clothes, Mrs Allen proves a foolish consumer' (15). In a short but revealing scene in the third chapter, she and Henry Tilney discuss shopping for muslins. Her own muslin gown, she lets slip, was bought as 'nine shillings a yard', an extravagant purchase. Henry reveals himself as a more able consumer, bragging that 'I always buy my own cravats, and am allowed to be an excellent judge; and my sister has often trusted me in the choice of a gown' (28). His latest purchase was 'a prodigious bargain' as he gave but 'five shillings a yard for it', and it a 'true Indian muslin'.[8] Moreover, on being asked for an opinion, Henry praises the material of Catherine's gown as 'pretty' but adds 'I do not think it will wash well; I am afraid it will fray'. Catherine finds his interest in the female domain of fabric purchase to be 'strange', though she catches herself from saying so (28). Henry further reveals his interest in fabric by noting that frayed muslin can be recycled into a handkerchief, cap, or cloak (his sister practices such economies, he notes). Henry seems a model consumer, if somewhat at odds with gender presumptions of the day that held that men were to know nothing of the practical side of female fashion.[9]

His father the General provides a signal contrast to Henry's thrift. We do not see the General shopping, but his home, the former abbey, is replete with modern luxury goods and furnishings, and the tour he gives Catherine provides him full opportunity of detailing the 'costliness' and 'elegance' of the rooms. The General leads Catherine through a dizzying array of large rooms, splendidly furnished with the newest of Regency interior design. During her visit at the abbey, Catherine will be called upon to note such then-modern luxuries as Wedgwood porcelain, satin furniture, japanned armoires, Rumford stoves, mahogany wardrobes, cocoa, and hothouse pineapples (Miskin 14). Catherine is marked as a good girl, relatively immune to this peacock display, partly because, as a novice consumer, she has an 'indiscriminating eye' (183). Catherine herself shows the usual probity of Austen's heroines in terms of shopping; we are told early on in the novel that while Mrs Allen spends several days preparing her inaugural outfit for Bath, Catherine only 'made some purchases herself' (20). The flatness of the narration implies that her shopping was sensible and modest.

Sense and Sensibility also features heroines whose desires, like Catherine's, are romantic, not consumerist, though even the unworldly Marianne can fall into the delicious fantasy of coming into wealth. In chapter seventeen, there is a long conversation among members of the Dashwood family and Edward Ferrars about what one would do with a windfall. Young Margaret begins with a simple statement of visionary greed: '" I wish", said Margaret, striking out a novel thought, 'that somebody would give us all a large fortune apiece!' This most un-novel of thoughts is followed by her elder sister: '"Oh that they would!" cried Marianne, her eyes sparkling with animation, and her cheeks glowing with the delight of such imaginary happiness' (92). The full somatic response (for those sparkling eyes and glowing cheeks have earlier been called forward only by Willoughby) shows Marianne's spontaneous investment in this dream of plenty, one Elinor tries to bat down with a statement about reality: 'We are all unanimous in that wish, I suppose … in spite of the insufficiency of wealth' (92). Edward joins in with a loving catalogue of all the cultured and virtuous purchases the family would make were they to become rich: 'What magnificent orders would travel from this family to London … in such an event! What a happy day for booksellers, music-sellers, and print-shops!' (92). Edward in fact manages to do what Elinor could not, change the topic of conversation, by reminding Marianne and Margaret of the higher values they hold. Furthermore, he implies that the sisters would not seek out the shopping experience as such but merely order such things as volumes of 'Thomson, Cowper, and Scott' from their cottage in the English countryside.

As the novel shifts its scene to London, the hub of commerce, Austen brings Elinor and Marianne to Gray's in Sackville Street. Gray's was the most fashionable jewelry shop in London, and Thomas Gray, its owner, was favored by the Prince Regent (for instance, Gray made the future George IV a 'spectacularly lavish' jewelled badge for his Order of the Garter sash in 1787—and for it received the princely sum of £403 15s. 6d [Lesser]). Elinor and Marianne are on a modest errand, exchanging some of their mother's 'old-fashioned' jewels, but they find themselves waiting behind a fop ordering a jewelled toothpick-case (this figure will later be revealed as Robert Ferrars, Edward Ferrars' vain and foolish brother). Robert Ferrars takes an inordinate amount of time before deciding on 'the ivory, the gold, and the pearls' of the case (221). His purchase could not be more frivolous. Jewelled toothpicks had been luxury items since the seventeenth century; a jewelled case for one's jewelled toothpicks seems to reside at an even higher level of inane conspicuous consumption! Ferrars's priorities are broadly satirized in this scene, especially as he does not deign to give the Dashwood sisters more than 'three or four very broad stares' 'as seemed rather to demand than express admiration' (220–21). Given that both sisters are attractive, and Marianne indeed is beautiful, his disregard for them helps underscore his self-absorption and vanity. As Elinor perceives him, he is 'of a strong, natural, sterling insignificance, though adorned in the first style of fashion' (220–21).

'Sterling' refers to the pound sterling, the silver coin of the realm, though often counterfeited or debased with impurities in Austen's day, and thus 'sterling insignificance' is an appropriate oxymoron to capture the mode of this vapid consumer. Robert Ferrars is succeeded in the shop by John Dashwood, and he too is there on a revealing errand, purchasing a seal for his arrogant wife (she evidently needs an expensive wax seal to put the final touch of display on her letters). It is also noteworthy that John Dashwood meets his sisters here in this shop for luxury goods; though they have been in London several days, he has not called on them yet (for which he makes apologies), but he has found the time to do a spot of high-end shopping.

Austen evidently hated shoppers who dithered in their purchases, as Robert Ferrars does here, or who bought without discrimination. Mrs Palmer seems to be another offender against decorous and rational shopping, here found on Bond Street (Bond Street is the London nexus of *Sense and Sensibility* where elite shopping can be conducted; here at one point or another are Mrs Palmer, the Dashwood sisters, Willoughby, Mrs Jennings, and Colonel Brandon). Mrs Palmer is described as 'tedious' because 'her eye [is] caught by every thing pretty, expensive, or new; [she] was wild to buy all, could determine on none, and dawdled away her time in rapture and indecision' (165). Harriet Smith in *Emma* is another ditherer. One of Austen's great narrative set-pieces is Harriet's performance in Mrs Ford's shop. Like Mrs Palmer, Harriet, being 'tempted by every thing and swayed by half a word, was always very long at a purchase' (233). After having described how Emma forces Harriet to make up her mind, working to 'convince her that if she wanted plain muslin it was of no use to look at figured; and that a blue ribbon, be it ever so beautiful, would still never match her yellow pattern' (235), Austen gives the reader the full force of Harriet's ensuing exchange with Mrs Ford in direct dialogue:

> 'Should I send it to Mrs Goddard's, ma'am?' asked Mrs Ford.—'Yes—no—yes, to Mrs Goddard's. Only my pattern gown is at Hartfield. No, you shall send it to Hartfield, if you please. But then, Mrs Goddard will want to see it.—And I could take the pattern gown home any day. But I shall want the ribbon directly—so it had better go to Hartfield—at least the ribbon. You could make it into two parcels, Mrs Ford, could not you?'
> 'It is not worth while, Harriet, to give Mrs Ford the trouble of two parcels'.
> 'No more it is'.
> 'No trouble in the world, ma'am', said the obliging Mrs Ford.
> 'Oh! but indeed I would much rather have it only in one. Then, if you please, you shall send it all to Mrs Goddard's—I do not know—No, I think, Miss Woodhouse, I may just as well have it sent to Hartfield, and take it home with me at night. What do you advise?'
> 'That you do not give another half-second to the subject. To Hartfield, if you please, Mrs Ford'.
> 'Aye, that will be much best', said Harriet, quite satisfied, 'I should not at all like to have it sent to Mrs Goddard's'. (235)

Like the delightful outpourings of Miss Bates in the same novel, this colloquy is rendered in such full detail precisely so that the reader will be as impatient for Harriet to make up her mind as Emma is.

Pride and Prejudice features more foolish shoppers, Lydia and Kitty. Their shallow minds are fixated on men and fashion, or, rather, fashion and men, as this description of the two in the Meryton street makes evident: 'Their eyes were immediately wandering up in the street in quest of the officers, and nothing less than a very smart bonnet indeed, or a really new muslin in a shop window, could recall them' (72). Later in the novel, they meet Jane and Elizabeth at an inn, where their fecklessness is amply displayed. They have ordered a mid-day meal, 'such cold meat as an inn larder usually affords', and demand praise and gratitude, 'exclaiming, "Is not this nice? Is not this an agreeable surprise?"' The two elder Bennet sisters soon find that there is no particular cause for gratitude, as Lydia explains that she meant to treat them to the meal, 'but you must lend us the money, for we have just spent ours at the shop out there'. Lydia perhaps rivals Robert Ferrars as the worst of Austen's shoppers, for she has bought a bonnet she does not like and means to tear apart: 'Look here, I have bought this bonnet. I do not think it is very pretty; but I thought I might as well buy it as not. I shall pull it to pieces as soon as I get home, and see if I can make it up any better'. Jane and Elizabeth condemn the bonnet as ugly, but Lydia is unconcerned: 'Oh! but there were two or three much uglier in the shop' (219).

There are no scenes of shopping in *Mansfield Park* (we never even see the village of Mansfield where shopping would presumably take place), though it is clear that Maria Bertram finds compensation for her dullard spouse, Mr Rushworth, in the displays of wealth marrying him will make possible, the 'new carriages and furniture' which are her reward (202). Mrs Norris is not a shopper, but she is a genteel sponger and thief. Her day at Sotherton, while painfully consequential for the romantic desires for Fanny, Edward, Maria, and both Mary and Henry Crawford, is a success for Mrs Norris because she makes off with a variety of treasures: a heath plant, a cream cheese, and some pheasant eggs. Her plans for the eggs involve more sponging, as she intends to have the Mansfield Park dairymaid get them hatched under 'the first spare hen', whereupon she will 'borrow a coop' to put the chicks in (106). Most memorably, the green baize purchased as a curtain for the ill-fated theatricals ends up in Mrs Norris's clutches: 'The curtain over which she had presided with such talent and such success, went off with her to her cottage, where she happened to be particularly in want of green baize' (195).

As mentioned before, Fanny's only commercial activity takes place at Portsmouth, where she has been banished by Sir Thomas. Her shopping is exemplary, as she makes only two purchases, each of which is to help someone else. The first occasion remedies her two sisters' continual competition over a silver knife, left by another sister on her deathbed to Susan but appropriated by the younger Betsy: 'It had very early occurred to [Fanny] that a small sum of money might, perhaps, restore peace for ever on the sore subject of the silver knife, canvassed as it now was continually, and the riches which she was in possession of herself, her uncle having given her 10 [pounds] at parting, made her as able as she was willing to be generous'. (396). Austen focuses on Fanny's great hesitancy over becoming a consumer: 'she was so wholly unused to confer favours, except on the very poor, so unpractised in removing evils, or bestowing kindnesses among her equals, and so fearful of appearing to elevate herself as a great lady at home, that it took some time to determine that it would not be unbecoming in her to make such a present' (396). This hesitance marks Fanny as an unwilling participant in the bustling Regency marketplace, even though her purchase of a second silver knife is a thoroughgoing success, removing a bone of contention from the Price family life. Austen also endorses her second use of her purse, a subscription to a circulating library to help Fanny educate the ill-read Susan through books. Again, the narrator's emphasis is on Fanny's audacity in participating in the marketplace as well as the virtue of her doing so: 'wealth is luxurious and daring, and some of hers found its way to a circulating library. She became a subscriber; amazed at being anything in *propria persona*, amazed at her own doings in every way, to be a renter, a chuser of books! And to be having any one's improvement in view in her choice!' (398). Austen knows that ten pounds is not exactly 'wealth', but that any spending by Fanny is a daring enterprise.

There are also no scenes of shopping in *Persuasion*. Though Bath is a commercial mecca filled with fashionable shops, Anne has no interest in shopping, another sign of her intrinsic worth. Shopping does, however, play a role in the plot, because the party from Uppercross comes to Bath so that Henrietta and Mrs Musgrove can buy Henrietta's trousseau. Bath also draws the Crofts, but here the excuse is the Admiral's gout. Captain Harville and Captain Wentworth come too, with the errand of re-setting Captain Benwick's miniature for Louisa, and it is the letter enacting this commercial commission that Wentworth interrupts to write his much more important letter of love to Anne. Nonetheless, the air of vogueish display pervades Bath, its sociability underwritten by the weak moral fiber of most of the town's inhabitants and visitors. One final judgment of such flawed moral values occurs in the last chapter, as we read of Mary's jealousy of Anne's 'very pretty laudalette' (250) and her sorrow in losing her 'seniority' when Anne marries Wentworth; her consolation is to reflect that Anne 'had no Uppercross-hall before her, no landed estate' (250). Many critics have followed Alastair Duckworth's convincing case in *The Improvement of the Estate* that by *Persuasion* Austen has come to the realisation that the corroded values of the landed estate are perhaps not worth inheriting, and that what Mary values is of less value than she thinks.

Sanditon, as so many of its readers and critics have noted, seems to open up new territory for Austen's narrative art. Written as Austen was dying in 1817, this fragment of a novel features broader satire and a less subtle technique. Characters such as Lady Denham, Sir Edward, and the hypochondriacal Parker siblings are caricatures, almost burlesques, and the narrative features more direct dialogue in contrast to the abundance of free indirect discourse evident in the later novels such as *Persuasion*.[10] However, since the work was unfinished, it is not possible to draw conclusions about whether Austen truly intended to move to a more robust, less understated style, because the final work might have revised, for instance, the treatment of dialogue. However, while we cannot be sure of what the upheaval in Austen's style portends, we can certainly note that her theme is social and economic upheaval. As a Tory whose sympathies lay with the landed gentry represented here by the Heywoods, Austen satirizes what she sees as a rush by her own class to destroy its probity through speculation and chasing after profits, here through the mechanism of a new sea resort.[11]

Mr Parker and Lady Denham represent those in the landed class who are abandoning the old ideals in pursuit of profit and novelty. As Michael Biddess notes, 'Austen [suggests] that [the] threat to the old order comes from within, via an honest but naively optimistic member [Parker] of that established landowning class whose weaknesses she had just highlighted so perceptively within *Persuasion*' (244). For Mr Parker, Sanditon as speculative prospect overshadows things of real value such as family and property:

> Sanditon was a second Wife and four Children to him—hardly less Dear—and certainly more engrossing.—He could talk of it forever.—It had indeed the highest claims;—not only those of birth place, property, and home,—it was his mine, his lottery, his speculation and his hobby horse; his occupation, his hope, and his futurity. (372)

Lady Denham is less naïve and more grasping: she 'seeks greedily to monetize to her own advantage just about everything in life … [including] literally liquid assets flowing from her lactating donkeys' (Biddiss 244). A confirmed speculator, she has already parlayed two marriages into her current position; the first husband left her a fortune and the second a title, so she is well-positioned to grasp even more wealth and power.[12]

The novel's beginning depicts the Tory world of agricultural verities, represented by the Heywoods, invaded by the new ideals of advertising and speculation, represented by Mr Parker. Led by the lures of advertisements to the narrow lane which causes his carriage to be upset, Mr Parker will soon be revealed a walking and talking advertisement himself, while all round him the old pursuit of bringing in the hay continues unimpeded.[13] Mr Parker pays no attention to the world he interrupts, instead intent on his errand to find a medical man for Sanditon and armed with not one but two newspaper advertisements. Despite Mr Heywood's assertion that there is no surgeon in the region, Mr Parker overrules local knowledge: he insists that the advertisements prove him right, and only relents when Mr Heywood explains that he has brought his carriage and himself to grief in the wrong Willingden.[14] Mr Parker's pursuit of a medical man to make Sanditon more attractive to resort-goers has ironically yielded nothing but his own sprained ankle. Nonetheless, Mr Parker's reliance on advertising continues, for self-advertisement, we learn, is the rule with him. His conversation burbles with puffery and parodies Regency advertising language with its superlatives and hyperbole: 'everybody has heard of Sanditon,—the favourite—for a young and rising Bathing-place, certainly the favourite spot of all that are to be found along the coast of Sussex;—the most favoured by Nature, & promising to be the most chosen by Man' (368). The adherence to the rhetoric of Regency advertising includes what the period called 'knocking copy' (Biddiss 247), Mr Parker's robust disparagement of competitive resorts such as Brinshore: 'A most insalubrious Air—Roads proverbially detestable—Water Brackish beyond example, impossible to get a good dish of Tea within 3 miles of the place—and as for the soil—it is so cold and ungrateful that it can hardly be made to yield a Cabbage' (*Sanditon* 369). As Sheila Minn Hwang has noted in relation to Mr Parker's effusions, 'to create a fashionable and profitable destination, one must build physical and *imaginative* constructions—constructions that appeal to the dreams and desires of prospective visitors' (250). Mr Parker's attempts to draw richer and higher status visitors relies on assertions which are really only aspirational constructions: 'the sure resort of the very best Company, those regular, steady, private Families of thorough Gentility and Character, who are a blessing everywhere, excite the industry of the Poor and diffuse comfort and improvement among them of every sort' (368). This is but one example of Mr Parker's praxis as a promoter, calling 'attention to the resort town's future potential while making that potential sound to his audience like it is the tangible present' (Hwang 263), for as Mr Parker finds on his return from his pointless jaunt to Willingden, Charlotte Heywood in tow, the list of subscribers at the lending library is 'not only without Distinction, but less numerous than he had hoped' (389).

The rational Charlotte is the witness to the considerable gap between Mr Parker's promises and Sanditon's current state. The various new lodgings, meant to be full of distinguished visitors, have plenty of vacancies. Charlotte also witnesses the deflation of Diana Parker's promised new visitors, a large Ladies Seminary and a multitudinous family from Surrey. The seminary and the family turn out to be one and the same, arriving in 'two hack chaises' (420) and leaving Diana with a large empty house she has rented entirely on speculation. The new visitors include merely three young ladies, a Miss Lambe and two Misses Beaufort. As Sara Dustin points out, the Miss Beauforts are also speculators in the town, buying six dresses for a three-day visit and adorning themselves more elegantly than they can afford to nab a wealthy husband (84). They wear white because white was a fashionable color and signified affluence (white was a mark of conspicuous consumption, because white clothes were easily dirtied and laundry costs were not inconsiderable—thus the wearer of a white gown is parading her non-participation in labor [Hafny-Lany 141]). The Beaufort sisters employ the same technique for catching a husband as Mary Crawford used in *Mansfield Park*, conjoining a harp (here, just a rented one) and a window-view to attract 'many an eye upwards' and to make 'many a Gazer gaze again' (422). They evidently consider themselves figures in a marketplace, on display. One or the other of them were perhaps meant to be modestly successful as the plot unfolded, for Austen suggests that the indolent and self-indulgent Arthur Parker has been attracted by the ladies on view: 'Mr Arthur Parker, though little disposed for supernumerary exertion, always quitted the Terrace, in his way to his Brothers by this corner house, for the sake of a glimpse of the Miss Beauforts, though it was quarter of a mile round about, and added two steps to the ascent of the Hill' (423).

The presence of these sisters emphasizes how *Sanditon* is, as Rebecca Richardson notes, 'newly aggressive in applying the logic of the marketplace [to the workings of the] marriage plot and romantic desire' (203). Austen is one of many writers during this period of economic change who satirizes her society's entanglement of economic and sexual motives, working, in Ruth Perry's words, 'to parse the relation between property and sexual exchange, to establish what could and could not be commodified' (242). One of the three young ladies newly arrived in those hack chaises, the intriguing figure of Miss Lambe, also seems to be destined to serve as a commodity in the Sanditon marital marketplace, marked, as her name implies, to be a victim, like a lamb to the slaughter. We never meet Miss Lambe in person, 'a young West Indian of large fortune, in delicate health', who is 'about seventeen, half mulatto, chilly and tender' (421), but she seems to be the only actual invalid in the town amid a sea of hypochondriacal poseurs. As such, Miss Lambe is to be fleeced. As Anthony Lane notes, here the predators size up the prey: '"No people spend more freely, I believe, than West Indians", Parker observes, and one can picture the leonine gleam in his eyes' (Lane).[15] Jocelyn Harris has traced the origin of the striking phrase, 'half mulatto, chilly and tender' to Lavache the clown's speech in *All's Well that Ends Well*: 'I am for the house with the narrow gate, which I take to be too little for pomp to enter. Some that humble themselves may, but the many will be too chill and tender, and they'll be for the flowery way that leads to the broad gate and the great fire' (V.v.50–55). The narrow gate leads to heaven, the broad gate leads to hell, and thus the 'chill and tender', choosing the 'flowery' or easy way, will damn themselves. If Austen was indeed thinking of Shakespeare here, Miss Lambe is a sheep who will deserve her fate (Harris 239–40). The last we hear of Miss Lambe is that she is about to take 'her first dip' in the ocean; the idea that she is slated for a sheep dip is, however, unfortunately anachronistic, as the first sheep dip was not invented until 1830.

In Austen's day, the opportunity to dip oneself in the ocean at a sea resort was a relatively new and popular inducement, drawing consumers eager for novelty and health. The explosion in new and augmented sea resorts, lampooned in *Sanditon*, was yet another mode by which the Regency urge for fashion and display manifested itself. Austen herself visited various seaside resorts, among them Sidmouth, Teignmouth, Dawlish, and Lyme, and by all accounts loved the sea.[16] She holds the sea blameless for the apparatus of human greed and vanity these resorts inspirited; when Charlotte herself sees the sea for the first time, she surely sees it as Austen saw it: 'dancing and sparkling in Sunshine and Freshness' (384). Sanditon as a resort is just beginning to have all the proper lures for those with leisure and money seeking a fashionable place for display. As Brian Southam notes, more fully developed resorts like Sidmouth had an array of enticements such as ice cream shops, milliner's shops, places to play cards and billiards, theaters, circulating libraries, tea-rooms, bathing machines, and even horse-racing. A good gravel promenade was also essential, so that invalids in bath chairs could be rolled along (Southam, 'Jane Austen beside the Seaside: Devonshire and Wales' 132). Of these, Sanditon has a 'broad walk, aspiring to be the Mall of the Place', a billiard room, fashionable shops, a tea-room, bathing machines, and a circulating library—as well as Lady Denham's donkeys for hire (if they are not required for their milk, they could be employed to draw bathing machines) (384).

All here is governed by commerce, or hopes of commerce, whether in the marital market (as we have seen with the Misses Beauforts and Miss Lambe) or in the shops. Mr Parker is sent into ecstasies on seeing the picture window of one of Sanditon's shops:

> Civilization, Civilization indeed!—cried Mr P—, delighted—. Look my dear Mary—Look at William Heeley's windows.—Blue shoes and nankin Boots! Who would have expected such a sight at a Shoemaker's in old Sanditon!—This is new within the Month. There was no blue Shoe when we passed this way a month ago.—Glorious indeed!—Well, I think I have done something in my Day. (383)

'I think I have done something in my Day': Mr Parker's triumph is ludicrous. Picture windows were part of the new commercialism of the Regency age—the exhibition of goods carefully arranged was meant, then and now, to whet the shopper's appetite. As Porter notes, the new displays in shops reveal the Regency 'desire to turn shopping into style, [its] drive towards the aestheticisation of the high street' (10). What is displayed here—'blue shoes and nankin Boots'—were also then both in vogue. Blue shoes were fashionable in part because it was difficult to keep their colour bright; like the white dresses of the Sanditon misses, the impracticability of the fashion augments its appeal. The nankin boots were made of cotton imported from Nanking, and while they had some practical use for ladies' walking, they were not nearly as sturdy as the leather boots worn by workmen. Everything we see for sale in Sanditon is fashionable but not particularly useful. Charlotte confronts the array of 'pretty Temptations' when she first visits the circulating library, but her good sense keeps her from extravagance:

> The Library of course, afforded everything; all the useless things in the World that could not be done without, and among so many pretty Temptations, and with so much good will from Mr Parker to encourage Expenditure, Charlotte began to feel that she must check herself—or rather she reflected that at two and Twenty there could be no excuse for her doing otherwise—and that it would not do for her to be spending all her Money the very first Evening. (390)

Unlike Fanny Price at the lending library in Portsmouth, choosing books for her sister's edification, Charlotte at Sanditon's lending library sees nothing to buy that is needed or useful, just 'pretty Temptations'. In fact, this 'library' has only a few books and seems instead to function primarily as a gift shop. In keeping with the rest of Austen's heroines, Charlotte is not seduced by the lures of fashionable spending.

Even the nomenclature of the buildings in Sanditon is meant to enhance fashionable consumerism. The sting of Austen's satire is particularly sharp when we learn that Mr Parker regrets naming his new house Trafalgar House, and that he plans to name the 'new crescent', if one is ever built, Waterloo Crescent: 'Waterloo is more the thing now' (380). Austen was deeply loyal to the British navy for reasons both familial and patriotic, so when Mr Parker commodifies arguably the most significant naval battle in British history that had taken place only a dozen years before the action of the novel, he is demonstrating his shallow regard for things that matter. As Clara Tuite argues, 'Mr Parker's speculative Waterloo bubble links patriotic nostalgia with commercialism' (615); what is commercialised loses much of its value, and neither Trafalgar nor Waterloo, the latter an equally momentous battle only *two* years previous, are honoured in this rush to use their names as advertising.

The other form of fashionable display in Sanditon is illness, feigned or not. As John Wiltshire has noted, *Sanditon* is a 'manic satire on medical consumerism' (197).[17] The chief 'sufferers' in the novel are the three Parker siblings; their illnesses are marked by exhibitionism, exorbitance, and theatrical display, whether of tooth-pulling or of a cornucopia of phials and salts. There does not seem to be anything in fact physically wrong with them, and their hypocrisies are demonstrated repeatedly, as when Arthur claims he cannot have much butter but then puts on a 'great dab' when he thinks no one is watching (418). Such hypochondria is also a symptom of fashionable leisure, as Charlotte properly diagnoses: 'Disorders and Recoveries so very much out of the common way, seemed more like the amusement of eager Minds in want of employment than of actual afflictions & relief' (412). Illness for Diana, Susan, and Arthur Parker is an avocation for amusement, the 'enjoyments of invalidism' (Wiltshire 198).

The parade of fools in Sanditon displays how the logic of consumerism, fashion, and vanity leads to rampant unreason and exploitation. As is true of all of Austen's fiction, here characters reveal their quality by their every action and speech, including shopping and other consumerist commitments. The shift in *Sanditon* from the earlier novels is one of scale and intensity. Here Austen suggests that an entire society has been traduced by the logic of speculation and fashion. We do not know how *Sanditon* was to end, but as Biddiss suggests, Sanditon's new crescent was probably meant to be Mr Parker's own Waterloo (253). In all likelihood the promise of the title would be redeemed in accord with Jesus's prophecy in Matthew 7: 24–27:

> Therefore everyone who hears these words of mine and puts them into practice is like a wise man who built his house on the rock. The rain came down, the streams rose, and the

winds blew and beat against that house; yet it did not fall, because it had its foundation on the rock. But everyone who hears these words of mine and does not put them into practice is like a foolish man who built his house on sand. The rain came down, the streams rose, and the winds blew and beat against that house, and it fell with a great crash.

Sanditon, built on the sand of speculation (the sand of the beach itself is held innocent), will indeed 'crash' as so many speculations of the period did. Consumerist desire, Austen suggests, must be reined in by humility and good sense in order for a virtuous society to flourish—*Sanditon* seems to express Austen's scepticism that such constraint in her society will ever develop.

Notes

1 As Mary Poovey notes in *Genres of the Credit Economy*, the economic instability during Jane Austen's adult life created a great deal of insecurity in the British public; she argues that one function of '[Austen's] fiction [was] to manage the anxieties it caused' (370). See also Katherine Toran's 'The Economics of Jane Austen's World'. Frank Trentman's 'Knowing Consumers—Histories, Identities, Practices: An Introduction' notes the eighteenth-century conservative suspicion of the then-modern shopper; by the nineteenth-century, such suspicions had generally waned and consumers were instead valorized, as they are today (3).

2 This argument has been elaborated by Elsie B. Michie in her *The Vulgar Question of Money: Heiresses, Materialism, and the Novel of Manners from Jane Austen to Henry James* (2011).

3 For more on Jane Austen's economic situation and the state of money in the Regency, see especially Edward Copeland, *Women Writing about Money: Women's Fiction in England, 1790–1820*; his chapters on 'Money' in *The Cambridge Companion to Jane Austen*, pp. 131–48; Janet Todd (ed.), *Jane Austen in Context*, pp. 317–26; and J. A. Downie, 'Who Says She's a Bourgeois Writer? Reconsidering the Social and Political Contexts of Jane Austen's Novels'.

4 As Edward Copeland has noted in his 'The Austens and the Elliots: A Consumer's Guide to *Persuasion*', Austen's 'memorandums at the End of the Year 1806' testify to her moderation and genteel propriety with their very carefully budgeted list of household and personal expenses (151).

5 Several critics have provided details on Austen's own consumerist behaviour. Susan Allen Ford's '"To Be above Vulgar Economy': Thrifty Measures in Jane Austen's Letters' canvases the details of Austen's thrift with clothes and her presiding interest in looking as fashionable as she could with the little she had to spend. Ford also notes Austen's letter to Cassandra of 25 September 1813 in which she shows her awareness of the role of maturity in purchasing clothes; she tells her sister that their niece Fanny Knight has made a poor choice in a new cap but softens her criticism by describing such foolishness as 'one of the sweet taxes of Youth to chuse in a hurry & make bad bargains' (216). Ford argues that Austen has a propensity to vivify her apparel, as if the garments have taken on a life of their own, as when in a crowded carriage Austen writes that 'I and my boa were of the party' (15 June 1808; 218). Tatiana Holway's 'Money in Jane Austen' provides many details about Austen's penny-pinching and argues that her pervasive economic anxieties left a deep mark on her psyche. Sara Tavela's '"I have Unpacked the Gloves": Accessories and the Austen Sisters' focuses on Austen's caps and gloves. Caps in particular could be modified with new dressings and thus gave women the opportunity to change fashions without considerable expenditure. Tavela also notes how interested Austen was in the vogues of color, buying a coquelicot cap, for instance, just as coquelicot (the red-orange of the wild corn poppy) was all the rage (6). Mary Hafner-Lany's '"I was tempted by a pretty coloured muslin": Jane Austen and the Art of Being Fashionable' explores how Austen's letters 'are a veritable treasure trove of fashion gossip, some serious, some facetious, like her advice to Cassandra in 1813: "You really must get some flounces"' (137). Hafner-Lany also includes a list of the places in London where Austen shopped.

6 Bond Street is also where Willoughby lodges in London. As Rachel Brownstein has shown, Bond Street had associations in this era with sexual license, spectatorship, and the marriage market. She suggests that these associations inform Austen's choice of this locale for Willoughby's hideout in *Sense and Sensibility*. In keeping with these associations, we should note that Frank Churchill in *Emma* has his haircut in Bond Street (and presumably purchases the mystery piano there as well).

7 A new edition of *The Beautifull Cassandra*, with an afterword by Claudia Johnson, features ink illustrations by Leon Steinmetz which capture the sense of the narrative's speed and anarchy; the human figures seem dashed off, Rorshachian blots depicting the tempo of Cassandra's dashes from scene to scene.

8 See Miskin on the difference between the more expensive colonial product, the 'true Indian muslin', and the cheaper British version, what Mrs Allen is presumably wearing. Miskin argues that Henry's wisdom about muslins shows his participation in a 'particular mode of imperial connoisseurship, a masculine aesthetic taste that performed an important regulatory function both within the metropole and abroad' (6).

9 Henry's perspicacity about fabrics and shopping, a seemingly feminine preoccupation, matches his ready interest in Gothic novels, a genre whose readership was mostly female. Both interests are at odds with the usual male pursuits of the day, but perhaps Austen is trying to create a hero for Catherine who will break various models of the Gothic hero. Henry's wry but knowledgeable view of women's doings at any rate sets him apart from the swashbuckling figures of romance. The intimations of gender-bending in Henry disappear, however, once the narration moves to the Abbey, where Catherine's tour briefly takes her past Henry's room, with its 'litter of books, guns, and greatcoats' (183), and to the rectory in Woodston, which features 'manly' pets, 'a large Newfoundland puppy and two or three terriers' (212).

10 See especially Gregory Tate's 'Austen's Literary Alembic: *Sanditon*, Medicine, and the Science of the Novel': 'Throughout *Sanditon* ... direct speech, rather than free indirect discourse, is the formal device that the text uses to enable its readers to analyse the reactions between its various characters. *Sanditon* aims to establish an impartiality of form instead of character: it is the novel itself, rather than a privileged protagonist, that secures unbiased knowledge through observation and experimental comparison' (242). Clara Tuite also comments on the newness of Austen's stylistic approach: '[*Sanditon*] dispenses with Austen's carefully cultivated protocols of free-indirect narrative witnessing in favour of a comparatively deracinated and disembodied third-person narrator, and one furthermore that shares the stage with a noisy and unruly cast of caricatures' (627).

11 See Sheryl Bonar Craig's *Jane Austen and the State of the Nation* (2015), which details Austen's Tory sympathies. See also Sara Dustin's '*Sanditon* at 200: Intimations of a New Consumerist Society', which shows how people like the Heywoods, the stalwart Tories of the novel, were faced with serious economic difficulties throughout the 1810s because of a series of agricultural depressions. Mary Jane Curry's 'A New Kind of Pastoral: Anti-Development Satire in *Sanditon*' shows that in Austen's day the very idea of the upper classes trying to make money ran contrary to the gentry ethos.

12 See Maggie Lane's 'Lady Susan and Other Widows: Merry, Mercenary, or Mean' for a thoroughgoing review of the precise details of how Lady Denham acquired her current status and wealth.

13 In *Mansfield Park*, Austen had earlier illustrated the contrast between the old land-owning ways and the intrusion of modernity through the trope of bringing in the hay, for Mary Crawford is frustrated in her desire of carting her harp to the Mansfield rectory because it is harvest time and no carts are available. The harp is itself a fashionable tool for advertising marriageable young women: 'a young woman, pretty, lively, with a harp as elegant as herself; and both placed near a window, cut down to the ground, and opening onto a little lawn, surrounded by shrubs in the rich foliage of summer, was enough to catch any man's heart' [65]). We will see the misses Beaufort in *Sanditon* use a harp similarly, as marriage-bait.

14 Hwang has noted that Austen had parodied the effects of false advertising very early on in writing career, in her 'A Tale' from *Volume the Second*, in which one Wilhelminus is attracted by an advertisement of 'a neat Cottage on the borders of an extensive forest ... ready furnished except two rooms & a closet' (*Minor Works* 177). On arrival Wilhelminus finds that there are *only* two rooms and a closet, indeed not furnished; he has been the victim of a neat advertising trick (Hwang 252–57).

15 Harris also draws a possible parallel between Miss Lambe and Sara Baartman, the so-called Hottentot Venus of the day, an African woman of short stature whose Regency celebrity gave rise to multiple caricatures. Harris argues that perhaps Austen's portrayal of Miss Lambe is in response 'to caricatures that purported to show the cash-strapped Duke of Clarence proposing to ... Sara Baartman' (250). If so, Sir Edward Denham, cash-strapped and without scruple, might have had a comparable fate in his narrative future.

16 See Southam, both 'Jane Austen Beside the Seaside: An Introduction' and 'Jane Austen beside the Seaside: Devonshire and Wales', for details about Austen's experiences seaside. Southam explains in the first of these that 'the seaside resort [was] a wholly British invention of the 1730s' (168).

17 Several critics have treated Sanditon's fashionable invalidism in the context of the rising professionalisation of medicine. See for example Amy Mallory-Kani's '"What Should We Do with a Doctor Here?": Medical Authority in Austen's *Sanditon*', Anita O'Connell and Clark Lawlor's 'Fashionable Discourse of Disease at the Watering-Places of Literature, 1770–1820', and Rebecca Richardson's '"Sent Here for Her Health"': Accounting for Sanditon's Economies'.

Works Cited

Austen, Jane. 'A Tale.' *The Works of Jane Austen, Vol. VI, Minor Works*, edited by Robert William Chapman, 3rd ed. OUP, 1932, pp. 176–177.

Austen, Jane. *Emma. The Novels of Jane Austen, Vol. IV*, edited by Robert William Chapman, 3rd ed. OUP, 1932.

Austen, Jane. *Mansfield Park. The Novels of Jane Austen, Vol. III*, edited by Robert William Chapman, 3rd ed. OUP, 1932.

Austen, Jane. *Northanger Abbey. The Novels of Jane Austen, Vol. V, Northanger Abbey and Persuasion*, edited by Robert William Chapman, 3rd ed. OUP, 1932.

Austen, Jane. *Persuasion. The Novels of Jane Austen, Vol. V, Northanger Abbey and Persuasion*, edited by Robert William Chapman, 3rd ed. OUP, 1932.

Austen, Jane. *Pride and Prejudice. The Novels of Jane Austen, Vol. II*, edited by Robert William Chapman, 3rd ed. OUP, 1932.

Austen, Jane. *Sanditon. The Works of Jane Austen, Vol. VI, Minor Works*, edited by Robert William Chapman, 3rd ed. OUP, 1932, pp. 363–427.

Austen, Jane. *Sense and Sensibility. The Novels of Jane Austen, Vol. I*, edited by Robert William Chapman, 3rd ed. OUP, 1932.

Austen, Jane. *The Beautifull Cassandra*, edited by Claudia Johnson, illustrated by Leon Steinmetz. Princeton UP, 2018.

Austen, Jane. *The Beautifull Cassandra. The Works of Jane Austen, Vol. VI, Minor Works*, edited by Robert William Chapman, 3rd ed. OUP, 1932, pp. 44–47.

Biddiss, Michael. '*Sanditon* and the Pursuit of Health.' *Persuasions: The Jane Austen Journal*, vol. 39, 2017, pp. 243–254.

Brownstein, Rachel. 'Austen's Bond Street.' The International Conference on Romanticism. Unpublished presentation, New York City, 6 Nov. 2009.

Copeland, Edward. *Women Writing about Money: Women's Fiction in England, 1790–1820*. Cambridge UP, 1995.

Copeland, Edward. 'The Austens and the Elliots: A Consumer's Guide to *Persuasion*.' *Jane Austen's Business: Her World and Her Profession*, edited by Juliet McMaster and Bruce Stovel. Macmillan, 1996, pp. 136–153.

Copeland, Edward. 'Money.' *The Cambridge Companion to Jane Austen*, edited by Edward Copeland and Juliet McMaster. Cambridge UP, 1997, pp. 131–148.

Craig, Sheryl Bonar. *Jane Austen and the State of the Nation*. Palgrave, 2015.

Curry, Mary Jane. 'A New Kind of Pastoral: Anti-Development Satire in *Sanditon*.' *Persuasions: The Jane Austen Journal*, vol. 19, 1997, pp. 167–176.

Downie, J. A. 'Who Says She's a Bourgeois Writer? Reconsidering the Social and Political Contexts of Jane Austen's Novels.' *Eighteenth-Century Studies*, vol. 40, 2006, pp. 69–84.

Duckworth, Alistair. *The Improvement of the Estate: A Study of Jane Austen's Novels*. The Johns Hopkins UP, 1971.

Dustin, Sara. '*Sanditon* at 200: Intimations of a New Consumerist Society.' *Persuasions: The Jane Austen Journal*, vol. 39, 2017, pp. 78–87.

Ford, Susan Allen. '"To Be above Vulgar Economy": Thrifty Measures in Jane Austen's Letters.' *Persuasions: The Jane Austen Journal*, vol. 30, 2008, pp. 216–221.

Hafner-Lany, Mary. '"I was tempted by a pretty coloured muslin": Jane Austen and the Art of Being Fashionable.' *Persuasions: The Jane Austen Journal*, vol. 32, 2010, 135–143.

Harris, Jocelyn. *Satire, Celebrity, and Politics in Jane Austen*. Bucknell UP, 2017.

Holway, Tatiana M. 'Money in Jane Austen.' *Review of English Studies*, vol. 64, no. 264, 2013, pp. 289–310.

Hwang, Sheila Minn. 'Praising and Puffing: Advertising, Identity, and Illusions of Illness in Sanditon.' *Global Economies, Cultural Currencies of the Eighteenth Century*, edited by Michael Rotenberg-Schwartz and Tara Czechowski. AMS, 2012, pp. 249–273.

Lane, Anthony. 'Reading Jane Austen's Final Unfinished Novel.' *The New Yorker*, 13 Mar. 2017. https://www.newyorker.com/magazine/2017/03/13/reading-jane-austens-final-unfinished-novel. Accessed 15 Jun. 2019.

Lane, Maggie. 'Lady Susan and Other Widows: Merry, Mercenary, or Mean.' *Persuasions: The Jane Austen Journal*, vol. 34, 2012, pp. 71–82.

Leffel, John C. 'Jane Austen's Miniature Novel: Gender, Politics, and Form in "The Beautifull Cassandra."' *Persuasions: The Jane Austen Journal*, vol. 32, 2010, pp. 189–195.

'Lesser George, 1787–78.' The Royal Collection Trust. https://www.rct.uk/collection/441151/lesser-george. Accessed 10 Oct. 2019.

Mallory-Kani, Amy. "'What Should We Do with a Doctor Here?'": Medical Authority in Austen's *Sanditon*.' *Nineteenth-Century Contexts*, vol. 39, no. 4, 2017, pp. 313–326.

McKendrick, Neil, John Brewer, and John Harold Plumb. *The Birth of a Consumer Society: The Commercialization of Eighteenth-Century England*. Europa, 1982.

Michie, Elsie B. *The Vulgar Question of Money: Heiresses, Materialism, and the Novel of Manners from Jane Austen to Henry James*. Johns Hopkins UP, 2011.

Miskin, Lauren. "'True Indian Muslin' and the Politics of Consumption in Jane Austen's *Northanger Abbey*.' *Journal for Early Modern Cultural Studies*, vol. 15, no. 2, 2015, pp. 5–26. Project Muse. https://muse.jhu.edu/article/576758/pdf. Accessed 10 May 2019.

O'Connell, Anita, and Clark Lawlor. 'Fashionable Discourse of Disease at the Watering-Places of Literature, 1770–1820.' *Journal for Eighteenth-Century Studies*, vol. 40, no. 4, 2017, pp. 491–501. Online Library. https://onlinelibrary.wiley.com/doi/full/10.1111/1754-0208.12513, Accessed 10 May 2019.

Perry, Ruth. *Novel Relations: The Transformation of Kinship in English Literature and Culture, 1748–1818*. Cambridge UP, 2004.

Poovey, Mary. *Genres of the Credit Economy: Mediating Value in Eighteenth- and Nineteenth-Century Britain*. Chicago UP, 2008.

Porter, Roy. 'Pre-Modernism and the Art of Shopping.' *Critical Quarterly*, vol. 34, no. 4, 1992, pp. 3–14.

Richardson, Rebecca. "'Sent Here for Her Health": Accounting for *Sanditon*'s Economies.' *Studies in Romanticism*, vol. 56, no. 2, Summer 2017, pp. 203–222.

Southam, Brian. 'Jane Austen beside the Seaside: An Introduction.' *Persuasions: The Jane Austen Journal*, vol. 32, 2010, pp. 167–172.

Southam, Brian. 'Jane Austen beside the Seaside: Devonshire and Wales.' *Persuasions: The Jane Austen Journal*, vol. 33, 2011, 125–147.

Tate, Gregory. 'Austen's Literary Alembic: *Sanditon*. Medicine, and the Science of the Novel.' *Nineteenth-Century Literature*, vol. 70, no. 3, 2015, pp. 336–362.

Tavela, Sara. "'I have Unpacked the Gloves": Accessories and the Austen Sisters.' *Persuasions On-Line*, vol. 38, no. 1, Winter 2017. http://jasna.org/publications-2/persuasions-online/vol38no1/tavela

Todd, Janet. editor. *Jane Austen in Context*. Cambridge, 2005.

Toran, Katherine. 'The Economics of Jane Austen's World.' *Persuasions: The Jane Austen Journal On-Line*, vol. 36, no. 1, 2015. http://jasna.org/publications-2/persuasions-online/vol36no1/toran/

Trentman, Frank, 'Knowing Consumers—Histories, Identities, Practices: An Introduction.' *The Making of the Consumer: Knowledge, Power, and Identity in the Modern World*. Berg, 2006, pp. 1–27.

Tuite, Clara. '*Sanditon*: Austen's Pre-Post Waterloo.' *Textual Practice*, vol. 26, no. 4, 2012, pp. 609–629.

Wiltshire, John. *Jane Austen and the Body*. Cambridge UP, 1992.

15

'BRINGING HER BUSINESS FORWARD': JANE AUSTEN AND POLITICAL ECONOMY

Sarah Comyn

UNIVERSITY COLLEGE DUBLIN

Elinor and Marianne Dashwood, protagonists of Jane Austen's *Sense and Sensibility* (1811), enter Gray's jewellery store in London to carry out the 'exchange of a few old-fashioned jewels' on behalf of their mother (250). Anxious for Marianne's emotional well-being, Elinor is keen to finish her transaction quickly, but is thwarted by a gentleman choosing a 'toothpick-case for himself, and till its size, shape, and ornaments were determined, all of which, after examining and debating for a quarter of an hour over every toothpick-case in the shop, were finally arranged by his own inventive fancy' (251). The reader, with Elinor, later discovers that this figure is Robert Ferrars, brother to her love interest, Edward. Why does Austen choose this scene and setting to introduce the character of Robert? What can his deliberation over the 'horrors of the different toothpick-cases presented to his inspection' (251) reveal about Robert's character before we as readers have been formally introduced to him? A strong contrast between Elinor and Robert's behaviour, wealth, and status is immediately drawn in this brief scene, with Elinor presumably seeking to supplement the family's reduced wealth through the sale of unnecessary and unfashionable jewels, while Robert is fastidiously pursuing the ornamentation of such a trifling object as that of a toothpick case.[1] Elinor loses 'no time in bringing her business forward', while Robert vacillates with a face of 'sterling insignificance' (251). Austen's novels abound with moments such as these where the relationships between wealth and character, purchase and duty, sense and expense are subtly foregrounded.

Austen's narrative pursuit of the pecuniary and social consequences of the economic system is evident, for example, in the opening of *Pride and Prejudice* (1813). The most famous of opening lines to an Austen novel emphasises the 'truth universally acknowledged' that wealth most frequently governs marriage prospects and that, therefore, Mr Bingley must be secured as 'the property' of one of society's daughters (3). A passing comment in *Lady Susan* (wr. 1794)—'when a Man has once got his name in a Banking House he rolls in money' (10)—hints at the proliferation of banks and the credit economy surrounding them during the late eighteenth century. While in Austen's last and unfinished novel, *Sanditon* (wr. 1817), an uneasiness accompanies an economy of property rather than marriage speculation, with the carriage accident beginning the narrative suggestive of financial crashes to follow. In recent years, Austen's novels have caught the attention of economists, such as Thomas Piketty and Morton Schapiro, eager to consider the illustrations and explanations of economic principles—an 'economic way of thinking' (Deyo 171)—that such examples from her work can provide. But literary scholars, such as Mary Poovey, Claudia L. Johnson, and Edward Copeland, to name just a few, have long noted the economic and political discernment present in Austen's work. Drawing on this literary scholarship, this chapter explores Austen's participation in the

DOI: 10.4324/9780429398155-15-18

economic debates that animated the political economists Adam Smith and David Ricardo. In considering the changing political economic context Austen was writing in, this chapter examines how Austen's novels implicitly engage with and critique the relationship between economic and moral values; events such as the Bank Restriction Act of 1797 and its consequences for monetary value; and the effects of parliamentary enclosure acts and improvement activities on the landscape and society of Britain.

Reading and Judging Value

Economic theory and Jane Austen's writing share a preoccupation with the concept of value and the ability of individuals to assess and judge value. While contemporary economics might be primarily concerned with value expressed in monetary terms, directed by cost-benefit analyses undertaken by a rational and self-interested *homo economicus* (or economic man), the origins of economics as a modern discipline can be traced back to eighteenth-century political economy and moral philosophy. Most (in)famous for the creation of the 'invisible hand' of the market—the theory that an individual's self-interested participation in the market was frequently more beneficial for society than actions motivated by altruistic reasons—Adam Smith's *Wealth of Nations* (1776) is considered the foundational text of political economy. Smith was, however, first and foremost a moral philosopher, author of *Theory of Moral Sentiments* (1759), and, as Claudia Klaver has shown, conceived of the individual within his economic system as 'intricately tied to a moral social vision' (9). Read together, Smith's *Theory of Moral Sentiments* and the *Wealth of Nations* show that while he believed the pursuit of wealth was beneficial to society, he was determined to construct a responsible, ethical, and civically minded economic actor (Comyn; Pocock).[2] For Smith, like Austen, the idea of value was not only an economic, but also a social and moral question. Qualities such as prudence and judgement were highly regarded by Smith because they offered a critical balance in his economic theory governing the wealth of nations and, in particular, the *virtuous* pursuit of wealth by individuals (Michie). While acknowledging that the 'misconduct of individuals' in economic transactions can occur, Smith argues that the 'imprudence of some' is 'always more than compensated by the frugality and good conduct of others' (*Wealth* 323; vol. 1, bk. 2, ch. 3).

We cannot know for certain that Austen read Smith, but his theories regarding wealth, prudence, judgement, and virtuous conduct in a rapidly commercialising society were widely circulated, and as Elsie B. Michie has convincingly shown, concepts and arguments similar to those expounded by Smith's *Theory of Moral Sentiments* were published in *The Spectator* which Austen is known to have frequently read.[3] It is, therefore, not far-fetched to assume that Austen was at least familiar with Smith's idea that the creation of a prosperous nation and society can occcur without the loss of qualities regulating the moral, economic, and social conduct of individuals. Austen and Smith are 'wrestling with the [same] ambivalence', Michie argues, about the benefits and potential harm caused by the 'desire for wealth' in a fast-evolving society and both attempt to imagine 'psychological and social mechanisms' that will restrain the potential excesses of this desire (6).

The moral implications of wealth, social status, and economic activities is a subject frequently explored by Austen. It is often through the economic actions and behaviours of her characters that Austen reveals significant and telling qualities and characteristics which the reader is encouraged to evaluate and judge. When, for instance, a pianoforte is anonymously purchased for Jane Fairfax in *Emma* (1815), it causes no want of speculation among the inhabitants of Highbury about who the possible benefactor could be. The episode encourages Emma's conjectures about Jane's romantic connections with the Dixons, but not all the characters look upon the gift favourably. Mr Knightley, who (though not infallible) is positioned by the text as the primary ethical and prudential judge of behaviour in the novel, questions the wisdom of such a gift, given without notice: 'Surprizes are foolish things', he unequivocally states, concluding that '[t]he pleasure is not enhanced, and the inconvenience is often considerable' (247).

Mr Knightley's negative appraisal of the 'gift' encourages the reader, with Emma, to question the character of the person responsible for the pianoforte's arrival. When Jane is forced by her circumstances to seriously consider becoming a governess, Mr Knightley's assessment gains support, with the potential loss of the instrument underscoring the pain Jane experiences and her social and economic losses more generally. Whoever bought the pianoforte is shown to have only thought of the pleasure of giving the gift and not of the consequences for the receiver. The revelation that Frank Churchill is responsible for Jane's pianoforte emphasises the deception he has perpetrated on the community of Highbury, his selfishness, vanity, and impetuosity. As Mr Knightley states: 'That was the act of a very, very young man, one too young to consider whether the inconvenience of it might not very much exceed the pleasure. A boyish scheme, indeed!' (486). Emma judged Frank's rash decision to travel to London 'merely to have his hair cut' as a sign of 'vanity' and 'extravagance' (221), but his true motivations of going to London so as to order the instrument are just as revealing. All the clues to Frank's true character were present in the act of the anonymous gift, and by making the episode such a scene of speculation and evaluation in the novel, Austen instigates the reader's assessment of this economic activity. With Mr Knightley, we judge Frank's character, and his purchase, as a poor and imprudent one.

A brief episode depicting a burst of economic activity by Lydia Bennet in *Pride and Prejudice* is equally informative about her character. Like Frank Churchill, Lydia and Kitty Bennet decide to surprise their sisters, Jane and Elizabeth, with lunch on their return to Meryton. 'Is not this nice? Is not this an agreeable surprise?', Lydia asks before she reveals that her sisters will in fact have to pay for their 'treat': '"And we mean to treat you all," added Lydia; "but you must lend us the money, for we have just spent ours at the shop out there"' (242). Lydia has spent all her money on a bonnet which she confesses she does not even find 'very pretty', but merely for the sake of buying it rather than not: 'Oh! but there were two or three much uglier in the shop' (242). Through this behaviour, Lydia reveals her irresponsibility and selfishness, as instead of foregoing the purchase of a bonnet she does not even care for, she forces her sisters into an expense they did not foresee. This episode also foreshadows the implications Lydia's carelessness will have on her family, especially her sisters' income and marriage prospects. Making her sisters responsible for her debt at the inn in Meryton forms but a miniature of the networks of debt she will involve her family in when she runs away with Wickham.

In contrast, Charlotte Heywood in *Sanditon* is shown to have more sense than Lydia and is able to resist the 'pretty temptations' of the circulating library, reflecting that 'at two and twenty there could be no excuse for her doing otherwise—and that it would not do for her to be spending all her money the very first evening' (167). Economic transactions can also portray moments of agency and assertion, particularly by women characters. When Fanny Price returns to Portsmouth in *Mansfield Park* (1814) she delights in her ability to resolve the ongoing quarrel between her younger sisters through the purchase of a silver knife: 'Her influence, or at least the consciousness and use of it, originated in an act of kindness by Susan, which, after many hesitations of delicacy, she at last worked herself up to' (459). Given £10 by her uncle, Sir Thomas, Fanny is initially hesitant about buying the knife because she was 'so wholly unused to confer[ring] favours' (459), but growing in confidence following the success of this purchase she proceeds to the circulating library: 'wealth is luxurious and daring—and some of hers found its way to a circulating library. She became a subscriber—amazed at being any thing in *propria persona*, amazed at her own doings in every way; to be a renter, a chuser of books! And to be having any one's improvement in view in her choice!' (461). Through her 'wealth', Fanny experiences an independence of spirit and influence she has never before felt. It is in these small moments, seemingly unnecessary to the overarching plot of the novel, that Austen demonstrates the potential power, responsibilities, and duty attached to wealth.

Characters like Miss Bates and Jane Fairfax in *Emma* and Mrs Smith in *Persuasion* (1818) also portray the extreme difficulties, dependencies, and vulnerabilities experienced by women without wealth, and their treatment by other characters in the novel comes under intense scrutiny by the narrative. It is Mr Elliot's past treatment of Mrs Smith, for instance, that gives Anne Elliot and the reader the first sense of the extent of his deceit and maliciousness.

Austen uses a character's entrance into economic territory as a means of underscoring their positive and negative attributes and their moral qualities, and thereby encourages her readers to assess the economic behaviour of the characters populating her novels. In doing so, Austen teaches her readers many of the skills necessary to evaluate their own economic decisions from a pecuniary, moral, and social standpoint. The ability to judge value became a crucial skill as people, property, and commerce became more mobile throughout the eighteenth century and when, following the Bank Restriction Act of 1797, Britain's economy became dependent on a paper currency.

Forging Currency, Forging Trust

The French invasion of a beach close to Fishguard in Wales in February 1797, though quickly defeated by the British, caused a panic in London that prompted the Bank of England governors and William Pitt's government to take radical action in the financial system of the country. Meeting on 26 February, the Privy Council suspended the convertibility of Bank of England's notes from paper to specie (coin). Noting that in 'Consequence of ill-founded or exaggerated Alarms in different Parts of the Country, it appears that unless some Measure is immediately taken, there may be Reason to apprehend a Want of a sufficient Supply of Cash to answer Exigencies of the Publick Service', the Council ordered it as 'indispensably necessary for the Publick Service, that the Directors of the Bank of England, should forbear issuing any Cash in Payment until the Sense of Parliament can be taken on that Subject' (Bank). The next day, the Bank of England attempted to maintain calm and reassure the 'Proprietors of BANK STOCK, as well as the PUBLIC at large, that the general Concerns of the BANK are in the most affluent and prosperous Situation, and such as to preclude every Doubt as to the Security of its Notes' (Bank), while still enforcing the suspension of note convertibility. Officially passed on 8 May 1797, the Bank Restriction Act was initially only intended to be in force for a few weeks, but remained in place for nearly 25 years, until 1821. The Bank Restriction Period (1797–1821), as it came to be called, therefore coincides both with the 'traditional dates marking "high" Romanticism' (Dick 696), and with an extensive period of Austen's writing and publishing career.

The Restriction Period provoked a critical assessment of the nature of and relationship between value and representation. The Bank of England notes were a representation of a certain value of gold, but since their conversion to specie was suspended people were forced to question whether the notes as a *representation* of value, still intrinsically held that value (Poovey). As Kevin Barry argues: 'The promise to pay, inscribed on the note, became a promise to pay promises with promises' (55). Or as the radical commentator William Cobbett exclaimed:

> The notes of the Bank of England bear, upon the face of them, a promise that the Bankers, or Bank Company, who issue the notes, will *pay* the notes upon *demand*. Now, what do we mean by *paying* a note? Certainly we do not mean, the giving of *one note for another note*. Yet, this is the sort of payment, that people get at the Bank of England. (3)

Engaged in the act of representation, works of fiction became a crucial site for investigating the evolving relationship between value and representation (Comyn; Poovey).

Mary Poovey was one of the first literary scholars to draw the connections between the Bank Restriction Act of 1797 and Austen's fiction, particularly *Pride and Prejudice*. Pointing to the original composition dates (1796) and the preparation of *First Impressions* for publication by Cadell and Davies in 1797, Poovey finds in the 'breach of promise Elizabeth [Bennet] associates with her resolution to thank Darcy' for his intervention on behalf of Lydia, the same 'breach of promise' plot that characterised the now suspended Bank of England notes (257). Poovey notes that the amount of breaches in the novel—'not one, but *three*' (257)—deemed necessary by Austen in order to achieve the novel's happy ending, underscore the social anxiety about the deferred payment installed by the Bank Restriction Act. Sheryl Craig has subsequently traced the effect of the Bank Restriction Act on *Northanger Abbey,* first published in 1818 but written in the year that followed the Restriction Act's passing. *Northanger Abbey* is 'a novel about truth versus artifice' where characters such as Isabella Thorpe and General Tilney can prove themselves untrustworthy, but their damage can nonetheless be contained (Craig 74). Equally, Catherine Morland's exaggerated fears and speculations about General Tilney not only parody the traditions of the gothic novel, but the 'exaggerated alarms in different Parts of the Country' that prompted the Act's passing (Bank; Craig 83).

The consequences of the Restriction Act extended beyond the anxieties associated with the representational nature of notes and their redeemable value, and had profound and unexpected social consequences. Ian Haywood argues that the Restriction Act was a 'misleading title, as it actually led to a massive expansion of paper money'. In order to replace the suspended specie no longer circulating, the 'Act authorized the mass production of new £1 and £2 banknotes', that were of reduced quality which meant they could easily be forged. With 'a class of people wholly unfamiliar with paper credit' using these notes for the first time and on a daily basis, they were frequently unknowingly given and consequently passing on fake notes (Handler, 'Forging' 252). They thereby became liable for prosecution as 'utterers' because they circulated counterfeit currency. The poor quality of the new notes and the inability of many people who used them to read and correctly establish whether they were genuine, combined with the Bank of England's strict pursual of convictions, led to a 'steep rise in prosecutions and executions' for forgery during the Restriction Period (Handler, 'Forgery' 690). Whereas there were 'only four prosecutions for forgery' between 1783 and 1797, there were 972 in the twenty years following the Restriction Act, and over 2000 prosecutions and 300 executions over the entire Restriction Period (Handler, 'Forgery' 690; Haywood). The controversy surrounding the Restriction Act was heightened when the suspension of convertibility continued despite peace with France being achieved in 1815. With the arrival of peace, the 'question of a possible return to cash payments became a key political issue', and the persistence of Restriction after the Napoleonic Wars had ended, combined with the increase in counterfeit notes and executions for forgery, caused a significant amount of anger and mistrust to be directed at the Bank of England as it was so strongly associated with the 'system of paper money' (Handler, 'Forging' 252).

Just as we find Austen exploring the anxieties about value and representation in *Pride and Prejudice* and *Northanger Abbey*, we can trace the anxiety and social repercussions of the process of 'uttering' in Diana Parker's behaviour in *Sanditon*. Writing to Mr Parker, who has relinquished his inherited land in order to speculate in the property and leisure economy of 'modern Sanditon' (156), Diana claims 'we are doing our utmost to send you company worth having; and think we may safely reckon on securing you two large families, one a rich West Indian from Surrey, the other a most respectable girls boarding school, or academy, from Camberwell' (164). Although using the language of surety—'safely', 'securing', 'rich', 'respectable'—Diana's description of the method she uses as 'wheel within wheel' (164), gives readers a clue of the true state of security her 'two families' may be held in. Upon arriving in Sanditon, Diana describes in more detail the 'wheels' through which her information has circulated, which include a Miss Capper, a Fanny Noyce, and a Mrs Darling. Forming for Diana but 'a *short* chain' (187), the information they circulate amongst one another has been corrupted and results in the calamitous situation where the two families are reduced to one and the same: 'Not all that the whole Parker race could say among themselves, could produce a happier catastrophe than that the family from Surrey and the family from Camberwell were one and the same' (200). Diana and the circuitous network of gossips and messengers she engages can all be accused of a process similar to uttering as they pass on false information that replicates the false notes circulating in Britain during the Restriction Period. The value of the information Diana has shared is in fact as worthless as the easily counterfeited Bank of England notes and her misinformation has disastrous consequences for Mr Parker's speculative leisure economy in Sanditon. It is Mr Parker who is left to bear the brunt of the false economy started by Diana's initial circulation of paper through letter writing. Like the banknotes, the value of Diana's papers is called into question.

Diana's mistaken doubling of the families is also suggestive of another fear associated with the Restriction Act: monetary inflation. Writing to the *Morning Chronicle* in 1809, the political economist David Ricardo issued a warning about the consequences of the Restriction Act for the price of gold and the overissue of paper money. 'When the Act restricting the Bank from paying in specie took place, all checks to the over issue of notes were removed', Ricardo wrote, concluding that it is 'evident that all the evils in our currency were owing to the over-issues of the Bank, to the dangerous power with which it was entrusted of diminishing at its will, the value of every monied man's property, and by enhancing the price of provisions'. There are echoes of this alarm regarding inflation in Lady Denham's warning to Mr Parker that people 'who scatter their money so freely, never think of whether they may not be doing mischief of raising the price of things' (170). As the concerns and anxieties associated with the Restriction Act were reanimated following peace in 1815, it is not surprising that *Sanditon*, though begun twenty years after the Act was passed, returns to these themes and potential consequences. The bank failure and subsequent bankruptcy of Austen's brother, Henry, in 1816 may have compounded the disquiet associated with paper promising to pay paper (Comyn 70).[4]

The exchange of gossipy letters by Diana and her friends demonstrates, moreover, the ways gossip can operate as its own form of speculative economy in Austen's work. The paper chain of gossip in Austen's epistolary novel, *Lady Susan*, places the eponymous Lady Susan as a 'discursive object' in a 'gossip economy' in which all the other characters are trying to assess, devalue, and/or re-evaluate her moral and economic value (Gaston 407). In *Northanger Abbey*, Catherine's economic value in the marriage market is misjudged by General Tilney due to the gossip economy surrounding potential heiresses, such that Catherine's 'expressed value fluctuates depending on the fiction being told' (Hall 120). The circulation of false and damaging information in the marriage economies of Austen's novels demonstrates not only the vulnerabilities of young women participating in this market but also the susceptibilities of the British economy and the Bank of England, in particular, to depreciating speculations about the value of circulating paper.

A Question of Improvement

If economic transactions give insight into the moral qualities and failures of characters, then those economic actions or inactions relating to land and estates carry perhaps the most significant weight in Austen's works, as the choices landholders and owners make could have profound consequences not only for their immediate families, but for their descendants, surrounding communities, and society more generally. Estates in Austen's fiction do not merely function as the backdrop or setting for the romantic action or the marriage plot to unfold but, as Alistair Duckworth argues, 'as indexes to the character and social responsibility of their owners' (38). As J. G. A. Pocock has shown in his foundational study of the changing relationship between property, virtue, and political economy in a philosophic tradition extending from Aristotle to John Locke: property and propriety have a related etymology and property therefore 'appears as a moral and political phenomenon, a prerequisite to the leading of a "good life," which is essentially civic' (103). Thus, when Elizabeth, upon visiting Pemberley in *Pride and Prejudice*, thinks to herself that 'to be mistress of Pemberley might be something!' (271), her reaction is both a response to the wealth and beauty of the property she encounters *and* to the careful and tasteful management of the estate that in turn reflects Darcy's character. Taking the view of Pemberley in, Elizabeth notes that there is a 'stream of some natural importance [...] but without any artificial appearance', and that the 'banks were neither formal nor falsely adorned', concluding that 'she had never seen a place [...] where natural beauty had been so little counteracted by an awkward taste' (271). Elizabeth's new and favourable assessment of Darcy's taste, propriety, and judgement is supported by his housekeeper's testament of his good and generous nature, confirming that like his father, Darcy is 'affable to the poor' (275). Elizabeth's reconsideration of Darcy's character during her visit to Pemberley is, therefore, due in part to the management of his estate and staff. His actions with regards to his property present signs of the strong ethical and prudential foundations informing his character that Elizabeth had been unconscious of before.

John Dashwood's management of Norland Park in *Sense and Sensibility* is cast in a very different light when he complains to Elinor about the 'enclosure of Norland Common' that he is pursuing, an activity that proves to be 'a most serious drain' on his wealth (255). Insensitive to the economic pressures placed on the Dashwood family by his own failure to fulfil the obligations made to his dying father, John continues to describe the improvements he is making to Elinor's previous home which include felling the 'old walnut trees' in order to replace them with a green-house (257). Elinor is able to keep 'her concern and her censure to herself' (257), but the text's condemnation of John's plans for Norland is explicit despite Elinor's silence. Escaping the confines of Elinor's controlled and polite dialogue, the free indirect discourse of the narration denounces John with cutting irony: 'Having now said enough to make his poverty clear, and to do away with the necessity of buying a pair of ear-rings for each of his sisters, in his next visit at Gray's, his thoughts took a cheerfuller turn' (257). Dispossessed by their brother and the realities of strict settlement in marriage, the Dashwood sisters are portrayed as profoundly 'affected by the patrilineal agenda that enclosure movements served' (Park 237). This negative portrayal of John Dashwood's enclosing activity at Norland Park, therefore, points to a larger societal debate regarding the need for and consequences of parliamentary enclosures in Britain, and the rhetoric of improvement that accompanied them.

The process of enclosure involved the delineation of borders and boundaries across land through the erection of walls, fences, and/or hedgerows and arguably 'did more than any other development to alter the face of the countryside' as it initially sought to support a growing population by transforming poor arable land into pasture (Brown 59). Although approximately 'half of the cultivated areas in Britain had already been enclosed or had never known open field cultivation' by 1700 (Brown 59), the period 1760–1815 saw a change and intensification to enclosure practices in Britain as enclosure by a private Act of Parliament became the norm. During the Revolutionary and Napoleonic Wars (1793–1815), the enclosures sought were frequently requests to enclose common or waste land (Turner 86, 106). Through these enclosures what was previously open to the community became inaccessible and 'cottagers and non-landowners' were 'excluded from practices' such as picking berries, gathering fuel, and grazing their pigs, sheep, and cattle (Easton 74; Kelly).

Parliamentary enclosures increased the cost in legal fees both for supporters and opponents of enclosure and, as Celia Easton argues, changed 'the nature of the propaganda regarding enclosure and the response to enclosure made by lawyers, landholders and members of the clergy' (73). Whereas earlier propaganda in favour of enclosure had still recommended support for those displaced by the process, by the late eighteenth century the pro-enclosure movement was arguing that it would be beneficial for everyone, including the poor. The enclosure movement also gained the support of the clergy as clergymen were given a portion (frequently one-fifth) of the land enclosed which meant it was no longer necessary for them to collect tithes to support themselves (Kelly). Helena Kelly argues that clergymen 'were not merely incidental beneficiaries of enclosure; they were centrally implicated in it' and that the Church of England 'gain[ed] 28,000 acres of land in

Northamptonshire' out of the enclosure movement. J. M. Neeson's study of enclosures in Northamptonshire (the setting of *Mansfield Park*) has shown, however, that opposition to enclosure continued despite 'cottagers and landless commoners' being 'shrewd realists' about the costs involved (116). Neeson finds that 'in some parishes local petitions were turned into parliamentary petitions and presented by sympathetic gentry' who may have been concerned by the prospects of 'a more dependent poor' population in their communities (122–23). A number of Austen's family members were clergyman, including her father and her brother Henry (who became a clergyman following his bankruptcy), and she would therefore have been aware of the impact enclosures could have on the living of a clergyman and the positive and negative consequences for the wider community. Given how long-lasting the debates over enclosure were, it is therefore unsurprising that it is a subject that Austen repeatedly returns to, often taking a different approach to the enclosed view.

Mr Knightley, a landowner and magistrate, who as we have already seen is portrayed as the primary moral agent in *Emma*, is also an improver and encloser. As Kelly argues, the novel is 'dense with references to parish boundaries, hedges and agricultural improvement'. In conversation with his brother, Mr Knightley is described as pursuing change: 'the plan of a drain, the change of a fence, the felling of a tree, and the destination of every acre for wheat, turnips, or spring corn' are all discussed by the brothers (107). When their conversation is interrupted by Mr Woodhouse, Mr Knightley is intent upon returning to the former topic of conversation: 'But John, as to what I was telling you of my idea of moving the path to Langham' (114). Brief in nature, the conversation nonetheless suggests, as Kelly argues, that the changes to the landscape and signs of enclosure that mark the text are of a recent nature and seem driven by Knightley. Knightley is cognizant of the effects on his neighbours and community and adds to his brother that he 'should not attempt [the change to the path], if it were to be the means of inconvenience to the Highbury people' (114), but there is evidence of hardship in Highbury, such as the 'distresses of the poor' (93) that Emma tries to relieve, the 'gipsies' possibly emboldened by need to attack Harriet and her friend, and John Abdy's son struggling to take care of his ill father. Kelly traces these instances of poverty to Knightley's door: 'As the major landowner, it must be Knightley who has enclosed Highbury and Donwell, and the local poverty and desperation lie at his door.' Yet any outright condemnation of Knightley's action is simultaneously undercut by his many benevolent actions on behalf of his community. It is Knightley, for instance, who reminds Emma of her duties to those less fortunate than herself. George Knightley may be an improver and encloser, but he is no John Dashwood.

Austen's most sinister treatment of the subject of enclosure and the concomitant debate concerning improvement occurs in *Mansfield Park* where the prospects of land enclosure, the profits of slavery, the economic dividends of marriage, and the price of an improvable 'girl now nine years old' (6) are all intertwined. The opening chapter of *Mansfield Park* introduces the questions that are to dominate the novel: what will Fanny Price cost the Bertram family, what price will they obtain for her on the marriage market, and what will her ultimate value be? In recommending the patronage of Sir Thomas, Mrs Norris states: 'Give a girl an education, and introduce her properly into the world, and ten to one but she has the means of settling well, without farther expense to any body' (7). Fanny's value is, therefore, immediately tied to her ability to 'improve', to be educated, to gain from her association with the Bertrams' status, and to achieve a favourable marriage. Worried about the potential risks to his daughters by association with Fanny, Sir Thomas argues: 'We shall probably see much to wish altered in her, and must prepare ourselves for gross ignorance, some meanness of opinions, and very distressing vulgarity of manner, but these are not incurable faults' (11). It is essential for Sir Thomas's investment to be successful that Fanny, unlike her mother, follows the example of Lady Bertram and marries suitably.

Dependent on her marriageability prospects, the question of Fanny's improvement is also tied to the two land improvement debates framing the novel: the consequences and future of Sir Thomas's estate in the West Indies, and the improving and enclosing designs of Henry Crawford. Although initially prepared to support Fanny, Sir Thomas expects Mrs Norris to ultimately 'claim her share in their niece' (27). As Fanny has, by now, improved in age and as 'his own circumstances were rendered less fair than heretofore, by some recent losses on his West India Estate, in addition to his eldest son's extravagance, it became not undesirable to himself to be relieved from the expense of her support, and the obligation of her future provision' (27–28). This passage emphasises the dependence of the Bertram family's wealth on this estate, which as Marcus Wood argues, exerts a 'constant pressure [...] on every character at Mansfield' and while 'avoid[ing] direct allusion to slavery', the account of Sir Thomas's thoughts regarding Fanny nonetheless reveals 'the network of dependencies which the plantation income generates' (305). A disturbing parallel is, therefore, drawn between Fanny's future improvement and the fate of the 'West India Estate', and when Sir Thomas is forced to leave Mansfield Park for the 'better arrangement of his affairs' in Antigua (36), his disappointment in his investment in Fanny clearly corresponds to that of his overseas estates. Addressing Fanny at his departure, Sir Thomas states: 'I hope you may be able to convince [William] that the many years which have passed since you parted, have not been spent on your side entirely without improvement—though I fear he must find his sister at sixteen in some respects too much like his sister at ten' (38). The declining profits of his colonial estates necessitate that Fanny, at least, show some signs of profit.

In a deft rereading of Duckworth's *Improvement of the Estate* (1971) and Edward Said's *Culture and Imperialism* (1994), Wood argues that *Mansfield Park*'s treatment of Fanny's improvement, and the broader implications for the Mansfield community, provides a similar critique to that found in Adam Smith's examination of Britain's colonial trade monopoly, particularly its trade with the colonial sugar plantations in the West Indies that relied on the labour of enslaved people (302–03). In the *Wealth of Nations*, Smith argues that the 'monopoly of the colony trade, therefore, like all the other mean and malignant expedients of the mercantile system, depresses the industry of all other countries', and while monopoly 'chiefly' depresses the industry within the colonies, it also diminishes 'that of the country in whose favour it is established': Britain (111; vol. 2, bk. 4, ch. 7). Monopoly, for Smith, ultimately 'discourages the improvement of the land' (112), and while bringing affluence to 'a single order of men, is in many different ways hurtful to the general interest of the country' (114), with the 'fatal' effect of making 'sober virtue seem superfluous' (113; Wood 303).

In Austen's depiction of Sir Thomas, Wood finds inflections of Smith's critique of the planter class whose monopolistic investments actually impede rather than promote improvement and whose pursuit of a 'high rate of profit seems every where to destroy the parsimony which in other circumstances is natural to the character of the merchant' (Smith 113; Wood 303). 'Careful not to present Sir Thomas as immediately conforming to the stereotype of the decadent planter', Wood argues, however, that Austen 'certainly does present the Bertram family as morally degenerate' (303). Thus, while Sir Thomas initially believes he instils and maintains a strict moral foundation in his household that only dissipates with his absence, he is, as he later realises, ultimately responsible for the moral 'infection' that spreads through and almost destroys Mansfield Park. That Sir Thomas's economic self-interest and his morally corrupt investment in the sugar plantations contaminates the Park is most clearly evident in his encouragement of Maria Bertram's marriage to Mr Rushworth despite recognising that 'Rushworth was an inferior young man, as ignorant in business as in books, with opinions in general unfixed, and without seeming much aware of it himself' (*MP* 233). Unsettled by his disappointment in Rushworth, Sir Thomas nonetheless approves the marriage, motivated in part by Maria's reassurances but also by the knowledge that he and Rushworth share the 'same [political] interest' (46) and 'an alliance which [Sir Thomas] could not have relinquished without some pain' (234), possibly alluding to Sir Thomas's interests in the slave trade.

As Fanny is the character to which the reader is given the most interior access, the reader is witness to her educational and moral improvement in contrast to the potential and actual moral degradation of the other characters in the novel, including even Fanny's primary educator, Edmund Bertram. It is one of the strongest ironies of the novel that while Sir Thomas laments his investment in Fanny's improvement until her value on the marriage market is unmistakeable, her exposure to a moral education at Mansfield Park eventually allows her to form the strongest opposition both to Sir Thomas's will and to the greatest 'capital improver' (284) and encloser in the novel, Henry Crawford. Fanny's feelings of dismay towards the improving tendencies of characters like Rushworth and Crawford is first registered in response to the felling of trees at Sotherton—'Cut down an avenue! What a pity!' (66)—but her resistance, increasing with the disruption brought on by the theatricals, becomes more adamant in response to Crawford's attentions to her.

Detecting in Fanny a 'wonderful improvement' that none of the others 'seemed sensible of' (267), Crawford sets a course of action to improve her through an association with himself. He attempts first to make Fanny love him, then to improve her situation and happiness through an offer of marriage and by assisting her brother William's naval career, and ultimately tries to use her to improve himself. The necklace he deceptively gives to Fanny through his sister performs the same attempts at enclosure and improvement that he fantasises performing at Thornton Lacey: 'The farm-yard must be cleared away entirely, and planted up to shut out the blacksmith's shop', a 'new garden' must be planted, and if the timber 'sprinkled' in the surrounding meadows is not part of the living, they must be purchased (281–82). Fanny successfully resists and rejects Crawford's efforts to improve and enclose her, and her marriage to Edmund secures a different improvement in the future of Thornton Lacey. The improvements planned by the Crawfords are 'distrusted in *Mansfield Park*' because, as Duckworth argues, they 'signal a radical attitude to a cultural heritage', one that takes 'no account of society as an organic structure' and that seems instead 'to favour a widening of the gap between church and house, religion and the landed order' (54). Through Fanny's rejection of Henry Crawford, the novel critiques and rejects 'a particular mode of "improvement"' (Duckworth 42), but Fanny's indebtedness to the Bertrams for her upbringing and her endogamous marriage to Edmund implicate her in the morally contaminated wealth of the plantations. Is the silver knife she purchased for Susan equally tainted? Can we trust the success of Fanny's moral resistance and her own mode of improvement? Or are we left, as Wood argues, 'to ponder the full loss in her ethical status that this absorption into a sugar fortune indicates'? (322).

Austen's approaches to the debates of land improvement and enclosure vary across her novels, but they always foreground the moral and gendered implications of economic change and the social consequences of individual actions. In exploring both the positive and negative effects of the enclosure and improvement movement, Austen reveals the complexity of these economic debates that had profound implications for all members of society.

★★★

'You know how interesting the purchase of a sponge-cake is to me', Jane Austen wrote to her sister Cassandra on 15 June 1808 (*Letters* 128). Both playful and sincere, this sentence captures Austen's fascination with the social and economic implications of acquisitions. Whether the purchase of a sponge-cake or a piano, Austen asks questions about the value to be had through the process of buying, giving, and receiving. She frequently asks and teaches her readers to evaluate the moral and social qualities of characters as they participate in economic transactions, pushing them to question the value of the paper promises within her novels and the currency circulating in society. Placing her characters within, outside, and crossing the boundaries of estates, Austen prompts her readers to examine the consequences, particularly for women, of transforming those boundaries and to consider carefully the value of and price to be paid for 'improvement'. Read alongside the works

Jane Austen and Political Economy

of political economists such as Adam Smith and David Ricardo and within the context of the economic debates defining her period, it is clear that, like Elinor Dashwood does in Gray's, Austen wastes no time in sensitively but adeptly 'bringing her business forward'.

Notes

1   For an excellent account of the 'toothpick case and its personification in Robert' Ferrars (17), see D. A. Miller, 9–20.
2   Smith nonetheless promoted Enlightenment's stadial theory of civilisational and economic progress that viewed society as progressing from 'primitive' hunting and gathering to what he saw as more complex and developed forms of economic production such as agriculture and commerce. For an excellent account on this theory and the impact on global thinking and trade, see Evan Gottlieb, especially 11, 19–27.
3   There is no copy recorded of the *Wealth of Nations* or the *Theory of Moral Sentiments* in the surviving 1818 catalogue of Austen's brother Edward Knight's library at Godmersham, for instance. There is, however, a three-volume 1814 edition of the *Wealth of Nations* 'with notes and an additional volume by David Buchanan' at Chawton House Library which features the Edward Knight bookplate and is recorded in the 1908 Godmersham library catalogue. The 1818 catalogue is accessible online, and the Godmersham Library has been recreated at Reading with Austen: https://www.readingwithausten.com/index.html.
4   Henry Austen was a partner in three country banks (in Alton, Petersfield, and Hythe), his firm Austen & Co. was involved in a 'network of country banks', and he became the Receiver General for Oxfordshire in 1813, a prestigious position that required substantial financial backing which he received from both friends and family (Clery 5, 189; Caplan 74–75). Many country banks suffered during the post-war depression and, sensing financial trouble in 1815, Henry 'severed ties' with the Alton country bank, Austen, Gray & Vincent which failed in November 1815. His firm (Austen & Co.) and his London bank (Austen, Maunde & Tilson) were nonetheless vulnerable to the rumours of financial irregularities at Alton and could not be extricated from the dense network of debts circulating Henry and the other banks (Clery 261, 265–66; Caplan 86). The London bank was declared bankrupt in March 1816. The shock of Henry's bankruptcy would ripple through the Austen family and friendship circle as many relations held deposits with the banks and his brother and uncle stood surety for his receivership (Clery 268–69; Caplan 87).

Works Cited

Austen, Jane. *Emma*, edited by Richard Cronin and Dorothy Mcmillan. Cambridge UP, 2005. *The Cambridge Edition of the Works of Jane Austen*, general editor, Janet Todd, 2005–2008.

Austen, Jane. *Jane Austen's Letters*, edited by Deirdre le Faye, 3rd ed. Oxford UP, 1995.

Austen, Jane. *Lady Susan. Later Manuscripts*, edited by Janet Todd and Linda Bree. Cambridge UP, 2008, pp. 3–78. *The Cambridge Edition of the Works of Jane Austen*, general editor, Janet Todd, 2005–2008.

Austen, Jane. *Mansfield Park*, edited by John Wiltshire. Cambridge UP, 2005. *The Cambridge Edition of the Works of Jane Austen*, general editor, Janet Todd, 2005–2008.

Austen, Jane. *Pride and Prejudice*, edited by Pat Rogers. Cambridge UP, 2006. *The Cambridge Edition of the Works of Jane Austen*, general editor, Janet Todd, 2005–2008.

Austen, Jane. *Sanditon. Later Manuscripts*, edited by Janet Todd and Linda Bree. Cambridge UP, 2008, pp. 137–209. *The Cambridge Edition of the Works of Jane Austen*, general editor, Janet Todd, 2005–2008.

Austen, Jane. *Sense and Sensibility*, edited by Edward Copeland. Cambridge UP, 2006. *The Cambridge Edition of the Works of Jane Austen*, general editor, Janet Todd, 2005–2008.

Bank of England. *Bank of England, February 27th, 1797. In Consequence of an Order of His Majesty's Privy Council Notified to the Bank Last Night*. London: Gale, 1797, Eighteenth Century Collections Online.

Barry, Kevin. 'The Aesthetics of Paper Money: National Differences during the Period of Enlightenment and Romanticism.' *Scotland, Ireland, and the Romantic Aesthetic*, edited by David Duff and Catherine Jones. Bucknell UP, 2007, pp. 55–76.

Brown, Richard. *Society and Economy in Modern Britain, 1700–1850*. Routledge, 1991.

Caplan, Clive. 'Jane Austen's Banker Brother: Henry Thomas Austen of Austen & Co., 1806–1816.' *Persuasions*, no. 20, 1998, 69–90.

Clery, E. J. *Jane Austen: The Banker's Sister*. Biteback Publishing, 2017.

Cobbett, William. *Paper against Gold; or, the History and Mystery of the Bank of England, of the Debt, of the Stocks, of the Sinking Fund, and of the Other Tricks and Contrivances, carried on by the Means of Paper Money.* London: WM. Cobbett, 1828.

Comyn, Sarah. *Political Economy and the Novel: A Literary History of 'Homo Economicus.'* Palgrave Macmillan, 2018.

Copeland, Edward. *Women Writing about Money: Women's Fiction in England, 1790–1820.* Cambridge UP, 1995.

Craig, Sheryl. *Jane Austen and the State of the Nation.* Palgrave Macmillan, 2015.

Deyo, Darwyyn. 'Jane Austen and the Economic Way of Thinking.' *International Journal of Pluralism and Economics Education,* vol. 7, no. 2, 2016, pp. 170–182.

Dick, Alexander. 'British Romanticism and Paper Money.' *Literature Compass,* vol. 10, no. 9, 2013, pp. 696–704.

Duckworth, Alistair. *The Improvement of the Estate: A Study of Jane Austen's Novels.* John Hopkins UP, 1971.

Easton, Celia. 'Jane Austen and the Enclosure Movement: The Sense and Sensibility of Land Reform.' *Persuasions,* vol. 22, 2002, pp. 71–89.

Gaston, Lise. 'Gossip Economics: Jane Austen, *Lady Susan,* and the Right to Self-Fashion.' *European Romantic Review,* vol. 27, no. 3, 2016, pp. 405–411.

Gottlieb, Evan. *Romantic Globalism: British Literature and the Modern World Order, 1750–1830.* Ohio State UP, 2013.

Hall, Lynda A. *Women and 'Value' in Janes Austen's Novels: Settling, Speculating and Superfluity.* Palgrave Macmillan, 2017.

Handler, Phil. 'Forgery and the End of the "Bloody Code" in Early Nineteenth-Century England.' *The Historical Journal,* vol. 48, no. 3, 2005, pp. 683–702.

Handler, Phil. 'Forging the Agenda: The 1819 Select Committee on Criminal Laws Revisited.' *The Journal of Legal History,* vol. 25, no. 3, 2004, pp. 249–268.

Haywood, Ian. 'Paper Promises: Restriction, Caricature and the Ghost of Gold.' *Romantic Circles,* Feb. 2012, np, http://www.rc.umd.edu/praxis/forgery/HTML/praxis.2011.haywood.html

Johnson, Claudia L. *Jane Austen: Women, Politics and the Novel.* U of Chicago P, 1988.

Kelly, Helena. 'Austen and Enclosure.' *Persuasions On-Line,* vol. 30, no. 2, Spring 2010, np.

Klaver, Claudia. *A/Moral Economics: Classical Political Economy and Cultural Authority in Nineteenth-Century England.* Ohio State UP, 2003.

Michie, Elsie B. 'Austen's Powers: Engaging with Adam Smith in Debates about Wealth and Virtue.' *Novel,* vol. 34, no. 1, Fall 2000, pp. 5–27.

Miller, D. A. *Jane Austen, or The Secret of Style.* Princeton UP, 2003.

Morson, Gary Saul, and Morton Schapiro, *Cents and Sensibility: What Economics Can Learn from the Humanities.* Princeton UP, 2017.

Neeson, J. M. 'The Opponents of Enclosure in Eighteenth-Century Northamptonshire.' *Past & Present,* vol. 105, no. 1, 1984, pp. 114–139.

Park, Julie. 'The Poetics of Enclosure in *Sense and Sensibility.*' *Studies in Eighteenth-Century Culture,* vol. 42, 2003, pp. 237–269.

Piketty, Thomas. *Capital in the Twenty-First Century.* Translated by Arthur Goldhammer. Belknap P of Harvard UP, 2014.

Pocock, J. G. A. *Virtue, Commerce, and History: Essays on Political Thought and History, Chiefly in the Eighteenth Century.* Cambridge UP, 1985.

Poovey, Mary. 'From Politics to Silence: Jane Austen's Nonreferential Aesthetic.' *Companion to Jane Austen,* edited by Claudia L. Johnson and Clara Tuite. Blackwell Publishing, 2009, pp. 249–260.

Ricardo, David. 'The Price of Gold Three Contributions to the Morning Chronicle 1809.' *The Works and Correspondence of David Ricardo,* edited by Piero Sraffra with Maurice H. Dobb, vol. 3, Pamphlets and Papers, 1809–1811. Liberty Fund, 2005, 11 vols.

Said, Edward W. *Culture and Imperialism.* Vintage P, 1994.

Smith, Adam. *An Inquiry into the Nature and Causes of the Wealth of Nations.* 1776, edited with an Introduction, Notes, Marginal Summary and an Enlarged Index by Edwin Cannan. Methuen & Co., 1904. 2 vols, https://oll.libertyfund.org/titles/smith-an-inquiry-into-the-nature-and-causes-of-the-wealth-of-nations-cannan-ed-in-2-vols

Turner, Michael. *Early Parliamentary Enclosure: Its Historical Geography and Economic History.* Dawson Publishing, 1980.

Wood, Marcus. *Slavery, Empathy and Pornography.* Oxford UP, 2002.

16

MATERIAL GOODS IN AUSTEN'S NOVELS

Sandie Byrne

OXFORD UNIVERSITY

Although Austen rarely gives detailed specific descriptions of material objects, houses, land, and consumer goods are all invested with significance for her plots, themes, and characterisation. Property, in the senses of both goods and ownership, is foregrounded in the opening of each of the major novels. The most famous iteration is of course in *Pride and Prejudice*, which makes play with the terms possession, possessions, and property. *Sense and Sensibility's* back-story introduces a will, an entail, and an inheritance; the words 'estate' and 'property' appear in the second sentence, and 'owner' in the third. *Mansfield Park's* marriage mathematical formula:

Handsome woman + £7000 < baronet with a handsome house and large income

Handsome woman + £10,000 = baronet with a handsome house and large income

makes a young woman (presumably possessed of good looks and good reputation) who has £10,000 the equal of a baronet with a good house and income (*MP* 3). Miss Maria Ward, with 'only seven thousand pounds', is acknowledged in the local gossip represented in free indirect style, to be 'at least three thousand pounds short of any equitable claim to it' (*MP* 3). The gossips respectfully reference the opinion of 'her uncle, the lawyer, himself', and thus introduce early in the novel a legal register. In Mrs Bennet's calculation, an income of £10,000 p.a. = a man of higher rank: 'Ten thousand a year, and very likely more! 'Tis as good as a Lord!' (*PP* 290). Mrs Jenkins similarly balances an equation of marriage mathematics when she regrets the ill-usage of 'such a pretty girl': 'when there is plenty of money on one side, and next to none on the other' (*SS 144*). The first sentence of *Emma* uses 'rich' as one of the three descriptors of its protagonist, and Emma Woodhouse is subsequently revealed to be the daughter of a cadet branch of an ancient family and to have a fortune of £30,000 (3, 107–8).

This chapter will argue that although in Austen's time a woman's legal status was that of property, Austen's novels illustrate the ways in which both *feme sole* and *feme covert* could choose, purchase, and retain property, how this was managed, why this was important, and why it should not be all-consuming. The novels set this theme within the wider subject of the ways in which law and social practice reduced a woman's right to choose more generally, giving them restricted power of decision in matters such as inheritance, ownership, proposal of marriage, travel, and even choice of dance partner. While not contending that the novels present a radical, proto-feminist agenda, the essay will suggest that they criticise social and legal systems, participate in contemporary debates, and, like the works of Mary Wollstonecraft, assert that women can be rational, sensible, and capable.[1] Austen took

DOI: 10.4324/9780429398155-16-19

care to get the details of inheritance law correct.[2] Ever the realist, she shows that the *feme sole* had 'a dreadful propensity for being poor',[3] the *feme covert* little autonomy and few rights to property, and neither much power, but that women could negotiate and ameliorate both law and custom.

Women's rights to ownership under the legal codes of England in the long eighteenth century were limited but did exist. Both custom and law gave women from both high- and low-ranking families opportunities to acquire, keep, and circulate goods, and women were important engines of consumerism. How objects are depicted in relation to women in Austen's fiction is important in the context of the significant terms 'possession' and 'property', but also 'taste'. Terms such as 'goods' and 'chattels' will be used in preference to 'property', however, to refer to objects held but not necessarily legally owned by women, and to distinguish consumer goods from real estate.[4]

In the major novels, the perception and aesthetic appreciation of objects are related to memory, feeling, and the characterising presence or absence of taste; the imposition of one's taste, and the ownership and circulation of goods are related to autonomy and identity. Fanny Price's feelings about the Mansfield estate, and Anne Elliot's about Kellynch, show their appreciation and nostalgia for their homes, and their good taste in enjoying nature (*MP* 338, 351, 372; *P* 43). Neither, however, has the power to employ her good taste in the aesthetics of estate management, as the well-off males such as Fitzwilliam Darcy and George Knightley do (*PP* 185, *E* 281, 283). Robert Ferrars shows terrible taste in over-embellishing a toothpick case, but money affords him the choice (*SS* 165–66). Power can trump taste, but on occasion female power prevails, albeit temporarily. While General Tilney believes Catherine Morland to be a desirable wife for Henry, he defers to her taste (*NA* 157–58). Finding her taste in china to match his, he hints that he will give her a similar set as a wedding present (*NA* 127–28). His autocratic behaviour and control over the spaces and artefacts of Northanger Abbey, however, lead the reader to suspect that a daughter-in-law's taste and wishes will be given no more weight than his daughter's. Once Catherine's value is diminished by the report of her lack of fortune, her wishes, even as to the disposition of herself, are disregarded (*NA* 165–66). Maria Bertram, 'pledged to Sotherton', not its owner, has greater power than Fanny or Anne because she is to marry a weak and pliable man (*MP* 157). After she is married and in London, her taste will have 'fairer play'; she will impose it on the family's carriages and furniture (*MP* 158). After her divorce, she is returned to her father's authority, and is subject to his confinement (*MP* 365).

Austen lived long before the Married Women's Property Acts of 1870 and 1882, at a time when women's hold on possessions was tenuous. In theory, the unmarried woman, *feme sole*, had the same legal status as a man, but as Gillian Skinner points out, that equivalence was only in private law, there was no place for them in public law (91). The married woman, *feme covert*, as property, could hardly own property. William Blackstone's *Commentaries* state that 'by marriage the very being or legal existence of a woman is suspended' (442). Rather than having a separate legal existence, she is subsumed under that of her husband, 'under whose wing, protection and cover she performs every thing' (442). A 1738 treatise defines 'The Nature of a Feme Covert' as

> *tegere* in Latin and is so called for that the Wife is *sub potestate viri*. The Law of Nature hath put her under the Obedience of her Husband [....] she wants Free-will as Minors want Judgement [....] Baron and Feme are commonly said to be one Person in Law; the Consequents [*sic*] of which are, that a Man cannot grant Lands and Tenements to his Wife'. (*Baron and Feme* 7–8)

The money and goods that women brought to, and that they earned during, marriage were generally the property of the husband, with exceptions. 'Marriage is an absolute Gift of Chattels Personal in Possession of her own Right', yet women could and did have money and goods allocated to them by marriage settlements, usually an allowance of pin money during the husband's lifetime and a widow's inheritance, a dower house, and/or income after his death (*Baron and Feme* 63). This did not, however, mean that they invariably received either. Lack of knowledge or understanding of the law, lack of funds to go to law, or simply *force majeure* might preclude a woman from securing her rights.

Emma Woodhouse's comfortable home, and her management of it, is early made significant, and discussion soon moves to the importance to Miss Taylor of having a house of her own, yet Hartfield will ultimately belong to one or other of the Knightley brothers, and Randalls is Mr Weston's (*E* 7). The preference of the law for primogeniture and the practice of entailing an estate on heirs male meant that a woman might furnish, care for, and administer a house and household for decades yet on her husband's death lose the home that she would have considered hers, as does Mrs Dashwood in *Sense and Sensibility*. This mostly applied in the case of the upper classes and middling sort, as Amy Louise Erickson notes: 'strict [equitable] settlements to preserve property in the male line were used only by the wealthy, different types of prenuptial settlements to preserve the wife's property interests were implemented by all levels of society, albeit often without the technical legal terminology' (150–51). Entails and primogeniture inheritance aimed to keep the acreage of estates intact rather than divided and progressively morcellated. Lady Catherine de Bourgh, whose husband's estate was not entailed, is unusual. Entailment was less important when the inheritance was not land but capital, and so more often partible. Female heirs and heirs apparent to investments, such as Emma, Mrs Ferrars, and Lady Denham, are more fortunate than Mrs Dashwood. Though Jane Bennet may be pleased that her husband has finally purchased an estate (*PP* 295), when it passes to his heir she may wish that he had kept his fortune in the government funds, unless, like Mrs Jenkins, she has an ample jointure (*SS* 28), but even that may be administered by a male trustee. These practices derived from feudal law, which excluded women from ownership of the manor because land was held under the king in return for military service. Joan Thirsk shows that in England, primogeniture was increasingly applied to aristocratic estates from the early sixteenth century (183–84); Christopher Hill dates strict settlement to 1647 (115). By the eighteenth century the practice had spread from the aristocracy to the gentry and yeomanry (Thirsk 191). Even after the end of feudal forms of tenure, the strict settlement preserved the patriarchal hierarchy and, Hill asserts, fostered the consolidation of landed property which made the Whig oligarchy of the eighteenth century (116).

Persuasion's opening phrase: 'Sir Walter Elliot of Kellynch-hall', repeated in the embedded heading from the *Baronetage*: 'ELLIOT OF KELLYNCH-HALL', immediately ties the Elliot identity to the estate and house (10). The narrative soon moves to the consequences of the failure of the custodian of Kellynch and the efficacy of his tenant, and therefore to the question of right and rights of ownership. Conceited and silly men such as Sir Walter, hypochondriac and silly men such as Mr Woodhouse, detached, lazy men such as Mr Bennet, and weak selfish men such as John Dashwood own houses and have power over women such as Anne Elliot, Emma Woodhouse, Elizabeth Bennet and Elinor Dashwood because of their legal rights to possessions. As Margaret Kirkham notes: 'Such is the man upon whom the laws and customs of England confer the control and protection of wives and daughters' (150).

Mr Dashwood, a life tenant in the entailed Norland estate, aims to provide for his wife and children, and initially his heir, John, acquiesces, until otherwise persuaded by his wife, who ensures that he will have the estate and income unfettered, and that their son will inherit it all (*SS* 4). Mr Bennet, whose Longbourn estate is also held in 'tail male', has failed to make provision for his wife and their five daughters, who, unless they married well, would rely on familial charity and the income from Mrs Bennet's £4000 (*PP* 20). Sir Walter Elliot has been such a spendthrift that on Anne's marriage 'he could give his daughter at present but a small part of the share of ten thousand pounds which must be hers hereafter', a sum presumably hers through the marriage settlements of Sir Walter and Lady Elliot (*P* 200). In this, the men become less conventionally masculine, failing in the requirements of independence and authority, marked by John's domination by his wife, and benevolent paternalism, marked by Mr Bennet's and Sir Walter's abnegation of their responsibilities. Each of these men has inherited rather than made his fortune or purchased his estate; it is the hyper-masculine Wentworth who will support his wife with the prize-money that he has earned and who can bequeath his wealth as he wishes. The root of this inequitable distribution of goods and power is not overtly criticised, but the novels show the system's flaw in privileging men without consideration of their ability or disposition to administer goods and power.

The law of primogeniture did not necessarily entail the beggaring of younger sons or females. As Thirsk shows, in Continental Europe there was an expectation that the testator or heir would provide for the heirs general in the form of small estates or income, since it would be likely that part at least of an estate would be held under 'tail general' rather than 'tail male' (182). Though this was not enshrined in law in England, it was not unusual for younger sons to be provided for in the will of the father, nor for daughters to receive portions, which were often derived from the dowry brought to the marriage by their mother. When no provision was made in the patriarchal will, there might be felt to be a moral obligation on the fortunate heir to provide for his siblings. George Wickham tacitly alludes to this in presenting himself as an honorary brother to Darcy, on the basis that Mr Darcy Senior was his godfather (*PP* 60). He suggests that he had a right to expect that Darcy would honour his father's wishes, which Darcy has done, but also to continue to provide for him after he has spent the equivalent in money to the promised living, which Darcy does not. Though the Dashwood and Bennet women have no rights of ownership in the respective estates, they could reasonably have expected a share of the income and/or shelter that those provided. The first edition of *Sense and Sensibility*[5] noted that Mr Dashwood was unable to provide for his second wife and daughters by any 'division' of the estate, a correct statement about the English preference for primogeniture. The second edition changes this to 'charge on the estate',[6] referring to the possibility of an income being reserved for the women, an option also ruled out.[7] John's suggestions, rejected by Fanny, are an annuity, or a lump sum, both acceptable ways for the heir to provide for siblings, but non-contractual ways were also common (*SS* 8–9). The Austen brothers, none of whom inherited much from the Reverend George Austen, nonetheless fulfilled expectations through informal non-contractual means, Edward Austen Knight allowing his mother and sisters to live in the cottage in Chawton, the other brothers voluntarily contributing to the women's upkeep without any legalised obligation. James Austen himself benefitted from belief in the superior rights of an eldest son. The family had expectations of large bequests from the will of their uncle by marriage, James Leigh Perrot, but in the event, Mrs Austen was left nothing, most of the siblings £1000, and James £24,000, none of these bequests payable until after the death of Mrs Leigh Perrot, which did not happen until 1836.

Mr Woodhouse, a descendant of the cadet branch of an ancient family (*E* 108), may have solved the problem of the younger son's line by marrying an heiress. His capital is invested, enabling it to be partible, so that his daughters can inherit, and as primogeniture doesn't apply, they can receive equal amounts. The Donwell estate is not likely to be partible and has been inherited by the elder son, George Knightley, so that his younger brother, John, has been required to take up a career. Nonetheless, it is clear from Mr Knightley's intervention in conversation (to distract John from his irritation at Mr Woodhouse) that the elder consults the younger about the estate and feels that he has a rightful interest in it.

> 'But John, as to what I was telling you of my idea of moving the path to Langham, of turning it more to the right that it may not cut through the home meadows [....] I shall see you at the Abbey to-morrow morning I hope, and then we will look them [the maps] over, and you shall give me your opinion'. (*E* 85)

This could relate to a section of the estate from which John derives an income, but the 'home meadows' would be likely to belong to the entailed estate.

The Watsons supplies a diatribe on the folly of entrusting money to women and might be taken to reflect the conventional view in support of entails and trustees, but it is put into the mouth of Robert Watson, the self-satisfied, stupid, and greedy attorney brother of the heroine.

> 'A pretty peice [*sic*] of work your Aunt Turner has made of it! By Heaven! A woman should never be trusted with money. I always said she ought to have settled something on you, as soon as her Husband died'. 'But that would have been trusting *me* with money', replied Emma, 'and *I* am a woman too.—' 'It might have been secured to your future use without your having any power over it now'. (*The Watsons* 282; emphasis and layout original)

In spite of his sister's protestations against speaking disrespectfully of her aunt and uncle, Robert continues:

> 'I thought Turner had been reckoned an extraordinarily sensible, clever man.—How the Devil came he to make such a will? [...] He might have provided decently for his widow, without leaving every thing that he had to dispose of, or any part of it at her mercy'. (*Watsons* 283)

Women, then, were disadvantaged by prejudice as well as by *coverture* and primogeniture, but the law was far from simple, and more than one legal system was active in England in the long eighteenth century. Erickson explains that 'common law 'is best known because it is used as a shorthand for 'the system which, through colonization, came to dominate nearly one third of the globe' (5). Roman civil law was more egalitarian than the common law, and ecclesiastical law, which regulated the division of personal property, followed Roman civil law, thus advocating

> a form of community property within marriage and the equal division of parental wealth among all children. Manorial or borough law varied locally, affecting the inheritance of land within the manor or borough. In many places this land was partible among all sons rather than impartible to the eldest son. Finally, parliamentary statutes, made by common lawyers sitting in parliament, also played a crucial role in regulating property transmission, principally by intervening in ecclesiastical law. (Erickson 5)

The system of equity originated to ameliorate the perceived harshness of the common law, and throughout its history a considerable part of the business of equity cases in Chancery consisted of cases involved the property of married women, which the common law did not recognise. Equity enabled married women through trusts to own property and have some protection under the law. That the system was complex can be seen in the length—236 pages—of James Clancy's 1815 'An Essay on the Equitable Rights of Women', which explains the system and aims to refute two judgements on the issues involved.[8]

Although in civil law married women in the long eighteenth century owned nothing, common law—custom—enabled them to garner and keep goods, not only through marriage settlements managed by trustees who would almost certainly be male, but on their own behalf. By custom, household goods were regarded as a woman's own and did not pass to her husband on marriage. Mrs Dashwood Senior, though bereft of the house and estate of Norland, is able to keep her personal household goods from the clutches of her step-daughter-in-law and successor. Having whittled down her husband's proposed generosity to almost nothing, Fanny (Mrs John) Dashwood prevents him from making any gifts of furnishings.

> [O]ne thing must be considered. When your father and mother moved to Norland, though the furniture of Stanhill was sold, all the china, plate, and linen was saved, and is now left to your mother. Her house will therefore be almost completely fitted up as soon as she takes it'.

> 'That is a material consideration undoubtedly. A valuable legacy indeed! And yet some of the plate would have been a very pleasant addition to our own stock here'. (*SS* 10–11)

Fanny's subsequent comments demonstrate her ridiculous resentment that it was in the older Mr Dashwood's power to enable his wife and daughters to inherit anything; that the entail did not extend to personal household goods brought into the entailed estate. It is worth noting that Mrs Dashwood Senior did not have an automatic right to the plates, silver, and bedding that she has used and cared for, and which she may have purchased, it has been bequeathed to her. Fanny Dashwood is a comic monster and her cupidity is consequently exaggerated, but she illustrates the problem for women of entailed property. She is secure in having a good settlement, but, like the older Mrs Dashwood, has only a temporary use of Norland and its income, and it is in her interest to shore up unentailed goods and income against her widowhood, when her son will take over the estate. It may be she who has encouraged John to purchase the land he mentions to Elinor, hoping to annex this unentailed property for her future use (*SS* 169). Austen here demonstrates the dilemma of women attempting to gain possession of material goods and thus secure their future: to fail to do so is unfortunate at best and irresponsible and catastrophic at worst, but to do so is frequently at the cost of other (rival) women, and far from permanent.

The extent to which *coverture* was a legal premise but a social fiction can be seen in Erickson's evidence of wives who 'managed finances on their own behalf and jointly with their husbands' (225). Even civil law allowed loopholes in property rights; since a wife's duties included ensuring that the household was properly supplied, she could with impunity spend her husband's money in ordering goods: 'where the Wife cohabiting with the husband takes up Goods in his Name, this prima facie is to be presumed the Contract of the Husband, for it is presumed that the Husband will trust so near a Relation to act for him' (*Law* 183). Elizabeth Bennet may be taking this into account when she practices some economies in order to send relief to Lydia. 'It had always been evident to her that such an income as theirs, under the direction of two persons so extravagant in their wants, and heedless of the future, must be very insufficient to their support'(*PP* 296). The phrase 'under the direction of two persons' indicates that Lydia as well as Wickham has spending power. Darcy, the arranger of their marriage, may have insisted on a water-tight settlement which gives Lydia pin money, or she could be running up the debts which Jane and Elizabeth are called on to pay through their allowances for household expenses. The law of necessaries permitted wives to purchase goods, though with an important proviso.

> The husband's consent to his wife supplying herself with necessaries suitable to his own station in life is implied [....] whether she lives with him, or parts under circumstances which justify her in so doing, provided she be chaste, since a husband is bound to maintain and protect his wife, seeing that he acquires all her available property (if any) by force of his marital right. (*Baron and Feme* 274)

Since Lydia maintains 'all the claims to reputation which her marriage had given her' (*Baron and Feme* 274), we assume that she is considered chaste.

Which goods and funds the Musgrove sisters will take with them when they marry, respectively, Captain Benwick and Charles Hayter, may differ, since cousin Charles is unlikely to afford a legal advisor and likely to accept whatever Mr Musgrove has proposed, whereas Benwick, having won prize-money, may expect a substantial dowry (*P* 81). Unlike daughters of less well-to-do families, they will not need to be given pots and pans to get their households started, but are likely to take their instruments and other personal items (*P* 45). Further down the social scale, Harriet Smith will have little to take with her, something noted unintentionally but brutally by Emma when she (wrongly) predicts of the vicarage: 'There go you and your riddle-book one of these days' (*E* 67). Mary Crawford has, among other things, a harp and a lot of jewellery (*MP* 202–3), and the £20,000 settled on her is likely to play a part in gaining her a spouse (32). Her family solicitors will arrange marriage settlements which will specify that which is to be at her disposal, probably held in trust by her uncle or brother. Used to spending freely, she is surprised to find that not everything is available for ready money (*MP* 46–47). What property Fanny Price would take to a marriage as her own would depend on her father and uncle, on the definition of household goods, and on the extent to which her future husband might extend his rights. Lieutenant Price will have nothing to contribute to Fanny's settlements, and though we might assume that had Fanny married Henry Crawford her uncle might have been expected to dower her, there is no obligation on him to do so, and he may feel that Edmund's living should support the couple. Fanny may find herself without an established regular income, and so entirely dependent on gifts or bills sent to her husband.

In Austen's fiction, women's spending and acquisition can be seen as defiant gestures of possession and appropriation of both material goods and spaces, though this may be regulated by men. Catherine Morland is given ten guineas by her father and by her mother a little book in which she is to keep an account of her spending (*NA* 9). Fanny Price similarly receives a gift of £10 from Sir Thomas when she returns to Portsmouth to visit her family (*MP* 311). In both cases, the sums donated enable the girls to enter the consumer economy. Fanny mediates in the squabble between Susan and Betsy by buying the latter a silver knife (*MP* 312) and Catherine buys the accessories needed to take her place in Bath society (*NA* 10). Fanny's purchases are made to benefit the family, whereas in *Pride and Prejudice*, the heedless, selfish Lydia spends the extra funds given to her by her mother on ribbons and bonnets for her own use, and though she 'treats' her older sisters to luncheon, they have to pay (167).

Fanny Price, the poor relation who is measured by her female cousins on the basis of her material goods, specifically her few sashes, and fobbed off by them with some of their least favoured toys, can find no congenial space at Mansfield Park in which to cry (*MP* 11–12). It is years later that she quietly appropriates a space, and makes it her own, significantly by bringing in some plants and other objects (*MP* 119). Most of those objects have been impersonal gifts of the kind given to most girls and with little thought: work-boxes and netting-boxes. Others are things considered too shabby or poorly executed for the principal rooms of the house: the faded foot-stool, the silhouettes, and the no longer fashionable transparencies. That Fanny has not chosen nor purchased these herself is indicative of her status, yet she has chosen and collected books 'from the first hour of her commanding a shilling', which, as discussed below, is a puzzle (*MP* 119). The East Room is doubly removed from Fanny's ownership by virtue of her sex and status, even though it may be finally accepted for her use. Sir Walter's reference to the flower garden at Kellynch as his daughter Elizabeth's is of a different order (*P* 21). Kellynch is held in entail male, so there is no legal sense in which Elizabeth Elliot can own the garden, and it will pass to Mr William Elliot along with the house and estate. Custom and usage, however, would denote a flower garden as a female space, and Sir Walter's demarcation of it as under the authority of his favoured elder daughter, marks Elizabeth's place in the family hierarchy just as the white attic and unwanted East Room do for Fanny. Fanny's tenancy of Mansfield spaces, and her possession of even the white dress with glossy spots given to her on her cousins' marriage (*MP* 174), is at Sir Thomas's will or whim. He (temporarily) expels Fanny, just as he does the disgraced Maria (*MP* 365), and until she marries she remains legally the property of Lieutenant Price.

For Gilbert and Gubar, the heroines of Austen's novels each marry a man

> whose house can provide her with shelter and sustenance and at least derived status, reflected glory. Whether it be parsonage or ancestral mansion, the man's house is where the heroine can retreat from both her parents' inadequacies and the perils of the outside world: like Henry Tilney's Woodston, Delaford, Pemberley, Donwell, and Thornton Lacy are spacious, beautiful places almost always supplied with the loveliest fruit trees and the prettiest prospects. (154)

Though this does, as Gilbert and Gubar assert, involve the heroines' accommodating themselves to men and the spaces they provide, the women set about modifying those spaces to suit themselves. Arranging the parsonage may be both a compensation for and a distraction from Charlotte Lucas' pragmatic marriage to Mr Collins: 'every thing was fitted up and arranged with a neatness and consistency of which Elizabeth gave Charlotte all the credit' (*PP* 121). Soon after encountering Mansfield Park, Mary Crawford considers the house and estate with a proprietary air. She weighs up the advantages of marrying Tom Bertram in terms of the house and estate he will inherit. The value of the former is inextricably bound up with the other, and it is significant that the house is considered as to its deserving of being blazoned in a publication which would display her acquisition to the envious multitude.

> She looked about her with due consideration, and found almost every thing his favour, a park, a real park, five miles round, a spacious modern-built house, so well placed and screened as to deserve to be in any collection of gentleman's seats in the kingdom. (*MP* 38)

Mary's thoughts quickly turn to furnishings, and she finds that Mansfield is 'wanting only to be completely new furnished' (*MP* 38). Lower on the social scale, Louisa and Henrietta Musgrove are putting their stamp on a space over which they have limited control in rehearsal for their futures in spaces over which they may have less.

> [T]he old-fashioned square parlour, with a small carpet and shining floor, to which the present daughters of the house were gradually giving the proper air of confusion by a grand piano forte and a harp, flower-stand and little tables placed in every direction. (*P* 37)

The reader imagines that notwithstanding the astonishment of the portraits of 'gentlemen in brown velvet and the ladies in blue satin', the sisters have cajoled their parents into permitting what seems to the older generation 'such an overthrow of all order and neatness', just as they cajole them into accepting short engagements (*P* 185). Austen depicts furnishing and refurbishing a room, or oneself, as acceptable ways for married women to pass the time, however quickly these might pall. Mary Crawford's half-sister, Mrs Grant, is pleased to be asked to take in Mary, 'having by this time run through the usual resources of ladies residing in the country without a family of children; having more than filled her favourite sitting-room with pretty furniture, and made a choice collection of plants and poultry' (*MP* 32). Elizabeth Elliot has a collection of plants, which she requires Anne to organise for donation to Lady Russell (*P* 36) and Mrs Weston keeps turkeys (*E* 380). In spite of Elizabeth's having left and Mr Collins being *in situ*, Charlotte is content.[9] 'Her home and her housekeeping, her parish and her poultry, and all their dependent concerns, had not yet lost their charms' (*PP* 165). Women's dressing and arranging interiors, then, while not creating legal ownership, can be seen as their marking territory, staking a claim to their home and denoting female spaces, while either the savings from keeping domestic fowls or the profits from the surplus might provide money which the woman could consider truly hers.

Habituated to this narrow domestic focus, both silly and sensible women in the novels observe details of furnishings or clothing almost before anything else. Harriet Smith, looking at Mr Elton's vicarage, echoes Miss Nash's admiration of the yellow curtains (*E* 67). While Anne Elliot keeps Captain Wentworth in view for the length of a street, Lady Russell is looking in vain for some handsome drawing-room curtains that have been recommended to her (*P* 145). The narrative voice shows the drawing-room of Uppercross Cottage through the eyes of Anne Elliot, noting that the furnishings ordered by Mary on her marriage are growing faded and shabby (*P* 35). The narrative does not condemn this occupation provided that it does not become all-in-all to the character and that she retains some strength of mind and inner resources. Without inner resources, characters who are no longer entertained by buying trappings for the house or the body, or keeping poultry, turn their energies to bossiness (Mrs Norris, Lady Catherine de Bourgh), or match-matching (Mrs Grant), or become enervated (Lady Bertram).

When a character's main occupation becomes useless decoration she is generally far from sensible. Lady Bertram's yards of fringe and carpet work (*MP* 140) and her desire for shawls and 'any thing else worth having', outweighing her concern for her sailor nephew's safety (239), place her as precisely as do the comments of the narrative voice. Mrs Allen's focus on clothing to the exclusion of much else is such that she considers the disadvantage of Catherine's riding in John Thorpe's gig to be the danger of her being splashed and wind-blown rather than the danger to her reputation (*NA* 75), and her only contribution to the question of whether her charge should call on Eleanor Tilney is to advise Catherine to wear white (65). Mrs Allen's conversation with Henry Tilney on the subject of muslins represents him as interested in women and women's interests, specifically his sister's but is also perhaps a rather condescending amusement at Mrs Allen's expense, as noted by Catherine, who reflects that he indulges himself too much with others' foibles (*NA* 16–17).[10] The narrative voice subsequently intervenes to pronounce that dress is 'a frivolous distinction' and that 'excessive solicitude' about dress may destroy its aim (*NA* 52). Catherine has been lectured on this yet remains awake (for a whole ten minutes) debating her choice of two dresses, and had she had time would have purchased a new one.

> This would have been an error in judgement, great though not uncommon, from which one of the other sex rather than her own […] might have warned her, for man only can be aware of the insensibility of man towards a new gown. It would be mortifying to the feelings of many ladies could they be made to understand how little the heart of man is affected by what is costly or new in their attire (52).

This seemingly conventional and even moralising statement might suggest that men are indifferent to or above interest in women's dress. It continues, however, to suggest that men do notice what women wear, and seek to influence it, as well as to suggest that for women dress is an aspect of rivalry. 'Woman is fine for her own satisfaction alone. No man will admire her more, no woman like her better for it', but men are said to require '[n]eatness and fashion'. The assertion of men's indifference to fine accoutrements might seem parallel to Catherine's belief about novels—that gentlemen have better things to do than to read them (*NA* 77). If so, Henry Tilney's entering into the conventionally feminine interests of novels and fabrics, would make him exceptional. The only occasions on which we see Edmund Bertram show an interest in dress are when he remarks that a woman dressed all in white cannot be too fine, and when he should be admiring Fanny but commits the solecism of saying: 'has not Miss Crawford a gown something the same?' (*MP* 174). Just as Austen distinguishes between women who immerse themselves in necessary domestic duties and have an innocuous interest in clothes, and those who think of nothing but domesticity or fashion, so she draws a distinction between men who involve themselves in domestic or conventionally feminine chattels, and those over-much interested. Henry Tilney is approved for his admission that he enjoys novels (*NA* 77), as is Captain Harville for his 'ingenious contrivances and nice arrangements' in the family's rented house (*P* 83), but Robert Ferrars is condemned for the 'puppyism' (*SS* 165). Sir Walter Elliot is characterised by his many looking-glasses which, like Elizabeth, reflect his image back at him (*P* 104), and his interest in clothes and cosmetics (118) further condemns him.

Austen's women are similarly characterised through their attitudes to other possessions. Mrs Bennet's pleasure in the news of her second daughter's engagement comes from anticipation of Elizabeth's receiving not love, but money and goods: 'Oh! my sweetest Lizzy! how rich and great you will be! What pin-money, what jewels, what carriages you will have!' (*PP* 290) Mrs Elton enters the novel (she is spoken of but not shown earlier) speaking incessantly of her brother-in-law's house and grounds (*E* 213). In drawing attention to possessions: carriages, rout-cakes, ice, card tables, unbroken packs (*E* 227), lace, pearls (229), gown and trimmings, white and silver poplin (236, 254), bonnet and be-ribboned basket (279, 282), she shows herself to belong to the consumerist, commercial Bristol merchant-class. This is in contrast to Emma and Mr Knightley, whose wedding demonstrates that they have 'no taste for finery or parade' (381). Mrs Elton's spending on goods is very different from Fanny Price's feeding the inner woman through subscribing to a circulating library and the outer woman through buying biscuits and buns (*MP* 324). Significantly, in becoming a subscriber, Fanny thinks of herself as acting 'in *propria persona*' (*MP* 313), in her own person, rather than represented by another; 'to be a renter, a chuser of books!' is to have some sense of autonomy, even if this is funded by the £10 provided by Sir Thomas. The puzzle here is that earlier in the novel the phrase 'her books' is used of Fanny's reading-material in the East Room, and she is said to have been a collector 'from the first hour of her commanding a shilling' (*MP* 119). The term 'commanding' indicates the sense of empowerment which the ability to choose how to spend would confer on an otherwise dependent woman, but it seems unlikely that the pin money given to Fanny would have enabled her to afford to purchase books, and her subsequent amazement at being able to choose and hire them suggests that this is a new experience. Perhaps her shillings have been spent under the watchful eye of others. In any case, the point made by '*propria persona*' is the close connection for women between spending power and an identity not subsumed under that of a man.

Baron and Feme acknowledges that by common law, a woman's clothing, defined as '*bona paraphernalia*', could be seen as her own and not the property of her husband. 'The wife by the Common Law ought to have her necessary Apparel for her Body after the Death of the Husband', but in the case of the death of a husband, a piece of cloth given to the woman to make a garment remains hers, with the proviso that 'against the Debtee, of the Husband the Wife shall have no more apparel than is convenient' (79). In other words, women's clothes could be taken against debts of her husband, the amount left to her a matter to be decided by law. This could be extended to her jewellery, but the number of cases quoted in which jewels were attempted to be defined as the property of the husband shows that this was not undisputed. This again seems in part to hang on the question of necessity. A case is quoted of a chain of diamonds and pearls worth £370 usually worn by a woman. 'The Lords Hastings and Douglas, Richardson and Crook thought the Wife shall not have them as *Bona Paraphernalia*, because they were not necessary for her, but only convenient' though all agreed that 'she shall have her necessary Apparel' (*Baron and Feme* 79). The law seems to have decided in favour of this particular woman, but *Baron and Feme* also shows that jewels given to a wife could be willed away from her, and that her possession of them was precarious (80).

Heirlooms are clearly different from personal chattels, and should not be disposed of, and a husband could give his wife permission to wear jewels but not necessarily make them at her absolute disposal.[11] It is Mr Churchill who permits Jane Fairfax to have his late wife's jewels; they are evidently not included in Mrs Churchill's will, and they come to Jane via Frank Churchill, who does not consult Jane about their resetting, or even whether she would want them.

'You will be glad to hear [...] that my uncle means to give her all my aunt's jewels. They are to be new set. I am resolved to have some in an ornament for the head. Will it not be beautiful in her dark hair?' (*E* 377)[12]

Two extreme versions of the *feme sole* exist in the same Austen novel. The differences between the situations of Emma Woodhouse and Miss Bates are age and money, Miss Bates being poor and no longer of marriageable age, Emma being still marriageable in terms of years and fortune. Emma's life as *feme sole* is more comfortable materially, and her prospects better; initially she believes that her unentailed fortune precludes the need to marry and insulates her against old-maidhood. She describes women who reach middle age without money or marriage as predestined to contracted minds and soured tempers, the 'proper sport of boys and girls' (*E* 69). Yet in Miss Bates Austen depicts an older unmarried woman who may be silly but is entirely respectable, forbearing, and contented. Emma's confusion of fiscal and social worth, and her assumption of Miss Bates' insensibility leads to her appalling rudeness at the picnic, and the need for Mr Knightley's correction (*E* 291, 296).

Emma is in some ways no less restricted than Miss Bates. Neither seems to have left Highbury for a considerable time; we see that Emma has never been to the coast (*E* 81), nor London, nor even Box Hill (277). Lacking the regular companionship of anyone her equal in quickness, and rejecting that of Jane Fairfax, Emma is bored and unfulfilled. Unlike Mrs Elton, she does not fill the void with decorating and dress, but like Mrs Bennet and Mrs Grant, with match-making schemes. More laudably, in the conventional view put by Mr Knightley (*E* 11), she also takes on charitable concerns, entering into an important part of the social economy, gift-giving. Miss Bates and her mother have to be on the receiving-end of these. The sensible Austen women's attitude to donation of goods is the antithesis of the squabbles over chattels of the silly (Betsy and Susan, before she is improved by Fanny), the lack of altruism of the insensible (the Bertram sisters' towards Fanny; Kitty's resentment of Lydia's good fortune [*PP* 175–76]) and the meanness of the nasty (Mrs Norris preferring to receive than to give). The Bates women receive gifts of food from the Woodhouses and Mr Knightley, as do the poor of Highbury, but Mrs and Miss Bates are not categorised with the 'poor sick family' visited by Emma and Harriet (*E* 67). The money given from Emma's purse, and the broth fetched from Hartfield by a cottage-child (*E* 70–71) are different in kind from the apples sent by Mr Knightley and the pork sent by Emma. Each of these can be represented as a speciality of the home: Mr Woodhouse's home farm has recently killed a pig, and 'Hartfield pork is not like any other pork' (*E* 135). Donwell Abbey's apples are 'the very finest sort for baking [...] there never was such a keeping apple anywhere as one of his trees' (*E* 187). The Bateses can be fed at a social occasion such as a dinner, or with gifts of such specialities and surplus, and still retain the status of gentlewomen, significantly because of the status of Mrs Bates as *feme covert*, widow of a clergyman, and of Miss Bates as his daughter. It was as wife and daughter that they will have once lived in the vicarage, and as his relicts to have lost it. It is Emma's task, as highest-ranking lady of the neighbourhood, to ensure that the right goods are distributed to the right recipient. As Mr Knightley's wife, lady of the manor, she will be expected to continue that duty, and is likely to have enough pin money and enough control over the household budget to be lady bountiful. In the same way as Emma, according to their abilities, Fanny Price, Anne Elliot, and Anne's friend Mrs Smith practice charitable giving, in spite of slim resources. In Nurse Rooke's teaching Mrs Smith to knit 'threadcases, pin-cushions and card-racks' to be sold to wealthy invalids for the good of the poor (*P* 126), we can see women's collaboration, pastimes, and charity in one set of small artefacts, and an assertion of Mrs Smith's slender claim to gentility in spite of her relative poverty.

Austen's demonstration of mature female characters' capacity for fiscal responsibility is understated yet clear. Emma has inherited from her mother the quickness and capability that has made her mistress of Hartfield since she was 12 years old (*E* 30), and has a practical, pragmatic, view of charity (70). Elinor Dashwood's cool judgement and strength of understanding qualify her at 19 to be her mother's counsellor (*SS* 6), and she manages money prudently, saving her mother and sister from overspending (*SS* 11). Elizabeth Bennet shows her understanding of marriage mathematics in her conviction that 'handsome young men must have something to live on' (*PP* 116) and what Mr Darcy's act of benevolent paternalism has meant in rescuing Lydia from ruin (279), and she helps to provide for her feckless sister (296).[13] Anne Elliot, like Mrs Croft, will run the family while her husband is at sea. Perhaps most significantly, the sensible mature women characters have confidence, not only when they have a strong sense of their worth and status, as Emma does, but even when they are relatively inconsequential or conventionally obedient and docile. Their belief in their own judgement enables them to refuse a convenient marriage (Elizabeth), stand up to a domineering patriarch (Fanny, Anne) or confront a wrong-doer (Elinor). Claudia L. Johnson refers to the moral lives of the characters who have 'rich and unapologetic senses of self-consequence' (xxiii). Perhaps in acknowledgement of that maturity, moral sense, and confidence, Austen makes the ending of *Persuasion* send a different message about women and goods from those of the other novels. The heroine is rewarded not with a solid house and land, and a husband taking on the same role of ownership as her father, but with mobility (*P* 201).[14] The value of the gift of a landaulette [*sic*] is clear from both the novels and Austen's letters, which depict women left like parcels awaiting deposit and collection by men (or wealthy widows).[15] Rather than ties of blood, particularly between sisters, the focus of the ending is on ties of shared experience, trust and loyalty forged by an energetic, self-made, and mobile group. Anne Elliot's prize is not a Pemberley or a Donwell Abbey, but 'belonging to that profession', the Navy (*P* 203). Women's tenancy of houses and temporary ownership of goods has become less important than purpose; lineage than merit; inheritance than 'domestic virtues' and 'national importance'. Nonetheless, though an equivalence is posited between the war tax paid by men and women, men pay in substance, specie, and women in insubstantial anxiety.

Like Anne, Elizabeth Bennet may gain mobility, but Mrs Gardiner's fantasy of rides in a low phaeton is significantly restricted to going around the Pemberley estate (*PP* 247). Austen's employment of fairy-tale *topoi* goes so far and no further. Her women characters do not attain autonomy and ownership. There are no overt protests in her work about the laws and customs relating to the *feme sole* and the *feme covert*, but there are examples of women who clearly could and should have control over their money, their possessions, and themselves, *in propria persona*.

Notes

1 This is not to suggest that Austen read Wollstonecraft's work. See Wollstonecraft (1792) and (1798) in Kelly (2009).
2 See, for example, Austen's letter to Cassandra Austen dated 25 April 1811 (*Letters* 190).
3 'Single Women have a dreadful propensity for being poor—which is one very strong argument in favour of Matrimony'. Letter to Fanny Knight (13 March 1817; *Letters* 332).
4 For a discussion of women's custodianship of and dispossession from houses, See Byrne.
5 Published by Thomas Egerton in November 1811.
6 Published by Egerton in November 1813.
7 See note to 4, Austen, *Sense and Sensibility* (302).
8 Skinner shows that equity was less beneficial for widows in its gradual erosion of rights to dower in favour of jointure (94).
9 Oliver MacDonagh discusses this 'career marriage' (33).
10 Lauren Miskin argues that Henry Tilney's interest in Indian Muslims represents a 'particular mode of imperial connoisseurship, a masculine aesthetic taste' (6).
11 See Marcia Pointon (19).
12 Kirkham regards this as Churchill's objectifying Jane (142).
13 Richard A. Posner argues that Elizabeth in refusing Mr Collins is curiously insensitive to her family's financial plight, yet concurs that for her to marry Mr Collins would be impossible. Elizabeth is all-too aware

of marriage mathematics and the law of primogeniture, as she shows when she does not censure Wickham's plan to marry an heiress (91–92).

14 Landaulets were not driven by the passenger, however, so Anne's mobility may be still due to male agency, a coachman.

15 See, for example, letters dated 23 August 1796, 15–16 September 1796, 18 September 1796 (*Letters* 5–7, 9–11, 11–13). See also *Sense and Sensibility* (210, 235); *Pride and Prejudice* (212); and *Mansfield Park* (322, 338).

Works Cited

Anon. *The Law of Evidence*. London, 1760.

Austen, Jane. *Emma* (1815, dated 1816), edited by James Kinsley. Oxford World's Classics, 2008.

Austen, Jane. *Jane Austen's Letters*, edited by Deirdre Le Faye. Oxford UP, 1997.

Austen, Jane. *Mansfield Park* (1814), edited by James Kinsley. Oxford World's Classics, 2008.

Austen, Jane. *Northanger Abbey* (1817 dated 1818) in *Northanger Abbey, Lady Susan, The Watsons, Sanditon*, edited by James Kinsley and John Davie. Oxford World's Classics, 2003.

Austen, Jane. *Persuasion* (1817 dated 1818), edited by James Kinsley. Oxford World's Classics, 2008.

Austen, Jane. *Pride and Prejudice* (1813), edited by James Kinsley. Oxford World's Classics, 2008.

Austen, Jane. *Sense and Sensibility* (1811), edited by James Kinsley. Oxford World's Classics, 2008.

Austen, Jane. *The Watsons, in Northanger Abbey, Lady Susan, The Watsons, Sanditon*, edited by James Kinsley and John Davie. Oxford World's Classics, 2003.

Blackstone, William. *Commentaries on the Laws of England*, 4 vols. Clarendon Press, 1765–69.

Byrne, S. *Austen's Possessions and Dispossessions: The Significance of Objects*. Palgrave Macmillan, 2014.

Carter, Samuel. *Baron and Feme: A Treatise of Law and Equity Concerning Husbands and Wives*. London, 1738.

Clancy, James. *An Essay on the Equitable Rights of Married Women: With Respect to their Separate Property, and also on their Claim to a Provision Called the Wife's Equity*. Reed and Hunter, 1815.

Erickson, Amy Louise. *Women and Property in Early Modern England*. Routledge, 1993.

Gilbert, Sandra, and Susan Gubar. *The Madwoman in the Attic: The Woman Writer and the Nineteenth-Century Literary Imagination*, 2nd ed. Yale UP, 2000.

Hill, Christopher. *Reformation to Industrial Revolution 1530–1780*. Penguin, 1969.

Johnson, Claudia L. *Jane Austen, Women, Politics and the Novel*, 2nd ed. U of Chicago P, 1990.

Kirkham, Margaret. *Jane Austen, Feminism and Fiction*. Athlone P, 1997.

MacDonagh, Oliver. *Jane Austen, Real and Imagined Worlds*. Yale UP, 1993.

Miskin, Lauren. '"True Indian Muslin" and the Politics of Consumption in Jane Austen's *Northanger Abbey*.' *Journal for Early Modern Cultural Studies*, vol. 15, no. 2, 2015, pp. 5–20.

Pointon, Marcia. 'Women and their Jewels.' *Women and Material Culture 1660–1830*, edited by Jennie Batchelor and Cora Kaplan. Palgrave Macmillan, 2007, pp. 11–30.

Posner, Richard A. 'Jane Austen: Comedy and Social Structure.' *Subversion and Sympathy: Gender, Law and the British Novel*, edited by Martha C. Nussbaum and Alison L. LeCroix. Oxford UP, 2013, pp. 84–96.

Skinner, Gillian. 'Women's Status as Legal and Civic Subjects: "A Worse Condition than Slavery Itself"?' *Women and Literature in Britain 1700–1800*, edited by Vivien Jones. Cambridge UP, 2000, pp. 91–110.

Thirsk, Joan. 'The European Debate on Customs of Inheritance 1500–1700.' *Family and Inheritance*, edited by Jack Goody, Joan Thirsk, and Edward Palmer Thompson. Cambridge UP, 1976, pp. 177–191.

Wollstonecraft, Mary. *A Vindication of the Rights of Woman* (1792). Harmondsworth: Penguin, 2004.

Wollstonecraft, Mary. The Wrongs of Woman (1798). *Mary and the Wrongs of Woman*, edited by Gary Kelly. Oxford World's Classics, 2009.

17

JANE AUSTEN AND MUSIC

Laura Vorachek

UNIVERSITY OF DAYTON

As readers of Jane Austen's novels are aware, music played a large role in women's lives in the late-eighteenth and early-nineteenth centuries. During the period in which Austen wrote, the piano became a popular domestic instrument and, as a result of its increased affordability, music became a common component of girls' education and social lives. A young woman's musical accomplishments were not only an important source of home entertainment but also signalled her class status. Critics have argued that music was further valued because it was thought to instill social mores through its regular practice and to reify gender roles, since men were discouraged from playing.[1] Music's disciplinary function, I argue, was especially apparent in music instruction material directed at a female audience. With instructions on practicing, physical decorum, and music selection, keyboard method books ordered women's conduct in accordance with Regency gender norms. Music performance was also gender performance. However, method books' attempts to contain women indirectly communicated the possibility that limitations placed on female musicians could be exceeded. Reading late-eighteenth- and early-nineteenth-century keyboard instruction manuals in conjunction with Austen's novels illuminates the ways her characters refuse or subvert cultural dictates about gender and music.

While other instruments were available for domestic music making, the piano became the predominant choice not long after its introduction to the English public.[2] Johann Zumpe produced the first English piano in 1766 and other manufacturers soon followed suit. John Broadwood, one of forty-five piano manufacturers in London in the late-eighteenth century 'made 6,000 square pianos and 1,000 grand pianos between 1780 and 1800, a large number when the size of the cultured population is taken into consideration' (Sumner 51). Production may have been driven by the firm's launch of the square piano in 1780. Retailing at between eighteen guineas and £30 (Hoover 40), the square piano was more amenable in size and cost to middle-class households than harpsichords or grand pianos.

As the piano became more affordable, lessons became an important part of middle-class girls' education. Elizabeth Appleton, author of *Private Education: or a Practical Plan for the Studies of Young Ladies* (1815), suggested a number of reasons girls might learn to play: 'to gratify the musical fondness of parents; the unfolding taste of childhood; to avoid the shame of being outdone in fashion; to open another source of amusement; or to add to feminine attraction' (135–36). While personal enjoyment of music was one motivation, equally important were the social incentives. Indeed, some argued that musical skill improves 'a young lady's chance of a prize in the matrimonial lottery' (Edgeworth and Edgeworth 6).[3] In addition to home entertainment, keeping *au courant*, or hedging one's bets on the marriage market, musical accomplishments signalled one's class. Lady Catherine delineates the link

218

DOI: 10.4324/9780429398155-17-20

between music and socioeconomic status in *Pride and Prejudice* when she interrogates Elizabeth Bennet about her family. When Elizabeth tells Lady Catherine that only one of her sisters besides herself plays piano and sings, Lady Catherine responds, 'Why did you not all learn?—You ought all to have learned. The Miss Webbs all play, and their father has not so good an income as your's' (*PP* 126–27). As Lady Catherine's consternation makes clear, all girls of a certain socioeconomic standing were expected to learn how to play the piano. As Appleton put it: 'I know not of any gentleman's or nobleman's daughter who had not attempted, at one period in her life, to learn music' (136). The Bennets, with only two of five daughters who play, deviate from this cultural expectation.[4]

Surprisingly, neither Lady Catherine nor her daughter, who are of a higher socioeconomic standing than either the Bennets or the Webbs, knows how to play the piano. However, this does not stop Lady Catherine from making authoritative pronouncements on music. She insists that 'If I had ever learnt, I should have been a great proficient. And so would Anne, if her health had allowed her to apply. I am confident that she would have performed delightfully' (*PP* 133). Her assertion of her daughter's and her own hypothetical proficiency at the piano demonstrates just how ingrained was the expectation that women play. Lady Catherine's confidence in her untried abilities manifests itself in her 'many instructions on execution and taste' during Elizabeth's performance (*PP* 135). Although Lady Catherine has no knowledge of music, she adopts the pose of expert, suggesting that she cannot bear to be thought ignorant about a subject so central to an upper-class woman's education.

At the other end of the social spectrum, the upwardly mobile Cole family in *Emma* signal their improved socioeconomic status with a piano. Originally 'of low origin, in trade, and only moderately genteel', the Coles experience a considerable increase in income and, in addition to other expenditures, they purchase a grand pianoforte (*E* 162). A grand piano cost £84 at this time (Hoover 40)—three times as much as a square piano—indicating their wealth has increased substantially. Nevertheless, a grand piano is an extravagant expense for a family with no musicians; as Mrs Cole tells her guests, 'I do not know one note from another, and our little girls, who are but just beginning, perhaps may never make anything of it' (*E* 169). While Mrs Cole has never learned, likely due to her lower social origins, she is making sure her daughters have a musical education to match the family's newfound wealth and social position.

Music education was considered *de rigueur* for genteel young ladies, but contemporary commentators differed as to its importance. Some felt that music enriched women's lives. Thomas Gisbourne, in *An Enquiry into the Duties of the Female Sex* (1797), argued that music was a useful accomplishment as it could 'supply [a woman's] hours of leisure with innocent and amusing occupations' (80). Similarly, Allston Burgh, in the prelude to *Anecdotes of Music, Historical and Biographical; in a Series of Letters from a Gentleman to His Daughter* (1814), argued that music 'may be the means of preventing that vacuity of mind, which is too frequently the parent of libertinism; of precluding the intrusion of idle and dangerous imaginations' (vi). For some, music's utility lay in its ability to occupy a woman, structuring her time and ordering her mind.

However, moralists and educators such as Hannah More, Maria Edgeworth, and James Fordyce felt that the 'phrenzy of accomplishments' expected of women, including music, were detrimental to their education (More 62).[5] They worried that the young woman focused on music 'will imbibe frivolous ideas, from her studies not being of sufficient weight to exercise the mental faculties' (Cambrianna 203). Thus, some felt that music could occupy too much of a young lady's leisure, leaving little time for serious subjects. Despite their concerns that music was insufficient to discipline young minds, these commentators agreed that music was a 'modern and *now absolutely necessary* acquirement' for women, if practiced in moderation (Cockle 242). The popularity of the piano and its function as a class marker made it difficult to escape.

Late-eighteenth- and early-nineteenth-century keyboard instruction material presented a different set of concerns about women and music. While most method books from this timeframe are gender neutral, indicating through text and image that the pupil could be either male or female, some specifically target women, reflecting women's growing provenance over keyboard instruments. Instruction manuals typically offered a mix of written instruction and music, to illustrate concepts and for practicing, though some contain only text. These text-only manuals, which would supplement other music books and instruction, are exclusively addressed to a female audience, suggesting their authors felt that women needed more discipline at the piano than men. Indeed, keyboard instruction material aimed at women often focuses on their physical decorum and is dotted with extra-musical lessons on fibbing, interrupting, and other indecorous behaviour.[6] As I will show, these manuals attempt to regulate women's time, physicality, and performance, reflecting cultural attitudes toward women and domestic music making. As music was central to middle-class girls' education, many would have encountered these ideas.

Austen, a pianist herself, was certainly familiar with keyboard instruction manuals. She owned J. Jousse's *Pianoforte Made Easy to Every Capacity* and, in 1813, went shopping with her niece Fanny Knight for method books on Martha Lloyd's behalf. In a letter to her sister Cassandra she wrote: 'Fanny desires me to tell Martha with her kind Love that Birchall assured her there was no 2d set of Hook's Lessons for Beginners—& that by my advice, she has therefore chosen her a set by another Composer. I thought she w[oul]d rather have something than not.—It costs six shillings' (*Letters* 233). Thus, in addition to Jousse, Austen was acquainted with James Hook's *Guida di Musica: being a complete book of instruction for beginners on the Harpsichord or Piano Forte* (1810) (for which there is no second set) and likely other keyboard instruction manuals. Austen's novels engage ideas about women and music expressed in these keyboard method books with characters who adopt or challenge their precepts.

For example, music could indeed take up a considerable portion of a woman's day. Piano method books and conduct manuals recommended that women practice for two to four hours a day, and some commentators contended that women were spending as much as five or six hours a day at the instrument.[7] Austen, however, disputes the idea that all women welcomed the emphasis on music in their education with characters who are not interested in learning or practicing keyboard instruments. In *Northanger Abbey*, Catherine Morland's 'mother wished her to learn music; and Catherine was sure she should like it, for she was very fond of tinkling the keys of the old forlorn spinet, so, at eight years old she began. She learnt a year, and could not bear it;—and Mrs Morland, who did not insist on her daughters being accomplished in spite of incapacity or distaste, allowed her to leave off' (*NA* 6). Catherine's experience reveals that the discipline of music was not agreeable to all women; some might find the expectation that they develop competency on an instrument a hardship. Moreover, as Austen is burlesquing the highly accomplished heroines of Gothic novels in her depiction of the very ordinary Catherine, she implies that it is perfectly natural for women to be unable or averse to learning to play an instrument.

William Steetz might as well be addressing Catherine in his *Treatise on the Elements of Music in a Series of Letters to a Lady* (1812). Referring to a previous letter in his book, he writes:

> You see, dear Cecilia, that you cannot read my letters straight forward, as you may Ann Radcliffe. It is perfectly indifferent to you, whether the *silver moon*, which she orders to shine through the gratings of a Northern Tower, be the same as that which reflected on the murmuring brook forty or fifty pages before; or whether the Nightingale, that enchants a lover's ear in the third volume, be the same bird which she made to warble in the *middle of January*, in the preceding. This is not the case with my rules. (61)

Acknowledging the popularity of Gothic authors like Radcliffe, Steetz informs his pupil that music requires more attention to detail than fiction. Cecilia's indifference to accuracy and continuity in a Gothic novel, a genre noted for high emotion, suspense and fear, suggests the very 'vacuity of mind' commentators hoped music instruction would prevent (Burgh vi). Therefore, Steetz admonishes his pupil to focus on her lessons. More sympathetically, he provides tips for what to do when 'your mind is so much taken up with the pleasures of the preceding night's ball, that you have forgotten which is the Major key requiring five sharps' (74–75). Steetz's allusions to activities competing for young ladies' attention reflects the view that music could discipline a woman's mind more effectively than frivolous occupations like reading and dancing. Perhaps this is why 'The day which dismissed the music-master was one of the happiest of Catherine's life' (*NA* 6).

Elizabeth Bennet and Emma Woodhouse get farther along with their lessons than Catherine Morland, but they too fall short of the musically accomplished woman envisioned by piano instruction manuals and some conduct books. Elizabeth admits, 'My fingers do not move over this instrument in the masterly manner which I see so many women's do. They have not the same force or rapidity, and do not produce the same expression. But then I have always supposed it to be my own fault—because I would not take the trouble of practising' (*PP* 135). Likewise, Emma 'played and sang … but steadiness had always been wanting; and in nothing had she approached the degree of elegance which she would have been glad to command and ought not to have failed of' (*E* 35). Both Elizabeth and Emma lack discipline when it comes to music. While Elizabeth is unconcerned by her shortcomings at the piano, Emma laments neglecting music when her skills are put into contrast with Jane Fairfax's at the Coles' dinner party. Then, Emma 'did unfeignedly and unequivocally regret the inferiority of her own playing and singing. She did most heartily grieve over the idleness of her childhood—and sat down and practiced vigorously an hour and a half' (*E* 182). It takes comparison with a superior musician to prompt Emma to practice, suggesting that her pride is at the root of her renewed (and temporary) dedication rather than an authentic interest in music. And she still falls short of the recommended two hours of daily practice. Elizabeth and Emma remind us that becoming an accomplished pianist requires 'the trouble of practicing', 'steadiness' of application when one might prefer to be idle, and perhaps a love of music, something young women do not always possess. Instead, Austen depicts young women resisting attempts to structure their leisure and their imaginations with music practice. Of course, Austen's novels also include women whose enjoyment of music is evident, such as Marianne Dashwood, Mary Bennet, Jane Fairfax, and Anne Elliot. But, as we shall see, they flaunt music's disciplinary function too.

In addition to structuring women's time, keyboard method books also attempted to discipline women's bodies. Most method books address posture at the instrument, advising performers to sit upright in the centre of the keyboard with arms and wrists in a straight line, fingers gently rounded over the keys. Additional directives on physical decorum were usually aimed at women. For example, Daniel Gottlob Türk, in his *School of Clavier Playing* (1789), advises:

> distorted facial expressions, writhing, grimaces, or whatever you might want to call them, as well as beating time with the feet, dividing each measure by a motion of the entire body, shaking or nodding of the head, snorting during a trill or during a difficult passage, and the like, must never be permitted by the pupil, regardless of social position or sex. In this respect politeness or permissiveness toward one of the fairer sex is very much to be reprimanded, for although music is perceived only through the sense of hearing, the sense of sight should not be offended in the process. (30)

While Türk admonishes any movement that might distract from the music regardless of the sex or station of the performer, such motion is especially offensive in women. By linking the sense of sight with 'the fairer sex', Türk recognizes that musical performance had social functions for women beyond music making. Francis Tatton Latour, 'Pianiste to his Royal Highness the Prince Regent', similarly counsels young ladies in his *New and Improved Method of Instruction on the Pianoforte* (1827) to avoid 'all unnecessary motion' including making 'wry faces' (11).[8] Indeed, 'Nothing is more ungraceful than to see the head of the performer constantly on the move or bent forwards—besides it produces round shoulders' (11). Latour warns that movement will make the pianist appear awkward and ungainly, thereby deterring young ladies hoping to attract potential suitors with their musical skills. Method books required the performer keep her face and body still ostensibly to keep listeners focused on the music. But this restriction precluded any motion that might indicate the performer was expending mental or physical effort or was emotionally responsive to the music she was playing. Rather, the female pianist is directed to perform as if an automaton.

Women's choice of music was also restricted. 'Let our daughters', the author of *Euterpe; or Remarks on the Use and Abuse of Music* (1780), advises '*perform* no more than what falls within the *easy* compass of their *execution*; nor ever attempt any thing but *select pieces* of *familiar, easy, simple* construction, such as may delight the *ear* of their friends' (13). Emma Woodhouse follows these guidelines when asked to play at the Coles' dinner party. She plays a couple of 'little things which are generally acceptable' (*E* 178), and Harriet tells her the next day that 'every body last night said how well you played' (*E* 182). Emma recognizes her limitations, acknowledging that her 'playing is just good enough', but her choice of easy, familiar songs earns her praise from her listeners (*E* 182). Jane Fairfax also performs according to her abilities, but her choice of music does not please everyone at the party. Harriet says of Jane: 'I hate Italian singing.—There is no understanding a word of it. Besides, if she does play so very well, you know, it is no more than she is obliged to do, because she will have to teach' (*E* 182). While Harriet's musical understanding is certainly deficient, Jane's performance nevertheless opens her to commentary that she plays too well for a lady.[9] While Emma regrets not playing as well as Jane Fairfax, she does model class-appropriate behaviour with her musical selections.

Indeed, method book authors discouraged any attempt to individualise one's performance through a demonstration of advanced abilities. The author of 'Desultory Remarks on the Study and Practice of Music, Addressed to a Young Lady' recommends 'a chaste, correct and expressive delivery' since it 'evinces Judgement in the Performer as well as skill, and argues a deference to the Composer' (180). Such a performance corresponds to traits valued in women—innocence, docility, and decorousness. He elaborates that 'an eager endeavor at embellishment with an earnestness to display dexterity of Finger, without regard to the text of the Lesson, shews that Conceit and Vanity predominate in the Performer, who plays not to give pleasure, but is labouring to extort applause' (180). Warning against musical flourishes that would demonstrate a woman's capability and bring attention to her own musical artistry, the author advises focusing on the (often male) composer's score. The penalty for going beyond the score is the appearance of traits castigated in women—conceit, vanity, and selfishness. Latour provides an equally damning scenario: 'it is often said that such a lady is a very great or dashing performer, Why? Because she rattles away on the keys and often raises her hands as high as her head; but often strikes her knuckles against the desk of the Instrument and dashes the lights into the middle of the room' (11). He warns that an overly expressive performance invites social embarrassment and is a potential fire hazard. Thus, piano method books cautioned against deviating from the script, whether composers' scores or social norms, thereby affirming the construction of women as modest and self-effacing.

Austen depicts the pitfalls of defying this prescription in *Pride and Prejudice*. At a party at Lucas Lodge, Mary Bennet plays with 'a pedantic air and conceited manner, which would have injured a higher degree of excellence than she had reached. Elizabeth, easy and unaffected, had been listened to with much more pleasure, though not playing half so well' (*PP* 17). Comparing the two sisters' performances, Austen affirms the perils of playing to 'extort applause', as Mary does with her affected manner and display of skill. Elizabeth, on the other hand, reifies gendered expectations, obliging others by playing to 'give pleasure'. However, both Elizabeth and Emma exploit limitations on what and how women play, relying on low audience expectations to mask the fact that they do not practice regularly. The reception of Mary Bennet's and Jane Fairfax's performances likewise reinforces and challenges method book precepts as they alert readers to women's potential to surpass those artificial limits.

Music may have been considered a draw on the marriage market because a woman could perform her feminine propriety at the instrument, and Austen's novels accentuate the ways that music making could give women some agency in the courtship process. For instance, music created opportunities for men and women to meet and advance their intimacy. In *Mansfield Park*, Mary Crawford enchants Edmund Bertram with her harp playing: 'one morning secured an invitation for the next, for the lady could not be unwilling to have a listener, and every thing was soon in a fair train' (*MP* 51).[10] In addition to demonstrating her obliging nature, modesty, and musical skill, the performer also displays her body to the male gaze. The title character of *Lady Susan*, though sceptical of the range and depth of accomplishments expected of a genteel young woman, understands this benefit of music education. Lady Susan reasons that 'Grace and Manner after all are of the greatest importance' and more likely to add 'Lover[s] to her list' than the more academic subjects of a girl's education (*LS* 199). Therefore, she wants her daughter 'to play and sing with some portion of Taste, and a good deal of assurance, as she has *my* hand and arm' (*LS* 199). Since Lady Susan never learned to play, it is Frederica's physical resemblance to her that she wants potential suitors to notice. Frederica is too meek to exert much agency in courtship, but Lady Susan demonstrates her ability to attract and manipulate men throughout the novella and is alive to the seductive possibilities of music performance. Thus, despite piano method books' attempts to depersonalise a woman's performance, Austen notes that a female musician draws notice, at the very least, to her hand and arm.

Lady Susan's confidence that a woman at an instrument would attract men's admiration is born out in *Pride and Prejudice*. Mr Darcy's gaze is often drawn to Elizabeth when she is at the piano. At Rosings when Elizabeth sits down to play at Colonel Fitzwilliam's request, Darcy 'walked away from [Lady Catherine], and moving with his usual deliberation towards the piano forte, stationed himself so as to command a full view of the fair performer's countenance' (*PP* 133). Darcy is more interested in Elizabeth's face than the music she plays, despite what method books would suggest. Indeed, this scene shows that music making could create opportunities for men and women to flirt with each other in near privacy. Darcy and Colonel Fitzwilliam follow Elizabeth to the piano, an arrangement that separates them from the rest of the company and allows Elizabeth to banter freely with both men. She teases Darcy about his reticence at the Meryton assembly, but does not forget Colonel Fitzwilliam, playfully asking him at the end of her first song, 'what do I play next? My fingers await your orders' (*PP* 134). Elizabeth takes advantage of the space music provides—and the brief reprieve from Lady Catherine's officiousness—for flirtatious conversation in a semi-public drawing room.

Austen imagines how music might enable further deviation from courtship conventions with the Broadwood square pianoforte that mysteriously arrives for Jane Fairfax in *Emma*. Its arrival causes much gossip in Highbury. Emma suspects the piano is from Mr Dixon; Mrs Weston thinks it is from Mr Knightley; and we later learn it is, in fact, a gift from Frank Churchill. In all three scenarios, the piano is understood as 'an offering of love' from a man to a woman (*E* 172). All three could also be considered illicit romances: Mr Dixon is married to Jane's best friend; Frank and Jane are secretly engaged; and Emma feels an alliance between Mr Knightley and Jane would upset the rightful inheritance of the Donwell estate and, though she is not aware of it yet, her claim to Mr Knightley's affections. In each case, the piano is a sign of affection in a secret, unsanctioned relationship. Moreover, as Frank and Jane have a difficult time contriving to be alone in Highbury society, they must communicate through music. Frank shows Jane his 'true affection' with the gift of instrument and sheet music, and Jane reciprocates by playing significant songs—a tune they danced to at Weymouth and '*his* favourite', Robin Adair (*E* 191). Music allows the couple to continue a relationship that circumvents parental authority and social norms.[11]

Music's connection to courtship was reinforced by the commonplace notion that women gave it up upon marriage. Commentators lamented that music 'seems only acquired to be forgotten' ('Old Woman' 99). Lady Middleton in *Sense and Sensibility* and Mrs Elton in *Emma* are prime examples of this. Lady Middleton 'had celebrated that event [her marriage] by giving up music' (*SS* 27), and Mrs Elton is 'determined upon neglecting her music' now that she is married (*E* 217). They demonstrate their agency in the courtship process by discarding the attraction of music once their object has been obtained. Since neither Lady Middleton nor Mrs Elton are sympathetic characters, Austen may have had little affinity for women who felt music offered social utility only in winning a husband.

Austen's novels provide a primer for other 'off book' uses of music, showing how women could use it to manipulate the rules of conduct in polite society. Lady Susan, for example, uses music to keep her daughter away from Catherine Vernon while at Churchill. Mrs Vernon writes to her mother that 'the small Pianoforte has been removed these few days at Lady Susan's request, into her Dressing room, and Frederica spends great part of the day there; *practising* it is called, but I seldom hear any noise when I pass that way' (*LS* 214). Lady Susan takes advantage of the popular view that girls should spend several hours a day practicing the piano to keep Frederica separated from her aunt. Although Mrs Vernon is aware of the ruse, she cannot graciously refuse Lady Susan's request since it conforms to social expectations for young women's use of time.

Music also could be used to distract company from unpleasant topics. In an early scene in *Sense and Sensibility*, Mrs Jennings pries into Elinor's love life. When Margaret comes dangerously close to revealing the name of the man Elinor likes, Lady Middleton makes a comment about the rain, Colonel Brandon takes up the subject, and 'Willoughby opened the pianoforte, and asked Marianne to sit down to it; and thus amidst the various endeavours of different people to quit the topic, it fell to the ground' (*SS* 47). While changing the subject is a group effort, Marianne's music provides a visual and aural distraction from the uncomfortable moment.

Not surprisingly, Marianne Dashwood is often involved in scenes where music plays a socially subversive role. For example, she uses music to escape group activities. When Lady Middleton proposes a card game, Marianne 'exclaim[s], "Your ladyship will have the goodness to excuse me—you know I detest cards. I shall go to the piano-forte; I have not touched it since it was tuned". And without farther ceremony, she turned away and walked to the instrument' (*SS* 107). Marianne is able to refuse her hostess's request, though with less tact than is required, because her alternate choice of activity is an acceptable one for young women and will provide enjoyment for others at the party.

Caroline Bingley manages a similar situation with more finesse in *Pride and Prejudice*. While Darcy and Elizabeth are sparring at Netherfield, Miss Bingley, 'tired of a conversation in which she had no share' interjects: 'Do let us have a little music' (*PP* 43). Her proposal disrupts the exchange between Darcy and Elizabeth and distracts him from her rival. As we have seen, Caroline's suggestion may also have the benefit of drawing Darcy's attention to herself while she plays and sings at the piano.

Because the piano created sound and a focal point for listeners' gazes, music could also generate space for an intimate exchange among those not interested in the performance. Marianne's piano playing provides opportunities for Elinor to have private conversations on more than one occasion. At a gathering at the Middleton's, the pianoforte 'was luckily so near [Elinor and Lucy Steele] that Miss Dashwood now judged, she might safely, under the shelter of its noise, introduce the interesting subject, without any risk of being heard at the card-table' (*SS* 108). Under cover of Marianne's playing, Elinor can chat with her rival about their mutual love interest without rousing the curiosity of others. There is the danger of hiatuses in the music, as Elinor and Lucy discover when Miss Steele, 'whose ear had caught those words by a sudden pause in Marianne's music', makes an impertinent remark (*SS* 110). However, for the most part discretion while discussing Lucy's secret engagement is not necessary as 'Marianne was then giving them the powerful protection of a very magnificent concerto' (*SS* 111).

Austen comically demonstrates what such a private discussion might look like from an observer's standpoint later in the novel. In London, Mrs Jennings witnesses a conversation between Elinor and

Colonel Brandon, the topic of which she mistakes because of music. 'She was too honourable to listen, and had even changed her seat, on purpose that she might *not* hear, to one close by the piano forté on which Marianne was playing' (*SS* 212). She thinks she is observing a romantic *tete-a-tete*, and 'still farther in confirmation of her hopes, in the interval of Marianne's turning from one lesson to another, some words of the Colonel's inevitably reached her ear' that seem to support this interpretation (*SS* 212). 'They talked on for a few minutes longer without her catching a syllable, when another lucky stop in Marianne's performance brought her these words in the Colonel's calm voice, "I am afraid it cannot take place very soon"' (*SS* 212). This snatch of conversation convinces Mrs Jennings that Colonel Brandon has proposed to Elinor, when in fact he is offering the living at Delaford to Edward. Austen shows that music could create privacy for delicate conversations in semi-public settings, defying method book expectations of attentive listeners. However, music scores come to an end, dropping the screen of sound. Thus, Austen cautions her readers with comic effect as to the partial efficacy of music to mask private conversations in the company of others.

Austen also probes the common notion that music could help women control their emotions. As Leslie Ritchie remarks, music was thought to create social harmony, in part by helping women 'regulat[e] their own moods' (31). Anton Bemetzrieder, for example, tells his female pupil in *Music Made Easy to Every Capacity* (1779) that she 'will find [music] a constant balm for your vexations (things we are all more or less subject to) and the more sweet, as you will draw it wholly from yourself' (217). Music, then, was a form of self-discipline, one that Georgianna Darcy appears to employ in *Pride and Prejudice*. The text shares little about Georgianna beyond her musical accomplishments; when she is spoken of by other characters, it is in relation to her musical proficiency. Darcy tells Lady Catherine that 'She practises very constantly' (*PP* 133), and Mrs Reynolds, the housekeeper at Pemberley, likewise says that Georgianna 'plays and sings all day long' (*PP* 187). Allowing for Darcy's and Mrs Reynolds' possible exaggeration, their praise indicates that Georgianna spends a good deal of time at the piano. As her devotion to music comes after her thwarted elopement with Wickham, she may be practicing constantly in order to contain her emotions. Darcy's gift of a new piano at this time suggests he endorses her use of music as means of self-control.

In *Persuasion*, Anne Elliot similarly relies on the multiple functions of music to cope with her emotions in a semi-public drawing room. When Captain Wentworth, her former fiancé, returns to England, she finds herself playing the piano while he dances with the Musgrove girls: 'The evening ended with dancing. On its being proposed, Anne offered her services, as usual, and though her eyes would sometimes fill with tears as she sat at the instrument, she was extremely glad to be employed, and desired nothing in return but to be unobserved' (*P* 62). The social utility of music allows her to provide entertainment for others and check her tears at the same time. As the focus is on the dancing, her grief escapes notice. Indeed, playing music allows her to indulge in private thoughts in the midst of a full drawing room. She reflects on Captain Wentworth's enjoyment of the admiration of all the young ladies present 'while her fingers were mechanically at work, proceeding for half an hour together, equally without error, and without consciousness' (*P* 62). Anne adopts to her advantage piano instruction manual directives that turned the female performer into an automaton. She is able to canvass painful ideas about Captain Wentworth finding new love without disrupting her performance or making any mistakes.

While Georgianna and Anne employ music to discipline their broken hearts, Austen indicates that women may also use it to indulge their emotions. The sentimental Marianne Dashwood expresses and amplifies her feelings through music after Willoughby abruptly leaves Barton. She

> played over every favorite song that she had been used to play to Willoughby, every air which their voices had been oftenest joined, and sat at the instrument gazing on every line of music that he had written out for her, till her heart was so heavy that no farther sadness

could be gained; and this nourishment of grief was every day applied. She spent whole hours at the pianoforte alternately singing and crying; her voice often totally suspended by her tears. (*SS* 63)

Marianne, like Georgianna and Anne, redirects her emotional energies with music, but she does so in a way that challenges piano instruction manual precepts. Rather than soothing her 'vexations' with music, Marianne exacerbates and prolongs her emotional pain. As wallowing in heartbreak disrupts the social harmony at Barton Cottage by giving pain to her mother and sister, the text is somewhat critical of this use of music. Nevertheless, Austen depicts possibilities for women's self-expression via music that test social norms.

After Willoughby's marriage and her own illness, Marianne resolves to exert self-restraint, in part, through music. She tells Elinor, 'I mean never to be later in rising than six, and from that time till dinner I shall divide every moment between music and reading' (*SS* 260). However, Austen raises doubts about Marianne's plan as the rigid schedule she sets reflects her characteristic lack of moderation. Elinor notes this irony, 'smiling to see the same eager fancy which had been leading her to the extreme of languid indolence and selfish repining, now at work in introducing excess into a scheme of such rational employment and virtuous self-controul' (*SS* 260). While Elinor commends her sister's plan as 'rational' and 'virtuous', music's efficacy for emotional temperance with a woman like Marianne is questionable. Nonetheless, Austen's characters exercise their own agency whether they use music to indulge or discipline their emotions.

Criticism on Austen has generally considered how music is used to convey character in the novels or examined how Austen's own music collection may have influenced her craft. Investigating the cultural contexts of domestic music making, in particular keyboard instruction material, shifts our focus to the social utility of music in Austen's era: as status marker, disciplinary activity, gender performance, and tool to manipulate behavioural codes. Austen's novels demonstrate how piano method book precepts about women's performance could be subverted or manoeuvred to allow women a degree of agency in courtship and other social situations. The extra-sonoric meanings of music performance resonate throughout Austen's body of work.

Notes

1 Critics Richard Leppert and Leslie Ritchie, in particular, discuss the ways music was perceived as a means of social control in the late-eighteenth century.

2 Other keyboard instruments Jane Austen and her contemporaries likely would have been familiar with include the spinet, virginal, clavichord, and harpsichord. However, the pianoforte surpassed them all in popularity by the end of the eighteenth century. The last harpsichords were manufactured in about 1800 (Selwyn 124).

3 Maria and Richard Lovell Edgeworth acknowledge but disapprove of this popular understanding of music's utility in *Practical Education*.

4 Critics have explored the relationship between music and character in Austen's novels, but no consistent message emerges. Some of her most morally upstanding characters, such as Elinor Dashwood and Fanny Price, do not play, yet neither does one of her most morally questionable characters, Lydia Bennet. Austen's proficient musicians also run the gamut of moral rectitude from Anne Elliot to Mary Crawford. For more on music and character, see Dubois, Shanks Libden, Selwyn, Wells, and Wood.

5 See for example, chapter 2 of More's *Strictures on the Modern System of Female Education*, chapter 20 of Edgeworth and Edgeworth's *Practical Education*, and Sermon VI of Fordyce's *Sermons to Young Women*.

6 See, for example, Bemetzrieder.

7 For recommendations on practice time, see Türk (19), Appleton (160), Vetus (423), and 'On Music' (95). For claims that women were spending five or six hours a day practicing, see Cockle (241) and Cambrianna (202).

8 The Austen family music collection contains five compositions for piano by Latour.

9 Professional women pianists at the end of the eighteenth and beginning of the nineteenth centuries were almost always from the lower orders. For more on professional female musicians, see Salwey.

10 See Wells for an extended discussion of the significance of Mary Crawford's harp playing.

11 For more on the symbolic significance of this piano, see Shanks Libden and Vorachek.

Works Cited

Appleton, Elizabeth. *Private Education: Or a Practical Plan for the Studies of Young Ladies*. London: Henry Colburn, 1815.

Austen, Jane. *Emma*. Oxford UP, 2008.

Austen, Jane. *Jane Austen's Letters*, 4th ed., collected and edited by Deirdre Le Faye. Oxford UP, 2011.

Austen, Jane. *Lady Susan. Northanger Abbey, Lady Susan, The Watsons*, and *Sanditon*. Oxford UP, 2008, pp. 189–249.

Austen, Jane. *Mansfield Park*. Oxford UP, 2008.

Austen, Jane. *Northanger Abbey*. Oxford UP, 2008.

Austen, Jane. *Persuasion*. Oxford UP, 2008.

Austen, Jane. *Pride and Prejudice*. Oxford UP, 2008.

Austen, Jane. *Sense and Sensibility*. Oxford UP, 2008.

Bemetzrieder, Anton. *Music Made Easy to Every Capacity, in a Series of Dialogues; Being Practical Lesson for the Harpsichord*, vol. 3, Translated by Giffard Bernard. R. Ayre & B. Moore, 1779.

Burgh, Allston. *Anecdotes of Music, Historical and Biographical; in a Series of Letters from a Gentleman to His Daughter*, vol. 1. London: Longman, 1814.

Cambrianna. 'Letters of Cambrianna. Letter VII. To Miss M★★★★★ on her intended Marriage.' *New British Lady's Magazine*, Nov. 1819, pp. 202–204.

Cockle, Mrs. *Important Studies for the Female Sex, in reference to modern manners*. London: C. Chapple, 1809.

'Desultory Remarks on the Study and Practice of Music, Addressed to a Young Lady while Under the Tuition of an Eminent Master. Written in the Years 1790–1 and 2.' *The European Magazine*, vol. 30, 1796, pp. 114–115, 179–81, 270–3, 357–8, 405–7.

Dubois, Pierre. *Music in the Georgian Novel*. Cambridge UP, 2015.

Edgeworth, Maria, and Richard Lovell Edgeworth. *Practical Education*, 2nd ed. Woodstock Books, 1996.

Euterpe: Or Remarks on the Use and Abuse of Music, as a Part of Modern Education. London: J. Dodsley, 1780.

Fordyce, James. *Sermons to Young Women*. Philadelphia: Carey, 1809.

Gisbourne, Thomas. *An Enquiry into the Duties of the Female Sex*. Garland, 1974.

Hook, James. *Guida di Musica: Being a complete book of instruction for beginners on the Harpsichord or Piano Forte*. London: J. & G. Balls, 1810.

Hoover, Cynthia Adams. 'The Workshop.' *Piano Roles: Three Hundred Years of Life with the Piano*, edited by James Parakilas. Yale UP, 1999, pp. 37–41.

Jousse, Jean. *Pianoforte Made Easy to Every Capacity*. Jenkyns 07—Binder's volume of printed keyboard and harp music, c. 1780–c. 1815. https://archive.org/details/austenfamilymusicbooks

Latour, T. Francis *T. Latour's New and Improved Method of Instruction for the Piano-Forte*. London: F. T. Latour, 1827.

Leppert, Richard. *Music and Image: Domesticity, Ideology and Socio-Cultural Formation in Eighteenth-Century England*. Cambridge UP, 1988.

More, Hannah. *Strictures on the Modern System of Female Education*, vol. 1. Garland, 1974.

'Old Woman No. CII.' *Lady's Monthly Museum*, vol. 2, Mar. 1807, pp. 99–102.

'On Music.' *La Belle Assemblee*, Feb. 1807, pp. 94–96.

Ritchie, Leslie. *Women Writing Music in Late Eighteenth-Century England: Social Harmony in Literature and Performance*. Ashgate, 2008.

Salwey, Nicholas. 'Women Pianists in Late Eighteenth-Century London.' *Concert Life in Eighteenth-Century Britain*, edited by Susan Wollenberg and Simon McVeigh. Ashgate, 2004, pp. 273–290.

Selwyn, David. *Jane Austen and Leisure*. Hambledon P, 1999.

Shanks Libden, Kathryn L. 'Music, Character, and Social Standing in Jane Austen's *Emma*.' *Persuasions*, vol. 22, 2000, pp. 15–30.

Steetz, William. *A Treatise on the Elements of Music in a Series of Letters to a Lady*. London: Smith, 1812.

Sumner, W. L. *The Pianoforte*. Macdonald, 1966.

Türk, Daneil Gottlob. *School of Clavier Playing*, Translated by Raymond Haggh. U of Nebraska P, 1982.

Vetus. 'To the Editor.' *Quarterly Musical Magazine and Review*, Oct. 1818, pp. 421–428.

Vorachek, Laura. '"The Instrument of the Century": The Piano as an Icon of Female Sexuality in the Nineteenth Century.' *George Eliot-George Henry Lewes Studies*, vol. 38–39, 2000, pp. 26–43.

Wells, Juliette. 'A Harpist Arrives at Mansfield Park: Music and the Moral Ambiguity of Mary Crawford.' *Persuasions*, vol. 28, 2006, pp. 101–113.

Wood, Gillen D'Arcy. *Romanticism and Music Culture in Britain, 1770–1840: Virtue and Virtuosity*. Cambridge UP, 2010.

18

'ALL THE EGOTISM OF AN INVALID': HYPOCHONDRIA AS FORM IN JANE AUSTEN'S *SANDITON*

Sarah Marsh

AMERICAN UNIVERSITY

When Princess Charlotte Augusta died on November 6, 1817, within hours of her first son's stillbirth, the British Regency was plunged into a period of acute constitutional crisis. Because neither Princess Charlotte nor her famously estranged parents had any other children, Britain had lost its heirs apparent, as well as the dynastic stability they promised. Perhaps worst of all, Britain had lost a beloved national plotline: in which a self-actualized young woman marries the man of her choice, on her own terms, ushering in an era of social renewal with the promise of a new generation of children.[1] After her parents' notorious debauches inflicted against propriety and marriage itself, Charlotte's loss was taken particularly hard. Harriet Martineau, reflecting on the deaths of Charlotte and her son some thirty years later, called it 'the great historical event of 1817'; 'never', she continued, 'was a whole nation plunged in such deep and universal grief' (qtd. in Behrendt 1).

Jane Austen, whose genius had popularised stories of social renewal through companionate marriage, was not alive to witness Britain in the wake of Charlotte's death. She had died on the 18th of July, 1817, a little more than three months before the woman who was to be her queen. At her death, however, Austen left behind a strange, unfinished manuscript now known as the *Sanditon* fragment, which follows a young woman named Charlotte Heywood (another Charlotte H., like the princess) from her country home at Willingden to the fictional seaside resort of Sanditon. Here, she plays a healthy antithesis to a cast of self-absorbed hypochondriacs in a nation sliding quickly toward social and economic dysfunction. Charlotte Heywood's exceptionalism in *Sanditon*, and the contrasting discourses of hypochondria that surround her, suggest that Austen was developing her seventh major novel as an extended satire on the condition of Regency-era Britain.

As Margaret Ann Doody and Jocelyn Harris recently have shown, Austen infrequently placed real historical actors in her novels, but nevertheless used name play to connect her fiction with the concerns of national politics (Doody 53–65; Harris 272). *Pride & Prejudice* and *Persuasion* respond to the evolving pressures of the Napoleonic wars; Austen (mordantly, some commentators reckon) dedicated *Emma* to the Prince Regent; and *Mansfield Park* engages Britain's involvement in the Atlantic slave trade. In *Sanditon*, Austen turns her political attention to Britain's extended accession crisis represented by the Regency itself: the corrupt Prince Regent, the embattled Princess Caroline, and the insane King George III, each their own sign of national decline and constitutional imbalance

DOI: 10.4324/9780429398155-18-21

229

(Clark 1–5).[2] Like Austen's Charlotte Heywood, whose patterns of discursive reserve in *Sanditon* differentiate her from a society of verbose solipsists, Charlotte Hanover was imagined as an alternative to her parents' adulterous, often self-serving, transgressions, which were well-publicised to the British public. Princess Charlotte thus became for Britons a crucial public figure, standing for the possibility that the Hanoverian line, and Britain with it, might recover from the decline signified by the older members of the royal family. As Stephen Behrendt has shown, Charlotte's ideological importance to her subjects became most apparent in the wake of her unexpected death. As royal daughter, heir apparent, and mother of the future king, Charlotte was mourned as a woman, a mother, and a monarch; as the art collector and novelist William Beckford attested in a letter: 'I consider her loss pretty great, a sad and dire accident calculated to fill with tears the eyes of almost all the people, a fatal event pregnant with confusion, and, in time, with civil war' (qtd. in Behrendt 2). The foreclosure of a young woman's marital and maternal destinies is continuous with national fracture.[3]

Here, however, the similarities between Charlotte Heywood and Charlotte Hanover end: in contradistinction to the British public's hopeful feelings about their future Queen Charlotte, Austen's manuscript is deeply ambivalent about its heroine's capacity for ascendency in a postwar society that can no longer perpetuate itself through land-based, dynastic plotlines that, in Austen's earlier fiction, had power to mend tears in the social fabric wrought by modernity. In *Sanditon*, rather, the comedic narrative structures made possible by real property, so critical in novels like *Sense and Sensibility*, *Pride and Prejudice*, *Mansfield Park*, and *Emma*, are eroded by postwar inflation, the persistent reflux of Britain's empire, and the ascendency of un-landed classes under capital. In *Sanditon*'s biting satire, the collapse of the country-house system thus produces not the endogamous inland retrenchments of *Mansfield Park* nor *Persuasion*'s exogamous removal of domestic virtue to seagoing navy families—but rather an unsociable society on England's coastline overrun by people for whom Britain is not real property, but a last resort.

Hypochondria is the figure Austen adopts to describe this national collapse. Importantly, hypochondria's cultural meanings, which included genuinely low spirits as well as obsession with imagined bodily disorder, allowed Austen to develop an extended critique of what J. G. Barker-Benfield has called 'the culture of sensibility'. Once figured satirically in peripheral characters like Mrs Bennet and Mr Woodhouse, the *Sanditon* hypochondriacs overrun the manuscript with speech patterns that defer to no one, suggesting a nation of Britons attending only to themselves and away from the organising principles of inland country life: primogeniture, strict settlement, and highly coded systems of social deference and paternalism. *Sanditon* enacts these new social patterns in the fragment's asyndetic form, a long series of disassociated monologues. These patterns also are signalled in the fragment's narrative structure by its lack of landed, marriageable men—who, in Austen's early fiction, are the very forms that afford social cohesion, national ascendency, and the comedic novel itself. The well-known patrician flourish that announces *Pride and Prejudice*—'that a single man in possession of a good fortune must be in want of a wife'—is foreclosed in *Sanditon* by men without fortune who think not of wives, but of themselves (Austen 1).

Instead of positioning her *Sanditon* heroines for social elevation in marriage, Austen seems instead to imagine a companionate relationship between Charlotte Heywood and Clara Brereton. The result is a structural innovation in the novel, which emphasises homosocial relations between women, not the consolidation of class power through the companionate marriage of women and men whose social differences are slight. Austen already had plotted this arrangement in *Sense and Sensibility* under the more traditional guise of sisters' double marriage. While Elinor and Marianne eventually are secured in their social and financial conditions through their respective marriages, it remains clear in the novel's final paragraph that friendship between the sisters outruns nuptial happiness:

[b]etween Barton and Delaford there was that constant communication which strong family affection would naturally dictate; and among the merits and the happiness of Elinor and Marianne, let it not be ranked as the least considerable, that, though sisters, and living almost within sight of each other, they could live without disagreement between themselves, or producing coolness between their husbands. (380)

This lack of 'coolness between [...] husbands'—as strange as two sisters living 'without disagreement'—suggests that Edward and Brandon may not even mind that their wives go elsewhere to find the kind of close companionship that James Thompson has called 'intimacy' (159–80). Though the reading that follows must remain speculative in view of *Sanditon*'s fragmentary nature, it seems likely that Austen was pulling taut in *Sanditon* the thread she had touched in the female relations of *Sense and Sensibility*, *Pride and Prejudice*, and *Emma*. Unlike Elinor, Marianne, Elizabeth, and Jane, whose consanguinity is the foundation of their friendship—and unlike Emma and Harriet, whose relationship is circumscribed by class—Charlotte Heywood and Clara Brereton's relationship transcends these categories. *Sanditon*, as critics frequently observe, remains deeply pessimistic, even fatalistic, about the future of Britain; Charlotte and Clara stand apart from this decline because their relationship is not based on family or rank, a sign of the novel's, and the nation's, burgeoning modernity.

★★★

Sanditon begins in the world-turning tumult of post-Waterloo Britain. On the way to Willingden to contract a surgeon to live at Sanditon, the fragment's eponymous (and fictional) seaside resort, Mr Thomas Parker overturns his carriage, spilling himself and his wife, Mary, into the road, injuring his ankle, and revealing his obsession with the commoditization of health. As John Wiltshire notes, 'Mr Parker has privatised the sea air'—and is eager that others buy in to this developing market on the coast (205). At Mr Parker's Sanditon home, Trafalgar House, Britain's costly naval victory is remade as personal luxury, playing up Mr Parker's belief that his financial interest in the health-promoting qualities of Britain's coast is a matter of his nationally minded beneficence, an early sign of psychically entrenched capitalism that would be described years later by Theodore Adorno. This, for example, is how Mr Parker assesses the effect of Sanditon's high society on the local poor: Sanditon is 'the sure resort of the very best Company, those regular, steady, private Families of thorough Gentility & Character, who are a blessing everywhere, excite the industry of the Poor and diffuse comfort & improvement among them of every sort' (368). Sanditon, on Mr Parker's view, advances a kind of proto-trickle-down economics, whereby 'private Families of thorough Gentility & Character' improve Britain's body politic by healing the social pathologies of other sorts of people, particularly the working poor.

Mr Parker's opinion—that the health-promoting qualities of Britain's coast were a sociological boon to Britain—was common historically as well. The January 1816 *Gentleman's Magazine* eagerly explained, for example, that

[i]t is now universally advised to have recourse to that Ocean, at once the safeguard and the glory of the Nation, whose healing properties cannot be too much extolled [...]. The numerous places on the coast that now, at each returning summer, vie with each other in tempting the invalid of the interior to try the efficacy of Sea-Air and Sea-Bathing, are solid and convincing proofs of the importance of the offered remedy. (qtd. in Wiltshire 206)

Very like this passage's circuitous rhetoric—in which the asserted 'healing properties' of a nationalist Atlantic become proof of 'the importance of' its 'remedy'—Mr Parker's self-interest and his nationalism amount ideologically to the same thing, the novel's first sign of things collapsing in on themselves.

Thus, for Mr Parker, 'Sanditon [is] second Wife & 4 Children to him—hardly less Dear', the narrator discloses, '[Sanditon] had indeed the highest claims;—not only those of Birthplace, Property, and Home,—it was his Mine, his Lottery, his Speculation & his Hobby Horse; his Occupation his Hope & his Futurity' (372). As the commas fall finally out of this litany, Austen's line enacts the breathless ardour of Mr Parker's general patterns of speaking about Sanditon, which often discourage others from responding. Trafalgar House is Austen's late counterpoint to Pemberley, both aesthetically and politically: Darcy's estate symbolizes and undertakes the maintenance of a multigenerational family structure that supports a flourishing local community (as Mrs Gardiner's memories of Derbyshire attest); even Darcy's servants believe him to be the 'best landlord, and the best master that ever lived' (248). Sanditon, by contrast, represents Mr Parker's investment in a health resort whose financial success will require the (real or imagined) decline of Britons everywhere.

The variety of *Sanditon*'s landscapes (the old and the new; the sturdy and the decaying; the real and the ersatz) together with a honed textual confusion about Sanditon's location (is it at the Parkers' old inland home of that name, in the village of Sanditon, or on the developing coast?) suggest the geo-social instability of Sanditon's populace, which is an effect of commercial imperialism. In addition to the Hilliers, tenants who have moved into the Parker's old manor house by invitation, Austen gives us a variety of characters whose class and familial identities are increasingly, and openly, mixed. The most suggestive of these characters is Lady Denham, Sanditon's resident dowager and Mr Parker's 'Colleague in Speculation', whose significant fortune of more than £30,000 is even more significantly encumbered by relations and legal heirs she has incurred through her multiple marriages—the first to a wealthy Mr Hollis and the second to an impoverished Sir Harry Denham, whom she widely is rumored to have married for his title (375). Lady Denham's mercenary interests in Sanditon, however, are tempered by her seemingly kind attentions to Miss Clara Brereton, a poor young relation from an unfashionable part of London whom she has invited to stay with her: Mr Parker 'gave [to Charlotte] the particulars which had led to Clara's admission at Sanditon, as no bad exemplification of that mixture of Character, that union of Littleness with Kindness with Good Sence [sic] with even Liberality which he saw in Lady D'. Lady Denham thus emerges as a figure for Britain's increasingly homogenous and moveable society: here is the 'Kindness' and 'Liberality' of noblesse oblige typical of Darcy and Knightley mixed with the social 'Littleness' and greed of a rising capitalist (378).

Sanditon's society is no less mixed—and this poses a dire challenge to Mr Parker and Lady Denham's joint venture to make Sanditon among the most fashionable of Britain's bathing places: after all, Mr Parker already has turned the resort's society into a marketable commodity in his promise to Mr Heywood that Sanditon's is a homogenous society of 'private Families of thorough Gentility & Character'. We later learn that Mr Parker has not let the facts get in the way of his sales pitch to Mr Heywood, as evinced by this very disappointing 'List of Subscribers', who are in Sanditon for the season:

> The Lady Denham, Miss Brereton, Mr and Mrs P—Sir Edw: Denham & Miss Denham, whose names might be said to lead off the Season, were followed by nothing better than—Mrs Mathews—Miss Mathews, Miss E. Mathews, Miss H. Mathews.—Dr & Mrs Brown—Mr Richard Pratt.—Lieut: Smith, R.N. Capt: Little,—Limehouse.—Mrs Jane Fisher. Miss Fisher. Miss Scroggs.—Rev: Mr Hanking. Mr Beard—Solicitor, Grays Inn.—Mrs Davis. & Miss Merryweather. (389)

Behind Austen's primary cast of characters, 'whose names might be said to lead off the Season', is a disheartening litany of miscellaneous people with unpromising last names—Miss Scroggs registering particularly as a proto-Dickensian marker of social mediocrity. Accordingly, Lady Denham assesses

Sanditon's situation: 'if we could but get a young Heiress to S[anditon]! But Heiresses are monstrous scarce! I do not think we have had an Heiress here or even a Co—[heiress] since Sanditon has been a public place. Families come after Families, but as far as I can learn, it is not one in an hundred of them that have any real Property' (401). Sanditon society is less distinguished than its chief speculators wish—and 'real Property', the old site of land-based social value and paternal care, is missing in Sanditon's consumer culture of moveable people and moveable goods (401).

Underwriting Lady Denham's exclamations about an heiress is the fact that postwar inflation has, at Sanditon and across Britain, outrun the conservation of wealth once guaranteed by strict settlement, a seventeenth-century development that consolidated family wealth by guiding its inheritance intact via primogeniture. 'Under strict settlement', Mary Poovey explains, 'each man was the only life-tenant of the family estates. Generally, the essential articles governing property were settled on the eldest son's marriage: the amount of his maintenance, his wife's jointure […] and the form and amount of portion that the younger children of the marriage would receive' (12). Lady Denham is familiar with this process because it has governed the inheritance of the dwindling Denham estate since the death of her most recent husband: after Sir Harry's decease (prior to the beginning of *Sanditon*), Lady Denham returned with her £30,000 per annum to Sanditon House, the home she enjoyed as Mrs Hollis, leaving behind an impoverished Denham Park for her nephew and his sister, Miss Esther Denham, as Sir and Lady Denham have had no children of their own. Heiresses, therefore—or co-heiresses, as Lady Denham allows—are necessary to raising the fortunes of penurious heirs like her nephew, the baronet Sir Edward, whose estate has long exceeded its income in spite of Sir Harry's efforts: in a mutually convenient effort to re-establish the Denham family, Sir Harry is supposed to have married Lady Denham for her fortune just as she is believed to have married him for his title. Economic fluctuations thus transvalue the country-estate gender codes of Austen's earlier fiction: in *Sanditon*, single men in possession of titles are in want of wives of good fortune.

Though the Denham estate has passed from Sir Harry to Sir Edward undivided, its yearly income is unequal to the Denhams' new style of life at Sanditon and Denham Park; as Mr Parker discloses, Sir Edward Denham is 'a poor Man for his rank in Society' and has not enough money to be a patron of the resort (377). Lady Denham and her nephew therefore find themselves in an ahistorical arrangement in which Lady Denham, herself an heiress not having had the inclination to enrich the 'ancient' Denham family with her new money, supports Sir Edward in his baronetcy according to her whim. She explains to Charlotte: 'for though I am only the *Dowager* my Dear, & he is the *Heir*, things do not stand between us in the way they commonly do between those two parties.—Not a shilling do I receive from the Denham estate. Sir Edw: has no Payments to make *me*. He don't stand uppermost, beleive [sic] *me*.—It is *I* that help *him*' (400). In Sanditon, money thus flows in the wrong direction: dowagers prop up heirs instead of enjoying the beneficence of the heir's excess. Sanditon's society is thus the strange shadow cast by deflating feudal incomes, rising capitalist markets, postwar inflation—and, in the foreground, not a missing male heir as in the Dashwood and Bennet families, but an heir without a fortune to inherit.

The heiress who arrives in Sanditon, at length, is the West Indian Miss Lambe: 'here was the very young Lady, sickly & rich, whom [Lady Denham] had been asking for; & she made the acquaintance for Sir Edward's sake, & the sake of her Milch asses', whose milk Lady Denham hopes to offer, or perhaps sell to, Miss Lambe for her constitutional improvement. Described as 'about 17, half Mulatto, chilly & tender', Miss Lambe has been, in spite of her brief appearance in the fragment, a magnet for the attention of literary critics because of her racial identity (421). D. A. Miller attributes Miss Lambe's racial characteristics to Austen's projected anxiety about the dermatologic symptoms of her own illness, which she characterizes as 'black and white and every wrong colour' in a late letter to her niece, Fanny Knight (55–56). Clara Tuite has argued that 'Miss Lambe is for Lady Denham what Maria Edgeworth's Lady Delacour in *Belinda* refers to as "the heiress lozenge"—the consolation of a rich wife for a ruined aristocrat', noting that '*Belinda* (1801) also has a West Indian intertext, and was revised in 1810 to occlude interracial marriage' (178–79). In Tuite's view, Miss Lambe, according to her sacrificial name, becomes in Lady Denham's imagination an offering to her penniless nephew: the wealthy offspring of imperial miscegenation will be sacrificed on the crumbling altar of the English aristocracy. Fortunately for Miss Lambe, Lady Denham's plan is checked by Miss Lambe's aunt, Mrs Griffiths, who 'would not allow Miss L. to have the smallest symptom of a Decline, or any complaint which Asses' milk c^d possibly relieve [sic]' (422). This interaction forecloses Lady Denham's marriage plot, but it seems unlikely that Austen would have introduced Miss Lambe into Sanditon's heiress-starved scene without a narrative purpose.

Clara Tuite's reading of Miss Lambe brings to light a critical imperial discourse in *Sanditon* on the social precarity of a decayed country-house system. Wealthy West Indians are, 'for the locals', as Tuite explains, 'a monstrous inbred parvenu class, persecuted for eliminating difference' through their immense wealth. '[B]ecause they have full purses', Lady Denham observes, 'West-injines' 'fancy themselves equal, may be, to your old Country Families'; 'they who scatter their Money so freely, never think of whether they may not be doing mischief of raising the price of Things' (Tuite 179; *Sanditon* 392). Here, Lady Denham reduces what Tuite identifies as a 'persecution text around the West Indians' to the market's absolute measure: 'the price of Things'. And, while Lady Denham broadcasts many unflattering prejudices against the West Indians in *Sanditon*, she notably has no compunction that Miss Lambe should become the next Lady Denham, suggesting that wealth now trumps absolutely Lady Catherine de Bourgh's myth of racialized aristocratic purity—not surprising, considering that Lady Denham herself married Sir Harry from outside the British aristocracy. Finally, Mr Parker convinces Lady Denham by this same logic that West Indians ought not to be persecuted, but welcome in Sanditon: '[m]y dear Madam, they can only raise the price of consumable Articles, by such an extraordinary Demand for them & such a diffusion of money among us, as must do us more Good than harm', an observation which largely quells Lady Denham's classist and racist concerns (392). Thus, the British and West Indian populations that constitute Sanditon society along the human fault lines of empire are as stable as the local markets of commoditized health. In Austen's formulation of postcolonial relations in *Sanditon*, the bottom line tends to, as Tuite says, 'eliminate difference' of race, class—even bodily wellness—thereby emptying social categories of their complex narrative meanings.

Indeed, *Sanditon*'s most programmatic discursive technique, enacted one way or another in all of the above examples, is to demonstrate *not* that Britons are in bodily decline per se (maybe some of them are—though who?), but that bodily health no longer maintains a direct, or even a predictable, relationship with narrative form, which is the central rhetorical function of hypochondriasis. While Austen's early novels reward good health with social ascendency and conversely yoke its decline to social ruin, there seems to be no such relationship in *Sanditon*, which persistently erodes the reader's ability to make judgments or predictions about the health of people, or the story's narrative progress. 'Austen', Sutherland notes, 'seems to have little energy for characters who require some probable development'. In her analysis of the *Sanditon* holograph, Sutherland finds evidence that Austen was working to achieve precisely this effect: '[t]ime and again, revision clears the text of information and works to counter the temptation of first thoughts to over-direct the reader's response and anticipate evaluation' (178, 180). This energy, which foils the mutual responsiveness of reader and text, is precisely the discursive tendency of the hypochondriac: as Mr Parker's hypochondriac sister, Diana, exclaims in a letter: 'We have entirely done with the whole Medical Tribe. We have consulted physician after physician in vain, till we are quite convinced that they can do nothing for us and that we must trust to our own knowledge of our own wretched constitutions for any relief' (386). Again, these discursive implosions—trusting only '*our own* knowledge of *our own* wretched constitutions'—enact the hypochondriacal structuring principles of *Sanditon* as a central figure for the inward-turning condition of the English in the early nineteenth century (my emphasis).

Austen uses the forms of hypochondria—set throughout the fragment at the levels of setting, character, plot, and literary allusion—to explore the medical and socio-historical meanings of the condition itself. Hypochondria, George C. Grinnel explains, was produced during the Romantic period by an 'unprecedented fascination with well-being combined with greater investments in the construction of the body as an object of knowledge' (14). For Austen, hypochondria also indicates the ways these 'fascination[s]' and 'greater investments' work against other modes of living, particularly those social patterns associated with real property and the British country estate. Sanditon, in fact, is the very world to which the uncontrollable physiological, social, and discursive symptoms of hypochondria go when they diverge from the established, hereditary order of the country-house system.

Austen's location of hypochondria on the coast of Britain also invokes important medical revisions of this condition's meaning. Originally identified by ancient practitioners as a somatic disorder of the hypochondrium (an area just anterior to the rib cage in the Galenic body), hypochondria had a long and well-documented cultural history in England, which

> begins with forms of melancholia or what became known as the English Malady. The Renaissance deemed melancholia to be a rapidly spreading disorder imported from Europe. The melancholic was a figure of foreignness and disordered well-being who became a stock malcontent in the literary and medical texts of the Elizabethan era. (Grinnel 16)

As Grinnel notes, the early-modern melancholic was not yet purely a figure of Englishness, but a foreign presence whose disordered well-being set him apart from the healthy Englishman.[4] It was not until 1733 that George Cheyne would offer a dramatic revision of the foreign splenetic sufferer in *The English Malady: A Treatise of Nervous Diseases of all Kinds, as Spleen, Vapours, Lowness of Spirits, Hypochondriacal and Hysterical Distempers*. In his widely influential study, the Bath physician (and lifelong hypochondriac) observed, in opposition to earlier formulations, that hypochondria was not a foreign disorder at all, but rather produced by English geography, climate, and ways of life:

> the moisture of our air, the variableness of our weather, (from our situation amidst the ocean) the rankness and fertility of our soil, the richness and heaviness of our food, the wealth and abundance of the inhabitants (from their universal trade), the inactivity and sedentary occupations of the better sort (among whom this evil mostly rages), and the humour of living in great, populous and consequently unhealthy towns, have brought forth a class and set of distempers with atrocious and frightful symptoms, scarce known to our ancestors, and never rising to such fatal heights, nor afflicting such numbers in any other nation. These nervous disorders being computed to make almost one third of the complaints of the [...] condition in England. (i–ii)

What is so striking about Cheyne's explanation of hypochondria is that, while he sees it first and foremost as the English malady his title asserts, he also acknowledges that this disorder was 'scarce known to our ancestors', suggesting that hypochondria, though a constitutional problem of the English, has no hereditary component. Rather, hypochondria represents the coincidence of 'universal trade', 'sedentary occupations of the better sort', and overcrowding with English climes and social habits—a set of characterizations which suggest that, even in the eighteenth century, hypochondria was understood to be historically and culturally bound (i–ii).

Austen presses this history into the service of her satire. The English malady—once a constitutional problem affecting nearly one third of all English people in Cheyne's estimation—is now moved to the coast of Britain, back in the direction of the continent from whence it is alleged to have come during the sixteenth century. Making possible this relocation is Mr Parker's vigorous contradiction of what Cheyne had earlier called England's unhealthy 'situation amidst the ocean'. On Mr Parker's view, nothing in England is healthier than Sanditon's geographic situation, which boasts '[t]he finest, purest Sea Breeze on the Coast—[...]—Excellent Bathing—fine hard Sand—Deep Water 10 yards from the Shore—no Mud—no Weeds—no slimey rocks—Never was there a place more palpably designed by Nature for the resort of the Invalid' (369). Aggressive commercialisation of the coast's salubrity was common historically, too, with new resorts springing up during Austen's lifetime and attracting an increasing number of patrons. As Wiltshire observes, it was common for British proprietors of one resort or another to slander neighbouring resorts, as Mr Parker does in running down Brighton, Worthing, and Eastbourne. This example from Dr Anthony Relhand's *Short History of Brighthelmston* (1761), sets Brighton apart from competitors at Baiae and the ancient city of Bath:

> Brighthelmston, thus free from the insalutary vapour of stagnant water, distant from [...] noxious steams [...] and every other cause aiding to produce a [...] putrid atmosphere, seldom sees its inhabitants labouring under those disorders which arise from a relaxed fibre and a languid circulation. Yet, from the vicinity of the sea, and the abundant, but salutary vapour it affords, it is as certain that the complaints that arise from a too rigid and tense fibre are equally unknown. Hence neither dropsical, nor Chlorotic complaints; Pleurisies, nor Quincies, nor any other inflammatory ones prevail here. (Qtd. in Wiltshire 206)

Mr Parker is similarly convinced that Sanditon's salubrious atmosphere and landscape, along with its 'Buildings', 'Nursery Grounds', and growing markets ('the demand for every thing' is Mr Parker's phrase), set it apart from every other resort on Britain's coast (368). What Cheyne had identified as the poison—of the British weather, overcrowding, and commercialisation—is here being offered in the bottle of the cure.

Herself a resident of Bath for several years during her mid-twenties (Charlotte Heywood is twenty-two), Austen had plenty of experience in this consumer culture of alienation and paradox.[5] In December of 1800, when Austen had just turned 25, her parents announced their plan to remove to Bath from their longtime home at Steventon, where Austen had spent almost all of her life. The choice seems to have been as unexpected to Austen as it was unwelcome. As Austen's biographer Claire Tomalin notes, 'Cassandra destroyed several letters Jane wrote to her immediately after hearing her parents' decision, which suggests they made her uncomfortable, too full of raw feeling and even anger' (171–73). It seems likely that Austen's scathing characterisation of the Parkers' heartless abandonment of their old home in favour of new Sanditon is a reworking in fiction of what she experienced when her parents moved to Bath: '[a]ll the Austen children were affected by it', Tomalin explains, 'every one of them who was absent and could possibly return to Steventon—Edward, Henry, Frank and Charles—made a point of doing so before their parents left—"while Steventon is ours", as Jane put it'. The sudden disruption of her family's steady life in her beloved childhood home is one that Austen learned to deflect with parody. As Tomalin explains, letters from this period show Austen using her 'established comic tone for Mrs Austen', who, as Jane Austen saw it, was leading the move to Bath for the sake of her own health and comfort: '[m]y Mother looks forward with as much certainty as you can do to our keeping two Maids—my father is the only one not in the secret', she noted in a letter to Cassandra (171–73). Long before Austen ever set to work on *Sanditon*, therefore, she seems to have been poised by her mother's indulgences to see formal linkages among hypochondria, consumerism, and the erosion of English families' geo-social stability.

Austen found Bath not much different from what she was expecting it to be. A place of 'vapour, shadow, smoke & confusion', Bath is, in Austen's letters, aesthetically similar to the disorienting place Sanditon would become in fiction. The society at Bath was as intolerable as its weather: she writes to Cassandra of 'stupid' parties, confessing finally that she 'cannot anyhow continue to find people agreable [sic]'. Other characterisations from the letters bespeak Austen's disdainful boredom with the women in her society: a Miss Langley, 'like any other short girl with a broad nose & wide mouth, fashionable dress, & exposed bosom', and a Mrs Chamberlayne, who prompted this bitter line to Cassandra: '[a]s to Agreableness [sic] she is much like other people'—a stunning rebuke when we consider that Cassandra had recommended Mrs Chamberlayne to Austen as a 'suitable friend' (Tomalin 171–73). These acerbic characterisations are, perhaps, the original kernels of the caricatures Austen would accomplish later in *Sanditon*.

Tomalin suspects that Austen's intense dissatisfaction with Bath society was underwritten by her 'stinging sense of humiliation at any idea of being paraded' by her parents in the Bath marriage market. Her parents had met and married in Bath, as had her Aunt Jane: it was not difficult for Austen to see the plan her parents had in mind. Austen rebelled against this arrangement, Tomalin suggests, by driving 'up and down Kingsdown Hill in a phaeton and four with a man she could not be suspected of setting her cap at, Mr Evelyn, who was both married and thought more of horses than anything else', a little like Captain Tilney in *Northanger Abbey*. Because the letters from Bath stop in May of 1801, just before Cassandra joined her family on the coast, we have little else with which to characterise Austen's life in Bath, except that she seems to have stopped writing altogether while she lived there. Tomalin concludes that, while Austen never wrote of being depressed in the way of Johnson or Boswell, her treatment of Fanny Price's 'permanent low spirits after a childhood trauma' in *Mansfield Park*—so different in its psychic complexities from her relatively clichéd figuration of Marianne Dashwood suffering as a heroine of sensibility—suggests how well Austen had come to understand other forms of emotional suffering during her residence at Bath (Tomalin 174–76).

It was not Austen's experience of depression, however, but her energetic irony that, once practiced on her mother in Bath, would finally direct her characterisations of hypochondria in *Sanditon*. As John Wiltshire has noted, 'the hypochondriacs who dominate the uncompleted novel *Sanditon* are presented with an amazing inventiveness, brio and zest. There is not just one 'sad invalid' here, but at least three, a trio of health-obsessed people', who are given much more attention than the hypochondriacs of *Pride and Prejudice*, *Emma*, and *Persuasion*, with the possible exception of Mrs Bennet, whose nervous complaints are mocked with considerable endurance (198). Sutherland notes that, in this vein, *Sanditon* 'seems to recall the spirit of the early, finished fragments of juvenile burlesque' rather than any of the finished works (176). Mr Parker's sister Diana, who is introduced through her long and bizarre letter read aloud by Mr Parker to Charlotte, is the fragment's most extended indulgence of this characterological form. In Diana's letter we learn the extreme measures by which she and her siblings, Arthur and Susan, maintain their 'wretched Constitutions' against all manner of ailments: 'Spasmodic Bile', '[deranged] Nerves', 'Headache' (for which Susan has had three teeth drawn), 'cough', and so on (386–87). This, Wiltshire explains, highlights 'the way all three Parkers suffer in concert, reflect and amplify, act and react upon each other's symptoms', suggesting that hypochondria is in *Sanditon*, as in Austen's letters, primarily a social problem (214).

Like her oeuvre's other suspected malingerers, none of the Parkers are observably sick; Diana, the avid inventor and narrator of the Parkers' ills, is especially busy upon her arrival in Sanditon and seemingly very healthy. Instead, hypochondria presents in *Sanditon* as a disordered family, Austen's version of what one day would be called *folie en famille*,[6] and a tableau of the broader social conditions at the Sanditon resort. 'Nothing', Wiltshire concludes, 'is too amazing to be true [in Sanditon] about a person's relation to their body: the body is an infinitely labile and plastic medium for the living through and projection of desires and symptoms and ideas, an expandable arena for the imagination and culture to collaborate in the creation of subjective phenomena' (214–15). Because bodies like the Parkers' can be illimitably destabilised through the actions of hypochondria, individuals in *Sanditon* begin to have a pathologic effect on each other, and on the novel itself.

The text of the fragment enacts this pathologic consequence primarily in a series of asyndetic monologues by Mr Parker, Lady Denham, Diana Parker, and Sir Edward Denham; in fact, only Charlotte Heywood and her father, from 'so healthy a family', seem consistently to speak in response to others, a lingering sign in *Sanditon* of a more cohesive society born of meaningful community bonds in the British countryside. As Sutherland notes, '[t]he unusual range of strongly drawn characters' who 'occupy the foreground, serially and in so short a space—Mr Parker, Diana Parker, Sir Edward Denham, Lady Denham, Arthur Parker—each one adrift in their own language-loop, deny by their robust self-absorption an underlying principle of consensus. There is none' (194). The asyndetic discourse of the unfinished novel is that of a society rendered diffuse and disorganised by its members' self-obsession.

In *Sanditon*, excessive care of the self becomes, at its worst, an isolating body horror, which Austen accomplishes most explicitly in 'those 3 Teeth' Susan Parker has had drawn in an appalling attempt to relieve a headache (388). More isolating still is the narrator's departure from the consciousness of the characters; as Sutherland notes, Austen's minimal use of free indirect discourse is divided in *Sanditon* almost equally between Charlotte and Mr Parker, one of *Sanditon's* 'leading eccentrics', and is hesitant to declare sympathy with any of the characters (175). This brings to light an important distinction between the discursive patterns of *Sanditon* and the early novels. Textual over-exposure (like going out in the rain or appearing in conversation to be too sexually available) tends to produce illness in Marianne Dashwood (and even Jane Bennet) while the textual composure of Elinor and Elizabeth, in combination with the narrators' sympathy with them, works narratively to fortify these characters' constitutions. The converse is true in *Sanditon*, where the narrator is ambivalent about characters who are persistently over-exposed by their own discourse, but not sick at all.

Thus, the *Sanditon* fragment is Austen's exploration of what a character like Charlotte Heywood—similar to Elizabeth Bennet in her constitutional vigor, ready prejudice, and early interest in a man whose 'great object in life was to be seductive'—will do in a world where society, and narrative itself, are increasingly destabilized by pathologic forms of individualism (Austen 405). As Alistair M. Duckworth notes: '[t]his is a world, it would seem, so far removed from traditional grounds of moral action that its retrieval through former fictional means is no longer possible, a world in which the heroine, though she remains a fundamentally moral figure, can no longer be an agent of social renewal'—perhaps especially because no other character bothers to hear Charlotte above her or his own monologue (221). The best example of this is Charlotte Heywood's conversation with Sir Edward Denham about the work of Sir Walter Scott, Robert Burns, James Montgomery, Thomas Campbell, and William Wordsworth. Resonant with Colonel Brandon's 'fallen woman' narrative to Elinor Dashwood; Henry Tilney and Catherine Morland's discussions of gothic novels in *Northanger Abbey*; and Anne Elliot and Captain Harville's debate about history in *Persuasion*, Charlotte and Sir Edward's conversation engages the commonplaces of contemporary genres.[7] However, instead of using conversation and listening among characters to expand their psychological complexities, as she tends to do in similar scenes from the earlier fiction, Austen absorbs other genres and forms into Sir Edward's monologue. This way of speaking, a parody of the Romantic man of feeling whose discourse collapses everything else into himself, is remarkably like the inward-turning discursive effects of hypochondria in the text.

In fact, Sir Edward appears in the *Sanditon* fragment primarily as a dilettante's idiolect. He repeatedly 'stagger[s]' Charlotte Heywood 'with the number of his Quotations, & the bewilderment of some of his sentences'. Because this lengthy passage enacts Sir Edward's views on literature, which counterpoint Austen's, it is necessary to quote at long length (length, which itself is much of the point):

'Do you remember', said he, 'Scotts' [sic] beautiful Lines on the Sea?—Oh! what a description they convey!—They are never out of my Thoughts when I walk here.—That Man who can read them unmoved must have the nerves of an Assassin!—Heaven defend me from meeting such a Man unarmed.—'What description do you mean?—said Charlotte. I remember none at this moment, of the Sea, in either of Scotts' Poems'.—'Do you not indeed?—Nor can I exactly recall the beginning at this moment—But—you cannot have forgotten his description of Woman.—

'Oh! Woman in our Hours of Ease—'

'Delicious! Delicious!—Had he written nothing more, he w^d have been Immortal. And then again, that unequalled, unrivalled address to Parental affection—

'Some feelings are to Mortals given

'With less of Earth in them than Heaven' &c.

'But while we are on the subject of Poetry, what think you Miss H. of Burns [sic] Lines to his Mary?—Oh! there is Pathos to madden one!—If ever there was a Man who *felt*, it was Burns.—Montgomery has all the Fire of Poetry, Wordsworth has the true soul of it—Campbell in his Pleasures of Hope has touched the extreme of our sensations—'Like Angel's visits, few & far between'. Can you conceive of anything more subduing, more melting, more fraught with the deep Sublime than that line?—But Burns—I confess my sense of his Pre-eminence Miss H.—If Scott *has* a fault, it is the want of Passion.—Tender, Elegant, Descriptive—but *Tame*.—The Man who cannot do justice to the attributes of Woman is my contempt.—Sometimes indeed a flash of feeling seems to irradiate him—as in the lines we were speaking of—'Oh! Woman in our hours of Ease'—. But Burns is always on fire.—His Soul was the Altar in which lovely Woman sat enshrined, his Spirit truly breathed the immortal Incense which is her Due.— (396–97)

He continues in this manner for several additional paragraphs, but Austen has achieved her point: just as there is a problem with the self-absorbed readings of one's own body, there is a problem with self-absorbed reading of literature. Sir Edward's character is a highly ironised form of this problem, his musings foreclosing the possibility that he will communicate with Charlotte at all. More disconcerting still is that Sir Edward, heir of Sanditon House and the proper steward of the estate and its surrounding community, is instead fully absorbed by himself. In this way, Sir Edward Denham consolidates the ridiculous frivolity of a Reverend Collins with the social station (and attendant civic responsibilities) of a Mr Darcy—a kind of social paradox that is corrosive to the national social order represented by the country-estate system and the dynastic narrative structure of the English novel.

Coming under Austen's particular scrutiny in *Sanditon* is what Keats would, the following year in a letter to Richard Woodhouse, call the 'Wordsworthian or egotistical sublime', or the tendency of Wordsworth's poetry to stand 'alone' in excessive self-reflexivity (387). Absorbed by their own narratives, or deflected as Charlotte is by the self-interest of her company, Austen's characters find themselves alone in the landscapes of their own imagining: '[a] little of our own Bracing Sea Air will soon set me on my feet again.—Depend upon it my Dear, it is exactly a case for the Sea. Saline air & immersion will be the very thing.—My sensations tell me so already', pronounces Mr Parker after injuring his ankle (367). Though he is comforted by the certainty he attributes to his own 'sensations', he hears no reply from his wife, Mary, whom Austen places in the position of the silent auditor of 'Tintern Abbey', Wordsworth's sister, Dorothy, or the Mary of Robert Burns's poems, who nearly vanish amidst each speaker's commentary on himself.

It is not my point to suggest that Austen disliked the poetry of Wordsworth, Burns, Montgomery, Scott, and Campbell. What is borne out by the text of *Sanditon*, however, is that self-absorbed readers of bodies and literature endanger English community life. At the commercial lending library on Sanditon's Mall, for example, novels regularly are subjected to 'that vast, unknown mass of buyers or renters and readers', who, like Sir Edward, constitute 'the most trea-cherous and unpredictable audience' (Thompson 10). In *Sanditon*, genre itself is under the hard sway of expanding British markets, as in Sir Edward's imperial designs on Clara Brereton:

> [i]f she could not be won by affection, he must carry her off. He knew his Business.—Already had he had many Musings on the Subject. If he *were* constrained so to act, he must naturally wish to strike out something new, to exceed those who had gone before him—and he felt a strong curiosity to ascertain whether the Neighborhood of Timbuctoo might not afford some solitary House adapted for Clara's reception;—but the Expense alas! of Measures in that masterly style was ill-suited to his Purse, & Prudence obliged him to prefer the quietest sort of ruin & disgrace for the object of his Affections, to the more renowned. (405–6)

Sir Edward's appearance in his own imagination as a rake in the style of Richardson's Lovelace is encouraged by the empire's expansive narrative possibilities; fortunately for Clara, Sir Edward's personal finances, deteriorating in the postwar economy, will prevent his taking action on any of them.

What becomes so striking, then, about the *Sanditon* fragment is that it seems a formulation of Austen's idea that literature (especially when read with excessive self-reflexivity) is insufficient to promoting human sympathy and the national cohesion such sympathy implies. This is how Austen frames Sir Edward's belief that novel-reading promotes human sympathy: '[t]he Novels which I approve', Sir Edward begins,

> hold forth the most splendid Portraitures of high Conceptions, Unbounded Views, illi-mitable Ardour, indomptible [sic] Decision—and even when the Event is mainly anti-prosperous to the high-toned Machinations of the prime Character, the potent, pervading Hero of the Story, it leaves us full of Generous Emotions for him;—our Hearts are paralyzed—. [...] These are the Novels which enlarge the primitive Capabilities of the Heart, & which cannot impugn the Sense or be any Dereliction of character, of the most anti-peurile [sic] Man, to be conversant with. (403–4)

Sir Edward's over-elocuted opinions about sympathy prevent Charlotte from sympathizing with him at all: '[i]f I understand you aright [...] our taste in Novels is not at all the same', she replies to him flatly (404). Austen suggests through Sir Edward's monologues to the mostly silent Charlotte that some methods of reading, produced in this case out of the idle lifestyle of an impoverished Regency aristocrat, make sympathy not only impossible but unfavourable, and the prospect of marriage to such a person more impossible and unfavourable still. Sir Edward is not the only ex-emplar of such reading in Sanditon. Mrs Whitby, the proprietor of Sanditon's lending library, appears at the beginning of the fragment's sixth chapter 'in her inner room, reading one of her own Novels, for want of Employment'. (389) At the centre of Sanditon's busiest social venue—and its repository of literature—sits a solitary, idle female novelist: a writer and a reader collapsed in a lonely dystopia of boredom.

After beginning this critique of hypochondria in *Sanditon*, Austen remained aware of her own illness's tendency to isolate her from her friends, or to make her socially ridiculous. In a letter written from Chawton on May 22, 1817 to Anne Sharp, Austen wittily admits to being 'really a very genteel, portable sort of an Invalid' in an account of her travel to the hospital at Winchester to receive treatment during the worst bout of her illness to date. The incongruent pairing of the languid adjective 'genteel' with the staccato notes of the word 'portable' suggest aurally that Austen cheerfully directed her irony at herself as eagerly as she had applied it to Mr Parker and his hypochondriac siblings. Later in this letter is another striking personal reference to the kind of monologue she had been developing among the *Sanditon* hypochondriacs: 'Beleive [sic] me', Austen assures Sharp, 'I was interested in all you wrote, though with all the Egotism of an Invalid I write only of myself'. After serially lampooning the *Sanditon* characters who speak only of themselves, she admonishes this tendency in herself—but, in another twist of her persistent irony, not until after she has permitted herself the indulgence. In Austen's last letters, there are more difficult moments as well, particularly Austen's constant worry that she is burdening Cassandra, and the rest of her family, with her care (494–95, 497). Thus we can see that, while Austen was sometimes engaged in the wry narration of her own illness, she was careful to check this mode not only with self-mockery but with a persistent sense of her own social obligations to her relatives, particularly her sister. In Austen's own experience of illness, therefore, family obligation was a critical and comforting protection against the 'Egotism of an Invalid' and *folie en famille*, a protection that she purposefully had written out of *Sanditon* altogether.

In *Sanditon*, in fact, there only seem to be the relatively undeveloped Charlotte and, less developed still, Clara Brereton, standing against the solipsism of the other characters, who exhibit what R. W. Chapman called 'a certain roughness and harshness of satire [...] due in part to lack of revision'. As Sutherland observes, 'Chapman [...] felt sure (following a hint from Anna Lefroy) that Austen would have toned down the caricatures of Mr Parker, his sister Diana, Lady Denham, and Sir Edward: "she would have smoothed these coarse strokes, so strikingly different from the mellow pencilings of *Persuasion*"' (Chapman qtd. in Sutherland 175). Critic Francis Warre Cornish discouraged altogether critical interpretation of *Sanditon* because of these rougher sections: while the fragment 'contains some promising sketches', on his view, 'it would be useless, if not impertinent, to pass an opinion on a work so obviously incomplete' (231). These more conservative approaches to the manuscript—and the caution they urge to critics who would take advantage of the suggestive power of fragments—are important to bear in mind when interpreting Charlotte and Clara: a fragment cannot support notions of authorial intention in the ways a published novel can.

But other critics suggest that Austen was not drastically off her mark in the manuscript she left at her death: 'a degree of savagery would, I think, have persisted', Chapman added, in his explanation of *Sanditon*'s satirized characters (208). As Brian Southam has argued, 'the modifications to the characters, especially to the four eccentrics, are not in the direction of toning down, of de-carricaturising, but tend to enforce and heighten their traits and eccentricities' (130). Sutherland notes more generally of the *Sanditon* holograph that 'every page is filled, implying that no large-scale revision of the draft in this form was contemplated' (172). The textual features we have assessed—development of hypochondria as a figure for Regency life, the lack of viable would-be husbands (and the dynastic narratives they afford), the formalisation of solipsism into asyndetic monologues, even a theory of reading—tend to corroborate these views of a more 'finished' *Sanditon* manuscript.

If Austen intended the caricatures of the Parkers and the Denhams, then we can see Charlotte and Clara as providing a kind of textual relief from the exhausting self-involvement of the others. That *Sanditon* was calculated to explore what a heroine might do under the relatively serious narrative pressure of being unable to speak (like Dorothy Wordsworth at Tintern Abbey, or Mary in Robert Burns's poem) is made astonishingly manifest in the dynamic Austen achieves briefly between Charlotte and Clara toward the fragment's end. Although short, it remains *Sanditon*'s most psychologically developed relationship. As Charlotte is making the approach to Lady Denham's home at Sanditon House, this is what she sees:

> [the] Entrance Gates were so much in a corner of the Grounds or Paddock, so near one of its Boundaries, that an outside fence was at first almost pressing on the road—til an angle *here*, & a curve *there* threw them to a better distance. The Fence was a proper park Paling in

excellent condition; with clusters of fine Elms, or rows of old Thorns following its line almost everywhere.—*Almost* must be stipulated—for there were vacant spaces—& through one of these, Charlotte as soon as they entered the Enclosure, caught a glimpse over the pales of something White & Womanish on the other side;—it was something which immediately brought Miss B. into her head—& stepping to the pales, she saw indeed—and very decidedly, in spite of the Mist; Miss B— seated, not far before her, at the foot of the bank which sloped down from the outside of the Paling & which a narrow Path seemed to skirt along;—Miss Brereton seated, apparently very composedly—& Sir E. D. by her side. (426)

Like the approach to Sotherton in *Mansfield Park*, which illuminates Fanny Price's place in the web of attractions and sexual jealousies suspended among the members of the party in transit, the approach to Sanditon House elaborates Charlotte's position in Sanditon, which is marked by her desire for clarity in the midst of uncertainty. While the odd composition of this scene might tend at first to suggest a lack of clarity and redundancy of detail that would have been removed from the passage in revision, Sutherland has shown that the reverse is true: as in other revisions to the fragment, Austen's manuscript shows her heightening, rather than reducing, the passage's 'roughness of finish, perceptual opacity, and the leveling of relevant and non-relevant information' (184). Through these disorienting discursive techniques, as well as a morning mist that threatens further to obscure her perceptions, Charlotte receives a series of vague impressions that make her think of Clara Brereton, who is finally confirmed to be seated next to Sir Edward, as if in a sketch or painting 'very composedly'. 'Like Alice in Wonderland', Sutherland notes, '[Charlotte] experiences the loss of peripheral vision that inhabiting a strange world entails' (190). It is notable, therefore, that she achieves a pronounced perceptual clarity when she encounters Clara—even in spite of the 'Mist', which overthrows the perceptive faculties of *Sanditon*'s other characters; Mrs Parker, who is travelling to Sanditon House with Charlotte, sees 'nothing' of the scene.

Earlier in the fragment, Clara has similar effects on Charlotte's consciousness. On their way from Willingden to Sanditon, when Charlotte is by turns overwhelmed and confused by Mr Parker's effusions on the resort and its inhabitants, he also speaks

warmly of Clara Brereton, & the interest of his story increased very much with the introduction of such a Character. Charlotte listened with more than amusement now;—it was solicitude & Enjoyment, as she heard her described to be lovely, amiable, gentle, unassuming, conducting herself uniformly with great good sense, & evidently gaining by her innate worth, on the affections of her Patroness.—Beauty, Sweetness, Poverty & Dependence, do not want the imagination of a Man to operate upon. With due exceptions—Woman feels for Woman very promptly & compassionately. (377–78)

Clara is the only person in *Sanditon* for whom Charlotte exhibits any kind of fellow feeling. In fact, for characters like Lady Denham, Charlotte finds it 'impossible even to affect sympathy' (401). Early in the fragment, Charlotte's sympathy for Clara is figured as an intense attraction that is related to genre: 'Charlotte could see in [Clara] only the most perfect representation of whatever Heroine might be most beautiful & bewitching [...].—Perhaps it might be partly owing to her having just issued from a Circulating Library' (391). Like Catherine Morland's tendency to expect the gothic everywhere in *Northanger Abbey*, Charlotte is eagerly prepared to find heroines in *Sanditon*.

Charlotte's rather superficial fascination with Clara becomes much more complicated, however, when she discovers Clara in a compromising situation alone with Sir Edward. At first, the view 'could not but strike [Charlotte] rather unfavourably with regard to Clara', but this assessment dissipates when Charlotte concludes that Clara's poverty is 'a situation which must not be judged with severity' (426–27). Then a striking thing happens: Charlotte, suspending even her disdain for Sir Edward, cannot 'but think of the extreme difficulty which secret Lovers must have in finding a proper spot for their stolen Interviews' (426–27). In addition to feeling sympathy for Clara (in spite of her own aversions to Sir Edward), Charlotte is eager for Clara's reputation to remain intact: '[Charlotte] was glad to perceive that nothing had been discerned by Mrs Parker; if Charlotte had not been considerably the tallest of the two, Miss B.'s white ribbons might not have fallen within the ken of *her* more observant eyes' (426). Charlotte, normally ruled by her first impressions like Elizabeth Bennet, is willing to make a long series of exceptions for Clara, whom she barely knows.

One reading of these scenes is that Charlotte Heywood, like Sir Edward, is just another bad reader of literature, all too eager to see opening in front of her the seduction of a Clarissa by a Lovelace, or far too enamoured of Clara to judge her honestly. But this does not square with what we know of Charlotte's willingness to revise for herself the impressions she receives from others: 'She is thoroughly mean', Charlotte concludes of Lady Denham, '[Mr Parker] is too kind hearted to see clearly.—I must judge for myself. (402) Nor does this reading work with a detail from Clara's consciousness, that she 'had not the least intention of being seduced' by Sir Edward, for it would require *Sanditon*'s narrator, in this rare example of free indirect discourse, to be wrong (405).

It seems more likely that these interactions between Charlotte and Clara are the fragment's tentative attempt to represent intimacy, a burgeoning love, between Charlotte and Clara, which Austen had once longed for herself in Bath's tedious society: '[t]he distance between Charlotte and the world she encounters and attempts to analyse is rarely bridged', Sutherland notes, but these rare occasions of understanding are almost always marked by Clara's presence (190). This is compelling evidence that Austen was beginning to establish bonds between these two young women as a viable alternative to the forms of hypochondriasis in *Sanditon* and the failing country-house system.

Tentative though it must remain, this reading sets the *Sanditon* manuscript as a site of competing notions of the future of English society: fellow feeling, and the national cohesion it implies, is embodied by young women and set in contradistinction to those who would erode social relations through excessive attention to the self alone. Charlotte's attempt to identify with Clara in the final pages of the fragment suggests that Austen may have been working out a narrative mechanism, similar to Wollstonecraft's in *Maria, or The Wrongs of Woman* (1792), through which two women might constitute a community apart from the pathologic individualisms of Sanditon. Critically, the sympathy Charlotte shows for Clara at the end of the *Sanditon* fragment marks a connection categorically different from friendships between related sisters in *Sense and Sensibility* and *Pride and Prejudice*, and the extra-familial friendship in *Emma* between Emma Woodhouse and Harriet Smith—which, founded on Emma's belief that Harriet is the daughter of an aristocrat, must end when the difference between their social positions is at last revealed. Instead, Charlotte's intimacy with Clara would seem to transcend categorical barriers of family and class: in fact, these characters have no more in common than their unfortunate situation in a nation and narrative made strange by hypochondria, where marriage seems at least highly undesirable, if not structurally impossible. What begins in *Sanditon* to constitute a heroine, therefore, is not Elizabeth Bennet's (or Princess Charlotte's) highly gendered capacity to break from her family in self-actualising companionate marriage and motherhood by which she (with the nation) will be reconstituted. Rather, Austen envisions in Charlotte Heywood a heroine whose primary psychological inclination is to cultivate homosocial bonds between women and see in another the possibility of a heroine.

Notes

1   So important was it for Britons to separate Charlotte from the rest of her family that something of a public campaign to this purpose became visible in literary and print media dating from 1812 to 1815, the years when Charlotte was in the process of selecting a husband. Lord Byron, in the 1812 poem 'Lines to a Lady

Weeping', characterised Charlotte's treatment at her father's hands as 'a Sire's disgrace, a realm's decay', drawing in these two possessive clauses the ready analogy between the 'disgrace' of George IV and the 'decay' of Great Britain while setting Charlotte apart from these deficiencies. After Charlotte's death, Byron would emphasize Charlotte's singularity in Canto IV of *Childe Harold's Pilgrimage*, calling her 'The fair-hair'd Daughter of the Isles' and 'The love of millions!'—appositives which hail the princess and elide her family: 'the Isles' of Britain stand clearly in the place of her parents (Behrendt 24–25). Accordingly, Charlotte's wedding—to Leopold of Saxe-Coburg, whom she chose over the Hereditary Prince William of Orange, whom her father had selected—inspired hopeful acclimation of a renewed national wholeness at a time otherwise marked by widespread social unrest; the *Augustan Review*, for example, proclaimed in June of 1816: '[Our rejoicings on the occasion] spring out of an event auspicious to the royal family, because it is so to the nation at large' (qtd. in Behrendt 11). Charlotte's refusal of William in favour of Leopold, which marked a royal young woman's ability seriously to contravene at least one of her parents, had acquired nationalistic resonance as well. The public reason Charlotte provided for ending her relationship with William was her nationalist aversion to spending any part of the year outside of Great Britain. This was grist to the mill of the anti-Regent Whig press, who characterized Charlotte's prospective marriage to William as the tyranny of a father who was trying to get her out of his political way, and, worse, 'an assault on British liberty' (Behrendt 18). Particularly poignant for many Britons was the idea that Charlotte, strongly identified as the queen under whom the British nation would cast off despotic power while retaining its monarchy, would be forced by that same despotic power to leave her people and her beloved homeland.

2 See Anna Clark's study, *Scandal: The Sexual Politics of the British Constitution* for a full account of these events and their relationship to Britain's constitutional monarchy, particularly: the dementia of George III, the financial excess of George IV, the sex scandals of George IV and Caroline of Brunswick, and Princess Caroline's resistance to her father.

3 Austen is at least partly responsible for this cultural effect. Her early fiction had posited women's self-actualisation in marriage as a method for imagining the future of the nation: the marriages of Elizabeth Bennet and Emma Woodhouse dramatise renewed community cohesion in the country-house system that implies an ascendent national future. Even in the marriage of the Bertrams, compromised by Mansfield Park's ongoing connection to Antigua enslavement, or the Wentworths, who take to the sea instead of the country estate to seek their fortune, Fanny and Anne are the vessels of a meaningful national future in their break from compromised circumstances into companionate marriage.

4 For a full-length study of nineteenth-century gendering of mental illness, see Elaine Showalter.

5 Strangely, critics hardly mention Austen's residence in Bath in their readings of *Sanditon*, tending instead to set the fragment in the context of Austen's final illness and death. We must remember, however, that this is a context that Austen very likely did not share, especially because she left off writing *Sanditon* several months before her final decline. Even Austen's last letters from May of 1817, which we will consider at the end of this chapter, suggest her belief that she might be getting better.

6 *Folie en famille* is a form of group psychosis (similar to the better-known *folie à deux*) in which family members, like the Parkers, share, and by sharing amplify, a set of psychotic tendencies.

7 Here, I am drawing on Caroline Levine's distinction between genre and form, in which genres are historically contingent, but forms are portable across genres and history (13–14).

Works Cited

Austen, Jane. *The Novels of Jane Austen*, edited by Robert William Chapman, 6 vols. Oxford UP, 1923–74.

Barker-Benfield, Graham John. *The Culture of Sensibility: Sex and Society in Eighteenth-Century Britain*. U of Chicago P, 1992.

Behrendt, Stephen. *Royal Mourning and Regency Culture: Elegies and Memorials of Princess Charlotte*. St. Martin's P, 1997.

Chapman, Robert William, *Jane Austen, Facts and Problems*. Oxford UP, 1948.

Cheyne, George. *The English Malady*, edited by Roy Porter. Routledge, 1991.

Clark, Anna. *Scandal: The Sexual Politics of the British Constitution*. Princeton UP, 2004.

Cornish, Francis Warre. *Jane Austen*. 'English Men of Letters' series. Macmillan, 1913.

Doody, Margaret. *Jane Austen's Names: Riddles, Persons, Places*. U of Chicago P, 2015.

Duckworth, Alistair M. *The Improvement of the Estate: A Study of Jane Austen's Novels*. Johns Hopkins UP, 1994.

Grinnel, George C. *The Age of Hypochondria: Interpreting Romantic Health and Illness*. Macmillan Palgrave, 2010.

Harris, Jocelyn. *Satire, Celebrity, and Politics in Jane Austen*. Bucknell UP, 2017.

Keats, John. *The Letters of John Keats: 1814–1821*, edited by Hyder Rollins. Harvard UP, 1958.

Levine, Caroline. *Forms: Whole, Rhythm, Hierarchy, Network*. Princeton UP, 2015.

Miller, David A. 'The Late Jane Austen.' *Raritan*, vol. 10, 1990, pp. 55–80.

Poovey, Mary. *The Proper Lady and the Woman Writer: Ideology as Style in the Works of Mary Wollstonecraft, Mary Shelley, and Jane Austen*. The U of Chicago P, 1984.

Southam, Brian Charles. *Jane Austen's Literary Manuscripts*. Oxford UP, 1964.

Showalter, Elaine. *The Female Malady: Women, Madness, and English Culture, 1830–1980*. Pantheon Books, 1985.

Sutherland, Kathryn. *Jane Austen's Textual Lives: From Aeschylus to Bollywood*. Oxford UP, 2005.

Thompson, James. *Between Self and World: The Novels of Jane Austen*. Pennsylvania State UP, 1988.

Tomalin, Claire. *Jane Austen: A Life*. Vintage Books, 1997.

Wiltshire, John. *Jane Austen and the Body*. Cambridge UP, 1992.

Wordsworth, William. 'Lines Written a Few Miles above Tintern Abbey, on Revisiting the Banks of the Wye during a Tour.' *Lyrical Ballads and Other Poems*, edited by James Butler and Karen Green. Cornell UP, 1992.

19

JANE AUSTEN AND THE WHITEWASHED PAST

Olivia Murphy

UNIVERSITY OF SYDNEY

In the months leading up to the bicentenary of Jane Austen's death controversy arose from an unexpected quarter. In the *Chronicle of Higher Education*, Nicole Wright detailed her research into Austen's popularity—or at least the frequent referencing of Austen's name and novels—on the blogs and social media fora of the so-called 'Alt-Right'.[1] Wright discovered that, amongst the posturings of avowed misogynists, neo-Nazis, and fellow travellers, Austen has become an icon of racial and sexual purity, feminine obedience, and whiteness. Wright saw that Austen's popularity was being used by right-wing extremists in order to make their fascist ideology more palatable and attractive to the unconverted:

> By comparing their movement not to the nightmare Germany of Hitler and Goebbels, but instead to the cozy England of Austen—a much-beloved author with a centuries-long fandom and an unebbing academic following—the alt-right normalizes itself in the eyes of ordinary people. It also subtly panders to the nostalgia of the Brexiters, with their vision of a better, bygone Britain. Such references nudge readers who happen upon alt-right sites to think that perhaps white supremacists aren't so different from mainstream folks. (Wright)

'Austen', here, is crucially not—or not just—the Jane Austen who lived 1775–1817, the author of six complex and endlessly fascinating novels, but rather a collapsed metonym for a particular time and place that never existed, an aesthetic mediated more through screen adaptations than through any engagement with the novels themselves. Wright details in her article the various ways in which this 'Austen' is being deployed in the new fascist imaginary, outlining three chief uses to which the novelist's name is put. 'Venturing into the mire', she explains, 'I found that there are several variations of alt-right Jane Austen: (1) symbol of sexual purity; (2) standard-bearer of a vanished white traditional culture; and (3) exception that proves the rule of female inferiority' (Wright). Even in the world of white supremacists and *soi disant* Men's Rights Activists, it appears, Austen must still do double and triple duty as all things to all people. In Wright's view, Austen's rhetorical role in this milieu can be reduced to the novelist—or what is often irritatingly referred to as the 'world' of her novels—as a readily understood shorthand for a sort of vanished utopia of racial and sexual purity that might be realised once more, and a guide for how to behave in the event. 'On the popular blog of the alt-right publisher Counter-Currents, Wright notes as an example,

> the world of Austen's novels is extolled as a prototype for the 'racial dictatorship' of tomorrow. One commentator wrote, 'If, after the ethnostate is created, we revert back to an

Austen-like world, we males ought to endure severe sacrifices as well … If traditional marriage à la P&P is going to be imposed, again, in an ethnostate, we must behave like gentlemen'.

Wright's analysis of the popularity of Austen within the far-right blogosphere focuses on the ways in which such commentators and misogynistic fantasists repurpose Austen as an ideal, anti-feminist figurehead. Wright's very brief article offered a glimpse into how persistent misogynistic readings of canonical texts can be, even when those texts were written by an author who has been championed by every wave of feminism to date. Her findings are suggestive of a range of fundamental problems with how Austen—and perhaps even literature more generally—operates in a patriarchy. The reception of Wright's article, however, almost entirely ignored analysis of Austen-themed misogyny, to focus exclusively on questions of racism.

This was, in part, a matter of context. In March 2017, when the article appeared, President Donald Trump had recently taken office after a bitter election campaign in which racial tensions were overtly and at times exuberantly aggravated (the article was illustrated with a picture of Austen in a red 'Make America Great Again' cap). The Black Lives Matter movement, protesting against the killing of overwhelmingly young black men by police, was well established.[2] In the UK, anti-European, anti-immigration, and white nationalist sentiment had renewed visibility after the plebiscite to leave the European Union ('Brexit') and in efforts by the Home Office to restrict immigration through mass deportations, which would later be found to have disproportionately affected black residents.[3] While Wright's analysis succinctly demonstrated the ways in which racism and misogyny intersect in alt-right discussions of Austen, when her article came to the attention of *The Guardian, The New York Times,* and other *bien pensant* organs, their attention was reserved for the bloggers' racist rather than their sexist comments, and specifically the far-right's praise of Austen as a model of whiteness and racial purity (that is, only the second of Wright's three major points).

It was references to Austen in these frightening, abhorrent online discussions that became the central concern of articles written in response to Wright's findings. 'Jane Austen has alt-right fans? Heavens to Darcy!' ran the headline in the *New York Times*, its author claiming that 'many Janeites responded to the notion of an alt-right Austen as if they had been personally trolled' (Schuessler). Eminent scholars of Austen were consulted, although in a rush to stir up further controversy their comments were clearly taken out of context by journalists eager to reinscribe Austen's stereotypical connection to all things middle class and unobjectionable.[4] Thus the *New York Times* quoted Elaine Bander's objection that all the Janeites she knows are 'rational, compassionate, liberal-minded people'—an observation with which I can only concur (Schuessler). In the *Guardian* Bharat Tandon made the excellent—if largely ignored—point that it was unlikely the far-right community had much actual knowledge of Austen's novels, a point that this chapter will further investigate (Kean).

In this chapter I wish to address why Jane Austen has become so vulnerable to co-option by would-be and actual Nazis, and how Janeites and journalists alike might struggle to defend her reputation. To be perfectly clear, there is no evidence whatsoever to suggest that Jane Austen was ever a white supremacist. Such racist doctrines were evolving during her lifetime, but they remained very much subject to debate, and were far from universally accepted. The ideology of racism lagged behind the practice of violent, systematic, and internationalised racial oppression. The eminent historian of the slave trade, Catherine Hall, notes that approximately '12 million African captives were forcibly transported to the Americas in the early modern period', well before any coherent discourse of racism can be identified (Hall). In the later eighteenth century, racist ideology was constructed in order to provide moral justification for the fantastically profitable, almost unimaginably murderous, and increasingly unpopular slave trade: as Peter Fryer succinctly notes, 'English racism was born of greed' (8). Writers extolling white supremacist viewpoints were inevitably in the pay of the West Indian lobby or, like John Locke, had their own money invested in the slave trade

(Fryer 151). Science was yet to offer its unqualified support for racism (as it would from the mid-nineteenth to mid-twentieth centuries); while the taxonomist Carl Linné tried to claim an inherent white superiority, the comparative anatomist Johann Friedrich Blumenbach, in a report much quoted in England, declared that the mental capacities of black people 'are not inferior to the rest of the human race' (qtd in Innes 24). There were many other writers in the period, white and black, who contested nascent racist ideology and campaigned for the abolition of the slave trade. Austen herself, who is difficult to catch in anything resembling a political opinion, wrote to her sister that she was 'in love with' the abolitionist campaigner Thomas Clarkson (24 January 1813; *Letters* 207).

What this minor scandal over Austen's popularity amongst the far right suggests is that Austen—or rather the fictional 'world' of her novels—has for many people come to be a kind of shorthand for an all-white England of conservative values and decorous feminine behaviour. Consider, for example, the first comment appended to Wright's original article. In a post that becomes increasingly more disturbing as it progresses, Joshua Strodtbeck writes that 'the reason Jane Austen's characters don't have thoughts about hyperdiversity [by which neologism Strodtbeck seems to indicate any society deviating from 'racial purity'] is the same reason they don't have thoughts about the internet'. Strodtbeck's point appears to be that cosmopolitan societies have only existed since the late twentieth century, and that therefore all of Austen's characters are white, just as her 'world' is white.

This is, simply, wrong. The white England of these assumptions is a myth, and always has been. It is a myth that has been allowed to stand only through racist assumptions and a determined ignorance about the past. Peter Fryer points out that there 'were Africans in Britain before the English came', with imperial Roman soldiers from the African provinces stationed in Britannia from at least the third century. Black people appear again in Scottish and English records—albeit in small numbers—from the fifteenth to seventeenth centuries. Elizabeth I's mercenary attempts to rid England of its black inhabitants were wholly unsuccessful. From the 1650s the black population of Britain began to grow steadily, and it was still growing in Austen's time.[5]

I use the term 'black' here largely because it is the most common term in use both by Austen's contemporaries, in histories of black British experience, and in the critical literature responding to black people's writing. While this unfortunately sets up exactly the black/white binary that re-inforces racist thinking, my chief concern here is to make visible what racist interpretations of the past consistently make invisible.[6] 'Black' people in Britain at the turn of the eighteenth century included people of recent sub-Saharan and North African descent, people from the Indian sub-continent and from Sri Lanka, and, increasingly, indigenous peoples from various parts of the world. This far-from-homogenous population fluctuated greatly throughout the eighteenth century, in response to its changing legal status in Britain and to geopolitical events. Contemporary estimates in the 1770s range between ten and twenty thousand, out of a total population of less than ten million, but this was essentially guesswork.[7] Some, but not all, eighteenth-century black Britons were or had been slaves (including those bought and sold in London and the powerful slave ports of Bristol and Liverpool). In the earlier part of the eighteenth century the vast majority had been taken from their families as children and brought to Britain against their will (Fryer 58–60). Nevertheless, they formed a flourishing and mutually supportive community, especially in London: Peter Fryer writes that from 'about the middle of the eighteenth century there is ... evidence of cohesion, solidarity, and mutual help among black people in Britain. They had developed a lively social life. And they were finding ways of expressing their political aspirations' (67). Those who remained in bondage were also finding ways to effect their emancipation. By the 1790s, when Austen was beginning to write her novels, 'black slaves in Britain voted with their feet', running away from their owners and establishing new lives, 'encouraged, and to some extent protected', by unclear laws and, in London at least, the support of white working class allies who since the mid-eighteenth century had made it 'not merely difficult but dangerous for masters to try to recapture' runaways (Fryer 142, 71). It was not only the London mob that sought to protect the lives and liberties of black people in the period. The movement to abolish the slave trade was the largest mass political movement Britain had ever seen, involving tens of thousands of men and women and transcending class and sectarian lines to launch hundreds of petitions over decades of frustrated effort.[8]

As Britain's involvement in the triangular slave trade increased, so did the number of black people living in Britain, their cultural contribution to British life, and, above all, their economic impact. The exploitation of black people provided the economic basis for much of Britain's Industrial Revolution and its most conspicuous wealth, wealth that would continue to drive Britain's imperial expansion long after slavery was officially abolished in her colonies.[9]

By the time Austen was born no Briton could ignore the presence of black people in what was indubitably an ethnically diverse society. Only the ways in which the Regency period is mediated to us make it relatively easy to maintain ignorance of its ethnic diversity. We know very little about what most Regency-era people looked like. Only the wealthiest and most famous had their images memorialised in oil paints and marble busts, and only the most famous of these remain on accessible display in institutions such as London's National Portrait Gallery. Our available images of Austen herself exist only because of her sister's amateur interest in watercolour portraits, which the author's small lifetime fame and greater posthumous celebrity led her family to preserve after her death. For the vast majority of people, no image and little other indication of their racial or ethnic identity survives. We do not know very much about the lives of black people living in Regency Britain, just as we know very little about the great majority of people living in Britain in this period. What is true of most Regency Britons is likewise true of black Regency Britons: only when they come to the attention of historians—usually through becoming famous in their lifetime, or by being related to the famous—do we take note of them.

In eighteenth- and early-nineteenth-century England, a significant number of black people worked in the service industry, as servants to wealthy households, as shopkeepers, and as publicans, none of which are professions much studied by historians or literary historians. David Dabydeen has studied images of black people in contemporary prints, where they appear as 'footmen, coachmen, pageboys, soldiers, sailors, musicians, actresses, prostitutes, beggars, prisoners, pimps, highway robbers, street-sellers, and other similar roles' (Dabydeen 19–20). Although after 1731 black people in London were theoretically forbidden to learn trades, they also worked as cabinetmakers, actors, cooks, political activists, librarians, fencing masters, agricultural labourers, hairdressers, botanists, laundrymaids, seamstresses and nursery-maids (Fryer 74–76, 60). Most famously of all, black people served in almost all military divisions as musicians: the 'review' that Mr Bennet promises as a reward for militia-mad Kitty in *Pride and Prejudice* would certainly have included the 'astounding', crowd-delighting black drummers, forerunners of modern-day military spectacles such as the Edinburgh Tattoo (Fryer 87, *PP* 331). Black people in eighteenth-century England did tend to be upwardly mobile, but scholarship of this period typically ignores anyone outside of the fractionally small upper middle classes (in contemporary terms, the wealthy gentry). Unless black Britons were very up-wardly mobile indeed, that is, they remain all but invisible. We know almost nothing about the workers at the two exclusively black London brothels, for instance, but there have been books on the subject of Sarah Baartman, Dido Elizabeth Belle, and Samuel Johnson's heir Francis Barber, all well-known black people living in England during Austen's lifetime.[10]

One point worth making is that we may well be studying works by black writers from this period without realising. Just as Virginia Woolf suggested that 'Anon., who wrote so many poems without signing them, was often a woman', we would do well to discard assumptions about authors' racial or ethnic identity (63). There are of course well-known black writers from this period, such as Olaudo Equiano or Ignatius Sancho, both of whom were prominent in late-eighteenth-century literary circles. There are still many writers from the period whose names are uncertain, and whose ethnic and racial backgrounds are wholly lost to us. To assume, implausibly, that all of these writers were white is simply to impose our own racist expectations upon the past, further whitewashing history.

Racism itself can sometimes look rather different from an eighteenth-century perspective. As Fryer notes, 'ethnocentric generalizations about dark skinned people' were available to ease 'English consciences about enslaving Africans', generalizations that eventually would be 'woven into a more or less coherent racist ideology' (7). Where racist statements do appear in eighteenth-century letters, however, they are as likely to focus on anxieties surrounding class mobility as on anything that a twenty-first century reader would immediately recognise as racialised discourse. Hester Thrale Piozzi (always reliably rude about everyone) noted that, in London,

> Men of colour in the rank of gentlemen: a black Lady, covered with finery, in the Pit at the Opera, and tawny children playing [in] the Squares,—the gardens of the Squares I mean,—with their Nurses, afford ample proofs [of the abolitionist leaders] Hannah More and Mr Wilberforce's success in breaking down the *walls of separation*.

Thrale Piozzi's concern here is not so much with race *per se*, but with the ways in which these black people's enjoyment of elite eighteenth-century sociability suggested, in her words, 'all ranks, all customs, all religions, *jumbled together*' (original emphasis, 243–44). Ambivalence about 'jumbling' can be seen in Maria Edgeworth's revisions to her second novel *Belinda*, in which she capitulated to the racist qualms of her father and professional critics. As Kathryn Kirkpatrick notes, in 'the 1801 edition Edgeworth had not only brought her heroine to the brink of marriage with the Creole gentlemen Mr Vincent, she had also married that gentleman's black servant Juba to an English farm girl. The lengthy cuts and revisions which Edgeworth made in her 1810 edition censored both relationships' (331–48). For those less sneeringly fastidious than Thrale Piozzi and Richard Lovell Edgeworth, however, what we would think of as Regency Britain's cosmopolitanism—partly, of course, the sequel of its rapidly and often brutally expanding trade and political empires—was seen by many as proof of the nation's growing global importance. In Anna Letitia Barbauld's radical poem *Eighteen Hundred and Eleven*, for instance, the 'mighty city' of London is characterised by streets on which 'the turban'd Moslem, bearded Jew,/and woolly Afric, me[e]t the brown Hindu' (152–61: 157, ll. 159, 165–66). William Wordsworth makes the same point in *The Prelude*, finding in London

> Among the crowd all specimens of man,
> Through all the colours which the sun bestows,
> And every character of form and face:
> The Swede, the Russian; from the genial south,
> The Frenchman and the Spaniard; from remote
> America, the Hunter-Indian; Moors,
> Malays, Lascars, the Tartar, the Chinese,
> And Negro Ladies in white muslin Gowns. (540, qtd in Innes 12)

White muslin gowns were the height of fashion: Wordsworth's 'Negro Ladies' belong to the up-wardly mobile black population that so annoyed Piozzi, those (including wealthy heiresses and schoolchildren sent to England by their well-to-do African families for a European education) that belonged to the social and economic strata from which Austen draws her characters.

The slippage I have used here, between the imagined settings of the novels Austen wrote and the historical world in which she lived, is deliberate. It imitates the ways in which, both for scholars, fans, and those who know little about Austen's works, the realist scenes of her literature are all-too-easily conflated with the realities of Regency-era England. Austen's realism, however, is a carefully stylised invention: it is far from a mimetic representation of lived experience. While it is thus historically implausible that Austen never encountered black people, it does not necessarily follow that her version of realism was accurate in this sense. Let us consider the evidence of the novels.

Much has been made of Miss Lambe, the young 'half Mulatto' heiress who appears in Austen's unfinished last novel, which we know by the name of 'Sanditon'. A close reading reveals that we are told little about Miss Lambe's appearance: in fact, nothing at all. We do learn that she is rich, a fact that was apparently far more important to Austen than the colour of her skin. Her social status seems clear: of the 'young ladies' boarding with Mrs Griffiths, she is 'beyond comparison the most important and precious, as she paid in proportion to her fortune' and is 'always of the first consequence in every plan' (*Later Manuscripts* 201–2). There is little else about Miss Lambe, as the narrative soon breaks off. Austen, like many of her contemporaries, refrains from offering readers much in the way of descriptions of her characters' appearance. The sort of minute, highly racialised, phrenologically inflected description we think of as belonging to the realist novel would not become established until the Victorian period. Austen actually provides far *less* description of her characters than was typical in novels of the long eighteenth century, especially in respect to her heroines. We know, seeing through Darcy's eyes, that Elizabeth Bennet has a 'light and pleasing' (but slightly asymmetric) figure, and 'fine eyes' (*PP* 26). What colour those eyes are we never learn, let alone what colour Elizabeth's skin or hair might be. As for Darcy, we know only that he is tall. *Northanger Abbey*'s Catherine Morland has 'sallow skin … dark lank hair, and strong features' (*NA* 5). Of all Austen's characters, Marianne Dashwood of *Sense and Sensibility* attracts the most specific description. She is taller than her sister Elinor, and 'a beautiful girl', with 'very brown' skin, and 'eyes, which were very dark' (*SS* 55). There is no compelling historical or textual basis for casting these coveted roles as white.

Why, then, do so many people assume that Austen's world is so white? Arguably this failure of historical imagination is due largely to Austen's astonishing success as a source of adaptation. Her novels' popularity as raw material for film and television means that, for decades now, most people—including, as Tandon surmises, the white supremacists pressing her into service—have experienced her 'world' largely, if not exclusively, through the medium of the screen. On the screen the long eighteenth century (let alone the more distant past) has, most certainly, been whitewashed. To date, no screen adaptation of an Austen novel set in something like its original time and place has featured any black actors. *Pride and Prejudice and Zombies* only briefly gestures towards connections between the slave trade and the zombie infestation of England in its opening, nor does it explore the Haitian *zonbi* tradition in any depth. It has no black actors in major or supporting roles.[11] Even Patricia Rozema's 1999 adaptation of *Mansfield Park*—the first adaptation to engage seriously with the source of the Bertram family's wealth in its slave plantations in Antigua—did so only through images of enslaved Africans and offscreen chanting (sketches of slaves being whipped and raped, a wooden side-table in the shape of a black waiter).[12] Ethnic and racial diversity was an historical reality throughout the anglophone world and beyond in this period, and yet popular representations of the past, with very few exceptions, exclusively feature white actors. It is easy to assume that Austen's world is all-white when all our best-known images of her period suggest just that.

There is a great deal that scholars and creative writers and artists can do to redress this damaging and unhistorical imbalance. We can ensure we teach the work of black eighteenth-century British writers such as Equiano and Mary Prince and that of anti-racist scholars such as Peter Fryer's *Staying Power: The History of Black People in Britain* (1984) and, more recently, David Olusoga's *Black and British: A Forgotten History* (2016). There are several comprehensive works on black British writers from the period, such as *A History of Black and Asian Writing in Britain, 1700–2000* (2002) by C. L. Innes, Helena Woodard's *African-British Writings in the Eighteenth Century* (1999), and *Black Writers in Britain, 1760–1890* (1995) edited by Paul Edwards and David Dabydeen.[13] We can protest when film and television productions set in the periods we study make inappropriate casting choices. And we can, finally, make recommendations about how to redress this injustice. There are a number of recent models for how this might work.

Ideally, screen producers would introduce 'colour-blind' casting for works set in the past. This has been standard practice in opera for decades and has lately become customary in many theatre companies. It is now routine for Shakespeare-focused companies like Australia's Bell Shakespeare and the UK's Royal Shakespeare Company to have their early modern plays performed by ethnically diverse casts. Lin-Manuel Miranda's *Hamilton: An American Musical*, playing on Broadway since 2015, based on a non-fiction biography of American 'founding father' Alexander Hamilton (c. 1755–1804), and a recent musical adaptation of part of Tolstoy's *War and Peace, Natasha, Pierre and the Great Comet of 1812*, both used colour-blind casting in their productions.

The extraordinary success of *Hamilton*—one of the most important and productive interventions in the reception of eighteenth-century history to date—shows what is at stake in representations of the past. *Hamilton* is distinct from the other examples considered here, as its characters are historical subjects known to have been white, played by, for the most part, non-white actors.[14] This casting is, moreover, central to the meaning of the musical's narrative. *Hamilton* uses American musical forms—hip-hop and rap, blues, R&B, and soul—forms developed by and principally identified with black musicians. It would not make *musical* sense with an all-white cast. The musical's emphasis on Hamilton's immigrant experience would, similarly, be far less legible to a contemporary audience if enacted by a cast more closely resembling portraits of its historical *dramatis personae*. The diverse casting of *Hamilton* allows for the crimes of American colonialism and federation to remain in the cast's—and the audience's—consciousness, despite the narrative spending little time explicitly engaging with them. It seems enough, instead, for the lyrics to insistently rhyme 'slavery' with 'bravery', to have Christopher Jackson, the (black) actor playing the slave-owning president George Washington, silently hang his head in shame in the final scene's accounting of the founders' successes and failures. *Hamilton*'s overwhelming commercial, critical, and cultural success is clearly, in part at least, owing to the decisions made in its writing and its casting to reflect the diversity of the United States now as a way of visualising its diversity then, at the turn of the nineteenth century.

One would hope that *Hamilton*'s success might go some way towards redressing the whitewashing of eighteenth-century narratives. Screen adaptations of novels and stories from the pre-photographic past have conspicuously lagged behind theatre in presenting an historically realistic diversity of cast.[15] Part of the difficulty appears to reside in lazy reading on the part of those making adaptations, and the 'default' of whiteness in an ideological climate that insistently preferences it over all other races and ethnicities. In 'Western media', writes Richard Dyer, 'whites take up the position of ordinariness, not a particular race, just the human race', racially invisible through the sheer, taken-for-granted ubiquity of our visibility (47). As Austen and many of her contemporaries simply did not mention details of their characters' appearance or comment on their ethnic or racial heritage, it has been too easy for adaptations to overlook the diversity present in the historical background to realist fiction. This imposes twenty-first century racism on eighteenth-century texts. Nonfiction works based on historical subjects perform somewhat better: there have been films made about Sarah Baartman and Dido Elizabeth Belle, for instance. Belle and Baartman, however, were real women whose real lives happen to be well documented, and of whom multiple images survive attesting to their appearance.

When popular novels are adapted for screen, racist assumptions imposed upon those novels by readers are made manifest. This is equally true of fictions set more or less in our own times. Controversy and racist vitriol accompanied the casting of Mos Def as Ford Prefect in the screen adaptation of science fiction novel *The Hitchhiker's Guide to the Galaxy* (2005) and Noma Dumezweni as an adult Hermione Granger in the play *Harry Potter and the Cursed Child* (debuted 2016).[16] In both cases, nothing in the source texts indicates the characters' ethnic identities: Ford

Prefect is an extra-terrestrial, his name a ridiculous alias. This demonstrates a 'compulsory' whiteness for fictional characters akin to Adrienne Rich's concept of 'compulsory heterosexuality', one which requires a concerted effort to redress.

Contemporary fiction is perhaps the most successful medium for recognising the historical diversity of the pre-photographic past and bringing it insistently to light in the explicit manner that seems to be required for modern audiences to overcome 'compulsory whiteness' and accept any fictional character as anything other than white. Recent novels set in the eighteenth century appear to have taken this entrenched readerly bias into account and are explicit in their inclusion of ethnically diverse characters as a means of realising a convincing historical realism.

Susanna Clarke's 2004 novel *Jonathan Strange and Mr Norrell*, which recasts the clashes between first- and second-generation Romantic poets as a battle between magicians for the soul of 'English magic' includes a central character who is explicitly portrayed as black—for emphasis, his name is Stephen Black—who was portrayed by Ariyon Bakare in a 2015 screen adaptation. Stephen Black is butler to a Member of Parliament: this was a typical profession for black men in Regency-era London, and it is implied that his employers have connections or investments in slave plantations, a group over-represented among MPs.[17] There are principal characters specifically identified as black in Emma Donaghue's *Slammerkin* (2000), set in London and Wales in the 1760s; Francis Spufford's *Golden Hill* (2016), set in mid-eighteenth-century New York; and in Jo Baker's *Longbourn* (2013), an imaginative re-telling of *Pride and Prejudice*. These novels work to bring to light, with impressive historical sensitivity, the lived experience of black people in the eighteenth-century anglophone world.

In the case of *Longbourn*, this is explicitly Austen's world, the world of *Pride and Prejudice*. Told from the perspective of Sarah, the Bennets' maid, when Mr Bingley arrives at Netherfield it is with a 'distressingly handsome' footman, who carries on much of the epistolary intercourse between Longbourn and Netherfield. Sarah thinks:

> So he was what they called a black man, then, even though he was brown? An African? But Africans are cross-hatched, inky, half-naked and in chains. That plaque she had seen at the parsonage, hanging in the hallway: *Am I not a man and a brother?* (54)

The plaque—they were mass-manufactured by Wedgwood and sold as fundraisers for the movement to abolish the British slave trade—gestures to slavery as an abstract political and religious issue. The handsome footman, who becomes Sarah's first suitor, does not fit later stereotypes of the freed slave, but is instead as individuated as any other character in Baker's novel. Like those other characters he reflects the novel's historical context, which is Austen's context, but one that is deliberately made legible to a twenty-first century reader. Baker's novel deftly shows how inescapably enmeshed in history is the life of every individual. In the footman's case this is revealed not through his skin, but through his name:

> 'Ptolemy Bingley. At your service'.
> His first name was strange enough, but: 'How can you be a Bingley?'
> 'If you are off his estate, that's your name, that's how it works'. (97)

Ptolemy, it is implied, is the illegitimate son of the late Mr Bingley senior and one of his sugar-producing slaves. He is thus—at least genetically—a brother to the Mr Bingley of *Pride and Prejudice*. In this 'downstairs' world of Longbourn's servants, his unusual degree of courtesy and self-confidence mark him out, to repurpose a term from *Emma*, as a 'half-gentleman', and his presence in the novel gestures towards the complexities of racial and class identity that conventional historical accounts typically overlook (*E* 213).

Race is even more central to the plot of *Golden Hill*, which is set immediately prior to the American War of Independence, at a time when the abolition movement was only just beginning in Britain. It is, among other things, a mystery novel, and many of its plot twists hinge on issues of race, and strategic 'passing'. 'You will be surprised, if you come with me', says the novel's protagonist, the mysterious Mr Smith to Tabitha, the woman he loves,

> and perhaps you will be shocked, and the—complexion of things—might seem very different to you, from what you had expected; but I swear, I swear to you with utmost seriousness, that you would not learn anything about me that made any essential difference to what you know of me now. I am as you see me. You may trust what you know.

Tabitha is unable to fully 'see' Smith, and unable to trust, but her enslaved maid, Zephyra, sees more clearly:

> There was Smith […] with a tension falling from his face—no, more than that, with a whole role falling from it, in flakes and pieces and cascading blocks, like a collapsing wall—that had been maintained in place without a pause since he landed. […] Smith looked at her again; again held out his hand. The messenger of her new fortune had indeed arrived; if she was willing to hear him.

> Which she was. Zephyra dropped the rag she was still holding, and without looking back, without even closing the door, clasped her hand across her belly and walked out of the house on Golden Hill for ever. (Spufford 322, 326)

The most difficult challenge in accommodating cultural and racial diversity in contemporary works set in the eighteenth century is the representation of slavery. With the exception of *Golden Hill*, the texts that are the principle focus of this chapter are set in England, and set after Lord Mansfield's 1772 judgement in *Somerset v Stewart*, widely if mistakenly interpreted as confirming earlier rulings that legally there could be no slaves in England.[18] In the poet Cowper's words:

> We have no slaves at home.
> …
> Slaves cannot breathe in England; if their lungs
> Receive our air, that moment they are free;
> They touch our country, and their shackles fall. (147)

A much clearer Scottish judgement, *Knight* v. *Wedderburn*, definitively prohibited slavery in Scotland. As we have seen, during Austen's lifetime slaves in Britain were increasingly able to emancipate themselves—*de facto* if not *de jure*—and make new, free lives. Away from British soil, of course, it was a very different matter. The transatlantic slave trade was not outlawed until 1807, and in Britain's colonies slavery continued beyond the 1830s (in the United States legal slavery was not abolished until the 1860s).[19]

The challenge of representing the lived experience of slavery is one that has been fraught with difficulties since the eighteenth century itself, when black writers increasingly turned to print to publicise accounts of their own experiences.[20] These were often deployed as propaganda by the abolition movement. This was sometimes successful, but just as often such accounts exposed black writers to criticisms of factual inaccuracy, melodramatising, and sheer fabrication. Works by formerly enslaved women were particularly liable to criticisms of exaggeration or falsehood, which were only made worse by the generic conventions that made it nearly impossible for women to write about the sexual violence that was an inescapable aspect of women's slavery. These difficulties didn't end in the nineteenth century. Octavia Butler's time-travel slave narrative *Kindred* (1979) is harrowing reading, but in eschewing representations of rape it plays down the violence routinely experienced by enslaved women, largely because Butler based her novel on first-person women's slave narratives from the eighteenth and nineteenth centuries, accounts that were themselves heavily censored.[21]

Another novel set in the Romantic period, *The Book of Night Women* (2009) by the Jamaican writer Marlon James, shares many affinities with Butler's *Kindred*, not least of which is its sensitive exploration of the complexity of race relations in a time of endemic sexual violence committed by white men against black women. Rape was often deployed as a deliberate strategy by slaveowners to propagate more slaves (a baby born to an enslaved woman was in law the property of the woman's owner). Robert Wedderburn wrote impressively of the economic benefits of raping women like his mother:

> My father ranged through his whole household for his own lewd purposes [...] if any one proved with child—why, it was an acquisition which might some day fetch something in the market, like a horse or pig in Smithfield. In short, among his own slaves my father was a perfect parish bull; and his pleasure was the greater, because he at the same time increased his profit.[22]

As a result, many enslaved people were, if only biologically, the children, grandchildren, and siblings of their owners. Both James and Butler consider the ambiguity of enslaved women forced into coercive relationships, with James expressing his heroine's difficulties in stark terms:

> She start to doubt her true womanness. She wonder what kind of nigger she be and why her stomach don't go sick every time the Irishman drop him drawers and suck her titties. [...] Lilith hate him, she know she do, she just didn't know that hate was goin' be just like what Homer say love be like. That she would have to guard it, lock it up in a pen like wild animal, for every chance hatred get, it flee. More times she have to just tell herself that she hate the man, she hate the man, she hate the man, goddamn.
>
> He touch her back in him sleep. Lilith curse herself. She is the one who get whip but he is the one she feel sorry for. She must be the most crossed and mixed-up nigger ever. But it is a diabolical thing when a white man show kindness. (282–83)

One striking aspect of both *Kindred* and *The Book of Night Women* is the sheer complexity of their representations of race and racism. James's narrator, for one, reverses the racist double-standard that allows whiteness individuality and even ethnic diversity, but homogenises blackness:

> White man is white man is white man, but not every nigger be the same nigger. And if she just come from the ship, more so be the difference. If the negro is a Igbo or she be born to a Igbo, sooner or later she goin' to kill herself. If she come from or born to an Angolan, then she goin' be lazy till her dying day. If she come from or born to a Popo or Ibibio, then she goin' work hard and laugh and merry and thank God for the massa. If she be Akan, her hand working as hard as her mind plotting. But lord help you if you get an Ashanti, what the white people call Coromantee. Not even massa whip can tame she. Coromantee blood that never know slavery mix with white blood that always know freedom and race through Lilith body like a brush fire. (49)

Novels like these, that perform anti-racist historical imagining for a modern-day readership, can help keep us attuned to the presence of racial and ethnic diversity in the lives of Romantic writers and in the canonical texts of the period. They are also rich literary material available for adaptation, adaptations that could work to destroy, for a wide audience, the troubling association of the Anglophone past with racial homogeneity. This work, however, is yet to be done.

In an interview on his appointment as a programming advisor to the BBC, the British actor Idris Elba explained:

> 'There's definitely a particular lens on the type of period dramas that we make', he says, choosing his words carefully. 'You tend to see stories about well-to-do Victorians and not the stories outside London, the history of Bradford, Birmingham, Newcastle. Make period pieces more diverse. Look at England's multicultural history. There's a lot more stuff to unearth in period drama. I'm not a massive fan of it ...'
> You mean you don't like watching it?
> 'If I'm going to watch TV it wouldn't be a period drama, put it that way.' (Jones)

Elba here notes, ever so politely, both the problems with our current way of selecting and producing popular entertainment set in the past, and also the opportunities that have been missed through making predictably racist choices. Better historical accuracy would improve the lot of actors and audiences alike.

As a white girl growing up in Canberra, if I were going to watch TV it usually *was* a BBC period drama, which were serialised over the Sunday evenings of my childhood and adolescence. Like most people alive today, my first encounter with the works of Austen (and Eliot, Thackeray, Dickens, and Gaskell) was through screen adaptations. These adaptations led me to read the novels of, and then to study a culture that, while alien to me as an Australian living in a different century, nevertheless always seemed relatively accessible, even welcoming. If it is true that 'you can't be what you can't see', then the overwhelming, ahistoric whiteness of literary adaptations is a force for excluding everyone who isn't white from a heritage and culture which by rights belongs to everyone; from a past that belongs to everyone.

It is long past time that representations of the pre-photographic past started to actually *look* like that past, just as images of our own society need to reflect the true composition of that society. By whitewashing the Regency—by erasing the traces of black lives and turning literary adaptations into racially homogenous simulacra of an imaginary all-white world that never existed—the Austen industry has unthinkingly created fuel for grotesque racist fantasies.

The black lives of past centuries matter, too. They must not be made invisible.

Notes

1 This is a loose and increasingly powerful collection of self-acknowledged racist, sexist and (mostly) homophobic right-wing extremists, 'the right wing stripped of any superstitious belief in human equality' (Main 4).

2 In contrast, the feminist #metoo movement would not gain significant momentum until late in 2017.

3 The Home Office's 'Hostile Environment Policy', which led to the deportations, was instituted in 2010, but the 'Windrush Scandal', which saw many elderly black Britons deported to Commonwealth countries they had left as children, would not be brought to light until early 2018 (Consterdine).

4 Notably, Claire Tomalin was quoted as stating that Austen liked the poet William Cowper, and that Cowper was opposed to hunting, a perplexingly out-of-place comment that suggests thoughtfully presented literary and historical nuance was quickly jettisoned by newspapers concerned more with maintaining controversy than accurately presenting their interviewees' views (Schuessler).

5 See Fryer (10–14).

6 See Woodard (xiii).

7 See Innes (11).

8 See Innes (12).

9 Detailed analysis of the (enormous) compensation paid to slave owners and its investment, often in colonial infrastructure projects such as railways, is being done by the Centre for the Study of the Legacies of British Slave-ownership established by Catherine Hall at University College, London.

10 Rachel Holmes, *African Queen: The Real Life of the Hottentot Venus* (New York: Random House, 2007); Paula Byrne, *Belle: The Slave Daughter and the Lord Chief Justice* (London: Harper Collins, 2014); and Michael Bundock, *The Fortunes of Francis Barber: The True Story of the Jamaican Slave Who Became Samuel Johnson's Heir* (New Haven: Yale University Press, 2015).

11 Given the amount of effects used to create Regency zombie hordes, it is possible the film has black actors in heavily made-up extras parts.

12 Edward Said had raised this point (69 ff); many critics have since responded by exploring the abolitionist discourse of the novel. *Mansfield Park*, dir. Patricia Rozema (Miramax, 1999).

13 See also Kathleen Chater, *Untold Histories: Black people in England and Wales during the period of the British slave trade, c. 1660–1807* (Manchester: Manchester University Press, 2011); Gretchen Holbrook Gerzina, *Black London: Life Before Emancipation* (New Brunswick: Rutgers University Press, 1995); Cassandra Pybus, *Black Founders: The Unknown Story of Australia's First Black Settlers* (Sydney: University of New South Wales Press, 2006).

14 This was 'raised to a principle' in the musical's development and production, with the historian Ron Chernow, on whose biography the musical is based, becoming 'what he calls a "militant" defender of the idea that actors of any race could play the Founding Fathers' (Miranda and McCarter, 33).

15 A recent exception is Disney's live action musical *Beauty and the Beast* (2017) set in a fairy-tale eighteenth-century France, which featured a number of black actors in secondary and extra roles, including Audra McDonald as a wardrobe and Gugu Mbatha-Raw as a feather duster (Ian McKellen plays a rococo clock). As this was, in essence, a filmed version of a Broadway musical, it is unclear how far it can be read as an indicator of casting diversity in film more generally.

16 See 'Don't Panic' and McLeod.

17 Susanna Clarke, *Jonathan Strange and Mr Norrell* (London: Bloomsbury, 2004). See 'Political Legacies' database, Centre for the Study of the Legacies of British Slave-ownership.

18 Lyn Innes notes that Mansfield's judgement was not intended to free enslaved people living in Britain, and indeed for 'years afterwards, notices of sales and wanted notices for runaway slaves continued to appear in newspapers, coffee shops, and other public gathering places' (13).

19 See Innes (11).

20 I do not here include Aphra Behn's *Oroonoko: or, The Royal Slave. A True History* (1688) which, while it does consider the lives and conditions of enslaved people does so through the highly stylised conventions of seventeenth-century romance and is in this respect outside of realist attempts at representation (however compromised). *Oroonoko*, especially in various stage adaptations—which, by making Oroonoko's wife white, linked the play with another eighteenth-century crowd-pleaser, *Othello*—remained very popular well into the eighteenth century (Innes 14).

21 See Octavia E. Butler, *Kindred* (1979) (Boston: Beacon Press, 2003); Lisa Long, 'A Relative Pain: The Rape of History in Octavia Butler's *Kindred* and Phyllis Alesia Perry's *Stigmata*'. *College English*, 64.4 (2002), 459–83, 465.

22 Robert Wedderburn, *The Horrors of Slavery* (1824), quoted in Innes (57).

Works Cited

Austen, Jane. *Emma*, edited by Richard Cronin and Dorothy McMillan. Cambridge UP, 2005.

Austen, Jane. *Jane Austen's Letters*, edited by Deirdre Le Faye, 4th ed. Oxford UP, 2011.

Austen, Jane. *Later Manuscripts*, edited by Janet Todd and Linda Bree. Cambridge UP, 2008.

Austen, Jane. *Northanger Abbey*, edited by Barbara M. Benedict and Deirdre Le Faye. Cambridge P, 2006.

Austen, Jane. *Pride and Prejudice*, edited by Pat Rogers. Cambridge UP, 2006.

Austen, Jane. *Sense and Sensibility*, edited by Edward Copeland. Cambridge UP, 2006.

Baker, Jo. *Longbourn*. Doubleday, 2013.

Barbauld, Anna Letitia. 'Eighteen Hundred and Eleven: A Poem.' *The Poems of Anna Letitia Barbauld*, edited by William McCarthy and Elizabeth Kraft. U of Georgia P, 1994.

Cowper, William. '"The Task" Book II, ll.37.' *The Poetical Works of William Cowper*, edited by Humphrey Sumner Milford. Oxford UP, 1911.

Dabydeen, David. *Hogarth's Blacks: Images of Blacks in Eighteenth-Century English Art*. Dangaroo P, 1985.

Dyer, Richard. *White*. Routledge, 1997.

Fryer, Peter. *Staying Power: The History of Black People in Britain*. Pluto P, 1984.

Hall, Catherine. 'Mother Country.' *London Review of Books*, vol. 42, no. 2, 2020.

Innes, Catherine Lynette. *A History of Black and Asian Writing in Britain, 1700–2000*. Cambridge UP, 2002.

James, Marlon. *The Book of Night Women*. Riverhead, 2009.

Jones, Ellen E. 'Idris Elba: "If I'm Going to Watch TV It Wouldn't Be a Period Drama, Put It That Way".' *The Guardian*, 25 Mar. 2017, www.theguardian.com/tv-and-radio/2017/mar/25/idris-elba-diversity-bbc-takeover-five-by-five-wire-luther

Kean, Danuta. 'Pride and Racial Prejudice – Why the Far Right Loves Jane Austen.' *The Guardian*, 22 Mar. 2017, www.theguardian.com/books/shortcuts/2017/mar/21/pride-and-racial-prejudice-why-the-far-right-loves-jane-austen

Kirkpatrick, Katherine J. '"Gentlemen Have Horrors upon this Subject": West Indian Suitors in Maria Edgeworth's *Belinda*.' *Eighteenth Century Fiction*, vol. 5, no. 4, 1993, pp. 331–348. https://www.lrb.co.uk/the-paper/v42/n02/catherine-hall/mother-countryKirkpatrick

Olusoga, David. *Black and British: A Forgotten History*. Macmillan, 2016.

Piozzi, Hester. 'Hester Thrale Piozzi to Penelope Pennington, 19 June 1802.' *The Intimate Letters of Hester Piozzi and Penelope Pennington 1788–1821*, edited by Oswald G. Knapp. Bodley Head, 1913.

Schuessler, Jennifer. 'Jane Austen has Alt-Right Fans? Heavens to Darcy!' *New York Times Online*, 25 Mar. 2017, p. C6. www.nytimes.com/2017/03/20/books/jane-austen-alt-right.html

Spufford, Francis. *Golden Hill*. Faber and Faber, 2016.

Woodard, Helena. *African-British Writings in the Eighteenth Century*. Greenwood Press, 1999.

Woolf, Virginia. *A Room of One's Own. 1929. A Room of One's Own* and *Three Guineas*, edited by Morag Shiach. Oxford UP, 1998.

Wordsworth, William. 'The Prelude, Book 7.' *Wordsworth: Poetical Works*, edited by Thomas Hutchinson. Oxford UP, 1969.

Wright, Nicole M. 'Alt-Right Jane Austen.' *The Chronicle of Higher Education*, 12 Mar. 2017, www.chronicle.com/article/Alt-Right-Jane-Austen/239435

20

THEY CAME BEFORE *AND* AFTER OLIVIA: CATS, BLACK LADIES AND POLITICAL BLACKNESS IN EIGHTEENTH-CENTURY BRITISH LITERATURE AND AUSTEN

Lyndon J. Dominique

LEHIGH UNIVERSITY

It's remarkable to think that the anonymous novel, *The Woman of Colour* (1808), could have been written by a person of colour and thus, may be the first novel of this kind. But even without the certainty of this attribution, the novel's heroine still makes a bold literary statement in her own right. The main title of this essay riffs off Ivan Van Sertima's fascinating and controversial Africana Studies book, *They Came Before Columbus* (1977), because I consider Olivia, *The Woman of Colour*'s heroine, as part of a group of black ladies who have the potential to make a substantive contribution to the way in which we rethink our approaches to Jane Austen's work as well as the landscape of British literature from a unique black perspective.

The Woman of Colour ends with a concluding dialogue between the 'Editor' of the novel and a 'Friend' that conveys a profoundly political message about Olivia's characterisation. The Friend tells the Editor: 'You have not rewarded Olivia ... with the usual meed of virtue—a husband' (189). This notion that 'a husband' should be the 'usual meed' for a virtuous woman comes, presumably, from the most famous plot of that kind: Samuel Richardson's *Pamela; or, Virtue Rewarded*—a plot in which a lower-class white heroine's rigid virtue is ultimately rewarded with marriage to the upper-class gentleman who has repeatedly tried to rape her. By evoking the strains of the *Pamela* marriage plot, yet denying the virtuous Olivia Pamela's ultimate prize, the Editor attempts to diminish the literary appeal of Richardson's skewed take on marriage and instead presents Olivia as a rather fascinating alternative for all women to consider. Freedom from marriage and the return of her inheritance offers this woman of colour the opportunity to participate in efforts to abolish slavery as well as participate in social advocacy for slaves and free people of colour in Jamaica. This is a remarkably progressive political position for a rich black lady to be associated with in British literature.

At the same time, however, Olivia wasn't the first black lady in literature to identify and politicise a need for liberation within British society. Although the Renaissance era provides numerous examples of intriguing black ladies in fictional texts that precede Olivia's appearance on the British literary landscape,[1] this essay puts *The Woman of Colour* in conversation with two relatively unknown

DOI: 10.4324/9780429398155-20-23

texts from the early eighteenth century—texts that convey their important political messages about liberation in ways that are quite distinct and distinctive. Ultimately, I conclude that they benefit immensely from being read alongside *The Woman of Colour* and under an all-inclusive umbrella of eighteenth-century political blackness.

After I explain what 'political blackness' is, how it is used in contemporary British popular culture and one of its main, seemingly insurmountable, problems, I propose that the term might have more relevance and usefulness when applied to the eighteenth century. To explore political blackness in this more favourable setting, I turn to Aphra Behn and John Dunton, two white writers who politicise both cats and black ladies in their popular texts *The Adventure of the Black Lady* (1698) and *A Cat May Look on a Queen* (1705). I demonstrate that the cats and black ladies in both of these texts are depicted either in terms of effusive praise or bawdy jokes in order to convey consciousness-raising class and gender messages about liberation to readers which prove to be, at once, progressive yet ultimately problematic. At the end, I briefly connect Behn's and Dunton's political messages to *The Woman of Colour* and two Austen novels to explore, in broad terms, the benefit we gain from reading these texts and their depictions of cats and black ladies against Austen as well as under the umbrella of political blackness.

If one heard the phrase 'political blackness' uttered publicly in American popular culture during the four years of the Donald Trump administration, a wealth of diverse images and possibilities might come to mind, from the Black Lives Matter movement and Kanye West to Kamala Harris and even Rachel Dolezal.[2] However, during this same period of time, articles have appeared in popular newspapers and journals like *The Guardian* and *Quartz* that provided a more specific sense of the term as it has been used in popular British culture.[3] Most recently, esteemed philosopher Kwame Anthony Appiah's opinion piece about it in *The New York Times* states that this term 'may have lessons for us today'.[4] So what is it?

As a term, political blackness emerges during the 1970s, a time of extreme racial turbulence in Britain due to anti-immigrant fervour, a rise in racist attacks on British streets, and increasing support at the ballot box for the far right, fascist, political party the National Front. The subtitle to Appiah's article explains that political blackness was Britain's 'own inclusive concept for nonwhite people',[5] and as Aamna Mohdin has observed, the term comes out of 'a lot of shared experiences of racism and discrimination [from] many who came from former British colonies [and] were lumped together as "coloreds"'.[6] These 'coloreds' fell under an all-inclusive umbrella that, Appiah says, was capacious enough to encompass 'minorities with family origins in Asia and the Middle East as well as in Africa and its diaspora'.[7] Under this umbrella, sociologist Claire Alexander states that, 'young people of color identified as black and campaigned together to fight racial discrimination'.[8] And that, in a nutshell, is the essence of political blackness: 'the idea that anyone from a group affected by racism could identify as politically black to form a united group'.[9]

1970s Britain, however, is also marked as a time when white people were actively involved in challenging systemic racism on a popular scale, as seen in the documentary *White Riot* (2019), Rubika Shah's homage to the Rock Against Racism movement, and the 1978 Victoria Park concert that served as the centrepiece for the movement's antiracist political message. From the slogans that they used ('Love Music, Hate Racism') to the messages they conveyed ('We want rebel music. Street music. Music that breaks down people's fear of one another'[10]), it is clear that Roger Huddle and Red Saunders, two of the organisers featured in Shah's documentary, saw Rock Against Racism as an opportunity to articulate their own dissatisfaction with a racist British system. These white men needed black people and black musical genres as allies in order to liberate themselves from the ways in which the state appeared to be conditioning them as white men to accept racism and fear of change as norms.

They Came Before and After Olivia

It's this creative and liberatory train of thought that Shah tries to capture in her documentary—the title of which is taken from the song 'White Riot' written by the punk group, The Clash, and performed during the 1978 Rock Against Racism concert. The song's lyrics are:

Black man gotta lotta problems
But they don't mind throwing a brick.
White people go to school
Where they teach you how to be thick.
And everybody's doing
Just what they're told to,
And nobody wants
To go to jail.
White riot, I want to riot
White riot, a riot of our own.
White riot, I want to riot
White riot, a riot of our own.

If they are read out of context, these repeated musical chants for a 'white riot, a riot of our own' might well sound like a cause for alarm. But The Clash's front-man, Joe Strummer, made it clear that the song and his group were in no way advocating violence or racism in 1970s Britain. Rather, 'White Riot' expresses the group's position that young white people should be as outraged over their oppressive government as black people are, and that young whites should demonstrate their disaffection through direct action and protest as black people had done not only in the 1976 Notting Hill riots but in numerous peaceful marches thereafter.[11] As he explained in the journal *New Musical Express*: 'The only thing we're saying about the blacks is that they've got their problems and they're prepared to deal with them. But white men, they just ain't prepared to deal with them—everything's too cozy. They've got stereos, drugs, hi-fis, cars. The poor blacks and the poor whites are in the same boat'.[12] From Strummer's perspective, 'the blacks', as he calls them, are models of progressive action for white people—they are a consciousness-raising force capable of compelling white musical creatives and their listeners out of their 'cozy' complacency, not to fight in opposition to black people, but to fight alongside them against a state that is failing them both. This is the very definition of allyship. Most importantly, The Clash's and Rock Against Racism's creative wake-up calls for white liberation are expressed and communicated by a popular genre: music; and these wake-up calls are centred around and framed by a specific acknowledgement of black action, black music, black culture, and black protest.

I have traced the broad outlines of these separate yet obviously related forces from 1970s British culture in order to establish a premise: if, on one side, people of colour are organising around political blackness to fight racism and, on the other, antiracist whites are being inspired by black action to become creatively engaged in the same fight, it seems worth asking if these forces are connected in any way under the umbrella of political blackness. What, if any, role do white creatives play in our popular understanding of the term? Is it wrong to think of political blackness as capacious enough to include not only Asians and blacks, but also creative antiracist whites?

This capacious sense of political blackness is definitely a *big* problem. And the problem arises because of how the term lumps racial groups together without specifically acknowledging their unique experiences of racism. In other words, when it is used as an all-encompassing panacea for people of colour who have experienced racism, political blackness threatens to conflate and flatten the specific racial prejudice experienced by each individual racial group. This was the concern expressed by the Asian sociologist Tariq Modood in his 1994 article 'Political Blackness and British Asians',

261

which presents seven different ways that 'the concept [of political blackness] harms British Asians' (859). Hanif Kureishi's 1995 novel, *The Black Album,* also reflects this decade's popular move away from pluralism and toward essentialism when the author writes: 'These days everyone was insisting on their identity, coming out as a man, woman, gay, black, Jew—brandishing whatever features they could claim, as if without a tag they wouldn't be human' (102). Kureishi's Asian protagonist Shahid is no exception to the decade's essentialist lure. He wants to 'belong to his people ... to know them, their past and what they had hoped for' (102). And Kureishi's novel charts Shahid's struggle to confront the problem of racism as Asians in England experience it and without conflating this problem under the all-encompassing umbrella of liberating blackness like that embodied by the musician Prince whose album serves as the title of Kureishi's text.

This problem of racial conflation reemerged in 2016 when students from the University of Kent used pictures of the Asian mayor of London Sadiq Khan and One Direction singer Zayn Malik to promote Black History Month, a move that diminished the importance of people of African descent during this celebratory period.[13] So, to return to my earlier premise, it seems unlikely that creative antiracist whites can find a home under the umbrella of political blackness, at least in contemporary popular culture. Political blackness threatens to conflate racial groups and deny their experiences specific individual attention; adding white antiracist allies and their specific desires for liberation to the concept only exacerbates this problem.

Yet these conversations about the possibilities and impossibilities of political blackness and liberatory creative whiteness still intrigued me enough to posit a new question: if racial conflation makes political blackness less useful if not irrelevant in a contemporary British society where racial categories are fixed and essentialised, might the concept of political blackness and its persuasive call for an umbrella of unity find more relevance and use during a period where race is viewed very differently, where categories like blackness and whiteness are much more fluid, where people with different complexions are mobilising around literary tropes of blackness, where identifying as black was capacious enough to include anyone including white people, and where political black bodies of various kinds are capable of being read without the danger of racial conflation? This period is the eighteenth century.

In numerous texts, eighteenth-century critics such as Roxann Wheeler, Derek Hughes, and Katy Chiles have all argued in favor of the need for more specificity when talking about the different ways eighteenth-century people thought about race.[14] Wheeler's book, *The Complexion of Race*, contends that clothing and religion were more predominant categories of difference than skin color at the beginning of the century (14–21), meaning that Britons put more weight into distinguishing how people dressed and prayed than what skin colour they were. More recently, Katy Chiles has built on Wheeler's formulations to propose that eighteenth-century Americans as well as Britons understood the term 'complexion' not simply as it referred to one's skin colour but also in distinctly mutable ways. Using the phrase 'Transformable Race',[15] Chiles argues that one's complexion could change based on a whole host of things: one's geographic location, climate, food, mode of living, politics, humours, even religion. We see evidence of this in Olaudah Equiano's *Interesting Narrative* (1789) when an Indian man compares the obviously black-skinned African to other white men serving onboard a ship. This Indian sailor asks Equiano: 'How comes it that all the white men on board who can read and write, and observe the sun, and know all things, yet swear, lie, and get drunk, only excepting yourself?' (220). Chiles reads this as a moment where 'the Indian thinks of Equiano as white not because of his appearance but because of the things Equiano does' (162). Her reading offers an explicit example that concepts like blackness and whiteness were a lot more fluid than we might understand them today and that there is a more complex way of reading and understanding what we think of as a racialised black body during this time. As Wheeler herself states, '*black* had a range of meanings unavailable to us today ... the only way to discover the meaning ... is to consider the context' (3). With this in context mind, I have been intrigued by the instances in which white writers use literary tropes of blackness—specifically tropes of blackness that involve black and white women—in ways that do not directly relate to antislavery, yet are still doing the work of undoing systemic forms of oppression. In his article on political blackness, Appiah remarks, 'Blackness, like whiteness, has never not been political'.[16] Having already identified the political message about freedom from marriage and for social advocacy in *The Woman of Colour*, I want to bring this text in conversation with others that use and politicise black ladies and advocate for other kinds of liberation before Olivia appears in English literature.

1660 marks not only the start of the Restoration period, but also the beginning of the decade in which Britain develops a more concerted involvement in the black Atlantic trade with the formations of the Company of Royal Adventurers Trading into Africa and its more explicit slave trading incarnation, the Royal African Company. But I want to propose that the year 1670 also marks a significant shift in the popular literary conception of black ladies in Britain with the appearance of *The Forced Marriage*, the first play by the celebrated yet infamous Aphra Behn. To have a woman making writing her profession, Dawn Lewcock states, 'was remarkable at a time when virtually all the accepted dramatists were men and men from a very narrow social class most of whom wrote for pleasure and not for profit' (66).[17] By presenting herself as a professional writer, Behn publicly marks herself as a nontraditional white woman and she also stigmatizes herself as scandalous for entering this public, male dominated domain.[18]

The late 1680s to 1690s also prove to be another important moment in the history of literary representations of black ladies with the publications of a series of Behn's prose fictions. Critical studies over the last forty years have made readers familiar with the black African women Imoinda and Onahal from Behn's 1688 novel *Oroonoko; or the Royal Slave*. But in *The Unfortunate Bride*, published in 1698, long after Behn's death in 1689, we find Mooria, another powerful woman of African descent whom Catherine Gallagher has called a 'black lady...more designing than the narrator and more adept than any other character at achieving her designs' (236). Women of African descent are not the only black ladies Behn was interested in toward the end of her life, however. Tropes of blackness heavily inform many of her depictions of white women in prose fictions. For instance, Behn's novella *The Fair Jilt* (1688)[19] gives us only a brief glimpse of the heiress Alcidiana, a white woman who develops a 'face black and all deformed' (77) after she is poisoned with mercury in what ultimately turns out to be a thwarted murder-plot orchestrated by her sister, Miranda. As the main protagonist and instigator of violence perpetuated not only against her sister, but also her male servant Van Brun, her husband Tarquin, and her spurned male love interest Henrick, Miranda is *The Fair Jilt*'s consummate black lady. Her evil intent is, perhaps, best evoked by the 'black dress' (11) and 'black velvet gown' (83)[20] she wears which both offset her beautiful external appearance while also evoking the foulness associated with her nefarious thoughts and actions. The complexion of blackness in white women takes a spiritual turn in Behn's *The History of the Nun* (1688) and its plot involving the lapsed nun Isabella who becomes 'filled with thoughts all black and hellish' (134) and ultimately, brings about 'a deed so black' (134) as the murders of her two husbands. These examples provide enough of a pattern to acknowledge that Behn had both a keen interest in blackness and that she wanted to explore this complexion as it relates to different types of women, black and white.

Behn's interest in displaying the black complexions of black as well as white women is also seen in the literary work of John Dunton, a writer who is more often talked about in relation to Daniel Defoe and Jonathan Swift.[21] It's clear, however, that while Behn's work directly influenced him, similarities in their life experiences also suggest some indirect parallels between them. As a gentleman-like tradesman, Dunton was somewhat of a peripheral figure in literary circles in terms of his rank just as Behn was in terms of her gender. And, like Behn, he was a very prolific professional writer, motivated to write for money. By his own measure, he produced and published six hundred projects on popular topics as varied as a condemnation of female prostitutes, a lampoon of homosexuals, and his admiration for women's posteriors.[22] He is also credited with writing the first autobiography in a post-modern style akin to Laurence Sterne's *Tristram Shandy*.[23] These tawdry and quirky projects weren't the only outcomes from his innovative mind. He was the originator of what Lucy Mangan calls the first advice column,[24] remarkable in its day for the way it made a point of soliciting questions on any subject from readers of any rank.[25] And he published the first periodical and the first dictionary directed exclusively at women, at a time when women readers were not an especially prolific or profitable target audience.

It is his work on black ladies, however, that I find most intriguing because he seems to return to them in a totally obsessive way. Take, for instance, his Paradox 22 from *Athenian Sport* (1707), the title of which is addressed 'to a Lady exceeding fair' to prove to her '[t]hat a Black-a-Moor woman is the greatest Beauty'. In this paradox, Dunton uses Behn's Imoinda as the example the fair lady should follow:

> Oh that every English lady wife had one of 'em [a black woman] in her house for an example, or would often look upon Behn's Imoinda for the same reason…Then, Madam, would you gaze more on our Black-a-moor beauties, it may be it might work some good upon ye, and the poor heathens might shame ye into duty and obedience. (105)

Dunton's interest in black women of African descent doesn't end with this sole reference to Behn's Imoinda. Remarkably, he returns to this theme many times in *Athenian Sport*, as this list of titles attests: Paradox 54 'Proving Black's White' (252), Paradox 57 'In Praise of a wife who is Black, Wrinkled, crooked and dumb' (268), Paradox 106 'A Fair Nymph Shaming a Black by Courting her' (465), and Paradox 114 'That the Whole world and all things in it are Black, Prov'd in a letter sent by a black maid to a fair boy with whom she was deeply in love' (485). These paradoxes and the venue in which they appear suggest that Dunton uses black ladies of African descent as integral parts of intellectually stimulating, literary play designed to delight and amuse white readers with the author's capacity for witty thought and repartee.

Dunton's literary work is also as keenly aware as Behn's of a distinction between black ladies of African descent and white ones with black complexions and he obsesses about one in particular in his 1705 satire *A Cat May Look on a Queen*.[26] Dunton creates a male speaker who talks incessantly about the black beauty of one of the most powerful women England had ever seen: the last Stuart monarch, Queen Anne. While acknowledging that Anne's uncle, Charles II, was known as a 'Handsome Black Man' (11), Dunton's speaker celebrates Anne's physical black beauty in effusive terms with numerous phrases like these: 'A Black Lady (when advanced to the royal dignity) is more perfect than other women' (9–10); 'besides her charms as a Black woman, her person dazzles us yet more as she is a Queen' (11); 'Black (or what but inclines to it) was ever esteemed lovely in common persons; what then must it be in a queen, where there is both virtue and majesty to innoble (sic.) the colour' (11); and finally:

> our Royal Anne, not only conquers with her gracious speeches…but commands all our hearts, as her hair and complexion has the first place in the rank of beauty…I never thought any woman handsome, but was just of her majesty's colour—I don't know how the ladies of the red complexion will like this, but I am able to prove there is no beauty but what is found in a black woman—Nay, there's such matchless charms in hair that resembles jet (or is dark Brown) that the lady that has it may pass for a beauty, let her person be what it will. (11–12)

It is very clear that Anne is not being depicted as a woman of African descent. Yet these repeated references over three pages of text are undoubtedly striking. They indicate that Dunton's speaker is making a deliberate point of constructing Anne as an attractive black woman to his readers. What, besides flattery, might be at the core of such exaggerated praise?

I read this speaker's deliberate and effusive praise of Queen Anne as a serious political move on Dunton's part. Although, the sheer frequency and detail of these quotes suggest that the speaker is going to extreme lengths to paint the white Queen's black femininity in a commendatory light, this speaker's praise actually diminishes Anne's importance as a monarch by exaggerating her appearance as a woman. The roots of the speaker's diminishing perspective of the Queen are evoked in the phrase that underlies Dunton's title. 'A cat may look at a king' is a fascinating proverb with a long history in popular print dating back to at least John Heywood's 1555 use of it.[27] During the Interregnum, it appeared as the title of an anonymous historical text which Alistair Bellamy and John D. Staines agree was staunchly antimonarchical.[28] The proverb itself speaks to the idea of a lower-class person having the right to look at the aristocracy with the unintimidated perspective common to a house cat. By doing so, this lower-class person's consciousness and status are raised as he or she hones their ability to appraise their aristocratic authority figures as humans rather than divine-right deities.[29]

In the preface to *A Cat May Look on a Queen*, the text's speaker reveals this sense of an emerging class consciousness when he expresses his connections to the cat and the queen evoked in Dunton's title. He exclaims, 'If Mrs Puss may be so honour'd [with the privilege of looking directly at a monarch], my Sex may be admitted (at least) to an equal Privilege with that purring and contemptible Animal' (Preface). Here, the speaker claims a genuine right—'an equal Privilege' to regard the queen with the unintimidated perspective enjoyed so effortlessly by the cat. Even the queen's lowest subjects should be free to enjoy this 'privilege'.[30] But it is the way in which he claims this freedom that proves problematic. His ostensibly flattering use of personification in the female honorific 'Mrs Puss' is swiftly undermined by the condescending manner with which he refers to this female cat as nothing more than a 'purring and contemptible Animal' (preface). And this false flattery extends itself further to his depictions of the 'Black Lady' queen, whose physical beauty he openly acknowledges, but whose power and status he staunchly dismisses with the suggestion that 'our sovereign Lady is no angel, but a woman'—nothing more than a 'monarch in petticoats' (2). At the beginning of this text, then, Dunton's anonymous male speaker articulates his genuine right to face and critique authority, but he also claims two ascendant positions over a female house cat and a reigning queen by virtue of nothing more than the power attributed to his 'sex'. Essentially, he identifies a problem: using a cat to raise the consciousness of lower-class white men in England and liberating them from submission to the monarchical authoritarianism represented by a black queen doesn't come about, apparently, without a good helping of misogyny.

Reading the effusive celebration of Anne's black beauty as Dunton's speaker's misogynistic attempt to colour and admire the queen as an ordinary, sod-of-the-earth woman rather than the powerful sovereign she is, makes visible the social and political conundrum about gender and class that this queen's sovereign status presented to *all* Englishmen. Anne was a powerful threat to them because, as Mary Beth Norton has shown, she was quite the contradiction: '[Anne] was a queen whose husband was not the king…England was thus confronted with a monarch who on the one hand was a wife, legally subject to her husband under the law and who on the other was the supreme ruler of the land, in which her husband had no political authority' (100). To resolve a contradiction that threatened to destabilise masculine 'privilege' in every household throughout the nation, Dunton's male speaker elects to view Anne as more of the beautiful black former ('wife, legally subject') and much less of the threatening latter ('supreme ruler'). His catlike, effusive praise of Anne's beautiful blackness indicates not only his own intent to look boldly at the queen's body and complete this diminishment of her authority, but also, by speaking on behalf of his 'sex', Dunton's low-ranking speaker suggests that *all* men of any rank should be free to enjoy this catlike 'privilege' too.

In her marvellous essay 'Reading Race and Gender: Jonathan Swift', Laura Brown identifies Swift 'as an explicit misogynist and also an explicit anti-colonialist'. She continues, 'Swift's texts lend themselves equally well to a negative and a positive hermeneutic' (121), yet she ultimately concludes that 'the unpromising materials of misogyny [depicted in Swift's life and work] enable us to perceive the critique of racism' (138). In my reading of the misogynistic and anti-aristocratic speaker in *A Cat May Look on a Queen*, I detect the same negative and positive hermeneutic, but one that's focused on class and gender instead of race and gender. Dunton's speaker's unpromising portrayal of misogyny helps us to perceive genuine challenges to aristocratic authority as well as the cost that such challenges of class submission threaten to have on the status of women. Like Brown, I agree that the sacrifice of women might seem a high price to pay for the problematisation of class or racial difference. Nevertheless, *A Cat May Look on a Queen* is an important marker for measuring the limits and problems of political blackness as white men like Dunton and Swift use it in the British Isles.

But what about the first professional woman writer? What political message about liberation do her literary black women convey? And do they convey this message with or without the overt misogyny that comes so naturally to men like Dunton and Swift? To explore this, I want to turn to a novel that has been attributed to Behn but without an ironclad assurance that it was actually written by her. *The Adventure of the Black Lady* first appears posthumously in a 1698 collection of Behn's *Histories and Novels*. But Leah Orr's essay 'Attribution Problems in the Fiction of Aphra Behn', does a stellar job of bringing into doubt Behn's authorship of it as well as many other works that were included in collections published long after Behn's death.[31] Despite this doubt about its attribution, Margaret Ferguson offers the approach to the text that I favour. Rather than wrestle with questions of authenticity, Ferguson states that she is more 'concerned with the economic politics limned in and by a set of texts, printed and in manuscript, that circulated *as* Behn's during her lifetime and thereafter' (8). Where Ferguson's interest is in 'economic politics', I concern myself with *The Adventure of the Black Lady*'s engagement with black ladies and the political message about women's sexuality that this text also attributes to Behn's literary legacy.

The rough outlines of *The Adventure of the Black Lady*'s plot are immediately recognisable if we consider a visual text published over three decades after Behn's novel first appears. William Hogarth's *A Harlot's Progress* (1731) charts the story of Moll Hackabout, an innocent country girl who arrives in London looking for work. But, instead, Moll encounters an older woman who introduces her to a life of prostitution. Once on this road, Moll's descent into poverty, single parenthood, disease and ultimate death is described in vivid visual detail. Behn's novel also has an innocent, virtuous country girl arriving in London. But this heroine is a lady—the suggestively named heiress, Bellamora[32]—who is looking for a safe haven rather than employment. Bellamora is eight months pregnant and unmarried when she arrives in town searching for her cousin, Madam Brightly, with whom she wants to hide out during her lying in. Madam Brightly can't be found, however, and even worse, Bellamora's trunk containing all of her money and jewels is stolen during her trip. It's in this moment of imminent financial and social ruin that Bellamora meets an older woman—a 'landlady' (498) who is never named in the text and is only described as a 'good, discreet, ancient gentlewoman…fallen a little to decay' (493). This landlady and another unnamed woman who is also referred to as a 'lady' (493–96),[33] work together to house Bellamora, retrieve her trunk, and orchestrate the reunion and ultimate marriage between Bellamora and the gentleman, Fondlove, whose presumed sexual assault is the reason for Bellamora's secret pregnancy and her furtive trip to London. Because they inhabit and act within this powerful space of lady anonymity, we can think of these women as black ladies.

From this synopsis, it seems that this text's gender politics may not be as misogynistic as that found in Dunton's text. Yet, they are still problematic. The landlady and her unnamed lady accomplice save Bellamora from penury only to facilitate her marriage to a man who may have sexually assaulted her. It is important to recognize, however, that Behn chooses to end this story not simply with Bellamora's problematic marriage to Fondlove, but with an intriguing coda that conveys a larger political message about gender politics in the eighteenth-century world.

While Bellamora and her new husband, Fondlove, are at the shops, the parish authorities or, as Behn's narrator calls them, 'the vermin of the parish (I mean the overseers of the poor, who eat the bread from them)' [came,]

> to search for a young Black-haired lady (for so was Bellamora) who was either brought to bed or was just ready to lie down. The landlady showed them all the rooms in the house, but no such lady could be found. At last she bethought herself and led them into her parlor, where she opened a little closet door and showed them a black cat that had just kittened; assuring them that she should never trouble the parish as long as she had rats or mice in the house; and so dismissed them like loggerheads as they came. (499–500)

Coincidentally, this scene provides another consciousness-raising, literary interaction between a cat and a black lady. But where Dunton's cat in a *Cat May Look on a Queen* is designed to liberate his male speaker from aristocratic subservience as well as empower others of his sex and rank to raise their class status and consciousness, Behn's cat is involved in another distinct form of liberationist politics directly aimed at black ladies. There's definitely some sort of economic triumph conveyed in this scene where the landlady reproduces a 'just kittened' black cat instead of the 'Black-haired lady' that the parish authorities had come to find. This 'fallen' landlady is somehow getting her own back against a parish that clearly exploits the poor and eats their 'bread'.

But there's something else being communicated by this scene in which the local parish forces are aggressively searching for a heavily pregnant and unmarried woman who has, possibly, been sexually assaulted. These 'overseers' appear to undertake this search merely to castigate Bellamora or to make money off her, or to parade her around as an example of their commitment to rooting out vice within the community, rather than to actually oversee and provide aid for her during her almost rapid descent into the state of penury that Hogarth graphically visualized for Moll Hackabout. In other words, because of her pregnant and unmarried condition, the parish authorities presume that Bellamora is a vice-ridden black woman who has lost control of her genitalia and their aggressive efforts to search for her imply that they want to gain control over it for their own financial, moral, or political benefit. *The Adventure of the Black Lady* ends with the landlady not only dismissing these parish authorities and denying them this kind of sexual control and social victory over Bellamora, but her actions are also reflective of a small victory for all of the text's other known and unknown black women—the unnamed London lady as well as the lost Madam Brightly—that are unfairly stigmatized, shamed, exploited, and discarded by a system that's only designed to police women's bodies and their sexuality rather than understand the conditions of their oppression. This small victory has much larger contemporary political overtones, as one of my graduate students pointed out in particularly graphic terms that I'll paraphrase: 'Behn is creating a bawdy black political joke[34] in this ending. If the parish authorities are so keen to grab a pussy and exert their control over a black lady's body and sexuality, Behn makes the landlady lead them to the only one they deserve to have power over: a *literal* black cat'.[35]

This essay has navigated the terrain of political blackness in two distinct historical periods. In the eighteenth-century portion, I've introduced five important literary black ladies who came before Olivia in two texts—Queen Anne in Dunton's *A Cat May Look on a Queen* and Bellamora, Madam Brightly, the anonymous landlady, and the unnamed London lady in Behn's *The Adventure of the Black Lady*. These texts contain distinctly anti-establishment political messages about class and gender. I've proposed that Behn and Dunton are centering both a political blackness that's distinguished in white women as well as politicised perspectives that are conveyed by cats in order to develop anti-establishment messages that are designed to elevate the class and gender positions and consciousnesses of their respective British readers. Read together, they proclaim that *all* ranks of Englishmen should be free to scrutinize authority at the highest level of British society and *all* English ladies, even those in the lowest ranks of British society, should be free to protect and control their own bodies. But these progressive messages ultimately prove problematic since we can clearly see the misogyny in Dunton's speaker who wants to elevate his lower-class consciousness in a way that ensures the continued domination of men over all women in society. And even though Behn's landlady and her lady accomplice protect access to Bellamora's black body and they save her from the parish forces that seek to unfairly stain and exploit her, they still conspire to throw the heroine, unprotected, into the precarious safety of marriage to a man who may have sexually assaulted her. So, there's a gap between the progressive messages about freedom that Behn's and Dunton's use of cats, black ladies, and political blackness convey and the ways these literary devices and strategies still manage to support and maintain other forms of oppression like marriage and male hegemony. I have also mentioned that these white writers are, themselves, on the peripheries of their cultures: Behn as the first professional woman writer in a male dominated environment, and Dunton as somewhat of a first-of-a-kind himself—a gentleman-like bookseller and printer whose influence in literary circles was perhaps limited by his low-ranking class position as well as his penchant for tawdry and quirky projects.

But how does all of this knowledge of Behn's and Dunton's lives and an awareness of the cats and black ladies that they politicise enable us to rethink both Austen's work as well as the landscape of British literature as I claimed so grandly in the opening to this essay? To answer this question, I must make a third and final recourse to cats, black ladies, and political blackness, but this time in Austen. Rebecca Smith has observed that, 'cats are conspicuous by their absence in Jane Austen's work, with barely a mention apart from Mrs Jennings in *Sense and Sensibility* saying [to Colonel Brandon]:'[36] 'Ah! Colonel, I do not know what you and I shall do without the Miss Dashwoods…Lord! We shall sit and gape at one another as dull as two cats' (292).[37] Cats may well be dull when they're looking at 'one another', as Mrs Jennings attests, but Behn's and Dunton's texts have shown that when eighteenth-century literary cats focus attention on authority figures, the messages they convey can be politically (if problematically) consciousness-raising, providing male and female readers enough justification to stare boldly in the face of aristocratic as well as abusive parish power. Emboldened white readers and writers like Behn and Dunton who are situated on the peripheries of British culture are, perhaps, best positioned to examine and expose the flaws of these authority figures because of the benefit of a distanced perspective. We see this in *Sense and Sensibility*'s depiction of Mrs Jennings, whose class status as 'the widow of a man who had got all his money in a low way' (245) makes her peripheral in John Dashwood's eyes, yet whose kindness and generosity to Elinor and Marianne expose the stark, cold, and selfish authoritarianism that John and Fanny Dashwood display toward their sisters.

We also see another peripheral Austen figure shaking up authoritarianism to even greater effect in *Mansfield Park*'s lower-class heroine, Fanny Price. In an essay that purports to defend Austen's least-liked heroine, Tara Isabella Burton calls Fanny 'unabashedly mousy'.[38] Yet, Burton's description of her puts me in mind of a very different animal when she writes: '[Fanny] spends most of the novel creeping around the periphery of the titular park, taciturn … she looks down on her wealthier cousins for engaging in flirtatious amateur theatrics; and…she refuses to voice her long-held love for her cousin Edmund'.[39] Reading Burton's descriptions of Fanny displaying cat-like rather than mouse-like proclivities allows us to envisage Fanny's 'taciturn' refusal to 'voice' her feelings, her 'creeping around the periphery' of the Mansfield Park domus, and, in particular, her tendency to look 'down on her wealthier cousins' as indications of her mercurial, wide-ranging, and bold visual acuity rather than the simple reserve which critics usually attribute to her characterisation. During the course of the novel, Fanny's moral perspicacity develops to such a large extent that she is able to face and judge the authoritarian slaveholder, Sir Thomas Bertram, with a boldness that is directly in keeping with the consciousness-raising proverb 'a cat may look at a king'. This moral face-off with Sir Thomas even has a connection to blackness. I have argued elsewhere that literary references about Fanny's dull complexion and her inability to glow align her with black people and their inability to blush: 'While Fanny clearly isn't Negro in any literal sense, her unchanging complexion

They Came Before and After Olivia

indicates that she is marred by the same stigmas that Negroes faced: ugliness and especially use-lessness'.[40] It is this reading of Fanny as a blackened white woman with a catlike perspective capable of challenging authority that compels me to list *Mansfield Park* as another text of political blackness—only, one that comes *after* Olivia's. It serves as a reminder that the black complexion of a white Austen heroine is just as integral to a discussion about race and liberationist politics as any conversation about *Sanditon*'s Miss Lambe would be.

Considering Fanny as part of the unique literary history that this essay has begun to construct around Dunton and Behn is also an opportunity to put on display Austen's role in raising the consciousness of her readers by encouraging them to scrutinize authority. We see this at the end of *Mansfield Park* when Edmund reflects on everyone's bad behavior during the time of the *Lovers' Vows* play: 'Maria was wrong', he remarks, 'Crawford was wrong, we were all wrong together; but none so wrong as myself' (237). In response, Fanny modestly acknowledges the power of her perspicacity. She tells Edmund: 'As a bystander…Perhaps I saw more than you did' (237). Austen is not merely privileging Fanny's righteousness as a perspicacious 'bystander' here, she is also en-couraging readers to acknowledge the active power of this bystander's peripheral perspective. *Readers* also saw more than Edmund throughout the novel; *our* moral consciousness was raised *only* because we saw Mansfield Park and the abuses of moral authority that happen there through Fanny's peripheral, judgmental, blackened, catlike eyes.

To return, though, to the cats, black ladies, and political blackness we find in texts that came *before* Olivia's, it is clear that these devices and strategies are used to articulate each authors' interest in a liberationist politics. Messages about liberating women from a state's moral control over their bodies and their sexuality and those that seek to liberate lower-class men from aristocratic in-timidation and submission put these texts in conversation with *The Woman of Colour*, the novel I described at the beginning of this essay as consciously attempting to liberate women from popular conceptions of the marriage plot. Putting all of these texts under an umbrella of political blackness allows for us to witness the broad spirit as well as the successes and failures of a popular liberationist politics. A second way in which these texts can be read under an umbrella of political blackness relates to their anonymity. *A Cat May Look on a Queen* and *The Woman of Colour* were anonymous when they were initially published. And as I mentioned earlier, we don't know for sure if Behn actually wrote *The Adventure of the Black Lady*. But I want to think of the anonymity and uncertainty of authorship surrounding these texts as a collective strength that unites them. They are each using the bold, black spaces of either anonymity or ghost authorship in order to push forward political messages that focus less on the individual author and more on the cause that each text conveys. The final way in which I am beginning to bring these three distinct and distinctive literary re-presentations together under an umbrella of political blackness involves considering them as a part of coalition of texts that can represent the roots of a united eighteenth-century literature of social justice—one that does not compartmentalise or conflate the individual oppressions of women, people of African and Asian descent, sexual and class minorities—but one that, instead, tries to find the threads around which mutual oppressions are connected and the conversation that connection elicits. In this essay, I have outlined an eighteenth century political blackness that's mobilised against questionable authority and abusive authoritarianism as one way of connecting those threads—one way of creating a united coalition of literary texts that have the potential to make readers see and discuss what a liberation for all who want it might look like as well as what the real obstacles and enemies to liberation might be for all who need it.[41]

Notes

1 Examples include Dunbar's 'Ane Blak Moir' (1507), Jonson's *Masque of Blackness* (1605), the 'Dark Lady' in Shakespeare's *Sonnets* (1609), and even *Love's Labour's Lost* (1598) which contains Biron's statement that

Rosaline is 'born to make black fair/ Her favour turns the fashion of the days' (IV.iii.258–59). Also see classic works of criticism about race, gender, and the renaissance by Kim Hall and Joyce Green Macdonald.

2 Kanye West is an American rapper and Trump supporter; Kamala Harris is the first black and Asian American Vice President of the United States; Rachel Dolezal is a former NAACP chapter president whose story went viral when it was discovered that she was a white woman posing as black.

3 See Wilson et al. and Mohdin.

4 See Appiah.

5 Ibid.

6 See Mohdin.

7 See Appiah.

8 Claire Alexander quoted in Mohdin's *Quartz* article above.

9 Wilson et al. For more on how academics have defined and understood political blackness see Tariq Modood's 'The Rise and Fall of Anti-Racism' (168–81) and Rob Waters's 'Political Blackness: Brothers and Sisters', (51–92).

10 Red Saunders quoted in the *White Riot* trailer, www.youtube.com/watch?v=Fj9WXw_W1dc

11 For more on the Notting Hill riots see 'The Notting Hill Race Riots', chapter 16 in Ian Hernon's *Riot! Civil Insurrection from Peterloo to the Present Day* (170–84). And for more on racial tensions between blacks and whites that preceded the 1976 Notting Hill Riots, see David Olusoga's *Black and British: A Forgotten History* (509–15) for a brief account of the 1958 Notting Hill riots as well as the policy and political slogans around which the 1976 riots were a response.

12 Quoted in Jack Whatley's 'The Story Behind The Song: "White Riot"'.

13 For more on this incident at the University of Kent and its outcomes see the Mohdin, Appiah, and Wilson et al. articles.

14 See, for instance, Wheeler's *The Complexion of Race: Categories of Difference in Eighteenth-Century British Culture*, Chiles's *Transformable Race: Surprising Metamorphoses in the Literature of Early America* and Hughes's 'Blackness in Gobineau and Behn: *Oroonoko* and Racial Pseudo Science'.

15 For Chiles's definition and use of this term, see her chapter 'Transformable Race: Surprising Metamorphoses in the Literature of Early America' in *Transformable Race* (2014). Also see Wheeler's *Complexion of Race* (2–14) for more discussion about complexion.

16 *New York Times*, 7 October 2020.

17 'More for seeing than hearing: Behn and the use of theatre', in *Aphra Behn Studies* (1996) 66.

18 Rob Baum's 'Aphra Behn's Black Body: Sex, Lies and Narrativity in *Oroonoko*' offers an intriguing reading of Behn's black body as seen through the lens of *Oroonoko*.

19 *The Fair Jilt; or, The History of Prince Tarquin and Miranda*. London: R. Holt, 1688. All subsequent references taken from this edition.

20 As an image, Miranda's black dress has a symbolic connection to Van Brun's black velvet prayer book and Tarquin's hat and coffin.

21 Dunton knew both of them. He published Swift's first poem, 'An Ode to the Athenian Society', in 1691 and his question-and-answer publication, *Athenian Oracle* (1703), competed with Defoe's own version of this format, the *Review* (1704), in the literary marketplace.

22 See Dunton's *Bumography* (1707), *He-Strumpet* (1707), and *NightWalker* (1696).

23 *Life and Errors* (1705).

24 'A Brief History of Agony Aunts', *The Guardian,* 12 November 2009.

25 See, for instance, *The Athenian Oracle*.

26 *A Cat may look on a Queen* (1708). All subsequent references refer to this edition.

27 In *Two hundred epigrammes, vpon two hundred prouerbes*, Heywood writes: 'A cat may loke on a kynge, and what of that. /When a cat so lookth: a cat is but a cat'. His innocuous interpretation of the cat's perspective changes considerably 100 years later.

28 Although they differ about who wrote it (Bellamy thinks Marchamont Nedhum is the author; Staines thinks it's Anthony Weldon), Bellamy and Staines are in agreement about the tone of *A Cat May look upon a King* (1652). 'From its title page onward', Bellamy calls this text 'a thoroughly anti-monarchical work … [one that] chronicled centuries of sexual, political and fiscal oppressions visited upon the English by their kings' (269). And Staines explains that the text uses 'the life of Mary Queen of Scots not only to stain the Stuart family but to destroy the legitimacy of the entire institution of the monarchy' (211).

29 This idea of the proverb as a potential consciousness-raising and threatening challenge to authority appears in numerous texts such as Lewis Carroll's *Alice's Adventures in Wonderland* (1865) when the Cheshire-Cat's head appears at the Queen's croquet ground. '"Don't be impertinent," said the King [to the Cheshire-Cat], "and don't look at me like that!" "A cat may look at a King", said Alice. "I've read it in some book, but I

don't remember where". "Well, it must be removed" said the King very decidedly', (68) and a Wikileaks webpage (Mathews and Assange).

30 Despite referring to himself as a 'gentleman', it's quite evident that Dunton's male speaker is neither noble nor intimately connected to Anne. In the 'Preface', he openly admits that he has had to 'enquire of persons that stand in the royal presence' for insider information about the queen, thereby acknowledging that he is, at least, once removed from her intimate circle.

31 For a brief discussion of Behn's posthumous works and problems of attribution also see Margaret Ferguson (33n19).

32 Bellamora is a suggestive name because it doesn't only imply beautiful love in French and Italian, (belle amor, bella amore), it's flexible enough to also indicate beautiful blackness (bella moor).

33 Bellamora also refers to this woman as 'your ladyship' (496). During the course of the novel, we discover that this unnamed London lady is actually Fondlove's married sister. But even with this discovery, her Christian and marital names are not revealed.

34 The Black Joke (sometimes spelled 'Joak') was a popular early eighteenth-century song that made reference to female genitalia. See Roberts.

35 My sincere thanks both to Arianna Vailas for this spot-on articulation of Behn's concluding message and all of my graduate students at Lehigh University and the Middlebury Bread Loaf School of English who helped me work through readings of Behn's and Dunton's works.

36 'A day in the life of Jane Austen', *History Extra: The official website for BBC History Magazine, BBC History Revealed and BBC World Histories Magazine*, www.historyextra.com/period/georgian/a-day-in-the-life-of-jane-austen/

37 *Sense and Sensibility*.

38 In this article, Burton quotes C.S. Lewis calling Fanny mouse-like in *The Screwtape Letters*.

39 Ibid.

40 See Dominique (243).

41 Here, I'm riffing off Red Saunders's call for a 'Music that knows who the real enemy is' quoted in the *White Riot* trailer (Shah).

Works Cited

A Cat May look upon a King. London, 1652.

Appiah, Kwame Anthony. 'What We Can Learn From the Rise and Fall of "Political Blackness."' *The New York Times* 7 Oct. 2020. https://www.nytimes.com/2020/10/07/opinion/political-blackness-race.html

Austen, Jane. *Mansfield Park*, edited by Claudia L. Johnson. Norton, 1998.

Austen, Jane. *Sense and Sensibility*, edited by Kathleen James-Cavan. Peterborough: Broadview, 2001.

Baum, Rob. 'Aphra Behn's Black Body: Sex, Lies and Narrativity in *Oroonoko*.' *BRNO Studies in English*, vol. 37, 2011, pp. 7–29.

Behn, Aphra. *All of the Histories and Novels Written by the Late Ingenious Mrs Behn, Entire in One Volume*. London: R. Wellington, 1705.

Behn, Aphra. *Oroonoko, or the Royal Slave*, edited by Joanna Lipking. Norton, 1997.

Behn, Aphra. *The Fair Jilt; or, The History of Prince Tarquin and Miranda*. London: R. Holt, 1688.

Behn, Aphra. *The History of the Nun*. London: A. Baskervile, 1689.

Behn, Aphra. 'The Unfortunate Bride.' *Oroonoko and Other Writings*, edited by Paul Salzman. Oxford UP, 1994, pp. 198–208.

Bellamy, Alistair. *The Politics of Court Scandal in Early Modern England: News Culture and the Overbury Affair, 1603–1600*. Cambridge UP, 2007.

Brown, Laura. 'Reading Race and Gender: Jonathan Swift.' *Critical Essays on Jonathan Swift*, edited by Frank Palmeri. Macmillan, 1993.

Burton, Tara Isabella. 'In Defense of Fanny Price.' *The Paris Review* 10 July 2014. www.theparisreview.org/blog/2014/07/10/in-defense-of-fanny-price/

Carroll, Lewis. *Alice's Adventures in Wonderland*, edited by Donald J. Gray. Norton, 1992.

Chiles, Katy. *Transformable Race: Surprising Metamorphoses in the Literature of Early America*. Oxford UP, 2014.

Dominique, Lyndon J. *Imoinda's Shade: Marriage and the African Woman in Eighteenth-Century British Literature, 1759–1808*. Ohio State UP, 2012.

Dunbar, William. 'Of Ane Blak-Moir.' *The Poems of William Dunbar*, edited by H. Bellyse Baildon. Cambridge UP, 1907, pp. 97–98.

Dunton, John. *A Cat May Look on a Queen: Or, a Satyr on Her Present Majesty. Attempted by John Dunton, author of the Satyr on King William. The second edition. To which is added, a distinct account of the several jewels in the crown of England*. London: John Morphew, 1708.

Dunton, John. *Athenian Sport*. London: B. Bragg, 1707.

Dunton, John. *Bumography: Or, a Touch at the Lady's Tails, Being a Lampoon (Privately) Dispers'd at Tunbridge-Wells, in the Year 1707. By a Water Drinker*. London, 1707.

Dunton, John. *The Athenian Oracle*. London: A. Bell, 1703–4.

Dunton, John. 'The He-Strumpets: A Satyr on the Sodomite-Club.' *Athenianism: Or, the New Projects of Mr. John Dunton*. London: Tho. Darrack, 1710, pp. 93–99.

Dunton, John. *The Life and Errors of John Dunton*, edited by John Nichols, 2 vols. Cambridge UP, 2014.

Dunton, John. *The Night-Walker: Or, Evening Rambles in Search After Lewd Women, with the Conferences Held with Them*. London: J. Orme, 1696.

Equiano, Olaudah. *The Interesting Narrative of the Life of Olaudah Equiano*, edited by Angela Costanzo. Peterborough: Broadview, 2004.

Ferguson, Margaret. 'Conning the "Overseers": Women's Illicit Work in Behn's "The Adventure of the Black Lady".' *Early Modern Culture: An Electronic Seminar*, vol. 5, 2006, pp. 1–40.

Gallagher, Catherine. 'Oroonoko's Blackness.' *Aphra Behn Studies*, edited by Janet Todd. pp. 235–258. Cambridge: Cambridge UP, 1996.

Hall, Kim. *Things of Darkness: Economies of Race and Gender in Early Modern England*. Cornell UP, 1995.

Hernon, Ian. 'The Notting Hill Race Riots.' *Riot! Civil Insurrection from Peterloo to the Present Day*. Ann Arbor: Pluto P, 2006, pp. 170–184.

Heywood, John. 'Of a Cattes Looke, cxvii.' *Two Hundred Epigrammes, Vpon Two Hundred Prouerbes With a Thyrde Hundred Newely Added and Made by Iohn Heywood*. London: T. Berthelet, 1555.

Hogarth, William. *Engravings By Hogarth*, edited by Sean Shesgreen. Dover Publications, 1973.

Hughes, Derek, 'Blackness in Gobineau and Behn: Oroonoko and Racial Pseudo Science.' *Women's Writing*, vol. 19, 2012, pp. 204–221.

Jonson, Ben. *The Masque of Blackness. The Works of Ben Jonson*. Boston: Phillips, Samson and Co., 1863, pp. 660–663.

Kureishi, Hanif. *The Black Album*. Simon and Schuster, 1996.

Lewcock, Dawn. 'More for Seeing Than Hearing: Behn and the Use of Theatre.' *Aphra Behn Studies*, edited by Janet Todd. Cambridge UP, 1996, pp. 66–83.

Macdonald, Joyce Green. *Women and Race in Early Modern Texts*. Cambridge UP, 2002.

Mangan, Lucy. 'A Brief History of Agony Aunts.' *The Guardian* 12 Nov. 2009. https://www.theguardian.com/lifeandstyle/2009/nov/13/agony-aunts

Mathews, Daniel, and Julian Assange. 'A Cat May Look Upon a King, but Not at Gitmo.' Wikileaks, https://wikileaks.org/wiki/A_Cat_May_Look_Upon_a_King,_but_Not_at_Gitmo

Modood, Tariq. 'Political Blackness and British Asians.' *Sociology*, vol. 28, 1994, pp. 859–876.

Modood, Tariq. 'The Rise and Fall of Anti-Racism: From Political Blackness to Ethnic Pluralism.' *New Left, New Right and Beyond: Taking the Sixties Seriously*, edited by Geoff Andrews, Richard Cockett, Alan Hooper, and Michael Williams. St. Martin's P, 1999, pp. 168–181.

Mohdin, Aamna. '"Political Blackness": A Very British Concept with a Complex History.' *Quartz*, 3 Mar. 2018. qz.com/1219398/political-blackness-a-very-british-concept-with-a-complex-history/

Norton, Mary Beth. 'John Dunton and the Invention of the Feminine Private.' *Separated by their Sex: Women in Public and Private in the Colonial Atlantic World*. Cornell UP, 2011, pp. 79–104.

Olusoga, David. *Black and British: A Forgotten History*. Macmillan, 2017.

Orr, Leah. 'Attribution Problems in the Fiction of Aphra Behn.' *Modern Language Review*, vol. 108, 2013, pp. 30–51.

Richardson, Samuel. *Pamela; Or, Virtue Rewarded*. Oxford UP, 2001.

Roberts, Edgar V. 'An Unrecorded Meaning of "Joke" (or "Joak") in England.' *American Speech*, vol. 37, 1962, pp. 137–140.

Sertima, Ivan Van. *They Came Before Columbus: The African Presence in America*. Random House, 1977.

Shah, Rubika. *White Riot* trailer. *YouTube*, uploaded by Film Movement, 22 Sep. 2020, www.youtube.com/watch?v=Fj9WXw_W1dc

Shakespeare, William. *Love's Labour's Lost*, edited by George Richard Hibbard. Oxford UP, 1990.

Shakespeare, William. *Sonnets*. Lerner, 2018.

Smith, Rebecca. 'A Day in the Life of Jane Austen.' *History Extra: The Official Website for BBC History Magazine, BBC History Revealed and BBC World Histories Magazine* 15 Dec. 2016. www.historyextra.com/period/georgian/a-day-in-the-life-of-jane-austen/

Staines, John D. *The Tragic Histories of Mary Queen of Scots, 1560–1690*. Ashgate, 2009.

Swift, Jonathan. 'Ode to the Athenian Society.' *The Works of Jonathan Swift*, vol. 8. Edinburgh: John Donadlson, 1774, pp. 257–266.

The Woman of Colour, A Tale, edited by Lyndon J. Dominique Peterborough: Broadview P, 2007.

Waters, Rob. 'Political Blackness: Brothers and Sisters.' *Thinking Black: Britain 1964–85*. U of California P, 2019, pp. 51–92

Whatley, Jack. "The Story Behind The Song: 'White Riot' The Clash's Misunderstood Punk masterclass." *Faroutmagazine* 18 Mar. 2020. faroutmagazine.co.uk/the-clash-white-riot-the-story-behind-the-song/

Wheeler, Roxann. *The Complexion of Race: Categories of Difference in Eighteenth-Century British Culture*. U of Pennsylvania P, 2000.

Wilson, Amrit, Kehinde Andrews and Vera Chok. 'Is Political Blackness Still Relevant Today?' *The Guardian* 27 Oct. 2016. www.theguardian.com/commentisfree/2016/oct/27/political-blackness-black-history-month-zayn-malik-sadiq-khan

PART III

Critical Approaches to Austen: A Sampling

21

HEARING VOICES IN AUSTEN: THE REPRESENTATION OF SPEECH AND VOICE IN THE NOVELS

Adela Pinch

UNIVERSITY OF MICHIGAN

Introduction

Austen's novels are full of voices. The characters impress themselves on us as memorable talkers, many with distinctive voices and patterns of speech. They talk a lot: it is as if, in liberating herself from the epistolary form of her early assays at fiction, Austen turned the novel form into a chatter-box, a forum for face-to-face encounters, out loud. Showcasing chapters consisting of virtually nothing but dialogue, Austen's novels sometimes seem rooted in the play script. And equally, they seem destined to have found afterlives as audible forms, from Victorian dramatizations of the talky bits (Looser 85–94), to film, to audiobook. Alongside character voices, moreover, Austen herself is paramount, in many reader's apprehension, for what seems like her own distinctive voice: it is a tone, a style, a sound, felt like 'quite the voice of a friend' (*MP* 318). In her 1871 appreciation of Austen, for example, Anne Thackeray likened discovering Austen to one of those moments when 'come pressing onward in the crowd of life, voices with some of the notes that are wanting to our own part—voices tuned to the same key as our own, or to an accordant one'. 'To few of us there exists any more complete ideal', she enthused (quoted in Southam 167). Contemplating how central voices are to Austen's fiction and reception may make us wonder anew what a novel truly is: is it the record of a narrating voice? Or, a set of instructions for a vocal performance? These questions estrange us from one of the most basic truisms of literary history: that the novel emerged as Europe's preeminent literary form only with the advent of silent reading (Hunter 1977, 1990; Siskin; Jajdelska).

To focus on speech and voice in Austen, therefore, affords us an opportunity to reopen some fundamental questions about her place in the history of the novel, a history to which she is rightly seen as central. It may also allow us to use Austen as a testing ground for key moves in narrative theory. Voice has been a central concept in theories of the novel, from M.M. Bakhtin's influential account in *The Dialogic Imagination* of the novel as an interwoven fabric of many voices, to Gérard Genette's categories of narrative voice in *Narrative Discourse*. Yet, as I will discuss below, classical narrative theory—powerful as it is—may fail to capture readers' sense that there are distinct voices in Austen. Now, I contend, is a good time to use Austen to explore not only gaps, but also new developments in narrative theory. After a few decades of emphasis—in the study of the novel in general and of Austen in particular—on the representation of character's minds, an exciting conversation about the techniques for representing dialogue in fiction is now taking place. In this context, my essay assesses the significance of the astonishing diversity of Austen's methods for representing speech and voice. It seeks to understand small moments when Austen makes a voice

DOI: 10.4324/9780429398155-21-25

emerge against the background of larger histories: a media-centred history of the novel as part of a longer history of media designed to capture sound; and the cultural history of Romantic-era Britain, a culture attuned to the glamour of the human voice.

Addressing both 'voice' and 'speech' requires some justification. Readers will have noticed that thus far I have tacked back and forth between the narrative voice of the novels—a voice that seems to emanate from, or be a quality belonging to, Austen herself—and the speech of her fictional characters. For much of what follows below, these two categories will be disaggregated, defined, and discussed separately. However, students of Austen know that one of the key pleasures and puzzles of her novels lie in the passages where the voices of narrator and character overlap. Austen's extraordinary use of free indirect discourse—the technique by which a character's words or thoughts seamlessly speak through a novel's narrator—is rightly seen as one of the distinguishing features of Austen's fiction, and one of her key contributions to the development of the novel. But the vast scholarly debate about Austen's use of free indirect discourse tends to emphasize its role in her delineation of thinking: we have, especially recently, been preoccupied with Austen in relation to the mental sciences.

Indeed, it is in part because narrative-theoretical approaches to Austen have tended to prioritize her representation of mind that I have chosen to emphasize how some of her distinctive technical achievements—including free indirect discourse—also raise huge theoretical questions about the form of the novel in relation to voice and sound. And yet, the distinction between thought and speech—like the distinction between narrative voice and character speech—needs to be broken down. "'Here have I", said she, "actually talked poor Harriet into being very much attached to this man'" (*E* 108). This is Emma alone in her room, in an extended episode in which her agonized thoughts are mostly represented through free indirect discourse, but then erupt into something that looks like speech. How do readers apprehend this 'said she'? Is Emma truly exclaiming out loud, or is this a moment where thought takes the form of speech? Under what conditions do thoughts seem like voices? Where are the voices? As we shall see by the end of this essay, Austen's novels turn inside out our sense of the difference between inside voices and outside voices.

The Author's Voice

In 1870, the unnamed author of an appreciative essay on Austen's work in the *St. Paul's Magazine* begins his or her assessment by noting that it is now 'more than half a century' since 'her pleasant voice ceased to charm the ears' (Southam 226). Another Victorian critic referred to Austen as a 'voice of common sense and dry wit' (Southam 214). The tendency to conflate Austen's writing with the voice of the person herself is so commonplace that it takes some effort to pause and unpack it. And indeed the concept of voice in literary criticism—and in novel studies in particular—has a complicated history, with some twists and turns in which Austen has been implicated.

In general, to speak of an author's voice is to refer to a distinctive set of features—tone, attitudes, linguistic patterns, but also recognizable positions and opinions that allows a reader to feel with some conviction that they know where a piece of text is coming from. It is an aural fingerprint—or pretends to be. One of the challenges of studying 'voice' in fiction is that it is, at bottom, a 'heuristic metaphor' (Aczel, 494 46; see also St. Clair, 357; Walsh, 37). Novels do not come with buttons that, when pushed, produce sounds perceptible to the outer ear. But the figure of voice is a metaphor that causes its users to forget, constantly, that it is a metaphor. Angela Leighton observes that reading for sounds—reading 'with the ears'—involves a 'slightly comic juggling of fact and figure, matter and metaphor .... the ear hovers somewhere between a literal and a metaphorical faculty in the work of reading, between a sense perception, alert to real noises, and a figure for hearing that might pay attention to sounds on the page that are self-evidently inaudible' (Leighton 2).

The study of voice in fiction—as opposed to poetry—has, moreover, a relatively recent history, sculpted by the crosscurrents of twentieth-century literary criticism. Andrew Elfenbein has argued that the concept of voice only emerged in the literary criticism taught in schools and universities once the arts of the voice—elocution, oratory, reading aloud—passed out of literary education, at the end of the nineteenth century (Elfenbein 202). The New Critics enshrined 'voice' in poetry studies—as in T.S. Eliot's 'Three Voices' and Reuben Browers' 'The Speaking Voice'—and read poetry for irony and tone. While the impact of the New Criticism on the study of the novel was muted, its emphasis on voice appeared in the work of Austen critic Mary Lascelles, whose 1939 *Jane Austen and Her Art* sought to identify 'the tone of Austen's voice' (Lascelles 59). She identifies what she calls the 'youthful, high-spirited voice' of the opening chapters of *Northanger Abbey*, and declares, after a chorus of characters respond to Louisa Musgrove's fall in *Persuasion*: 'a familiar voice penetrates the babble of the poor Musgroves, a voice which no one who has heard it before can fail to recognize for Austen's own' (77).

Yet Lascelles' insistence on the recognizability of 'Austen's own' voice rubs up against a concept she seems to offer as a contrast: at times she distinguishes Austen's voice from the 'narrative' voice. In distinguishing Austen's voice from the narrative voice, Lascelles introduces a question that became central to narrative theory: is it necessary to postulate that the voice of a novel emanates from a narrator—a fictive being of some kind who is distinct from the actual person of the author? Whose voice are we hearing? Theorists took different paths. Continental, structuralist narratologists of the 1960s and 1970s such as Roland Barthes and Gérard Genette always removed the actual person of the author from the equation, in order to analyse different forms of narrative voice. Wayne Booth suggested that we call the voice that narrates a third-person novel an 'implied author', distinct from the real author herself (Booth 57). In her feminist-narratological approach to Austen and other women writers, Susan Lanser singled out a particular mode of narration she called 'authorial voice'—overtly public, opinionated—through which we can track a woman writer's struggles to achieve authority (Lanser 15–18). Indeed, in discussions of voice, voice is often a figure for authority, identity, and agency: to have a voice is to be a specific kind of person (Keane; Walsh 37). 'Studies of "voice" in literature are far more likely to be figurative investigations of identity projections than anything to do with aurality', laments one sound scholar (St. Clair 357).

The advantages of approaches to fiction that use voice as a figure for identity, distinguishing the voice telling the story from the actual mouth of the flesh-and-blood author, are many. It avoids a naïve empiricism that attributes a novel to the personal perspective of an individual; it makes us aware of the constructedness of fictional narratives in their telling as well as in their tales; and it provides us with a starting point for attending to different kinds of narration, even with in a single work. But more locally, as readers of Austen, we tend to agree that there are passages of the novel where we feel we are experiencing something like Austen's 'own voice'. Who says, towards the end of *Persuasion*, 'this may be bad morality to end with, but I believe this to be truth' (199)? Who exclaims, about Mrs Price in *Mansfield Park,* 'Poor woman! She probably thought a change of air would agree with many of her children' (*MP* [2003] 10). Why are we more likely to say we hear Austen speaking at such moments, more so than when we read the more strictly narrative parts of the novels ('It was the beginning of February....'. [*P* 131])? Is that a narrator's voice? Are the concepts of 'narrator', and 'voice' the best way to describe such readerly experiences?

In recent years, some scholars have suggested that perhaps the different taxonomies of persons and voices of classical structuralist narratology do not correspond to reader's experiences. In an article called 'Does Austen Need Narrators? Does Anyone?' Bryan Boyd's answer is, in a word, 'no'. Boyd dismantles the stipulation of classical narratology, that we must always postulate a narrative voice distinct from the author. Using *Emma* as his test case, he argues that insisting on a narrator commits us to a curiously two-stepped understanding of this novel, in which Austen first invents the story-world, and then a narrator tells it. In *Emma*, he demonstrates, the invention of the story-world and the narrating of it are clearly feeding on each other. 'The enforced division of responsibilities as author and a distinct narrator somehow reporting from the world of Highbury in the Necessary Narrator Thesis is ontologically and causally muddled', he concludes (Boyd 300). Boyd's pragmatic suggestion is that we dispense with 'narrative voice' altogether, and just talk about Austen, the writer. Perhaps a more nuanced way to honour our sense that there are passages in Austen that seem 'voicey' would be to dispense with taxonomies that ask us to discriminate between voices—author's? implied author's? narrator's?—and consider instead Seymour Chatman's proposal of a 'spectrum of possibilities, going from narrators who are least audible to those who are most so' (Chatman 146). There are not different persons telling the story; there are simply features—an 'I', an exclamation point—that create different voice-effects for readers.

Students and readers interested in the concept of voice in Austen will also find that classical narratology relies on a very particular conception of the term. In *Narrative Discourse*, Genette establishes different categories of voice that are not at all about vocal quality, tone, or sound, but are rather derived from grammatical categories that designate the position of a speaker. Under the umbrella of 'narrative voice' Genette developed taxonomies for identifying *the time when* a storyteller is situated in relation to the time of the events, the ontological level from which the story is being told (is the storyteller outside of the action, or inside?), and the nature of the person speaking. In 'Hearing Voices in Narrative Texts', Richard Aczel notes there is a kind of 'deafness to voice' in Genette's categories; 'his limited characterization of voice (and its attendant preoccupation with categorizing narrator types and levels) ultimately forecloses more insight into voice than it opens' (Aczel 469). Aczel advocates a pivot away from the Genettian structural-functional approach to voice in fiction towards one that is more pragmatic, more qualitative in approach, focusing on the textual features and signs that make readers feel they are hearing a voice (see also Walsh; Fludernik 'New Wine').

In the view of literary voice advocated by Aczel, voice is 'framed less as an ontological question than as a pragmatic aspect of reading' (494); it is an effect rather than 'the private property either of a character or of the author or narrator' (Ree 1045). Perhaps we should think of Austen's novels the way Mary Musgrove's drawing-room appears to Anne Elliot, on first seeing Captain Wentworth after eight years: 'the room seemed full—full of persons and voices' (*P* 52). It is worth dwelling on the peculiar phrase 'persons and voices', which separates voices from the persons from whom they presumably emanate with an 'and'. Is Austen using one of Shakespeare's favourite rhetorical figures, the hendiadys, in which something which might reasonably be one thing gets split into two by an 'and' (as in, 'food and diet' [*Hamlet* I.i.99], 'the view and knowing of these contents' [*Hamlet* V.ii.44]) for emphasis? Might Austen be using hendiadys to stress Anne's state of shock, her inability to perceive where the voices around her are coming from? Austen separates out voices from other aspects of person elsewhere: she uses a comparable, slightly hendiadic phrase to indicate the aural presence of unseen others in *Mansfield Park*, when Fanny strains to hear 'voices and feet' ([2003] 77). Here, as in 'persons and voices', the 'and' ought to remind us to pause, not to leap to conclusions about what a voice is, and where it comes from. Austen's novels are 'full of persons *and* voices', not persons *with* voices.

If we take a more qualitative approach to voice, then, as Richard Walsh notes, 'many of the discursive features commonly embraced by voice are equally, and perhaps better, understood as style' (50). Perhaps, then, to understand how and why reading Austen feels like hearing a voice, we should turn not to narrative theory but to an adjacent body of scholarship, the analysis of style. For D.A. Miller, 'voice' and 'style' are nearly synonymous. He opens *Jane Austen, or the Secret of Style* by appealing to the Austen-lover's seduction by a particular voice and casts the young Austen reader as an impressionable Harriet Smith to Austen's Emma Woodhouse: 'All of us who read Jane Austen early … were lost to the siren song of her voice. "How nicely you talk; I love to hear you. You understand everything"' (Miller 1). In moving seamlessly from his appeal to the power of the voice of the novels, to Harriet's love of Emma's speech patterns, Miller affirms the central metaphor—that reading and hearing, speaking and writing, are all self-evidently combined in the figure of voice. Miller's move here is not unlike Henry Austen's affirmation of the connection between his sister's skill as a speaker and writer: 'Her voice was extremely sweet. She delivered herself with fluency and precision … excelling in conversation as much as in composition' (5). As Miller continues, however, he distinguishes between the voice of a person, and the voice of Austen's fiction, which is fundamentally impersonal: 'Yet whereas Emma's talk merely held Harriet with the charm of a *person*, what Austen's writing channelled for us was the considerably more exciting appeal of no longer being one. Here was a truly out-of-body voice, so stirringly free of what it abhorred as 'particularity' or 'singularity' that it seemed to come from no enunciator at all''. 'Altogether', he declares, 'such thrillingly inhuman utterance was not stylish; it was Style itself' (2).

In this striking account, Miller leverages several assumptions about voice to further his distinctive account of Austen Style. First, Miller endorses a view of Austen's voice as definitionally distinct from 'person'. In seeing Austen's voice as 'truly out-of-body', detached, and impersonal, in fact, Miller's view of 'Austen Style' ultimately draws on a longstanding analysis of Austen's prose style heir to the syntactic patterns and moral and political values of the great Augustan and Georgian prose writers, in particular Samuel Johnson. This is a view of Austen style/voice that emphasizes her use of grammatical parallelism, as, for example, in this characterization of Mrs Norris in *Mansfield Park*: 'her love of money was equal to her love of directing' ([2003] 7); or this characterization of Mr Bingley's sisters in *Pride and Prejudice*: 'not deficient in good humour when they were pleased, nor in the power of being agreeable when they chose it' (10). These parallel structures seem to go hand in glove with an attitude, a worldview, a tone: an orderly detachment that gently mocks the folly and disorder of the world (see Yelland 93–122).

Close stylistic analyses of Austen's sentence structure can, indeed, go a good way towards defining what many readers identify as Austen's characteristic voice. There are, however, risks to this approach. It may be reasonably objected that language use and prose style belong firmly to the study of writing, and do not address the maddeningly difficult question of the complex metaphor of voice, when and how we apply that category to a book. Moreover, choosing a set of linguistic patterns and identifying them as Austen's 'voice' risks blanketing Austen's prose style with an expectation of sameness. Many attentive scholars of Austen's prose have demonstrated how wrong it is to see Austen's as an uncritical adopter of the Johnsonian sentence (Page *Language*; Bray; Elfenbein; Yelland); and how diverse and flexible Austen's prose is; how dramatically it morphed over the course of her novels.

Most compelling for the student of the relationship between style and voice in Austen may be the approach taken in Cris Yelland's *Jane Austen: A Style in History*. A 'micro-history' of Austen's style, Yelland's distinctiveness lies in situating changes in Austen's prose across time at the crossroads of two currents of ideas about language use in her era: on the one hand, the rise of prescriptive grammar focused on rules; and on the other hand, a culture of reading aloud that—as we shall discuss in the next section—prioritized prose that captured the rhythms of ordinary speech. Thus—in contrast to approach to the author's voice such as D.A. Miller's, that takes voice and style as synonymous—Yelland provides a detailed analysis of Austen's flexible style as shaped by historical practices and beliefs about the speaking voice. The cultures of the human voice during Austen's era is where we shall turn in the next section.

Romantic Voice Culture

Austen wrote her novels in an era that glamorized the presence and capacities of the human voice. Regency culture memorialized great voices caught in the act of talking, through a vogue for books such as Lady Blessington's *Conversations with Lord Byron,* and the *Table Talk* of Samuel Taylor

Coleridge; not far behind was the example of that 'Hercules of conversation recording', as Lennard Davis termed him, the John Boswell of *The Life of Samuel Johnson* (Davis 173). Theatregoers sought to capture in writing the great voices of the stage, such as Sarah Siddons and Fanny Kemble (Michaelson 117–123; Pascoe; Lynch). Romantic poetry celebrated the powerful voice, modelled on natural sound, as when, for example, Wordsworth eulogizes Milton's 'voice whose sound was like the sea' ('London, 1802'). Katie Trumpener, Ivan Kreilkamp, and Yopie Prins have emphasized that the context for nineteenth-century fascination with voice was the perception of a world that had become completely dominated by silent print. How did Austen and her contemporaries view the relationship between print and voice? Was the job of print to capture the human voice? Did print demand to be read aloud?

Jane Austen, writes Patricia Michaelson, 'almost certainly wrote her novels anticipating that they would be read aloud' (195; see also Sutherland 301). The evidence of her letters, and the recollections of her friends and family, points to a strong commitment to reading aloud, in particular of her own works. Her brother Henry Austen claimed that 'she read aloud with very great taste and effect. Her own works, probably, were never heard to so much advantage as from her own mouth' (5). Her nieces Anna Lefroy, Caroline Austen, and Fanny and Marianne Knight all recollected Austen reading aloud (Yelland 60; Michaelson 179; Le Faye 202). The Austen family read her novels out loud to each other and to friends, the novelist on one occasion sharply taking exception to her mother's failings as a reader: 'our 2d evening's reading to Miss Benn had not pleased me so well, but I believe [sic] something must be attributed to my Mother's too rapid way of getting on—& tho' she perfectly understands the Characters herself, she cannot speak as they ought' (4 February 1813; *Letters* 203). Michaelson and Yelland have fleshed out a historical context for the Austen family's commitment to reading aloud, a context in which the virtues of reading aloud, its ideal practices, and the ways in which texts could accommodate themselves to the exigencies of reading aloud, were elaborated by educators, performers, and elocutionists. The eighteenth-century elocutionary movement spawned numerous treatises training readers to perform text out loud with the cadences of natural, impassioned voices. For example, Joshua Steele's *Prosodia Rationalis* (1779) proposed an elaborate system of textual markings—akin to musical notation—to capture the detailed patterns of rhythm, pauses, and tones of speech. Gilbert Austin, the author of *Chironomia; or, a Treatise on Rhetorical Delivery* (1806), urged specific methods for dramatic readings of novels, which, he notes, frequently furnished the materials for family read-alouds (we might recall that Henry Tilney reads *The Mysteries of Udolpho* aloud to his sister, [*NA* 77]): 'Novels, or modern fictitious biography, are so frequently the subject of private readings … that they demand some notice. … In reading these works aloud to the private circle, the custom, arising from the eager desire of unravelling the story, has determined that the mere narrative should be read with unusual rapidity'. But, he continues—affirming Austen's complaint about her mother's 'too rapid way of getting on'—'the interesting scenes demand impressive reading, and many of the scenes, which are constructed like those in a regular drama, require to be read in a similar manner' (quoted in Michaelson 193).

Austen's characters sometimes distinguish between reading aloud and speaking, between—as Tom Bertram puts it—'conversing in the elegant written language of some respectable author' and 'chattering in words of our own' (*MP* [2003] 99). When she is pressed to help Edmund Bertram and Mary Crawford rehearse their scene in *Lovers' Vows*, Fanny Price protests that if she does, 'I must *read* the part, for I can *say* very little of it' (*MP* 132). But in practice, Austen's novels evoke a world in which human voices pour forth utterances that fall along a spectrum between reading and saying, between chattering one's own chatter and eloquently performing another's words. The elocutionists often explicitly lumped reading and speaking together: Michaelson observes that 'in a chapter of his *Liberal Education* entitled 'On Learning to Speak or Read with Propriety', Vicesimus Knox said bluntly, 'Under speaking I comprehend reading'' (Michaelson 143).

In her most extended treatment of reading aloud—the scene in *Mansfield Park* in which Henry Crawford reads aloud from Shakespeare's *Henry VIII*—reading and talking are layered together. Henry's reading serves as a kind of siren's call to Fanny, so vivid is it that she cannot resist becoming entranced:

> His reading was capital, and her pleasure in good reading was extreme. To *good* reading, however, she had been long used; her uncle read well—her cousins all—Edmund very well; but in Mr Crawford's reading there was a variety of excellence beyond what she had ever met with. … Whether it were dignity or pride, or tenderness or remorse, or whatever were to be expressed, he could do it with equal beauty. ([2003] 264)

After the reading ceases, an extended conversation *about* reading aloud ensues: Austen pointedly notes that 'the two young men' present—Henry and Edmund—'were the only talkers', and frames the conversation as an extension of Henry's performance, to which 'Fanny was listening *again* with great entertainment' , emphasis mine). Reading aloud, and the capacity to *talk* about reading aloud, are joined as a single cultural capacity; and listening to reading and listening to talking about reading are equally pleasurable, Austen suggests.

The terms of Edmund's and Henry's discussion of reading aloud come right from the elocutionist's manuals. They canvas the need for 'early attention and habit' to instil the skills of reading, of 'management of the voice, of proper modulation and emphasis, of foresight and judgment', of the need for 'distinctness and energy' in reading ([2003] 266). Thus, Austen makes clear how familiar she expected her readers to be with this discourse. The elocutionary movement stemmed in part from dismay about the lackluster speaking skills of many Anglican clergy. In *Mansfield Park*, with its focus on Edmund's vocation as a modern, evangelically inspired minister, the question of reading aloud is not surprisingly folded into Edmund's concerns throughout the novel of defending the sincerity of the ideal clergyman (on the Austen family's concern with the Anglican clergy's skills in reading and speaking, see *Mansfield Park* [Lynch] 372–373n5, 6). What is surprising—especially in the context of debates, both elsewhere in *Mansfield Park* and elsewhere in eighteenth- and nineteenth-century Britain about whether it was permissible for a clergyman to read a sermon authored by someone else rather than preparing his own—is the way in which Edmund seems to suggest there really is—or perhaps ought to be—no difference between reading and preaching. He contrasts modern clergy inspired by the current 'spirit of improvement' to older men of the cloth who, he says disparagingly, 'to judge by their performance, must have thought that reading was reading and preaching was preaching'. 'It is different now', he continues, curiously suggesting that for modern clergy the ability to read skilfully and to preach sincerely and effectively are part of the same set of skills ([2003] 266).

While Austen pokes gentle fun at both Henry and Edmund throughout their reading aloud discussion, the evidence of her concern with the reading aloud of her own fiction suggest that the concerns of the elocutionists—the vision of print as matter to be converted into sound—alluded to in *Mansfield Park* were central to her vision of the novel. It suggests that Austen's novels may be apt candidates for a view of the novel as a genre, not as the property of the individual, isolated silent reader, designed to facilitate a seamless interface between printed surface and the reader's brain, but rather something more like a script or prompt-book, awaiting activation through out-loud, sociable readings. This is a vision of the novel that prioritizes what one scholar calls 'transdiction' ('print becomes voice'; Sutherland 311), and this is also the provocation of Jonathan Ree, who argues:

> Having distinguished, perhaps too confidently, between performing and non-performing arts, theorists normally bundle literary fiction into the second category, grouping with painting or sculpture rather than with, say, plays and songs. This is rash. Many readers find

it almost impossible to avoid approaching novels as schemas for vocal performances, comparable to playscripts or vocal scores. (1046)

Ree continues, 'we imagine the words spoken in specific voices, male or female, young or old, and with particular timings, pitches, dynamics, and pronunciations. We gesticulate, chuckle, grunt, and sigh. Some of us, in fact, can get quite hoarse after a couple of hours of solitary absorption in the novel' (1046). Ree's impressionistic account is backed up by recent neuroscientific research, which provides evidence that perhaps, in fact, reading aloud and reading silently may not be cognitively distinct activities: silent reading activates the places in the brain also activated by hearing voices (Rubery 15–16). Literary historians and theorists influenced by media studies and sound studies have asked us to think about the novel as part of long history of voice reproduction technologies—from manuscript, to play script, to codex, that look forward to audiobook and film, and digital (Rubery; Keskinen; Sterne; Butler). In this view, novels are resonant blocks, 'full of persons and voices', and audiobooks are the fulfilment of the two-century's long dream that novels in fact talk. Judith Pascoe suggests that we 'look back to the years we call the romantic period in order to discover the moment when some not-yet-imagined mode of technology makes a preliminary, uncooked foray into the public sphere' (18). We might think of Austen's novels, as Pascoe thinks of Wordsworth's resonant 'Solitary Reaper', that they are 'part of a larger culture whose concerns would make sound recording technology conceivable' (18).

We can specify what it might mean to see Austen's novels in this long history by studying how her books incorporated some of the orthographic technologies designed by late eighteenth-century elocutionists to help books record and produce sound. To do so is to delve into her novels' place in the history of punctuation marks. Since its origins, punctuation in Europe has always been associated with sound reproduction; many of the marks emerged in medieval manuscripts alongside textual marks and variations for liturgical oratory and musical notation (Ree; Parkes). In late-eighteenth-century England, however, punctuation was the subject of debate between the elocutionists—devoted, as we have seen, to viewing text as script to be read aloud—and grammarians (Carlson 129–144, 150–160). In the works of grammarians such as Hugh Blair's influential *Lectures on Rhetoric and Belles Lettres* (1783), punctuation was always to follow rules of syntax and grammar. For the elocutionists, punctuation indicated spoken emphasis, stress, and rhythm; textual marks served as means of 'encoding speech in print' (Carlson, 182); in the words of John Rice, 'giv[ing] the Energy of the Living Voice to the Precision of the Dead Letter' (quoted in Carlson 155).

The relationship between punctuation and voice in Austen's novels is at the centre of Kathryn Sutherland's intriguing, controversial account of the textual history of the novels. Like Michaelson and Yelland, Sutherland sees Austen as deeply enmeshed in the culture of reading aloud. In Austen's negotiations with the publishers who produced her work, Sutherland sees the author as caught up in the differences between ideologies of textual marking, the grammatical and the elocutionary. Her test case is the one instance in Austen's lifetime in which two different publishing houses brought out editions of a single work: *Mansfield Park*. Comparing the 1814 edition published by Thomas Egerton, with the second edition of that novel brought out by John Murray in 1816, Sutherland identifies patterns of punctuation in both. She argues that the 1816 edition regularizes punctuation according to grammatical rules, replacing a looser punctuation in the 1814 edition that, according to Sutherland, was designed to reflect and to enable oral delivery; that text accommodates what she calls the 'acoustic trace' (Sutherland 298). In 1814, there is more use of commas that not only indicate a relation between grammatical units, but rather mark breathing space, a place where a speaker might catch her breath, a pause in the rhythm of what a listener would hear. For example, here is Edmund talking about Shakespeare—in *Mansfield Park*'s dialogue about reading aloud—in the 1814 edition: 'To know him in bits and scraps, is common enough, to know him pretty thoroughly, is perhaps, not uncommon, but to read him well aloud, is no every day talent' (*Mansfield*

Park [Penguin] 313). Here commas obey no grammatical rules; there is no distinction between punctuation for emphasis (such as the comma between 'scraps' and 'is') and punctuation separating grammatical units (such as the comma between 'enough' and 'to'). The heavy use of commas creates a rhythm of utterance, running-on, and pauses, as if Edmund is thinking his way through his position. In 1816, some of those commas have been replaced with more grammatically correct semi-colons: 'To know him in bits and scraps, is common enough; to know him pretty thoroughly is, perhaps, not uncommon; but to read him well aloud, is no every-day talent' (*MP 2003* 265). In this version, Edmund's speech reads more like a composed set of sententiae; he is guilty of the pomposity and priggishness that, indeed, some readers have accused him of.

Sutherland argues that Austen's own preference was for the looser, more aural/oral style of 1814 that made room for what she calls 'vocal encroachment' into the world of print (300). Furthermore, for Sutherland, the transition from the 1814 to the 1816 *Mansfield Park* is the story of the eclipse of a more flowing, feminine text by the more rigid, silent text governed by the masculine rules of modern grammar. She laments the legacy of 1816, which was the base text for the influential twentieth-century editor of the Oxford editions of Jane Austen, R.W. Chapman. In following the grammatical punctuation laid down by the house of Murray, she contends, Chapman solidified for modern readers the version of Austen as a 'conformant and prim stylistician' (Sutherland 295). Chapman's edition, in turn, provided the text for countless editions of Austen—including, of course, the Oxford World's Classics texts I am using as my base text for this essay, on account of their familiarity. But in Sutherland's account, in disseminating and normalizing the Chapman versions of the novels, the 'acoustic trace' of Austen's novels recedes.

We may ultimately be agnostic about Sutherland's claim that the evidence points firmly towards Austen's preference for punctuating with the 'acoustic trace' in mind (for the other side of the debate, see Wiltshire 'Editing "Mansfield Park"'; Wiltshire 'Introduction'; see also Gemmill's helpful discussion of punctuation and printers, 157n4). However, Sutherland's account demonstrates how the impression of a voice depends, paradoxically, on detailed textual markings, in the slender diacritical differences between one marking and another. A desire for voice leads the critic deep into the materiality of print. Sutherland prompts us to be mindful not only of the deeply engrained desire for voice that attends our reading of fiction, but also of the uneven, often contingent histories of the print technologies and practices that mediated Austen's representation of voice. Theories of literary voice, the study of Austen makes acutely clear, must be inseparable from book history. Some of those histories—especially the history of quotation marks—will be relevant in our next section, as we turn to Austen's representation of her character's voices.

Austen's Representation of Character Speech

How might we expand our thinking about Austen's representation of the other voices in her books? The 'eternal talker's' who populate them (*E* 130), their distinctive voices, the dialogues, the 'un-reserved conversation' (*SS* 16)? There have been numerous studies of the thematic significance of talk in Austen (Stovel), of the ethics of conversation (Tandon), of the politics of speech and silence, of hearing and listening to others (Gaylin; Nesbit). Given the centrality of conversation to Austen's novels, it seems not unreasonable to suggest that—rather than simply reflecting the era's conversational practices—they may have served as how-to 'conversation manuals' for readers (Michaelson 20); that they might be viewed as ideal instances of Lennard Davis' contention that the rise of the novel in fact created 'conversation' as a recognizable speech genre (Davis 162). This essay, however, has been suggesting that reframing both narrative voice and character speech within the overlapping frames of narrative theory and cultural history can return us to the more fundamental questions about how speech appears, and help us see what is rich and strange in Austen's practice. What can Austen's work teach us about what it means to represent a voice? What are its conditions and conventions? As we shall see, in many ways the decades right before Austen's writing saw a significant stabilization of the conventions for representing character speech in fiction, and in many ways, her novels bear witness to that normalization of techniques. However, her work also reveals an almost logic-defying diversity of modes of representing character speech. The remainder of this essay seeks to give a glimpse into the peculiarities of some of Austen's modes of representing speech; studying them, I hope to show, can provide another point of entry into debates in narrative theory, and can lead to a new way to understand our attachment to Austen.

Speech representation in the novel has largely been less extensively theorized than many aspects of novel form. And quoted character speech often seems to have an especially direct relation to the 'real', accorded transparent access to something that seems real, in both naïve—and not so naïve—theories of literary realism (Cohen and Green 130–31; Menon 161; for a sophisticated account of realism that sees quoted speech as bodily presence, see Jameson 98–99). There is a tendency to treat quoted discourse in fiction as very close cousin to quoted speech in other, nonfiction genres of writing. Quotation marks appear to readers as stamps of the veracity of what lies between them, conspiring to make us feel as if quoted speech is perfect recording of what was actually said. The opening quotation mark figures not unlike a 'press play' button on a recording device that captures the voice, until the closing quotation mark—called by eighteenth-century printer John Smith in *The Printer's Grammar* 'the mark of silence'—presses stop (Smith 89). Quoted speech in fiction seems thus 'maximally mimetic', exempted from some of the scrutiny that other aspects of realist fiction (character, plot, narration, description) have received (Patrick O'Neill quoted by Cohen and Green, 130). We tend to read quoted fictional speech according to a 'transcriptional' aesthetic (which presumes the text is a record of a voice), as opposed to a 'transdictional' one discussed in the last section of this essay.

Jane Austen, however, comments slyly on the particularly fictional status of quoted speech, and in so doing anticipates some recent narrative theory. It occurs in a dialogue about reading between Catherine Morland and Eleanor Tilney in *Northanger Abbey*. While Catherine is an avid reader of fiction, she confesses to Eleanor that she has no taste for reading history. Interestingly, one of her prime objections to history is the patent falseness of the speeches attributed to historical figures: "'I often think it odd that it should be so dull, for a great deal of it must be invention. The speeches that are put into the heroes' mouths, their thoughts and designs—the chief of all this must be invention, and invention'", she concludes, self-reflexively, "'is what delights me in other books'". Eleanor professes herself to be totally fine with the fictionality of represented speech, even in history: "'if a speech be well drawn up, I read it with pleasure, by whomsoever it may be made—and probably with much greater, if the production of Mr Hume or Mr Robertson, than if the genuine words of Caractacus, Agricola, or Alfred the Great'" (*NA* 79). For both Eleanor and Catherine, quoted dialogue—whether of real or imagined persons—is at bottom fundamentally fictional. That this discussion occurs between two fictional characters in the pages of a novel only underscores Austen's point.

Contemporary narrative theory has identified the particular contours of quoted speech's peculiar fictionality in part by disclosing the inadequacy of the categories with which character speech in fiction has traditionally been parsed. These are the three fundamental categories: 1) directly represented speech, which uses quotation marks to set off the character's utterance ("'I want no proof of their affection", said Elinor' [*SS* 60]; 2) indirectly reported speech, which attributes speech to a character yet subordinates the character's utterance to the grammar and logic of the writer's sentence ('yesterday he actually said, that he could not be surprised at any effect produced on the heart of Man by such Loveliness & such Abilities' [*Lady Susan*, 201]); and 3) speech indirectly reported through free indirect discourse, in which the writer assumes the voice of a character ('Why was not she to be as useful as Anne! And to go home without Charles too—without her husband! No, it was too unkind!' [*P* 96]). This tripartite division of modes of conveying the speech of a character remains a convenient starting place. But as we shall see below when we turn to examples from Austen, there are many character speech acts that fail to fall clearly into any of these three categories, many that have so many strange semantic, grammatical, and orthographic features that they defy categorization. A number of theorists, including Brian McHale and Monika Fludernik, have suggested replacing the tripartite taxonomy of speech representation with the concepts of either a sliding scale, or of adjacent 'zones', according to which instances of fictional speech could be placed as more or less direct-ish, or indirect-ish, according to their specific features and contexts (McHale; Fludernik 2001). The difficulty of determining in Austen's fiction what is free indirect discourse and what is direct presented speech is at the heart of the database 'Austen Said'; in meticulously seeking to answer 'who is speaking here?' for every word in every Austen novel, the site's authors confront the limits to our ability to categorize and ascribe a single speaker (White and Smith).

Acknowledging the complexity of speech representation in fiction, Fludernik and Meir Sternberg have explained why it is crucial to dispense altogether with the idea of the mimetic nature of quoted speech in fiction. Unlike quoted speech in nonfictional discourse, behind which there may actually be (pace the skepticism of Catherine Morland) a real person's utterance captured verbatim, behind the quoted fictional utterance there is nothing. Fludernik views fictional quoted utterances according to the logic of typicalification instead of mimesis. To simplify her argument drastically, she suggests that in practice we read fictional quoted utterances not as reproductions of what the character *said*, but as an instance of the *kind* of thing the character *might typically* say (Fludernik *Fictions of Language*). Viewing quoted fictional speech as typical rather than mimetic opens our ears and eyes to the ways in which Austen's practice may be seen as prioritizing the impression of voice, rather than simply documenting what was said.

Once again, however, theorizing acoustic traces of character speech in Austen comes up against the uneven, often contingent histories of the print technologies and practices that shape Austen's place in the history of the novel. When we assume that quoted speech is directly represented speech, we are assuming that quotation marks encase the discrete utterance of one individual. But the history of representing speech in fiction, and the history of quotation marks, is a complex one. 'Our current practice of using one quotation mark to open a quotation and another one to close it developed in fits and starts over the eighteenth and nineteenth centuries', notes one historian of punctuation (Estill, 3). Quotation marks as we know them emerged out of a range of textual markings for speech in medieval and early modern Europe—special marks, different fonts, indentations and paragraphing—that had their origins in early musical and liturgical notation; for many centuries, the familiar inverted comma shape (") was as likely to be a way of making a marginal notes to mark a favourite, or memorable passage in a text as it was to represent quotation (Parkes; Houston; Finnegan; Ree; Estill).

Most historians of punctuation agree that in English-language publishing, modern conventions of quoting speech had more or less stabilized in the decades right around when Jane Austen began writing, in the 1780s and 1790s, and that the rise of the novel in the eighteenth century provided crucial impetus for the establishment of a regularized form of representing people talking in prose (Gemmill; Mylne 59). In fact, among authors and printers alike, some ambiguity and flexibility concerning how to designate fictional speech extended into the first decades of the nineteenth century. As late as 1829, for example, Walter Scott made revisions to a new edition of his 1815 novel *Guy Mannering* explicitly to clarify which character was speaking, adding speech tags ('said Brown', e.g.,), and describing vocal tones ('his laugh sinking into a hysterical giggle'). His most recent editor speculates that these changes responded to ongoing shifts 'in the conventions of presenting fiction in the 1820s and/or the anticipation of a readership less adept at negotiating the kind of polyphonic diversity found in the original text' (quoted in Sutherland 305–6). Even in the flush of excitement on first seeing the first edition of *Pride and Prejudice* in 1813 ('I want to tell you I have got my own darling Child from London'), Austen herself betrays uncertainty about how her book marks character speech. While she notes that there are 'a few Typical [i.e., typographical] errors' in the book, the one flaw she specifies is the absence of speech tags in certain dialogues: '& a "said he" or a "said she" would sometimes make the Dialogue more immediately clear'. But she immediately walks this worry back, implying that it is the reader's failure if they can't follow the speakers:'—but 'I do not write for such dull Elves', she concludes (29 January 1813; *Letters* 201–202). The terms of the contract between reader and writer over what were the conventions of speech representation were not set in stone. The orthographic and lexical features of speech representation in fiction remains an aspect of fictional form where conventions and trends ebb and flow. For example, the contemporary writer frequently compared to Austen, Sally Rooney—in her talky, aptly titled *Conversations with Friends*—dispenses with quotation marks entirely. While scholars of modernism and postmodernism may seek to distinguish the innovations of modern fiction's modes of speech representation against a nineteenth-century 'standard' (e.g., Mepham), that 'standard' was never very standardized, as the variation of modes of representing speech in Austen discloses.

The following examples of some of Austen's modes of representing speech will serve to affirm that her practice of representing speech does not truly follow a transcriptional aesthetic, does not always sort neatly into direct-quoted-represented speech versus indirect modes of speech reporting, does not always attribute a voice as the individual possession of one person. The first set of examples that flies in the face of a transcriptional model of speech representation might be called gappy quotations: these are instances where quotation marks encase the words of a single speaker, but clearly omit parts of the spoken world they belong to. When Catherine Morland is anxiously waiting to see if the Tilneys will be true to their promise to come get her at twelve noon, we find the following quotation as soon as the clock strikes twelve:

> I do not quite despair yet. I shall not give it up till a quarter after twelve. This is just the time of day for it to clear up, and I do think that it looks a little lighter. *There, it is twenty minutes after twelve*, and now I shall give it up entirely. Oh! That we had such weather here as they had at Udolpho, or at least in Tuscany and the South of France!—the night that poor St. Aubin died!—such beautiful weather! (*NA*, emphasis mine, 59).

Norman Page comments, 'unblushingly, the novelist permits twenty minutes to elapse during the uttering of less than forty words' (Page 30). Clearly, we need to infer either that other words have been spoken—by Catherine, or by the others present in the room, Mr and Mrs Allen, or that there have been long periods of silence: the quotation makes no pretense of transcribing a single discrete utterance. In omitting things that may be imagined to have 'happened' in the interstices between some of these 'forty words', Austen creates not a represented utterance, but a Catherine-voice, with many of its obsessions, anxieties, and scatterbrainedness.

While this example from *Northanger Abbey* may surprise even attentive Austen readers, most readers will recognize that many quotations of Miss Bates' speech in *Emma* function much the same way: a single quotation contains marked or unmarked places where someone else must be imagined to have spoken; quotation is not a transcription of an imagined speech event, but a 'Miss Bates voice effect'. But, perhaps the most astonishing instance of this phenomenon is Austen's use of quotation as Mrs Elton rambles on in Mr Knightley's strawberry beds:

> The best fruit in England—every body's favourite—always wholesome.—These finest best and finest sorts.—Delightful to gather for one's self—the only way of really enjoying them.—Morning decidedly the best time—never tired—every sort good—hautboy infinitely superior—no comparison—the others hardly eatable—hautboys very scarce—Chili preferred—white wood finest flavor of all—price of strawberries in London—abundance

about Bristol—Maple Grove—cultivation—beds when to be renewed—gardeners thinking exactly different—no general rule—gardeners never to be put out of their way—delicious fruit—only too rich to be eaten much of—inferior to cherries—currants more refreshing—only objection to gathering the strawberries the stooping—glaring sun—tired to death—could bear it no longer—must go and sit in the shade. (*E* 282)

In this remarkable passage of quotation, not only are any other hypothetical speakers omitted, but also, we infer, most of Mrs Elton's 'actual' words. Extrapolated from the fragmentary phrases represented must balloon out even longer phrases and sentences, as Mrs Elton's satisfactions and dissatisfactions wax and wane. In this passage and others like it, Austen forces us to think of quotation not from the point of view of the speaker, but from the point of view of those who hear: in this instance, the fragments between the quotation marks indicate what other members of the strawberry-picking party hear as they intermittently attend to, and attempt to tune out, Mrs Elton's irritating chatter. It is the impression of a voice, not what the voice says. We can confirm this by noting, further, that some of the fragments have the grammatical third-person, past-tense form of reported speech rather than the first-person, present-tense grammar of directly represented speech (so, for example '*could* bear it no longer' instead of '*can* bear it no longer'). As we shall discuss further below, Austen's tendency to put reported third-person speech between quotation marks is one of the most fascinating aspects of her speech representations; here, that 'could' puts the speaker at a distance, as her auditors seek to minimize the aural assault of Mrs Elton. Representing voice can invoke the presence of a person, but it can also be a form of—as in this case, when Austen makes such a show of erasing her words—of absenting them. This technique seems crazily modern, and indeed when we find a contemporary novelist doing this—there are pages of this technique, for example, in Anna Burns' *Milkman*—we take it in stride (Burns 270–71, 338–39).

Austen also uses quotation for unattributed, corporate, or group speech. She uses this technique to convey the opinions of the town gossip in *Emma* ('I suppose you have heard of the handsome letter M. Frank Churchill had written to Mrs Weston?' says nobody, 15), but also more radically in this passage from *Persuasion* when the members of the Elliot household are surprised by a late night visitor:

Anne was considering whether she should venture to suggest that a gown, or a cap, would not be liable to any such misuse, when a knock at the door suspended every thing. 'A knock at the door! And so late! It was ten o'clock. Could it be Mr Elliot? They knew he was to dine in Lansdown Crescent. It was possible that he might stop in his way home, to ask them how they did. They could think of no one else. Mrs Clay decidedly thought it Mr Elliot's knock'. Mrs Clay was right. With all the state which a butler and foot-boy could give, Mr Elliot was ushered into the room. (*P* 116)

The historian of punctuation M.B. Parkes notes that here, 'inverted commas are placed round what the reader accepts as a chorus of voices all reacting to that moment and commenting on it'. Utterances by several undifferentiated speakers are mushed together into one quotation, and, as Parkes also notes, 'the language between the inverted commas … represents both direct and indirect speech as well as statements that could be neither' (Parkes 93–94).

These examples reveal that one feature that makes Austen's speech representation so challenging is her use of quotation marks to encase indirect reporting—the kind of speech representation we normally think of as an alternative to direct quotation. Truly defying categorization is her tendency to combine the orthographic sign of direct quotation with the grammatical forms of indirect speech. We saw instances of this in the examples of corporate or group quotation, above, but it happens with single speakers with striking frequency:

The general was flattered by her looks of surprise, which told him almost as plainly, as he soon forced her to tell him in words, that she had never seen any gardens at all equal to them before; and he then modestly owned that, 'without any ambition of that sort himself—without any solicitude about it—he did believe them to be unrivalled in the kingdom. If he had a hobby-horse, it was that. He loved a garden. Though careless enough in most matters of eating, he loved good fruit—or if he did not, his friends and children did. There were great vexations, however, attending such a garden as his. The utmost care could not always secure the most valuable fruits. The pinery had yielded only one hundred in the last year. Mr Allen, he supposed, must feel these inconveniences as well as himself'. (*NA* 130)

One's first impression is that General Tilney is speaking about himself in the third person and in the past tense—in a way that some self-important, self-memorializing public figures have been known to do. But in Austen, characters considerably meeker than the pompous General Tilney 'speak' this way, even innocent Catherine Morland herself. The slim amount of scholarly comment on this particular mode of speech representation tends to look first at the grammatical form of the sentences, and thus to identify them as instances of free indirect discourse. In this view, the quotation marks are 'redundant' (Fludernik 1993, 230), a symptom of 'uncertainty' about how free indirect discourse works (Ree 1048), or a 'wrong' use of quotation marks (Finnegan 105–6). The quotation marks are, in this view, a little extra 'talk signaling' sprinkled around free indirect discourse, like pepper on a dish that doesn't really need it. But in fact, a simple thought-experiment with instances of this technique reveals that the quotation marks hardly feel redundant. For example, when Charles Musgrove's enthusiasm for Captain Wentworth bubbles over, while an un-quotation-marked version of his utterance might conform to our expectations of what Austen could accomplish with free indirect discourse, the quotation marks here lift the passage into a prime instance of Charles' repetitive, small-minded, limited habits of speech:

Charles 'had never seen a pleasanter man in his life; and from what he had once heard Captain Wentworth himself say, was very sure that he had not made less than twenty thousand pounds by the war. Here was a fortune at once; besides which, there would be the chance of what might be done in any future ware; and he was sure Captain Wentworth was as likely a man to distinguish himself as any officer in the navy. Oh! It would be a capital match for either of his sisters'. (*P* 99)

The quotation marks stamp personality features around the edges of the character that the character himself may not be aware of.

What if we took in (as I believe most readers actually do), when reading such passages, the quotation marks first, and the grammatical form of such utterances, next? Doing so increases our sense of the oddity and distinctiveness of the form: such phenomena cease to be rationalized as 'free indirect discourse with redundant quotation marks', and can be termed instead, 'quotations in the third person'. Responding to the quotation marks first prioritizes the aurality at stake in this phenomenon. These quotation-marked, third-person pseudo-utterances are 'unspeakable sentences' more profoundly and paradoxically even than the free indirect discourse that Ann Banfield identified as 'non-speech', in that they are marked as speech but ridiculous as enunciations (Banfield 'Where Epistemology, Style, and Grammar Meet', 449).

While occasional instances of this technique can be found in earlier novelists (Mylne, 58, mentions an instance in a novel of 1739, and Page *Speech in the English Novel*, 29, cites this example from *Tom Jones*: 'Meeting the landlady, he accosted her with great civility, and asked "what could he have for dinner"'), it is surprisingly frequent in Austen. It is crucial to keep in mind, once again, that we don't really have enough evidence about either Austen's punctuation preferences in her composition of her novels, or her involvement in the preparation or correction of pages, to be able to make confident assertions about orthographic patterns. We can only observe the effects that instances of 'quotation in the third person' have, contextually and differentially.

In many instances, for example, 'quotation in the third person' seems to have a typifying effect. That is, the utterances that take this form tend to be set off from consequential, plot-driving dialogue; they tend to be instances of politeness or pleasantry, marked as the kind of thing that a character might be likely to say, suggesting that what was said was 'something like this'. Here is one of many instances, when General Tilney is exerting himself, against character, to be as solicitous of Catherine as he can:

> And when they had gone over the house, he promised himself moreover the pleasure of accompanying her into the shrubberies and garden'. She curtsied her acquiescence. 'But perhaps it might be more agreeable to her to make those her first object. The weather was at present favorable, and at this time of year the uncertainty was very great of its continuing so. Which would she prefer? He was equally at her service. Which did his daughter think would most accord with her fair friend's wishes? But he thought he could discern. Yes, he certainly read in Miss Morland's eyes a judicious desire of making use of the present smiling weather. But when did she judge amiss? The abbey would be always safe and dry. He yielded implicitly, and would fetch his hat and attend them in a moment'. (*NA* 129)

At other times, 'quotation in the third person' has the effect of shifting our attention away from what is being said, and toward what is being heard. The strained yet revelatory encounter between Anne Elliot and Captain Wentworth at the concert hall in Bath comes to an end when Anne 'finds' Wentworth saying goodbye to her:

She found herself accosted by Captain Wentworth, in a reserved yet hurried sort of farewell. 'He must wish her good night. He was going—he should get home as fast as he could'.

> 'Is not this song worth staying for?' said Anne, suddenly struck by an idea while made her yet more anxious to be encouraging. (*P* 154)

Here 'quotation in the third person' seems to effect an instantaneous conversion of Wentworth's words into an impression in Anne's mind: it is as if we are hearing her thinking 'oh no, he's going! He says he is going!'

Far from being 'redundant', 'quotation in the third person' jostles up against other modes of speech representation in Austen, creating micro-contrasts among what we could call layers of audibleness. The reader absorbed in her Austen novel may pass through these micro-contrasts and endless variations of speech representation without stopping to notice them, but they shape our desire to hear voices in her fiction.

Among the micro-contrasts that add to the sonic environment we feel we are in are crucial moments when the spigot of represented speech—whether quoted, indirectly represented, or the hybrid-between form we have just been examining—is switched off. There are moments where Austen creates the impression of voices speaking by withholding quotation, through the merest hint that reporting speech is going on. In a section of her recent study of *Pride and Prejudice* called 'Hearing Mr Collins', Elaine Auyoung demonstrates how Austen cognitively primes the reader to feel as if Collins is talking even when she's not quoting him. She does this, Auyoung argues, by featuring massive amounts of direction quotation of Collins' long-winded pompous, simultaneously subservient and arrogant talk in Chapter 14, followed by absolutely zero Collins-quotation in Chapter 15. Austen doesn't need to quote him, Auyoung argues; all we need to be told is that he is 'talking to Mr Bennet, with little cessation' (*PP* 53) for an impression of his voice to loom. Auyoung comments, 'the gerunds that Austen provides (talking with little cessation, describing, protesting, enumerating, and repeatedly fearing) are sufficient for readers to retrieve the impression they have acquired from the preceding chapter', making it 'possible for readers to feel as if they can hear him even in the face of total narrative silence' (Auyoung 43). While Austen's silencing of Collins is comic, it is in *Persuasion* that she most effectively pushes the 'mute' button on her characters in order to achieve sound and voice. *Persuasion* contains the greatest proportion of reported, as opposed to represented, speech, and—sinking character speech even further—engages in what Norman Page identifies as 'submerged speech': instances where we become aware that speech is happening even without the reporting of what has been said (Page *Speech in the English Novel*, 32). It is the novel 'full of persons and voices' (52), the 'buzz of words' (186). Anne and Wentworth are sounds—sometimes good sounds, sometimes painful—to each other ('while still hearing the sounds he had uttered' [*P* 182]; '"you sink your voice, but I can distinguish the tones of that voice"' [*P* 191]). But by submerging speech, paradoxically, Austen transforms *Persuasion* into a novel alive to the sheer sound of voice, a 'sounding box' (Lucey 282). *Persuasion* is a sounding box that is like Prospero's island, 'full of noises, / Sounds.../... and sometimes voices' (*Tempest* III.2.133–4, 136). This novel's sounds-effects are a symptom of the extreme innerness of its thoughtful heroine. In its emphasis on Anne's experience of consciousness, *Persuasion* renders her, in Kate Nesbit's phrase, a 'tool for sound' (Nesbit 451), a listening machine.

Indeed, the example of *Persuasion* prompts us to ponder where the sound of a voice should be thought to be: in the mouth of the character that speaks? In the atmosphere? Inside the listening character's cortex? In raising these questions, Austen models the problem of voice in the novel in its entirety: is 'voice' a term for a textual phenomenon, or something that happens in the reader's mind? 'Where should this music be? I'th'air, / or th'earth?' (*Tempest* I.2.391–2). I would like to conclude this essay by suggesting that one effect of bringing together Austen's representation of speech with a broader consideration of voice is to make us question the difference between 'outside' and 'inside' voices, the voices out in the world and those in our minds. Austen's novels reveal to us some of the psychological truths involved in the continuity between speech and thought, outside and inside voices.

My example is a passage from *Emma* which showcases Austen's ability to reveal detailed layers of audibility, micro-gradations between speech and thought. The passage begins, in free indirect discourse, as Emma is responding internally to her discomfort at the news of Jane Fairfax's imminent arrival in Highbury:

> Emma was sorry;—to have to pay civilities to a person she did not like through three long months!—to be always doing more than she wished, and less than she ought! Why she did not like Jane Fairfax might be a difficult question to answer; Mr Knightley had once told her it was because she saw in her the really accomplished young woman, which she wanted to be thought herself; and though the accusation had been eagerly refuted at the time, there were moments of self-examination in which her conscience could not quite acquit her. But 'she could never get acquainted with her; she did not know how it was, but there was such coldness and reserve—such apparent indifference whether she pleased or not—and then, her aunt was such an eternal talker!—and she was made such a fuss with by every body!—and it had always been imagined that they were to be so intimate—because their ages were the same, every body had supposed they must be so fond of each other'. These were her reasons—she had no better. (*E* 130–31)

By its second sentence, the passage has morphed from its close, gut-level, free indirect discourse rendering of Emma's annoyance, to report on a more deliberative, juridical mode of thought, a 'self-examination' before the jury of her 'conscience', which turns on a recollected, reported conversation with Mr Knightley. 'Mr Knightley had once told her': this is reported speech *wrapped inside* a thought. The passage then turns to 'quotation in the third person': 'But "she could never get acquainted with her!"'. Where is this voice? In spite of the quotation marks, it is clearly a continuation of Emma's thoughts: beyond the quoted passage, even into the next paragraph, we remain in Emma's head. If this were simply a return to the free indirect discourse of the beginning of the passage, why the quotation marks?

I suggest that in this instance, the local effect of the layering of modes of speech and thought representation is a highlighting of the ways in which thinking sometimes does take the form of remembered or imagined speech. If 'Mr Knightley had once told her' is reported speech *wrapped inside* a thought, the 'quotation in the third person' segment of this passage is too. While Emma is debating herself, with herself, by herself here, the passage in quotation marks must be an imaginary or remembered conversation with Knightley. The psychological truth is that thinking often takes the form of talking with a loved one in your mind. The cognitive literary critic Alan Palmer rightly argues that the novel as a literary genre captures aspects of mental life that cannot be accounted for by speech categories (Palmer 65). However, Austen's novels affirm that voices are heard not only out in the world, but also in pretty deep layers of the mind, and interleaved in deep pages of books.

The link that connects outside voices and inside voices—as in this passage, where Knightley speaking to Emma, and Emma speaking to Knightley, are at the heart of a thought-event—is love. 'Hearing', writes the soundscape theorist R. Murray Schafer, 'is a way of touching at a distance' (Schafer 11). In *Persuasion*, as we have seen, Anne Elliot and Captain Wentworth are sources of good sound for each other. Upon being thrown together after their separation of eight years, Anne notes that 'when he talked, she heard the same voice' (*P* 55); Wentworth can 'distinguish the tones of that voice, when they would be lost on others' (191). It is their internalization of the tones of each other's voices that spans the eight years between their separation and reunion. For the object-relations psychoanalyst Christopher Bollas, becoming a 'good sound' for a patient is a way he can become what he calls a 'transformational object' for the patient, activating the patient's internal relations to others and allowing them to grow. Of one patient he writes, 'I was to learn that what he wanted was to hear my voice, which I gradually understood to be his need for a good sound' (Bollas 21). In Bollas' view, books can also serve as 'transformational objects'. And, I would add, books by loved authors are especially resonant objects in the mind. Austen's revolutionary gradations of speech and voice representation in her novels, I have been arguing, suggest ways in which speech and voice in fiction cannot be automatically linked with individual identity, with personhood, with presence, with agency. But her particular ways of making voice multi-located, intersubjective, and affective may explain why so many readers turn to her novels as transformational objects, sources of deeply meaningful sound. 'I love to hear you', as Harriet says; our love of Austen causes us to want to hear her, in the pages of the novels, from the stage, in the movie theatre, in tiny earbuds in our ears.

Works Cited

Aczel, Richard. 'Hearing Voices in Narrative Texts.' *New Literary History*, vol. 29, no. 3, Summer 1998, pp. 467–500.

Austen, Henry. 'Biographical Notice of the Author.' *Persuasion*, by Jane Austen, 1818, pp. 3–8.

Austen, Jane. *Emma*, edited by James Kinsley and Adela Pinch. Oxford World's Classics, 2003.

Austen, Jane. *Jane Austen's Letters*, edited by Deirdre Le Faye, 3rd ed. Oxford UP, 1995.

Austen, Jane. *Mansfield Park*, edited by James Kinsley and Jane Stabler. Oxford World's Classics, 2003.

Austen, Jane. *Mansfield Park*, edited by Kathryn Sutherland. Penguin Classics, 1996.

Austen, Jane. *Mansfield Park*, edited by John Wiltshire. Cambridge UP, 2005.

Austen, Jane. *Mansfield Park: An Annotated Edition*, edited by Deidre Shauna Lynch. Harvard UP, 2016.

Austen, Jane. *Northanger Abbey, Lady Susan, The Watsons, Sanditon*, edited by John Davie and Claudia L. Johnson. Oxford World's Classics, 2003.

Austen, Jane. *Persuasion*, edited by John Davie and Deidre Shauna Lynch. Oxford World's Classics, 2004.

Austen, Jane. *Pride and Prejudice*, edited by James Kinsley and Fiona Stafford. Oxford World's Classics, 2004.

Austen, Jane. *Sense and Sensibility*, edited by James Kinsley, Margaret Anne Doody, and Claire Lamont. Oxford World's Classics, 2004.

Auyoung, Elaine. *When Fiction Feels Real: Representation and the Reading Mind*. Oxford UP, 2018.

Bakhtin, M. M. *The Dialogic Imagination: Four Essays*, edited and translated by Caryl Emerson and Michael Holquist. U of Texas P, 1983.

Banfield, Ann. 'Where Epistemology, Style, and Grammar Meet: The Development of Represented Speech and Thought.' *New Literary History*, vol. 9, no. 3, 1978, pp. 415–454.

Barthes, Roland. 'Introduction to the Structural Analysis of Narrative.' *New Literary History*, vol. 6, no. 2, 1975, pp. 237–272.

Bollas, Christopher. *The Shadow of the Object: Psychoanalysis of the Unthought Known*. Columbia UP, 1987.

Booth, Wayne. *The Rhetoric of Fiction*, 2nd ed., U of Chicago P, 1983.

Boyd, Brian. 'Does Austen Need Narrators? Does Anyone?' *New Literary History*, vol. 48, no. 2, Spring 2017, pp. 285–308.

Bray, Joe. *The Language of Jane Austen*. Palgrave Macmillan, 2018.

Brower, Reuben. 'The Speaking Voice.' *The Lyric Theory Reader*, edited by Virginia Jackson and Yopie Prins. Johns Hopkins UP, 2014, pp. 211–218.

Burns, Anna. *Milkman*. Greywolf, 2018.

Butler, Shane. *The Ancient Phonograph*. Zone Books, 2016.

Carlson, Julia S. *Romantic Marks and Measures*. U of Pennsylvania P, 2016.

Chatman, Seymour. *Story and Discourse*. Cornell UP, 1978.

Cohen, William A., and Green, Laura. 'Introduction: Revisiting Dialogue.' *Narrative*, vol. 27, no. 2, 2019, pp. 129–139.

Davis, Lennard. *Resisting Novels: Ideology and Fiction*. Methuen, 1987.

Elfenbein, Andrew. *Romanticism and the Rise of English*. Stanford UP, 2008.

Eliot, T. S. 'The Three Voices of Poetry.' *The Lyric Theory Reader*, edited by Virginia Jackson and Yopie Prins. Johns Hopkins UP, 2014, pp. 192–200.

Estill, Laura. 'Commonplace Markers and Quotation Marks.' *ArchBook: Architectures of the Book*, edited by Alan Galey et al. U of Toronto iSchool, 2014. http://drc.usask.ca/projects/archbook/commonplace.php

Finnegan, Ruth. *Why Do We Quote? The Culture and History of Quotation*. Open Book, 2011.

Fludernik, Monika. *The Fictions of Language and the Languages of Fiction: the Linguistic Representation of Speech and Consciousness*. Routledge, 1993.

Fludernik, Monika. 'New Wine in Old Bottles: Voice, Focalization and New Writing.' *New Literary History*, vol. 32, no. 3, Summer 2001, pp. 619–638.

Gaylin, Ann. *Eavesdropping in the Novel from Austen to Proust*. Cambridge UP. 2002.

Gemmill, Katie. 'Typography and Conversational Threat in Samuel Richardson's Clarissa.' *Narrative*, vol. 27, no. 2, 2019, pp. 140–159.

Genette, Gerard. *Narrative Discourse: An Essay in Method*. Translated by Jane E. Lewin, Cornell UP, 1980.

Houston, Keith. *Shady Characters: The Secret Life of Punctuation, Symbols, and Other Typographical Marks*. Norton, 2013.

Hunter, J. Paul. *Before Novels: The Cultural Contexts of Eighteenth-Century English Fiction*. Norton, 1990.

Hunter, J. Paul. 'The Loneliness of the Long-Distance Reader.' *Genre*, vol. 10, 1977, pp. 455–484.

Jajdelska, Elspeth. *Silent Reading and the Birth of the Narrator*. U of Toronto P, 2007.

Jameson, Fredric. *The Antinomies of Realism*. Verso, 2013.

Keane, Webb. 'Voice.' *Key Terms in Language and Culture*, edited by Alessandro Duranti. Blackwell, 2001, pp. 268–271.

Keskinen, Mikko. *Audio Book: An Essay on Sound Technologies in Narrative Fiction*. Lexington Books, 2008.

Kreilkamp, Ivan. *Voice and the Victorian Storyteller*. Cambridge UP, 2005.

Lanser, Susan Sniader. *Fictions of Authority: Women Writers and Narrative Voice*. Cornell UP, 1992.

Lascelles, Mary. *Jane Austen and Her Art*. Oxford Clarendon P, 1939.

Le Faye, Deirdre. *Jane Austen: A Family Record*. 2nd ed. Cambridge UP, 2004.

Leighton, Angela. *Hearing Things: The Work of Sound in Literature*. Harvard UP, 2018.

Looser, Devoney. *The Making of Jane Austen*. Johns Hopkins UP, 2017.

Lucey, Michael. 'On Proust and Talking to Yourself.' *Qui Parle*, vol. 26, no. 2, 2017, pp. 281–293.

Lynch, Deidre Shauna, 'The Unwritten History of the Woman of Genius (Austen, Stael, Siddons): What She Says, Goes.' Forthcoming, *Romanticism*, 2022.

McHale, Brian. 'Speech Representation.' *The Living Handbook of Narratology*, edited by Hühn, Peter et al. Hamburg: Hamburg U. 2014, http://www.lhn.uni-hamburg.de/article/speech-representation

Menon, Tara. 'Keeping Count: Direct Speech in the Nineteenth-Century British Novel.' *Narrative*, vol. 27, no. 2, 2019, pp. 160–181.

Mepham, John. 'Novelistic Dialogue: Some Recent Developments.' *New Developments in English and American Studies*, edited by Zygmunt Mazur and Teresa Bela. Proc. of the Seventh International Conf. of English and American Literature, 1997, pp. 411–431.

Michaelson, Patricia. *Speaking Volumes: Women, Reading, and Speech in the Age of Austen*. Stanford UP, 2002.

Miller, D. A. *Jane Austen, or the Secret of Style*. Princeton UP, 2003.

Mylne, Vivienne, 'The Punctuation of Dialogue in Eighteenth-Century English and French Fiction.' *The Library*, vol. s6-I, no. 1, March 1979, pp. 43–61.

Nesbit, Kate. '"Taste in Noises": Registering, Evaluating, and Creating Sounds and Story in Jane Austen's *Persuasion*.' *Studies in the Novel*, vol. 47, no. 4, 2015, pp. 451–468.

Page, Norman. *The Language of Jane Austen*. Blackwell, 1972.

Palmer, Alan. *Fictional Minds*. U of Nebraska P, 2004.

Parkes, M. B. *Pause and Effect: An Introduction to the History of Punctuation in the West*. Ashgate, 1992.

Pascoe, Judith. *The Sarah Siddons Audio Files: Romanticism and the Lost Voice*. U of Michigan P, 2011.

Prins, Yopie. 'Voice Inverse.' *Victorian Poetry*, vol. 42, no. 1, 2004, pp. 43–59.

Ree, Jonathan, 'Funny Voices: Stories, Punctuation, and Personal Identity.' *New Literary History*, vol. 21, no. 4, 1990, pp. 1039–1058.

Rooney, Sally. *Conversations with Friends*. Hogarth, 2017.

Rubery, Matthew, *The Untold Story of the Talking Book*. Harvard UP, 2016.

Schafer, R. Murray. *The Tuning of the World*. Knopf, 1977.

Shakespeare, William. *Hamlet*, edited by George Richard Hibbard. Oxford UP, 2008.

Shakespeare, William. *The Tempest*, edited by Stephen Orgel. Oxford UP, 2008

Siskin, Clifford. *The Work of Writing: Literature and Social Change in Britain, 1700–1830*. Johns Hopkins UP, 1998.

Smith, John. *The Printer's Grammar: Wherein Are Exhibited, Examined, and Explained, the Superficies, Gradation, and Properties of the Different Sorts and Sizes of Metal Types, Cast by Letter Founders*. London: Owen and Cooper, 1755.

Southam, B. C. *Jane Austen: The Critical Heritage*. 2 vols. Routledge and Kegan Paul, 1968.

St.Clair, Justin. 'Literature and Sound.' *The Routledge Companion to Sound Studies*, edited by Michael Bull. Routledge, 2019, pp. 353–361.

Sternberg, Meir. 'Proteus in Quotation-Land: Mimesis and the Forms of Reported Discourse.' *Poetics Today*, vol. 3, 1982, pp. 107–156.

Sterne, Jonathan. *The Audible Past: Cultural Origins of Sound Reproduction*. Duke UP, 2003.

Stovel, Bruce, and Lynn Weinlos Greg, editors. *The Talk in Jane Austen*. U of Alberta P, 2002.

Sutherland, Kathryn. *Jane Austen's Textual Lives: From Aeschylus to Bollywood*. Oxford UP. 2005.

Tandon, Bharat. *Jane Austen and the Morality of Conversation*. Anthem, 2003.

Trumpener, Katie. *Bardic Nationalism: The Romantic Novel and the British Empire*. Princeton UP, 1997.

Walsh, Richard. 'Person, Level, Voice: A Rhetorical Reconsideration.' *Postclassical Narratology: Approaches and Analyses*, edited by Monika Fludernik. Ohio State UP, 2010, pp. 35–57.

White, Laura Mooneyham, and Carmen Smith. 'Discerning Voice through *Austen Said*: Free Indirect Discourse, Coding, and Interpretive (Un)Certainty.' *Persuasions Online*, vol. 37, no. 1, Winter 2016, http://jasna.org/publications/persuasions-online/vol37no1/white-smith/

Wiltshire, John. 'Editing "Mansfield Park": A Work in Progress.' *The Cambridge Quarterly*, vol. 31, no. 4, 2002, pp. 293–305.

Wiltshire, John. Introduction. *Mansfield Park*, by Jane Austen, 1814, Cambridge UP, 2005, pp. xxv–lxxxiv.

Wordsworth, William. *The Major Works*, edited by Stephen Gill. Oxford UP, 2008.

Yelland, Chris. *Jane Austen: A Style in History*. Routledge, 2018.

22

BEING PLOTTED, BEING THROWN: AUSTEN'S CATCH AND RELEASE

William Galperin

RUTGERS UNIVERSITY

Jane Austen was no fan of plot. Even Walter Scott, who was bowled over by her unprecedented realism, recognized that the 'narrative of all her novels' (as he called it) was largely extraneous to their achievement (Southam *Jane Austen: The Critical Heritage*, 64). Maria Edgeworth went even further, complaining not just about the absence of plot in *Emma*, which she stopped reading after just one volume, but about the circumstantial filler that effectively substituted for story. 'There was no story in it', she wrote to Anne Romilly, 'except that Miss Emma found that the man whom she designed for Harriets lover was an admirer of her own—and he was affronted at being refused by Emma and Harriet wore the willow' (Butler 46). There's more to say about this particular 'exceptionalism', which, as Edgeworth suggests, involves a 'refusal' of the marriage plot until such time as it must be honoured however doggedly. For the moment it is worth noting that virtually everything that Austen felt about plot, if only on the evidence of her earliest readers, is embedded in her most famous sentence at the beginning of her most beloved novel. Here, beyond a matter of necessity or genre, plot is effectively reduced, telescoped, to a single word and teleology: the 'wife' to whom a heroine, as distinct now from a person, is destined, both as a condition of becoming representable and, as the sentence has it, real. To be sure, there is a consciousness—Mrs Bennet's—that is also being channelled in this declarative statement, along with its corollary, where a resistance to plot, as something in lockstep with wish fulfilment, is plainly nested: a truth so obvious that it can dispense with the rhetorical prop of universal acknowledgment. A single woman in possession of *no* fortune must be in want of a husband.

The depth of Austen's resistance, certainly to any plot that obscures or distracts from this latter truth through a fantasy of hitting the jackpot, is especially prominent in her early narratives, whose protagonists, or, perhaps better, thought experiments, are seemingly unaware of the need to relinquish personhood so as to become heroines, much less rich ones. There is the inscrutable Catherine Morland to whom *Northanger Abbey*'s satire (and the plot in which it is plainly invested) is demonstrably unequal and who only becomes a 'heroine', and by turns a wife, upon discovery that her 'real power'—that is, woman's power—'is nothing' (*NA* 182) More tellingly, there is Emma Watson in the unfinished and unpublished *The Watsons*, whose personhood has both a material basis (a fortune she was heir to prior to her aunt's remarriage) and a sustaining counterexample in her unmarried sisters whose desperation and deformation can be laid directly at the truth—the other plot—that the marriage plot on Mrs Bennet's model subserves. Nor is it any accident that at the very moment that Emma Watson discovers—empirically and by her brother's tutelage—that personhood is unsustainable: that she is destined, heroine or not, to be a deformation no matter what, the story

296

DOI: 10.4324/9780429398155-22-26

stops, refusing all plots, the marriage one *and* its social provocation, all of which are plots against people. No future, no marriage, no more.

Futurity, a fixed mark guiding the narrative, was the orientation generally missing for Austen's earliest readers and *The Watsons* (which they did not read) is an extreme example.[1] But in recognizing this absence and the unplotted, detail-laden present that takes over, early readers were not only forced to concede that Austen was doing something very different in substituting 'no story' for story; they were also practicing a jerry-built formalism in recognizing a fundamental distinction between what *happens* in an Austen novel and its plot—that is, between events in themselves and the mechanism, as Russian formalism has it, by which a reader is made aware of what is happening (Chatman 19–21). For Austen's early readers especially, awareness is rerouted, complicated—if not to the degree that one is completely ignorant of the import of events either to a marital trajectory, or to a developmental one where a heroine is 'turned wise by precept, example, and experience' (Scott 64), then to a degree that by the time that Catherine Morland or Marianne Dashwood or Elizabeth Bennet or Emma Woodhouse is taught the error of her ways it is impossible not to be struck by what Lady Bessborough, considerably in advance of Eve Sedgwick, called a 'stupid ending' (*Lord Granville Leveson Gower* 418).

The marriage plot, taken on its own, is a slightly different matter and although it is frequently twinned with the developmental plot in Austen, its refusal—figured, for example, by a person surprised, even shocked, by the attention of an admirer—is the more critical one by far. This is not only because one kind of awareness—the bearing of the future on what is happening—is overwhelmed by an awareness unencumbered by a marital teleology. It is also because the banality of the marriage plot, as distinct from the stupidity of the pedagogical plot, is also muted by certain contingencies, from precarity to celibacy, that its refusal brings to view. Commensurate, then, with an awareness of the present *as* the present, an awareness of what Anne Romilly, describing *Mansfield Park*, called 'real, natural every day life', is an awareness of someone—a human being—unmoored from plot, which turns out, through no small irony, to be as heroic as it gets for Austen (*Romilly-Edgeworth* 92).

This brings me to the most and least heroic of Austen's persons—*Persuasion*'s Anne Elliot who, having 'learned romance' following her initial rejection of Captain Wentworth in the narrative's prehistory, spends a good deal of the novel decoupling the pedagogical plot, which has reached conclusion prematurely, from a marriage plot in which she stands to lose despite knowing, despite having learned, that being plotted is what she apparently has wanted all along (*P* 30). 'Want' is not always easy to gauge where this character is concerned and we see it most visibly in her mysterious loss of bloom, whose effect (and purpose it would appear) is to prevent any man from admiring her without her knowledge or consent. This changes during Anne's famous walk at Lyme, where her bloom is restored under the triangulated gaze of two men, one of whom is Wentworth. While the net effect of this encounter is to alert Anne to what she already knows or thinks she knows—namely that she wants to be married and to Wentworth—it also marks her transformation from a person, someone in the moment, into the wife-to-be that Wentworth at this very juncture aptly calls 'something like Anne Elliot' (*P* 87). Becoming something in lieu of a person comes with dividends, of course, if not necessarily for Anne, who spends a good portion of the novel resisting the ends of pedagogy, then for Elizabeth Bennet somewhat earlier ('to be mistress of Pemberley might be something' [*PP* 159]) and for readers of *Persuasion* yearning for passages such as this one, where Anne reflects on Wentworth just after he has assisted her into a carriage:

> She was much affected by the view of his disposition towards her, which all these things made apparent. This little circumstance seemed the completion of all that had gone before. She understood him. He could not forgive her,—but he could not be unfeeling. Though condemning her for the past, and considering it with high and unjust resentment, though

perfectly careless of her, and though becoming attached to another, still he could not see her suffer, without the desire of giving her relief. It was a remainder of former sentiment; it was an impulse of pure, though unacknowledged friendship; it was a proof of his own warm and amiable heart....(77)

Adela Pinch has described this novel's affective lure as akin to being 'lost in a book' (Pinch 137–63) and something served by that description is plainly on offer here, where the 'book' is not necessarily *Persuasion* by Jane Austen, which joins with her other novels in standing outside of plot, especially when Anne is disowning what she has learned and the future (a sailor's wife) to which it is joined, but another narrative—call it *Persuasion* by Mrs Bennet or, maybe better, Harriet Smith—that Anne has introjected and that Austen is obligated (here and elsewhere) to record. The only difference is that by the time of *Persuasion* this is not only as bad as it gets, given the knowledge that continually resists learning where the protagonist is concerned, but, with the birth of the Harlequin Romance that this passage midwifes in annihilating personhood, producing in the process 'something like' an original cliché, as good as it gets as well.

★★★

There is, however, another kind of transport in Austen that is opposed to plot and to the 'progress', accordingly, of an individual. And it involves, or is characterized, by what Martin Heidegger, in reference to the everyday, describes as a 'groundless floating' (*Being and Time* 213–14). One of Heidegger's examples here is gossip or 'idle talk'—an Austenian event if ever there was—where one is 'thrown proximally', as he puts it, 'into the publicness of the they' in ways that for his part are inauthentic and unhinged (*Being and Time* 210). But even here the situation is far from clear. For as 'the least differentiated and determinate expression of Being's existence' (Harootunian 113), thrownness or publicness encapsulates to a very great degree—and in the hands of someone like Austen—the ideal of Being or of being-with that Heidegger famously promotes. It stands opposed, in other words, to the isolation, the self-sufficiency and, most important of all, the overall *interest* of characters such as Fanny Price or Anne Elliot or Elizabeth Bennet, whose very progress, whose very importance, is the obverse of a world elsewhere and, as it happens, one close at hand.[2]

Consider, for example, this 'idle talk' into which *Pride and Prejudice* immediately falls and into which the reader is reciprocally thrown:

'What is his name?'
'Bingley'.
'Is he married or single?'
'Oh! single, my dear, to be sure! A single man of large fortune;
four or five thousand a year. What a fine thing for our girls!'
'How so? How can it affect them?'
'My dear Mr Bennet', replied his wife, 'how can you be so
tiresome! You must know that I am thinking of his marrying one of
them'.
'Is that his design in settling here?'
'Design! nonsense, how can you talk so! But it is very likely
that he *may* fall in love with one of them, and therefore you must visit him
as soon as he comes'.
'I see no occasion for that. You and the girls may go, or you may
send them by themselves, which will be still better, for as you are as
handsome as any of them, Mr Bingley might like you the best of the
party'.

Being Plotted, Being Thrown

'My dear you flatter me. I certainly *have* had my share of beauty,
but I do not pretend to anything extraordinary now. When a woman has
five grown up daughters, she ought to give over thinking of her own
beauty'.
'In such cases, a woman has not often much beauty to think of'.
'But, my dear, you must indeed go and see Mr Bingley when he
comes into the neighborhood'.
'It is more than I engage for, I can assure you'.
'But consider your daughters. Only think what an establishment
it would be for one of them. Sir William and Lady Lucas are determined
to go, merely on that account, for in general you know they visit no new
comers. Indeed you must go, for it will be impossible for *us* to visit him,
if you do not'. (*PP* 3–4)

Apart from describing action and setting, free indirect discourse operates in two distinct registers for Austen: as a 'metalanguage' that puts conversation in quotations (see above) and as a representation of consciousness or interiority, whose joint operation, leading to what one critic terms 'perfect representation' (MacCabe 35), is in disarray here. This is true not only for the reader, who must track the dialogue in the absence of dramatic form, but also for the interlocutors (I was almost going to say dramatic personae), who are performing not as characters with depth but in a more outward and dynamic configuration. Their 'talk' is more directed, to be sure, than the gossip that, as Heidegger describes it, is 'everywhere and nowhere' (*Being and Time* 217). But it also 'floats' in a way that the more emplotted aspects of the novel—in a well-managed compact between an exceptional heroine and a narratorial intelligence—are prevented generally from doing.[3]

Such floating is especially evident in exchanges like the Bennets', which proceed with virtually no intelligence from a narrator confined (with one small interjection) to bearing witness. It is evident, too, in performances like Collins' or Miss Bates' or even Mrs Elton's, where the narrator is similarly disarmed and thereby thrown. And it is even present in the famous sentence that precedes the Bennets' dialogue, which, in channelling Mrs Bennet rather than representing her directly, is far from simply a joke, reaching critical mass or condensation in the inaugural 'it' to which a nameless, disembodied woman is subordinated prior to emerging in the only form or role she can. Unlike the stable irony we associate with Austen, where the reader is in on the joke, there is something in this famous sentence—in its contractibility to 'It is... wife'—that throws the reader or should, largely because also going on—with an assist from Mrs Bennet—is what Heidegger calls 'thinking': a procedure that 'withdraws' or is 'veiled' or that 'turns' toward 'what turns away' over and against the fantasy for which plot or story is another term (*Basic Writings* 350–58).

Around the time that Austen was channelling Mrs Bennet in the twenty-three most quoted words she would ever publish, she was also at work on a narrative that I have already touched on—*The Watsons*—which, in addition to containing numerous elements that reappear in her other works, remains, as the Cambridge editors remind us, the 'earliest extant work in the realist mode of the mature novels' (*Later Manuscripts* lxxvi). This mode (free indirect discourse) was clearly an advancement on the epistolary mode in which *Sense and Sensibility* (and quite possibly *Pride and Prejudice*) were initially conceived (Southam *Jane Austen's Literary Manuscripts* 45–62). But it was an advancement with particular problems in this case, some involving the marriage plot (as I have argued) but most involving personhood and individualism: specifically the separation of the heroine—and with her the story's narrator—from a 'world' ('the Watsons') into which they are either jointly thrown or radically exposed. In the great Austen novel, whose heroine is also named Emma, the problem is partly mitigated by juxtaposing Emma Woodhouse's view of things and the narrator's apparently broader view. However, in *The Watsons* there is virtually no daylight between these respective viewpoints, creating a disproportion from the outset between a character, whom the story revolves around, and the 'they'—Emma's father, her sisters, her brother, her sister-in-law, and several potential suitors—who, in all but a very few instances, she suffers as does the narrator.

The conversation between Emma and her older sister Elizabeth at the story's outset is a lopsided one in which Emma, who has just returned to her family after being raised and sponsored by her aunt, is primarily an auditor and the register, accordingly, of the scene overall. Thus, in lieu or in place of what might be called *narrative* intelligence, the weight of this conversation regarding Elizabeth's failure to secure a husband (which she blames on certain men and on the treachery of another sister Penelope) falls squarely on Emma, who is taking in, for perhaps the first time, her own likely fate as one of many. Much more than the affectionate exchange at the beginning of *Pride and Prejudice*—and it *is* affectionate—this 'idle talk', in which the heroine barely gets a word in, not only reproduces the effect of 'being thrown proximally into the... they'; it communicates it in a register that is stunning rather than simply disorienting.

> 'I was very much attached to a young man of the name of Purvis, a particular friend of Robert's, who used to be with us a great deal. Every body thought it would have been a Match'.
> A sigh accompanied these words, which Emma respected in silence—; but her sister, after a short pause, went on—
> 'You will naturally ask why it did not take place, and why he is married to another woman, while I am still single.—But you must ask him—not me—you must ask Penelope. —Yes Emma, Penelope was at the bottom of it all.—She thinks everything fair for a husband; I trusted her, she set him against me, with a view of gaining him herself, and it ended in his discontinuing his visits and soon after marrying somebody else.—Penelope makes light of her conduct, but *I* think such treachery very bad. It has been the ruin of my happiness. I shall never love any man as I loved Purvis.' (*Later Manuscripts* 81)

We do not yet know the circumstances surrounding Emma's return to her family on the occasion of her aunt's remarriage, which turns out to have been a treachery as well. But it is clear, if only by her interpositions here ('I can think of nothing worse ... than marry a man I did not like' or 'to pursue a man merely for the sake of situation—is a sort of thing that shocks me' [83]), that the one-sidedness of the exchange owes as much to Elizabeth's desperation as to the 'shocking' reversal that Emma is processing and that we are thrown, with the narrator, into processing with her. The confinement to Emma's consciousness is certainly in keeping with the affective individualism in her opinions regarding marriage. But crucial suddenly is the link between narrative practice and the sense of entitlement or singularity that underlies everything Emma does, including her singular decision, shortly after, to dance with a little boy rather than with a possible suitor.

There are many instances in Austen where the ideal of a companionate marriage is pursued by the heroine. But unlike Elizabeth Bennet's advocacy of such an arrangement in her debate with Lady Catherine—an advocacy leveraged by a 'situation' named Pemberley—Emma's behaviour reflects the destiny to which she feels entitled regardless of situation. When she reminds her sister Elizabeth—à propos of their brother Robert's good fortune—that '[w]e must not all expect to be individually lucky' or that the '[t]he luck of one member of a family is luck to all', she is being neither stoical nor especially altruistic (281). She is underscoring the exceptionalism that marks her, both in her understanding of herself as similarly deserving and in the narrative's collusion with her.

But this is just one aspect of Emma's individualism. The other aspect, buttressed by the story's form, is an exceptionalism that, like the narrative overall, is fraying. In addition to the fact that Emma is now an exile returned—and just one of 'the Watsons'—her sloganeering about luck and the difference it bespeaks stands in uneasy juxtaposition to her material circumstances, which are increasingly typical rather than unusual. The narrative may continue to represent the Watsons and their world as Emma construes them, particularly as something she could never have imagined for herself. But what it cannot avoid ultimately is the continuity between Emma's sense of betrayal and outrage and the selfishness that, by her own testimony, governs the behaviour of virtually everybody. Thus, even as there is a narrator present to confirm or reconfirm Emma's sense of things and the affront that these things generally represent, it is left mostly to the story itself and to the disproportion it promotes in pitting a singular protagonist against a blameworthy environment to founder on its own formal bias. This becomes especially clear in *The Watsons'* final stage when, closeted at last in her father's chamber, Emma rages against her environment and the 'inferior minds' to whose company she is condemned, which issues immediately in the story's suspension (135).

★★★

The Watsons is far from the only Austen narrative that juxtaposes the individual and 'the they' to the detriment of the latter. Nor is it the only narrative where this juxtaposition and the 'realist mode' it leverages encounters blowback and is thrown into disarray. There is the memorable (and for my undergraduates forgettable) example of *Emma*'s Miss Bates, whose 'talk', although seemingly 'idle', is anything but and whose strain on the narrative is marked both by the heroine, who eventually responds aggressively and defensively at Box Hill, and by the narrator who, for all her knowingness, turns out by comparison to be sequestered and blinkered.[4] There is also *Mansfield Park*, which is in many ways a *Watsons* in reverse, featuring a heroine whose entry into the narrative begins a rise rather than a fall, and a world more broadly (call it 'the Crawfords') where characters are not just thrown but where they effectively pitch themselves in a boundless performativity or publicness that, by comparison to Fanny's forbearance, is highly absorptive rather than an affront. But even here, in a plot that is presumably triumphalist for the heroine, the reversal of fortune that Fanny experiences when sent back to her parents' home in Portsmouth not only issues in a response similar to Emma Watson's upon return to her family; it also serves warning, in a way that Emma's shock and anger can't, that the individual had better get what she wants lest all hell break loose:

> she must and did feel that her mother was a partial, ill-judging parent, a dawdle, a slattern, who neither taught nor restrained her children, whose house was the scene of mismanagement and discomfort from beginning to end, and who had no talent, no conversation, no affection towards herself; no curiosity to know her better, no desire of her friendship, and no inclination for her company that could lessen her sense of such feelings. (306–7)

Unlike Emma's betrayal, which embeds a feminist argument—as individualism and the heroine's gender are a bad match in a world dominated by men—Fanny's outrage owes primarily to the fact that she is already or potentially one of the victors, not just in her establishment at Mansfield, which has been only temporarily interrupted, but in the history that she and others like her (notably her brother William) will help shape as servants of the empire.

By the time of this novel the game has changed. Victory or what might count as victory for an Austen heroine is no longer a question of franchise and autonomy, however much a fantasy they may have been, but simply a matter of assuming one's rightful and privileged role in the new Britain. For *Persuasion*'s Anne Elliot, to cite the most obvious example, this role is very close to the disembodied entity of *Pride and Prejudice*'s first sentence, which presupposes subordination along with a melancholic sense that women, far from agents with constructive control over their lives and environments, must 'belon[g]' *as individuals* to someone (*P* 203). Thus, while the later novels both resume and sophisticate the novelistic project inaugurated in *The Watsons* with its commitment to an individual, the particular union of narrator and character essential to this commitment, and to its disavowal of others, is forged increasingly by a sense of loss or resignation or perplexity rather than by the resentment onto which *The Watsons* opens in a 'realist mode' that is pulling in two directions.

In *Persuasion* the sense of loss is especially pronounced. However, in *Mansfield Park* it emerges reflexively in the particular surplus or publicness that takes precedence over the singular and increasingly isolated positions of the protagonist and the narrator, whose respective and mimetic miseries (in, for example, the dyspeptic account of Fanny and Edmund's union) prove a damper on a world into which the novel is deposited, where story and development are consistently secondary to what happens in the moment, which is to say 'real natural every day life'.

An example of this 'every day life', and the thrownness it honours, would be the frequently cited moment of Sir Thomas' encounter with John Yates in what was Sir Thomas's 'closet' prior to becoming the temporary stage for a theatrical, which pits privacy against publicness to the debit of the former:

> He stept to the door, rejoicing at that moment in having the means of immediate communication, and opening it, found himself on the stage of a theatre, and opposed to a ranting young man, who appeared likely to knock him down backwards. At the very moment of Yates perceiving Sir Thomas, and giving perhaps the very best start he had ever given in the whole course of his rehearsals, Tom Bertram entered at the other end of the room; and never had he found greater difficulty in keeping his countenance. His father's looks of solemnity and amazement on this his first appearance on any stage, and the gradual metamorphosis of the impassioned Baron Wildenhaim into the well-bred and easy Mr Yates, making his bow and apology to Sir Thomas Bertram, was such an exhibition, such a piece of true acting as he would not have lost upon any account. It would be the last—in all probability the last scene on that stage; but he was sure there could not be a finer. The house would close with the greatest éclat. (143)

In contrast to the models of free indirect discourse that bind the narrator and a protagonist in a state of differentiation or exception, or in what Leo Bersani (with Heidegger subliminally in mind perhaps) calls 'non-being' (77) this one morphs effortlessly, like Yates, from Sir Thomas's point of view to the narrator's and finally to Tom, who (as Heidegger might describe him) is 'thinking back' here 'to what is to be thought' (*Basic Writings* 352). For like the pleasure it produces, this distributed consciousness or thrownness not only devolves upon a truth in search of acknowledgment as opposed to one universally acknowledged and all-too probable; it also captures the floating, the lightness of being-there, where plot vanishes and where attention is suddenly proximal to the 'they' rather than to a moral or 'novelistic' order consolidated in the individual.

Attention ultimately goes both ways in *Mansfield Park*, pitting 'ontological floaters' like the Crawfords against a representational framework in which, as Bersani further observes, 'each episode contributes significantly to coherent portraits of personality' (76). There is both stability in this narrative, preeminently in Fanny, who operates along with the narrator as a 'center of judgment' (77). And there is the 'liveliness' or 'agitation' of 'beings without definition', in which the Crawfords in particular are 'actively ready to jump from one entertaining performance to the next' (76). This tension, as Bersani construes it, is a characterological matter, where the 'great threat... is precisely an improvised self or the possibility that there is no best self to which one must be true' (76). Still and all, what is true at the level of character in the capacity to threaten is even truer finally of the novel itself, whose episodic disposition remains the 'style of bein[g]' (76) in perhaps the fullest sense, throwing both judgment and its 'non-desiring center' (77) to a world on display where desire is requited in being serially attracted and attracted as a condition of being always satisfied.

Yet the question remains: exactly *whose* desire? In answering this it is important to distinguish again between the individual—Fanny Price, or Emma Watson, or Emma Woodhouse, or even Anne Elliot—who remains a centre of consciousness and judgment and what, on the example of a phenomenologist like Maurice Merleau-Ponty and, more immediately, a character like Tom, represents a mode of being best described as the 'first person'. For Merleau-Ponty, who repeatedly uses the first person singular in exploring the givenness of perception to the world (and vice versa [Marion])—a process he describes as gearing into (Merleau-Ponty 311)—this exemplary subject is precisely that: a placeholder through which (rather than through whom) an account of one's responsiveness or permeability is demonstrable. But what this also means, with attention specifically to Austen, is that the difference between the first-person singular and the first-person plural is at key moments in the novels—Emma Watson's immersive return, Tom's migratory subjectivity, the Bennets' verbal *pas de deux*—quite negligible. It is negligible for characters, who channel one another by listening or watching or mindreading (Vermeule). And it is negligible for the reader, whose exposure to Miss Bates amounts to a cohabitation: both with the character, who essentially speaks 'what' she 'see[s]', and with a consciousness (Emma's) through which Miss Bates is suddenly rendered. That this rendering is necessarily motivated, and desired, may be hard to grasp given how annoying Miss Bates can be. Nevertheless, in the consciousness experiment that is *Emma*, she remains a decentred and decentring figure: the opposite of Emma *after* Box Hill, whose 'progress', on the heels of her insult (or judgment), is not only to maturity, responsibility, and 'definition' but also to a citadel (and a marriage) overseen by the 'center of judgment' nonpareil, Mr Knightley.[5] But if this last is in many ways the plot of *Emma*, the story of Emma's capture, it is neither *Emma* in aggregate nor the world by extension to which the novel, as a manifestation of consciousness, is directed or released. We see this primarily through Miss Bates, again, whose monologues (unlike Elizabeth Watson's) are explicitly a matter of choice or receptivity rather than mere circumstance. Early on (Volume I, Chapter 3), when Emma's desire is fixated on Harriet Smith, Miss Bates, although plainly present, is necessarily invisible and, more importantly, inaudible. This changes in the novel's second volume and it changes not just because Miss Bates is seemingly always there. It changes because the world of the novel has expanded: circumstantially, with the arrival of new characters, and phenomenologically, with a protagonist who is suddenly more receptive and strangely passive. The most striking aspect of this receptivity, or thrownness, is the overwhelming spinster herself. But, as if to signal that Miss Bates is more properly a symptom of desire rather than its counterintuitive apotheosis, there is Emma's extraordinary view from Ford's store, which stakes out a position analogous to Miss Bates' that the *narrative* as a centring repository disavows:

> Much could not be hoped from the traffic of even the busiest part of Highbury;—Mr Perry walking hastily by, Mr William Cox letting himself in at the office door, Mr Cole's carriage horses returning from exercise, or stray letter boy on an obstinate mule, were the liveliest objects she could presume to expect; and when her eyes fell only on the butcher with his tray, a tidy old woman travelling homewards from shop with her full basket, two curs quarrelling over a dirty bone, and a string of dawdling children round the baker's little bow-window eyeing the gingerbread, she knew she had no reason to complain, and was amused enough; quite enough still to stand at the door. A mind lively and at ease, can do with seeing nothing, and can see nothing that does not answer. (183)

The second 'nothing' at the conclusion of this remarkable passage is partly a pun—'no thing'—because the point here (beyond amusement) is that for the mind on display— a mind open to the world and to any mind reading it—everything answers just as it answered to Tom Bertram.

Both moments are milestones in free indirect discourse, portending later manifestations—in, for example, Henry James—where consciousness is a 'centre'. But in Austen such moments are also about what's accessible to the first person: a plenitude that, from the perspective of both plot and the individual, looks a lot like 'nothing'. In contrast to the 'story', then, of which Mrs Bennet and Maria Edgeworth are 'in search', *Emma*'s fixation on Miss Bates, on the world according to her ('What is before me, I see' [138]), registers a different need: the desire of things answering, day by day and moment by moment, where 'a mind at ease', if also thrown, is presiding.

Notes

1 For a full discussion of the responses of Austen's earliest readers to her novels, see Galperin (*The Historical Austen* 44–81).
2 For an extended discussion of Austen's 'everyday', see Galperin (*The History of Missed Opportunities* 73–99).
3 There are exceptions to this tendency, chiefly in the byplay between Elizabeth and Caroline Bingley and, early on, between Elizabeth and Darcy. But in general the lightness of being is usurped by both a narrative and a narrative apparatus that chooses sides, pitting Elizabeth and Darcy against the 'they'. For more on this see Alex Woloch.
4 See, again, Galperin (*The Historical Austen* 180–213).
5 Although from the narrator's perspective Miss Bates has been the anti-Emma throughout, beginning with the initial description of her as 'a woman neither young, handsome, rich, nor married' (*E* 17), she is a consciousness that Emma repeatedly introjects, both in channelling her (it's from the heroine's perspective that we typically encounter Miss Bates) and in emulating her, if more relaxed, in the scene at Ford's. Eventually, Emma adds 'married' to her inaugural attributes ('handsome, clever, and rich' [5]) but until that point her consciousness is increasingly directed toward and through Miss Bates—that is, until Emma breaks with her at Box Hill, becoming (in Bersani's terms) both a centre of judgment, indeed of insult, and a non-desiring one.

Works Cited

Austen, Jane. *Emma*, edited by James Kinsley. Oxford UP, 2003.
Austen, Jane. *Later Manuscripts*, edited by Janet Todd and Linda Bree. Cambridge UP, 2008.
Austen, Jane. *Mansfield Park*, edited by James Kinsley. Oxford UP, 2003.
Austen, Jane. *Northanger Abbey and Other Works*, edited by John Davie. Oxford UP, 1980.
Austen, Jane. *Persuasion*, edited by James Kinsley. Oxford UP, 2004
Austen, Jane. *Pride and Prejudice*, edited by Donald Gray. W. W. Norton, 2001.
Bersani, Leo. *A Future for Astyanax: Character and Desire in Literature*. Little, Brown, 1976.
Butler, Marilyn. *Maria Edgeworth: A Literary Biography*. Clarendon P, 1971.
Chatman, Seymour. *Story and Discourse: Narrative Structure in Fiction and Film*. Cornell UP, 1978.
Galperin, William H. *The Historical Austen*. U of Pennsylvania P, 2003.
Galperin, William H. *The History of Missed Opportunities: British Romanticism and the Emergence of the Everyday*. Stanford UP, 2017.
Harootunian, Harry. *History's Disquiet: Modernity, Cultural Practice, and the Question of Everyday Life*. Columbia UP, 2000.
Heidegger, Martin. *Basic Writings*, edited by David Farrell Krell. Harper San Francisco, 1977.
Heidegger, Martin. *Being and Time*. Translated by John Macquarrie and Edward Robinson. Harper and Row, 1962.
Lord Granville Leveson Grower: Private Correspondence, 1721–1821, edited by Castalia Countess Granville, vol. 2. John Murray, 1917.
MacCabe, Colin. *Tracking the Signifier*. U of Minnesota P, 1985.
Marion, Jean-Luc. *Reduction and Givenness: Investigations of Husserl, Heidegger, and Phenomenology*. Translated by Thomas A. Carlson. Northwestern UP, 1998.
Merleau-Ponty, Maurice. *Phenomenology of Perception*. Translated by Donald A. Landes, Routledge, 2014.
Pinch, Adela. *Strange Fits of Passion: Epistemologies of Emotion, Hume to Austen*. Stanford UP, 1996.
Romilly Edgeworth Letters, 1813–1818, edited by Samuel Henry Romilly. John Murray, 1936.

Sedgwick, Eve. 'Jane Austen and the Masturbating Girl.' *Critical Inquiry*, vol. 17, no. 4, 1991, pp. 818–837.

Southam, B. C. *Jane Austen's Literary Manuscripts*. Oxford UP, 1964.

Southam, B. C., editor. *Jane Austen: The Critical Heritage*, vol. 1. Routledge, 1968.

Vermeule, Blakey. *Why Do We Care About Literary Characters?*. Johns Hopkins UP, 2010.

Woloch, Alex. *The One vs. the Many: Minor Characters and the Space of the Protagonist in the Novel*. Princeton UP, 2003.

23

AUSTEN'S LITERARY TIME

Amit Yahav

UNIVERSITY OF MINNESOTA, TWIN CITIES

In an early review of *Emma*, Walter Scott emphasizes the wide impact Jane Austen aims for with her novels. He classes her work among those writings that rely on 'the universal charm of narrative' (37), appealing to all people for pleasure and for the alleviation of suffering; 'hours of languor and anxiety, of deserted age and solitary celibacy, of pain even and poverty are beguiled by the perusal of these light volumes' (38), he writes. Scott also singles out Austen's novels as 'superior to what is granted to the ephemeral productions which supply the regular demand of watering-places and circulating libraries' (38), indicating that the impact of her writing should be measured not only by its popular appeal but also by its endurance. The superiority Scott identifies has been more recently explicated by scholars as the wholesomeness eighteenth- and nineteenth-century readers associated with those literary works worthy of re-reading—the choice few titles of popular productions that endure as beloved canonical literature, as Deidre Lynch argues.[1] But whether intended for a single read or for re-readings, for sociable young ladies or for lonely elder gentlemen, for the middling classes or for aristocrats, publishing fiction entailed competing for readers' leisure time. It is the kind of literature prescribed to Vicesimus Knox's Gentleman vacationer, who confesses 'I am forbidden by my physician to read any thing but what is called summer reading, and therefore I am a frequent lounger at the circulating library' (III.150); or the kind of reading Edward Byles, professor of Sanskrit at Cambridge, picked up before going to sleep—as Lynch recounts (*Loving Literature* 187); or the kind *Northanger Abbey*'s Catherine Morland and her friend Isabella Thorpe enjoy together on rainy days, or *Mansfield Park*'s Fanny Price takes refuge in at her east-room retreat.

Undertaken at off-times—summer vacations, low-key domestic evenings, or any minute in the day one can afford to get away—literature for leisure is literature designed as breaks from the mass connectivity and productive urgency of the world of social and economic obligations. William Wordsworth famously consecrates the Romantic lyric for such pauses from the ordinary business of 'getting and spending', and explains what such pauses mean to him in many writings, from his 'Preface to Lyrical Ballads' to passages in the *Prelude*. Romantic era verse, however, circulated primarily among the aristocracy and gentry, and insofar as Romantic poetry makes an emphatic case for the lyric as enshrining a humanist value of relaxation from economic acquisitiveness, it does so by transforming class privilege and financial means into professional privilege and cultural capital—the special skills of poets to cultivate capacities of the imagination. Novels, by contrast, circulated commercially among the middling classes as much as among groups of higher status, and as such were able to dispense leisure much more widely—time with literature as salutary breaks for a much larger and economically and culturally diverse readership.[2]

306

DOI: 10.4324/9780429398155-23-27

In proposing to explore Austen's literary time, this essay examines what Austen's novels tell us about the value of spare time for fiction readers. As I already began to suggest, and as scrutiny of Austen's novels and their publication histories will further elaborate, such value is various; it could mean 'the alleviation of suffering' one might find in sympathy for fictional characters, or the learning and cultural capital one might accumulate through the pleasing instruction of canonical literature, or it could mean the pure entertainment afforded by what Knox calls 'summer reading' or what Scott calls 'light volumes'. This essay considers how Austen's *Persuasion, Mansfield Park*, and *Northanger Abbey* develop all of these options, but it focuses on the cases made by the latter two for literature's pure entertainment value.[3] Austen-studies, as much as novel-studies more generally, tend to focus on the professional craft, the didactic mission, or the practices of knowledge conveyed in fiction. Lynch, for example, richly explores how literary leisure fosters an affective practice of knowledge; and Christina Lupton, in another recent example, beautifully examines how books offer a respite from work in fostering a slow inquisitiveness that contrasts with demands for efficient productivity. But even as these studies highlight leisure, they continue to privilege the palliative and didactic values of reading; Lynch focuses on the expectation that the teaching of literature be bound with the love of literature, and Lupton argues that ideal reading is most fully realized in the analytical and retentive practices of academic humanist education.[4] Here I highlight, by contrast, Austen's positive valuations of a kind of leisure reading that leaves few long-term traces, provides only temporary pleasures, and solicits its effects less on the mind or on the heart, than on the body.

We might identify such literary time as 'easy reading'—reading whose object, as Andrew Elfenbein explains, is not knowledge but experience.[5] Following Austen's lead, I call such literary time 'idling', invoking Samuel Johnson's essay series from the mid-eighteenth century, which Austen refers to in *Mansfield Park*. In Elfenbein's analysis of easy reading, transport is key. But in Johnson's *Idler* essays and in Austen's renderings of idle reading, the value of such transport depends less on how it takes readers elsewhere, and more on how it promotes an experience of 'ponderous bodies' (5), as Johnson calls it in *Idler* 1. According to Johnson's dictionary, 'to ponder' means to muse, but 'ponderous' means heavy, momentous, and impulsive. Austen explores such mentally equivocal and physically weighty literary idling both as a reading practice—a function of where, when, and how one reads—and as a writing technique—a function of specific formal elements that enable fiction to promote such experience. These formal elements, I suggest, constitute some key dimensions of the 'universal charm of narrative' that Scott flags in his review and that Austen highlights in her novels. And as relatively accessible reading materials—demanding comparatively light financial and intellectual resources—idle reading affords such leisurely literary time not only to educated and wealthy men, but also to women and domestic subordinates.

★ ★ ★

When Austen first achieved print publication in 1811 with *Sense and Sensibility*, she was entering a burgeoning book market. The circulation of books was limited and volatile, catering to a small luxury market for a small class of literate up-and-coming people; but both the book market and the group of people it served were constantly expanding and diversifying. Before 1700, some eighteen hundred titles were produced in Britain each year; by 1830 the annual production of titles rose up to six thousand (see Raven, *The Business of Books*).[6] Books were expensive and print runs were small; Austen's *Emma*, first published in 1815, sold at twenty-one shillings with a print run of 2,000 copies, in William St Clair's estimation. This was a relatively large run for the early nineteenth century, but *Emma* far from sold out—by the end of 1815, 750 copies remained available and by 1818, 565 copies remained unsold (St Clair 579).[7] But if few people bought books, many shared the same copies—with booksellers lending volumes as well as selling them, and with circulating libraries, book clubs, and reading societies constantly expanding their subscriptions and memberships (see St Clair, Chapter 13). Reading was becoming an increasingly popular way of passing one's time among diverse segments of the population—not only those who could afford amassing their own book collections, but also those who rented printed materials or shared them with others in any number of ways.[8]

Austen did not sell especially well—certainly not as much as Scott. Scott's *Guy Mannering,* published in the same year as *Emma* with a similar print run of 2,000 copies, sold out within 24 hours (St Clair 636). Scott was a breathtakingly effective operator in the book market. He was the principal owner of Ballantyne publishing and printing, who together with his London partners 'achieved an ownership of the whole literary production and distribution process from author to reader, controlling or influencing the initial choice of subjects, the writing of the texts, the editing, the publishing, and the printing of the books, the reviewing in the local literary press, the adaptations for the theatre, and the putting on of the theatrical adaptations at the theatre in Edinburgh which Scott also owned', St Clair explains (170). No other Romantic author could match Scott's savviness in the industry. As a woman, Austen could not even dream of being so active in the public economic sphere of print.[9] Nonetheless, she was very much invested in getting her manuscripts published (see Fergus, *Jane Austen*). Austen was furious when Crosby & Co. failed to publish her first completed manuscript, *Susan,* by 1809 after having purchased the copyright in 1803. She demanded immediate publication or release from copyright obligation in a letter she famously signed:

I am, Gentlemen, etc., etc.,

M.A.D.

Angry as she was, Austen let the manuscript languish at Crosby's for another seven years. She eventually bought it back in 1816 for the £10 of its original sale, revised some parts and renamed it *Catherine,* but then temporarily shelved it as she worked on *Persuasion* and *Sanditon. Catherine* was published posthumously in 1817 by the title *Northanger Abbey,* which Cassandra Austen chose for it (see Wolfson 5–12).

If novels seemed important to Austen, as her eagerness to get published suggests, then at least one of several likely reasons is that she deemed people's spare time vitally important and believed novels could fill such time especially well. Unlike Wordsworth, however, Austen never issued extensive or programmatic declarations of what the off-time of literary reading means to her—what spare time might be good for in her opinion, and how her specific art-form—not lyric, but novel—might cater to it. And yet, Austen's novels all feature the pastime of the leisure classes and comment on a range of leisure activities—from strolling and horseback-riding, to sociable conversations, playing cards, playing music, listening to reading aloud, and silent reading. How do Austen's novels, then, imagine what we do when we spend our spare time with literature?

In *Persuasion* Austen features characters who read for feeling—time with literature serving to reflect the inner workings of the heart, and serving to construct sympathetic bonds. *Persuasion's* Captain Benwick reads for the pleasure of finding himself reflected in someone else's words, devotedly immersing in poetry of 'a broken heart, or a mind destroyed by wretchedness' (100). Anne Elliot, for her part, thinks this is a dangerous pastime, telling Benwick that 'it was the misfortune of poetry, to be seldom safely enjoyed by those who enjoy it completely; and that the strong feelings which alone could estimate it truly, were the very feelings which ought to taste it sparingly' (100). Anne recommends prose instead of poetry, which she believes targets minds more than hearts; she 'mentioned such works of our best moralists, such collections of the finest letters, such memoirs of characters of worth and suffering, as occurred to her at the moment as calculated to rouse and fortify the mind by the highest precepts, and the strongest examples of moral and religious endurance' (101). Although Benwick listens to Anne intently, he ultimately opts for a different bookish cure to his narcissistic depression—not to replace reading for feeling with reading for learning, but to replace reading for feeling alone with reading for feeling with others. He invites Louisa Musgrove to peruse Scott and Byron together with him, and their subplot concludes when the two 'had fallen in love over poetry', as Anne puts it (164).

Mansfield Park's Fanny Price also loves to read in her spare time, but under Edmund's guidance such reading serves to cultivate taste and judgment. As in *Persuasion*, leisure reading in *Mansfield Park* assuages the soul, confirms and confers identity, and serves as the basis for bonding with others. But it also supports a program of aesthetic education—which in this novel seems like a worthy pleasure in and of itself. Edmund 'recommended the books which charmed her [Fanny's] leisure hours, he encouraged her taste and corrected her judgment; he made reading useful by talking to her of what she read, and heightened its attraction by judicious praise' (20). In the east room, where Fanny takes 'comfort ... in hours of leisure', she enjoys 'her books—of which she had been a collector, from the first hour of her commanding a shilling' (126).

Fanny is routinely denied access to many leisure activities featured in the novel, humble origins excluding her from the leisure class to which her wealthy relatives belong. In the estimation of Aunt Norris and most of the Bertrams, Fanny ought always to make herself useful. Thus, part of what is at stake in *Mansfield Park* is the right of a member of the lower middle classes to ascend into leisure. Indeed, in Portsmouth Fanny creates for herself and her younger sister Susan a similar upper level refuge as she had in *Mansfield Park*, designed for leisurely aesthetic cultivation:

> By degrees the girls came to spend the chief of the morning up stairs, at first only in working and talking; but after a few days, the remembrance of the said books grew so potent and stimulative, that Fanny found it impossible not to try for books again. There were none in her father's house; but wealth is luxurious and daring—and some of her's found its way to a circulating library. She became a subscriber—amazed at being anything *in propria persona,* amazed at her own doings in every way; to be a renter, a chuser of books! And to be having any one's improvement in view in her choice! But so it was. Susan had read nothing, and Fanny longed to give her a share in her own first pleasures and inspire a taste for the biography and poetry which she delighted in herself. (330)

Austen here emphasizes the celebratory nature of the occasion—the accomplishments involved in Fanny's ascending to the position of chooser of books and of guide in a program of aesthetic education. Fanny cherishes not only the pleasure of reading, but also the satisfaction of proprietorship—both of which cannot be taken for granted by a young woman of modest means such as herself. Here Austen identifies leisure reading as cultural capital in its intellectual and material dimensions—leisure time spent in accumulating knowledge and discerning capacities, which in turn enable one to advance in the world. Such intellectual enrichment materializes as increased financial privilege. And these gains of cultural capital are imagined in this passage to be achieved through reading biography and poetry. Here, unlike in Scott's review, circulating libraries supply not ephemeral products but serious works for study. Fanny may not be wealthy enough to buy books when she is away from her patrons, but the circulating library makes it possible for those with only modest financial means to rent such access to educated pleasures.

But *Mansfield Park* also identifies a kind of leisure reading that it seems to categorize neither as cultural capital nor as emotional palliative. Among the collection of books in the east room Edmund singles out a volume of Samuel Johnson's *Idler* essays—'at hand to relieve you if you tire of your great book' (130), he tells Fanny. If leisure reading in the east room affords Fanny a break from the social scheming and labour exploitation she suffers at the great halls of Mansfield, then the leisure reading of *Idler* essays affords her with a break from the aesthetic education that usually transpires on her leisurely breaks. Sometimes, Edmund acknowledges, one needs to pause all kinds of instrumental endeavours—even those projects that are pleasing and that support growth and autonomy. Sometimes one simply needs to do nothing, and doing nothing with an *Idler* essay seems better than doing nothing with nothing.

Doing nothing? This is no small suggestion. In fact, that Edmund Bertram or, even more, that Jane Austen may recommend doing nothing seems hardly imaginable within a culture that privileges so overwhelmingly self-improvement, productivity, and advancement. For many of us who have been thoroughly inducted into the values of productivity and growth, doing nothing necessarily seems like deficiency, weakness, and waste. Think of how disturbing Charles Dickens's Louisa Gradgrind's staring into the fire seems to readers of *Hard Times* (1854). However, I would like to suggest that along with advocating for the therapeutic and educational values delivered by leisure reading, Austen also makes the case for the importance of pure rest, and for the ways in which novels support it. Several decades before Dickens had presented his critique of hard times, Austen had presented defenses of easy times—pastimes that do not make one smarter, more ethical, or more powerful, but that are valuable nonetheless. A vital nothing that can be supported by reading a volume of what Edmund deems a less-than-great book. Here perhaps lies Scott's 'universal charm' of 'ephemeral productions' and Austen's commitment to publishing novels: promoting the value of pure leisure, or the worthiness of literature that aims not for canonization and study but, instead, aims to support idle relaxation.

The majority of Austen's academic readers have tended to prize agency and proprietorship as the best marks of worthiness, but in an exceptional study Anne-Lise François beautifully argues that for Austen inaction is not simply an instance of perversity or false consciousness but, rather, an instance of a Romanticism 'permissive of a differently lived relation to desire and plot' (228). My discussion joins François's positive assessments of inaction, but aligns Austen's writings less with the elitism of Romantic poetry and high modernism, as François does, and more with the best-sellers among which her novels had been grouped by nineteenth-century booksellers and circulating libraries. These populist dimensions of Austen's novels have tended to be minimized by scholars, partly as a way of making a feminist case for her intellectual calibre. My point, however, is that Austen's populist contributions are equally, albeit differently, profound.

Let's follow Austen's lead, then, into Johnson's *Idler* essays—a series of newspaper columns which was extremely popular during its first publication between 1758 and 1760.[10] Austen doesn't present a scene in which Fanny actually reads Johnson, but we can briefly turn to the *Idler* essays themselves to understand better what is at stake in reading them. In *Idler* 1 Johnson proposes that idling is a general characteristic of humanity within a scheme of differentiated time. He explains: 'Perhaps man may be more properly distinguished as an idle animal; for there is no man who is not sometimes idle' (4). Of these 'sometimes', the times of reading *Idler* essays are exemplary—'for who can be more idle than the reader of the *Idler*?' (4), he asks. This question invites simultaneous rhetorical and literal interpretations. *Idler* readers must be the idlest of the idlers—we may answer, thus interpreting the question rhetorically. And yet Johnson's essays deliver descriptions of varieties of idlers—not just readers, but also theatre goers, horse-back riders, people who stare out their windows, those who encroach on others' time, literary critics, and even scientists who perform experiments on animals.[11] The more we read Johnson's *Idler* essays, the more we are nudged to parse his initial question literally—as genuinely open; each essay offers its own idler supreme not so much helping us decide 'who can be more idle' as constituting our own idling as a kind of surfing of other idlers. Sometimes the essays are satirical, at others clichéd, at still others sympathetic of such spending of one's time; and sometimes all such different valences condense into a single discursive moment. This construes idling as reading that does not accumulate toward useful ends—unhelpful for ranking and judging. But these sketches muse and confuse without seeming wasteful or morally suspect; or even without seeming deconstructive—what Paul de Man values in the indeterminacy of literary language as it mobilizes incompatible rhetorical and literal meanings. If the *Idler* essays sometimes directly advocate and sometimes indirectly nudge their readers to suspend judgment, they do so not in the name of a skepticism of meaningful difference, but rather in the name of affirming an especially important difference: the difference between work and leisure—two complementary but incompatible values.

Sleep, daydreaming, or blank staring and meditative counting—to name a few of Johnson's examples—seem unworthy from the perspective of a culture of universal utility and efficiency, and yet must be positively valued from the perspective of our all-too-human idling tendencies, as we take necessary breaks from our work.[12]

Mansfield Park exemplifies such non-intellectual and non-useful literary value in Henry Crawford's reading aloud of Shakespeare. Here Shakespeare represents not an inexhaustible treasure of wisdom and insight, but the magnet of populist appreciation. Crawford explains that 'Shakespeare one gets acquainted with without knowing how. It is a part of an Englishman's constitution. His thoughts and beauties are so spread abroad that one touches them everywhere, one is intimate with him by instinct.—No man of any brain can open at a good part of one of his plays, without falling into the flow of his meaning immediately' (279). Such immediacy of embodied literary intimacy is certainly the clichéd version of Shakespeare, but when listening to Henry read Shakespeare aloud, Fanny instantiates such 'falling into the flow' rather than poses an exception to it: 'Not a look, or an offer of help had Fanny given, not a syllable for or against. All her attention was for her work. She seemed determined to be interested by nothing else. But taste was too strong in her. She could not abstract her mind five minutes; she was forced to listen; his reading was capital, and her pleasure in good reading was extreme' (278). And thus Fanny 'gradually slacken[s] in the needle-work' and becomes 'fixed on Crawford, fixed on him for minutes, fixed on him in short till the attraction drew Crawford's upon her, and the book was closed, and the charm was broken' (279).

Reading performances were a key activity of eighteenth-century sociable leisure, a cultivated skill popular not only with the elites but also with ascending classes who were especially aware of 'all the potential for social mobility that [it] brought' (22), as Abigail Williams establishes. 'Far from being a dying custom of preliterate communities', she emphasizes, 'reading out loud *well* was at the very centre of polite accomplishment' (34). Indeed, this reading scene in *Mansfield Park* continues with Edmund and Henry conversing about '[t]he subject of reading aloud' (280), with the young men complaining of 'the too common neglect of the qualification, the total inattention to it, in the ordinary school-system for boys, the consequently natural—yet in some instances almost unnatural degree of ignorance and uncouthness of men, of sensible and well-informed men, when suddenly called to the necessity of reading aloud' (280). This scene, then, realistically recreates a common activity of eighteenth-century domestic leisure, which often functioned not quite as a break for doing nothing but, rather, as an occasion to display cultural capital. But if Henry and Edmund assess the situation through this lens, imagining that Henry's skilful reading aloud favourably impresses Fanny with his polite accomplishments, Fanny and the narrator underscore how we might—and even how we might better—assess the pleasure of such reading aloud for its valuable nothingness. Austen does not offer an interior view of Fanny's consciousness in the absorptive situation of listening to Henry's Shakespeare; Fanny's mind may or may not be thinking—may or may not be realizing that she is loosening her guard or, at least, appears to be loosening her guard against Henry. But her body surely is in a state of relaxation, as she stops working and becomes immobile—'fixed on Crawford, fixed on him for minutes'. Henry may be absorbed less in Shakespeare than in impressing Fanny, and Edmund may mistakenly or truthfully interpret Fanny's absorption in the literature as evidence of a repressed attraction to Henry. But deciding between these options is beside the point according to the narration of this scene; for without free indirect discourse we cannot judge definitively. Instead, Austen flags in this passage how the pleasure of the moment is contingent upon reading—the breaking of the charm and the closing of the book coincide. She thus gently ironizes all its characters' limited understandings, and emphasizes how reading may yield little knowledge—little knowledge of self, of others, or of Shakespeare. But at the same time, and no less importantly, she underscores how such mindless absorption might nonetheless be valuable for the full relaxation it yields—Fanny's brief respite from useful needlework—within a circumscribed moment with no consequences.[13]

In *Mansfield Park* Austen endorses reading for relaxation delivered by a populist appreciation of Shakespeare or by the enjoyment of a less-than-great *Idler* essay, but she also reminds her readers that there are ways to read Shakespeare and there are selections from Johnson that could yield more enduring understanding. In *Northanger Abbey*, however, Austen focuses more undividedly on idle pleasures. In this novel, which spans her career from first completed manuscript to posthumously published book, Austen famously issues an appeal for novelists of the world to unite: 'Let us not desert one another; we are an injured body. Although our productions have afforded more extensive and unaffected pleasure than those of any other literary corporation in the world, no species of composition has been so much decried … . there seems almost a general wish of decrying the capacity and undervaluing the labour of the novelist, and of slighting the performances which have only genius, wit, and taste to recommend them' (102). Here Austen cites Frances Burney's *Cecilia* (1782) and *Camilla* (1796) and Maria Edgeworth's *Belinda* (1801) as examples of such productions. But it is Ann Radcliffe's *The Mysteries of Udolpho* (1794) that preoccupies *Northanger Abbey* most, not only in Austen's gothic spoofs but also in conversations among the characters, who all delight in reading it.

Radcliffe's gothic romances were the popular literary sensation of the 1790s in England, and Radcliffe was 'the first novelist to command huge fees from her publisher and the name-recognition of a middle-class reading public', Ian Duncan notes (35). According to St Clair, *The Mysteries of Udolpho* sold out its first print run of 1306 books in 1794, to be reissued the same year in another 1306 copies (631). This novel must also have been very popular at the circulating libraries, if we accept St Clair's argument about a clear pattern in the Romantic book market by which the higher the sales, the higher the demand at book-sharing venues (Chapter 13).[14] In *Northanger Abbey*, *Udolpho* instantiates popular literature that one must be careful not to learn from—hence the whiffs of Quixotic satire that run through Austen's fiction. But *Udolpho* is also a novel that characters read, and certainly not a book that should be avoided. Henry Tilney declares that 'The person, be it gentleman or lady, who has not pleasure in a good novel must be intolerably stupid'; and he continues: 'I have read all Mrs Radcliffe's works, and most of them with great pleasure' (179).

Austen underscores how *Northanger Abbey's* characters read Radcliffe's sensation. Henry explains that 'The "Mysteries of Udolpho", when I had once begun it, I could not lay down again; I remember finishing it in two days, my hair standing on end the whole time' (179–80). Indeed, Henry refuses all distraction while he reads *Udolpho*. When his sister Eleanor admits an interruption, he runs away with the book 'refusing to wait only five minutes' (180). This is not to say that he believes such reading materials demand solipsism; to the contrary—Henry reads aloud to his sister as eagerly as Catherine reads together with her friend Isabella. But the duration of reading—whether in society or in isolation, aloud or in silence—must be, according to Henry, fully devoted to this reading and nothing else. Henry reads Radcliffe, it seems, just like Janice Radway's twentieth-century American informants read dime romances—reading through the whole volume in one sitting, becoming intensely involved in it, and insisting that this is the only way such fiction can be read. Radway's groundbreaking ethnographic study calls attention to 'the complex social event of reading' (8), examining the values middle-class suburban mothers found in the 1970s in the romances they devotedly read. Radway's subjects revealingly explain their practice as 'simple relaxation'; 'reading is just for me; it is my time' (60), they insist.[15] Henry, of course, is not a twentieth-century American suburban homemaker, but an eighteenth-century English country gentleman, who can command much more of his time for himself than Radway's subjects can. Nonetheless, he also insists on reading gothic romances for pure leisure—reading these fictions as time off from the duties of social engagements, of learning, and of cultivating oneself towards a profession.

Catherine Morland similarly reads *Udolpho* in absorption. When she is finally 'left to the luxury of a raised, restless, and frightened imagination over the pages of *Udolpho*', and is 'lost from all worldly concerns of dressing and dinner, incapable of soothing Mrs Allen's fears on the delay of an expected dressmaker', she has 'only one minute in sixty to bestow even on the reflection of her own felicity in being already engaged for the evening' (121). No social vanities or self-congratulating bliss can distract Catherine from the pages of Radcliffe's novel. Catherine may not be as resolute in warding off distraction as Henry had been. Being a few minutes late to meet her friend Isabella, Catherine apologetically explains that she spent the morning immersed in *Udolpho*; 'I should like to spend my whole life in reading it, I assure you; if it had not been to meet you, I would not have come away from it for all the world' (107). But even as Catherine gives in to the interruptions of social obligations while reading her gothic romances, Austen's account of *Udolpho*'s effects on her evokes Johnson's 'ponderous bodies'. The 'luxury of a raised, restless, and frightened imagination over the pages of *Udolpho*' emphasizes the materiality of the book and physicality of the reader's response, drawing attention to the embodied effects of reading, rather than to any lessons of heart or mind that may be learned from this fiction.

The way Austen describes reading *Udolpho* suggests that not the content of the romance, but the absorptive idleness of its reading matters most. This draws attention to the very duration of reading, indicating that Radcliffe's gothic romance somehow disjoins its reading-time from other times, making this duration feel special and encouraging readers to safeguard its difference. Paul Ricœur argues that when we read fiction we are less compelled to evaluate how the representation mirrors reality, than we are to feel that our own real time of reading is shaped by the time-sense that structures the composition.[16] And Gérard Genette proposes that such activation of temporal experience arises from the way novelists mobilize literary techniques to create a sense of rhythm.[17] Radcliffe's gothic, as Austen knew well, amply manipulates such narrative duration. In her spoofs of gothic scenes in *Northanger Abbey*, Austen relies not only on the gothic's visual style of locked cabinets, mysterious trap doors, and long corridors all shrouded in darkness, but also on the genre's techniques of modulated durations. Often in gothic novels and in Austen's version of them there is 'no time to be lost' (e.g., 269) and no daring to 'waste a moment' (e.g., 242); there are 'ill-timed' coincidences (e.g., 242), such as the finding of a note at the same moment that a candle blows out; and, last but not least for ensuring distinctive rhythm, there are ominous pauses whereby the heroine is 'for a few moments … motionless with horror' (e.g., 247).

The gothic spoofs of *Northanger Abbey* underscore genre-fiction's reliance on techniques of rhythm. If Radway's subjects intuitively identify elements of plot and content as what promotes their immersive reading practices, Austen emphasizes how modulating between action and discursive dilations, between streamlined summaries and extensive scenes, and mobilizing sentence-level effects of rhythm is no less important in a fiction's ability to grip its readers.[18] Indeed, Austen uses such techniques of rhythm amply throughout her novels, borrowing from, no less than refining, the popular gothic writers who precede her. *Northanger Abbey* underscores how different plot situations afford different durational experiences to its characters, as well as how such varying durational experiences might be imparted to the novel's readers. On the one hand, we get many dialogues in Bath and then at the Abbey highlighting by way of scene the gradual process of Catherine's and Henry's growing intimacy. On the other hand, Austen uses summary to impart Isabella and Catherine's too-quick attachment—'they passed so rapidly through every gradation of increasing tenderness that there was shortly no fresh proof of it to be given to their friends or themselves' (100). Catherine's joy at visiting Henry's parsonage is summed up by observing that 'Never had any day passed so quickly' (292). And when General Tilney departs from the Abbey, the narrator reports: 'The happiness with which their time now passed—every employment voluntary, every laugh indulged, every meal a scene of ease and good-humour, walking where they liked and when they liked, their hours, pleasures and fatigues at their own command' (297). When General Tilney dismisses Catherine with extreme temporal compression—banishing her from the Abbey overnight—Austen underlines the inadequacy of this pace with meticulously detailed scenes of Eleanor and Catherine's parting. And when Catherine leaves Eleanor, the narrator emphasizes the temporality of their farewell, noting: 'the time of their remaining together' 'Short, however, was that time' was consummated with 'a long and affectionate embrace' (307). The duration of an embrace can tell volumes especially when time is short, indicating that at stake here isn't simply length but pace: in this case, the slowing down that certain attitudes may effect to stretch out a foreshortened duration.

In drawing on genre fiction's ample use of narrative rhythms, however, Austen not only promotes immersive reading; she also underscores techniques that promote release from 'the universal charm of narrative'. If, as I have been arguing, the value of literary time for Austen rests not only in its palliative and edifying qualities, but also in the pure leisure it can afford, she also suggests that such idle relaxation can only be temporary. Thus, the last chapter of *Northanger Abbey* includes a discursive comment that adroitly refuses readers continued absorption: 'The anxiety which in this state of their attachment must be the portion of Henry and Catherine, and of all who loved either, as to its final event, can hardly extend, I fear, to the bosom of my readers who will see in the tell-tale compression of the pages before them that we are all hastening together to perfect felicity' (326). Austen flags the technique of summary—'compression'—to emphasize that plotting must come to a close and that narrative duration cannot be interminable. Readers are hastened to see perfect felicity but not to feel it, nudged into the position of ones whose leisure time is up. At least, for a while—until we arrive at our next off-the-clock break for immersive leisure reading.

In *Mansfield Park* Austen also flags a homology between narrative compression and the plot's resolution in marriage. 'I purposely abstain from dates on this occasion, that every one may be at liberty to fix their own, aware that the cure of unconquerable passions, and the transfer of unchanging attachments, must vary much as to time in different people' (387), the narrator declares as she hurries to conclude with Fanny and Edmund's felicitous union. More generally, all of Austen's novels realize this homology through their commitment to the marriage plot. The form of the marriage plot undercuts duration by positioning the moment of union at the end, omitting all that may follow, resignifying all that precedes as a leading path (whether as cause or as error soon to be corrected), and representing the very moment itself in summary. In the marriage plot, marriage functions as an abstracted moment, rather than a durational one, marking the end of absorption in narrative duration and, thus, ejecting readers from their immersion in fiction. If gothic form is among the novel's most effective techniques for promoting idle immersion in literary time, then the marriage plot is its most easily visible form for promoting release, snapping readers out of the world of fiction and back into the real world of chronometric measures, productivity, and efficiency.

This is not to argue that Austen's literary time does not include chronometric consciousness. Austen's realism carefully simulates chronometric probabilities; as Anne Thackeray observes 'With Jane Austen days, hours, minutes succeed each other like clockwork' (qtd. in Lynch, 'Austen Extended', 235) and as Yoon Sun Lee notes 'in Austen a mile is always a mile a minute is always a minute' (192). But also crucial for Austen is how these days, hours, minutes, can vary widely in their experience and how literary time might not only represent such modulations, but also promote varieties in readers' own durational experiences. She recognizes the variability of time consciousness and the shortcomings of approaches that reduce human experience and human purposes solely to economic rationality.[19] Time is much more than money, Austen insists, just as Wordsworth does. And she adds to this insistence a celebration of durations for doing nothing as much as of durations for achieving something—promoting relaxation and entertainment as much as the edifying and palliative potentials of more elitist literature.

Barbara Benedict explains that Austen's 'intertextuality suggests that she conceived of her novels in the context of current fiction, as a part of popular literature, and designed her novels to reach the audiences who were reading contemporary novels' (64). Further developing this perspective, I have argued here that Austen's populist contributions are equally profound as her psychological, political, and professional insights. If, as St Clair finds, half the copies of the early editions of Austen's novels circulated not through sales but through lending libraries, this may not have been a bad thing in Austen's estimation (245). Her novels may have kept company with 'ephemeral productions', as Scott has it, but as such they contributed to an important socio-aesthetic program. Austen's novels made the vital pleasures of doing nothing available to less privileged readers—not just vacationers in Bath like Henry Tilney and Catherine Morland, but also lower middle-class subscribers to circulating libraries in Portsmouth like Fanny and Susan Price.

Notes

1 In addition to Lynch's work, also see Alan Richardson's and Richard Cronin's. For Austen's active engagement in carving a privileged position for her work among popular fiction, see Clifford Siskin.

2 For the elitist circulation of Romantic era verse vs. the populist circulation of Romantic era novels, see St Clair (172–76); for Romantic lyric's ideological transformation of class privilege into professional privilege, see Siskin.

3 My discussion here extends my exploration of Austen's positive valuation of fiction as a break from work and learning, which I began in 'Leisure Reading and Austen's Case for Differentiated Time'.

4 In *Loving Literature* Lynch explains how literary appreciation came to be laden with emotional underpinnings that make crossovers between reading for work and reading for leisure seem inevitable, and Lupton chronicles a desire for alternations between book time and work time and an imagined future in which access to reading would be equitably distributed.

5 Experiments in cognitive science demonstrate, according to Elfenbein, how literary techniques can activate networks of associations that load words with multiple resonances, supporting 'a sensation that does not produce paraphraseable meaning but a phenomenological feeling' (35). Easy reading, he demonstrates, prizes dense experience and imaginative transport, and is satisfied with gist—a minimal and imprecise retention of content. Elfenbein focuses on what easy reading has meant for the Victorians and how this aligns with cognitive studies of the automatic processes that underwrite much of our reading.

6 Novels only constituted a small fraction of these titles; Jan Fergus points out that in 1811 *Sense and Sensibility* was 'one of just 80 titles of novels for adults produced in the British Isles in that year' ('The Literary Marketplace', 41).

7 St Clair does not estimate the print runs of Austen's first three novels. He also explains that for most of the population 'a single volume of one new novel would have cost more than a week's income' and 'print runs were seldom above 500' (240).

8 Austen herself had the privilege of occasionally enjoying an especially well-stocked private library at Godmersham Park, the residence of her brother Edward Austen Knight. Typical of such wealthy private collections, its generic range was wide; atypically, however, it included a relatively large number of novels. See the Library of Godmersham Park website, https://www.readingwithausten.com/about.html

9 Byron's works also garnered phenomenal commercial success, and women novelists such as Ann Radcliff and Maria Edgeworth were effective and successful market operators. But Scott topped them all in both sales and overall activity. See St Clair, 159–76, 254, 585–90, 597, 631, as well as Susan J. Wolfson.

10 The *Idler* essays were first published as contributions to the *Universal Chronicle or Weekly Gazette*. Though this newspaper was not especially successful, Johnson's columns were very popular, with other periodical publications immediately pirating *Idler* essays in their own numbers.

11 The last are especially pernicious, Johnson suggests, for they are unaware of the frivolity of their activity, cruelly supporting their own pleasure at the expense of others' pain.

12 The essays often deliver anecdotes, sometimes narrated by Mr Idler, sometimes narrated by characters who write letters to Mr Idler, and these varying points of view often directly qualify one another. *Idler* 18 disputes the gentle satire of *Idler* 16; *Idler* 28 challenges the complaints levelled at a husband in *Idler* 15; *Idler* 21, a letter from Dick Linger, qualifies the critique of Jack Whirler from *Idler* 19. And if *Idler* 13 censures a woman who is 'an irreconcilable enemy to Idleness, and considers every state of life as idleness, in which the hands are not employed, or some art acquired, by which she thinks money may be got or saved' (43), then *Idler* 19 condemns those who believe that 'the highest degree of earthly happiness is quiet; a calm repose of both mind and body, undisturbed by the sight of folly or the noise of business, the tumults of public commotion, or the agitations of private interest' (59) for 'none have the right to withdraw from their task of vigilance, or to be indulged in idle wisdom or solitary pleasures' (59). Thus these essays repeatedly dramatize the precariousness of assessments of leisure, suggesting that perhaps our need for rest might also arise from a deep seated recognition of the limitations of our knowledge and judgments.

13 Alternatively, François emphasizes the privacy insisted upon in the narration of Fanny's absorption in Henry's reading. For François this occasion of undecidability exemplifies Austen's liberalism in its insistence on privacy. Such moments of avoiding interior monologue respect 'Fanny's predilection for remaining in public without being seen' thus 'make[ing] her a representative of the liberal fantasy of a public space hospitable to the unstated preferences of its members and defined not by formal contract, but by the implicit willingness of each to credit the others' powers of judgment and discretion over their own desires and pleasures, however publicly occasioned' (250).

14 St Clair doesn't provide precise numbers of copies of Radcliffe's novels acquired by circulating libraries.

15 According to Radway, one of her subjects picked up reading when her doctor told her that for her mental and physical health she must find an enjoyable leisure activity she could engage in for an hour a day (51); another subject recommended romance as 'good therapy and much cheaper than tranquilizers' (52). But if the doctor's initial prescription called for an hour a day, Radway's subjects report a different way of managing their doses—finding times (mostly when their kids arrive at school age) and appropriate reading materials (gripping romances) to gulp down during a single extended sitting; see page 59. Radway's account of the twentieth-century U.S. history of popular fiction publication resonates in very interesting ways with eighteenth-century British literary history. She highlights the importance of the gothic genre popular in America in the 1960s, and she underscores the landmark transformation of the market in 1972 by Kathleen Woodiwiss' *The Flame and the Flower*, which very much sounds like a version of a Radcliffian sensible gothic—long narratives that include not only sexual predations but also travel, ending with 'the heroine safely returned to the hero's arms' (34).

16 In a breathtakingly wide-ranging study, Ricœur explains that the referential significance of narrative representation has less to do with its better or worse mirroring of objects than with its activation of temporal experience constitutive of our actions and understanding.

17 Genette considers the difficult problem of assessing what the duration of a novel might feel like for readers, given the infinitely diverse conditions in which novels are read. His solution is to analyse ratios of action and narration and, thus, to formalize duration as rhythm which, he explains, conceives of novelistic time in terms of musicological models.

18 Radway's emphasis on plot and content is apparent throughout her study, but for an especially useful example see Table 2.2 of Chapter 2, p. 67.

19 Austen inherits her complex approach to literary time not only from Johnson, but also from the eighteenth-century culture of sensibility in novelists such as Samuel Richardson, Laurence Sterne, and Ann Radcliffe and essayists and philosophers such as Joseph Addison, Denis Diderot, and Edmund Burke (see my *Feeling Time*).

Works Cited

Austen, Jane. *Mansfield Park*, edited by Kathryn Sutherland. New York: Penguin, 1996.

Austen, Jane. *Northanger Abbey*, edited by Susan J. Wolfson. Belknap P, 2014.

Benedict, Barbara, 'Sensibility by the Numbers: Austen's Work as Regency Popular Fiction.' *Janeites: Austen's Disciples and Devotes*, edited by Deidre Lynch. Princeton UP, 2000.

Cronin, Richard. 'Literary Scene.' *Jane Austen in Context*, edited by Janet Todd. Cambridge UP, 2005.

De Man, Paul. 'Semiology and Rhetoric.' *Allegories of Reading*. Yale UP, 1979.

Duncan, Ian. *Modern Romance and the Transformations of the Novel: The Gothic, Scott, Dickens*. Cambridge UP, 1992.

Elfenbein, Andrew. *The Gist of Reading*. Stanford UP, 2018.

Fergus, Jan. *Jane Austen: A Literary Life*. Macmillan, 1991.

Fergus, Jan. 'The Literary Marketplace.' *A Companion to Jane Austen*, edited by Claudia L. Johnson and Clara Tuite. Wiley Blackwell, 2009.

François, Anne-Lise. *Open Secrets: The Literature of Uncounted Experience*. Stanford UP, 2008.

Genette, Gérard. *Narrative Discourse: And Essay in Method*. Translated by Jane E. Lewin. Cornell UP, 1980.

Johnson, Samuel. *A Dictionary of the English Language*, vol. 2. J. Knapton; C. Hitch and L. Hawes; A. Millar, R. and J. Dodsley, 1756; accessed on ECCO, 5/2/2020.

Johnson, Samuel, *The Idler and The Adventurer. Yale Edition of the Works of Samuel Johnson*, vol. 2. Yale UP, 1963.

Knox, Vicesimus. 'On Reading Novels and Trifling Books without Discrimination.' *Winter Evenings: Or, Lucubrations on Life and Letters*, vol. 3. London: Charles Dilly, 1788.

Lee, Yoon Sun. 'Austen's Scale Making.' *Studies in Romanticism*, vol. 52, no. 2, 2013, pp. 171–195.

Lupton, Christina. *Reading and the Making of Time*. Johns Hopkins UP, 2018.

Lynch, Deidre Shauna. 'Austen Extended/Austen for Everyday Use.' *Imagining Selves: Essays in Honor of Patricia Meyer Spacks*, edited by Rivka Swenson and Elise Lauterbach. U of Delaware P, 2008.

Lynch, Deidre Shauna. *Loving Literature: A Cultural History.* U of Chicago P, 2015.

Radway, Janice. *Reading the Romance: Women, Patriarchy, and Popular Literature*. U of North Carolina P, 1984.

Raven, James. 'Book Production.' *Jane Austen in Context*, edited by Janet Todd. Cambridge UP, 2005.

Raven, James. *The Business of Books: Booksellers and the English Book Trade 1450–1850*. Yale UP, 2007.

Ricœur, Paul. *Time and Narrative*. Translated by Kathleen McLaughlin and David Pellauer, 3. vols. U of Chicago P, 1984.

Richardson, Alan. 'Reading Practices.' *Jane Austen in Context*, edited by Janet Todd. Cambridge UP, 2005.

Scott, Walter. 'Review of *Emma*.' *Quarterly Review*, October 1815. *Jane Austen: Emma, a Casebook*, edited by David Lodge. Macmillan, 1968.

Siskin, Clifford. *The Work of Writing: Literature and Social Change in Britain 1700–1830*. Johns Hopkins UP, 1998.

St Clair, William. *The Reading Nation in the Romantic Period*. Cambridge UP, 2004.

Williams, Abigail. *The Social Life of Books: Reading Together in the Eighteenth-Century Home*. Yale UP, 2017.

Wolfson, Susan J. Introduction. *Northanger Abbey*, by Jane Austen, 1818, Belknap P, 2014.

Yahav, Amit S. *Feeling Time: Duration, Novels, and Eighteenth-Century Sensibility*. U of Pennsylvania P, 2018.

Yahav, Amit S. 'Leisure Reading and Austen's Case for Differentiated Time.' *The Eighteenth Century: Theory and Interpretation*, vol. 60, no. 2, 2019, pp. 163–183.

24
AUSTEN, MASCULINITY, AND ROMANTICISM

Sarah Ailwood

UNIVERSITY OF WOLLONGONG

Introduction

Jane Austen's men hold a central place in her literary and cultural legacy. Yet it is only in the last two decades that Austen's men have become a focus of scholarly attention. We are still in the process of describing, analysing, interpreting and evaluating Austen's men as textual constructions of masculinity and the contribution she made, through them, to the development of the novel as genre. The trajectory by which Austen's men have achieved the status of cultural icons, from the Romantic period through to the digital era, similarly demands scholarly exploration. Scholars are revealing in new ways the depth and complexity of Austen's male characters, including her male protagonists or 'romantic heroes' and also peripheral men, who play critical roles as fathers, sons, brothers and friends, to Austen's culturally embedded vision of Romantic masculinity. The myriad ways in which Austen's men have been reimagined across different times, places and cultures have triggered further new interest in Austen's men as complex and enduring subjects of adaptation and translation across form and genre. In this chapter I chart trends in the interpretation of Austen's men from Austen's earliest readers to the present. I also offer a new way of interpreting Austen's men as textual constructions of masculinity within the context of the Romantic era, with a particular focus on *Pride and Prejudice* (1813) and *Persuasion* (1818), illustrating that a focus on Austen's men not only illuminates the characters themselves, but also reveals new insights into Austen's broader engagement with prevailing cultural, political and social ideologies. Finally, I outline new directions for future research on Austen and masculinity.

Reading Austen's Men

Austen and Her Early Readers

Jane Austen (and her literary executor, her sister Cassandra) left to posterity few authorial insights into either her male characters or how she approached the task of writing masculinity. Austen's only surviving commentary on any of her male protagonists concerns Mr Darcy, whose character she references in a letter to Cassandra, describing her search for a portrait of Elizabeth Darcy in London galleries in 1813:

> We have been both to the Exhibition & Sir J. Reynolds', – and I am disappointed, for there was nothing like Mrs D. at either. – I can only imagine that Mr D. prizes any Picture

318

DOI: 10.4324/9780429398155-24-28

of her too much to like it should be exposed to the public eye. – I can imagine he w^d have that sort [of *omitted*] feeling – that mixture of Love, Pride & Delicacy.' (24 May 1813; *Letters* 213)

In describing Darcy as possessing 'that mixture of Love, Pride & Delicacy', Austen encapsulates his defining characteristic—his consuming love for Elizabeth Bennet—and exposes the depth of her admiration for, and pride in, the character who would become her stellar male protagonist, arguably transform the courtship romance genre and secure her legacy into the twenty-first century. Yet on the publication of *Pride and Prejudice* in 1813, Austen appears to have had some misgivings, at the very least, about his public reception. When the first set of volumes to arrive at Chawton were read aloud, Austen reflects on her neighbour Miss Benn's amusement with 'two such people to lead the way': 'she really does seem to admire Elizabeth. I must confess that *I* think her as delightful a creature as ever appeared in print, & how I shall be able to tolerate those who do not like *her* at least, I do not know' (29 January 1813; *Letters* 201). Austen's emphasis—'*her* at least'—has been interpreted as emphasising her delight in her heroine, but it simultaneously reveals her concern that readers may not 'like' *him*: that Darcy may be undervalued, misunderstood or unappreciated by readers, or that their value for him may not match Austen's own.

Commentary from Austen's early readers, however, reveals that any concern Austen felt about the reception of Darcy was misplaced. To Annabella Milbanke, the future Lady Byron, Darcy was a particularly striking character: 'I have finished the novel called *Pride & Prejudice*, which I think a very superior work … I really think it is the *most probable* fiction I have ever read. It is not a crying book, but the interest is very strong, especially for Mr. Darcy' (Elwin 159). Mary Russell Mitford would have disappointed Austen in her appraisal of Elizabeth, instead reserving all of her praise for Darcy:

> The want of elegance is almost the only want in Miss Austen. I have not read her "Mansfield Park;" but it is impossible not to feel in every line of "Pride and Prejudice," in every word of "Elizabeth," the entire want of taste which could produce so pert, so worldly a heroine as the beloved of such a man as Darcy. Wickham is equally bad. Oh! They were just fit for each other, and I cannot forgive that delightful Darcy for parting them. Darcy should have married Jane. He is, of all the admirable characters, the best designed and the best sustained. (Letter to Sir William Elford, December 1814; L'Estrange 300)

Maria Edgeworth similarly praised the 'natural' characters of Captain Wentworth and Anne Elliot, writing that *Persuasion*:

> appears to me, especially in all that relates to poor Anne and her lover, to be exceedingly interesting and natural. The love and the lover admirably well drawn; don't you see Captain Wentworth, or rather don't you in her place feel him taking the boisterous child off her back as she kneels by the sick boy on the sofa? And is not the first meeting after their long separation admirably well done? And the overheard conversation about the nut? (Maria Edgeworth to Mrs Ruxton, 21 February 1818; Barry (ed.) 232)

Edgeworth, Milbanke, and Mitford each praise the realism of Austen's work, and particularly of her male protagonists. Realism had indeed become a touchstone of literary excellence, achieved by the novelist who could create characters that were 'natural, 'well supported' and 'drawn to Life'—praise that Austen clearly valued, as she recorded it herself in 'Opinions of *Mansfield Park*' and 'Opinions of *Emma*' (Chapman (ed.) 431–39).

Austen's preference for realism in writing masculinity is also revealed, albeit as a tongue-in-cheek subterfuge, in her correspondence with James Stanier Clarke in the course of dedicating *Emma* to the Prince Regent. Austen deploys realism as a shield through which she can politely decline Clarke's self-serving suggestion that she model her next literary work on him:

> I am quite honoured by your thinking me capable of drawing such a Clergyman … But I assure you I am not. The comic part of the Character I might be equal to, but not the Good, the Enthusiastic, the Literary. Such a Man's Conversation must at times be on subjects of Science & Philosophy of which I know nothing – or at least be occasionally abundant in quotations & allusions which a Woman, who like me, knows only her Mother-tongue & has read very little in that, would be totally without the power of giving. (11 December 1815; *Letters* 306)

Austen's declaration to Clarke—'I must keep to my own style & go on in my own Way' (1 April 1816, *Letters* 312)—with her focus on 'pictures of domestic Life in Country Villages', is much more than a commitment to realism as an end in itself. Her literary advice to her niece Anna Lefroy the previous year reveals her explicit concern with the need for realism in the construction of literary masculinity, particularly in the courtship romance genre. Targeting Anna's character Henry Mellish—possibly the romantic hero of the piece—for being too stereotyped a vision of literary masculinity, Austen declares: 'Henry Mellish I am afraid will be too much in the common Novel style—a handsome, amiable, unexceptionable Young Man (such as do not much abound in real Life) desperately in Love, & all in vain. But I have not business to judge him so early' (28 September 1814; *Letters* 277). To Austen, writing realistic male characters who reflected men of 'real Life' separated her work from the 'common Novel' and its reliance on stock, stereotyped male characters: morally perfect romantic heroes, dastardly villains, rakes, fops and other figures inherited from her eighteenth-century predecessors. Her disdain for one-dimensional male characters is also evident in her 'Plan of a Novel', in which she lampoons 'some totally unprincipled & heart-less young Man, desperately in love with her Heroine, & pursuing her with unrelenting passion' and 'the Hero—all perfection of course—& only prevented from paying his addresses to her, by some excess of refinement' (Chapman (ed.) 429–30). To Austen, realism meant forging a new, richer and more complex vision of literary masculinity that could serve her literary agendas and ultimately advance the novel as a literary form.

As E. J. Clery argues, early reviewers evaluated Austen's novels through a gender-neutral lens, praising the realism of both her male and female characters and 'the compelling and diverse characterization of the heroes' (333). In his review of *Emma*, Walter Scott endowed equal praise on Austen's men and her women, championing 'a style of novel' concerned with 'the common walks of life, and presenting to the reader, instead of the splendid scenes of an imaginary world, a correct and striking representation of that which is daily taking place around him' (188). This approach was also taken by Richard Whateley in his 1821 critical essay, and indeed by critics throughout the nineteenth century.

Despite early praise for the 'natural' realism of Austen's men, across the waves of her fluctuating popularity, and through the trajectory of literary criticism in the nineteenth and twentieth centuries, there emerged an increasingly dominant interpretation of Austen's men as somehow lesser characters than her heroines. This perspective is encapsulated rather humorously in Sir Francis Darwin's essay 'Jane Austen', published in 1917. Darwin advocates a taxonomic classification of her male characters, who he categorises as 'Attractive' and 'Unattractive', and then subdivides within the 'Attractive' genus into 'Trustworthy' and 'Untrustworthy', with the 'Trustworthy' category further subdivided into 'Dull' and 'Interesting'. Within this scientific ordering, Darwin classifies Colonel Brandon and Edward Ferrars as Attractive, Trustworthy, and Dull, and Mr Darcy, Mr Knightley, Henry Tilney, and Captain Wentworth as 'Attractive', 'Trustworthy,' and 'Interesting'. Frank Churchill, Henry

Crawford, William Elliot, George Wickham, and John Willoughby are, needless to say, classified as 'Attractive' and 'Untrustworthy' (Darwin 71). Whereas Darwin's taxonomy of male virtue is an homage to Austen, with whom he is clearly enchanted, other twentieth-century critics earnestly peddled such a reductive interpretation of Austen's men in a phenomenon Clery describes as the 'sexing' of Austen as a 'feminine' novelist' (332–33). Harrison Steeves perhaps best reflects this gendered dismissal-en-masse of Austen's men, labelling them mere 'appendages' to the plot, claiming that 'while the world acknowledges a place for a "man's woman", we find less enthusiasm for the "woman's man"' (223) and attributing what he describes as their marginal position within her novels to her inability to create convincing male characters:

> The fact remains that Jane Austen's one plot (with a single exception) the capturing of a well-placed and well-to-do husband – approaches its problem, and solves it, from the point of view of a woman's thoughts, feelings, and interests. However the husband-to-be may look like the active mind in the transaction, as Knightley does in *Emma* and Wentworth in *Persuasion*, it is the woman's experience that Miss Austen submits to analysis, because she understands it and can voice it. (372)

Modern Interpretations

The chauvinistic view of Austen's men as no more than thin but necessary scaffolding for the courtship romance plot has been thoroughly trounced by a number of waves of critical re-evaluations of Austen, her place within eighteenth-century, Regency and Romantic contexts, and her literary legacy. Explorations of Austen's novels in the broader context of her life and times brought her men into focus in works such as Audrey Hawkridge's *Jane and her Gentlemen*, Brian C. Southam's *Jane Austen and the Navy,* Irene Collins' *Jane Austen and the Clergy,* and Alistair Duckworth's *The Improvement of the Estate*. In exploring the professions, estate management practices, and other kinds of 'work' undertaken by men within the historical context of Austen's novels, these scholars offered new ways of reading Austen's men beyond their necessary structural role.

Richer, more nuanced understandings of Austen's men and the complexity of their characterisation emerged in the last decades of the twentieth century, enabled by two distinct but related threads of Austen criticism: the recognition of Austen as a political writer and the emergence of feminist literary criticism and its powerful re-readings of Austen's novels through a specifically gendered lens. Works such as Marilyn Butler's *Jane Austen and the War of Ideas* (1975), Warren Roberts' *Jane Austen and the French Revolution* (1979), Tony Tanner's *Jane Austen* (1986), and Mary Evans' *Jane Austen and the State* (1987) revealed Austen to be a writer who was—either implicitly or explicitly—engaged with the great political questions of her time, whose works were capable of supporting conservative, progressive and even radical ideological affiliations. These and other explorations of Austen as a political writer offered new approaches to interpreting her male characters because, being male, they possess access to education, property, the professions and roles within national, imperial, and international contexts, all of which provide a platform for engagement with the politics of the public sphere. Their scope of agency encompasses national and global events and the ideological debates that dominated the post-revolutionary and Regency era. Austen's men are economic, social and political agents whose professional status, views, decisions, and actions are invested with some of the most contentious political issues of the day. Through her characterisation of men, then, Austen has been interpreted as engaging in politicised commentary on issues as varied as the enclosure of land, estate management, and 'improvement'; the rise of the professions, meritocracy, and class mobility; the role of the clergy, the status of the church and the rise of Evangelicalism; England's relationships with Scotland and Ireland; the French Revolution;

England's conflict with France throughout the Napoleonic Wars; the Regency crisis; and Britain's imperial project in India, the Caribbean, and beyond.

Indeed, Austen's characterisation of men has been interpreted—problematically, and not without risk—as offering insight into her own political views and opinions, with Austen's place on the political spectrum signified through the role that individual men play in the courtship romance plot. Through this lens, Austen's 'happy endings'—narrative resolution through the marriage of the heroine and her romantic hero—stamp Austen's approval of the political values embodied in the male protagonist and rejection of his (often dangerous) rival. *Mansfield Park* has attracted significant scholarly attention that illustrates this critical approach, although it has been used to draw out the political aspects of each of Austen's novels, particularly *Emma* and *Persuasion*. *Mansfield Park* is arguably Austen's most explicitly political novel, and its acute political context is inscribed in Austen's characterisation of men: the parliamentarian, estate patriarch, and absentee landlord Sir Thomas Bertram; the profligate, similarly absentee elder son Tom; the Evangelical, domestic clergyman Edmund; the shallow yet aspirational Rushworth; the patriotic, hard-working sailor William Price; and the Francophilic, intelligent yet superficial Henry Crawford. In *Mansfield Park* Austen foregrounds these men's professional identifications, scope of agency, and attitudes to their responsibilities—particularly the exercise of power—as key indices of their worth and value. Scholars have argued that the narrative resolution of *Mansfield Park*, in the marriage of Fanny Price and Edmund Bertram, represents political views as diverse as Austen's reactionary conservatism on one hand, and on the other her value for radically disruptive middle-class mobility through the triumph of the meritocracy.

Feminist literary critics have offered similarly innovative approaches that reveal the depth and complexity of Austen's men, by evaluating them through an explicitly gendered lens. In works such as Margaret Kirkham's *Jane Austen, Feminism and Fiction* (1983), Mary Poovey's *The Proper Lady and the Woman Writer* (1984), and Alison G. Sulloway's *Jane Austen and the Province of Womanhood* (1989), the politics of Austen's work are drawn inward to the arguably more important realm of the personal, enabling a shift in the evaluation of Austen's men from their roles as social, political, and economic actors to their roles as fathers, brothers, sons, lovers, and husbands. Feminist literary criticism, on Austen and other eighteenth-century and Romantic women writers, revealed the power of the courtship romance novel to interrogate relationships between women and men that were critical to women's lives and to elevate education, courtship, companionate marriage, idealised romantic love, domestic authority, and women's roles within and beyond the family as compelling political issues. Recognising the power of the courtship romance novel as a medium for women writers to overtly scrutinise men, feminist literary scholars were among the first to explore Austen's men as subjects in their own right, offering new critiques of her male protagonists, their rivals, and more peripheral characters—particularly fathers—through the lens of the heroine's consciousness, interests and agency.

Masculine Subjectivity: A New Approach to Interpretation

Indeed, feminist literary criticism has been critical to the evaluation of Austen's men not only because it offers a lens through which to interpret these characters, but also because feminist theory has revealed both the constructed nature of gender and the role of cultural texts in framing gender identity. This revelation of the power of text to engage with gender ideologies through form and genre—encompassing not only femininity but also masculinity, among other modes of gender identification—offers new ways of reading masculinity in literature, which have laid the foundation for new approaches to interpreting Austen's men as embodying masculine subjectivities. Scholarship by Joseph Kestner, Devoney Looser, and Claudia Johnson, emerging from or in tandem with feminist critical approaches to Austen, pioneered the interpretation of Austen's men as intentional and strategic literary and cultural constructions of masculinity. Underpinned by a theorisation of masculinity as being, like femininity, a culturally determined construct that encompasses a range of identities and practices, rather than a monolithic concept equated with patriarchal privilege, this mode of interpretation has triggered a new wave of scholarship on Austen's men that is ongoing and may yet be taken in a range of further directions.

Austen's men are now recognised not only as conduits for her political engagement—in the public and private realms—but also as Austen's direct intervention in eighteenth-century and Romantic debates about masculinity itself. Current and emerging scholarship investigates how Austen negotiates the construction of masculinity as a core aspect of her fiction that is deeply embedded in highly contested ideological debates of her time. By the time Austen was writing her juvenilia in the 1780s, masculinity had become a matter of fervent public debate. Countless works of male conduct literature were printed and reprinted throughout the eighteenth century, particularly aligned with the 'ideal' of male 'politeness', which then attracted controversy when it was unmasked as potentially deceptive, fraudulent and even dangerous by the publication of Lord Chesterfield's *Letters to His Son* in 1774. Masculinity was increasingly politicised in the wake of the French Revolution, the Napoleonic Wars and the Regency, and projected into discourses of English national character, well-being and survival. Indeed, Austen lived and wrote during a period that gender historians have described as witnessing a 'crisis' in masculinity, in which competing masculine discourses concerning refinement, work and professionalism, domesticity, nationalism and chivalry vied for social acceptance and cultural ascendancy. The breadth and depth of Austen's engagement with Romantic-era debates concerning desirable and undesirable masculinities has been illuminated by Michèle Cohen, E. J. Clery, Sarah S. G. Frantz, Tim Fulford, Michael Kramp, Jason D. Solinger, Meaghan Malone, and Megan A. Woodworth. The focus of these scholars on exploring Austen's men collectively across her work, rather than individually or within the parameters of specific novels, presents opportunities to chart threads of continuity and change across Austen's writing career as she responds to shifts in constructions of masculinity circulating within Romantic public culture. It is now apparent that Austen critiques, satirises, challenges and celebrates diverse and often conflicting models of masculinity with the same forensic precision she brings to her heroines and peripheral female characters.

In *Disciplining Love: Austen and the Modern Man*, Michael Kramp explores Austen's negotiation of diverse models of 'proper' masculinity in post-Revolutionary English society and argues that in the face of conflict and uncertainty her men relinquish the pursuit of individual desires to fulfil the greater demands placed upon them by the rapidly modernising nation. Kramp's work illuminates Austen's engagement with post-Revolutionary debate on desirable and undesirable masculine gender identities and concludes that her novels 'reveal that these men's efforts repeatedly compel them to relinquish their identities as lovers and discipline their sexual desire' (7). Megan A. Woodworth similarly explores Austen's negotiation of shifting models of culturally sanctioned masculinity in *Eighteenth-Century Women Writers and the Gentleman's Liberation Movement* and argues that Austen reinvents gentlemanly masculinity from its association with birth and inheritance to a new definition based on merit and substance. Kramp's splendid edited collection *Jane Austen and Masculinity* reveals not only the 'diversity of men who engage with complicated historical events such as the political debates of the 1790s, the Regency crisis, and the post-Revolutionary Wars', but also the diverse range of contemporary scholars turning their attention to Austen's engagement with masculinity, and the power of this interpretive lens to offer new interpretations and readings of Austen's work (1).

In my own book, *Jane Austen's Men: Rewriting Masculinity in the Romantic Era*, I advance this scholarship by refocusing Austen's engagement with Romantic-era debate on the desirable man on the critical relationship between the heroine and the male protagonist, which forms the crux of the courtship romance novel. I argue that Austen both deployed and developed the courtship romance genre to rewrite masculinity as an internalised, individual way of understanding the self that was measured by personal authenticity rather than external performance and social recognition. Liberated from the demands of performative modes of masculinity, Austen's male protagonists are capable of forging egalitarian relationships with her heroines, which in turn enable the expression of the Romantic feminine agency they crave. I further argue that in championing a new model of masculine subjectivity, Austen advanced the courtship romance genre to enable more complex, layered representations of textual masculinity, and was closely in dialogue with her immediate Romantic contemporaries, including Jane West, Jane Porter, Maria Edgeworth, Sydney Owenson, Hannah More, and Mary Brunton. Further work is needed to fully explore women's collective textual rewriting of masculinity, and networks of influence among them, in the Romantic era.

Austen's Men as Cultural Icons

In parallel with evolving scholarly inquiry into Austen's men as constructions of masculinity invested with political, social and cultural meanings is a distinct thread of criticism exploring Austen's men within literary and cultural history. Much early criticism on Austen's men sought to evaluate them in relation to their eighteenth-century predecessors, particularly Sir Charles Grandison, protagonist of the novel Austen once described as her 'favourite' and which she dramatised in her youth, and the male protagonists of Frances Burney's novels, particularly Lord Orville of *Evelina* (Barker; Gilmour). These connections must be revisited in the light of new approaches to interpreting Austen's men in terms of masculine subjectivity, to reveal new insights into the relationship between modes of male subjectivity and literary influence. Further, the influence of Austen's men on nineteenth-century fiction—icons of Victorian literature such as Rochester, Heathcliff, Lydgate, and Thornton—is asserted but has not been explored. In *Jane Austen and the Victorian Heroine*, Cheryl A. Wilson makes a compelling argument for Austen's influence on Victorian readers, writers and literary heroines, as the novel rose to dominate the literary field throughout the nineteenth century. A similar study is needed to explore Austen's influence on Victorian literary masculinity, although Patricia Menon has begun this process regarding an archetype she identifies as the 'mentor-lover'. Similarly, connections between Austen's male protagonists and the now-stereotypical 'romantic hero' of literary and popular romance are frequently drawn, though relationships of direct and indirect influence between Austen's Romantic-era male protagonists and the 'romantic heroes' of popular romance and the rom-com genre have been assumed rather than analysed and explored.

A second thread of criticism evaluating Austen's men as cultural icons has emerged since the period drama boom was ignited in the mid-1990s by Andrew Davies' BBC/A&E adaptation of *Pride and Prejudice* (1995). A key innovation of Davies' adaptation of *Pride and Prejudice* was the increased prominence he gave to Austen's male characters, particularly Darcy, through the inclusion of scenes beyond the narrative scope of the novels, and the use of cinematic techniques to enhance his symbolic characterisation and visual representation. Despite its polarising reception among fans and scholars either captivated by Davies' approach or critical of its unorthodox and allegedly unfaithful representation of the novel (Nixon; Belton), this pioneering visualisation of Austen's men on screen is reflected in each successive wave of Austen adaptations (and, indeed, period drama more broadly). The iconic status of Austen's men has in turn triggered new critical perspectives on the adaptation of Austen's novels, offering fresh modes of interpreting her men on page and screen (Ailwood 'What Are Men'; Cartmell; Gymnich and Ruhl, Voiret). Sarah Wootton's *Byronic Heroes in Nineteenth-Century Women's Writing and Screen Adaptation* is particularly notable among this new wave of criticism for not only combining both literary and cinematic representations of masculinity but also establishing connections between Austen's Byronic heroes and their nineteenth-century literary descendants.

Austen's Men, Romantic Love and Romanticism: *Pride and Prejudice* and *Persuasion*

Exploring Jane Austen's men as literary constructions of masculine subjectivity illuminates new ways of interpreting her novels—not only through new readings of the characters themselves, but also because of what Austen's negotiation of masculine subjectivities reveals about her broader cultural, political and social concerns. In this section I illustrate how exploring masculine subjectivity in *Pride and Prejudice* and *Persuasion*—two novels from different stages of Austen's writing career, emerging from different political contexts—can reveal in new ways Austen's explicit textual engagement with Romanticism, and particularly with the dialogic constructions of masculine and feminine genders in the Romantic era through the transformative power of romantic love. However, a focus on masculine subjectivity is certainly not limited to these novels, to male protagonists or to Romanticism; on the contrary, exploring masculine subjectivity has the potential to reveal in new ways a myriad different interpretations of Austen's work.

Reading *Pride and Prejudice* and *Persuasion* in parallel reveals Austen's exploration of romantic love and its effects on the male self, her deployment of the fraught and at times tortuous relationship between the male mind and body as a narrative device, and her advancement of the courtship romance novel through an explicit engagement with Romanticism. *Pride and Prejudice* is the first novel in which Austen takes the male protagonist as a subject in his own right, exploring the effects of romantic love on masculine identity by placing Darcy's personal transformation at the centre of the narrative. By dramatising Darcy's development of a new model of masculine identity in response to Elizabeth Bennet's desire for Romantic feminine agency and self-actualisation, Austen advances the courtship romance genre through an explicit projection into Romantic ideology. In dialogue with *Pride and Prejudice*, in *Persuasion* Austen dramatically expands this investigation by exploring in greater complexity the male experience of love, rejection, jealousy, and endurance, as Captain Wentworth's love for Anne Elliot triggers not only passion and devotion but also grief, anger, bitterness, resentment and envy. Given the impact of these powerful feelings on Wentworth's sense of self, Austen creates a fresh approach to masculine identity in her last male protagonist.

In both novels, Austen is deeply engaged with Romantic public culture in ways that are explicitly connected to her male protagonists, and to questions surrounding men and masculinity more generally. In the earlier novel, Elizabeth Bennet's exclamation 'What are men to rocks and mountains?' (152) both exploits Romantic ideology to register her disillusionment with the men she has encountered and satirises the Romantic promise of self-fulfilment through an emotive response to nature. In *Persuasion*, Austen clearly responds to contemporary Romantic poets, two of whom—Lord Byron and Walter Scott—she references throughout the novel, including in a discussion about romantic love between Anne Elliot and the grieving Captain Benwick. Locating these novels within the Romantic literary context, Austen offers an alternative vision of Romantic masculinity to the autonomous, socially detached vision of the male self lauded in the poetry of Byron and Scott and also Wordsworth and Coleridge. In each novel Austen offers a new approach to Romantic male subjectivity that is premised not on reflective solitude, but rather on the transformative effects of romantic love. Poetry, written by men who 'have had every advantage of us in telling their own story' and for whom 'the pen has been in their hands' (*Persuasion* 220), may extol a solitary, individual and isolated vision of the male self; but Austen demonstrates that 'a larger allowance of prose' (*P* 94)—courtship romance novels written by women—offer an alternative model of Romantic masculinity that serves both men and women.

Austen's particular concern with male textual subjectivity in these novels is revealed in the innovative techniques she develops in each novel to endow Darcy and Wentworth with his own narrative perspective. In the first half of *Pride and Prejudice*, Austen's narrative focus frequently roams away from Elizabeth as she uses free indirect discourse, dialogue and focalisation to offer the reader an omniscient perspective on Darcy. Austen's split narrative perspective between Elizabeth and Darcy creates a dissonance between the heroine and a critically engaged reader, who knows more about Darcy than Elizabeth does, to whom alternative interpretations of his behaviour are available and who can see the unfolding events through his eyes. In her next two novels, *Mansfield Park* and *Emma*, Austen refrains from drawing her male protagonists through these narrative techniques; their characterisation is driven instead by Austen's complex engagement with contemporary fictional genres including Evangelical fiction, the national tale and the historical novel. In *Persuasion*, however, Austen returns to the interrogation of male subjectivity through narrative technique. Drawing once again on focalisation and free indirect discourse, Austen destabilises the narrator from the central characters and offers the reader greater access to Wentworth's consciousness and—critically—his emotional state.

In both *Pride and Prejudice* and *Persuasion*, Austen exploits her narrative access to her male protagonist's interiority and consciousness to explore the profound impact of romantic love on the male self. For Darcy and Wentworth, the experience of falling in love with Elizabeth Bennet and Anne Elliot has an utterly transformative effect on their sense of self and how they understand their identities as men. Austen charts this transformation in Darcy through the seemingly irreconcilable conflict between his desire for a woman who is his social and economic inferior and his externalised masculine identity with its value for wealth, reputation, and display, a conflict that results in his explosive first marriage proposal and is only reconciled by his realisation of his fundamental need to become desirable to the woman he loves. In *Persuasion*, by contrast, Wentworth's transformation is triggered by rejection by his beloved and his deeply confused response to their reunion. For both men, Austen represents their responses to romantic love and the deep psychological and emotional challenges it presents through visualising the fraught and at times tortuous relationship between the body and mind.

Austen focuses Darcy's narrative perspective exclusively on revealing to the reader his growing attraction to and love for Elizabeth Bennet and the torment it costs him. The glimpses she offers the reader into his interiority reveal him to be consumed by his fascination with and desire for the heroine, as we see him fall further and further in love. Falling in love with Elizabeth is far from a welcome experience, however, as he becomes a site of contest between two alternative and competing masculine identities. Darcy's individualism, highly introspective personality and self-containment, which are bolstered by Austen's strategies for revealing his interiority and psychological complexity, align him with a masculine identity that is grounded in a sense of individual, internalised subjectivity and selfhood. Yet the pride that dominates his way of thinking about himself and others signifies his ongoing investment in a masculinity defined externally by the performance of social status and the work of maintaining a public reputation. Darcy may appear intellectually and emotionally detached from the people and society around him, but how he sees himself as a man is dominated by status, wealth, codes of social propriety, and above all reputation, the linchpins of an adult male identity defined by social performance rather than an internalised sense of self.

For Darcy, falling in love with Elizabeth Bennet intensifies the conflict between these two mutually exclusive approaches to masculine selfhood. Austen's focalisation through Darcy's erotic gaze as he is increasingly drawn to Elizabeth exposes the battle between his conscious pride and his attraction to a woman whose agency lies beyond her sexualised role within polite sociability:

> Mr. Darcy had at first scarcely allowed her to be pretty; he had looked at her without admiration at the ball; and when they next met, he looked at her only to criticise. But no sooner had he made it clear to himself and his friends that she had hardly a good feature in her face, than he began to find it was rendered uncommonly intelligent by the beautiful expression of her dark eyes. To this discovery succeeded some others equally mortifying. Though he had detected with a critical eye more than one failure of perfect symmetry in her form, he was forced to acknowledge that her figure to be light and pleasing; and in

spite of asserting that her manners were not those of the fashionable world, he was caught by their easy playfulness. (24)

Austen's focalisation through Darcy reveals both his attraction to Elizabeth and his resistance to it. Elizabeth—a woman of lower socio-economic standing who brings with her a family that exposes him to public embarrassment—presents a threat to Darcy's reputation and therefore to the externalised masculine identity in which he remains invested. His initial response is denial: 'He really believed, that were it not for the inferiority of her connections, he should be in some danger' (51). When denial is no longer plausible, he acknowledges his attraction and resolves to extinguish it:

> She attracted him more than he liked—and Miss Bingley was uncivil to *her*, and more teasing than usual to himself. He wisely resolved to be particularly careful that no sign of admiration should *now* escape him, nothing that could elevate her with the hope of influencing his felicity; sensible that if such an idea had been suggested, his behaviour during the last day must have material weight in confirming or crushing it. Steady to his purpose, he scarcely spoke ten words to her throughout the whole of Saturday, and though they were at one time left by themselves for half an hour, he adhered most conscientiously to his book, and would not even look at her. (59)

Matching Darcy's conflict between alternative masculine identities is the battle between the mind and the body as he seeks to control his desire: 'He wisely resolved', 'Steady to his purpose', and 'he adhered most conscientiously to his book'. Where Austen earlier reveals Darcy's attraction through the gaze, his resistance is signified through its absence: he 'would not even look at her'.

The heightened tension between Darcy's split masculine identity—the externalised value for reputation, status and wealth and the internalised, authentic self that is captivated by Elizabeth—finally detonates when he asks her to marry him. His elaboration on his 'sense of her inferiority—of its being a degradation—of the family obstacles which judgment had always opposed to inclination' (185) reveals that the challenge Elizabeth poses to his status and reputation, and thus to his gender identity, have protracted and all but prevented his proposal. He describes such feelings as 'natural and just', asking: 'Could you expect me to rejoice in the inferiority of your connections? To congratulate myself on the hope of relations whose condition in life is so decidedly below my own?' (188). Austen reveals his struggle to control the body through the mind: 'His expression became pale with anger, and the disturbance of his mind was visible in every feature. He was struggling for the appearance of composure, and would not open his lips, until he believed himself to have attained it' (186). Shocked by Elizabeth's rejection, and confronted with the knowledge of his fundamental deficiency in pleasing 'a woman worthy of being pleased' (349), Darcy is forced to acknowledge the thinness of a masculine identity defined by social performance and its justifiable repugnance to Elizabeth. He finally discards the externalised masculine subjectivity that Elizabeth loathes, and accepts in its place an internalised, authentic identity that is heedless of the demands of the establishment and the fashionable world.

In *Persuasion*, Austen once again takes men's experience of romantic love as her subject, exploring the range, depth and intensity of men's feelings in Captain Wentworth, her most expressive and emotionally volatile male protagonist. Austen expands the narrative techniques she developed in *Pride and Prejudice*, with an even greater emphasis on the relationship between the male body and the mind. Indeed, the intensity of men's feelings and their connection to the body become the focus of Anne's conversation with Captain Harville in the climactic scene at the White Hart Inn: 'I believe in a true analogy between our bodily frames and our mental; and that as our bodies are the strongest, so are our feelings' (219). What is extraordinary about Captain Harville's claim for his fellow naval officers is that it is made not in the context of their professional lives and a sense of fervent patriotic duty, or triggered by traditionally Romantic solitude in nature, but through their experience of romantic love: Admiral Croft and Captain Harville's love for their wives and pain at their separation; Captain Benwick's lost love and the difficulties others experience rationalising his dramatic change and engagement to Louisa Musgrove; and Wentworth's experience of rejection from his beloved, and unruly emotional state when peace is declared and he is reunited with Anne.

Where Darcy develops an authentic, internalised male subjectivity that enables him to fully embrace romantic love, Captain Wentworth's expression of such an identity ultimately leads to rejection, anger and resentment. Anne recalls the 'exquisite felicity' of their brief courtship as they felt 'rapidly and deeply in love': 'It would be difficult to say which had seen the highest perfection in the other, or which had been the happiest; she, in receiving his declarations and proposals, or he in having them accepted' (26). As Anne later reflects: 'there could have been no two hearts so open, no tastes so similar, no feelings so in unison, no countenances so beloved' (59–60). The quality Anne loves most—and she later finds William Elliot to utterly lack—is Wentworth's open expression of feeling: 'She prized the frank, the open-hearted, the eager character beyond all others. Warmth and enthusiasm did captivate her still' (151). Yet Wentworth's authentic, expressive self is a two-edged sword, for while it captivates Anne, it signals to Lady Russell a dangerous, untrustworthy character.

Wentworth's emotional response to Anne's rejection is equally expressive and volatile, and Austen uses focalisation to reveal that it endures over an eight year separation, on his return to Somerset:

> He had not forgiven Anne Elliot. She had used him ill; deserted and disappointed him; and worse, she had shewn a feebleness of character in doing so, which his own decided, confident temper could not endure. She had given him up to oblige others. It had been the effect of over-persuasion. It had been weakness and timidity. (57)

Reluctant to expose the authentic self already rejected, Wentworth retreats into stylised, performative codes of masculine behaviour. Polite sociability offers a refuge from his incapacity to confront and address his confused feelings, providing a conventional language for civilised behaviour between them that Anne finds loathsome, describing it as 'cold politeness' and 'ceremonious grace' (67).

This veneer is unsustainable, however, as Austen increasingly uses Wentworth's body to convey his emotional state. When he first encounters Anne by herself in the cottage, she writes: 'The surprise of finding himself almost alone with Anne Elliot, deprived his manners of their usual composure: he started ... he walked to the window to recollect himself, and feel how he ought to behave' (73). Austen equates masculine physical strength with an ethic of care and compassion as Wentworth releases Anne from her nephew's grip, and later secures her a place in the Crofts' carriage, betraying an ongoing tenderness that he can neither acknowledge nor express, but Anne clearly perceives:

> yes, – he had done it. She was in the carriage, and felt that he had placed her there, that his will and his hands had done it, that she owed it to his perception of her fatigue, and his resolution to give her rest ... She understood him. He could not forgive her, – but he could not be unfeeling. (84)

In the same way that Darcy's conflicted masculine identity implodes in his first proposal to Elizabeth, so Wentworth's emotional fragility is spectacularly revealed by Louisa Musgrove's fall from the

Cobb at Lyme. Austen represents his emotional crisis through physical weakness: "'Is there no one to help me?" were the first words which burst from Captain Wentworth, in a tone of despair, and as if all his own strength were gone' (102). His emotional turmoil—'He sat near a table, leaning over it with folded arms and face concealed, as if overpowered by the various feelings of his soul' (104)—is ultimately resolved through his protracted acknowledgement of Anne's superiority and his ongoing love for her.

For both men, Austen locates the power and possibility of romantic resolution, on which their sense of masculine selfhood ultimately depends, in the agency of her heroines. In this way, Austen uses the courtship romance plot to inextricably tie feminine agency to the construction of masculine subjectivity through romantic love. Austen focuses the second half of *Pride and Prejudice* not on Darcy's transformation of masculine selfhood, but on the question of whether Elizabeth will ultimately choose him. Austen dramatises a dialogue between a woman who embodies a rational, individualistic Romantic feminine subjectivity, and the psychological development of a man who is otherwise a conservative gentry ideal, to become the man she needs him to be. She presents female desire as a powerful, disruptive force that can—and should—trigger fundamental changes in masculine identities: how individual men understand themselves as men, in relation to women, and in relation to other men. Championing female desire as a driving force for male self-improvement, Austen rejects dominant discourses that motivate men to be what society demands, what their (male) peers and professions respect, and what the nation needs. In place of such social and political causes, Austen privileges the personal and the intimate, dramatising her stellar male protagonist—a bastion of idealised gentry manhood—changing himself for the sole purpose of becoming desirable to the woman he loves. Darcy tells Elizabeth quite plainly at the end of the novel that his return to Hertfordshire was 'to judge, if I could, whether I might ever hope to make you love me' (361). Although Darcy's change is often interpreted as a development from self-restraint to emotional display, as an essentially behavioural change from rudeness to politeness, or as a shift in values from social exclusivity to inclusiveness, these are the effects of a fundamental change in his gender identity. This change is triggered not by his desire for Elizabeth but instead by his fundamental need to become desirable to her.

In *Persuasion*, Wentworth's recognition of his enduring love for Anne and value for the agency she embodies leaves him incapable of acting to secure their reunion in Bath. When they meet by chance Anne notes: 'He was more obviously struck and confused by the sight of her, than she had observed before; he looked quite red. For the first time, since their renewed acquaintance, she felt that she was betraying the least sensibility of the two' (165). This Captain Wentworth is 'not comfortable, not easy, not able to feign that he was' (166). He again flounders when he sees Anne at the concert, lacking the language to discuss Captain Benwick's rapid recovery in contrast to his own loyalty to Anne – 'A man does not recover from such a devotion of the heart to such a woman! – He ought not – he does not' (173)—with 'sentences begun which he could not finish – his half averted eyes, and more than half expressive glance' (175). Unable to control his anger at the threat of rivalry presented by Mr Elliot, Wentworth's erratic behaviour convinces Anne 'that he had a heart returning to her at least … He must love her' (175). Although Anne initially resolves to 'leave things to take their course' (207), when she witnesses Wentworth's inability to act in the face of her family, it becomes apparent that if they are to be reunited it is she who must act. At the White Hart, she reaches out to him through her conversation with Captain Harville, declaring: 'All the privilege I claim for my own sex … is that of loving longest, when existence or when hope is gone' (221). It is only when Anne offers this reassurance that Wentworth can finally act, producing the most emotionally expressive marriage proposal in all of Austen's fiction:

> Tell me not that I am too late, that such precious feelings are gone for ever. I offer myself to you with a heart even more your own, than when you almost broke it eight years and a

half ago. Dare not say that man forgets sooner than woman, that his love has an earlier death. I have loved none but you. Unjust I may have been, weak and resentful I have been, but never inconstant. (222)

In the highly charged conversation that follows, Wentworth confirms that it was Anne's agency that overcame his jealousy of Mr Elliot: 'It had been gradually yielding to the better hopes which her looks, or words, or actions occasionally encouraged; it had been vanquished at last by those sentiments and those tones which had reached him while she talked with Captain Harville' (226).

In *Pride and Prejudice* and *Persuasion*, Austen offers a new vision of Romantic masculinity that functions as a counterpoint to the socially isolated, detached, solitary and contemplative masculinity that dominated the work of her Romantic contemporaries. Austen's model of Romantic male subjectivity is founded in authenticity and individualism, but also in connection and self-actualisation through romantic love. Austen realises this vision through her manipulation of the courtship romance plot and its privileging of feminine agency as a path to self-fulfilment for both men and women. In each novel, Austen explores the consequences of romantic love for masculine subjectivity and feminine agency, locating the process of gender formation at the heart of each novel's trajectory and staking a claim for the courtship romance as a key genre of Romanticism.

New Directions

Scholarship on Austen's men has emerged as a rich and innovative field that yet holds the promise of further new and exciting modes of interpreting Austen's novels and her literary and cultural legacy. Although there has been a focus on Austen's male protagonists in terms of masculine subjectivity, this interpretive lens has been less extended to more peripheral male characters who nevertheless play critical structural and thematic roles in her novels. There has also been a tendency to explore men's relationships with women, with comparatively little attention to men's relationships with other men. Attending to how Austen represents men within their male peer groups—how she constructs masculine subjectivity not only individually but collectively, and relationships between men as friends and rivals—is a potentially fruitful area for further exploration. Finally, we are only beginning to describe and analyse the influence of Austen's men as cultural icons. This influence tends to be stated or assumed, rather than rigorously analysed. Tracing the impact of Austen's men on nineteenth-century literature, on twentieth-century screen adaptations, and on the constant reworking of Austen texts in the digital era is key to fully understanding the scope and power of Austen's literary legacy.

Works Cited

Ailwood, Sarah. *Jane Austen's Men: Rewriting Masculinity in the Romantic Era.* Routledge, 2020.

Ailwood, Sarah. '"What Are Men to Rocks and Mountains?" Romanticism in Joe Wright's Pride & Prejudice.' *Persuasions On-Line*, vol. 27, no. 2, 2007, http://www.jasna.org/persuasions/on-line/vol27no2/ailwood.htm

Austen, Jane. *Jane Austen's Letters*, edited by Deidre Le Faye. Oxford UP, 1995.

Austen, Jane. *Persuasion.* 1818. Penguin, 2015.

Austen, Jane. *Pride and Prejudice.* 1813. Penguin, 2015.

Barker, Gerard A. *Grandison's Heirs. The Paragon's Progress in the Late Eighteenth-Century English Novel.* U of Delaware P, 1985.

Barry, F. V., editor. *Chosen Letters.* Jonathan Cape, 1931.

Belton, Ellen. 'Reimagining Jane Austen: The 1940 and 1995 Film Versions of *Pride and Prejudice*.' *Jane Austen on Screen*, edited by Gina MacDonald and Andrew MacDonald. Cambridge UP, 2003, pp. 175–196.

Butler, Marilyn. *Jane Austen and the War of Ideas*. Clarendon P, 1975.

Cartmell, Deborah. '*Pride and Prejudice* and the Adaptation Genre.' *Journal of Adaptation in Film & Performance*, vol. 3, no. 3, 2010, pp. 227–243.

Chapman, R. W., editor. *The Works of Jane Austen*, vol. VI, Minor Works. Oxford UP, 1954.

Clery, E. J. 'Austen and Masculinity.' *A Companion to Jane Austen*, edited by Claudia L. Johnson and Clara Tuite. Wiley-Blackwell, 2009, pp. 332–342.

Cohen, Michèle. '"Manners" Make the Man: Politeness, Chivalry, and the Construction of Masculinity, 1750-1830.' *Journal of British Studies*, vol. 44, no. 2, 2005, pp. 312–329.

Collins, Irene. *Jane Austen and the Clergy*. Hambledon P, 2003.

Darwin, Sir Francis. 'Jane Austen.' *Rustic Sounds and other Studies in Literature and Natural History*. John Murray, 1917, pp. 61–77.

Duckworth, Alistair. *The Improvement of the Estate: A Study of Jane Austen's Novels*. Johns Hopkins UP, 1971.

Elwin, Malcolm. *Lord Byron's Wife*. J. Murray, 1974.

Evans, Mary. *Jane Austen and the State*. Tavistock, 1987.

Frantz, Sarah S. G. 'Jane Austen's Heroes and the Great Masculine Renunciation.' *Persuasions*, vol. 25, 2003, pp. 165–175.

Fulford, Tim. *Romanticism and Masculinity: Gender, Politics and Poetics in the Writings of Burke, Coleridge, Cobbett, Wordsworth, De Quincey and Hazlitt*. Macmillan P, 1999.

Fulford, Tim. 'Romanticizing the Empire: The Naval Heroes of Southey, Coleridge, Austen and Marryat.' *Modern Language Quarterly*, vol. 60, no. 1, 1999, pp. 161–196.

Gilmour, Robin. *The Idea of the Gentleman in the Victorian Novel*. George Allen & Unwin, 1981.

Gymnich, Marion, and Kathrin Rhul. 'Revisiting the Classical Romance: *Pride and Prejudice, Bridget Jones's Diary*, and *Bride and Prejudice*.' *Gendered (Re)Visions: Constructions of Gender in Audiovisual Media*, edited by Marion Gymnich, Kathrin Ruyl and Klaus Scheunemann. Bonn UP, 2010, pp. 23–44.

Hawkridge, Audrey. *Jane and Her Gentlemen: Jane Austen and the Men in Her Life and Novels*. Peter Owen Publishers, 2000.

Johnson, Claudia L. *Equivocal Beings. Politics, Gender, and Sentimentality in the 1790s: Wollstonecraft, Radcliffe, Burney, Austen*. U of Chicago P, 1995.

Johnson, Claudia L. *Jane Austen: Women, Politics and the Novel*. Chicago UP, 1988.

Kestner, Joseph. 'Jane Austen: Revolutionizing Masculinities.' *Persuasions: The Jane Austen Journal*, vol. 16, 1994, pp. 147–160.

Kirkham, Margaret. *Jane Austen, Feminism and Fiction*. Harvester P, 1983.

Kramp, Michael. *Disciplining Love: Austen and the Modern Man*. Ohio State UP, 2007.

Kramp, Michael, editor. *Jane Austen and Masculinity*. Bucknell UP, 2017.

L'Estrange, A. G. *The Life of Mary Russell Mitford: Related in a Selection from Her Letters to Her Friends*, vols 3. Bentley, 1870.

Looser, Devoney. 'Jane Austen "Responds" to the Men's Movement.' *Persuasions: The Jane Austen Journal*, vol. 18, 1996, pp. 159–170.

Malone, Meaghan. 'Courting the Eye: Seeing Men in *Persuasion*.' *Nineteenth Century Gender Studies*, vol. 8, no. 1, Spring 2012, https://www.ncgsjournal.com/issue81/malone.htm

Menon, Patricia. *Austen, Eliot, Charlotte Bronte and the Mentor-Lover*. Palgrave Macmillan, 2003.

Nixon, Cheryl L. 'Balancing the Courtship Hero: Masculine Emotional Display in Film Adaptations of Austen's Novels.' *Jane Austen in Hollywood*, edited by Linda Troost and Sayre Greenfield, U of Kentucky P, 2001, pp. 22–43.

Poovey, Mary. *The Proper Lady and the Woman Writer. Ideology as Style in the Works of Mary Wollstonecraft, Mary Shelley, and Jane Austen*. U of Chicago P, 1984.

Roberts, Warren. *Jane Austen and the French Revolution*. Macmillan, 1979.

Sales, Roger. *Jane Austen and Representations of Regency England*. Routledge, 1996.

Scott, Walter. 'Unsigned Review of *Emma*.' *The Quarterly Review*, October 1815, pp. 188–201.

Solinger, Jason D. *Becoming the Gentleman. British Literature and the Invention of Modern Masculinity, 1660-1815*. Palgrave Macmillan, 2012.

Southam, Brian. *Jane Austen and the Navy*, 2nd ed. Hambledon P, 2005.

Steeves, Harrison. *Before Jane Austen: The Shaping of the English Novel in the Eighteenth Century*. Allen & Unwin, 1966.

Sulloway, Alison G. *Jane Austen and the Province of Womanhood*. U of Pennsylvania P, 1989.

Tanner, Tony. *Jane Austen*. Macmillan, 1986.

Voiret, Martine. 'Gender and Desire in Jane Austen's Adaptations.' *Jane Austen and Co: Remaking the Past in Contemporary Culture*, edited by Suzanne R. Pucci and James Thompson. State U of New York P, 2003, pp. 229–245.

Whatley, Richard. 'Northanger Abbey and Persuasion.' *Quarterly Review*, vol. 24, 1821.

Wilson, Cheryl A. *Jane Austen and the Victorian Heroine*. Palgrave Macmillan, 2017.

Woodworth, Megan A. *Eighteenth-Century Women Writers and the Gentleman's Liberation Movement: Independence, War, Masculinity and the Novel, 1778-1818*. Ashgate, 2011.

Wootton, Sarah. *Byronic Heroes in Nineteenth-Century Women's Writing and Screen Adaptation*. Palgrave Macmillan, 2016.

25

JANE AUSTEN LIKES WOMEN: SELF-WORTH, SELF-CARE, AND HEROIC SELF-SACRIFICE

Kathleen Anderson

I love Jane Austen because she likes women.

What does this mean? Austen's chosen representative of the universal human being in her novels is a woman, and women's daily concerns are presented as not only valid but of chief interest and importance. Moreover, her novelistic affirmation of women depends upon her presupposition of both genders' equal accountability for their characters in accordance to universal standards of virtue. Gender does not determine anyone's intellectual capacity, moral integrity, or human dignity; all characters will be judged on merit alone. Thus, Austen liberates female readers to enjoy her narratives without wasting energy bracing themselves for the possibility of being arbitrarily sullied by derogatory gender stereotypes. Neither will she exasperate readers by recycling the impossibly idealised 'pictures of perfection' she detests.[1] Though they strive to live up to their ideals, Austen's protagonists are multifarious, flawed, mutable. She tests them and they grow before attaining the rewards of that growth as paid in self-knowledge and happy alliances.

More importantly, the author at once insists on her heroines' earthly thriving—providing still-relevant strategies for its realization—and pays them the compliment of expecting more. She promulgates women's worth through their responsibility to engage in self-care of body, mind, and spirit and to assert truth to self in their relationships with especially men, providing guidelines on how to fulfil this prerogative.[2] Heroines must act upon their own conscience and conviction, doing what is right with no thought of a reward and even believing they will never obtain their heart's desire. Genuine giving can occur only from a position of liberty and wholeness; 'one must possess oneself in order to give oneself' (Giuffre 1). The protagonists' prioritization of principle and other people over themselves reflects a radical assertion of the individual will in which self-approval takes precedence over men's approval. Thus, Austen accentuates her heroines' transcendence of merely personal gratifications in favour of a sacrificiality that exemplifies a distinctly feminine form of greatness—a heroism that reflects the highest form of truth to self.[3] They are not to be bought for love or money. This is the profoundly logical paradox—consistent with an incarnational Christian worldview—that distinguishes Austen's feminist heroism and its simultaneous foundation and manifestation in self-nurture.

Austen's novelistic self-help books effectively communicate that women's innate worth requires their cultivation of optimal corporal, attitudinal, cerebral, and social wellness. Women are worthy of feasting; they have the right and obligation to pursue health and stamina for the productive, pleasurable life these assets enable. The author herself finds comic pleasure in the epistolary flaunting of

DOI: 10.4324/9780429398155-25-29

her gustatory enjoyments—whether of apple tart, chicken, asparagus, veal, lobster, toasted cheese, or wine—and relishes dancing and walks. She mocks the expectation of feminine abstemiousness as well as the trivialization and circumscription of female domesticity through her foodie persona, boasting to sister Cassandra that 'I always take care to provide such things as please my own appetite, which I consider as the chief merit in housekeeping' (17–18 November 1789; *Letters* 20) and, 'You know how interesting the purchase of a sponge-cake is to me' (15–17 June 1808; *Letters* 128). Austen empathizes with *Mansfield Park*'s Fanny Price when her parents greet her with poor fare on dirty dishes and deprive her of a meal entirely on her departure from Portsmouth: 'the breakfast table … was quite and completely ready as the carriage drove from the door. Fanny's last meal in her father's house was in character with her first; she was dismissed from it as hospitably as she had been welcomed' (*MP* 445).[4] Women must prioritize their own nourishment, while the extent to which their companions nourish them often demarcates their worthiness of the heroines' esteem. Austen depicts both delicate and robust women as beautiful, and their relative size does not define their appeal for either the author or the characters that love and variously feed them. Rather, heroines' corporeality delineates their figurative forward movement—their growth curve.

This pattern is especially evident in *Mansfield Park*, in which Fanny Price's initial frailty signifies passivity and social precariousness, and her bodily development correlates with personal progress and increasing self-assertion. As John Wiltshire aptly synopsizes in *Jane Austen and the Body*, 'Health is intimately related to enablement and fulfilment, illness to frustration, anger and defeat' (22). Fanny transforms from a cowering cringer self-obscured in silence to a wilful young woman who triumphs over abuse and attempted coercion to become patriarch Sir Thomas's central advisor and the stabilizing force of the Bertram family. Throughout the novel, the women incite while the men obstruct Fanny's movement. Lady Bertram and Aunt Norris both rely on her for a continuous round of tasks and errands; the former's dependency and the latter's rigorous training program spur the heroine's increasing strength. By contrast, Edmund, Sir Thomas, and Henry Crawford all thwart Fanny's freedom of motion. Edmund usurps her horse for flirty rides with Mary and insists on her prolonged rest during a walk, and Sir Thomas orders her to bed during the ball in her own honour. In these instances, Fanny desires to continue her activity, and its cessation is involuntary. As Aunt Norris reminds the guilty Edmund, though from self-justifying motives, 'If Fanny would be more regular in her exercise, she would not be knocked up so soon. She has not been out on horseback now this long while, and I am persuaded, that when she does not ride, she ought to walk' (*MP* 73). Fanny gains both outer and inner substance and ultimately becomes hardy enough to bear children, as implied in the denouement's allusion to her and Edmund's eventual need for 'an increase of income' (473). Her image shifts from that of maiden in distress to that of rescuer, as epitomized by her vision from Portsmouth of aiding Lady Bertram during Tom's illness, a comical forecast of Fanny's ultimate displacement of both aunts as Mansfield's matriarch: 'how many walks up and down stairs she might have saved her' (432). Lady Bertram reinforces this augury through her only active movement in the novel; when Fanny returns to Mansfield, her Aunt Bertram 'came from the drawing room to meet her … with no indolent step; and, falling on her neck, said, "Dear Fanny! now I shall be comfortable"' (447). Regardless of a woman's level of vitality, Austen expects her to maximize it through exercise and good eating, to her own and others' benefit.

Heartiness is undeniably sexy, and Austen portrays the universality of women's sex drive as a given and their sexual wellness as a critical component of their self-care. Flushed hiker Elizabeth Bennet sparks the admiration of both Darcy and Bingley and feels a strong attraction to the handsome Wickham. Bustling beauty Emma—Mrs Weston's ideal representative of the healthy, mature woman—enjoys flirting with both Frank Churchill and Mr Knightley, the latter of whom admits that he 'love[s] to look at her' (*E* 39). The ebullient Marianne infatuates both Colonel Brandon and Willoughby and rushes into a romance with Willoughby. The invigorated Fanny Price and breeze-blushed Anne Elliot draw the attention of two admirers each (Henry/Edmund and

William Elliot/Captain Wentworth, respectively) and subtly pursue the one they want. Women's and men's sexuality is portrayed as equally intense. Both genders participate in not only the narrative backdrop of affairs, seductions, and illegitimate offspring, but the sanctioned everyday flirtations with their electric glances, hints, and rare touches. Austen's women are agents of their own moral destinies who 'have only themselves ... to blame' when they make bad choices (Easton 133, 135). In an historical context in which law and custom abetted men's autocracy in marriage, however, the female characters must navigate the courtship minefield with special care to preserve their safety and sanity.[5] As Alison G. Sulloway points out, 'the law of femin[ine] *coverture*' still held, conflating the wife's identity with her husband's (36), and adultery laws favoured men, protecting their socio-economic interests in preserving their inheritance through the line of legitimacy. In addition, 'English common law ... ruled that whatever property a woman owned before marriage or might receive thereafter automatically became her husband's (Swords 77). Men's social sovereignty fostered private tyrannies as well and accentuates women's vulnerability and the magnitude of their marital decision in determining their future. Consistent with such realities, there is a dark side to the charm of Austen's love stories. Her heroines have few or no models of wholesome, happy relationships to emulate and know many cases of abused and neglected wives, such as: Mrs Tilney and Lady Elliot, who were likely driven to early graves, Mrs Price, Isabella Knightley, Mrs Palmer, Mrs Bennet, Lady Bertram, and Mary Musgrove. Yet even intelligent, righteous heroines Elizabeth Bennet, Fanny Price, Marianne Dashwood, and Anne Elliot come terrifyingly close to repeating history, magnetized toward men who mask selfish, sadistic, or downright evil natures. Amid a marital landscape littered with disastrous alliances founded on looks or economic gain, the heroine must reject or transform her connection with the most aggressive, misogynistic suitor in her social circle if she is to find a devoted husband who will best promote her happiness.

As Mary Bennet declares, a woman 'cannot be too much guarded in her behaviour towards the undeserving of the other sex' (*PP* 289). She must challenge her would-be hero to a difficult chivalric test—a pushback that challenges his ego and brings suspect values or motives into sharp relief. This test consists of an assertion of personal boundaries that I denote 'sexual orthodoxy'; Austen's heroines must act upon their own convictions, even when flawed or false, as an expression of their transcendent value in relation to the divine, apart from—as well as within union to—the opposite sex.[6] They must insist on truth to themselves as a moral imperative that overrules the pressures of physical passion, socioeconomic considerations, or the male lust for power.[7] This trial enables inexperienced young women to distinguish the suitors who are least or most likely to honour their discrete selfhood and partner in a marriage that would be most advantageous to the women's psychological and emotional well-being and, consequently, sexual fulfilment.

Effective strategic experiments include the pronouncement of adamant opinions, resistance to the man's asserted will, and insistence on his accomplishment of particular outcomes as preconditions of a potential romantic relationship—one that must be mutual. A simple but effective assertion of sexual orthodoxy consists of the right to liberty over one's movements. Fanny Price recognizes in Henry Crawford's unwelcome physical contact the impulsive sensuality and underlying lack of self-discipline that would most endanger her marital happiness with him. She feels relief when the servant's entrance disrupts his 'close neighbourhood' (*MP* 342) and 'deliver[s] her from a grievous imprisonment of body and mind' (344) and suffers shock on the Portsmouth walk when 'he would take her hand, he would not be denied it' (365), penetrations of the chastity of her personal space.[8] Fanny's determined denial throughout Henry's halfhearted reform outlives both his desire for conquest and his insufficient best intentions, ensuring her self-protection from a feckless cheater for a husband. In ironic contrast, Fanny hovers in Edmund's proximity until he learns to love her for her eyes as well as good character—with romantic passion as well as rational admiration of her virtue. In so doing, she upholds her right of marital/sexual choice, holding out for the man she wants (in his more enlightened, post-Mary form) or no one.

Catherine Morland obtains ample evidence of John Thorpe's controlling nature and even sadism when he ignores her demand for liberty and carries her away in his curricle, a parody of Gothic kidnapping that is nonetheless as tangible in its foreshadowing of severer violation. Despite her general obtuseness, Catherine recognizes in the horse-whipping Thorpe a potential abuser in the mould of General Tilney, whose shouting at Eleanor 'in his loudest tone' triggers in Catherine 'terror upon terror' and the impulse to hide in her locked room while 'deeply commiserating the state of her poor friend' (*NA* 192), a visceral response that overtakes any comedy as caricature collapses into nightmarish realism. By circumventing General Tilney's control over his domestic space, sneaking back to 'the forbidden door' of Mrs Tilney's prohibited room and exploring it, Catherine triggers a revelatory counter-scene with Henry. Rather than shouting upon discovering her investigative mission or enforcing his father's prohibition of her free exploration of the house, he calmly questions the logic behind her conjectures. He acknowledges his mother's suffering from his father's temper while also defending the General's honour, and treats Catherine with greater kindness rather than resentment after her humiliating revelation. Henry amply justifies Catherine's choice. Though he can be rather smug and condescending in his instructor role, he demonstrates gentleness rather than tyranny and presumes a woman's right to physical and intellectual self-determination. Henry also refuses to objectify his future wife economically. When her modest means are revealed, he places principle above material prosperity, risking his inheritance by displeasing his mercenary patriarch, declaring himself 'bound as much in honour as in affection to Miss Morland' (*NA* 247).

A man's attitude toward a woman's bodily autonomy signals his level of respect for her equally essential psychic liberty. Elizabeth Bennet and Emma Woodhouse love strong, self-assured men whose superiority complex must be dashed for them to become marriageable. The two heroines intuit the necessity to dare their love interests into husband-readiness at risk of losing them. Elizabeth Bennet dislikes and repulses her future spouse with a forceful rudeness that surpasses his, thereby motivating in him the introspection and self-improvement essential to her regard. Darcy's initial arrogant entitlement would have rendered him an unbearable husband who would expect her to perform the role of grateful subject rather than partner in life, a sure groundwork for the proliferation of inequities throughout their marriage. Elizabeth counters Darcy's every presumption of superiority with aggressive emphasis. After overhearing his dismissal of her as 'not handsome enough to tempt' him to dance and as 'slighted by other men' (*PP* 12), she twice rejects his offers to dance—rejections of his touch. In response to his spontaneous invitation to dance a reel at Netherfield, she is openly insulting. She pretends not to hear him and, when he repeats the request, claims that she 'always delight[s] in … cheating a person of their premeditated contempt … now despise me if you dare' (52), a fitting statement about her over-arching pushback test that parallels as well as instigates this refusal. Elizabeth dares Darcy to despise her, not for her taste in dances but for her reckless tongue, her independent voice, her blatant freedom to oppose him. The unexpected 'gallantry' of his reaction to what likely appears an arbitrary insolence (especially considering his ignorance that she overheard his unflattering remarks) manifests his potential for reform.

Yet Elizabeth must repulse Darcy even more vigorously during his first marriage proposal to succeed in launching his self-transformation. His frank assertion of qualms about 'her inferiority—of its being a degradation—of the family obstacles that judgment had always opposed to inclination' (*PP* 189) provokes her to make personal attacks in retaliation. She volunteers expansive explanations for her refusal; declares, 'You could not have made me the offer of your hand in any possible way that would have tempted me to accept it'; itemizes Darcy's character flaws; and concludes with the famous punchline, '… I had not known you a month before I felt that you were the last man in the world whom I could ever be prevailed on to marry' (192–93). Though this commentary is juvenile in its gratuitous vengefulness, it proves the essential antidote to Darcy's equally juvenile domination-masked-as-honesty, inspiring his voluntary dethronement and Elizabeth's love. She accepts him only after his desire for possession becomes a deeper longing for her approbation and companionship as a fully actualized human being.

The evolutionary paradigm of the Emma Woodhouse-Mr Knightley relationship and the heroine's self-protection tactics therein show remarkable similarities to the Elizabeth-Darcy pattern. Emma tests Mr Knightley for his intentions and attitude toward women—via both avatar Harriet Smith and self-referential manoeuvres—and especially for his capacity to tolerate differences of opinion from her. Once he surrenders the paternalistic advisor and jealous secret-crush roles in favour of the role of disinterested friend, she initiates the courtship of her deferential would-be lover.

Emma employs Harriet as her romantic surrogate to assess Mr Knightley's spouse potential, and Mr Martin functions as his corresponding surrogate in their tense negotiation of their own relationship. Claudia L. Johnson points out that in Emma's assumption of 'power over the destinies of others ... she poaches on what is felt to be male turf' (125). Yet Mr Knightley dislikes her friendship with Harriet primarily because he senses it represents a barrier between her and himself. Emma must establish that Mr Knightley does not view her as a sex object and, by extension, respects her right of marital choice. She experimentally dares him to love Harriet as symbol of her sexual self—'... what every man delights in—what at once bewitches his senses and satisfies his judgment.... Were you, yourself, ever to marry, she is the very woman for you'—and claims as her due the self-determination to 'pick and choose' and 'have time to look about her' (*E* 64). Mr Knightley responds with both the ire of frustrated desire and the confirmation she needs that he (as Mr Martin) is not motivated by 'selfish passion' (63) and 'Men of sense ... do not want silly wives' (64). Although Emma and Mr Knightley have multiple disagreements in which she proves as stubborn as he is by maintaining her position despite the force of his arguments and anger, they always reconcile because he always accepts her ultimate independence of his will. Not only does he show uniform consideration for all the women in their social circle, including the vulnerable Miss and Mrs Bates and Jane Fairfax, he scrupulously defers to Emma on her choice of mate. He even stifles his endearingly human, youthful jealousy of Frank Churchill beneath the selfless loyalty of a concerned longtime friend. He is always loyal to Emma but becomes more nobly so as his own hopes fade amid flashy Frank's flirtation with the heroine.

Through her portrayal of Emma's courtship journey, Austen makes a clear distinction between the physical chemistry essential to the woman as well as the man in a healthy marital partnership and the lusts—whether sensual, socioeconomic, or psychological—that lead to male despotism. Once convinced of Mr Knightley's honourable intentions toward women and herself, Emma acts on her attraction to him and invites his attraction to her. She surveils his sexy 'tall, firm, upright' physique (*E* 326), 'extremely good' dancing (328), and gallant treatment of Harriet as mediator of the couple's growing passion and esteem, and chooses him for herself. The two exchange looks while Mr Knightley dances with Harriet; agree on her superiority to Mr Elton in an intimate chat; and Emma initiates their first dance together as eligible adult singles by monarchically inviting him to ask her. The most significant symbolic moments in the couple's shift to an egalitarian relationship are his near-kiss of her hand and the confidential walk in the shrubbery, in both of which he submits to her will and its free expression. After learning of Emma's conciliatory post-insult visit to Miss Bates, Mr Knightley honours her integrity apart from himself even as it intensifies his love: he makes 'a little movement of more than common friendliness on his part.—He took her hand;—whether she had not herself made the first motion, she could not say—she might, perhaps, have rather offered it—but he took her hand, pressed it, and certainly was on the point of carrying it to his lips—when ... he suddenly let it go' (*E* 385–86). This moment provides a vivid contrast to the violation in Mr Elton's and Henry Crawford's aggressive hand-seizures, infringements that serve as reminders that regardless of a woman's wealth or status, thoroughly testing a man's character before giving him her heart and hand is critical in a treacherous patriarchal society; it could mean not only happiness or misery, but life itself. Emma's uncertainty over who initiated her and Mr Knightley's touch reflects the increasing mutuality of their relationship. Mr Knightley's forestallment of his hand-kissing impulse and Emma's resulting disappointment ('He would have judged better, she thought, if he had not stopped' [386]) as well as his shrubbery-scene surrender to Emma's lead showcases each one's prioritization of the other's feelings above his or her own hopes, reinforcing the virtue-attraction equation Austen advocates for both genders in selecting a spouse. Emma's and Mr Knightley's mutual suppression of their undeclared love when they think the other loves someone else poignantly accentuates their lovability.

In placing higher principles above a self-gratification that debases both their own and others' value, Austen's heroines demonstrate self-worth. Despite or because of their flaws and weaknesses, these women's adherence to truth and right is an assertion of self that reveals tremendous strength; it also communicates the expectation that their beloveds adhere to the same scrupulous moral standards. Thus, Austen depicts as a beneficial side-effect of female virtue the resistance to objectification and the concomitant ability to identify a good man by his devotion to her full selfhood. Regardless of the role chemistry, social suitability, or personality plays in a woman's romantic preference, she must insist on her beloved's total commitment to supporting her emotional wellness. Austen expects women to take charge of their emotional health in the manner of such surprising exemplars as Mrs Jennings and daughter Charlotte Palmer, who are 'determined to be happy' irrespective of circumstance (SS 112).[9] This hard-won equanimity supports and stems from the heroines' exercise of their duty to God and humanity, which produces the self-approval essential to self-worth.[10] Austen's women must employ their intellectual and spiritual gifts to bolster community, regardless of their personal situation and its most anguishing difficulties. A promising husband-candidate enhances a woman's giftedness and its positive influence through his appreciation of her talents and espousal of her self-investment in the greater good. Sense and Sensibility's narrator indicts Marianne for her narcissistic absorption in piano-playing and melodramatic theatrics at others' expense—while Colonel Brandon attentively listens to her music, admires Elinor's painted screens, and compassionates the feelings of both—and signals her moral elevation once she redirects her resources to intentionally enriching others' existence, thereby becoming 'the patroness of a village' (379).[11] Marilyn Butler avers that Austen critiques the 'sensibility' of 'the worship of self' that threatens society with 'the anarchy that follows the loss of all values but self-indulgence' (194). While the novelist does communicate this subtext through her portrayal of the pre-reformed Marianne, the character's caricature-like self-obsession reveals her loss of self in a dysfunctional emotionalism. Elinor Dashwood provides perhaps the most intriguing defence of a woman's crucial right to emotional health. Though she consistently invests her talents in others' welfare, her man, unlike Colonel Brandon, necessitates a thorough chastisement to comprehend the potentially devastating consequences of his careless exercise of male privilege at women's expense.

Like Darcy, Mr Knightley, Edmund Bertram, and Captain Wentworth, Edward Ferrars must reform his character to become a desirable husband. In exercising conscious deception, however, the seemingly sweet, benign Edward behaves worse than the rest, thus requiring a firmer corresponding punishment. Led by physical attraction to commit to a counterfeit relationship with an ignorant woman, he then commits a more egregious act by falling for Elinor while betraying both her and his secret fiancée. Edward must repent his unfairness and prove his trustworthiness to Elinor, ironically, by being true to the woman he no longer even likes. When finally free of his penitential engagement to Lucy, he proposes and confesses all to Elinor. She lectures him as Elizabeth does Darcy, as if to cement his reform and establish her expectations of her future husband's conduct: 'Your behaviour was certainly very wrong,' said she, 'because—to say nothing of my own conviction, our relations were all led away by it to fancy and expect *what*, as you were *then* situated, could never be' (SS 368). Even in her clear allusion to the sufferings Edward caused her, Elinor is outward-thinking and sensitive to the broader familial community. His comical demonstration of swift and absolute dependence on her judgment reflects both his recognition of his beloved's moral ascendancy and his commitment to a companionate marriage in which he will forevermore eschew the manipulative exercise of male privilege. Thus, when Elinor explains Lucy's likely reasons for her contradictory behaviour, 'Edward was of course immediately convinced that nothing could have been more natural than Lucy's conduct, nor more self-evident than the motive of it' (367).

Elinor is arguably the purest in pursuit of pure principle of all of Austen's heroines and best showcases the author's depiction of a distinctly feminine heroinism that is defined by sacrificial decorum toward even those who cause her the most suffering. Not only does Elinor honour her promise of confidentiality to Lucy, but she actively furthers Edward's fulfilment of his promise to Lucy, communicating Colonel Brandon's offer of the living that could accelerate the marriage. Yet significantly, Elinor is no angel, but a passionate person who has played mind games with Lucy to preserve her pride and who, once the engagement becomes public news, details her sufferings to Marianne at length. This foundation of human weakness, in conjunction with her belief that Edward and Lucy's marriage has transpired, is essential to readers' appreciation of Elinor's valiance in her greatest moment in the novel. '[T]hough fearing the sound of her own voice', she compels herself to the painful politeness of asking after the new 'Mrs Ferrars'; when Edward misinterprets her question as about his mother, '"I meant," said Elinor, taking up some work from the table, "to inquire after Mrs *Edward* Ferrars"' (359). This scene captures with beautiful simplicity Elinor's agonized effort to maintain her decorum toward the man she has lost and his undeserving wife, accepting the distressing consequences of the sacrifice she has already made while trying to avoid multiplying them for others.

All of Austen's heroines are or become, to varying degrees, warriors for politesse. Their courtesy to others shows heroic strength and is a central indicator of their self-worth.[12] From a present-day perspective, this paradigm and its feminist implications may be difficult to perceive, much less justly to appreciate. It is critical to understanding Jane Austen and her persistent popularity to discern that the heroic decorum demonstrated by Elinor Dashwood, Anne Elliot, Fanny Price, Emma Woodhouse, Elizabeth Bennet, and even somewhat Catherine Morland in the very face of their thwarted hopes requires a stalwart self. A self that chooses sacrifice from within a secret closet of self-knowledge that only God and conscience can see, where principle supersedes a Darwinian worldly gain and self-respect supersedes as it assists a healthy self-interest. Any discovery of these women's honourable conduct is a side-effect, never a hoped-for consequence, of their hard-fought decorum—their agentic self-sacrifice for their community. Through sacrificial civility, Austen's heroines insistently enact an autonomy that reflects truth to themselves as moral, spiritual, emotional, and physical beings whose self-care arises from knowledge of their transcendent value—beyond the claims of men but to the benefit of the entire village of humanity.

Notes

1 Austen famously stated in a letter to her closest niece, Fanny Knight, that 'pictures of perfection as you know make me sick & wicked' (23–25 March 1817). All quotes from Austen's letters are from Deirdre Le Faye's third edition of *Jane Austen's Letters*.

2 This chapter is a revised version of material drawn from my recent book, *Jane Austen's Women: An Introduction*, published by State University of New York Press, 2018. My book is a critical introduction to Austen's women that explores the heroines' relationships to body, mind, spirit, environment, and society; how they achieve greatness; and why their stories are still profoundly pertinent to today's readers. See also Anderson entries under Works Cited for original articles from which I incorporated material into the book and on which several chapters are largely based.

3 A number of scholars have produced incisive readings of women's issues in Austen's fiction from a range of thematic foci, including Alison G. Sulloway, Deborah Kaplan, Claudia L. Johnson, Margaret Kirkham, and Devoney Looser, whose work tends to emphasize the important historical influences on the author. Sulloway's book, *Jane Austen and the Province of Womanhood*, proved especially useful to my own approach. An explication of the novelist's satire in light of her family upbringing and the philosophical, literary, and educational inheritance she received from an era reactionary to 'women in general and women writers in

particular' (5), Sulloway's analysis traces Austen's use of the 'provinces' of a woman's life as frames for portraying her experiential joys and sorrows. Kaplan contributes a cultural study of the characteristics and effects of a communal 'women's culture' on Austen and other women of the period, and the ways in which her novels reflect the sometimes conflicting values and messages of both the dominant patriarchal gentry ideology and the women's culture that persists within it. Kirkham explores Austen's work as a reflection of and response to its diverse literary-ideological context in eighteenth-century Enlightenment feminism, and Johnson analyses the author's engagement in a 'progressive middle ground' of social criticism through the medium of 'conservative fiction' (166). Others offer astute discussions of more focused topics as applied to the author and her epoch, such as women and education or marriage.

4 All quotes from Austen's novels are taken from the third Chapman edition of *The Novels of Jane Austen*.

5 Hazel Jones cites correspondence in which wives debate how to respond to unfaithful and sadistic husbands. In a particularly horrifying case, a woman 'suffered blows to the head, often delivered unexpectedly, anxieties about being poisoned, imprisonment and starvation' (141).

6 It is a given that Austen's assumption that sex should occur only within marital commitment reflects the devout Anglican author's and her virtuous characters' Christian worldview, as well as her era's social mores for proper female conduct. What requires explication is Austen's illustration of the strategic utility of sexual orthodoxy to women's selection of a spouse.

7 Susan Morgan credits Austen for disregarding sexual experience as a factor in a woman's development: 'She erases the physical basis of character' and 'holds a heroine responsible for herself' (352).

8 Similarly, Emma Woodhouse obtains confirmation of Mr Elton's selfish opportunism (and unworthiness of Harriet) through his drunken seizure of her hand and 'violent' love-making in a confined carriage (*E* 129), but is protected from heartbreak at Frank Churchill's more skilled machinations only by an arbitrary disinterest in him.

9 See Chapter 3 of Anderson (*Jane Austen's Women*), an edited version of an article co-authored with Jordan L. Von Cannon ('Mrs Jennings and Mrs Palmer: The Path to Female Self-Determination in Austen's *Sense and Sensibility*', 135–48). We analyse the novel's promotion of women's emotional self-determination through a self-help program of willful positivity as the key to women's long-term psychological wellness.

10 Virtuous behaviour tends to produce the gratifications of 'self-approbation' and joy in aiding others' joy (Dadlez 61), but Austen expects her heroines to follow through on their convictions regardless of fickle emotional highs and lows. Elinor's veiled desolation continues through much of her righteous activity, and the same is true for Fanny Price and Anne Elliot.

11 See Chapter 4 of Anderson (*Jane Austen's Women*) for a detailed discussion of Austen's illustration of how women's intellects and their expression in such media as music and visual art can and should function in the performer's relationship to herself, her medium, and her audience.

12 I discovered this when composing the concluding chapter of *Jane Austen's Women*, '"Unpropitious for Heroism": Female Greatness in the Austenian Imagination'. I initially struggled over a mistaken desire to back-project contemporary ideals of success and empowerment onto heroines whose narratives do not, cannot and, arguably, should not contain them. An ironic hypocrisy of this impulse was my misappropriation as feminist a worldly fantasy of self-fulfilment founded in stereotyped masculine signals of achievement such as superior performance in measurable skills, social authority, and material acquisition. This conception of success depends on the elevation of oneself and the subordination of others, whereas the true achievement of Austen's heroines is the subordination of their baser to their best selves through voluntary elevation of others.

Works Cited

Anderson, Kathleen. 'The Jane Austen Diet: The Weight of Women in Jane Austen's Letters.' *Persuasions: The Jane Austen Journal*, vol. 27, 2005, pp. 75–87.

Anderson, Kathleen. 'Jane's "Wonder Women": Female Heroism the Austenian Way.' *Sensibilities: The Journal of the Jane Austen Society of Australia*, vol. 33, 2006, pp. 20–34.

Anderson, Kathleen. 'Lounging Ladies and Galloping Girls: Physical Strength and Femininity in *Mansfield Park*.' *Women's Studies: An Interdisciplinary Journal*, vol. 38, no. 3, 2009, pp. 342–358.

Anderson, Kathleen. *Jane Austen's Women: An Introduction*. State U of New York P, 2018.

Anderson, Kathleen, and Jordan L. Von Cannon. 'Mrs Jennings and Mrs Palmer: The Path to Female Self-Determination in Austen's *Sense and Sensibility*.' *Persuasions: The Jane Austen Journal*, vol. 30, 2008, pp. 135–148.

Austen, Jane. *The Novels of Jane Austen*, edited by R. W. Chapman, 3rd ed., vols. 1–5. Oxford UP, 1933–66.

Austen, Jane. *Jane Austen's Letters*, edited by Deirdre Le Faye, 3rd ed., Oxford UP, 1995.

Butler, Marilyn. *Jane Austen and the War of Ideas*. Clarendon P, 1975.

Dadlez, E.M. *Mirrors to One Another: Emotion and Value in Jane Austen and David Hume*. Wiley-Blackwell, 2009.

Easton, Celia. 'Austen's Urban Redemption: Rejecting Richardson's View of the City.' *Persuasions: The Jane Austen Journal*, vol. 26, 2004, pp. 121–135.

Giuffre, Giulia. 'Sex, Self and Society in *Mansfield Park*.' *Sydney Studies in English*, vol. 9, 1983–84, pp. 76–93.

Johnson, Claudia L. *Jane Austen: Women, Politics, and the Novel*. U of Chicago P, 1988.

Jones, Hazel. *Jane Austen and Marriage*. Continuum, 2009.

Kaplan, Deborah. *Jane Austen among Women*. 1992. The Johns Hopkins UP, 1994.

Kirkham, Margaret. *Jane Austen, Feminism and Fiction*. Barnes & Noble Books, 1983.

Looser, Devoney. *British Women Writers and the Writing of History, 1670–1820*. Johns Hopkins UP, 2000.

Looser, Devoney. *Women Writers and Old Age in Great Britain, 1750 1850*. Johns Hopkins UP, 2008.

Morgan, Susan. 'Why There's No Sex in Jane Austen's Fiction.' *Studies in the Novel*, vol. 19, 1987, pp. 346–356.

Sulloway, Alison G. *Jane Austen and the Province of Womanhood*. U of Pennsylvania P, 1989.

Swords, Barbara W. '"Woman's Place" in Jane Austen's England 1770–1820.' *Persuasions: Journal of the Jane Austen Society of North America*, vol. 10, 1988, 76–82.

Wiltshire, John. *Jane Austen and the Body*. 1992. Cambridge UP, 2006.

26

'QUEER AUSTEN' AND *NORTHANGER ABBEY*

Susan Celia Greenfield

FORDHAM UNIVERSITY

'I cast my lot with the queer Austen', proclaims Claudia L. Johnson in her pathbreaking essay, 'The Divine Miss Jane: Jane Austen, Janeites, and the Discipline of Novel Studies' (146). Published in 1996, the article may well be the first piece of literary criticism to juxtapose the words 'queer' and 'Austen'. At any rate, the pairing was prophetic. As Clara Tuite put it a few years later, there has been a 'recent', 'very exciting', and 'very tentative formation within Austen criticism which we could refer to as "Queer Austen"' (17). Now, more than a quarter of a century after the appearance of Johnson's article, queer Austen has become a well-recognised area of Austen studies.

The question of what queer Austen has come to signify, and the historical precedent for this association is the subject of the first section of this essay.[1] In the second section I offer a queer reading of Austen's first major novel, *Northanger Abbey* (1803, 1818).[2] Here I focus first on the heroine's and hero's resistance to gender norms and then on the heroine's reading of Ann Radcliffe's contemporarily famous gothic novel, *The Mysteries of Udolpho* (1794). Though both these features of *Northanger Abbey* have received substantial attention, no scholar I know has considered their joint relation to the queerness of the heroine's gothic obsessions. These obsessions are particularly evident in her desire to re-enact one of *Udolpho*'s most formulaic—and arguably most homoerotically charged—scenes.

Austen, Queer Theory, and Literary History

The term 'queer theory' was first coined by Teresa De Lauretis in 1990. Feminist scholars had long focused on signs of resistance to compulsory heterosexuality, and there was already a developing field of gay and lesbian studies. What would distinguish queer theory, De Lauretis proposed, was its attempt to 'problematize some of the discursive constructions and constructed silences in the emergent field of "gay and lesbian studies"' (iii). A few years later, Eve Kosofsky Sedgwick's 'Queer and Now' suggested that the word 'queer' could transcend identity categories like lesbian and gay without displacing 'same-sex sexual expression ... from the term's definitional center'.[3] Rather, Sedgwick adds in a much quoted passage, '"queer" can refer to: the open mesh of possibilities, gaps, overlaps, dissonances and resonances, lapses and excesses of meaning when the constituent elements of anyone's gender, of anyone's sexuality aren't made (or *can't be* made) to signify monolithically' (8). Queer, writes David Halperin, 'acquires its meaning from its oppositional relation to the norm. Queer is by definition *whatever* is at odds with the normal, the legitimate, the dominant' (62).[4]

342

DOI: 10.4324/9780429398155-26-30

This idea of opposition influenced the importance of another term—heteronormativity. As Melissa Sanchez explains, the definition of heterosexuality can be limited to the 'desire for genital contact exclusively with members of the opposite sex assignment' (24); heteronormativity is far more capacious, pointing to what Lauren Berlant and Michael Warner describe as 'the institutions, structures of understanding, and practical orientations that make heterosexuality seem not only coherent—that is, organized as a sexuality—but also privileged' (Sanchez 7, Berlant and Warner 548 n2). It points to the hegemonic forces that produce and enforce the idea that binary sexual difference and heterosexuality are normal. Perhaps the clearest way to define queer theory is to recognise heteronormativity as one of its 'most persistent targets of opposition and analysis' (Sanchez 7).[5]

Johnson's 1996 shout-out to queer Austen grows out of this theoretical development. More obviously, her article was influenced by two then recent series of events that have since become legendary in queer Austen criticism. The first occurred in 1989 with the programme listing of Eve Kosofsky Sedgwick's paper title for the Modern Language Association Convention: 'Jane Austen and the Masturbating Girl'. Soon after, knowing nothing more about Sedgwick's argument, Roger Kimball cited that title in his book *Tenured Radicals* to prove what he saw as the absurdity of—and the dangers posed to the humanities by—left wing academic extremists, proponents of 'women's studies, black studies, gay studies, and the like' (5, 219). From there, as Sedgwick puts it in her subsequent and identically named article, 'Jane Austen and the Masturbating Girl' became 'an index of depravity in academe' for the many journalists who 'righteously' recycled the phrase ('Jane Austen and the Masturbating Girl', 818).[6] For the many Austen scholars and/or queer theorists who actually read the article, on the other hand, the essay became canonical. In it, Sedgwick attends to the sister heroines' non-heteronormative desires in *Sense and Sensibility*. She describes 'the passion and perturbation of [Elinor and Marianne Dashwood's] love for each other', suggests that the 'erotic axis' of the novel is 'most obviously the unwavering but difficult love' of Elinor for Marianne, and outlines the many insinuations that Marianne is a masturbator, which was, in Austen's time, a 'long-execrated form of sexuality' (823, 826, 821).

The second series of events centred around Terry Castle's 1995 review of *Jane Austen's Letters* (edited by Deirdre Le Faye) in the *London Review of Books*. Like Sedgwick's essay, the review focuses on a 'passionate' sororal relationship, though in this case that involved Austen herself and Cassandra, her older sister (Castle, 'Sister-Sister'). Seeking provocation (and without Castle's advanced knowledge), *LRB* entitled the essay, 'Was Jane Austen Gay?'. A frenzy of media outrage followed as well as weeks of letters to the *LRB* editor. On the BBC Castle protested, 'Nowhere … did I state that Jane Austen was a "lesbian" … or that she had sex of some sort with her sister' ('Stanford University News Release'). What Castle did 'stand by' was her belief that 'Austen's relationship with Cassandra was unquestionably the most important emotional relationship of her life' and that this relationship had 'unconscious homoerotic dimensions' (Castle, 'Letters').

In 'The Divine Miss Jane', Johnson challenges the foundational status of these events. Though Sedgwick and Castle's outraged opponents responded as if 'no one had *ever* doubted Austen's normativity before', this was 'far from the case … Even Sedgwick and Castle … appear unaware that their positions have ample … precedent' (147, 162). But they do. Edmund Wilson, for instance, anticipates both Sedgwick's and Castle's claims by half a century when he describes the relationships between sisters in Austen's novels as 'certainly the most deeply felt'; singles out Elinor Dashwood's emotional reaction to her sister as the 'most passionate thing in Jane Austen'; and associates the 'relationships imagined' in the novels with Austen's own familial and 'peculiar "conditioning"' (Wilson 202–3).[7] Johnson charts the enduring and multifold history of such ideas, showing how Austen's biography, her readership, and her novels have long been queered.

For one thing, Johnson argues that '[b]ecause Austen's heterosexuality was not guaranteed by marriage' there have always been 'doubts about her sexuality' (148). As early as 1850, Charlotte

Brontë suspected her of frigidity and gender non-normativity, telling W. S. Williams, 'the Passions are perfectly unknown to her' and that 'Jane Austen was a complete and most sensible lady, but a very incomplete, and rather insensible … woman' ('Letter to W. S. Williams', 128).[8] In 1930, D. H. Lawrence called Austen 'mean' and an 'old maid' (qtd. in Southam, *Critical Heritage*, 2:107). And in 1952, Marvin Mudrick suggested that both 'Love and Freindship' and *Emma* reflected Austen's own 'fear' of the 'adult commitment of sexual love' (194, 19).[9]

Johnson pays special attention to the queering of Austen's readership. 'One of the biggest secrets of the literate world', she writes in her *LRB* letter about Castle's review, 'is that Austen is a cult author for many gays and lesbians' (Johnson, 'Letters'). 'The Divine Miss Jane' focuses particularly on Austen's male enthusiasts in the first half of the twentieth century, documenting the frequency with which they were accused of effeminacy.[10] Many decades later, D. A. Miller associated his own queerness and implicit effeminacy with his childhood love of Austen, proposing that '[a]ll' young male Austen lovers are fated to discover their 'wrong' relation to the 'sex system', and to find that they have made an 'asinine transvestite spectacle' of themselves (1, 3).

Miller also queers Austen's novels by associating her narrative style (with its consummate irony and free indirect discourse) with what he calls 'the Unheterosexual'. As 'though it were on an exemption from "sex"—in the old-fashioned sense … of both gender *and* sexuality', Austen's style, he says, is 'decidedly *neuter*' (29, 33). The passage, though admiring, is reminiscent of Brontë's sweeping complaint about the asexuality of Austen's writing, the incapacity of her 'mind's eye' to behold 'the heart of her race' (128). George Sampson offered a similar summation of the novels' sexlessness in 1924: 'In her world there is neither marrying nor giving in marriage, but just the make-believe mating of dolls … . Jane Austen is abnormal … because [her characters] have no sex at all' (qtd. in Johnson, 'The Divine Miss Jane' 149). Decades after Sampson, feminist critics began putting a different spin on such 'make-believe mating', viewing Austen's elliptical and (with the possible exception of *Persuasion*) notoriously unromantic marital finales as a pointed protest against the genre's requisite heterosexuality. As E. J. Clery summarises, Austen 'punishes' the novel-reader's addiction to a happily ever after ending 'by withholding some of the scenes that would most gratify, or by darkening the auguries of happiness with satire or skepticism'. The same kind of 'deep suspicion of the telos of romance' generally marks the 'queer perspective on Austen' (163).

Queer readings of individual novels are increasingly common and date back at least as far as 1944 when Edmund Wilson claimed that Emma Woodhouse 'is not interested in men', and is instead 'inclined to infatuations with women' (201, 202). A few years later, Marvin Mudrick echoed him: Emma is 'in love with [Harriet]: a love unphysical and inadmissible, even perhaps undefinable in such a society' (203, qtd. in Johnson, 'The Divine Miss Jane' 159).[11] After the rise of feminist literary criticism such interpretations became more frequent, positive, and sustained. In 1987, Ruth Perry argued that the action in *Emma* (1815) calls 'attention to the ways in which compulsory heterosexuality disrupts and distorts the relationships between women' (197–98). A decade later, Lisa Moore offered what she called an 'optimistic account of the novel's production of homosexual desire' (122). The same year, Susan Korba flatly asked, 'Why *shouldn't* Emma be a lesbian?' (141). By 2009, discussions of Emma's homoeroticism had become so common place that Fiona Brideoake could write, '[c]ritics have long acknowledged the same-sex desires evident in *Emma*' (463).

After *Emma*, *Mansfield Park* (1814) is the novel most frequently queered. Johnson emphasises Fanny Price's rejection of Henry Crawford, who wonders if the heroine is 'peculiarly resistant to normal heterosexual seduction' (Johnson, 'The Divine Miss Jane' 147) and bewilderedly asks: 'Is she queer?—Is she prudish?' (*MP* 158). Others have emphasised Fanny's incestuous love for her cousin Edmund, which Ellen Pollack describes as an 'alterity' that violates 'internal [and] external boundaries' (183). Fanny *is* queer, George Haggerty suggests, in that she nurtures a transgressive love that begins in 'shame and heartache' and that her 'family structure … forbids' ('Fanny Price' 187). Misty Anderson argues that like the threat of incest, the '[h]omoerotic attraction' between Fanny and Mary Crawford 'remains an unspoken possibility' in the novel (172). And a recent article by Erin Spampinato characterises Tom Bertram's 'social world … as potentially queer' (484).[12]

Such interpretations raise a basic question about history—a question that predates the rise of queer theory but continues to preoccupy it: Is it accurate to apply words like 'homosexual desire', 'homoerotic attraction', and 'queer' to novels produced at a time when these terms either did not exist or may have had different implications?[13] In *The History of Sexuality* Michel Foucault claims that male homosexuality did not become a Western identity category, or as he puts it, a 'species', until the second half of the nineteenth century (43). And it was not until the early twentieth century that a 'universally identifiable English term to define sexual love between women' emerged (Greenfield, *Mothering Daughters* 62). At the same time, historians like Randolph Trumbach have tracked the appearance of the word 'molly' to designate the eighteenth-century development of a 'new kind of [effeminate] sodomite', the 'first European men who might reasonably be called "homosexuals"' (77). In England, there was a rocketing rise in arrests for sodomitical behaviour. Beginning in 1806 an average of ninety men per year were indicted for sodomy and between then and 1861, 404 received the death penalty (fifty-six were actually executed [Cocks 109]). The criminalisation of women's same-sex love was not as widespread, but, as Susan Lanser documents, 'seventeenth- and eighteenth-century Europe … witnessed an intensified interest in lesbians', and the deployment of 'a score of labels' and innuendos to describe female 'homoerotic desire and behaviors'. In England, for instance, the term 'sapphic' became far more common (1, 16, 196).[14] Many scholars have also pointed to the eighteenth-century fame of the Ladies of Llangollen, Lady Eleanor Butler and Miss Sarah Ponsonby, who eloped from Ireland to North Wales in 1778 and cohabitated for the next fifty-one years. As Brideoake notes, they were 'plagued by persistent insinuations that their relationship was sexual' (*Ladies* xvi).[15]

It also makes sense to apply the broadest definition of queer (including all varieties of non-heteronormativity) to interpretations of the period's history. On the one hand, standards of gender and sexual 'normalcy' rigidified in the period. The brutal increase in sodomy indictments indicates this, as well as the idealisation of companionate marriage. More and more, Foucault argues, the legitimate couple, with its regular sexuality … [t]ended to function as a norm'. At the same time, enormous cultural attention was paid to non-normative behaviors and desires. Foucault describes this as a 'discursive explosion' with respect to 'the setting apart of the "unnatural" as a specific dimension in the field of sexuality … . People often say that modern society has attempted to reduce sexuality to the [legitimate heterosexual] couple … . [But] there are equal grounds for saying that it has, if not created, at least outfitted and made to proliferate, groups with multiple elements and a circulating sexuality' (38–39, 45). These elements included (but were not limited to) incest, sodomy, sadism, necrophilia, and seducing a nun, as well as 'the sexuality of children, mad men and women, criminals; the sensuality of those who did not like the opposite sex; [and] reveries, obsessions, petty manias, or great transports of rage' (38–39). In short, the intensification of heteronormativity was inextricably linked to all varieties of its antithesis. When Susan Lanser argues that the 'heteronormative order' of modernity simultaneously marks 'the emergence of the sapphic as an epistemic plausibility' she offers just one of many possible examples of the interdependence of heteronormativity and queerness (4–5).[16]

Other examples of their interdependence appear in English representations of the French Revolution. A comparison of Edmund Burke's attack on the revolution in *Reflections on the Revolution in France* (1790) and Mary Wollstonecraft's support of its ideals in *A Vindication of the Rights of Woman* (1792) offers a good case in point. Both authors defend their positions by associating them with heteronormativity, and both associate ideological opposition with sexual 'deviance'.[17] Burke, for instance, notoriously links pre-revolutionary France with an uber-feminised vision of Marie Antoinette, 'glittering like the morning-star, full of life, and splendor, and joy' (169); in contrast, the women who initiated the October March—described as 'the unutterable abominations of the furies of hell, in the abused shape of the vilest of women' (165)—epitomise gender deviance. Wollstonecraft reverses the strategy. For her, a revolutionary extension of individual rights and especially the rights of education to women would 'quickly' transform them into 'good wives, and mothers' (187). Meanwhile, she implies that women's current lack of rights fosters homoeroticism in both sexes; 'women are, in general, too familiar with each other', and men become 'lustful prowler[s]', some of whom 'attend the levees of equivocal beings, to sigh for more than female languor' (135, 147).

Of all the literary reactions to the period's heteronormativity none has more frequently been characterised as oppositional and queer than the late eighteenth-century gothic novel.[18] '[M]any scholars of the Gothic would probably agree' that 'much Gothic fiction is "queer"' writes Lauren Fitzgerald. '[G]othic fiction [is] always already queer', George Haggerty proposes, because '[t]ransgressive social-sexual relations are [its] most basic common denominator'.

> Terror is almost always sexual terror: fear and flight, as well as incarceration and escape, are almost always coloured by the exoticism of transgressive sexual aggression. It is no mere coincidence that the cult of gothic fiction reached its apex at the very moment when gender and sexuality were beginning to be codified for modern culture. In fact, gothic fiction offered a testing ground for many unauthorized genders and sexualities, including sodomy, tribadism, romantic friendship (male and female), incest, pedophilia, sadism, masochism, necrophilia, cannibalism, masculinized females, feminized males, miscegenation, and so on. ('The Horrors of Catholicism')

Centuries before the term queer theory was coined, Haggerty suggests, '[the gothic novel] offer[ed] an historical model of queer theory and politics' ('The Horrors of Catholicism').[19] In this respect, Michael O'Rourke and David Collings note, it is only fitting that before she became a 'queen of queer theory', Sedgwick wrote her doctoral dissertation and first book on the gothic novel ('Introduction'). The latter—in which Sedgwick describes the lack of an 'inherent' or 'original or private' personal or individual identity, 'including sexual identity', in the gothic novel—anticipates queer theory's resistance to fixed gender and sexual identity categories (*Coherence* 157, 142). So too, some of Sedgwick's descriptions in 'Jane Austen and the Masturbating Girl'—both of the ways masturbators were historically 'surveilled, punished, jawboned, imprisoned, terrorized, shackled, diagnosed, purged, and physically mutilated', and of the 'space of same sex tenderness, secrecy, longing, and frustration' signified by the bedroom scene in *Sense and Sensibility*—sound like they could be summaries of gothic conventions ('Jane Austen' 821, 823).

In *Northanger Abbey*, the heroine Catherine Morland relishes the gothic conventions in *The Mysteries of Udolpho* and responds to them with queer and obsessive fascination. Reading or thinking about Radcliffe's novel arouses and distracts her so much that she tends to forget her interest in the hero, Henry Tilney. Moreover, when she finally arrives at Northanger Abbey, the Tilney family's ancient (and Catherine hopes suitably gothic) estate, she tries to re-enact one of the most standard 'unheterosexual' plots in gothic fiction: she undertakes a desperate search for an absent and reputedly dead mother figure—in this case Mrs Tilney. Instead of busily desiring Henry, Catherine spends much of her time at the abbey fantasising about his female parent and hoping to find her in her mysteriously restricted bedroom. In short, Catherine is full of the kinds of 'reveries [and] obsessions' Foucault argues were associated with non-normative sexuality (38).

Queer *Northanger Abbey*

To various extents, all of Austen's major novels question both the broad social—and the particular novelistic—conventions of gender difference and heterosexual romance. But none of her subsequent completed novels do this as openly and exuberantly as *Northanger Abbey*. Perhaps this is because *Northanger Abbey* is closest chronologically to the unabashed literary satire of Austen's juvenilia. Perhaps in this first completed novel we see an early instantiation of an ironic voice that will later disguise its socio-political aims in a denser 'cover story', as Sandra Gilbert and Susan Gubar might have it (155). At any rate, in opening with the oft-quoted line that 'No one who had ever seen Catherine Morland in her infancy, would have supposed her born to be an heroine', followed by an entire chapter detailing first Catherine's early failure at achieving femininity, and later her deliberate attempt to conform to it, *Northanger Abbey* explicitly denaturalises gender difference. As a plain-looking child, who is fond of 'boy's plays', prefers cricket to dolls, and is 'noisy and wild' the young Catherine Morland is proof that there is nothing biologically deterministic about girlhood (37, 39). Catherine's behaviour and desires may seem non-normative, but they are, the narrator satirically suggests, neither surprising nor unnatural. When Catherine does become more feminine at age fifteen, when her 'love of dirt [gives] way to an inclination for finery', and she begins 'to curl her hair and long for balls' and grow '*almost* pretty', she does so because she is in 'training' to become a heroine, and reading 'all such works as heroines must read' (39–40). Catherine has, in other words, reached an age of indoctrination, in this case enforced by male authored literature and popular culture. In Judith Butler's terms, we might say she has begun a self-conscious process of gender imitations and performances, a '*stylized repetition of acts*' that create the 'illusion of an interior and organizing gender core' (*Gender Trouble*, 140, 136).

These implications, much discussed by Austen critics, are nicely summarised by Clery who calls *Northanger Abbey*'s first chapter 'a comic anticipation of Simone de Beauvoir's aphorism: "One is not born a woman, one becomes one"' (159). We can also look backward to some of Wollstonecraft's most progressive pronouncements in *A Vindication of the Rights of Woman*, as when she writes: 'I do earnestly wish to see the distinction of sex confounded in society'. The gender problem, Wollstonecraft suggests, begins in childhood when girls are not 'allowed to take sufficient exercise', and are 'confined in close rooms till their muscles are relaxed' (62, 67). Catherine, who 'hate[s] confinement' and loves 'nothing so well in the world as rolling down the green slope at the back of the house', is luckily free of these constraints (*NA* 39). Nobody makes her stay inside, especially not her mother who is ironically too busy bearing babies to instruct her daughters in proper womanhood. Even after she becomes more feminine, Catherine remains refreshingly non-normative. She gives up her 'love of dirt', but unlike Mrs Allen or Isabella Thorpe, she still says 'I never mind dirt'. She stops rolling down hills, but she continues to be 'out of doors' so much that, as she tells Henry, 'Mamma says, I am never within' (39, 99, 175).

Wollstonecraft's primary complaint in *Vindication* concerns the failure of women's intellectual education and their indoctrination in self-objectification. Instead of being trained in reason, they are mainly taught to beautify themselves for male sexual gratification. Women's subsequent ignorance and hyper-sexualisation are then attributed to female biology rather than to the socialisation that is their true source. Wollstonecraft attributes this 'false system of education' to 'books written ... by men' who, she says, in language that sounds remarkably like twentieth-century feminist theory, seek only 'to render [women] insignificant objects of desire' (10, 13). When Catherine herself turns to books by men to learn heroism, she reflects the potential danger of this gender lesson. Nevertheless, she is never consumed by it. Whereas Mrs Allen is obsessed with dress and Isabella with attracting male attention, Catherine is obsessed with neither.[20] She is happy when two men at the Upper Rooms 'pronounc[e] her to be a pretty girl' (*NA* 47). Yet when Isabella later suggests that they dress exactly alike at a dance because 'the men take notice of *that* sometimes', Catherine's disinterest is classic: 'it does not signify if they do' (64). She never becomes the 'insignificant object of desire' that Wollstonecraft despises.

In fact, Catherine's subjective experience of desire is one of the most oft-noted and anti-conventional details of *Northanger Abbey*. Every good novel reader knows, the narrator jokes, 'that no young lady can be justified in falling in love before the gentleman's love is declared' (52). But Catherine desires Henry first, and his subsequent affection, the narrator 'must confess' at the novel's end, originates 'in nothing better than gratitude' and 'a persuasion of her partiality for *him*' (233, my emphasis). Instead of being objectified by the male gaze, Catherine spends much of the Bath portion of the novel looking for and at the 'object' of Henry (80).[21] Henry memorably compares country dancing and marriage and announces, 'in both, man has the advantage of choice, woman only the power of refusal' (95). This is certainly true with respect to actions—Catherine can neither ask Henry to dance nor to marry her. But when it comes to the experience of desire, *she* chooses him, and *he* does not refuse. It is only because she finds Henry 'irresistible' that Catherine ultimately becomes irresistible to Henry (140). Their marriage may be heterosexual, but their route to it is queer.

This is perhaps not surprising given that Henry is at least as gender non-conforming as the heroine. Thus Sarah Eason argues that Henry's 'gender performance resists categorization' and that he is 'a queer literary character' ('Henry Tilney'); and Judith Wylie, invoking Butler, suggests that Henry's 'fluidity of identities [is] a parody of essentialist gendering similar to drag' (140). Henry's much-discussed expertise in muslin and female dress, for instance, shocks Mrs Allen because '[m]en commonly take so little notice of those things'. Nevertheless, Henry takes pride in how his sister trusts 'me in the choice of a gown'—a pride that, given the narrator's later insistence on the 'in-sensibility of man towards a new gown', smacks of possible transvestism (51, 92). Henry even refers to himself as 'queer' when he and Catherine first dance (49).[22]

Like the narrator, Henry also takes gleeful pleasure in satirising gender norms, especially as they tend to be articulated in the period's conduct books for women. The narrator mocks traditional expectations about women's talents in musicianship and drawing (Catherine is bad at both); Henry mocks a comparable expectation when he says: 'Every body allows that the talent of writing agreeable letters is peculiarly female' (38, 50). The narrator notes Catherine's disinterest in 'watering a rose-bush' and gathering flowers; Henry, tongue in cheek, tells her, 'a taste for flowers is always desirable in your sex' (38, 175). In Chapter 14, both the narrator and Henry make fun of men's claims to intellectual superiority. The narrator accuses men of viewing 'imbecility in females [as] a great enhancement of their personal charm'. Henry tells Catherine and his sister, 'I have no patience with such of my sex as disdain to let themselves sometimes down to the comprehension of yours' (125, 126).

And yet, as this last quotation suggests, Henry easily slides from satirising gender norms to ex-emplifying male power. Shortly after his speech above, for instance, Henry calls his sister 'stupid', complains about the 'weakness of the woman', and says that women never 'use more than half' of their understanding. His tone may be jocular, but the narrator is certainly describing Henry when she mocks the 'proportion of [men] too reasonable ... to desire any thing more in woman than ignorance'. If Catherine does not 'know that a good-looking girl, with an affectionate heart and a very ignorant mind, cannot fail of attracting a clever young man' (125), then Henry also does not know the extent to which her ignorance attracts him. '[A] teachableness of disposition in a young lady is a great blessing' (175) Henry tells Catherine, again satirically. But as his constant didacticism makes clear, Catherine's teachableness is a blessing to *him*. In this way Henry resembles D. A. Miller's description of the 'effeminate' Robert Ferrars in *Sense and Sensibility*: 'For all that [he] reveals the Woman in him[self] ... [it] fails to rob him of the smallest bit of male entitlement' (Miller 19).

The same tension between gender defiance and male privilege characterises Henry's discussion of the novel as a literary genre. The historical context here is important, since novels tended to be feminised and dismissed at the end of the eighteenth century, especially, the narrator suggests, by male critics. They were associated both with women readers like Catherine and Isabella Thorpe (who eagerly 'shut themselves up, to read novels together' [58]), and with women writers, like Frances Burney and Maria Edgeworth, to whom the narrator pointedly refers in Chapter 5.[23] Chapter 5 is famous for its aggressive defence of the novel genre and its tacit attack on literary sexism. 'Let us not desert each other', the narrator calls out to an implicit cohort of female novelists, 'we are an injured body. Although our productions have afforded more extensive and unaffected pleasure than those of any other literary corporation in the world, no species of composition has been so much decried' (59). The idea of a literally and explicitly female 'injured body' becomes more central to Catherine when she visits Northanger Abbey. Most important in these early chapters is how men typically attack novels, exemplified when John Thorpe proudly scoffs, 'I never read novels … . Novels are all so full of nonsense and stuff' (71). By the time Catherine takes her walk with the Tilneys in Chapter 14, she is convinced that 'young men despis[e] novels amazingly'. But Henry again defies gender norms: 'The person, be it gentleman or lady, who has not pleasure in a good novel, must be intolerably stupid', he says (120–21).

As is characteristic, Henry's claim is double-edged. 'Do not imagine that you can cope with me in a knowledge of Julias and Louisas' (popular names for contemporary heroines), he warns Catherine. 'If we proceed to particulars … I shall soon leave you … far behind me'. Even when it comes to this feminised genre, Henry assumes he is an intellectually superior man. His account of first reading *The Mysteries of Udolpho* points to other domineering tendencies. As he and Eleanor recollect during their walk, Henry had originally promised to read part of one of the volumes aloud to Eleanor. But when Eleanor was briefly called away (probably by their demanding father), Henry ran off to finish the volume by himself. He did this even though the book belonged to Eleanor and was, as Henry is 'proud' to note, 'particularly her own' (121). If in Chapter 5, the novel genre is particularly women's own, here it provides an opportunity for male appropriation.

Henry also never thinks the novel genre has any role as serious literature. For him a good novel provides 'pleasure' and entertainment and nothing more. In contrast, the narrator describes the novel's artistic supremacy in Chapter 5, singling out *Cecilia* (1782) and *Camilla* (1796) (by Burney) and *Belinda* (1801) (by Edgeworth) as models of intelligence, eloquence, and realism. They display 'the greatest powers of the human mind…, the most thorough knowledge of *human nature*, the happiest delineation of its varieties, [and] the liveliest effusions of wit and humour … to the world in the best chosen language' (60, my emphasis). When Henry reprimands Catherine in his mother's bedroom, which I discuss later, he emphasises the opposite, convincing her that '[c]harming as were all Mrs Radcliffe's works, … it was not in them perhaps that *human nature* … was to be looked for' (197, my emphasis). In fairness, the narrator partly agrees with Henry about the limits of gothic novels. Unlike *Cecilia, Camilla,* or *Belinda, The Mysteries of Udolpho* is not the place to look for verisimilitude, and as I will also discuss later (and is generally well-known) whenever Catherine expects 'real life' to conform to gothic fiction she is dutifully satirised.

At the same time, *The Mysteries of Udolpho* and gothic conventions in general offer Catherine a powerful alternative to heteronormativity. Henry, for all his queerness, lords his male authority over Catherine. The gothic novel, in all its queerness, and despite Catherine's interest in Henry, offers her both a logic for—and means of—escaping him. Marriage was, of course, the inevitable conclusion of most novels, gothic or not, including those by Austen. That is why the narrator jokes at the end of *Northanger Abbey* that readers 'will see in the tell-tale compression of the pages before them, that we are all hastening together to perfect felicity' (238). But in many gothic novels, the most memorable marriages lead to anything but felicity, and heterosexual relationships and desires are hazardous for female characters. The fantasies Catherine indulges speak to her absorption of—and compulsion to repeat—this message, as well as to the appeal of non-heteronormative desires.

349

From the moment Catherine starts reading *Udolpho* it undercuts her compliance with hetero-normative standards. Instead of beautifying herself for the men she will meet at an evening dance, for instance, Catherine pores 'over the pages of' Radcliffe's novel, 'lost from all worldly concerns of dressing' (74). Similarly, when Isabella assumes she is obsessing about Henry, Catherine not only corrects her by saying, 'you should not persuade me that I think so very much about him', but adds 'while I have Udolpho to read' nothing else matters (63). Even when Catherine becomes more preoccupied with Henry, her desire for him is often in competition with her gothic fantasies. Consider the train of free indirect discourse describing Catherine's dual pleasure when invited to visit the Tilney home: 'She was to be ... under the same roof with the person whose society she mostly prized—and ... this roof was to be the roof of an abbey!' At first, Henry seems to supersede her gothic fantasies: 'Her passion for ancient edifices was next in degree to her passion for Henry—and castles and abbies made usually the charm of those reveries which his image did not fill' (147). But then we learn that

> To see [Northanger Abbey] ... had been for many weeks a darling wish... too nearly impossible for desire. And yet, this was to happen ... . [A]nd she was to be its inhabitant. Its long, damp passages, its narrow cells and ruined chapel, were to be within her daily reach, and she could not entirely subdue the hope of some traditional legends, some awful memorials of an injured and ill-fated nun. (147–48)

By the end of the passage, Catherine's gothic fantasies have replaced Henry entirely and concluded not only with the image of a woman, but of an 'injured' one, echoing and literalising the 'injured body' of women novelists described in Chapter 5.

When Catherine finally reaches Northanger Abbey, the 'injured body' of a woman writer is at the heart of her first quest. En route to the abbey, Henry teasingly tells her she might find the memoirs of 'the wretched Matilda' (a suitably gothic name) in a 'cabinet of ebony and gold' in her bedroom (163). The fantasy is literary and polymorphous. It originates with Henry's words but leads Catherine to search for a woman's written narrative. True, the cabinet in her bedroom is not 'absolutely ebony and gold'. But that does not deter the gullible and aroused Catherine. In a compulsive exploration that makes her seem as much of a 'masturbating girl' as Sedgwick's version of Marianne Dashwood, Catherine 'applie[s] herself to the [cabinet] key, ... moving it in every possible way'; a 'door suddenly yield[s] to her hand: her heart leap[s] with exultation'; she discovers 'in the centre ... a cavity of importance', whose 'inner lock' she finally manages to 'unfasten'. And there, 'pushed back into the further part of the cavity', is a manuscript. Catherine's 'heart flutter[s], her knees trembl[e]', and 'her feelings' are 'indescribable' (170–71). The morning light brings an anti-climax; the manuscript, it turns out, is merely a laundry list, and a 'humbled' Catherine hopes Henry will never know about 'her folly'. And yet, she also realises, 'it was in great measure his own doing' (174).

This is notably the last time Henry has any narrative control over Catherine's gothic fantasies. The next morning he leaves the abbey for his parsonage in Woodston, and by lunchtime, Catherine has begun developing a new and more compelling fantasy, this one driven by her desire to find—or at least to find out more information about—Henry's reputedly dead mother, whom he has not mentioned. Unlike in all of Austen's subsequent novels, where the hero's absence or unavailability often prompts the intensification of the heroine's desire for him, Catherine almost never thinks about Henry after he leaves for Woodston. Instead, his absence disappears into his absent mother. Or, to put it another way, she forgets about his body and becomes obsessed with finding a maternal one. In this, Catherine is obviously influenced by contemporary gothic novels whose plots about missing mothers and their daughters' heroic quests for them were among the most popular and predictable of the period. In keeping with Catherine's earlier imaginings, many of the maternal characters are connected to nuns.

Such plots are often sexually charged. As I have written elsewhere, gothic novels routinely emphasise 'the power and potential eroticism of mother-daughter affection' ('Veiled Desire' 74).[24] Radcliffe's final novel, *The Italian* (1797), which Isabella is eager for Catherine to read next, offers a good case in point. In it the heroine, Ellena Rosalba, is kidnapped and imprisoned in a convent. There she meets her unrecognised mother, Olivia, who has become a nun. They are mutually attracted, Ellena watching the nun 'with a degree of interest which render[s] her insensible to every other object in the chapel' (86). Olivia, whose eyes are 'often fixed upon [Ellena's] face', blushes, grows pale, and has 'an air of such universal languor as precedes a fainting fit' (91). Later when the hero rescues and wants to marry the heroine, she weeps on Olivia's bosom, and is so reluctant to leave her that the hero has to 'disengag[e]' them. '[D]o I then hold only second place in your heart?' he asks her. 'I envy your friend those tears ... and feel jealous of the tenderness that excites them' (135–36). The threat that the women's love for each other poses to heterosexuality is clear.

Though there is no equally charged mother-daughter scene in *The Mysteries of Udolpho*, the connection between the heroine, Emily St. Aubert, and her two maternal surrogates as well as a third woman who is a nun, raises a comparable challenge. Each woman is in some way injured, ends up absent, and epitomises the hazards of heterosexual love and marriage. Emily's first maternal surrogate, her aunt and guardian, is imprisoned in a castle turret by her husband and the novel's villain, Count Montoni. He 'suffer[s] her to lie, forlorn and neglected, under a raging fever', until Emily finds her, emaciated, skeletal and on the verge of death (364–65). Towards the end of the book, Emily learns about another aunt and maternal surrogate, the Marchioness de Villeroi who, like Madam Montoni, was also murdered by her husband. Told she looks just like her, Emily develops a 'thrilling curiosity' to search the woman's former bedroom (529). There, Emily suggestively observes the 'articles of her dress ... scattered upon the floor, as if they had just been thrown off' (533). Catherine incorporates details about both the aunts into her search for Mrs Tilney. Like Madam Montoni, she thinks Mrs Tilney is perhaps being imprisoned and starved by her husband; and as with Emily and the Marchioness, Catherine is desperate to see her former bedroom.

In an earlier and especially famous scene, Emily cannot resist uncovering a picture concealed by a black veil. As soon as she does, she drops 'senseless on the floor' (248–49). At the novel's end, Radcliffe reveals why. Emily thinks she sees the worm-ridden corpse of Signora Laurentini, the former owner of Udolpho. In fact, all she really sees is a wax sculpture, and Signora Laurentini is still alive. The character dies at the novel's end after telling Emily her sordid history: In her youth, Laurentini was a fallen woman, desperately in love with the Marquis de Villeroi. He married Emily's aunt, but later agreed to Laurentini's violent plot to kill his wife so that he could marry Laurentini instead. As soon as the Marchioness was dead he changed his mind, and threatened to kill Laurentini unless she joined a convent. She complied, became a nun, and went mad. Whereas Emily's aunts become victims of heterosexual violence, Laurentini becomes violent because of heterosexual passion.

In the Bath portion of Austen's novel, Catherine is obsessed with Signora Laurentini and the black veiled picture. But by the Northanger Abbey portion of the novel, Catherine seems to have forgotten Laurentini. Perhaps this is because she does not identify with her heterosexual desire.[25] Laurentini warns Radcliffe's heroine: 'Sister! beware of the first indulgence of the passions; beware of the first! Their course, if not checked then, is rapid—their force is uncontroullable—they lead us we know not whither—they lead us perhaps to the commission of crimes ...!' (646). Catherine's 'first passion' may be for Henry. But the passion she indulges when he is gone, the one whose 'force is uncontroullable' and leads her she knows 'not whither' is for his missing mother. Her 'criminal behavior', Catherine later thinks, is the fantasy that provokes her to undertake this search (196).

That fantasy begins the morning Henry leaves for Woodston when Eleanor takes Catherine down the gloomy path that was once her 'mother's favourite walk'. At this first mention of the late Mrs Tilney, Catherine's 'interest [is] excited'. She encourages Eleanor to describe her 'great affliction' about the loss, then suspects General Tilney of having 'been dreadfully cruel' to his late wife (180–81). With an apparently abusive father and victimised mother, Eleanor (whose name begins with 'E' like both of the Radcliffe heroines described above) could be a gothic protagonist. Catherine effectively takes Eleanor's place, developing an increasingly violent fantasy about the General's behaviour and an increasingly passionate desire to enter Mrs Tilney's bedroom. The latter, as with Sedgwick's description of the bedroom in *Sense and Sensibility*, becomes a 'space of same sex tenderness, secrecy, longing, and frustration' (Sedgwick 823). Like many architectural details in gothic novels (and like the cabinet in Catherine's bedroom), the imagery sounds vaginal. Mrs Tilney's room is located behind an 'important lock' at the end of a narrow passage, beyond a pair of folding doors. That the General twice interferes with Eleanor and Catherine's attempts to probe the space together only makes Catherine more aroused, his 'evident desire of preventing' this providing 'an additional stimulant' (190, 185).[26]

After the first frustrated attempt, Catherine starts thinking about Mrs Tilney as 'an *injured* wife' and assumes General Tilney was her murderer (186, my emphasis). But that night, 'revolving these matters, while she undressed', Catherine excitedly adapts the plot to correspond more closely to *Udolpho*, deciding that Mrs Tilney may still be alive and 'shut up for causes unknown, and receiving from the pitiless hands of her husband a nightly supply of coarse food' (187). Catherine is 'hardly able to breathe' the next time she and Eleanor 'pass through the folding doors' and Eleanor puts 'her hand upon the important lock'. Again the General interrupts and separates them. Having failed twice with her friend, Catherine resolves to make 'her next attempt ... alone'. She breathlessly succeeds that afternoon, slipping at last through the 'forbidden door' (190–91).

The result is famously satiric. Instead of gothic horror, Catherine discovers a sunny and well-appointed bedroom with no sign of foul play. As when the manuscript in the cabinet turns out to be a laundry list, Catherine is seized with 'common sense' and 'shame'. When Henry appears, her shame gets far worse. With a few choice questions, he understands exactly why Catherine is in the bedroom and exactly what 'liberty ... her imagination ha[s] dared to take with the character of his father' (196). Appalled, Henry issues his humiliating reprimand.

> Dear Miss Morland, consider the dreadful nature of the suspicions you have entertained. What have you been judging from? Remember the country and the age in which we live. Remember that we are English, that we are Christian. Consult your own understanding, your own sense of the probable, your own observation of what is passing around you—Does our education prepare us for such atrocities? Do our laws connive at them? (195)

Henry's response is xenophobic and smug, swiping at Catholic (as distinct from 'Christian') France, whose revolution has generated all varieties of 'atrocities'. It is also heteronormative. How, Henry accusingly implies, could Catherine possibly imagine such evil of an English*man*—so much abuse from a husband 'in a country like this'? He significantly concedes that his father's 'temper *injured*' his mother (195, my emphasis). But he insists this is nothing compared to the heterosexual horrors she has fathomed. 'Dear Miss Morland, what ideas have you been admitting?' Henry asks, as if Catherine's mind needs a much stronger lock (196). For as with her bedroom (or her genitals), a woman must always be very careful about what comes inside.

The scene sucks Catherine into heterosexuality. From this point forward she gives up her 'craving to be frightened' and gives into a wholehearted desire for Henry. Instead of forgetting the hero when he next goes to Woodston, his absence becomes 'the sad finale of every reflection', and his parsonage displaces the abbey as the most 'charming to her imagination' (207). Soon after, she gets to visit Henry's property, her mind 'full' of hope for their domestic future, and her only 'anxiety' concerning Henry's 'wishes' (208, 210). Later, when the General expels her from the abbey and sends her back home, Catherine pines for Henry, convinced that she 'could never forget Henry Tilney, or think of him with less tenderness' (227). Her normative wishes are soon satisfied. Henry learns that Catherine was outcast only for being 'less rich than [his father] had supposed', and instead of complying with his father's orders 'to think of her no more', he goes to Fullerton and proposes. Soon after they are married and 'begin perfect happiness' (234, 240).

But as is so often the case in Austen's novels, the tone here is ironic, pointing to the arti- ficiality of yet another literary convention. Even more ironic, the conventionally horrifying gothic marriage has proven surprisingly realistic. As is commonly noted, when Henry tells Catherine why the General expelled her, she realises 'she had scarcely sinned against his character, or magnified his cruelty' in suspecting him 'of either murdering or shutting up his wife' (236). An English*man* can be a brutal patriarch, regardless of what Henry says the 'laws connive at' (195). Though he may have never physically abused his wife, who knows exactly how the General's 'temper injured' her or hastened her early death (195). Henry, we are meant to believe, is temperamentally his father's opposite, but we know he has demonstrated au- thoritarian tendencies with Catherine. In addition, his own heterosexual inclinations remain dubious. In proposing, Henry is 'sustained in his purpose by a conviction of its justice. He felt himself bound as much in honour as in affection to Miss Morland, and believing that heart to be his own which he had been directed to gain, no unworthy retraction of a tacit consent ... could shake his fidelity'. His feeling of obligation is strong. His feeling of 'affection', mentioned only once, pales in comparison to his sense of honour, gallantry and possession—his belief that Catherine's heart is already 'his own' (237).

And what of Catherine? After she returns to Fullerton and before Henry appears and proposes, she takes a sad walk to the Allens,

> all her thinking powers swallowed up in the reflection of her own change of feelings and spirits since last she had trodden that well-known road. It was not three months ago since, wild with joyful expectation, she had there run backwards and forwards some three times a-day, with an heart light, gay, and independent; looking forward to pleasures untasted and unalloyed, and free from the apprehension of evil as from the knowledge of it. Three months ago had seen all this; and now, how altered a being did she return! (228)

This passage is remarkably biblical. Before her journey Catherine had enjoyed a kind of Edenic innocence. With certain 'pleasures' yet 'untasted', she was as 'free from the apprehension of evil as from the knowledge of it'. Now, like Adam and Eve after the fall, she has become an 'altered ... being'. Of course, Adam's, and especially Eve's, consumption of the forbidden fruit is sexually charged. No sooner do they eat than they are ashamed, covering their genitals. Earlier in the Bible there are two creation stories, one which suggests a certain gender parity ('So God created man in his *own* image ...; male and female created he them' [Genesis 1:27]), and the better known and more sexist version where Eve is created from Adam's rib. But it is only after their fall that the biological and social terms of sexual difference are unequivocally articulated and enforced. Both Adam and Eve will suffer pain in labour, but for woman, that labour will be childbirth and for man it will be toiling the fields. In addition, a wife will forever be her husband's inferior: 'he shall rule over thee' (Genesis 3:16). The fall is a fall into sexual difference and female subjection.

The same is effectively true for Catherine. Though she had begun to act womanly even before her journey, heteronormative oppression was still largely unknown to her. Having reached 'the age of seventeen, without having seen one amiable youth who could call forth her sensibility' (41), Catherine had not yet been inducted into heterosexuality. Her 'heart' was still 'light, gay, and independent' (228). Even during her travels, Catherine's gothic desires marked her continued independence. But all that is forsaken with Henry's reprimand. For her happy ending, Catherine will be ruled both by her didactic husband and by the physical consequences of heterosexuality—the pain (and if her mother is any indication, the constancy) of reproductive labour. Catherine was once 'wild' and gender fluid, happy to explore a range of desires. Now she is not. This may well be Austen's version of paradise lost.

Notes

1 I am indebted to Corey McEleney for his wisdom and bibliographical advice about queer theory. Other excellent overviews of the queering of Austen can be found in Fiona Brideoake, 'Sexuality' and Vincent Quinn, 'Jane Austen, Queer Theory and the Return of the Author'.

2 *Northanger Abbey* is categorised as Austen's first major novel because it was accepted for publication in 1803, but it was not actually published until 1818, after Austen died. Claire Grogan provides a good summary of the history and possible causes of the novel's delayed publication (8–17).

3 All identity categories, Judith Butler suggests, 'tend to be instruments of regulatory regimes', even when (like lesbian, gay man, or homosexual) they are 'rallying points for a liberatory contestation of [heterosexual] oppression' ('Imitation', 308).

4 Also see Lee Edelmen whose definition of queer includes anyone 'stigmatized for failing to comply with heteronormative mandates', and above all the mandate of heterosexual reproduction (17).

5 Sanchez continues: 'Because "queer" is a relational and contingent term, it can illuminate the ideological work not only of sexual norms but also of the racial, ethnic, national, economic and legal categories often assumed to have nothing to do with sex or gender' (7). Though I am sympathetic to such readings, I restrict my analysis to sexual and gender non-normativity.

6 For instance, Roger Rosenblatt suggested that Sedgwick's title was 'claptrap' in his largely favourable *New York Times* review of Kimball's book ('Universities Under Attack').

7 I am drawing on Johnson's reference to Wilson, but I quote different passages; see Johnson ('The Divine Miss Jane', 158 and n33).

8 I am drawing on Johnson's reference to Brontë, but I quote different passages; see Johnson ('The Divine Miss Jane', 149).

9 See Johnson ('The Divine Miss Jane', 158–59).

10 In his 1928 address to the Royal Society for Literature, H. W. Garrod complained about Austen's 'feminine triviality' and accused the 'only' men who liked her of suffering an exceptionally unromantic middle age (Garrod 36), or, as Johnson puts it, of having 'unmanned themselves' ('The Divine Miss Jane', 149–50). '[M]odern Austenian criticism', Johnson suggests, was motivated by the suspicion that Janeites were 'not masculine enough'. Thus, Austen critics like D. W. Harding (in his 1940 'Regulated Hatred') and F. R. Leavis (in his 1954 *The Great Tradition*) attack the Janeites as part of a broader mission to 'clear themselves from the charge of effeminacy by making Austen safe for real men engaged in real study' (155, 157).

11 'As Mudrick himself acknowledges, his interpretation of Emma's lesbianism is indebted to Edmund Wilson's' discussion of Emma (Johnson, 'The Divine Miss Jane' 159n35).

12 Earlier, at the 2018 ASECS Conference in Orlando, Florida, I made the same argument about Tom in my paper, 'Another Queering of *Mansfield Park*; or, "Rears and Vices" and Tom and Fanny'.

13 For a good summary of the critical history of this question and related questions, see Gonda and Mounsey.

14 For a summary of other scholarly discussions of eighteenth-century female homoeroticism, see my *Mothering Daughters* (62).

15 Brideoake's introduction to *The Ladies of Llangollen* offers a very helpful explanation about the value of describing their relationship as 'queer'.

16 Also see Binhammer.

17 My analysis in what follows is influenced by Johnson (*Equivocal* 2–12). Also see Binhammer and Lanser (216–17).

18 The profusion and enormous popularity of English gothic novels in the 1790s are also commonly attributed to the cultural terrors raised by the French Revolution.

'Queer Austen' and Northanger Abbey

19 Similarly, Michael O'Rourke and David Collings suggest that in 'queering normative codes and narratives', the eighteenth-century gothic novel opened 'up the space now occupied by ... queer theory, and the politics of living otherwise'.

20 Unlike Catherine, Isabella also likes to make binary declarations about male characters whom she commonly refers to as 'you men' followed by a flirtatiously insulting generalisation, as when she tells Captain Tilney, 'You men have none of you any hearts' (152; also see 78, 79, 106). Her brother, John, also extremely binary in his discussions about gender, makes a similar pronouncement about 'you women' (84).

21 Catherine also gazes at or looks for Henry on 57, 75, 108.

22 Both Eason and Wylie (142) comment on Henry's use of the term.

23 As one male *Monthly Review* critic grumbled in 1790, 'Ladies seem to appropriate to themselves an exclusive privilege in this kind of writing' (qtd. in Greenfield, *Mothering Daughters*, 17).

24 In addition, see my chapter, 'Gothic Mothers and Homoerotic Desire', in *Mothering Daughters*, from which much of this paragraph is drawn.

25 On the other hand, it is possible that Catherine never finishes Radcliffe's novel and is thus unaware of this detail.

26 William Galperin argues that '[t]here are many examples of same-sex desire in *Northanger Abbey*' and that Catherine's 'attachment to Eleanor Tilney', not Henry 'is the motivating factor in her attachment to the Tilney family' (145–46).

Works Cited

Anderson, Misty G. '"The Different Sorts of Friendship": Desire in *Mansfield Park*.' *Jane Austen and Discourses of Feminism*, edited by Devoney Looser. St. Martins, 1995, 167–183.

Austen, Jane. *Mansfield Park*, edited by Claudia L. Johnson. Norton, 1998.

Austen, Jane. *Northanger Abbey*, edited by Claire Grogan. Broadview, 2004.

Berlant, Lauren, and Michael Warner. 'Sex in Public.' *Critical Inquiry*, vol. 24, 1998, pp. 547–566.

Binhammer, Katherine. 'The Sex Panic of the 1790s.' *Journal of the History of Sexuality*, vol. 6, 1996, pp. 409–434.

Brideoake, Fiona. 'Sexuality.' *A Companion to Jane Austen*, edited by Claudia L. Johnson and Clara Tuite. Wiley-Blackwell, 2009, 456–466.

Brideoake, Fiona. *The Ladies of Llangollen: Desire, Indeterminacy, and the Legacies of Criticism*. Bucknell UP, 2017.

Brontë, Charlotte. 'Extract from letter, 12 April 1850, to W.S. Williams.' *Jane Austen: The Critical Heritage*, 2 vols., edited by Brian Southam. Routledge, 1968, 1, 127–128.

Burke, Edmund. *Reflections on the Revolution in France*, edited by Conor Cruise O'Brien. Penguin, 1986.

Butler, Judith. *Gender Trouble: Feminism and the Subversion of Identity*. Routledge, 1990.

Butler, Judith. 'Imitation and Gender Insubordination.' *The Lesbian and Gay Studies Reader*, edited by Henry Abelove, Michèle Aina Barale, and David M. Halperin. Routledge, 1993, pp. 307–320.

Castle, Terry. 'Letters.' *London Review of Books*, 24 Aug. 1995, https://www.lrb.co.uk/v17/n15/terry-castle/sister-sister. Accessed 13 Nov. 2019.

Castle, Terry. 'Sister-Sister.' *London Review of Books*, 3 Aug. 1995, https://www.lrb.co.uk/v17/n15/terry-castle/sister-sister. Accessed 13 Nov. 2019.

Clery, E. J. 'Gender.' *The Cambridge Companion to Jane Austen*, edited by Edward Copeland and Juliet McMaster. Cambridge UP, 2010, pp. 159–175.

Cocks, H. G. 'Secrets, Crimes and Diseases, 1800-1914.' *A Gay History of Britain: Love and Sex Between Men Since the Middle Ages*, edited by Matt Cook. Greenwood, 2007, pp. 107–144.

De Lauretis, Teresa. 'Queer Theory: Lesbian and Gay Sexualities, an Introduction.' *Differences*, vol. 3, 1991, pp. iii–xviii.

Eason, Sarah. 'Henry Tilney: Queer Hero of *Northanger Abbey*.' *Persuasions On-Line*, vol. 34, 2013, http://jasna.org/persuasions/on-line/vol34no1/eason.html? Accessed 7 Sep. 2019.

Edelman, Lee. *No Future: Queer Theory and the Death Drive*. Duke UP, 2004.

Fitzgerald, Lauren. 'The Sexuality of Authorship in *The Monk*.' 'Queer Romanticism.' *Romanticism on the Net*, edited by Michael O'Rourke and David Collings, 27 Jul. 2005, https://www.erudit.org/en/journals/ron/2004-n36-37-ron947/011138ar/. Accessed 5 Sep. 2019.

Foucault, Michele, *The History of Sexuality, Volume I: An Introduction*. Translated by Robert Hurley. Vintage, 1980.

Galperin, William H. *The Historical Austen*. U of Pennsylvania P, 2003.

Garrod, H. W. 'Jane Austen: A Depreciation.' *Discussions of Jane Austen*, edited by William Heath. D.C. Heath and Co., 1961, pp. 32–40.

Genesis. *King James Bible Online*, https://www.kingjamesbibleonline.org/Genesis-Chapter-1/. Accessed 24 Jan. 2020.

Gilbert, Sandra M., and Susan Gubar. *The Madwoman in the Attic: The Woman Writer and the Nineteenth-Century Literary Imagination*. Yale UP, 1984.

Greenfield, Susan C. 'Another Queering of *Mansfield Park*; or, Incest and Sodomy and Fanny and Tom,' *The 49th Meeting of the American Society for Eighteenth-Century Studies*. 24 March 2018, Orlando, FL, Conference Presentation.

Greenfield, Susan C. *Mothering Daughters: Novels and the Politics of Family Romance, Frances Burney to Jane Austen*. Wayne State UP, 2002.

Greenfield, Susan C. 'Veiled Desire: Mother-Daughter Love and Sexual Imagery in Ann Radcliffe's *The Italian*.' *The Eighteenth Century: Theory and Interpretation*, vol. 33, 1992, pp. 73–89.

Gonda, Caroline, and Chris Mounsey. 'Queer People: An Introduction.' *Queer People: Negotiations and Expressions of Homosexuality, 1700-1800*, edited by Chris Mounsey and Caroline Gonda. Bucknell UP, 2007, pp. 9–37.

Grogan, Claire. Introduction. *Northanger Abbey*, by Jane Austen, 1818, edited by Claire Grogan. Broadview, 2004, pp. 1–24.

Haggerty, George E. 'Fanny Price: "Is She Solemn?—Is She Queer?—Is She Prudish?".' *The Eighteenth Century: Theory and Interpretation*, vol. 53, 2012, pp. 175–188.

Haggerty, George E. 'The Horrors of Catholicism: Religion and Sexuality in Gothic Fiction.' 'Queer Romanticism.' *Romanticism on the Net*, edited by Michael O'Rourke and David Collings, 27 Jul. 2005, https://www.erudit.org/en/journals/ron/2004-n36-37-ron947/011133ar/. Accessed 5 Sep. 2019.

Halperin, David M. *Saint Foucault: Towards a Gay Hagiography*. Oxford UP, 1995.

Johnson, Claudia L. 'The Divine Miss Jane: Jane Austen, Janeites, and the Discipline of Novel Studies.' *Boundary*, vol. 2, no. 23, 1996, pp. 143–163.

Johnson, Claudia L., *Equivocal Beings: Politics, Gender, and Sentimentality in the 1790s: Wollstonecraft, Radcliffe, Burney, Austen*. U of Chicago P, 1995.

Johnson, Claudia L. 'Letters.' *London Review of Books*, 5 Oct. 1995, https://www.lrb.co.uk/v17/n15/terry-castle/sister-sister. Accessed 13 Nov. 2019.

Kimball, Roger. *Tenured Radicals: How Politics Has Corrupted Our Higher Education*. Ivan R. Dee, 2008.

Korba, Susan M. '"Improper and Dangerous Distinctions": Female Relationships and Erotic Domination in *Emma*.' *Studies in the Novel*, vol. 29, 1997, pp. 139–163.

Lanser, Susan S. *The Sexuality of History: Modernity and the Sapphic, 1565–1830*. U of Chicago P, 2014.

Miller, D. A. *Jane Austen, or the Secret of Style*. Princeton UP, 2003.

Moore, Lisa L. *Dangerous Intimacies: Toward a Sapphic History of the British Novel*. Duke UP, 1997.

Mudrick, Marvin. *Jane Austen: Irony as Defense and Discovery*. Princeton UP, 1952.

O'Rourke, Michael, and David Collings. 'Introduction: Queer Romanticisms: Past, Present, and Future.' 'Queer Romanticisms: Past, Present, and Future.' edited by O'Rourke and Collings, *Romanticism on the Net*, 27 Jul. 2005, https://www.erudit.org/en/journals/ron/2004-n36-37-ron947/. Accessed 5 Sep. 2019.

Perry, Ruth. 'Interrupted Friendships in Jane Austen's *Emma*.' *Tulsa Studies in Women's Literature*, vol. 5, 1986, pp. 185–202.

Pollak, Ellen. *Incest and the English Novel, 1684–1814*. Johns Hopkins UP, 2003.

Quinn, Vincent. 'Jane Austen, Queer Theory and the Return of the Author.' *Women: A Cultural Review*, vol. 18, 2007, pp. 57–83.

Radcliffe, Ann. *The Italian*, edited by Frederick Garber. Oxford UP, 1981.

Radcliffe, Ann. *The Mysteries of Udolpho*, edited by Bonamy Dobrée. Oxford UP, 2008.

Rosenblatt, Roger. 'The Universities Under Attack.' *New York Times*, 22 Apr. 1990. https://www.nytimes.com/1990/04/22/books/the-universities-under-attack.html. Accessed 13 Nov. 2019.

Sanchez, Melissa E. *Shakespeare and Queer Theory*. Arden, 2019.

Sedgwick, Eve Kosofsky. 'Jane Austen and the Masturbating Girl.' *Critical Inquiry*, vol. 17, 1991, pp. 818–837.

Sedgwick, Eve Kosofsky. 'Queer and Now.' *Tendencies*. Routledge, 1994.

Sedgwick, Eve Kosofsky. *The Coherence of Gothic Conventions*. Methuen, 1980.

Southam, Brian, edited by *Jane Austen: The Critical Heritage, Volume 2, 1870–1940*. Routledge, 1987.

Spampinato, Erin A. 'Tom Became What He Ought to Be: *Mansfield Park* as Homosocial Bildungsroman.' *Studies in the Novel*, vol. 51, 2019, pp. 481–498.

'Stanford University News Release.' 16 Aug. 1995, https://news.stanford.edu/pr/95/950816Arc5119.html. Accessed 13 Nov. 2019.

Trumbach, Randolph. 'Modern Sodomy: The Origins of Homosexuality, 1700-1800.' *A Gay History of Britain: Love and Sex between Men since the Middle Ages*, edited by Matt Cook. Greenwood, 2007, pp. 77–105.

Tuite, Clara. *Romantic Austen: Sexual Politics and the Literary Canon*. Cambridge UP, 2002.

Wilson, Edmund. *Classics and Commercials: A Literary Chronicle of the Forties*. Farrar, Straus, 1950.

Wollstonencraft, Mary. *A Vindication of the Rights of Woman*, edited by Deidre Shauna Lynch. Norton, 2009.

Wylie, Judith. '"Do You Understand Muslins, Sir?": Fashioning Gender in *Northanger Abbey*.' *Styling Texts: Dress and Fashion in Literature*, edited by Cynthia Kuhn and Cindy Carlson. Cambria, 2007, pp. 129–148.

27

'A PERFECTLY SWELL ROMANCE'[1]: JANE AUSTEN AND FRED ASTAIRE: A CASE STUDY IN ANALOGY CRITICISM

Paula Marantz Cohen

DREXEL UNIVERSITY

In the 1970s and 1980s, many literary critics began to move away from the no-longer-new New Criticism and embrace a methodology known as Reader-Response Criticism. Reader-Response consciously incorporated the subjectivity of the reader into the interpretive process, calling into question the sacred integrity of the text. This approach led in a number of directions. One path led to Translation Studies, which, in an increasingly global literary context, has become a field of particular interest and innovation. Attention has now definitively shifted from the idea of a transparent original text that can be faithfully rendered into another language to the understanding that the translator and the language of the target culture are both important variables in the making of a translation. Another byproduct of Reader-Response Criticism was Adaptation Studies that looked at ways in which works were expressed in another medium. At first, this involved a unidirectional focus on the way literary works were adapted for the screen. But as cinema and digital media became more dominant and pervasive, the relationship of literature—most often, the novel—to film grew more theoretically complex, raising issues that doubled back to affect readers and viewers in a variety of ways. 'To be second is not to be secondary or inferior', Linda Hutcheon, one of the early theorists in Adaptation Studies, argued; 'likewise, to be first is not to be originary or authoritative' (xv). It has now become commonplace to give the adaptation equal status with the work that inspired it.

This idea has special relevance with regard to Jane Austen. Her name has become, as an editor I know put it, 'a best-selling brand',[2] her work known throughout world culture in a variety of media formats. New adaptations of her novels can sometimes seem to refer as much to earlier film and television adaptations as they do to the original novels. Likewise, readers of Austen nowadays often feel indebted to adaptations for initiating them into her work. Hutcheon again put it well: 'we may actually read or see that so-called original *after* we have experienced the adaptation, thereby challenging the authority of any notion of priority. Multiple versions exist laterally, not vertically' (xv). This is a truism more than ever in a mediascape where work is constantly being fed to us without respect to chronology or canonical status.

These observations prompt me to think about Austen with respect to a new kind of offshoot of Reader-Response Criticism—one that considers the relationship between and among works as

358   DOI: 10.4324/9780429398155-27-31

they operate within postmodern culture. This critical approach, which I will call *Analogy Criticism*, seeks to explain how two works with a less-than-obvious connection to each other exist in an analogous relationship that adds interest and resonance to both. This can be understood as a variation on what Lars Ellestrom, in referring to a more radical approach to adaptation, calls *transmediation*: '"picking out" elements from a medium and using them in a new way in another medium' (511). Taking Ellestrom's concept further, Analogy Criticism involves a 'picking out' by the critic (rather than the creator)—examining two seemingly *unlike* works and establishing a convincing connection between them.

In my effort at critical (rather than production-oriented) *transmediation*, my focus will be on Jane Austen and Fred Astaire. I will 'pick out' elements from both that echo each other in significant ways. This is not an arbitrary comparison but it *is* an emotional one at its origin. The spur comes from my intuition that there are important analogies to be drawn between these two artists' work and from the similar way they affect me as a reader and viewer. In establishing an analogy between Austen and Astaire, I have chosen to focus on Austen's six completed novels and the 10 films Astaire made with Ginger Rogers, nine for RKO between 1933 and 1939, and one final film, *The Barkleys of Broadway*, made for MGM in 1949. Despite the excellent work that Astaire would go on to do later, these 11 films constitute, in my opinion, an exceptionally coherent and cohesive oeuvre that presents an illuminating parallel to Austen's mature body of work.

Let me begin by clarifying Astaire's role in this discussion. The dancer/choreographer Hermes Pan (a great friend and look-alike of Astaire) is credited with choreographing most of the Astaire-Rogers films; four of these films were produced by Pandro Berman, and five were directed by Mark Sandrich. Creative responsibility was divided; film, unlike literature, is a communal medium. Nonetheless, it is well known that Astaire was the animating spirit behind these films. He was involved in all aspects of production, particularly the dance numbers that constitute their heart and soul, and was given final artistic control. As a result, he can be understood as these films' *auteur*, the term coined by the *Cahier du Cinema* critics to equate a filmmaker with the kind of guiding vision associated with the author of a literary work. It is now commonplace to see Astaire as worthy of inhabiting the cinematic pantheon alongside Alfred Hitchcock, John Ford, Orson Welles, and Howard Hawkes, figures who are considered on a par with our greatest canonical authors.

Astaire's *auteur*ist role is further supplemented by his positioning as a performer and star. If Austen created her heroines as imaginative extensions of herself, Astaire created his heroes by physically embodying them on screen. He honed a persona that was uniquely his own and helped to shape the films in which that persona was showcased. John Mueller, who has spent a lifetime studying Astaire's work, has called him 'one of the master artists of the century' (3), and Arlene Croce, the venerable dance critic, asserted that his 'dancing [with Rogers] was transformed into a vehicle of serious emotion between a man and a woman' (8). While Astaire's talent was recognised during his lifetime, his stature—not just as a dancer, but as a singer, musician, and brilliantly honed performer—has taken on mythic proportions since his death. His musicals, particularly those done with Rogers, are now seen as singular vehicles for the showcasing of his genius. Writes Croce: 'It never happened in movies again' (8). In short, the placement of Astaire alongside Austen, whose reputation has also increased with time, need not be viewed as an unequal or incongruous pairing. It is interesting, moreover, that while Austen's reputation has grown with a popular audience as her novels have been adapted to television and film, Astaire has supplemented his initial popular appeal with increasing critical acclaim.

In dealing with works separated in time by over a century, it is worth beginning by considering influence. Influence is not a necessary factor in Analogy Criticism—indeed, the point is to compare works that seem ostensibly unrelated—but influence can be oblique and cultural rather than direct and personal, and, acknowledging this, can bring to the fore important correspondences.

There is no indication that Fred Astaire was influenced by Jane Austen. He did not finish high school and was not a reader. And yet one can argue for influence of a generalised kind: Austen's work is fundamental to the so-called 'romance genre' through her development of the courtship plot. This plot involves the circuitous route by which a heroine finds her way to a hero by first taking a detour to the wrong suitor—or, at least, to a wrong view of the right one. Austen essentially invented this 'two-suitor convention' that has since become the tried and true structure of romantic comedy in both literature and film (Kennard). Perhaps even more than this structure—or at least contributing to it—is the way in which the hero and heroine move back and forth between attraction and resistance, eventually coming to agreement as a unified couple in the end.

Astaire-Rogers films, as Arlene Croce has noted, 'were romances' (7) and, as such, relied on the courtship plot. There is always a preliminary meeting of the heroine with the hero, followed by a misunderstanding and detour, often involving a secondary male character (or a male character to whom the heroine is initially linked), before the fated couple come together in a happy union. In the course of the narrative there is invariably the kind of back-and-forth of attraction and resistance that characterises this sort of romantic plot.

But if we can speak of a generalised influence of Austen on Astaire, we can also argue for a doubling back of influence. The pioneering dance numbers in Astaire-Rogers musicals must be said to exist behind the adaptations of Austen's novels into films. This is because dance figures significantly in the novels, as I shall discuss, and because dance is a visual and dynamic element well suited to cinematic representation. In dealing with two film adaptations of *Emma*, for example, Nora Foster Stovel has noted that the films take advantage of movement and music: 'Both film adaptations conclude the ball with a stately, but sensual, dance as the pair move gracefully together, suggesting their mutual attraction and physical compatibility' (7). Behind this description of two complementary figures in motion, one can see Astaire's pioneering work in crafting dance numbers that relay a narrative of the couple.

Central to the analogy I wish to draw concerns the way in which the back-and-forth of the courtship plot and the complementarity of dance function for these two artists. Both repartee and dance exist in both and, in some sense, are metaphors for each other, serving to move the narratives forward. However, the use and balance of these elements differ in ways that help us better appreciate both their respective medium and their positioning in time and place.

Deirdre Le Faye notes that there are dance scenes in all of Jane Austen novels because, in the period in which they were set, dances and balls were the best place to meet a future spouse. Austen herself puts this succinctly toward the beginning of *Pride and Prejudice*: 'To be fond of dancing was a certain step towards falling in love' (11). The most direct connection between dance and the larger courtship plot occurs in the conversation in Austen's earliest completed novel, *Northanger Abbey*, when Henry Tilney comments to Catherine Morland at the Bath ball:

> I consider a country-dance as an emblem of marriage. Fidelity and complaisance are the principal duties of both; and those men who do not choose to dance or marry themselves, have no business with the partners or wives of their neighbours. (74)

If dance is used as a metaphor for marriage in this novel, it also serves as a structural element in advancing the plot. 'Tilney's witty comparison of the country dance to marriage expresses the notion of dancing as being a form of trial marriage' (115), writes Jacqueline Reid-Walsh. This is also true, in a less felicitous sense, in *Sense and Sensibility*, where the fact that Marianne and Willoughby dance every dance without attention to others tells us something about problems in their character that will affect their relationship. In *Emma*, when Knightley graciously asks Harriet to dance at the Crown Inn Ball after she is snubbed by Mr Elton, Emma becomes aware of his exceptional qualities (and grows jealous). In *Mansfield Park*, Fanny's desire to dance with Edmund and not with Henry

Crawford at the Mansfield Ball forecasts her refusal of Henry's marriage proposal—a refusal that leads ultimately to her union with Edmund. Finally, in *Persuasion*, Anne Elliot's position at the piano while the others dance highlights her alienation and loneliness and makes the eventual happy ending seem all the more felicitous and hard-won.

But the most important example of dance as a structural component of narrative development occurs in *Pride and Prejudice*. We see Darcy first spurn the idea of dancing with Elizabeth at the Meryton Ball ('I am in no humour at present to give consequence to young ladies who are slighted by other men' [13]), thereby gaining her attention and scorn. He then disparages dance ('Every savage can dance' [26]). Finally, he dances with her at the Netherfield Ball where she gives him lessons on appropriate conversation ('It is *your* turn to say something now, Mr Darcy—I talked about the dance, and *you* ought to make some kind of remark on the size of the room, or the number of couples' [90]). The evolution is central to the evolution of Darcy from a self-centred snob to a more humble and generous personality, worthy of Elizabeth's love.

What must be observed here is not only the content but the form of these encounters. In *Northanger Abbey*, the conversation holds, on both counts, to a clear, hierarchical structure. Henry directs Catherine in a satirical manner, establishing himself as her affectionately indulgent superior. This will change with *Pride and Prejudice* when Elizabeth will assume the satirical tone with Darcy and school him in proper conversation on the dance floor.

In Astaire-Rogers movies, lively, satirical repartee is invariably a hallmark of their relationship, but dance, rather than talk, is central in a way it is not in Austen. The music to which they dance is a kind of addendum to their bodies in motion and serves in lieu of conversation—though in some cases, they sing to each other before they launch into dancing together. If in Austen, the characters always know how to talk eloquently, in Astaire-Rogers films, the principals know how to dance superbly[3]—they often play professional dancers, and the musicals are, by definition, built around the extraordinary physical skill of their stars. Yet though the dance numbers are spectacular (and have frequently been shown out of context as part of dance montages), they are also narratives of relationship. The dance serves not only as a metaphor for the progress of the couple but also as a catalyst for the relationship and a means of representing its progress in a sustained and direct way.

A wonderful example of the narrative of dance in Astaire's films occurs early in the 1935 *Roberta*, where Astaire and Rogers, sitting on the steps to the side of a band rehearsal, start by reminiscing about their past together in Indiana. The give-and-take involves a good number of taunts and jabs before segueing into their seemingly extemporaneous dancing to the tune of 'I'll be Hard to Handle'. The number involves escalating competitive steps, culminating in an exuberant pairing of the two figures in which they move off the small dance floor and collapse side-by-side where they began—to the applause of the band members who have supplied the musical accompaniment. The same sort of progress occurs again in that film (a wonderful counterpoint to the scene in which Elizabeth schools Darcy on the dancing floor) that begins with Astaire playing the piano (with both marvellous bodily and facial expression), then having Rogers sing to him and he respond: 'I Won't Dance'—but later in the film succumbing to her enticements and engaging in a perfect partnership on the dance floor. In *Top Hat*, there is a similar segue when Astaire sings to Rogers, 'Isn't This a Lovely Day?' in the midst of a rainstorm; he begins to move his body to the music; she joins him; and the lyrics give way to their spirited dancing.

In all of their films, Rogers varies in the degree of her self-assertion but, overall, she is more like Elizabeth Bennet in her 'genial resistance' (Croce 11) than like Catherine Morland or Marianne Dashwood, who are in thrall to their male partners from the beginning. Like Elizabeth, Rogers exudes an authority and self-possession that she never abandons. In *The Gay Divorcee*, she has to be seduced into the dance number 'Night and Day'. In *Top Hat*, the progression is equally pronounced: 'Cheek to Cheek' begins with Rogers reluctant to dance and ends with her willing participation. The number is noteworthy for the dress she wears that sheds its feathers as she moves as though shedding her opposition to Astaire as a partner. The plot backtracks afterward, with a misunderstanding that needs to be resolved before the two can finally come together in the joyful 'Piccolino' number.

Certain elements in the 'staging' of the couple—in conversation and on the dance floor—are also analogous in the work of both artists. Austen pioneered a certain kind of witty banter between her protagonists that has become the norm in good *rom-com* repartee. This represents a divergence from her predecessor, Samuel Richardson, who launched the genre of the domestic novel but created earnest, melodramatic plots, written in cumbersome epistolary form. Austen's plots are compact and direct, and her dialogue is sprightly. Where Richardson concentrated on the minutiae of familial and sexual oppression, Austen produced a soufflé of wit, manners, sense, and sensibility.

Astaire similarly deviated from his predecessor, Busby Berkeley, in his development of the movie musical. Berkeley's films for Warner Bros in the early 1930s featured kaleidoscopically arranged male and female bodies, the musical numbers inserted as staged performances inside the film, even as these numbers were highly contrived and could never have been presented live in a theatre. Astaire broke with this style in making the dance numbers emerge organically out of the flow of the plot. He also pioneered whole-body filming, the camera following the dancers' figures in a single, fluent take. This is in counterpoint not only to Berkeley's dance numbers but to many later numbers on film that rely on extensive camera-angle cutting to add excitement and cover the limited abilities of the dancers. Astaire's filming is not about showcasing spectacle or about highlighting individual athleticism (as with Gene Kelly) but about developing character and relationship. The films are, as Croce put it, 'chapters in a single epic romance' (7–8)—the dance numbers linked to narrative development and honest with regard to what is actually happening with the couple as they move rhythmically together. It helps, of course, that Astaire and Rogers are such expert dancers that nothing needs to be edited or covered up.

What Austen and Astaire share is an orchestrated quality to depicting the relationship of the couple that is at once mannered and natural. As Darrell Mansell observes, Austen's novels 'present the relationship between the sexes in a graceful, restrained and highly stylized form' (8). He goes on to describe how the romantic relationship parallels that of the country dance: 'The destined couples thread their way through an intricate design, to be united at the close' (8–9). Nora Foster Stovel takes this idea further in considering the pattern of back and forth between Darcy and Elizabeth in *Pride and Prejudice*: 'each time Darcy takes a step toward Elizabeth, she takes two steps back—the pattern of the mating dance imitated in the tempestuous tango' (193) The line evokes Fred and Ginger's back-and-forth dancing to 'Night and Day' in *The Gay Divorcee*. David Denby sums up the narrative element in this number when he describes Astaire leading Rogers, 'who has been resisting him, into a long dance of seduction, with heart-stopping episodes of aggression, temporary acquiescence, fierce pleading, and, finally, submission, all of it dramatized with dance *as* dance'. Many numbers are plotted in this way, with Astaire and Rogers engaging in a push and pull that leads eventually to the harmonious pairing of their bodies in movement. Their dancing demonstrates, in the most literal way possible, that they are compatible and worthy of each other, while the silly plots are excuses for allowing the dances to happen. This is the inverse of what occurs in Austen, where the dances and formal balls are excuses that allow the principals to be thrown together so that they can later become better acquainted through visits and talk.[4]

A further analogical connection between Austen's novels and Astaire's musicals can be found in the combined rigour and ease that characterises their work. Both were concerned with revision: Austen, reworking her juvenilia and early drafts into more mature, polished form; Astaire tirelessly rehearsing routines: 'Fred always worked seven days a week. He'd never stop' (Franceschina 52). The result, for both, seems effortless. There is a freshness and unpretentiousness to Austen's dialogue that explains why she finds avid first readers from as young as middle school and devoted re-readers into old age. Likewise, Astaire's seemingly effortless grace has made every woman imagine that she would be able to dance with him (the contrast is often made with Gene Kelly, who looks like he would be hard to dance with). Both artists are, by extension, triumphs of style:

Astaire, not only in his dancing but in his speech, singing, and dress; Austen, in the delightful fluency and wit of her writing that includes dialogue easily adaptable to film and television and characters who attract 'stylish' movie stars like Colin Firth, Gwyneth Paltrow, and Keira Knightley to play them.

It is, in part, owing to this stylish ease that both Austen and Astaire were denigrated or dismissed by readers/viewers at some point in history. Austen's novels were seen as frivolous by Mark Twain, Ralph Waldo Emerson, Charlotte Brontë, and George Eliot, among others. Astaire was famously dismissed after his first screen test with: 'Can't act. Slightly bald. Dances a little' (Thomas 78). None of his great RKO films were ever nominated for a Best Picture Academy Award. And, of course, the movie musical of the 1930s was long seen as a frivolous form of cultural expression and Depression-era uplift, branding Astaire as a mere entertainer rather than an artist. Yet he was eventually championed by professionals in his field (both Nureyev and Balanchine called him the greatest and most influential dancer of the twentieth century; Irving Berlin and Jerome Kern claimed that no one put over his songs better than Astaire [Cohen, 'Thoughts' 129, 138]). Austen similarly found a champion in Lionel Trilling, arguably the most important American critic of the twentieth century, who helped put her in the college curriculum and initiated a generation of serious scholars into her work.

Part of the reason why both Austen and Astaire were dismissed at earlier points in time is owing to the seemingly narrow worlds in which their work is set. Austen embraced the circumscribed domestic viewpoint of 'three or four families in a country village' (*Letters*, Brabourne Edition LXXXVII); Astaire's films appear similarly limited in scope and seriousness to an affluent, Art Deco world. John Mueller notes, 'The variety in Astaire's dances is particularly remarkable because he was working within considerable constraints, some of them self-imposed' (19). Yet in both cases, the constraints, which seem disconnected from a larger social context, also reference that context obliquely in ways that critics would eventually discern and appreciate. Austen was writing during the Regency period, a time of particularly dramatic social change in the wake of the Napoleonic Wars. Astaire was creating his musicals in the context of the Great Depression when movies had only recently acquired sound and had become a major source of entertainment for a mass public seeking escape from the hardships of daily life. The confined nature of the settings allowed for social critique by making small deviations from convention assume drama and importance. Austen's novels espouse what can be interpreted as a quietly disruptive relationship to societal norms. In the opening of *Pride and Prejudice*, we learn that the Bennet sisters must be uprooted if their father dies and the estate falls to the nearest male heir—an injustice that is given expression, albeit in the voice of the silly Mrs Bennet: 'I do think it is the hardest thing in the world, that your estate should be entailed away from your own children; and I am sure, if I had been you, I should have tried long ago to do something or other about it' (42).

David Daiches observes how well Austen critiques the mercenary tendencies of her society. In noting Willoughby's snub of Marianne in *Sense and Sensibility* when he realises the need to marry for money, Daiches writes, 'How ruthless is the clarity with which Jane Austen observes and records the economic realities underlying this graceful social dance!' (291). In *Pride and Prejudice*, Elizabeth's aunt and uncle 'in trade' are shown to have innate good sense and good manners, superior in this respect to Darcy's high-born aunt, Lady de Bourgh. Astaire's musicals, often set in transparently contrived foreign locales—a mock-Venice and London in *Top Hat,* for example—bring into relief the unpretentious way in which Fred and Ginger relate to each other. Both are often presented as Americans abroad and sometimes as pretend-Europeans who are eventually unmasked as their down-to-earth selves: Astaire pretends to be a Russian ballet dancer when he is actually an American song-and-dance man in *Shall We Dance*; Ginger pretends to be a Polish countess living in Paris in *Roberta* but is soon recognised by Fred who knew her in their native Indiana. The names of the characters in their films speak to their down-to-earth American identity: Huck and Lizzie, Guy and Mimi, Jerry and Dale, John and Penny, etc.

In keeping with this genial social critique, Austen and Astaire both make pretension and snobbism a focus of satire. There is the famous scene in *Pride and Prejudice* when Elizabeth visits her sister, taken ill at Netherfield, and arrives with a muddy skirt, having walked in the rain to get there. The snooty Bingley sisters are appalled, but their brother is touched by this sign of sisterly affection, and Darcy is attracted by Elizabeth's 'bright eyes'. For Astaire, a similar moment occurs at the beginning of *Top Hat*, when he explodes the sobriety of a British men's club with an exuberant tap dance. He embarrasses his friend, played by Edward Everett Horton, but we viewers (like Darcy) are meant to find his energy and irreverence delightful.

Astaire and Rogers' characters are frequently high-profile performers, contrasting the disdain with which performance is held in *Mansfield Park* (the one Austen novel that addresses this), but it also makes the analogical aspect of my comparison more pointed. When one considers the historical and social context of the novels versus the musicals, one sees that the marker of social importance has shifted dramatically as we move from late eighteenth- and early nineteenth-century England to 1930s America. In Austen, land ownership remains a major source of income and importance; in Astaire's world, celebrity has become a new form of status as a result of the widespread influence of movies. Astaire's talent seems 'both God-given and perfectible, rather than carried by hereditary bloodlines' (Boyer 7). The star has become the new aristocrat. This point was brought home to the world in the famous friendship that developed in the early 1920s between Lord and Lady Mountbatten, the cream of the British aristocracy, and Douglas Fairbanks and Mary Pickford, the first great American movie stars.[5] This was the period in which Astaire and his sister Adele, having performed on the London stage after their Broadway success in the teens, became friendly with the Prince of Wales in the 1920s. Indeed, Astaire went on to movies in the '30s because Adele left the theatre to marry an English aristocrat. In Austen's time, a stage performer and a nobleman would only have been linked in an illicit pairing.

In keeping with this evolution in cultural norms, gender roles that are gently tweaked in Austen's novels become more fluid in Astaire's musicals. Elizabeth Kendall notes that the sarcastic quips traded between Fred and Ginger reveal 'a trusting, needy, yet fiercely independent Rogers encountering a curiously shifty Astaire ... . lightweight, ingratiating, a little goofy, a little nasty—except when he danced. That's when he showed his "other" nature: the passionate lover' (98). I should add that Astaire's slight, dandyish appearance and mannerisms are often contrasted with the more strenuous and 'manly' Gene Kelly, while Rogers in her often extravagant costumes and often emphatic voice and gestures (making her a favourite among drag impersonators) have served the astute viewer as an oblique critique of conventional gender roles. Indeed, this is a new kind of complementarity, not entirely disconnected from the one that Austen relied on, but different in the range of characteristics allowed to the male and female protagonists.

Finally, there is a moral element central to both artists' work, though it is expressed with a different valence in keeping with their time period and the medium. The heroines in Austen's novels are invariably moral centres. We follow their progress knowing that eventually they will do the right thing and have a moral influence on those around them. Even in *Emma*, where the heroine strays from the right path, she eventually comes to comprehend her failings and improve her judgement. Moral seriousness may at first seem at odds with the silliness of the Astaire-Rogers musicals, yet a certain kind of soundness and good nature infuses these works. Despite the hubbub of the theatre world that surrounds the Fred and Ginger couple, they are represented as pure souls, sprung unsullied out of this dubious environment. There is something of the American sense of 'beginning the world again' that permeates the musicals—Astaire and Rogers are morally as well as romantically elevated in the act of dancing together. The films extol an idea of the couple as complements in character as well as physical compatibility.

If we are inclined to give short-shrift to the moral element in Astaire's films, we tend to do the same for the spontaneous, instinctive element in Austen's. Yet when the novels are read in the context of the Astaire musicals in which this element is paramount, we can see it more clearly, particularly in *Pride and Prejudice*, where Darcy and Elizabeth are not just moral complements (cancelling each other's respective flaws) but improvisational partners who seem to increasingly enjoy the spirited give-and-take associated with their encounters. Toward the end of the novel, Elizabeth notes that it was her 'impertinence' (359) that first attracted Darcy. There is no doubt that she can speak frankly to him without being intimidated, and he can accept this. Rogers interacts similarly with Astaire. For both, the woman provokes and charms the man. The famous quip about Astaire and Rogers, attributed to Katharine Hepburn—'He gives her class and she gives him sex'—could be attributed as well to Darcy and Elizabeth.

Arlene Croce has noted that Astaire's RKO films with Rogers can be read as a single romantic plot. The same can be said for Austen's six novels. In both cases, the works operate within the same kinds of constraints while finding ways to produce new variations with each rendering. In considering this idea of a whole, one can look at the trajectory of both the novels and the films and see a progression that reflects both a development in the authority of their creators and, by extension, of the liveliness and force of the characters they create.

For this purpose, *Northanger Abbey* compares well to Astaire-Rogers' first film, *Flying Down to Rio*. Both launch a vision of the couple that will be further elaborated in later work. *Northanger Abbey* uses the spoof of gothic romance as a narrative crutch on which to hang a novel of manners. This kind of structural aid will later be jettisoned as the shifting relationship of the couple carries the full weight of action and suspense. Similarly, in their early film, *Flying Down to Rio*, the relationship of Astaire and Rogers occupies a secondary position in support of the more conventional, less interesting couple, played by Gene Raymond and Dolores del Rio. In their subsequent musicals, this kind of subordination will be abandoned and the Astaire-Rogers interactions will take centre stage. I should also note that in *Roberta* and *Follow the Fleet*, Astaire and Rogers are part of a dual-couple plot, not unlike that in *Sense and Sensibility* and *Pride and Prejudice*. In these films and novels, the two couples complement each other much the same way that the male and female characters complement each other within the romantic relationship. Both artists have two works that represent the high point of their achievement: for Austen, *Pride and Prejudice* and *Emma*; for Astaire, *Top Hat* and *Swing Time*. All four of these works are 'light and bright and sparkling' ('Letters in Austen-Leigh's *Memoir*' ix)—exceptionally well-paced and full of joy. They have become enduring favourites with readers and viewers.

I want to end by considering works that, for both, serve as a coda rather than a high point: *Persuasion*, Austen's last, posthumously published novel, and *The Barkleys of Broadway*, Astaire and Rogers' last film together, made at MGM in 1949, ten years after their final RKO film. *Persuasion* has the bittersweet tone of a union that might not have been—a fortuitous and unlikely second chance for the heroine who was dissuaded from marrying the love of her life seven years earlier. *The Barkleys of Broadway* is about a married couple whose interactions have grown predictable and stale. They too need a second chance—and, as such, qualify for what Stanley Cavell has called 'the comedy of remarriage' where they must learn to see and appreciate each other anew.

It is interesting to think how the confined space of Austen's world, where her characters are thrown together and must navigate their renewed relationship, parallels the confines of the marriage represented in the last Astaire-Rogers movie. In both, the heroine is given centre stage, even as her dependency on the hero is emphasised. Anne Elliot announces, when she is finally reunited with Captain Wentworth, that she would have done the same again—owning her earlier decision to reject him in a way that I think Austen intends to be empowering. Rogers' character leaves the marriage and the musical comedy roles that she performs alongside her husband (which mirror Rogers' RKO roles with Astaire), to appear in a serious play where she is initially out of her depth. Astaire, disguising his voice, pretends to call her on the phone as her director, and builds her confidence so that she triumphs in the role. When she learns what he has done, they reconcile.

Both works can be said to turn on the difficulty of empowering the woman but reinforcing the couple. In a patriarchal context, this is a contradiction in terms. And yet both the novel and the movie try their best to resolve this contradiction. Both have a quality of sadness about them—a sense of having settled, after turmoil and disappointment, for a more realistic set of expectations. In the case of Astaire and Rogers, we have as well the physical fact of their bodies, still vital and in their way beautiful, but, nonetheless, ten years older, less resplendent than they were in their heyday (indeed, the very fact that they are now at MGM rather than the feistier, youthful RKO speaks to the issue of their aging). *Persuasion*, for its part, is meant to have us think about the aging of its heroine, even as we are told that her looks improve as she reunites with Wentworth. The novel was also published posthumously, which reminds us that its author never found—or re-found—her Wentworth. Still, for both Austen and Astaire, the works are testaments to an idea of the couple and of entertainment that has endured and uplifted us into the present.

Let me conclude by noting the larger framework in which I want this analogical discussion to be understood. The American movie musical, embodied by the Astaire-Rogers films, was, in my opinion, the thematic heir to the domestic novel, embodied by Austen. The films reflect the shift in cultural importance from Britain to America, from novel to film, from conversation to physical and visual performance. Both artists used their medium with exceptional grace, style, and moral force. Both created entertainments that would distil aspects of their culture and their historical moment. Both can be said to have drawn on the existence of the other, if not directly, then through cultural and formal kinds of cross-pollination. Both created work whose artistic value has become more apparent with time and that continues to delight readers and audiences and to inspire creative expression that borrows from and extrapolates on what they accomplished.

The value of Analogy Criticism, as I hope this essay demonstrates, is that it brings added interest to two works by considering them together. It makes possible new entryways for meaning and pleasure. I began this essay after realising that my *feeling* about Austen and Astaire was similar—a feeling of joy, combined with a sense that the artistry involved was exceptional and that the work, in both cases, contained elements that were aesthetically and morally profound. I allowed myself to be open to this feeling—this intuition of connection. I believe that this same sort of subjective, emotional starting point may work for other critics as a way to find connections among works that could enrich their personal appreciation and be made available to others in new ways. As we move further away from the kind of chronological, influence- and canonically-based assessment of artists and more toward the subjective and serendipitous, Analogy Criticism may become a way to open the cultural canon to more voices and more forms of expression.

Notes

1 The title is from the song, 'Never Gonna Dance' (Dorothy Fields and Jerome Kern) from *Swing Time* (1936).

2 This was said to me by my editor, the late Hope Dellon, at St. Martin's Press.

3 In *Swing Time*, Astaire *pretends* that he can't dance in order to take lessons from Rogers, who is a dance teacher. The way in which his contrived awkwardness segues into exceptional grace (when Rogers' boss enters and accuses her of being a bad teacher) is one of the great dramatic moments in cinema.

4 This point has been qualified by Edward Gallafent who argues for the importance of the frame: 'the density of the relation between the dance and what provokes it … their dramatic and comedic scenes, and the context of their supporting players, play an inescapable role in defining what their dance can be' (6–7).

5 I begin my book, *Silent Film and the Triumph of the American Myth*, with a photograph of these two couples in which it is clear that the movie stars eclipse the British aristocrats as the focal point of interest and style.

Works Cited

Austen, Jane. '*Letters of Jane Austen*—Brabourne Edition: Letters to her niece Anna Austen Lefroy, 1814–1816.' https://pemberley.com/janeinfo/brablt16.html

Austen, Jane. 'Letters of Jane Austen: Other excerpts from letters in Austen-Leigh's *Memoir*.' https://pemberley.com/janeinfo/auslet22.html#letter125

Austen, Jane. *Northanger Abbey*. Penguin Classics, 1995.

Austen, Jane. *Persuasion*. Penguin Classics, 1998.

Austen, Jane. *Pride and Prejudice*. Penguin Classics, 1995.

Boyer, G. Bruce. *Fred Astaire Style*. Abe Books, 2005.

Cavell, Stanley. *Cavell on Film*. State U of New York P, 2005.

Cohen, Paula Marantz. *Silent Film and the Triumph of the American Myth*. Oxford UP, 2001.

Cohen, Paula Marantz. 'Thoughts on the Centennial of Fred Astaire.' *Raritan*, vol. XX, no. i, Summer 2000, pp. 127–141.

Croce, Arlene. *The Fred Astaire and Ginger Rogers Book*. Galahad Books, 1972.

Daiches, David. 'Jane Austen, Karl Marx, and the Aristocratic Dance.' *American Scholar*, 1948, pp. 289–296.

Denby, David. 'Critic's Notebook.' *The New Yorker*, online, 23 Aug. 2010.

Ellestrom, Lars. 'Adaptation and Intermediality.' *The Oxford Handbook of Adaptation Studies*. Oxford UP, 2017, pp. 509–526.

Franceschina, John, and Hermes Pan. *The Man Who Danced with Fred Astaire*. Oxford UP, 2012.

Gallafent, Edward. *Astaire & Rogers*. Columbia UP, 2002.

Hutcheon, Linda. *A Theory of Adaptation*. Routledge, 2006.

Kendall, Elizabeth. *The Runaway Bride: Hollywood Romantic Comedy of the 1930s*. Alfred A. Knopf, 1990.

Kennard, Jean E. *Victims of Convention*. Archon Books, 1978.

Le Faye, Deirdre. Forward. *Dance and Jane Austen: How a Novelist and Her Characters Went to the Ball*, by Susannah Fullerton. Frances Lincoln, 2012.

Mansell, Darrell. *The Novels of Jane Austen: An Interpretation*. Macmillan, 1978.

Mueller, John. *Astaire Dancing*. Alfred A. Knopf, 1985.

Reid-Walsh, Jacqueline. '"Entering the World" of Regency Society: The Ballroom Scenes in *Northanger Abbey*, "The Watsons," and *Mansfield Park*.' *Persuasions*, vol. 16, 1993, pp. 115–124.

Stovel, Nora Foster. '"Every Savage Can Dance": Choreographing Courtship in the Novels of Jane Austen.' *Persuasions: Journal of the Jane Austen Society of North America*, vol. 23, 2001, pp. 29–49.

Thomas, Bob. *Astaire, the Man, The Dancer*. Weidenfeld & Nicolson, 1985.

Trilling, Lionel. 'Mansfield Park.' *The Opposing Self*. Viking, 1955.

28

TRANSLATING JANE AUSTEN: WORLD LITERARY SPACE AND ISABELLE DE MONTOLIEU'S *LA FAMILLE ELLIOT* (1821)

Rachel Canter

GEORGE WASHINGTON UNIVERSITY

In the English-speaking world, we know Jane Austen as, among other things, an important novelist of realism, a moralist, a feminist, and as a pop-culture icon. Among these Jane Austens are the many forged through various translations. Though still an emerging subfield, Jane Austen translation studies have increased in the twenty-first century through the work of Gillian Dow, Valerie Cossy, Lucile Trunel and others.[1] Much of the emerging scholarship on Jane Austen and translation has focused on the reception histories of Austen translations. Gillian Dow has written extensively on the reception of Austen's novels globally, while Valerie Cossy and Lucile Trunel have each published substantial studies of Jane Austen's French reception history. While refrains of the lack of existing work on Jane Austen translation and the notion that she 'doesn't travel well' remain common within these reception histories, critics such as Dow and Marie Nedregotten Sørbø have complicated such claims. Both argue that regardless of whether Austen travels well, she does seem to travel quite a bit. Sørbø references a number of Austen translations in a variety of languages, calling her one of the most translated British authors (Sørbø 2). Dow notes the embrace of Austen among 'common readers' in France, despite the neglect of Austen by French critics. On the whole, the majority of existing scholarship on Austen translations remains centred on establishing and often amending her reputation across the European continent and occasionally in Asia.

By contrast, Lance Hewson's *An Approach to Translation Criticism* uses Austen's *Emma*, alongside Flaubert's *Madame Bovary*, as a case study to establish a theoretical approach to translation criticism. While Hewson is not specifically interested in the implications of translation for Jane Austen as a literary entity, his choice of *Emma* as a literary 'classic' translated well enough to provide a relevant case study for his work is telling. In contrast to earlier translation criticism, Hewson moves away from the traditional approach of seeking equivalency between the source text and its translation. Instead, Hewson sees inequivalencies not necessarily as errors but as opportunities to pursue new possibilities for interpretation. For Hewson, analysing a literary translation requires reading it as a dual text with various interpretations available through the language choices made in the original and in the translation.

368   DOI: 10.4324/9780429398155-28-32

While these critics have developed substantial work on Jane Austen and translation, I argue that Isabelle de Montolieu's *La Famille Elliot, ou l'ancienne inclination* (1821), a French 'translation libre' of *Persuasion* (1817), is one version of Jane Austen that deserves more critical attention. While *La Famille Elliot* has often been dismissed as a text that submerges Austen's celebrated realism under sentimentalism, a close look at *La Famille Elliot* reveals that the translation actually retains a key element of Austen's realism—her interiority—through its use of free-indirect discourse.

Much of the existing work on *La Famille Elliot* has centred around its reception in France. Scholars such as Valerie Cossy and Lucile Trunel have argued that Montolieu's reputation as a popular sentimental novelist and her sentimental embellishments to Austen's texts created a more sentimental Austen in France than existed in England. For this reason, Austen remains primarily known as a sentimental novelist in France—even among recent literary critics. Cossy and Trunel attribute this neglect of Austen in French critical discourse both to the failings of Montolieu's translation and to the particular rules of the French literary hierarchy in the nineteenth century, which prized realism over sentimentalism. However, recent criticism has begun to question assumptions about *La Famille Elliot*'s sentimentalism. For example, Adam Russell's work on free-indirect discourse in Montolieu's translation reveals that this technique, often associated with Flaubert's form of psychological realism, remains present in several key passages of the translation.

Russell's work suggests that we should read Montolieu's translation not as an exclusively sentimental text but as a hybrid of sentimentalism and realism. Reading Montolieu's *La Famille Elliot* as a hybrid aligns her translation more closely with its source text, *Persuasion*. Aligning the texts as hybrid novels restructures Austen's reception history in a subtle but important way. Had French critics immediately recognised the presence of free-indirect discourse in translations of Austen's work, she may have become more closely associated with such a realist giant as Flaubert. Instead, she was largely cast off as a writer of sentimental fiction, a genre which did not gain critical prestige in the French literary context. But by the mid-twentieth century, Roy Pascal and Dorrit Cohn had published the first book-length studies in English on free-indirect discourse, identifying Austen as one of the earliest, if not the original, practitioner of the technique in the English language. Thus, the development of free-indirect discourse studies in English further established Austen as a novelist worthy of serious study, while free-indirect discourse studies in France have done nothing to expand Austen's reputation. Because free-indirect discourse had not yet been identified as a literary critical term at the time when Austen was first translated, Austen's use of this technique did not gain prestige for her in the French literary hierarchy. Not only, then, does Austen's reputation in France seem to suffer due to the particular rules of the French literary hierarchy, but it also suffers for having been translated too early.

Through the disjunction between Austen's reputation in England and in France, we see a peculiar phenomenon of literary hierarchies. In the English context, Austen's reputation has and continues to be defined in a variety of ways—notably as an important novelist of realism. Yet, in the French context, Austen studies have stalled around the project of amending her sentimental reputation. I contend that Pascale Casanova's theory of world literary space helps us think through this disjunction between Austen's English and French reputations in order to suggest that the construction of Jane Austen depends on the principles of the literary hierarchy in which she is situated. In Casanova's framework, authors can accrue 'literary capital' that impacts the way that they are received, regardless of whether the accrual of literary capital is actually tied to innate qualities of their work. Reading Austen's French reception through the lens of Casanova's theory, we see the construction of Jane Austen, as Devoney Looser has called it, as a 'fraught public process' (Looser 1). The Jane Austen we see evolves according to the rules of a given literary context. Through Casanova and Looser we can read Austen's authorship as unstable and dependent on relatively subjective factors, implying that our understanding of Jane Austen is often more of a construction based on specific literary principles than it is a stable reality.

La Famille Elliot's Reception History

In the 1820s, when Montolieu published *La Famille Elliot*, the sentimental genre was reaching its height of popularity, just before Stendhal and Balzac began forging what would become the realist genre in France (Cohen 6, 26). Margaret Cohen writes that critics considered the sentimental social novels written by romancières, such as Montolieu, 'to be the most important French novels, although they treated the novel as polite entertainment rather than as a preeminent literary form' (29). But polite entertainment soon traversed into literary seriousness, as Balzac and Stendhal began appropriating conventions from the sentimental genre and reshaping them into realist codes (31). Crucially, Cohen also argues that by obscuring the sentimental origins of the realist poetics that they developed, Balzac and Stendhal established a framework for thinking about French literary history that erased the significance of the sentimental genre for French literature (31). This framework persisted into the twentieth century, reinforcing the hierarchy that cast the sentimental as lesser and the realist as greater (31).

Cohen outlines several opposing criteria for the sentimental social novel and the realist novel. I will unpack two specific opposing criteria: the centrality of moral conflict in the sentimental social novel and the significance of descriptive detail to the realist novel. Within the French context, the sentimental and the realist are not only gendered as feminine and masculine respectively, but the narrative techniques associated with each are gendered as female versus male talents.

According to Cohen, protagonists in the sentimental social novel often find themselves caught between two moral imperatives: collective welfare versus individual freedom (34). Often, this conflict of moral imperatives takes the form of family obstacles to marriage (38). Cohen also remarks that the sentimental novel allows for the development of interiority in order to demonstrate the inner turmoil of the protagonist (41). Although interiority eventually becomes associated with Flaubert's form of psychological realism, which moves the novel towards the so-called inward turn, inner monologue was not a key feature of early French realism. Rather, the meticulous description of French realism had to be 'material' and 'visual' to fit into the standards developed by male novelists (115). French critics during the early nineteenth century often cast this descriptive convention in professional terms. Cohen writes that 'realism's encyclopaedic approach to social representation was characterised with reference to professions exercised overwhelmingly, if not exclusively, by men' (112). Through Cohen, we see that Austen's gender and her association with the sentimental genre would have contributed to her limited construction as a purely sentimental, and, by definition, lesser, novelist in the French context. Furthermore, although Austen has often been lauded for her development of interiority through free-indirect discourse, because the French realism of the nineteenth century eschewed interiority in favour of exterior description, the very technique that gained Austen prestige as a great realist in English would have excluded her from the realist category in French.

With this context in mind, the fact that Austen was translated by Montolieu, a famous sentimental novelist, becomes crucial for her situation in the French literary context. Cossy and Saglia interpret the significance of Montolieu publishing her translation of *Persuasion* in her own completed works in 1821. They argue that 'Austen's novel, consequently, had to accommodate the expectations of her translator's readership' (173). Austen had to become more sentimental in order to conform to Montolieu's established sentimental style.

For example, Valerie Cossy discusses how Montolieu alters the ending of *Persuasion* to allow Anne and Captain Wentworth to live at Kellynch Hall with their children (who do not exist in the original English text), eschewing the ambiguity of Austen's ending in English (Cossy *Jane Austen in Switzerland* 292). Cossy additionally remarks on Montolieu's 'restoration of Lady Russell's importance' (292). In Cossy's interpretation, restoring Lady Russell undermines Austen's social commentary, which 'cast doubt not only on the traditional values her character stood for but also on the function of the female advisor, and, by extension, on the author of didactic literature' (291). Through both of these decisions, Cossy argues that Montolieu shifts the novel towards a tidier moral conclusion, in which the female advisor regains her position and the importance of family is re-inforced through positioning Anne and Wentworth in Anne's ancestral home.

Cossy also acknowledges that even if Montolieu had not sentimentalised the novels, Austen's hybrid form of sentimental realism still would not have fared well within the confines of the French literary hierarchy:

> If we agree with Cohen that, in France, the realist novel establishes the legitimacy of the genre by publicly repudiating the sentimental subgenre and by obscuring—vide Balzac—its indebtedness to a sentimental origin, we understand better why Austen was completely ignored in nineteenth-century France. Her novels do indeed combine elements of moral sentimentalism and realism [...] The reception of Austen's novels is representative of how, in nineteenth-century France, the words 'sentiment' and 'realism' remained mutually exclusive. (294–95)

Both Cossy and Cohen suggest that these gendered distinctions between 'sentiment' and 'realism' in the French literary hierarchy did not exist in that of England. Referencing Cohen, Cossy writes, 'Cohen actually observes how this dichotomous poetics opposing the masculine to the feminine and the sentimental to the realist is alien to the English novel, especially to Austen's narrative' (Cossy 'Why Austen Cannot Be a Classique'). Although Austen does eventually gain prestige as an im-portant novelist of realism in the English context, it is an oversimplification of the history of the novel genre in England to suggest that oppositions between feminine and masculine and senti-mentalism and realism did not exist in the English context. In fact, Laurence Mazzeno's history of Jane Austen criticism suggests that gendered interpretation did significantly impact Austen's re-putation throughout the nineteenth century.

Mazzeno asserts that during the late Victorian age, critics considered Austen as:

> someone who, knowing her place both as a woman and artist, never attempted writing about subjects which she did not experience intimately. For the Victorians, this meant she was a pleasant and talented practitioner of a minor form of fiction, the novel of manners—perhaps the best to write in that genre, but certainly not a major literary figure. (21)

The Victorian interpretation of Austen aligns closely with Cossy's own summary of Austen's re-ception in early nineteenth-century France. Although Mazzeno references several other critics who, from an early point, praise Austen for her realism, he also argues that the sentimentalised view of Austen as 'dear aunt Jane' solidified with James Edward Austen-Leigh's *Memoir of Jane Austen* (1870). This version of Austen remained prominent until after World War I when literary criticism became established as an organised discipline (27, 60). Many of the late Victorians that Mazzeno cites seem concerned with determining why Austen continues to endure. In contrast, recent scholarship on the nineteenth-century reception of Austen in France has focused on why she has not endured.

Free-Indirect Discourse in *Persuasion* and *La Famille Elliot*

While Cossy has provided compelling reasons for why Austen's reputation did not take hold in France, Russell's work on Montolieu's translation of *Persuasion* lays the foundation for aligning Montolieu's version of Austen more closely with Flaubert and psychological realism. Russell's recent studies on Montolieu's free translation of *Persuasion* push back on the ubiquitous claims about how poorly Austen has been represented in French. Through close-reading several key passages of Austen's *Persuasion* and comparing them with Montolieu's *La Famille Elliot*, Russell finds that Austen's free-indirect discourse survives in several key passages of the French translation. Free-indirect discourse, as defined by Russell, is 'primarily concerned with the representation of a fictional character's inner life as well as his or her discourse, often recalling the very "melody" of the character's actual words' (Russell 'Isabelle de Montolieu' 233). Through free-indirect discourse, the narrator relays a character's inner thoughts without using quotation marks or other signals to indicate that the perspective has changed from the general point-of-view to the character's specific point-of-view. Importantly, Russell notes that Flaubert is often credited with bringing free-indirect discourse into French literature, and he suggests that there could be significant implications for literary history if free-indirect discourse can be identified throughout Montolieu's text (Russell 'French Translations' 15). By drawing an implicit similarity between Austen, as translated by Montolieu, and Flaubert, Russell implies that Austen's reputation in France may deserve reconsideration.

To begin the work of reconsidering Montolieu's translation, I will first pick up where Russell left off to establish the presence of free-indirect discourse in two key passages of Montolieu's translation. I will then discuss the history of free-indirect discourse in literary studies and apply it to Austen's reception history in France. I have copied below two passages from Austen's *Persuasion*, their equivalents in Montolieu's *La Famille Elliot*, and my English translations of the French:

> Frederick Wentworth had used such words, or something like them, but without an idea that they would be carried round to her. He had thought her wretchedly altered, and, in the first moment of appeal, had spoken as he felt. He had not forgiven Anne Elliot. *She had used him ill; deserted and disappointed him; and worse, she had shewn a feebleness of character in doing so, which his own decided, confident temper could not endure. She had given him up to oblige others. It had been the effect of over-persuasion. It had been weakness and timidity.* (Austen 57)

In the above passage, and in the following versions, I have italicised where the narration shifts to free-indirect discourse. Initially, the transition is slightly ambiguous. The narrator could be reporting that Wentworth has not forgiven Anne, or this sentence could function as a window into Wentworth's own thoughts. By the next sentence, the voice becomes clearer. We can infer that Wentworth, rather than the narrator, condemns Anne through this monologue. Austen's use of free-indirect discourse here reveals Wentworth's psychological interiority. Through Wentworth, Austen continues to provide commentary on persuasion and decision-making as central themes of the text.

Here is Montolieu's version of the passage in French:

> Frederich Wentworth avait en effet dit cela, ou quelque chose de semblable, mais sans aucune idée qu'on pût le répéter à miss Elliot. Il se faisait d'elle, lorsqu'il y pensait, une idée si charmante, qu'il la trouva excessivement changée, et dans le premier moment d'un appel à son jugement sur elle, il dit ce qu'il pensait. Alice telle qu'il l'avait vue en s'attachant à elle, était encore à ses yeux la première des femmes; pour le genre de figure et le fond du caractère, il n'en avait point trouvé qu'on pût lui comparer; mais son amour et son amour-propre blessés par un refus, et surtout huit ans d'absence, avaient détruit sa passion; il n'en restait plus la moindre trace ni dans son coeur ni dans son esprit au moment ou il la retrouva. Á l'exception d'un mouvement de curiosité qui l'avait amené chez Charles Musgrove, il n'éprouvait aucun désir de la revoir. Son attachement pour elle avait été très vif; mais plus il l'aimait véritablement, plus il s'indigna de la faiblesse de caractère qu'elle avait montrée lors de leur séparation; *elle le rejeta, l'abandonna pour complaire à des parens tyranniques et a une ami prévenue, qui lui persuadèrent qu'elle devait agir ainsi; elle céda à leurs avis*

contre le sien propre, contre la voix de l'honneur et de l'amour, puisqu'elle lui avait donné son coeur et promis sa main; cette faiblesse ou cette timidité étaient si opposées au caractère ferme, ouvert et décide de Frederich Wentworth, qu'il résolut de la bannir de son coeur, et il y avait reussi. (Montolieu 128–29)

Here is my English translation:

Frederick Wentworth had in effect said this, or something similar, but without any idea that someone could repeat it to Miss Elliot. He was done with her, when he thought about it, such a charming idea, that he found her excessively changed, and in the first moment of an appeal to his judgment of her, he said what he thought. Alice, such as he had seen her when attached to her, was still to his eyes the first among women; in type of face and the foundation of character, he had never found one that could compare to her; but his love and his injured pride, and above all eight years of absence, had destroyed his passion; not the slightest trace of it remained in his heart or in his spirit at the moment when he found her again. With the exception of a movement of curiosity that had led him to Charles Musgrove's house, he did not experience any desire to see her again. His attachment to her had been very short; but the more he had truly loved her, the more indignant he became at the feebleness of character that she had shown at the moment of their separation; *she rejected him, abandoned him in order to please tyrannical parents and a prejudiced friend, who had persuaded her that she had to act in this way; she ceded to their opinions against her own, against the voice of honour and of love, since she had given him her heart and the promise of her hand; this weakness or this timidity was so opposed to the strong, open, and decided character of Frederich Wentworth, that he resolved to banish her from his heart, and he had succeeded.*

Montolieu blends the passage in Austen's original text with the passage that follows it, which focuses on Wentworth's former attachment to Anne and her breach of that attachment. In Austen's organisation, she separates Wentworth's judgement on Anne's character from his sense of attachment to her. By combining the two, Montolieu blurs the lines between emotion and logical reasoning. Yet, even in Austen's original passage, Wentworth's condemnation of Anne's passivity rises to a considerable emotional pitch. Through these passages, we see that both Austen and Montolieu subtly shift from third-person narration into direct interiority through free-indirect discourse.

We additionally see in both passages a tension between allegiance to one's community versus allegiance to one's own heart. Wentworth's disgust at Anne's willingness to cede to Lady Russell's advice suggests his own commitment to independence over allegiance to the community. Here, Wentworth is aligned with the tropes of French realism through his ability to rise socially and financially in his military career. For the French, the sentimental novel charts the tension between the protagonist's personal desires and obligation to the community, while the realist novel '[traces] the progress and success of a male protagonist against the community' (Cossy and Saglia 174). Although Wentworth is highly committed to his friends and family throughout the novel, we can read his social and financial rise as a journey of independent progress in the wake of the breach of his engagement to Anne. He goes away from the community to undergo his hero's journey, whereas Anne stays connected within her family and circle of friends. As such, we can position Wentworth as a traditional masculine, realist hero (in the French sense of realism). Yet, by the end of the novel, Anne makes an independent decision to marry Wentworth; however, both she and Wentworth agree that it was right for her not to defy Lady Russell when she was young, indicating the novel's ambivalence towards independence versus commitment to community. Through these passages, we see both Austen's *Persuasion* and Montolieu's *La Famille Elliot* representing familiar sentimental-realist tensions.

Later in the novel, similar tensions arise between interior versus exterior expression and the individual protagonist versus her community. The following passage details Anne's reaction upon receiving Mary's letter, which informs her that Louisa Musgrove is engaged to Captain Benwick:

> Mary need not have feared her sister's being in any degree prepared for the news. She had never in her life been more astonished. Captain Benwick and Louisa Musgrove! *It was almost too wonderful for belief;* and it was with the greatest effort that she could remain in the room, preserve an air of calmness, and answer the common questions of the moment. Happily for her, they were not many. Sir Walter wanted to know whether the Crofts travelled with four horses, and whether they were likely to be situated in such a part of Bath as it might suit Miss Elliot and himself to visit in; but had little curiosity beyond. (Austen 156)

Here is the same passage from Montolieu:

> Ah! Oui certainement, Alice était étonnée; jamais elle ne l'avait été davantage; elle ne pouvait en croire ses yeux: c'est Bentick que Louisa épouse! *Wentworth est libre encore!* A cet article de la lettre de Maria, un cri de surprise lui échappa. Elisabeth daigna lui demander si un des enfans était malade.—Non, ma soeur—Pourquoi donc criez-vous? Pourquoi dites-vous, ah! Mon Dieu? Vous m'avez effrayée: que vous dit donc Maria? (Montolieu 100)

Here is an English translation of Montolieu's passage:

> Ah! Yes certainly, Alice was surprised; never had she been more so; she could not believe her eyes: it is Bentick that Louisa marries! *Wentworth is free again!* At this article of Maria's letter, a cry of surprise escaped from her. Elizabeth deigned to ask her if one of the children was sick.—No, my sister.—Then why did you cry? Why did you say, ah! My God? You scared me: what does Maria say to you then?

Both passages exhibit brief interjections of free-indirect discourse. In Austen's original version, we read Anne's excited thoughts: 'Captain Benwick and Louisa Musgrove! It was almost too wonderful for belief' and the narrator's transition back into the third-person: 'and it was with the greatest effort that she could remain in the room [...]' (28). Similarly, In Montolieu's version, we read, 'c'est Bentick que Louisa epouse! Wentworth est libre encore!' Here, Montolieu maintains free-indirect discourse as a stylistic feature, but she also adds a cry of surprise, which is completely absent from Austen's original text and which even characterises Alice differently than Anne. Through Anne's interiority throughout the novel, Austen demonstrates how Anne consistently works to control her inner thoughts and emotions and her outward display of those emotions.

This constant inner monologue also connects to the title *Persuasion* and a key philosophical theme of Austen's novel: if and how people can be convinced to change their minds. While Montolieu, on some level, maintains this theme by maintaining the interiority of Austen's heroine through free-indirect discourse, she also undoes the thematic power of this stylistic choice by making visible what Austen keeps strictly interior. Anne exclaims internally in Austen's text. Through her inner thoughts, we see how hard she tries to keep the news to herself, to figure out how to respond. But Montolieu breaks this facade, making Alice cry out in surprise, resulting in a string of questions from her sister that we do not have in the original text.

This moment embodies an intentional departure from Austen's text that Montolieu describes in her translator's note. To her, the title *Persuasion* seems 'trop vague' (too vague) in French (Montolieu Note du Traducteur). She changed the title to *La Famille Elliot* to indicate 'l'ensemble de la situation'. By forcing more of Alice's emotional turmoil to the exterior, Montolieu creates an ensemble situation. In Austen's English text, Anne's family ignores her while she internally struggles to understand and control her emotions. But when Alice cries out in Montolieu's version, she draws attention from her family, eliciting a reaction from them, even if unintentionally, and creating a moment of interaction with her family. Such emphasis on the family ensemble of the novel would have signalled sentimentalism to the French reader. While a French realist plot may have followed a track more similar to Wentworth's—going away from family and community in order to grow and gain success—Austen's plot follows a more nuanced track. Wentworth does go away to gain prestige and wealth, but he does not know his own heart until he returns to the community. Whereas Anne rejects independence by following Lady Russell's advice and only accepts Wentworth after he becomes a more attractive option in her community. In Austen's text, we see a tension between independence versus community that Montolieu diminishes by mitigating Anne's isolation from her family and adding new emphasis on family dynamics in the novel.

Yet, even though both Austen's *Persuasion* and Montolieu's *La Famille Elliot* exhibit elements of sentimentalism and the free-indirect discourse that marks psychological realism, the hybrid nature of Montolieu's text has gone largely unrecognised. This is likely due to the fact that, when Montolieu translated Austen's *Persuasion* in 1821, free-indirect discourse had not yet been discovered, so to speak, as a narrative technique. Roy Pascal identifies Swiss linguist Charles Bally as the originator of the term 'style indirect libre' (or free-indirect discourse in English). Charles Bally first coined the term in an article on linguistics published in 1912. But the technique had received some attention even prior to Bally's usage. Dorrit Cohn remarks that Flaubert comes close to identifying the technique in his own work without directly coining a specific term for it (114).

Ironically, given Austen's lacklustre reputation in France, Cohn even implies that when Flaubert developed this inward turning narrative technique, he was unconsciously inheriting a tradition first established by Jane Austen. Perhaps even more ironically, Pascal speculates that Marguerite Lips, a French critic and student of Bally's, was the first to identify Austen as a practitioner of free-indirect discourse. Lips claims that English novelists primarily use free-indirect discourse to report banal conversations, rather than to express interior thoughts, as in French literature, suggesting a lesser view of its usage in English (215). However, she also comments specifically on Austen's usage of the technique, marvelling that she likely had no 'influence étrangère' when she began using the technique in her novels (215). That Pascal, Cohn, and even such an early French critic as Lips all identify Austen as a practitioner of free-indirect discourse at such early stages of free-indirect discourse studies confirms Austen's importance to this branch of literary study and further solidifies her place as an innovative and important novelist in the Anglophone context. Yet, although Lips recognises Austen for her use of free-indirect discourse early in the history of free-indirect discourse studies, this recognition seems to have done nothing for Austen's reputation in France.

The history of free-indirect discourse, then, demonstrates that Austen entered the French literary context too early to have achieved critical acclaim for one of her most notable achievements. Had Austen been translated a century later, after Flaubert's indirect identification of the technique and after Bally first coined the term now used to describe it, Austen's use of free-indirect discourse may have been immediately identified. As it stands, however, free-indirect discourse was not yet a part of the literary critical vocabulary at the time when Austen was first translated. The lack of recognition for this technique further contributed to the many factors that prevented Austen from gaining prestige in the French literary context.

World Literary Space and Jane Austen's Reception Histories

We can further understand the disjunction between Austen's English reception history and her French reception history by thinking through the paradigms of literary prestige that Pascale

Casanova presents in *The World Republic of Letters*. Casanova argues that we must situate authors and their texts in world literary space: the entire set of literary production as it circulates across national borders. In this world literary space, critics and writers trade and compete for literary capital, creating a market whose medium of exchange is prestige (13). Casanova defines several metrics for measuring literary capital, including the material objects that constitute this capital, the age of a national literature, and what she calls the professional 'milieu', or the formal and informal gatherings of the literary elite (14–15). Translation into 'literary' languages also constitutes a key component of literary capital. In Casanova's formulation of literary capital, a translated author gains capital and belonging in world literary space through his or her translation into another language, particularly French.

But the network of literary prestige such as Casanova describes—one in which novels are considered a serious form of art—did not yet exist in France when Montolieu translated Austen into French. As Cohen has acknowledged, sentimental novelists such as Montolieu were regarded as the greatest practitioners of the novel form, but the novel in France at the time was still considered entertainment rather than art. So, although Casanova considers translation a form of *littérisation*, through which an author can gain prestige through translation into a literary language, Montolieu's translation of Austen could not have functioned as a *littérisation* (133). Admittedly, Montolieu translated Austen at a time when many English novels were being translated into French, indicating that transnational networks of prestige were already beginning to form by the early nineteenth century.[2] But these networks were still in a nascent state compared to what they would become in another hundred years when the novel would become established as a serious form of art.

By the time that transnational networks of prestige formed in the way that Casanova describes, Austen had already been cast aside as secondary literature. Without critics to recognise her achievements as a practitioner of free-indirect discourse, and in a system that erased the sentimental origins of the realist genre, Austen could not acquire value in the literary market. In this way, the literary market functions through self-reinforcing mechanisms: an author gains prestige, 'once it is believed that what [s]he has written has literary value' (Casanova 17). Casanova writes 'Literary capital so surely exists, in its very immateriality, only because it has—for all those who take part in the competition, and above all for those who are deprived of capital—objectively measurable effects that serve to perpetuate this belief' (17).

We know that literary capital exists, according to Casanova, by its effects. We can see such effects through Austen's limited construction in France. In contrast, critics in the English context such as Devoney Looser have emphasised the multiplicity of Austen's construction in the English context. Looser tracks the history of Austen's reception, often blurring the distinction between Austen's popular and critical reputation. In describing 'the invention of Jane Austen' as a 'fraught public process', Looser rejects the project of stabilising Austen (1). Instead, Looser demonstrates through her work on representations of Austen in a variety of contexts including theatre, film, and textbooks that Austen's identity has always been a subject of debate. Looser discusses a variety of Jane Austens embraced and contested by her fans and critics since the beginning of her public reputation. While some have touted 'dear Aunt Jane'—the domestic, moralising Austen—others have preferred Jane Austen as a political and feminist symbol. In Looser, we see that the popular embrace of Austen has defined as many enduring identities for Austen as her critical reception.

If we apply Looser and Casanova together, we see that the construction of Jane Austen always depends on context. Yet we also see that an author's reputation has measurable effects exhibited through his or her inclusion or exclusion from literary canon(s). Through Montolieu's translation, we see yet another version of Jane Austen: one that, with a heavy sentimental hand, still maintains Austen's complex representations of interiority. Cossy has argued that the Montolieu translation is worth studying primarily for what it reveals about the French literary hierarchy, rather than about Jane Austen herself (Cossy *Jane Austen in Switzerland*). But Montolieu's translation can also provide an avenue for re-examining the importance of French sentimentalism to networks of literary prestige, and in doing so, the Montolieu translation can remind English critics of Austen's own use of sentimental tropes. Through Jane Austen, we can explore the ways that sentimentalism and realism might blend, even in French, and perhaps develop new critical paradigms for describing them. Rather than writing off Montolieu's version of Austen as overly sentimental, we can view it as another multi-faceted version of Austen, one that has had significant effects on her reception in France and one that may yet provide a path towards appreciating Austen's hybridity as both a sentimental and a realist author who can sit rather comfortably alongside such seemingly divergent novelists as Isabelle de Montolieu and Gustave Flaubert.

Notes

1   See Valerie Cossy's *Jane Austen in Switzerland: A Study of the Early French Translations* and 'Why Austen Can Never be a Classique in French'; Valerie Cossy and Diego Saglia's 'Translations'; Gillian Dow's 'Uses of Translation: The Global Jane Austen', 'Criss-Crossing the Channel: The French Novel and English Translation', and 'Translations' in both the *The Cambridge Companion to Emma* and *The Cambridge Companion to Pride and Prejudice*; Anthony Mandal and Brian Southam's *The Reception of Jane Austen in Europe*; Marie Nedregotten Sørbø's *Jane Austen Speaks Norwegian: The Challenges of Literary Translation*; Lucile Trunel's 'Jane Austen's French Publications from 1815: A History of Misunderstanding'; and Ellen Moody's 'Continent Isolated: Anglocentricity in Austen Criticism'.
2   See Noel King's 'Jane Austen in France'.

Works Cited

Austen, Jane. *Persuasion*, edited by Gillian Beer. Penguin Classics, 2003.
Casanova, Pascale. *The World Republic of Letters*. Harvard UP, 2004.
Cohen, Margaret. *The Sentimental Education of the Novel*. Princeton UP, 1999.
Cohn, Dorrit. *Transparent Minds*. Princeton UP, 1978.
Cossy, Valerie. *Jane Austen in Switzerland: A Study of the Early French Translations*. Editions Slatkine, 2006.
Cossy, Valerie. 'Why Austen Cannot Be a "Classique" in French: New Directions in the French Reception of Austen.' *Persuasions: The Jane Austen Journal Online*, vol. 30, no. 2, 2010.
Cossy, Valerie, and Diego Saglia. 'Translations.' *Jane Austen in Context*, edited by Janet Todd. Cambridge UP, 2005, pp. 169–182.
de Montolieu, Isabelle, translator. *La Famille Elliot, ou l'ancienne Inclination*, T. 1, edited by Jane Austen. Arthus Bertrand, Paris, 1828.
de Montolieu, Isabelle, translator. *La Famille Elliot, ou l'ancienne Inclination*, T. 2, edited by Jane Austen. Arthus Bertrand, Paris, 1828.
Dow, Gillian. 'Criss-Crossing the Channel: The French Novel and English Translation.' *The Oxford Handbook of the Eighteenth-Century Novel*, edited by Alan Downie. Oxford UP, 2016.
Dow, Gillian. 'Translations.' *The Cambridge Companion to Pride and Prejudice*, edited by Janet Todd and Gillian Dow. Cambridge UP, 2013, pp. 122–136.
Dow, Gillian. 'Translations.' *The Cambridge Companion to Emma*, edited by Peter Sabor and Gillian Dow. Cambridge UP, 2015, pp. 166–185.
Dow, Gillian. 'Uses of Translation: The Global Jane Austen.' *Uses of Austen: Jane's Afterlives*, edited by Gillian Dow and Clare Hanson. Palgrave Macmillan, 2012, pp. 154–174.
Hewson, Lance. *An Approach to Translation Criticism*. John Benjamins, 2011.
King, Noel J. 'Jane Austen in France.' *Nineteenth-Century Fiction*, vol. 8, no. 1, 1953, pp. 1–26.
Lips, Marguerite. *Le Style Indirect Libre*. Payot, 1926.
Looser, Devoney. *The Making of Jane Austen*. Johns Hopkins UP, 2017.
Mandal, Anthony. Introduction. *The Reception of Jane Austen in Europe*, edited by Anthony Mandal and Brian Southam. A & C Black, 2007, pp. 1–33.
Mazzeno, Laurence. *Jane Austen: Two Centuries of Criticism*. Camden House, 2011.
Moody, Ellen. 'Continent Isolated: Anglocentricity in Austen Criticism.' *Re-Drawing Austen: Picturesque Travels in Austenland*, edited by Beatrice Battaglia and Diego Saglia. Ligouri Editore, 2004, pp. 329–338.

Pascal, Roy. *The Dual Voice: Free Indirect Speech and Its Functioning in the Nineteenth-Century European Novel.* Manchester UP, 1977.

Russell, Adam. 'French Translations of Jane Austen.' *AUMLA*, vol. 117, 2012, pp. 13–33.

Russell, Adam. 'Isabelle de Montolieu Reads Anne Elliot's Mind: Free Indirect Discourse in *La Famille Elliot.*' *Persuasions: The Jane Austen Journal Online*, vol. 32, 2010, pp. 232–247.

Sørbø, Nedregotten. 'Marie.' *Jane Austen Speaks Norwegian: The Challenges of Literary Translation.* Brill, 2018.

Trunel, Lucile. 'Jane Austen's French Publications from 1815: A History of Misunderstanding.' *Global Jane Austen: Pleasure, Passion, and Possessiveness in the Jane Austen Community*, edited by Laurence Raw and Robert G. Dryden. Palgrave Macmillan, 2013, pp. 21–35.

29

JANE AUSTEN AND THE SOCIAL SCIENCES

Wendy Jones

The *Oxford English Dictionary* defines social science as 'The study of human society and social relationships'. Most readers of Austen would agree that this definition suits her novels despite their status as fiction. Through her heroines and their experiences, Austen studies 'human society and social relationships', following the lead of social science in the variability of her focus—from specific to general, micro to macro, partial to universal. While Austen certainly portrays culturally distinctive, rule-bound practices, such as appropriate behaviour in polite society and the rituals of courtship, she also addresses the existential sociality of humans: our need to be included, to be respected, to be known, to be loved.

I will return to the idea of Jane Austen as a social scientist at the end of this essay, but first I offer a survey of literary scholarship that addresses Austen from a social science perspective. Given that a thorough survey would require a book rather than an essay, I will consider just one of the social sciences, psychology, primarily in its incarnation within literary studies as (the too narrowly named) cognitive literary criticism. Even within this restricted topic, my survey is by no means exhaustive; my goal is to offer an idea of the shape and scope of the field. To be sure, my choices reflect my judgements, and lack of world enough and time has inevitably led to my omitting valuable contributions.

Evolutionary Studies

Evolutionary literary criticism falls under the rubric of cognitive literary criticism because evolutionary theory is a cornerstone of cognitive approaches, which assume that human minds share certain fundamental characteristics. Brian Boyd, one of the founders of evolutionary literary criticism, provides a manifesto of its principles in 'Jane Meet Charles: Literature, Evolution, and Human Nature'. Like other critics writing at the advent of this sub-field, Boyd challenges the hegemony of poststructuralist theory (also known as 'Theory' and 'high theory'), especially the claim of cultural constructivism, the belief that culture determines all aspects of human thought and behaviour.

Boyd points out that the opposition genetics versus culture (or nature versus nurture) posits a false distinction, one rejected by most scientists, who speak more accurately of nature *through* nurture (Prinz; Ridley; Sapolsky, *Monkeyluv*, *Behave*); there is no separating the two inputs because the majority of our genes depend on the environment to control how and even if they will exert their influence. Not only is biology a product of culture, but culture is a product of biology for it would not exist at all without a brain that is organised and functions in ways that facilitate its development:

DOI: 10.4324/9780429398155-29-33

Evolution has fashioned the mind in highly specific modes, not simply in what ways we see and hear, but even in terms of the ways we feel, think, and interact (Boyd 2).

Grounding his argument in the existence of such human universals, Boyd argues that one reason Austen's work appeals so widely is that it demonstrates behaviour that resonates with our ways of thinking and behaving that were formed 'deep into the evolutionary past' (16), and so can be recognised by people everywhere: 'Their [Austen's novels'] power depends on the universal and central human problem—a problem we share with most of the animal kingdom—of choosing and winning the right sexual partner' (16). This quest derives from the more inclusive wish for intimacy; humans and other mammals are social beings whose survival and well-being depend upon closeness and companionship.

Boyd observes that theory of mind, a capability that involves inferring the thoughts, feelings, and intentions of others (also known as 'mindreading'), is crucial to choosing one's mate wisely in Austen's novels, as demonstrated by Fanny Price in *Mansfield Park*. She 'lands the best man around, the staunchest partner, through her superior ability to read the minds of others—to see Henry's weaknesses, to see that no one else comes close to matching Edmund's strengths—and through Edmund's ability in turn to read her superior capacity for reading others' (22). Boyd is truly a pioneer, for within a few years of the publication of 'Jane Meet Charles', theory of mind would become a central issue within the emerging field of cognitive literary criticism. Boyd is likely the first scholar to have cited its significance in Austen's work. Theory of mind has also remained a central topic in social psychology and social neuroscience.

Boyd not only introduced the topic of theory of mind in Austen criticism, but also linked mindreading to Austen's 'invention' of free indirect discourse. Austen's characters need to watch each other carefully, put together what they observe with information they already possess, and calibrate their own responses to what they hear, know, and observe. To portray 'this interplay of external and internal, of mouthspeaking and mindreading' (22), Austen used free indirect discourse, which had not yet appeared in prose fiction to the extent or skill she demonstrates 'because no one before Austen paid such minute attention to the way we monitor ourselves and each other so finely' (22).

To illustrate, here is Fanny's response to Henry Crawford's refusal to take no for an answer to his proposal of marriage:

> Now she was angry. Some resentment did arise at a perseverance so selfish and ungenerous. Here again was a want of delicacy and regard for others which had formerly so struck and disgusted her. Here was again a something of the same Mr Crawford whom she had so reprobated before. How evidently was there a gross want of feeling and humanity where his own pleasure was concerned—And alas! How always known no principle to supply as a duty what the heart was deficient in. (379)

By reporting Fanny's responses using free indirect discourse (the language is Fanny's), the narrator conveys both Fanny's thoughts, her reasons for disapproval, and her emotional responses, which include not only anger and resentment, which are mentioned, but also her distress at Henry's behaviour and her own position. Free indirect discourse is able to convey the totality of Fanny's state of mind accurately, succinctly, and in a way that not only tells but also shows her distress—readers witness the breathless, agitated quality of Fanny's thought through the breakdown in syntax. Boyd's linking of theory of mind to free indirect discourse, and his understanding of theory of mind in the context of the social skills of Austen's characters, render his essay relevant decades after it was written.

In the course of his discussion of evolution, Boyd references a theory that has conversely failed to be validated by subsequent research: parental investment theory. Formulated by the evolutionary scientist Robert Trivers in 1972, and based on the findings of Angus John Batemen, who famously worked with fruit flies in the 1940s, the theory proposes that the larger an investment a parent makes in their offspring, the more they will exercise discretion in choosing a mate. Beginning with gestation and nursing, female mammals tend to invest far more in reproduction and care than males. For this reason, so the logic goes, women look for men with resources and other desirable qualities that promise stability for themselves and their children, while men look for women who exhibit signs of fertility such as health and beauty.

It is easy to see the appeal of applying parental investment theory to Jane Austen's novels, which depict a society in which marriage is the primary source of income for women. The only problem is that the theory is inaccurate: the scientific community has largely discredited parental investment theory (Fine 2018, 29–45). Neither human nor non-human animals conform to this template for mate choice, and alternative resources for support and help in raising offspring also abound, even among humans (Hrdy). The primary tenets of parental investment theory are not even consistently applicable to Austen's novels. Emma does not marry Mr Knightley for his resources, for she has plenty of her own, and Austen suggests, in the decorous way available to her, that Emma finds Mr Knightley sexually attractive. Watching him at the ball, she notices '[h]is tall, firm, upright figure [which] … must draw every body's eyes … there was not one among the whole row of young men who could be compared with him' (352), a moment akin to Darcy's watching Elizabeth as she walks around the drawing room and 'begins to feel the danger of paying Elizabeth too much attention' (64). And Austen's men certainly seek mates for their resources above all else, as seen with Willoughby and Mr Elton.

Boyd does not draw on parental investment theory in his actual reading of Austen's work, but unfortunately, others have taken up the cause. Given the deficits of this theory, their claims lead to contradictions and qualifications, as we see in Joseph Carroll's 'Human Nature and Literary Meaning: A Theoretical Critique Illustrated with *Pride and Prejudice*' (2005). As a chapter in *The Literary Animal*, this essay constitutes one of the inaugural texts in the sub-discipline of evolutionary literary studies.

Carroll asserts that the findings of parental investment theory apply to *Pride and Prejudice*, that 'the women want wealth and status in their men and the men want youth and beauty in their women' (95). But he wisely avers that motivations of this kind do not have direct innate triggers (already a diminution of the theory), but rather that they result from complex systems that are themselves mediated by higher-order thinking, such as conscious goals. Yet his reading of *Pride and Prejudice* contradicts this claim; Carroll views such higher-order cognitive phenomena as *competing* with rather than *mediating* parental investment theory. Characters weigh potential resources and beauty (criteria of value in parental investment theory) against attention to mind and character (evidence of higher order thinking), a phenomenon that Carroll describes as 'a conflict between the mating system and the cognitive behavioral system' (95). This account of competition between systems not only undermines the deterministic force that Carroll claims for parental investment theory, but also adds little to what readers since Austen's day have observed about her novels: her heroines must weigh various factors, pragmatic and emotional, in deciding whom to marry.[1] Carroll's insights that are not wedded to parental investment theory are astute, such as his observation that Austen conveys 'quality of mind' through style: Those characters who display the 'precision, incisiveness, and acuity of Austen's own style (as seen especially in Darcy's letter), possess the most desirable qualities of mind; style is the expression and the marker of cognitive superiority' (96).

In 'Sexual Selection and Female Choice in *Northanger Abbey*' (2018), Beth Lau provides a useful summary of evolutionary literary criticism that acknowledges the influence of parental investment theory. Yet, as with Boyd, the reading that follows is connected to the broad evolutionary claim that people seek partners for sex and companionship, and that social intelligence is an adaptive skill for attracting desirable mates. Lau is also clear that there are many cultural determinants for the match in goals between Austen's novels and parental investment theory. From this evolutionary, cognitive perspective, Lau engages with a question pertinent to Austen criticism more generally, whether Catherine Morland is worthy of status as an Austen heroine. Catherine appears to have so little social acumen at the start of the novel that she appears somewhat stupid and certainly unlike Austen's other heroines.

Lau argues that Catherine's naivety, her 'guilelessness and inability to detect other people's ulterior motives' (478) might actually be an asset because such artlessness tags people as harmless, not only unwilling but unable to pose a threat to their superiors. Such transparency is also an effective sexual strategy, for not only is Henry charmed by Catherine's ingenuousness, but he is also put off his guard because Catherine is so unlike Isabella and other husband-hunting young ladies. While Catherine's strategies and motives might be opaque, even to herself—Lau cites evolutionary psychologist David Buss, who notes that adaptive strategies for mating are not always conscious—this lack of awareness does not render her behaviour any less effective or intelligent. Catherine knows that she likes Henry, and she is smart enough to understand how to actively pursue opportunities to be in his company, as well as to learn to overcome obstacles, such as John Thorpe's machinations. After he causes her to miss an engagement with the Tilneys, she outmanoeuvres his attempts to thwart a second appointment.

Such learning is the topic of a companion piece to this essay, 'Catherine's Education in Mindreading in *Northanger Abbey*' (2018). Here, Lau shows that Catherine's intelligence is not simply subconscious, for by the end of the novel she has become adept at the very skills she lacked at the start. Her initial naivety can be explained by a sheltered life and parents who appear to take everything at face value. Catherine lacked both practice and models for detecting deception or disingenuousness. But she encounters both in abundance at Bath and, as a result, her theory of mind develops incrementally. By her second meeting with John Thorpe, she is already beginning to distrust him, and by the end of the novel, she has advanced sufficiently to recognise Isabella's lies, and to dismiss her plea for help repairing her relationship with Catherine's brother. Catherine is well on the way to developing the superior social intelligence that 'qualifies her to be considered a worthy Austen heroine' (46).

Attention to mate choice is not the only way to engage in evolutionary criticism, as we see in Olivia Murphy's 'A Future to Look Forward to?: Extinction and Evolution in Jane Austen's *Persuasion*'. Murphy offers an astute account of how ideas about geology and past extinctions that were current in the scientific milieu of Austen's day influenced her writing of *Persuasion*. This discourse included arguments that past extinctions had occurred (contrary to biblical doctrine), which Austen would have encountered in Goldsmith's *History of the Earth*, which she owned, as well as in the works of Georges Cuvier; an account of his views was published in the widely-read *Edinburgh Review*.

Murphy observes that Sir Walter Elliot is thematically aligned with a view of genealogy that assumes an unbroken line of descent (and so no extinction) through his obsession with bloodlines and the marriages that sustain the status of his socioeconomically elite family. The Musgroves, conversely, do not concern themselves with good breeding but rather allow their children to marry as they wish, leaving everything to chance; this attitude aligns with recent theories of extinction, for it portends that lineages will be vitiated thereby precluding the possibility of pure descent and introducing the risk that some lineages will not survive. In addition, the various plotlines of *Persuasion* implicitly comment on Cuvier's observation that we do not know why some species survive and others do not: '*Persuasion*'s interest in the workings of "luck"' and "Providence"' (164) suggests that contingency, an inherent part of nature, often dictates the fate of species and of families. However, we might note that this is a contradictory but also cleverly guarded answer to the problem of extinction on Austen's part (perhaps a Pascal's wager!) because luck and Providence imply different versions of causality: Providence suggests divinely guided outcomes that appear contingent to blinkered human intelligence. But from a limited earthly point of view, *Persuasion* suggests that contingency dictates both survival and extinction.

Persuasion is clearly linked to evolution through its setting of episodes in Lyme Regis. The new geology was supported by the fossil found in Lyme of an ichthyosaurus, a giant animal that resembled no living creature, and which therefore suggested that extinctions had indeed occurred. Lyme Regis was already famous for its fossils at the time of this discovery, but these smaller samples resembled living animals. The ichthyosaurus was different, evidence of a break in the great chain of being and the end of a lineage. The setting of key scenes of the novel in Lyme Regis metonymically foregrounds the novel's evolutionary theme while also suggesting that Sir Walter and his kind are 'dinosaurs', as we would say today.

Theory of Mind

Austen has attracted the attention of cognitive literary critics because she so clearly concentrates on the workings of the mind-brain in her characters. As many readers have noticed, she offers few descriptions of people or places, but rather focuses on her fictional people's feelings, thoughts, and behaviour. Foremost among such processes is theory of mind. Many scholars have followed Boyd's lead in addressing its significance in Austen's work; in fact, it has been the topic most frequently addressed in cognitive literary criticism. Theory of mind is a complex process that draws on diverse aspects of our mental capabilities. Literary scholars have addressed this diversity within Austen's novels, following the lead of mind-brain scientists as they discover new information about the ways we understand others' thoughts and feelings.

Early theorists (in addition to Boyd, discussed above) include George Butte and David Lodge. In *I Know That You Know That I Know*, Butte explores the representation of deep intersubjectivity, the embedding of the contents of other people's minds within a given character's mind. For instance, in the scene in *Persuasion* set in Molland's bakery shop, in which Anne Elliot witnesses the meeting between Wentworth and Elizabeth, Anne perceives and is distressed by Elizabeth's recognition and hostility and by Wentworth's disappointed expectation of a greeting. Such complexity in the representation of minds is an innovation: 'When Anne Elliot watches Wentworth and Elizabeth negotiating complex force fields of memory and protocol, the enabling strategy of her story is a new layering of human consciousnesses, or a new representation of those subjectivities as layered in a specific way … [S]omething new in narrative is transpiring in that bakery shop in Bath, among Anne and Elizabeth and Wentworth' (4). Lodge in *Consciousness and the Novel: Connected Essays* similarly focuses on Austen's portrayal of theory of mind, while further linking it to her innovative use of free indirect discourse. Developing the potential of this narrative technique allowed Austen to make 'a smooth, seamless transition' (48) from one mind to another, including the transition from the narrator's mind to that of a character (focalisation). As a result, Austen can dispense with narrative tags (he said, she said), which can be clumsy and intrusive.

In 'Why Jane Austen Was Different, And Why We May Need Cognitive Science to See It', Lisa Zunshine explores the implications of the issues raised by Butte and Lodge in depth, while also showing how Austen's different innovations work together to produce a quantum leap in narrative technique. Zunshine begins by pointing out that we can describe the deep intersubjectivity discussed by Butte with the sentence, 'Anne realises that Wentworth understands that Elizabeth pretends not to recognize that he wants to be acknowledged as an acquaintance' (279). This interplay of perceptions attains four levels of embedment: (level 1) Anne understands that she understands (one's knowledge of one's own thoughts counts as a level of embedment) that (level 2) Wentworth's thoughts about (level 3) Elizabeth's thoughts about (level 4) Wentworth's wish for recognition.

Zunshine explains that Austen's experimentation with deep subjectivity allowed her to innovate new modes of representing embedded thought in the novel that avoid not only clumsiness (Lodge), but more important, the self-consciousness and prolixity of the attributions of thought found in sentimental fiction, which Austen disliked and mocked mercilessly in her juvenilia. Austen shows Anne thinking and feeling without deictically signalling these mental processes. While multiple levels of embedment can be found in sentimental fiction, a crucial difference between Austen's novels and texts such as Rousseau's *Émile* and Sterne's *A Sentimental Journey* is that in the latter, the activity of observing body language such as tears or gestures is described whereas Austen's narratives take the reading of non-verbal cues for granted. Austen does not describe Anne as watching Wentworth and Elizabeth but rather conveys the results of her heroine's observation.

By getting rid of this first layer of embedment, the reference to a character's observation, Austen frees up a level of intentionality (the contents of minds) which can then be used to add an extra layer of embedment that we are able to follow without confusion. Austen thereby creates deeply emotional scenes by conveying intensity of emotion through social dynamics whose meaning depends on our understanding of the ways that characters mindread one another, as in taking for granted the observation of body language. Austen's genius is evident in that a level of embedment cannot be removed without changing the meaning of a given scene.

Zunshine concludes that we pay attention to the levels of embedment in Austen, even though they might require thought and attention, because the emotional stakes of understanding these complex relays of thought and perception are high—perhaps as high for the reader as they are for characters. What fan of Austen has not read *Persuasion* with almost the same intensity of hope and attention as its heroine? Readers who deal with decoding the complicated dynamics of deep intersubjectivity in novels might well acquire an enhanced sense of confidence in their ability to function among the non-fictional people they encounter in the real world. Reading Austen exercises our minds, especially their capacity for theory of mind.

In *The Neural Sublime* (2010), Alan Richardson recapitulates the crucial goal of cognitive literary scholars who had written about Austen thus far: to demonstrate 'the signal role of Jane Austen in the history of fictional representations of consciousness' (80), which includes above all her use of theory of mind. His own contribution focuses on *Emma*, 'the novel that features her [Austen's] most deft and penetrating social observation' and in which she '[places] her characters in situations that force them to guess and guess again one another's intentions, beliefs, and emotional states' (81). Richardson traces the interplay of theory of mind among different characters, which often includes embedded thought, such as what Emma thinks Frank is thinking about Jane as he stares pointedly at her.

In asserting the pertinence of theory of mind to Austen, Richardson corrects a critical emphasis on the cerebral in cognitive literary criticism that shortchanges the complexity of Austen's representations. Literary scholars have tended to emphasise the perception of beliefs in considering theory of mind, whereas mindreading includes 'the full range of mental states (beliefs, desires, intentions, imaginations, emotions, etc.) that cause action' (Belmont, qtd. in Richardson 85), and which are often conveyed by facial expressions and body language. Richardson corrects this bias with close readings of scenes in *Emma* that highlight the signalling and perception of non-verbal cues, 'the role of gestures, the face, and especially the eyes in conveying mental states and intentions' so that the ball (Volume 3) consists not only of dances but also of an 'equally elaborate dance of looks, expressions, and pointed glances' (91). These bodily signs encode emotions and desires.

Richardson is as much a historicist as a scholar of mind-brain studies, and he argues that choosing between a cognitive or historical approach, as scholars have tended to do, diminishes our understanding of Austen. Accordingly, his work consistently relates mind-brain research that we use to read authors of the past with texts that are contemporaneous with the authors he considers. Tracing sources for Austen's emphasis on nonverbal communication, he cites Samuel Richardson, Thomas Reid, and Edmund Burke, among others (95). The position of women in Regency society provided an equally important motive for Austen's focus on social signals and body language. Taught to be reticent and self-effacing, their speech limited by the dictates of propriety, non-verbal modes of communication allowed women to express that which could not be said: 'The conduct book tradition … focused the attention of women writers … on the very activities—meaningful looks, unspoken displays of interest and assent in conversation, silently "reading" others through tracking their nonverbal behaviors—that would encourage the discrimination and representation of theory of mind phenomena' (95).

In her two-part essay 'Metarepresentation and Decoupling in *Northanger Abbey*', Barbara McMahon foregrounds another crucial aspect of theory of mind, metarepresentation, the process of being aware of the source of a thought or an utterance and using that awareness to evaluate the information conveyed. Metarepresentation is central to successful mindreading because some sources are more trustworthy than others. McMahon is clear that she does not offer an original reading of *Northanger Abbey* but rather uses traditional readings to explain metarepresentation in both social and literary contexts. People who possess a functioning theory of mind metarepresent automatically most of the time.

McMahon's discussion draws on both relevance theory, an account of cognition developed by Dan Sperber and Deirdre Wilson and on work on theory of mind by Leda Cosmides and John Tooby. Both approaches distinguish between literal and non-literal statements; the latter include all remarks (including thoughts) that are not strictly literal such as paraphrase, irony, general belief, speculation, fantasy, and other common modes of articulating perceptions. In relevance theory, these are called 'interpretive' statements; Cosmides and Tooby refer to them as 'decoupled statements' because they are held safely in an 'offline area', where they do not necessarily influence behaviour (523). In terms of relevance theory, a novel can be defined as an extended interpretive utterance (and so the creation of a possible world); in terms of decoupling, a novel is a narrative of events decoupled from the real world.

Casting *Northanger Abbey* in terms of these cognitive theories, McMahon points out that 'a number of characters … fail to understand one another' (part 1, 532) because they cannot make the distinction between literal and interpretive/decoupled statements; they fail to accurately metarepresent. This is especially true of Catherine, who has 'problems with both mindreading and with decoupling the world of fiction from her real world' (part 1, 532). For instance, when Henry teases her about what she can expect to encounter at *Northanger Abbey*, he predicts events that he knows are interpretive/decoupled from reality, and he expects Catherine to realise that he is joking.[2] But she does not realise this—at least not fully—because she does not adequately decouple Gothic fiction from reality, as readers from 1817 through today have realised.

To make matters yet more complicated, Catherine's intuition about the General turns out to be correct. He might not have murdered or imprisoned his wife, but he prioritises wealth above his children's happiness, he puts Catherine in danger by sending her travelling with no money, and he is all round not a very nice person—in fact, he is not all that different from a typical Gothic villain. Catherine's 'failure' to metarepresent Henry's joke accurately might well signal that her capacity for judging character is superior to Henry's, for despite her naivety about the Gothic, she does not accept that General Tilney's benevolence is genuine. By our very understanding of this situation, we demonstrate that people are able to process very complex metarepresentational embeddings without specific or conscious learning, a quality that we use while engaged with real as well as fictional people.

Discussions of Austen's representation of theory of mind have generally elucidated its undeniably positive value. It is certainly foundational to the extraordinary and unprecedented social intelligence of humans as compared to all other mammals, even our great ape cousins; many believe it is an exclusively human capability. Because theory of mind enables us to understand what others are thinking without actually being inside their minds, it has come to be called 'mindreading', in academic as well as informal circles. But we cannot truly read minds; we can only infer their contents, and inference is subject to error.

In '"To Know What You Are All Thinking": Riddles and Minds in Jane Austen's *Emma*,' Jeanne Britton demonstrates Austen's awareness and representation of this fallibility. Building on the now-familiar claim that free indirect discourse is the formal correlative of theory of mind, Britton calls attention to Austen's use of this narrative device to convey not only the narrator's mindreading of characters but characters' mindreading of one another. This point has been taken for granted in scholarly discussions (of course the narrator reads characters' minds and characters read one another's minds!), but Britton shows that layering characters' free indirect discourse within that of the narrator is crucial in terms of thematizing theory of mind—calling attention to people thinking about other people thinking. The narrator's free indirect discourse formally imitates the characters' attempts to read other people's thoughts through 'grammatical structure, imaginative embodiment, and affective imitation' (660), the same formula for representing the thoughts of characters that is used by the narrator. For example, here is Emma as she helps Harriet compose a rejection of Robert Martin's proposal: 'The looking over his letter again, in replying to it, had *such a softening tendency that it was particularly necessary to brace her up with a few decisive expressions ...* ' (emphasis mine). To this point the narrator has been using free indirect discourse to convey Emma's thoughts, but as the passage continues, Emma does the same to express Harriet's thoughts: ' ... and she was so very much *concerned at the idea of making him unhappy, and thought so much of what his mother and sisters would think and say, and was so anxious that they should not fancy her ungrateful,* that Emma believed if the young man had come in her way at that moment, he would have been accepted after all' (emphasis mine, 57–8).

These attempts at mindreading, and the free indirect discourse that expresses them, often appear in scenes involving riddles and games and therefore suggest metonymically that uncertainty and guesswork are involved in theory of mind. Both processes, solving puzzles and reading minds, depend on interpreting clues, verbal ones for the games and social signals for theory of mind. And in both cases, one can come up with the wrong answer. The narrative sequencing of events is often significant in this network of identifications and commentary: the episodes featuring riddles and games begin with wordplay, then focus on instances of theory of mind, and end with passages of free indirect discourse that mimic the process of mindreading, as in the scenes involving Mr Elton's courtship charade. His riddle ostensibly encodes a verbal puzzle, but the more important interpretive challenge refers to decoding the object of its flattery, a case involving mindreading. When Mr Elton later declares his love to Emma, solving that particular riddle, the narrator shifts into free indirect discourse, tracing Emma's thoughts, both her realisation of her failure to mindread correctly and her regret for her mistakes: Emma 'would gladly have submitted to feel yet more mistaken—more in error—more disgraced by mis-judgment than she actually was, could the effects of her blunders have been confined to herself' (qtd. in Britton 665). Theory of mind is at best a sophisticated form of puzzle solving.

The limitations of mindreading are conveyed by another issue in *Emma* that has received critical attention, the lack of narrative omniscience. Just as the narrative demonstrates that people often fail in their attempts to mindread, so the narrator does not display the omniscience associated with third-person narrators. The narrator's limited omniscience 'parallels the limits of human knowledge about other minds' (674). This chain of equivalences among theory of mind, free indirect discourse, mindreading failures of *Emma*'s fictional people, and limited narratorial omniscience, 'challenges the influential assessments of the coercive force attributed to free indirect discourse' (675) and by analogy to theory of mind, assessments found in both literary studies and cognitive science. Austen's most substantial stylistic contribution to the novel as a genre is also a consideration of the boundaries between minds, boundaries that protect as well as obscure.

Austen and Social Science Methodology

The essays discussed so far have involved the application of social-science theory and research to Austen's novels. Some scholars have ventured further into interdisciplinary territory, applying social-science methodologies in their research. I will look at two studies that take this approach: *Graphing Jane Austen: The Evolutionary Basis of Literary Meaning* by Joseph Carroll and his research team, grounded in evolutionary literary studies, and 'Literary Neuroscience and History of Mind: An Interdisciplinary fMRI Study of Attention and Jane Austen' by Natalie Phillips, which uses neuroscience to explore the perceptual and neural qualities involved in different modes of reading.

Carroll et al. studied Austen's novels by analysing the results of a widely distributed questionnaire. The questionnaire is a familiar quantitative method used in the social sciences, and it is generally believed to yield evidence-based—and hence reliable—results. However, the method has its dangers; among the pitfalls of surveys are first, that one can skew results through biased input, such as leading questions or the omission of questions that might yield undesirable results, and second, that the results of any computation must be interpreted. In *Graphing Jane Austen: The Evolutionary Basis of Literary Meaning*, the problematic conclusions of these authors with respect to gender demonstrate the weak points of quantitative research methods.[3]

Carroll et al. asked responders to select among a list of characters from various novels and then to assess these characters by giving them numerical ratings pertaining to a range of traits and aspirations. Among these qualities were valence, whether a character had laudable values in line with those of the novel as a whole, and salience, how important the chosen character was in the text (for instance, protagonist, antagonist, minor character, etc.). They found that male and female characters, especially protagonists, held laudable values in common, and they therefore concluded that the significance of gender has been exaggerated by literary scholars of the nineteenth-century novel, including Austen scholars: although 'many of Austen's critics have taken gendered power relations as the central organizing theme of her work, this contention clearly cannot be taken as self-evident' (109).

To begin with, this observation proposes odd criteria by which to assess the importance or even the presence of gender issues in Austen's work because a focus on gender need not necessarily take the form of conflicting values between or among characters. Rather, the lack of difference in the moral values of Austen's male and female protagonists proves rather than undermines the significance of gender for Austen. In Austen's era, sexual and gender differences were often invoked to justify male domination and privilege, rendering challenges to the gendering of traits an ineluctably progressive, feminist stance, as we see in the era's most famous feminist text, Mary Wollstonecraft's *A Vindication of the Rights of Women* (Jones, *Consensual Fictions* 51–60). Moreover, Austen's characterisations of female characters accord with Wollstonecraft's ideas of women's rationality and morality. Her thoughtful heroines who assert themselves to do the right thing or point out injustices are a far cry from the docile, self-effacing proper ladies of conservative ideology, as seen, for instance, in Hannah More's *Coelebs in Search of a Wife* (Johnson 1–27). Even Fanny Price, Austen's most self-effacing heroine, opposes the wishes of her guardian and refuses to marry Henry Crawford because she does not love or trust him. To miss the defiance of patriarchal views conveyed by representations that portray women's morals, values, and attitudes as similar to those of men requires ignoring the intellectual, political, and social milieu in which Austen wrote.

Phillips organised a research team comprising literary scholars and neuroscientists to investigate differences in brain function between reading for pleasure and close reading. Pleasure reading was defined as reading as if one had casually picked a book from a bookshelf; close reading was defined as reading as if one were going to write an essay, paying attention to literary phenomena such as tone, characterisation, plot structure, characterisation, and so forth.

The study used graduate students as subjects, and the reading material was the second chapter of *Mansfield Park*, a novel chosen because it is one of Austen's lesser-known works to all but fans and scholars of Austen. A relatively unfamiliar text was likely to show typical results about brain activity that occurs with each kind of reading strategy—familiarity might have distorted these patterns. Subjects read within an fMRI (functional Magnetic Resonance Imaging) scanner that shows which areas of the brain are active, and which also used fMRI-compatible eye-tracking, which records how subjects move their eyes as they read. The fMRI allowed the comparison of cognitive patterns that emerge when subjects read a literary work with these different kinds of focus (casual or analytical), while the eye-tracking told whether pace of reading increased or decreased by registering the amount of time people spent on a passage. The chapter was divided into sections, and instructions at the beginning of each section told the reader whether to read for pleasure or to engage in close reading.

Results indicated that close reading activates regions of the brain that govern our sense of touch and that initiate voluntary movement as well as language processing areas, whereas pleasure reading tends to confine itself to the latter. The kind of neural integration (combining of input from different brain areas) that close reading induces is good for the brain, helping it to function flexibly and optimally; because the brain is a dynamic system, it gains in complexity and capability when multiple and diverse areas activate (Siegel). As literary scholars have long suspected, close reading is exercise for the brain that results in cognitive benefits for the mind.

In addition to proving the cognitive benefits of literary study, Phillips expanded research on the neuroscience of reading and attention. Until Phillips's experiment, research trials in the study of attention and the neuroscience of reading considered words, phrases, and, at most, sentences. Changing the object of study to a chapter from a novel yielded results that could not have been obtained with the usual brief samples. Knowing that the brain changes according to how one is asked to read, and that these changes involve significantly distinct brain patterns, adds to our knowledge about how the brain works neurologically, which is of course, the goal of research in neuroscience.

The study prompted Phillips to ask if research that we do today might shed light on reading in the past. I find that this question leads to another: What mechanisms involved in reading remain constant across times and cultures? Of course, these questions might be largely unanswerable because we have limited access to knowledge about eighteenth-century brains. But we can use studies of the neurology of reading to explore questions that might well have answers: are characters more likely to be perceived as fictional people (not words on a page) according to our reading approach? Does reading style affect the degree to which we transpose the empathy engendered by reading to real-life situations?[4] Whatever issues in the neurology of reading we choose to explore, Phillips and her team have demonstrated that collaboration between literary scholars and mind-brain scientists can yield findings valuable to both fields. What is true about the brain is true about thinking at larger, disciplinary levels: integrating input from different areas can benefit the whole.

Austen and Attachment Studies

Much of the work on Austen that falls under the rubric of cognitive literary studies has focused on theory of mind and evolutionary studies, an emphasis I have followed in this survey. This was especially true of the aughts; more recently, however, the field has diversified. In 'Austen and Autism: Reading Brain, Emotion, and Gender Differences in *Pride and Prejudice*' (2014), Mikhal Dekel explores whether Mr Darcy might qualify for a diagnosis of Autism Spectrum Disorder. Matt Lorenz discusses *Pride and Prejudice* with respect to social identity theory, the tendency of people to identify to differing degrees with the groups to which they belong in '*Pride and Prejudice* and Social Identity Theory'. Christopher R. Miller's *Surprise: The Poetics of the Unexpected from Milton to Austen* examines how attitudes toward surprise, considered by many to be an innate, basic emotion, changed in the course of the long eighteenth century. Although spoiled for choice with the proliferation of topics among cognitive literary scholars, I have chosen to focus on work grounded in attachment theory. I do so in the interest of authentic interdisciplinarity which, if it is to truly reflect the relationship between Austen and the social sciences, should address issues that are current and germane to both approaches.

Studies involving theory of mind and evolution as well as other topics in cognitive literary studies fulfil this requirement. But in the area that has traditionally attracted literary scholars, psychotherapeutic theory, literary study continues in the direction it has taken for the last thirty or so years, incorporating, building on, and critiquing classic Freudian and Lacanian psychoanalysis from a poststructuralist perspective.[5] For instance, while affect theory shares the focus on feeling that has also transformed psychology and cognitive studies, this subfield tends to consider the topic in the context of Theory rather than current research on the emotions (Hogan 2016). This focus is not truly interdisciplinary because it continues to draw on a tradition that belongs to literary scholarship (and other work in the humanities) and not to scholarship on emotion and feeling relevant to contemporary scholarship in the *social sciences*.

Attachment theory is currently one of the most influential paradigms in psychology, including neuroscience, social psychology, and developmental psychology. Attachment theory emphasises that attachment is crucial to brain development, that attachment relationships of various kinds can reshape the brain throughout the lifespan, and that well-being throughout our lives depends to a great degree on the quality of attachment we experience. Attachment theory is also vital to current psychotherapeutic theory and practice, and in fact grounds all current approaches insofar as the therapeutic alliance—the quality of attachment between therapist and client—as been shown to be the most significant factor in a successful therapeutic outcome (Wachtel 103). Attachment theory is strongly evidence-based, using both quantitative and qualitative data. Yet few literary scholars have recognised its paramount significance.[6] The long association of literary studies with psychotherapy—we gave a home to psychotherapy during the dark days of behaviourism, when emotion was banished from academic psychology and the brain was thought to be an advanced if organic supercomputer—and the central place of attachment theory in psychology argue for its inclusion in literary studies. But the most cogent reason stems from its capacity to provide a vital, organising discursive frame for reading. This is especially true for work on Austen, whose novels revolve around the ways that people relate and attach, or fail to attach, to one another.

Kay Young writes on Austen from an attachment-studies perspective. In chapters on Austen in *Imagining Minds: The Neuroaesthetics of Austen, Eliot, and Hardy*, Young reads *Emma* and *Persuasion* as narratives about healing from dissociation, which she refers to in its neurological aspect as a lack of neural integration within the brain; both attachment and neural integration are key concepts within attachment studies and social neuroscience. As noted above, the brain is a dynamic system, which means that the more of its parts that work together, the better it functions; such benefits extend both to the capacities of the mind and to well-being more generally. Rendering dissociated aspects of the mind available for processing and reflection involves reintegrating the neural patterns that generate these aspects of mind and thought within the wider network of neural activity from which they have separated. The quality of one's relationships, past and present, influences the extent to which thoughts and feelings are connected and neural areas integrated. Security fosters the development of neural integration in babies and children's brains, and it facilitates neural interconnectivity in those of adults.

Emma's imaginative turn is symptomatic of dissociation and so a lack of neural integration. Living in her imagination far too much of the time, Emma cuts herself off from perceptions outside her own inventive mind, and so she misses readily available information, such Mr Elton's wish to marry her. She also dissociates from her own feelings, especially her love for Mr Knightley. In short, she lacks what Young calls 'self-consciousness' (41), awareness of herself in terms of her relationship to others, and so she inhabits an enclosed and imaginative interiority. She is not unhappy (she is 'lively and at ease') (251), or without feeling (she certainly has desires and ambitions), but the impetus for much of her feeling comes from her imagination, as does her sense of reality. And when the perception of feelings—her own or others'—interferes with the imagination, Emma is blinkered. Emma 'lives in a narrative state of self-imagining and self-reflection—there is very little to "distress or vex" that narrative state of inward turn' (41).

That vexation comes when incidents at Box Hill jolt Emma into awareness that she lives in a world of other people, so that she becomes 'at last cognizant of the world beside her not of her design, and of herself in relation to others over time' (48). Feelings motivate this knowledge, and they are indeed feelings of vexation to begin with. Although Emma does not yet realise that she loves Mr Knightley, his disapproval matters intensely. And she is ashamed of her witty quip at Miss Bates's expense, which came purely from wit dissociated from context—perhaps funny in and of itself but not when it is a statement that causes pain to its target. Vexation and humiliation upset the equilibrium of Emma's closed and defensive system, causing the flow of (neural) energy between sequestered parts of the brain, and information across dissociated parts of her mind. After this, Emma begins to know herself more fully, becoming cognizant of her attachments to other people and of the threat posed to those attachments by her dwelling too much in her own mind.

Dissociation, a lack of neurally integrated brain areas, is also the problem in *Persuasion*. Like Emma, Anne lives far too much in her head, but unlike Emma, she is acutely aware of her feelings. The dissociation in her case involves a disconnect from her bodily, physical self, which she suffers because of a total lack of 'relational objects', people (called 'objects' when represented within our own minds) who affirm our existence through the process of relating. Young observes that 'having oneself be represented by another as an object … [is] necessary to the emergence and maintenance of one's own feeling of being known and knowable as well as knowing' (58). But Anne has been a 'non-object' in the eyes of her family for so long that she has been erased in their minds and in her own, an erasure expressed by her dissociation from her body, as if she were slowly disappearing altogether. She lives a kind of ghostly existence, taking herself out of the way of lively activities (such as playing the piano instead of dancing), and accepting that her bloom has faded, as if her body is dead or dying in many respects. She is withdrawn and rarely speaks. Her erasure further includes being invisible as a sexual, desirable woman. Young observes that '[t]he felt-quality of loss throughout the opening [of *Persuasion*] is what we experience as what outwardly remains of Anne registered through her body—faded, thin, quiet—traces of a consciousness that has lost its relational objects' (60). She no longer knows herself as a person whose opinions and desires—whose very life—matters in the least.

Anne had lost the 'feeling [of] her own presence' (83) after the death of her mother, who enabled her to feel worthy of being considered by another, a feeling she also had enjoyed during her brief (first) engagement to Wentworth, and which she has lost again by the time *Persuasion* begins. It takes Wentworth's return, which gradually becomes a return to *her*, to reconnect Anne with her bodily existence. This process begins by his actual closeness in taking Anne's annoying nephew off her back and then later in handing her into a carriage. Not only does Wentworth's proximity bring bodily awareness to Anne, but his consideration demonstrates his attunement to her feelings, that he holds her in his mind (he becomes once again a 'relational object'). When Wentworth suddenly sees Anne as attractive through the mediation of Mr Elliot's admiration—an indication that she has recovered her bloom—Anne recovers the feeling and knowledge of her own body, feeling 'fully conscious because fully embodied … [Wentworth is] the relational object that enables that [bodily and self-aware] representation' (63).

Young's readings show that neural integration, and the kinds of secure relationships that foster it, lead to emergent states of well-being. That is to say, the well-being of each of the characters Young discusses increases far more than might have been predicted as the consequence of any of the precipitating events Austen portrays. Take Anne. After Wentworth hands her into the carriage, we begin to see that her depression has lifted. Even if this moment works in tandem with other events that have bettered Anne's situation (such as spending time with the Musgroves), none of these, nor all of them together, could have been expected to effect the global change we see in Anne—to produce the Anne of Lyme, 'no one, so proper, so capable' (123). However, each of these positive events intervenes in the mind-brain-body system that is Anne, and as with all dynamic systems, a small change can ripple through its various parts, causing emergent change—a change that is greater than the sum of its parts. Emergent changes that accompany tweaks to the system recursively and geometrically lead to even greater changes, and these produce the well-being felt by each of these characters.

In her essay '"My Fanny": The Price of Play', Bethany Wong also draws on attachment theory, especially the work of paediatrician and psychotherapist D. W. Winnicott, to consider Fanny Price's inability to play, a trait that has alienated many readers of *Mansfield Park*. Winnicott argues that play is essential to both creativity and well-being: 'It is in playing and only in playing that the individual child or adult is able to be creative and to use the whole personality, and it is only in being creative that the individual discovers the self' (qtd. in Wong 137). Developing the capacity for play depends on the sense of security engendered by adequate care on the part of attachment figures.

Fanny has lacked such security for much of her life. Born to a mother who did not particularly want her, and encountering relatives who dismiss and undermine her at Mansfield Park, Fanny inhabits a 'world where she is never in control, can never be secure, and can never stop being afraid or in pain—a setting where she cannot play' (142). However, Fanny has felt loved and supported by William and Edmund; she was actually a playfellow for her brother when they were young, and Edmund's contribution to Fanny's life as a watchful and protective friend as well as loving mentor mitigates the evils that come her way. The love and care of these two slowly enable Fanny to acquire the capacity for play, which emerges as her circumstances improve. When William visits Mansfield Park and Fanny enjoys both his and Edmund's company, it takes very little—the offer of a ball by Sir Thomas (and so an acknowledgement of her worth on his part)—to set in motion the urge and ability to play that has been so lacking in Fanny's life. The narrator suggests that Fanny will acquire even greater resources for play and playfulness in the future. *Mansfield Park* aligns with research showing that secure attachment and its benefits can be acquired later in life, a process designated by the term 'earned secure attachment'.[7]

Wong concludes that not only William and Edmund, but also the narrator supports Fanny, watching over her as 'the good enough mother' (Winnicott) who enables the child to play without feeling abandoned. The narrator of *Mansfield Park* breaks the fourth wall in a way unseen in Austen's other major novels, referring to Fanny as '[m]y Fanny' (533). In much the same extradiegetic fashion, Austen provides a space in which readers can also play: 'With all the heroism of principle and duty, we may seize Austen's novel and play in spite of ourselves with these fictional friends, who offer unlimited presence in our imagination. We play with the fiction in order to learn how to be alone with someone, to gain the resources to play, and to acquire the security to be creative individuals through our engagement with Austen's textual world' (152).

Jane Austen, Social Scientist

Austen approached the world from a scientific perspective, and she wrote like a scientist in the sense of insisting on accuracy and precision in her fictional worlds. Peter Knox-Shaw details Austen's scientific habits of observation noting, 'she was perhaps of all great creative writers of her generation the one most easily associated with an empirical habit of mind' (17). Such an approach came easily; Austen grew up in a family that loved science, and the children were exposed to its methodologies and findings from an early age. The Austen family even owned a microscope. At some point in her childhood, Austen's brother Edward gave her a copy of Thomas Percival's *Tales, Fables, and Reflections* (1775), a manual on science in the form of a conduct book; conduct literature was a typical way for ladies to learn about science (Williams 258–274). Knox-Shaw observes that *Tales* provides a thorough introduction to the discipline of science not only through its report of the work and findings of individual scientists and telling of the wonderful creations and mechanisms of the universe to be discovered in daily life, but also to the value of empirical habits of mind: Percival insists in *Tales* that 'a strict attention has been paid to truth and nature ... the narrations are conformable to the usual course of things, or derived from the records of history' (qtd. in Knox-Shaw, 19).

That Austen applied this scientific, empirical approach to writing is indicated in her advice to her niece Anna, who was writing a novel. Austen tells Anna not to write of Lyme because she has not allowed her characters sufficient time for travel there. Similarly, Anna should not write about her characters' trip to Ireland 'as you know nothing of the manners there .... You will be in danger of giving false representations' (qtd. in Knox-Shaw, 22). Austen famously did not write of scenes in which men talk amongst themselves because she could never have witnessed such scenes; she has Mr Knightley observe to Emma that Mr Elton might 'talk sentimentally' when women are around, but he voices very different opinions when 'talking in unreserved moments, when there are only men present' (70). Critics in Austen's day as well as our own recognised this scrupulous faithfulness to reality. One reviewer wrote, 'Austen's characters come to life as individuals because of the way they are surveyed in this microscopic detail' (qtd. in Knox-Shaw 23). Her most famous reviewer, Walter Scott, credits Austen with inventing a new kind of fiction characterised by its 'copying from nature' (qtd. in Knox-Shaw, 23).

It might have been Austen's scientific outlook that rendered her attractive to the greatest social scientist of the nineteenth century, Charles Darwin, her admirer throughout his life. Elizabeth Bankes suggests that Austen's 'empirical approach ... [which] emphasizes the need to look at particular details, to question "universal truths", and to be always ready to revise opinions in the light of new evidence' constitute 'journeys of interpretation [that] might well have appealed to the mind of a man who elsewhere was engaged in the ongoing process of examining evidence, drawing tentative conclusions, and questioning fundamental assumptions about the origins of life' (1–2). Along similar lines, Peter Graham suggests the shared scientific outlook of these two writers: Austen and Darwin were 'perhaps the great English empiricists of the nineteenth century' (xii). Graham further notes similarities in their interests 'such as sibling relationships and marriage' and in the scope of their studies: 'The microenvironment of the Galapagos island is similar in scale to Austen's "3 or 4 families in a country village"' (1).

Olivia Murphy (2017) takes the similarities between Darwin and Austen beyond resonance and admiration to suggest that it is possible that Austen actually influenced Darwin. Murphy speculates that Austen's representation of female choice in her marriage plots might well have inspired Darwin's ideas about sexual selection, although ironically, he would not accord human females this much social power, and humans remain an exception to the theory. It would be a nice ironic touch if the evolutionary theorists who turn to Austen's work to demonstrate human universals of mate selection were actually calling on Darwin's own source.

Finally, Austen might actually be considered a social scientist as well as a pioneer of mind-brain science because she so precisely captures the workings of various aspects of thought and feeling in a social context. Cognitive literary scholarship on Austen works with this assumption, and some scholars make the claim outright. Alan Richardson describes Austen as 'an early theorist of ... theory of mind' (81). Patrick Hogan suggests that Austen so accurately depicts the workings of theory of mind that her novels 'might contribute to our understanding of sociocognitive understanding ... [W]hen contextualized by current cognitive scientific research, Austen's finely nuanced observations of interpersonal understanding and misunderstanding convey insights about the nature, operation, and functions of social cognition' ('Lessons' 180–181).

In *Jane on the Brain: Exploring the Science of Social Intelligence with Jane Austen*, I turn to Austen's novels to illustrate the social and embodied mind-brain. In the spirit of Austen's own writings and of the various societies dedicated to her (my own is the Jane Austen Society of North America), the book addresses an audience of fans as well as scholars. I begin with a question germane to both populations of readers: what accounts for Austen's tremendous popularity? I offer two answers. To begin with, we care about Austen's characters because it is our biological destiny to be interested in people and their stories; the human brain is a social brain. As Alan Palmer argues in *Fictional Minds*, we tend to think of literary characters as real people and to engage with 'fictional minds' just as we do with real ones. Austen's characters are so believable, so life-like, that for many of us, they are not just imaginary beings but tantamount to friends whom we know and love.

This ability to create true-to-life fictional people yields the second reason for Austen's popularity. I believe that we love Austen because she understands the breadth and depth of human psychology so thoroughly that we feel that she empathises with us, her readers. I follow Decety and Meyer in defining empathy as the ability to think and feel from someone else's perspective, and this capacity means not only understanding another's thoughts and feelings (theory of mind) but actually feeling their emotions, although recognising them as separate from our own.

Humans have a profound need for empathy. When we read Austen's novels, we know that she understands us because she understands 'human nature', those characteristics found across human cultures, such as the need for support, caring, and above all empathy, which tells us we are present to others. Answering just what it is that Austen gets so right provided the occasion for me to offer an introduction to social intelligence, an account of the psychological and neurological processes that enable our prodigious social abilities as a species.

I use Mr Darcy's contemptuous glance at Elizabeth to present basic information about brain anatomy and function, tracing how a glance travels from eyes to consciousness—and judgment!—while Elizabeth Bennet's reactions show that emotions are appraisal systems that tell us how to deal with other people and situations. *Sense and Sensibility* supports research in neuroscience that discredits the dichotomy between reason and passion, so virulent a binary in Western philosophy and culture. Psychotherapeutic concepts receive attention in a chapter considering the subconscious and other analytic concepts that have stood the tests of time and research (turning here to *Pride and Prejudice* again). A chapter on *Sense and Sensibility* explains how and why the brain is capable of change, and so therefore amenable to the influence of psychotherapy. The relationships in *Mansfield Park* point to neurological systems that govern relationships of all kinds—with family, friends, and intimate partners.

Mansfield Park and *Sense and Sensibility* illustrate attachment styles, distinct and predictable ways of relating to close others, and the influences that tend to produce them. The brain's development, emotional and social as well as cognitive, depends on a baby's relationship with caregivers. Receiving empathy instills a sense of security and self-esteem, key components of a secure attachment style (a confident, relaxed approach to relationships); social intelligence, including the ability to read social signals and form positive relationships; and the ability to extend empathy to others. As neuroscientist Simon Baron-Cohen says, secure attachment is a 'pot of gold' (72). Nor do we ever outgrow the need for recognition and affirmation. Adults as well as children and babies need people who provide a 'secure base' (Bowlby), a person whom they can depend on for emotional support and 'refueling' (Mahler), the replenishment of emotional reserves that enables us to endure the 'slings and arrows' of being out there in the world.

I discuss empathy, the crown jewel of the social brain, in a chapter on *Emma*, explaining how its components, cognitive perspective-taking (theory of mind) and emotional resonance, are conveyed to others, as well as some of the neurology that might be essential to empathy, such as mirror neurons. I focus on the vital role of empathy in human connection by tracing Emma's moral awakening, her realisation that to be truly kind and good, she must understand the perspectives and situations of others. *Persuasion* and *Northanger Abbey* provide abundant material to discuss personality disorders, which can be considered as empathy disorders (Baron-Cohen), and which tend to result from traumatic experience—either sins of omission (neglect or an absence of affection, resonance, and affirmation) or commission (abuse). Empathy and attachment share centre stage as the organising principles of my book.

Jane on the Brain concludes with a summary of the social brain through a discussion of Austen's last and best heroine, Anne Elliot. Attention to all the factors of mind, brain, body, and environment that have contributed to her prodigious social intelligence account for why there is 'no one so proper, so capable, as Anne'. We can trace the experiences that make Anne who she is. This is less true for her creator, about whom we have scant personal information, especially regarding her personal thoughts and feelings. But whatever miracle of contingency—of the mixture of nature and nurture, biology and culture, genes and the environment—that produced Jane Austen, her profound understanding of human psychology has been appreciated by readers from her day to our own.

Notes

1 Other scholars who assert the universality of parental investment theory also encounter problems with justifying their claim. Stasio and Duncan cite parental investment theory as a determinant of mate choice in Austen, but then state that they also see mate choice as influenced by the 'historically relevant qualities Austen and her audience would have found most appealing' (138). Krueger et al. observe that Austen's characterizations of women's mating strategies are remarkably similar to depictions in the modern literature of evolutionary psychology. This observation explains why evolutionary literary critics like to write on Austen, it does not prove cause and effect between human mating patterns and literary representation.
2 Jocelyn Harris has suggested an alternative reading: Henry does not expect Catherine to understand that he is joking, and he is actually setting her up for subsequent humiliation. This motive would be in character given Henry's relish of his superiority over Catherine and his more generalised disdain for women and their concerns.
3 For an extensive critique of applying computational, quantitative methods to literary analysis, see Da.
4 The extent to which reading fosters empathy is a topic of interest in cognitive literary studies. See, for instance, Vermeule, Keene, and Jones, *Jane on the Brain*.
5 Many of Freud's insights have been incorporated into current psychotherapeutic theories—denial, for instance—rendering all psychotherapy Freudian to some degree. I use the word 'classic' to refer Freud's theories as he originally articulated them, many of which have been revised or rejected by the majority of psychotherapeutic theorists and practitioners.
6 Psychotherapy has always been largely about neural integration, even if it was not—could not be—spoken of in these terms. The well-known psychological concept of dissociation can be described as a lack of neural integration in neurological terms. For an excellent and detailed account of neural integration, see Siegel.
7 The concept of earned attachment security was formulated by Mary Main, the originator of the Adult Attachment Interview, and her research team. For an early instance of the concept see Main et al.

Works Cited

Austen, Jane. *Emma*. Cambridge UP, 2005.
Austen, Jane. *Mansfield Park*. Cambridge UP, 2005.
Austen, Jane. *Northanger Abbey*. Cambridge UP, 2006.
Austen, Jane. *Persuasion*. Cambridge UP, 2006.
Austen, Jane. *Pride and Prejudice*. Cambridge UP, 2013.
Austen, Jane. *Sense and Sensibility*. Cambridge UP, 2006.
Bankes, Elizabeth. '"Read and Reread until They Could Be Read No More": Charles Darwin and the Novels of Jane Austen.' *Pesuasions: The Jane Austen Journal On-Line*, vol. 30, no. 2, 2010, https://search.proquest.

com/openview/c5efe81c2364cb6d2a49013e9b07ac37/1?pq-origsite=gscholar&cbl=4462234. Accessed 7 Mar. 2021.

Baron-Cohen, Simon. *The Science of Evil: On Empathy and the Origins of Cruelty*. Basic Books, 2011.

Bateman, Angus John. 'Intrasexual Selection in Drosophilia.' *Heredity*, vol. 2, no. 3, 1948, pp. 249–368.

Belmonte, Matthew. 'Does the experimental Scientist Have a "Theory of Mind"?' *Review of General Psychology*, vol. 12, 2008, pp. 192–204.

Bowlby, John. *A Secure Base: Parent-Child Attachment and Healthy Human Development*. Basic Books, 1988.

Boyd, Brian. 'Jane Meet Charles: Literature, Evolution, and Human Nature.' *Philosophy and Literature*, vol. 22, no. 1, 1998, pp. 1–30.

Britton, Jeanne M. '"To Know What You Are All Thinking": Riddles and Minds in Jane Austen's *Emma*.' *Poetics Today*, vol. 39, no. 4, (December), 2018, pp. 651–678.

Butte, George. *I Know that You Know that I Know: Narrating Subjects from Moll Flanders to Marnie*. Ohio UP, 2004.

Carroll, Joseph et al. *Graphing Jane Austen: The Evolutionary Basis of Literary Meaning*. Palgrave Macmillan, 2012.

Carroll, Joseph et al. 'Human Nature and Literary Meaning: A Theoretical Critique Illustrated with *Pride and Prejudice*.' *The Literary Animal*, edited by Jonathan Gottschall and David Sloan Wilson. Northwestern University Press, 2005.

Cosmides, Leda, and John Tooby. 'Consider the Source: The Evolution of Adaptations for Decoupling and Metarepresentations.' *Metarepresentations: A Multidisciplinary Perspective*, edited by Dan Sperber. Oxford UP, 2000, pp. 53–116.

Da, Nan Z. 'The Computational Case against Computational Literary Studies.' *Critical Inquiry*, vol. 45, no. 3, 2019, pp. 601–639.

Decety, Jean, and Meghan Meyer. 'From Emotion Resonance to Empathic Understanding: A Social Developmental Neuroscience Account.' *Development and Psychopathology*, vol. 20, 2008, pp. 1053–1080.

Dekel, Mikhal. 'Austen and Autism: Reading Brain, Emotion, and Gender Differences in *Pride and Prejudice*.' *Nineteenth-Century Gender Studies*, Issue 10, 2014, http://ncgsjournal.com/issue103/dekel.htm.

Fine, Cordelia. *Testosterone Rex: Unmaking the Myths of Our Gendered Minds*. W. W. Norton & Company, 2017.

Goldsmith, Oliver. *An History of the Earth and Animated Nature*. J. Nourse, 1744.

Graham, Peter. *Jane Austen & Charles Darwin: Naturalists and Novelists*. Routledge, 2008.

Harris, Jocelyn. 'Magnificent Miss Morland.' Annual General Meeting of the Jane Austen Society of North America, 4 October, 2019, Williamsburg, VA, Plenary: Williamsburg Lodge.

Hogan, Patrick Colm. 'Affect Studies.' *Oxford Research Encyclopedia: Literature*. August, 2016. https://oxfordre.com/literature/view/10.1093/acrefore/9780190201098.001.0001/acrefore-9780190201098-e-105?result=1&rskey=s1wN09&mediaType=Article. Accessed 2 Jun. 2020.

Hogan, Patrick Colm. 'Lessons in Sociocognitive Understanding.' *Jane Austen and Sciences of the Mind*, edited by Beth Lau. Routledge, 2018, pp. 180–199.

Hrdy, Sarah Blaffer. *Mothers and Others: The Evolutionary Origins of Human Understanding*. The Belknap Press, 2011.

Jones, Wendy. *Consensual Fictions: Women, Liberalism, and the English Novel*. U of Toronto P, 2005.

Jones, Wendy. *Jane on the Brain*: Exploring the Science of Social Intelligence with Jane Austen. Pegasus, 2017.

Johnson, Claudia. *Jane Austen: Women, Politics, and the Novel*. U of Chicago P, 1988.

Keen, Suzanne. *Empathy and the Novel*. Oxford UP, 2010.

Knox-Shaw, Peter. *Jane Austen and the Enlightenment*. Cambridge UP, 2004.

Krueger, D. J. et al. 'Variation in Women's Mating Strategies Depicted in the Works and Words of Jane Austen.' *Journal of Social, Evolutionary, and Cultural Psychology*, vol. 7, no. 3, 2013, pp. 197–210.

Lau, Beth. 'Catherine's Education in Mindreading in *Northanger Abbey*.' *Jane Austen and Sciences of the Mind*, edited by Beth Lau. Routledge, 2018, pp. 37–57.

Lau, Beth. 'Sexual Selection and Female Choice in *Northanger Abbey*.' *Studies in the Novel*, vol. 50, no. 4, 2018, pp. 465–482.

Lodge, David. *Consciousness and the Novel: Connected Essays*. Harvard UP, 2002.

Lorenz, Matthew. '*Pride and Prejudice* and Social Identity Theory.' *Jane Austen and Sciences of the Mind*, edited by Beth Lau. Palgrave: Macmillan, 2018, pp. 115–135.

MacMahon, Barbara. 'Metarepresentation and Decoupling in *Northanger Abbey*: Part 1.' *English Studies*, vol. 90, no. 5, 2009, pp. 528–544.

MacMahon, Barbara. 'Metarepresentation and Decoupling in *Northanger Abbey*: Part 2.' *English Studies*, vol. 90, no. 6, 2009, pp. 673–694.

Mahler, Margaret. *The Selected Papers of Margaret S. Mahler, Volume Two: Separation-Individuation*. Janson Aronson, 1979.

Main, Mary et al. 'Security in Infancy, Childhood, and Adulthood: A Move to the Level of Representation.' *Monographs of the Society for Research in Child Development*, vol. 50, no. 1, pp. 66–104. Mary-darwinists.html. Accessed 7 Mar. 2021.

Miller, Christopher R. *Surprise: The Poetics of Unexpected Form from Milton to Austen*. Cornell UP, 2015.

Murphy, Olivia. 'A Future to Look Forward to? Evolution and Extinction in Jane Austen's *Persuasion*.' *Eighteenth-Century Life*, vol. 4, no. 2, 2017, pp. 154–170.

Palmer, Alan. *Fictional Minds*. University of Nebraska Press, 2008.

Phillips, Natalie M. 'Literary Neuroscience and History of Mind: An Interdisciplinary fMRI Study of Attention and Jane Austen.' *The Oxford Handbook of Cognitive Literary Studies*, edited by Lisa Zunshine. Oxford UP, 2015, pp. 56–81.

Prinz, Jesssie J. *Beyond Human Nature: How Culture and Experience Shape the Human Mind*. W. W. Norton & Company, 2012.

Richardson, Alan. *The Neural Sublime: Cognitive Theories and Romantic Texts*. The Johns Hopkins UP, 2010.

Ridley, Matthew. *Nature Via Nurture: Genes, Experience and What Makes Us Human*. Harper Collins, 2003.

Sapolsky, Robert M. *Behave: The Biology of Humans at Our Best and Worst*. Penguin Press, 2017.

Sapolsky, Robert M. *Monkeyluv: And Other Essays on Our Lives as Animals*. Scribner, 2005.

Siegel, Daniel. *The Developing Mind: How Relationships and the Brain Interact to Shape Who We Are*, 3rd ed. The Guilford Press, 2020.

Sperber, Dan, and Deirdre Wilson. *Relevance: Communication and Cognition*. Oxford UP, 1995.

Stasio, Michael J., and Kathryn Duncan. 'An Evolutionary Approach to Jane Austen: Prehistoric Preferences in *Pride and Prejudice*.' *Studies in the Novel*, vol. 39, no. 2, 2007, 133–146.

Trivers, Robert. 'Parental Investment and Reproductive Success.' *Natural Selection and Social Theory: Selected Papers of Robert Trivers*. Oxford UP, 2002. Pp. 56–110.

Vermeule, Blakey. *Why Do We Care About Literary Characters?* Johns Hopkins UP, 2010.

Wachtel, Paul. *Therapeutic Communication: Knowing What to Say When*. The Guildford Press, 2011.

Williams, Abigail. *The Social Life of Books: Reading Together in the Eighteenth-Century Home*. Yale UP, 2017. 258–274.

Winnicott, D. W. *Playing and Reality*. Routledge Classics, 2005.

Wong, Bethany. '"My Fanny": The Price of Play.' *Jane Austen and Sciences of the Mind*, edited by Beth Lau, Routledge, 2018, pp. 136–155.

Young, Kay. *Imagining Minds: The Neuroaesthetics of Austen, Eliot, and Hardy*. Ohio State UP, 2010.

Zunshine, Lisa. 'Why Jane Austen Was Different, And Why We May Need Cognitive Science to See It.' *Style*, vol. 41, no. 3, 2007, pp. 275–299.

PART IV

Austen's Communities:
A Sampling

30

PERSUASIONS: THE JANE AUSTEN JOURNAL AND *PERSUASIONS ON-LINE*: 'FORMED FOR [AN] ELEGANT AND RATIONAL SOCIETY'

Susan Allen Ford

DELTA STATE UNIVERSITY

At the end of 1979, a modest newsletter was mailed to the members of the newly constituted Jane Austen Society of North America (JASNA). Beneath an ornamental header reading 'PERSUASION' is an image of Jane Austen, based on Cassandra's watercolour but drawn by Pamela Susan Koppel, the fifteen-year-old daughter of a member (and future editor). Jane looks out steadily—though, because of the different sizes of her two eyes, somewhat quizzically. The thirty-two saddle-stapled pages include a photograph of two of the three founders of the organisation (Joan Austen-Leigh and J. David Grey, who also edited the issue), a report from the president (chiefly announcements), minutes of the meeting, an appeal for assistance in releading and reglazing the windows of St. Nicholas Church at Steventon, an account of 'Our First Dinner', a congratulatory telegram from the Committee of the Jane Austen Society (of the U.K.), a quiz, and a list of members organised by postal code (Figure 30.1).

A bit fewer than fourteen full pages contain what in hindsight we would now define as the heart of the publication: the two talks from JASNA's first meeting, Donald Greene's summary of his slide-illustrated 'Pemberley, Revisited' (694 words) and A. Walton Litz's 'The Picturesque in *Pride and Prejudice*' (2392 words); and three other contributions, Hilma D. Barrett's 'A Member's First Pilgrimage to Winchester' (702 words), Cathy Fried's 'Some Notes on the "Parish Business" in *Emma*' (502 words), and a letter to J. David Grey from the late novelist James T. Farrell, defining his admiration for Jane Austen (394 words). These contributions provide a welcome to JASNA's discussion of Jane Austen.

Henry Austen's 1818 description of his sister as 'formed for elegant and rational society' (5) might apply as well to *Persuasions* in its initial and ideal manifestation. Just as our understanding of Jane Austen has become more complex than Henry's words would seem to allow, however, so the journals of the society have outgrown that definition. From a newsletter with a distribution of approximately 450, mostly focused on building relationships among the members of the new organisation, *Persuasions: The Jane Austen Journal* and its complement *Persuasions On-Line* have grown into two refereed journals, one published in print and as ebook, with a circulation of approximately 5500, and the other published electronically on the organisation's website and accessible to all. Paradoxically, as the reach and audience of *Persuasions* have widened, it has become more scholarly in nature.

DOI: 10.4324/9780429398155-30-35

Figure 30.1   Persuasions No. 1 1979. Photo by Kim Rushing.

Joseph Weisenfarth speculates that in choosing a title for their newsletter Joan Austen-Leigh and J. David Grey 'first thought of the singular noun because they were persuaded to found the Society by Denis Mason Hurley, Joan's husband', who 'had been denied the use of a washroom at Chawton by Sir Hugh Smiley of the English Jane Austen Society' (1). By the second issue, the title had changed: according to a statement on the inside front cover, 'In order to avoid confusion with the one and only *Persuasion*, it has been decided to retitle our journal *Persuasions*'. Later, there was another explanation: a member mistakenly referred to the publication as '*Persuasions*', and Austen-Leigh and Grey recognised a superior title (Weisenfarth 1; Austen-Leigh, Editorial [1986] 2).[1] Printed at the bottom of the cover was 'The Jane Austen Society of North America', and, starting with issue No. 2 (1980), the interior publication information contained some version of '*Persuasions*, Journal of the Jane Austen Society of North America' (Figure 30.2). In an attempt to identify more

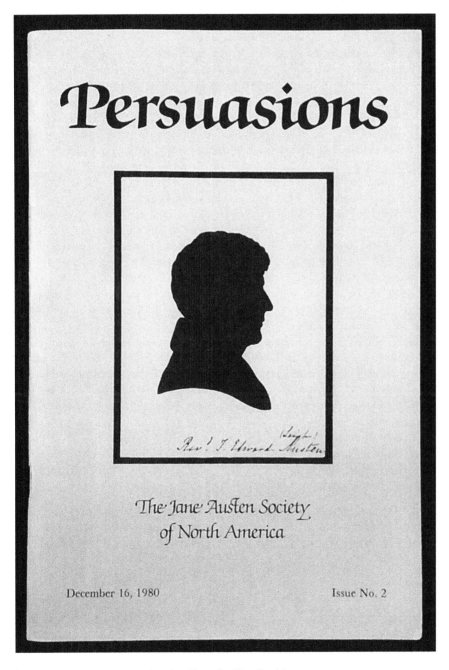

Figure 30.2 *Persuasions* No. 2 1980. Photo by Kim Rushing.

clearly the focus of the journal for non-members, in 1987 Juliet McMaster added the subtitle 'The Jane Austen Journal' to editorial stationery (McMaster), but due to a concern by the president, Lorraine Hanaway, and founders that 'another publication's sponsors across the water' (i.e., the JAS) would be offended (Hanaway), it was not added to the journal itself. Not until the 1998 redesign, under the editorship of Laurie Kaplan, did the subtitle—added without permission, fanfare, or comment—appear. While in 1987 Hanaway argued for the need for JASNA's members to 'feel[] that Persuasions is their journal' and against 'diluting this identification' (Hanaway), Kaplan's intent—like McMaster's (though in ignorance of that previous discussion)—was to define the journal as something more than a publication for members only.

The change from a newsletter for members to a journal that serves a complex audience that is both academic and non-academic was a gradual, though not an entirely smooth, one. An April 1979 letter to JASNA's patrons (mainly academics) and potential members announced a newsletter that would report the proceedings of the annual meeting and also solicited contributions 'that you think might interest the membership': 'They should not exceed 500 words in length unless absolutely necessary' (Austen-Leigh and Grey 2). In the early issues, many of the pieces representing the proceedings of the annual meetings were summaries. Financial contributions were made in 1982 so that two speeches (by Juliet McMaster and Enid Hildebrand) could be published at length (Austen-Leigh [1982] 2). Early issues also included reprints of relevant articles from periodicals such as the *New York Times* and the *Los Angeles Times*.

The early years of the journal show an attempt to figure out what readers wanted and needed as the organisation was built. From the beginning, the editorial position was defined partly in resistance to the academic world. Early correspondence between Joan Austen-Leigh and J. David Grey expresses Austen-Leigh's resentment of the academic: 'I think our function is to amuse our readers and let them express themselves in print. The likes of Ian Watt have any number of academic journals in which to publish their stuff. Ian Watt is a charming man, and famous, but altogether too long-winded in this case' (Letter [18 December 1981]). At almost 5000 words, Watt's talk—which begins with an apology for not preparing something special for the occasion of his address but instead 'fall-[ing] back onto a theme from a work in progress' (14)—is long even by the standards of today's journal. The note appended must, for Austen-Leigh, have added insult to injury: 'Since this address was prepared in haste, and for a very particular occasion and audience, Ian Watt wishes it to be considered not as a "publication" but merely as a printed souvenir for the members of the Jane Austen Society of North America' (14). For the following issue, *Persuasions* 4 (1982), Austen-Leigh set down a statement of editorial policy:

> First, what is *Persuasions* not. It is not an academic sounding board. Abstruse dissertations on recondite themes do not belong here.... Neither is *Persuasions* a reviewer of books. Other journals exist for that purpose....
>
> No, the object of *Persuasions* is to entertain: to amuse; to delight; to please; to publish new articles and to reprint old ones that many of our readers may not have seen. In short we aim to make this journal as 'light, and bright and sparkling' as it is possible without Jane, herself, to write for us.
>
> Speaking of Jane, this editor has a very pronounced dislike of hearing our author referred to as 'Austen,' as if she were her father, her brother or her nephew. This rather recent vogue—of calling women by their surnames without title—indulged in by feminists and provincial newspapers, is seldom, I am happy to say, followed by the *New York Times* or *The Times* of London, and never, by that doyen of all Jane Austen scholars, R. W. Chapman. Henceforth in these pages, Jane Austen, the woman who has inspired this

society, and engendered this journal, will be referred to as Jane Austen, J.A., or Jane, for Miss Austen she was not. (2)

Such a policy, however, proved difficult to enforce. Soon afterward, Austen-Leigh complained again to Jack Grey about academic papers, looking forward to an AGM where members would be speaking: 'After all they are likely to know far more about JA than any academic hack simply making his living' (Letter [8 January 1984]).[2]

The prejudice against admitting 'Austen' represented a convention that saw the use of a lady's surname unmodified by a Christian name or honorific as impolite, an affront to gentility. (And, of course, 'Miss Austen' would have referred to her elder sister, Cassandra.) Even the familiar 'Jane' seemed preferable as a way of referring to 'our author'. By the time the decade was out, however, change was afoot: JASNA's President Eileen Sutherland wrote to editor Gene Koppel with a carbon copy to her friend Joan Austen-Leigh: 'I have changed my mind about the use of "Austen"—I would *prefer Jane Austen* or even *JA*, but never *Jane*; however I think the use of "Austen" in a scholarly article puts her properly in the top rank of writers' (Sutherland). Although the controversy subsided, in some quarters the sentiment remained. The 2012 obituary for David Selwyn, editor of the *Report* of the U.K.'s Jane Austen Society, mentions that as editor he 'silently and mischievously changed every academic use of "Austen" that he came across to the more respectful, as he saw it, "Jane Austen"' (Lane 11).

There was a contradiction between eschewing academic control (and, sometimes, even participation) and the desire for scholarly recognition and academic buy-in. The first step in organising JASNA, after all, was inviting more than forty Austen scholars to serve as patrons, listing them along the left margin of the stationery (Austen-Leigh and Grey). During that initial year, one member contributed $100 'for the purpose of sending a mailing announcing our existence to one thousand departments of English' (Grey 4). JASNA's officers tracked (and publicised) standing orders of *Persuasions* by academic libraries (see, for example, Doudna). In *Persuasions* No. 5 Joan Austen-Leigh celebrated its growth:

> Now a sturdy five-year-old, it has graduated from where it was an honour for anyone to notice it (even the likes of Robert Martin) to being acknowledged as an established member of literary society. It has achieved the dignity of having an ISSN (International Standard Serial Number) bestowed upon it, and been indexed by the *Modern Languages Association* for the *Bibliography*. (2)

Copy for a 1989 flyer developed by Juliet McMaster to advertise *Persuasions* to university libraries quoted Norman Page, A. Walton Litz, and B. C. Southam. Page defined *Persuasions* as 'a substantial scholarly journal containing a wide range of critical and biographical essays'. Litz described it as 'a full-scale annual indispensable to Austen scholars and university libraries,… a pleasant mixture of the light-hearted and the serious' (JASNA, Library flyer).

What was imagined for both JASNA and its journal was oxymoronic: sportive thought or serious fun. Or, as brochures devised in 1987–1988 put it,

> The Jane Austen Society of North America brings scholars and enthusiasts, amateurs and professionals together on equal terms to study and celebrate the genius of Jane Austen…. We are a serious but not a stuffy group. Major libraries and educational institutions recognize our literary journal *Persuasions*, as an important source for Jane Austen studies, and our meetings include presentations of scholarly papers. Equally important, however, are lessons in eighteenth- and nineteenth-century card games and dancing, and fanciful debates over favorite characters or possible dinner conversations between Elizabeth Bennet and

Henry Tilney. Our inquiries delve into Jane Austen's life, her writings, and the era that gave shape to both. We may examine architecture, manners, humor, the military, religion, money, law, or dress. Jane Austen's interests were unlimited, and so are ours. (JASNA, Membership brochure)

In response to a reader's suggestion that *Persuasions* had strayed from Joan Austen-Leigh's editorial principles, Gene Koppel, editor from No. 10 (1988), offered a defence and an explanation of his editorial principles, pointing out that 'we… carry serious scholarly material (and have all along)':[3]

> Different readers will disagree about which essays should come under the 'interesting' and 'boring' headings. There is simply no way to avoid this. But one thing I *will* promise you. As long as I draw breath as editor (and I know the two other editors will back me up in this promise), I will *never* try to transform *Persuasions* into an imitation (or even real) scholarly journal. I can't imagine anything worse happening to the journal. There will continue to be overlap in the kind of articles we use, but we will also use pieces the scholarly journals would never consider…. [T]hese articles will continue to appear in *Persuasions* because we believe that JA's readers will find them useful and informative. We will also continue to publish purely light and personal pieces simply because we and our fellow JASNA members enjoy them. (Letter [5 April 1991])

Increasingly, as the annual general meetings became longer and larger, the scholarly contributions increased, and the 'light and personal pieces' migrated to the newsletter, which was established by Lorraine Hanaway in 1985. An editorial board was added with issue No. 16 in 1994 but was not used consistently until Laurie Kaplan's editorship, beginning in 1998.

The bibliographer David J. Gilson, in a letter to JASNA's third co-founder Henry Gershon Burke, captured a partial reason for JASNA's dependence on scholars, making a distinction between JASNA as a literary society and JAS as a society defined in terms of maintaining Austen's residence at Chawton as a memorial: 'your society began as a literary society with a high proportion of academics among its founder members, so that meetings of an academic cast are natural' (17 November 1980, qtd. in Wells 217). Deidre Shauna Lynch has remarked on divisions in somewhat different terms, citing the 'tensions' in what she terms Jane Austen cults, between the devotion of fandom and the dispassion of the scholar (111), 'between a popular audience and an academic one, between readers for whom Austen represents domestic privacy, leisure and sometimes shopping and professional scholars/teachers/readers for whom Austen represents career and a connection to the public sphere' (113).

While such a distinction has some validity, it does not wholly capture the complex readership of *Persuasions*. Laurie Kaplan's description, since No. 20 (1998) printed on the journal's second page, does the best job, describing the audience not in terms of difference but in terms of identity:

> The Editor welcomes submissions that offer original insights into the writing of Jane Austen and the period in which she lived. With clear and expressive language appropriate for both academic and informed general readers, articles should consider issues and concepts that open up the writings on a variety of levels, leading toward our common goal of becoming better readers and interpreters of Austen's works.

Kaplan's definition of the journal enforces a common language and encourages a common purpose. It has opened the way to a wide range of subjects and approaches while determining an inclusive clarity of expression.

Laurie Kaplan began her editorship with a redesign of the beige or tan-coloured 8½" by 5 ½" *Persuasions*, taking advantage of changes in publishing technologies. *Persuasions* No. 20 was a 9½" by

6½", startlingly handsome journal (with book, cover, and typography designed by Margaret Re). The multiple typefaces used (Monotype Bell, Trade Gothic, Snell Roundhand, and Arabesque Ornaments) mimicked the Regency's typographical emphasis on 'variety, energy, and symbolic complexity' as well as combining the traditional and the modern (Kaplan, Editor's Note 9). Extra-wide margins were provided for marginalia, encouraging active reading and further discussion among the members. The debossed cover featured a witty letter by Jane Austen to her sister, Cassandra, of 14 September 1804, in which she 'crossed' text in order to get more content on the page, giving greater value to her reader, who had to pay the postage. Gold (or more specifically Turner Yellow), a newly fashionable colour during Austen's life, evoked 'tradition', 'harmony', and the 'great brilliance that defines Jane Austen's place in literary history' (10) (Figure 30.3).

In another use of evolving technology, Laurie Kaplan issued JASNA's first online journal in the summer of 1999 (*Persuasions On-Line*). The idea was born of immediate necessity—a superfluity of publishable essays that year leading to not enough space (as finances dictated)—but also a sense of timeliness: 'We hope to expand the community of readers and continue the intimacy that JASNA offers a cohort of Janeites—that is, the community of readers of Jane Austen's novels who share a love of the texts and an interest in ideas' (Editor's Note). President Elsa A. Solender underscored the role of *POL* in 'advanc[ing] our mission,… "to foster among the widest number of readers the study, appreciation and understanding of Jane Austen's works, her life and her genius." We welcome to our website fellow enthusiasts, especially students and other young readers, and cordially invite them to join us' (President's Message).

Persuasions On-Line, open access, indexed by the *MLA Bibliography*, and included in a number of databases to which libraries subscribe, has certainly expanded the reach of JASNA's journal.

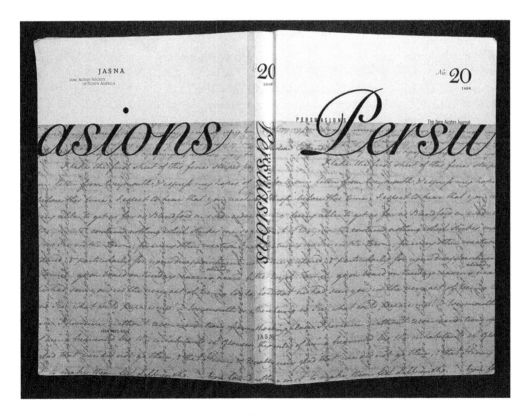

Figure 30.3 *Persuasions* No. 20 1998. Photo by Kim Rushing.

Although early on there was resistance from many authors to online as opposed to print publication, that disposition has changed for most authors. As editor, in 2006 Susan Allen Ford initiated a modest redesign of the *POL* pages. Since 2007, at the urging of webmaster Carol Medine Moss, *POL* has capitalised on its capacity to include highly illustrated pieces as well as audio and film clips. The range of topics included in the online journal has grown: film, music, cultural contexts (carriages, churches, etc.), and the yearly Jane Austen bibliography. *POL* has also published catalogues of exhibits at Chawton House Library and the libraries of King's College, Cambridge, and Cambridge University, bringing rich collections of artefacts to readers around the world. Further, in a time when essay collections have become increasingly difficult to market, *POL* has offered an opportunity for special issues on topics like Joe Wright's *Pride & Prejudice* (2007), Global Jane Austen (2008), and Teaching Austen and Her Contemporaries (2014). Indeed, the special issue on *Sanditon* [2018] marked the first collection of criticism on the fragment since *Persuasions* 19 [1997]. Such projects have offered readers well beyond JASNA's borders access to new perspectives.

Even though *Persuasions* has become more academic in nature, it has always, because of its wide and complex audience, avoided highly theoretical and jargon-laden approaches. Many developments in academic literary criticism over the forty-odd years of *Persuasions* and *Persuasions On-Line* have proved well suited to the interests of JASNA members. In addition to formalist approaches, essays have branched out to explore Jane Austen's connection to her world, through feminist and gender-related methodologies, historical and historicist investigation, cultural materialism, reception history, adaptation study, political perspectives, and attention to celebrity culture.

A recent special issue of *Texas Studies in Language and Literature* edited by Janine Barchas and Devoney Looser addressed the question 'What's Next for Jane Austen?' JASNA's president, Liz Philosophos Cooper, defines the organisation's mission as 'foster[ing] among the widest number of readers the study, appreciation, and understanding of Jane Austen's works, her life, and her genius' (483). The first of three areas she specifies is 'JASNA's major role in fostering Austen scholarship by publishing two peer-reviewed journals'. The circulation of *Persuasions* is currently just below 5000, including 74 institutional subscriptions (64 in the U.S., 5 in Canada, and 4 international); essays from the journal can also be downloaded from the databases of Gale, EBSCO, and ProQuest. *Persuasions On-Line* is, as Cooper notes, 'an educational resource free to the public' (483). In the fiscal years 2014–2019, essay pages on the JASNA website were viewed 1,256,152 times. Geographically, in 2019, a representative year, 65.2% were users from the U.S.; 8.0% from the U.K.; 3.9% from Canada; 3.7% from India; 3.4% from Australia; 1% from Germany; and 14.8% from 204 other countries or territories. The reach of the two journals is wide.

The history of *Persuasions* and *Persuasions On-Line* reveals an extension outward to other communities. *Persuasion* began as an exercise in organisation building: providing a sense of the conference proceedings, sharing opinions, news, and quips. Not only has JASNA *News* taken over most of those functions, but in an internet age there's no need for members to share newspaper or magazine articles in print: those who do not have news feeds set to Jane Austen stay current through JASNA's Facebook page, Austen-related listservs, and JASNA email blasts. The focus of *Persuasions* and *Persuasions On-Line* has shifted over the years to JASNA's contribution to Jane Austen studies, disseminating an understanding of all things Jane among the widest readership possible.[4]

Notes

1 Yaffe attributes the title change to a printer's error (172). For more on the 'persuasion' exerted by Denis Mason Hurley see Yaffe (163–65).
2 For more on this tension—or to use Bander's term 'the anxiety of affiliation', see Bander (esp. 150–55) and Yaffe (172). Claudia Johnson addresses the anxiety from the scholarly side:

Even though lectures by academic Austenian scholars are featured at Jane Austen Society and Jane Austen Society of North America conferences, and even though JAS's *Collected Reports* and JASNA's *Persuasions* often publish a tremendous amount in the way of sheer information, most academics I know take a rather dim view of these galas, where enjoyment rather than hermeneutic mastery is assumed to be the reward of reading, where reading is sociable rather than solitary, and where the stuff of erudition itself seems so different.... We sometimes suffer the additional mortification of discovering our own papers becoming yet another relatively undifferentiated, unhierarchicalised item in the great repository of Austeniana assiduously collected by Janeites and compiled in newsletters and reports, printed somewhere between recipes for white soup and the latest word jumble (223). That description (published in 1997) is outdated.

3 Almost from the beginning of JASNA, Koppel had pushed for a scholarly journal. On 7 May 1982 he wrote to JASNA President Joseph J. Costa: 'Mary Millard called me and asked me to take charge of a *Persuasion* (newsletter, not novel) discussion section. I was very happy about this—I think the possibility of turning *Persuasion*(s) into a small, twice-a-year journal that deals with all aspects of Jane Austen's worlds—fictional and real—is certainly worth talking about'. And then on 10 September 1982 he reported: 'My own pet idea is to expand our annual *Persuasions* into a full-scale journal (though still published only once a year). It would consist of our present *Persuasions* + articles. The articles would be *both* literary and non-literary (women's studies, historical, sociological, history of ideas, etc.). I believe all the college and university libraries would subscribe to such an annual journal, and we could make expenses'.

4 I'm very grateful to Tara Olivero, curator of special collections and archives at Goucher College; to JASNA's president, Liz Philosophos Cooper, for providing additional materials about the early history of JASNA, including a copy of Joseph Weisenfarth's unpublished manuscript; to Iris Lutz, JASNA's website manager, and Isa Schaff, JASNA's database manager, for information and statistics; to Laurie Kaplan and other previous editors of *Persuasions* for their efforts and their vision; and to JASNA for supporting its mission of 'foster[ing] among the widest number of readers the study, appreciation, and understanding of Jane Austen's works, her life, and her genius' (JASNA, 'About JASNA') and for recognising the crucial role *Persuasions* and *Persuasions On-Line* play in that mission.

Works Cited

Austen, Henry. 'Biographical Notice of the Author.' 1818. *Northanger Abbey and Persuasion*, 3rd ed., edited by R. W. Chapman. Oxford UP, 1933, pp. 3–9.

Austen-Leigh, Joan. 'Editorial.' *Persuasions*, vol. 4, 1982, p. 2.

Austen-Leigh, Joan. 'Editorial.' *Persuasions*, vol. 5, 1983, p. 2.

Austen-Leigh, Joan. 'Editorial.' *Persuasions*, vol. 8, 1986, p. 2.

Austen-Leigh, Joan. 'Letter to J. David Grey.' 18 Dec. 1981. JASNA Series XII, Joan Austen-Leigh papers: Correspondence with Jack Grey. 1979–80 (and n.d.); Box 1, Folder 2, Goucher College Library Special Collections.

Austen-Leigh, Joan. 'Letter to J. David Grey.' 8 Jan. 1984. JASNA Series XII, Joan Austen-Leigh papers: Correspondence with Jack Grey. 1981–82 (and n.d.); Box 1, Folder 5, Goucher College Library Special Collections.

Austen-Leigh, Joan, and J. David Grey. 'Letter to Patrons and Members of the Jane Austen Society of North America.' Apr. 1979. Collection of Joseph Weisenfarth.

Bander, Elaine. 'JASNA and the Academy: The Anxiety of Affiliation.' *Persuasions*, vol. 39, 2017, pp. 147–162.

Cooper, Liz Philosophos. 'The Jane Austen Society of North America.' *Texas Studies in Literature and Language*, vol. 61, no. 4, Winter, 2019, pp. 482–485.

Doudna, Eileen B. 'Report of Publications Secretary,' Nov. 1984–Sep. 27, 1985. JASNA Records MS 0028 Series V, Subseries A, Folder 1, Goucher College Library Special Collections.

Gilson, David J. 'Letter to Henry Burke.' 17 Nov. 1980. Burke Collection, container 2, folder 8, Goucher College Library Special Collections.

Grey, J. David. 'From the President…' *Persuasions*, vol. 2, 1980, pp. 3–5.

Hanaway, Lorraine. 'Letter to Juliet McMaster.' 28 Jul. 1987. JASNA Records MS 0028 Series V, Subseries B, Folder 8, Goucher College Library Special Collections.

JASNA. 'About JASNA.' *JASNA: Jane Austen Society of North America*. 2020. http://www.jasna.org/about/

JASNA. Membership brochure. [1987–1988?] JASNA Records MS 0028 Series IV, Subseries B, Folder 2, Goucher College Library Special Collections.

JASNA. Library flyer. [1989–1990?] JASNA Records MS 0028 Series V, Subseries B, Folder 5, Goucher College Library Special Collections.

Johnson, Claudia L. 'Austen Cults and Cultures.' *The Cambridge Companion to Jane Austen*, edited by Edward Copeland and Juliet McMaster. Cambridge UP, 1997, pp. 211–226.

Kaplan, Laurie. 'Editor's Note.' *Persuasions*, vol. 20, 1998, pp. 9–11.

Kaplan, Laurie. Interview with the author. 10 Jan. 2020.

Koppel, Gene. 'Letter to Deborah B. Brennan; cc to Joan Austen-Leigh.' 5 Apr. 1991. JASNA Records MS 0028 Series V, Subseries B, Folder 12, Goucher College Library Special Collections.

Koppel, Gene. 'Letter to Joseph J. Costa.' 7 May 1982. JASNA Records MS 0028 Series II, Subseries B, Folder 2, Goucher College Library Special Collections.

Koppel, Gene. 'Letter to Joseph J. Costa.' 10 Sept. 1982. JASNA Records MS 0028 Series II, Subseries B, Folder 2, Goucher College Library Special Collections.

Lane, Maggie. 'David Selwyn: 21 Nov. 1951–9 Apr. 2013.' JAS *Report*, 2012, pp. 11–12.

Lynch, Deidre Shauna. 'Cult of Jane Austen.' *Jane Austen in Context*, edited by Janet Todd. Cambridge UP, 2005, pp. 111–120.

McMaster, Juliet. 'Letter to Lorraine Hanaway.' 29 May 1987. JASNA Records MS 0028 Series V, Subseries B, Folder 8, Goucher College Library Special Collections.

Persuasion, vol. 1, 16 December 1979.

Persuasions, vol. 2, 16 December 1980.

Persuasions, vol. 16, 1994.

Persuasions, vol. 20, 1998.

Persuasions On-Line, vol. 20.1, 1999.

Solender, Elsa. 'President's Message.' *Persuasions On-Line*, vol. 20.1, 1999.

Sutherland, Eileen. 'Letter to J. David Grey; cc to Joan Austen-Leigh.' 29 Apr. 1991. JASNA Records MS 0028 Series V, Subseries B, Folder 12, Goucher College Library Special Collections.

Watt, Ian. 'Jane Austen and the Traditions of Comic Aggression: *Sense and Sensibility*.' *Persuasions*, vol. 3, 1981, pp. 14–15, 24–28. Also at www.jasna.org.

Weisenfarth, Joseph. 'Persuasion: Founding the Jane Austen Society of North America.' Unpublished manuscript. 26 Apr. 2017. 6 pp.

Wells, Juliette. *Everybody's Jane: Austen in the Popular Imagination*. Continuum, 2011.

Yaffe, Deborah. *Among the Janeites: A Journey through the World of Jane Austen Fandom*. Houghton Mifflin, 2013.

31

'IT IS SUCH A HAPPINESS WHEN GOOD PEOPLE GET TOGETHER': JAS AND JASNA

Alice Marie Villaseñor

MEDAILLE COLLEGE

Introduction

This essay provides an overview of the UK Jane Austen Society (JAS) and the Jane Austen Society of North America (JASNA). Although there are multiple Austen societies around the globe, I am focussing on the two I have personal experiences with: the oldest (JAS) and the largest (JASNA). The two organisations share many common goals and interests, and I will discuss how the two Societies have stayed connected over the years. However, one of the goals of this essay will be to explain the differences between the two Societies, as the groups were founded in different eras for distinctly different purposes. I will also discuss recent scholarly and popular representations of Janeites in a variety of genres.

Jane Austen Society

Founded in 1940, the oldest Austen Society is the UK-based Jane Austen Society (JAS), which aims to 'foster the appreciation and study of the work, life and times of Jane Austen, and the Austen family' ('Welcome'). Jane Austen biographer Elizabeth Jenkins records her first-hand accounts of the group's origins in her introduction to *The Collected Reports of the Jane Austen Society, 1949–1965*. Jenkins relates how Dorothy Darnell, with the help of a small group of recruits, founded the Society with the explicit mission to acquire the cottage in Chawton, Hampshire, where Jane Austen had lived, in order to convert it into a museum open to the public (vii and ix). In December 1946, the Society took out an advertisement in *The Times* asking for support to purchase Jane Austen's cottage, which generated only £1,400 in donations that were eventually put towards the building's repairs because the sum was insufficient to meet the purchase price (x). However, in July 1948, Mr Thomas Edward Carpenter, J.P., purchased the house in his own right for £3,000 from the Knight family (who were descendants of Jane Austen's brother Edward Austen Knight) in memory of his son Lieutenant John Philip Carpenter who was killed in action in Italy (Carpenter 18–19; Jenkins x).

In the end, the Jane Austen Society never took on the 'financial and administrative burden' for managing the museum, as Carpenter founded The Jane Austen Memorial Trust, which ran the museum until a new Jane Austen House Museum Charitable Incorporated Organisation (CIO) was formed in 2014 (Jenkins x; Carpenter 24). However, the Society has supported the work of the museum in many ways. As Maureen Stiller, Honorary Secretary of the Jane Austen Society, notes, in

DOI: 10.4324/9780429398155-31-36

409

the early days, some JAS committee members served on the Management Committee of the Jane Austen Memorial Trust ('Eighty' 56). JAS also organised a General Meeting when Jane Austen's House officially opened to the public on 23 July 1949 (Jenkins x). The Jane Austen Society printed an eight-page programme titled 'Jane Austen and Jane Austen's House' to commemorate the occasion, featuring pieces by R.W. Chapman, Elizabeth Jenkins, and John Simpson. Selwyn Duruz proposed a 'Design for a Garden for Jane Austen's House', which was implemented immediately (JAS, 'Jane Austen Society: Report for the period' 16). On 14 May 1953, 90 members of the Society gathered to celebrate the opening of additional rooms in the museum, where members of the Society and museum Trustees spoke (JAS, 'Opening of Additional Rooms' 41). More recent support has focused on helping to sponsor school groups' participation in the Education Outreach Programme, which is a partnership between the museum and Chawton House, a library for British Women Writers (1660–1830) housed in an estate once owned by Jane Austen's third brother, Edward Austen Knight (Carpenter 19).

The most important contribution the Society has made to the museum is related to one of the goals that occupied the organisation's formative years: to track down objects related to Jane Austen to display in the house (Jenkins ix). The Society *Reports* reflect the flurry of activity around the acquisition of 'relics' that were either purchased by the Society, or loaned or donated by individuals. For example, in 1950, the Society made its 'first major purchase' with the help of the National Art-Collections Fund: 'a walnut escritoire and two Hepplewhite chairs, which formed part of the furniture of Steventon Rectory when Jane Austen lived there' (JAS, 'Jane Austen Society: Report for the period' 15). The same year, JAS also managed to borrow from Windsor Castle the three volumes of *Emma* that John Murray sent to the Prince Regent on behalf of Jane Austen (JAS, 'Jane Austen Society: Report for the period' 15). At the 2019 Annual General Meeting (AGM), the Society announced its intention to transfer its assets to Jane Austen's House, including 'Jane and Cassandra's topaz crosses and gold chain, family portraits, and furniture and furnishings, including Jane Austen's table and patchwork quilt' (Stiller, 'Transfer' 11). As Maureen Stiller explains in a formal announcement published in the Autumn 2019 JAS *Newsletter*, Jane Austen's House 'has always assumed total responsibility for their care and it is particularly fitting, in celebration of the 80th anniversary of the Society in 2020 and the 70th anniversary of the Museum this year, to transfer the ownership of the assets outright to the Museum under Deed of Gift' ('Transfer' 11).

Society members continue to maintain other connections with Jane Austen locations, as they convene in the village of Chawton every July for the AGM held on the grounds of Chawton House. The day consists of a morning business meeting, a picnic lunch, an afternoon talk that is printed in the Society's *Reports*, and a pleasant tea ('Society Events'). The event is open to all members, which currently number about 1,400, although past membership numbers have been closer to 2,000 (Stiller, 'JAS Information for Publication'; Lane 492). The Society also sponsors an Annual Study Day in London and an Annual Conference, which is held in various locations and comprised of lectures and outings ('Society Events').[1] While most of these conferences take place in the United Kingdom over a three-day period, they do sometimes occur abroad, such as the 2005 'Jane Austen and the North Atlantic' conference held in Halifax, Nova Scotia, Canada, and a subsequent week-long conference in the same location in 2017 ('Society Events'). Further activities of the Society include undertaking fundraising in support of specific projects as well as an educational outreach programme providing free talks to community groups (Stiller, 'Draft'; 'Talks for Outside Groups'). Currently, there are also five Branches of the Society that host their own events throughout the year (Stiller, 'Draft'); information about them is provided on the Society's website and their activities are documented in the annual Society *Reports* ('Branches').

In addition to the related early goals of establishing a museum and filling it with Austen relics, a third primary aim of the Society, as documented by Jenkins, was to track down 'local traditions about Jane Austen' (ix). This mandate is clearly reflected in the organisation's various publication projects.

Their annual journal, which I have previously referenced, *The Jane Austen Society Reports*, features lectures given to the Society as well as articles relating to Austen's works, the Austen family (and their circle of acquaintances), and local history related to Austen family members and their acquaintances ('Jane Austen Publications'). The Society has republished and indexed the majority of these *Reports* in six volumes of *Collected Reports*, covering the years 1949–2005 ('Jane Austen Publications'). A bi-annual newsletter provides timely updates about recent and upcoming events; news from Austen-related sites, such as Jane Austen's House and Chawton House; book reviews; reports about other Austen societies around the globe; and other items of interest, such as information about film adaptations of Austen's novels or acquisitions of Austen family relics ('Newsletter'). The Society also publishes books related to Austen and the Austen family circle, such as letters and poems written by the Austen family (e.g., Fanny Knight's letters and James Austen's poems) as well as information about particular locations Jane Austen knew (e.g., Bath and Godmersham Park) ('Jane Austen Publications').

Jane Austen Society of North America

The largest literary Society devoted to Jane Austen, the Jane Austen Society of North America (JASNA), was founded almost forty years after JAS ('About JASNA'). The mission of this non-profit organisation is 'to foster among the widest number of readers the study, appreciation, and understanding of Jane Austen's works, her life, and her genius' ('About JASNA'). In *Everybody's Jane: Austen in the Popular Imagination*, Juliette Wells details how the 1975 JAS AGM prompted Denis Mason Hurley (who was married to one of JASNA's founders, Joan Austen-Leigh), to first verbalise the idea of creating a more democratic version of JAS for North Americans (215). Austen-Leigh (author and descendant of Jane Austen's brother, James) recalls that a series of bi-centennial events in North America allowed the initial idea of JASNA to percolate—offering opportunities for her to develop a friendship with another JASNA founder: J. David (Jack) Grey of New York City (a junior-high vice-principle and Austen collector) (7–8). The relationship grew over the next four years, but the founders were hesitant to move forward. Austen-Leigh notes that she and Grey were both engulfed in writing projects, and they were also daunted by the enormity of the task at hand:

> It was not an idea to be taken seriously. There was, at that time, in the entire world only the one society: the Jane Austen Society which met for one afternoon, once a year, in July, in a tent at Chawton, to hear a speech, drink tea and go home again. Yet here was my absurd husband proposing that we, in North America, Jack living in New York, and I living in the far side of the continent in another country—well, the idea was preposterous. (8)

Grey's correspondence to Austen-Leigh, written during JASNA's first year, highlights the distance from Austen's Hampshire, as one of the reasons he had to doubt JASNA's success. In a 15 March 1980 letter, Grey lamented, 'It's not the same as Chawton, is it? The cottage is a constant reminder of [the UK Jane Austen Society's] existence and we have no such similar hook to hang our hat on' (qtd. in Austen-Leigh 11).

Eventually, the two friends decided to move forward. In early 1979, they began by contacting Sir Hugh Smiley, the Chairman and Honorary Secretary of JAS, for a list of North American members (Austen-Leigh 9). Austen-Leigh recalls that Grey also invited academics to be patrons of the Society: 'they didn't even have to join, only to allow their names to be printed on the stationary. Jack felt that these names, thus displayed, would lend an air of credibility to what seemed to us both at the time an extremely shaky enterprise' (9). The duo also invited Henry Burke, lawyer and Austen collector, to join them as the Society's third co-founder (Austen-Leigh 9). In March 1979, 'acknowledged admirer[s] of J.A.' received letters inviting them to join 'the new Jane Austen Society of North America' (Grey and Austen-Leigh). The letter announced that the first meeting would take place in New York City, where 'we will dine, exchange ideas, and have the pleasure of being able to "talk Jane" with others similarly afflicted' (Grey and Austen-Leigh). Lorraine Hanaway, one of the Society's original board members, records that these efforts resulted in forty-four patrons and 335 members joining in the first six months ('Brief Highlights' 7). Thirty-six Society members and four members of the press attended the inaugural JASNA meeting in New York City (Hanaway, 'Brief Highlights' 7), while 100 members attended the dinner featuring two talks and a toast to 'the incomparable Jane' ('Our First Dinner' 11). In her summary of the dinner, Hanaway characterises attendees as 'scholars and students, collectors and booksellers, librarians and scientists; all admirers' ('Our First Dinner' 10).

Subsequent AGM summaries show a sharp increase in meeting attendance and membership during the early years. 170 people registered for the third AGM in San Francisco (Hanaway, 'The Meeting'). By the five-year mark, the Society membership had grown to 1,300 (Parker 27), and 240 people participated in the Philadelphia AGM (Hanaway, 'Who Attended'). Ten years on, Sallie R. Wadsworth reports 400 people attending dinner at the 1989 Sante Fe AGM, with membership numbers totalling 2,221 US members and 260 Canadian members. In her published reflections on the 1993 AGM at Lake Louise, Juliet McMaster recalls that meeting as a kind of growth spurt for JASNA: 'The rooms filled up, to the maximum of 600, which was by far the biggest AGM attendance so far in JASNA's history' ('Revisiting'). The Lake Louise trend of selling out AGMs has resurfaced in recent years. For example, all 850 slots for the 2019 AGM in Colonial Williamsburg sold out right away; on the same day that the online registration opened, JASNA's Vice President for Conferences, Linda Slothouber, communicated to all members by email that hopeful registrants 'began to be routed to the waitlist almost immediately'.

Today, the Society boasts more than 5,000 members from all over the globe, although the majority come from the United States and Canada ('About JASNA'). Given these large numbers and the vast geographical area that this organisation covers, publications and JASNA Regions play key roles in keeping members connected with one another throughout the year.[2] The Society started with eight Regions (Grey 5). Today, the number of JASNA Regional groups has swelled to 80, requiring a dedicated Vice President of Regions who supports the work of the Regional Coordinators ('Regional Groups'). JASNA also recently launched its first virtual Region to support members who do not live close to an established Region (Cooper, 'The Jane Austen Society of North America' 484).

JASNA requires membership in the main organisation to participate in Regional activities ('Regional Groups'). Some Regions, however, do sponsor outreach events that are open to the public, one of the largest being the annual, multi-day Jane Austen Festival sponsored by the Greater Louisville Region ('About Us'). The size of Regional Groups—and, consequently, the kinds of activities that they organise—are highly variable. Regions are able to keep up with one another through updates in *JASNA News* and an event calendar on the JASNA website, as well as through social media postings and email blasts put out by the Regions themselves ('Event Calendar'). JASNA also includes Regional activities and spotlights Austen-related news in its *JASNA Update* monthly email blast (Cooper, 'Draft'). The Society encourages all Regions to invite the JASNA President to a meeting during his/her term to deliver a talk—at the expense of the Society. And JASNA recently expanded some of its Regional Grant Programs, including the J. David Grey Fund (to support programming) and the Travelling Lecturer programme (which identifies three speakers spanning different geographical areas who are prepared to deliver Regional talks) (Cooper, 'President's Column' 3).

JASNA also directly sponsors outreach activities that are in line with its mission. For example, the organisation coordinates an annual Essay Contest for high school, undergraduate, and graduate students ('Essay Contest Winning Entries').[3] Students write essays that tie into each year's AGM theme. JASNA has also run several J. David Grey Young Writers' Workshops, providing opportunities for students who are local to the city where each AGM is taking place ('J. David Grey'). Recently, the 2017 AGM in Huntington Beach, CA, used this fund to support a Young Filmmakers Contest ('Call for Films'). In the 1990s, the Society also sponsored Henry G. Burke Grants, to support research and creative projects on Jane Austen 'that will help to bring Jane Austen's name before the public' (JASNA, 'Henry G. Burke Grants' 4). Winning proposals included Joan Pawelski's one-act opera based on *Lady Susan*, Joan Austen-Leigh's novel *Letters from Highbury*, a two-act musical drama of *Sense and Sensibility* written by Paula Schwartz and Neil Moyer, and a guide to the Burke Collection of Jane Austen Materials at Goucher College's Julia Rogers Library (JASNA, '1991 Awards' 4; JASNA, '1992–1993 Henry G. Burke Grants' 4).

In addition to outreach to new readers of Austen in North America, JASNA, like JAS, has a history of supporting Austen-related sites in England. At the first meeting, members voted to endorse maintenance and restoration efforts of St. Nicholas Church in Steventon, Hampshire, pledging to raise $1,500 (Tucker 8–9). This philanthropic impetus continues today in the Churches Committee, which supports the churches affiliated with Austen through grants ('Austen Family Churches'). Jean Bowden, previous Curator of Jane Austen's House, writes that her trip to the 1990 JASNA AGM to deliver a talk resulted in 'closer links' being forged between JASNA and the museum, adding 'I have been asked to contribute a twice-yearly "Letter from Chawton" to the JASNA Newsletter. There are now complete sets of JASNA's journal, *Persuasions*, and Newsletters in the library at Jane Austen's House' (173). Tom Carpenter, who has previously served in the roles of Curator and Head Trustee, estimated in his 2015 Jane Austen Society *Report* article that JASNA had made annual donations to the museum totalling £39,000 (20). This money has been used towards conserving exhibits, including the restoration of Jane's Donkey Carriage (Carpenter 20).

Chawton House also benefits from JASNA affiliations. After hearing about the Chawton House estate at the 1992 AGM, JASNA member Sandy Lerner, an entrepreneur and philanthropist, bought a 125-year lease from Richard Knight in 1993 and restored the estate into a library that was opened in 2003 (Yaffe 53–54; Cole 6). Chawton House, a registered charity, recently credited JASNA for various charitable contributions. Two JASNA Regions—the North Texas and the New York Metropolitan Region—donated enough money to the Flag-Raising Campaign to have their state flags flown over Chawton House ('Flag-Raising'). Many JASNA members and several JASNA Regions have also contributed to the #BrickbyBrick fundraising campaign ('With Thanks'). More recently, JASNA Regions contributed to the Jane Austen Garden Trail effort organised by North American Friends of Chawton House and opened in 2019 ('The Jane Austen Garden Trail').

Cross-Continental Connections

Although JAS and JASNA were founded in different eras for distinctly different purposes, the two organisations have maintained formal and informal connections. As has been discussed, several members of JAS and JASNA have been members of both organisations over the years. And from the beginning, the JAS Committee showed support for JASNA by sending a telegram to Jack Grey offering their 'best wishes' for JASNA's inaugural meeting (Committee of JAS 19). Several years later, when the Honorary Secretary of JAS, Anthony Trollope, was invited to the 1987 JASNA AGM to speak at the formal dinner and propose the toast, he concluded by talking about 'a special chain of friendship and partnership in the spreading of the legacy of great literature which Jane Austen has bequeathed to the world' (56 and 58). Since that time, the two organisations have worked together on several cross-continental projects.

I have already mentioned that JAS has held some of their conferences in North America; likewise, JASNA has worked with JAS to develop opportunities for its members to visit England. For example, JASNA sponsors an annual Tour of England for a small group of its members. Although every year features a different theme, certain landmarks are highlighted in all tours, including St. Nicholas Church in Steventon, Jane Austen's House in Chawton, and Winchester Cathedral ('Tours of England'). The tradition of including the JAS AGM as a highlight of the trip dates back to the 1998 'Jane Austen, Great Homes & Gardens' Tour (Solender 75). In October 2003, JAS helped to welcome an even larger group of North Americans, as the 2003 JASNA AGM, 'Homecoming: The Importance of Home and Family in Jane Austen's Life and Works', took place in England ('Annual General Meeting Winchester England'). Although the New York Metropolitan Region of JASNA organised the AGM, the Jane Austen Society helped to plan the day at Chawton (JAS, 'Minutes of the Annual General Meeting held on Saturday 17 July 2004' 289).

In order to keep up the relationships between JASNA and Austen-related institutions in England, which were strengthened by the 2003 AGM, the New York Metropolitan Region allocated money to set up a JASNA International Visitor Program ('International Visitor Program'). More recently, the Washington, D.C. Metropolitan Region also donated funding to this programme (Cooper 'Draft'). At the time of writing this piece, 12 JASNA members since 2005 have travelled to England for several weeks over the summer to work on their self-defined Austen projects, which have included studying manuscripts, rare books, and estate records; creating musical compositions; working in gardens; and interviewing museum visitors about their experiences ('International Visitor Program'). A unique aspect of this fellowship is that there is a service component to the programme; the International Visitor has worked with the Jane Austen Society as well as Jane Austen's House, Chawton House, and/or St. Nicholas Church to provide service to the Austen-related institutions ('International Visitor Program'). Mary Guyatt, former Director of Jane Austen's House, discusses the benefits of the programme from the museum's point of view:

> We have enjoyed the talks and tours they have presented, and we always benefit from their readiness to lend a hand, whether stewarding visitors through the house or out gardening in the summer sunshine. Because we have a chance to get to know each visitor, and they us, the program has a further, lasting value. Each annual program fosters new networks within the worldwide Janeite community and greatly strengthens the support that Jane Austen's House, here at its very centre, depends upon.

Representations in Academic Writing & Popular Culture

University of Edinburgh Professor George Saintsbury first used the term 'Janite' interchangeably with 'Austenian' in his 1894 preface to *Pride and Prejudice*. And Rudyard Kipling modernised the spelling in his short story, 'The Janeites', appearing in *Debits and Credits* in 1926. But, although the concept of Janeitism pre-dates the founding of both JAS and JASNA, the term 'Janeite' is often used to describe members of both Societies. One reason for this may be that, from the start, both JAS and JASNA have embraced the concept of an emotional bond with Austen. For example, R.W. Chapman's foreword to the previously mentioned 'Jane Austen and Jane Austen's House' pamphlet, published by JAS to mark the formal opening of the museum, exclaims that 'the house is now made free to lovers of Jane Austen' (2). And the previously mentioned letter authored by Grey and Austen-Leigh inviting potential JASNA members to '"talk Jane" with others similarly afflicted', suggests the new organisation will welcome personal sentiments. These kinds of intimate expressions help to explain why discussions of JAS and JASNA members are often bound up with larger conversations about Janeites.

The 1990s was a watershed moment in the history of Janeitism due to the so-called Jane Austen film craze of the mid-90s, which brought Jane Austen (and her readers) into the limelight in new ways. The films sparked what Rachel Brownstein's book *Why Jane Austen?* (2011) deems 'Jane-o-mania'—'the belated vogue for Jane Austen' (6). Janeites are not simply admirers of Jane Austen—they are true fans who often claim a personal connection with Austen's novels, with Austen's characters, and even with the author herself. But since the 1990s, the increased attention to Jane Austen's readers has conjured representations—and misrepresentations—in popular media and in academic publications alike.

Readers having a kind of personal relationship with Austen hints at why the term 'Janeite', rather than 'Austenite', is still employed by critics referring to the most enthusiastic of Austen's readers. A word like 'Austenian' is more in line with the terminology used to refer to readers of other canonical British writers with a popular following (e.g., Shakespearian, Dickensian, and Trollopian). But using Austen's first name, rather than her last, implies a friendship with the author while also emphasising her gender. Several critics, including Deidre Lynch in the introduction to her edited collection on *Janeites: Austen's Disciples and Devotees* (2000), have also observed this phenomenon:

> 'Janeite' works, as corresponding terms do not, to highlight the author's gender and to imply that the reader's is the same. The intimacy of the reading situation the epithet evokes is enhanced by the suggestion that Jane and the Janeite share their gender and more: lately, indeed, some of the annoyance critics express when confronting the spectacle of Janeitism seems motivated by their suspicion that the novels provide cultural spaces where we girls can all be girls together. (14)

Additionally, in her 2008 *Persuasions* article, 'Jane Austen, Samuel Johnson, and the Academy', scholar and long-time JASNA member and regular speaker, Jocelyn Harris, discusses the significance of the word's suffix: 'the suffix "ite" in "Janeite" denotes followers of a movement, says the *Oxford English Dictionary*, and often in a derogatory way, as in "Luddite"' (34). Harris goes on to discuss the relationship between Austen's gender and her reception in academic communities: 'I believe that Austen's popularity among women actually counts against her, for even in these so-called post-feminist days, literature by and about women is still regarded as less significant than literature by and about men' (34).

In her introduction to *Jane Austen's Cults and Cultures* (2012), Claudia Johnson also discusses the link between the assumed gender of most contemporary Janeites and the condemning of traditional Janeite activities (10). Johnson points out that since World War II, 'the public adoration of Jane Austen, along with her vigorous marketing in the form of print, television, and motion pictures, has been [feminised], and Janeites are likelier to be seen as batty ladies than as supremely discerning connoisseurs' (10). For Johnson, the term 'Janeite' and the activities Janeites participate in both suggest a 'tendency to collapse distance':

> Sometimes this distance is personal, as in the familiarity of first-naming her. At other times, the collapse of distance is historical. [...] Janeites themselves are the time travelers, taking themselves back into Austen's world by staging Regency costume balls, devising quizzes drawn from minutiae in Austen's novels, knitting Regency reticules, preparing banquets out of late-eighteenth- and early nineteenth-century cookbooks, discussing how a character from one novel might converse with a character from another, and setting tables according to the protocols of Austen's time, all with a distinctive combination of gaiety, fervor, and exactitude. Most of these activities can seem trivial, unprofessional, and even chastening to academic scholars—how mortifying to encounter one's own earth-shattering essay on Austen printed alongside a recipe for white soup, as somehow equivalent exercises—but they also produce real information and knowledge along with a sort [sic] pleasure that Clara Tuite has brilliantly described as 'period euphoria'. (10–11)

Scholars Juliette Wells and Elaine Bander, long-term members of JASNA who have served on the JASNA Board as well as held the JASNA International Visitor Program position, have both discussed the divide between academic and non-academic readers in the Society. In *Everybody's Jane*, Wells warns, 'newcomers to JASNA from both the fan and academic world must adjust to the [organisation's] lively, participatory tone as well as to the range of activities at its annual meetings' (218). She further elaborates by drawing from her own experiences:

> Having myself presented at several JASNA annual and regional meetings beginning in 2001, when I was still a graduate student, I can attest that the cultural differences between the academic world and JASNA are profound. In particular, seeing fans and even some scholars attired in Regency dress takes some getting used to. So too do comments like one I received from an audience member after my first JASNA presentation: 'I feel sure,' announced an elderly man, 'that Jane Austen knew she was a genius!' Doctoral-level literary study does not prepare you to follow up on such a remark. (219)

While Bander's 2017 *Persuasions* article, 'JASNA and the Academy: The Anxiety of Affiliation', also rehearses these kinds of tensions, she does not see the concepts of loving Austen and approaching Austen through an academic lens to be quite so distinct:

> I am, on the one hand, an enthusiastic Janeite (which I define as someone who loves and studies the works of Jane Austen) and a long-time JASNA member: by profession a teacher and writer rather than a professor or scholar. … On the other hand, I wrote a PhD dissertation on Austen, and I attempt to research, write, and publish to the highest scholarly standard. These activities have never seemed incompatible to me, nor do they to the many scholars who are proud JASNA members and who have enriched my understanding of Austen as well as my life. Nor would they to Austen herself. She, after all, lacked formal credentials. (151)

The divide between academic and non-academic (i.e., Janeite) readers analysed by Lynch, Harris, Johnson, Wells, and Bander, is key to understanding the dynamics of modern-day critiques of Janeites. And yet, the 'mortification' Johnson expresses, as well as the 'annoyance' regarding the 'spectacle' of Janeitism to which Lynch refers are, I believe, somewhat unfairly proliferated by popular culture representations that suggest Janeites are incapable (or unwilling) to separate fact from fiction and are likewise unable to read Austen's novels through a critical lens. The British television miniseries *Lost in Austen* (2008), for example, portrays a modern-day Londoner transported into the plot of *Pride and Prejudice* who is constantly surprised by the gritty reality of the world of her favourite Austen novel. And the plot of the feature film *Austenland* (2013) relies on the inherent inability of the heroine—a love-starved American woman in her thirties who spends her life savings on an Austen-inspired immersive experience on an English estate—to separate authenticity from imagination. Moreover, as revealed by Jeanne Kiefer, in her analysis of her own 2008 *The Jane Austen Survey* results, sometimes even self-proclaimed Janeites are guilty of stereotyping fellow fans. Kiefer concludes her summary of the survey by admitting that, after sifting through 4,501 responses, she can 'no longer sum up the "typical Janeite" in a few easy phrases'.

Similarly, journalistic representations of Janeite gatherings highlight stereotypically feminine activities like dressing for costume balls and practising Regency embroidery. To be sure, the kinds of activities authors list are certainly on offer at many JASNA AGMs and Regional events (much less so at JAS events). In fact, during a panel about JASNA's history held during the 2019 AGM in Colonial Williamsburg, Juliet McMaster recalls that the first JASNA Regency Ball took place in 1986, and 1987 was the first conference where attendees were invited to come in period dress

('The Company'). And in their summary of the 1987 meeting published in *Persuasions*, Judith Terry and Sallie Wadsworth emphasise the 'great numbers' of Regency costumes (7). But even though such living history pursuits are only part of the agenda at such gatherings, these are the activities journalists tend to emphasise the most when covering Jane Austen events. For example, Jennifer Schuessler's *New York Times* coverage of the 2012 JASNA AGM offers a more balanced approach to the conference than most journalists publish. While the piece starts by claiming, 'the daytime dress code for many ran to pale Regency dresses, demure bonnets and straw baskets to hold anything that wouldn't fit into a period-correct reticule', the story quickly goes on to emphasise that the conference is 'also a place to go back to the texts'. And yet, the only two pictures that run with the online version of the article are of women in costume, despite the fact that for the majority of the conference the majority of attendees were dressed in 2012 clothing. Although the ostentatious Regency costumes make for a better headline, the vast majority of Jane Austen conference goers are usually less formally attired.

I would like to encourage readers to seek out a more balanced approach to Janeites by focusing on texts—in a variety of genres—that are produced by Janeites themselves, or in which Janeites' voices are heavily represented. For example, the recent 'JASNA Recap' episode of the *First Impressions* podcast focused on the authors' experiences attending their first AGM. Referencing the 2019 Colonial Williamsburg AGM focused on *Northanger Abbey*, Maggie and Kristin report that 'JASNA sort of takes an academic conference and a fan convention and mashes them together', further explaining that there is 'daytime formality and night-time frivolity'. They describe many of the workshops offered before the conference—such as the cravat tying workshop and the English country dancing lesson—as being 'a little more on the fan side'. But the duo also spends a significant amount of time discussing the ideas at the breakout session talks that they attended. This balanced point of view is also featured in a short film on *YouTube* called 'Jane Austen Society of North America 2015 AGM'. The film features interviews with several members of JAS and JASNA from a variety of backgrounds, including several who have already been referenced in this piece. The interview with Claire Bellanti, who was then serving as the JASNA President, emphasises the diverse nature of JASNA AGMs: 'Janeites cannot be put into a box. There are all kinds of people who come to this conference … The variety of people who come is just astonishing'.

Another take on JASNA is presented in Deborah Yaffe's *Among the Janeites: A Journey Through the World of Jane Austen Fandom* (2013). Relying heavily on interviews of contemporary Janeites who are members of JASNA, Yaffe's non-academic study weaves together the personal stories of Janeites (including her own adventures in Janeite costuming) in order to cover topics like literary tourism and fan fiction.[4] The text culminates in a final chapter on 'The Tribe' chronicling the 2011 JASNA AGM on *Sense and Sensibility* (see esp. 201–227). This same AGM features prominently in the 2011 BBC documentary titled *The Many Lovers of Miss Jane Austen* (2011). The documentary includes interviews with some of Austen's fans in the United States and the United Kingdom (such as Cheryl Kinney, one of the Coordinators of the 2011 JASNA AGM) as well as academic perspectives on Jane Austen's readers over the ages (including interviews with Katie Halsey, John Mullan, Kathryn Sutherland, and Janet Todd).

Conclusion

While this piece has focused on JAS and JASNA, it is important to note that there are several other societies across the globe, with more being formed all of the time. Links to eleven other Austen societies can be found on the JASNA website ('Other Resources'), and news articles about many of these groups are often printed in *Jane Austen's Regency World Magazine*, a bi-monthly magazine dating back to 2003. In the coming years, we can expect more discussions of Austen societies—including newer groups founded in countries where English is not the dominant language. In his introduction to

The Reception of Jane Austen in Europe (2007), Anthony Mandal explains that Austen's popularity has taken off in several European countries as a result of the 1990s film adaptations, spurring 'no fewer than sixty-four new translations' of Austen from 1995–1999 (8). These translations are begetting new Austen fans, who will continue to form their own approaches to Austen. Moreover, *All Roads Lead to Austen* (2012)—Amy Elizabeth Smith's memoir of reading Austen with book clubs in Guatemala, Mexico, Ecuador, Chile, Paraguay, and Argentina—includes a brief discussion of her meeting with the Jane Austen Society of Buenos Aires (JASBA) (see esp. 304–307). I look forward to learning more about societies across the globe in the coming years.

Acknowledgements

I would like to thank Maureen Stiller, Honorary Secretary of the Jane Austen Society, and Liz Philosophos Cooper, President of the Jane Austen Society of North America, for the time they spent providing helpful feedback on this piece.

Notes

1 No conference took place in 2018 (JAS, 'Minutes of the 62nd Annual General Meeting' 4).
2 For more information about JASNA publications, please see Susan Allen Ford's chapter in this volume titled '*Persuasions: The Jane Austen Journal* and *Persuasions On-Line*: "Formed for [an] Elegant and Rational Society"'.
3 The first annual contest began in 1988, and it was only open to undergraduate students (JASNA, 'Jane Austen Society of North America First Annual Literary Competition' 45). The annual contest was cancelled in 1993 and later reinstated (Marshall).
4 In the interest of full disclosure, I should point out that my husband and I are two of the Janeites briefly featured in Yaffe's book (212–13).

Works Cited

'About JASNA.' *Jane Austen Society of North America*, 2020, jasna.org/about/. Accessed 1 June 2020.
'About Us.' *Jane Austen Society of North America Greater Louisville Region*, 2019, jasnalouisville.com/about-us. Accessed 5 Dec. 2019.
'Annual General Meeting Winchester England October 9–13 2003.' *Jane Austen Society of North America*, n.d., www.jasna.org/agms/england/index.htm. Accessed 16 Dec. 2019.
'Austen Family Churches.' *Jane Austen Society of North America*, 2019, jasna.org/about/. Accessed 6 Dec. 2019.
Austenland. Directed by Jerusha Hess, Sony Pictures, 2013.
Austen-Leigh, Joan. 'The Founding of JASNA.' *Persuasions*, vol. 15, Dec. 1993, pp. 7–13.
Bander, Elaine. 'JASNA and the Academy: The Anxiety of Affiliation.' *Persuasions*, vol. 30, 2017, pp. 147–162.
Bowden, Jean. 'News from Chawton.' *Report for 1990. Collected Reports of the Jane Austen Society 1986–1995*, vol. 4, The Jane Austen Society, vols. 6, 1997, pp. 172–173.
'Branches and Groups of the Society.' *The Jane Austen Society of the United Kingdom*, n.d., www.janeaustensoci.freeuk.com/pages/branches.htm. Accessed 21 Nov. 2019.
Brownstein, Rachel M. *Why Jane Austen?* Columbia UP, 2011.
'Call for Films.' *Jane Austen in Paradise: Intimations of Immortality JASNA AGM 2017*, n.d., www.jasna.org/agms/huntington/call-for-films.html. Accessed 6 Jan. 2020.
Carpenter, Tom. 'The Jane Austen Memorial Trust: A Brief History 1949 to 2015.' *Jane Austen Society Report for 2015*, 2015, pp. 18–24.
Chapman, R.W. 'Foreword.' 'Jane Austen and Jane Austen's House,' by the Jane Austen Society, 23 July 1949, *Collected Reports of the Jane Austen Society 1949–1965.* William Dawson & Sons, 1967. Reprint, vol. 1, The Jane Austen Society, vols. 6, 1996, p. 2.
Cole, Helen. *Chawton House Library.* Scala Arts & Heritage Publishers Ltd, 2016.
Committee of the Jane Austen Society. 'Telegram to Jack Grey.' *Persuasion*, vol. 1, 16 Dec. 1979. Reprint, First Folio Printing Co., n.d., p. 19.

JAS and JASNA

Cooper, Liz Philosophos. 'Draft of Villaseñor Essay on JAS & JASNA.' Received by Alice Villaseñor, 24 Feb. 2020.

Cooper, Liz Philosophos. 'President's Column.' *JASNA News*, vol. 35, no. 4, Winter, 2020, p. 3.

Cooper, Liz Philosophos. 'The Jane Austen Society of North America.' *What's Next for Jane Austen*, special issue of *Texas Studies in Literature and Language*, vol. 61, no. 4, Winter, 2019, pp. 482–485.

Duruz, Selwyn. 'Design for a Garden for Jane Austen's House.' 'Jane Austen and Jane Austen's House,' by the Jane Austen Society, 23 July 1949, *Collected Reports of the Jane Austen Society 1949–1965*. William Dawson & Sons, 1967. Reprint, vol. 1, The Jane Austen Society, vols. 6, 1996, pp. 9–11.

'Essay Contest Winning Entries.' *Jane Austen Society of North America*, 2019, www.jasna.org/publications/essay-contest-winning-entries/. Accessed 9 Dec. 2019.

'Event Calendar.' *Jane Austen Society of North America*, 2019, jasna.org/conferences-events/event-calendar/. Accessed 6 Dec. 2019.

'Flag-Raising Campaign.' *North American Friends of Chawton House*, 12 July 2019, www.nafch.org/post/flag-raising. Accessed 20 Mar. 2021.

Grey, David J. 'From the President.' *Persuasion*, vol. 1, 16 Dec. 1979. Reprint, First Folio Printing Co., n.d., pp. 3–7.

Grey, David J., and Joan Austen-Leigh. 'Letter of Invitation to Join JASNA.' 1979 March. 'JASNA Turns 40.' *The Jane Austen Society of North America*, 22 Apr. 2019, jasna.org/about/jasna-post/jasna-turns-40/. Accessed 3 Dec. 2019.

Guyatt, Mary. 'Re: Quotation for Publication?' Received by Alice Villaseñor, 13 Nov. 2019.

Hanaway, Lorraine. 'Brief Highlights of the Minutes of the Meeting (not recorded elsewhere in this Newsletter).' *Persuasion*, vol. 1, 16 Dec. 1979. Reprint, First Folio Printing Co., n.d., p. 7.

Hanaway, Lorraine. 'Our First Dinner.' *Persuasion*, vol. 1, 16 Dec. 1979. Reprint, First Folio Printing Co., n.d., pp. 10–11.

Hanaway, Lorraine. 'The Meeting.' *Persuasions*, vol. 3, 16 Dec. 1981, pp. 17–18.

Hanaway, Lorraine. 'Who Attended the Philadelphia Meeting?' *Persuasions*, vol. 5, 16 Dec. 1983, p. 25.

Harris, Jocelyn. 'Jane Austen, Samuel Johnson, and the Academy.' *Persuasions*, vol. 30, 2008, pp. 27–37.

'International Visitor Program.' *Jane Austen Society of North America*, 2019, jasna.org/programs/international-visitor/. Accessed 13 Dec. 2019.

'J. David Grey Young Writers' Workshop.' *Persuasion: 200 Years of Constancy and Hope*, JASNA Metropolitan Kansas City Region, n.d., jasna.org/agms/kansascity/workshop.html. Accessed 9 Dec. 2019.

'Jane Austen Publications.' *The Jane Austen Society of the United Kingdom*, n.d., janeaustensoci.freeuk.com/pages/publications.htm. Accessed 21 Nov. 2019.

Jane Austen Society. 'Jane Austen and Jane Austen's House,' 23 July 1949. *Collected Reports of the Jane Austen Society 1949–1965*. William Dawson & Sons, 1967. Reprint, vol. 1, The Jane Austen Society, vols. 6, 1996, pp. 1–8.

Jane Austen Society. 'Jane Austen Society: Report for the period 1st Oct., 1949–31st Dec., 1950.' *Collected Reports of the Jane Austen Society 1949–1965*. William Dawson & Sons, 1967. Reprint, vol. 1, The Jane Austen Society, vols. 6, 1996, pp. 15–18.

Jane Austen Society. 'Minutes of the Annual General Meeting held on Saturday 17 July 2004 at Chawton House, Hampshire (by courtesy of the Chawton House Library).' *Report for 2004. Collected Reports of the Jane Austen Society 2001–2005*, vol. 6, The Jane Austen Society, vols. 6, 2008, pp. 289–292.

Jane Austen Society. 'Minutes of the 62nd Annual General Meeting held at Chawton House on Saturday 14 July 2018.' *Jane Austen Society Report for 2018*, 2018, pp. 2–6.

Jane Austen Society. 'Opening of Additional Rooms in Jane Austen's House: Visit to Steventon and Manydown.' *Report for the Year 1953. Collected Reports of the Jane Austen Society 1949–1965*. William Dawson & Sons, 1967. Reprint, vol. 1, The Jane Austen Society, vols. 6, 1996, p. 41.

Jane Austen Society of North America. 'Henry G. Burke Grants.' *Persuasions*, vol. 12, 16 Dec. 1990, p. 4.

Jane Austen Society of North America. 'Jane Austen Society of North America First Annual Literary Competition.' *Persuasions*, vol. 9, 16 Dec. 1987, p. 45.

Jane Austen Society of North America. '1991 Awards.' *Persuasions*, vol. 13, 16 Dec. 1991, p. 4.

Jane Austen Society of North America. '1992-1993 Henry G. Burke Grants.' *Persuasions*, vol. 14, 1992, p. 4. *The Jane Austen Society of North America*, Mar. 2014, www.jasna.org/assets/Persuasions/No-14/e200b548fd/burke.pdf. Accessed 10 Dec. 2019.

'Jane Austen Society of North America 2015 AGM.' Directed by Brandon Hess and Tara Tucker, interview of Claire Bellanti, 2015, *YouTube*, uploaded by Rick King, 10 Jan. 2016, www.youtube.com/watch?v=arRYQ_h17oE. Accessed 20 Mar. 2021.

Jane Austen's Regency World Magazine, 1–105 to date (2003–2020).

Jenkins, Elizabeth. 'Introduction.' *Collected Reports of the Jane Austen Society 1949–1965.* William Dawson & Sons, 1967. Reprint, vol. 1, The Jane Austen Society, vols. 6, 1996, pp. vii–x.

Johnson, Claudia L. *Jane Austen's Cults and Cultures.* U of Chicago P, 2012.

Kiefer, Jeanne. 'Anatomy of a Janeite: Results from *The Jane Austen Survey 2008.' Persuasions On-Line*, vol. 29, no. 1, 2008. 11 Aug. 2015, jasna.org/persuasions/on-line/vol29no1/kiefer.html.

Kipling, Rudyard. 'The Janeites.' *Debits and Credits.* Macmillan and Co., Limited, 1926, pp. 147-174.

Lane, Maggie. 'The Jane Austen Society (United Kingdom).' *What's Next for Jane Austen*, special issue of *Texas Studies in Literature and Language*, vol. 61, no. 4, Winter, 2019, pp. 491–493.

Lost in Austen. Directed by Dan Zeff, ITV, 2008.

Lynch, Deidre. 'Introduction: Sharing with Our Neighbors.' *Janeites: Austen's Disciples and Devotees*, edited by Deidre Lynch. Princeton UP, 2000, pp. 3–24.

Maggie and Kristin. 'JASNA Recap.' *First Impressions Podcast*, Ep 44, Podbean, 24 Oct. 2019, firstimpressionspodcast.podbean.com/e/ep-44-jasna-recap/.

Mandal, Anthony. 'Introduction.' *The Reception of Jane Austen in Europe*, edited by Anthony Mandal and Brian Southam. Continuum, 2007, pp. 1–11.

Marshall, Mary Gaither. '"The Company of Clever, Well-Informed People": Personal Reminiscences of JASNA's First 40 Years.' Annual General Meeting of the Jane Austen Society of North America, 4 Oct. 2019, Williamsburg Lodge, Virginia. Panel Presentation.

McMaster, Juliet. 'Revisiting Lake Louise 1993.' *Persuasions On-Line*, vol. 39, no. 1, Winter, 2018, jasna.org/publications/persuasions-online/volume-39-no-1/revisiting-lake-louise-1993/.

McMaster, Juliet. '"The Company of Clever, Well-Informed People": Personal Reminiscences of JASNA's First 40 Years.' Annual General Meeting of the Jane Austen Society of North America, 4 Oct. 2019, Williamsburg Lodge, Virginia. Panel Presentation.

'Newsletter.' *The Jane Austen Society of the United Kingdom*, n.d., www.janeaustensoci.freeuk.com/pages/newsletter.htm. Accessed 21 Nov. 2019.

'Other Resources and Links.' *Jane Austen Society of North America*, 2020, jasna.org/austen/resource-links/. Accessed 8 Jan. 2020.

Parker, Keiko. 'St. Louis 1984—A Personal Account.' *Persuasions*, vol. 6, 16 Dec. 1984, pp. 26–29.

'Regional Groups.' *Jane Austen Society of North America*, 2020, jasna.org/about/regions/. Accessed 1 June 2020.

Saintsbury, George. Preface. *Pride and Prejudice*, by Jane Austen, George Allen, Ruskin House, 1894. Reprint, Dover Publications, 2005, pp. ix–xxiii.

Schuessler, Jennifer. 'Lots of Pride, a Little Prejudice,' *New York Times*, 8 Oct. 2012, www.nytimes.com/2012/10/09/books/jane-austen-society-of-north-america-meets-in-brooklyn.html?pagewanted=all&_r=0.

Slothouber, Linda. 'AGM Registration Update.' Received by Alice Villaseñor, 12 June 2019.

Smith, Amy Elizabeth. *All Roads Lead to Austen: A Yearlong Journey with Jane.* Sourcebooks, 2012.

'Society Events.' *The Jane Austen Society of the United Kingdom*, n.d., www.janeaustensoci.freeuk.com/pages/society_events.htm. Accessed 21 Nov. 2019.

Solender, Elsa. 'The Jane Austen Society of North America (JASNA).' *Report for 1997. Collected Reports of the Jane Austen Society 1996–2000*, vol. 5, The Jane Austen Society, vols. 6, 2005, pp. 75–76.

Stiller, Maureen. 'Draft of Villaseñor Essay on JAS & JASNA.' Received by Alice Villaseñor, 16 Feb. 2020.

Stiller, Maureen. 'Eighty Years Young.' *Jane Austen's Regency World*, Mar./Apr. 2020, pp. 56–57.

Stiller, Maureen. 'JAS Information for Publication.' Received by Alice Villaseñor, 16 Jan. 2020.

Stiller, Maureen. 'Transfer of Society Assets.' *News Letter: The Jane Austen Society*, no. 53, The Jane Austen Society, Autumn 2019, p. 11.

'Talks for Outside Groups.' *The Jane Austen Society of the United Kingdom*, n.d., www.janeaustensoci.freeuk.com/pages/outside_group_talks.htm. Accessed 1 June 2020.

Terry, Judith, and Sallie Wadsworth. 'Notes on the Ninth Annual Meeting.' *Persuasions*, vol. 9, 16 Dec. 1987, pp. 7–11.

'The Jane Austen Garden Trail.' *Chawton House*, n.d., chawtonhouse.org/visit/more-about-the-garden/the-jane-austen-garden-trail/. Accessed 6 Dec. 2019.

The Many Lovers of Miss Jane Austen. Directed by Rupert Edwards, written by Amanda Vickery, BBC, 2011.

'Tours of England.' *Jane Austen Society of North America*, 2019, jasna.org/conferences-events/tour/. Accessed 13 Dec. 2019.

Trollope, Anthony. 'A Scotchman at Overton: Jane Austen's North Hampshire.' *Persuasions*, vol. 9, 16 Dec. 1987, pp. 56–58.

Tucker, George Holbert. 'St. Nicholas Appeal.' *Persuasion*, vol. 1, 1 Dec. 1979. Reprint, First Folio Printing Co., n.d., pp. 8–9.

Wadsworth, Sallie R. 'Santa Fe Meeting.' *Persuasions*, no. 11, 1989, pp. 4–6. *The Jane Austen Society of North America*, n.d., www.jasna.org/persuasions/printed/number11/wadsworth.htm. Accessed 5 Dec. 2019.

'Welcome to the Website of the Jane Austen Society.' *The Jane Austen Society of the United Kingdom*, n.d., www.janeaustensoci.freeuk.com/index.htm. Accessed 1 June 2020.

Wells, Juliette. *Everybody's Jane: Austen in the Popular Imagination.* Continuum, 2011.

'With Thanks to Our American Supporters.' *Chawton House*, 30 May 2018, chawtonhouse.org/2018/05/with-thanks-to-our-american-supporters/. Accessed 20 Mar. 2021.

Yaffe, Deborah. *Among the Janeites: A Journey Through the World of Jane Austen Fandom.* Mariner Books, 2013.

32

LIVE AUSTEN ADAPTATION IN THE AGE OF MULTIMEDIA REPRODUCTION

Christopher C. Nagle

WESTERN MICHIGAN UNIVERSITY

> I am convinced that Jane Austen *as a play-wright* will fascinate her audiences as much as she has her readers *as a novelist*.
>
> —*Rosina Filippi (1895)*

Why Is Jane Austen On Stage?

When Rosina Filippi first made her bold claim in the preface to her successful and pioneering editions of 'duologues', excerpted from the novels and 'arranged' by Filippi (with some emendations) for amateur performance, she scarcely could have imagined that after little more than another century Jane Austen's works would have proliferated on stages across the globe. Though mostly for English-speaking audiences, a mix of amateur and professional stagings of Austen adaptations, continuations, spin-offs, and tributes have multiplied exponentially since the turn of the twenty-first century, dwarfing the productions of cinema and television that continue to emerge. As I have noted elsewhere, this surprisingly rapid expansion is also a global one, with theatrical productions, including some world premieres, appearing in Australia, Brazil, Germany, Ireland, Japan, New Zealand, Russia, Sweden, and the United Kingdom. Unsurprisingly, Austen's homeland represents the majority of non-U.S. productions, but the overall impression one should take away from a closer look at the data is that—as in the realms of fan-fiction and film reception—Austen on stage is a global commodity, and one that calls for the kind of sustained critical attention that her novels have enjoyed.[1]

Perhaps more curiously, the performance genres into which Austen's fiction is incorporated—and to a lesser extent, her life—vary quite widely, too. Out of the nearly 150 distinct adaptations I have identified thus far, straight plays make up the majority of adaptations (ca. 64%), but there is a significant and growing body of musicals (ca. 17%), and a small but fascinating expansion into opera (3.5%), ballet (1.4%), and a variety of difficult-to-classify works. The latter include things such as solo (usually 'one-woman') shows, parodies, and light 'diversions', many of which seem to take themselves less seriously than those productions aspiring to professional standards. Indeed, some published or reported works show no evidence yet of being staged at all. For the productions mounted in the United States, to take the example which dominates statistically (ca. 70% of all twenty-first-century productions), the split between amateur and professional productions is roughly even. A number of the most prolific living writers, such as Jon Jory, who has adapted all six of Austen's completed novels into plays (and an additional musical in collaboration with Peter Ekstrom, *Pride & Prejudice: A Musical Romantic-Comedy*[2]), have found particular success in community and school productions. But it is also true that in several cases—the plays of Kate Hamill and those of Lauren Gunderson, or the musicals of Paul Gordon—professional productions have been consistently successful in filling houses and winning awards, and I will return to such examples for greater attention below.

One last category has gone without mention, a special case that I will address at the end of this essay: improvisational comedy. A distinct example in that it relies on unscripted material and is necessarily loose in its adaptive relation to the source texts, improv is nevertheless a real presence in the Austen performance scene: I have found at least five different troupes who have been dedicated either exclusively or in part to 'doing' Austen for a live audience, in Boston, Chicago, Los Angeles, Minneapolis, and the United Kingdom (in London, and currently touring more widely). Having explored the work of three of these groups, I will speculate a bit on what this surprising offshoot of the staged Austen boom might add to our understanding of Austen's deep resonance and wide appeal for English-speaking audiences, and I will also conclude with consideration of what all of this weirdly diverse and wildly creative adaptation work offers to those of us interested in Austen's legacy for the current century. One thing seems clear: however committed some might be to the primacy of the novels, the popularity, proliferation, and innovative richness of the new Live Austen makes it increasingly likely that more people than ever will encounter her work for the first time in an adapted form. I would also argue that such a circumstance is felicitous and enriches rather than diminishes the worlds of both fandom and scholarship.

Staging Austen

Biographers and critics have often discussed the history of family theatricals performed while Austen was growing up, as well as her practice of reading dramatically from her own novels in progress, in addition to her limited experimentation with 'joke-playlets', as Brian Southam calls them, and her one longer attempt at adapting (for presumably amateur performance) her favourite novel, Samuel Richardson's *Sir Charles Grandison*.[3] If the history of Austen's work being transformed for performance has its roots in the Austen household, then one looks to the Rosina Filippi 'duologues' as the first significant example of adaptation for a broader audience. As Devoney Looser has illuminated, the influence of this frequently reprinted and widely disseminated collection led to an amateur theatrical expansion that had unprecedented significance for Austen's reception. Designed for performance in private homes, schools, or other community settings, this book would have allowed for untold numbers of young women to have their introduction to Austen come through reading and then watching and listening to live performances of scenes from her novels. Even more remarkably, Looser notes, the selections chosen by Filippi for the remarkably successful collection of her duologues focus on 'moments in which Austen's female characters are most direct and rebellious'.[4] Foregrounding comedy through female-focused excerpts, with the arranger's hand actively highlighting both the humour and the assertive voices of women speaking their own minds, Looser shows that Filippi's scenes function as subtle political as well as pedagogical tools in an age of the New Woman's rise in the early twentieth century.

Clearly, the innovative work of this foremother of stage Austen opened up possibilities for all later, more formal adaptations, such as Helen Jerome's very successful play, *Pride and Prejudice: A Sentimental Comedy in Three Acts* (1935), which ran for over 500 performances on Broadway and London's West End, before touring further and eventually providing the basis for MGM's famous 1940 film starring Greer Garson and Laurence Olivier.[5] In both of these cases as well as in other, lesser-known early productions, Looser demonstrates compellingly that early adaptors do much more than fangirl; the implicit (and sometimes, explicit) political reverberations of these creative works opened up new ways of reading Austenian source texts while also fitting them to suit the rapidly shifting cultural contexts of their day. Creative translation of Austen into theatrical material always has brought with it the potential for newly vibrant female empowerment, which continues in our own time. In recent decades, there has been a remarkable resurgence in staging Austen for playgoing audiences varying from school and community performances to full-fledged professional companies mounting critically acclaimed and even award-winning productions. These twenty-first century adaptations also reflect the cultural crosscurrents of our tumultuous age, and they most commonly elaborate on the feminist extensions of earlier versions of Austen on stage, allowing for a breadth of provocative incarnations that firmly place women's lives and experiences at the centre of the production—still uncommon in a theatre world perpetually dominated by men's voices, experiences, and perspectives.[6] Several of the most interesting recent examples give a state-of-the-art snapshot of the best of new Austen theatrical productions. These forms of live adaptation testify to a seemingly inexhaustible source of innovation that precedes historically—and exceeds in number—its recorded (cinematic, televisual, and internet-based) siblings, while promising a vibrant and durable body of performance-based works that are likely to provide a new canon for students and scholars of Austen.

For Whom the Bell Tolls: Kate Hamill's Pride and Prejudice

Much like her first Austen adaptation of *Sense and Sensibility* (2016), Kate Hamill's *Pride and Prejudice* (2018) is a brashly innovative and distinctly feminist transformation of what is still the most popular and frequently adapted of all Austen works.[7] Premiering under the inspired direction of Amanda Dehnert in an off-Broadway collaboration with the 2017 Hudson Valley Shakespeare Festival, Hamill's play features elements familiar to fans of her previous award-winning show: broad comedy extending into farce; the doubling and tripling of characters, some cross-dressed; simple, creative staging to make efficient use of a constrained space; and a distinctly contemporary mash-up of periods that we might call 'Regency-adjacent', with popular twentieth-century music and pop culture references punctuating the mostly early nineteenth-century feel of a production with typical period costumes and furnishings. Both of the latter were creative approximations of Austen's era, and there is no specific indication of period in the script (as there is, for example, about maintaining at least a 50% female-identified cast, and the option to forego doubling). Blending contemporary idioms with a true sense of Austenian characters and plot allows for a production that is equal parts recognisable and refreshed. As a playwright, Hamill has shown herself to be a master of inhabiting the text authentically while finding clever ways to jolt audiences awake to see unexpected connections to our own day.[8]

For this reimagining of the story, Hamill makes games central to the production. 'The Game of Love' would work as a fitting subtitle for her *Pride and Prejudice*: the theme is sounded consistently throughout the script by multiple characters—in fact the premiere opened with the cast singing Wayne Fontana's 1960s hit of the same name (no music is specified in the script)—while games are literally being played on stage, influenced by Hamill's research into Regency amusements. And yet as light-hearted and often farcical as much of this action is, we also see how clearly serious the consequences of the love-game are for everyone, especially for women in Austen's age. As Lizzie explains to Lydia in the first scene, 'Playing games keeps one sane, when the stakes involved threaten to drive one MAD' (14). This idea generates a productive debate throughout the script between the Bennet sisters as well as their parents. Act One begins with the Prologue featuring formal dance that leads to a dreamlike game of Blind Man's Bluff. Described in the script as 'sexy and naughty' playfulness (9), the dance becomes more tense as it builds to an intimate confrontation of blindfolded

Lizzie alone with Darcy. Just as they both reach for the blindfold on her face, with hands about to touch, the scene is punctuated by a cacophonous ringing bell that first marks their dangerously intimate proximity and then bleeds into the first scene: Mrs Bennet is ringing a bell to gather the household for news about Netherfield Park's newest tenant.

This auditory feature, which recurs consistently throughout the play, is perhaps the boldest and most interesting creative choice in this adaptation. Widely varied kinds of bells play a central role within the production, providing punctuation, sounding alarm, marking the time, and highlighting the metaphorical significance for key moments—as if the characters sense the importance of them even if they do not literally hear the sound as we do. Both individually and also through their cumulative effect throughout the performance, they guide us toward what is inexorably out of the characters' control.[9] As one of many examples of Hamill's Regency-adjacent world, we encounter features appropriate to the period—dinner bells, servant call bells, traditional church bells, wedding bells—but we find characters voicing DINGS and BONGS unconventionally in absurd or farcical use as well. For example, at the Long's ball which introduces the Bingley party, bells ding sharply when Bingley first sees Jane and also when Lizzy and Darcy first confront each other face to face. Unlike the realistic examples just noted, these clearly seem to be extra-diegetic uses that underscore the importance of certain moments in the story for the audience—but perhaps they are ringing like some internal psychic alarm for the characters as well. If these bells serve as obvious symbolic markers it is nevertheless uncertain how the actors will interpret and respond to them, which leaves the audience in a similar position of heightened attention and suspense.

This complexity and the rich uncertainty that bell ringing provides for the audience is heightened at the conclusion of Act 1. After the dual disasters of Lizzy rejecting Collins' proposal and Bingley seeming to jilt Jane by leaving suddenly for London, the Bennet household struggles to regain equilibrium. As the act reaches its concluding emotional crescendo, Lizzy attempts to placate Jane by insisting, with uncharacteristic sunniness that rings hollow, that 'everything will be perfect' (56). At the same time, both sisters are subjected to a 'cacophonous' attack of bells from the ensemble circling them, drowning them in a sea of sound that seems more like an externalised reflection of internal emotion and anxiety in the face of each sister's true desperation.[10] But this darker moment is a rare interruption of the screwball comedy that pervades the play, and it also effectively sets up the genuinely moving proposal scenes to come. Both romantic proposals are compressed within the equally frantic pace of the second act, but both also bear the potential to be surprisingly effective in their scripted awkwardness with stellar performances by actors such as those featured in the premiere.

Although the script captures much of what makes this adaptation successful, the strikingly fresh, authentic performances that brought the characters to life in the Primary Stages production—especially Hamill's Lizzy and Jason O'Connell's Darcy (the only two actors not to double)—made this transformation possible. Both actors tapped into unexpected dimensions of each character through their respective emotional vulnerability and repressed desire—as well as an equal disgust with the prospect of their entry into the marriage market—while leading the production to its necessary but nevertheless unexpected conclusion. Remarkably, the famous nuptial resolution with which Austen tales nearly always conclude—even more familiar, perhaps, than this novel's perpe- tually quoted opening line about universal truths—never seems inevitable throughout the course of Hamill's play. Despite marking each of the crucial moments that spur Lizzy to reassess Darcy's character (his stewardship of Pemberley, bribing Wickham to marry Lydia, bringing Bingley back to Jane)—and all of this in a very short span of three successive scenes—the realisation that they are in love does not guarantee they will reconnect. This element of suspense alone is a triumph, with Lizzy and Darcy's *rapprochement* saved for the last page of the script and their final moments on stage. It is also part of the playwright's subtle feminist ethos, as both characters stumble with an equal measure of uncertainty and commitment to embrace each other, finally, after having tried so hard to resist the pull of each other and of the Austenian storyline. As they playfully agree to dance, the show ends as it must, with the ringing of a bell as they embrace.

Of Karaoke and Bonnets

Billed as an adaptation like no other, Isobel McArthur's *Pride and Prejudice* (*sort of)* is an even more remarkably free-wheeling new production. First produced in Glasgow in 2018 and subsequently touring the United Kingdom throughout 2019, this adaptation is not as loose as its premise (and its title) might suggest. McArthur and her cast reimagine the familiar tale framed and punctuated by six female servants, who the script describes as characters who 'steer the course of the action in ways unnoticed by the Master characters' (10). Indeed, in this play, even the novel's famous opening line is given not to Lizzie (as in Hamill's play) or to Mrs Bennet (as is often the case in others) but to a servant named Clara—which certainly upends all previous conventions of centreing this Austenian theme, whether more or less ironically, since it is delivered by a character from outside the novel. But this is far from the most surprising liberty taken with the source text. If Hamill's liberal embrace of farce shocked some theatregoers, McArthur's rollicking house-party of an adaptation would send such people to an early grave. *Pride and Prejudice* (*sort of)* embeds the creatively anachronistic use of karaoke at the heart of the play, with characters periodically exposing themselves on the microphone either by simply giving speeches or by singing pop songs appropriate to the mood of the moment. When Jane and Bingley first dance, for example, the party includes a karaoke performance by Jane singing The Shirelle's 'Will You Still Love Me Tomorrow'; after being spurned by Darcy at the same event, Elizabeth sings Carly Simon's 'You're So Vain', and it is clear who is the target of her vocal assassination.

This meta-performative conceit brings to life the social anxiety of such occasions and literalises the element of performance that we usually see as metaphorical. Of course, there are literal performance occasions in the novel—Mary's attempt to shine by singing at the Netherfield Ball, Elizabeth's mediocre piano skills on display at Rosings—so this seemingly wild deviation into the world of karaoke might be seen as intuitive despite its obvious twentieth-century roots. Both forms of performance are also smart ways to update the variety of embarrassing social performances that occur in the novel, almost inevitably leading to public shame here, too. A drunken Mrs Bennet literally broadcasts her plans for Jane and Bingley's future marriage through the microphone. Darcy is forced by Bingley not simply to dance with someone but to perform 'on stage', and he fails doubly: first by making a spectacle of his refusal to perform and then by erupting into a much more public insult than intended over the mike: 'You'd have me paired with the plainest woman in the entire room just to entertain her idiotic family?!' (32). Both instances heighten the comic effects engendered by putting a character in the spotlight, whether one who always seeks it—thereby shaming her family—or one who never wants it—thereby shaming himself. It is a funny but also astutely *levelling* ploy. As the framing of this tale staged by servants suggests, class status provides obvious advantages and yet guarantees one very little when navigating social spaces successfully—or ultimately, in finding happiness. Anyone can, and likely will, make a fool of themselves at some point in front of others.

Moreover, McArthur's strategy of multi rolling (as she calls it) the all-female cast creates exponentially more hilarity and complication for audiences, as individual actors must shift between anywhere from 3–5 different roles, including the leading male roles. The sole exceptions are reserved for the actor who plays the demanding role of Elizabeth, doubling only as the servant Effie, and the role of Mr Bennet, which is 'played by an armchair facing upstage' (10). One is less surprised, perhaps, that Kitty is maintained in this adaptation; usually a casualty of compression, the least essential Bennet daughter remains here in a retelling that is happy to expand its cast into chaotic excesses of kind as well as number.[11] Although the servants close the story as they opened it, providing ironic commentary that bookends the famous tale, the 'finale' interrupts even that much tidy closure to this decidedly untidy play: Mary emerges as the last character standing, taking the stage when no one remains to prevent her from performing. As she breaks into the opening verses of Candi Staton's 1976 disco classic 'Young Hearts Run Free', the servants return to join her in a rousing chorus before the final blackout. As amusing as it is to see Austen's underdog find her voice at last, the servant's joyous collaboration with her is perhaps the most important touch of all. We end with a reminder that none of this story could have been told to begin with were it not for the invisible labour making possible its circuitous but ultimately happy ending. Or, as Flo, Annie, Maisie, and Tillie put it more memorably: 'You can't write a novel without— / Someone to empty the chamberpot. / Or, to have a whirlwind romance without— / Clean bedding' (14).

Emma, Interrupted

In Phil Timberlake's adaptation of Austen's *Emma* (2019) for Chicago's Lifeline Theatre, the most distinctive element of the production was the ensemble's tripling or quadrupling of roles for everyone but the heroine herself. This choice served both to highlight the comic potential of the story and also to draw attention to its titular heroine and to what is distinctive about her character, what makes her special in Austen's eyes. At some point, for example, everyone but the actress playing Emma took a turn at elderly hypochondriac Mr Woodhouse—whether male or female, old or young—and a single distinctive prop was used to signify his identity, a cane. Though perhaps no one provided as great a challenge for each actor as Mr Woodhouse, this ploy was also used to great effect with other characters of Highbury: a pair of prominent gold spectacles for Mr Weston, a simple fan for Mrs Elton, and a dressmaker's dummy to represent Mrs Bates, which also signified that whoever was wheeling her around at the moment was playing the voluble Miss Bates. One of the best examples of a brilliant innovation here was the deployment of the Bateses for subtle exposition. Drawing from the novel's comic pairing of Mrs Bates' near-deafness and Miss Bates' logorrhoea, the actor who plays the latter must frequently repeat discussions, summarise current activities, or recall past contexts of the Highbury community. In addition to heightening the comedy by directing this information to a 'character' represented by a dummy (the two seem fittingly interchangeable, we intuit), the running commentary serves to clue in an audience potentially less attuned to the nuances of Austen's multilayered plot.

Occasionally this back-and-forth made for especially challenging conversions between roles, such as when the brilliant actress who played virtually everyone but Emma was forced to jump up and down to play both sides of an interchange between Miss Bates and Harriet Smith during Emma and Harriet's visit to the Bates' lodgings. Perhaps nothing requires as dramatic a shift as moving from the warmth of an older Mrs Weston to the reserve of a younger Jane Fairfax to the hilariously grotesque Mrs Elton; the latter was exactly as painful as we find in the novel, without quite straining into parodic excess. The play demands an impressive versatility of the men as well. Converting effortlessly between a more one-dimensionally gregarious Mr Weston and the more subtle warmth and strong attachment of our hero Mr Knightley might seem impressive enough, until the same actor takes a turn at both Miss Bates and Mr Woodhouse. Another actor shares a turn at the latter two minor characters before bringing the awkward Mr Elton and the flirtatious Frank Churchill plausibly and distinctly to life. In addition to showcasing the talents of its cast, the play's stellar performances remind one that it is possible with sufficient subtleties to make clear how radically different these potential suitors are, despite being played by the same actor in the same costume.

Taking its cue from the familiar conventions of candlelit heritage film, Lifeline's production supplemented the Regency style of the costumes with its lighting. The set was flanked by faux candles, and several scenes made excellent use of this suggestion by mirroring as closely as one can the effects of dim nineteenth-century illumination with the lighting design. This tone was especially effective during the ball scene when Knightley saves Harriet from the indignity of standing without a partner after being snubbed by the 'old, married man', Mr Elton. After their turn together ended, Emma and Knightley followed with the lights dimmed, producing a beautifully dramatic, shadowed effect for this couple who for the first time are visually foregrounded for the audience as a prospective romantic pair. This especially skilful scene allowed for even greater tension, setting up a parallel foreshadowed sense of romance which poor, mistaken Harriet shortly would misconstrue and share with Emma (as with us), demonstrating just how difficult it is to read the social cues meant to convey the heart's affections and intentions. Both actresses, shrouded in the intimacy of candlelight with Austen's leading man, are thus primed—one more quickly, one much more slowly over time—to revisit the romantic echoes of this scene later in the play.

As a work of adaptation, Timberlake skilfully compressed a long and complex novel, maintaining the most crucial episodes. The only obvious absence was the consistent gameplay that threads through the novel, but the element of mystery and detection centred on Jane Fairfax (and ultimately, Frank Churchill) was maintained as clues drop for attentive audience members whether they know Austen's tale or not. And one questionable choice emerged in the infamous Box Hill scene for which all readers patiently wait: painfully rushed, everything was over seemingly before the scene began, undercutting significantly the impact of Emma's crucial blunder. Her insult came too quickly, as soon as the characters assembled on blankets for their picnic, and the gross impropriety of Frank's public flirtation with Emma was reduced to inconsequence. This scene is perhaps one that cannot benefit from the same frenetic, multi rolling pace that enlivened so many others. Overall, the use of the ensemble and the quick-paced comic staging of the scenes worked marvellously, keeping the action moving and the tone light-hearted. But those who have seen Hamill's more balanced approach to adaptation—juxtaposing scenes that allow a slower-paced contrast to the full-throttle farce of others surrounding it—would be likely to notice this less effective approach to *Emma* maintained at breakneck speed.

As a contrast to the previous two recent adaptations, Timberlake's *Emma* pushes the comedy of the source text to its maximum without actually committing to full-on farce as in Hamill and McArthur. Counterintuitively, perhaps, the game-playing that is actually central to the novel disappears, but the intensity of constant multi rolling contributes to a pace that vies with both of the other plays for sheer energy and exuberance, even if it is a traditional play in every other sense. Since the social world of Highbury is famously Austen's most narrowly constrained in setting while also being its most richly elaborated in detail, the novelistic intimacy she creates necessitates a comparable sense of intimacy in adaptation. On stage it would be difficult to imagine a better solution to this challenge than to adopt the multi rolling strategy of Timberlake's play, especially if comedy is the focus. Characters are not merely close to each other in kinship and in physical proximity, but also in their literal and unpredictable interchanging of roles, showing us just how much they—and perhaps we, too—ultimately share with each other.

Making Austen Musical: From Burrows to Taylor to Today

Another development in this performance history that Rosina Filippi likely would not have anticipated is the birth of the Jane Austen musical. Although this surprising conjunction has become much more familiar over the past decade, the tradition began inauspiciously with a Broadway flop from 1959 called *First Impressions*. Abe Burrows, famous for his more successful production of *Guys and Dolls*, directed and wrote the book for this new musical, drawing from the widely acclaimed Helen Jerome stage play of 1935. One of its most distinctive elements is its retooling of the play as a vehicle for aging star Hermione Gingold, an established British Shakespearean actor recently transplanted to America who certainly was not a singer. The result is a show that could have been called *Mrs Bennet and Her Daughters*, featuring Gingold in six of fifteen vocal numbers and revising the story to make the matriarch a central character. Here Mrs Bennet is not only anxious to marry off her daughters, but also laments having been duped by Mr Bennet into expecting a more lavish lifestyle, and in one of her featured songs giddily fantasises about the prospect of 'A House in Town' once one of her daughters finally marries into wealth and privilege.

Andrew Wright sums it up best: 'the play [sic] as a whole is a sad decline from Helen Jerome—not to mention Jane Austen'.[12] In fact very little about the show is memorable, largely thanks to the lacklustre score co-authored by George Weiss, Robert Goldman, and Glenn Paxton, but it does establish one tradition worth noting: the theme of 'Five Daughters'. A featured number in adaptations to come, such as those by Bernard J. Taylor and by Rita Abrams and Josie Brown, this innovation—in concert with the decision to make Mrs Bennet central to the story—is significant artistically, setting in motion a more balanced narrative that does not revolve solely around the Lizzie-Darcy love story. Resisting the gravitational orbit of the romantic leads has also been difficult for both cinema and television adaptations of Austen works, and stage versions choose different ways of expanding the field of creative options, as we can see in the examples that follow.

There is little sign of interest in a Jane Austen musical between the brief, two-month run of *First Impressions* and the Austen renaissance of the 1990s.[13] The same year that brought the cinematic boom of Austen to mass audiences—Andrew Davies' epic, five-hour *Pride and Prejudice* mini-series for the BBC, Ang Lee's *Sense and Sensibility* film, and the smaller-scale Nick Dear-Roger Michell *Persuasion*—also introduced composer Bernard J. Taylor's *Pride and Prejudice*.[14] Taylor's approach scarcely could be more different from Burrows', producing a beautiful score that blends the influence of Regency keyboard styles and contemporary musical theatre stylings from the age of Andrew Lloyd Webber and Tim Rice. Indeed, one of the most striking stylistic features in the production is that several pieces counterbalance the expected ballads of the romantic leads with authentically angry, frantic, and emotionally intense interchanges that would be at home in a musical like the 1980s cult favourite *Chess*.[15]

The first example of the latter is Taylor's rendition of Elizabeth and Darcy's exchange after the latter's original, insulting proposal. Although the tone of Darcy's offer is significantly different from the novel—his soaring profession of love in 'Don't Ask Me Why' is one of the show's strongest, most moving songs—there is still enough lyrical nuance to communicate the condescension of his imagined sacrifice. The authenticity of Darcy's effusive heart is simultaneously countered by pragmatic acknowledgement that 'the cost of loving you is high.' Thus Elizabeth's truly irate response ('Should I Be Flattered?') still has motivation, despite the paradox of beautiful melodic lines conveying Darcy's insults, a complexity superadded to the original fictional scenario. The second example of this dynamic interchange occurs more predictably in Lady Catherine's confrontation with Elizabeth ('My Dear Miss Bennet'). Although this brief piece easily allows Elizabeth to outmatch the spoken-sung performance of her nemesis, it is emotionally effective and also contributes a literal musical reprise of her part in the earlier duet-battle with Darcy. As one of the central themes recurring in the score, it helps Taylor to weave a distinctly contemporary style to great effect, highlighting Elizabeth's own modernity—her bold independence and self-assertion—in contrast to the more traditional, conservative musical styles of those who represent the upper class strata of Austen's source text.

Taylor's other important innovation comes from his decision to foreground Jane and Bingley's romance. Both leads have featured solos and the drama of their relationship comes first, setting up the central romantic pairing that follows. In fact Elizabeth is not featured until the ninth song of the score, well after Jane's first solo as well as her first duet with Bingley. As is customary with many adaptations to follow, Mr Collins is also featured in his own piece ('A Woman Who Knows Her Place'), and Wickham, though excluded in the original script, earns one in the expanded score. Unlike many other versions, all five Bennet daughters appear, and perhaps more surprising, Lydia is

Christopher C. Nagle

featured toward the end in a group celebration of her shotgun wedding ('Thank God They're Married!'). Overall, Taylor's musical is one of the finest adaptations to date, yet regrettably seems less widely known than it deserves despite some measure of success: more than 40 productions worldwide are reported from 1995–2012, but I have yet to encounter another soul who knows or discusses it.[16]

Further attempts after Taylor's would be a long time coming, and all of them to my knowledge emerge in the twenty-first century. At present count, there have been at least 24 Austen musicals of all kinds, including at least nine different *Pride and Prejudice* musical adaptations and an 'improvised Austen musical'. There has also been interest in narrativising Austen's life in musical form—two musicals taking her as their subject but not directly adapting her work emerged in 2006 (Geetika Lizardi and Michelle Lord's *Jane – The Musical*) and 2017 (Rob Winlow's *Austen The Musical*), respectively. The only biographically grounded musical that has realised significant success to date has been a stirring and inventive non-traditional hybrid of Austen's life, letters, and the composition of *Pride and Prejudice*, Lindsay Warren Baker and Amanda Jacob's *Austen's Pride*. I have written about this stellar show elsewhere, so I simply will note here that its central innovation—imagining the process of the story's creation and revision over time, rather than slavishly adapting the novel itself—seems key to its richly deserved success.[17]

From the current perspective, it appears that the same boom in stage plays during the first two decades of the twenty-first century helped to usher in the contemporary Austen musical's coming of age. For this reason I want to look now at two different examples of contemporary Austen musicals, the notably successful productions of Paul Gordon, with a focus on his adaptation of *Emma* (available via the pioneering Streaming Musicals website), and Harold Taw and Chris Jeffries' *Persuasion: a new musical*, which had its premiere in Seattle and a San Diego production, and which is the sole traditional musical adaptation of the novel to date.[18] Gordon is a special case because he has executed an 'Austen trilogy', with *Sense and Sensibility*, *Emma*, and *Pride and Prejudice* musicals, all of which have been staged successfully and are planned for streaming access. I have written elsewhere about Gordon's *Sense and Sensibility*, which tilts the focus to Elinor at Marianne's expense, while in tone privileging sensibility over sense.[19] Unlike that show's more two-dimensional, melodramatic characters and pleasant but largely unmemorable score, Gordon's *Emma* is a masterly exploration of the genre.

Thoroughly Modern Emma

The first element that strikes one when watching Paul Gordon's adaptation is the choice of setting, which places *Emma* in a mid-century modern environment (ca. 1961) while leaving the language of Austen intact.[20] The second is our heroine addressing us directly at the beginning of the show: 'Oh, Hello. I'm Emma Woodhouse. I enjoy the best blessings of existence and I find there is very little to vex or distress me'. As she will do on various occasions throughout the show, Emma establishes intimacy with her audience by breaking the fourth wall, but she does so sparingly and usually—unlike this opening gesture, which invites us in—with a sense of speaking out-loud to herself rather than confessing or conspiring with the audience. While this first address evacuates the ironic tone of Austen's displaced narrator—here there is no 'seeming' to qualify Emma's enjoyment or her blessings, as in the novel—the company soon fills in a note of dramatic irony while literally singing her praises along with the rest of the novel's famous opening: 'Isn't she clever, rich, and pretty ... always a wonder to behold ... she is pure perfection / the mistress of the house / she needs no correction'. The effect is to support rather than to undermine Emma's model qualities and her universal appreciation by everyone in Highbury.

That is, until Mr Knightley's entrance, and from their first interaction we see that the force of contradiction, opposition, and correction will come only from him—especially on the topic of her matchmaking skills, or as he calls it, 'meddling where you *do* not belong'. This mostly friendly friction, later to develop into something more deeply intimate, is the source of most of the 'action' in this retelling of Austen's tale. Since the subplot of Jane Fairfax and Frank Churchill's secret engagement is radically abridged here, apart from Emma's failed attempts to match Harriet to Mr Elton and then (after flirting with the idea of a match for herself) to Mr Churchill, little arises to compete for attention with the central focus on Emma and Knightley. Another result of the necessary compression of a long novel into a two-hour musical is that the plot must be revealed sooner, quite unlike the slow, cagey drip of information for Austen's readers. And of course, with compressed exposition of the story comes a stronger and sometimes less subtle delineation of character: Emma, despite her faults, is consistently winning, kind, and well-intentioned; Knightley is not just a pedagogue for Emma but comically rude to others—not merely Emma's painting skills, but also Mr Elton's judgement and even his eyesight are called out, and Mrs Elton is burned by his withering rebuke when she attempts to dictate his own plans for him; Mrs Elton is truly grotesque in her over-the-top narcissism and interference in other peoples' lives; Harriet is hilariously naïve, eager, awkward, and also a much bigger character overall (the comic highlight of the show); Jane Fairfax and Frank Churchill, both central to the mystery of the narrative, are subordinated dramatically, and their relationship is revealed to the audience before the rest of the cast learns of it.

Another key consequence of compression is that Emma's dramatic realisation—that the match most important to her is her own—comes at the end of Act One. Readers might find that this clarity arises so soon and with so much emphasis that it risks clouding and competing with the later revelation of her love for Knightley. The epiphanies seem to have a kind of structural parity, seeing each act to its dramatic close. As in the novel, Knightley seems right for the heroine, of course, but not because only he ever really was; he is the second in a sequence of matches she imagines for herself, and what most clearly sets Knightley apart is his timing (once Frank Churchill's unavailability is exposed). Nor is Frank ever given any opportunity to 'expose' himself as he does in the novel during the Donwell picnic. His flirting is also less egregious here, and his reaction to Emma's Box Hill incident makes him seem as shocked—and therefore in at least this one sense, as morally upstanding—as everyone else at the picnic. With Knightley as the sole match still available in the end, the romantic inevitability for their final pairing might seem compressed, but it surely is not forced. The simple, elegant beauty of Gordon's scoring turns their already strange near-familial ties—one of many comic elements of the show's exploration of 'Relations' (a wry song featuring the whole company)—into a nuptial resolution likely to please readers and non-readers alike.

Another happy consequence of the show's brisk pace is that one of Emma's key beliefs—'fate improvises if we don't step in' ('The Recital')—is heightened especially effectively. Emma's practice of matchmaking is more than simple daydreaming; it insists on the value of taking an active hand in shaping fate, rather than sitting back and hoping that life will turn out for the best. This shaping hand, of course, is seen as meddling and invasive by Knightley, and is likely to work for ill if the matchmaker does not see other people as clearly as she imagines. But Emma's imagination is precisely what makes her so charming in this adaptation. She clearly derives profound pleasure from the idea of other people being made happy together, and this feminist incarnation of Austen's 'heroine whom no one but myself will much like' is consistently foregrounded at the expense of other characters.[21] This contrast includes the 'perfect Mr Knightley'—ironically punctured by this label from Emma—who in Gordon's production is also a harsher, more acerbic, brandy-swilling version of Austen's leading man, never afraid to be rude in public. For this reason, we are less likely to be alienated by Emma's privilege, or her persistent failure to get things right, or even her misdirecting poor Harriet not once but twice, when her best chance for happiness lies simply with Mr Martin.

So if Gordon's Knightley becomes less gentle as a gentleman, this edge allows Emma as a consequence to commit less 'badly done' blunders as well. The exception to both of these truths, interestingly, comes in the famous Box Hill debacle. In this scene Emma's insult is bigger, clearer, and more intense than it is usually played in adaptations—everyone, including Frank Churchill, is agape in response to her cruelty—and yet Knightley's response is kinder and gentler than I have ever seen it played in film or on stage. This is still the Great Humiliation for our heroine, but it does not require an angry, scolding Knightley to drive home the point. Emma herself sings 'Badly Done', a piece written for her to reflect and self-correct alone. As with other scenes in the streaming production, given to us as 20 'chapters', this one seems designed to help set up a less difficult and more readily imagined romantic *rapprochement* for the leads: Emma is clearly good in her intentions and able to self-regulate without needing a strong male pedagogue; Knightley is more attractive to Emma (despite his age) and less prey to toxic masculinity than in some adaptations that overplay the shaming scene in which he berates her for being unfeeling to a socially marginal friend deserving her empathy. These are wise decisions for a contemporary audience, and if they distort some key dynamics from this complex, popular, and critically regarded novel, then they also succeed in raising Emma up as a less problematic feminist icon for an age in which strong female leads are desirable.

Cinderella for a New Age

In Harold Taw and Chris Jeffries' inspired adaptation of *Persuasion* (2017), a rare choice for the stage in any form, we find some of the best music and most effective adaptation for the stage of any Austen musical. Moving seamlessly across the more varied landscapes of the novel—a decided production challenge compared with staging *Emma*—the writers take us from Kellynch Hall to Uppercross Manor to Lyme to Bath in the span of two acts. Most of the novel's characters are maintained, and so are both the original and revised endings of the book (cleverly recast here for greater dramatic effect on stage). Perhaps best of all, the social context of Austen's imagined world is brought to rich comic life through use of a Hamill-like feature of Gossips, particularly in the Bath scenes of Act 2, allowing not only for laughs but also for a stronger sense of the very real pressures felt by the characters in their milieu. This social world also balances the polished world of balls and spa treatments with the rugged world of the navy's 'Glory and Gold' (a key song featured in the score), and provides ample opportunity for its heroine to navigate each setting.

The framing conceit for this sophisticated adaptation is the power of fairy tales to shape the narrative of adult lives. Anne's voice opens the show and introduces the musical score, in distinct contrast to her significantly delayed introduction in Austen's novel. Her brief moment of soliloquy for recollection of the lost love of her life ('Prologue') is punctuated by flashback, and we hear interchanges from eight years ago capturing the conflict between Anne and Wentworth, between Lady Russell and Anne, and finally Wentworth's angry last words before heading off to sea: 'when I return with title and fortune, the last person I'll call upon will be Anne Elliot!' This bit of interpolated narrative imagines the pre-history of the novel's events and sets up the adaptation with impressive economy and considerable emotional charge, priming the audience to meet the characters where they now are with the added benefit of where they have been. It also tilts the blame for this separation farther away from Anne's persuadable nature and closer to the side of Wentworth's ego and impatience. The script implicitly suggests that their romance might simply have paused and resumed if only he had been willing to wait.

But despite this fairy-tale framework, Anne understands full well that life is less reliable than the fantasies generated by fiction. Anne sees her last eight years through the eyes of a 'spell in which I am bound', one that 'someone forgot to lift'. Her fate has been to see a near-perfect romance interrupted by her family's persuasions, and to suffer continually ever since. More than missing out on her happy ending, she has been confined to a nightmarish substitute. Is this a tale, then, of Cinderella inverted? Her abandonment is only part of the story, since Wentworth's peevish behaviour shows that 'he wasn't quite a prince', and this twist of the narrative turns out to be perhaps the most crucial one of all (as it is arguably in the novel as well). The difficulties of reconnecting old lovers are manifestly increased over those of connecting two people for the first time. If it is hard for two unmarried people to take advantage of the limited opportunities to connect, to get to know each other, to fall in love while balancing both sensibility and sense, how much worse is it for two aging, former lovers, whose broken engagement would require generous reconciliation, to re-connect? The deep pathos of Austen's most moving narrative is heightened by setting up a seemingly impossible scenario: for Anne and Wentworth's fate to be a happy one now would be like lightning striking twice in the same spot.

Throughout the score Taw and Jeffries capture the uncertainty, the envy, the game-playing, but also the tenderness and slow process of reconnecting lost loves who do not necessarily realise that the fire still burns within them. Anne is distracted not only by Wentworth's return and his seeming courtship of young Louisa Musgrove but also by Benwick's interest in her (and their shared interest in poetry), and eventually by the mysterious, long-lost relative, Mr Elliot. And although the musical's incarnation of a more powerful, expressive heroine is never voiceless—that simply cannot exist in this genre—she is not wholly self-assured, and we see and hear the inner turmoil she experiences. The best example of her uncertain future, and her place in a narrative with a possible happy ending, is rendered beautifully in her signature song, 'Only Anne'. Her theme captures directly from the novel the mixed, ironic sense in which this phrase rings true: to some, like her abysmal, pretentious, unfeeling family, she is 'only Anne' in the sense of 'just Anne, and nothing more'—insignificant; to others who see and feel as fully human beings, such as her friends (Benwick, the Harvilles, and eventually Wentworth), there is no one like her, no one better, 'only Anne'.[22]

The famous scene at Lyme on the Cobb is precisely where we see Austen's genius for misdirection before the ultimate resolution, contributing to a sense that what we want to see is not at all inevitable, and much of this original complexity is maintained in the musical. We begin with two overlapping triangulations of romantic potential: Benwick-Anne-Wentworth and Louisa-Wentworth-Anne. But this configuration itself is complicated further with the surprise arrival of the stranger who turns out to be Mr Elliot, another potential suitor interested in Anne's newly visible 'bloom' as she comes alive by the seaside, and a new competitor for the renewed attentions of Wentworth. The captain is himself triangulating attention in the musical between Louisa's dangerous flirtations: dangerous to *him* as we eventually see, since he has committed too much attention to her as a love interest, and more immediately, dangerous to *her* because she is risking life and limb to playfully jump from the sea wall into his arms below. Distracted as he is by Anne's increasingly evident beauty, reawakening his own desire, he attends only partly to Louisa, who plummets too quickly for him to catch, initiating the key shift in the story and the directions of each character in the wake of her tragedy. As in the novel, Anne's cool head prevails and she directs the response to this emergency, while Wentworth comes to see again how worthy of respect—and perhaps also of his love—she truly is. The stage directions are explicit that each character wonders about the other, unable to read with certainty their respective feelings. And as they separate, Anne heading off for Bath and Wentworth staying behind, Act One closes with their duet in shared but separate space onstage—'each lost in private reverie' reprising the theme of 'Only Anne' (Taw 61)

Through the brisk pacing of the second act everyone converges in Bath, and we come to see a transformation from the novel's focus on Anne's inner life and the consequent opacity of Wentworth's true feelings and intentions, to an openly expressive counterpoint of feeling—marked decisively by the musical score—that traces Anne's greater autonomy of self in tandem with Wentworth's increasing reinvestment in her inherent value, her inner beauty sustained over the course of their long separation.[23] But the previous barrier of his apparent interest in Louisa has shifted now to Anne's possible interest in Mr Elliot's unmistakable romantic overtures. Compounding his uncertainty, Lady Russell confronts Wentworth at the concert—here is the adaptation of the novel's original ending—and declares Anne's match to Mr Elliot to be established. His soaring ballad-monologue follows ('The Concert') with self-awareness and the generous resolve to give her up: 'what fool would dare / hold out his hand for love /he's proved himself so utterly unworthy of ...be happy, Anne / forget me' (Taw 87).

Committed to leaving a letter behind for her with Harville as he leaves Bath, Wentworth is surprised by Anne's visit to the Musgroves' lodging where he is taking his leave, and the famous revised ending of the novel is here revised again: he crumbles his letter up after listening to Anne and Harville discuss men's and women's constancy, and accepts her invitation to the entire company to attend the next evening's ball. Denied the opportunity for a private audience with Anne upon his arrival at the ballroom, he declares his intentions publicly to everyone assembled (including Mr Elliot, whose kneeling proposal posture has just been rebuffed by Anne), with the song that replaces the novel's private letter, 'Half Agony, Half Hope'. To everyone's surprise, and against the vocal protestations of Lady Russell and Mr Elliot, Anne finally chooses Wentworth and uncertainty over the conventional vision of a happy ending that would also mean 'no surprises, every day the same/ no adventures waiting' ('That's Home'). Her new vision, shared fully with her ideal partner, is a home that embodies 'giv[ing] the world new tales to talk about' (Taw 98). Claiming her own happiness on her own terms, unconcerned with gossip or persuasion, Anne chooses to write over the passive master narrative of fairy-tale endings, and in so doing offers a model for heroines to come.

'Fighting for the Future': Improvised Austen

Improvisational comedy, a form that by definition is a mix of spontaneity and structure, may seem like a bizarre outlier, tenuously connected to the world of Austen adaptation. Few forms could seem less fitting for channelling the spirit of a writer who was so attentive to her craft, so little herself inclined to improvise. So why, then, would so many different groups find the challenge of translating Austen's fiction to the improv stage appealing? Susan Civale's recent analysis of the popular U.K. ensemble called *Austentatious* suggests convincingly that the inevitable mix of old and new not only generates laughs but also 'lampoons the textually and temporally promiscuous nature of modern Austen adaptations'—not just Austen's originals, but the culture of Austen adaptation itself.[24] An important correction to what might be flip assumptions about the mindlessness of Pop Culture Austen, Civale's work also highlights the crucial aspect of these live performances as collaborative engagements between the performers and the audience. Along with each performance's distance from any particular source text—at most, the cast will take its cue via a suggested title for a new ('lost') novel of Austen, before launching into more random Regency-style story-telling—this cooperative aspect is surely one of the most distinctive elements of improvised live Austen.

My experience with such performances is similar. Having watched live recordings of *Austentatious* performances from different years as well as recorded and live-streamed performances by Impro Theatre's *Jane Austen Unscripted* from Los Angeles (including an unbelievably ambitious improvised Austen musical), and having attended live performance by the Chicago-based all-female group Improvised Jane Austen, it seems clear to me that it is as much the distance from Austen as it is the imagined closeness to her original work and world that pleases each audience. Surely some attendees have little or no idea of what to expect when they attend something labelled 'Austen improv'. But most are likely to begin with some sense of what they think a typical 'Jane Austen story' consists of: the common themes of money, marriage, and morals, perhaps rural comfort and cosmopolitan scandal—all of which come into play while being extended or exaggerated in the improvisational space of actors creating a tale for a live audience in real time.

The ladies of Improvised Jane Austen in Chicago cleverly refer to their genre of performance as 'Obstinate Headstrong Girlprov', which makes them a fitting choice with which to cap this exploration of twenty-first century live adaptation of Austen and its increasing focus on woman-centred performance.[25] When I attended a show they were still performing in a tiny black box space in Rogers Park, with seating limited to about 40 people, a set consisting of two chairs and a settee, and simple costumes that conveyed a sense of Regency England without being overly fussy about details. In some cases, performers blended traditional elements of both male and female attire for flexibility—a blouse and jacket over riding pants and boots, for example. The troupe gamely spun a tale of romance and intrigue amidst a cast of invented characters who successfully ruined cuisine, hunting, and relationships in equal, hilarious measure.

At the ladies' request the audience began by choosing two key words that started with 'q'—they were *quickly* and *quail*—and the performers found little difficulty in turning such inauspicious materials into long-form improvisational gold. True comic professionals, each troupe member offered something clever and very funny in turn, with excellent timing and tone. Most scenes featured three characters at a time, with a focus on period-believable if not period-specific scenarios that largely conformed to the language, style, and type of events one could imagine finding in a 'lost' Austen novel. The results of comedic improvisation, however, often took us much closer to the exuberant juvenilia than to the more subtle fiction of her maturity. A gender-transgressive young lady recounted her education: original failure as a cook led to manlier attempts at hunting (another failure after accidentally shooting both horses and humans), and ultimately culminated in her schooling in 'the deceptive arts' in order to attract a husband. Three gentlemen made a friendly wager on which was the most likely to marry first, leading to the exposure of one bachelor's tragi-comic history with a vicar's daughter who jilted him, leaving him with nothing but a bust to weep over (i.e., a work of memorial sculpture, but a joke that played heavily on the innuendo).

There is mostly limited discussion in Austen's fiction of the details of meals and shooting parties, successful or not, but the comic dilation on these daily banalities was precisely what made much of the live comedy so effective. Slapstick, pratfalls, and broad humour were used sparingly. Instead, household duties, social gatherings, and romantic prospects were folded together in separate but ultimately interconnected vignettes that tested the wits—and respective memory—of each performer. Troupe members were adept and intuitive about knowing when to shift scenes and players to keep the performance lively, and although no official audience participation was solicited after the show began, the appreciative responses of a delighted crowd obviously fed the merriment on stage. So while the distance between carefully crafted narrative and improvised dialogue might seem vast, the elusive but widely sought 'spirit' of Austen's work—and the investment in this ineffable substance by so many twenty-first-century Janeites—might also find a home here, in a space of unpredictable, female-centred performance that actively includes its audience in the shared enterprise of bringing Austen's world to life.

Coda: Some Concluding Thoughts

So the crucial question remaining is this: what does the recent prolific expansion of staged Austen demonstrate? More than simply confirming her enduring popularity or contemporary relevance, what live performance of Austen shows us is the active desire to have closer, more immediate, emotionally charged engagement with her life and work. Whether these productions are artistically brilliant or commercially successful—some are one or the other, occasionally they may be both—is less the point than understanding that audiences crave an experience beyond reading the novels, watching films, TV, and web series, or attending Regency cosplay events. Live Austen continues to proliferate because so many of us want something more—not to replace or to improve upon what exists, but to add what theatre and live performance alone can offer: Austen narratives alive and embodied in real time, with affective intensity and elements of unpredictability, yet still experienced as ephemeral (this time limit, and the unique quality of each performance, is crucial). Fittingly, for many of the same reasons that Austen loved the experience of theatre in her own day, Janeites want Austen onstage at the theatre today as well.[26]

The desire to be in intimate proximity to the action is crucial, but so too is sharing this space *at a distance*. The experience of theatre—immersive, unpredictable, transitory, and at its best, both intense and revelatory—is one for which the audience is usually only indirectly a part. An important exception occurs in the interaction common to certain moments of improv comedy, and in some plays such as Hamill's which, depending on their staging (as with the 2016 production of *Sense and Sensibility*), might break the fourth wall and directly engage with individual theatregoers seated at the edge of the performance space, bringing the audience in more fully. But the convention is for us to watch, to listen, to empathise, and to do so anywhere from several feet to several hundred feet away from the action. Importantly, this engagement also comes in the company of (and thus often in concert with, or occasionally in opposition to) others with whom we are sitting or standing in close proximity. These responses—whether they are like or unlike our own, whether we are more or less conscious of them—contribute to the shared intimacy of the theatrical experience. Our private experience of the show is manifested publicly as we laugh, cry, gasp, moan, and when it feels appropriate, applaud the performers in front of us. In other words, this experience is always embodied, affectively engaged, and to some meaningful extent interactive, regardless of what is taking place on stage.

Perhaps the main point to take away is that Janeites intuitively understand what Amanda Price, the time-travelling heroine from ITV's 2008 mini-series *Lost in Austen,* slowly comes to realise to her own surprise: first and foremost, love of Austen means love of her work as it is written, as we each know it most intimately. Even when given access to the greatest fan fantasy of all-time—to enter into the narrative itself of, say, *Pride and Prejudice*, as a character—the risk is great that altering the story-world will diminish what we have come to know and love, even (or especially) if the Janeite herself is the one to initiate this alteration. It is not necessarily that adaptation is doomed to ruin the 'Sacred Text', but rather that some kinds of changes may distort beyond all recognition what we are already intimately a part of, or what is better understood as a part of us.

The key, then, lies in the way that we know the text, and how effectively a good adaptation might shift our own previous understanding. Change can also expand and enrich, not just diminish or deplete. It is possible for the creative liberties taken by an adaptation to bring us, unexpectedly, even closer to the source text, allowing us to see things we had not yet realised are present.[27] Writers and performers who are truly intimate with Austen, who hear her narrative voice as clearly as their own after years of reading and rereading, can add layers of meaning and affective richness without erasing what lies beneath. With intelligent, intuitive, deeply feeling adaptations, we might learn from Amanda Price's example: instead of running from change, we might adapt to it and open ourselves up to the unlimited intimacies that reimagined Austen has to offer us, living simultaneously in her time and in our own.

Notes

1 See Nagle, 'Austen's Present Future Stagings'. In what follows I will be discussing a mix of shows, including some that I have seen performed live or in recorded form, or for which I have had access to scripts, or both when possible, and in all cases I have consulted existing reviews of performances as well. This admittedly heterodox approach has been necessary given the limitations of access to live performances. Special thanks to Briana Asmus, Chuck Bentley, and Donna Kaminski for vital discussion of these works over many years.
2 This show had its world premiere in Russia at the Moscow Art Theatre Chekov in September 2016.
3 See Southam (13).
4 Looser 92.
5 The script is credited to Aldous Huxley and Jane Murfin, but it is based on the original Jerome play and went through a dizzying array of other writers and rejected scripts throughout the process. See Looser (124–37).
6 For a recent perspective and some statistics on the trends for male-authored and female-authored productions, see Weinert-Kendt. Hamill has noted in many interviews that her original motivation for turning to Austen novels for adaptation was the demonstrable lack of strong, central roles for women in theatre.
7 My research suggests that about 35% of all recent Austen-themed adaptations are devoted to *Pride and Prejudice*, with three times as many plays as musicals, and a significant portion of the total exploring sequels,

continuations, or other offshoots of the original. The next closest in number are *Emma* and *Sense and Sensibility*, each of which account for about 12%, respectively, followed closely by *Persuasion* with 11%. The other finished novels, *Mansfield Park* and *Northanger Abbey* each average only about half of that, 5–6% apiece.

8   As she has noted in interviews, the sense of newness comes from treating each play as a distinct work with its own point of view, rather than approaching the adaptation process as yet another 'copy and paste' affair like many existing Austen plays. See Hamill and Dehnert (Interview).

9   See Hamill.

10 Hamill's *Sense and Sensibility* has a parallel scene in which the Dashwood sisters are surrounded and buffeted by the menacing sounds of The Gossips, a Greek chorus-like manifestation of Regency social life, judging, abusing, and constraining the life choices of the heroines.

11 McArthur's Introduction notes: '[t]he joke that we are all in on (that there are only just enough pairs of hands to pull this off) forms a big part of the overall presentation ... and much of an audience's enjoyment can be derived from seeing which performer will next pop up as which character, if they will make their costume changes in time for their next entrance, etc.' (5).

12 Wright (438).

13 Wright notes the exception of a South African musical adaptation from 1964, co-authored by Nico Carstens and Mark Eldon (438–439, 445). His study ends at 1975, but thus far I have found nothing to add to this timeline prior to the 1990s. Surely there are more to be discovered, but my focus lies with twenty-first-century innovations.

14 According to his Wikipedia entry, the show premiered in January 1995 at the Public Theatre Company in Peoria, Illinois. The concept album with which I am working was recorded in the same year.

15 With lyrics by Webber's frequent collaborator Tim Rice and music by ABBA's Benny Andersson and Björn Ulvaeus, the musical began as a concept album in 1984, followed by a West End stage premiere in 1986 and a radically altered Broadway version in 1988.

16 I am especially grateful to Bernard Taylor for generously sharing the most recent libretto, as well as scoring and recordings not otherwise available to me.

17 See Nagle, 'Problem'. The official website for this show, considered to be still in development before a possible Broadway debut, includes four tracks recorded from previous stagings.

18 The Chicago Chamber Opera has been performing a chamber opera-style production with a touring group since 2013, mostly throughout the United Kingdom. They describe the productions as 'a musical drama' featuring a chamber orchestra and Irish step dancers. Usually a chamber opera suggests a smaller cast and orchestra, and thus a more scaled-down production from what one expects in a traditional opera performance. Note that the distinction between chamber opera and stage musical is not always clear, as the description of 'a musical drama' here suggests.

19 See Nagle, 'Problem'. Gordon's personal website includes a video montage from the 2014 Chicago Shakespeare Theatre production.

20 Gordon clarifies in the liner notes to the original recording the reasons for this choice as twofold: first, the expense of period costuming was prohibitive for the small budget devoted to this soundstage musical (filmed in a theatre, without an audience, explicitly for online streaming); second, he saw a profound connection between Emma and Holly Golightly, the heroine of Truman Capote's *Breakfast at Tiffany's*. I should add that a subsequent live production at the Chicago Shakespeare Theatre (2020) shifted the musical to its more traditional Regency setting, and was equally successful.

21 This famous quote derives from Austen-Leigh (140).

22 Mrs Smith, of course, would be another key example from the novel, but this adaptation only alludes to her without including her in the cast.

23 In an interview, Harold Taw argues for precisely these elements of musical adaptation making an ideal fit for this novel: 'Music is the heart's compass, pointing us toward the true north of submerged grief or tremulous joy. Anne and Captain Wentworth are immersed in mutual nostalgia, unable to let go of regret to embrace the present. Is there a better vehicle for reliving nostalgia and regret in the here and now than song? It is an axiom in musical theatre that when a character's emotions become too overwhelming to speak aloud, she must sing. Throughout the novel, Anne and Captain Wentworth scrupulously hide their passion from themselves and each other. But in counterpoint and harmony, they can lose and find each other again'. ['Why Adapt']

24 Civale (417). Thanks to Beth Bradburn for additional consultation on improv training and performance.

25 The group's aim is explained on their Facebook page: 'As an ensemble made up of women, we perform in the familiar world of our chosen literary genre, but we are also able to play a multitude of characters, men and women found in Jane Austen's world, that audiences may find to be both surprising and refreshing. Our best shows should leave the audience laughing and thinking about the status that women (and men) hold in

society—both then and now. IJA can comment slyly on modern issues in what seems to be a form that celebrates the past, but actually is fighting for the future' (Improvised Jane Austen [Facebook page]).

26 This paragraph borrows some phrasing from Nagle, 'Austen's Present Future Stagings'. As O'Quinn notes, theatre was in Austen's day 'the primary locus where representation and sociability came together on a nightly basis', but analysis of its effects is perpetually challenged by the very 'transience of theatrical and conversational performance' (378).

27 Part of this phenomenon might be the result of what Scheinman describes as the paradox of 'engaging with others' conceptions of Austen [which] brings you closer to the real thing' (128).

Works Cited

Austen-Leigh, J. E. *A Memoir of Jane Austen*. 2nd ed. Folio Society, 1989.

Civale, Susan. '*Austentatious*: Comedy Improv and Austen Adaptation in the Twenty-first Century.' *Women's Writing*, vol. 25, no. 4, 2018, pp. 416–428.

'Emma.' By Phil Timberlake, directed by Elise Kauzlaric, performance by Emma Sipora Tyler, Lifeline Theatre, Chicago, IL, 24 May 2019.

Filippi, Rosina. *Duologues and Scenes from the Novels of Jane Austen: Arranged and Adapted for Drawing-Room Performance*. J. M. Dent, 1895.

Gordon, Paul. *Emma: A New Jane Austen Musical (Original Soundstage Recording)*. Broadway Records, 2019.

Hamill, Kate. 'Five Burning Questions With *Pride and Prejudice* Star and Creator Kate Hamill.' Interview conducted by Josh Ferri. *The Daily Scoop*, 20 Dec. 2017, www.broadwaybox.com/daily-scoop/5-burning-questions-with-pride-and-prejudice-i-star-kate-hamill/.

Hamill, Kate, and Amanda Dehnert. 'Kate Hamill and Amanda Dehnert on Adapting Jane Austen for the Stage.' Interview conducted by Sarah Rebell. *The Interval*, 12 Dec. 2017, www.theintervalny.com/interviews/2017/12/kate-hamill-and-amanda-dehnert-on-adapting-jane-austen-for-the-stage/.

Hamill, K. *Pride and Prejudice*. Dramatists Play Service, 2017.

Hamill, K. *Sense and Sensibility*. Dramatists Play Service, 2016.

Improvised Jane Austen. *Facebook* page. www.facebook.com/events/io-chicago/improvised-jane-austen/883794215352961/.

Improvised Jane Austen. Performance. McKay Theater, Chicago, 16 June 2017.

Looser, Devoney. *The Making of Jane Austen*. Johns Hopkins UP, 2017.

McArthur, Isobel. *Pride and Prejudice* (*sort of)*. Nick Hern Books, 2019.

Nagle, Christopher. 'Austen's Present Future Stagings.' *Texas Studies in Literature and Language / special issue: What's Next for Jane Austen?* edited by Janine Barchas and Devoney Looser, vol. 61, no. 4, 2019, pp. 472–474.

Nagle, Christopher. 'The Problem of the Jane Austen Musical.' *Women's Writing*, vol. 25, no. 4, 2018, pp. 499–511.

Nicholson, Kent, and Tim Kashani, directors. *Emma: A New Jane Austen Musical*, edited by Paul Gordon. *Streaming Musicals*, 2018, www.streamingmusicals.com/

O'Quinn, Daniel. 'Jane Austen and Performance: Theater, Memory, and Enculturation.' *A Companion to Jane Austen*, edited by Claudia L. Johnson and Clara Tuite, Blackwell, 2009, pp. 377–388.

'Pride and Prejudice.' By Kate Hamill, directed by Amanda Dehnert, performance by Hamill and Jason O'Connell, Primary Stages, Cherry Lane Theatre, New York, NY, 6 Jan. 2018.

Scheinman, Ted. *Camp Austen: My Life As An Accidental Jane Austen Superfan*. Farrar, Straus and Giroux, 2018.

'Sense and Sensibility: A New Musical.' By Paul Gordon, directed by Barbara Gaines, performance by Sharon Reitkerk and Megan McGinnis, 23 Apr. 2015, Chicago Shakespeare Theatre, Chicago, IL.

'Sense and Sensibility.' By Kate Hamill, directed by Eric Tucker, performance by Hamill and Andrus Nichols, Bedlam Company, 6 Mar. 2016, The Gym at Judson, New York, NY.

Southam, Brian, editor. *Jane Austen's 'Sir Charles Grandison.'* Clarendon Press, 1980.

Taw, Harold. 'Why Adapt Persuasion for Musical Theatre?' *Jane Austen News*, 6 June 2017.

Taw, Harold, and Chris Jeffries. *Persuasion: A New Musical*. Taproot Theatre Company, 2017.

Taw, Harold, and Chris Jeffries. *Persuasion: A Musical in Two Acts*. Theatrical script, 2015–17.

Taylor, Bernard J. *Pride and Prejudice: a musical based on the novel by Jane Austen*. First Stage Records/Dress Circle, 1995.

Weinert-Kendt, Rob. 'This Year's Gender and Period Count.' *American Theatre*, 25 Sep. 2018.

Wright, Andrew. 'Jane Austen Adapted.' *Nineteenth-Century Fiction*, vol. 30, no. 3, 1975, pp. 421–453.

33

'YOU DO NOT KNOW HER OR HER HEART': MINOR CHARACTER ELABORATION IN CONTEMPORARY AUSTEN SPIN-OFF FICTION[1]

Kylie Mirmohamadi

LA TROBE UNIVERSITY

The project of re-imagining Jane Austen's characters outside the narrative context of the original novels dates back at least to Austen's own 1813 letter to her sister, Cassandra, in which she recounts finding a portrait of Mrs Bingley in a London art exhibition. Her hope to locate similarly a Mrs Darcy is unrealised, she writes, speculating that 'Mr D. prizes any Picture of her too much to like it should be exposed to the public eye' (*Letters* [24 May 1813] 220, 222; see Yaffe 2018). Austen's nephew and first biographer wrote that his aunt 'would, if asked, tell us many little particulars about the subsequent career of some of her people', and so they learned that while Kitty managed matrimony with a clergyman near Pemberley, Mary 'obtained nothing higher than one of her uncle Philip's clerks, and was content to be considered a star in the society of Meriton' (Austen-Leigh 148).

The speaking of an extra-diegetic existence for Austen's characters is also a long-standing and ongoing publishing phenomenon, ranging from the publication of Sybil G. Brinton's sequel to the novels on the cusp of the First World War (1913) to the contemporary digital outpourings of online Jane Austen Fan Fiction [JAFF] (Mirmohamadi). In 2019, Devoney Looser extended the accepted timeline of JAFF by some ninety years when she published an article on a fictional letter written to the editors of *The Lady's Magazine* on 30 April 1823, which she identifies as 'the first known piece of Austen-inspired fan fiction, and the first featuring Austen as a character' (Looser 'Fan Fiction').

The past decade or so has seen a publishing upturn in the type of Austen spin-off fiction that Jeremy Rosen calls 'minor character elaborations'. Such novels, as genre texts, 'subsist … at the nexus of form, cultural history, and material conditions of production and consumption' (Rosen viii). Responding to publishing trends, market demands, cultural shifts, and the textual desire for constant reiteration that characterises Austen fandom (see, e.g., Wells; Yaffe *Among the Janeites*; Mirmohamadi; Malcolm; Looser *Making of Jane Austen*), as well as ongoing and emerging cultural renegotiations around representation and visibility, these narratives work to re-situate minor characters as key protagonists or narrator/protagonists by centralising a figure that had hitherto been

DOI: 10.4324/9780429398155-33-38

439

on the periphery of the narrative action, dramatic thrust, and emotional economy of a canonical novel.

Elizabeth Bennet remains the focus of many of the prequels, coquels, and sequels that proliferate on publishers' lists as well as in the less commercial realm of fan fiction (Parey).[2] However, contemporary historical fiction that re-imagines, recasts, or recalibrates Austen's most re-worked novel, *Pride and Prejudice*, through the perspective of minor characters claims a growing share of the print and digital publishing market. The intent is often identified as recuperative (see Rosen 51), part of the project to highlight the subjectivity and experience of a marginalised group such as the servant class (e.g., Baker), but it is also to do with the politics of characterisation. In these novels, neglected or underdeveloped characters who have received a relatively limited share of diegetic visibility and of the attention and affection of narrators, readers, and adapters, finally 'have their day' (Rosen). In this way, while not every reader of Austen spin-off fiction is necessarily familiar with the source texts, all these novels implicitly invite their readers to contemplate the respective 'attention and neglect' allocated to the characters in *Pride and Prejudice* (see Woloch 2).

This chapter considers a small group of contemporary historical novels that re-work *Pride and Prejudice*. While a limited number of alternative narratives have been constructed around the other 'minor' sisters, Kitty and Lydia (e.g., Kablean; Farrant), the chapter will focus on novels which re-imagine the character of Mary Bennet (e.g., McCullogh; Paynter; Fleming; Chen; Kessel; Hadlow).[3] It highlights how the novels' authors develop the character of Mary Bennet—conventionally positioned as the background for her sisters' happy endings, or as fodder for ridicule from characters, narrator, readers, and adapters alike—in new directions by providing her with an enhanced literary and intellectual sensibility and a trajectory towards feminist enlightenment.

The Mary Bennet of *Pride and Prejudice* is shifted, in these later texts, into the centre of the narrative, elbowing her sisters out of the spotlight and making room for an expanded explication of this minor character. When the reader encounters Mary in the beginning of Janice Hadlow's *The Other Bennet Sister*, she is plain and overlooked: 'but her sisters shone so brightly that they seemed to cancel out her failure and, indeed, eclipse her presence altogether' (Hadlow loc 85). By the end of the novel, however, some years after Mr Bennet has died and Charlotte and William Collins have taken possession of Longbourn, the focus is on a newly-enhanced Mary, residing in London with the Gardiners, and the marriage of equals that is promised her with Tom Hayward. Just as this Mary makes her own proposal of sorts, rather than passively waiting for an offer, Mary Bennet is, in these novels, given the opportunity to speak for herself. The use of first-person narration in Katherine Chen's *Mary B*, for example, highlights this enhanced scope. Chen's Mary directly addresses contemporary readers, stating her own case, in the declaration that gives this article its title: 'So to anyone who has ever doubted that the sour little creature sitting on the sidelines of the ball isn't capable of the same purity of love as her two esteemed sisters, I say you do not know her or her heart' (Chen 19). The 'new' Mary's ability to speak wisely and judiciously in her own defence and on other topics recasts her as a different type of character from the source Mary, who famously 'wished to say something very sensible, but knew not how' (*PP* 9).

These novels all build on a shared motif of development, in which Mary is depicted as having moved beyond her limited understanding and experience in the source text to an enhanced sexual, gendered, intellectual, and religious world view. Mary's (original) spinsterhood also functions to generate commentary on the position of women in early-nineteenth-century England, and especially the debates and literature around women's education, female authorship, and economic independence.

The ideas of spinsterhood and marriage shape much of these novels' implied commentary about the position of women, even though Mary is given various alternative matrimonial fates and sexual experiences across the range. When *Mary B* concludes, she is living alone in a cottage near

Pemberley, penning novels and enjoying a chaste relationship with her unhappily-married mentor and patron, Darcy. The conclusion of the expanded mash-up (with *Frankenstein*), *Pride and Prometheus,* sees her also in a cottage, with a lone servant, in Lyme Regis, where she fossil-hunts with her friend, Mary Anning.[4] In *The Independence of Miss Mary Bennet*, Mary is rewarded with an offer of marriage (and some pre-marital sex) with Angus Sinclair. *Perception* ends with Mary's marriage to Sebastian Montagu and a dowry from his aunt, which 'may be used as you see fit' in recognition of Mary's 'intellect' and 'energy'. In a reference to the emphasis on inheritance in *Pride and Prejudice*, Lady Sandalford further stipulates that 'any residual is to remain in the female line at your discretion and that of the daughter or other lady you choose to inherit' (Fleming loc 4623). At the end of *Mary Bennet*, Mary is married to Peter Bushell, the son of the woman who wet-nursed her as an infant, and living in Australia, apparently, in this colonial context, freed from the trammels of class-consciousness. Here she names her first daughter 'Elizabeth', pointedly for the Governor's wife, Mrs Macquarie, and not her sister (Paynter loc 5300). For all their variations in denouement, Mary's life begins in these novels in singleness, giving their writers scope for an exploration of and commentary on the politics of spinsterhood that extends far beyond her resigned status, at the end of *Pride and Prejudice,* as 'the only daughter who remained at home' (*PP* 310).

By furnishing Mary with a 'happily ever after' outside the boundaries of conventional romance and marriage, *Mary B* subverts the marriage plot that dominates so much of Austen spin-off writing. Mary begins her own account of herself in *Mary B* with the promise of providing the other side of the story of tragic spinsterhood: 'Because I am plain, others have always assumed in me a disinterest to the opposite sex, to romance, and, accordingly, to marriage. But I will write here, as if with my own life's blood, that I have indeed loved. I have loved not once or twice but three times, which is three times more than anyone would believe of me' (Chen 19). Through the events of the novel arising from her attraction to Mr Collins and her fully consummated relationship with a caddish Colonel Fitzwilliam, Mary finds in her eventual chosen spinsterhood financial independence and intellectual companionship with Darcy, whose marriage to Elizabeth survives in conformity to convention only. Mary's non-matrimonial fate in *Pride and Prometheus* is equally subversive in the implied contentment she finds in the (almost) solitude of the life of an established 'aging spinster' who has 'only herself to please', and its suggestion of the primacy of female relationship, with 'queer' Mary Anning (Kessel 364, 354, 351).

Just as the idea of the uses and abuses of literature and reading is a prominent theme within Austen's original oeuvre and autobiographical gleanings (Trumpener 444; Newey), in these novels it is through correct and corrective reading practices that Mary's intellectual development from spinster nobody to independent, or married, somebody is most often and overtly achieved. The development of Mary's literary sensibility, which unfurls throughout *The Other Bennet Sister*, is signalled by the cover image, which depicts a woman reading a book. In these novels, the libraries at Pemberley and Longbourn are reimagined as sites of Mary's educative, or re-educative, reading, rather than the 'thread-bare morality' (*PP* 53) contained in the conventional feminine literary fare of sermons and conduct books.[5] The Mary of *Pride and Prometheus*, for example, is described by Kitty as 'the queen of the library' at home, and she herself comments on her book-buying habits in London (Kessel 13). In this novel, which develops the transformation trope at full throttle, Mary attains knowledge rather than the mere wish to say something sensible, vocation rather than accomplishment, literary sensibility rather than bookishness. She builds an integrated, applied, and systematic understanding of the world using the scaffolding of books and reading, fuelled by her curiosity about and research into natural philosophy as well as fiction.

In *Mary B* she is self-educated, again through the library at Longbourn, where she writes that her parents' laxity 'had given me ample opportunity to consume all the plays by our revered Bard, the great poems and epics of antiquity, manuscripts of human anatomy and natural science, and much more scandalous fare in the form of novels borrowed from the circulating library, which, luckily for me, Papa enjoyed with as much relish as I'. With this broader literary background, she consumes Fordyce's Sermons as a strategic move in her attempt to attract Mr Collins, even though she 'possessed a low opinion of the work' (Chen 41). In *The Independence of Miss Mary Bennet*, Mary is encouraged by her beloved nephew, Charlie, to 'give up reading Christian books, as he called them, in favour of great thoughts'. Instead, she reads every book in the library at Shelby Manor and reads in such a way as to change her outlook on life. They made her, she says, 'tired of delicacy about subjects that lie so close to our female fates!', as is evidenced by her assertion that Bingley should 'plug it with a cork' after Jane has eight living and four dead babies, as well as, it is later revealed, additional children by his mistress in Jamaica. Mary reflects on these corrective, and corrected, reading practices, when she tells Elizabeth that 'I thought you and Jane were obsessed with making rich marriages, while Kitty and Lydia were too undisciplined, too wild. I modelled my own conduct on the books I read—how dreadfully prosaic I must have been! Not to mention boring, for the books I read were boring' (McCollough loc 270, 367, 364, 2864, 404).

Mary's more rational approach to reading in Fleming's *Perception* takes the form of an adjusted sense of the appropriate role of books and reading in a woman's life. She initially opines that the domestic cares and responsibilities of marriage had wasted her sisters' intelligence: 'Imagine having the wonderful library at Pemberley at your disposal. One could become really immersed in that magnificent room's treasures. The old Lizzy would have revelled in such a room but the married Lizzy had so many other claims on her time and seemed not to mind at all' (Fleming loc 83). However, over her character evolution she comes to value other, socially grounded endeavours. While she retains a love of books and reading and her library work is key in her finding a husband, she declares that 'I think that the old Mary was rather a poor creature. True wealth is surely happiness and a life well-lived' (Fleming loc 4637).[6]

In *Pride and Prometheus,* when Mary Bennet cites Mary Wollstonecraft in critique of Charles Woodleigh's observation that 'it is more common, I believe ... for young ladies to study the foibles of their neighbors than natural philosophy' (Kessel 13),[7] Kessel is employing a familiar shorthand for Mary's burgeoning feminist consciousness. In their pursuit of a feminist trajectory for this character, a number of the novels name-check traditions of women's philosophical writing. Hadlow's Mary comes across Catharine Macaulay's *History of England* in the Longbourn library, at the beginning of her long, and sometimes circuitous, arc towards feminist and literary understanding, and seeks out other female-authored history texts. 'When she found none', the reader is told, 'she was absurdly disappointed' (Hadlow loc 401).

In particular, Wollstonecraft's books, and especially *A Vindication of the Rights of Woman,* act upon Mary as protagonist. The Mary of Paynter's novel complains to her friend, Cassandra Long, that her elder sisters, upon hearing that Netherfield Park is let, 'are exactly like the girls Miss Wollstonecraft writes of in her *Vindication* ... Marriage is the grand feature of their lives, although they would never admit it', and it is to the same text that this friend sends Mary when she is disturbed by viewing, and her responses to, pornographic images with which Wickham had supplied Lydia (Paynter loc 1444, 3578). In *Mary B*, Mary, abandoned by her married sisters and left wounded after her pursuit of Mr Collins has ended in his marriage to Charlotte Lucas, spends a year at Longbourn reading books such as Wollstonecraft's *The Wrongs of Woman* 'voraciously' and 'with monastic zeal' (Chen 136). By placing Wollstonecraft's books in their protagonists' armoury of ideas, these writers are acknowledging the intellectual and ideological context she shared with Austen, as well as her broad cultural and literary influence, to which Austen must have been exposed (Reiff 276n1; Poovey).

Mary's transformation in her afterlife is effected most powerfully through an enhanced intellectual development, but the changes are not in understanding alone. Her body, face, and manner are also sometimes redeemed to conform to notions of female beauty. Some authors seem unable to imagine a more positive fate for Mary that does not involve an improvement in her physical appearance. In *The Independence of Miss Mary Bennet*, McCullough describes a process of unlikely medical interventions, akin to contemporary cosmetic surgery, through which Elizabeth Darcy's apothecary, Kitty notes to Mary, 'has cured your suppurating spots and her dentist has dealt with your tooth' (McCullough loc 245). Perhaps reflecting the ubiquity of the makeover narrative in current lifestyle media (Raisborough 4), Fleming also splices the cultural trope of the makeover into *Perception*. In this novel, Elizabeth and Jane effect a transformation in Mary by making over her hairstyle and wardrobe and she comes into the understanding that, as she sassily observes to the woman who is to become her mother-in-law, '[t]hey do say clothes maketh the man, but it seems to me they are of even greater importance to ladies' (Fleming loc 3453). Hadlow's Mary carries out a form of self-makeover in London, under the tutelage of her Aunt Gardiner, but in this novel, her physical transformation indicates deeper, more philosophical shifts in understanding about what constitutes human happiness.

In their project to re-write the experiences of Mary Bennet, many of these novels revisit her most humiliating scene in *Pride and Prejudice,* the interrupted performance on the pianoforte at the Netherfield Ball. While some of these novels refuse to offer her complete redemption from this social and artistic failure,[8] the narratives all hold out to Mary the possibility of sympathy, and a number of them offer her redemption from her humiliation. In *Mary Bennet*, a slightly inebriated Mary repeats her ill-judged performance on the pianoforte, complete with her father's rebuke, but this account is given from Mary's perspective, and she herself realises the inappropriateness of the song she performs and is therefore grateful for the distraction of Mr Collins's 'sermonising on the duties of a clergyman' (Paynter loc 2511). Other novels go further in their reference to the fateful events at the Netherfield ball. In *Pride and Prometheus*, the memory of her performance even thirteen years later 'reawakened' pain for Mary, but it is also evidence of this new character's self-awareness, distinguishing her from the Mary of *Pride and Prejudice*. 'From that day on', we are told, 'she began to notice how nobody in the family listened to the things she said', and, in retrospect, 'Mary felt the justice of their indifference'. Vocal music becomes, in this new context, a redemptive force for Mary. Her early study of 'thorough base', a subject of narratorial mockery in Austen's novel, is the key to a moving scene in which she and Adam, Frankenstein's monster, who Mary has accepted as a result of her enlightened attitudes and enhanced education, sing and harmonise together (Kessel 11, 260–63).

Themes of growth and redemption can be tracked across the whole body of spin-off writing focused on Mary Bennet. Moreover, in both *Pride and Prometheus* and *The Independence of Miss Mary Bennet*, Mary's development towards independence and enlightenment is mirrored in an actual journey, akin to the archetypal hero's quest, or monomyth, in folklore (Campbell).[9] In *Pride and Prometheus,* Mary Bennet embarks on a journey to Scotland in search of Kitty's corpse, which has been stolen by Frankenstein in order to create a bride for his creature.[10] Her hero's reward at home, at the end of her quest and the novel, as we have seen, is to attain an independence, intellectual stimulus, and the support of female friendship. In McCullough's more chaotically-plotted novel, Mary, inspired by the radical writing of a journalist known only as 'Argus' in the *Westminster Chronicle*, sets out to travel through the north of England to research and write a book on poverty. However, she is captured on the way and finally falls into the hands of a crazed religious zealot, who has started a murderous sect called The Children of Jesus, and who imprisons her in the underground cave systems of Derbyshire. These misadventures culminate in a successful rescue mission led by Darcy, who, up until almost the end of the book, is a bitter bore who only cares about his ambition to become Prime Minister, who is tired of Lizzy and her family, who terrifies his son because he sees him as too effeminate, and who constricts his three daughters, whose femaleness he reads as 'the Bennet curse'. Darcy is joined in the rescue mission by his son Charlie, his murderous but loyal giant of a friend Ned Skinner (who turns out to be his unacknowledged half-brother), and his friend Angus Sinclair, editor of the *Westminster Chronicle* and, secretly, the radical writer 'Argus', who eventually marries Mary.

Mary Bennet's journeys in these novels, of all types, are depicted in the historical detail that is a genre expectation shared by all readers of historical fiction and viewers of period drama adaptations. She uses quill pens, reads and writes by candlelight, travels in carriages, and wears bonnets, ribbons, gloves, and pelisses. However, it is a truth almost universally acknowledged that historical fiction reveals as much about the time in which it is written as it does about the era in which it is set (Southgate 8). The novels that re-situate Mary Bennet into the centre of the world of Austen's novel, and beyond, work from contemporary cultural, literary, and market trends, and also operate within the ever-changing parameters of fan activity. They signal a desire for loved stories, literally, never to end; to go on, in endless variation, imagining alternative destinies for characters, different plots, other dialogues. Spin-off fiction offers a perpetual potential for recuperation in its repeated renovations of the familiar plots and characters of classic texts. In this capacity, minor character elaborations denote a generic susceptibility to the redemption plot. By refusing to limit Mary Bennet to her original role—as one of the three silly sisters—subsequent authors re-write her with optimism, holding out an ever-present possibility of growth and transformation beyond the borders of *Pride and Prejudice*.

Notes

1. I use the term 'spin-off' here to define a text that continues, re-works, or claims an intertextual relationship with a canonical literary work. Following Birgit Spengler's characterisation, the texts discussed here 'establish this primary intertextual relationship to a literary pre-text very plainly in the title, by other paratextual markers, and/or at the beginning of the text, in a way that seeks to draw the reader's attention to intertextuality as a basic principle of construction and a major dimension of the spin-off's efforts at meaning-making' (Spengler 33).
2. Parey claims that 'novel expansion'—'when the plot and characters from a finished novel are retrieved to be developed in new adventures set before, after or during the narrative time of the source text'—is 'a key phenomenon in contemporary fiction' (Parey 11).
3. Other texts featuring Mary Bennet, and falling within two of the major streams of Austen spin-off writing, erotica and religious or 'Inspirational' writing, include Mary's narrative in *Sex Comes to Pemberley* (Bennet 2014), and *A Match for Mary Bennet* (Ward 2009), which is described by its publisher as a sequel 'that will resonate with all readers who can relate to Mary Bennet's determination to live according to God's wishes'.
4. In Mary Anning's fossil shop, Mary has a chance meeting with a Captain Walton, who tells her of the fate of Victor Frankenstein. This is just one example of the deft intertextual weaving in this novel, including a tangential moment in Lyme Regis in which Mary learns that '[a] young woman who had stopped there the day before with a party of visitors from Uppercross had fallen from the Cobb' (Kessel 12).
5. Katherine Newey argues in regard to Mr Collins's reading of Fordyce's Sermons that 'Austen is in agreement with Mary Wollstonecraft's damning critique of Fordyce' (Newey 88).
6. In both Chen and McCullough's novels, Mary's literary destiny is enhanced when she also becomes an author.
7. Readers of *Pride and Prejudice* would recognise Elizabeth Bennet in this account, thus affording Mary a small victory over her more glamorous sibling.
8. In *Mary B,* this performance is drunken and even more excruciating, culminating in Mary vomiting and receiving rebukes from a servant and Darcy (Chen 116–20). Hadlow also refuses to offer her Mary complete consolation. When, during her aborted stay at Jane's house, after their father's death, Mary applies her developing sensibility and re-plays the Scottish air from the Netherfield Ball 'with a tremendous attack quite unlike her usual precise style', she is overheard by Caroline Bingley, who reminds her of Mr Bennet's intervention and words (Hadlow loc 2598).
9. Hadlow's Mary is more peripatetic in her search for a home, and her journey is more circuitous than others in this group, but she is also allowed to make Elizabeth's aborted trip to the Lakes District.
10. The fact that Mary, after she is robbed by highwayman, is joined on her journey by Adam refers to another folktale archetype, the Beauty and the Beast narrative (see Sherman 3).

'You do not know her or her heart'

Works Cited

Austen, Jane. *Jane Austen's Letters*, edited by Deirdre Le Faye. Oxford UP, 2011.

Austen, Jane. *Pride and Prejudice*. Penguin, 1996.

Austen-Leigh, James Edward. *A Memoir of Jane Austen*. London: Richard Bentley & Son, 1871.

Baker, Jo. *Longbourn*. Doubleday, 2013.

Bennet, Mary. *Sex Comes to Pemberley*. Kindle ed. Bedroom Books, 2014.

Brinton, Sybil B. *Old Friends and New Fancies: An Imaginary Sequel to the Novels of Jane Austen*. Holden and Hardingham Adelphi, 1913.

Campbell, Joseph. *The Hero with a Thousand Faces*. Meridian Books, 1956.

Chen, Katherine J. *Mary B*. Kindle ed. Penguin Random House, 2018.

Farrant, Natasha. *Lydia: The Wild Child of Pride and Prejudice*. The Chicken House, 2016.

Fleming, Terri. *Perception*. Kindle ed. Orion, 2017.

Hadlow, Janice. *The Other Bennet Sister*. Kindle ed. Pan Macmillan, 2020.

Kablean, Carrie. *What Kitty Did Next*. RedDoor, 2018.

Kessel, John. *Pride and Prometheus*. Simon & Schuster, 2018.

Looser, Devoney. 'Fan Fiction or Fan Fact?: An Unknown Pen Portrait of Jane Austen.' *Times Literary Supplement*, 13 Dec. 2019, p. 14.

Looser, Devoney. *The Making of Jane Austen*. Johns Hopkins UP, 2017.

Malcolm, Gabrielle, editor. *Fan Phenomena: Jane Austen*. Intellect Books, 2015.

McCullough, Colleen. *The Independence of Miss Mary Bennet*. Kindle ed. Harper Collins, 2008.

Mirmohamadi, Kylie. *The Digital Afterlives of Jane Austen: Janeites at the Keyboard*. Palgrave Pivot, 2014.

Newey, Katherine. '"What think you of books": Reading in *Pride and Prejudice*'. *Sydney Studies in English*, vol. 21, 1995, pp. 81–94.

Parey, Armelle, editor. *Prequels, Coquels and Sequels in Contemporary Anglophone Fiction*. Routledge, 2018.

Paynter, Jennifer. *Mary Bennet*. Kindle ed. Penguin, 2012.

Poovey, Mary. *The Proper Lady and the Woman Writer: Ideology as Style in the Works of Mary Wollstonecraft, Mary Shelley, and Jane Austen*. U of Chicago P, 1984.

Raisborough, Jayne. *Lifestyle Media and the Formation of the Self*. Palgrave Macmillan, 2011.

Reiff, Marija. 'The "Fanny Price Wars": Jane Austen's Enlightenment Feminist and Mary Wollstonecraft'. *Women's Studies*, vol. 45, no. 3, 2016, pp. 275–290.

Rosen, Jeremy. *Minor Characters Have Their Day: Genre and the Contemporary Marketplace*. Columbia UP, 2016.

Sherman, Howard J. *World Folklore for Storytellers: Tales of Wonder, Wisdom, Fools and Heroes*. Routledge, 2009.

Spengler, Birgit. *Literary Spinoffs: Rewriting the Classics – Re-Imagining the Community*. Campus Verlag, 2015.

Southgate, Beverley C. *History Meets Fiction*. Taylor & Francis, 2009.

Trumpener, Katie. 'Jane Austen in the World: New Women, Imperial Vistas.' *A Companion to Jane Austen*, edited by Claudia L. Johnson and Clara Tuite. Basil Blackwell, 2009, pp. 444–455.

Ward, Eucharista. *A Match for Mary Bennet*. Kindle ed. Sourcebooks Inc, 2009.

Wells, Juliette. *Everybody's Jane: Austen in the Popular Imagination*. Continuum, 2011.

Woloch, Alex. *The One vs. the Many: Minor Characters and the Space of the Protagonist in the Novel*. Princeton UP, 2003.

Yaffe, Deborah. *Among the Janeites: A Journey Through the World of Jane Austen Fandom*. Mariner, 2013.

Yaffe, Deborah. 'On this day in 1813,' 2018. http://www.deborahyaffe.com/blog/4586114521/On-this-day-in-1813.-.-./11301676

34

JANE GOES GAGA: AUSTEN AS CELEBRITY AND BRAND

Marina Cano

VOLDA UNIVERSITY COLLEGE

The title of this chapter might, at first sight, seem perplexing. After all, what does Lady Gaga, a modern Italian-American pop singer, have to do with Jane Austen, a British novelist from the Regency period? I am borrowing the first half of my title from Jack Halberstam's book *Gaga Feminism: Sex, Gender, and the End of Normal* (2012). There Halberstam argues that pop star Lady Gaga functions as an avatar for a new kind of feminism, 'a sign of a new world of disorder', in the twenty-first century (xii). Lady Gaga's outlandish performances, free rhythms and lyrics and eccentric outfits, Halberstam continues, push cultural boundaries, pointing to wider sociocultural changes in the West (137). Halberstam uses the terms 'gaga' and 'going gaga' in the sense of going crazy, becoming wild, anarchic and out of control. He notes that the word 'gaga' precedes Lady Gaga herself and has similar sensibilities as the word 'queer', in that both evoke the spirit of anarchy and allude to an anti-normative world order—or rather disorder (6).

My use of the term 'gaga' in this chapter departs slightly from Halberstam: I am first evoking Lady Gaga as diva and cult figure to argue that in the late 2010s and early 2020s Austen has entered the world of celebrity. Austen has become a celebrity idol to whom we expect round-the-clock access—as we do to Lady Gaga, Beyoncé and other notables of their generation. Yet some of Halberstam's meaning of gaga as the outrageous and preposterous also applies—for instance, one Austen event I analyse below invited fans to re-enact the pond scene from the BBC *Pride and Prejudice* (1995) in their backyard. Halberstam's sense of gaga as something culturally wild, anarchic and excessive is present in the recent Austen events and popular manifestations that I examine in this chapter. I am proposing a Gaga Austen: as celebrity, brand and object of endless scrutiny, contemporary Austen is going gaga.

The sources I use for my examination of Gaga Austen are exhibitions, events and online platforms from the 2010s, many of which were part of the 200th anniversary celebrations of Austen's death in 2017. They include the exhibitions *Which Jane Austen?* at the Bodleian Library, Oxford (June–October 2017), which presented Austen as war novelist and savvy businesswoman; and *Jane Austen by the Sea* at the Royal Pavilion, Brighton (June 2017–January 2018), which explored Austen's connection with coastal towns. Other sources are the Austen wax figure unveiled in 2014 (The Austen Centre, Bath), and Chawton House's fundraising campaign *Reimagining Jane Austen's 'Great House'*, which aims to save the manor house belonging to Austen's brother Edward. Recent e-spaces also receive attention: the project *Reading with Austen* (launched in 2018) recreates Edward Austen Knight's library at Godmersham, and *What Jane Saw* (launched in 2013) reconstructs the London art gallery Austen visited, or might have visited, in 1796 and 1813. The instability and

446

DOI: 10.4324/9780429398155-34-39

ephemeral quality of some of these spaces and events—either made of pixels or with a short lifespan—add to the anarchic and unpredictable quality of what I am here calling Gaga Austen.

By necessity my archive of Austen-related events is not exhaustive, but focuses on British and sometimes North American celebrations. An inspiring event in the United States that advanced some of the ideas explored here was the Folger Library exhibition *Will & Jane: Shakespeare, Austen, and the Cult of Celebrity* (Folger Shakespeare Library, Washington D.C., 6 August–6 November 2016). Curated by Janine Barchas and Kristina Straub, the Folger exhibition proposed that Jane Austen and William Shakespeare are, at present, literary celebrities of similar calibre. Their cultural status is the result of material production and reproduction, which has been ongoing since the late eighteenth century. The items on display proved this point: from portraits of the authors, biographies and editions of their works, to kitsch objects, films and modern continuations.[1] Here I build upon Barchas and Straub's exploration of Austen and celebrity culture; I follow up this idea after the 2017 anniversary celebrations and bring it to the level of gaga.

Celebrity fascinates and perhaps always has. Yet celebrity scholars recognise that we are currently going through a new era: the advent of mass communications means that fans can sometimes access their favoured star 24/7 (Cashmore; Rojek, *Fame*). In the age of the internet, the iPhone, the iPad, Instagram, Facebook, Twitter (and whatever platforms and devices come next), celebrities have become extremely accessible and domestic. They sometimes choose to communicate with their fans directly through social media. On 14 July 2017, Beyoncé posted a photo of her one-month-old twins on her personal Instagram, to the delight of 10,334,207 followers ('Sir Carter and Rumi'). As Chris Rojek notes, 'vicariously, you can always be in the company of your star' now, for the internet 'gives stargazers unprecedented opportunities to participate, in conjunction with stars, in building celebrity brands' (*Fame* 12). This is what I am calling the gaga moment in Jane Austen studies and Austen popular culture, and what I examine in the present chapter. But, first of all, let us go gaga and make Lady Jane's acquaintance.

Lady Jane

Rojek observes that the public image and its dissemination are essential in the making of a celebrity (*Celebrity* 125). And so this section focuses on recent images of Jane Austen and the way they depict her as a star, closer to Marilyn Monroe than to any literary figure of Austen's generation. My first port of call is Chawton House, the country estate owned by Austen's brother Edward in Alton (Hampshire), now a tourist destination and a research facility for eighteenth-century scholars. In 2017 Chawton House Library launched the fundraising campaign *Reimagining Jane Austen's 'Great House'*, with the aim of obtaining enough money to remain open and expand visitors' facilities. Promotional materials depict Austen and the manor house in Warholian style (Figure 34.1). Theirs is a pop art version of the writer, which not only recalls Andy Warhol's silkscreens immediately, but also the iconic figure of Marilyn Monroe. In the 1960s, Warhol selected a widely known image of Monroe—the publicity stills from her film *Niagara* (1953)—and used it as the base for a series of painted prints. Similarly, Chawton graphic designers have chosen a well-known portrait of Austen, the engraving made for Evert A. Duyckinck's *Portrait Gallery of Eminent Men and Women of Europe and America* (1873). This portrait was based on the engraving in James Edward Austen-Leigh's *Memoir of Jane Austen* (1869), and shows the author sitting by a table with a book in her hand and (surprisingly) a ring in her finger (Figure 34.2).

The images of Austen and Monroe are presented as a serial: three panels across and three more below. Their shared metallic colours further assimilate both pictures. Warhol's Marilyns bear non-naturalistic tones, shifting from quadrant to quadrant: red, pink, green and blue are alternately applied to Monroe's face; blue, black, red and green to her lips. The Chawton poster gives Austen analogous psychedelic treatment. The author is depicted wearing heavy eye shadow, in tones that

Figure 34.1 Poster of Fundraising Campaign *Reimagining Jane Austen's 'Great House'*. Courtesy of the designer Jackson Bone and Chawton House Library.

shift from fuchsia to bright blue; and the collar of her gown is alternately straw yellow, fuchsia and aquamarine. Like Monroe's lips sometimes, Austen's are bright red, which together with the Monroe connection, adds an erotic undertone to the public image of the writer—after all, Monroe was voted 'sexiest woman of the century' by *People Magazine* (People Staff).

Figure 34.2 Jane Austen engraving in Evert A. Duyckinck's *Portrait Gallery of Eminent Men and Women of Europe and America* (1873).

All these similarities assimilate Austen into celebrity culture, linking her to twentieth-century megastar Marilyn Monroe. Warhol is also well-known for his interest in brands. His mass-produced paintings of soup cans, ketchup bottles and soap boxes took the art world by storm in the early 1960s. One of his best-known series, the Campbell's Soup Cans paintings, sold for $100 each at the time (Kerrigan et al. 15). In Warhol's hands, celebrities received similar treatment, as products to be printed, serialised and consumed. To guarantee recognition—essential for the success of a brand—Warhol emphasised Monroe's features and facial expression, simplifying the details of the original photograph (Whiting 58). Likewise, the simple lines and bold colours of Austen's face minimise the traits of the Duyckinck engraving: her mouth, eyes and face are exaggerated to heighten recognition. Incidentally, her face, like that of a modern celebrity, has been photoshopped, for the eye bags of the original are gone and the double chin is in shadow.

There is something gaga about the Chawton pop Austen. She is portrayed in the style associated with a punk artist of the mid-twentieth century, a key figure in the New York gay circles, notoriously prone to eccentricity—such as sending a look-alike to Columbia University, where he had been invited to speak. Could this be anything but gaga? Isn't this the 'wild thinking, and imaginative reinvention' that Halberstam calls 'the art of going gaga'? (xv). Halberstam reads Lady Gaga herself as a Warholesque figure, one who is as much in control of her public image as Warhol was in the last century (xii). Such Warholesque quality is present in another recent image of Austen: the poster of the exhibition *Which Jane Austen?* (The Bodleian Library, Oxford, 23 June–29 October 2017). Curated by Kathryn Sutherland, this exhibition and tie-in talks and events presented a bold Jane Austen: one concerned with war, the empire and, above all, a professional author.

The exhibition poster, also in the pop art tradition, is a collage of five different Austen portraits (Figure 34.3). Five vertical stripes—of different width and in different colours—combine to form Austen's face: the first piece (on the left) is taken from the frontispiece of Austen-Leigh's *Memoir*, but given a new background in acid green tones; the second stripe is much narrower and shows a lithograph of Austen in heavy black ink against a fuchsia backdrop. Next comes the standard Victorian image of Austen from the *Memoir* in its original colours. This is followed by an eighteenth-century-style portrait, exposing Austen's left cheek and some of her hair in pastel colours. The final stripe, more Warholian than the rest, shows the end of Austen's cap in tones that recall the Marilyns: a bright orange cap with a deep blue outline and a fuchsia backdrop.

At first sight, the Bodleian poster, which combines new and old Austen images in various colours and artistic styles, looks broken, outlandish—gaga. It evokes some of the wildness of gaga culture: the poster pours acidic tones onto the Victorian, sacrosanct image of Austen (that of the *Memoir*); and it mixes pastel colours, evocative of Joshua Reynolds, with the metallic tones of Warhol's pop art. This is punk Jane Austen: the 'proper' image of Austen is fiddled with and made 'improper;' Austen's face is broken and fragmented. Yet there is also continuity between the lines that compose Austen's face. The contours have been adjusted so that they fit seamlessly. Like the Chawton poster, the Bodleian image guarantees instant recognition: Austen might look fragmented and even outrageous; but her cap, gown and muslin dress collar leave no one in doubt of the subject's identity. Like the Chawton Austen, the Bodleian poster presents Austen as celebrity and brand.

The dissemination of Austen's image, like that conducted through the Bodleian and Chawton posters, is part of the celebrity production process. Austen's extended moment in the limelight is confirmed by an earlier artwork: the wax figure of the author unveiled in 2014. Designed by forensic artist Melissa Dring and sculptor Mark Richards, the wax figure gave Austen Madame-Tussauds treatment for the first time. At Madame Tussauds Hollywood, fans can view the wax effigies of Lady Gaga, Madonna, Marilyn Monroe and Elvis Presley, among many others; similarly, at the Jane Austen Centre in Bath, enthusiasts can now see the wax figure of the writer. Madame Tussauds Hollywood has carefully replicated Lady Gaga's white lace hairdress and mask outfit; and Melissa Dring has painstakingly studied contemporary descriptions of Austen and Austen family portraits. What is more, Austen's hair has been done by former Madame Tussaud's artist Nell Clarke, who worked, for instance, on a wax figure of Elizabeth Taylor in the 1990s. Austen's outfit was in charge of award-winning designer Andrea Galer, recipient of a Bafta and an Emmy—a British Academy Film Award and an American Television Award, respectively. Such red-carpet treatment

Figure 34.3 Poster for Jane Austen Bodleian Libraries Exhibition. The Bodleian Libraries, The University of Oxford.

Figure 34.4 Moment of unveiling the Austen wax figure at The Jane Austen Centre in Bath, 2014. Photograph courtesy of ITV West Country.

was corroborated at the moment of unveiling the figure. As soon as the curtain was withdrawn, the wax Austen found herself under the siege of journalists, fans and photographers, in a moment that reproduced the razzmatazz of Hollywood ceremonies (Figure 34.4). Austen was on the red carpet, and indeed the walls of the room where the figure was placed had bright red wallpaper.

Soon fans started to debate the accuracy of the wax figure. Through blogs and social media, some complained that her face was too long or too angular, that her expression was too placid or not satirical enough, and that her gown was too revealing or even ahistorical. Well-known Austen blogger Margaret C. Sullivan observed that 'she needs a chemisette before she catches a cold, or scandalizes the neighbourhood', and Austenesque author Diana Birchall added 'it looks too modern, with a suspicious nod to Keira Knightley' (Sullivan, Birchall). Similar debates have surrounded recent wax figures of Lady Gaga and Beyoncé. When Madame Tussauds New York unveiled a white-looking Beyoncé (2017), protests online went viral. Like Birchall, one Beyoncé fan said on Twitter: 'This looks nothing like Beyoncé but more like Lindsey Lohan with a tan. Just bad & sad' (@Ms_Addertongue). Celebrity followers feel strongly about their favoured star—be it Beyoncé, Jane Austen or Lady Gaga, whose Peruvian rendition attracted even more violent complaints (Tesema). Many fans take their commitment seriously and wish to be near their idol—spend time with them, be with them, at all times and in all sorts of places. This is why my next section takes us on a date with celeb Jane Austen.

A Date with a Celeb

In *Fame Attack*, Chris Rojek explains such cultural fascination by noting that celebrity 'provides the overwhelming majority of ordinary men and women with access to intimations of elevated existence'. Celebrity furnishes us with 'role models or inspirational lifestyle leaders', and sets us on a 'highway to transcendence' (Rojek 1). Rojek's language of elevation and transcendence intimates that celebrity worshipping is the modern-day equivalent of the eighteenth-century sublime. This idea is corroborated by the Austen Memorial Book compiled by JASNA (the Jane Austen Society of North America) on the bicentenary of Austen's death. During 2017, the Society invited fans to send their personal reflections about the author which would then be compiled and posted online. Like letters or messages to a celebrity, most of these reflections are written in the second person, communicating their admiration directly to the author. In January 2018, JASNA member Sharon E. Strong wrote: 'you have provoked my curiosity, inspired my wonder, provided me with consolation, and compounded my appreciation for your life and work. You have become for me a magnificent obsession, my secular saint' (Memorial Book).

Along similar lines, Beyoncé fan 'Flawlessbeyoncexo' posted the following on her idol's Instagram: 'You light up my life with everything that you do and your smile brings me so much joy and happiness! You are utter perfection and beauty! You are amazing in every single way! I love you loads! Xoxo' (Flawlessbeyoncexo). Both messages use very similar language—the language of romance, devotion and obsession (e.g., 'You have become for me a magnificent obsession', 'You light up my life'). They present their favoured celebrity as a major source of happiness and guidance (you have 'inspired my wonder', or brought 'me so much joy and happiness'). In this sense, another JASNA member wrote, even more emphatically: you 'are my compass and I view the world that is and the world that was, through different eyes because of you' (Memorial Book). This message was sent on the first day of the year 2018, which suggests that this fan regards Austen as an intimate friend, someone to be contacted on January the 1st and wished Happy New Year, as one might to close friends and family.

The desire to be close to Austen, to have access to her at all times (New Year's Day included) and also to all Austen-related places is typical of twenty-first-century celebrity culture. In the 1990s, Austenmania, the popular phenomenon which emerged around the BBC *Pride and Prejudice* and other screen adaptations, allowed Austen to preserve a certain aura of mystery and remoteness—no generally available world wide web as yet. In contrast, the present ubiquity of social media platforms means that most public figures are extremely accessible, and the urge for more about social icons, Austen included, has become increasingly insatiable. On her 37th birthday (September 2018), Beyoncé shared some personal reflections with her fans on Instagram. She summarised the year gone by and expressed her gratitude for her twin sons (born that year), her husband and her work, even recording that she had breastfed the twins ('At 36'). Not fully satisfied with such a personal tirade, a fan replied: 'I wish you opened up more so we your people could learn and be inspired to grow' (Propheticprophetess).

More and more, fans feel the right to insider information about their idols and their personal lives. As Ellis Cashmore notes, 'there can never be too much information'—not even breastfeeding details—for nowadays 'to be a celebrity means to be willing to go public with the minutiae of what might, at another time in history, be known as a private life' (43). This culture of excess in which we live is the culture of gaga—of the extravagant, the frivolous and the superfluous. Austen celebrity culture is indeed excessive and extravagant, and as with Beyoncé, star-struck fans expect access to the minutia of her life: to her person, her home, her beach holidays and her most personal objects—all of which I examine in what follows.

The Austen celebrations in Oxford granted fans time with their idol. As part of the exhibition *Which Jane Austen?* the Bodleian Library organised a series of talks and events. One of them was 'A day with Miss Austen' (10 September 2017), which invited enthusiasts on an outing with the author. The first event on the day's schedule was, logically, to 'Meet Jane Austen & her companions' ('A Day with Miss Austen. Entertainments in Blackwell Hall'). There fans encountered actors in full Regency attire, and in their company, engaged in typical Regency activities: dancing, learning eighteenth-century etiquette, learning how to write with a quill and read the language of the fan. The day out concluded at the playhouse, with the performance of *Yours Ever, Jane*, a play based partly on Austen's letters and her novel *Pride and Prejudice*.

If going to the theatre in the vicarious company of Jane Austen is not enough, another option is a visit to the art gallery. The project *What Jane Saw* permits such time travelling feat: in May 2013, the University of Texas at Austin and Professor Janine Barchas launched the website Whatjanesaw.org. This online platform recreates the London venue at 52 Pall Mall, where Austen might have seen a Shakespeare exhibition in 1796, and where she did see a Sir Joshua Reynolds retrospective in 1813. Now fans can follow Austen into the electronic art gallery and all but visit it in her company. Theirs will be a fully immersive experience: the introductory screen states 'You are invited to time travel to two art exhibitions witnessed by Jane Austen', and hovering over a drawing of each exhibition with the mouse, fans are told to 'ENTER' (Whatjanesaw.org). As part of the explanation of the project's genesis, a Google SketchUp Video Animation is available for viewers. The video, being in motion, propels viewers up the staircase and into the gallery, as if they were actually accessing 52 Pall Mall, London. It then guides visitors through the venue: beginning in the North Room, whose North wall visitors would have first encountered when coming up the stairs, and then moving clockwise around the space (Barchas 'About What Jane Saw in 1796').

What Jane Saw illustrates how modern technology can grant us access to a celebrity's world. Fans can see exactly what Austen might have seen in 1796 at the Shakespeare Gallery: Joseph Wright's rendition of *The Tempest* (act 4, scene 1) on the North wall, Henry Fuseli's scenes from *A Midsummer Night's Dream* and Thomas Stothard's from *Othello* on the East wall, to mention a few examples (Figure 34.5). Clicking on the desired painting, they can read the relevant Shakespeare passage, also provided to the original visitors in 1796 (Barchas 'About What Jane Saw in 1796'). Austen's sightseeing experience is recreated in minute detail for the modern viewer. The venue has been painstakingly reconstructed following a watercolour drawing from 1808 and a visitor's account from 1860. The University of Texas at Austin has carefully considered the potential size of each of the three rooms, the height of the ceiling, the size of the paintings and the distance between them on the wall (Barchas 'About What Jane Saw in 1796'). The same efforts apply to the 1813 Sir Joshua Reynolds exhibition included on the site. Paintings here include Reynolds's portraits of George III, nobles such as Lord Richard Cavendish and Lady Melbourne, and famous actors David Garrick and Sarah Siddons. In fact, the Prince Regent, Siddons, and Lord Byron were guests of honour at the opening reception in May 1813; and Barchas notes that Austen's interest in this high profile exhibition—with high profile subjects and guests—shows her own sustained interest in the celebrity culture of her time (Barchas 'About What Jane Saw in 1813').

Figure 34.5 The 1796 Shakespeare Exhibition, North Wall. Part of the e-gallery *What Jane Saw*. Courtesy of Janine Barchas, creator of *What Jane Saw*.

The question still remains of why so much time and effort have been lavished into the accurate reconstruction of what Austen saw, or might have seen. I believe the answer lies in modern celebrity culture. Audiences are no longer satisfied with being mere observers of celebrity life (if they ever were), but wish to be active participants. In the words of Cashmore, 'the pleasure in being in celebrity culture is that the consumer observes, secure in the knowledge that he or she is actually not just an observer, but a player too' (4). Fans wish to spend time with Austen, walk with her around the streets of Oxford and go with her to the theatre or the art gallery. This time with their icon—even if imaginary, even if by proxy—is what might lead them to transcendence, as Rojek notes, or to twenty-first-century sublimity, as I prefer to call it.

Like all the famed and the celebrated (from Elizabeth Taylor and Richard Burton in the 1960s to the Kardashians in the 2010s), Austen has been followed up to the beach on vacation. To mark the bicentenary of her death, the Royal Pavilion, Brighton, hosted the exhibition *Jane Austen by the Sea* (17 June 2017–8 January 2018). This was an exploration of Austen's connections to the sea and coastal towns, Brighton in particular. The historical Austen is not known to have ever visited Brighton, but curator Alexandra Loske observes that 'given she used Brighton to such great effect in her works, it suggests that she at least came through the city' (Moss). And that is precisely what the Royal Pavilion exhibition does: it brings Austen to Brighton (as if on vacation) and follows her around town (as if she were being pursued by paparazzi).

In photo reportage style, the exhibition first documents Austen's imaginary arrival in Brighton. One of the items on display is Jacob Spornberg's watercolour *Old Steine, Brighton, from the North* (1796) (Figure 34.6). The Old Steine was originally a green open space, which became fashionable in the late eighteenth century with the increasing arrival of visitors. Spornberg's watercolour shows some of the early constructions in the area (the Pavilion, Grove House) as well as the open fields. There is a military encampment, where red-coated soldiers are getting ready for their drill. From the right, a long line of carriages is entering the picture, no doubt new arrivals in town. One of them, seemingly a stage coach, must certainly bring more holiday-makers to the sea. And could Austen not be one of them? Might this not be the way the Royal Pavilion is documenting her imaginary visit?

Figure 34.6 *Old Steine, Brighton, from the North*, 1796, by Jacob Spornberg. Watercolour painting. Courtesy of The Royal Pavilion & Museums, Brighton & Hove.

Figure 34.7. Walking Dress, seafront, 1818. Hand-coloured aquatint. From Rudolph Ackermann's *The Repository of Arts, Literature, Commerce, Manufactures, Fashions and Politics*. Courtesy of the University of Sussex.

There are, of course, no images—no stolen pictures—of Austen by the sea. But the exhibition holds the next best thing. Among the images on display is *Walking Dress, seafront, 1818*, a fashion plate from Rudolf Ackermann's *The Repository of Arts, Literature, Commerce, Manufactures, Fashions and Politics* (Figure 34.7). The print depicts a young woman sitting on a rock by the sea, which in the context of the exhibition, can be read as the equivalent, or the closest, to an image of Austen herself by the sea. (The fact that Ackermann's fashion plate is the image chosen for the promotional poster reinforces such a reading). The sitter wears a white cotton pelisse, or walking dress, with the typical empire line and some frills around the bottom of the skirt. Her auburn hair, with curls poking out of a large cream-coloured bonnet, recalls Cassandra's sketch of Austen and family descriptions of the author (Austen-Leigh 70). Ackermann's subject sits placidly by the sea, with the cliffs, a bathing machine, a boat and other holiday-makers delineated in the background as mere silhouettes. As if unaware that she is being observed until now, the sitter has just turned her head towards the viewer. This could be Jane Austen caught during a promenade by the sea. Hijacked by the artist, she has had her privacy invaded, like a modern celebrity under the siege of paparazzi. Maybe they have

Figure 34.8 Bathing Machines, 1790, Aquatint by Thomas Rowlandson, Tinted by Henry Alken. Published by Messrs Robinsons Paternoster Row. Courtesy of The Royal Pavilion & Museums, Brighton & Hove.

interrupted her thoughts on *Sanditon*, her unfinished seaside novel whose manuscript was also displayed at the Royal Pavilion, opened precisely to a description of the beauties of the sea.

If paparazzi chase celebrities, normally against their will, the Royal Pavilion exhibition follows Austen's imaginary footsteps around town. Had she visited Brighton, Austen would have probably stopped by the circulating library. This is 'documented' by two original library cards from Pollard's and Wilkes's in the Marine Parade, the Steine, dated 1796 and 1811. She would have also used the bathing machines, intended to help eighteenth-century bathers access the ocean while keeping their bodies from prying eyes. One of the prints on display is Thomas Rowlandson's *Bathing Machines* (1790), where as many as five machines align on the shore, waiting for the eager visitors. Holidaymakers rush towards them, as if afraid the machines will be all gone by the time they reach the sea (Figure 34.8). Again the implication is that one of these visitors could be Austen, for the adjacent text panel makes it clear that she enjoyed bathing in the sea. The historical Austen used similar machines in Lyme Regis, and as the letter quoted on the panel stresses, she sometimes stayed too long in the water: 'The Bathing was so delightful this morning & Molly [her bathing helper] so pressing with me to enjoy myself that I believe I staid in rather too long' (qtd. in Loske). Wouldn't she have used one of the Brighton bathing machines too?

Holiday over, Austen is followed back home. Celebrity homes have long fascinated the public. *Hello! Magazine* has a fixed section named 'Inside Celebrity Houses', where readers are regularly invited into the homes of Catherine Zeta-Jones or former Spice Girl Geri Halliwell, to mention but two examples (Best 'Catherine Zeta-Jones' and 'Geri Horner'). As the magazine's website announces, 'Ever wondered what it's like inside the homes of the A-list? From their bedroom to their bathrooms, get a closer look inside the homes of the rich and famous—prepare to get serious interiors inspiration' ('Inside Celebrity Houses'). Sometimes celebrity homes become places of pilgrimage when the celebrity is deceased: Elvis Presley's mansion in Graceland, Tennessee, receives around 750,000 visitors a year, apparently more than the White House (Rojek, *Celebrity* 59).

Austen's Cottage at Chawton, near the 'Great House' owned by her brother Edward, and where Austen spent the last eight years of her life, receives an average of 35,000 visitors a year, 60,000 in the case of the Jane Austen Centre in Bath.[2]

The fascination with Austen's places is nothing new. In 1946, one year before Chawton Cottage was purchased by T. Edward Carpenter for the British nation, the *Times* noted that 'acquisition of the property would assure the use of a large room (identified by the blocked-up window) to be used for housing relics of the novelist, and form the nucleus of a place of pilgrimage' ('An Appeal' 6). This semi-religious devotion for Austen, as for Elvis, is not a twenty-first-century phenomenon. What is new is the level of such devotion: it is fans' desire to be there with Austen, sit with her, read with her, and even own part of her house that encapsulates the modern spirit of gaga.

This type of excess can be discerned in the project *Reading with Austen*, unveiled in October 2018 (Readingwithausten.com). Similar to *What Jane Saw*, *Reading with Austen* recreates Edward Austen Knight's library at Godmersham Park, Kent (Figure 34.9). The result is an electronic library that looks as it would have done when Austen visited her brother. Introductory information on the website makes this point clear: 'Here you can explore the Library as Jane Austen might have seen it, and browse photographs of and bibliographic information for the very editions she may have handled' ('Introduction'). Language matters here: note the intensifying adverb 'very' and the preposition 'with', in *Reading with Austen*. The goal is to get closer and closer to celebrity, so close that fans can all but handle the same books ('the very editions') that Austen did, and what is more, read them in the company of their idol.

As with the e-gallery, visiting the Godmersham virtual library is an immersive experience. Modern technology allows fans to browse the shelves at leisure and select their own reading—as if they were to spend the evening there with Austen. Hovering over the hand-drawn spines with the computer mouse, a small window appears indicating the title of the book, its author and publication date. With one click, fans can select their own reading materials; a larger window then pops up

Figure 34.9 Landing page of the e-library *Reading with Jane*. Courtesy of the artist Jessica Irene Joyce.

containing photographs of the leather binding, the title page and a few extra pages. Often, there is a link to free sites with the full text (archive.org, HathiTrust, Google Books). This is, in short, the online equivalent of going through the library and, indeed, reading with Austen.

The library has also been recreated in minute detail. The physical space has been reproduced following Austen's own description in a letter to Cassandra (3 November 1813), and the reading material following an extant catalogue conveniently dated in 1818 ('The 1818 Catalogue'). As with the art gallery, this involved a meticulous process, where researchers from Chawton House Library and McGill University (Canada) needed to consider the height of the shelves, the size of the volumes, the space taken by them and the way they would have been distributed ('Digitally Recreating the Library'). Researchers are still trying to identify missing volumes, which has led to the creation of the Godmersham Lost Sheep Society, just as the University of Texas is on the lookout for missing Shakespeare paintings to complete the 1796 Gallery ('Finding the Lost Sheep of Godmersham'; Barchas 'About What Jane Saw in 1796').

As well as pointing to contemporary celebrity culture (as one of participants rather than by-standers), these two online projects belong to what Halberstam calls 'the art of going gaga': they are excessive in their minuteness, in the lengths they go to in order to recreate early nineteenth-century spaces, and in the desire to replicate and share Austen's *exact* experience. (As many as ten people are credited and eleven more acknowledged on the *Reading with Austen* website). *What Jane Saw* and *Reading with Austen* are part of what Halberstam describes, and celebrates, as the modern 'move toward the insane, the preposterous, the intellectually loony and giddy, hallucinatory visions of alternative futures' (25–26). To be sure, excessive enterprises like these might still hold apparent intellectual value—e.g., tracing Austen's literary and artistic influences—but they no longer have to. Gaga Austen practices break the conventional categories of scholar and fan, never distinct in the case of Austen, and now fully dismantled at last.[3]

The turn towards the crazy, the anarchic and the nonsensical is present in another recent Austen project of perhaps lesser scholarly 'use': *Sitting with Jane*, which allows fans not only to read with her at the library, but also to sit outdoors in the company of their idol. *Sitting with Jane* was part of the anniversary celebrations of Austen's death in her native Hampshire, *Jane Austen 200—A Life in Hampshire*. To honour the author, 24 public benches, each shaped as a book, were distributed around Hampshire during the summer of 2017—including Chawton, Steventon, Basingstoke and Winchester. Previously, the book-benches had been hand-painted by an artist, according to an Austen-inspired theme of their own design. The resulting art works, each unique and by a different artist, were on location between 17 June and 31 August 2017. This public art trail was accessible to all, making Austen herself accessible to fans by extension. Everyone could sit *with* Jane in one of the benches, in a quasi anarchic turn that democratises both celebrity culture and the art world. *Sitting with Jane* ties in with the gaga revolution that Austen is currently undergoing. If something gaga 'borrows promiscuously, steals from everywhere, and inhabits the ground of stereotype and cliché all at the same time' (Halberstam 5), the Austen book-benches, as gaga manifestations, plundered the hyper canonical: the world of Jane Austen, her life and novels, as well as fairy tale, classical Asian art, pop art and manga.[4]

The designs of the book-benches show this type of gaga promiscuity. The bench *Once Upon a Time in Steventon*, by artist Sian Storey, depicts St Nicholas Church in Steventon, where Austen's father preached (Figure 34.10). Storey's is a fairy-tale reimagining of the church with a nod to the Brothers Grimm. The church stands at the centre of the 3D canvas, but the surrounding colourful wildlife is what catches the viewer's eye: giant mushrooms with polka dots, sprigs of lavender, irises and lilies. In the background, behind the pointed church tower, the sun is setting in bright yellow and orange tones. Storey mixes the well-established world of Jane Austen with fairy-tale clichés, in a gaga work of art that takes the viewer to the early years of their icon. Another book-bench brings the viewer even closer to the author. *A Fine Day to Sit and Look Upon Verdure*, by Lynsey Brecknell and Kieron Reilly, depicts a bench within a bench (Figure 34.11). The design shows a white-painted iron bench that takes up the whole 3D canvas. The seat of this drawn-up bench is wooden;

Figure 34.10 Austen book bench *Once Upon a Time in Steventon* by Sian Storey. Part of the project *Sitting with Jane*. Image courtesy of the organisers Destination Basingstoke.

Figure 34.11 Austen book bench *A Fine Day to Sit and Look Upon Verdure* by Lynsey Brecknell and Kieron Reilly. Part of the project *Sitting with Jane*. Image courtesy of the organisers Destination Basingstoke.

the back is decorated with Austen's bust in silhouette. This means that Hampshire tourists can literally sit in the company of Jane Austen. As the project's title indicates they can sit *with* Jane, and in this case, look upon the verdure inside and outside—the drawn bench being set against a lush green backdrop and the actual bench being placed in the middle of Basingstoke's wildlife, outside the Viables Craft Centre.

Jane Goes Gaga

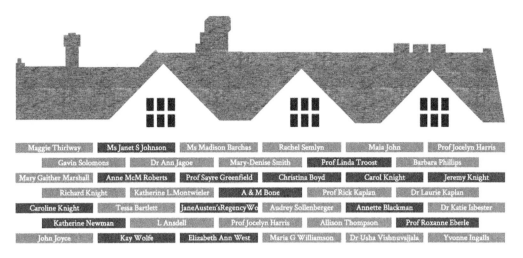

Figure 34.12 E-wall from the fundraising campaign *Brick by Brick*. Courtesy of Chawton House.

This experience might not be enough for star-struck fans who, not satisfied with being in the company of the author and scrutinising her places, also wish to possess part of them. One of the fundraising appeals by Chawton House Library allows for such a feat. As part of their plea to save Edward Knight's mansion, the 'Great House', Chawton House has conducted the campaign *Brick by Brick* since November 2017. Their motto is to save the building 'one brick at a time'. In practice, this means that fans are invited to purchase one brick of the manor house for £25 ($40), a full row of bricks for £100 ($150) or an entire wall (£2,500, $3,500). Once the brick or bricks are bought, donors' names appear on a virtual wall, in a brick-looking box. The online wall, on the Chawton Library website, is topped by the hand-drawn roof of Edward Knight's mansion, emphasising the idea of ownership by making the e-house and wall look as real as possible (Figure 34.12). This astute campaign evokes the idea of possession: owning a brick of Austen's home (even if not really her home) becomes a way of owning a bit of Jane Austen by association. Donors even receive a personalised certificate acknowledging their contribution, which, as the official record of their ownership, all but resembles a property deed.

What is more, generous fans—those purchasing at least one full row of bricks—are promised more lasting recognition. Their names will be included in a drawing permanently housed at Chawton in the future (#BrickbyBrick). These fans, in other words, will forever inhabit the house of Jane Austen, with Jane Austen. The promise is that their names will live forever with that of their idol and under the same roof. Yet the fact that this special recognition is offered as a bonus, an incentive, highlights the ephemeral quality of the campaign. *Brick by Brick*, like some of the other appeals and events, brings to the fore the intangibility and impermanence of gaga Austen: exhibitions are temporary (only a few months); the internet is unstable; events take just a few hours and then are gone. That is gaga Austen.

The *Brick by Brick* appeal takes Austen celebrity culture further by allowing fans to possess part of her house. Like gaga for Halberstam, this approach might seem silly, childish and, altogether, a bit loony—one can buy a brick but can never take it home, and is it really possible to possess one brick of the house anyway? Yet, in its lunacy, the campaign comes close to undoing the type of interaction to which fans are generally restricted: the parasocial. Coined by Donald Horton and R. Richard Wohl in 1956, the parasocial has become a staple term in celebrity studies. It refers to the remote or mediated interactions that most fans will ever have with stars: seemingly intimate but always beyond the social, rarely face-to-face (Cashmore 39). Through campaigns such as *Brick by Brick*, however, fans are permitted to breach the parasocial. By purchasing a brick of Austen's house, reading or sitting outdoors with her, they attempt to escape the limitations of the parasocial and move, to some extent, into the fully social, doing things *with* their favoured celebrity.

Another way of closing the distance between fans and stars is through personal objects. Rojek observes that commodities acquire value when they are known to have belonged to celebrity and to have been touched by them. For example, President Kennedy's rocking chair was sold for $453,000 at auction, and the desk where he signed the 1963 Nuclear Test Ban Treaty for $1.43 million (Rojek, *Fame* 2). Jane Austen's objects, used and touched by her, fetch high prices and captivate stargazers in equal measure.[5] Recent anniversary exhibitions, such as *Jane Austen in 41 Objects*, foregrounded some of these personal items. *Jane Austen in 41 Objects*, an exhibition at the Jane Austen's House Museum (Chawton, March–December 2017), told the story of Austen's life through a selection of objects. One of them was the small walnut table where she wrote *Emma*, *Mansfield Park* and *Persuasion* while living at the Cottage. Former marketing and events manager Madelaine Smith records fans' reactions to the artefact: 'Standing by the table, fingers itching to touch it, as if the wood itself contains something of Jane, some visitors hold their breath. Others cry' (Smith).

Like a celeb, and probably more than JFK, Austen has become larger than life. Many fans develop a psychic and physical attachment for the author, like the one Smith describes. A similar commodity, frequently displayed during the bicentenary celebrations, is Austen's portable desk. This foldable mahogany desk had been a present of Austen's father, which she used while travelling or visiting relatives. During 2017, it was displayed at *Which Jane Austen?* (The Bodleian Library) and *Jane Austen Among Family and Friends* (The British Library, 10 January–19 February 2017). Both exhibitions emphasised notions of exclusivity, implying that they were granting visitors VIP access to Austen and her world. The British Library boasted about displaying the three notebooks of Austen's Juvenilia, together for the first time in 40 years (Norledge). The Bodleian Library showcased the manuscripts of Austen's fragment novels, *The Watsons* and *Sanditon*, in Austen's own hand, and stressed its 'extraordinarily rich Austen holdings', which constitute 'one of the world's three most significant collections of Austen materials' ('War, Empire and Business').

This type of exclusive access to Austen and her objects is another way of breaching the parasocial. Much more personal items were displayed in 2017, bringing the devoted fan close to Austen's body. *Jane Austen in 41 Objects* (Chawton) showcased Austen's gold ring, set with a turquoise stone, and the topaz crosses (one Jane's, one Cassandra's), presented by their sailor brother Charles (Figure 34.13). *Which Jane Austen?* (Bodleian) displayed a replica of Austen's silk pelisse,

Figure 34.13 Austen's gold ring, set with a turquoise stone. Courtesy of Jane Austen's House Museum, Chawton.

reconstructed with the methods and materials available in the 1800s. About the brown silk pelisse, curator Kathryn Sutherland noted that, given the measurements derived from the reconstruction, Austen was 'between 5' 6" and 5' 8"—and thinner than Kate Moss' (Maitland). Sutherland's comment, quoted in *Vogue Magazine*, and her comparison of Austen with top model Kate Moss place the writer, once again, in the world of glitz and glamour.

Branding Jane

The consequence of such excessive celebrification is that, in the 2010s and early 2020s, Austen has fully become a brand. Cashmore connects the rise of celebrity and consumer culture, observing that 'the cast of characters that make up today's generation of celebrities couldn't be more saleable if they had barcodes' (2). The branding of celebrity might be nothing new, but there is something distinctive about contemporary celebrity culture: 'the celebrities have become products themselves', Cashmore continues; 'they are now commodities in the sense that they've become articles of trade that can be bought and sold in a marketplace' (3). One can buy a replica of Austen's turquoise ring for £139.99 ($176.62) at the Jane Austen Centre in Bath. Also for sale are earrings, pendants, wristwatches, leggings, plaited skirts, dressing gowns, socks, baby clothing, slippers, mugs, pillowcases and so on—all with the image of Jane Austen, her characters, the cover of her novels, or a caption from the latter.

More than ever before, Austen nowadays functions as a brand, detached and disassociated from her works—for one does not have to read the novels to participate in brand and celebrity culture. Brands are based on instant recognition; for a brand to be successful, it must be easily identifiable, as Monroe and Austen are emphatically made in their pop art renditions. What enables such immediate recognition is 'a name, term, design, symbol or any other feature that identifies one seller's good or service as distinct from those of other sellers' (AMA Online Dictionary). In Austen's case, a typical mechanism to ensure recognition is that of reduction and simplification. Her canon is reduced to one single work, *Pride and Prejudice*, and her world to a simple list of elements, which consumers can immediately identify and connect with the brand name Jane Austen.

These trends can be observed in the work of improv theatre group Austentatious, an Improvised Jane Austen Novel.[6] In their show, Austentatious improvise a play based on an Austen-sounding title provided by the audience. Recurrent elements include a ball, a pair of young unmarried sisters, soldiers in red coat, cantankerous fathers and aloof gentlemen. The troupe's Facebook page lists as their personal interests: 'Bonnets, turns about the room, swooning, sewing, staring wistfully and collecting militia jackets'.[7] Jane Austen, her novels and her world are, tongue-in-cheek, scaled down to a list of ingredients or menu. Likewise, Austen's oeuvre is reduced to one single novel recognisable to all, *Pride and Prejudice*. In the preface to the show, one member of Austentatious explains to the audience: 'Jane Austen, what a woman. Over the course of her short life, this quiet, modest, unassuming woman wrote six novels, which between them revolutionised the state of English literature. I'm referring, of course, to *Pride and Prejudice* and—the others' (Austentatious). This might be a joke that regularly elicits the laughter of the audience, but the implication is that *Pride and Prejudice* is the only Austen novel that most people would recognise.

The centrality of *Pride and Prejudice* is confirmed by yet another fundraising appeal: *The Darcy Look* (Summer 2017), part of Chawton House Library's wider campaign *Reimagining Jane Austen's 'Great House'*. *The Darcy Look* called for men willing to get drenched while wearing a white shirt, in imitation of the celebrated pond scene in the BBC *Pride and Prejudice* (1995). The experience should be recorded and uploaded on social media; this would then be followed by a text message to donate £3 to Chawton House and a nomination of three friends to replicate the experience. The branding of Austen comes here not only from the equation of Austen and *Pride and Prejudice*, but also from the fact that the BBC pond scene was of scriptwriter Andrew Davies's invention. This moment, now regarded as quintessentially Austen, is nowhere in *Pride and Prejudice* the novel. If the connection with the television adaptation was not clear, the promotional material stressed this point. On their Facebook page, Chawton House encouraged participants to 'channel his inner Colin Firth!' and on their website, they asked, 'Are you a man who could give Colin Firth a run for his money?' Firth too has become synonymous and interchangeable with Fitzwilliam Darcy. No need to mention Mr Darcy by name in any of these calls.

Branding or not, there is something very 'gaga' about this whole enterprise. The politics of 'wild thinking and imaginative reinvention', which Halberstam identifies as the 'art of going gaga', are present in the resulting videos (xv). In his Darcy Look video, Mark Brownlow starts by delivering Darcy's line 'In vain have I struggled my feelings will not be repressed. You must allow me to tell you how ardently I admire and love you' (@markbrownlow). This passage belongs to Darcy's first, and failed, marriage proposal to Elizabeth Bennet. In Brownlow's rendition, the speech is followed by a squirt of water coming from the left and directed to the performer. 'So this is your answer?' Brownlow declaims, again quoting (or rather misquoting) Darcy: 'Can you explain to me why with so little attempt at civility you reject me so?' What comes next is a full splash of water, like a bucketful being emptied on the performer. And if this is not wild and gaga, what is? For Halberstam, gaga will take us 'to a new understanding of anarchy and to the road to unlearning', for 'mutation is possible, and insurrection is here' (148). Brownlow reinvents *Pride and Prejudice*. His video is giddy, frivolous and slightly crazy, and for this reason, culturally anarchic. It weaves in one moment from novel and film (Darcy's failed proposal) and one moment from the adaptation (the pond scene), both of which are totally unconnected (in the TV series, they are two episodes apart). In so doing, Brownlow undoes and redoes Jane Austen, and sets us—the more than 1,000 viewers of the video—on the 'road to unlearning'.

Other Darcy Look videos change and 'unlearn' Austen in different ways. On 23 August 2017, Josh Hasdell did The Darcy Look to the soundtrack of the *Baywatch* TV series (O'Sullivan). Previous to the upload, the video was edited and Jimi Jamison's song 'I'm always here' added as soundtrack. As the theme song that opened every episode of *Baywatch*, Jamison's score conjures up images of sandy beaches and suntanned bodies in California, of David Hasselhoff and Pamela Anderson (perhaps the Marilyn Monroe of the 1990s) running along the shore, red float in hand. All this seems very far removed from the Regency England of Austen's novels, seemingly green and placid. Like the Marilyn Monroe connection, the video adds an erotic undertone to Austen, the modern celebrity. It is also another example of how gaga Austen 'borrows promiscuously' from all sources of popular culture.

The gaga spirit of anarchy of *The Darcy Look* has yet another manifestation. On 18 July 2017, the campaign was launched by the mayor, some local councillors and fire fighters of Alton (the town to which the village of Chawton belongs) (Figure 34.14). They led through example, volunteering to get drenched in a white shirt and so help save Chawton House. Not only did local authorities stand impassive to receive the watery tribute, what is more anarchic about the whole campaign is that it allowed anyone to impersonate Austen's wealthiest hero. *The Darcy Look* breaks down power hierarchies and social distinctions, by allowing anyone to pose as Fitzwilliam Darcy, owner of Pemberley and £10,000 a year. If to be gaga is to be crazy and unpredictable, to 'celebrate variation, mutation, cooperation, transformation, deviance, perversion, and diversion' (Halberstam 143), then *The Darcy Look* fulfils all the criteria of gaga Austen.

These gaga processes of unruly reinvention are embraced, epitomised and celebrated in 2010s Austen events. Public art trails have allowed fans to sit with their icon *al fresco*; websites invite them to read or attend an art gallery in her company; exhibitions have spotted her sitting on the beach, displayed her most intimate objects and portrayed her as a Warholian muse—a celebrity, a commodity and an object of desire. In the twenty-first century, Jane Austen operates as a megastar, like Lady Gaga, Beyoncé or any other notables. Despite the current branding of celebrity, which in the case of Austen condenses some aspects of her work and amplifies others (romance, Darcy), there is

Figure 34.14 The Darcy Look enacted by the local authorities of Alton, Hampshire, in July 2017. Photograph courtesy of Chawton House.

something outlandish in what I have here called the gaga turn of Austen and popular culture. Towards the end of *Gaga Feminism: Sex, Gender, and the End of Normal*, Jack Halberstam notes that 'a gaga feminism does not need to know and name the political outcome of its efforts' (143). I too would like to conclude that a gaga Austen does not need to serve a purpose, have intellectual 'value' or be academically useful. Gaga Austen is unpredictable; it refuses to conclude or be fully defined. And the variety of activities examined in this chapter makes it hard to pinpoint the specific future of Austen culture. One can only join in the 'ongoing gagapocalypse' (132) which, following the 2017 anniversary celebrations, has fully reached Jane Austen.

Notes

1. An account of the process of curating the Folger exhibition can be found in Barchas and Straub's article 'Curating *Will & Jane*', and an updated version in *Jane Austen and William Shakespeare: A Love Affair in Literature, Film and Performance*. The latter collection also explores the figures of Austen and Shakespeare as literary celebrities (Cano and García-Periago).
2. According to their annual report, in 2017 Jane Austen's House Museum at Chawton received a record number of 55,000 visitors ('2017: a Year to Remember').
3. The line between Austen fans and scholars, Janeites and Austenites, has always been blurry. Even E. M. Forster—novelist, intellectual and author of works of literary criticism—declared himself 'slightly imbecile about Jane Austen', and said to read her novels indiscriminately, with 'the mouth open and the mind closed'. See Cano, *Jane Austen and Performance*, 9–12.
4. See benches such as *Girl Power* by David Graham and *Willow Pattern* by Julia Brooker. Photographs available at http://www.sittingwithjane.com/book-benches. Accessed 20 January 2019.
5. In 2012 Austen's turquoise ring sold for £150,000 at a Sotheby auction. It was bought by American pop singer Kelly Clarkson and later resold to the British nation. Now it belongs to the exhibit *Jane Austen in 41 Objects*.
6. For a more extensive analysis of the work of improv group Austentatious, see Cano, 'Austen and Shakespeare: Improvised Drama'.
7. Austentatious! An Improvised Novel, https://www.facebook.com/austenimpro. Accessed 4 March 2018.

Works Cited

'A Day with Miss Austen. Entertainments in Blackwell Hall,' Bodleian Libraries, University of Oxford. www.bodleian.ox.ac.uk/__data/assets/pdf_file/0008/239714/A-Day-with-Miss-Austen-timetable-for-poster. pdf. Accessed 20 Jan. 2019.

'An Appeal for Jane Austen's Home.' *Times* 10 Dec. 1946, p. 6.

Austen-Leigh, James Edward. *A Memoir of Jane Austen, and Other Family Recollections*, edited by Kathryn Sutherland. Oxford UP, 2002.

Austentatious. *Jane Austen's Married to a Cad and Bounder*. BBC Radio 4 Extra, 18 Jun. 2017.

Barchas, Janine. 'About What Jane Saw in 1796.' *What Jane Saw*. The University of Texas at Austin. www. whatjanesaw.org/1796/about.php. Accessed 20 Jan. 2019.

Barchas, Janine. 'About What Jane Saw in 1813.' *What Jane Saw*. The University of Texas at Austin. www. whatjanesaw.org/1813/about.php. Accessed 20 Jan. 2019.

Barchas, Janine, and Kristina Straub. 'Curating Will & Jane.' *Eighteenth Century Life*, vol. 40, no. 2, April 2016, pp. 1–35.

Barchas, Janine and Kristina Straub. 'Curating Will & Jane' (Updated). *Jane Austen and William Shakespeare: A Love Affair in Literature, Film and Performance*, edited by Marina Cano and Rosa García-Periago. Palgrave, 2019, pp. 357–398.

Best, Chloe. 'Catherine Zeta-Jones' New York Home Is Just as Dreamy as her Others.' *Hello! Magazine* 10 Sep. 2018. www.hellomagazine.com/homes/2018091062129/catherine-zeta-jones-living-room-new-york-home. Accessed 19 Jan. 2019 .

Best, Chloe. 'Geri Horner is Giving Fans Serious Home Envy with her Surprising Bedroom Décor.' *Hello! Magazine* 26 Sep. 2018. www.hellomagazine.com/homes/2018092662768/geri-halliwell-bedroom-decor. Accessed 19 Jan. 2019 .

Beyoncé. 'At 36.' *Instagram* 7 Sep. 2018. www.instagram.com/p/BnY7IFDFj_2/

Beyoncé. 'Sir Carter and Rumi 1 month today.' *Instagram* 14 Jul. 2017. www.instagram.com/p/BWg8ZWyghFy/

Birchall, Diana. 'A Beautiful Statue, Waxing Wicked on the Waxwork.' *Light, Bright, and Sparkling*, 11 Jul. 2014. lightbrightandsparkling.blogspot.com/2014/07/a-beautiful-statue-waxing-wicked-on.html. Accessed 20 Jan. 2019.

#BrickbyBrick #BrickbyBrick. *Jane's 'Great House.'* janesgreathouse.org/fundraising. Accessed 21 Jan. 2019.

Cano, Marina. 'Austen and Shakespeare: Improvised Drama.' *Jane Austen and William Shakespeare: A Love Affair in Literature, Film and Performance*, edited by Marina Cano and Rosa García-Periago. Palgrave, 2019, pp. 239–268.

Cano, Marina. *Jane Austen and Performance*. Palgrave Macmillan, 2017.

Cano, Marina and García-Periago Rosa, editors. *Jane Austen and William Shakespeare: A Love Affair in Literature, Film and Performance*. Palgrave Macmillan, 2019.

Cashmore, Ellis. *Celebrity/Culture*. Routledge, 2006.

'Digitally Recreating the Library.' *Reading with Austen*. Burney Centre, McGill University/Chawton House Library. www.readingwithausten.com/about.html#about_making. Accessed 20 Jan. 2019.

Duyckinck, A. *Portrait Gallery of Eminent Men and Women of Europe and America*, vol. 1. New York: Johnson, Fry and Company, 1873.

'Finding the Lost Sheep of Godmersham.' *Reading with Austen*. Burney Centre, McGill University/Chawton House Library. www.readingwithausten.com/about.html#about_lost-sheep. Accessed 20 Jan. 2019.

Flawlessbeyoncexo. 'Response to Beyonce, At 36.' *Instagram* 7 Sep. 2018. www.instagram.com/p/BnY7IFDFj_2

Halberstam, Jack. *Gaga Feminism: Sex, Gender, and the End of Normal*. Beacon Press, 2012.

'Inside Celebrity Houses.' *Hello! Magazine*. www.hellomagazine.com/tags/celebrity-homes/2. Accessed 19 Jan. 2019.

Horton, Donald, and R. Richard Wohl. 'Mass Communication and Para-Social Interaction: Observations on Intimacy at a Distance.' *Psychiatry*, vol. 19, no. 3, 1956, pp. 215–229.

'Introduction.' *Reading with Austen*. Burney Centre, McGill University/Chawton House Library, www. readingwithausten.com/about.html#about_popup. Accessed 20 Jan. 2019.

Kerrigan, Finola, et al. '"Spinning" Warhol: Celebrity Brand Theoretics and the Logic of the Celebrity Brand.' *Journal of Marketing Management*, vol. 27, no. 13–14, 2011, pp. 1504–1524.

Loske, Alexandra. 'Sea Cures, Text Panel.' *Jane Austen by the Sea*. Brighton: The Royal Pavilion, Jun. 2017–Jan. 2018.

Maitland, Hayley. 'Five Things You Didn't Know About Jane Austen.' *Vogue Magazine* 14 Sep. 2017. www.vogue.co.uk/gallery/five-things-you-didnt-know-about-jane-austen. Accessed 20 Jan. 2019.

@markbrownlow (Mark Brownlow). 'The Darcy Proposal Recreated for #TheDarcyLook Fundraising Campaign.' *Twitter* 24 Jul. 2017, 10:51 pm. twitter.com/markbrownlow/status/889362340075974656?ref_src=twsrc%5Etfw%7Ctwcamp%5Etweetembed%7Ctwterm%5E889362340075974656&ref_url=https%3A%2F%2Fwww.bustle.com%2Fp%2Frecreate-mr-darcys-iconic-wet-shirt-scene-you-could-help-save-jane-austens-old-library-72106

'Memorial Book. Jane Austen: 1775–1817.' *JASNA* 12 Jun. 2017. www.jasna.org/about/memorial-book/celebrating-a-life. Accessed 21 Jan. 2019.

Moss, Richard. 'Jane Austen didn't Hate Brighton Says Royal Pavilion Curator.' *Museum Crush*, 7 Apr. 2017. museumcrush.org/jane-austen-didnt-hate-brighton. Accessed 19 Jan. 2019.

@Ms_Addertongue. 'Replying to @STRAWBERRYradio.' *Twitter* 21 Jul. 2017, 12:48 pm. twitter.com/Ms_Addertongue/status/888485766262902784

Norledge, Joanna. 'Jane Austen Among Family and Friends, Curated by Sandra Tuppen.' *English and Drama Blog.* The British Library, 10 Feb. 2017. blogs.bl.uk/english-and-drama/2017/02/jane-austen-among-family-and-friends.html. Accessed 20 Jan. 2019.

O'Sullivan, Clio. 'Josh Hasdell Doing #TheDarcyLook to Save Jane's "Great House."' *Facebook* 23 Aug. 2017, 13:00. www.facebook.com/clio.osullivan. Accessed 21 Jan. 2019.

People Staff. 'People Poll of the Century.' *People*, vol. 52, no. 25, 31 Dec. 1999. https://people.com/archive/people-poll-of-the-century-vol-52-no-25. Accessed 19 Jan. 2019.

Propheticprophetess. 'Response to Beyonce, At 36.' *Instagram* 7 Sep. 2018. www.instagram.com/p/BnY7IFDFj_2

Rojek, Chris. *Celebrity*. Reaktion, 2001.

Rojek, Chris. *Fame Attack: The Inflation of Celebrity and Its Consequences.* Bloomsbury Academic, 2012.

Smith, Madelaine. 'Object 1: Jane Austen's Writing Table.' *Jane Austen in 41 Objects.* Jane Austen's House Museum, Chawton. www.jane-austens-house-museum.org.uk/1-jane-austens-writin<underline>g</underline>-table. Accessed 20 Jan. 2019.

Sullivan, Margaret C. 'Jane Austen Centre at Bath Unveils Wax Figure of Jane Austen.' *Austen Blog* 9 Jul. 2014. austenblog.com/2014/07/09/jane-austen-centre-at-bath-unveils-wax-figure-of-jane-austen. Accessed 20 Jan. 2019.

Tesema, Martha. 'Lady Gaga's Latest Wax Figure is Straight out of a Nightmare.' *MashableUK* 25 Oct. 2017. mashable.com/2017/10/25/lady-gaga-wax-figure/?europe=true#Nefumzj9EPqg. Accessed 19 Jan. 2019 .

'The 1818 Catalogue.' *Reading with Austen.* Burney Centre, McGill University/Chawton House Library. www.readingwithausten.com/about.html#about_catalogue. Accessed 20 Jan. 2019.

'2017: A Year to Remember at Jane Austen's House Museum.' Jane Austen's House Museum, Chawton, Hampshire. docs.wixstatic.com/ugd/862090_5331f6610e6249269a6fdc52190da7d0.pdf. Accessed 22 Jan. 2019.

'War, Empire and Business: An Exhibition on Jane Austen's Unexplored Life.' Bodleian Libraries, University of Oxford, 3 Jun. 2017. www.bodleian.ox.ac.uk/news/2017/jun-03. Accessed 20 Jan. 2019.

Whiting, Cécile. 'Andy Warhol, the Public Star and the Private Self.' *Oxford Art Journal*, vol. 10, no. 2, 1987, pp. 58–75.

35

GLOBAL JANE AUSTEN: OBSTINATE, HEADSTRONG PAKISTANIS

Laaleen Sukhera

(This essay is dedicated to the memory of Melissa van der Klugt)

My late friend Melissa's obituary began with a quote from a memorable editorial feature that she had published in *The Times* (Van der Klugt):

> *When Melissa van der Klugt, a tall, elegant journalist known as 'Missy', met 'the Lizzie Bennets of Lahore', she had an instinctive understanding of their place in Pakistani society. 'They are gathering to sip cocktail glasses, swap their shalwars (sic) for little black dresses and stilettos, and gossip about the men in their life', Van der Klugt wrote in The Times in 2017, describing the young Muslim women who had converged at a discreet country club in the capital. 'Outspoken, affluent and as well-heeled as they are well-read, these women are not the typical face of Pakistan. This couldn't be farther from the quiet parsonages of eighteenth-century England depicted in Jane Austen's novels, yet the names that come up in conversation are straight out of her best-known works: Darcy, Knightley, Wickham. Meet Pakistan's first Jane Austen Society'.* (Melissa van der Klugt Obituary)

Missy was a British journalist who had been in touch from Delhi and flew over to Lahore to interview me and work on a few other stories. We became good friends in the process. In true Pakistani style, there was a covert bomb threat at the literary festival we were attending, so I whisked her away from her hotel and brought her home to stay. In between spa treatments, socialising with friends from the Jane Austen Society of Pakistan (JASP) for afternoon tea, and attending a soirée, we swapped stories and nicknamed our romantic interests Mr Tilney and Capt Wentworth.

Missy's coverage was one of many noteworthy features on JASP during this time period. I had submitted a manuscript to Bloomsbury for an anthology called *Austenistan*, written by JASP members, and photos of our last tea–party had gone viral among Janeite circles on Facebook and Twitter. There was sudden buzz about us and it felt quite surreal. Author and satirist Moni Mohsin's *Austenistan* essay on us in *1843* magazine was nominated for an FPA Media award, while episodes of NPR's *Morning Edition* and *Rough Translation* (Hadid and Warner) both featured my sister Mahlia S. Lone and myself in very intimate portrayals. Our critically acclaimed *Rough Translation* podcast turned out to cover reporter Diaa Hadid's own Austenesque romance while she was working on the podcast, and she became part of the story too.

Most journalists, instead of merely focusing on our anthology, seemed equally, if not more, interested in our personal lives. Why us, I wondered. And why me? What was so special about my

468

DOI: 10.4324/9780429398155-35-40

views and my experiences and my social bubble? Imposter syndrome kicked in and I haven't been able to shake it off since. It seemed to these journalists that we were more intertwined with Austen's world than we thought. In some ways, we seemed to embody it as much as the characters we'd written about.

In writing this essay, I found myself getting in touch with *Austenistan*'s writers, key JASP members in Pakistan and around the world, and various friends I had interacted with in the Janeite universe to make sense of all this, and to enrich this composition with their perspectives. I did not want to impose a single experience or interpretation—mine—on theirs. In what follows, therefore, I feature their individual voices by way of illustrating the variegated array of perspectives in and around the topic of 'Global Jane Austen'.

Farzana Baduel runs a PR firm and was part of our JASP meet-up with Giles Coren for his Sky Arts documentary in London called *I Hate Jane Austen* (I'm convinced he never did hate her). 'The media fascination with *Austenistan* arises from the narrow world-view of Pakistan due to the media stories dominating the narrative' she tells me.

> It was quite a surprise for some that in between indulging in a spot of terrorism or shooting schoolgirls, there's a penchant for nineteenth century English literature. The world forgets that a country is not the sum of a few media bylines but has a complex fabric of over 200 million stories living out their day under the national banner of Pakistan. The Pakistan that I witnessed in 1989 as a young girl living in the country for a year was a society of power dynamics through marriage and tribalism, class obsession and bribing servants for gossip from other households. Austen spoke to me of my experience in Pakistan more than CNN reminding the world of a state gone rogue. (Baduel)

Renee M. Powers, founder of the Feminist Book Club Box + Podcast in Minneapolis, once featured *Austenistan* as its book of the month and we participated in an enjoyable podcast over Skype. 'Audiences have grown up with reality television', she says, when I asked her what prompted readers' interest in us on a personal level.

> We're primed to be a little bit nosy. It would be fascinating to see how the truth of *Austenistan*'s stories echo into the personal lives of the members of JASP. In *Austenistan* as in Regency society, many of the women feel constrained to the roles and expectations of their families. They have agency but the society's and their families' influences are always taken into consideration. Of course, *Austenistan* is modern, so it's especially interesting to see how those social mores play out with the use of technology and social media. (Powers)

Amy L. Patterson is a journalist from Ohio and a bookseller at Jane Austen Books. We met at the Jane Austen Society of North America (JASNA) AGM (Annual General Meeting) in Washington, D.C., in 2016. 'Austen is relevant in any part of the world, because her characters transcend time and setting', she says.

> But there are parts of the world in which arranged marriage, the pressure to overlook a man's faults if he can provide an income, and the push to submit a woman's goals and wishes to those of her family seem to more closely resemble the structure of Austen's fictional world. In the U.S., outside of some isolated religious groups, we don't really have a formal culture with rules about courtship or honour. We do have unwritten and unspoken rules about those things, but we have a cultural narrative of independence and self-sufficiency that tells women we should be able to make it on our own. Especially in the U.S., the images we see of women in countries like Pakistan are skewed towards showing

us victims of an oppressive culture who must be 'liberated'. But I have friends in the U.S. who have also dealt with pressure from family to get or stay married, or the need to tiptoe around angry or unpredictable men in their family or workplace. (Patterson)

She continues:

Reading fiction—even when it closely resembles reality—allows us to engage only with the fictional world presented. It's easy to compartmentalise what you've read as 'just a story'. But engaging with a whole person 'in real life' allows you to go deeper than the fictional story and realise that we share many more similarities than we may think. So many of us yearn for that connection with Austen herself, whether by reading every biography we can get our hands on or making a pilgrimage to her home in Chawton. We want to connect to her works in every way possible, and I think we sometimes see stories like those in *Austenistan* as another conduit for understanding her entire world, instead of just the part that we identify with in our own day-to-day lives. Austen captures so much of a woman's experience, whether that's being undervalued and ignored, or being expected to be perfectly composed at all times. Sometimes all it takes is being friends with someone who grew up in a different culture to realise we all have similar problems. (Patterson)

'It's not just because Austen's novels are fantastic—many people find them long-winded and a bore', explains Shazaf Fatima Haider, a novelist from Karachi who lives in London.

It's because of Empire—she's on the curriculum in almost every English department in every university where literature is taught. And it's because of the emergence of the Austen industry—she forms a loose launching pad for other writers to revise, modernise, improvise her works. It's business and publishers know that any adaptation of her stories will sell well because after all those movies and mini-series, one may not have read Austen but one is familiar with her world and her characters. She's big business and spin-offs and variations of her books earn money and garner much interest. So JASP is a part of that world and gathers international interest because it allows Westerners to see our world through their lenses. (Haider)

'JASP provides an insight into the lives of women who are usually behind closed doors in Pakistan', says Zeina Toric Azad, a journalist and activist who attended JASP's last meet-up in Karachi and now lives in Kent. 'JASP allows the world to see a society through a lens that is well loved and well understood. As we all know, Jane Austen's voice can bridge worlds easily'.

It's no secret that publishing our stories was a fairy-tale experience. The concept alone got me inquiries from agents and publishers, before we even had a manuscript ready. Faiza Sultan Khan, who works as a Consulting Publisher at Bloomsbury Publishing in London, acquired *Austenistan*. I'd call her a major force in mainstreaming commercial fiction, in addition to more highbrow literary fiction, by writers of colour. 'I love Austen, I love good Austen adaptations, of which *Austenistan* is definitely one', she tells me. 'And Austen aside, I'm always looking to publish witty, romantic, contemporary stories from urban Pakistan, especially ones that reflect women's lives' (Khan).

'My first instinct when I received this anthology', Khan shared, 'was to ask for a nonfiction account of JASP—it sounds irresistible, a group of women discussing their partners in a café in Pakistan.'

I think the anthology stands on its own as a very entertaining and often elucidating work but for the outside world, who appear to have their own strong notions of what Pakistan is, what normal means in Pakistan and how divorced women gossiping in cafés is not that, I can imagine they have an anthropological curiosity in who has written it! (Khan)

'Jane Austen stories have become familiar and comfortable', says Lone. 'It's like meeting an old friend that you don't have to explain yourself to. And the stories never become stale. Always funny and light with characters that never age'.

'I find that the work of Austen resonates with me immensely', says Afshan Shafi, a poet who was featured in our first BBC News story, 'because it centres around the lives of women expected to navigate a patriarchal society with as much elegance as possible! The various pressures and demands that we are subjected to are, sadly, still as oppressive as they were in Austen's time' (Shafi).

I asked Dr Bharat Tandon, a notable British Indian Austen scholar who I was introduced to at JASNA's AGM in 2016, about his early experiences with the author.

> I recall that in my teens, when I first discovered Austen, the parts of the novels that felt odd to so many of my peers at school were those which spoke most directly to me: knowing exactly how you were related to people at extraordinary degrees of biological separation; the sophisticated combinations of code-switching and innuendo that allowed private lives to be conducted and articulated in the large social gatherings that so often took up the significant part of weekends; the ability to personalise to your own advantage a social environment that couldn't be completely dismantled or abandoned. (Tandon)

Mohsin, who also moderated our book launch party at the British Council Library in Lahore, tells me,

> It may seem more apposite in socially conservative societies where differences in 'station' are still stumbling blocks to marriage or where women do not inherit property or indeed need parental consent to marry. That said, it is not for its social relevance alone that one reads Austen. She is a consummate stylist, a great satirist, an exquisite writer of dialogue and her characters are so vivid they leap off a page. (Mohsin, Personal interview)

There is so much that has been said about Jane Austen as a contemporary global icon, yet it feels that there is so much more we have yet to discover.

'Jane Austen remains relevant today as her writing explores social hierarchies which are very much alive today as they were in the late eighteenth century', says Baduel.

> Although the technocracy has largely supplanted the aristocracy, the Mr Darcys of this world can still be found at Frieze art fair VIP viewings or pontificating about climate change at Davos! Jane Austen has the remarkable ability to write as an outsider and through reading her works, we are the voyeur in a bygone era which still draws parallels with our lives. When the protagonist in her novel is rejected by a man due to her family's lack of social position, we feel empathy as we experience rejection when he swipes left. After all, we are still social animals craving acceptance. (Baduel)

I asked Dr Adriana Sales her opinion; she runs the Jane Austen Society of Brazil and has translated Austen into Portuguese.

> In the past, Austen had more social relevance in English speaking countries, but since Austen is an icon around the world due to foreign language translations and television adaptations, she goes beyond the language barrier. Here in Brazil, people are really

interested in her because she's accessible in six different Portuguese editions. More and more academics are studying her work at Brazilian universities. (Sales)

Tamara Chestna is a writer and producer based in Los Angeles and we've had some interesting discussions. Incidentally, her film *After* featured direct references to *Pride and Prejudice*.

> I believe Jane Austen speaks to the hearts and minds of women around the world and her work cuts through many different cultures. The notion that against all expectations, rules and barriers women may be able to cut their own paths, find true love and equals in their relationships—I think that remains a dream and aspiration for even the most modern women. After all, even in 'modern' society, women who are unmarried are 'the exception', not the rule.

> However, in terms of where Austen may have more societal relevance, there are certainly cultures where women of today face the same overt pressures and obstacles that Austen's characters faced. Laws where women cannot divorce their husbands. Laws where women cannot work. Laws that prevent women from driving or voting or being educated. In these places, a woman's future is still defined by the man she marries. Even in places where it may not be strictly written in the law, a woman's reputation and her future among her peers may be at stake depending on her marriage. And that is why *Austenistan* is so poignant and relevant. It points out that we are still holding women in these binds—but, and this is the most important, beautiful part, women still dream. And love. And find hope wherever they can. It's why Austen lives on—and why it's so important to acknowledge that her work still parallels our world today. (Chestna)

Powers agrees. 'Jane Austen's work is timeless in a lot of ways, but I think for certain parts of the world, the social norms and especially the gendered expectations resonate more deeply. Even in the United States, I imagine many Southern debutantes can identify with the norms and practices Austen writes about'.

'That's part of her popularity, isn't it, that so many of us can relate to Austen from different parts of the world?' asks Khan.

> The more traditional, shall we say, a society is, the more it often resembles Regency England with its focus on marriage for women, tightly-knit communities, and keeping up appearances. A lot of these things feel very familiar in Pakistan, though I don't want to overstate the similarities as women are doing amazing things in the workplace in Pakistan too, and increasingly the average age of people getting married is going up as is the divorce rate. There may be no Mr Darcys out there but there are also less compelling reasons to marry Mr Collins. (Khan)

Over the past few years, I've had the immense good fortune to speak to global audiences about this anthology: publications, news channels, podcasts, literary festivals, and university symposiums in Australia, Britain, Brazil, the United Arab Emirates, the United States, Ireland, Italy, India, and of course, Pakistan. In the process, I've discovered that our social world has proved fairly fascinating to the press, far beyond the pages of our anthology. There's been a healthy curiosity about how outwardly twenty-first-century Pakistani women are obliged to navigate between the old world ('rich yet repressive domestic and colonial heritage') with the new ('emerging feminists in a patriarchal system') in the context of the all-powerful marriage mart perennially occupying the apex of Pakistani high society as it did in England's Regency era. Seen in this light, juxtaposing our world with Jane's is logical, relatable, and enjoyable, if at times as frustrating as it must have been two centuries ago.

Journalist Mashaal Gauhar, who now lives in Muscat, felt sufficiently inspired to write an editorial, 'Austen's Relevance in Pakistan'.

> I think you invoke fascination for your spirited and courageous adaptations and interpretations of her stories'. I think that many women have had similar experiences and the fact that JASP writers have shared their stories has struck a chord with so many women. I was so inspired by the stories of these women who face the same challenges as a lot of Jane Austen's heroines, how very often there is no Mr Darcy to save them from their circumstances and they end up saving themselves, how they live courageously amid social stigmas surrounding divorce, being unmarried, financial difficulties, and the social repercussions of living life on your own terms as a woman. (M. Gauhar, Personal interview)

Writer and independent publisher Mehr F. Husain explains,

> Since the 1980s (Soviet-Afghan war), Pakistan has been viewed with a critical lens. What is shocking is despite all the books, articles, and analyses written about Pakistan, Pakistani women have by and large been ignored in terms of what they think, who they are, what they feel. This is sheer ignorance. So when *Austenistan* came out and the authors were these articulate, bold, independent women, it brought on a wave of curiosity—where were the burqas? They could speak English? They wore stylish, modern clothing? Who were these women? Frankly, it started a conversation that should have been conducted decades ago. While the world stayed in the past, these women showed they were the future. (Husain)

Ours might be the first South Asian fictional tribute to Austen, but it is by no means the only one. As editorial features in *The Atlantic* (Smith) and *The Economist* ('Fame and Favourability') have mentioned, this seems to be a growing subgenre. 'It is only natural for writers from India, Pakistan and other parts of South Asia to join the horde of Austen adaptors', wrote Nilanjana Roy in *The Financial Times*.

'I think recent re-imaginings of her work have focused on Austen's matrimonial themes; however, there is much to learn from how she depicts coming-of-age as a young woman', says Shafi. 'For example in *Emma*, we see how the lead protagonist evolves past much of her vanity and begins to realise the subtleties of human nature, with almost epiphanic force, by the end of the novel'. My friend Saniyya Gauhar, JASP's first member, is a barrister who lives in Islamabad. 'The thing that strikes me the most about contemporary re-imaginings of her work is how seamlessly and beautifully her stories fit into a modern reinterpretation', she tells me.

> They can be set almost anywhere in the world with little change or deviation from the original story. It is incredible that *Emma* can be effortlessly reimagined as a spoilt though delightful high school girl attending an exclusive private school in Los Angeles (*Clueless*), and Miss Bingley finds herself as a snobby, rich magazine editor in Islamabad dealing with the 'mortification' of Darcy's wedding to Elizabeth. (S. Guahar)

'With so many adaptations and re-imaginings, one would think the stories would get old, but when the new *Emma* (2020) film rolled around, I for one was so excited to watch it', Lone tells me. 'Visually, the film was gorgeous and I liked the slight pantomime element of the depiction'.

'Victorian Janeite men such as Thomas Macaulay and Archbishop Whately were fond of comparing Austen to Shakespeare', recalls Tandon.

> While this may have had a good degree of critical hyperbole to it, the irony is that the comparison also has a good deal of truth behind it, not least because Austen, like Shakespeare, can be re-worked by generation after generation to speak to and for them. But the real genius of both Shakespeare and Austen in this context is one which reveals the true bluntness of modern terms such as 'relatability': both authors can reveal extraordinary affinities between the psychological dynamics of the original and those of the world in which they are reimagined, even while that original stands back in its own space and keeps its distance. (Tandon)

'Take *Clueless*, for example: still, to my mind, the great modern version of Austen'. Tandon continues, 'Even as one marvels at the ingenuity with which the novel's concerns have been re-directed to the social anxieties of Beverly Hills, the original remains what it is; and so the best translations and transitions of Austen have the peculiar additional quality of sending one back to the original texts as if for the first time'.

And then, of course, there are the inevitable historical links between England and her former colony. Author and journalist Catriona Luke makes a fascinating case for Austen's association with the Indo-Pak subcontinent in her 2020 essay, 'Jane Austen's Pride and Prejudice and East India Company Connection', explaining how the funds used to publish *Pride and Prejudice* came from her family's links with the East India Company!

A journalist at *The Daily Beast*, Jasmin Malik Chua, quoted me in 'The Battle Over Jane Austen's Whiteness'. I asked Chua for her personal take on Austen's relatability.

> I think Austen's world of drawing-room intrigue has particular resonance in parts of the world where classism still reigns and in communities that share the same tight-knit (and gossipy!) village mentality reflected in her version of Regency England. Marrying well and within your station is still an important consideration in countries in South Asia; so is the desire to adhere to familial expectations—perhaps more so than in the contemporary West, where individualism and social mobility are the dominant mores. (Chua)

'The culture that Jane Austen writes about—mothers fretting over their daughters' marriages, the courtships, the "viewings" of prospective partners—it is all very applicable to South Asian, especially Pakistani culture', reveals Husain.

> The feelings she documents, the concerns and worries are not just a 'fictional story'—for millions of Pakistanis it is their very existence. Her work validates our own culture and shows that at the end of the day, mankind is one and the same no matter the geography, culture or timeline. Her world is very much applicable to mine. Hailing from a conservative family, I am proud to see the younger girls in my family take control of their destinies much like Austen's heroines. Austen's contemporary work, whether in series or film, carry same themes of feminism, marriage, patriarchy that women today still grapple with. Her work will always remain relevant as long as the patriarchy stays. (Husain)

'We really enjoy dark humour', quips author and scholar Faiqa Mansab. 'Austen's circumscribed world of women, where the happily ever after was marriage, reflects Pakistani society so well. The gossip, scandals, loves and triumphs of the subculture of women is very relatable. I also feel her wit and satire are akin to Pakistani sensibilities'.

Mohsin opines, 'The elite is tiny and interconnected and often related to each other. Thanks to masses of domestic help, everyone in this class has plenty of time for leisure, much of which is used up in gossiping about each other'.

'We still have staff in the middle to upper income households in South Asia', agrees Lone. 'That's one similarity to Regency England that still exists here today'.

'As a white American Midwestern mom, when I watch a period Austen film with big manor houses and everyone in elaborate fashions, it feels foreign, exotic, and a little romantic', reveals Patterson.

> I wonder what it must be like to have a maid to help me dress in the morning and change again for a party later in the day. Most of what I wear is casual and off the rack of a local department store. I live in a place where I wear my 'nice jeans' to get dressed up. It's fascinating to imagine living in a more formal time or place where I would be able to showcase my fashion sense more than once a year for the office Christmas party. *Austenistan* captured some of that exotic, yet recognisable feeling. The world in the stories is familiar, but different enough from my own that it allows me to see what other women face while re-evaluating my own struggles and triumphs in comparison. (Patterson)

'South Asia has yet to recover from its painful and expensive history, and that has left society in this region mirroring less the modern day world and more England in the 1800s', observes Azad. 'Pakistan's issues around marriage, dignity (*izzat*), and inheritance could have been taken directly out of Regency England'.

'Jane Austen first of all writes from a woman's perspective, living in a patriarchal society in which her options are limited due to society pressures and familial judgement', says Mishayl Naek, an economist and entrepreneur in Karachi who contributed to *Austenistan*.

> This is still a reality for the majority of Pakistani women, regardless of class, financial status and country of residence. For me, and perhaps many women, reading and empathising with characters who struggle with domestic and emotional issues makes me feel less alone. (Naek)

'I think Jane Austen's work continues to resonate in South Asia as the social mores of Jane Austen's era are still prevalent in South Asia', agrees S. Gauhar.

> Society's unsparing judgement of women, the pressure to get married, the fact that social prestige in Pakistan is almost a form of currency, the hierarchical structure of a patriarchal society and how a woman is expected to navigate these complex dynamics to her advantage and often for her survival. Even Jane Austen's outcomes for her characters reflect that judgement, when Mary Crawford dared to defy social conventions with a suitor when she had the chance. She pays a price for it in the book. And Kitty and Lydia are often seen as the giddy and wild sisters who also don't fare as well in marriage. (S. Gauhar)

Kamila Rahim Habib lives in Karachi and runs a delivery-based library, *My Bookshelf*.

> Matchmaking is reminiscent of most mothers in South Asian culture who have daughters of a marriageable age. Their primary pursuit in life is to arrange a match, preferably a sound one, by which we mean rich, of course, for their daughters which will ensure their social standing, economic future and subsequent lifelong happiness. Women see themselves in Austen's stories. The constant tussle between decency and craving a sense of liberation,

between education and too much education making you matrimonially undesirable is all too familiar. We also see the pitfalls of placing the entire burden of a family's honour on the fragile shoulders of a teenage woman. The elitist mentality, the scandalous gossip, the incessant falling from grace and ups and downs of heartbreak, Austen showed us all of it in a humorous way which perhaps helps us laugh at ourselves and not take life too seriously. (Habib)

'Jane Austen is universal because love, the problem of finding the right person to marry, the issues of convenience and compatibility have always been negotiated in different ways by all cultures', explains Haider.

> Her novels may feature small towns and a few people, but those characters are in themselves individuals as well as tropes and we all know a dependent parent who interrupts their child's advancement like Mr Woodhouse or headstrong girls jumping to wrong conclusions about people like Elizabeth Bennet. I think the need to marry for social advancement and financial stability are common to the characters of Austen and to people in South Asia and the games people play to 'settle well' are very similar in this regard—hence, the relatability factor.

> Her social world and mine were very similar in that they were little 'bubble groups' of the same kind of folk. What strikes me upon re-reading her is the mind-numbing boredom of that world where dances, day visits and marriages offer a welcome distraction from the sheer tedium of life. It's remarkable how she captures life in that tedium and there is a gloom which her humour is often able to dispel. I hadn't noticed it when reading it as a young girl, or perhaps it's reading Austen in Covid lockdown that has made me realise how narrow and repetitive respectable life for women was in the nineteenth century (Haider)

'Despite women entering into the workforce in many countries, there remains a gender pay gap alongside a lack of women present at senior levels in the worlds of business, media and government', explains Baduel.

> Therefore, access to wealth via marriage remains a pathway for women. A quick scan of the rich list shows sources of wealth for a number of women via their husbands or fathers remains a depressing reality. We like to think we have moved on from the Austen era, but systemic barriers exist for women to achieve economic parity with men. Jane Austen resonates in conservative cultures, particularly in Pakistan where there is a significant proportion of women who echo the eighteenth-century lifestyle of women staying at home and not entering the workplace. The arranging of marriages is therefore of critical importance and has been elevated to a national sport. if not a national obsession, underpinned with a marathon of week-long wedding parties being the norm. (Baduel)

'Austen is the snarky sapient single aunt we all have in the family', says Ayesha Rehman, an entrepreneur and writer in Karachi. 'You know, the one who's known for making sharp comments about people or situations that others find "unexceptionable"'.

> The older people regard her with a tolerant eye, the married woman with exasperated condescendence, the younger lot with admiration tinged with apprehension. The men alternately feel threatened or supported, leaving them with a lingering sense of insecurity in their dealings with her. To many South Asian women, Austen's world is very familiar:

a family-oriented existence, full of household minutiae. Sedate walks are considered 'exercise'. The days are spiced with 'society' gatherings, social gossip and news of extended relatives. We even have a 'Season'. Major events in the outside world—like general elections, tax policies or the government's prolonged war on terror—are of peripheral importance. Men, on the other hand, get to lead exciting lives. A woman's status in society is determined by the man she marries. While a man with a provincial or unpolished wife is acceptable, the reverse is cause for comment because of the relative social weightage.

Also familiar is the formality and unspoken etiquette governing interaction between the sexes. For example, even in an office setting in Pakistan, it is often improper for a man to extend his hand to a women in expectation of a handshake. At a CPR course I organised, the trainer taught us a 'mouth-free' method because he said the physical contact taboo is so strong that people are unable to overcome it even in life or death situations. Similarly, during official Zoom meetings, no one would dream of asking 'ladies' to switch their cameras on. I once bumped into an old family friend at a work training. He and I greeted each other with our usual double peck on the cheek. Only belatedly did I realise my staff was struck dumb with horror! (Rehman)

'There's a precision to the way in which Austen's novels play with quantities, whether the size of a character's income or the duration of a social visit, which is very much to do with what Austen could take for granted in what she intimated to her readers', reveals Tandon. 'So it's entirely natural that the resonances of numbers are more obliquely intimated in these modern retellings'.

Merging Jane Austen's work—and her world—with Pakistani society came naturally to us when we took a stab at *Austenistan*. We fictionalised social settings and characterisations, elements we found inspirational yet relatable from our favourite novels, and tied them in with our surroundings to create an homage to Austen. Balls and weddings continued to remain key in our narratives, while letters between characters were naturally updated with comparable forms of communication, namely social media and phone apps. Characters were re-explored, renamed and re-introduced, all with a tongue-in-cheek Pakistani Janeite lens. The whole process felt organic and it happened astonishingly quickly.

'In *Emaan Ever After,* I adapted Emma Woodhouse into a contemporary Karachi girl', Mishayl Naek tells me,

who enjoyed matchmaking but had given up on love herself post-divorce. I wanted the character to reflect Emma as a person more than strictly stick to the original storyline. For me, Emma was about the relationship between the two main characters, based on friendship and respect, and so I attempted to recreate that dynamic. My inspiration was the original Austen novel and of course Karachi high society. I used to sit in the places I referenced in my story and spied on people around me, trying to understand the nuances that made them unique to my city. (Naek)

'So many of Jane Austen's memorable characters can easily be transplanted to other cultures and time periods', observes Nida Elley, a writer and college instructor based in London who wrote 'Begum Saira Returns' in *Austenistan*.

Austen's characters feel universal. Lady Susan, as a strong older woman and widow, keeps her own self-interests as a priority in a male-dominated society where marriage is everything. It felt like an archetype for many of the women I'd grown up seeing. It was such a treat for me to bring that character to life in a familiar, Pakistani setting. (Elley)

Dr Gayathri Warnasuriya is a research scientist who currently lives in Glasgow and penned 'The Autumn Ball' in *Austenistan*. 'My inspiration was my love for *Pride and Prejudice*', she tells me.

I read and reread it as a teenager, mainly for the love of Elizabeth as I could relate to her railing against the expectations of a well brought up young lady. I always had a vague suspicion that, in spite of the happy ending in the book, Darcy would revert to his boring non-dancing self once the honeymoon was over. My story is based on a contemporary imagining of a snippet of Elizabeth and Darcy's life, a little after the first flush of youth and love. (Warnasuriya)

Saniyya Gauhar goes into detail about the inspiration for her contribution, 'The Mughal Empire':

My story has reimagined Caroline Bingley as the editor of a society magazine in Islamabad who is dealing with her 'mortification' over Darcy's wedding to Elizabeth. Austen's Miss Bingley, albeit wealthy, was born into the fringe of England's aristocracy and her Pakistani counterpart, Kamila Mughal, hails from one of the richest families in Pakistan. Like Caroline, Kamila is a snob. And also like Miss Bingley, she made her adoration for Pakistan's answer to Mr Darcy (and her jealousy of Elizabeth aka Erum) all too obvious. As a high society socialite, Kamila is extremely embarrassed at being snubbed in favour of someone whom she considered beneath her in the social hierarchy. 'The Mughal Empire' imagines Miss Bingley's story after the Darcy wedding and explores her wounded pride, her prejudice towards Erum or anyone 'middle class', her materialistic motivations as well as the nature of jealousy and social snobbery.

I was intrigued by the line towards the end of *Pride and Prejudice* that Miss Bingley was 'very deeply mortified by Darcy's marriage'. I thought that 'mortified' was such an interesting world to use as it means 'to feel embarrassed or ashamed'. I wondered why she would have felt embarrassed. If she had indeed loved Darcy, wouldn't 'heartbroken' have been a more appropriate word? I realised that because she had made her feelings for Darcy so glaringly obvious, a proud character like her would have felt embarrassed and humiliated and would do her utmost to rehabilitate herself in society. Her ability to move on and heal would have been made more difficult by the fact that the Darcys would have been a couple that she would have had to see very often or at least hear about through mutual friends. How would she deal with it every time someone gushed about them? How would she feel every time she saw them? I thought that this was something that could translate so well into modern day Pakistan, which is a very social society.

Jealousy is not only a lonely emotion, it's an embarrassing one too, and one that nobody likes to admit to. I am convinced that her pride and ego were a lot more wounded than her heart, which is something I hope comes across in my version of the story. In terms of the writing process, once Miss Bingley stormed into my mind, she stormed onto the page too. It was very easy to recast her in contemporary Pakistan and her story almost effortlessly told itself. So many characters 'appeared' and at one point I felt as if I were a mere fly on the wall as I struggled to get their dialogue down fast enough. 'The Mughal Empire' was written in two days, and the writing process was a pleasure from start to finish. (S. Gauhar)

I have an increasingly personal connection with Jane Austen. In many ways, she has inspired me and even saved me; she has helped me become a stronger version of myself. She has pulled me out of the toughest time of my life. I grew up reading her, my college honours thesis analysed Austen screen adaptations, I even heard her name bizarrely cited in courtrooms as I struggled to gain custody of

Global Jane Austen

my children. My university alumni magazine chronicled this in 'Pride v. Prejudice: Clark Alumna Fights for Women's Rights In Pakistan' (Lynch). I could suddenly understand why she had published her novels anonymously when some of us began to experience a backlash.

Saniyya Gauhar explains our bewilderment:

> Interestingly, *Austenistan* came in for some criticism in Pakistan for being 'elitist' and its characters drawn from amongst the upper and upper-middle elite class. Where were the honour killings? Where was the poverty? Where was the terrorism? It was felt that *Austenistan* was not an accurate depiction of Pakistan. These were comments I personally found quite baffling. *Austenistan* was a reimagining of Jane Austen's stories and her characters were also part of the upper and middle echelons of society. Jane Austen was in fact criticised in her lifetime for not including politics or social issues in her stories. There was poverty in her time as well. There was patriarchy. There was war. There was social injustice. However, she chose to focus solely on the story itself, which mainly took place in ballrooms, drawing rooms and grand country homes. This does not and cannot mean for a second that she was oblivious to what was happening in the wider world outside of Pemberley any more than any of our writers are unaware of issues in our society or the world at large. To make such an accusation is frankly absurd. However, we chose not to focus on them because firstly, these were short stories and there was a word limit and secondly, we wanted to stick as faithfully as possible to the spirit of Jane Austen.

> At no time did *Austenistan* purport to be an all-encompassing depiction of Pakistani society. Like Austen, the characters in *Austenistan* are from amongst a particular segment of society, which is also a part of the Pakistani fabric. My story in particular had a heroine from a very privileged and rarefied strata of society and because she is a very materialist character, she at one point envies the Elizabeth character's trousseau which was assembled from amongst the top designers in Pakistan as well as from an array of designer shops on Sloane Street. This is the character's thought process, not my own, and was used to demonstrate how her feelings for Darcy were motivated more by materialistic considerations. (S. Gauhar)

'JASP has been under fire by embittered critics recently', recalls Shafi. 'I find their vitriol to be against the very spirit of literature! The policing of Cosplay and the disdain directed towards the individual members of the society has been absurd to witness. All we aim to do as a society is to celebrate the freedom, wit and feminine power inherent in this great novelist's oeuvre!'

Television presenter Mina Malik-Hussain cited some of the backlash in her newspaper column:

> Apparently talking about Austen means a group of people are letting Pakistan down. No matter if most of those people are journalists, media professionals, activists, teachers, poets and writers—they are all bad and irresponsible. It's shirking one's patriotic duty to drink tea and natter about literature… The idea that literature and people inclined towards it wield this immense power to vex and bewilder, far more so than tax evaders and the destruction of heritage sites and people who steal electricity and the smog epidemic. It seems you are a national disgrace only if you are an English-speaking woman who likes to have a bit of fun over tea and Mr Darcy. How quaint! How super! Pass the crumpets!

This entire experience, with JASP, publishing *Austenistan*, feeling part of the Janeite world, has brought with it inspiration, exhilaration, myriad connections, even a support system. I feel that we have helped demonstrate Jane Austen's global status from our neck of the woods with continued relevance in today's multicultural, cosmopolitan world. And that our tribute to her in the form of commercial fiction, intended for entertainment purposes rather than an accurate representation of all the ills in our society, helps to illustrate the universality of human experiences beyond colour and ethnicity.

Works Cited

Austen, Jane. *Pride and Prejudice*, edited by Robert P. Irvine. Broadview, 2002.

Azad, Zeina Toric. Personal interview. 29 Jun. 2020.

Baduel, Farzana. Personal interview. 28 Jun. 2020.

Chestna, Tamara. Personal interview. 28 Jun. 2020.

Chua, Jasmin Malik. 'The Battle over Jane Austen's Whiteness.' *The Daily Beast.* 20 Feb. 2020. https://www.thedailybeast.com/the-battle-over-jane-austens-whiteness

Chua, Jasmin Malik. Personal interview. 28 Jun. 2020.

Elley, Nida. Personal interview. 28 Jun. 2020.

'Fame and Favourability,' *The Economist.* https://www.economist.com/books-and-arts/2017/07/13/jane-austen-200-years-on

Gauhar, Mashaal. 'Austen's Relevance in Pakistan.' *Pakistan Daily Times.* 1 Nov. 2018. https://dailytimes.com.pk/316935/austens-relevance-in-pakistan/

Gauhar, Mashaal. Personal interview. 28 Jun. 2020.

Gauhar, Saniyya. Personal interview. 29 Jun. 2020.

Habib, Kamila Rahim. Personal interview. 28 Jun. 2020.

Hadid, Diaa, and Gregory Warner. 'Austenistan.' *NPR: Rough Translation.* 11 Jul. 2018. https://www.npr.org/transcripts/627779858

Hadid, Diaa, and Gregory Warner. '2 Sisters in Pakistan Find They Have a Lot in Common with Jane Austen.' *NPR: Morning Edition.* 22 Jan 2018. https://www.npr.org/2018/01/22/579629339/2-sisters-in-pakistan-find-they-have-a-lot-in-common-with-jane-austen

Haider, Shazaf Fatima. Personal interview. 28 Jun. 2020.

Husain, Mehr Fatima. Personal interview. 29 Jun. 2020.

Khan, Faiza Sultan. Personal interview. 29 Jun. 2020.

Lone, Mahlia S. Personal interview. 28 Jun. 2020.

Luke, Catriona. 'Jane Austen's Pride and Prejudice and East India Company Connection.' *Samaa.* 27 Feb. 2020. https://www.samaa.tv/culture/2020/02/jane-austens-pride-and-prejudice-and-the-east-india-company-connection/

Lynch, Melissa. 'Pride v. Prejudice: Clark Alumna Fights for Women's Rights in Pakistan.' *Clark Now.* 29 Mar. 2019. https://clarknow.clarku.edu/2019/03/29/pride-v-prejudice-clark-alumna-fights-for-womens-rights-in-pakistan/

Malik-Hussain, Mina. 'On Cakes and Ale.' *The Nation.* 1 Jan. 2018. https://nation.com.pk/01-Jan-2018/on-cakes-and-ale

Mansab, Faiqa. Personal interview. 28 Jun. 2020.

'Melissa van der Klugt Obituary.' *The Times.* 11 Sept. 2019.

Mohsin, Moni. 'Austenistan.' *1843 The Economist.* Oct./Nov. 2017. https://www.1843magazine.com/features/austenistan

Mohsin, Moni. Personal interview. 28 Jun. 2020.

Naek, Mishayl. Personal interview. 28 Jun. 2020.

Patterson, Amy. Personal interview. 28 Jun. 2020.

Powers, Renee M. Personal interview. 28 Jun. 2020.

Rehman, Ayesha. Personal interview. 28 Jun. 2020.

Roy, Nilanjana. 'Why Do We Still Love Jane Austen So Much?' *The Financial Times.* 10 Aug. 2018. https://www.ft.com/content/9d675b3a-9b26-11e8-9702-5946bae86e6d

Sales, Adriana. Personal interview. 29 Jun. 2020.

Shafi, Afshan. Personal interview. 28 Jun. 2020.

Smith, Rosa Inocencio. 'Austen in South Asia.' *The Atlantic.* 23 Jul. 2017. https://www.theatlantic.com/notes/2017/07/austen-in-south-asia/533820/

Sukhera, Laaleen. *Austenistan.* India: Bloomsbury, 2017.

Tandon, Bharat. Personal interview. 28 Jun. 2020.

Van der Klugt, Melissa, 'Meet the Lizzie Bennets of Lahore.' *The Times* 6 Nov. 2017. https://www.thetimes.co.uk/article/meet-the-lizzie-bennets-of-lahore-l5mw8vgkb

Warnasuriya, Gayathri. Personal interview. 29 Jun. 2020.

36

RACE, CLASS, GENDER REMIXED: REIMAGINING *PRIDE AND PREJUDICE* IN COMMUNITIES OF COLOUR

Sigrid Michelle Anderson

UNIVERSITY OF MICHIGAN

Soniah Kamal's 2019 novel *Unmarriageable,* subtitled *Pride and Prejudice in Pakistan,* begins with Alys Binat—the Lizzie Bennet character who teaches English literature at a local girls' high school—asking her students to imagine themselves in Austen's novel by writing their own version of the famous opening line. The version that serves as the chapter's epigraph—'It is a truth universally acknowledged that a girl can go from pauper to princess or princess to pauper in the mere seconds it takes for her to accept a proposal' (11)—and the variations on this theme that follow, reflect the importance of marriage as a means for economic security in the lives of these young Pakistani women. Making a poor choice can lead to poverty and remaining unmarried is unthinkable. When Alys expresses her plan to stay single, her most conservative student chides her that 'marriage is a cornerstone of our culture' (20).

This opening scene establishes how Kamal builds on the framework of *Pride and Prejudice* to explore contemporary gender roles for young women in Pakistan, especially in the context of a patriarchal society where women depend on men for social status and economic security. As Nora Foster Stovel observes, modernisations of Austen's novels raise the question 'that perhaps women haven't come such a long way since the Regency after all' (110). Defying expectations and enraging her mother, Alys Binat, like Lizzie Bennet, is determined not to put her community's expectations ahead of her own inclinations, even if it means remaining a 'forever career woman' (18).

Much has been written about the global reach of Austen fandom and the many adaptations of her novels that have appeared in different media. Adaptations of Austen's novels have offered critiques of class (Jo Baker's *Longbourn,* for example) and empire (*Bride and Prejudice*), as well as offered a feminist take on the Bennet sisters (as in Curtis Sittenfeld's *Eligible*). The continued proliferation of Austen spin-offs and Austen-themed collectibles has inspired a subgenre of Austen criticism focused on the fandom itself, including studies such as Deborah Yaffe's *Among the Janeites*, Devoney Looser's *The Making of Jane Austen*, and most recently Holly Luetkenhaus and Zoe Weinstein's *Austentatious: The Evolving World of Austen Fans*. These, and other studies, take seriously the question of what Austen has meant to millions of fans, arguing that fandom is not a debasement of her work. As Looser reassures us, 'What the history of Austen's legacy shows us is that, as long as her fiction morphs in meaningful ways from

DOI: 10.4324/9780429398155-36-41

one fresh popular medium to the next—those very transformations that have been so repeatedly fretted over or decried by the guardians of high culture—she'll probably stick around' (223).

This essay turns a critical eye towards another subgenre of Austen adaptations that has picked up momentum in the last few years: modern retellings, written by authors of colour, that switch ethnicity and cultural context. The most famous and most-studied example is Gurinder Chadha's 2004 film *Bride and Prejudice,* which, Cheryl Wilson has noted, uses the Bollywood form to 'achieve a contemporary social critique which, incidentally, is not terribly different from Austen's own' (324). While scholars have written about global adaptations of Austen's novels, most particularly what Suchitra Mathur has described as examples (like *Bride and Prejudice*) of 'the colony "talking back" to the metropolis', this chapter focuses on the ways that race has been reseen or remixed (as one adaptation puts it) in several recent novels and short stories that have updated and recast *Pride and Prejudice.* Specifically, it examines the ways that writers of colour have used Austen's plots as an opportunity to explore racialised, gendered, and cultural identity within their communities in the early twenty-first century. Whether it is Ibi Zoboi's rendering of class tensions within a gentrifying African-American neighbourhood in *Pride: A Pride and Prejudice Remix*; clashes between conservatism and a more liberal reading of Muslim identity, especially as it pertains to women's life choices, in Uzma Jalaluddin's *Ayesha at Last*; the experience of second-generation Japanese Americans in Karen Tei Yamashita's *Sansei and Sensibility*; or limitations on women's lives and options in Pakistani society in Kamal's *Unmarriageable*, these novels use the framework of *Pride and Prejudice* to explore and resist social, religious, racial, gender, and class prejudice both within and towards communities of colour. If, as Stella Butter asserts, 'one of the factors that fuels Austen's popularity is the transformation of her work into a site for negotiating contemporary cultural identities' (167), *Pride and Prejudice,* the most frequently adapted text, opens up a space for articulating racialised cultural identities across a range of contexts.

While little critical work has been done yet on these texts, studies of Shakespeare and *Robinson Crusoe* adaptations offer a framework for understanding the cultural work that Kamal and others undertake in retelling *Pride and Prejudice.* Shakespeare's plays and *Robinson Crusoe* are canonical texts that have been adapted and rewritten in multiple settings and from a wide range of points of view. The subversive and revisionist power of these adaptations hinges on the status of these two authors in the Western canon. Shakespeare, in particular, is seen through the lens of literary greatness, as well as the primacy of white colonial rule. To recast Shakespeare from a postcolonial point of view is to direct the playwright's high culture status towards expressing local concerns. According to Sandra Young, this 'indigenisation' of Shakespeare's plays 'would seem to accord agency to local cultural forms which are imagined as powerfully reshaping the original into a form that is locally recognizable' (374).

Likewise, Defoe's *Robinson Crusoe* has offered a rich terrain for rewriting, so much so that its adaptations have their own genre designation, the Robinsonade. In describing postcolonial Robinsonades, such as J.M. Coetzee's *Foe* (1986) and Derek Walcott's *Pantomime* (1978), Andrew O'Malley underscores how the Robinsonade allows readers and authors 'to explore questions of identity' (xiv). Likewise, Ian Kinane sees the Robinsonade as engaging readers 'with contemporary socio-political and cultural issues, such as gender politics and postcolonial concerns' (1). Ann Marie Fallon points out that '[b]ecause *Robinson Crusoe* is often considered the first English novel, retelling it allows writers to create alternative histories of colonialism, racism, and other forms of oppression' (208). In other words, postcolonial authors have used the Robinsonade to reimagine and rewrite histories that have been dominated by the white Western perspective.

What connects the analyses of Shakespeare adaptations and Robinsonades to *Pride and Prejudice* is the flexibility of these firmly canonical texts' plots—and the advantages of their familiarity—in exploring new questions about identity, culture, and power relations through a racialised lens. Contemporary *Pride and Prejudice* rewrites by writers of colour are writing against the idealised

Race, Class, Gender Remixed

British cultural heritage version of Jane Austen, beloved symbol of white, middle-class womanhood. At the same time, choosing this highly canonical text offers a chance not only to draw on its cultural capital and boost sales, but also to make it their own and write themselves into the narrative. As Fallon points out in the case of Robinsonades, '[t]he references to *Robinson Crusoe* in these titles function as both marketing tool and touchstone' (208).

Retellings of *Pride and Prejudice* also use the plot framework to explore change in their heroines' communities, the choices available to them, and their relationship to community expectations. Most of all, the characters in these novels make racial and gender bias visible by illustrating the difference between how outsiders see them and their communities and their own identities. 'Prejudice' in the title takes on new meanings of racial, class, and gender prejudice, with 'pride' encompassing pride in community and one's identity. The characters demand to be seen for who they are, rather than through the lens of stereotypes. They negotiate their desire to be seen through personal relationships and through literary texts that are woven through all these novels, emphasising the acts of rewriting and revisioning. As Valentine Darsee tells Alys in *Unmarriageable*, 'We have been forced to see ourselves in the literature of others for too long' (136). The writers of colour discussed in this essay have used *Pride and Prejudice* as a framework for writing themselves and their protagonists into the larger culture.

Pride in racial identity and a community under siege takes centre stage in Ibi Zoboi's *Pride*, set in Bushwick, a working-class, black neighbourhood in Brooklyn. When an affluent family moves into the house across the street from the Benitez sisters, the Lizzie character, Zuri, sees it as an un-welcome gentrification that threatens her strong connection to her community. As she explains, 'For the last few months, construction crews have been giving that abandoned house an Extreme Makeover: Bushwick edition. They gutted and renovated the best thing on our block—that run-down, weed infested, boarded-up house. Now it looks like something that belongs in the suburbs, with its wide double doors, sparkling windows, and tiny manicured lawns' (1–2). Zuri objects to the change that this renovation represents for her neighbourhood, wanting to hold her block 'a little bit tighter and for a little bit longer, as if it's slowly slipping away' (14).

Gentrification and the erosion of community are not the only sources of tension for Zuri; the changes to her neighbourhood highlight class differences that go beyond those implied by gentrification. As they watch the new family arrive, the sisters take bets on whether it will be a white family, given the mini-mansion that has been constructed. When it turns out that the family is black, their arrival highlights class tensions in the black community. The new family includes two sheltered, private school-educated brothers, Ainsley and Darius Darcy. Much like Mr Darcy, Darius is unimpressed by the corner of Bushwick that Zuri holds so dear. Just as Darcy irritates Lizzy by dismissing her as 'not pretty enough to tempt me', Darius immediately angers Zuri by describing the move to Bushwick as 'an….adjustment' (9). In Zuri's eyes, his ellipses show that he considers the move to her neighbourhood as an adjustment because of the chasm between his social and economic position and that of his new neighbours. In his disdain for Bushwick, Zuri sees disdain for her and her sisters as well because they are rooted in the community.

As in many of these adaptations, romance—and certainly not marriage—are not the end goals of the story, although romance is a significant plot point. Zuri's main goal throughout the story is to be accepted at Howard University, and she devotes her creative attention to composing her application essay. At the same time, Zoboi's narrative uses the romance between Zuri and Darius to explore Zuri's attachment to her neighbourhood and her Haitian-Dominican roots—two elements that are inextricable from her sense of identity. The threat of change, critique, and gentrification that Darius and his family represent, bound up with her reluctant attraction for him, leads to a personal crisis, which she processes through poetry. In one poem, entitled 'How to Save the Hood', she describes wanting to 'steal the tight corners/Where hope meets certainty/To form perfectly chiseled bricks/Stacked high to make walls/Surrounding my Bushwick' (34). In these lines she expresses a desire for the certainty of knowing Bushwick, which she identifies with hope, will never change, and she wants to use 'perfectly chiseled bricks' to form a wall around her community to keep out new-comers who will bring change. As Viet Thanh Nguyen has written, 'The appearance of the white hipster in neighbourhoods that white people abandoned long ago reminds the current residents that they don't truly own where they live. Their lives are subject to economic forces they don't control and to the desires of people wealthier than they are' (6). Although the Darcy family is black, their appearance in the neighbourhood, and the changes that it signals, show Zuri how powerless she is to prevent the more wealthy and powerful from transforming it.

Her affection for Bushwick takes in and savours all the elements that someone like Darius would see as scruffy or 'sketchy', racialised markers for black neighbourhoods. She describes the process of gentrification as losing what gives the neighbourhood character:

> I don't see any more homeless pets
> Like the ones that used to gather
> In the junkyard on Wyckoff Avenue
> Beneath the overhead train tracks
> Like marks on the arms of junkies
> Who used to stumble down Knickerbocker
> Boxing the air, fighting the wind
> Suckerpunching a time
> When those graffiti-covered walls
> Used to be background canvases
> For old ladies in house slippers
> Pushing squeaky shopping carts
> Around tight corners
> Where hope meets certainty (34–35)

The old ladies in house slippers, the junkies, and the homeless pets are all part of the backdrop of home for her, and she wants to hold onto the Bushwick that she loves 'where hope meets certainty'. For Zuri, gentrification is a threat to whiten up this neighbourhood and make families like hers—black, poor, and deeply comfortable in their own sense of self and community—unwelcome. Rather than seeking the elevation in economic and social status that Jane and Lizzie achieve in *Pride and Prejudice,* Zoboi uses the novel's framework to explore the tight connections between gentri-fication and losing a black community's identity.

On the other hand, *Ayesha at Last* by Uzma Jalaluddin explores the cultural conflict within a Muslim community in Toronto. Ayesha, an immigrant from India, wears the hijab and stays closely connected to her neighbourhood mosque, but she also avoids and criticises those in her community who take part in and organise *rishtas*, the formal meetings between two potential marriage partners who have already been carefully vetted by each other's parents. The question for her is how to reconcile her independence with her attachment to the community and faith in Islam. She is caught in between, as she puts it, 'Part of both worlds, yet part of neither' (6). Like Zuri, she is also a poet and finds poetry an outlet for exploring her identity. She does not know what to do with her life, especially having just graduated from teachers' college, in debt, and hating her first job as a substitute teacher. She is filled with uncertainty about what she wants to do and be, but she is also certain about her commitment to Islam *and* to independence.

While Ayesha struggles to reconcile her desire for independence with community expectations, Khalid, the Darcy character, must learn to reconcile his strict adherence to Muslim practices with a hostile workplace. Khalid encounters friction from his decidedly non-inclusive boss because of his traditional attire, including a full-length robe, skullcap, and beard, and his refusal to shake hands with women. He resists compromise, even if it would make his life easier, because he 'had long ago decided to be honest about who he was: an observant Muslim man who walked with faith both outwardly and inwardly' (14).

Prejudice in *Ayesha at Last* takes many forms, but in particular it emerges in the first impressions that each character's outward appearance suggests to the other. When Khalid first sees Ayesha, she is at a 'lounge' that a friend has dragged her to because there's an open mic poetry event. Already annoyed by what she thinks of as 'veil chasers', i.e., men who take her hijab as a romantic challenge, she is incensed by Khalid who, like Darcy, refuses to be introduced to her, although in this case it is because of his strict religious conservatism. As he tells his friend, 'I stay away from the type of Muslim who frequents bars' (40). Ayesha is infuriated by the gendered double-standard that this represents—i.e., that a female Muslim in bars is offensive, while it is acceptable for him to be there.

Ayesha processes her response to Khalid's words through a spontaneous poem that she recites to the crowd:

> What do you see
> When you think of me,
> A figure cloaked in mystery
> With eyes down-cast and hair covered,
> An oppressed woman yet to be discovered?
> Do you see backward nations and swirling sand,
> Humpbacked camels and the domineering man?
> Whirling veils and terrorists
> Or maybe fanatic fundamentalists? (42)

In these lines, she lists stereotypes about Islamic women as oppressed victims, forced to stay behind a veil, and Islamic men as domineering, backward terrorists and fundamentalists. 'What do you see/ When you think of me' suggests that the observer does not really see her, but rather conjures up a series of stereotypes. She invokes the way outsiders see women in the hijab as a 'mystery', or a void, that they fill with their assumptions that she is oppressed and waiting to be 'discovered' by them. The language of discovery conjures up images of 'unexplored' continents that colonising nations long saw themselves as discovering, despite the presence of inhabitants who had lived there for centuries. Women wearing the hijab, Ayesha tells her audience, are considered unconquered territory to observers steeped in cultural stereotypes about the exoticism and oppression of the Muslim faith.

In her next stanza, she demands to be seen as herself and asserts that the inability to see beyond stereotypes says more about the observer than the observed.

> Yet...
> You fail to see
> The dignified persona
> Of a woman wrapped in maturity.
> The scarf on my head
> Does not cover my brain.
> I think, I speak, but still you refrain

From accepting my ideals, my type of dress,
You refuse to believe
That I am not oppressed.
So the question remains:
What do I see when I think of you?
I see another human being
Who doesn't have a clue. (42–43)

Looking directly at Khalid while she recites, Ayesha uses this poem to pour out her frustration with the assumptions that people make about her because of her appearance. These assumptions keep them from seeing her as she is, dignified, mature, thoughtful. These observers likewise do not consider what she thinks of them based on their inability to see past her hijab. Although Khalid and Ayesha wind up together at the end of the novel, they both have to learn to see beyond their outward appearance and understand the complexity of each other's identity and connection to the Muslim faith.

Also drawing on ideas of community and identity, Karen Tei Yamashita's short story collection, *Sansei and Sensibility* (2020), uses Jane Austen's novels as a framework to represent the experiences of sansei, Japanese Americans whose grandparents immigrated to the United States. The stories are set in 1960s Southern California and completely rewrite each of Austen's novels (including *Lady Susan*) while keeping to their essential framework. Sansei, Yamashita makes clear, live with a sense of cultural dislocation, as well as the inherited trauma from their parents' generation's (the niseis') experience of internment camps and incarceration during World War II. As Yamashita explained in an interview, she's capturing her own early years in Southern California during a time when 'our parents and our community were trying to start their lives again after the war, but they didn't talk to their children about what happened during the war—that they had been interned and incarcerated' (Westenfeld par. 6). Their parents' silence about their experiences during the war, along with their determination to move past it, left sansei surrounded by trauma that they did not fully understand. Yamashita chose this setting because she wanted to write about a time right before the Asian American movement of the 1970s, when '[w]e lived in a very confined and provincial space in which our social contracts and our relationships were all contained within the Japanese American community. I liken that to Jane Austen's milieu' (Westenfeld par. 7).

Set in this tightly knit community of Japanese Americans, 'Giri and Gaman' recasts the characters of *Pride and Prejudice* as high school students. The story's title comes from the Japanese concept of duty or obligation (giri) and patience and endurance under adversity (gaman), which directly relates to the sansei sense of inherited trauma and the silence and stoicism of their parents' generation. The community where the characters in this story live is small and insular: 'this was a suburb gerry-mandered by nisei real estate brokers turned politicians; it was, well, let's say, postcamp, a safe place where sansei had the opportunity to grow up in camp without being in camp' (124). In other words, nisei carved out this section of the city to allow their children to grow up in the kind of isolated community that the internment camps represented but transformed it into a space where they could protect their families.

Rather than searching for advantageous marriages, the quest in this community is more tightly knit to identity. Like Kamal's *Unmarriageable*, Yamashita's story begins with a rewriting of Austen's opening line, changing it to 'The truth of the matter is that despite what you may think, sansei do have a sense of humor' (123), omitting Austen's reference to either marriage or a 'good fortune'. This rewriting reflects a feeling of being misunderstood as sansei, that they do have a sense of humour, despite the atmosphere of sadness and silence that permeates their community. Strikingly, this rewriting of the opening line erases the question of marriage and economics entirely and re-places it with a different ethos connected to sansei experience. There is some slippage, however,

Race, Class, Gender Remixed

about who it is who holds this misconception, and Yamashita's narrator suggests that sansei are equally unsure about who they are and what they are supposed to be. As the narrator explains:

> growing up sansei was very confusing. Fortunately no one has to do this again. Your parents' generation, the nisei, were generally closed-mouthed, diffident people who had been burned big-time. Everything that should have been obvious about American society and its promises of freedom and the future was on a standby basis, depending on you. And everything the nisei passed on to sansei was unspoken innuendo about what kind of people you were supposed to grow up to be. (209)

What the nisei generation had learned in the experience of the internment camps and anti-Japanese racism was that the promise of American society could be taken away at any moment. When the country turned on them, they had been 'burned big-time'. For sansei, their parents' reluctance to describe these experiences and explain what they had taken away from it caused deep confusion. In a community of silence and innuendo, sansei learn that 'freedom' in the United States is contingent on following unspoken rules that they had to figure out on their own.

On the edges of this community are outsiders who see the sansei as objects of study whose story they can tell for them—and thus control the narrative. The sansei high school students are treated as source material by their high school principal, Miss Catherine Borg, and the school librarian, Mr Collins. Borg is a YA (young adult) author who writes under the pseudonym C. Borg, and she has decided to locate her most recent novel in Japan, a country she has never visited. Instead of doing research on the country, however, she decides to send Mr Collins to spy on the students to gather information because, in her mind, capturing the social lives of sansei is the same as researching Japan. She's hoping for scandalous behaviour and is disappointed when Mr Collins fails to gather anything more exciting than some students smoking in the bathroom. What makes his task impossible is that 'these were well-behaved Japanese Americans as featured in *Time* magazine, still corralled in a cultural bubble that C. Borg meant to appropriate before the onslaught of pot, reds, LSD, sex, and rock "n" roll' (128). This 'cultural bubble' is a product of the nisei 'gerrymandering' of the neighbourhood to create a protected space.

While the story includes plenty of flirting amongst the characters, and the Lizzy and Darcy characters begin by disliking each other, romance is not the culmination of this story. Lizzy and Darcy discover the tape recorder that Mr Collins has planted under a bench and stage a false romantic conversation in Japanese. Their relationship goes no further, however, and the story ends with Lizzy skipping prom and going to the movies with her father. In fact, most of Yamashita's rewritings in this collection conclude with anti-romantic endings where the main characters are pursuing their own lives without any concern for the character who is their love match in Austen's version. In the afterword, Yamashita speculates on the nature of romance in Austen novels, declaring that it is:

> a romance without romanticism; it's antiromantic, all about calculating your chances to make the right choice, which for most of the characters, except the heroine, is the wrong choice. Marriage is like [making] marmalade—you could miss 220 [degrees] and reject Mr Knightley or Mr Darcy or Captain Wentworth, and, well, c'est la vie. (208)

As Yamashita describes it, Austen's novels are not romantic, and the marriages are the result of calculations that can go awry. The outcome for the characters in Yamashita's stories is the opportunity to pursue their own desires alongside their commitment to their community.

This chapter has gestured towards the potential critical work to be done in accounting for reworkings of Austen's plots in communities of colour. For many of these authors, *Pride and Prejudice* is a means for reclaiming and positioning people of colour in the canon and in the lineage of one of the best-loved novels. Further, as I have argued, *Pride and Prejudice* as a novel offers a framework for thinking about communities in transition, gender roles, and racialised tensions.

Alongside the novels discussed above, Corrie Garrett, a white writer, takes up the issue of un-documented immigration in her self-published novel *Pride and Prejudice and Passports*. This novel focuses on a mixed-status Mexican-American family living in California. The parents are un-documented, the eldest daughter (Noa) is DACAmented, and the younger daughters are U.S. ci-tizens because they were born after their parents immigrated. The Bingley character—Ben Lee—is a Republican politician, and Darcy, who heads a Republican political action committee, is concerned about Ben's political future. The novel is told through Elisa's (Lizzie's) point of view and offers the family's story in the context of immigration reform, inviting sympathy for the family's vulnerable immigration status. Ben's and Darcy's relationships with Noa and Elisa cause them to rethink their opposition to immigration reform.

Garrett uses the narrative framework of *Pride and Prejudice* to educate readers and argue for immigration reform. At the same time, her representation of the experiences of a Latinx family raises uncomfortable questions and directly relates to the preceding discussion about who gets to tell which stories. Recent critical conversations have questioned whether and how white writers should assume the perspective of people of colour in their work and when it ranges into cultural appropriation. Issues of cultural appropriation and authenticity have been highlighted recently by Jeanine Cummins's novel *American Dirt*, which has been sharply criticised for trading in stereotypes about Mexican culture and Cummins's claims to be speaking for the voiceless. While part of the craft of writing is to imagine people other than oneself, the use of communities of colour as subjects for fiction is particularly fraught when non-white writers are underrepresented in the publishing in-dustry. As Nguyen has argued, 'It is possible to write about one not like oneself, if one understands that it is not simply an act of culture and free speech but one that is enmeshed in a complicated, painful history of ownership and division that needs to be addressed responsibly—that is to say, with great artistry—in one's own writing' (6). In other words, authors who write experiences and points of view outside their own have to acknowledge the complicated history the act engages in and the extra work required to do it thoughtfully and responsibly. While Garrett's reliance on self-publishing indicates that she has also struggled to make her voice heard in the publishing industry, her use of Latinx characters nevertheless raises the issue of owning one's story, especially when Latinx writers feel shut out of publishing in the United States. The #OwnVoices and #digni-dadliteraria movements have emerged to advocate for writers from marginalised communities being heard and telling their own stories.

The novels discussed in this essay are part of a larger conversation about making space for writers of colour, representation, and cultural capital, alongside the impulse to use fiction as a means to create understanding in readers. In a moment when our fractured political landscape has revealed that there is a wide swath of the public that does not see people of colour as individuals, but rather as invaders, criminals, and disease carriers, there is a real need to make space for and amplify texts representing diverse points of view. The #OwnVoices movement calls for writers from marginalised communities to write their own stories and for the publishing industry to publish more writers of colour. As this essay has suggested, works by writers of colour that revise and remix Austen's novels open up opportunities for new voices and new stories. As Nguyen puts it, for many years

> the job was easier for white writers who could get published and say anything they wanted about anyone. Now those people who were written about are writing back and speaking out. They demand a conversation, they criticise, and sometimes they are too sensitive. But they are not silencing anyone. The ones who are truly silenced are the ones who cannot get published. (6)

Race, Class, Gender Remixed

Retelling Austen's novels has provided both the cultural capital to find a place in the publishing industry and a useful framework for making space for new voices and points of view.

Works Cited

Butter, Stella. 'Jane Austen Meets Bollywood: Forms and Functions of Transcultural Adaptations.' *Pride and Prejudice 2.0: Interpretations, Adaptations and Transformations of Jane Austen's Classic*, edited by Hanne Birk and Marion Gymnich. Vandenhoeck & Ruprecht, 2015, pp. 167–188.

Chadha, Gurinder. *Bride & Prejudice*. Miramax Home Entertainment Distributed by Buena Vista Home Entertainment, 2005.

Cummins, Jeanine. *American Dirt*. Flatiron Books, 2020

Fallon, Ann Marie. 'Anti-Crusoes, Alternative Crusoes: Revisions of the Island Story in the Twentieth Century.' *The Cambridge Companion to Robinson Crusoe*, edited by John Richetti. Cambridge UP, 2018, pp. 207–220.

Garrett, Corrie. *Pride and Prejudice and Passports: A Modern Retelling*. Kindle Direct Publishing, 2018.

Jalaluddin, Uzma. *Ayesha at Last*. Berkley, 2019.

Kamal, Soniah. *Unmarriageable: Pride and Prejudice in Pakistan*. Allison and Busby, 2019.

Kinane, Ian. 'Introduction: The Robinsonade Genre and the Didactic Impulse: A Reassessment.' *Didactics and the Modern Robinsonade*, edited by Ian Kinane. Liverpool UP, 2019, pp. 1–52.

Looser, Devoney. *The Making of Jane Austen*. Johns Hopkins UP, 2017.

Luetkenhaus, Holly, and Zoe Weinstein. *Austentatious: The Evolving World of Austen Fans*. U of Iowa P, 2019.

Mathur, Suchitra. 'From British "Pride" to Indian "Bride": Mapping the Contours of a Globalised (Post?)Colonialism.' *M/C Journal*, vol. 10, no. 2, 2007. http://journal.media-culture.org.au/0705/06-mathur.php. Accessed 15 Mar. 2020.

Nguyen, Viet Thanh. 'The Appropriation of Culture: Fights over Pho, Music and Writing across Race Have Deep Roots in Our Unequal Past. How to Move Forward?' *Los Angeles Times* 2 Oct. 2016: F6. *ProQuest Historical Newspapers*. https://www-proquest-com.proxy.lib.umich.edu/newspapers/book-review-appropriation-culture-fights-over-pho/docview/1824953174/se-2?accountid=14667. Accessed 2 Jun. 2020.

Stovel, Nora Foster. 'Welcome to the Twenty-First Century!: Modernising Jane Austen in the HarperCollins Project.' *After Austen: Reinventions, Rewritings, Revisitings*, edited by Lisa Hopkins. Switzerland: Palgrave Macmillan, 2018, pp. 105–125. *ProQuest Ebook Central*. https://ebookcentral-proquest-com.proxy.lib.umich.edu/lib/umichigan/detail.action?docID=5598631. Accessed 15 May 2020.

Westenfeld, Adrienne. 'Karen Tei Yamashita Wants to Know What Happened to the Servants in Jane Austen's Novels.' *Esquire.com* 31 May 2020. https://www.esquire.com/entertainment/books/a32711261/karen-tei-yamashita-sansei-and-sensibility-jane-austen-interview. Accessed 3 Jun. 2020.

Wilson, Cheryl A. '*Bride and Prejudice*: A Bollywood Comedy of Manners.' *Literature/Film Quarterly*, vol. 34, no. 4, 2006, pp. 323–331.

Yaffe, Deborah. *Among the Janeites: A Journey through the World of Jane Austen Fandom*. Mariner, 2013.

Yamashita, Karen Tei. *Sansei and Sensibility*. Coffee House P, 2020.

Young, Sandra. 'Beyond Indigenisation: *Hamlet, Haider*, and the Pain of the Kashmiri People.' *Shakespeare*, vol. 14, no. 4, 2018, pp. 374–389. doi: 10.1080/17450918.2017.1351486

Zoboi, Ibi. *Pride: A Pride and Prejudice Remix*. Balzer + Bray, 2018.

37

WRITING COMMUNITY: SOME THOUGHTS ABOUT JANE AUSTEN FANFICTION

Melanie Borrego

BRANDMAN UNIVERSITY

As everyone who has read Deborah Yaffe's *Among the Janeites* knows, the Jane Austen Society of North America (JASNA) holds a national conference each year. This conference is uncommon in academic circles because it is composed of both scholars and fans. The day before the conference officially begins there are additional workshops that teach Georgian and Regency-era games, crafts, and dances. There are those who attend strictly as sharp-eyed anthropologists of Austen, her time, and the other participants. They are juxtaposed against those who give themselves over to the fan experience entirely, including wearing period clothing and attending the Saturday night ball. Most fall somewhere in between. It is an academic conference where the boundaries between scholar and fan are unusually porous. Positioned along these boundaries are the many works of fiction inspired by Austen's work, known broadly as Jane Austen Fan Fiction, or JAFF.

Each year at this conference, I hear someone ask a version of the following questions: 'Why would anyone want to rewrite Jane Austen? What's the point?' They then declare, 'They are ruining her work. It will never be better than Jane'. The answer to these inquiries is complex, but it begins with some simple facts. First, borrowing characters and plots from previous works to create a new story is a long-standing practice among writers—William Shakespeare was a master of the craft. More particularly, the strength of Austen's characters and yet the sparse attention to some portions of her stories that modern readers desire or even expect to see leaves those spaces in the text ripe for fanfiction authors.

What, precisely, *is* fanfiction? It is a loaded question. As Juliette Wells diplomatically points out in her book *Everybody's Jane*, definitions of fanfiction 'do not always coincide' (J. Wells 178). There are many who claim only work that remains unpublished and free deserves the title. Wells points to Sheenaugh Pugh's broader definition, however, as most relevant to those studying Austen: 'writing, whether official or unofficial, paid or unpaid, which makes use of an accepted canon of characters, settings and plots generated by another author or writers' (qtd. in J. Wells 178).

Pugh's definition of fanfiction encompasses writing that borrows from but does not necessarily admire its source material. These works often attempt to respond to or elucidate a part of the story that seems incomplete, culture-blind, or simply out of tune with current mores. Some of these works are written by established authors, and many take minor characters from an established text to give them their own narrative. For example, Jean Rhys' 1966 *Wide Sargasso Sea* might be termed a fanfiction in the sense that it uses Charlotte Brontë's 'canon of characters' to give the marginalised Bertha Antoinetta Mason her own voice. It quite stunningly and comprehensively turns the original narrative on its head.

490

DOI: 10.4324/9780429398155-37-42

This creative impulse to explore gaps in the original text is very common in fanfiction, though of course Rhys' masterful writing sets her novel apart from much of fanfiction's more amateur efforts. She is hardly the only well-known author, however, who has felt compelled to fill in the details of a minor character or characters from another story. For example, in Tom Stoppard's 1996 *Rosencrantz and Guildenstern Are Dead*, he pens a philosophical script for two minor characters who are pawns of the royal family in Shakespeare's *Hamlet*. John Gardner's 1971 *Grendel* offers the villain of *Beowulf* his own novel. Jo Baker's *Longbourn* undermines the narrative of *Pride and Prejudice*'s Elizabeth Bennet; the book is written about and from the perspective of the servants, several of whom are obliquely referred to in Austen's novel.

As Holly Luetkenhaus and Zoe Weinstein claim in the opening chapter of *Austentatious*, 'Fans want to be involved … But fans want *more*. They want to be the creator. And so they … have taken the text into their own hands' (19). No matter the strength of the canonical text, there are always parts of the story missing that a reader may wish to know. When the original narrative is as compelling as Austen's, the reader often wishes to keep reading, to remain in the world the author has imagined. However, Austen died at 41—the books we have, in the format we have them, will never change.

Austen was not much for descriptive detail unless it was essential for the story—readers are never told what Elizabeth Bennet looks like beyond the 'beautiful expression of her dark eyes' and the reference to her 'light and pleasing' figure (*PP* 42). Mr Darcy is a 'fine, tall person', with 'handsome features', and has a 'noble mien' (*PP* 16). In *Persuasion*, readers are never privy to Anne and Wentworth's first engagement or the details of how it was broken. In *Sense and Sensibility*, readers do not witness the duel between Colonel Brandon and John Willoughby. If readers want to fill in the scenes that have stirred their curiosity, or if they simply wish for more time with their favourite characters, they must look to other writers or create those stories themselves. The development of Internet communities as repositories for fan production, including Jane Austen-specific sites such as The Republic of Pemberley's Bits of Ivory, Beyond Austen, The Derbyshire Writers Guild (Dwiggie), DarcyAndLizzy, and A Happy Assembly (also known as The Meryton Assembly), has simply expanded opportunities for individual fans to connect with one another; what had long been more or less a local endeavour now has a consistently international reach. Therefore, the visibility of fanfic, along with other expressions of fan devotion, has increased exponentially, encouraging many nascent writers to engage with Austen's texts.

However, the Jane Austen fandom began long before the Internet or Colin Firth's Mr Darcy rose from a pond and encountered Elizabeth Bennet in an embarrassing state of dishabille. The term 'Janeite' was coined by George Saintsbury more than one hundred years earlier in his Preface to the 1894 edition of *Pride and Prejudice*. In it, he used two Walt Whitman terms to explain what had already been made apparent: that Jane Austen was among those few authors who were not 'loved by allowance' but instead by 'personal love' (Saintsbury ix). Given the way in which Austen's novels have been performed on stage, adapted for television and films, turned into year-long transmedia events, and yes, spun into thousands of fanfics, the 'personal love' of readers for Jane Austen that Saintsbury identified does not appear to have faded.

The continuing interest in Jane Austen's life and work following her death resulted in James Edward Austen-Leigh's *A Memoir of Jane Austen: And Other Family Recollections* (originally published in 1869 and again in a revised edition in 1871). In it, he explained that Austen continued to think about her characters even after her books were published. In fact, if Austen-Leigh is to be believed, Austen indulged her family by fashioning 'after-stories' for some of them. Of course, even if Austen herself did not assign these fates to her characters, Austen-Leigh has—thereby demonstrating, at the least, an awareness of his readers' desires to remain within the Austen universe beyond the conclusions of the novels themselves.

We learned that Miss Steele never succeeded in catching the doctor, that Kitty Bennet was satisfactorily married to a clergyman near Pemberley, while Mary obtained nothing higher than one of her uncle Philips's clerks, and was content to be considered a star in the society of Meriton (sic); that the 'considerable sum' given by Mrs Norris to William Price was one pound; that Mr Woodhouse survived his daughter's marriage, and kept her and Mr Knightley from settling at Donwell about two years; and that the letters placed by Frank Churchill before Jane Fairfax, which she swept away, unread, contained the word, 'pardon'. (Austen-Leigh)

There is some evidence, however, that supports the veracity of Austen-Leigh's claims, because Austen herself did imagine her characters leading lives outside of her novels. In a letter dated May 24, 1813, she was pleased to tell her sister Cassandra that she had located a portrait of *Pride and Prejudice*'s Mrs Bingley at an exhibition in Spring Gardens:

Mrs Bingley's [portrait] is exactly herself,—size, shaped face, features, and sweetness; there was never a greater likeness. She is dressed in a white gown, with green ornaments, which convinces me of what I had always supposed, that green was a favorite color with her. I dare say Mrs D. will be in yellow. (Brothers 190)

Later in the same letter, she had to admit that she had been unable to locate a portrait of 'Mrs D.' although she had searched for one:

Monday evening.—We have been both to the exhibition and Sir J. Reynolds'; and I am disappointed, for there was nothing like Mrs D. at either. I can only imagine that Mr D. prizes any picture of her too much to like it should [it] be exposed to the public eye. I can imagine he would have that sort of feeling,—that mixture of love, pride, and delicacy. (Brothers 193)

When Austen herself ruminates so deliciously about her characters in this letter, it cannot be surprising that her readers, particularly those who feel and demonstrate that 'personal love' Saintsbury mentions, might wish to do the same.

Although one of the earliest pieces of published JAFF was *Old Friends and New Fancies*, written by Sybil Grace Brinton in 1913, Emily Friedman of Auburn University explained in a 2017 JASNA presentation that there was a culture of fanfiction occurring in a tradition of 'circulated manuscripts', some of them very finely done with hand-drawn, coloured illustrations. These texts remained in the private domain and have been largely, but not completely, lost to posterity. Given the strong interest in Jane Austen's novels, and as relatively inexpensive copies had been available since at least 1833 (Barchas), it is not difficult to imagine that some of those circulated manuscripts may have been early versions of Austen fanfiction.

With contemporary JAFF narratives numbering in the thousands, we do not have to imagine the kind of creative production occurring around Austen's books today. In addition to the Austen-focused fanfiction sites, there are a number of fanfiction sites online of which Austen fanfics are a part, such as fanfiction.com, wattpad.com, and Archive of Our Own. In terms of published books, Meredith Esparza at Austenesque Reviews keeps a running tally and the most recent completed list for 2019 (Part One) has 193 published titles for *Pride and Prejudice* variations alone. Why are so many people reading and writing fanfic in general and JAFF in particular? There are many reasons, but one of the most important comes, Anne Jamison claims, from Austen herself.

Jane Austen … makes the stakes clear in *Persuasion*: when men are the only ones telling the story, only certain stories get told … Online fan communities evolved to give as much space as possible to all the different stories people wanted to tell. (Jamison 156)

Writing fanfiction, particularly with the more immediate response of an online audience, offers fans of a text an important opportunity. It allows, even encourages, those who may not normally consider themselves writers to create the stories they not only want but often need to tell. Austen's world is made up of characters who are primarily well-off if not wealthy, Anglican, and white. While many readers today have fallen in love with that world, they cannot imagine themselves there. Through fanfic, they stake a position in this universe they have grown to love, even if they must consciously write themselves into it.

There are many examples of this in JAFF. A few include AmyA's paired short stories 'Love Across the Ages' and 'Christmas Eve Through the Ages', which depicts a modern interracial romance set against the backstory of a white Darcy in love with an African American Elizabeth in 1912. The 1912 couple do not marry—Elizabeth instead goes on to become a suffragist; Darcy marries a society wife. Riana Everly's published fanfic *Through a Different Lens* is a *Pride and Prejudice* story about autism. Because one of Elizabeth's Gardiner nephews is on the spectrum (these modern phrases are not used), she recognises Darcy's inability to 'read' the emotions of others and offers to help him learn. Elizabeth Bennet is an Irish dancer suffering from lupus in the 'BernadetteE' Austen mashup of all the novels, 'An Even Path' (currently offline for editing). Daniella Harwood's 'Marry in Haste, Repent at Leisure', explores issues of domestic abuse (Elizabeth is married off against her will a few years before the Meryton Assembly).

A number of stories also have characters who must hide their sexual preferences. One is Linda Wells' epic Work in Progress (WIP), the WWII-era 'Keeping Calm', in which Anne de Bourgh and Charlotte Collins begin a romantic relationship while Mr Collins is away at war. 'Connections Redux' by HarveyS, depicts Darcy's great uncle, a duke, whose valet has been his lover for nearly twenty years. While none of the younger men in his family are precisely comfortable with the knowledge, they do not condemn him. In L.L. Diamond's fanfic novel *Undoing*, the Duke of Leeds marries Elizabeth Bennet in part to hide a long-standing sexual relationship with his valet. In many of these fanfics, then, writers use characters with whom readers are comfortable in order to restore visibility to relationships and identities that have been historically erased.

A Happy Assembly, like other Austen-specific fanfiction sites, seeks to foster a fan community, not only to exist as a repository for fanfic. The site has promoted group readings of Austen's texts, where a comment thread is set up and members read the same chapters each week before participating in the discussions. There are introduction forums and forums where members can arrange to meet in real life (IRL). There is also a forum that encourages historical questions and education. Conversations here range from items such as the recent discovery of the Matthew Tomlinson journal (Couglin) to the details of inheritance laws and even the likely location or locations of Mr Darcy's London home. Answers often require a great deal of research through primary documents such as newspapers, letters, drawings, books, and maps from the early 1800s. Members do the work to answer these questions simply because they are interested in the topic. Their reward, in many cases, is that the historical details which most interest them appear in future stories.

There are benefits to the writer as well. Writing is generally done in isolation, with little feedback from readers until the entire manuscript is written, edited, and put on the market, generally a year or so after it has left the author's hands. The ability to receive reader feedback immediately is a real draw for authors posting stories, but the way in which that feedback is delivered is also crucial. At AHA (A Happy Assembly) the comment threads are monitored. Comments must be positive—all criticism must be about the story and it must be constructive—the site rules require that more specific critiques be sent via private message directly to the author, and that critics think carefully before they send. In this kind of an environment, new writers are bound to flourish. In some ways, then, the writing of fanfic is larger than Austen. In others, particularly in the rare sense of community building that can be found in both in the novels and the Austen fandom, writers of JAFF are exactly where they feel safest in a world that is often dismissive of or even hostile to them.

This reflects the kind of community that exists in Austen's own novels. While there are female antagonists in each novel, there are also communities of women, often family but also friends and acquaintances, who support the heroines. Mrs Smith and Nurse Rooke's penchant for what is revealed to be rather useful gossip in *Persuasion* comes to mind. In *Pride and Prejudice*, Charlotte Lucas is the first to notice that Mr Darcy does not appear to disapprove of her friend and is also the presumably unintentional agent of their reunion in Kent. Emma assists Mrs and Miss Bates, and by extension Jane Fairfax. She believes she is supporting Harriet Smith in her search for a husband, though her efforts amount, in the end, to little more than ineffectual interference. It is not difficult to see that those who are attracted to these kinds of communities might also be interested in helping to build them.

Legally, Austen's books are in the public domain, which must account for some portion of her popularity among fanfiction writers, but there does seem to be a sense among many Austen purists that to engage in writing fanfiction is to engage in some sort of theft. Instead, the predominantly women writers of JAFF engage in the same sort of complicated community building that occurs in Austen's novels, because the culture and experience of contemporary women (and many men) around the world is not yet entirely divorced from the situations of dependency that populate the canonical texts. How better to challenge that paradigm than using Austen's work as a platform for or even a springboard to texts of their own?

Fanfic is often derided for the quality of its writing, but I would suggest that such concerns are not the primary concern of the genre, and that readers of those books will serve as the natural arbiters of excellence. As an instructor of undergraduate writers, I am instead rather awed by the kind of organic education taking place in the Austen fandom. Like the communities of women in Austen's novels, fanfic writers and readers work together in an excellent example of what Henry Jenkins has called 'participatory culture' (Jenkins 7). Amber Nicole Pfannenstiel, a professor of digital literacy at Millersville University, explains that 'Co-creation allows both authors and readers to participate in the use of a familiar narrative to work through complex cultural ideas. This is why I think fanfiction is so pervasive, it feels both comfortable and empowering at the same time' (Pfannenstiel). That comfort and empowerment is created through a recursive process over which readers have a voice, but the author has ultimate control. For instance, many writers will stipulate in an Author's Note (AN or A/N) what level of critique they desire. Often, an AN will tell readers that the story was written 'for fun' and should not be taken seriously, or explains that English is the author's second, third, or fourth language and offers apologies in advance for any errors. On the other end of the spectrum, an author might ask for historical critique or grammar notes because there are eventual plans to publish.

The writing ecosystem in JAFF makes peer review in a college classroom look nothing short of artificial. Writers have 'betas', other fanfic community members, who read and edit each chapter of the story before it is posted. They are generally reading serially, but ahead of the main audience. The writer accepts or does not accept the feedback, makes the changes she wishes, and posts. Concurrently, each chapter has a comment thread where readers can offer their thoughts on the characters, the plot, the writing, and where they often speculate about where the story might take them next. Often those posting have side conversations about the story without requiring any input from the author. For those who intend to publish, once the entire manuscript is finished, there are generally one or two 'cold readers'. These are editors or other authors who read the now-completed manuscript for continuity issues and plot holes. All of this is done voluntarily, in a communal process of creating the best possible tale. Readers who frequent the comment threads become closer, more analytical readers. Writers cannot help but improve their craft in such a system, even if they never intend to publish at all.

Writing Community

The numerous film and web adaptations of Austen's novels continue to bring new readers to her work, and those readers often make their way to JAFF sites. Many of them are inspired to write fanfic themselves. Are all JAFF stories well-written? No, but many are. Do they disrespect Austen or honour her? JAFF is born out of the 'personal love' so many feel for Jane Austen's stories and characters—while that love might not always be sophisticated or scholarly, it is difficult to see it as disrespect. Were Austen alive today, she would likely say something wickedly witty about fanfiction writers, the good and the bad, and then enquire about her percentage of the royalties.

Why would anyone want to rewrite Jane Austen's novels? When handled in the way A Happy Assembly has done, the Austen fandom and its fanfiction can echo the kind of communities that Austen depicted with honest appraisal and affectionate, though sometimes biting, humour—where none of us are perfect, but we are trying to be better, where those who were invisible can write themselves into visibility, and where those who seek to challenge the limitations of their culture or society can do so through the written word.

Works Cited

Amy, A. 'Christmas Across the Ages.' *A Happy Assembly*, 24 Dec. 2017. https://meryton.com/aha/index.php?/topic/18940-christmas-eve-across-the-ages/

Amy, A. 'Love Across the Ages.' *A Happy Assembly*, 12 Dec. 2017. https://meryton.com/aha/index.php?/topic/18895-love-across-the-ages-rated-t-complete/

Austen, Jane. *Emma*, edited by David Shapard. Anchor Books, 2012.

Austen, Jane. *Persuasion*, edited by David Shapard. Anchor Books, 2010.

Austen, Jane. *Pride and Prejudice*, edited by David Shapard. Anchor Books, 2012.

Austen, Jane. *Sense and Sensibility*, edited by David Shapard. Anchor Books, 2011.

Austen-Leigh, James Edward. *A Memoir of Jane Austen: And Other Family Recollections*, edited by Kathryn Sutherland, Kindle ed., Oxford UP, 2002.

Baker, Jo. *Longbourn*. Vintage, 2013.

Barchas, Janine. *The Lost Books of Jane Austen*. Kindle ed., Johns Hopkins UP, 2019.

Brothers, Roberts, editor. *The Novels of Jane Austen: Lady Susan; The Watsons; A Memoir; Letters*. Cambridge, USA: John Wilson and Son, 1892.

Coughlan, Sean. 'The 200-Year-Old Diary that's Rewriting Gay History.' *BBC News* 10 Feb. 2020. https://www.bbc.com/news/education-51385884

Diamond, L.L. *Undoing*. L.L. Diamond, Mar. 27 2020.

Esparza, Meredith. 'Pride and Prejudice Releases for 2019, Part One.' *Austenesque Reviews: Jane Austen Book Blog* 13 Mar. 2020. https://austenesquereviews.com/2020/03/pride-and-prejudice-releases-for-2019-part-1-a-comprehensive-guide.html

Everly, Riana. *Through a Different Lens*. Bay Crest P, 2019.

Friedman, Emily. 'Jane Austen, Fangirl: Austen Among the Amateur Authors.' Jane Austen Society of North America Association Annual General Meeting, The Hyatt Regency, Huntington Beach, California. 6 Oct. 2017. Conference Presentation.

Gardner, John. *Grendel*. Vintage, 1998.

Harvey, S. 'Connections Redux.' *A Happy Assembly*, 26 Dec. 2009. https://meryton.com/aha/index.php?/topic/5612-connection-redux/

Harwood, Daniella. 'Marry in Haste, Repent at Leisure.' *A Happy Assembly*, 12 Dec. 2013. https://meryton.com/aha/index.php?/topic/14776-marry-in-haste-version-1/&tab=comments#comment-464603

Jamison, Anne. *Fic: Why Fanfiction is Taking Over the World*. BenBella Books, 2013.

Jenkins, Henry. 'Confronting the Challenges of Participatory Culture: Media Education for the twenty-first century.' MacArthur Foundation. 2006. https://www.macfound.org/media/article_pdfs/JENKINS_WHITE_PAPER.PDF

Luetkenhaus, Holly, and Zoe Weinstein. *Austentatious: The Evolving World of Jane Austen Fans*. U of Iowa P, 2019.

Pfannenstiel, Amber Nicole. 'Re: Academics and Fanfiction.' Received by Melanie Borrego, 5 Feb. 2020.

Pride and Prejudice. Directed by Simon Langton. BBC, 1995.

Pugh, Sheenagh. *The Democratic Genre: Fan Fiction in a Literary Context*. Poetry Wales P, 2015.

Rhys, Jean. *The Wide Sargasso Sea*. W. W. Norton and Company, 2016.

Saintsbury, George. 'Preface.' *Pride and Prejudice*. London: George Allen, 1894.

Stoppard, Tom. *Rosencrantz and Guildenstern are Dead*. Grove P, 2017.

Wells, Juliette. *Everybody's Jane: Austen in the Popular Imagination*. Continuum, 2011.

Wells, Linda. 'Keeping Calm.' A Happy Assembly, 30 Dec. 2012. https://meryton.com/aha/index.php?/topic/13470-keepingcalm/&tab=comments#comment-403852

Yaffe, Deborah. *Among the Janeites: A Journey through the World of Jane Austen Fandom*. Houghton Mifflin Publishing Company, 2013.

PART V

Teaching Jane Austen: A Sampling

38

TEACHING JANE AUSTEN IN THE TWENTY-FIRST CENTURY

Michael Gamer[1] *and Katrina O'Loughlin*[2]

[1]UNIVERSITY OF PENNSYLVANIA
[2]BRUNEL UNIVERSITY

Of the many words haunting twenty-first-century classrooms, 'relatable' is not one of our favourites. Although part of common usage for at least three centuries, it appeared in our own seminar discussions a little over a decade ago, when suddenly it seemed everywhere at once. Stories were 'relatable' to the degree that students could imagine themselves into them, as were situations, settings, and especially characters. 'Relatability' became a reason to read or not to read, to finish or not finish, a novel. Identification with characters and scenes became a central criterion of value, sometimes the only form of value students would recognise in fiction. That a portion of students might not finish an assigned reading—or might judge a book's interest by the degree to which it spoke to their own experience—is hardly new. But that 'relatability' might function as a basis—even *the* basis—for judging literary value, or other forms of instrumentality that have replaced literary value for contemporary students, strikes us as a shift worth taking seriously. It seems particularly relevant to the question of teaching Jane Austen, who, far from suffering the fate of most authors in becoming less relevant with the passage of time, has achieved a new currency in the last quarter century.

Given the growing prevalence of 'relatable', 'relatability', and Austen in popular culture, it seems worth mapping their genealogies. While 'relatability' is of fairly recent circulation—the *Oxford English Dictionary*'s first cited usage is a 1937 issue of the *Burlington Magazine*—'relatable' has a longer history reaching back to the early seventeenth century. Originally denoting the ability of something to be described or put into words—literally that 'may be narrated'—it came in the later nineteenth century also to denote the ability of one concept or idea to be connected to another. An emerging political scandal might be relatable to a particular scandal of the past, as might be a given company's monopolistic dominance of a specific market to earlier monopolies. Half a century ago the word took on a further meaning, one far closer to current popular usage: rather than describing the ability of one idea to be connected to another, it came to signify the power of any object or person to inspire a sense of recognition and empathic connection in another.

It is important, we think, to keep all these orders of meaning in play—narration, the connection between ideas and concepts, and the sense of empathetic connection or identification that 'relatability' also describes—as they all, in their different ways, speak to the shared cultural and emotional vocabularies that make fictional representation meaningful. Instead of seeing 'relatability' and 'relatable' as frustrating markers of modern disengagement or self-referentiality, we want to recognise it here as contemporary shorthand for those complex navigations that constitute an encounter with

DOI: 10.4324/9780429398155-38-44

historical and cultural difference in a two-hundred-year-old novel. When readers remark relatability (or its failure), they are describing the possibility and problems of achieving the connective cultural-emotional vocabulary on which storytelling depends. In this sense, relatability acts as a kind of currency within the scene of reading, identifying certain texts as capable of resonating with readers in the present moment, and therefore as valuable. At once 'current' and 'coin', it marks specific novels (or specific scenes, characters, or devices within novels) as prized sites of emotional exchange. These markers, we argue, can prove powerful allies for energising discussion, since they at once allow readers to recognise one another and provide specific vehicles for making connections. But there also is the sense of relatability's *coin* that we wish to emphasise here, the sense of property and ownership that comes with recognition of, and connection with, a novel. How should we understand (and support) the experience of readers whose expectations of ownership are frustrated by their inability to bond with a given text: where an investment in the novel—its ideas, importance, or cultural prestige—is not reciprocated by the reading experience? Even more urgently, how do we address the hesitations of those who believe they could not or should not dare claim such a privilege? 'Relatability' thus also reveals avenues of sympathetic and ideological access to the otherworlds of nineteenth-century fiction. In this sense, it strikes us as a powerful vehicle for teaching.

This seems especially the case for Austen, whose popularity has soared in the wake of the film adaptations of the past quarter century. The successes of *Sense and Sensibility* (1995), *Pride and Prejudice* (1995), *Clueless* (1995), *Emma* (1996), *Persuasion* (1996), *Mansfield Park* (1999), *Bride and Prejudice* (2004), *Pride and Prejudice* (2005), *Emma* (2009), *Love and Friendship* (2016), *Pride and Prejudice and Zombies* (2016), and *Emma* (2020) have fuelled not just further film adaptations but also a flurry of parodies, sequels, and versions in other media, including board and video games, the stage, podcasts and vlogs, specialty tours, and, most recently, notes of currency. Austen's recent appearance on the ten-pound note in many ways marks the culmination of this process of adaptation and commodification, where the appearance of each new product posits a new connection between her world and ours. This proliferation has proven all the more rapid thanks to Austen's residence in the public domain, which has made her especially attractive to adaptors, whether writers of fan fiction or sellers on eBay and Etsy. Their combined activities have changed how and where we encounter Austen, whose rise as a popular author and pop-culture icon means that our students are likely to come to the original novels later—after, rather than before, they have encountered her in other forms.

This newly mediated engagement with Austen's novels strikes us as an opportunity for an audience-based pedagogy based in adaptation and analogical thinking that addresses 'relatability' directly. Such an approach seems all the more important given the profound differences that exist between Austen's time and our own, and among twenty-first-century readers themselves. Teaching Austen effectively, we want to suggest, requires both foregrounding these differences and recognising the power of analogical thinking to create points of entry and overlap. With this in mind, we propose exploiting the question of 'relatability' as a step toward subsequent and more fruitful questions centreing on historical and cultural difference and the imaginative experiment that is reading. This approach is based in two premises: first, that twenty-first-century readers of Austen are far more likely than readers of previous generations to encounter Austen first through adaptations rather than through her novels; and second, that popular adaptations and appropriations of Austen frequently carry with them implicit readings of her and her work that inform our first encounters with her fiction. If students come to Austen expecting her stories and characters to be 'relatable', it is in part because so many cultural forms and commodities have made it their business to present her as such. Brand Austen is everywhere, and our students encounter it not only through adaptations, parodies, prequels, sequels, and games, but also as a form of cultural nostalgia—the investment of an older generation (that of these authors at least!) in the 1990s 'golden age' of Austen adaptations and in the Austen kitsch it fostered.

Part of our reason for co-writing this essay arises from the diversity of Austen's readers and their engagements with her, since discussing this diversity has enriched and transformed our personal teaching. Our experiences in university classrooms, both more and less elite, have ranged from majority-minority student bodies to largely homogeneous ones, from pre-freshman programs to evening courses for mature students in North America, Australia, Turkey, and Britain. Beyond the university we have also discussed Austen in book clubs and reading groups, secondary school classrooms and educational support programs, film societies, theatre post-show Q&A sessions, literary associations, alumni webinars and other online forums, and gaming conventions. Whatever the venue, the question of relatability inevitably finds its way into discussion, with discussants usually divided into those who find Austen 'relevant' and those who don't. Often these discussions shift quickly to include questions of ownership, with similar divisions emerging between those who expect to have some ownership in Austen, and those who do not. The consistency of these frames of reference stems in part from the span of years dividing the Regency from our own present, and in part from that equally fundamental question of what we want when we read. Both are shaped not just by identity but also by degrees of literacy, privilege, and cultural access. Within the rich mosaic of Austen students, we have found readers who expect to see themselves in every character and those who anticipate the opposite. The majority, however, report a combination of recognition and surprise: moments of unexpected resonance and radical differences difficult to fathom. Whether pleasant or unpleasant, these moments can often jump-start conversations, since they invite us to recognise the cultural and historical specificity of supposed universals like emotion and to acknowledge that what we bring to books can inform our experience of them.

Teachers inevitably reflect on classroom successes; many of the most illuminating readings we have encountered in our own seminars and tutorials have come from students recognising and identifying with the processes of social restriction and enforcement described in Austen's fiction. Even if details and precise forms are unfamiliar, or students find it difficult to understand all of the competing forces whirling around a scene of Austenian courtship, they directly recognise how propriety functions as a form of social enforcement: its real and ongoing force in their own families or communities. Moments of recognition like these are not ends in themselves, but powerful beginnings. They can energise discussion by turning plots into complex allegories and by transforming details into speaking objects. In the pages that follow, we introduce several ideas for group exercises and assignments that have proven successful in our own classrooms (in person and virtual) and those of our colleagues. Most of them begin, either directly or indirectly, by asking students to find points of recognition or analogy in a given work of Austen before moving to more detailed discussion of the text. Their aim is, in the first instance, to build familiarity with the novels, particularly where reading and comprehension of the novels might be limited or where students might not be confident in their own abilities. Done well, they can produce intimacy and a sense of ownership with the details of the novels while deferring questions of 'deeper meaning' or interpretation that can be intimidating to many new readers.

It is an old maxim of the writing classroom that students are energised more by speaking and writing than by reading and listening, although both kinds of activity are necessary for learning. The majority of our activities bring with them the virtue of placing students' ideas, and very often their text, at the forefront of discussion. The aim is to hear from as many students as possible as early as possible. Importantly, these tasks also ask students to do preliminary work—either before class meets or in small groups during class—and then to share their work as a way of opening discussion. In each case, we ask participants to locate their ideas in one or more passages or scenes from Austen—not just to substantiate their claims but also to provide opportunities for in-class analysis, comparison, and reflection. We then offer two exercises that place close reading itself at the forefront. The first asks students to consider which objects speak most eloquently in Austen's fiction—and, by extension, which objects are sold in the marketplace today under the Austen brand. The second focuses on those scenes in the novels where characters (and readers) are confronted with documents—usually, but not always, epistolary correspondence—and forced to read beyond the words in front of them. What are we to make of Austen's fondness for dramatising scenes of extended textual interpretation? Does she, in fact, model close reading for us?

Prelude: 'First Impressions'

This is not so much an exercise as a tactic: that of asking, at the beginning of a class meeting, for students' initial impressions of the novel up for discussion. At first blush a rather lame-sounding opening gambit, asking students for their first impressions in fact authorises them to *have* first impressions, and to speak to them. More profoundly, it licences readers to notice details: to voice unformed (and as yet uninformed) opinions; to wonder about things; and to have questions. Granting those first reactions and questions a status in the classroom, it allows people to participate, particularly in cohorts where students find their experience of alienation from a canonical novel evidence not of the novel's 'failure', but of their own. It also opens up discussion to the (potential) gaps between expectation and experience of reading Austen. This kind of opening is invaluable for gathering information in new classes on how students have encountered Austen before (who is reading Austen for the first time, who is reading the novel of a film they already know, and how is it different?), and of introducing into discussion the nature and diversity of encounters with Austen (ours personally were confused and somewhat alienated). Perhaps most powerfully, such an exercise can create open and welcoming conditions for discussion because every member of the discussion is made equally a Reader of Austen. We use this opening in two variations: asking for first impressions in discussion; or asking students (in a quick writing exercise often set at the beginning of seminar meetings) to jot down 'three things you noticed and a question, or something you found yourself wondering about'. The latter, in particular, gives students time for reflection at the beginning of class, a chance to write, and an opportunity to refer to those notes while discussing their impressions.

Case 1: Mapping

Our first activity asks students to map the novel under discussion. It calls for paper and pens and pairs students for ideas and discussion. In it we encourage students to think as broadly and laterally as possible about 'mapping', and to be creative with their maps. (This is often really productive for students who prefer to think visually and spatially, and can unlock some great insights). Students are invited to map homes, landscapes, and regions, or to represent spatially the hierarchies and relationships within them. They might include sketches of rooms, gardens, shrubberies, parks, and walks; the proximity or distance of neighbours, villages, assembly rooms, regional cities, London and beyond. We encourage rereading and detective work, as students rifle back through their novels to find important details. With familiarity comes confidence: textual knowledge grows in a way that seems to lead naturally to larger questions and connections in discussion. Where lies the 'center', and where the 'periphery', in each student's map? Does this change over the course of the novel? Where is the action located and to what degree does it depend on mobility and transport? What does it mean for Mrs Bennet to withhold the carriage from Jane in *Pride and Prejudice*, for Lizzie to walk through 'dirt' to care for Jane when she is ill, or for the small child Fanny to travel alone in a public conveyance from Portsmouth to the great house at Mansfield?

We have found that asking students to navigate and map *Mansfield Park*—a novel that many of them find strange and unlikeable—to be especially generative. Even the relatively mundane act of marking which characters get to 'own' rooms and which do not—or considering the relative significance of various rooms to one another—inevitably generates further discussion about the (mis) appropriation of Sir Thomas's study as a green room, Mrs Norris's desire always to keep a spare room vacant for a friend, or Fanny's achievement of a room of her own in the East attic. Mapping over time can also be revealing here, showing how Fanny's peripheral rooms gradually assume a centrality and moral authority over the course of the novel as other characters are drawn there. It can reveal the parsonage as a space of quiet but intense contention between the Norrises, the Grants, and its eventual possessors Edmund and Fanny Bertram. Mapping also reveals other kinds of geographies that are contained in (and burst out of) Sir Thomas Bertram's estate domestic. These in turn can point both to constitutive regional and global geographies, and to the powerful class geographies inscribed within the layout not only of Mansfield but also via Mr Rushworth's estate at Sotherton and Lieutenant Price's house in Portsmouth. This constant movement between ideas and details, between physical and conceptual fields, can be especially powerful as students consider just how far Mansfield lies (literally and conceptually) from Antigua, or Portsmouth, or even Thorton Lacey. To consider these distances is to invite students to think about larger questions that recur in the novels: about patronage and local attachment, about different kinds of nationhood, and about the networks of trade and trafficking that underwrite life at the Park.

One of the reasons we like this activity (and those that follow) is its flexibility and repeatability: it can be done more than once, alone or in groups, virtually or in person, in advance or in class. The sheer wealth of scenes from the novels themselves that can be used to introduce the exercise is also an asset. Thinking through the many balls, card parties, and crushes that punctuate the novels, for example, students might map the physical space of Catherine Morland's first ball in *Northanger Abbey*, or consider the series of rooms through which Marianne Dashwood must pass before she can confront John Willoughby at a London party, or anxiously plan with Mrs Weston in *Emma* how to make the rooms of the Crown Inn fit both for dancing and for the exacting eye of Mr Woodhouse. All of these scenes testify to how carefully social and physical geographies are plotted in the novels. Exploring class and status differences between Darcy, Bingley, and the Bennets through their homes, for example, asks that we understand the difference between not just owning and renting but also between a clear estate and an entailed one, since each property differently maps its inhabitants in the social order. One of our recent students, for example, placed the chapel at the centre of a map of Sotherton in order to foreground Fanny's response to that space as a key moment of character development in *Mansfield Park*, and a predicate for the more marked transgressions into park and wilderness that follow. Another constructed a more conceptual map of the novel's characters: arrows moving back and forth between various pairs marked which of the two possessed comparative moral and class authority over the other and in relation to the whole, revealing a kind of spider web and beautifully capturing the complex interplay of power cathected by the novel. In both cases too, what was *absent* from each map—the avenue of oaks in the former and Tom Bertram in the latter—prompted further fruitful discussion.

This back-and-forth between space and ideas means that student maps will vary—a good thing—and we encourage students to be as literal or as lateral as they like. Some maps will be primarily geographical; others will become downright conceptual as geography comes to signify more than location and relative distance. Nearly all will have inscribed into them fundamental assumptions and deeper questions worthy of further discussion. The connotations that come with the Elliots relocating to Bath, or Elizabeth Bennet 'touring' at Pemberley, can invite subsequent debates concerning what is the 'world' of the novel, how it is constituted, and where breached. What does it mean for Lydia and Wickham to run away to London rather than Gretna Green, or for Frank Churchill to travel sixteen miles to the metropole for a haircut? And how are we to read the difference between a woman travelling escorted (as Elizabeth is during her trips to Kent and Derbyshire) and one travelling alone (as Catherine Morland does when she returns home from Northanger Abbey)? In some ways, asking students to 'map' a novel or scene encourages them simply to reconceive relationships in a way that makes sense to them, making use of both adaptive and analogical reading. It interrupts the (almost irresistible) authority of Austen's written line, and very often has the effect of revealing her complex spatialisation of power in rooms, homes, and regions in a way that may not be immediately recognisable, but is almost always familiar to all of us.

Case 2: Pitching

This exercise gives students the opportunity to imagine a film adaptation of a given Austen novel. Working in groups of three or four, students are given 15 to 20 minutes to develop a pitch and then to make it to the 'producers' (the rest of the class). In our instructions, we advise them to fully block out their proposed production—when and where will it be set, how will it be shot, what will be its major narratives and who its target audience—and then to choose a key scene to illustrate concretely the nature of their adaptation. Often we ask students after this initial pitch to extend their thinking into casting decisions; if assigned as homework for presentation in the next class, students can even assemble a slideshow of images to present their casting call.

Like mapping, an exercise like this encourages students to begin to find their own ways into the novels. They are exercises in translation, adaptation, and analogous thinking, capable of making a novel's social dynamics and power relationships visible by recasting them in modern or specific cultural terms. One of the most exciting examples of pitching and casting was created by a British student who recast *Pride and Prejudice* in the terms of 2019 Bollywood. Obviously riffing off *Bride and Prejudice*, this reformulation was at once more intelligent and more critically illuminating than that film. Using her extensive knowledge of the culture and gossip of the Indian film industry, the student not only granted roles that built on traditions of representation within Bollywood (this actress is always given 'girl next door' roles; this actress is considered transgressive and is often highly sexualised in the press), but also used her casting to explore analogous social and cultural constraints within two genres that, however historically and geographically distant from one another, nevertheless share a powerful preoccupation with the marriage plot and with social enforcements of power. During our class session, the student's decision to focus on the cultures of Bollywood—and on its extensive economic and social power—energised discussion of the cultural capital of Austen in the nineteenth century and in our own period.

Pitching and casting are fundamentally exercises in translation and adaptation, and the process swiftly opens up discussion to the politics of reading (where every reading is a kind of imaginative adaptation) and of representation. We have had some fascinating discussions on historical and cultural standards of beauty, for instance, and how these work toward characterisation in Austen and in our own period. These in turn have led to conversations about historical and cultural difference and the critical importance of developing a shared vocabulary of detail when reading other times and places. As these examples make clear, the presentation aspect of the assignment also helps foster accessibility, providing a range of ways that readers can find their way into a novel and helping a class to develop a common vocabulary for discussion. The process of finding shared terms in each class is also critical, since it helps students to discover gaps of understanding not only between themselves and the text at hand, but also between one another. This is particularly true of very diverse classrooms, where finding shared and transferable experiences between students can be as challenging as finding them with the fiction.

Case 3: Financial Dossiers

In this exercise we ask students to assemble a detailed financial dossier of individual characters in a given novel, from the most prominent to the least conspicuous. Students then compare notes in small groups and, having marshalled the relevant details from the text, are able to assemble a complex and comparative picture of a group of characters that prove—in true Austenian style—highly revealing of not only class, social, and financial status, but of personality, sociability, and mien. Austen is remarkably detailed about financial matters, a feature of her work that readers often find curious or jarring. Directly and systematically tackling these details challenges students to trace the arrangements of inheritance and entailment; of property, assets, and ready money; of the relative cost of living; and of character economy and extravagance. The dossier asks them to do so, moreover, not through abstract historical patterns, but rather through the conditions that materially shape the lives, choices, and foreseeable futures of a range of characters, particularly those of women. What does it mean for Charlotte Lucas to choose to accept Mr Collins, or for Mrs and Miss Bates and Jane Fairfax to be confined to 'two rooms' when Emma is, at twenty-one, already mistress of her own home? Why does Mr Knightley choose *not* to keep a carriage when Mr Woodhouse does? More speculatively, how might Mr Knightley and Robert Martin's shared interest in farming methods and modest living connect them, producing the possibility of friendship as well as patronage? Or, to cite a final example, how does Captain Wentworth's prize money—earned in a prosperous and still active naval career—allow him to reconcile the differences of rank between himself and a baronet's daughter over a critical eight-year interim? And can money alone ever fully erase this gap?

Having students assemble and study this level of financial detail can help bring Austen's own analyses of micro-social class identities and movements to the forefront of discussion, not to mention the wider social and economic transformations of the Regency. It also has the added benefit of placing us as readers in the same position as those characters—Mrs Bennet, John and Fanny Dashwood, and John Thorpe, to name but a few—who talk openly about money. In our own classes, inviting students to carefully consider the material circumstances of Austen's characters has proven especially fruitful to creative writers, since few authors are more explicit or nuanced about how the presence or absence of money can dictate situations and plotlines. Comparing Mrs Bennet's dowry of five thousand pounds to the radically diminished portions of each of her daughters reveals their relative prospects in a stark light. And in our own age of soaring tuition and university fees, asking students to think analogically about dowries can be powerful. Are they, for example, like college funds? Or are they more like assistance with the down payment on a house, or a first car, or first and last month's rent? In what, or whom, should parents invest? Here Lady Catherine de Bourgh's questioning of Elizabeth about her upbringing and education, while impertinent, snaps at least one factor into focus: if Mr and Mrs Bennet's income has not been spent on masters to instruct their daughters, then on what has it been spent? This line of questioning into household conduct can easily extend to other households like Lucas Lodge (where the disjunction between Sir William's knighthood and his daughter Charlotte's lack of dowry becomes a powerful testimony to his vanity and mismanagement) and even to Rosings and Pemberley, which Austen explicitly contrasts to one another as extensions of their owner's respective characters.

Case 4: Speaking Objects

In narratives so powerfully shaped by the conditions of wealth, students are often surprised at the relative absence of *things* in Austen. Where they do appear, however—Lucy Steele's ring, Lydia Bennet's torn muslin, Harriet Smith's nub of pencil and bit of plaster, Lady Bertram's pug, Mrs Morland's copy of *The Spectator*, or Admiral Croft's shaving mirror, to name just a few memorable examples—they can speak volumes. In our fourth activity, we ask students to consider the objects that compose Austen's fictional worlds, and to choose one that carries significant and multiple meanings. In our instructions, we encourage them to consider either an especially speaking object (such as those listed above) or an everyday article (bonnets, carriages, shoe-roses, particular kinds of fruit, etc.) that over multiple scenes comes to take on a particular meaning or larger symbolic role. As with other activities, we encourage students to research contextual materials needed to understand their chosen object fully and to consider whether there exist modern equivalences. Is their object particular to Regency England, or is it something we still use? We also ask them explicitly to think about location, function, and cultural status. Where does the object first appear and is it associated with a particular character? Do we know its cost? Does Austen present it as beautiful, ugly, quotidian, useless?

As with the financial dossier exercise, the resulting discussions often have led to questions of narrative function, since certain kinds of objects (letters especially) frequently propel Austen's plots forward. We have found, however, that often the most fruitful conversations have arisen from objects and details that do *not* have to be there. These are the objects we would never miss but that tell us much, such as the shelves installed by Lady Catherine de Bourgh into Mr Collins' parsonage, or Robert Ferrars's toothpick case, or Captain Harville's shelves, handmade toys, and fishing net. Where apparently insignificant details seem to say so much, they invite students to begin thinking synecdochically: either to connect their chosen object to other things in the text, or to ask how its small part might suggest a larger whole. They can also provoke more fundamental questions about the workings of narrative *beyond* plot, and about how authors wield satire and where they deploy social commentary. Like most of our exercises, 'Speaking Objects' asks students to engage in a thought experiment: to choose a lens through which to view a given novel and to ask what aspects become suddenly visible when considered through a chosen object, or from a specific perspective. We hope that, along the way, it also teaches the pleasures of interpretation and the power of *play*: that illuminating a text begins with noticing details and wondering about them.

Case 5: Documents

Like most classroom exercises, the mapping, pitching, dossier, and speaking object activities aim to create footholds for students into Austen's worlds, which can otherwise seem alien to first-time readers. Each invites students into a given novel by asking them to articulate parallel ideas and imagine modern equivalents and experiences. Encouraging this kind of imaginative experimentation—the creation of a kind of 'double register' of sympathetic identification or 're-latability' that recognises analogous human experiences without eliding historical and cultural differences—is one of our cherished goals as humanists and teachers. It is also fundamental, we believe, to that essential act of textual analysis, close reading.

Our final class activity thus directs readers to the very moments in Austen's fiction where her own characters must grapple with the meaning of a text, and must likewise become readers and interpreters. Sometimes these scenes involve printed matter, as when Fanny Price and her father both respond to the newspaper report of Maria Bertram's elopement with Henry Crawford; even as one witnesses its impact at the house in Portsmouth, so one must also imagine (with Fanny) its impact at Mansfield Park. Usually, however, such document-scenes feature personal letters. These are sometimes provided in full (as with Isabella Thorpe's letter to Catherine at Northanger Abbey, in which she begs Catherine's 'kind offices' to repair her relationship with James) and sometimes not (as when *Sense and Sensibility*'s Mrs Jennings speculates on the contents of the message that has driven Colonel Brandon to London).

Most famously, of course, there is Mr Darcy's post-proposal letter, which Austen provides in its entirety in one chapter and then, in the next, narrates Elizabeth's varied and evolving interpretation of it across two hours of repeated reading and rereading. In courses where a majority of students are encountering the original text of these chapters for the first time, we sometimes ask them to write about Darcy's letter *before* reading Elizabeth's response to it, and then to compare their impressions of its tone, style, emotional candour, and arguments to those of Elizabeth. Where do their own responses to Darcy's letter converge or diverge? And did their impressions change after watching Elizabeth respond to the very same letter? Such questions can provide a platform for further insights into Austen's narration: given her fondness for free indirect discourse, where does Austen choose to merge or not merge her narrator's consciousness with that of Elizabeth? Do these moments correspond with their own moments of engagement? At the very least, canvassing a class's responses can help students to pinpoint key moments of identification with, or alienation from, given characters and one another. More powerfully still, they show Austen modelling textual interpretation for readers, as her characters confront what a given piece of writing denotes and connotes, says and implies. Showcasing these moments, we believe, can infuse a classroom with new energy and urgency. Close reading, it turns out, is not just something one does in English courses; it is a staple activity of characters trying to make sense of their surroundings. Such scenes thus powerfully foreground the power of context to interpretation. Elizabeth, after all, cannot peruse Darcy's letter without a host of other considerations attending her reading. There is her attraction to Mr Wickham, her resentment of Darcy's interference in the courtship of Jane and Mr Bingley, and her anger at the impoliteness of his proposal—not to mention the aftereffects of a migraine headache. Yet, as our various activities make clear, the same can be said for students' varied experiences of Austen's fiction, which they encounter in ways—and on media—she could never have foreseen. These inevitable mediations also are worth talking about, at least in passing, since they help to foreground the very issues of situation and narration that constitute most acts of reading.

Conclusion

While acknowledging our scepticism toward the terms 'relatable' and 'relatability' at the beginning of this essay, we have nevertheless argued for their power as pedagogical concepts for teaching Austen today—particularly the older sense of 'relatable' as denoting the ability of something, whether concept or experience, to be narrated. Given the diversity of students peopling our classrooms, our first challenge as teachers of Austen is offering ways into her fiction. We need to provide not only a possibility of engagement, even ownership, but also the option of *not* buying into a given novel or specific worldview. Each case provided has thus sought to acknowledge what it means to want—more than anything—a strong sense of connection to fictional characters, while also asking students to give time and thought to the myriad differences between Austen's world and our own. Much of what is creative about teaching stems from the many analogies we offer to students who, confronting what appears to them to be a blank wall, have yet to spot the footholds available to them. The more footholds offered, the greater the numbers able to navigate a path.

As teachers who have spent their lives trying to make the past at once legible and pleasurable, we believe that expanding the canon has at least two components: increasing the range of texts students encounter, and increasing the range of students encountering texts. On the one hand, students demanding relatability from texts represents a positive and even egalitarian development: a more diverse group of readers at university levels asking for fictions and characters that speak to their own experience. On the other hand, these same demands for self-recognition threaten to erase, or at least grossly undervalue, historical and cultural differences—and thus risk reinstating the same politics of self-identification that we fought so hard to dismantle in masculinist and racist literary canons. Hence our insistence that every attempt to find a path to student engagement lead to more nuanced, and eventually reflective, considerations of difference, and that discovering these differences might be the most fun of all. Is there a middle ground, a way of reading and teaching, that honours readerly desire for identification while recognising, even celebrating, the many immense, strange, and uncanny distances between Austen's world and our own?

As a way of answering this final question (and in the spirit of Austen's decision to introduce a new character in the final chapter of *Northanger Abbey*, namely the 'charming … man of fortune and consequence' who marries Eleanor Tilney), we conclude by introducing a new term ourselves, one complementary to 'relatability': 'propriety'. Most fundamentally, propriety denotes social obligation, convention, and conformation; Austen wields the term usually to denote those forms of politeness demanded of us across a range of situations. To behave with propriety is to acknowledge the particularities of a social scene and to adjust one's behaviour to meet its varying demands. While some situations—institutional rituals and ceremonies, for example—demand high levels of conformity, most social scenes require what we might call 'adjustment'—a nice metaphor for reading Austen—because one's presence within a scene also alters that scene. To behave with propriety in Austen's fiction, then, is to understand how a given social situation might have to adjust to one's presence even as one adapts to that scene. Some of Austen's most durable set-pieces involve this fundamental negotiation: a character (usually young and female) enters, takes the temperature of the room, adjusts her countenance, and does the best she can. Whether Catherine Morland, Eleanor Dashwood, or Emma Woodhouse, the fundamental pressures remain largely the same. (Interestingly, Austen's most gothic scenes simply vary this formula by having the young woman navigating social codes encounter someone who changes the rules without informing her.) If Austen still has the power to resonate with younger readers, it is in these scenes of social navigation and adjustment, where every participant must also be a reader. Even where her details have only been partially legible to students, larger structures of social obligation and negotiation remain visible and resonant. If the exercises we have offered in this essay share one principle, it is that good teaching first invites, and then fosters, similar exercises in propriety and adjustment between novels and readers. In this way, a conversation with Austen can begin.

39

CLOSE READING AND CLOSE LOOKING: TEACHING AUSTEN NOVELS AND FILMS

Martha Stoddard Holmes

CALIFORNIA STATE UNIVERSITY, SAN MARCOS

A twenty-first century literature class can sometimes look like a film class, whether film is the focus or simply a mode of delivery. Either way, the inclusion of film in secondary and post-secondary literature curricula has meant a wonderful expansion of access to Jane Austen's novels. Some 25–30 adaptations of the major novels, many easily accessible in DVD or streaming video, invite the use of film, video, or television as gateways to the novels or even substitutes for them, as an abridgment might have been used in the past.[1] With a host of engaging screen versions of Austen novels and more appearing, many teachers supplement their teaching of Austen with excerpts from film or television, in part simply to get ahead of the fact that most students are turning to the screen—for some, a more comfortable place than the page—to keep up with the reading. Including film does not necessarily mean teaching film, except in an implicit way, with unintended messages about the relationship between novel and film; or, teachers may want to engage the richness of that 'repetition with a difference' that film versions invite, but lack a clear sense of how to weave that thread into the classroom discourse.[2] This chapter draws on my own experience engaging this challenge with the help of a number of print and video resources, six groups of enthusiastic students over twelve years of teaching, and supportive colleagues at my university and elsewhere.

In the wake of my own enjoyment of Austenmania (a popular term for the 1990s proliferation of screen versions of Austen), I created a course on Austen Novel to Film as one of a series of Film and Literature courses my department offers, serving literature and writing studies majors and other students across our five colleges seeking to fulfil their upper-division general-education humanities requirement. After the first offering in 2008, the department has gradually increased the course's frequency from every few years to once or twice a year. As I finalised this chapter in 2020, I had just 'Zoomed' with 80 students in my first fully online iteration of this course after teaching it face-to-face five times. I suspect the fill of the course has little to do with Austen's popularity, her excellence, my passion, and the vigour of our active local chapter of JASNA notwithstanding. Our students have generally never encountered Austen in any form before and are in the class to meet a requirement. Further, some of them may not enjoy the process of interpreting literature and/or may be actively resistant to it, having experienced classmates coming up with 'deep meanings' whose sources seem mysteriously unavailable to others. As a choice for reluctant readers, Austen novels are pedagogically challenging. Even the literature majors may not have focused on 'older' texts and may be taking this class because it was available at the right time for their work/life schedule. Bringing film into this mix of motivations—as more than just a 'sweetener' for the 'medicine' of literature,

DOI: 10.4324/9780429398155-39-45

509

that is, or a way to make the course seem easier to students who do not like to read—surely creates conceptual and logistical challenges for teachers and students.

Despite these very real challenges, I advocate here for the benefits and delights of using film not just as a sweetener, transitional object, supplement, or conversation starter, but also to deepen students' ability to observe, read, and write critically and deeply. As well as offering multiple forms of access to the novels, teaching the films plus some basics of 'close looking' (to accompany the skill of 'close reading' students practice with the print text) can reawaken the beginner's mind of most 'expert' literature majors. Teaching even a bit of film analysis invites all students to try out a manageable approach to analysing craft that transfers back to the analysis of all kinds of texts. Further, making screen literacy part of the course gives non-majors a place to shine, allowing for a more inclusive classroom. All of these effects can generate a more engaged learning space—physical or virtual—in which active learning and multiple forms of intelligence are invited. Students can see themselves as more than consumers of teacherly and writerly knowledge and as makers of knowledge in their own right.

My particular approach has not yet been shared in print, as far as I know. The recent history of scholarship on Austen on screen features a post-Austenmania surge followed by a quieter afterlife. Two monographs, two collections, and a number of individual essays on screen translation were published in the 1990s and early 2000s, most focused on what David Monaghan, Ariane Hudelet, and John Wiltshire in *The Cinematic Jane Austen* term 'Austen adaptation studies' (2). The essays in the important 1998 collection *Jane Austen in Hollywood,* edited by Linda Troost and Sayre Greenfield, share a feminist and/or gender studies inflection but represent a variety of critical stances towards the screen versions. Sue Parrill's *Jane Austen on Film and Television: A Critical Study of the Adaptations* offers a thorough discussion of each novel and the screen versions available at the time, providing a filmography as an appendix. *Jane Austen on Screen*, edited by Gina Macdonald and Andrew Macdonald, invites readers to sample the ongoing critical debates about various screen versions, framing the collection by tracing and exemplifying the positions of 'literary purists' anchored to 'fidelity' to the novels and 'film enthusiasts' who celebrate the films as creative works in their own right. (It is worth nothing that the latter group includes one of our most celebrated scholars of Austen's writing, Jocelyn Harris.) As Monaghan, Hudelet, and Wiltshire observe, most of these texts were generated by literary scholars and anchored to the written text's characteristics and the challenges of translation (1–2). The overall focus is not on cinematic techniques per se but rather on broad issues such as compression, supplementation, production values, and cinematography writ large, with selected observational gems on mis-en-scène, camera angles, setting, and/or lighting. I note also John Wiltshire's *Recreating Jane Austen*, which takes a substantially different approach than any of the above by examining selected versions as 'recreations' of Austen, viewed through a psychoanalytic lens informed by the work of D.W. Winnicott.

In *The Cinematic Jane Austen*, David Monaghan, Ariane Hudelet, and John Wiltshire observe that, after a surge of studies focused on the 'Austenmania' of 1990s film and television adaptations, there has been less critical work generated while works continue to be generated 'in the post-Austenmania period' (2). Their book was published after *Masterpiece's* Complete Jane Austen film festival in 2007–8, which included new productions of *Northanger Abbey, Sense and Sensibility, Mansfield Park, Emma,* and *Persuasion* (several written by Andrew Davies), but left the iconic 1995 ITV *Pride and Prejudice* no further disturbed than it was by Joe Wright's very popular 2005 film. *The Cinematic Jane Austen* addresses these more recent productions and also focuses on the cinematic and cinematographic aspects of the films in and of themselves, not eliding the relationship to the novels but not enshrining the written text. In a substantially different approach from most earlier criticism, the book examines the aspects of Austen that work in ways similar to the dynamic of cinema, while not necessarily lending themselves at all to screen adaptations. Further, the text often flips the 'page-to-screen' emphasis of most earlier criticism and begins with screen productions as keys to aspects of

Austen's novels. In contrast to the earlier books, the emphasis is absolutely on the 'auditory and visual dimensions' of cinematic technique as well as the cinema history of certain threads in Austen productions, such as the technically challenging goal of approximating natural light. In addition to these books, a host of excellent individual essays and book chapters continue to emerge, such as Kathryn Sutherland's chapter on Austen on screen in the second edition of the *Cambridge Companion to Jane Austen's* Novels (2011) and Jodi L. Wyett's 'Sex, Sisterhood, and the Cinema: Sense and Sensibility(s) in Conversation' in *The Cinematic Eighteenth Century*. Scholars' modes of apprehending Austen on screen keep developing and deepening, especially given the opportunity to examine the aesthetic conversations among screen versions rather than anchoring relationships solely to the print originals.

None of the aforementioned texts is strictly focused on pedagogy (although Macdonald and Macdonald include discussion questions to guide the book's use by teachers or discussion leaders). In contrast, Louise Flavin's monograph, *Jane Austen in the Classroom: Viewing the Novel/Reading the Film,* makes extensive use of Troost and Greenfield's collection to provide a practical and useful guide for teaching. For each of the novels, she provides 'questions for analysis and discussion', followed by a summary of key aspects of one or more screen versions and 'questions for discussion and writing'. The slight difference between these headings indicates something of the book's emphasis on film as a bridge helping students approach a deeper understanding of the written text rather than a focus in its own right. While each film has a 'cinematic elements' section devoted to it, most of these discussions of cinematic details are—with the exception of the discussion of the 1995 miniseries of *Pride and Prejudice*—relatively short and not particularly granular; they are appropriate to her emphasis on film as '"adaptation" and transference of the novel' (2). Flavin's book precedes the remakes broadcast in 2007-8, as well as the Joe Wright *Pride and Prejudice* (2005).

Other resources for teaching Austen novels and film include several essays in *Persuasions*, as well as some of the four MLA *Approaches to Teaching Austen* volumes—two edited by Marcia McClintock Folsom, and two by Folsom and John Wiltshire. The series illuminates the increasing attention to screen versions as a doorway to studying Austen; the 1993 volume on *Pride and Prejudice*, published before the iconic miniseries starring Colin Firth and Jennifer Ehle, does not address screen versions. The 2004 volume on *Emma* includes a full chapter on screen versions, and the 2014 volume on *Mansfield Park* (not surprisingly, given the controversies surrounding Patricia Rozema's 1999 film) includes in its introduction a useful section on the three screen versions then available. The 2021 volume on *Persuasion*, co-edited by Folsom and Wiltshire, includes not only an introductory section but also one full chapter on film, and its instructor survey specifically asked about film.[3] All of the essays in the series are treasure-troves of teaching ideas, whether or not they specifically address film.

What is largely missing in these very useful texts are the nuts and bolts of how to scaffold film into courses that are primarily focused on literature, practical guidance on how to bring film into the classroom in a way that is integral to the process by which we teach students the skills of critical analysis of literary works. Texts that focus on pedagogy make implicit the assumption that we all know how to use film well enough, possibly because the point is Austen, not the films themselves. We know that popping in a DVD or accessing the many versions is quite a bit different than teaching film, but if we are already working to teach or reinforce basic literary analysis along with Austen's novels, the prospect of also teaching basic film analysis may seem unfeasible and be-wildering. Even the most practical texts on pedagogy (like Flavin's) do not describe *how* to cultivate the basic visual literacy many students already possess into a more precise form of analysing the cinematic frame.

In this chapter, I offer an example for guiding students to develop skills of close looking to parallel the close reading skills most are also struggling to develop. Specifically, I suggest how to scaffold learning outcomes to build close looking in concert with close reading; approaches to providing basic film training even if you lack this expertise; and handling the challenge of screen time vs. lecture/discussion time. I focus on face to face teaching, but include a note at the end on the ways I modified these approaches in Fall 2020, when I began teaching in a blended online format.

In my state university, budgets dictate offering general-education classes serving the entire university—some of them large lectures and others medium-sized classes like this one—to fund smaller classes for students in our major and MA programme. My current group is representative—students from 4 colleges, about half literature and writing majors and the rest distributed across STEM fields, business, social and behavioural sciences, humanities, and health/human services majors such as kinesiology. Many of our students are from underserved communities. About 55% are the first in their generation to attend college. They arrive in our classrooms with substantial burdens that include not only family aspirations but also family care and work responsibilities. They often take an over-full course load to maximise the enrolment their tuition purchases. In the COVID-19 context, they struggle to do their homework in the midst of close quarters and in the presence of others who may fully support their degree goals but not fully understand what 'studying' looks like or demands in terms of time and focus. My course, 'Austen: Novel into Film' asks them to read and discuss six novels and some of their versions over a fifteen-week semester. They are not eager readers of Austen right out of the gate, and I suspect some of them enrol thinking we will just watch movies in class, but there are long waiting lists for general-education courses and they stay in the course despite initial worries about what they have gotten themselves into. My goal is for all of them to succeed in this course at the level to which they aspire.

Beginning the Class

While assigning reading before the first day may work for some teachers, in my context it is both impractical and inequitable, since many students spend their breaks working to pay for their education. So, while I provide suggestions for students who want to read (or listen) ahead, I open with a discussion of the opening chapters of *Northanger Abbey* and a screening of one of the screen versions—in either order.[4]

The 1987 and 2007 *Northanger Abbey* films, as Ellen Moody discusses in her enormously helpful blog entry on 'The Three Northanger Abbeys', both indulge in the gothic to the degree that they 'endorse what Austen critiques', a recurrent pattern in the film versions shaped by expectations about twentieth- and twenty-first-century viewers as well as perhaps by interpretative energies. The films' rebalancing of pleasure and didacticism, however, serves the first week of a general-education class very well. Even the reluctant students are drawn in, laughing and paying attention, and they enter the novel receptive to taking on the challenge of reading something written in language several describe as 'old English' and picturing the environment they are reading about. The 1988 film is particularly effective in engaging students because of the Bath scenes, which, though not entirely historically accurate, invite readers into the strangeness of the past and incline them to spend the next fourteen weeks in a similar imaginative space.

Our discussion of what film and novel, respectively, offer in the way of themes, questions, and possible contexts leads to comparisons of the two imaginative modes and their relationships. This opens an opportunity to introduce adaptation theory and ways of thinking about adaptation: as imitation, translation, interpretation, version, and criticism—setting them up to go home and read part of the novel. (Alternately, I have devoted the first class session to reading a few of Austen's short, information-packed chapters followed by extracts of their rendering in the introductory moments of film versions. Both *Northanger Abbey* and *Sense and Sensibility*—my two options for starting the course—lend themselves beautifully to this.) I model the use of some basic film terminology for shot distance and editing, just to lay a bit of groundwork for what happens next.

Close Reading

Our next class returns to the print text, not only to discuss the first half of the novel but specifically to introduce or recall the process of annotation and close reading. In my recent teaching experience, students find close reading a challenge. What most students bring from their high school training suggests an emphasis on summary and the big picture, to the extent that students are very uncomfortable and uncertain about how to address the small picture, the details of a writer's craft, except in a general way. Many students are diligent highlighters, but may not dive deeper into why they highlighted a phrase or what language enacts at that point in the text. Referring them to studies of how longhand note-taking asks the brain to do 'heavier lifting', but acknowledging that handwritten notes may not work for everyone, I begin many of our classes with reading quizzes that ask them to *annotate a passage* from the text and then *write about what they noticed* (see Mueller and Oppenheimer). The first time we do this, I annotate the passage, prompted by them, on a document camera so that they can see exactly how wild, disorderly, but engaged the process might look when we are using it for our own purposes.

Close reading—a learning outcome for our major—is something I do in all of my classes, and selecting the passages is part of that learning outcome. For 'Austen: Novel into Film', however, I tend to curate the passages we discuss as ones we can also explore in a screen version. A favourite example is, of course, the famous first line of *Pride and Prejudice*. Annotating a single sentence tends to stymie them at first until I ask them to annotate by circling and highlighting places that generate questions, such as

- Who says this?
- In what group is this universally acknowledged?
- Why no mention of a single woman and what she might need?
- Does a single man really need a wife?
- What about a single man without a fortune?
- What is a 'good' fortune?
- What does 'fortune' mean here?
- What is the tone of this statement?

With all of these questions on the board, we discuss how many, many questions are raised and which ones we can explore just on the basis of this sentence.

As I review close reading quizzes, I invariably notice that those who annotate bring in more specifics than those who do not; those who write have more evidence than those who only highlight; and just about every student who annotates notices more interesting things than ever end up in the resultant paragraph, something I share with them as an observation. The move to summarise, reduce, and unify seems to be overpowering, but continual practice at close reading has the potential to dislodge it a bit, if we also spend a bit of time in metacognitive discussion about how it worked (or didn't), what was challenging, and how to try it differently. Because this is a formative practice and not a summative result, and to try to maintain an inclusive classroom, I do not penalise students who make an effort but find that it is not generative for them because of their situations of body or mind; alternate modes may work better for them, such as a voice memo 'note-taking' process, typing margin notes, or even taping an interactive and collaborative reading session with a partner.

Close Looking

Close reading sends us back to the screen and the beginning of a series of close looking practices. After we have spent some time in discussion of the *Pride and Prejudice* passage, I show them the first few minutes of the 1995 and 2005 screen versions and then ask them if they noticed that first line of the novel showing up anywhere. As they observe, in the 1995 miniseries, the line is shortened a bit and uttered by Elizabeth in a snarky response to a conversation between her mother and father as the family walks from church services. Her comment that 'a single man of good fortune must be in want of a wife' generates her mother's emphatic rejoinder, 'yes, he must!' Students also point out that the 1995 miniseries provides a prologue to this scene that is not in the novel; in the miniseries opening, Darcy and Bingley on horseback assess Netherfield Hall and—unknowingly—are themselves assessed by a smiling Elizabeth, out walking. This visual frame sets up our understanding of the sentence.

As part of unfolding these layers of this filmic translation and interpretation, we look at this brief sequence a few times. I ask them to start taking notes in an unusual (for most of them) way: I hand out a double-sided storyboard template with nine frames on each side of the paper (easily found as a free download) and tell them that this format—more commonly used to plan sequences of images for films, presentations, and the like—is something we will use to record what we see: a sequence of shots that already exist. Some notice that it looks like a comics template, which is right on track and something more are familiar with because of many recent courses that use graphic novels.

Few students are surprised by a request to annotate, but most are a bit shocked by the request to do a storyboard. This is a good thing because it places just about everyone in the destabilised situation of beginners. Their first concern tends to be artistic ability, which I have to address immediately, firmly, and repeatedly. Because these are notes to help and document our process, stick figures are the norm: we want to capture as much as we can about what's in the frame for each shot and ultimately, record every one of the shots that makes up a shot sequence (or part of it). I introduce the assumption that they all notice many things as they watch a film or other screen production, and that we'll focus those observations with some basics on terminology and things to notice and then practice ways to capture what they see. If I can reduce the performance anxiety of the group, there is room for the pleasure of note-taking in a different mode, as well as, for some, the pure pleasure of drawing. (Inevitably, some produce beautiful storyboards that may or may not offer measurable evidence of their progress towards the course earning outcomes.)

We do the first storyboard very slowly, sketching the first shot with the video or stream on pause, then noting where it ends—as if the camera blinked. (I sometimes run through the entire sequence and ask them to clap or thump on the table whenever the shot changes.) We pause the next shot and keep sketching, inching our way through a minute or so comprised of around six individual shots—*many* fewer than usually comprise a movie trailer. Students handle shots of long duration, featuring a camera that follows ('tracks') the family as Mr Bennet leads them on their walk, either by drawing diagrams that indicate where the camera goes or by sketching more than one frame and marking them with arrows or notes to show they are all part of the same 'take'.

We do this without sound so that we can focus on what's in the frame—then try it again with sound to add things we have missed or things we now notice, which can extend to what words are spoken in each frame, whether anyone's speech bleeds into anyone else's image, whether there is noticeable symmetry in one shot, and so on. While some students only record a few frames and others fill both sides of the page, it is hard and impressive work all around. They are stunned by how much there is to note, even in a brief sequence with few shots, and how each viewing reveals additional details they did not notice or weren't able to capture. (They are still worried about bad art even if I assure them that this is not the purpose and show them what my drawings look like.)

Scaffolded storyboarding as training in 'close looking' is, like close reading, an effective way to both communicate the process of film analysis and assess what is actually happening for students, who are often polite, conciliatory, desirous of passing as accomplished, or simply not wanting to take on the difficulty and awkwardness of learning how to do something unfamiliar and hard.

After we do the first storyboard in class, I collect and scan their first attempts so that I have a record (and give them credit for one quiz grade). In the next class, we add on Dave Monahan's video on composing the frame and *mise en scène* (in the ancillary materials for *Looking at Movies* by Barsam and Monahan, a recommended text for my course); then, I return their storyboards with feedback, run the sequence again, and invite them to add more detail. These efforts form another quiz grade.

To guide the next session, I show them Monahan's videos on shot types and camera angles. Both are short (5–8 minutes). Then we watch a very short shot sequence from whichever book we are now on. As well as opening scenes and closing scenes, there are many, many good choices in all of the screen versions, so that finding something short enough to be manageable as well as rich is not incredibly challenging. The paper focuses on a major or minor turning point that both occurs in one of the early novels and is translated into a screen version. (See appendix for a list of ideas.)

We return to this process at least two more times before their first paper, which requires a page-to-screen comparative analysis AND a storyboard, is due a third of the way through the course. (Their knowledge of this deliverable definitely sharpens their attention.) As I explain to them, the storyboard is not a 'product' that needs to be beautiful but a record (for me) of their process and a record (for them) of their observations, to make writing the paper easier because they have evidence in a retrievable form.

We move back and forth from building reading skills for literature and reading skills for film, doing a close reading or a close looking every week. There are striking parallels between the two scaffolded activities: When I have them annotate and then write about what they notice, they invariably have details IF they annotate. Some do not annotate at all, or highlight but do not write to say what they are noticing. Similarly, with the storyboards, if I ask for specific things—distance, some aspect of lighting, etc.—they will have evidence, if minimal in some cases. We need practice in this and in talking through what we do and why. Challenges remain: those who have notes don't build them into their analyses; those with cinematographic evidence may leave out their most interesting observations. In both cases, they tend to reduce it to the big picture, not seeing that the small, messy one is more valuable. This last message is one I need to reiterate throughout the course and also take care to reinforce with my assessment of work, as when a student takes a risk with an idea and ends up with an unwieldy and uneven paper full of exciting ideas.

The second paper takes a deeper dive into film by asking them to compare two screen versions of the same important textual moment, deepening their attention to the relationships among imaginative products both across and within genres (getting more practice at allusion as well as ekphrasis). Austen film scholars have amply noted the rich comparisons invited by the two prominent versions of *Pride and Prejudice* on screen (1995 and 2005) and their enactment of Darcy's proposal, his letter after Elizbeth's refusal, and the meeting between Elizabeth and Darcy at Pemberley; there are many other great choices to explore with students as they embark on papers, such as Marianne's fall in *Sense and Sensibility* (1995 and 2008) or Anne's frantic search for Wentworth at the end of *Persuasion* (1995 and 2007). The opening and closing shot sequences in any two versions are as far as we need to look for a fascinating discussion of comparative framing. In some cases, the relationship between two screen versions is more intense than either's relationship with the novel.[5]

Comparison of visual media and indeed, the repetition of images for the purpose of analysis, generates insights that are meaningfully and sometimes painfully shaped by their own contexts. While students' discussions of the carriage scenes in two 1996 *Emma*s along with the car scene in *Clueless* (1995) are always intense, their analyses of the scene (in which Cher/Emma is left without resources in an unfamiliar part of the city after an unwanted sexual advance) were focused in the #metoo era in ways that they had not been in previous semesters when they lacked a clear language for public discussion of sexual aggression. This focus, in turn, spurred engagement in historical material on the situation of women in carriages, the dangers so legible in Austen's novels, if only temporarily, peripherally, or as worries instead of events.

By the end of this course, we work up to other issues such as lighting, the moving camera, and editing, each presenting unexpected entry points for students. John Wiltshire's excellent chapter on lighting in Austen films spurred a memorable point of connection with one of my recent students, who thought of her grandmother's stories of driving home in the dark and the horse knowing the way that the riders could not see. Suddenly the alterity of Austen's past merged with the more familiar alterity of her family heritage, and she spoke up in class.

Camera motion is central to one of the most delightful threads to explore in Austen on screen, as the rendering of the dances that are so illuminating about the social dynamics of the novels have been handled in distinctively beautiful ways, something any viewer of the 2005 *Pride and Prejudice* is likely to notice without necessarily considering how it happened. One of my students took on the monumental project of tracing, diagramming, and storyboarding the camera and dance patterns from the ball at Netherfield Hall. Editing is a rich entry point for teachers to engage the concept of representation as a purposeful act, and an occasion for students who have edited their own videos before posting to social media to consider the connections between that process and the work that professionals do—and both of these, potentially, with what could happen in the process of revising a novel (or a paper for class).

While students clearly find their own connections to films without being prompted by a teacher who is a film expert, DVDs with the director's commentary are invaluable guides for both teachers and students in understanding more intricately how a team of professionals met the challenges of filming before, during, and after filming. Aspects of the collaborative business of film, for instance, can be a topic in which business majors may be moved to bring their disciplinary training to the discussion.

Outcomes

One obvious but uncertain (in terms of its actual outcomes) benefit of using film to teach Austen is that film provides a pathway or at least opening for reluctant readers who may find early nineteenth-century literature daunting. As Louise Flavin puts it, film can address the reality that students may struggle with Austen's diction and cultural references and help 'transition students to the novels' (11). Once they see from the film that Austen is engaging, witty, applicable, and complex, they will (the argument goes) want to read the novels that catalysed the films; films are thus a form of training wheels, or perhaps a gateway drug to the greater and more positive addiction of Austen novels. When well-researched films with big production budgets picture the eighteenth century through location shoots and with period accuracy, students get a feel for 'Austen's world', even if that world is more or less National Trust or 'muddy hem' history (Sutherland, 'Muddying'); when they read the books, their imaginations will be stocked with appropriate images for visualising the Bennet home, Bath, or Pemberley, and they may have sutured those images to aspects of their own lives that Austen makes less visible. Distinctive shots of servants hauling elaborate picnic items up a steep slope for the Box Hill picnic (*Emma* dir. Diarmuid Lawrence, 1996) connects to students who work themselves in service industries or whose parents are agricultural or domestic workers.

Other, more certain, benefits include enhancing the analytical skill of close reading through the 'close looking' at film translations, as well as learning more about the novels *and* the films through comparative analysis of novel and screen to illuminate what each offers through the constraints and opportunities of its medium. An analysis of the visual, verbal, and auditory grammar of a filmed scene leads us back to the page with a heightened appreciation of how Austen unfolded it in words alone. More substantially, if we consider film not only as adaptation or imitation but also as an interpretive act of translation, response, or critique, we stand to learn much about the novels through the films.[6] Further, as *The Cinematic Jane Austen* argues, despite the fact of the novels being written a century before the invention of cinema, the dynamics of the novels are readily described as 'cinematic', which may not mean that they are easily transferred to film versions but rather that they can help us understand not simply how Austen works, but also how narrative cinema works.

We can also consider new imaginative works, not only in relation to a revered original but also on their own merits, modelling for (and learning from) our students in practicing open reception of what we read and see from a framework of attributes rather than deficits. 'Jane Austen's World' is both the title of a popular and useful blog and a convenient concept I find myself referencing (with an inner *mea culpa*) when I speak to undergraduates about the novels and their contexts. In actuality, the organism that is Austen's world is far more amorphous and boundaryless. Readers, devotees, scholars, critics, and various *translators* all sustain and grow Austen's world, in the process transforming it with their own interpretive acts.

Perhaps more so than other authors, Austen seems to have invited a sense of ownership or possession, so that readers are particularly aware of having a 'my Jane Austen' or 'my Jane' and of enjoying community with others who have personal Janes who complement their own.

This sense of community—with 'Jane' or with other Janeites—is wonderfully generative of many positive things, including, in some cases, a loyalty to the primacy of the novel (or, as one of my students observed, to 'the experience of reading the novel', which is even more intimate a loyalty). But few of my students enter my class with that loyalty to Austen and thus they are wide open both to considering the relationships between novel and film in various models—imitation, adaptation, translation, version, conversation, interpretation, critique, and as another student framed it, challenge (this in connection with Rozema's *Mansfield Park*). The film challenges the novel: to say more; to say it to this audience; to say it more quickly or with more visual description. This openness to Austen films may invite them to be less dogmatic about those reading or viewing experiences to which they feel emotionally sutured and treat as 'originals' toward whom 'fidelity' is owed. They may be willing to consider the merits, for example, of a live action version of Disney's animated *Little Mermaid* (which for them is the ur-text of this story, as most have not read Hans Christian Anderson's text).

Further, changes in cultural and historical contexts and attitudes among groups of students continually inform the kinds of conversations we are invited to have about the films (and new films keep appearing). If resistance to Fanny Price's 'creepmouse' tendencies in the novel informed the two most recent screen versions' revision of Fanny, Fanny of the novel found staunch supporters in several of my classrooms from 2008 to 2012 (around the same time as the publication of the *Twilight* Series, with its emphasis on abstinence) for her stubborn virtue in a morally lax and sexually coercive climate, a resistance that took on new layers in the context of #metoo and Jeffrey Epstein's crimes.

Supported attention to cinematographic elements gives students a way into craft, just as an exercise that asks them to locate the similes in a paragraph will be less paralyzing than a request to mark all distinctive literary techniques. Learning how to identify and write about film evidence is useful cross-training for literary analysis as well as providing an area in which students across the disciplines may excel as local experts. And indeed, by four novels in, students have the pleasure of feeling expertise in patterns of various kinds, and in this case, those patterns invite a wider range of intelligences. As well as opening up another way to engage the novel for students whose interests and learning styles tend toward the visual, the multiple languages of film create equally rich invitations for students across the disciplines to *make things*.

Students' final projects in this course have included deeper analyses of a single film version in relation to an Austen novel, a comparative analysis of multiple films and their relationship to the novel and each other, and more evolved historicisations of certain threads in the novels. In addition to the dance project, discussed earlier, musical compositions inspired by the novels, garment research and construction (dresses and bonnets), and a memorably delicious Georgian wedding cake exemplify projects that have given students not only more understanding of Austen's historical context but also a window on the complexity and duration of the collaborative process of making a film. Screen adaptations of scenes NOT addressed by the major films and free adaptations of certain scenes (a screenplay that moved the Elliots to Santa Monica after the real estate crash, for example) have also been effective learning activities. With the addition of expertise in digital writing in my department, a number of my students used Twine to create digital translations of the theme Austen often provides of possible outcomes that do not occur (often in the context of narrative irony about genres such as the gothic). Another popular project has been the creation of lesson plans for a single day or a week of teaching at the middle or high school level. A number of my students intend to be teachers, though not necessarily of literature. In doing these projects, they have generated fun products like board games, but also and more fundamentally, gained a deeper understanding of lesson planning from objectives to assessment that hopefully serves them well in their later training. These projects may seem lightweight in terms of training literary scholars to prepare them for graduate programmes, but students with this goal can be guided appropriately. Two essential elements of all projects are a critical introduction that explains the rationale for the project and a metacognitive reflection on what they learned from doing it and what they would do differently given another week. While this wide range of culminating projects is certainly possible without ever seeing a single Austen-based film, I would argue that seeing the film and foregrounding alternative forms of reading and looking opens up a livelier invitation to do so. There have definitely been projects that did not take the invitation seriously (a popsicle-stick carriage languishes in my abandoned university office as I write, unaccompanied by any rich historical grounding in carriage taxonomies or analysis of the language of carriages in Austen), but these have been the exceptions.

My students come into this course on Jane Austen and film with a sense that they are going to get something: a requirement, a grade, and whatever I have to teach them. If they know anything about Austen, they may enter the class thinking that what they have to contribute is enthusiasm, eagerness, perhaps knowledge, like the student who had treasured hardbound copies of the books and had read them multiple times. Few think that their specific expertise, which may be anchored to Southern California and/or Mexico or even just to the county we live in, transfers to something meaningful to say about Austen; but they may realise that they have something to say about film, and not only because many have grown up so near to the geographic heart of the industry. By the end of the course, they realise that they have something to say about both Austen and film. My hope is that they will not only continue to watch each new production as it emerges (and email me to tell me their thoughts on it) but also consider returning to read the novels. I wish it especially in the context of COVID-19 and the daily experience many of my students are having—of life in close quarters with those who find it hard to understand or support the practice of silent reading, or that of reading a novel aloud to the entire family, as much as they support the attainment of a college degree. Elizabeth Bennet, Anne Elliot, and Austen herself would understand.

Acknowledgements

I would like to acknowledge the kind help of Drs. Marcia Folsom, John Wiltshire, and Robin Keehn in the preparation of this chapter.

Close Reading and Close Looking

Notes

1 A useful source of information on screen versions is the Jane Austen Society of North America's 'Austen on Screen' page, http://jasna.org/austen/screen/.
2 Linda Hutcheon's foundational work *A Theory of Adaptation* theorizes a range of ways that adaptation is 'repetition without replication' (7) whose differences signify in various ways.
3 Personal communication from the editors. I am indebted to Drs Folsom and Wiltshire for their kind and collegial conversations with me about this chapter.
4 The timing of *Northanger Abbey*—first accepted for publication, last published (with *Persuasion)* of the six novels—creates some options in a course with the chronological structure I use. While I've tried it both first and last, first is what I have stayed with because of the film component of the course. Excerpts from the teenage writings are also an excellent way to get students surprised and engaged by Austen early on, and they will hear echoes of them in Rozema's *Mansfield Park*.
5 An example of this is the 2007 *Northanger Abbey* (dir. Jon Jones) whose opening sequence draws directly on Austen's narration but then moves, via a parental discussion of the dangers of reading (not in the book) to a touchstone scene of gothic-inspired adolescent fantasy: exactly where the 1987 *Northanger Abbey* (dir. Giles Foster) begins.
6 I am indebted to Kamilla Elliot's concepts of 'adaptations as criticism' and adaptations as 'editions' (126, 127).

Works Cited

Austen on Screen. Jane Austen Society of North America. http://jasna.org/austen/screen/

Barsam, Richard, and Dave Monahan. *Looking at Movies*, 6th ed., Norton, 2018.

Elliott, Kamilla. 'Teaching Wuthering Heights through Its Film and Television Adaptations.' *Approaches to Teaching Emily Brontë's Wuthering Heights*, edited by Sue Lonoff and Terri A. Hasseler. MLA, 2006, 126–135.

Flavin, Louise. *Jane Austen in the Classroom: Viewing the Novel/Reading the Film*. Peter Lang, 2004.

Folsom, Marcia, editor. *Approaches to Teaching Jane Austen's Pride and Prejudice*. MLA, 1993.

Folsom, Marcia, editor. *Approaches to Teaching Jane Austen's Emma*. MLA, 2004.

Folsom, Marcia, and John Wiltshire, editors. *Approaches to Teaching Jane Austen's Mansfield Park*. MLA, 2014.

Folsom, Marcia, and John Wiltshire, editors. *Approaches to Teaching Jane Austen's Persuasion*. MLA, 2021.

Hutcheon, Linda. *A Theory of Adaptation*, 2nd ed., Routledge, 2013.

Lonoff, Sue, and Terri A. Hasseler, editors. *Approaches to Teaching Emily Brontë's Wuthering Heights*. MLA, 2006.

Macdonald, Gina, and Andrew F. Macdonald, editors. *Jane Austen on Screen*. Cambridge UP, 2003.

Monaghan, David, Ariane Hudelet, and John Wiltshire. *The Cinematic Jane Austen*. McFarland, 2009.

Moody, Ellen. 'The Three Northanger Abbey Films.' Jane Austen's World 6 Apr. 2008, https://janeaustensworld.wordpress.com/2008/04/06/the-three-northanger-abbey-films/

Mueller, Pam A., and Danie M. Oppenheimer. 'The Pen is Mightier than the Keyboard: Advantages of Longhand over Laptop Note Taking.' *Psychological Science*, vol. 25, 2014, pp. 1159–1168. doi: 10.1177/0956797614524581.

Parrill, Sue. *Jane Austen on Film and Television*. McFarland, 2002.

Sutherland, Kathryn. 'Jane Austen on Screen.' *The Cambridge Companion to Jane Austen*, 2nd ed., edited by Edward Copeland and Juliet McMaster. Cambridge UP, 2011, pp. 215–231.

Sutherland, Kathryn. 'Muddying the Hem: How to Make the Great Jane Austen Movie – From Makeover to Minimalism.' *Times Literary Supplement* 3 Apr. 2007, pp. 20–21.

Thompson, Emma. *The Sense and Sensibility Screenplay & Diaries: Bringing Jane Austen's Novel to Film*, 2nd ed., Newmarket, 1996.

Troost, Linda, and Sayre Greenfield, editors. *Jane Austen in Hollywood*, 2nd ed., UP of Kentucky, 2001.

Wiltshire, John. 'By Candlelight: Jane Austen, Technology, and the Heritage Film.' *The Cinematic Jane Austen*, edited by David Monaghan, Ariane Hudelet, and John Wiltshire. McFarland, 2009, pp. 38–56.

Wiltshire, John. *Recreating Jane Austen*. Cambridge UP, 2001.

Wyett, Jodi. 'Sex, Sisterhood, and the Cinema: Sense and Sensibility in Conversation.' *The Cinematic Eighteenth Century*, edited by Srividaya Swaminathan. Routledge, 2017, pp. 154–169.

Appendix: Resources

Preparing the Teacher

My limited background in film, beyond a lifelong love of it and one cinematography course as an undergraduate, expanded in the way that many of us develop as teachers: I gained most of my knowledge of film terms when I was assigned an elements of cinema course for my teaching load in my very first year in a tenure track job. I learned on the job, mentored by another teacher who had been teaching film for years. More to the point, however, I regularly draw on other teachers who have created invaluable resources for teaching my students the basics of cinematic analysis so that I can draw on that shared language without having to prepare in ways that may not be comfortable to me.

While I originally cobbled together a basic primer of film terms—the kind of thing that is now very easy to find online through the generosity of the internet—I suggest a good film textbook as a recommended resource for students. Assigning additional readings and screenings is not appropriate for the emphasis of my course, but a teacher who chooses to focus more on film analysis by narrowing the focus to a few novels might well assign the entire book. After trying several, I am particularly happy with Richard Barsam and Dave Monahan's *Looking at Movies* (Norton) and even happier with the online (and DVD) tutorials prepared by Dave Monahan (not to be confused with Austen scholar David Monaghan).

As noted, another invaluable preparation tool for me as a teacher are the directors' commentaries available on some of the DVDs of Austen films and miniseries. Emma Thompson's *Sense and Sensibility: Screenplay and Diaries* is another wonderful resource to get a sense of the collaborative process of making an Austen film from the perspective of someone with multiple roles in that process.

Preparing the Resources

In increasing access to Austen or any other text by using screen versions, it is crucial to attend to a range of issues of access. I name a few I have encountered and the institutional supports that have been essential to meeting them.

Access to screen versions in the classroom:

> For instructors with access to DVD projection equipment or other forms of streaming, screening Austen in class time may be the best option provided there is enough time for screening and discussion of the film and the book. (In some cases, discussing the film alone may be what teachers choose, with reading the book an extra credit activity spurred on by the experience of screening.) I note that providing closed captioning and other accommodations students need to participate is both a legal and ethical obligation to our students. I would also suggest that all students benefit from closed captioning; its UDL (universal design in learning) benefits supersede the visual interference with the frame. Potentially, individual students can turn off captions for re-screening and study as desired (videos prepared for streaming by my university's media library are required to be captioned and these captions cannot be removed). My students and I tend to appreciate captions in multiple contexts, including trying to follow and digest fast-paced dialogue, as well as many of the difficult listening situations produced by COVID-19, such as trying to continue our studies while meeting the ever-present demands of family life or while roommates are sleeping. Audio description is a concern I have yet to have the opportunity

to learn about in the context of this course as no visually impaired students have taken it with me.

Access outside the classroom through library reserve and video on demand:

My university is able to prepare and make accessible streaming video of materials they or I own as fair use items provided that the physical copies are also on reserve for students to check out. This was for years the only way students had access outside of class without purchasing their own copies. Some of these procedures have been shaped by COVID-19 and our shift to a virtual campus. Students without the level of internet access to screen films online at home may have relied on the school library and now be faced with yet another challenge. These are all issues that anyone undertaking a sustained use of film in an Austen class would ideally explore in advance to consider alternate options.

Private access through subscription services:

While my students have often supplemented institutional access with a range of private approaches including personal copies of DVDs, access through excellent local libraries, and (increasingly) online subscription services like Netflix and Amazon Prime or Masterpiece, I have been able to avoid requiring additional purchases because of my university's excellent support for multimedia teaching. However, given that Austen novels are readily available as e-texts, I can imagine that some instructors requiring screenings outside of class might choose to require that students purchase their own copies of selected films; with an author in the public domain, there are at least many options for reducing the cost of textbooks, even if that may mean reduced access to the benefits of edited volumes with explanatory notes.

Taking the course online

In Fall 2020 I taught Austen: Novel into Film online for the first time. Eighty in two sections of the course attended either or both of two 75-minute synchronous Zoom sessions I led each week. Because online learning in Fall 2020 was planned for (as opposed to the sudden shift to virtual learning in March 2020), I had the summer to think through which parts of the class (background lectures and film screenings, for example) could be rendered in an asynchronous, self-paced form; which parts could be modified for online synchronous learning (breakout group discussions, group annotations of google doc passages, storyboarding practice with YouTube clips, Zoom panel discussions of final projects); and which parts invited reinvention, such as the notion of firm deadlines and printed papers.

Many of these changes improved students' learning and my teaching, and will be part of all future courses, regardless of mode. The self-paced aspect of the asynchronous learning was both a given and an ethical choice during COVID-19, given how many serious disruptions students were fielding at home, at work, and in the process of juggling multiple online courses for the first time. It resulted, however, in various forms of feasible course customisation to help students gain confidence in the unfamiliar and/or uncomfortable skills of close reading and close looking. By creating a few deeply humbling short videos demonstrating my process of close reading and close looking, I was able to give students a model they could watch in their own time frame. Similarly, when students screened and answered questions about two video clips of the same textual moment in an asynchronous, online Moodle 'lesson', rather than during a synchronous class, they were able to schedule the lesson for a good time, take as much time as they needed, and repeat the lesson for a higher score—essentially choosing their own Austen adventure. Multimodal options were another plus; the pandemic spurred me to be more flexible with formats for readers' journals and accept them in neat handwriting, video, or graphic notes/comics as well as traditional formats. Not only are multimedia journals a perfect fit with the course content, but students were also more likely to be able to actually think about them and more likely to complete them. Also, with more time at home and less commuting, students seemed to take on some richer final projects—dresses, reticules, and an epistolary dear Jane video involving period dress and quill pens. The course, in short, proved productively customisable to lives lived in close quarters with some and socially distanced from others (not unlike the situation of Austen characters).

For my part, I could automate some grading and offer voice or video comments to facilitate the rest. I got to know more students' thinking processes better through our expanded epistolary relationship (another suggestion of Austen) than I might have in a large live class. Given the generosity of various Austen societies in shifting to online access, I was not only able to attend all of the JASNA Meeting, but also able to connect my students to online events such as JASNA lectures and Austen Wednesdays. Like many teachers, then, I found that the constraints of online learning during COVID-19 forced me both to focus on essential learning (and what that really means) and to create more inclusive ways for students to meet the learning outcomes of this course and all of my courses.

40

MYTH, REALITY, AND GLOBAL CELEBRITY: TEACHING JANE AUSTEN ONLINE

Gillian Dow and Kim Simpson

UNIVERSITY OF SOUTHAMPTON AND CHAWTON HOUSE

Introduction: The Business of Bicentenaries

Walking across the wide lawn, fringed on one side by the deep green at the lower edge of the wilderness and with the red bricks of Chawton House catching the afternoon sun behind them, are two women. On the left, the younger cuts an elegant figure in a white tea gown printed with pretty blue flowers. The feather in her straw bonnet bobs gently with her step. She is accompanied by her mother, bedecked in heavier purple silk, red-faced in the heat and waggling a fan. In front of them a chubby baby coos in the latest Silver Cross pram, entertained by a clip-on electric mobile emitting a tinny lullaby. They stop for a selfie, trying to fit the whole house into the background, whilst not losing the baby's head from the frame. It is Regency week, 2018, and the village of Chawton—containing Jane Austen's House Museum and Chawton House, the Elizabethan manor house once owned by Austen's brother Edward and now home to a considerable library—is a focal point for the annual pilgrimage of Jane Austen fans, many of whom show up in full Regency costume to walk in Jane's footsteps.

Scholarly responses to both Austen fandom and affective responses to her literature that involve re-enactment have, in the past, ranged from the mildly baffled to the outright scornful. The sense that such behaviour is not 'serious' has been carefully interrogated by many, including Deidre Lynch in her compelling introduction to her edited collection, *Janeites*, first published in 2000. Lynch wrote of 'contemporary codes of scholarly conduct' which 'would warn the career-conscious critic against letting the wrong people know of her desire to, for instance, wear Regency costume and dance at a Jane Austen Literary Ball' (14). Times have changed. This is an academic age of public outreach, which enforces the necessity of demonstrating tangible impact for one's research and engaging with public humanities in the broadest sense. As a result, there has been ever-more attention paid by numerous scholars to embracing and engaging all readers of Austen and viewers of adaptations of her works. A recent co-authored book entitled *Engaging the Age of Jane Austen: Public Humanities in Practice* defends the continuing relevance of Austen's work, and of the humanities more broadly, to our current moment, suggesting ways to engage broad-based communities with Austen's writing.[1] Engagement can certainly involve wholehearted participation in fan communities—dancing, dressing up, embroidery workshops, and performance more generally. One 'community' where there is considerable overlap between professional critics and fans is found amongst visitors to places connected with Austen and the world of her novels. Claudia Johnson reminds us in a chapter

DOI: 10.4324/9780429398155-40-46

523

on Jane Austen's House in her 2012 study, *Jane Austen's Cults and Cultures,* that 'the *treasures* we might cherish for their power to conjure Austen's presence can also *bewilder* us into a false sense of the fullness of her being' (179). But there is no denying that literary tourism can provoke a genuine sense of proximity to a much-loved author. At Chawton House, one of the only authentic pieces of furniture that remains from the days when Jane Austen used to dine there with her brother Edward is a dining table. Some visitors take time to sit at each place at the table so they can say that they sat exactly where Jane Austen once sat. Engaging with this community of visitors, and with their affective investments in material culture, is now an important part of the work of curators and scholars in the heritage industry.

The literary-tourist community is large. In 2018 alone, the Jane Austen House Museum welcomed 41,124 visitors and Chawton House welcomed 14,200; these numbers are growing each year, and both houses have increasing footfall embedded firmly in their strategic and resilience planning for the future. Despite the struggle faced by many heritage houses to survive in an unfavourable economic climate, their popularity is not waning; indeed, the very conditions that threaten the old estates and country manors also make them havens for those wishing to escape the troubled present. Austen, her houses, and the genteel British past that she—for some, at least—represents, is no exception. The National Trust has done a great deal of 'branding' of their properties for lovers of Austen and adaptation: as their website puts it, it's 'easier to follow in the footsteps of Lizzie and Darcy or Elinor and Marianne than you might think'.[2] One can visit Lyme Park, Basildon Park, Belton House, Laycock Village, or Montacute House in the hunt for these beloved characters. There's no evidence at all that Jane Austen did, but—as a volunteer put it when interviewed about Stourhead's starring role in the 2005 *Pride and Prejudice*—she should have done (Seal).

The village of Chawton, and neighbouring Alton, have invested significantly in 'reclaiming' Austen from Bath in recent years: the Alton Regency Week—now in its twelfth year—is part of this endeavour. Investment in 'Hampshire's Jane' has been key, too, for the wider region. 2017 and 2018 were big years in the Jane Austen heritage industry. 2017 marked 200 years since Austen's death, and 2018 was the last of a slew of bicentenaries of her novels—200 years since the posthumous publication of *Persuasion* and *Northanger Abbey*.[3] Events were put on across the country at sites with even the loosest connection to the author, or in some cases, no connection at all. At the beginning of 2018, Hampshire County Council commissioned an economic impact evaluation of the Jane Austen 200 commemorations, drawn together by the Hampshire Cultural Trust. Tourism South East's report, which analysed attendance at key Jane Austen attractions in Hampshire, including Chawton House, Jane Austen's House Museum, and Winchester Cathedral, proved the profound effect of Austen tourism on the heritage and hospitality sectors, estimating the impact at close to £21 million ('Jane Effect').

At Chawton House, as Executive Director (2014–2019) and Postdoctoral Fellow (2016-present), we arranged a series of events to participate in key Austen bicentenaries. In 2017, our overarching project was titled 'Reimagining Reputations: Austenmania and What We Forgot'. We explored Jane Austen's immense popularity, but also aimed to introduce women writers who have been lost, written out of history, or neglected except in universities. Our primary exhibition, which ran from 12 June to 24 September 2017, was entitled 'Fickle Fortunes: Jane Austen and Germaine de Staël', and it explored Austen alongside one of her most famous European contemporaries, seeking to interrogate the reversal of fortune that saw a moderately successful English author overtake a European superstar to become the most famous woman writer in the world.[4] Alongside the exhibition, we organised a programme including evening lectures by visiting scholars and authors, concerts that recreated the music Austen would have enjoyed, a study day, 'Jane Austen in Chawton', Regency week curator's tours, and a large international conference. Wherever Jane Austen's name appeared in the programming, events would sell out, with audiences eager to hear about all things Austen, from punctuation and amateur theatricals to *Sanditon* and the Regency Ball industry. The 2018 Gothic exhibition at Chawton House, 'The Art of Freezing the Blood', continued to draw on Austen, exploring Gothic influences on two very different bicentenary novels: Austen's *Northanger Abbey* and Mary Shelley's *Frankenstein*.

The intense public appetite for learning about Austen, coupled with our personal interest in her extraordinary rise to become one of the world's most canonical writers, led us to take the step from the physical to the virtual by creating a free two-week Massive Open Online Course (MOOC) on the Future Learn platform: 'Jane Austen: Myth, Reality and Global Celebrity'. The course sought to situate Jane Austen in her local Hampshire context, whilst examining what she means to a global audience today. We wanted, from the outset, to challenge some persistent myths surrounding Austen's writing and her life, myths that have concerned us in our public-facing roles at Chawton House. Devoney Looser, in her coda to *The Making of Jane Austen* puts it neatly when she worries about the tendency of 'keeping intoning the limiting stories about Austen, her fiction, and her cultural legacy ("she was hesitant to publish!" "Darcy became sexy in 1995")' (221). We share Looser's concern about these limiting stories, and we take her call to arms seriously. In our teaching we wanted to challenge our participants' preconceptions by inviting them to go back to some source material and encouraging them to think about how we know what we think we know.

The course was designed to make the most of existing links between the University of Southampton and Chawton House and to attract visitors to the latter, and indeed to the Jane Austen House Museum, by showcasing resources at both institutions and simply by demonstrating the beauty of each place. Course content, created in collaboration with the University's Digital Learning Team, covered Jane Austen's education and reading; influences on her writing, including theatre, music, gardens and landscaping, money and capital; reputation and biography; and translation, adaptation, and legacy. We touch on issues of curation and on variant editions and paratextual presentations of Austen's novels through the ages. Content was delivered in a variety of ways designed to appeal to different learners, from video discussions and interviews with specialists to short articles, from audience polls and close reading exercises to Padlet walls on which participants could share artwork or recordings of their performances of music from the Austen family music books. We were fortunate in being able to draw on the expertise of colleagues across the Faculty of Humanities, notably from the departments of English, Film and Music.[5] Indeed, another of the objects of the course was to highlight the University of Southampton as a hub of expertise on the long eighteenth century, adaptation, and on Jane Austen's writing more specifically. Our new MA in Jane Austen has recruited some participants via this route, and we hope to see more in the future.

As a potentially lucrative opportunity for genuine outreach and public engagement with academic research, and for fruitful collaborations between academic and heritage institutions, these sorts of online pedagogical tools are becoming increasingly vital for universities contending with ever-changing technological advancements and financial challenges. Indeed, although subject to anxieties about scholarly rigour that are reminiscent of the academic disdain for Janeite engagements with Austen, and which often turn out to be rooted in broader anxieties about the digital future of higher education, MOOCs can be progressive and responsive learning tools which challenge the traditional higher education paradigm. As one article on the impact of MOOCs puts it:

> At their core, MOOCs are simply academic courses. What makes them innovative and potentially game-changing is the 'Massive' and 'Open' aspects of their approach. [...] The promise of MOOCs is that they might democratize higher education, break down historic and well entrenched class and geographical barriers, and tackle woeful higher education access, quality, and relevance outcomes. This in turn will allow people to gain skills that will make them more employable and more productive in their employment or at least more knowledgeable, informed, and connected in the knowledge economy. (Nath et al. 157)

Arguably, this overstates the revolutionary impact of courses that carry no formal, 'marketable' qualifications, that are not widely taken up in the developing world, and that tend to attract older/retired learners drawn by interest alone. However, MOOCs are almost certainly having an effect on the wider shifts towards the digital and are paving the way for new forms of distance learning that universities are increasingly interested in. There were pragmatic, indeed financially-driven, motives for offering a free Jane Austen course as a 'taster' of the University of Southampton's general offer. However, neither of us would have done this had it not been for a belief in the power of public humanities to inspire, and to do so for free. Ultimately, the course design, and each run of the course, had to be fun, both for us and for the participants.

In April 2018, the course went live, and drew an audience of almost 10,000. A second run extended the course to three weeks, responding to the feedback of initial participants and ensuring that the subject matter remained responsive. This grew the audience to well over 15,000. Learners included subject specialists—academics, librarians, and heritage workers—autodidacts, students, retirees, full-blown Janeites who knew her novels and letters inside out, and those who had yet to read any Austen at all, curious to see what the fuss was about. The course drew these people together from all over the world, and every continent—Europe and America, but also countries as diverse as Libya, Iceland, Peru, Kenya, and Indonesia—a testament to Austen's remarkable and continuing global reach. The active message boards, in which participants converse with each other and the course tutors, yielded 37,366 messages in total over the first two runs. Three further runs of the course were held in both 2019 and in 2020. Our intention is to continue to run the course as long as there continues to be a demand for it.

In the rest of this chapter, we reflect on the process of creating and curating material for the course, drawing from our experience and from data and audience responses from the initial runs of the course. How do you take a writer as well-known as Jane Austen and design a course with something for everyone? How do you differentiate learners, ensuring that each is satisfied? What is important in teaching Jane Austen and her context? What are the specific benefits and disadvantages of the online learning space? What is it that people want to know? How do you remain scholarly, or negotiate sensitively between the popular and the scholarly? Here, we outline some of the challenges posed by online learning, sharing our practice of translating our research for a non-specialist audience, engaging with participants on the message boards, and responding to feedback in subsequent iterations of the course.

Texts in Context: Recreating Austen's World

Our primary approach to Austen and her writing on the course is to set her within her historical context. This was informed by our own research, as well as by the remit of Chawton House to promote Austen's female contemporaries and predecessors. Is Austen a gateway drug to all things long eighteenth century? She can certainly be made to be so, and participants often request reading lists of other eighteenth-century women writers, delighting to learn of Ann Radcliffe, Charlotte Smith, and Mary Robinson, in addition to writers they may have heard of like Frances Burney and Maria Edgeworth. An historicist approach is further legitimised by a great many recent volumes of 'Companions' to Austen, including this one. In her Preface to the 2005 edited collection *Jane Austen in Context*, published by Cambridge University Press alongside the new scholarly editions of all of Austen's novels, Janet Todd points out that the collection 'necessarily speaks to the interests of the twenty-first century' by addressing 'issues of nationalism and empire as well as transport and the professions' (xxii). Alongside essays on Austen's life, works, and critical fortunes, the section on historical and cultural context includes agriculture, print culture, dress, manners, and religion. Our coverage, on the online course, is by no means comprehensive, but we do invite historicisation, with articles on location, education, and reviewing in week one, which focuses on education and reading, and articles on theatre, music, landscape, money, and celebrity in week two, where the focus is on influences on Austen.

There is, on each run of the course, some interesting and productive resistance to this approach, even whilst participants express their enjoyment of the source material. In the introductory video to week two—which we designed to be light and engaging in tone—Gillian claims 'we cannot read a novel in isolation', which proves somewhat controversial. Yes we can, many participants observe in their comments; it is the text that matters. The comment about literature in isolation was always designed to be provocative. Whilst a fuller discussion of historicist and formalist critical approaches to Austen's work cannot take place on a short, accessible course of this nature, we can certainly point participants towards further reading. Ultimately, we want to get participants thinking about influences on Austen's writing. It is one way of challenging an important myth—that Austen doesn't engage with the politics or events of her period, that her writing springs forth from a country village, untroubled by the broader concerns of the age.[6] So whilst we certainly do not claim, on the course, that Austen's novels are *about* female education (or gardens, or music, or money, or the theatre, or the slave trade, or the revolutionary and Napoleonic Wars), we do look in quite some detail at how she might be providing commentary on such topics in her writing.

We benefit here from some extremely useful online resources that enable participants to look up information themselves. In a section on what Austen read, we get participants thinking about the breadth of her reading, and in particular her reading of fiction, inviting them to think about what her response to Mary Brunton's 1811 *Self-Control* might have meant: 'I am looking over Self Control again, & my opinion is confirmed of its being an excellently-meant, elegantly-written Work, without anything of Nature or Probability in it'. Questions about what this last phrase means lead participants to discuss the construction of the perfect heroine, but also to consider genre, providing a space to talk about romance, realism, and the rise of the novel. We also, in more recent iterations of the course, introduce them to readingwithausten.com, a new collaborative project led by Peter Sabor at the University of McGill in collaboration with Chawton House. This website recreates the library of Jane Austen's brother Edward Knight at Godmersham Park in Kent, using the 1818 catalogue and the extant Knight collection, today on deposit at Chawton House. Here, participants can browse the shelves of a gentleman's country house library, noting its contents. They observe large quantities of sermons, works on estate management, and diverse fiction. They are mostly surprised by the amount of material in French in the collection, and on the inclusion of 'radical' authors such as Voltaire and Rousseau. We encourage thoughts on what Austen may have read on her visits to her brother—she spent around ten months at Godmersham in total—whilst pointing out the speculative nature of any conclusions we may come to.

Part of the emphasis on Austen's reading in week one of the course is to draw out contemporary thoughts on education, and by extension, the education of her characters. We frame the debate on female education as something that united women writers of the long eighteenth century. We also provide participants with extracts from Mary Wollstonecraft's *Vindication of the Rights of Women* (1792) and Hannah More's *Strictures of the Modern System of Female Education* (1799). By encouraging them to think about the similarities and differences between both writers—each standing to represent the radical, and the conservative, viewpoint—we get them to engage with key concepts in feminist thought and then to consider how these might appear in extracts that address accomplishments and education from *Pride and Prejudice, Mansfield Park,* and *Emma*. The discussion can be lively, and polarising. Some participants are extremely resistant to ideas that Austen herself may have been in any way 'radical' in her response to the position of women in her society, or 'proto-feminist' in her outlook. Others, influenced perhaps by the film adaptations of the 1990s and 2000s, are quick to read Austen and some of her characters (particularly Elizabeth Bennet, but also Marianne Dashwood, Emma Woodhouse, and Mary Crawford) as outspoken, pioneering feminists.

In week two, we move to broader potential influences on Austen and her writing. We look at Austen's love of the theatre, inviting participants to think about her engagement with Shakespeare's plays in life and in her writing. We point them towards the Folger Shakespeare Library 2016 exhibition that compared Austen and Shakespeare's Global Literary celebrity. We give links to the digitised Austen family music books and encourage those who can play an instrument to record their own version of one of the pieces in the books and to post the results in a 'virtual drawing room'. The idea is to interrogate our own twenty-first-century ideas of female accomplishment and to think about what it might mean, in Austen's novels, to be an accomplished woman, thus continuing the discussion over from week one. Many participants are, of course, aware of the discussion on the topic between Darcy, Miss Bingley, and Elizabeth Bennet in *Pride and Prejudice*, not least because of memorable adaptations of the scene. This section is designed to enhance their understanding of this much-loved passage and to think about the changing education debate in the long eighteenth century more generally.

A section on gardens and landscape includes an interview with Southampton colleague Professor Stephen Bending, who explains some of the landscape features that appear in Austen's fiction—the wilderness, the walled garden, and the ha-ha—as well as outlining the eighteenth-century landscape improvements led by Capability Brown and Humphrey Repton. Participants also hear about Gilpin's picturesque, divisions between country and city, and how the outside spaces of the country estate are gendered. Extracts from *Mansfield Park* (particularly Chapters 9 and 10) then invite participants to explore how Austen's descriptions of landscape aim to produce national identity, how they make use of symbolism to aid plot development and characterisation, and how they engage with contemporary writers, in particular Romantic poets. Feedback on the course suggests that the participants relish the chance to exercise their analytical skills and focus closely on Austen's prose: more close reading activities may well be one way of expanding the material and learning activities in the future.

One of the most enduringly popular sections on the MOOC is one written for the second run of the course by a graduate student in the department of English. Alison Daniell designed a series of tasks enabling participants to think about variations of wealth within Austen's novels, from inheritance, estates, and income to social capital. These sections look at Austen's own finances (including a link to her 1807 year-end account) and outline the complexities of capital in relation to the eighteenth-century marriage market. Participants are introduced to the currency converter measuringworth.com, and asked to consider what Austen's characters are worth today, providing insight into the wider economic background against which she was writing, and enabling discussions of social class distinctions, too. The Google Books version of *A Master-Key to the Rich Ladies Treasury, or, the Widower and Bachelor's Directory* proves shocking to a great many participants, used to thinking of Georgian and Regency Society as genteel and refined. We invite comparisons with modern 'rich lists', and the transactional nature of marriage both in Austen's own age, and now.

All teachers of literature must have engaged with concerns about the 'relatability' of texts in our classrooms, whether they be virtual classrooms like the MOOC environment, or smaller seminar groups on various university campuses across the globe. This is much more the case for literature of earlier periods: the eighteenth century feels, in the twenty-first century, increasingly remote. Our aim in drawing comparisons between Austen's time and our own in the first part of the course is not to make her 'relatable', but rather to draw out the nuances in her writing in an intelligible way, and to explain and illuminate the historical specificity of the period in which her fiction was first composed, published, and read. The second half of the course moves on to consider the afterlife of Austen's fiction and biography and the way that subsequent generations 'made' her into the Austens that are recognised by modern readers and scholars.

Making Jane Austen: Biography, Adaptation, Myth

At the outset of the course, we ask participants the question 'what does Jane Austen mean to you?' Their answers cast light on their various motivations for taking the course. Whilst many express a desire to learn more about the historical moment, others, seeing Austen as an inspiration, want to understand her life. 'She was a voice in her time for all women', writes one. Another is rather less celebratory: 'At the moment she is simply the preacher's daughter who wrote some material that I and many others over the years have found to be entertaining. I await more information on her character and personality as the course progresses'. Whilst the earlier sections of the course aim to explore how Austen came to write what she did, and what literary and cultural influences she was drawing on, the later sections turn to look at the making of her reputation in the years after she died and to scrutinise our obsession with Jane Austen as a person. Asking such a question at the outset throws into sharp relief the different readerly investments in what John Wiltshire calls 'Jane Austen', as opposed to Jane Austen—a collection of fantasies adhering to a name, a discourse rather than a person (3). The familiar web of contradictory versions emerges out of participant responses: polite and retiring Aunt Jane, creator of quaint and apolitical worlds into which we can escape from our busy twenty-first century lives; Austen, the acerbic social critic eager to demonstrate the difficulties her heroines faced in a brutal Regency marriage marketplace; Jane, old friend and writer of romances, which thrill whilst also comforting.

Our section on biography aimed to help participants understand the making of Jane Austen as an ongoing process. We start, naturally, with Henry Austen's 1817 biographical note, which prefaced her posthumous novels, and ask readers to reflect on his agenda. A video discussion between Emma Clery, whose dual biography of Jane and Henry Austen came out in 2017, and Rebecca Smith, herself an Austen descendent and novelist, then fleshes out the development of her early biography, from Henry Austen's enlarged memoir in the 1833 Bentley edition of Austen's complete works, through James Edward Austen Leigh's 1870 memoir, to the first edition of Jane Austen's letters, edited by Lord Brabourne in 1884. Clery and Smith bring to light the ways in which different strands of the family had different investments in their posthumous presentations of Jane Austen, both protective and commercial. They open up for participants the ways in which the destruction of papers and excisions made in a bid to control the family legacy might have left us with a partial, curated, or sanitised version of the author, which nonetheless remains strangely fixed. Participants enjoy considering the ethics of these practices on the message boards. We wanted them to grasp, as Kathryn Sutherland (quoting Susan Sontag) put it in a chapter on biography in *Jane Austen's Textual Lives*, that:

> [t]he kinds of truths biographies and portraits deal in are not the replicable truths to be found in head moulds, death masks, or photographs but the truths of conversation, changing with its participants. Biographies, Jane Austen's included, are 'statements about the world', not 'pieces of it'. (117)

The filming took place at Chawton House, and includes early editions of the biographies in question, including a beautifully-bound first edition of *Northanger Abbey* and *Persuasion*, giving a sense of the material dimensions of an immaterial reputation and foregrounding later sections on heritage and curation.

Articles on the various portraits posited as Jane Austen and on the history and theory of celebrity culture prompt participants to examine their own investments in Austen—to interrogate the sense of intimacy or even kinship produced by biographies, letters, and objects. This section also opens up considerations of adaptation as one of the mechanisms, with no less of an agenda than Henry Austen's original biography, for proliferating Austen's celebrity, this time by blurring boundaries between Austen's life and fiction, and by spinning the biographical gaps and omissions so carefully produced by Austen's relatives into a saleable persona in keeping with current ideals of femininity. If our aim, by exploring representations of Austen, was to see her as the product of early family biographies, we aimed, in our sections on adaptation, to explore how the modern moment is making Jane Austen again.

Recent years have seen a wealth of Austen adaptations in the United Kingdom alone: Whit Stillman's 2016 adaptation of 'Lady Susan' starring Kate Beckinsale was generally well-received, whilst in August 2019, Andrew Davies' eight-part series adaptation of *Sanditon* was first aired on ITV and proved predictably controversial. It met with unfettered enjoyment from some quarters—fans on Twitter celebrated the introduction of a woman of colour into a whitewashed period drama world—and outraged dismay from others—the *Independent* dismissing it as 'Jane Austen meets Love Island' (Harrison). A new and much-anticipated adaptation of *Emma*, written by Eleanor Catton and directed by Autumn de Wilde, appeared in February 2020. The theatre saw Laura Wade's completion of Austen's unfinished *The Watsons* meet with critical acclaim when it was staged in Chichester in November 2018, and London the following year. The improvised comedy play *Austentatious*, which boasts titles such as 'Strictly Come Darcy' and 'Mansfield Shark' has been touring since 2012, whilst Isobel McArthur's 'Pride and Prejudice* (*sort of)', described by the *Guardian* as a 'Jane Austen karaoke romcom' in which 'Love-struck pop hits punctuate the regency matchmaking in this raucous, yet surprisingly faithful, all-female adaptation', was first enjoyed by audiences in 2018, returning to theatres all over the United Kingdom in 2019 and 2020 (Fisher). In books, 2020 is clearly the year for sibling recovery; January alone saw the publication of two no-velistic adaptations, with Gill Hornby's Cassandra-focused *Miss Austen* (Penguin), and Janice Hadlow's defence of Mary Bennet in *The Other Bennet Sister* (Mantle).

The ongoing interpretation of Austen's fiction and her life leads, on the MOOC, to a very lively—and different—dialogue each run, although discussion often gets derailed by a fixation on questions of fidelity or faithfulness.[7] In our adaptations section, we wanted to move the discussion beyond which are 'good' and 'bad' adaptations, whilst also enabling participants to share their opinions on both classic and more recent films, series, and books. A video discussion between academics from the University of Southampton English and Film departments opened up several theoretical areas of consideration for participants, including what, exactly, counts as adaptation, and what makes something 'Austenesque'. Clips from Whit Stillman's 1990 film *Metropolitan* are used to prompt a consideration of the ways in which Austen's 'essence' might be said to carry beyond her historical or geographical origins, opening up the tension between Hampshire's Jane, and Jane Austen in Hollywood, or Bollywood. In considering how adapters across the globe have 'written back' to Austen, the video conversation aims to frame adaptation as a conversational practice, unpicking the notion that, as Shelley Cobb puts it in the discussion, 'the film or the adaptation always has to be submissive to the original'. This global version of Jane Austen also enables a discussion of her relationship to imperialism. Our question—'is *Mansfield Park* Austen's most radical novel?'—asks participants to consider the 'present absence' of slavery in the novel, pointing them towards Patricia Rozema's 1999 adaptation, in which the intersections between the scholarly and the popular are particularly marked. Whilst some par-ticipants are resistant to postcolonial readings, insisting Austen would have had no experience of the slave trade, others enjoy the detective work of unearthing clues left by Austen's suggestive use of names.

Our consideration of how Austen's story is told ends with a snapshot of the way in which modern archivists and curators tell the world about Jane Austen. In an interview with Mary Guyatt, former Curator at the Jane Austen House Museum, Gillian discusses the creation of a space that feels authentic in the cottage where Jane Austen lived and considers how museums and galleries ought to negotiate the knowledge that visitors bring with them, a consideration that proved important in putting together the MOOC itself. Special items in the collection are displayed, including Jane Austen's hair, her ring, and a manuscript in her hand, prompting participants to consider the ways that, as Nicola J. Watson writes in her recent book on writers' house museums, 'authorial remains, possessions, and spaces [...] evoke the simultaneous materiality and immateriality of the author' (5). The final task for participants involves creating their own fantasy exhibition, following a video example in which Gillian uses a manuscript journal, a late Victorian biography, and the Austen £10 note to plot a brief narrative of Austen's spectacular rise to fame.

Global Jane Austen

From the outset, we knew that the course would contain several sections on how Austen is translated—and indeed packaged by publishers—for audiences for whom English is not their mother tongue. This is one of Gillian's research interests, explored in her co-edited collection *Austen's Afterlives: Uses of Jane*, and in several articles she has published since.[8] Academic interest in translations and the foreign reception of Austen has been something of a hot topic—in 2018 alone, two book-length studies were published, on Austen in Bulgaria and in Norway, and there are now studies of Austen's reception in most European countries, as well as outside the European Union in Japan.[9] Our experience has taught us, however, that a 'lay' reader very rarely considers what the translation process changes, or indeed adds, to an understanding of any author. In these sections of the course we drew on Gillian's classroom experience of teaching literature in translation to undergraduate students at the University of Southampton.[10]

It generally comes as something of a surprise to the MOOC participants that all of Jane Austen's published novels appeared on French bookshelves in her lifetime, the products of leading Paris-based publisher Arthus Bertrand. Introducing course participants to one of Jane Austen's first translators, Isabelle de Montolieu (1751–1832), enabled us to think further about the waxing and waning of the literary reputations of women writers. Montolieu was by far the greater literary celebrity in the eighteen-teens, in her native Switzerland, in France (where she published), and indeed across Europe, working closely with Arthus Bertrand in bringing her publications to fruition. She was one of the most prolific translators of fiction in the period, publishing over one hundred volumes of translations and adaptations from English and German.

During her lifetime, Montolieu was known for the 1786 sentimental novel *Caroline de Lichtfield*, translated into English by Thomas Holcroft in the same year. This novel was a Europe-wide literary sensation: a sort of beauty and the beast tale of love conquering all. It may well have inspired Austen in her writing of *Sense and Sensibility*—she certainly read it. Throughout the nineteenth century, Montolieu was equally well-known for her translation of *Le Robinson Suisse* from the German of Johann David Wyss: it was this French version that provided the source text for the popular English translation of the same period. It says something about Austen's celebrity that if Montolieu is now known, she is known for her translations of *Sense and Sensibility* (*Raison et Sensibilité*, 1813) and *Persuasion* (*La Famille Elliot*, 1821). Montolieu's translation methods, for Austen, as for the other writers she tackled, were to 'improve' on the originals. This was entirely typical for the period. Montolieu used what is now referred to as the domesticating model, changing her source texts to fit the horizon of expectations of her readers in her target language, French. The effect, in Montolieu's translation of *Sense and Sensibility*, is to make the novel much more a novel of sensibility. She changes the novel's conclusion to give Marianne Dashwood and Colonel Brandon a much more unproblematic happy ending, whilst simultaneously redeeming Willoughby's character by having him marry the second Eliza, thus legitimising their bastard child. It's Austen, then, but not as we know her!

As in our adaptations section, our aim in the translation section was to interrogate the sense that there is a 'true' author, the owner of the creative property on one hand, and then there is a lesser practitioner, the translator, whose work cannot have an autonomous textual identity. As theorist Emily Apter has put it, 'translation throws into arrears the whole idea that authors of "originals" are the sole owners of their literary property' (93). In the case of such a canonical and revered author as Austen, such ideas seem like sacrilege. Our participants were, on the whole, extremely indignant that anyone would dare to change Austen's prose, let alone her plots: we wish to challenge their indignation. Here, we were assisted by participants who had first—or indeed only—encountered Austen via translations into their mother tongue, and by several translators who grapple with translation at the sentence level in their professional lives and who have returned to the course on each iteration thus far. These participants helped us to think through the myth that there can be a perfect translation of any author and to see the first translations as creative adaptations; to think, that is, of the film and television adaptations and first and later translations as working in similar ways. On the whole, we find this section of the course works extremely well: it introduces participants to an aspect of Austen's reception that they find surprising and new, and those who comment tend to express their appreciation of their preconceptions being challenged in this way.

One final thought on the Global Austen is a political one. England's Jane has often been co-opted for conservatism with a small—and indeed with a large—'c'. It is, perhaps, one of the lasting myths of Austen's writing that she champions the status quo, and the War of Ideas (defined so memorably and influentially in terms of the politics of the late eighteenth and early nineteenth centuries by Marilyn Butler in her landmark study of Austen, first published in 1975) is by no means over in academic writing. The course design and runs coincided with the 2016 Brexit vote and the subsequent polarisation of politics in the United Kingdom—indeed Conservative politician Michael Gove, one of the key figures in the Leave camp of the vote, claimed in 2017 that Austen's *Sense and Sensibility* was the book most like the Conservative party manifesto.[11] We were—and remain—concerned about the rise in nationalism, and a new populism globally, and this informs our teaching and course design. It would be too much to claim that we changed any perceptions on current affairs. Indeed, steering somewhat clear of this kind of controversy is necessary to remain inclusive on the discussion boards, especially when there is no clear sense of who the silent majority of participants are, nor indeed how they are responding to the source material. But we hope we encouraged, and will continue to encourage, participants to think about a more radical Austen than a Little England Jane. Certainly, we wanted to demonstrate that English readers by no means have a monopoly on Austen or her writing, by complicating and contextualising her place in world literature, both in her own lifetime, and today.

Conclusion

In putting together our MOOC, then, we tried to provide a balance of historical context, biographical detail, and adaptation theory, providing participants in a vast classroom with the opportunity to discuss the Jane Austen they knew from perspectives they recognised, but also to learn about other, less familiar Jane Austens, with classmates from across the globe. Despite remaining largely anonymous and faceless, the MOOC community has, over subsequent runs, emerged as one both deeply committed and deeply engaged. The message boards have yielded a fascinating diversity of conversations, which lead in different directions each run. Indeed, these conversations are reflective of the dynamic and changing environment of Austen studies more broadly, which continues to explore new and exciting angles.[12] As the future of university funding streams become increasingly uncertain, so innovative, and digitised, teaching methods like this are now an absolute necessity. MOOCs are an integral part of a future vision of the university in which digital education is the norm. They enable teaching to take centre-stage, which is surely important in light of the TEF (Teaching Excellence and Student Outcomes Framework: a new government-run metric to assess teaching excellence in the United Kingdom). MOOCs also necessitate an increased consciousness in university staff about different manners of delivering education, enabling engagement with pedagogical theories on course design and learning science. They provide a huge audience to disseminate research to, and a chance to draw together expertise in departments with tech specialists, but also to connect HE institutions and heritage institutions, developing team-based approaches. Because of the nature of audience feedback, MOOCs also enable fast experimentation and changes with course content and learning tools that the institutional structures of the university necessarily slow down. As Michele Palmer notes:

Myth, Reality, and Global Celebrity

Separated from traditional organizational process and structures—and coupled with the team-based approach—teams at our institutions have begun to question inherited assumptions about higher education. It's something about MOOCs, we decided, that gives us permission to imagine what's possible along each vertical of the acronym—the massive, the open, and the online (or, digital).

CODA

We put the finishing touches to this chapter in June 2020, as the COVID-19 pandemic swept through the Western World, changing life for so many. The mainstream press has seen a small crop of articles about (re)reading Austen in a time of social distancing; if she was 'relevant' before, she is depicted as all the more 'relevant' now.[13] The run of the course that started on 16 March, 2020, was planned long before the impact of the novel coronavirus became apparent, and—as tutors—it has been heart-warming, and sometimes extremely poignant, to see participants joining from across the globe. They come online seeking solace, from self-isolation or shielding, because they have been furloughed from their jobs, or because they are looking for distraction from positions as nurses or carers. Although we tried, in the comments and end-of-week video roundups, to point out that Austen is not always comforting, or safe, it is clear, from comments by participants in the March 2020 run, that they are finding comfort in her. And who are we to argue? As one participant commented, the course has 'taught me, in such unprecedented times of uncertainty, that "there's an Austen for that"'. For our part, as we grapple with homeschooling and caregiving, cleaning and grocery shopping, it's Austen's line from her letter of 1816 that rings true: 'Composition seems to me Impossible, with a head full of Joints of Mutton & doses of Rhubarb'. The 'Myth, Reality, and Global Celebrity' participants have provided a much-needed sense of community for us, too.

Notes

1 Draxler and Spratt.
2 See https://www.nationaltrust.org.uk/lists/jane-austen-film-and-tv [Accessed 10 Feb., 2020].
3 The novels were, of course, actually published in late Dec. 1817, but the frontispieces read 1818, and the heritage industry welcomed the stretch of another year.
4 An online version of the 2017 exhibitions at Chawton was published in *Persuasions* 38.1 (2017), and can be accessed at http://jasna.org/publications/persuasions-online/vol38no1/dow-simpson-seth-intro/
5 We remain grateful to Stephen Bending, Joe Brett, Kate Borthwick, Jeanice Brooks, Emma Clery, Shelley Cobb, Stephanie Jones, Will May and Rebecca Smith for their contributions, either on film, in writing, or at the level of course design and filming.
6 Donald Greene noted Austen's seclusion from the turbulent political and ideological world of Regency Britain in 1975 as a myth: 'the one steady landmark in the swirling waters of Jane Austen criticism', and whilst scholarly criticism has, of course, moved on, taking leads from Greene and others, the idea of Austen as an apolitical and therefore 'safe' writer, writing in rural seclusion, has persisted amongst many of her readers.
7 Shelley Cobb has written compellingly about the persistence of the gendered language of fidelity in adaptation studies, and its tendency to see adaptations as feminine and therefore degraded forms.
8 See Gillian Dow 'Uses of Translation' (154–74); 'Translations', *The Cambridge Companion to* Pride and Prejudice; and 'Translations', *The Cambridge Companion to* Emma.
9 See Sørbø; Kostadinova.
10 Dow, 'Translation for beginners'.
11 See Picciuto.
12 See, for example, Looser and Barchas (335–44).
13 See, for example, Gil; Tovey; Goldstein.

Works Cited

Apter, Emily. 'What is Yours, Ours and Mine: On the Limits of Ownership and the Creative Commons.' *October*, vol. 126, Fall, 2008, pp. 91–114.

Cobb, Shelley. 'Adaptation, Fidelity, and Gendered Discourses.' *Adaptation*, vol. 4.1, Mar. 2011, pp. 28–37.

Dow, Gillian. 'Translation for Beginners, or, Teaching the 'Dangerous.' in *Les Liaisons Dangereuses.*' *Romantic Circles Pedagogies* Jul. 2014. romantic-circles.org/pedagogies/commons/translation/commons.2014.translation.dow.html

Dow, Gillian. 'Translations.' *The Cambridge Companion to Pride and Prejudice*, edited by Janet Todd. Cambridge UP, 2013, pp. 122–136.

Dow, Gillian. 'Translations.' *The Cambridge Companion to Emma*, edited by Peter Sabor. Cambridge UP, 2015, pp. 166–185.

Dow, Gillian, and Clare Hanson, editors. *Uses of Austen: Jane's Afterlives*. Palgrave Macmillan, 2012.

Dow, Gillian. 'Uses of Translation: The Global Jane Austen.' *Uses of Austen: Jane's Afterlives*, edited by Gillian Dow and Clare Hanson. Palgrave Macmillan, 2012, pp. 154–174.

Draxler, Bridget, and Danielle Spratt. *Engaging the Age of Jane Austen: Public Humanities in Practice*. U of Iowa P, 2018.

Fisher, Mark. '"Pride and Prejudice * (*sort of)" Review – Jane Austen karaoke romcom.' *The Guardian* 1 Jul. 2018. https://www.theguardian.com/stage/2018/jul/01/pride-and-prejudice-sort-of-review-tron-jane-austen-karaoke. Accessed 5 Sep. 2019.

Green, Donald, 'The Myth of Limitation.' *Jane Austen Today*, edited by Joel Weinsheimer. U of Georgia P, 1975, pp. 142–175.

Harrison, Ellie. 'Sandition Review: Jane Austen Meets Love Island in This Sexed up, Cringe-worthy Adaptation of Her Last, Unfinished Novel.' *The Independent* 24 Aug. 2019. https://www.independent.co.uk/arts-entertainment/tv/reviews/sanditon-review-jane-austen-itv-anne-reid-andrew-davies-cast-a9075871. Accessed 5 Sep. 2019.

Johnson, Claudia. *Jane Austen's Cults and Cultures*. U of Chicago P, 2012.

Kostadinova, Vitana. *Jane Austen Translated: Cultural Transformations Across Space and Time*. Plodiv UP, 2018.

'Letter to Cassandra Austen, 8–9 September 1816,' *Jane Austen's Letters*, edited by Deirdre Le Faye, 4th ed., Oxford UP, 2011.

Looser, Devoney, *The Making of Jane Austen*. Johns Hopkins UP, 2017.

Lynch, Deidre, editor. *Janeites: Austen's Disciples and Devotees*. Princeton UP, 2000.

Nath, Asoke, Abhijit Karmakar, and Totan Karmakar, 'Moocs Impact in Higher Education Institution: A Pilot Study In Indian Context.' *Journal of Engineering Research and Applications*, vol. 4, no. 7, Jul. 2014, pp. 156–163.

Palmer, Michele. 'Impact of MOOCS on Higher Education.' *edX* 27 Oct. 2014. blog.edx.org/impacts-moocs-higher-education/. Accessed 3 Aug 2019.

Sabor, Peter, editor. *The Cambridge Companion to Emma*. Cambridge UP, 2015.

Seal, Jeremy. 'Jane Austen: Stourhead, Bath, Chawton Mark Bicentenary of Her Death.' *The Australian* 17 Jun. 2017. https://www.theaustralian.com.au/travel/jane-austen-stourhead-bath-chawton-mark-bicentenary-of-her-death/ news-story/ea3891ce0eff57b496f1c46bc99218fb. Accessed 9 Sep. 2019.

Sørbø, Marie Nedregotten. *Jane Austen Speaks Norwegian*. Brill Rodopi, 2018.

Sutherland, Kathryn. *Jane Austen's Textual Lives: From Aeschylus to Bollywood*. Oxford UP, 2005.

'The Jane Effect: Jane Austen 200 Gives Hampshire a £21 Million Boost.' *Hampshire Cultural Trust* 11 Jun. 2018. https://www.hampshireculture.org.uk/news/jane-effect-jane-austen-200-gives-hampshire-ps21-million-boost. Accessed 5 Aug. 2019.

Todd, Janet, editor. *Jane Austen in Context*. Cambridge UP, 2005.

Watson, Nicola J. *The Author's Effects: On Writer's House Museums*. Oxford UP, 2020.

Wiltshire, John. *Recreating Jane Austen*. Cambridge UP, 2001.

41

EPISTEMIC INJUSTICE IN *PRIDE AND PREJUDICE* AND *MANSFIELD PARK*; OR, WHAT AUSTEN TEACHES US ABOUT MANSPLAINING AND WHITE PRIVILEGE

Tim Black and Danielle Spratt

CALIFORNIA STATE UNIVERSITY, NORTHRIDGE

What can Jane Austen teach us about social justice?

Most new readers of Austen have no ready answer, and for good reason. Images of Austen's world—teatime chats, country dances, candlelit proposal scenes, gauzy empire waist dresses—can seem, well, awfully basic: the nineteenth-century equivalents of today's pumpkin spice latte. To put it another way, the plots, characters, and the overarching setting of Austen and her novels have come to function as peak (if historical) signifiers of heteronormative white women, white culture, and white privilege. As Patricia A. Matthew puts it, 'With Austen as, often, the primary literary lens into her time period, it can be all too easy to forget how deeply invested English culture was not only in curtailing women's choices, but also in enslaving millions of people'. For some students, the details that constitute Austen's world seem largely ignorant of and divested from any broader sociopolitical meaning, except perhaps on the matter of valuing a particular kind of middle-class women's experiences. Others, who are aware of how these associations have been co-opted in horrifying ways by white supremacist groups to support their racist, sexist agenda, might see Austen's works as cultural products that at best continue to resist, and at worst purposely run counter to, the very forms of social justice we so desperately need. So when we ask students to think about how Austen's novels are at all relevant to either historical or contemporary issues of social and political equity, they are rightly sceptical.

We recently posed this question to a group of students at California State University, Northridge, when we had the rare opportunity to team teach an upper-level seminar in the English Department on Austen and philosophy. As colleagues at a large, public, Hispanic-serving institution of about 40,000 students per year, we are lucky to work with students who bring a vast array of diverse and innovative perspectives: most of our classes are filled with first-generation students of colour who, especially in the wake of events like the 2016 US presidential election, the 2017 white supremacist violence in Charlottesville, Virginia, and the 2020 protests of police brutality and the killings of

DOI: 10.4324/9780429398155-41-47

535

George Floyd and Breonna Taylor, became all too aware of how systemic forms of heteronormative white privilege inform racist, sexist, anti-LGBTQ+ hate speech and violence.

As part of our collaboration, each week we paired an Austen novel with relevant readings from moral and epistemological philosophy. One specific concept that provided a welcome and liberating key to considering the nuances of Austen's writing about systemic oppression came from Miranda Fricker's work on what she calls 'epistemic injustice', or the idea that people can be wronged 'specifically in their capacity as a knower' (1). Fricker identifies two forms of epistemic injustice, testimonial injustice and hermeneutical injustice. 'Testimonial injustice occurs when prejudice causes a hearer to give a deflated level of credibility to a speaker's word', as when 'the police do not believe you because you are black' (1). Throughout the semester, as a class we discussed how Austen's works are intensely perceptive to this form of injustice; even as she herself did not have recourse to this philosophical terminology, Austen's novels offer many examples of this category as a fully *thinkable* form of experience, particularly for women, and indeed as a necessary requirement informed by her society's ties to paternalism, empire, and colonialism.[1]

'Hermeneutical injustice', Fricker says, 'occurs at a prior stage, when a gap in collective interpretive resources puts someone at an unfair disadvantage when it comes to making sense of their social experiences' (1), as when someone is sexually harassed in a society or culture that lacks the concept of sexual harassment. There are acts of injustice in Austen, some of which we discuss in detail in what follows, that we and Austen and her characters actively identify as unjust. Contemporary readers can make sense of some of these acts as, say, sexist since we now have that concept. Austen and her characters, on the other hand, can't do this since there was no such concept in Austen's time: there is for them a hermeneutical lack. Students and other readers might initially see Austen's failure to characterise sexist acts *as sexist* as a failure on her part to acknowledge sexism, which might in turn contribute to the perception that she doesn't care to confront sexism or even that she means to promote the sexist status quo. The notion of hermeneutical injustice is helpful here: to suppose that Austen has or should have the concept of sexism, to hold her and her characters to that standard, is to run the risk of treating her in a hermeneutically unjust way. And so we talk to students about the conceptual resources they have—and even take for granted—but that Austen and her characters lack, and about how we should not hold Austen to a standard that requires her to have conceptual resources she lacks. We remind our students, too, that we should not let the fact that Austen has a different and in some respects more limited set of conceptual resources obscure her confrontation of sexism or lead us to think that her work reinforces sexist systems of her day.

For the purposes of this essay, we will focus on testimonial injustice, especially because the pervasiveness of certain hermeneutical injustices in Austen's work can make it difficult to address them effectively in the classroom, and because they signal *differences* between our students and Austen, when we are hoping to find spaces where our students can find some common ground with her work. The texts we have found to be most difficult to teach in a survey of Austen's writing, *Pride and Prejudice* and *Mansfield Park*, are exceptionally helpful in this regard. As teachers of Austen well know (it's tempting to say something like 'It is a truth universally acknowledged'), each of these novels presents its own set of interpretive obstacles. Some combination of film adaptations and readerly sentimentality often makes it hard for student Janeites to disengage themselves emotionally from *Pride and Prejudice*: whether because Darcy seems like a dream partner, because they identify with or aspire to Elizabeth's self-confidence in the face of Lady Catherine de Bourgh's threats, or because the novel seems lifted entirely from historical time in a way that promotes a kind of adult fairy tale, affording as it does a distinctive kind of pleasurable, immersive reading experience. By contrast, students initially read Fanny Price and the world of *Mansfield Park* as a dour foil to the 'light & bright & sparkling' (4 February 1813; Jane Austen's *Letters* 212) scenes of Pemberley and Longbourn; Fanny's seeming victimhood, divested from the (justified) rage-fuelled interiority of fictional successors like Jane Eyre, seems an affront both to their expectations as readers and to their

OG Austen hero, Elizabeth Bennet. For the non-Austen-anointed, the novels seem at best like a series of boring white people problems, and at worst an example of why we need to decolonise the literary canon yesterday.

To address these issues, we argue that teachers of Austen can productively pair these two novels alongside Fricker's category of testimonial injustice to provide a useful pedagogical framework that both historicises the very real sociopolitical issues of the early nineteenth century and contextualises them as of a piece with ongoing matters of racism, sexism, ableism, and heteronormativity that seek to repress or silence voices from marginalised groups in our own twenty-first century moment. While the takeaway is certainly not that Austen is above reproach on these matters, this focus demonstrates for students the continuing relevance of her novels for their scholarly and social lives for two reasons. First, we hold that Austen's novels offer productive models that develop Fricker's points in ways more instructive and representative than some of Fricker's own literary examples, a point that shows students how literary works can contribute to philosophy and other disciplinary forms of knowledge-making. Second, and significantly for student audiences, we show how deploying these concerns within a public humanities context—in our case, the class's culminating experience was for students to design and host a podcast series—values the concerns, ideas, and experiences of our students as forms of knowledge and expertise, thus redressing the many ways that our own students frequently experience epistemic and other social injustices in their academic and day-to-day lives.

Method and Theory

Before we expand on the relationship between epistemic injustice and forms of privilege in Austen's novels, we would be remiss if we did not acknowledge our own: the privilege of team teaching a class at all. One of the most immediately noticeable benefits of this team teaching was that we both felt equal parts student and teacher in the course, bringing our own expertise and learning from each other's. This pedagogical upshot rippled outward to our students, allowing them to share their own expertise: as readers of pop culture or queer theory and as members of a generation of students who are more attuned to systemic injustices than we can claim at parallel moments of our educational experience. This levelling of authority across forms of knowledge and expertise is a crucial aspect of what Danielle and Bridget Draxler have written about elsewhere as a form of 'activist presentism', a principled pedagogical and scholarly method that, in bringing together matters of the past and the present with public-facing projects that equally acknowledge and value the expertise of all participants—faculty, students, community partners, and the public—'seeks to redress the inequities within our individual fields and in and beyond the academy. When we reread the past to rewrite our future, we begin to do the work of activist presentism' (Spratt and Draxler). We were excited to bring public-facing projects and a public humanities component into this team-taught class, giving students the chance to enact activist presentism by working with a local non-profit or working in groups to create a podcast series about issues that groups found important over the course of the semester.

One of the things we knew we wanted to focus on was to cover some parallels Tim has seen between Søren Kierkegaard's moral philosophy and the moral philosophy that comes through in some of Austen's novels, and we also wanted to cover some of the ways we noticed Austen's work interrogating both the notion of epistemic injustice and the conditions that cultivate and support such injustices. Our choices for the class, equal parts strategic and serendipitous, chimed with Tim's inspiration for bringing Austen into conversation with Fricker. Tim first taught Fricker's *Epistemic Injustice* in the fall semester of 2017 in an advanced epistemology course that used the book as its primary text. The book represents an exploration of the intersection of ethics and epistemology, engaging a distinctively epistemic type of injustice, in which someone is wronged specifically in their capacity as a knower. In studying the issue of epistemic injustice, the book examines related issues such as social power, prejudice, intellectual virtue, the genealogy of knowledge, and epistemic injustice's place in the broader patterns of social injustice. Tim suggested Fricker's book in part because it has been remarkably influential in philosophy and in many other disciplines that address and interrogate issues of social injustice.[2]

One of the interdisciplinary appeals of Fricker's book is that it often uses literature—novels, in particular—to illustrate its points. So, for example, Fricker makes pointed use of scenes from Harper Lee's *To Kill A Mockingbird* as illustrations of what she (Fricker) calls testimonial injustice, which occurs when someone is wronged in their capacity as a knower and, more specifically, when a speaker receives a credibility deficit—that is, when she is taken to be less credible than she deserves to be taken—owing to a prejudice in the hearer against people the hearer takes to belong in a specific social group, e.g., women or African Americans. In Lee's novel, a young black man named Tom Robinson is accused of raping a white girl, but as he is tried for this crime, he is wronged in his capacity as a knower by almost every white person in the courtroom, with the notable exceptions of Atticus Finch, Robinson's attorney, and Finch's daughter, Scout. Robinson is denied credibility by the judge, by opposing counsel, and by the jury: every reasonable explanation of his behaviour is rejected in favour of explanations provided by prominent white people, and his testimony is written off as unreliable unless it can be seen as confirming explanations provided by prominent white people. Robinson suffers a testimonial injustice, an identity-prejudicial credibility deficit, as Fricker designates it, which happens when a hearer gives less credibility to a speaker than the speaker deserves and does so because the speaker is seen by the hearer as belonging in a certain social group against which the hearer has a prejudice.

In another example, this time from Anthony Minghella's screenplay of Patricia Highsmith's novel, *The Talented Mr. Ripley*, Fricker draws our attention to a man's rejecting a woman's testimony. Herbert Greenleaf says to Marge Sherwood, in the context of Marge's saying that she suspects that Tom Ripley has murdered Greenleaf's son, 'Marge, there's female intuition, and then there are facts'. In saying this, Greenleaf commits an epistemic injustice, wronging Marge in her capacity as a knower. Marge suffers a testimonial injustice—here too in the form of an identity-prejudicial credibility deficit—since Greenleaf gives less credibility to Marge than she deserves and does so because of a bias against women and against Marge as a woman.

These examples are helpful, we think, in bringing philosophy out of its usual haunts, which some see as formal, staid, and impersonal. But each of these examples is set in the context of suspected or alleged criminal activity. The example from *To Kill A Mockingbird* is in fact set in a courtroom, which could really complicate matters by introducing a confusion between *epistemic* injustice, which is the sort of injustice that the example is meant to foreground, and a more familiar sort of injustice, a *legal* or *judicial* injustice. So, even though these examples help us to see Fricker's philosophy as applying in and to the world, the world of these examples might be pretty far removed from the world her readers inhabit and might even introduce complications and confusions that we wanted to avoid in the classroom.

Given this, Tim thought it might help our Austen class to consider some other examples. The sort of examples that would be most helpful, Tim thought, would be set in contexts that are less exceptional, that are easy to understand, and that are more universally relatable. An example from Jane Austen's *Pride and Prejudice*—Volume I, Chapter 19 of the novel, where Mr Collins proposes marriage to Elizabeth Bennet—seemed to fit the bill perfectly. In addition, Tim suggested that the example from *Pride and Prejudice* is a better and clearer example of identity-prejudicial credibility deficit, since Elizabeth is reporting on her own preferences and her own state of mind, with respect to which she is the foremost authority, while Marge Sherwood and Tom Robinson are each reporting on events that occurred (or that are suspected or alleged to have occurred) in the external world.

538

Epistemic Injustice

Volume I, Chapter 19 presents the infamous scene of Mr Collins' blundering and blustery marriage proposal to Elizabeth. Once the proposal has been made, Elizabeth responds by saying that 'it is impossible for [her] to do otherwise than decline' it (*PP* 77). This does not discourage Mr Collins, however. Instead, he takes Elizabeth's resistance as an opportunity to mansplain: he insists that it is typical for women who mean to accept a marriage proposal to play at rejecting it once, or even two or three times. Elizabeth then asks Mr Collins explicitly to 'give [her] leave to judge for [her]self, and [to] pay [her] the compliment of believing what [she] say[s]' (78). Still, he says in reply, 'I know it to be the established custom of your sex to reject a man on the first application' (78), and he goes so far as to say that he is in fact *encouraged* by Elizabeth's rejections. Now feeling frustrated, Elizabeth says that she 'would rather be paid the compliment of being believed sincere' (78), and she struggles to reject Mr Collins in a way that he will not see as tantamount to acceptance. Mr Collins, even in the end, insists on being 'persuaded that when sanctioned by the express authority of both [of Elizabeth's] excellent parents, [his] proposals will not fail of being acceptable' (78).

This is a clear example of testimonial injustice, in the form of an identity-prejudicial credibility deficit. Elizabeth Bennet is the foremost, if not the sole authority on her own preferences and states of mind; her word will settle any and all questions about these matters. Yet Mr Collins refuses to believe her reports, giving her far less credibility here than she deserves, precisely because of a prejudice that he has against women and against Elizabeth as a woman.

This example is a teachable one for several reasons. First of all, it is a straightforward and un-controversial case of testimonial injustice, of the sort that Fricker has in mind. It can therefore be used to help students see just what testimonial injustice is. In addition, the example is not exceptional—it shows that testimonial injustices can happen in any context, not just in those that involve reports of unusual or even criminal behaviour in the external world. The example also involves one of literature's most beloved characters, Elizabeth Bennet, for whom readers feel a strong affinity. Readers, we think, can really connect with Elizabeth here and, perhaps, are better able to internalise her frustrations, since we are witnessing such a beloved character being treated in an epistemically unjust way with regard to her reports of her own preferences, something that many readers will have experienced for themselves to some degree or other.

This example also helps us show students that Austen's works are not—or are not on the whole—to be seen as cultural products that perpetuate sexist forms of social injustice, even though, of course, the concept of sexism did not exist in Austen's time. On the contrary, this part of *Pride and Prejudice* makes a certain form of social injustice palpable, and it has Elizabeth stand up to and resist the testimonial injustice that she suffers, on an interpersonal level, at least, if not also on a larger, societal level. Unlike other examples that we explore later, this failed proposal scene is one that Elizabeth—and thus the reader—does not take entirely seriously, or as a seriously coercive threat to her future: Elizabeth must restrain herself from laughing at Collins. Yet even under these less-than-dire circumstances, the passage nevertheless reminds its readers that Elizabeth sees this as an injustice and recognises the societal conditions that contextualise this interaction and that render her, ulti-mately, silent:

> To such perseverance in wilful self-deception Elizabeth would make no reply, and im-mediately and in silence withdrew; determined, that if he persisted in considering her repeated refusals as flattering encouragement, to apply to her father, whose negative might be uttered in such a manner as must be decisive, and whose behaviour at least could not be mistaken for the affectation and coquetry of an elegant female. (*PP* 79)

Here, we can see Elizabeth processing how her status as a woman in a society organised around paternalism and primogeniture allows Collins selectively to overrule her rejections. What we get, then, in this part of *Pride and Prejudice*, is a real-world instructive example of how to identify, understand, and resist a certain sexist form of testimonial injustice. To this extent, then, we can use the example to help students see Austen in a way they might not be inclined to see her, as someone who recognises certain forms of social injustice, recognises them *as* forms of injustice, understands the conditions that sustain them, and speaks out against them by having her characters resist their advancement.

Yet *Pride and Prejudice* does not end its engagement with testimonial injustice here. The novel overtly redresses these wrongs to Elizabeth through the courtship plot with Darcy, allowing her to establish epistemic equality with him. When Darcy mirrors Mr Collins' botched proposal in his reluctant declaration of love, Elizabeth proclaims, 'You are mistaken, Mr Darcy, if you suppose that the mode of your declaration affected me in any other way, than as it spared me the concern which I might have felt in refusing you, had you behaved in a more gentleman-like manner .... You could not have made me the offer of your hand in any possible way that would have tempted me to accept it' (*PP* 134). Darcy takes Elizabeth's refusal seriously: he believes that she properly represents her own feelings, a perspective that Elizabeth has already shown us she cannot necessarily take for granted. Elizabeth's assertion of epistemic privilege in fact becomes one of the ways in which the novel resolves the marriage plot between the two characters. As Darcy later discloses to Elizabeth after his far more successful proposal scene, 'Your reproof, so well applied, I shall never forget: "had you behaved in a more gentleman-like manner". Those were your words. You know not, can scarcely conceive, how they have tortured me;—though it was some time, I confess, before I was reasonable enough to allow their justice' (251).

Likewise, in the penultimate chapter of the novel, Darcy builds on this respect for Elizabeth when he tells her he admires her 'for the liveliness of her mind' (*PP* 260). Darcy's comment here is especially important: we know from earlier in the novel that after reading his post-proposal rejection letter, Elizabeth begins to doubt her own understanding of self, lamenting, 'Till this moment, I never knew myself' (144). Rather than attempting to override Elizabeth, in these instances, Darcy shows how he loves and values her specifically in her capacity as a knower. While many of our students bristle at Darcy's haughtiness and class snobbery, they find it helpful to identify moments like these to see how he demonstrates a pattern of granting credibility to Elizabeth even when those around him, as well as broader systemic conditions, do not require or even encourage such sanctioning.[3]

There is a connection to be made here, we think, with another of Jane Austen's novels, *Mansfield Park*, whose protagonist, Fanny Price, does not typically receive the warm reception of her literary predecessor, in part because her experiences of testimonial injustice are so pervasive in the novel.[4] In rejecting a marriage proposal from Henry Crawford, Fanny experiences a testimonial injustice that is very much like the one experienced by Elizabeth Bennet. When we appeal to these similarities, along with the fact that readers see the testimonial injustice in Elizabeth Bennet's case and sympathise with her as she grows more and more frustrated with being denied the credibility she deserves, we can make a strong case for the claim that there is testimonial injustice in Fanny Price's case too and that we should see her many silences not as examples of passivity, but rather as small acts of resistance in response to being denied the credibility she deserves. Making these connections can help readers to develop an appreciation for *Mansfield Park* as they see how the layers of epistemic injustice that Fanny faces complicate the common position that Fanny is ultimately too passive or too malleable.

Like Elizabeth, Fanny offers a clear rejection of Henry Crawford's marriage proposal:

No, no, no!' [Fanny] cried, hiding her face. 'This is all nonsense. Do not distress me. I can hear no more of this. [...] I do not want, I cannot bear, I must not listen to such—No, no, don't think of me. But you are *not* thinking of me. I know it is all nothing. (*MP* 206)

After rejecting Henry in this way, Fanny finds herself hoping that Henry's proposal had not been a serious one and wants 'to feel and appear as usual' when he joined the Bertrams for dinner. Yet there was 'no consciousness of past folly in his voice' (*MP* 207) as he delivered to Fanny a note from his sister, Mary. Her note made it even clearer to Fanny that Henry's proposal was no joke: Mary's note offered Fanny 'a few lines of general congratulation' and gave her Mary's 'most joyful consent and approval' (207).[5] Fanny deserves to be seen as credible, just as credible as Elizabeth: Fanny, like Elizabeth, is unquestionably the foremost authority on her own preferences and states of mind. Yet like her brother, either Mary Crawford fails to believe what Fanny has said about her preferences and states of mind, or Mary puts undue trust in Henry's epistemically unjust characterisation of what Fanny has said about her preferences and states of mind.

There's some reason to believe that it's the latter, as Henry seems also to have misrepresented Fanny's response to Sir Thomas. Sir Thomas tells Fanny that he understands Henry to have 'received as much encouragement to proceed as a well-judging young woman could permit herself to give' (*MP* 213), a reaction on Henry's part that recalls Mr Collins' response to Elizabeth's rejection. For Henry to represent Fanny's answer to Sir Thomas in this way is for him to give her less credibility than she deserves, due to a prejudice or set of prejudices that he has. It is likely that Henry has a prejudice against women and against Fanny as a woman, and it might also very well be the case that he has a prejudice, one that Mary Crawford likely shares, given how she feels about Edmund Bertram's financial prospects and his decision to join the clergy, against people like Fanny who are less privileged socioeconomically.

Fanny eventually experiences a testimonial injustice at the hands of a far more powerfully paternalistic figure: Sir Thomas himself. When Fanny insists that she means to reject Henry's proposal, Sir Thomas says to her, 'I am half inclined to think, Fanny, that you do not quite know your own feelings' (*MP* 214). Here, Sir Thomas gives Fanny a credibility deficit while also granting himself an excess of credibility, as do both Henry and Mary Crawford, precisely because of a prejudice he harbours against women and likely against those in Fanny's less privileged socioeconomic position. Fanny finds it disappointing that Sir Thomas won't just take her at her word about how she feels: 'She had hoped that to a man like her uncle, so discerning, so honourable, so good, the simple acknowledgment of settled *dislike* on her side, would have been sufficient. To her infinite grief she found it was not' (215). She realises that Sir Thomas is treating her in a testimonially unjust way—and that he might not be quite so good and honourable as she wants to believe—and this is made worse by her understanding that her epistemic position with respect to Henry and his character is much better than Sir Thomas': she has seen Henry's inappropriate flirtation with both Maria and Julia. Fanny strongly suspects that if she were to share her observations with Sir Thomas, he would not believe her about Henry either, just as he does not believe her about her own preferences and states of mind: 'her heart sunk under the appalling prospect of discussion, explanation, and probably nonconviction' (215). Fanny knows that Sir Thomas does not and will not afford her the credibility she deserves, but she refuses, in her characteristically inward and quiet way, to give in to his epistemic demands. While this moment of resistance is not as overt as that of Elizabeth's confrontation with Lady Catherine de Bourgh, for instance, Austen presents us here with a moment where Fanny refuses to allow Sir Thomas to discredit her as a knower, as someone who has knowledge of and who in fact occupies a superior epistemic position with respect to both empirical and emotional truths.[6]

There is thus ample reason to conclude that Fanny Price experiences testimonial injustices that are structurally similar to and at least as egregious as the one experienced by Elizabeth Bennet. It might nonetheless be the case, especially since Fanny is widely viewed as particularly unlikeable, that some readers will not be as sympathetic to Fanny as they are to Elizabeth, a reaction that we have seen with our students on multiple occasions. We take this as an opportunity to examine this reaction. Are we more likely to see testimonial injustices in cases involving the privileged and likeable? Are we more likely to see testimonial injustices in cases involving unlikeable and unappealing offenders? Should the likeability or socioeconomic status of the targets of testimonial injustices make a difference when it comes to our willingness to acknowledge the presence of testimonial injustice? Should the unlikability of the perpetrators make a difference? Should the relative socioeconomic positions of the perpetrators and the targets of testimonial injustice make a difference? That is, should it make a difference that the perpetrator is wealthy but the target is not?

Attempts to answer questions like these, perhaps especially in the context of a classroom discussion, can help us learn how to use Austen's examples in building on Fricker's system. So, Mr Collins can treat Elizabeth in a way that is testimonially unjust only because he is presumed, both by himself and by his and Elizabeth's society, to be a higher epistemic authority than she is, even where it concerns Elizabeth's own preferences and states of mind! Elizabeth's *diminished* epistemic authority is possible only because of a different but intimately related epistemic injustice: Mr Collins is unjustly afforded an *elevated* epistemic authority, or a credibility excess, in his and Elizabeth's world.[7] There is also the matter of how treating women in epistemically just ways might be seen as threatening in and to an unjust society. To give Fanny the credibility she deserves would be to see her, a less-privileged woman, as more reliable and more trustworthy than Henry Crawford, which is anathema to the hetero-patriarchal classist order of their world—and of *ours*, as it turns out. Women owe testimonial deference to men, even in cases where their own preferences and states of mind are at issue. Women who do *not* pay such deference are therefore seen as threatening in and to the hetero-patriarchal classist order.[8]

When culturally established unjust credibility assignments are disrupted—by, for example, Fanny's refusal both to give Henry Crawford more credibility than he deserves and to accept the diminished credibility that she is expected to accept—certain individuals can be made more vulnerable to 'downfall in the existing social hierarchy' (Manne 194). That's because, as Kate Manne reminds us, patterns of testimonial injustice 'often serve the function of buttressing dominant group members' current social position' and, correlatively, of keeping them safe from being slighted or outdone 'by those over whom they have historically been dominant' (194). We see, in fact, in *Pride and Prejudice*, just how entrenched these protections can be, so entrenched that women themselves sometimes help to enforce a society's systemic injustices. We can read Mrs Bennet in this way, as she says, knowing that Mr Collins means to propose to Elizabeth, 'Lizzy, I *insist* upon your staying and hearing Mr Collins' (*PP* 75). And then, after learning that Elizabeth has rejected him, Mrs Bennet tells Mr Collins that Elizabeth 'is a very headstrong, foolish girl, and does not know her own interest but I will *make* her know it' (80). Eventually, Mrs Bennet resorts to threatening Elizabeth in an attempt to get her to change her mind about Mr Collins. As we discuss this with students, all of this can be read as Mrs Bennet's working, even if she does so unwittingly, in the interests of the established hetero-patriarchal classist order and its systemic injustices.

While Mr Bennet ultimately endorses Elizabeth's ability to know her own mind and preferences (both for Collins and, at the novel's end, for Darcy), the male figures of authority in *Mansfield Park*—as mentioned above, Henry, Sir Thomas, and even Edmund—routinely disregard Fanny's ability to know better: not just her own mind, but also the characters of others. As opposed to the ending of *Pride and Prejudice*, which further endorses the value and validity of Elizabeth's knowledge, the ending of *Mansfield Park* cedes the majority of its narrative perspective to that of Sir Thomas. As Martha Folsom and John Wiltshire note, in the last chapter of the novel, nine of the thirty paragraphs are explicitly devoted to Sir Thomas's thoughts (Folsom and Wiltshire 45–46). As we discussed with our class, however, we might plausibly expand the territory of this narrative dominance if we understand that the majority of the final chapter of the novel uses free indirect discourse to express not the operations of Fanny's mind, but rather those of Edmund and Sir Thomas. After Austen's narrator famously interjects herself by noting that 'I purposely abstain from dates' (*MP* 319) when Edmund's romantic interests shift from Mary to Fanny, she explores Edmund's thoughts about the source of his affection for Fanny. He takes credit for 'her mind in so great a degree [being] formed by his care' (319). And while it is true that Edmund repeatedly refers to Fanny as a better moral arbiter than himself in the post-*Lover's Vows* moments of the novel, he never fully believes that her observations or knowledge are more just than his own: it is only when he sees Mary's reaction to Maria and Henry's elopement that he agrees with Fanny. Like his father, Edmund grants himself more credibility than Fanny in action, if not in words.

If *Pride and Prejudice* ends with a vision of Pemberley that affords testimonial and epistemic justice to its novel's heroine, *Mansfield Park* presents a more complicated scenario. Describing Sir Thomas's plan to help Fanny realise her error in refusing Henry Crawford's proposal by sending her to her working-class family home in Portsmouth, Austen's narrator indicates his epistemic coerciveness: 'It was a medicinal project upon his niece's understanding, which he must consider at present diseased. A residence of eight or nine years in the abode of wealth and plenty had a little disordered her powers of comparing and judging' (*MP* 250). Fanny finds her childhood home no less epistemically coercive. The Price home is 'the abode of noise, disorder, and impropriety' (264), and her core complaint about Portsmouth is how her family, especially her parents, generally ignore her.

While in Portsmouth, Fanny infamously reflects on Mansfield Park as a kind of utopia: 'no sounds of contention, no raised voice, no abrupt bursts, no tread of violence was ever heard; all proceeded in a regular course of cheerful orderliness; every body had their due importance; every body's feelings were consulted' (*MP* 266). Although students and critics alike tend to read this passage as a form of Stockholm Syndrome, it is also worth noting that Fanny's status as a knower is underrecognised in all spaces available to her, despite her apparent failure to see that this is so at Mansfield Park. This is clear in the novel's last two paragraphs, which double down on the oppressive paternalistic forces in the novel by channelling Sir Thomas's perspective rather than either Fanny's or the narrator's:

> With so much true merit and true love, and no want of fortune or friends, the happiness of the married cousins *must appear* as secure as earthly happiness can be…. [T]hey removed to Mansfield, and the parsonage there, which … soon grew as dear to her heart, and as thoroughly perfect in her eyes, as every thing else, within the view and patronage of Mansfield Park, had long been. (*MP* 321, emphasis added).

With language like 'must appear' and a summary that denies the longstanding terror that Fanny felt in her uncle's home, these last sentences build on the sense of knowing superiority that Sir Thomas feels in the successes of the Price family, alluded to directly in the previous paragraph ('Sir Thomas saw repeated, and for ever repeated reason to rejoice in what he had done for them all' [321]). Rather than endorsing Fanny's epistemic ascension, *Mansfield Park* ends by subsuming her mind and thoughts with those of Edmund and Sir Thomas. Read this way, we show students how the novel potentially performs—and perhaps subtly critiques, without yet having the language to do so—the many forces that cohere to perpetuate Fanny's experience of testimonial injustice.

Austen's Epistemic Injustice, Beyond White Privilege

While our students found the details of epistemic injustice relevant to understanding issues of sexism within the novel, they still had lingering questions about the white privilege of Austen's world. Many students found it problematic, if not overtly racist, that Austen's novels did not directly confront the atrocity of slavery or promote the cause of abolition. How could *Pride and Prejudice* remain all but silent on these issues? Perhaps this is another case in which Austen has a hermeneutical lack, creating a gap between Austen's ability to categorise and articulate these injustices and the tools that we have as contemporary readers. But we see in *Mansfield Park* that Austen does in fact have the conceptual resources to be conversant with the issues and injustices surrounding slavery and the slave trade: for example, the novel pointedly invokes the Mansfield Decision as a means of critiquing Sir Thomas's colonial landholdings.

Why then would *Mansfield Park* so tepidly address slavery in Fanny's tentative question to her uncle about the slave trade and the ensuing, uncomfortable silence of the Bertram family?[9] Students are further puzzled by this passage when we discuss how Austen's extant correspondence shows that she read abolitionist writing and even admitted to being 'in love' with Thomas Clarkson, the abolitionist activist and author of the *History of the Abolition of the Slave Trade* (1808) (24 January 1813; Jane Austen's *Letters* 207). We suggest that this silence, as well as *Pride and Prejudice*'s, calls to mind the uneasy and, as Sarah Marsh has shown, deeply contradictory post-Abolitionist moment, where abolishing slavery on British soil did not end the violence of the British Empire or its other structural oppressions. Even some of those who advocated for the end of the slave trade remained silent about their true motives, which were not necessarily anti-racist or even explicitly anti-slavery—some, for example, were informed by concerns about the working conditions for white crewmembers on slave ships.[10] The silences in the novels can be seen as Austen's acknowledgement of, and, at least publicly and overtly, her complicity with the gentry's refusal to recognise the injustices associated with slavery, perhaps because shrouding these issues in silence helped to preserve the status quo, which in many ways was beneficial to socioeconomically privileged white people. So, although Austen's novels do not explicitly call for abolition, we can read them as documenting a society that must rely on silence as a means of maintaining entrenched paternalistic hierarchies of gender, class, and race.

In her own time and in our own, this silence signifies Austen's white privilege: the lived experiences of Austen and her community largely permitted the suppression or dismissal of these human rights violations. Rather than ending the conversation here, however, we take this opportunity to think about, and ideally read in detail, authors from the period who *did* actively engage with slavery and abolition, and authors who include characters of colour. As Matthew reminds us, 'Unlike Austen, many of her contemporaries wrote stories about interracial marriage and biracial women …. They also used their fiction and poems to contribute to debates about abolition, in concert with women who circulated petitions, raised funds for the cause, and boycotted sugar from the West Indies' (Matthew). In addition to encouraging our students to read more deeply in the period, our students' critiques of Austen's privilege can move us forward in time and allow us to consider how forms of paternalistic, white, western privilege continue to rely on myriad forms of oppression today.

Conclusion

When we support our students' concerns over the way that Austen fails to denounce what we understand as systemic and social injustice, we validate their own need for testimonial and epistemic justice. Rather than telling them they are being ahistorical and presentist, that they are imposing standards on a text that are unfair, we endorse these critiques as valid and valuable forms of observation and knowledge that help us better understand the fraught social dynamics in Austen's time and our own. Assignments that mirror this kind of activist presentism—that allow for students, community partners, and faculty to have equal resources and forms of knowledge and expertise—take as their cornerstone an advocacy for epistemic justice.

For our recent class on Austen, this assignment was a podcast series, which the students gleefully named *Pod and Prejudice*. This assignment allowed them to choose topics about Austen that were relevant and important to them; as the writers, producers, and hosts of these episodes, they also assumed authoritative roles that allowed them to share their insights, questions, and analyses as forms of worthwhile, publicly consumable knowledge. Students hosted episodes on film adaptations of the novel, on Austen's philosophical positions, and even mused about how to queer Austen's novels. In the next iteration of this course, we plan to pair a multimodal assignment like podcasting with other public humanities projects, like the transcription and annotation of archival materials on the lived experiences of people in the eighteenth and nineteenth centuries, especially those documents that capture the lives of people who have traditionally been marginalised in academic archives and in the broader western imagination. We hope that Austen's narrative of epistemic injustice in *Pride and Prejudice*, and her depiction of the near-perpetual challenges to Fanny's capacity as a knower, can bring us and our students closer to achieving epistemic justice in our own time.

Notes

1 David Scott Kastan notes that literary works can demonstrate how ideas were thinkable, even if they were not widely held or clearly defined (50).
2 Work on epistemic injustice now extends well beyond philosophy into, just to name a few disciplines, social science and psychology (see the collection of essays in Sherman and Goguen), medicine and healthcare (Carel and Kidd), mathematics (Rittberg et al.), and disability studies (Tremain).
3 Sarah Emsley suggests that '*Pride and Prejudice* is concerned with the social virtue of ... the problem of how to be truthful and civil simultaneously' (83) and 'how to get from sin to justice' (85).
4 Paula Bromberg has argued that Fanny's voice emerges in Vol II (63–64); we agree that the novel traces the way she attempts to assert her moral authority throughout the novel, although we do not believe that those surrounding her ultimately grant her sufficient credibility.
5 Monica Cohen suggests that Mary routinely attempts to silence Fanny with maxims (92–94).
6 Juliet McMaster has argued that Elizabeth is given the task of 'slaying' Lady Catherine verbally (168). Emsley notes that Fanny's resistance suggests 'strong, independent judgment coming from someone long used to submission' (111).
7 See Medina, 23–24 and Manne, 188–93.
8 See Manne 191.
9 Paula Loscocco has called *Mansfield Park* 'Austen's preimperial novel in a postcolonial context' (223). While many critics have followed Edward Said's influential reading of the silence as part of a broader representation of the west silencing the non-European world, other critics, like John Wiltshire and George E. Boulukos, have argued that the novel is either far less politically committed to engaging in a debate about the slave trade (the former) or that the novel is explicitly ameliorationist in perspective.
10 See, for instance, Scott, 82–83.

Works Cited

Austen, Jane. *Jane Austen's Letters*, edited by Deirdre Le Faye. Oxford UP, 2011.
Austen, Jane. *Mansfield Park*, edited by Claudia L. Johnson. Norton, 1998.
Austen, Jane. *Pride and Prejudice*, edited by Donald Gray and Mary A. Favret. Norton, 2016.
Boulukos, George E. 'The Politics of Silence: *Mansfield Park* and the Amelioration of Slavery.' *Novel*, vol. 39, no. 3, 2006, pp. 361–383.
Bromberg, Paula. '*Mansfield Park*: Austen's Most Teachable Novel.' *Approaches to Teaching Jane Austen's Mansfield Park*, edited by Marcia McClintock Folsom and John Wiltshire. MLA, 2014, pp. 60–69.
Carel, Havi, and Ian James Kidd. 'Epistemic Injustice in Healthcare: A Philosophical Analysis.' *Medicine, Health Care and Philosophy*, vol. 17, no. 4, 2014, pp. 529–540.
Cohen, Monica. 'The Price of a Maxim: Plausibility in Fanny's Happy Ending.' *Approaches to Teaching Jane Austen's Mansfield Park*, edited by Marcia McClintock Folsom and John Wiltshire. MLA, 2014, pp. 90–96.
Emsley, Sarah Baxter. *Jane Austen's Philosophy of the Virtues*. Palgrave, 2005.
Folsom, Marcia McClintock, and John Wiltshire, editors. *Approaches to Teaching Austen's Mansfield Park*. MLA, 2014, pp. 21–49.
Fricker, Miranda. *Epistemic Injustice*. New York: Oxford UP/Clarendon P, 2007.
Kastan, David Scott. *Shakespeare After Theory*. Routledge, 1999.
Loscocco, Paula. '"You Do Not Know Me": Reformation and Rights in *Mansfield Park*.' *Approaches to Teaching Jane Austen's Mansfield Park*, edited by Marcia McClintock Folsom and John Wiltshire. MLA, 2014, pp. 223–232.

Manne, Kate. *Down Girl: The Logic of Misogyny*. Oxford UP, 2018.

Marsh, Sarah. 'Changes of Air: The Somerset Case and *Mansfield Park*'s Imperial Plots.' *Eighteenth-Century Studies*, vol. 53, no. 2, Winter 2020, pp. 211–233.

Matthew, Patricia A. 'On Teaching, but Not Loving, Jane Austen.' *The Atlantic* 23 Jul. 2017. www.theatlantic.com/entertainment/archive/2017/07/on-teaching-but-not-loving-jane-austen/534012/. Accessed 11 Oct. 2019.

McMaster, Juliet. 'Talking about Talking.' *Approaches to Teaching Jane Austen's Pride and Prejudice*, edited by Marcia McClintock Folsom. MLA, 1993, pp. 167–173.

Medina, José. 'The Relevance of Credibility Excess in a Proportional View of Epistemic Injustice: Differential Epistemic Authority and the Social Imaginary.' *Social Epistemology*, vol. 25, no. 1, 2011, pp. 15–35.

Rittberg, Colin Jakob, Fenner Stanley Tanswell, and Jean Paul Van Bendegem. 'Epistemic injustice in mathematics.' *Synthese*, vol. 197, 2018, pp. 1–30.

Said, Edward. *Culture and Imperialism*. Knopf, 1993.

Scott, Julius C. *The Common Wind: Afro-American Currents in the Age of the Haitian Revolution*. Verso, 2018.

Sherman, Benjamin R., and Stacey Goguen, editors. *Overcoming Epistemic Injustice: Social and Psychological Perspectives*. Rowman & Littlefield, 2019.

Spratt, Danielle, and Bridget Draxler. 'Pride and Presentism: On the Necessity of Public Humanities for Literary Historians.' *Profession* Spring 2019. profession.mla.org/pride-and-presentism-on-the-necessity-of-the-public-humanities-for-literary-historians/. Accessed 11 Oct. 2020.

Tremain, Shelley. 'Knowing Disability, Differently.' *Routledge Handbook of Epistemic Injustice*, edited by Ian James Kidd, José Medina, and Gaile Pohlhaus Jr. Routledge, 2017, pp. 175–184.

Wiltshire, John. 'Decolonising Mansfield Park.' *Essays in Criticism*, vol. 53, no. 4, Oct. 2003, pp. 303–322. doi: https://doi.org/10.1093/eic/53.4.303

42

RACE, PRIVILEGE, AND RELATABILITY: A PRACTICAL GUIDE FOR COLLEGE AND SECONDARY INSTRUCTORS

Juliette Wells

GOUCHER COLLEGE

A young African-American woman asks what relevance Jane Austen's novels can possibly have for her, since Austen depicts no characters of colour. A first-generation college student from a working-class family points out that Austen concentrates on the lives of the economically privileged, making only passing references to labourers and servants. A young man who self-identifies as being on the autism spectrum responds strongly to Mr Darcy's awkwardness in public and obliviousness to social cues, traits this student is well aware of in himself.

Each of these reactions to Austen's novels occurred in one of my courses within the last several years, since I joined the faculty of Goucher College in 2012. Goucher is a small, private liberal-arts institution focused primarily on undergraduates, whose mission emphasises social justice and global education. The college's campus is located in Towson, Maryland, USA, just north of Baltimore City. In April 2015, Goucher students joined Black Lives Matter protests in Towson and Baltimore following the death in police custody of Freddie Gray.[1]

Demographically, Goucher's undergraduate population is diverse in terms of race, ethnicity, socioeconomic status, and home state or country.[2] Before arriving in my classroom, my students have been educated variously in public, private, and parochial schools. Some have been home-schooled for all or part of their pre-college education. Some have transferred from two- and four-year colleges; of these, some are older than the typical undergraduate age of 18–22. Entering my courses, some students have already read an Austen novel, either for class or on their own; more have seen a screen adaptation or two. (Broadly speaking, the USA's Common Core national curriculum in public schools has de-emphasised literature in favour of nonfiction texts.)

Goucher's faculty have recently reconceived both the college's general-education curriculum and many major programmes of study in order to promote student-directed learning and cultivate interdisciplinarity. Among our reinvented majors is my home programme of literary studies, formerly known as English. My literature courses typically interest students who are majoring in literary studies, creative writing, or women's, gender, and sexuality studies. I teach *Pride and Prejudice* in a survey course on the English novel and also offer an upper-level seminar, 'Jane Austen and Her Readers'.[3] Few of my undergraduates plan to study literature or other academic fields at the

DOI: 10.4324/9780429398155-42-48

547

postgraduate level, though many will eventually pursue master's degrees in creative writing, library science, education, law, or other professional fields.

All these factors and contexts both contribute to the expectations my students bring to Austen's novels and also help shape their interpretations. My own perspective continues to evolve after nearly two decades of work in undergraduate teaching; research on Austen in popular culture, Austen's reception, and Austen's historical readers; and public-humanities writing and speaking on Austen and book history to a wide range of audiences.[4] In this essay, I continue the endeavour I began in my 'reader-friendly' editions of *Emma* and *Persuasion* for Penguin Classics: to welcome the widest possible audience and to support them with accurate information presented in an accessible manner, free of academic jargon. In keeping with the pedagogy of 'universal design', this approach acknowledges that all readers are worthy of respect, whether or not they proceed to become scholars.

Austen, I well know, is not for everyone, in spite of the tendency of her fans to claim her, familiarly, as 'everybody's Jane'.[5] I have written elsewhere about the pedagogical advantages of integrating adaptations and reception in undergraduate teaching of Austen (Wells, 'A Place at the (Seminar) Table'). Presently, I welcome the entire continuum of my students' reactions to Austen's novels: from confusion and hostility to unabashed fandom and professions of 'relatability'. The latter term, which once made me cringe, I have come to value as affording a new entry point for fostering students' original, critical thinking about Austen's writings.

Existing resources for teaching Austen, such as the volumes in the MLA Approaches to Teaching World Literature series, tend to stress imparting essential content in order to direct students away from mere responses towards informed academic inquiry.[6] My aim here is quite different: to provide a practical guide for navigating the real-life challenges and opportunities for connection that arise in secondary and undergraduate classrooms once students are comfortable speaking freely about their experiences of reading Austen. Throughout, I explain matters as straightforwardly as possible, for the benefit of teachers who are not Austen specialists, as well as to enable sections of this essay to be usefully shared with students at introductory and intermediate levels. (Advanced students may well be better served by other chapters in this volume, which provide more complex scholarly accounts of the same issues.)

After summing up some of the challenges that students often articulate, I focus on two especially hot-button topics: race and ethnicity, followed by socioeconomic status. I offer brief overviews of contexts in history, biography, intertextuality, adaptations, and readers and fan communities, each pegged to a question or questions that students frequently ask. In the section on race, I also include a roundup of Austen's descriptive language that today's readers may interpret as racialised. I cite and recommend selected academic sources as well as pertinent films, contemporary novels, and other popular-culture resources that address, appealingly and often quite imaginatively, concerns and questions frequently raised by students. Next, I discuss, more briefly, aspects of Austen's novels that students often declare to be relatable: her innovations in characterising heroines and heroes; her depictions of courtship culture; and her attentiveness to socially awkward behaviour and to psychology more generally. I conclude with a call to invent new kinds of writing assignments that allow students to engage in personal ways with Austen's novels.

The suggestions and strategies I present are applicable to a variety of courses and student populations. Teachers, your knowledge of your own students best equips you to meet them where they are, to bridge gaps in their understanding, and to think through assumptions about the importance of novels considered 'great' or 'classic'. I hope that you will each find something here that can help transform moments of confrontation or uncertainty into rich conversations about Austen's artistry, influences, and legacies. Perhaps you work among traditionally minded colleagues who scoff at efforts to reduce barriers to students' comprehension of, appreciation of, and capacity to analyse Austen. If so, I also encourage you to take heart and continue to teach in a capacious, responsive manner.

Let me begin by asking you to reflect on what you find difficult about teaching Austen to your particular students, as well as on what your students report is challenging for them about reading Austen. If you are not sure how your students would respond to this question, consider asking them directly. If you do so, be sure that they can weigh in anonymously, unless you have an exceptionally forthcoming and unintimidated group.

When I ask my students what they find challenging about reading Austen, I receive a variety of answers, all of which are worth honouring and talking through. Some students say that Austen's prose is too hard to read: they find her vocabulary archaic and her sentences and paragraphs long and complex. To this, I express sympathy. Austen's prose does demand a lot from today's readers, especially those for whom English is not their first language or who have read little written before the twentieth century. I share some of the tips that I include in my Penguin Classics editions of *Persuasion* and *Emma*. Read slowly, not too much all at once. Read out loud as much as possible or listen to an audiobook while simultaneously reading. Consider film adaptations as a way to be introduced to Austen's characters and to envision her milieu.

Other students reply that reading Austen is tough because 'nothing happens'. I reply that they are in good company: many of Austen's contemporaries had the same complaint. The popular novels of her day were stuffed with plot and peril. She deliberately chose a different course by penning her uneventful tales involving (relatively) ordinary people. It takes time to acclimate to what Austen and her characters consider to be significant, as well as to the nuances of her style. Only when we do so can we ascertain how acutely she observes and how subtly she critiques her society.

Depending on the gender balance in my classroom, I may also hear that Austen's novels are 'for chicks'. This, I explain, is a relatively recent phenomenon. Male Austen fandom was very strong through the mid-twentieth century. The wave of 1990s screen adaptations, led by the BBC mini-series of *Pride and Prejudice* starring Colin Firth, rebranded Austen in the popular imagination as appealing chiefly to audiences of women. I note, too, the persistent tendency for novels written by men to be celebrated as being of universal importance, while women's writing is thought to interest mainly women. I tell the story of Sam, a male student of mine from several years ago, who attended an all-boys Catholic high school in which virtually no writing by women was assigned in literature classes. Sam found much to appreciate in Austen's depictions of male characters and their interactions with family members, friends, and potential mates. At the conclusion of our course, he declared his resolve to urge his high-school friends, who were by then majoring in aeronautical engineering at a large state university, to read Austen.

So far, so good. But what if a student responds that Austen's novels are off-putting because all of her characters are white? First, acknowledge that, indeed, Austen focuses on characters who take for granted their own and each other's identities as white English people, so much so that race or ethnicity are not mentioned by either the characters or the narrator in any of her six major novels.

The next step in your discussion might go in one of several directions. Depending on your students' prior knowledge and the goals for your course, you could draw on the collective expertise in your classroom, or on the brief overviews I provide below. Alternatively, you could assign students to research answers to the questions with which these overviews begin; to view and report back on the popular-culture sources I suggest; or to creatively respond in writing, or in another artistic medium, to what they find thought provoking about these questions. (These avenues of exploration apply as well to my subsequent treatment of socioeconomic status.)

History: What roles did people of colour have in the England of Austen's day? What legal status did enslavement have, and what views about enslaved people were held?

People of colour lived and worked in England's cities, especially populous London. Dark-skinned servants to wealthy families appear in family portraits and other artworks. Mixed-race or multiracial people were present as well. The 2014 film *Belle* imagines the experience of one such person: the multiracial woman Dido Belle, a young ward of a wealthy English family in the late eighteenth century.

In 1807, the international slave trade was abolished in Britain. Not until 1833, however, were enslaved people in the British Empire freed (White 1). Indigenous inhabitants of European colonies were often referred to and treated in dehumanising, prurient ways. A prime example is the 1810–12 exhibition in London of Sara Baartman, the so-called 'Hottentot Venus'.[7]

In addition, hierarchies were present within groups of Britons that are now viewed as white. Colonial attitudes of the English elite towards the Scots and Irish peoples resulted in denigration of those ethnicities. The English themselves had as forebears both the indigenous, Anglo-Saxon peoples and the Normans who conquered the island in 1066.

Biography: Was Austen personally acquainted with any people of colour?

Her surviving letters do not refer to seeing, meeting, or knowing anyone of a different race or ethnicity, although she may have done so. As Sheila Johnson Kindred has shown, Austen's sister-in-law Fanny Palmer Austen grew up in Bermuda in households with enslaved servants, in a system less harsh than the West Indian plantations; Fanny Austen may well have discussed her experiences with Austen.

Intertextuality: In which of Austen's writings does she directly address race, ethnicity, or enslavement, and how does she do so? What descriptors does Austen employ that, to our eyes, have potentially racialised overtones?

Sanditon, the novel Austen began in her last year of life, and which she left unfinished, introduces a character whom the narrator identifies as a 'half mulatto' (*Later Manuscripts* 202). As Jocelyn Harris has pointed out, Austen seems to have coined this puzzling term (262). *Mansfield Park* contains Austen's most direct references to the enslavement of people in British colonies, through discussions of the dependence of the Bertram family on the profits of their plantation in Antigua. Noteworthy too is the 'gypsies' episode in *Emma*, which represents the supposed threat to an orderly English village, and to virginal Harriet Smith in particular, posed by the Romany people, who had been present in England for centuries.

Austen also treated the topic of enslavement figuratively and via implication. In *Emma*, Jane Fairfax, who is beautiful and talented but penniless, objects to working as a governess as being a form of slavery (325). Critics have pointed out that the moneyed but vulgar Mrs Elton, who professes to be appalled by Jane's comparison, comes from the city of Bristol, formerly a major port in the international slave trade. New research, furthermore, has illuminated the significance of the phrase 'pride and prejudice' in abolitionist rhetoric during and after Austen's lifetime, in both Britain and the USA (Burns; Favret, 'Frederick Douglass' Pride and Prejudice').

In *Pride and Prejudice*, the narrator portrays the appearance and behaviour of Lydia, the youngest Bennet sister, in ways that parallel how people of colour have historically been denigrated. Lydia has 'high animal spirits'; she is 'wild' (49, 348).

Occasionally, too, Austen's narrator describes a character's complexion using words that, to us, seem suggestive of colourism. Such language appears in reference to both male and female characters, and its significance varies according to context. Miss Bingley of *Pride and Prejudice* sneers that Elizabeth's face has become 'brown and coarse'—we might say, tanned—from being outdoors (299). Yet Mary Crawford of *Mansfield Park* is no less beautiful for having what that novel's narrator describes as a 'clear brown complexion' (51). So too does Marianne Dashwood of *Sense and Sensibility*: 'Her skin was very brown, but from its transparency, her complexion was uncommonly brilliant' (55). Readers who recall Mr Darcy as tall, dark, and handsome are misremembering. The narrator of *Pride and Prejudice* states only that Darcy has a 'fine, tall person, handsome features, [and] noble mien' (10). Several other male characters, however, present a dark appearance, though whether in terms of skin tone, hair colour, eye colour, or a combination of these traits is not necessarily clear. Henry Crawford of *Mansfield Park* initially strikes the Bertram sisters as being 'black and plain' (51). The narrator of *Persuasion* introduces Captain Harville as 'a tall, dark man' (105). Henry Tilney of *Northanger Abbey* earns an exceptionally detailed description—'"a brown skin, with dark eyes, and rather dark hair"' (36)—albeit via a complicated route: Isabella Thorpe is quoting Catherine Morland's words back to her, presumably accurately.

Adaptations: How have adaptors of Austen's works addressed race and ethnicity?

To date, no period screen adaptation of one of Austen's six major novels has included people of colour in central or noticeable roles. By contrast, many stage plays, musicals, and operas based on Austen's novels have featured performers of colour.

Among period film adaptations, Patricia Rozema's *Mansfield Park* (1999) stands out for its explicit, sustained treatment of enslavement and abuses. Among adaptations set in the present day, Gurinder Chadha's Bollywood-inspired *Bride & Prejudice* (2004) most fully imagines Austen in an international context, with characters hailing from India, London, and the USA. The three YouTube series *The Lizzie Bennet Diaries*, *Emma Approved*, and *Welcome to Sanditon*—all set in twenty-first century America—prominently feature characters and actors of colour.

Most professionally and fan authored fiction inspired by Austen's novels steers clear of race and ethnicity. Thought-provoking exceptions include Ibi Zoboi's 2018 *Pride*, a young-adult 'remix' of *Pride and Prejudice* set in the gentrifying Bushwick neighbourhood of Brooklyn with a socio-economically diverse cast of Haitian- and Dominican-American characters. Soniah Kamal's witty *Unmarriageable* (2019) transposes *Pride and Prejudice* to present-day Pakistan, appending metafictional musings about what it means to appreciate Austen in the postcolonial era. More loosely, Sonali Dev's *Pride and Prejudice and Other Flavors* (2019) suggests connections between Austen's world and that of a prosperous Indian-American family.

Austen's unfinished novel *Sanditon*, with its 'half mulatto' character Miss Lambe, has been completed by several novelists and fans. Most recently, and most prominently, a fanciful, greatly expanded miniseries version by Andrew Davies aired in the United Kingdom in 2019 and in the USA in 2020. Publicity for Davies' *Sanditon* highlighted the role of Miss Lambe, played by Crystal Clarke. A survey of such media coverage (perhaps researched by a student) could open a useful classroom conversation about ideas concerning Austen and race, as could screening scenes featuring Miss Lambe.

Finally, as a quick and productive discussion-starter, I recommend showing students Amy Sherald's portrait of a young everyman of colour, titled 'A single man in possession of a good fortune', part of the artist's recent exhibit at the Hauser & Wirth gallery in New York.[8]

Readers and fan communities: In what ways is racial and ethnic diversity present in Austen's readership and fandom today?

How readers outside the Anglo-American context respond to Austen's novels has been explored by, among others, Azar Nafisi, in *Reading Lolita in Tehran* (2003); Bee Rowlatt and May Witwit, in *Talking about Jane Austen in Baghdad* (2010); the members of the newly formed Jane Austen Society of Pakistan, who have been interviewed by the BBC and NPR; and Soniah Kamal, in her essay 'Pride and Prejudice and Me', at the conclusion of her novel *Unmarriageable*. Elements of Austen's novels that resonate with all these readers include the strict social hierarchy and mores she depicts, as well as the struggles of women characters to attain self-actualisation within a patriarchal society.

As this book goes to press, an unprecedented amount of discussion is taking place on social media among Austen fans who identify as people of colour. Interested students could survey current and recent conversations on this topic and share their findings with the class.

Addressing Privilege

Perhaps some of your students respond that what distances them from Austen's novels is her focus on characters that are economically privileged. The money anxieties of the Bennet family in *Pride and*

Prejudice, for example, might well grate on a student who is taking on significant debt to finance undergraduate education. And the woes of Emma Woodhouse might seem like 'first-world problems' indeed.

Here, too, I encourage you to begin by acknowledging the students' responses. Austen's novels certainly centre on characters who have many privileges, including adequate (and sometimes grand) housing; access to at least some forms of education; and, in most cases, a modicum of personal wealth, though not necessarily enough to ensure independence. Moreover, the comfortable, leisured lives of Austen's main characters result from the work of many whom she leaves largely invisible, from servants to estate tenants.

It is worth pointing out, too, that in class terms, few of us can realistically 'see ourselves' in an Austen novel. If we had been alive in her time, we would most likely have been servants, labourers, or other working people, not ladies or gentlemen.

History: How do Austen's characters fit into the status hierarchy of her day? In terms of depicting privilege, how does she compare with her contemporaries and successors?

Austen chose to portray the experiences of characters that occupy the middle levels of the British status hierarchy: below royals and high aristocrats (dukes, earls, etc.) and above ordinary working people. It is essential, I find, to stress the distinction between these intermediate levels and how the terms 'middle-class' or 'middle classes' are variously understood today. Everyone in Austen's novels, like their historical counterparts, is keenly status-conscious and well aware of the intersecting importance of monetary wealth, proper manners and conduct, and family respectability. In Austen's novels, as in her world, social roles are gendered: a father, for instance, is thought to hold different obligations towards his children than a mother. A strong double standard governs sexual behaviour before marriage. Men can enjoy themselves, or err and repent, but women have to guard their reputations.

Though few of Austen's major characters occupy truly precarious economic positions, many experience threats to the stability of their lives. Austen returns again and again to the challenges faced by young people of comparatively modest means in a marriage market that places great value on inherited wealth. Her female characters have virtually no options for earning money of their own. Austen shows sympathy, too, towards those of her male characters who must make their way in the world in one of the few professions considered appropriate to them, principally the clergy and the military. Moreover, she explores the pressures of the traditional gentlemanly role, through characters such as Mr Darcy. The courtship plot that anchors all of her novels enables her to emphasise the serious consequences for both women and men of choosing a marriage partner. With divorce virtually unobtainable, ill-suited spouses were essentially trapped with each other until death.

Many of Austen's predecessors and contemporaries in the English novel took an interest in the predicament of a young, well-brought-up woman with little money as she entered the marriage market. Frances Burney's bestseller *Evelina* (1788) is one such tale. Other authors of realistic novels depicted characters of roughly the same social ranks as those in Austen. Not until the 'condition of England' novels of the 1840s and 1850s, including those of Charles Dickens and Elizabeth Gaskell, would the lives of the poor receive sensitive—albeit sentimental—literary treatment.

Biography: What was Austen's own social and financial position? What were her personal attitudes towards marriage and professional authorship?

Austen's family occupied much the same 'middling' ranks of society that we find in her novels. Her father was a clergyman, educated though not personally wealthy, while her mother's extended family included landowners. The professions pursued by Austen's brothers mirror those of the male characters in her novels: the clergy, the navy, banking. One of Austen's brothers was adopted by rich distant relations and became the heir to their estates, an experience somewhat comparable to that of Frank Churchill in *Emma*. After Austen's father's death in 1805, which occurred when she was twenty-nine, she—along with her widowed mother and elder sister—essentially depended on the support of her married brothers. A glimpse of Austen's restricted personal finances can be found in the list she kept of her expenses in the year 1807: she spent a total of £44.10s.6d on essentials including clothing, laundry, postage, and servants' wages, plus charity and tithes to the church, and a few indulgences such as renting a pianoforte (*Autograph Memorandum*).

Austen received at least one marriage proposal, from the brother of close friends, and may have received more. She opted not to marry and instead spent her prime writing years, her thirties, living with her mother, sister, and a woman friend; her wealthy brother supplied the house. She was proud of what she earned from the novels she published in her last decade of life and kept careful track of her investments, as can be seen from her handwritten 'Profits of my novels' (*Autograph Note*). However, the amount that she earned from her publications was not enough to support herself, much less her entire household. In her novels and letters, she repeatedly commented on the indignities of poverty for unmarried women: for instance, she remarked to her niece Fanny Knight in 1817 that '[s]ingle Women have a dreadful propensity for being poor' (*Letters* 347).

Intertextuality: In which of Austen's novels does she focus most on the experience of socially or financially marginalised characters? Where and how does she criticise privilege?

Austen consistently commends characters that are truly cheerful in spite of narrow circumstances. Most memorably, she exalts Miss Bates of *Emma*, a fortyish spinster who lives in rented rooms with her widowed mother, as possessed of 'universal good-will and contented temper': 'The simplicity and cheerfulness of her nature, her contented and grateful spirit, were a recommendation to every body and a mine of felicity to herself' (36).

Mansfield Park offers Austen's most unsparing depiction of the difficulties of impoverishment. Fanny Price's father, Lieutenant Price, who is disabled from active duty and dependent on alcohol, makes life a misery for his wellborn but now downtrodden wife and their numerous children. Sensitive Fanny suffers both at home and, differently, while under the patronage—and patronisation—of her mother's wealthier sisters, who bring her up from the age of nine.

By contrast, *Persuasion*, the final novel Austen completed before her death, celebrates the capacity of the human spirit to flourish even in circumstances of penury and disability. The injured Captain Harville and his wife, who must make do on very little, are nevertheless generous and open hearted, while the titled landowner Sir Walter Elliot is vain and selfish in the extreme. Austen singles out for praise, too, the intelligence of a workingwoman, Nurse Rooke, who makes up for her lack of formal education with shrewd observations of human nature. Among Nurse Rooke's patients is the chronically ill Mrs Smith, who earns the narrator's admiration by remaining optimistic and eager to connect with people, despite being confined to living in two small rooms.

Every Austen novel includes characters that are menaced by disgrace and ignominy. In *Sense and Sensibility*, two generations of women named Eliza, mother and daughter, are seduced and abandoned in turn. *Pride and Prejudice*'s Lydia Bennet risks her reputation and safety by gleefully eloping (so she thinks) with Wickham. Without the protection of privileged patrons, the illegitimate Harriet Smith and the talented Jane Fairfax in *Emma* would both be vulnerable to predators. *Northanger Abbey*'s Isabella Thorpe places herself in danger through her attraction to the unscrupulous Captain Tilney.

In no sense does Austen advocate class revolution. Nevertheless, she firmly counters the notion that rank ought to be respected no matter what. She applies some of her strongest satire to condescending, power-hungry titled people, from overbearing Lady Catherine de Bourgh of *Pride and Prejudice* to Sir Walter Elliot of *Persuasion*. Contrary to popular belief, Austen does not depict the social hierarchy as rigid or unchanging. In *Pride and Prejudice*, Mr Darcy accepts as a friend the well mannered, warm-hearted Mr Bingley in spite of the recent origins of the latter's wealth. With the Martin family in *Emma*, Austen shows how trustworthy tenants can steadily rise in prosperity and respectability. Most importantly, the naval men of *Persuasion*, from the now-wealthy Captain Wentworth to the financially struggling Captain Harville, demonstrate a new kind of honour, in contrast to the self-absorbed Elliots (excepting Anne).

Adaptations: Which novels and films based on Austen offer the most thought-provoking depictions of social class and financial privilege?

By far the most imaginative reworking of Austen from a class perspective is Jo Baker's 2013 novel *Longbourn*, a film version of which is currently in production. Baker imagines the life of Sarah, a servant in the Bennet household, who pursues her own happiness in spite of bigger obstacles than those confronting the young ladies whose petticoats she launders. An unvarnished, even déclassé view of the Bennets themselves is present in Joe Wright's 2005 feature film of *Pride & Prejudice*, in which livestock move freely in and out of the family's cluttered, crumbling house. Autumn de Wilde's 2020 feature film *Emma.* is notable for Mia Goth's sensitive portrayal of Harriet Smith as capable of being not only silly but also, ultimately, self-possessed.

Most screen adaptations of Austen show servants at work much more frequently than the novels themselves do. In Roger Michell's 1995 telefilm *Persuasion*, the camera accords great dignity to working people. De Wilde goes even further in *Emma.* by giving the servants at Hartfield both names and opportunities for (nonverbal) critique. In another vein, Patricia Rozema's *Mansfield Park* feature film, which I recommended earlier with respect to race, is again of interest because Rozema endows Fanny Price with the ambition to become an author. Emma Thompson's screenplay for Ang Lee's 1995 *Sense and Sensibility* spells out for a turn-of-the-millennium audience why the Dashwood sisters cannot just go earn a living.

As I previously mentioned, Ibi Zoboi's young-adult novel *Pride* 'remixes' *Pride and Prejudice* along socioeconomic as well as racial lines. The five Benitez sisters and their parents live in a tiny apartment; their father works nights at a hospital cafeteria.

Readers and fan communities: Countless novels feature present-day Austen fans of moderate means engaging with ersatz or real Austen characters, or with the author herself, via time travel, role-playing, or magic. Of these, the most insightful on the subject of class differences is Shannon Hale's 2007 novel *Austenland*, which was made into a 2010 film directed by Jerusha Hess. In both versions, an American fan travels to England to participate in a kind of live-action enactment of a pseudo Austen novel. Among the country-house cast are Darcy and Wickham types, played by actors whose roles conceal the men's very different true identities.

I highly recommend, too, the television miniseries *Lost in Austen* (2008), which proceeds from a frankly ridiculous premise. Amanda, a modern-day London office worker who adores *Pride and Prejudice*, finds her way into the world of that novel via her bathroom wall, thereby switching places with Elizabeth Bennet. While the defiantly non-posh Amanda fakes Regency behaviour in an apparently doomed effort to pass, Elizabeth makes herself comfortably at home in the life of a self-supporting single woman in our century.

Points of Connection

As the foregoing examples demonstrate, attending to Austen's representations of gender uncovers points of possible connection for today's readers. In particular, the question of Austen's feminism always rewards investigation. While no radical like Mary Wollstonecraft, Austen nevertheless promoted women's self-determination in a way that can be seen as progressive. Elizabeth Bennet refuses Mr Collins on the grounds that neither would make the other happy. Charlotte Lucas accepts Mr Collins because his offer matches her own pragmatic goals of leaving her family home and gaining the independence of a married woman. In *Persuasion*, Mrs Croft robustly demonstrates women's physical courage and stamina, while gentle Anne Elliot voices her objections to men's assumed authority: 'the pen', she memorably declares, 'has been in their hands' (255).

Austen decisively influenced the genre of the novel, moreover, by establishing new kinds of both heroines and heroes. This contribution is clearest in *Pride and Prejudice*, whose characters debate the qualities of the so-called accomplished woman. Such a person is faultlessly behaved, artistically well trained, perfectly beautiful, and successfully endures trials to her virtue. By contrast, an Austen heroine is someone who thinks for herself and develops self-knowledge. Thus, *Pride and Prejudice* centres not on the trusting and lovely Jane Bennet—who would have made an ideal eighteenth-century heroine—but on the sparkling, overconfident Elizabeth. An Austen heroine, far from changing herself to become more attractive to a man, concentrates on her moral self: her personal growth, as we would say today.

An Austen hero is not static either. He examines himself, identifies his faults, and works to remedy them. Especially in *Sense and Sensibility* and *Persuasion*, Austen airs the conventional view that a flawed man can be improved or redeemed by the love of a 'good' woman, but she does not endorse this notion. Her heroes and heroines enter marriage having already made themselves worthy of each other.

Austen follows the norms of her era in investing men with the power to propose marriage, while granting women the power only to accept or refuse such an offer. Though many students guess that marriages in Austen's era were arranged, in fact her emphasis on the importance of love accords with prevailing views of her time. Her celebration of truly companionate marriage, however, sets her apart.

I often hear from my students that the world Austen depicts reminds them of their own experiences in high school, full of flirting, crushes, and romantic rivalries (minus, of course, social media). Discussions about parallels and differences between Regency and present-day dating cultures can lead to valuable insights. Adaptations of Austen's novels to college and university settings, such as Green and Su's *The Lizzie Bennet Diaries*, likewise open up questions of perceptions of conduct, especially women's, then and now. My students have found especially thought provoking the transformation of Lydia in *The Lizzie Bennet Diaries* from a heedless hedonist to a victim of an abusive relationship.

Other aspects of Austen's novels that resonate with today's students include her treatment of social awkwardness, which they perceive as analogous to the experiences of neuroatypical young people navigating a baffling world. As an example of how works of literature might be interpreted outside of traditional academic frameworks, I often share Phyllis Ferguson Bottomer's analyses of Austen's novels in light of current understandings of the autistic spectrum. Those students who are familiar with Matthew Macfadyen's performance in Joe Wright's 2005 *Pride & Prejudice* film can comment, too, on his portrayal of Darcy as being less proud than deficient in social skills.

More generally, psychological explorations of Austen's characters greatly interest many of my students, who are all too aware of the prevalence in their generation of anxiety, depression, and other forms of mental illness. Marianne Dashwood's excessive sensibility, for example, can be approached both via medical theories of Austen's day and also as a cautionary tale of refusal to engage in acts of self-care. By contrast, Elinor Dashwood assiduously manages her own symptoms of distress, in large part by doing what we would now call setting boundaries with her mother and sister. Anne Elliot, too, well aware of her tendency towards emotional overwhelm, capably looks after herself and her needs, often by seeking solitude and reflection. Furthermore, Anne sensitively counsels Captain Benwick regarding his painful grief. Robustly healthy herself, Emma Woodhouse patiently and sympathetically copes with her father's moods and hypochondria. Altogether, Austen's depictions of emotional resilience, which Kay Young has recently illuminated, hold strong appeal for young people who seek to cultivate wellness in a world full of stressors.

Finally, Austen's astute analysis of gendered power dynamics holds new relevance in the wake of the #MeToo movement. Valuably, Austen depicts not only verbal and physical assaults on women but also acts of effective resistance. Elizabeth Bennet laughs off minor insults, including of course Mr Darcy's judgement that she is 'tolerable, but not handsome enough to tempt me' (*PP* 12). Moreover, Elizabeth asserts herself in response to the arrogance of first Mr Collins and then Mr Darcy, as each man in turn not so much proposes marriage as demonstrates his certainty that he cannot be refused. As Celia A. Easton has explored, students' unfortunate familiarity with sexual assault and alcohol abuse leads them to appreciate the real dangers of the tête-à-tête carriage ride in *Emma*, during which Emma firmly resists the advances of the wine-drunk Mr Elton. Meek Fanny Price stalwartly refuses to bow to Sir Thomas Bertram's overbearing authority, Edmund Bertram's efforts at persuasion, and Henry Crawford's blandishments. Austen endows all her heroines with the certainty that they deserve happiness and respect. What's more, she celebrates her characters' commitment to their personal integrity, rather than their maintenance of their sexual virtue per se.

In addition to being open to classroom discussions of the relatability and relevance of Austen's novels, I encourage you who are instructors at the secondary and undergraduate level to design at least one course assignment in a non-traditional mode, in order to allow your students to investigate connections and contexts that are of particular concern to them. In my experience, young writers exceed expectations at every level, from research to writing style, when they are free to pursue their own curiosity, draw on their unique expertise, and address their chosen audience.

My favourite example from my own courses is the project completed by the student whom I mentioned at the beginning of my introduction: the African-American woman who felt that her own experience was not at all reflected in Austen's novels. She decided to write a personal essay recounting her reactions and responses to our readings, which eventually led her to appreciate certain aspects of Austen's artistry. This student wanted to share her insights with others who, like her, live in the city of Baltimore and use its public libraries. So she designed and formatted her essay in the form of a booklet, made copies of it using curriculum-support funds, and placed one of the booklets in each of the library branches in and around the neighbourhood where she grew up.[9] She hoped that a curious young reader might pick up her essay and be inspired to give Austen a try.

Notes

1 My thanks to Cheryl A. Wilson and Maria Frawley for their invitation to contribute to this volume, and for their enthusiasm about this topic. I gratefully acknowledge the opportunity, made possible by Professor Anna Paluchowska-Messing, to present work in progress to English literature students at the Jagiellonian University, Krakow, Poland, in April 2019. I appreciate the inspiration of my own students, especially those in my LIT 335 course, Jane Austen and Her Readers. I drafted and revised this essay in a rapidly changing world, which will have changed still further by the time you read it. I completed final revisions in August 2020, several months into the COVID-19 pandemic and the next wave of the Black Lives Matter movement, with the critical US Presidential election a few months in the future.

2 Goucher's 1400 or so undergraduates include approximately 40% students of colour, a proportion that has been steadily rising in recent years ('Fall 2018 Fact Sheet'). Collegewide, the gender balance is officially 69% women, 31% men, although an increasing proportion of students identify as nonbinary ('Fall 2018 Fact Sheet'). The overwhelming majority of students in my literature classes identify as women, nonbinary, and/ or trans. Approximately 25% of incoming students are first-generation, i.e., the first members of their immediate family to attend a four-year undergraduate institution ('Class of 2022 Infographic').

3 In Fall 2020 I launched a new course in Goucher's general-education curriculum: a first-year seminar titled '*Pride and Prejudice*, Here and Now'.

4 See in particular Wells, 'Austen in Public'.

5 Patricia A. Matthew has incisively analysed how Austen's novels, thanks to fervent fans, tend to eclipse other worthy works, including the anonymously published 1808 novel *The Woman of Colour: A Tale*. Teaching Austen in conjunction with *The Woman of Colour* is an approach taken by instructors at America's historically black colleges and universities (Favret, 'Jane Austen at 200').

6 In addition to the chapters in this volume, recommended resources for imaginative Austen pedagogy include Olivera Jokic's illuminating article 'Teaching to the Resistance: What to Do When Students Dislike Austen', which includes quotations from her undergraduates at John Jay College of the City University of New York; Michael Verderame's reflections on teaching *Persuasion* to incarcerated students; and Bridget Draxler and Danielle Spratt's treatments of public-humanities and community-based-learning approaches. More valuable work is on the way, including the forthcoming summer 2021 special issue of *Persuasions*

On-Line, the open-access journal of the Jane Austen Society of North America, titled 'Beyond the Bit of Ivory: Jane Austen and Diversity'.

7   For a thorough consideration of the degree of likelihood that Austen herself saw Sarah Baartman, see Harris, chapter 7.

8   A digital image of Sherald's portrait is included in Schjeldahl.

9   The curriculum-support funds that made it possible for my student to produce multiple copies of her booklet came through the generosity of Betty Applestein Sweren, Goucher class of 1952, to Goucher's pioneering Book Studies programme. Together with her husband Edgar Sweren, Mrs Sweren has recently endowed the college's Marcie Sweren Wogan Institute for the Study of the Book.

Works Cited

Austen, Jane. *Autograph Memorandum of Personal Accounts*. Dec. 1807, The Morgan Library & Museum, MA 2911.2.

Austen, Jane. *Autograph Note Concerning the 'Profits of my Novels, over and above the £600 in the Navy Fives.'* Ca. March 1817, The Morgan Library & Museum, https://www.themorgan.org/collection/literary-and-historical-manuscripts/81568

Austen, Jane. *Emma*, edited by Richard Cronin and Dorothy McMillan. Cambridge UP, 2005.

Austen, Jane. *Jane Austen's Letters*, edited by Deirdre Le Faye, 4th ed. Oxford UP, 2011.

Austen, Jane. *Later Manuscripts*, edited by Janet Todd and Linda Bree. Cambridge UP, 2008.

Austen, Jane. *Mansfield Park*, edited by John Wiltshire. Cambridge UP, 2005.

Austen, Jane. *Northanger Abbey*, edited by Barbara M. Benedict and Deirdre Le Faye. Cambridge UP, 2009.

Austen, Jane. *Persuasion*, edited by Janet Todd and Antje Blank. Cambridge UP, 2006.

Austen, Jane. *Pride and Prejudice*, edited by Pat Rogers. Cambridge UP, 2006.

Austenland. Directed by Jerusha Hess, screenplay by Shannon Hale and Jerusha Hess, Sony Pictures Classics, 2013.

Baker, Jo. *Longbourn*. Doubleday, 2013.

Belle. Directed by Amma Asante, screenplay by Misan Sangay, Fox Searchlight Pictures, 2014.

Bottomer, Phyllis Ferguson. 'A Speech Language Pathologist Journeys to Highbury.' *Persuasions: The Jane Austen Journal*, vol. 29, 2007, pp. 155–166.

Bottomer, Phyllis Ferguson. '"Conversation, or Rather Talk": Autistic Spectrum Disorders and the Communication and Social Challenges of John Thorpe.' *Persuasions: The Jane Austen Journal On-Line*, vol. 30, no. 1, 2010. jasna.org/publications/persuasions-online/vol30no1/bottomer.html?

Bottomer, Phyllis Ferguson. *So Odd a Mixture: Along the Autistic Spectrum in Pride and Prejudice*. Jessica Kingsley, 2007.

Bride & Prejudice. Directed by Gurinder Chadha, screenplay by Paul Mayeda Berges and Gurinder Chadha, Miramax, 2004.

Burns, Margie. '"Pride and Prejudice" and Slavery in America.' *Persuasions: The Jane Austen Journal On-Line*, vol. 40, no. 1, 2019. http://jasna.org/publications/persuasions-online/volume-40-no-1/burns/

Caldwell, Joshua. *Welcome to Sanditon*. YouTube, uploaded by Pemberley Digital, 9 May 2013 to 12 Aug. 2013. www.youtube.com/playlist?list=PL_ePOdU-b3xeIJZtHVbO2rtSkoNp63bjR

'Class of 2022 Infographic.' *Goucher Research Intelligence Dashboards*. Goucher College. www.goucher.edu/institutional-effectiveness/grid/

Dev, Sonali. *Pride and Prejudice and Other Flavors*. New York: William Morrow, 2019.

Draxler, Bridget, and Danielle Spratt. *Engaging the Age of Jane Austen: Public Humanities in Practice*. Iowa City: U of Iowa P, 2019.

Easton, Celia A. '"The Encouragement I Received": *Emma* and the Language of Sexual Assault.' *Persuasions: The Jane Austen Journal On-Line*, vol. 37, no. 1, 2016. jasna.org/publications/persuasions-online/vol37no1/easton/

Emma. Directed by Autumn de Wilde, screenplay by Eleanor Carron, Focus Features, 2020.

'Fall 2018 Fact Sheet.' *Goucher Research Intelligence Dashboards*. Goucher College. www.goucher.edu/institutional-effectiveness/grid/fact-sheet-fall-2018

Favret, Mary A. 'Frederick Douglass' Pride and Prejudice.' Jane Austen Symposium, Peabody Conservatory, Baltimore, MD. 23 Nov. 2019. Lecture.

Favret, Mary A. 'Jane Austen at 200.' Modern Language Association, Philadelphia, PA. 6 Jan. 2017. Panel Presentation.

Green, Hank, and Bernie Su. *The Lizzie Bennet Diaries*. YouTube, uploaded by Pemberley Digital, 9 Apr. 2012 to 28 Mar. 2013. www.youtube.com/user/LizzieBennet/videos?disable_polymer=1

Hale, Shannon. *Austenland*. Bloomsbury, 2007.

Harris, Jocelyn. *Satire, Celebrity, and Politics in Jane Austen*. Bucknell UP, 2017.

Jokic, Olivera. 'Teaching to the Resistance: What to Do When Students Dislike Austen.' *Persuasions: The Jane Austen Journal On-Line*, vol. 34, no. 2, 2014. http://jasna.org/persuasions/on-line/vol34no2/jokic.html

Kamal, Soniah. *Unmarriageable*. Ballantine, 2019.

Kindred, Sheila Johnson. *Jane Austen's Transatlantic Sister*. McGill/Queens UP, 2017.

Lost in Austen. Directed by Dan Zeff, screenplay by Guy Andrews, Mammoth Screen, 2008.

Mansfield Park. Written and directed by Patricia Rozema, Miramax, 1999.

Matthew, Patricia A. 'On Teaching, But Not Loving, Jane Austen.' *The Atlantic* 23 Jul. 2017. https://www.theatlantic.com/entertainment/archive/2017/07/on-teaching-but-not-loving-jane-austen/534012/

Nafisi, Azar. *Reading Lolita in Tehran*. Ballantine, 2003.

Persuasion. Directed by Roger Michell, screenplay by Nick Dear, BBC Films, 1995.

Pride & Prejudice. Directed by Joe Wright, screenplay by Deborah Moggach, Focus Features, 2005.

Pride and Prejudice. Directed by Simon Langton, screenplay by Andrew Davies, performances by Colin Firth and Jennifer Ehle, BBC, 1995.

Rowlatt, Bee, and May Witwit. *Talking about Jane Austen in Baghdad*. Penguin, 2010.

Sanditon. Created by Andrew Davies, ITV, 25 Aug. 2019 to 13 Oct. 2019.

Schjeldahl, Peter. 'The Amy Sherald Effect.' *New Yorker* 16 Sep. 2019. https://www.newyorker.com/magazine/2019/09/23/the-amy-sherald-effect

Sense and Sensibility. Directed by Ang Lee, screenplay by Emma Thompson. Columbia Pictures, 1995.

Su, Bernie, and James Bushman. *Emma Approved*. YouTube, uploaded by Pemberley Digital, 7 Oct. 2013 to 23 Aug. 2014. www.youtube.com/watch?v=aeeXkf8LZ_8&list=PL_ePOdU-b3xcKOsj8aU2Tnztt6N9mEmur

Verderame, Michael. 'Austen Unbound: Teaching *Persuasion* in Prison.' *Teaching Jane Austen*, special issue of *Romantic Circles Pedagogies Commons*, Apr. 2015. romantic-circles.org/pedagogies/commons/austen/pedagogies.commons.2015.verderame.html

Wells, Juliette. 'A Place at the (Seminar) Table for Austen's Popular Readers.' *Teaching Jane Austen*, special issue of *Romantic Circles Pedagogies Commons*, Apr. 2015, romantic-circles.org/pedagogies/commons/austen/pedagogies.commons.2015.wells.html

Wells, Juliette. 'Austen in Public.' *Objects of Study: Teaching Book History and Bibliography Among the Disciplines*, edited by Barbara Heritage and Donna Sy, in preparation.

Wells, Juliette, editor. *Emma*. by Jane Austen, 1815, Penguin Classics, 2015.

Wells, Juliette. *Everybody's Jane: Austen in the Popular Imagination*. New York: Bloomsbury Academic (formerly Continuum), 2011.

Wells, Juliette, editor. *Persuasion*. by Jane Austen, 1817, Penguin Classics, 2017.

White, Gabrielle D. V. *Jane Austen in the Context of Abolition: 'A Fling at the Slave Trade.'* Palgrave Macmillan, 2006.

Young, Kay. 'Resilience and Jane Austen.' *Jane Austen and Sciences of the Mind*, edited by Beth Lau. Routledge, 2018, pp. 200–221.

Zoboi, Ibi. *Pride*. Balzer + Bray, 2018.

43

AUSTEN'S BELIEF IN EDUCATION: SŌSEKI, NOGAMI, AND SENSIBILITY

Kimiyo Ogawa

SOPHIA UNIVERSITY, TOKYO

Jane Austen's novels have always been popular among Japanese university students interested in British culture and literature. This chapter derives from my experience of teaching her novels at an undergraduate level, and, in that capacity, of having repeatedly encountered difficulties in making certain aspects of Austen's novels comprehensible. Having been heavily influenced by New Historicism, I have taught my literature classes focusing on a historical awareness of how an author might have written a literary text in a culturally specific context. For example, I have taught Austen's ambiguous political attitude through introducing discourses on the French Revolution which were deployed by Thomas Paine, William Godwin, Mary Wollstonecraft and Edmund Burke. I have also looked at particular social codes and 'proper' behaviour exemplified by various characters in Austen's novels. When I offered a course called 'Japanese Reception of Jane Austen's Novels' in 2018, however, I made a conscious effort to go beyond that cultural boundary—I tried to teach the rhetoric deployed in service of the so-called cult of sensibility represented in Austen's writing and expressed through Japanese novels.[1] This was a conscious effort on my part to raise students' awareness about their own cultural legacy from the Meiji period (1868–1912) onwards.

In other words, I changed my teaching objective from trying to pursue culturally specific themes within the bounds of British Romanticism to finding more common grounds between Austen and Japanese writers. Since I myself was once in their position—I did A-level English Literature as an exchange student in Britain many years ago[2]—I gathered that they encountered stumbling blocks just as I had. For example, in *Sense and Sensibility*, Sir John Middleton's hospitality is shown in his willingness to bring 'a present of game' to the Dashwoods (36). A lack of cultural literacy hinders Japanese students from making a link between 'game' and the animal meat, thereby preventing them from understanding why this was a hospitable act—they had thought that 'game' meant amusement. Immersing oneself in Austen's fictional world is truly a bliss, if you can trace her mental footsteps, as it were, but even for readers who share the characters' feelings or experiences, or who understand the remote setting of the British countryside and the gentry classes of the Regency period, this may not be easy. For non-British readers, it is much harder.

A breakthrough came when I read Barbara K. Seeber's *Jane Austen and Animals* which sheds light on the juxtaposition of the body and animals and examines the 'physiological and psychological effects' of being in an inferior status—as some female characters suffer emotionally and physically from being mistreated by men (77, 29).[3] Just then I was working on an article on *Machiko* (1931), a Japanese adaptation of *Pride and Prejudice*, written by Nogami Yaeko (1885–1985), which chimed with many of these ideas. Seeber's analysis of Austen's metaphors, such as 'a small hole' which Henry

DOI: 10.4324/9780429398155-43-49

559

Crawford tries to make in 'Fanny Price's heart' in *Mansfield Park,* may be reliant on a cultural understanding of hunting as sport and its implied male aggression. But beyond this cultural specificity, the students can see something more universal, such as Fanny's acute pain and her sensibility which are also expressed through Nogami's female characters. In both of these authors' works, the body is represented as the site of social injustice (*MP* 267). Of course, no one was so articulate about social injustice against eighteenth-century women as Mary Wollstonecraft, and we also know that the maltreatment of animals was used as an allegory of the victimhood of women. For example, in *Maria, or the Wrongs of Woman* (1798), Wollstonecraft put in the mouth of Jemima her ideas about degraded women, 'I was the filching cat, the ravenous dog, the dumb brute, who must bear all' (109–110). Seeber recuperates the same political vocabulary from Austen's novels. In order for women to gain 'human' status, Wollstonecraft had recommended education, and in Austen's novels too 'discussions of education frequently form the backdrop and sometimes the central action' (Halsey 430).

In Japan, those who were eager to gain knowledge entered women's 'higher schools' (*kōtō jogakkō*) during the late nineteenth century and the early twentieth century, and Nogami was one of these girls. We can say that this was the time of Wollstonecraftian Enlightenment for Japanese women. The term 'New Women' (*shin fujin*), which was associated with a group of female writers contributing to a magazine called *Seitō,* became current during this period.[4] Many of these New Women wore fashionable Western dress, were intellectually aware, socialised with men in public, and those women who refused to marry a man of their parents' choice had their romantic partners (Ogawa 298). Nogami lived through the Meiji and Taishō Eras (and through to the Showa Era) when two opposing values, traditionalism and the new ethic of Western individualism, collided. To look at this rhetoric of the body and animals as something more 'universal', which therefore can straddle between two different cultural contexts, does not necessarily mean that the historical knowledge becomes less valuable. On the contrary, I believe that particular discourses which find their momentum in different temporal and spatial zones bear even greater importance in comprehending the issues that are more pressing, but not necessarily articulated by the author. In this course, I elaborated on Seeber's argument about eighteenth-century British culture that associated women with animals and observed the Japanese reception of this culture in the Meiji period. In *Seito,* an article about the problematic gender representation in Havelock Ellis's *Studies in the Psychology of Sex* (1897–1928) was published by Hiratsuka Raichō (1886–1971), a feminist writer and political activist. Seizaburo Ogura's translation of Ellis's *Man and Woman: A Study of Human Secondary Sexual Characteristics* (1904) was also advertised in *Seito* magazine in 1913. One of Ellis's implicit points, that women's bodies came very close to that of animals, is relevant to an important feminist issue.[5] Since Nogami also contributed some translations to *Seito* around the same time, it is likely that she was also aware of this discussion. By excavating what unsaid statements in Austen's or Nogami's novels could have implied through close reading these periodicals, students came to see that there is shared discrimination and also the rhetoric of sensibility which was deployed to counter that discrimination.

By introducing Nogami and her mentor and a literary giant, Natsume Sōseki (1867–1916), as one of the first readers of Austen's novels in Japan, I could provide my students with a kind of 'scaffolding' to make Austen's novels more relevant and attractive to them. Sōseki was the source of inspiration for many Japanese writers and also for Nogami.[6] Sōseki was able to introduce Western literature in *The Theory of Literature* (1907) to his disciples because he was one of the first to be sent to England at government expense to study English literature.[7] Students who enter Sophia University to study English language and literature are predominantly female, and this tendency is prominent among those who take my course on gender and literature. Although only a few male students register with this course, they are very keen to understand and trace the genealogy of Japanese feminism, which has its roots in Western Enlightenment thought. Therefore, I designed my course so that they could trace Austen's ideas not just through learning about Nogami's gender representation in her novels, but also through understanding Sōseki's sense of modernity, which is synonymous with his idea of individualism as elaborated in his prose and also in his novels. What is unique about *his* concept of individualism is that it is deeply embedded in an individual's 'sense of justice' and his/her capacity to sense what others are feeling, as he states, 'I am firmly convinced that if we look at things fairly and if we have a sense of justice, as we develop our own individuality to attain happiness we must at the same time guarantee to others the same freedom as we grant to ourselves' (Sōseki 'My Individualism' 46). This chapter will look at the way in which sensibility defined newly discovered subjectivity in Meiji and Taishō Japan. I followed three steps in my syllabus in order to illustrate the continuity from Austen's works to modern-day Japan: (1) how Sōseki's literature bore the marks of its rapid transition to modernity (2) how women's education impacted female writers such as Nogami (3) how Nogami's *Machiko* reiterates the same language of sensibility as Austen's *Pride and Prejudice*.

Natsume Sōseki as a Marker of Modernity

If the body divested of Cartesian rationality were compared to animals or women in eighteenth-century novels, interrogating the idea that women lack a measure of social power and standing because they are 'feeling' beings, the same thing can be said about Japanese novels in the early twentieth century. This course at Sophia University began with the introduction of Nogami's mentor, Sōseki, and his individualism especially in his later novels. Almost everyone in my class knew who he was and had read at least one of his major works such as *I am a Cat* [Wagahai wa neko de aru] (1905), *Sanshiro* (1908) or *Light and Dark* [Meian] (1916), although no one had ever read Nogami's novels. Sōseki has clearly earned a privileged place in the literary canon in Japan because his literature in the aggregate is 'both a reflection of and commentary on the new social, political and cultural order' (Marcus 37). Interestingly enough, very few of my students knew that he had cross-disciplinary interests. For my pedagogical purposes, it was essential that I introduce this canonical figure as someone who had suggested that Nogami read Austen's novels, and also as an intellectual who embraced then-contemporary Western scientific ideas about the physiological body, which had psychological and moral ramifications.

Sōseki singles out Austen as the leading authority in the world of realism, and he was not just imitating her psychological approach. There is a reason why Sōseki was drawn to Austen's realism. As John Mullan argues, Austen's narrative anticipated the psychological realism of the Modernist age: 'though little noticed by most of the pioneers of fiction…, [Austen's realism] belongs with the great experimental novels of Flaubert or Joyce or Woolf'. Not much has been said by Austen critics, but her novels are filled with stylistic innovations that resemble the psychological/physiological approaches of William James and Henri Poincaré, French philosopher of science and physicist of the early twentieth century. She explores not just a character's feelings, but her deep ignorance of her own feelings, and perhaps Catherine's delusion in *Northanger Abbey* (1817) is a typical example (see Mullan). Coincidentally, the early twentieth century was when Sōseki was studying in London (and also in Cambridge for a very short while) where he even attended the classes of a renowned physiologist, Michael Forster (Komori). His interest in sensibility and realism are deeply rooted in the contemporary scientific discourses. Among many theorists, Sōseki was greatly influenced by Henri Poincaré, who elaborated on the complexity of the human mind, and he even mentions the name 'Poincaré' in *Light and Dark*, which is his last, unfinished novel.[8]

Rather than characterising some features of Sōseki's literature, in my classes I wanted to pay closer attention to those factors that can be characterised as 'modern' by both Western and Japanese commentators. *Light and Dark* significantly echoes Western cutting-edge science and also Austen's narrative approach.[9] The fact that Western commentators have assessed *Light and Dark* negatively may also be partially explained by its 'modern' features. Donald Keene, for example, critiqued the 'modern' attitude of O-Nobu, the heroine of *Light and Dark*, and Jay Rubin even states that the novel is 'one of the most tedious exercises in the Japanese language' (Auestad 237). Unlike these Western commentators, major Japanese intellectuals have been much more welcoming of this 'modern' aspect of *Light and Dark*. For example, Jun Eto, a proponent of the 'pro-O-Nobu faction', praises *Light and Dark* for its 'realism' and its dramatisation of the heroine's psychology (Auestad 246). I want to emphasise that it is no coincidence that O-Nobu's psychological depth is revealed in *Light and Dark* and that could be a reason for her unpopularity among Western intellectuals—possibly misjudging or underestimating Sōseki's endorsement of modern women. Indeed, it may have been puzzling for any critics who knew Sōseki's didactic attitude towards or even condemnation of New Women who challenge paternal authority. Perhaps, O-Nobu is starkly different from Sōseki's typical, or earlier, female characters exemplified by Fujio in *The Poppy* [Gubijinso], but she is an individualist in that she is not afraid to confront the 'agents' with patriarchal power. What is different is Sōseki's treatment of Fujio, a New Woman, who disobeys her brother's recommendation and expresses her wish to marry Ono who does not belong to the same social class. In a letter to Takahama Kyoshi dated 16 July 1907, a month and a half before he completed the novel, Sōseki wrote, 'I am tired of *The Poppy*. I simply want to kill off the woman [Fujio] quickly and finish it off. It is hot and noisy, and I feel insane', and that is exactly what he does—this female character commits suicide (Hajime 35). Although we do not know the ending of the novel, unlike his earlier novels such as *The Poppy*, O-Nobu in *Light and Dark* is *not* condemned for demanding what she wants, namely, exclusive love from her husband, Tsuda. She does not flinch even when she feels the pressure from Mrs Yoshikawa, the wife of her husband's boss, who uses her influence to educate O-Nobu to be a reticent and humble wife. Mrs Yoshikawa, a meddler, represents the voice of Japanese 'tribalism', or someone who tries to prevent anyone from challenging the social conventions (Auestad 232–33). Here, Sōseki is applying his own idea of individualism to critique Mrs Yoshikawa's use of 'power' in somehow infiltrating 'into the head of someone else'—he criticises the wrong kind of individuality, that is, 'enlarging the field of one's own individuality by seducing or suborning others' (Sōseki, 'Individualism' 43).

O-Nobu marries Tsuda whom she loves, but she eventually finds out that there is something he is hiding from her, his lingering affection for his former lover, Kiyoko. Funnily enough, it is Mrs Yoshikawa, conspiring with Tsuda's egotism, who suggests that he visit a hot spring town [onsen] where Kiyoko is staying. Sōseki's psychological realism in telling O-Nobu's story lies in his capacity to meticulously portray her misconception about Tsuda's character and have her *gradually* discover his selfishness. I agree with Reiko Abe Auestad that O-Nobu's '"modern" sense of self-hood…which defies traditional assumptions, ought to have received more recognition in the West' (242). The reader comes close to the heroine's perspective. One example is when she is accompanying Tsuda to the hospital. She wears something which, she thinks, looks nice to please him, but when he sees her outfit, he remarks, 'it feels as if waltzing into the clinic as a couple with you in that get-up would be a little—', and when she responds to him, 'Excessive?', he starts to 'laugh' aloud. Sōseki does not describe how O-Nobu feels. He simply hints at her annoyance, describing what the reader can see on the surfaces of her body: 'eyebrows briefly arched' (Sōseki, *Light* 97). The narrator explains that O-Nobu's first impression of Tsuda was wrong, and she admits that she had 'misjudged the man' (Sōseki, *Light* 149). The reader is invited into O-Nobu's point of view, enabling him or her to share how she may be feeling: she learns that '[i]n the little more than half a year that had passed since her marriage, O-Nobu's thoughts about Tsuda had changed' (Sōseki, *Light* 152). Sōseki's empathetic narrative that describes the sensibility of the powerless may have much to do with his witnessing the powerful Meiji oligarchs who adopted a conservative agenda, and also with being exposed to liberal ideas from reading Western literature and scientific books.[10]

As I have shown, Sōseki dexterously portrays the function of the mind even to the level of the unconscious, which is beyond what the brain, in transient moments, registers through the five senses—vision, sound, taste, touch and smell. He was aware of the complex workings of bodily sensibility which could even temporarily delude itself.

> But we do not know ... to what extent the senses complicate matters. The things that we cannot see today with the naked eye, that we cannot touch with our hands, or even those things that go beyond the five senses, are progressively, I think, entering into our field of awareness. And so, it seems to me, the best thing for us is to take our time and wait. (Sōseki, 'Philosophical' 72)

His notion of the 'senses' through the eye, hands and other bodily organs signifies something that is highly complex, which reminds us of Austen's realism which also depicts similar uncertainty about one's psychological responses.

The mishmash of the feigned sensibility of fashionable practice and the genuine sensibility of suffering creates the comedy and irony that surrounds Austen's depiction of characters. Especially from the point of view of the reader, things that characters sense as 'real' or 'true' do not always turn out to be so, because even they are deceived by their own senses. *Pride and Prejudice* exemplifies this very complexity of brain-experiences. The reader of Austen novels can see these emotions through her description of bodily signs, and this is akin to the way in which eighteenth-century empirical scientists and philosophers observed the ever-changing state of life through exterior manifestations such as the countenance, sounds of the voice and gestures of the body. A number of early neuroscientific accounts of mind, including Charles Bell's, make these exterior signs integral to their accounts of pervasive mind-body interaction. According to Alan Richardson, what is characteristic about their writings is that they establish a neurological basis (93). For example, Elizabeth Bennet, who is initially charmed by the 'countenance, voice and manner' of Mr Wickham, comes to see that for a very long time she was aware of his vices, although it never surfaces or catches her attention, until she learns of his past selfish and ill-intentioned conduct from Mr Darcy.

> She tried to recollect some instance of goodness, some distinguished trait of integrity or benevolence [in Mr Wickham], that might rescue him from the attacks of Mr Darcy.... But no such recollection befriended her. She could see him instantly before her, in every charm of air and address; but she could remember no more substantial good than the general approbation of the neighbourhood, and the regard which his social powers had gained him in the mess. (*PP* 228).

Now that she hears about Mr Wickham's 'extravagance and general profligacy' (228), all the memories she has stored up in her mind are pieced together as one, pointing to something that is quite solid and reliable. Indeed, as Sōseki states, 'the best thing for us is to take our time and wait'. Austen's fascination with the workings of the human mind is expressed through the following sentence which describes Elizabeth's thoughts about the first conversation she had with him: 'She was now struck with the impropriety of such communications to a stranger, and wondered [why] it had escaped her before' (229). Austen is here interrogating the condition of self-deception. Elizabeth wonders why she never saw Mr Wickham's approach as improper. All the while, deep in the psyche there lay something truthful, and that is what gives rise to her sense of being morally right or just.

We can also locate a scientific analogue of such an inspiration in the psychological theories of Sōseki's time. Poincaré states in his book, *Science and Method*, 'only [those things] which are interesting find their way into the field of consciousness'. According to him, '[i]t is certain that the combinations which present themselves to the mind in a kind of sudden illumination after a somewhat prolonged period of unconscious work are generally useful and fruitful combinations'

Women's Education and Nogami Yaeko

As we saw, the process of Japanese intellectuals in the Meiji and Taishō Eras adopting Western philosophical, scientific and medical theories became an important part of Japan's modernising project. It was through Austen's novels (and perhaps also Sōseki's works) that Nogami was introduced to women's independence of mind in the West and how education could promote it. We can say that she was one of the female writers who represented the life of modern women such as O-Nobu. She follows Austen's views that women's domestic education in acquiring accomplishments was not only 'pointless', but also 'actively destructive' (Halsey 439). Katie Halsey has argued that Austen shows Maria and Julia, two daughters of the Bertrams in *Mansfield Park*, as bad examples of the 'total abnegation of responsibility' of Lady Bertram and 'superficial accomplishments' acquired from their flattering aunt Norris. Austen clearly shows that 'mere seclusion from the "world"' does not educate women to become virtuous (Halsey 440). Wollstonecraft's statement in *A Vindication of the Rights of Woman* that '[n]ature, or, to speak with strict propriety, God, has made all things right; but man has sought him out many inventions to mar the work' has profound bearing on Austen's satire against instrumental or exploitative characters (100). Seeber, in arguing that Austen draws a radical connection between women and animals, illuminates how such an interventionist approach could have a negative effect on women. Perhaps, in this context, the animal/meat metaphor would have dual meanings: women are not just consumed or commodified but also tampered with. Wollstonecraft encourages women to become moral agents and to improve themselves and argues that this should not be impeded by male characters or meddlers who want to manipulate women as commodities. Aunt Norris's interventionist 'education' is perhaps an exemplar case.

Also, the belief that women are endowed with natural sympathy enjoyed important currency in the eighteenth century. Analogously to La Mettrie's argument in *Man a Machine* (1747), that animals 'give us enough evident marks of their repentance and understanding, ... and [seem] to feel the law of nature' (39), Wollstonecraft states that there is a recurrent theme of sensibility as the touchstone of women's ethical capacity: '[t]he world cannot be seen by an unmoved spectator; we must mix in the throng and feel as men feel, before we can judge of their feelings' (Wollstonecraft, *Vindication* 181). Nogami believed that, like men, women could potentially develop not just rationality but also ethical capacity, and leaving home to be educated could help them achieve that end. Halsey's remark that education was increasingly becoming a signifier in fiction that was 'deployed in ways that reflect a much broader concern about women's changing roles in the public and private spheres' is also very apt (442). The earlier assumption that girls would be best educated at home was no longer the norm among affluent middle- and upper-class Japanese families. No wonder Austen's novels had an exceptional appeal to Japanese readers during the Meiji and Taishō period. According to Kuwabara, in 1882 there were only five female higher schools in Japan with a total number of 286 students, but in 1898 the number increased to thirty-four with 7,154 students (93, 113). Educated women came prevalently from upper-middle-class families, namely those women whom the government was targeting with its education aimed at *ryōsai kenbo*—good wives and wise mothers (Patessio 558).[11]

This very incongruity of the new and the old was in the fabric of Meiji society which was reflected in the work of its writers and intellectuals (Marcus 37).[12] Questions about how to 'fix particular meanings onto bodies' not only related to gender issues, but also to the newly introduced discussion of Social Darwinism which was a huge influence on Nogami—in that the focal point of the novel *Machiko* is class struggle and social justice. For example, acclaimed novelist Shimazaki Tōson (1872–1942), who happened to be an instructor at Meiji Women's School [*Meiji Jogakkō*] where Nogami studied, wrote *Hakai* [*The Broken Commandment*] (1906), a reading of Darwin, critiquing feudal remnants that hindered the birth of true equality in Meiji society (Bourdaghs 177). It is a story about a school teacher who struggles with a commandment that was given to him by his father, that is, he is never to reveal his background as Burakumin. Burakumin were originally members of outcast communities in the Japanese feudal era. Through the influence of Social Darwinism Tōson came to perceive human beings as 'part of nature' (Noma 16). This gave rise to questions such as 'Can only the "fittest" survive in the existing power relations?', which echo the animal/woman metaphors through which Austen critiqued the greed of the powerful.

Literature became the key player in that these scientific and sociological debates were allegorised in many Japanese novels, and it was an effective means through which authors criticised the social injustice of the marginalised including women.[13] It is not widely known, even among Japanese people, that major Western literary texts, including Austen's novels, were used in the modernising process after the Meiji Restoration. The value of social progress and civil rights for women was taught in Japanese society through educational institutions, translations, or entertainments such as drama. This was only possible because after ending the isolationist policy Japan opened up to the world, importing Western art, science and literature. Of course, women were not all of the progressive type, but a small group of New Women appeared: competing discourses over women's education, therefore, coexisted. Nogami was one of those ambivalent types who positioned themselves in the middle. She entered a very liberal school with many intelligent women who would be playing an active role in literary, educational or political arenas in the future, but at the same time, did not dare transgress the moral code and pursue 'free love'. Nogami's life was an amalgam of such complex social contexts. Her conservative attitude towards marriage, since she remained faithful to her husband until the end, is probably owing to her upbringing in her conservative hometown, Usuki, but after entering Meiji Women's School where Tōson and many other intellectuals such as the poet Kitamura Tōkoku (1868–1894) taught, she came to hold liberal ideas. What is more, the wife of the school principal, Iwamoto Yoshiharu (1863–1942) was Wakamatsu Shizuko, a well-known intellectual who translated works by Charles Dickens, Frances Hodgson Burnett, and Alfred Tennyson. These Meiji intellectuals were all Nogami's role models who taught the importance of thinking independently. In her autobiographical novel *The Forest* [Mori, 1972], Nogami describes the excitement her alter ego Kane felt when, looking back on her early days at Meiji Women's School, she first learned that the headmaster's late wife was actually the famous translator of Frances Hodgson Burnett's *Little Lord Fauntleroy* [1939], 'Tatsumatsu Shizuko', a name that is almost identical with 'Wakamatsu Shizuko': 'Now Kane [alter ego of Nogami] could understand why everyone always said Headmaster Okuno's wife was such a remarkable person. She felt a new wave of respect wash over her heart. How lucky she was to have entered this school!' (Nogami 158–161).[14] After publishing her first work, the short story 'Ties of Love' [Enishi] (Nogami, 1907), Nogami began to submit poems, short stories and translations to the mainstream magazines, such as *Chuōkōron*, *Shinchō* and also a feminist magazine, *Seitō*, in the 1910s.

Incidentally, it was also in the 1910s that Sophia University, where I teach, was founded. Although the institution has no relations with Nogami or Sōseki, the fact that the university and these intellectuals were contemporaries had an impact on my students. Also, Sophia is one of the few universities in Japan that has had a strong emphasis on internationality since it was founded in 1913, just like the school where Nogami was exposed to diverse thoughts and ideas. Our university's faith in internationality and the global exchange of ideas can be traced back to 1549 when St. Francis Xavier (1506–1552) came to Japan to spread Christianity: the Jesuits (Rev. Joseph Dahlmann, Rev. Henri Boucher, Rev. James Rockliff, Rev. Hermann Hoffmann, and Rev. Yachita Tsuchihashi) who had backgrounds in various areas of Western learning started this university (Shibata 452). And with this piece of information, I brought my students' attention back to Nogami's upbringing. As a child, her father told her tales of the history of the region, including the missionary work of St. Francis Xavier who landed in Kyushu in 1549, disembarking at Usuki (Iwahashi 27).[15]

My students' learning process, as it were, parallels that of Nogami and many other students who gained knowledge about foreign countries in these newly emerging schools and universities. In Japan, 'the concept and the operation of comparative education' correlated with Japan's enthusiasm to investigate, adapt and absorb a foreign education system as a 'crucial means of the formation of a modern state' (Iwahashi 451).

Nogami's Creative Adaptation of Austen's *Pride and Prejudice*

As Eleanor Hogan has pointed out, adhering to the model of influence studies and simply stating that Nogami was 'influenced' by Austen relegates Nogami to a marginal status, thus making her somehow 'lesser' than Austen. But as recent adaptation studies have shown, not all adapted novels or films are simple attempts to reproduce the original. Furthermore, as J. Scott Miller has explained, Japan has inherited a 'traditionally broad definition of what constitutes originality', which means that 'there has been a much greater tolerance for derivative elements in art' (17). He describes the Meiji period as follows:

> Against the backdrop of tremendous cultural difference, Western thought rose to the fore as one of the keys to understanding and catching up with the West, and subsequently the number of Japanese translations of Western philosophy, scientific writing, and literature increased year by year. Most literary histories of modern Japan pay homage to the early translations of Western literature, since they played an important role in the development of modern Japanese poetry, narrative, and drama. (13)

I chose Nogami's *Machiko* as a novel to be taught alongside Austen's novels because I thought that doing so would stimulate the students' imagination about our predecessors in the early twentieth century who absorbed, adapted, or translated Western works. They may feel the excitement which the first readers of *Machiko* must have had in comparing the eponymous heroine with Elizabeth Bennet. Machiko will soon be twenty-four and is independent-minded. Nogami's concern for women's education is expressed through her heroine's education: Machiko audits sociology at the university after graduating from a women's college, presumably like the one Nogami used to go to. Likewise, Elizabeth is an intelligent and witty young woman who is going to be twenty-one years old. She is one of the five daughters of the Bennets, living in southern England. Her father's property will pass to his relative, Mr William Collins, since he has no son to inherit it. Both heroines are of marriageable age, and they also belong to the leisure class (Enomoto 247).

Nogami follows Austen's plot in that the story of Machiko begins with the description of her mother, who tries to get her married, which clearly reminds us of Mrs Bennet's effort as a matchmaker. Just like Elizabeth who marries a wealthy landowner, Mr Darcy, Machiko in the end rejects the political activist, Seki, who aspires to change the society by joining the left-wing movement, but turns out to be egotistic, and comes to accept Kawai, a Darcy-like character, as her future partner. She realises the generosity and sensitivity of Kawai, although she initially avoided him because of his wealthy background: 'I can say one thing clearly. Even if I perceive a marriage just as I think of food some day, I will never seek a partner in your class' (Nogami *Machiko* 248). Thus, in writing *Machiko*, Nogami followed Austen's *Pride and Prejudice* fairly faithfully, but there are subjects which she deliberately expanded on—themes that she probably pondered much longer than others. There are mainly three aspects of Nogami's adaptation which I focused on in my course.

The first theme is her criticism of treating marriageable women as commodities. There is a scene in *Pride and Prejudice* where Austen portrays Mrs Bennet critically for promoting the economic exchange of the marriage market. Mrs Bennet uses the word 'haunch' to boast of her dinner saying that it was 'as well dressed as any I ever saw'. This is later followed by compliments to Jane, 'And, my dear Jane, I never saw you look in greater beauty' (*PP* 379). The descriptions of meat—'[t]he venison ... roasted to a turn', 'so fat a haunch', or 'the partridges' which were 'remarkably well done'—are conflated with the image of Jane's beauty (*PP* 379). Her eldest daughter is a desirable bride for Mr Bingley and Austen's irony is that the word 'haunch' metaphorically means a feast to be consumed by him (Ogawa 304). Mrs Bennet, a meddler just like Mrs Yoshikawa in *Light and Dark*, is treating a young woman as if they have no agency. Nogami's headstrong heroine reverberates with Elizabeth who condemns the abuse of such 'power', and also with O-Nobu's individualism in persisting to have her own way. In *Machiko*, Nogami takes issue with men's objectification of women by parodying Mr Collins who decides to marry one of the five daughters to ease the guilt of getting their property. At first Mr Collins plans to marry Jane, but as soon as he learns that she is soon to be engaged, he changes from her to the second daughter, Elizabeth, who flatly rejects him. Machiko is also irritated when she sees how Takeo approaches her. With an intention to court her, he behaves as if casually buying 'a suitcase or a wool blanket' (Nogami, *Machiko* 33). A blanket is a suitable metaphor for a marriage of convenience which Takeo envisions. Takeo resembles Mr Collins in that he is finding a marriage partner in the same way as he would purchase a commodity at a store.

The second aspect of Nogami's adaptation is her focus on the heroine's body and its sensibility. When Machiko encounters a stranger for the first time, she trusts her feelings, as opposed to the social standing which her parents had more faith in. Machiko's verbal banter with her sister, Tatsuko, about the proposal made by Takeo is perhaps reminiscent of Elizabeth's rebellious attitude to her mother's persistent advice. It is interesting that Nogami observes Machiko's emotive aspect: she cannot 'feel anything special' towards Takeo (Nogami 33). Machiko's 'feeling' is not always right; Elizabeth's judgement erred about Wickham. Just as Austen interrogated the condition of self-deception in *Pride and Prejudice*, Nogami follows Sōseki's individualism—her heroine too is deceived by her own senses.

The last important aspect of Nogami's adaptation is the moral strength of the heroine with her empathy and ethical capacity. She is perhaps more fierce than Austen when it comes to defending social injustice. The very reason why Machiko admires Seki, for whom she gradually develops intense feeling, is because of his revolutionary stance (Hogan 253); the theme of social injustice is foregrounded in this adaptation. In 1928, when Nogami was writing this novel, '1,600 suspected communists and radicals were arrested; in 1929, there were 700 more arrests' (Hisamori). Seki is, therefore, risking his life to fight for the cause. 1928 was also marked by a series of workers' strikes and efforts by the police to suppress the left-wing movement. Nogami had 'intimate friends among the activists who had visited for themselves the glorious post-Revolutionary Russia' (Hisamori). However, Nogami does not depict her heroine as an idealist. For Machiko, friendship with Yoneko is more valuable than her romance with Seki. After she has premarital intercourse with Seki, which may be perceived as a typical act of defying patriarchal marriage, she receives a visit from Yoneko. Yoneko confesses to Machiko that she became intimate with Seki through her political activities, and is now pregnant: she says, 'I would have kept it a secret if Seki was only my husband and not the father of this child' (Nogami, *Machiko* 314). Yoneko is prepared to withdraw if Machiko is not disappointed in Seki about his relationship with Yoneko. But when Machiko sees Yoneko's tears, suddenly 'a feeling of compassion filled her heart, and [she] is deeply moved by Yoneko's friendship' (Nogami, *Machiko* 316). After this scene, Machiko understands that she has loved Seki's commitment to the 'public' cause, but not his 'individual' self. Machiko's choice of a personal friend, Yoneko, is reminiscent of Sōseki's individualism which is summed up in his statement, 'When we take the country as a basis of assessment and envisage it as a monolithic entity, we must be calm and content ourselves with a low level of morality. On the other hand, if we take the perspective of individualism, then the importance of morality increases considerably' (Sōseki, 'Individualism' 57).

Conclusion

Reading the novels by Austen and Nogami side by side enabled me and my students to see that there is a 'universal language' of sensibility which has the value of ethical obligation to defend the rights of the marginalised. Those with the power to feel and understand the weak, such as animals and women, are more positively depicted in Austen's novels. Henry Crawford, certainly, is not a good decoder of Fanny's feelings. My course was created based on the idea that Nogami adapted the theme of modernity and women's rights from reading Austen's works and understanding Sōseki's individualism. It centred on the theme of bodily desire conflicting with the social convention of marriage, and how this imagination fed into Nogami's feminism. My students showed a very keen interest in Austen's depiction of sensibility as a prototype of modernity. This idea of modernity continues to influence our political attitude and how we wish to behave towards others. Adaptation is an innovative form of artistic expression which is not only entertaining, but also profoundly educational. Even those students who were initially confounded by Austen's diction and cultural references could empathise with Elizabeth Bennet's predicament through the channel of Sōseki's O-Nobu and Nogami's Machiko.

Notes

1 It was a literature course primarily designed for third- and fourth-year students in the Department of English Studies at Sophia University.
2 In the United Kingdom, the A Level (Advanced Level) is for students completing secondary or pre-university education.
3 Seeber's argument is based on John Wiltshire's argument that the 'body is normally merely enabling, transparent, taken for granted: it is only when it becomes painful or dysfunctional that its workings become disclosed to consciousness', and that Austen's narratives make use of this dysfunction where characters are acutely aware of 'others' faces and bodies and their symptoms' but are not always correct decoders (8, 6).
4 'Seito' means 'Blue Shoes', a translation of 'Blue Stockings' (Bardsley 1).
5 See Ogawa's 'Nogami Yaeko's Adaptations of Austen Novels' for this discussion.
6 She had a more remarkable career than her husband, Toyoichirō Nogami, also Sōseki's disciple, but it was he who first translated Austen's *Pride and Prejudice* in 1926. Nogami also proofread her husband's translation of *Pride and Prejudice* (Hiroshi et al.).
7 After spending two years in London from 1900 to 1902, he returned to Japan. He brought back Austen's novels and lent *Pride and Prejudice* to Nogami Yaeko.
8 In *Light and Dark*, Tsuda thinks to himself: 'No doubt our marriage happened because I chose to take her. But I have never once felt that I wanted her. Chance? Poincarre's so-called zenith of complexity? I have no idea' (Sōseki, *Light and Dark* 28).
9 It was first published in the *Asahi Newspaper* beginning on May 16, 1916, and is an incomplete novel, since he fell ill half way.
10 For discussions on the female body and eugenics, see Otsubo; Terazawa.
11 Mara Patessio argues that with the promulgation of the Constitution in 1889, of the Imperial Rescript on Education in 1890, of the Civil Code in 1898 and of the various legislations against male but especially female political participation, Japanese women lost the rights and freedom hitherto acquired. The loss of rights and the access to education happened alongside each other, with the purpose of education being old-fashioned roles for women.
12 Please see my argument on Havelock Ellis and his influence on Itō Noe (Ogawa).
13 This theme can be found also in Japanese novels such as Shimazaki Toson's *Hakai* [*The Broken Commandments*]. Those characters with the capacity to feel and understand others' pain are more positively depicted by Austen. Since more than 80% of my students in this course were female students, I imagined that many of them would be interested in the education of women in Meiji and Taishō periods.
14 See also Copeland (158).
15 With a Jesuit outlook of expanding the worldwide network of education, Sophia University increased its network over time since its founding, with more than 400 partner institutions in the world.

Works Cited

Auestad, Reiko Abe. 'The Critical Reception of Sōseki's *Kojin* and *Meian* in Japan and the West.' *The Journal of the Association of Teachers of Japanese*, vol. 27, no. 2, 1993, pp. 229–257.

Austen, Jane, *Mansfield Park*, edited by John Wiltshire. Cambridge UP, 2005.

Austen, Jane. *Pride and Prejudice*, edited by Pat Rogers. Cambridge UP, 2006.

Austen, Jane. *Sense and Sensibility*, edited by Edward Copeland. Cambridge UP, 2006.

Bell, Charles. *Idea of a New Anatomy of the Brain: Submitted for the Observations of His Friends*. London, 1811.

Bardsley, Jan. *The Bluestockings of Japan: New Woman Essays and Fiction from Seitō, 1911–1916*. U of Michigan Center for Japanese Studies, 2007.

Bourdaghs, Michael. 'Shimazaki Tōson's Hakai.' *Transformations of Sensibility: The Phenomenology of Meiji Literature*. U of Michigan Center for Japanese Studies, 2002.

Copeland, Rebecca L. *Lost Leaves: Women Writers of Meiji Japan*. University of Hawai'i Press, 2000.

Enomoto, Yoshiko. 'Machiko and *Pride and Prejudice*.' *Comparative Literature Studies*, vol. 28, no. 3, 1991, pp. 248–258.

Hajime, Seki. 'The Poppy as a Melodrama' [Mero-dorama toshite no Gubijinso].' *Sōseki Studies*, vol. 16. Kanrin Shobo, 2003.

Halsey, Katie. 'The Home Education of Girls in the Eighteenth-Century Novel: "The Pernicious Effects of an Improper Education."' *Oxford Review of Education*, vol. 41, no. 4, 2015, pp. 430–446.

Hiratsuka, Raichō. 'Introduction to Havelock Ellis, Same-sex Love between Women [Dōsei Renai].' *Seitō*, Apr. 1914.

Hiroshi, Ebine, Amano Miyuki, and Hisamori Kazuko. 'Jane Austen in Japanese Literature: An Overview.' *Persuasions On-line*, vol. 30.2 (Spring), 2010. http://www.jasna.org/persuasions/on-line/vol30no2/introduction.html?

Hisamori, Kazuko. 'Elizabeth Bennet Turns Socialist: Nogami Yaeko's Machiko.' *Persuasions-Online*, vol. 30, no. 2, 2010. http://jasna.org/persuasions/on-line/vol30no2/hisamori.html

Hogan, Eleanor J. 'Beyond Influence: The Literary Sisterhood of Nogami Yaeko and Jane Austen.' *U.S. Japan Women's Journal*, vol. 29, 2005, pp. 77–98.

Iwahashi, Kunie. *Hyōden; Nogami Yaeko* [*Critical Biography: Nogami Yaeko*]. Shinchosha, 2001.

Kuwabara, S. *Koto jogakko no seiritsu: Koto jogakko shoshi—Meiji hen*. Takayama Honten, 1982.

La Mettrie, Julien Offray de. *Machine Man and Other Writings*. Translated and Edited by Ann Thompson. Cambridge UP, 1996.

Marcus, Marvin. 'Natsume Sōseki and Modern Japanese Literature.' *Education About Asia*, vol. 20, no. 2, 2015, pp. 37–40.

Miller, J. Scott. *Adaptations of Western Literature in Meiji Japan*. Palgrave, 2001.

Mullan, John. 'How Jane Austen's Emma Changed the Face of Fiction.' *The Guardian, Guardian News and Media* 5 Dec. 2015. www.theguardian.com/books/2015/dec/05/jane-austen-emma-changed-face-fiction

Natsume, Sōseki. *Theory of Literature and Other Critical Writings*, edited by Michael K. Bourdaghs, Atsuko Ueda, Joseph A. Murphy. Columbia UP, 2009.

Nogami, Yaeko. *Machiko* [1931]. *Complete Novels*, vol. 7. Iwanami, 1981.

Nogami, Yaeko. 'Mori.' *Nogami Yaeko zenshū, dai ni ki*, vol. 28, Iwanami Shoten, 1972, 1991, pp. 158–161.

Noma, Hiroshi. 'Hakai ni tsuite.' *Gunzō Nihon no Sakka 4: Shimazaki Tōson*. Shōgakukan, 1992, pp. 115–121.

Ogawa, Kimiyo. 'Nogami Yaeko's Adaptations of Austen Novels: Allegorizing Women's Bodies.' *British Romanticism in Asia: The Reception, Translation, and Transformation of Romantic Literature in India and East Asia*. Palgrave Macmillan, 2019.

Otsubo, Sumiko. 'The Female Body and Eugenic Thought in Meiji Japan.' *Building A Modern Japan: Science, Technology and Medicine in the Meiji Era and Beyond*, ed. Morris Low. Palgrave Macmillan, 2005.

Patessio, Mara. 'Women getting a "university" education in Meiji Japan: Discourses, Realities, and Individual Lives.' *Japan Forum*, vol. 25, no. 4, 2013. pp. 556–581.

Poincaré, Henri. *Science and Method*. T. Nelson, 1914.

Richardson, Alan. *The Neural Sublime: Cognitive Theories and Romantic Texts*. Johns Hopkins UP, 2010.

Seeber, Barbara. *Jane Austen and Animals*. Ashgate, 2013.

Shibata, Masako. 'Contextualisation of the Development of Comparative Education and Intercultural Education in Japan: The Eras of Colonialism, War and their Legacy.' *Intercultural Education*, vol. 23, no. 5, 2012, pp. 451–463.

Shimazaki, Toson. *Hakai [The Broken Commandments]*. Iwanami bunko, 1905, 2002.

Sōseki, Natsume. *Light and Dark: A Novel*.Translated and with an Introduction by John Nathan. Columbia UP, 2014.

Sōseki, Natsume. 'My Individualism.' *My Individualism and The Philosophical Foundations of Literature*. Translated by Sammy I. Tsunematsu. With an Introduction by Inger Sigrun Brody. Tuttle Publishing, 2004.

Sōseki, Natusme. 'The Philosophical Foundations of Literature.' *My Individualism and the Philosophical Foundations of Literature*. Translated by Sammy I. Tsunematsu. Tuttle Publishing, 2004.

Terazawa, Yuki. 'Racializing Bodies Through Science in Meiji Japan: The Rise of Race-Based Research in Gynecology.' *Building A Modern Japan: Science, Technology and Medicine in the Meiji Era and Beyond*, edited by Morris Low. Palgrave Macmillan, 2005.

Wiltshire, John. *Jane Austen and the Body: 'The Picture of Health.'* Cambridge UP, 1992.

Wollstonecraft, Mary. *A Vindication of the Rights of Woman* [1791]. *The Works of Mary Wollstonecraft*, edited by Janet Todd and Marilyn Butler, vol. 5. William Pickering, 1989.

Wollstonecraft, Mary. *Maria, or, the Wrongs of Woman*. *The Works of Mary Wollstonecraft*, edited by Janet Todd and Marilyn Butler, vol. 1. William Pickering, 1989.

Yoichi, Komori. *Re-reading Sōseki* [Sōseki o yominaosu]. Iwanami Shoten, 2017.

44

TEACHING JANE AUSTEN THROUGH PUBLIC HUMANITIES: THE JANE AUSTEN SUMMER PROGRAM

Inger S. B. Brodey, Anne Fertig, and Sarah Schaefer Walton

UNIVERSITY OF NORTH CAROLINA, CHAPEL HILL

When first exploring the idea of starting a public humanities outreach program centred on Jane Austen, Inger Brodey and James Thompson made a pilgrimage to attend the annual Dickens Project at UC Santa Cruz in the summer of 2012. Inspired by Jill Lepore's article about the 'Dickens Universe', Brodey and Thompson enjoyed the atmosphere of the two-week program that had earned Lepore's praise and were particularly struck by the combined academic and pedagogical programming that attracts Dickens scholars and fans alike year after year to Santa Cruz.[1] The two professors took the opportunity to share their vision for bringing a similar program about Austen to life. One attendee—a British actress and longtime Dickens lover—expressed her scepticism at the idea, claiming 'that would draw a different *clientèle*', suggesting that Austen was too elitist to draw the same, tolerant crowd as that great champion of the working classes, Charles Dickens.

This actress's response to the idea of a community-based Austen 'universe' speaks to a long-standing cultural perception of Austen—and Austen fans—as elitist and exclusive. This vision of Austen-lovers situates Austen firmly in the ivory tower, the darling of elbow-patched intellectuals with hyphenated surnames. It stands in sharp contrast with another image of a Janeite:[2] the merchandise-collecting, Darcy-crazed (and generally female) fan, perhaps as enthusiastic about *The Jane Austen Book Club* as *Mansfield Park*. This seemingly irreconcilable gulf between approaches to Austen is not new, as Rachel Brownstein shows in *Why Jane Austen?* Her book opens with a cartoon from the late 1940s that juxtaposes an effusive 'Janie' pep band against snooty Austen scholars (Figure 44.1). In the cartoon, Jane herself seems to lean away from her more effusive followers. Seventy years later, this gulf is rearticulated in the debate over whether to feature Austen on the ten pound note; whether to consider her a feminist, proto-feminist, or conservative; and whether to market her novels as YA fiction, romance, or 'classic' literature.

Dickens runs into no such problems. But then, Dickens fans do not generally call their hero by his first name, unlike many followers of Austen. There is both an intimacy and vehemence found among Austen fans that is unlike that of any other extant literary group.[3]

And yet, as early as 1924, Rudyard Kipling could imagine a society of Austen enthusiasts spanning social classes, education levels, and gender. In 'The Janeites', set in the gloomy trenches of the Great War, officers and enlisted men turn to Austen's world to escape the war's brutality:

DOI: 10.4324/9780429398155-44-50

Figure 44.1 Carl Rose, 'The Two Camps of Austen Devotees', *New York Times*, October 23, 1949

'There's no one to touch Jane when you're in a tight place' (242). Invoking Austen, these men identify aspects of her work that transcend her historical moment and speak to a common human experience. The Kipling story shows the nostalgic view of Austen, consecrating a domestic ideal of the English countryside, comforting at such a time of upheaval. By naming military cannons and other weapons after her more irritating characters, they also simultaneously acknowledge the power of her satire to disrupt.

Austen's works have managed to stand up to and even benefit from being translated across cultures, time, and media form. There have been over 30 film and TV adaptations of her novels and juvenilia, more than half of which were released in the last twenty-five years, and Fanfiction.net maintains an archive of over 4,600 stories based on *Pride and Prejudice* written by community members. Many of these adaptations speak to the diverse populations drawn to Austen's work. Recent novel adaptations of *Pride and Prejudice* are set in contemporary Muslim Toronto (*Ayesha at Last,* Uzma Jalaluddin), an Afro-Caribbean community in New Jersey (*Pride,* Ibi Zoboi), and early 2000s Pakistan (*Unmarriageable,* Soniah Kamal). Film adaptations have been set in a Mormon community in Utah, in various parts of India, and in Los Angeles; there are stage plays that foreground Austen characters as LGBTQ and musicals that set *Sense and Sensibility* to modern dance music and roller skates. It is not simply the adaptations that speak to Austen's global and surprisingly malleable appeal: there are a great many national organisations dedicated to the author around the world, most of which both focus on scholarly engagement with her texts and involve a degree of costumed historical reenactment. The Jane Austen Society of North America (JASNA) and the original Jane Austen Society in England are the largest, but the Jane Austen Societies of Australia, Brazil, Japan, Italy, and Pakistan (among others) indicate that Austen is not, in fact, limited (by her novels or her fans) to the drawing rooms of the southern half of England.

Indeed, Austen has become so universal that the fan base itself has attracted critical and scholarly attention. *Janeites: Austen's Disciples and Devotees*, edited by Deidre Lynch, contains nine essays by scholars who explore a range of Austen's adaptations and seek to account for her enduring popularity in contemporary culture. Deborah Yaffe's *Among the Janeites: A Journey through the World of Jane Austen Fandom* investigates the complex world of Austen fandom, while Ted Scheinman's prominently reviewed *Camp Austen: My Life as an Accidental Jane Austen Superfan* humorously narrates Scheinman's involvement in our own very first Jane Austen Summer Program (known as 'JASP'). In many ways, rather than representing a homogenous community of Austen readers, this trend demonstrates the gap between academia and popular readership. A popular topic in these works has been the tendency of fans to dress in period costume at these events, while academics generally show disdain for this practice. As a result, as Deidre Lynch points out in *Janeites: Austen's Disciples and Devotees,* local chapters of groups like JASNA often ask for 'readers, not academics' (3). Despite this supposed divide among audiences, however, the founders of the Jane Austen Summer Program hoped to demonstrate that it is possible to create dialogue and productive discourse among scholars, teachers, and (other) enthusiasts. We argued that, despite these perceived differences, her omni-presence and cultural capital are strengths rather than liabilities for such a public humanities enterprise. So far, this has indeed proven to be the case.

Austen in the Southern Part of Heaven

The current momentum towards public humanities coincides with widespread populist scepticism about the value of a college education, particularly in the humanities. As Peter Brooks writes, 'the very value of a university education, for so many decades a central article of American faith, now has been put into doubt. [...] In this 'crisis', the humanities are made to appear a kind of zombie wandering in a world that should be producing technocrats and entrepreneurs' (Brooks and Jewett 2). The public humanities are most often anti-elitist at core, and indeed it could be said that the 'act of reading literature is itself an act of civic participation' (Draxler and Spratt 223). Because of Austen's strong presence in popular culture and all contemporary media, we see her as an ideal bridge between past and present, and between scholars and popular audiences, and between older and younger readers. The latter is confirmed by Danielle Spratt's public humanities venture in-volving *Emma*. Spratt reports that in her project, '[w]hile Austen's reputation as a novelist interested in manners and morals drew a group of elderly community members to the public library, the novel's tough backbone of social issues from women's economic needs to slavery produced inter-generational discussions that transformed older and younger readers' (Draxler and Spratt xii). Austen is therefore also an ideal tool for public humanities and the defence of the value of literary study. Most individuals in the public will recognise her name—even if it is from more recent inter-pretations of her work. Undeterred by Austen's complex cultural network, Brodey and Thompson founded the Jane Austen Summer Program in 2013. They were confident in their mission in part because of their own context: both are Austen scholars as well as fans, with a deep appreciation of adaptations like *Clueless* and *The Lizzie Bennet Diaries* as well as being English professors at the University of North Carolina, Chapel Hill (UNC), who regularly publish, speak, and teach courses on Jane Austen.

Any college town would be a natural fit for hosting a community-based literary event, but UNC and the town of Chapel Hill are particularly well-suited to public humanities programming because of the history of the community. As the United States' first public university, commissioned in 1789, the University of North Carolina at Chapel Hill has a long history of trailblazing public programs and serving the educational needs of the local community. The establishment of the institution dates to the founding documents of North Carolina, requiring that the university provide 'for the con-venient instruction of youth, with such salaries to the masters, paid by the public, as may enable them to instruct at low prices' (NC Const., Article XLI). UNC has adhered to its founding mission: to serve as an 'educational and economic beacon for the people of North Carolina and beyond' ('Visitor's Guide' 6). UNC, in short, is a community-oriented research institution with a legacy of excellence in the liberal arts.

The university's investment in the public humanities is not merely implied or historical: the Carolina Public Humanities Program is an institutional initiative dedicated to extending the re-sources available at UNC to 'all citizens and community members of North Carolina'. In their words, Carolina Public Humanities provides programming that 'draws upon the humanities to nurture a deeper understanding of history and culture, enrich the life of the mind, and contribute to the development of a more humane world' (https://humanities.unc.edu). Some of their projects include Carolina K-12, which offers professional development opportunities to NC teachers, and the Humanities for the Public Good (HPG) endeavour, a four-year, $1.5-million initiative funded by the Mellon Foundation, intended to recognise and catalyse publicly engaged scholarly activity among humanists and humanistic social scientists at UNC-Chapel Hill. HPG is, in a sense, an articulation of UNC's public mission and engagement: according to their website, it 'relies upon and complements the long-standing work of UNC-Chapel Hill's array of programs, centres, institutes, and initiatives which have served as bridges between the university and its many internal and external publics' (https://hpg.unc.edu/about/).

The surrounding community in Chapel Hill and Carrboro also includes many artistic institutions that have collaborated and cosponsored JASP events. These include PlayMakers Theatre, the Ackland Museum, Wilson Library Rare Books Collection, Ayr Mount Preservation Society, Carolina Performing Arts, Carolina Arts Everywhere, and the dancers of the North Carolina Assembly and the Sun Assembly of Durham. For the success of the Jane Austen Summer Program, it has been important to engage representatives of these organisations; our involvement with these institutions has helped us recruit additional members of the community at large to attend and help organise JASP. We agree with Matthew Kirschenbaum's assessment that work in the public humanities is fundamentally 'a social undertaking' with 'an unusually strong sense of community and common purpose' (qtd. in Draxler and Spratt 171). Central to JASP's success has been ensuring that it did not resemble a classroom setting with the professors teaching the public; instead it has been a joint venture among a group of individuals both from within the university and without.

JASP and Its Format

The cofounders of JASP felt that their Carolina home was the ideal space to start an Austen-centric literary community modelled, as already noted, on the Dickens Universe as well as on the Annual General Meeting (AGM) of the Jane Austen Society of North America. For thirty-eight years, the Dickens Universe has drawn a large number of attendees comprised of readers from inside and outside the academy. It has evolved into a beloved institution that meets the needs and interests of a heterogeneous group of established scholars, graduate students, advanced undergraduate students, and general readers passionate about Charles Dickens, as well as high school teachers who earn course credits through the UC Santa Cruz summer school. Similarly, the AGM has for decades also drawn its attendance from both scholars and general readers, mixes academic formats like panels with a ball and hands-on workshops, and generally offers a mixture of new scholarly research and general appreciation for large crowds of up to 800 or 1000 attendees. Both the AGM and the Dickens Universe demonstrate the desirability and potential of sustaining a high level of intellectual discourse about literature among public groups, without jargon or condescension.

A special attribute of the Jane Austen Summer Program is its blend of scholarly discourse and hands-on experiences within a social environment that brings together multiple audiences and ages. In 2018, for example, the age range of attendees was 11–81. JASP achieves this broad range by creating a network of readers centred around their love of Jane Austen. Many mother-daughter pairs (at all age ranges) have attended JASP, for example, perhaps attracted to the interesting mother-daughter relationships in the novels themselves. For the first six years of its existence, the symposium focused on one of Jane Austen's major novels each year, taking advantage of the bicentennial of many of the titles. We have since added subsequent programs on additional texts (such as Austen's letters and her teenage writings). JASP's emphasis spans major themes within each novel, the history and material culture of her time, issues in pedagogy and student engagement with Austen, as well as contemporary literary research by leading scholars.

Over time, we have developed a basic format for our annual symposiums that we believe best facilitates this blend of scholarly and fan engagement with Austen's work.

The key structural components of our symposium are: (a) all formal presentations are plenary, to encourage a sense of a shared experience, and (b) all plenary sessions are followed by break-out discussion groups, so that participants get the chance to process the information in smaller groups of 10–15 people. These groups stay constant in membership for the whole symposium so that a close-knit community is formed. Each discussion group is a cross-section of all the types of attendees in terms of career, age, expertise, etc.; these groups address historical and contextual issues on material culture, music, dance, science, religion, and the politics of Regency society, as well as topics in English and comparative literature.

Speakers for panels to talks include scholars, writers, playwrights, historical costumers, and archivists; they may be professors, teachers, graduate students, undergraduates, book collectors, lawyers, novelists, or stay-at-home parents. Talks range from 45-minute lectures with a hefty dose of Q&A, to discussion panels, to 10-minute 'context corners' that provide historical context to key elements of the novel. We make sure to provide lots of time for Q&A during all plenary sessions, and we sometimes even have 'open' plenary sessions that are devoted to audience discussion. We strive throughout to cultivate a sense of shared adventure (in the style of Admiral and Mrs Croft) and avoid a top-down sense of hierarchy (in the style of Sir Walter or Lady Catherine).

We also have additional opportunities for community building, including meals such as the opening banquet and a final English tea, daily elevenses, and a pub crawl. In addition, during the four days there are theatrical performances (generally by our graduate students), readings, concerts of period music, exhibits of rare books, visual art tours, and screenings of films based on Austen's work. Concluding the JASP symposium is a grand Regency ball held in either Gerrard Hall on the UNC-CH campus or the Carolina Inn, complete with costumed attendees and musicians playing period music. Occasionally a local bartender with an interest in historic drinks has prepared historically accurate beverages for the occasion as well.

A significant number of our attendees enjoy historical costumes, and we subsequently include a presentation on costume and other material culture each year by an expert in the field. These experts generally are also willing to lead a workshop, where 20–40 participants get hands-on experience writing a letter with quill, sewing a reticule or workbag, trying on a corset or cravat, learning how to make ink, or creating shoe ribbons. Similarly, in order to avoid creating a division in the group between those with know-how and materials to wear Regency costumes to the ball and those who don't, we also provide very inexpensive Regency clothing for rent. Throughout these events, we ensure that a sense of fun prevails, and that participants aren't judged for their level of skill or knowledge.

JASP also makes use of its community resources by touring local historical houses, art museums, and archives. These activities somewhat resemble the pastimes of the groups of families in her novels, engaged with domestic crafts, reading, music, and visiting other country estates. The community aspect of JASP allows both general readers, scholars, and teachers from within the state of North Carolina and readers across the country to meet, socialise, and bond within a central location. This social angle fosters a personal interest in Austen's works while creating communities of readers that are often maintained through social media long after the symposium ends. Participants of JASP take away not just this deeper interest, however; they carry with them a renewed critical apparatus for interpreting the works of Austen and the cultural impact of Austen's works in our own historical moment.

JASP has for the past several years included special pedagogical workshops for middle and high school teachers who might be interested in adding Austen (or her period) to their curriculum. Discussions are held during the symposium specifically for teachers on teaching Austen's work at all academic levels in order to help them engage younger audiences with knowledge of late eighteenth and early nineteenth-century literature and culture. We use essay contests to draw in middle and high school attendees who might not otherwise come.

JASP Content/Themes

The table below shows the topics of all the JASPs to date, including their topic, selected speakers and workshops, as well as special events for the year's theme. We had initially thought that we would attract participants more easily to the JASP on *Pride and Prejudice* and have more difficulty with the lesser known and denser works, like *Mansfield Park*. This has not been our experience, however. Our events sell out more quickly each year, and people come as much for the sense of community and general learning as they do for the specific theme (Table 44.1).

Pedagogy, Teachers, and Education Advocacy

Despite the boom of Janeite fan culture and adaptations over the last twenty years, Austen is being read less in high schools. Teachers who come to JASP often share their difficulties in convincing high schoolers to give Jane Austen and other historical writers a chance. Male students, in particular, often reject Austen as merely a romance writer and struggle to identify with her work. JASP actively works to create mediums through which Austen's texts become more accessible for the high school classroom. Our workshops and discussions accomplish this by generating ideas for critical discussion, lesson plans for historical context, learning through adaptations, and plans for multidisciplinary classroom activities. The teachers who attend JASP offer their successes in teaching these texts and later transfer new strategies and lessons to their students. These pedagogical strategies are not just limited to teaching Austen but can transfer to a wide variety of texts and subjects, especially since our focus is often as much on Austen's historical context as on her novels. While the pedagogical aspects of our program are also tailored to fulfil particular state educational standards within North Carolina, teachers from other states often can easily adapt them for their own local requirements as well.

Our education advocacy has been key to our mission and has helped us apply for grants from the North Carolina Humanities Council (NCHC). It is also something that many people outside academia are interested in supporting. Silent auctions and small NCHC grants have helped us provide special scholarships for NC teachers to attend JASP. This opportunity allows teachers of both urban and rural schools to participate within the program and to lend their unique voices to our wider discourse on Austen's continuing legacy within modern culture. Over the past several years we have brought teachers from many different counties within North Carolina, including counties with vastly different socioeconomic and demographic profiles. See Map of North Carolina counties in Figure 44.2.

This success in our teacher education programs resulted in JASP winning NCHC's annual Joel Hardin Gradin Award for creativity and excellence in the public humanities in 2018.

There is a clear need for this type of pedagogy within the American education system. According to the National Endowment for the Arts Annual Arts Basic Survey (2013–2015), only 43.1% of U.S. adults read a novel, short story, poem, or play not required for work or school each year. This decline in personal reading has often been attributed to the competition among forms of entertainment, such as television or games, but it signals something deeper within the collective consciousness of the nation. It is backed up by a decline of literacy in middle and high school students.[4] Proficiency in reading has been dropping among high schoolers in the last 25 years. According to the National Assessment of Educational Progress, 40% of high schoolers in 1992 read at a 'proficient' level while in 2017 only 37% did ('Reading Practices'). One study found that only 30% of high school teachers use close reading techniques when teaching literature, preferring to have students write reflections or personal responses (Stotsky et al. 3). Nonetheless, the tangible benefits of literature have often been noted in the media. Studies list benefits such as increased empathy, more active civic participation, and stronger critical reasoning skills. Yet rarely discussed are the ways in which greater readership and literary engagement can be achieved within communities.

Table 44.1 Overview of JASP Content and Size

Year	Number of Participants	Theme	Selected Speakers	Special Events	Workshops
2013	50	200th anniversary of *Pride and Prejudice*	'The Networked Novel and what it did to Domestic Fiction' by Nancy Armstrong (Duke University), 'Education and Experience in *Pride and Prejudice*' by Jessica Richard (Wake Forest)	An exhibit of *Pride and Prejudice* editions from approximately 30 different languages	Fashion demonstration by Jade Bettin (UNC).
2014	65	*Sense and Sensibility*	'Making Sense of Sensibility' by Inger S.B. Brodey (UNC–Chapel Hill); 'Political Economy and *Sense and Sensibility*' by Robert Clark (University of East Anglia)	Romance author Kathleen Gilles Seidel; Historic games played and taught during elevenses	Session on how to read free indirect discourse.
2015	75/sold out	200th anniversary of *Emma*	'Waterloo, Austen, and the Duchess of Richmond's Ball' by Peter Graham (Virginia Tech); 'Learning to Read with Emma' by Deborah Knuth Klenk (Colgate University)	A strawberry picnic at Ayr Mount House, a historical manor built in the same year Emma was published. Duchess of Richmond's Ball	Info on men's dress with Jade Bettin, and a teacher's forum on Austen for high school and middle school.
2016	95/sold out	200th anniversary of *Mansfield Park*	'Lord Mansfield and the Slave Ship *Zong*' by Danielle Christmas (UNC–Chapel Hill) and '*Mansfield Park* and Sheridan's *Art of Reading*' by Susan Allen Ford (Delta State University)	Historical tour of local cathedral; fashion exhibit with lecture	Reticule making workshop; whist instruction
2017	100/ sold out	200th anniversary of *Persuasion*	'Finding Captain Wentworth:Reflections on *Persuasion*' by Jocelyn Harris (University of Otago); 'War and Fashion' by Hope Greenberg (University of Vermont)	Rare book exhibit at Wilson Library; Austen and Art exhibit at the Ackland Art Museum	Penmanship, calligraphy, and letter folding workshop with R.B. Bartgis
2018	111/ sold out	200th anniversary of *Northanger*	'Horror and the French Revolution' by Lloyd Kramer (UNC–Chapel		Mask making workshop

(Continued)

Table 44.1 (Continued)

Year	Number of Participants	Theme	Selected Speakers	Special Events	Workshops
		Abbey and *Frankenstein*	Hill); 'Gothic Fashion' by Samantha Bullat (Jamestown-Yorktown Foundation)	A masquerade ball in the 'Well Room' of the historic Carolina Inn.	
2019	120/ sold out	*Pride and Prejudice* and its Afterlives	Speakers included writers of recent adaptations: Sonia Kamal (*Unmarriagle*); Uzma Jalaluddin (*Ayesha at Last*); and Sonali Dev (*Pride, Prejudice, and Other Flavors*)	Screenings of the *Lizzie Bennet Diaries* and *Bride and Prejudice*; book signings with invited authors	Piloted a writing workshop that encouraged participants to think deeply about the process of adaptation
2020 [postponed to 2021]	N/A	Jane Austen and Her World (Austen's collected letters and Claire Tomalin's *Jane Austen: A Life*)	The symposium panels will focus on her historical context, the relationship between her life and fiction, and film and media interpretations of her biography.	Events may include games from Austen's era as well as new art and rare book exhibits.	Workshops include hands-on exposure to material culture from her period, such as letter-writing and the influence of the Ottoman Empire on fashion.
2022	N/A	Austen's Teenage Writings	We will have speakers on a variety of Austen's youthful works, including 'Love and Freindship' (sic) and 'The History of England'.	Special activities will be planned in conjunction with the International Society for Literary Juvenalia	We will expand out writing contests and workshops for middle and high school students in honour of the topic

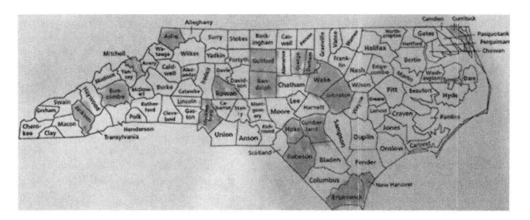

Figure 44.2 NC Counties. Counties represented by JASP Teacher Scholars are shaded

The absence of Austen in the high school curriculum is part of a larger trend in English pedagogy at the high school level. The 'literary canon', as taught to high schoolers currently, fails to address the diverse and complex nature of material written in the English language. Syllabi are often dominated by white male authors, with Shakespeare being heavily over-represented (Stotsky et al. 14–17.). One study compiled from over 200,000 students shows that while multiple Shakespearean plays are taught each year, high schoolers are reading few other texts written before the twentieth century (Renaissance Learning 58–59). Of the pre-twentieth-century texts listed, only one (*Frankenstein*) is written by a woman. Austen does not appear on the list for any grade level, despite the fact that national Common Core Standards lists *Pride and Prejudice* as an 'exemplar' of fiction for grades 11–12 (Common Core State Standards Initiative 142; National Governors Association 11). Pedagogical training on how to access older texts and historical periods can be particularly important for public education, now that the only 'old' literary work that is required of public school students in North Carolina is one work by Shakespeare.

Our special mission to train North Carolina middle and high school teachers encourages discussion on how Austen is received by younger generations and generates new ideas on both the university and secondary levels for making older texts more accessible to students. This is not so much professional training as it is a forum for teachers, professors, and other education workers to share ideas for encouraging higher-level literacy in students. They can also gain CEU credits for participating. Our teacher testimonials have revealed that teachers appreciate our unique venue for learning about history, art, and literature. They report afterwards that they build on these ideas in their subsequent teaching. As part of this mission, it is crucial that teachers and students participate not only in the symposium but in the larger organisation and outreach efforts of JASP. Our planning committees thus include current and former NC middle and high school teachers, university professors, graduate students, college students, and middle and high school students.

As JASP grows, we are interested in attracting more high school and undergraduate students into the fold to help foster a lifelong love of reading and participation within the humanities. In 2018, we welcomed two high school essay winners to the symposium, and the following year a middle schooler won the essay contest and attended free of charge. In both of the past two years, undergraduates from UNC's summer ENGL 340 class on Jane Austen also produced original research on Jane Austen and presented posters during the event. Beginning also in 2018, JASP has offered two for-credit internships for undergraduate students at UNC each year, with the goal of providing them experience in marketing, event logistics, and public humanities work. Going forward, we hope to attract more students through exhibits and volunteer opportunities that help make Austen pertinent

The Anatomy of the JASPer

As mentioned, JASP appeals to North Carolina middle and high school teachers and students, college professors, graduate students, Janeites, and history buffs. This audience includes both specialists and non-specialists, but the event is designed to be accessible, welcoming, and inclusive for all attendees. Some who attend JASP are self-taught historical costumers, country dancers, or amateur critics while others come to explore a burgeoning interest in history, women's literature, or Jane Austen. While most of the teachers who attend are from North Carolina, other attendees come from all around the United States, and occasionally from distant locations such as Brazil or Hong Kong. We have also succeeded in drawing from a wide range of rural areas as well as urban, and from a range of NC counties with broad diversity in socioeconomic standing. The varied perspectives from different ages, occupations, regions, cultures, and stages in life create rich and interesting conversations during break-out discussion groups, Q&A panels, and social events. Attendees often remark in their evaluations that JASP provides an open and welcoming forum for discussion among people with different worldviews.

For four years in a row (2015–2018), JASP applied for and received a GrassRoots Grant from the NCHC to support our outreach to North Carolina teachers. These annual awards ranged from $2500 to $3500 to bring middle and high school teachers to JASP with full scholarships. We brought 22 NC teachers to JASP with the full tuition scholarship over the course of these four years and also supplemented a discounted price of tuition for 20 more teachers. These participants have consistently been more ethnically diverse than the rest of our non-teacher participants. In 2017, 25% were African American; in that same year 50% of scholarship attendees had only an undergraduate education, while the other 50% had additional graduate school experience. Half of the winners were from rural communities. Looking at all the teacher scholarship recipients for the past four years: The 22 winners teach in 19 different counties, spanning the state geographically and also socioeconomically. (Our teacher-scholars came from the counties shaded on the map in Figure 44.2.) As a point of comparison, the child poverty in some of the represented counties is as high as 33.2% in Ashe County and even 44.0% in Robeson County. Median household income in these same two counties are $35,155 and $30,248, respectively. In contrast, Orange County (the location of UNC-CH) has 13.4% child poverty rate and a median household income of $59,472; and the wealthiest county represented, Wake County, has 14.5% child poverty and a median household income of $65,433, more than twice the average of Robeson County (Data based on the 2013 Poverty and Income Estimates for North Carolina's 100 Counties, by the Budget and Tax Center). The NCHC funding can only be spent on NC citizens, and we consider ourselves to be a regional conference for the Southeastern United States, so we applied to Oxford University Press and received a $800 grant to support teacher-scholars from outside NC.

While JASP has been very successful in drawing a diverse crowd, it has remained largely female (93% in 2019). It has also not been as diverse as we would like in terms of race and ethnicity, as Figure 44.3 shows. In this sense, we have had difficulty overcoming some of the stereotyping discussed at the beginning of this chapter. For our program in 2019 on 'Pride and Prejudice and its Afterlives', we consciously tried to counter these expectations. We invited perhaps the most diverse set of speakers at a North American Austen event to date: our three speakers all had written South Asian and Middle Eastern adaptations of Pride and Prejudice. Soniah Kamal retells Pride and Prejudice

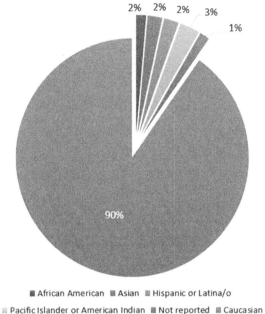

Figure 44.3 Demographic Breakdown from JASP 2019—Race & Ethnicity

set in modern Pakistan in *Unmarriageable*; Uzma Jalaluddin takes the plot and characters to a Muslim community in Toronto in *Ayesha at Last*; and Sonali Dev takes the story to Indian immigrants in California in *Pride and Prejudice and Other Flavors*. All three of these authors came to JASP and presented ideas on their adaptations across time and culture. It is fascinating that these adaptations all came out within a year of each other, along with Ibi Zoboi's *Pride*, which sets the story in an AfroCaribbean suburb of New Jersey. Perhaps this outpouring of multicultural and multiethnic adaptations will help turn the tide of Austen's monoethnic associations (Figure 44.4).

'Who Could Be in Doubt of What Followed?'

As the longevity of the event indicates, JASP has successfully created an annual literary event that connects scholars, teachers, and Janeites through engaged public discourse. The number of attendees has increased each year, and for the last four years (*Mansfield Park, Persuasion, Northanger Abbey*, and *Persuasion*), the program has sold out. JASP has a core group of attendees who return year after year. In fact, many praise the inclusive but thoughtful atmosphere created by JASP through its educational programming and social events.

As JASP moves forward and continues to develop its programming, it is also looking to create new avenues to expand the diversity of its participants. We are considering expanding our programming beyond the four-day symposium to include smaller public events. JASP has already launched a new free public book series focusing on female historical authors contemporaneous to Jane Austen, such as Phillis Wheatley and Maria Edgeworth. This series, called 'Jane Austen & Co.', contextualises these historical texts and provides a forum for critical community discourse through local public libraries in the Triangle Region of North Carolina. During the COVID-19 pandemic of 2020, this same outreach branch will be hosting Zoom conferences featuring several of our past and future speakers. JASP is also looking to strengthen its already strong educational mission by

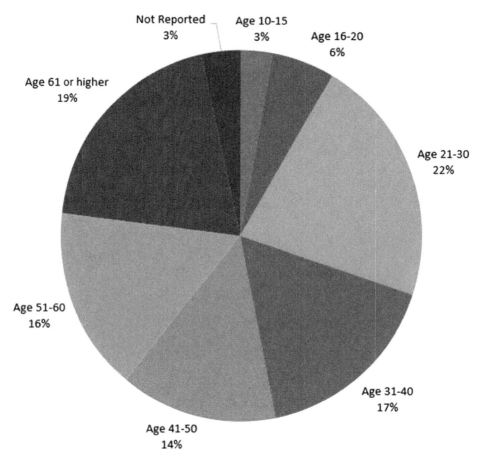

Figure 44.4 Demographic Breakdown from JASP 2019—Age

performing more research into the needs of local high school teachers. This includes visiting rural schools to survey instructors on what they teach and would like to teach and increasing the attendance of high school and middle school students at the annual symposium. Most recently we have a new partnership with the National Humanities Center, who are helping us create additional digital programming for our teacher continuing education programs, starting in 2020 (postponed until 2021).

Satisfaction surveys from JASP participants have been increasingly enthusiastic. Following the 2019 '*Pride and Prejudice* and its Afterlives' symposium, participants praised the inclusive activities and the range of content. One attendee stated in their exit survey that they were 'Surprised at just how much content there was and how high quality it was. I learned so much and was made to think about and reassess so much'. Another stated that they 'particularly liked that facilitators were guided by what we wanted to discuss'. Repeat attendees claim that the sense of community from JASP brings them back year after year. One attendee reported: 'Always enjoy reconnecting with fellow attendees at earlier JASPs; seeing and hearing the newer crop of graduate students present research (and the undergraduates with their posters, too); and building gradually on my bits of knowledge about Regency dance'. The focus on adaptation was

The Jane Austen Summer Program

also appreciated, with one attendee stating that 'the three assigned novels (the *P&P* retellings) introduced me to communities completely new to me'.

Teachers in particular report satisfaction with the teacher forums, with some asking for more forums in each JASP. Teachers appreciate that JASP provided them not just with pedagogical sessions but allowed them to participate in a wider range of interactive, social, and academic sessions with non-teachers as well. One teacher, who had reported attending previous JASPs, stated that 'The chance to meet, connect with and learn from other teachers is the biggest attraction for me, but I appreciate the new insight each year on a personal level as well'.

Furthermore, the participation of graduate and undergraduate students draws praise from participants. One participant praised the undergraduate poster presentations, stating: 'Can the awesome ENGL 340 students please get some respect…This was the first year I've made it to the poster session, and it was terrific. Their work was interesting and the students were very generous in talking about it. I had a great time with them and will be looking out for the poster session at future JASPs'. Others noted that they enjoyed the graduate student-led theatrical skit.

The surveys also noted room for improvement. With the growth of JASP, the venue tends to become more crowded. When asked if they wanted JASP to increase in size, many attendees stated that they preferred the small, intimate atmosphere of JASP; expanding would threaten the sense of community that they so enjoyed. While participants nearly unanimously rate both what they learned and how much they enjoyed JASP as either 'Excellent' or 'Good', the scores were slightly lower in 2019 (Tables 44.2 and 44.3). This may be because the 2019 program focused less on Austen's works and more on contemporary adaptations. Further data is required to understand these trends. Furthermore, the increasing cost of JASP creates logistical challenges to provide the highest value of content while still maintaining accessibility for a diverse population. While JASP receives small

Table 44.2 Answers to: How Much You Learned?

	Excellent	Good	Average	Below Average	Poor
2015	78.43%	21.57%	0.00%	0.00%	0.00%
2016	75.68%	21.62%	2.70%	0.00%	0.00%
2017	80.00%	20.00%	0.00%	0.00%	0.00%
2018	76.00%	18.00%	2.00%	0.00%	0.00% [*]
2019	65.00%	28.33%	1.67%	1.67%	0.00% [*]

Notes

[*] *3.33% chose Not Applicable in 2019; 4.00% in 2018*

Table 44.3 Answers to: How Much You Enjoyed?

	Excellent	Good	Average	Below Average	Poor
2015	90.20%	7.84%	1.96%	0.00%	0.00%
2016	86.49%	10.81%	2.70%	0.00%	0.00%
2017	90.00%	10.00%	0.00%	0.00%	0.00%
2018	90.20%	9.80%	0.00%	0.00%	0.00%
2019	83.05%	13.56%	1.69%	0.00%	0.00% [*]

Notes

[*] *1.69% chose N/A in 2019*

grants from various parts of UNC to help cover costs, such help has been unpredictable, and it has been difficult to keep costs down sufficiently to make JASP accessible to all.

As JASP progresses, we hope to work with other Austen-related organisations like JASNA to revise the scene in the cartoon from the 1940s with which this article started. In the revised cartoon scene, the academics would also be capable of enjoying the fun and revelry of the people on the left side, and the cheerleaders for 'Janie' might also be carrying about some of her books, like the dour academics on the right. One hopes that the statue might wink favourably upon this improved scene of combined erudition and enthusiasm.

Notes

1   For the experience of Harvard historian Jill Lepore at the Dickens Universe, see Lepore.
2   Rudyard Kipling first used the term 'Janeites' in his short story about Austen readers in the trenches of WWI.
3   This is not to say that other authors don't also attract mixed crowds: Shakespeare companies all over the United States, including the Great River Shakespeare Festival, Chesapeake Shakespeare Company, and Marin Shakespeare Company, strive to engage their home communities in the arts; this last company in particular emphasises annual events, including 'year-round classes for students of all ages [and] Shakespeare for Social Justice programs' (marinshakespeare.org). In Ireland, the annual Bloomsday Festival, officially hosted by the James Joyce Centre, celebrates Ulysses and draws fans and scholars alike into performances, readings, and reenactments of Leopold Bloom's busy day in Dublin.
4   Data suggests that these trends are not just limited to the United States. Renaissance Learning, which conducts statistical analysis of Accelerated Reading Tests in various countries, reports that British students in years 9–11 on average 'were reading at least three years below their chronological age' (Topping and Clark 23). Another study completed by the National Literacy Trust states that young people's enjoyment of reading is declining, but interestingly, those young people who enjoyed reading tend to read at a higher reading level than their chronological age (Clark and Teravainen-Goff 1–2).

Works Cited

Brooks, Peter, and Hilary Jewett. *The Humanities and Public Life*. Fordham UP, 2014.
Brownstein, Rachel. *Why Jane Austen?* Columbia UP, 2011.
'Carolina Public Humanities.' https://humanities.unc.edu
Clark, Christina, and Anne Teravainen-Goff. 'Children and Young People's Reading in 2019: Findings from Our Annual Literacy Survey.' *National Literacy Trust*, 2020.
Common Core State Standards Initiative. 'Appendix B: Text Exemplars and Sample Performance Tasks.' *English Language Arts & Literacy in History/Social Studies, Science, and Technical Subjects*, 2010. www.corestandards.org/assets/Appendix_B.pdf
Draxler, Bridget, and Danielle Spratt. *Engaging the Age of Jane Austen: Public Humanities in Practice*. U Iowa P, 2018.
'Humanities for the Public Good.' https://hpg.unc.edu/about/
Jalaluddin, Uzma. *Ayesha at Last*. Harper Avenue, 2018.
Jane Austen Summer Program. www.janeaustensummer.org
Kamal, Soniah. *Unmarriagable*. Ballantine Books, 2019.
Kipling, Rudyard. 'The Janeites.' *Debits and Credits*. Macmillan, 1924.
Lepore, Jill. 'Dickens in Eden.' *New Yorker* Aug. 29 2011, pp. 52–61.
Lynch, Deidre, editor. *Janeites: Austen's Disciples and Devotees*. Princeton UP, 2000.
National Endowment for the Arts. 'To Read or Not to Read: A Question of National Consequence,' Research Report #47, Nov. 2007. https://www.arts.gov/sites/default/files/ToRead.pdf. Accessed 19 Oct. 2019.
National Governors Association Center for Best Practices and Council of Chief State School Officers. 'Appendix B: Text Exemplars and Sample Performance Tasks.' *English Language Arts & Literacy in History/Social Studies, Science, and Technical Subjects*, 16 Oct. 2015. http://www.corestandards.org/assets/Appendix_B.pdf. Accessed 19 Oct. 2019.

'Reading Practices.' *The Condition of Education – Preprimary, Elementary, and Secondary Education – Assessments – Reading Performance – Indicator May (2018).* National Center for Education Statistics, May 2018. nces.ed.gov/programs/coe/indicator_cnb.asp. Accessed 19 Oct. 2019.

Renaissance Learning. 'What Kids Are Reading, Annual Report,' Wisconsin, 2018. www.renaissance.com/wkar/

Scheinman, Ted. *Camp Austen: My Life as an Accidental Jane Austen Superfan.* Farrar, Straus, and Giroux, 2018.

Stotsky, S., J. Traffas, and J. Woodworth. *Forum 4: Literary Study in Grades 9, 10, and 11: A National Survey.* Washington DC: Association of Literary Scholars, Critics, and Writers, 2010.

'The Constitution, or Form of Government, Agreed To, and Resolved Upon, by the Representatives of the Freemen of the State of North-Carolina, Elected and Chosen for that Particular Purpose, in Congress Assembled, at Halifax, the Eighteenth Day of December, in the Year of Our Lord One Thousand Seven Hundred And Seventy-Six.' *Documenting the American South,* U of North Carolina at Chapel Hill. docsouth.unc.edu/unc/uncbk1017/uncbk1017.html

Topping, Keith, and Christina Clark. 'What and How Kids Are Reading: The Book-Reading Behaviours of Pupils in British and Irish Schools.' Renaissance Learning UK, London, 2020.

'Visitors' Guide.' U of North Carolina, Chapel Hill, 2018. www.unc.edu/visitors/guide.pdf

Yaffe, Deborah. *Among the Janeites: A Journey through the World of Jane Austen Fandom.* Mariner Books, 2013.

Zoboi, Ibi. *Pride: A Pride and Prejudice Remix.* Blazer and Bray, 2019.

INDEX

abolition 3, 63, 64n2, 129, 248, 250, 254, 257n12, 543–544, 558; *see also* Thomas Clarkson; slavery and slave trade
Ackermann, Rudolf 456
Aczel, Richard 278, 280
Adams, Carol 2
adaptations 2, 3, 4, 6, 7, 23, 65, 71, 245, 252–256; passim 257n20, 308, 324, 330, 358, 360, 411, 414–415, 418, 422–436, 436n6, 444, 453, 470, 471, 473, 478, 481–483, 509–510, 519n5, 522–523, 527–532, 533n7, 536, 544, 548, 549, 551, 554, 572–573, 576, 580, 582–583; *see also* fanfiction, retellings, and spin-off writing
adaptations, film: *Austenland* (2013) 416, 554; *Bride and Prejudice* (Chadha 2004) 481, 482, 500, 504, 551, 578; *Clueless* 23, 473, 474, 500, 515, 573; *Emma* (1996 Lawrence) 515, 516; *Emma* (2020 de Wilde) 473, 530, 554; *Mansfield Park* (1999 Rozema) 251, 257n12, 282, 511, 517, 519n4, 530, 551, 554; *Lady Susan* (2016 Stillman) 529–520; *Northanger Abbey* (1987); *Northanger Abbey* (2007 Jones) 519n5; *Persuasion* (1995); *Persuasion* (2007); *Pride and Prejudice* (1995 Davies) 324, 429, 446, 463, 510, 511, 514, 549; *Pride and Prejudice* (2005 Wright) 406, 510, 511, 514, 516, 524, 554, 555; *Pride and Prejudice and Zombies* (2016, Steers) 251, 275; *Sense and Sensibility* (1995 Lee) 23, 24, 34, 429, 515, 554; *Sense and Sensibility* (2008) 515
adaptations, improv 434–435; *Austentatious* 434, 463, 465n7, 530
adaptations, musicals 428–430; *Persuasion: A new musical* 430; *Pride and Prejudice* (Taylor) 429–430
adaptations, stage 7 422–436; *Emma, Interrupted* (2019) 427–428; *Pride and Prejudice* (Hamill, 2018) 424–426, 428; *Pride and Prejudice* (McArthur 2018) 426, 428; *Pride and Prejudice: A Musical Romantic-Comedy* (423); *Pride and Prejudice: A Sentimental Comedy in Three Acts* (1935) 423; *Sense and Sensibility* (Hamill, 2016) 424, 436, 437n10; *Yours Ever, Jane* 453
adaptations, television and YouTube; *Emma, Approved* (551); *Lizzie Bennet Diaries, The* 551, 551, 573; *Lost in Austen* (2008) 416, 420, 436, 554, 558; *Many Lovers of Miss Jane Austen, The* (2011); *Persuasion* (Mitchell, 1995) 554; *Sanditon* (2019 Davies) 530, 551; *Welcome to Sanditon* (551)
Addison, Joseph (*The Spectator*) 161
Adventure of the Black Lady (A Behn) 260
Adventures of Jemima Russell, an Orphan 68–69
Adventures of John Wetherell, The 81
advertisements and advertising 164, 165, 185, 186, 188, 190, 191
aesthetics 90, 203, 206, 389, 396
affect theory 389
Agitation, or Memoirs of George Woodford 68
Ahern, Stephen 155n4, 155n6
Ahmed, Sara 86
Aiken, John 152
Ailwood, Sarah 6, 8, 318–332
Alexander, Claire 260
Alphonsine 67
Amy, Helen 104n1
analogy criticism 358–367
Anderson, Howard 100
Anderson, Kathleen 6, 8, 33, 333–341
Anderson, Misty 344
Anderson, Sigrid Michelle 3, 7, 8, 481–489
Angelica; or Quixote in Petticoats 67
Anglican clergy and beliefs 283, 340n6, 493
anonymity 266, 269; *see also* pseudonyms and pseudonymity
Antigua 58, 62, 64, 200–201, 244n3, 251, 503, 550

Antoinette, Marie 346
Appiah, Kwame Anthony 260, 263
Appleton, Elizabeth 218, 226n6
Apter, Emily 531
Ariosto 160–61
aristocracy (*see also* class system) 47, 54n6, 56n21, 56n23, 75, 83–91, 133, 137, 142, 207, 234, 265–269, 306, 364, 471, 478
Aristotle 83, 84, 88, 91, 198
Armstrong, Nancy 67n2
Astaire, Fred 6, 359–366; *Barkleys of Broadway, The* 359; *Flying Down to Rio* 365; *Follow the Fleet* 365; *Gay Divorcee, The* 361, 362; *Roberta* 361, 365; *Shall We Dance* 363; *Swing Time* 365, 366n1, 366n3; *Top Hat* 361, 363, 364, 365
attachment theory 388–391
Auden, W. H. 34, 41
Auerbach, Emily 4
Auerbach, Nina 59, 76–80, 79, 86
Austen, Anna: *see* Knight, Anna
Austen, Caroline Mary (JA's niece) 95, 100, 101, 103, 106–107, 111, 118, 122n3, 134, 282
Austen, Cassandra-Elizabeth (JA's sister) 11, 12, 25, 27, 67, 95–105, 107, 113–114, 134, 136, 145–147, 158–159, 160, 166, 168n4, 178n2, 181, 189n5, 191, 202, 216n2, 220, 236–237, 241, 308, 318, 334, 343, 403, 405, 439, 456, 459, 492, 530; *see also* letters, as source material
Austen, Cassandra-Leigh (JA's mother) 25
Austen, Charles 107, 236
Austen, Edward (JA's brother, later Knight) 12, 25, 46, 203n3, 208, 236, 392, 409–410, 447, 457–458, 461, 523, 552 (*see also* Godmersham and Godmersham Library)
Austen, Francis Williams (JA's brother) 46, 98, 107, 147, 236
Austen, Reverend George (JA's father) 25, 34, 42, 145, 159, 161, 200, 208, 462, 552
Austen, Henry (JA's brother) 3, 11, 12, 46, 95, 107, 133, 145, 159, 161, 168n4, 180, 200, 281, 282, 529; *see also* 'Biographical Notice of the Author'
Austen, James Edward (Austen-Leigh)(JA's nephew) 12, 13, 65, 95–97, 107, 111, 127–130, 143, 145, 158, 161–162, 168n4, 371, 411, 447, 450, 491–492, 527, 529
Austen, Jane: aphorisms 40, 139; bank note 530; books owned by 160–161, 392; characterisations of 11, 16, 45, 80, 109, 110, 127, 130, 131, 246–247, 371, 403, 529, 532, 548; childhood 122n2, 134, 236, 392; celebrity status 3, 446–467, 531–532, 548; donkey carriage 413; handwriting 98, 100, 102, 103–104; health, illness, and death 244n5; homes: *see* Bath, Chawton, Stevenson, Southampton; income and finances 553; influences 5, 14, 28, 110, 158, 160, 339n3, 459, 469, 525–529, 548; jewelry 410, 462, 463, 465n5; 'Opinions of *Emma*' 151, 319; 'Opinions of *Mansfield Park*' 151, 154, 319; pen names 12;

reading 5, 141, 145–46, 151, 158–169, 194, 216n1, 527; romantic attachments and attitudes toward marriage 46, 553; '3 or 4 Families in a Country Village' formulation 154, 392; writing table and portable desk 96, 100–101, 104n8, 112, 222, 46; *see also* Austen family members, Chawton and Chawton House, individual works (*The Beautiful Cassandra, Catherine, or the Bower Emma, Juvenilia, Lady Susan,* "Letter from a Young Lady" *Letters, Love and Freindship, Mansfield Park, Persuasion, Pride and Prejudice, Sanditon, Sense and Sensibility, Susan, The Watsons*), manuscripts
Austenistan (Sukhera) xvii, 6, 468–480 passim
Austen-Leigh, Chomoley 129
Austen-Leigh, James Edward: *see* Austen, James Edward
Austen-Leigh, Joan 399–404, 411–414
Austen-Leigh, Mary Augusta 97–99, 128, 129–130
Austen-Leigh, Richard Austen 97
Austen-Leigh, William 97–98
Austin, Gilbert 282
Auyoung, Elaine 291–292
Azad, Zeina Toric 470, 475

Baartman, Sara ('the Hottentot Venus') 164, 190n15, 249, 252, 550, 557n7
Baduel, Farzana 469, 476
Bage, Robert 160
Baker, Jo 253
Baker, William 2
Bakhtin, M.M. 277
Ballantyne (publisher) 130, 308
Ballaster, Ros 147, 155n5, 155–156n13
Bally, Charles 375
Balzac, Honoré de 370, 371
Bander, Elaine 3, 5, 145–157, 247, 406n2, 416
Banfield, Ann 290
Bank Restriction Act of 1797 194, 196–199
Bankes, Elizabeth 392
Barbauld, Anna Laetitia 152, 250
Barber, Francis 249
Barchas, Janine 16, 158, 162, 164, 167, 406, 447, 453, 454, 459, 465n1, 492
Baretti, Joseph 160
Baron-Cohen, Simon 393, 394
Barrett, Eaton Stannard 135, 151, 160
Barrett, Hilma D. 399
Barry, Kevin 196
Barsam, Richard 520
Batchelor, Jennie 164, 169n6, 169n7
Bath 12, 15–16, 19, 20, 25, 50, 53, 76, 84, 86, 89, 109, 115–116, 142, 154, 156, 161, 164, 172, 176, 181–184, 211, 231, 236–237, 243, 244n5, 291, 313, 315, 329, 348, 351, 360, 374, 382–383, 411, 432–433, 446, 450, 452, 463, 467, 503, 516, 524, 534
Baum, Rob 270n18
'Beautifull Cassandra, The' 107, 113–114, 181, 189n7

Index

Beauty and the Beast (2017 film) 257n15
Beckford, William 230
Behn, Aphra 147, 155n5, 257n20, 260, 263, 266, 270n17, 270n18; *Fair Jilt, The* 263; *Forced Marriage, The* 263; *History of the Nun* 263; *Oroonoko; of the Royal Slave* 263; *Unfortunate Bride* 263
Behrendt, Stephen 229, 230, 244n1
Bell, John 160
Bellamy, Alistair 265
Bellanti, Claire 417
Belle, Dido Elizabeth 249, 252, 549–550
Belmonte, Matthew 384
Bemetzrieder, Anton 225, 226n6
Benedict, Barbara M. 12, 14, 15, 155n2, 314
Benis, Toby R. 16
Bentham, Jeremy 81
Berkeley, Busby 362
Berlant, Lauren 343
Bersani, Leo 302
Bertrand, Arthus 531
Bessborough, Lady 297
Beyoncé 446, 447, 453
Bible, The 51, 128, 353, 356, 382; *see also* religion
Bildungsroman 17, 36, 365
Bilger, Audrey 111
Binhammer, Katherine 155n2, 354n17
'Biographical Notice of the Author' (Henry Austen) 3, 11, 12, 54n9, 95, 107, 133, 168n4, 203n4, 236, 399, 529; *see also* Austen, Henry
Birchall, Diana 452
Black, Tim 3, 7, 535–546
Black Lives Matter Movement 247, 260, 547, 556n1
Blackstone, William 206
Blair, Hugh 53, 56n37, 61
Blessington, Lady 281
Blower, Elizabeth 68
Blumenbach, Johann Friedrich 248
Bollas, Christopher 293
Borrego, Melanie 6, 490–496
Bottomer, Phyllis Ferguson 555
Boulukos, George E. 545n9
Bowden, Jean 413
Boyd, Brian 279–280, 379–380
Brabourne, Lord (Edward Hugessen Knatchbull Hugessen) 96–97
Bredar, Trish 170–171, 177, 178n7
Bree, Linda 3, 4, 5, 106, 133–144
Bride and Prejudice film (Chadha 2004) 481, 482, 500, 504, 551, 578
Brideoake, Fiona 344, 345, 354n1, 354n15
Brighton 455, 457
Brinton, Sybil G. 439, 492
British Critic 12, 45
Britton, Jean 386
Brodey, Inger 7, 26, 571–585
Bromberg, Paula 545n4

Brontë, Charlotte 343–344, 354n8, 363, 490; *Villette* 92
Brontë, Emily; *Wuthering Heights* 92
Brooke, Henry 147
Brookes, Charlotte 161
Brooks, Peter 573
Brophy, Brigid 131n1
Brothers, Robert 492
Brower, Ruben 41–42
Brown, Laura 265
Brown, Lloyd 13
Brownlow, Mark 464
Brownstein, Rachel 6–7, 164, 189n6, 415, 571
Brunton, Mary 136, 146, 159–160, 324; *Self Control* 136, 146, 159–160, 527
Buchanan, Claudius 160
Buchanan, Douglas 2
Buffon, Comte de 161
Bundock, Michael 257n10
Burgess, Miranda 64n2
Burgh, Allston 219, 220
Burke, Edmund 47–48, 76, 79, 118, 121, 149, 316n19, 345–346, 384, 404, 559
Burke, Henry Gershon 404, 411, 413
burlesque 11, 14, 67, 106–108, 110, 118, 122, 123n17, 135, 146, 151, 237; *see also* comedy, humor
Burnett, Frances Hodgson 565
Burney, Frances 5, 14, 17, 18, 23, 66, 108, 133–143, 147–148, 151–154, 160, 161, 170, 178n6, 349, 526; *Camilla* 66, 71, 119, 133–135, 142, 143n2, 148, 150, 152, 155n9, 160, 312, 349; *Cecilia* 66, 71, 116, 133, 134, 136, 152, 153, 312, 349; *Evelina* 17, 19, 66, 67, 133–136, 149, 324, 552; *Wanderer, The* 170, 172, 178n6
Burney, Sarah Harriet 136, 146
Burns, Anna 289
Burns, Robert 160, 238, 239, 241
Buss, David 382
Butler, Eleanor 345
Butler, Judith 86, 354n3
Butler, Marilyn 16, 63, 65, 77, 79–80, 86, 168n4, 169n10, 321, 338, 532
Butler, Octavia 255, 257n21; *Kindred* 255, 257n21
Butte, George 383
Byrne, Paula 4, 257n10
Byrne, Sandie 205–217
Byron, Lord, 34, 41, 46–47, 51, 55n33, 121, 142, 143, 160, 164, 173, 178n2, 233–234n1, 281, 308, 319, 325, 454; *Childe Harold's Pilgrimage* 244n1; *Don Juan* 121
Byronic heroes 324, 332

'Cambrianna' 210, 226n7
Campbell, Thomas 238, 239
Cano, Marina 6, 7, 446–467
canon and canonicity 2, 3, 28, 76, 77, 83, 155n8,

Index

366, 376, 424, 463, 482, 488, 490, 507, 537, 561, 579

Canter, Rachel 6, 8, 368–378

Caplan, Clive 203n4

Carlson, Julia 284

Carpenter, Edward Thomas 409

Carpenter, Tom 413

Carroll, Joseph 381, 387

Carroll, Lewis 270–271n29; *Alice in Wonderland* 270–271n29

Casanova, Pascale 369, 376

Cashmore, Ellis 453, 461

Castle, Terry 343, 344

Catherine 12, 75, 108, 110, 150, 308

'Catherine, or the Bower' 107, 118, 147–48

Cecil, David 96

celebrity 6, 51, 162, 164, 165, 190n15, 249, 364, 406, 446–465, 523–533

Celestina 149

Centlivre, Susanna 160

Cervantes, Miguel D. 122; *DonQuixote* 122n11, 150

Chamberlain, Shannon 35–36

Chapman, R. W. 12, 31, 96, 98, 109, 162, 164, 168n5, 178n1, 241, 285, 320, 409, 414

Charlotte Augusta, Princess 229–230, 243–244n1

Chater, Kathleen 257n13

Chatman, Seymour 280

Chawton House and Chawton House Library 12, 25, 99, 101, 161, 169n9, 203n3, 208, 400, 406, 409, 410–411, 413–414, 446, 447, 457–458, 463, 464, 465n2, 523–526, 529

Cheltenham 164

Chen, Katherine 441

Chernow, Ron 257n14

Chesterton, G.K. 108–109

Chestna, Tamara 472

Cheyne, George 235–236

childhood 75, 136, 218, 221, 237, 256, 344, 347, 395, 543; *see also* Jane Austen, childhood

Chiles, Katy 262, 270n14, 270n15

Chua, Jasmin Malik 3, 474

circulating libraries 15, 20, 53, 56n36, 56n38, 143n1, 145, 164, 180, 187, 188, 242, 306, 309–312, 315, 316n14

Clancy, James 209

Clarentine 136, 145

Clark, Anna 244n2

Clarke, James Stanier 320

Clarke, Susanna 253, 257n17; *Jonathan Strange and Mr Norrell* 253

Clarkson, Thomas 160, 248, 544

class system 16, 58, 71, 85, 87, 218, 263k, 267, 268, 426, 505, 528, 554, 562; *see also* aristocracy, clergymen, economics, gentry and gentry classes, inheritance, labouring classes, rank, servants

clergymen 34, 199; *see also* religion

Clery, E. J. 16, 18, 203n4, 320, 321, 323, 344, 347, 529, 533n5

Cobb, Shelley 533n7

Cobbett, William 196

Cockle, Mrs, 219, 226n6

Coetzee, J. M. 482

Cohen, Margaret 370, 371

Cohen, Michelle 168n2, 323

Cohen, Monica 545n5

Cohen, Paula Marantz 3, 6, 358–367

Cohn, Dorri 369, 375

Cole, Helen 413

Coleridge, Samuel T. 81, 281–282, 325

Collings, David 346, 354n19

Collingwood, R. G. 81

Collins, K. K. 90

colonialism and imperialism xiv, 24, 15, 62–63, 64n2, 76, 201, 204, 232, 252, 482, 530, 536, 546

comedy 53, 61, 77, 111, 113, 117, 122, 123n17, 133, 134–136, 164, 336, 360, 365, 423, 434–436, 530, 563; *see also* burlesque, humor, irony, juvenilia, parody, satire

commodities 30, 32, 181, 205–217, 462, 463, 500, 564, 566

Companion to the Altar, A 161

companionate marriage 35, 52, 155n6, 229, 230, 243, 244n3, 300, 322, 338, 345, 555; *see also* marriage

Comyn, Sarah 5, 193–204

conduct books 37, 111, 121, 122n7, 123n18, 158, 160, 161, 220, 221, 348, 392, 441

consumerism and consumer culture vi, 5, 15, 35, 180–192 passim 205, 206, 211, 214, 233, 236, 455, 463, 510

Cooper, Edward 160

Cooper, Liz Philosophos 406, 412, 414, 418

Copeland, Edward 2, 164, 169n7, 189n3, 189n4, 193

Corman, Brian 156n15

Cornish, Francis Warre 241

Cossy, Valerie 368, 369, 370, 376

Costa, Joseph J. 407n3

courtship and courtship plots 55n33, 78, 138, 146–148, 153–154, 167, 223–224, 319–330, 335, 337, 379, 386, 433, 469, 501, 540, 548, 552

Cowper, William 81, 148, 158, 160, 168n4, 182, 256n4

Crabbe, George 158, 160, 168n4

Craig, Sheryl Bonar 190n11, 197

Critical Review 44–45, 52, 53, 138

Croce, Arlene 359–365; passim

Crosby, Richard 11, 12, 16, 308

Croskerie, Margaret Case 155n13

Cross, John 143

Curry, Mary Jane 190n11

Cuvier, George 382

Da, Nan Z. 394n3

Dabydeen, David 249, 251

Index

Dadlez, E.M. 340n10

Dames, Nicholas 2

dance and dancing 19, 95, 117, 205, 359–366

D'Arblay, Madame: *see* Burney; *see* Fanny

Darnell, Dorothy 409

Darsee, Valentine 483

Darwin, Charles 29, 129–130, 392, 564–565

Darwin, Sir Francis 320–321

Davis, Lennard 73n2, 282, 285

death, from serial childbirth 46, 55n18

deBeauvoir, Simone 347

De Feuillide, Eliza, née Hancock, later Austen)

Defoe, Daniel 151, 263; *Moll Flanders* 151; *Robinson Crusoe* 158, 482

Dekel, Mikhal 388

De Lauretis, Teresa 342

Dellon, Hope 358, 366n2

De Man, Paul 310

DeMontolieu, Isabelle 368–378; *La Famille Elliot* 368

DeQuincey, Thomas 52

Derrida, Jacques 78, 83–85, 92n1

Desmund 149

Devine, Jodi A. 3, 5, 95–105

Deyo, Darwynn 193

Dickens, Charles 109, 232, 256, 310, 415, 551, 565, 571

Dickens University 574

disability and disability studies 174, 178n8, 545n2, 553

D'Israeli, Isaac 161

Dodsley, Robert 159

Dolezal, Rachel 260

domesticity 81, 213, 227, 323, 334

Dominque, Lyndon 3, 5, 259–273

Donogue, Emma 253

Doody, Margaret 26, 38n1, 55n21, 106, 110, 121, 122n1, 146, 155n1, 155n12, 170, 229

Dow, Gillian 7, 368, 523–534

Downie, J.A. 189n3

Drabble, Margaret 110

Draxler, Bridget 537, 556–557n6, 573

dress and clothing 117, 214, 216n10; *see also* fashion

Dryden, Robert 161

Duckworth, Alistair 15, 41, 54n14, 54n31, 76, 78, 86, 201, 238

Dunbar, William 269n1

Duncan, Ian 312

Duncan, Kathryn 394n1

Dunton, John 260, 263–273; *Athenian Sport* 264; *A Cat May Look on a Queen* 260, 263–273; passim

Dustin, Sara 190n11

Duyckinck, Evert A. 447, 449

Dyer, Richard 252

Eason, Sarah 348, 355n22

East India Company 474

East Indies 117

Easton, Celia A. 556

economics 5, 23, 24, 32–35, 41, 43, 58, 112, 116, 127, 180, 185, 189n3, 190n11, 193–202, 203n2, 229, 233, 249, 250, 266–267, 306, 308, 314, 321–327, 335, 354n4, 363, 440, 475–476, 481–484, 505, 524, 528, 566, 573; *see also* class system, class system, political economy

Edelman, Lee 354n4

Edgeworth, Maria 5, 14, 66, 133–44, 218, 219, 226n3, 226n5, 296, 304, 324, 526, 581; *Absentee, The* 142; *Belinda* 66, 133, 137, 138, 151, 152, 233–234, 250, 312, 349; *Castle Rackrent* 137, 141; *Letters for Literary Ladies* 136, 137; *Maria Edgeworth's Letters* 142, 143; *Patronage* 142

Edgeworth, Richard Lovell 137, 143n5, 218, 226n3, 226n5, 250

Edinburgh Magazine 12

Edinburgh Review 139, 382

education 29, 43, 45, 50, 55, 73, 90, 91, 93n4, 118, 120, 155n2, 250, 258, 282, 307, 321, 322, 340n3, 410, 435, 476, 493–494, 505, 512, 525–528, 547–548, 552; *see also* Jane Austen, education

education, theme in JA's fiction 15, 18, 117, 139, 200, 202, 309, 382, 443, 505, 553

education, women's 123n23, 218, 220–221, 346–347, 440, 527, 564–566

Edwards, Paul 251

Enquiry into the Duties of the Female Sex, An 219

Egerton, Thomas 216n5, 216n6

Ehrenpreis, 100

Elba, Idris 256

Elfenbein, Andrew 279, 307

'Elinor and Marianne' 12, 23, 25, 26

Eliot, George 80, 143, 256, 363; *Middlemarch* 92

Eliot, Simon 164–165, 169n8

Eliot, T.S. 279

Ellestrom, Lars 359

Elley, Nida 477–478

Elliot, Kamilla 519n6

Ellis, Havelock 560

elocution and elocutionists 8, 282–284

elopement and clandestine marriages 37, 50–51, 55n24, 55n31, 55n33, 225, 506, 543

Elwin, Malcolm 319

Emerson, Ralph Waldo 363

Emma 5, 12, 20, 46, 65–74, 86, 108, 136, 137, 142, 143, 146, 151, 152, 162, 167–168, 180, 183, 189n6, 194–195, 200, 205, 206, 207–219, 221–223, 229–231, 237, 243, 253, 278–281, 288–293, 296, 303, 306–307, 320, 336–339, 340n8, 344, 360, 364–365, 368, 381, 384, 386, 389–39, 393–394, 410, 437n7, 477, 510, 527, 548, 549; *see also Emma* adaptations, film, and, stage

Emmeline 15

Empson, William 43, 54n9

Emsley, Sarah 30, 545n3

Index

English Malady, The 235
epistemic injustice 535–545
epistemology 18
epistolary form and conventions 12, 14, 21, 25, 27, 28, 61, 91, 93n8, 100, 104n6, 110, 115, 133, 136, 149, 153, 161, 176, 198, 253, 277, 299, 333, 362, 502, 521–522
Equiano, Oloudah 249, 251
Erickson, Amy Louise 207, 209
Erickson, Lee 15
Eudemian Ethics 83
evangelical clergy and beliefs 38, 120, 128, 322, 326
Evans, Mary 321
Everly, Riana 493
evolutionary studies 397–383
exhibitions: *Austen by the Sea* (Brighton 2017-2018) 446, 455; *Chawton* (2017) 533n4; *Reading with Austen* (Godmersham 2018) 203n3, 458–459, 527; *What Jane Saw* (2013) 446, 453, 454, 458–459; *Which Jane Austen?* (Bodleian Libraries 2017) 446, 450, 451, 453, 462; *Will & Jane: Shakespeare, Austen, and the Cult of Celebrity* (Folger Library, 2016) 447, 465n1, 527–528

Fallon, Ann Marie 482–483
fandom 404, 423, 548–549, 554, 571, 574
fanfiction, retellings, and spin-off fiction 3, 7, 439–445, 481–489, 490–496, 551, 572; *see also* adaptations *Ayesha at Last* (Jalaluddin) 482, 484–486, 572, 578; *Emma Ever After* 477; *Independence of Miss Mary Bennet* (McCullough) 441, 442–443; *Longbourn* (Baker) 253, 481, 491, 536, 554; *Machiko* (Nogami) 559; *Match for Mary Bennet, A* (Ward) 444n3; *Mary B* (Chen) 440–441, 444n6, 444n8; *Mary Bennet* (Paynter) 442, 443; *Miss Austen* (Hornsby); *Old Friends and New Fancies* (Brinton) 492; *Other Bennet Sister, The* (Hadlow) 440, 442, 444n9, 530; *Pride and Prejudice and Passports* (Garrett) 488; *Pride and Prejudice and Zombies* (Grahame-Smith 2009) 251, 275; *Pride and Prometheus* 441–443; *Pride: A Pride and Prejudice Remix* (Zoboi) 482, 483–484, 551, 554, 572; *Pride, Prejudice, and other Flavors* (Dev) 578; *Sansei and Sensibility* (Yamashita) 482, 486, 487; *Sex Comes to Pemberly* (Bennet) 444n3; *Through a Different Lens* (Everly) 493; *Unmarriageable* (Kamal) 481, 482, 483, 486, 551, 572, 578, 580
Farrell, James T. 399
fashion 15, 49, 101, 104, 162, 180–182, 187–188, 189n5, 213, 218, 250, 270n1, 455–456, 475, 577, 578; *see also* dress
fashions, literary 28, 137, 391
Favret, Mary 27, 80–81, 82, 100, 103, 104n4, 550, 556n5
Fay, Elizabeth 99
female inheritance (*see also* fortune hunters) 46–49, 54n10, 55n24
Female Quixote, The 15, 67, 68, 135, 150

feminism and feminist criticism 5, 8, 13, 16, 19, 31–34, 36, 41, 66, 76–77, 79, 82–83, 93–94, 110–112, 131, 147, 155n5, 160, 170, 205, 247, 256n2, 279, 301, 310, 321–322, 333, 339, 340n12, 342, 344, 347, 368, 376, 387, 402, 406, 415, 424–425, 431–432, 440, 442, 469, 476, 481, 510, 527, 565, 568, 571
femininity 265, 322, 323, 340, 347, 529; *see also* domesticity
Fergus, Jan 3–4, 15, 308
Ferguson, Margaret 266
Fertig, Anne 7, 571–585
Fielding, Henry 18, 23, 66, 80, 108, 122n11, 133, 145, 147, 156n15, 160, 161, 168n4; *Amelia* 66; *Joseph Andrews* 122n11, 133; *Tom Jones* 122n11, 150, 290; *Tom Thumb* 160
Filippi, Rosina 422, 423, 428
'First Impressions' 12, 23, 25, 197, 243, 417, 428, 429, 485, 502
Firth, Colin 2, 6, 23, 363, 464, 511, 549
Fitzgerald, Lauren 346
Flaubert, Gustave 368, 371, 372, 377, 561
Flavin, Louise 511, 516
Fletcher, Loraine 148
Fludernik, Monika 287, 290
Folsom, Marcia McClintock 27, 511, 518n3
Ford, John 349
Ford, Susan Allen 6, 181, 189n5, 399–408, 577
Fordyce, James 15, 152, 160, 219, 226n5
Forster, E. M. 73n2, 467n3
fortune 41, 43–47, 55m16; *see also* fortune-hunters
fortune-hunters 44, 46, 48–49, 51, 55n24, 55n33
Foucault, Michel 345, 346
Franceschina, John 362
François, Anne-Lise 59, 310
Frantz, Sarah S. G. 323
Frawley, Maria 1–8
Frederic and Elfrida, a novel 117, 143n3
free indirect discourse 12, 14, 28, 39, 65, 69, 70, 73n1, 74, 172, 185, 190n10, 199, 205, 238, 243, 278, 286, 287, 290, 292–293, 302–304, 311, 325–326, 344, 350, 369–378, 383, 386, 506, 542, 577
French Revolution 16, 49, 89–90, 120, 137, 170, 321, 323, 345, 354n18, 559, 577
Freud, Sigmund 389, 394n5
Fricker, Miranda 536–545; passim
Fried, Cathay 399
Fryer, Peter 247–248
Fulford, Tim 323
Fuseli, Henry 454

Gallafent, Edward 366n4
Gallagher, Catherine 263
Galperin, William 6, 8, 14, 35, 36, 42, 54n3, 54n15, 55n23, 55, 90, 93n8, 99, 296–304, 355n26
Gamer, Michael 7, 499–508
Garrett, Corrie 488

Garrod, H.W. 354n10
Garson, Greer 423
Gaskell, Elizabeth 256, 552
Gaskell, Philip 105n9
Gauhar, Mashaal 473
Gauhar, Saniyya 473, 475, 478, 479
Gay, Penny 15
gender 11, 13, 15, 16, 19, 75, 80, 82–85, 88, 90, 111, 114, 119, 121, 122n10, 127, 149, 162, 168n2, 171, 172, 177, 182, 190, 202, 218–219, 226, 243, 244n4, 260, 263, 265–267, 270n1, 301, 320, 323, 325, 327, 329–330, 333, 334, 338, 344–349, 354, 354n5, 355n20, 370, 371, 387–388, 415, 435, 440, 446, 465, 476, 481–485, 487, 528, 533n7, 544, 547, 549, 552, 554–556, 556n2, 564, 571; *see also* femininity, femininity, gender ideology, gender roles, gender studies, masculinity, queer, and queer studies, sexuality
gender ideology 6, 18, 36, 81, 218, 222–223, 266, 342, 472, 555
gender roles 25, 63, 64n3, 218, 364, 488
gender studies 8, 16, 76, 406, 510
Genette, Gerard 277, 280, 313
Gentleman's Magazine 12, 20, 231
Gentry and gentry classes 41, 47, 49, 50, 54n6, 55n26, 55n27, 96, 99, 100, 133, 137, 153, 171, 185, 190n11, 200, 207, 249, 306, 329, 340n3, 544, 559
Gerzina, Grethen Holbrook 257n13
Gesch, Kelly 2
Gibbon, Edward 161
Gilbert, Sandra 8, 16, 32, 33, 41, 48, 55n23, 77, 79, 90, 110, 122n10, 212; *see also The Madwoman in the Attic*
Gilpin, William 528
Gilson, David 159, 404
Gisbourne, Thomas 219
Gladstone, William Ewart 128, 131
Godmersham Park 101–103, 315n8, 411, 527
Godmersham Park library 158, 159, 162, 168n3, 203n3, 458–349; *see also* exhibitions, *Reading with Austen*
Godwin, William 160, 559
Goethe 143
Goldsmith, Oliver 158, 160, 161, 168n4, 382; *History of the Earth,* 382; *Vicar of Wakefield, The* 161
Gonda, Caroline 354n13
Gordon, Paul 423, 437n20
gossip 48, 50–53, 72, 90, 99, 100, 104, 153, 165, 189n5, 198, 205, 223, 289, 298–299, 434, 468, 469, 474, 476, 477, 494, 504
gothic conventions and fiction 4, 6, 11, 13, 14–20, 26, 71–72, 79, 134, 135, 145, 148, 151–153, 155, 160, 164, 190n9, 197, 220, 238, 242, 312–313, 316n15, 336, 342, 346, 349–353, 354n18, 3354n19, 365, 385, 508, 512, 518n5, 525, 578; *see also* Radcliffe, Ann
gothic architecture 164

Gove, Michael 532
Graham, Peter 4, 23–39, 392
Grant, Elizabeth 159
Greenburg, Hope 577
Greene, Donald 111–112, 533n6
Greenfield, Susan 6, 8, 342–357
Greenfield, Sayre 510, 511
Gregory, Dr. John 46, 55n16, 111
Greiner, Rae 81–82, 90
Gretna Green 50, 51, 503; *see also* elopement
Grey, J. David 2, 399, 401, 402, 411–414
Griffith, Richard 172
Grinnel, George C. 235
Grogan, Claire 354n2
Grundy, Isobel 146, 155n1, 158
Gubar, Susan 8, 16, 32, 33, 41, 48, 55n23, 77, 79, 90, 110, 122n10, 212; *see also The Madwoman in the Attic*
Gunderson, Lauren 423

Habib, Kamila Rahim 475–476
Hadid, Diaa 468
Hadlow, Janice 440
Hafner-Lany, Mary 189n5
Haggerty, George 344, 346
Haider, Shazaf Fatima 470, 476
Halberstam, Jack 446, 450, 459, 465
Hall, Catherine 247, 257n9
Hall, Lynda A. 35, 36
Halperin, John 3, 342
Halsey, Katie 3, 5, 8, 15, 158–169, 417, 564
Hamill, Kate 423, 424–426, 428, 432, 436m, 437n8
Hamilton 252
Hanaway, Lorraine 402, 404, 412
Handler, Phil 197
handwriting 98, 100, 102, 103
Harding, D.W. 13, 43, 54n9, 64n1, 354n10
Hardwicke, Lord 50
Harris, Jocelyn 15, 23, 28, 38, 158, 162, 164, 187, 190n15, 229, 394n2, 415, 510, 550, 577
Harris, Kamala 260, 270n2
Hawkins, Laetitia-Matilda 136
Hayley, William 160
Hays, Mary 170
Haywood, Eliza 147, 151, 155n5, 155n13
Haywood, Ian 197
health 1, 17, 53, 115, 121, 174, 175, 187, 190n17, 219, 231–238, 316n15, 333–334, 337–339, 381, 512, 545n2, 555; *see also* hypochondria, resorts, sea-side resorts
Heidegger 299, 302
Henry and Eliza 106, 107, 112
Hermsprong; or, Man as he is not (R. Bage) 160
Hernon, Ian 270n11
Heroine, The (E. S. Barrett) 135, 151, 160
Hewson, Lance 368
Heydt-Stevenson, Jillian 15, 111, 123n18, 123n20, 155n11

Index

Highsmith, Patricia 538
Hill, Christopher 207
History of England, The 107, 110, 148, 155n12, 578; *see also* Juvenilia
Hitchcock, Alfred 359
Hoeveler, Diane 14
Hogan, Eleanor 566
Hogan, Patrick 389, 392
Hogarth, William 266
Holmes, Martha Stoddard 7
Holmes, Rachel 257n10
Holway, Tatiana 189n5
Honan, Park 3
Hook, James 220
Hoover, Cynthia Adams 218
Hopkins, Robert 16
Hornsby, Gill 530
Horrocks, Ingrid 170–173; passim 177
Hudelet, Ariane 510
Hughes, Derek 262, 270n14
Hume, David 33–34, 76, 79, 81, 134, 158, 159, 160, 161, 168n4, 286; *History of England* 160
humor: *see* burlesque, comedy, irony, juvenilia, parody, satire
Hurley, Denis Mason 400, 411
Husain, Mehr F. 473, 474
Hutcheon, Linda 358, 518n2
Huxley, Aldous 436n5
Hwang, Sheila Minn 190n14
hypochondria 5, 188, 207, 229, 237–244, 555

imagination 13, 17, 41, 43, 65, 66, 71, 73, 80, 92, 115, 123n18, 234, 237, 240, 242, 251, 277, 306, 312, 313, 340n12, 352, 353, 389–391, 416, 431, 545, 549, 566, 568
inheritance 14, 31–34, 43, 47, 54n10, 55n25, 205–207, 209, 216, 223, 233, 259, 323, 335–336, 339n3, 441, 475, 493, 505, 528
Innes, C.L. 251, 257n18
irony 15, 17, 19, 31, 38, 41–43, 48, 50, 64n1, 70, 85, 97, 109, 112, 139, 155n2, 168, 199, 226, 237, 240, 241, 279, 297, 299, 344, 385, 430, 474, 518, 563, 567

'Jack and Alice' 107, 116, 117, 143n2, 153, 167, 169n9
Jackson, Christopher 252
Jalaluddin, Uzma 482
James, Henry 110, 303
James, Marlon 255; *Book of Night Women, The* 255
Jameson, Frederic 286
Jamison, Anne 492–493
Jane Austen Book Club 571
Jane Austen Society (JAS) 6, 409–421; passim 572
Jane Austen Society of Brazil 471
Jane Austen Society of North America (JASNA) 6, 65, 106, 399–408, 409–421, 452–453, 469, 471, 490, 492, 509, 518n1, 522, 572, 574, 584

Jane Austen Society of Pakistan (JASP) 6, 468–480, 551, 572
Jane Austen Summer Program (Durham, NC) 571–584
Janeites 40, 43, 54n9, 109, 247, 354n10, 405, 414–417, 435–436, 439, 465n3, 468, 474, 477, 479, 481, 490, 496, 517, 523, 526, 571–573, 580, 581, 584n2
Jarvis, Robin 171, 177
Jenkins, Elizabeth 409–410
Jerinic, Maria 14
Jerome, Helen 423
Jewett, Hilary 573
Jockic, Olivera 556n6
Johnson, Claudia L. 2, 16, 26, 34, 37, 47–48, 53n30, 54n5, 54n8, 55n30, 63, 65, 78–80, 84, 86, 93n4, 106, 112, 118, 121, 123n18, 189n7, 193, 216, 322, 339n3, 342, 343, 344, 354n8, 354n10, 354n11, 406n2, 415, 416, 523–524
Johnson, Freya 131n1
Johnson, Samuel 17, 79, 149–150, 158,168n4, 249, 281, 311, 313, 415; *Dictionary* 41, 43; *Idler* 161, 307, 309, 310; *Rambler* 149–150, 161, 162; *Rasselas* 160
Jones, Hazel 340n5
Jones, Wendy 370–396
Jonson, Ben 269n1
Jordan, Dorothy 164
Jouse, J. 220
Joyce, James 561, 584n3
Justice, George 4, 5, 8, 15, 65–74
juvenilia vi, 4, 5, 12, 13, 67, 72, 106–122, 122n3, 122n9, 122n10, 136, 143n3, 146–148, 150, 153, 161, 181, 323, 347, 362, 384, 435, 462, 572, 580

Kamal, Soniah 481, 482, 483, 486, 551, 572, 578, 580–581
Kaplan, Deborah 99, 100, 339n3, 404
Kaplan, Laurie 402, 404–405
Kastan, David Scott 545n1
Kean, Edmund 164
Keats, John 42, 239
Kearful, Frank 13
Kelly, Gary 16, 216n1
Kelly, Gene 364
Kelly, Helena 4, 199–200
Kennard, Jean 360
Kestner, Joseph 322
Kettle, Arnold 49, 55n26
Khan, Faiza Sultan 470–471
Kidd, Jordan 33
Kierkegaard, Soren 537
Kimball, Roger 343
Kinane, Ian 482
Kindred, Sheila Johnson 550
King, Noel 377n2
Kipling, Rudyard 414, 571–572, 584n2
Kirkham, Margaret 16, 207, 216n12, 322, 339n3

Index

Kirkpatrick, Kathryn 250
Kirschenbaum, Matthew 574
Klaver, Claudia 194
Knight, Anna 98, 136, 137, 141–142, 146, 178n2, 282
Knight, Edward Austen (JA's brother): *see* Austen, Edward (later Knight)
Knight, Fanny, Lady Knatchbull 11, 90, 96, 98, 108, 189n5, 216n3, 220, 233, 282, 339n1, 411, 553
Knight, Marianne 282
Knight, Richard 413
Knox-Shaw, Peter 131n1, 158, 159, 391–392
Knox, Vicemous 306–307
Koppel, Gene 407n3
Korba, Susan 344
Kowaleski-Wallace, Beth 16
Kozaczka, Edward 92n2, 93n5
Kramp, Michael 323
Kreilkamp, Ivan 282
Kureishi, Hanif 261

Labbe, Jacqueline 155n8
labouring class 49–50, 55n26
LaBruyere, Jean De 152
Lacan 389
Lacelles, Mary 14, 279
Lady Emma Melvill 68
Lady Gaga 446–467
Lady's Magazine 164, 439
Lady Susan, 2, 67, 69–70, 73, 96, 108, 109, 122n3, 136, 141, 147, 190n11, 193, 198, 223–224, 286, 413, 477, 486, 529
Lambdin, Laura C. 2
Lambdin, Robert T. 2
Lane, Maggie 190n12
Lanser, Susan 345, 354n17
Lathom, Francis 145, 160
Latour, T. Francis 221–222, 226n8
Lau, Beth 381–382
Lawlor, Clark 190n17
Lawrence, D.H. 344
Lazzaro-Weis, Carol 36
Leavis, F. R. 354n10
Lee, Ang 23, 24, 34, 429, 554; *see also* adaptations, film, *Sense and Sensibility*
Lee, Harper 538
Lee, Yoon Sun 176
LeFaye, Deirdre 4, 12, 14, 23, 53, 98–104, 104n3, 162, 282, 339n1, 343, 360
Leffel, John 5, 106–124, 181
Leighton, Angela 278
Lefroy, Anna: *see* Knight, Anna
Lefroy, Tom
Leigh-Perrot, James 102
Leighton, Angela 278
Lennox, Charlotte 15, 67, 135; *Female Quixote* 15, 67–69, 135, 150

Leppert, Richard 226n1
Lerner, Sandy 413
'Letter from a Young Lady, A' 111–12
letters and correspondence 3, 4, 5, 27–28, 65, 69, 74, 95–105, 107–110, 115,117, 123n16, 134, 145–147, 149, 152–153, 160, 162, 165, 168n4, 181, 183, 189n5, 198, 216, 236–237, 241, 244n5, 250, 282, 308, 315n12, 339n1, 348, 411–412, 430, 453, 477, 493, 506, 526, 529, 536, 550, 553, 574, 578
Letters, as source material 5, 16, 40, 51, 53, 54n2, 55n18, 90, 95–105, 134–137, 142–143, 145–147, 150–154, 158–162, 168, 171, 178n2, 202, 216n2, 261n3, 271n15, 220, 248, 282, 288, 319–320, 334, 343–344, 363, 439, 544, 553
Letters from the Mountain (E Grant) 159
Levine, Caroline 86, 244n7
Levine, George 14
Lewcock, Dawn 263
Lewis, Matthew "Monk" 18, 134
Lewis, Michael 5, 75–94
Liasons Dangereuses, Les 158
libraries: *see* circulating libraries
Linné, Carol 248
literary tourism 417, 524
Litvak, Joseph 16
Litz, A. Walton 2, 13, 59, 109–110, 399, 403
Lloyd, Martha 159, 164, 220
Locke, John 198, 247
Lodge, David 73n2, 383
Lone, Mahlia S. 468, 471, 473, 475
Looser, Devoney 3, 4, 5, 15, 18, 23, 64n3, 127–32, 322, 339n3, 369, 376, 406, 423–424, 436n4, 436n5, 439, 481–482, 525
Lorenz, Matt 388
Loscocco, Paula 545n9
Lost in Austen (2008) 416, 420, 436, 554, 558
'Love and Freindship' 75, 83, 85, 108,109, 110, 112, 122n10, 135, 344, 578
'Lover's Vows' (Inchbald) 269, 282, 543
Luetkenhaus, Holly 481, 491
Luke, Catriona 474
Lupton, Christina 307
Lyme-Regis 67, 80, 81, 88, 93n5, 102, 142, 154, 158, 164, 171–177, 187, 297, 329, 383, 392, 432–433, 441, 444n1, 457, 524
Lynch, Deidre 104n8, 306, 307, 314, 404, 416, 523, 572, 573
Lynch, Melissa 478–479

Macaulay, Catharine 442
Macaulay, Thomas 474
MacDonagh, Oliver 216n9
MacFadyen, Heather 152
Mackenzie, Henry 82, 147
Madwoman in the Attic (Sandra Gilbert and Susan Gubar) 8, 16, 32, 48, 77, 110

Index

Magee, William 155n8
Mahler, Margaret 393
Main, Mary 394, 7
Malcom, Gabrielle 439
Malik-Hussain, Mina 479
Mallory-Kani, Amy 190n17
Malone, Meaghan 323
Mandal, Anthony 377n1, 417–418
Manley, Delarivier 147, 155n5
Mansab, Fariq 474
Mansell, Darrell 362
Mansfield Park 1, 5, 7, 12, 24, 58–64, 67, 71, 86, 139, 140, 145, 151, 154, 162, 170, 174, 178n2, 180, 184, 186, 190n13, 195–196, 200–202, 205–206, 223, 227n10, 229, 230, 237, 242, 244n3, 268–269, 277, 280, 282–285, 298–302, 306–314, 322, 334, 335, 339, 360–361, 380, 387, 388, 391, 393, 437n7, 510, 517, 527, 535–546, 560, 564, 568, 571, 576, 577, 581; *see also* adaptations, film; Rozema, Patricia
manuscripts (JA's) 4, 11, 12, 23, 25, 95, 96, 107, 109, 118, 120, 122, 148, 161, 165, 169n9, 229, 230, 241–243, 308, 350, 352, 456, 462, 530, 550
Marcus, Marvin 561
Margiana: or, Widdrington Tower 135
marriage 3, 4, 36, 37–38, 42–46, 50, 55n24, 61, 70, 71, 80, 84, 86–87, 90–92, 93n8, 107, 112, 115, 118, 122n7, 131, 134, 138, 140, 149, 155n6, 171, 176, 190n13, 193, 195, 199–200, 202, 223, 226, 229, 230, 233–237, 240, 243, 244n1, 244n3, 247, 250, 259, 263, 268, 322, 326, 329, 335, 336, 339, 340n3, 343–353, 360–361, 370, 392, 425, 426, 434, 440, 442, 464, 469, 471–477, 483, 484, 486, 492, 528, 538, 544, 552, 555, 562, 565–566; *see also* companionate marriage, elopement, Gretna Green
marriage, economics of 32, 38, 40, 54n10, 131, 198, 205, 208–217, 381, 481; *see also* marriage market; marriage, female status in
marriage, female status in 30, 44, 47–47, 566
marriage market 13, 30, 52, 116–117, 122n15, 180, 189n6, 198, 200, 202, 218, 223, 237, 425, 528, 552, 566
marriage proposals 59, 61, 326, 329, 336, 361, 464, 539, 540, 55
marriageability 24, 29, 80, 116, 190n13, 215, 230, 336, 475, 566; *see also* companionate marriage, courtship and courtship plots
Married Women's Property Acts 206
Marsh, Sarah 5, 8, 229–245, 544
Martineau, Harriet 229
masculinity 6, 8, 36, 76, 82–83, 318–332
material culture 15, 33, 96, 104, 439, 505, 524, 574–575, 578; *see also* consumerism and consumer culture, commodities
Matthew, Patricia 3, 54n2, 535, 544, 556n5
Mauer, Shawn Lisa 36, 38

May, William 99
Mazzeno, Laurence 371
McArthur, Isobel 426–427, 437n11
McHale, Brian 287
McKendrick, Neil 180
McMan, Barbara 385
McMaster, Juliet 2, 106, 110, 402, 403, 416, 545n6
medicine 185, 190n10, 190n17, 509, 545n2; *see also* health, sea-side resorts
Melbourne, Lady 51
melodrama 136, 137, 160
Memoir of Maria Edgeworth 141
Menon, Patricia 324
Mepham, John 288
Merleau-Ponty, Maurice 302–303
Merret, Robert 15
metafiction v, 4, 11–22, 79, 90, 155n2, 551
#MeToo movement 2, 3, 256, 516, 517, 555
Micahaelson, Patricia 282, 282
Michie, Elsie 189, 194
Midnight Bell, The 145
Mijares, Jackie 32
Milbanke, Anne Isabella (later Lady Byron) 51, 319
Millard, Mary 407n3
Miller, Christopher 388–389
Miller, D.A. 61–62, 80, 91, 93n7, 203n1, 233, 280–281, 344, 348
Miller, J. Scott 566
Millgate, Jane 173
Milton, John 167
Miranda, Lin-Manuel 252
Mirmohamadi, Kylie 7, 439–445
Miskin, Lauren 15, 181, 190n8, 216n10
Mitchell, David 174
Modert, Jo 95, 98
Modood, Tariq 261–262, 270n9
Mohdin, Aamna 260
Mohsin, Moni 468, 471
Moler, Kenneth 167
Monaghan, David 510, 515
Monaham, Dave 520
money: *see* class system, consumerism, economics and inheritance
Montaigne 83
Montgomery, James 238, 239
Monthly Review 137, 355n23
Montolieu,Isabelle de 6, 368–377, 531; *Caroline de Lichfield* 531; *La Famille Elliot* 369–377, 531
Moody, Ellen 377, 512
Mooneyham, Laura 15
Moore, Lisa 344
More, Hannah 76, 118, 120–21, 160, 219, 250, 324, 387, 527; *Coelebs in Search of a Wife* 120–121, 387; *Strictures on the Modern System of Female Education* 527
Moretti, France 101

Index

Morgan, Susan 30, 340n7
Moritz, Karl Phillip 171
Morning Chronicle 160, 198
Moshin, Moni 475
Moss, Carol Medine 406
Moss, Stephanie 96,104n2
Mounsey, Chris 354n13
Mudrick, Marvin 14, 64n1, 344, 354n11
Mueller, John 359, 363
Mullan, John 417, 561
Murfin, Jane 436n5
Murphy, Olivia 3, 5, 158, 167, 246–258, 382, 392
Murray, John 12, 159, 162, 284
music 5, 34, 92n1, 182, 218–228, 260, 261, 271n41,
  292, 308, 338, 340n11, 360–361, 406, 424, 432,
  437n15, 443, 524, 528, 572, 575

Naek, Mishayl 475, 477
Nafisi, Azar 551
Nagle, Chris 7, 422–438
Napoleon Bonaparte 53
narrative technique and narrative voice 14, 18, 27, 32,
  40, 58, 60–62, 70, 80, 140, 213, 277, 280, 285,
  326, 375, 383, 436; *see also* free indirect discourse
National Portrait Gallery 249
navy and naval officers 72, 77, 78, 88, 89, 92, 98,
  188, 202, 216, 230–231, 290, 321, 328, 505, 552,
  553
needlework 162, 164, 311; *see also* samplers
Neeson, J.M. 200
Neill, Edward 131n1
Neill, Natalie 14
Nelson, Lord 164
Nesbit, Kate 292
new criticism 279, 358
new woman figure, new women 560, 562, 565
Newey, Katherine 441, 444n5
Newman, Karen 42, 54n4
newspapers 99, 128, 141, 158, 162, 164, 167, 256n4,
  257n18, 260, 402, 493
Nguyen, Viet Thanh 484, 488
Nietzsche 83, 84
Nogami, Yaeko 559–568
North American Friends of Chawton House 413
Northanger Abbey 1, 3, 6, 8, 11–22, 24, 67, 72, 107,
  133, 136, 139, 142, 145, 150, 151–154, 155n6,
  161, 162, 164, 167, 181, 197, 198, 220, 237,
  238, 251, 279, 282, 286–291; passim 296,
  306–308, 312–313, 336, 337, 346–354, 360,
  361, 381–382, 385, 394, 437n7, 510, 511, 524,
  525, 561
Norton, Mary Beth 265
novel, development of 6, 13, 15, 18, 92, 106–122,
  133, 137, 145–155, 156n15, 278, 318, 360, 369,
  370, 528; epistolary fiction; *see also* free indirect
  discourse, gothic fiction, realism, sentimentalism

O'Connell, Anita 190n17
Ogawa, Kimiyo 8, 559–570
Olivier, Laurence 423
Oliviero, Tara 407n4
O'Loughlin, Katrina 7, 499–508
Olusoga, David 251, 270n11
O'Rourke, James 26–27
O'Rourke, Michael 346, 354n19
Orr, Leah 266
Owenson, Sydney (Lady Morgan) 160, 324; *Ida of
  Athens* 160
Oxford English Dictionary 66

Page, Norman 292, 403
Paine, Thomas 559
paintings 164, 167, 449, 454, 459; *see also* portraits
Palmer, Alan 293
Palmer, Michael 532–533
Palmerston, Lord 128
Parey, Armelle 444n2
Parkes, M.B. 289
parody 14–17, 52, 106, 108, 110, 118, 146, 150, 160,
  197, 236, 238, 336; *see also* burlesque, comedy,
  humor, irony, juvenilia, satire, style
Parrill 510
Pascal, Roy 369, 375
Pascoe, Judith 284
Pasley, Charles 160
Patchias, Anna C. 155n13
patriarchy and patriarchal culture 14–20, 27, 31, 32,
  53, 76, 78, 83, 85, 87, 90, 122, 207, 208, 323, 337,
  340n3, 366, 387, 471, 472, 475, 481, 542, 551,
  562, 567; *see also* gender, inheritance,
  primogeniture
Patterson, Amy L. 469–470
Paul et Virginie 153
Paulson, Ronald 16
Peel, Robert 128
Percival, Thomas 392
Perry, Ruth 344
Persuasion 3, 5, 12, 24, 58, 66–67, 72, 75–94, 107,
  133, 140, 142, 170–179, 184–18, 196, 206, 207,
  221, 225, 229, 232, 237, 238, 279, 280, 290–292,
  297, 301, 307, 308, 318, 319, 325–330, 335, 339,
  344, 365–366, 369–377, 382, 383, 389–391
  passim, 394, 399–408, 430, 432, 492–493, 494,
  510, 517, 524, 531, 548, 549, 575, 577, 581;
  see also adaptations, film
*Persuasions: the Jane Austen Journa*l 6, 399–408
Persuasions Online 399–408
Pettit, Alexander 155n13
Pfannenstiel, Amber Nicole 494
Phillips, Natalie 387–388
Pike, Holly 175
Piketty, Thomas 193
Pinch, Adela 6, 8, 79–82, 86, 277–295, 298

596

Pinion, R. B. 2
Piozzi, Hester Thrale 250
Plato 83, 84, 91
Pocock, J.G.A. 194, 198
Poincare, Henri 563
Pointon, Marcia 216n11
political economy 193–204, 577
politics and political environment 5, 27, 90, 118, 127–32, 137, 151, 160, 167–168, 190n11
Pollack, Ellen 344
Ponsonby, Sarah 345
Poovey, Mary 37, 41–42, 64n1, 189n1, 193, 196, 233, 322
Pope, Alexander 161, 165, 167
Popham, Sir Home 164
Porter, Jane 324
Porter, Roy 180
portraits of Jane Austen 90, 318–319, 447, 449, 450, 551; *see also* National Portrait Gallery
Posner, Richard 216–217n13
Powers, Renee M. 469
Pride and Prejudice 1, 4, 7, 12, 14, 19, 23, 24, 25, 29, 40–57, 58, 65, 67, 71, 86, 92, 108, 136, 140, 142, 143, 145, 152–54, 164, 171–172, 178n2, 183–184, 193, 195, 198–199, 206, 207, 218–219, 221–226, 229–232, 237, 243, 244n3, 247, 249, 251, 253, 287, 291, 296, 318–319, 321, 325–330, 334, 335, 338, 360–365, 381, 388, 393, 424–425, 436–437n7, 440–443, 444n7, 472, 478, 481–489, 491, 494, 513, 514, 517, 527, 528, 535–545, 547, 549, 561, 563, 566–568, 575, 576, 577, 579, 580, 581; *see also* adaptations, fanfiction
Pride and Prejudice and Zombies 251, 275
primogeniture 38, 85, 205–216, 230, 233, 560, 562, 565; *see also* class system, economics patriarchy and patriarchal culture
Prince, Gerald 48, 49, 52
Prince, Mary 251
Prince Regent 182, 229, 244n2
Prins, Yopie 282
Private Education: or a Practical Plan for the Studies of Young Ladies 218
psychology 6, 54n9, 79, 151, 379–394, 394n1, 545n2; *see also* attachment theory
public humanities ix, 7, 523, 526, 537, 545, 548, 571–584
publishers: *see* Ballantyne, Crosby, Egerton, Murray
Pugh, Sheenagh 490
Pybus, Cassandra 257n13

Quarterly Review 44, 49, 51, 143, 160
queer (elements in JA's fiction) 6, 8, 13, 15, 16, 83, 86, 146, 342–354, 441, 446
queer studies and theory 82, 83, 86, 92n3, 93n5, 346, 354n1, 354n4, 355n19, 537, 544
Quinn, Megan 176

race 3, 5, 7, 127, 174, 234, 246–258, 259–269, 269n1, 481–488, 535–545, 547–550, 580–581; *see also* abolition, slavery and slave trade
Radcliffe, Ann 14, 135, 151, 152, 220, 352, 526; *The Italian* 351; *The Mysteries of Udolpho* 18, 72, 153, 282, 312–313, 342, 346, 349–351, 355n25; *The Romance of the Forest*
Radway, Janice 312
Rambler, The (Johnson) 17, 149
Raven, James 307
readers and reading 6, 8, 15, 18, 100, 134, 306–315; *see also* exhibitions, Reading with Jane Austen; Godmersham Park Library
reader-response criticism 358
readerships and book history 2, 137, 178n2, 190n9, 287, 306, 343–344, 370, 404, 406, 551, 572, 576
reading aloud 2, 130, 134, 277, 279–284, 308, 311–312
reading, silent 277, 284, 308, 518
reception 2, 3, 8, 11, 13, 99, 104n2, 106, 108, 155n8, 222, 240, 247, 252, 277, 319, 324, 368–377, 377n1, 306, 415, 418, 423, 454, 517, 531–532, 540, 548, 559, 560
Ree, Jonathan 283–284, 290
Reeve, Clara 136
Reflections on the Revolution in France 47, 149
Regency Era 23, 30, 36, 38, 82, 95–97, 104n5, 105, 164, 169n8, 180–187, 189n3, 190n15, 218, 229, 240–241, 244, 249–253, 256, 257n11, 281, 316, 321–323, 331, 363, 384, 405, 415–418, 446, 453, 464, 469, 472–475, 481, 490, 501, 505, 523–523, 528–530, 533n6, 575, 582
Rehman, Ayesha 476–477
Reid-Walsh, Jacqueline 360
Relhand, Anthony 236
religion 2, 96, 111, 120, 151, 172, 202, 262, 404, 526, 575; *see also* Anglican, clery and beliefs; Bible, Evangelical clergy and beliefs
Reliques of Irish Poetry (C Brookes) 161
Repton, Humphrey
resort towns 11, 15, 37, 180, 185–187, 190n16, 229–233, 236–237, 242
Reynolds, Sir Joshua 164, 450, 454
Rhys, Jean 490, 491
Ricardo, David 194, 203
Rich, Adrienne 253
Richards, Anne 37–38
Richardson, Alan 123n23, 384, 392, 563
Richardson, Rebecca 16, 27–28, 186, 190n17
Richardson, Samuel 23, 66, 100, 108, 123n16, 133, 145, 147, 150, 156n15, 158, 160, 161, 259, 362, 384, 423; *Clarissa* 28, 66, 100, 150, 153, 162; *Familiar Letters on Important Occasions* 100; *Pamela* 28, 66, 100, 153, 162, 259; *Sir Charles Grandison* 18, 28, 153, 160, 165–166, 169n9, 324, 423

Ricoeur 313
Rios, Alexandra 68
Ritchie, Leslie 226n1
Roberts, Bette B. 14
Roberts, Robert 321
Roberts, Warren 16
Robinson, Mary 526
Rock Against Racism (movement and concert) 260, 261
Rogers, Ginger 359; *Gay Divorcee, The* 361; *Top Hat*
Rohrbach, Emily 5, 58–64, 82
Rojek, Chris 447, 452, 457
Romilly, Ann 296–297
Ronell, Avital 112
Rooney, Sally 288
Rosanne: Or, a Father's Labour Lost 136
Rosen, Jeremy 439, 440
Rosenblatt, Roger 354n6
Ross, Josephine 2
Rousseau, Jean Jacques 152, 161, 527
Rowlandson, Thomas 457
Rowlatt, Bee 551
Roy, Nilanjana 473
Rozema, Patricia 251, 257n12
Rubery, Matthew 284
Rumbold, Kathryn 169n11
Russell, Adam 369, 371–373

Sabor, Peter 106, 122n9, 158, 527
Saglia, Diego 370
Said, Edward 62–63, 201, 257n12
Saintsbury, George 414
Sales, Adriana 471–472
Sales, Roger 96–97, 99, 104n5
Salwey, Nicholas 227n9
samplers 158, 162, 167, 168, 169n6
Sanchez, Melissa 343, 354n5
Sancho, Ignatius 249
Sanditon 5, 11, 67, 73, 162, 180, 185, 193, 197–198, 229–245, 251, 269, 308, 456, 462, 551; *see also* Adaptations, *Sanditon*, film
satire 4, 17, 19, 42, 46, 52, 53, 71, 77, 99, 109–112, 117–118, 122, 148, 149, 158, 162, 164, 168n4, 181, 185, 186, 190n11, 229, 230, 235, 241, 264, 296, 312, 315n12, 339n3, 344, 346, 364, 474, 506, 553, 564, 572; *see also* burlesque, comedy, humor, irony
Schafer, R. Murray 293
Schapiro, Morton 193
Scheinman, Ted 572
Schmidt, Jane 37
School of Clavier Playing 221
Schorer, Mark 41, 54n11, 55n34
Schuessler, Jennifer 247
Scott, Walter 5, 53, 82, 108, 130, 131, 137, 142, 143, 168n4, 182, 238, 239, 287, 296, 302, 306–307, 309, 310, 325; *Guy Mannering* 287, 308; *Heart of Midlothian* 170–179; *Waverly* 137, 151, 178n2

Scudéry, Madeleine de 147, 151
seaside resorts 185–187, 190n16, 190n17; *see also* resorts
Sedgwick, Eve Kosofsky 297, 342, 343, 346, 350, 352, 354n6
Seeber, Barbara K. 559–560
Self-Control (M Brunton) 136, 146, 527
Selwyn, David 226n2, 403
Sense and Sensibility 1, 12, 14, 23–39, 71, 86, 135, 136, 138, 141, 149, 155n6, 162, 180, 182–183, 189n6, 193–194, 199, 205, 207, 221, 223–226, 230–231, 237, 243, 251, 268, 297, 301, 307, 321, 335, 338, 339, 343, 348, 350, 352, 360, 365, 393, 413, 417, 437n7, 510, 511, 531, 532, 559, 572, 577; *see also* adaptations
Sense and Sensibility (Ang Lee film, 1995) 23, 24, 34, 429, 515, 554
sensibility, ideals and fictional conventions 17, 19, 24, 26, 43, 45, 49, 55n16, 83, 110, 112, 140, 149, 155n6, 230, 237, 316n19, 329, 338, 354, 362, 430, 440, 444n8
sentimental conventions, modes, genres 11, 15, 17, 18, 19, 35, 37–38, 50, 71, 82, 108, 110, 113, 135, 146–150, 153, 155n2, 155n6, 160, 168, 225, 369–371, 376–377, 384, 423, 531, 552
sentimentalism 155n4, 369, 370, 371, 375, 377
Sermons to Young Women (Fordyce) 15, 152, 226n5
Sertima, Ivan Van 259
servants 49, 89, 177, 232, 249, 253, 301, 426, 427, 469, 491, 516, 547, 549, 550, 552–554
sexuality 86, 111, 121, 123n18, 124, 153, 174, 253, 266, 267, 269, 295, 342, 343–346, 351–354, 354n1, 547
Shafi, Afshan 473
Shah, Rubika 260
Shanks Libden, Kathryn 227n11
Shakespeare, William 65, 161, 164, 169n11, 187, 252, 269n1, 284, 311, 415, 447, 474, 482, 490, 527, 579, 584; *Hamlet* 50, 280, 491; *Henry VIII* 282; *Love's Labour's Lost* 269n1; *Midsummer Night's Dream, A* 167, 454; *Othello* 257n20, 454; *Sonnets* 269n1; *Tempest, The* 49, 292, 454
Shaw, Narelle 12
Shelley, Mary 38, 92n1; *Frankenstein* 441, 525, 579
Sherlock, Thomas 160, 161
Sherman, Howard 444n10
shopping: *see* commodities, consumerism and consumer culture
Short History of Brighthelmston 236
Showalter, Elaine 244n4
Siddons, Sarah 164
Simpson, Kim 7, 523–534
Siskin, Clifford 15
sketches 107, 161, 241, 251, 310, 502
Skinner, Gillian 206, 216n8
slavery and the slave trade 58, 62–63, 127, 164, 200, 201, 217, 229, 244n3, 247, 249–256, 259, 263, 527, 530, 543–544, 545, 549–550, 573
Slothouber, Linda 412

Index

Smiley, Sir Hugh 400, 411
Smith, Adam 76, 81, 82, 152, 159, 193–194, 203, 203n3, 203n4; *Theory of Moral Sentiments* 194, 203n3; *Wealth of Nations* 194, 203n3
Smith, Amy Elizabeth 418
Smith, Charlotte 15, 148, 151, 155n6, 155n10, 178n7, 526; *Celestina* 149; *Desmund* 149–150, 155n11, 156n15; *Emmeline, the Orphan of the Castle* 148–149m, 156n14; *Etheline, or the Recluse of the Lake* 148–149
Smith, Goldwin 130
Smith, John; *Printer's Grammar, The* 286
Smith, Rebecca 529
Smollett, Tobias 147, 151
Snyder, Sharon 174
social sciences 379–396; *see also* attachment theory, psychology
Socrates 83
Soderman, Melissa 175
Solender, Elsa A. 405
Solinger, Jason D. 323
Sontag, Susan 529
Sorbo, Nedregotten 368
Sōseki, Natsume 559–568
Southam, B. C. 2, 14, 109–110, 113m, 122n2, 123n17, 148, 187, 190n16, 241, 277–278, 296, 299, 344, 377n1, 403, 436n3
Southampton 100, 159, 161, 164, 523, 525, 528, 530, 531
Spacks, Patricia Meyer 54n6, 54n12, 54n22, 56n37, 95, 99, 100
Spampinato, Erin 345
Spectator 161, 162, 167
Spengler, Birgit 444n1
spinsters and spinsterhood 19, 41, 45–46, 80, 171, 303, 440–441, 553
Spratt, Danielle 3, 7, 535–546, 556–557n6, 573
Spufford, Frances 253
Staines, John D. 265
Stasio, Michael J. 394n1
Steele, Richard (*The Spectator*) 161
Steele, Joshua 282
Steetz, William 220–221
Steeves, Harrison 321
Steiner, Enit Karafili 28
Stendhal (Marie-Henri Beyle) 370
Sterne, Laurence 147, 167, 264
Steventon v, 12, 25, 34, 100–103, 134, 159, 236, 399, 410, 413–414, 459–460
St. Clair, Justin 278, 314–315
St. Clair, William 307, 312
Stiller, Maureen 409–410, 418
St. Nicholas Church 413, 414
St. Paul's Magazine 278
St Pierre, Jacques-Henri Bernadin 152
Straub, Kristina 447, 465
Strodtbeck, Joshua 248

Strong, Sharon E. 453
Stoppard, Tom 491
Stovel, Nora Foster 360, 481
style 2, 6, 8, 13, 14, 27, 37, 48, 50, 56n37, 61–64, 64n1, 67, 75, 79–80, 88, 93, 96, 98, 103–104, 106, 110, 133, 135, 150, 151, 182, 185, 240, 264, 277, 280–281, 285, 290, 313, 320, 244, 362, 366n5, 370, 381, 393, 427, 429, 434–435, 447, 450, 506, 549, 556; *see also* burlesque, free indirect discourse, Miller, D.A., handwriting, irony, narration and narrative voice, voice)
Sukhera, Laaleen 6, 8, 468–480
Sulloway, Alison G. 322, 335, 339–340n3
Susan, ms of *Northanger Abbey* 11, 12, 16, 23, 71, 308
Sutherland, Kathryn 2, 23, 104n8, 106, 108, 146, 151, 158, 165, 234, 237, 238, 241–242, 284–285, 28, 417, 450, 463, 510, 516, 529
Swift, Jonathan 263, 265–266, 270n21
Swisher, Clarice 2
Swords, Barbara 335
Sykes, Henrietta 135

Tandon, Bharot 14, 17, 247, 251, 471, 474
Tanner, Tony 14, 78, 81–82, 93n4, 321
Tate, Gregory 190n10
Tave, Stuart 54n14
Tavela, Sara 189n5
Taw, Harold 437n23
Teachman, Debra 2
Tennyson, Alfred Lord 565
Terry, Judith 417
Thackeray, Anne 314
Thackeray, William Makepeace 80, 256
theatre 6, 7, 68, 164, 252, 293, 308, 310, 362, 364, 376, 422–438, 453, 455, 463, 501, 525–527, 530, 574; *see also* adaptations, film, stage
theatricals 59, 63, 184, 202, 423, 525
Therese, Anne, Marquise de Lambert 161
Thomas, Bob 78
Thompson, Emma 30, 520, 554
Thompson, James 160, 178n5, 182
'Three Sisters, The' 114
Tieken-Boon Van Ostade, Ingrid 95, 100, 103–104
time and temporality 6, 306–317
Todd, Janet 2, 15, 93n3, 106, 122n7, 189n3, 417, 526
Tolstoy 252
Tomalin, Claire 4, 236–237, 256n4
Toran, Katherine 189n1
Tovey, Josephine 3
travel and travelling 1, 62, 78, 95, 100, 104, 114, 145, 176, 242, 303–304, 385, 412, 436, 462, 503
translation 6, 8, 161, 318, 358, 368–377, 424, 468, 504, 510, 512, 514, 517, 525, 531–532, 533n7, 568n6
transportation 217n14
Treatise on the Elements of Music in a Series of Letters to a Lady 220

Index

Trentman, Frank 189
Trilling, Lionel 41, 43–44, 363
Trollope, Anthony 415
Troost, Linda 510, 511
Trumbach, Randolph 345
Trump, Donald 247, 260, 270n2
Trumpener, Katie 282, 446
Trunel, Lucile 368, 369, 377n1
Tuite, Clara 2, 123n18, 188, 190n, 233–234, 342, 415
Turk, Daniel Gottlob 221, 226n7
Turner, Michael 199
Ty, Eleanor 14
Tylney-Long, Catherine 164

Uphaus, Robert 15

Van der Klugt, Melissa 468
Verderame, Michael 556
Victim of Prejudice, The (M Hays) 170
Villaseñor, Alice 6, 409–421
Vindication of the Rights of Woman (Wollstonecraft) 31
voice 277–293; *see also* elocution and elocutionists, narrative voice
Voltaire 161, 527
Von Cannon, Jordan 340n9
Voracheck, Laura 5, 218–228

Wadsworth, Sallie 417
Walcott, Derek 482
Waldron, Mary 15, 121, 122n8, 123n18
Walker, Eric 55n16
walking 170–179
Wall, Cynthia 13
Wallace, Anne 171, 177
Wallace, Tara Goshal 5, 14, 170–179
Walle, Taylor 82–83
Walsh, Richard 278, 280
Walton, Sarah Schaefer 7, 571–585
war 75, 76, 80–82, 89–90, 92, 98, 164, 170, 180, 203n4, 216, 290, 446, 450, 462, 479, 486, 493, 559, 571; American Revolution or War of Independence 199, 254, 527; American Civil War 131; Napoleonic Wars 49, 80–82, 89, 98, 164, 171, 180, 188, 197, 199, 229, 321–323, 363, 527; *see also* The French Revolution
Ward, Eucharist 444n3
Warhol, Andy 447–450
Warhol, Robyn 79–80
Warnasuriya, Gayathri 478
Warner, Michael 343
Warner, Richard 161
Waterloo 82, 188, 231, 577; *see also* wars, Napoleanic wars
Waters, Rob 270n9
Watsons, The 2, 104, 209, 296–301, 462, 530

Watt, Ian 73n2, 402
Wedderburn, Robert 257n21
Weinstein, Zoe 481, 491
Weisenfarth, Joseph 400
Welles, Orson 359
Wells, Juliette 3, 4, 7, 227n10, 416, 439, 490, 547–558
West, Jane 160, 324
West, Kanye 260, 270n2
West, Rebecca 12
Westenfeld, Adrienne 486
Whately, Richard 320, 474
Whealler, Susan 99
Wheatley, Phillis 581
Wheeler, Roxann 262, 270n14
White, Laura Mooneyham 5, 180–192
Whitman, Walt 491
Wilberforce, Bishop Samuel 129
Williams, Abigail 392
Williams, Helen Maria 160
Williams, Raymond 55n27
Wilson, Cheryl 324, 482
Wilson, Edmund 344
Wilt, Judith 14
Wiltshire, John 174, 231, 236–237, 334, 510, 511, 518n3, 529, 545n9
Wilwerding, Lauren 32
Winchester 414, 524
Winnicott, D.W. 510
Witwit, May 551
Wolfson, Susan 4–5, 11, 40–57, 3–8
Wollstonecraft, Mary 14, 31, 32, 38, 43, 44, 46, 49, 53, 56, 73, 76–77, 79, 82, 118, 170, 205, 216n1, 346–348, 387, 442, 554, 560, 564; *Maria: Or the Wrongs of Woman* 170, 243, 442, 560; *Vindication of the Rights of Woman, A* 44–46, 345, 387, 442, 527, 564
Woloch, Alex 41–42, 54n12, 55n34, 304n3, 440
Woman of Colour, The 259
Wonder, The: A Woman Keeps a Secret (S Centlivre 160;)
Wong, Bethany 391
Wood, Marcus 201–202
Woodard, Helena 251
Woodsworth, Megan A. 323
Woolf, Virginia 41, 92, 93n7, 109, 111, 249, 561; *Common Reader* 92, 109; *Room of One's Own, A* 92
Wootton, Sarah 324
Wordsworth, Dorothy 241
Wordsworth, William 81, 143n4, 238, 239, 250, 282, 306, 308, 314; *Preface to Lyrical Ballads* 306; *Prelude, The* 250, 306
Works of James Thompson 160
Wright, Andrew 429, 437n13
Wright, Joseph 454
Wright, Nicole 246–247

Index

writing table and portable desk 96, 100–101, 104n8, 112, 222, 462
Wyett, Jodi 4, 11–22, 156n14, 510
Wylie, Judith 355n22

Yaffe, Deborah 406n2, 413, 417, 439, 481, 490, 572
Yahav, Amit 6, 8, 306–317
Yamashita, Karen Tei 482, 486, 487

Yates, Samuel 178n8
Yelland, Chris 281, 284
Young, Kay 389, 555

Zlotnick, Susan 15
Zoboi, Ibi 482
Zunshine, Lisa 383–384

Printed in Dunstable, United Kingdom